D0049104

On His Own Terms

On His Own Terms

A Life of Nelson Rockefeller

RICHARD NORTON SMITH

RANDOM HOUSE

New York

ISBN 978-0-375-50580-5
eBook ISBN 978-0-8129-9687-6

Printed in the United States of America on acid-free paper

www.atrandom.com

2 4 6 8 9 7 5 3 1

FIRST EDITION

Book design by Simon M. Sullivan

For Brian Lamb
and
the C-SPAN *family*

I celebrate myself, and sing myself,
And what I assume you shall assume,
For every atom belonging to me as good belongs to you. . . .
I harbor for good or bad, I permit to speak at every hazard,
Nature without check with original energy.

—WALT WHITMAN, "Song of Myself"

There is no problem that cannot be solved.

—NELSON A. ROCKEFELLER

Note to the Reader

Nelson Rockefeller suffered from dyslexia, the genetic reading disorder whose most obvious manifestations include the visual scrambling of letters and numerals. One side effect of the condition, not surprisingly, is poor spelling skills. The portrait of Rockefeller that follows is based, among other sources, on thousands of pages of private correspondence, much of it only recently available to researchers. I have deliberately left Rockefeller's words as he wrote them, while dispensing with the obligatory (*sic*) as both intrusive and, through the very number of citations called for, self-defeating. The result, I hope the reader will agree, compensates in authenticity for whatever it may lack in orthographic rigor.

Contents

Part Four: The Limits of Power (*1965–1971*)

Part Five: Out of Step (*1972–1979*)

Prologue: July 1964

"This Is Still a Free Country,
Ladies and Gentlemen"

*There came down upon Rockefeller from those galleries a howl of hatred
which was not of an opinion but of a human being who embodied
everything these people had hated for 20 years. . . . He just stood there
and began his prose in the armor of a magnificent contempt. Who cares
what he said; it was what he was that night.*

—Murray Kempton

1

NELSON ROCKEFELLER IS not a patient man. For the most powerful member of the most powerful family in the most powerful nation on earth, time is a commodity, like wealth, women, art, and talent, to be experienced on his terms. To a staff assistant with the temerity to point out that he is running late for an event, Rockefeller replies tartly, "That's your problem, not mine." As good as his word, on a 1963 European trip, the obligatory Grand Tour for would-be presidents, Rockefeller left both British prime minister Harold Macmillan and the newly crowned Pope Paul VI to cool their heels while he dallied in art galleries.

Tonight, however, is different. On this second night of the 1964 Republican convention, a slot reserved for debate over the party platform, even Rockefeller is a clock-watcher. It is a little after six o'clock in San Francisco, nine o'clock in the East. Sidelined by convention managers who hope by delaying his appearance to diminish his national television audience, Rockefeller exhibits the restlessness of a caged animal. It is a familiar stance to those who know him. "He is like a perfect engine," explains his friend architect Wallace Harrison. "It starts acting up if you don't keep it right in the groove of creating something." As with an engine, some part of Rockefeller is perpetually in motion. Journalists unable to match his dervish energy ask whether the governor eats Benzedrine for breakfast. They recall how, at the conclusion of an exhausting campaign, the victorious candidate flew to his fourteen-thousand-acre Venezuela ranch. There he relaxed by scaling a five-thousand-foot mountain on horseback, a five-hour round-trip followed by a punishing swim.

His approach to politics is just as intense; his wooing of voters has been likened to a fullback crashing the line. Rarefied background notwithstanding, Rockefeller may be the best retail campaigner in America. Upon alighting from his private plane, he crosses the airport tarmac with a loping stride of entitlement, all the while offering mechanics and baggage handlers his signature greeting: "Hiya, fella." This cheery salutation, improvised to conceal his inability to remember names, is delivered in a voice of gravel sanded to a patrician softening of consonants. The same faux intimacy is accorded, less successfully, to people who have been around him for years.

"You don't know my name, do you?" a grizzled New York reporter once demanded of the governor.

"Yeah," said Rockefeller, "it's some kind of Polish name, isn't it?"

Inside the terminal, Nelson approaches a man cradling a pay telephone to his ear. "Who are you talking to?" he asks the startled stranger. Not waiting for an answer, Rockefeller seizes the phone and introduces himself to the man's wife. To passersby, he flashes the jack-o'-lantern grin familiar to Oregon lumberjacks, jostling street crowds in Spanish Harlem, French-speaking millworkers in northern New Hampshire, and children of all ages. Rockefeller has discarded the battered fedora, evocative of his lifelong hero Franklin Delano Roosevelt, worn in his early campaigns. But he remains indifferent to clothes, favoring double-breasted suits bought off-the-rack for $150 and proudly displaying tags from outfits worn twenty years or more. The candidate's baggy pants and scuffed shoes are of a piece with his cast-iron stomach and exuberant fondness for Coney Island hot dogs and onion rolls from a Lower East Side delicatessen. An equal opportunity snacker, Rockefeller devours tacos, cannoli, knishes, mulligatawny soup—described by one associate as "a WASP minestrone"—salsa, and soul food with the same gusto he exhibits scooping up caviar or dining on whitebait and oyster crabs at the 21 Club.

To cabdrivers, bartenders, and tabloid readers alike, he is Rocky, the uncommonly wealthy patrician with the common touch. Those who know better avoid the familiar moniker. Those who know best acknowledge their emotional distance. "I only wish we knew him as well as the voters of New York do," Rockefeller's daughter Mary has said of her father. "Gregarious and outgoing," claims William J. Ronan, for eight years his chief deputy in Albany and for many more a close collaborator. "Yet other parts of him were impenetrable." To longtime personal assistant Joe Canzeri, Rockefeller resembles a sixteen-slice pizza pie, with no one besides his second wife, Happy, having access to more than three or four slices. Casual observers assume his life is defined by a single-minded pursuit of the presidency. This overlooks another Rockefeller passion, more consuming than the quest for delegates. "When most politicians are in campaign mode, all they do is campaign and sleep," according to R. W. "Johnny" Apple of *The New York Times*. "Some of them drink. A few of them chase women. But Rockefeller would get museum directors to open their museums at ten o'clock at night, or six o'clock in the morning, because he wanted to look around."

On a long flight to the West Coast, the candidate exchanges briefing books for art catalogs, a favorite way to unwind for a connoisseur who is never happier than when redeploying his vast array of spiky Calder stabiles or two-headed Picasso women. Legislators scratch their heads when Rockefeller fills Albany's ramshackle Executive Mansion with works by Franz Kline, Jackson Pollock, and Jasper Johns. Press secretary Bob McManus worries out loud that American voters might not be ready to elect a president who collected modern art. His boss went on buying. Showing off his treasures is, for Rockefeller, a source of pleasure second only to their acquisition or rearrangement, as fellow governor Mark Hatfield can attest. The forty-two-year-old Oregonian, who doubles as temporary chairman of this week's convention, shares with Rockefeller a strict Baptist upbringing and a moderate-to-liberal slant on domestic issues. On one visit to New York, Hatfield enjoyed a personally conducted tour of his friend's sumptuous apartment on Fifth Avenue. After viewing the thirty-two-room triplex where displays of African jewelry and Mexican pottery compete for attention with Picasso's cubist masterpiece *Girl with Violin*, Giacometti lamps, and a living room fireplace embellished by Henri Matisse, Hatfield couldn't resist asking which of his collections afforded Rockefeller the most pleasure.

"My china," his host replied unhesitatingly. "Sometimes I get up in the middle of the night just to set the table."

No one observing him greeting Hatfield and others in the wings of the Cow Palace would guess that Nelson is suffering from sleep deprivation, the consequence of harassing phone calls from political tricksters over the last two nights. Rockefeller appears younger than his fifty-six years, despite flecks of gray in his thick brown hair and the battle scars etched in what he disdains as his "Aldrich skin . . . you look like you just crawled out from under a stone." At 190 pounds, he retains the narrow-hipped, broad-shouldered build of the collegiate soccer player. His square face and blocky torso, both seemingly chiseled from granite, add nothing to his claimed height of five feet ten inches. Magnifying his charisma is a gaze of almost startling intensity. In a receiving line ("*So glad you could come*"), Rockefeller never looks bored or distracted, never peers over anyone's shoulder to see if someone more important might be lurking nearby.

Women, especially, respond to his blatant virility. On the road, aides warily accept trinkets from female admirers not above sharing phone numbers or room keys.

An electrifying street campaigner, Rockefeller is less adept at formal speech making, his dyslexia causing him to stumble through texts typed in 24-point letters. In private moments, he admits to being "petrified" of the printed word. In its place he has developed alternative means with which to establish audience rapport. These include the most expressive eyebrows in American politics. The Rockefeller repertoire of winks and nods is on a par with the elbow-grabbing, shoulder-crunching *abrazos* variously known as the quarter Nelson, half Nelson, and full Nelson. There are limits, however, even to his crowd-pleasing informality. When ardent fans treat his coat buttons as collector's items, Rockefeller snatches them back, as if to do anything less would yield his dignity as well.

2

A MAN WHO RETRIEVES his buttons is unlikely to surrender his principles. Although outnumbered and outmaneuvered by conservative forces supporting Arizona senator Barry Goldwater for president, Rockefeller has come to San Francisco to register a very public protest of the direction his party is taking. Convention organizers are just as determined to smother dissent in tedium. By shoving tonight's duel over the platform past the eleven p.m. prime-time window in the East, the governor's enemies can figuratively achieve what Goldwater had once proposed literally—to saw off the eastern seaboard and let it float out to sea. This was no mere figure of speech. In the closing days of the deadlocked 1960 campaign between John Kennedy and Richard Nixon, the Arizonan had offered GOP chairman Thruston B. Morton some characteristically pungent advice. Forget the urban East, said Goldwater; Nixon should concentrate his remaining efforts in Illinois and Texas. "I'd like to win this goddamned election without New York," Goldwater rasped. "Then we could tell New York to kiss our ass and we could really start a conservative party."

Now, four years later, he is tantalizingly close to his objective, an achievement all the more impressive for its cultural backdrop. Little about the famously cosmopolitan city by the bay suggests fertile ground for a conservative uprising. While Goldwater girls in sombreros and tasseled boots flood hotel lobbies and drape cable cars with banners extolling their hero, few of the lawyers, farmers, small-business owners, undertakers, and housewives attending the twenty-eighth convention of the Grand Old Party are to be spotted in the swinging nightspots of North Beach, where topless dancers writhe happily to "the swim," primly described by *Time* magazine as "a stationary wriggle cum Australian crawl." At the nearby hungry i, black comic Dick Gregory cracks wise at Goldwater's expense. ("He's so square," says Gregory, "he's up in his hotel room right now watching *radio*.")

Barely eight years have elapsed since Republicans assembled in this same city to renominate Dwight Eisenhower for a second term. Ike's mantra of Modern Republicanism had accepted much of the welfare state improvised by Franklin D. Roosevelt, while casting off the isolationist dogma of hard-shell conservatives led by Robert Taft. To Goldwater, the Eisenhower years represent "a dime-store New Deal," as evanescent as the morning fog over Alcatraz. Rejecting the accommodationist views of those he scorns as Me Too Republicans, the senator has suggested making Social Security voluntary, repealing the graduated income tax, and suspending American financial support of the United Nations should the world body admit Communist China. Goldwater frowns upon foreign aid, farm subsidies, and federal assistance to education. He tells *Newsweek* that as president he won't hesitate to drop a low-level atomic bomb on Chinese supply lines in North Vietnam or "maybe shell 'em with the Seventh Fleet." With equal pugnacity, he would direct Fidel Castro to turn on the water supplying the American base at Guantánamo, "or we're going to send a detachment of Marines to turn it on and keep it on."

Defanging these harsh pronouncements is a self-mocking humor more reminiscent of salty Harry Truman than glum Bob Taft. After a meeting with supporters this morning, Goldwater yields to photographers asking him to pose in the center of California Street. "Hurry up," he teases the cameramen. "I don't want to stand in the middle of the road too long." His followers are less bemused. Populists in pinstripes, these middle-class revolutionaries mirror the migration of talent and industry from the moneyed East to the burgeoning Sun Belt. To *Atlanta Constitution* editor Eugene Patterson, the Goldwater legions are "a federation of the fed up," as dismayed by the moral laxity of North Beach as the greed of the tax collector and the erosion of yesterday's individualistic, aspirational culture by social engineers and legislators masquerading as judges. Outside the candidate's suite at the Mark Hopkins, one proverbial little old lady in tennis shoes is gently turned away, but not before trilling, "I just wanted to tell Senator Goldwater to be sure and impeach Earl Warren."

A decade after the Warren Court banned racial segregation in the nation's schools, this is carrying coals to Newcastle. Two weeks ago, Republicans on Capitol Hill provided the margin of victory for the 1964 Civil Rights Act outlawing discrimination in public accommodations. Goldwater cast one of six GOP votes against the landmark legislation. Anything but a racist, in the 1940s the senator had taken the lead in desegregating his family's department store, as well as the

Arizona National Guard. Yet his brand of rugged individualism recoils from anything that smacks of federal coercion at the expense of local sovereignty.

Rockefeller hails from a very different tradition. The struggle for racial equality is as much a part of his family lineage as oil wells and art museums. In the nineteenth century, his grandfather, otherwise stigmatized as the prototypical robber baron, had endowed Atlanta's Spelman College to educate black women. Nelson's father, John D. Rockefeller, Jr., supported the Urban League and United Negro College Fund. As an adolescent, Nelson paid the tuition of a youngster attending Virginia's historically black Hampton Institute. When the Reverend Martin Luther King, Jr., hero of the Montgomery bus boycott, was stabbed by a crazed assailant during a 1958 visit to Harlem, the preacher's medical bills were quietly paid by Nelson Rockefeller. More recently, Rockefeller has helped rebuild Negro churches burned to the ground by southern bigots and furtively supplied bail money to sustain Dr. King and his Children's Crusade against the rigidly segregated power structure of Birmingham, Alabama. Rockefeller's New York has banned racial discrimination in the sale or rental of apartments, commercial space, and private housing developments.

On hearing it said that Goldwater is in the mainstream of their party, Nelson replies acidly that it must be a meandering stream indeed. In any event, it flows to the right if the party platform is any indication. Written to Goldwater's specifications, the document nods dutifully in the direction of "full implementation" of the new civil rights law, though avoiding the politically charged word *enforcement.* Instead, the party credo denounces what it calls "federally sponsored reverse discrimination," language seen by Goldwater's opponents as a crude appeal to resentful whites, whose existence in the millions is confirmed by a casual glance at the day's newspapers. *The New York Times* reports that the owner of the Hotel Martha Scott in Opelika, Alabama, is closing his establishment rather than "bow to tyranny" by admitting Negroes. A few days ago, three Negro youths attending a Fourth of July rally at the Atlanta fairgrounds were beaten with metal chairs. At the White House, meanwhile, President Lyndon Johnson is assigning fifty FBI agents to lawless Mississippi, where northern civil rights workers have been murdered and white-sheeted Klansmen roam at will.

White backlash is by no means restricted to the South. Goldwater backers read into the recent strong showing of Alabama's segregationist governor George Wallace in northern Democratic primaries the stirrings of a political realignment that will dissolve at last the old New Deal coalition that for thirty years has dominated American politics. It is a prospect that holds little appeal for Rockefeller Republicans. The day before the convention opened, to chants of "Goldwater must go!" Rockefeller addressed forty thousand civil rights demonstrators outside San Francisco City Hall. He shared the platform with Pennsylvania governor William Scranton, a late entrant to the nomination sweepstakes, to whom Rockefeller has turned over virtually his entire organization. Lacking any realistic prospect of victory, those who would stop Goldwater hope to provoke an incident—any incident—that might somehow reverse his momentum. In challenging his rival to a last minute debate, Scranton has issued a brutally worded letter accusing the front-runner of treating 1,308 convention delegates as "little more than a flock of chickens whose necks will be wrung at will." For good measure, Scranton flays the Arizonan for letting himself be used by "radical extremists."

"Bill Scranton didn't write this," Goldwater sputters in disbelief. He is right, although the letter does carry Scranton's signature—forged by the same overzealous staffer who was its author. Emblematic of their plight, the episode leaves party moderates looking inept and, worse, extreme. Still they press on. At yesterday's opening session of the convention, anti-Goldwater forces questioned the credentials of any delegate selected through racially discriminatory practices. "Forces are at work to expel Negroes from positions of leadership in our party," one speaker claimed. "Yeah," snarled an opponent in an unmistakable Dixie drawl, "and next convention there won't be no niggers to expel!"

The resolution was crushed on a voice vote. Undaunted, Rockefeller, Scranton, and company have devised a trio of planks taking issue with the platform as currently worded. These affirm the constitutionality of the new civil rights law—Rockefeller would go further, to demand federal voting rights legislation—denounce political extremism, and reassert, in contradiction of Goldwater's recent claim, that only the president of the United States can order the use of nuclear weapons. Under a tenuous agreement between the warring camps, the civil rights plank will be accorded the dignity of a formal roll call; the others will be shouted up or down. The ghostly Henry Cabot Lodge, Jr., Richard Nixon's running mate four years ago, compares tonight's scrimmage with the "Fair Play" amendment he and other moderates cooked up at the 1952 convention. That last minute sleight of hand had overturned a Taft majority and produced a first-ballot victory for Dwight Eisenhower.

Publicly, Lodge professes confidence in the party of Abraham Lincoln. "A Republican National Convention could never vote against a strong civil rights plank on a roll call vote, particularly on national television," he maintains. Others are less sanguine. Shaming the Goldwater legions before a mass audience requires both the audience and a sense of shame. Time, in more ways than one, is bypassing Lodge and his allies. No one understands this better than Rockefeller. At a low point in this spring's California primary campaign against Goldwater, political operative Stuart Spencer had pressed his candidate to summon that fabled nexus of money, influence, and condescension known as the Eastern Establishment.

"You're looking at it, buddy," Rockefeller told Spencer. "I'm all that's left."

3

O UTSIDE THE COW Palace, a fraying concrete vault originally built as a livestock pavilion by Franklin Roosevelt's Works Progress Administration, 150 demonstrators from the Congress of Racial Equality attempt unsuccessfully to block delegate entrances. Inside it is Thruston Morton's job, as permanent chairman of the convention, to guard against the unexpected. When the bibulous senator from Kentucky repairs to a nearby trailer command post to quench his thirst, his place behind the podium is taken by Mark Hatfield. Less than twenty-four hours ago, Hatfield made history as the first keynote speaker ever to be booed by his own party's delegates. His offense? Lumping the right-wing John Birch Society—whose leader Robert Welch, Jr., has linked Dwight Eisenhower and John Foster Dulles to the international Communist conspiracy— with the Ku Klux Klan and the Communist Party USA in a denunciation of political extremism.*

It is on the extremist issue that Rockefeller has chosen to make his stand, just as soon as those dictating the convention schedule allow him five minutes to address the nation. If left to platform committee chairman Mel Laird, a forty-one-year-old Wisconsin congressman with the proverbial elephantine memory, that won't be anytime soon. Laird has not forgotten his very public humiliation of four years earlier, when, unknown to him, the party's prospective nominee, Vice President Richard Nixon, agreed to an eleventh-hour meeting at Rockefeller's Manhattan apartment. There the New Yorker had extracted major concessions on defense spending and civil rights. The resulting "Treaty of Fifth Avenue" enraged Eisenhower and infuriated conservatives for whom Nixon was already ideologically suspect. It had fallen to Laird to placate Eisenhower and calm rebellious colleagues.

Now, with Rockefeller spurning his latest offer of compromise, the Wisconsin lawmaker is in a position to exact revenge. Laird decrees that the entire draft platform, all eighty-five hundred eye-glazing words of it, must be read out before delegates and a stupefied television audience. This alone, it is calculated, will consume ninety minutes of airtime. Convention managers have other delaying tactics up their sleeves. Even before the platform marathon, they have scheduled a pitch for unity from the last Republican president. Nothing about Dwight Eisenhower is more moderate than his admiration for Rockefeller. Earlier this year, in advance of the pivotal California primary, campaign aides had urged Nelson to pose for pictures with the old soldier, who spends part of every winter on the golf links around Palm Springs.

---

* At its peak in 1965, the Birch Society was estimated to number ten thousand members in California alone, enough to control the California Republican Assembly.

"Forget it," said Rockefeller. "That guy hates my guts." In the end, the photographs to which both men had reluctantly submitted were unusable. In private, Ike criticizes the governor for excessive reliance on problem-solving experts—hiring too many brains, he mutters, to rely on his own. Rockefeller is just as offended by Eisenhower's refusal to enter the fray on behalf of the moderate principles to which he pays lip service. For months he has dropped tantalizing hints that Goldwater is unacceptable. On more than one occasion he has called for an "open convention," without explaining the meaning of that delphic term. Now, yielding to the inevitable, Eisenhower is resolved to paper over the divisions Rockefeller would dramatize.

His speech text is intended to pour oil upon troubled waters. The unity he achieves is not what he had in mind. Foreshadowing by nearly three decades Pat Buchanan's inflammatory declaration of culture wars, Eisenhower denounces switchblade-wielding criminals, then adds a throwaway line assailing "those outside our family, including sensation-seeking columnists and commentators . . . who couldn't care less about the good of our party." Roused to fury, hundreds of delegates leap to their feet. Some stand on chairs and shake their fists at the network anchormen in their skyboxes. At the North Dakota standard, one man directs his rage at a figure more ominous than the John Birch Society or KKK. "Down with Walter Lippmann! Down with Walter Lippmann!" he bellows. The convention band pipes Eisenhower off to the buoyant strains of "We love the sunshine of his smile . . ."

4

"I NEVER LOOK BACK," Rockefeller asserts. "I'm only interested in the future." Relegated to the wings as the platform reading drones on, he disproves his claim by reminiscing about the first Republican convention he attended, the bruising 1952 conclave at which Senator Everett Dirksen of Illinois had pointed an accusing finger at Governor Thomas E. Dewey—another pillar of the Eastern Establishment—as the architect of twin defeats in 1944 and 1948. Rockefeller wonders if history will repeat itself tonight. His disquiet is shared by Arch Gillies, a delegate hunter in his mid-twenties whose unenviable task it is to sell Rockefeller south of the Mason-Dixon line. As an uphill climb, this far exceeds the forty-five-degree angle conquered by San Francisco's cable cars. At a meeting of North Carolinians, one woman, on learning the identity of his candidate, had spat at Gillies. His reception elsewhere strained the region's famed hospitality to its limits. In the end, Gillies obtained the support of exactly three southerners, one of them Rockefeller's brother Winthrop.

As the hour hand sweeps past eight, tensions inside the Cow Palace rise perceptibly, with access to the hall disputed by combatants on both sides. "I had a hell of a time getting past the goons," recalls Bill Ronan, the former dean of New York University's School of Public Administration, now Rockefeller's *chef du cabinet* in Albany. "I got through finally by showing my credentials. My credentials were a New York City police badge." Prior to going to work for the newly elected governor in 1959, Ronan had asked Rockefeller to define his duties. "Bill," he was told, "you make the spitballs and I'll throw them." Tonight it is a verbal missile that Ronan has prepared, a bristling text originally written for Theodore Roosevelt McKeldin, the Marylander scheduled to place his gubernatorial colleague in nomination tomorrow evening. The speech has been appropriated by Rockefeller himself for its punchy, alliterative prose targeting extremist tactics.

It is a subject on which he has considerable personal experience. Earlier this year, Oregon voters were showered with literature accusing the Rockefellers of aiding Russian Communists in exchange for access to that country's Baku oil fields. At a California reception, an armed man was removed from a receiving line moments before he could shake hands with, or get off a shot at, the governor. Shards of glass were dumped into the punch at another Rockefeller event. And the candidate himself is still fuming over the last minute cancellation of a speaking invitation from Catholic Loyola University in Los Angeles. Coming days before the California primary—and the birth of Nelson Rockefeller, Jr.—the action by James Francis Cardinal McIntyre was clearly timed to remind voters of the governor's divorce from his wife of thirty-two years and his subsequent remarriage to the former Margaretta Fitler "Happy" Murphy, eighteen years his junior.

Meeting the new Mrs. Rockefeller for the first time, journalist Theodore H. White is reminded of "tennis, not nightclubs; soap, not perfume; sailing, not sport cars." Shy, athletic, and outdoorsy, she is hardly a femme fatale. But Happy Rockefeller is also the mother of four youngsters, aged two through fifteen—abandoned, according to the popular press, so that she could marry her multimillionaire lover. Typical of the fallout was a late night phone call from an Associated Press reporter to Caspar Weinberger, then chairman of the California GOP and a closet Rockefeller supporter. Californians were too sophisticated to be influenced by such personal matters, said Weinberger. "I'm sure it won't affect their willingness to vote for Rockefeller."

On hanging up, Weinberger was confronted by his wife, Jane.

"I don't know about that," she said. "*I'm* a California voter, and I'm not too sophisticated to be influenced by it. In fact, *I* wouldn't vote for him."

Bill Ronan, envisioning millions of Jane Weinbergers, had delivered a blunt warning against the divorce and remarriage, telling his employer, "I don't think you're ever going to be president of the United States if you do it." Unmoved, Rockefeller replied, "This is a personal thing, I want to do it. This is *me*." The alternative was to prolong the deception of decades, denying himself the emotional support that made tolerable the brutalities of public life. His will is as formidable as his desire for validation. "If you're a Rockefeller, you never know if people agree with you because of your money," contends William Rusher, a founding father of modern American conservatism, whose reflexive opposition to the governor of New York doesn't preclude a sneaking admiration for an adversary whose entry into politics poses a unique test of character.

For the presidency is one of the few things beyond Rockefeller's purchasing power. Once, invited by a television reporter to estimate his personal fortune, Nelson likened his wealth to the silverware in the kitchen cabinet: unsure how many forks and spoons he has, he knows he has enough. Yet money is no substitute for power, still less for purpose, and Rockefeller retains enough of his Baptist heritage to regard idleness as a sin. Conceding that he could have grown up to become either a gigolo or governor, he says that the former occupation would have left him "bored to death." Only the demands of his job compel Rockefeller, a stranger to New York's theaters and concert halls, to sit through a Yankees or Mets game. "If he hit a few golf balls, it was part of the work process," says a close associate. "He worked a party much like he worked a political room." Flying from Westchester to Albany one night, Rockefeller grudgingly permitted the pilots to darken the cabin so that his fellow passengers might briefly observe the northern lights. The little group on board watched transfixed as brilliant plumes of orange, purple, and McIntosh red danced over the horizon. A minute passed. "Okay," said Rockefeller. "You can turn the lights back on, and get back to work."

5

"NELSON IS LIKE a polar bear," says George Hinman, the governor's courtly emissary to the Republican National Committee. "You shoot at him, and he just keeps coming on." His Panglossian optimism is grounded in a lifetime of beating the odds. Raised to believe himself at an intellectual disadvantage with other children because of his dyslexia, at Dartmouth Rockefeller earned a Phi Beta Kappa key through sheer application. Three decades later, he takes pride in returning within twenty-four hours every staff memo, most limited to a single page in deference to his reading disability. Not satisfied to inhabit his family's legend, Rockefeller determined at an early age to create a surpassing one of his own. Amid the economic devastation of the 1930s, when millions of square feet of Manhattan office space went begging, he found tenants for Rockefeller Center at the expense of its taller, poorer cousin on Thirty-fourth Street, soon derided as "the Empty State Building." Envious competitors likened him to his piratical grandfather John D. Rockefeller, Sr. Nelson took it as a compliment.

Appointed coordinator of inter-American affairs by FDR in 1940, the rich man's son outmaneuvered such battle-tested infighters as Cordell Hull and Colonel William "Wild Bill" Donovan. At the organizing conference of the United Nations, Rockefeller stared down the Soviet delegation, and most of his own, to enact Article 51, guaranteeing member nations the right to form mutual security alliances like NATO. Trusted advisers had counseled him against running for governor of New York in 1958. It looked to be a Democratic year, with incumbent Averell Harriman heavily favored to win a second term. As a consolation prize, a patronizing Tom Dewey had offered to make Rockefeller postmaster of New York City. Defying the kingmakers, the political upstart who couldn't pronounce the words *bar mitzvah* or explain the meaning of take-home pay, snatched the crown for himself.

Anticipating John Kennedy's restless call to "get this country moving again" following the recuperative Eisenhower years, Rockefeller converted a $400 million deficit into a $5 million surplus, albeit at the cost of higher taxes on personal income, gasoline, cigarettes, and estates. Not content to pass a groundbreaking minimum wage law, he made it state business to protect migrant workers from exploitation, even as he blocked popular demands for welfare residency requirements. Under its hyperactivist governor, New York is the first state in the nation to have its own arts council and atomic energy authority. Rockefeller's government devotes more resources to elementary and secondary education in sixty-two counties than Uncle Sam does in fifty states. The same holds true for housing and mass transit.

His youthful desire to be an architect thwarted by family expectations, Rockefeller finds compensation in a pharaonic construction program. His current preoccupation is a characteristically audacious rebuilding of frowzy Albany. Soon one hundred acres of gleaming office towers will rise atop subterranean galleries lined with the work of Rockefeller's favorite abstract expressionists of the postwar New York school. The same *folie de grandeur* will feature a performing arts center popularly dubbed the Egg, conceived one morning over breakfast as the governor placed half a grapefruit atop an empty milk carton.

"That's what I want," said Rockefeller.

Accustomed to getting what he wants, he has little patience with co-workers bold or foolhardy enough to question his priorities. "I'm not interested in what I can't do," he tells them. "I want to know how I can do what I want to do, and it's your job to tell me how." Occasionally, a lone voice is raised in objection to his latest building project or administrative innovation.

"Governor, it's a great program, but the problem is money."

"No," Rockefeller shoots back, "the solution is money. The problem is where do we get it?"

As a politician or patron, Rockefeller recognizes few limits. After a round of gallery hopping with the governor, his resident art expert Dorothy Miller remarks to a friend, "There's not enough money in the world for Nelson to buy what he would like to own . . . the fact is, he can't afford his own taste." Wooing a party distrustful of government, Rockefeller believes that the surest way to become president is to demonstrate a genius for governing. A policy wonk long before the term gained currency, Rockefeller accumulates experts, according to one of them, Henry Kissinger, the way other politicians amass delegates. In the campaign now ending, he has offered a smorgasbord of detailed proposals ranging from the space race—which he opposes, surprisingly, as a $40 billion boondoggle—to U.S. policy toward Thailand.

The basic function of government, says Rockefeller, is to transform problems into opportunities. Having the best ideas, the boldest innovations, and the brainiest associates inspires comparisons to such earlier Albany trailblazers as Theodore Roosevelt, Charles Evans Hughes, and Al Smith. It gains Rockefeller endorsements from *The New York Times* and the New York State Labor Council, as it generates unprecedented support among blacks, Jews, Hispanics, and other voting blocs off-limits to more conventional Republicans. What other GOP presidential hopeful would join forces with David Dubinsky, president of the International Ladies' Garment Workers' Union, and Jacob Potofsky, his counterpart in the Amalgamated Clothing Workers, to finance construction of seven thousand low-cost homes in Israel? In Harlem, Count Basie introduces his jazz-loving friend as someone rich enough to air-condition a cotton field, and it is hard to tell who laughs louder, Rockefeller or the tenement dwellers jiving at the Apollo Theater.

Yet his very success at home alienates the governor from Republicans nationally. Asked why he hasn't simply changed his party registration, something first urged on him by FDR, Rockefeller replies that he would much rather be pushing the GOP elephant forward than holding the Democratic donkey back. Until now, his need to woo conservatives in the hinterlands has acted as a brake on Rockefeller's free-spending instincts, producing a "pay as you go" liberalism that supplants racially charged talk of states' rights with a muscular federalism grounded in states' responsibilities. Fiscal prudence and social conscience: These are the building blocks of Rockefeller Republicanism. To many on the right, the term is an oxymoron. Already they detect in the governor's creative use of state bonding authority the seed corn of future bankruptcy. Eliminate the restraints of a presidential campaign, they argue, and there is no gauging the financial consequences of Rockefeller-style activism untethered to ideology.

From boyhood he has learned how to manipulate people, applying to his starchy father the same persuasion and guile later employed to cajole tax increases disguised as "fees" out of the New York State Legislature. Charm, however, has its limits. Addressing a breakfast gathering of straw-hatted Republican matrons in San Diego, the heart of Goldwater country, Rockefeller appeared to be making noticeable headway—until out of the corner of one eye he spotted a black waiter removing dishes. For months, would-be handlers had cautioned him to avoid the topic of open housing, an explosive issue on the California ballot and one unlikely to gain him many votes in a Republican primary. This failed to reckon with a candidate who cannot be handled. The sight of the waiter triggered an abrupt shift in Rockefeller's message. Courtship turned to confrontation, as the governor of polyglot New York extolled the virtues of color-blind neighborhoods achieved, if necessary, by state action. The room temperature plummeted. Boarding his campaign plane afterward, the candidate observed to Stu Spencer, "I guess I really blew it, didn't I?" He did not sound notably contrite.

Small wonder that a friendly onlooker, invited to assess his mercurial ally, adapts the immortal rationalization of Henry Clay: "He would rather be Nelson Rockefeller than president." In truth, he sees no reason to choose.

6

I T IS A few minutes after nine o'clock, midnight in the East, when Rockefeller bounds up to the platform to second the motion of Hugh Scott, a stocky Pennsylvanian whose bushy mustache gives him the appearance of an elegant walrus. Carrying his speech is Joe Boyd, a loyal factotum since the day in September 1958 when, during a visit to Colgate University, gubernatorial candidate Rockefeller spontaneously designated Boyd chairman of Students for Rockefeller. Boyd pleaded scheduling conflicts, an obstacle quickly resolved after Rockefeller convinced a nearby dean of the educational benefits accruing from life on a campaign bus. Boyd told the candidate he didn't have on him so much as a toothbrush. "Here's five dollars," replied Rockefeller. "You can get what you need." A slightly dazed Boyd boarded the bus; he has never looked back.

Completing the little entourage now making its way toward the podium is Major Edward Galvin, a personable New York state trooper who serves as the governor's one-man security detail. At the moment, Galvin could use some reinforcements, as people in the galleries take things into their hands. Literally. "They were throwing paper at him," Boyd recalls. Fearing more lethal projectiles, an angry Boyd hands Rockefeller's speech to Galvin and charges off into the stands. Seizing one of the ringleaders, the diminutive Boyd lifts him out of his seat. "Okay, who's next?" he shouts. An uneasy quiet is restored.

On the platform, an even nastier confrontation is only narrowly averted as Thruston Morton, professing concern for Rockefeller's safety, urges him to postpone his remarks. To drive his point home, Morton resorts to a little body language.

"You try to push me again," Rockefeller snaps, "and I'll deck you right in front of this whole audience."

His introduction elicits a thin chorus of cheers from the New York delegation, quickly lost in a swelling chant of "We want Barry!" A tight smile, not extending to his slitted eyes, creases Rockefeller's handsome face. Impassively he scans the seething hall, until his glance comes to rest upon his wife, occupying a box high above the delegates. Less than six weeks after giving birth to their first child, Happy Rockefeller wears a stricken look. A similar expression, prompted by very different emotions, spreads across the face of Goldwater's chief delegate hunter, F. Clifton White. From his fifty-five-foot trailer parked just off the floor, White can communicate simultaneously with more than two dozen separate outposts. This state-of-the-art system in turn feeds into a rooftop antenna secretly installed to prevent jamming by the other side. Now, as the heckling of Rockefeller intensifies, to the thumping accompaniment of a bass drum, White dispatches a stern order to his troops: *Cut it.*

But emotions are running too strong for White or anyone else to restrain them. Inflamed by the Scranton letter, the new Republican majority is in no mood to be lectured by Nelson Rockefeller. Having cooked his own goose, conservatives reason, Rockefeller is now serving it up stuffed with sour grapes. "Remember he was waging war on a platform they had written," explains Doug Bailey, then a Rockefeller policy researcher. "They were absolutely convinced that the only reason he was doing what he was doing was to hurt Barry Goldwater in the general election. They knew that. They *knew* that to the marrow of their bones."

Taking advantage of a lull in the derisive chorus, Rockefeller begins to speak. "During this past year I have crisscrossed this nation fighting to keep the Republican Party the party of all the people and warning of the extremist threat—" Outraged voices interrupt him. Below and to the left of the podium, Californians in bright orange Mae West jackets jeer their nemesis. Their catcalls are taken up by red-faced Republicans from Texas, Ohio, and Washington State. Over Rockefeller's shoulder, Mel Laird is scowling, though whether at the speaker or his unruly audience is impossible to tell. As the decibel count rises, Thruston Morton spreads his hands helplessly. The governor should be allowed to speak his piece, says Morton. "It's only fair and right."

The hall begs to differ. Rockefeller's mention of his Loyola speech and its "cancellation by coercion" drives a tall blond woman on the floor over the edge. "You lousy lover!" she shrieks. "You lousy lover!" A youthful Goldwater runner chimes in, "You goddamned Socialist," before adding, less than eight months since John Kennedy's assassination, "I wish somebody would *get* that fink. Maybe it would save this country."

Yet it is the man at the microphone with whom Mel Laird is fast losing patience. "That's it," he snaps. "We're going to shut him off." Morton springs for the podium, eager to bring down the curtain on what is rapidly degenerating into a national embarrassment.

Rockefeller isn't going anywhere. He doesn't control the audience, he reminds Morton. It's up to the chair to impose order. Only then, he mutters into the live microphone, can he finish what he came here to say. Congressman John Lindsay, waiting his turn to speak on behalf of the moderate civil rights plank, is astonished by the rage enveloping his fellow New Yorker. Not so a Louisiana alternate delegate who points to the explosive galleries and directs his neighbor, "Look at that. It's America up there." Glancing around him, Doug Bailey observes a deputy of the San Mateo County Police booing Rockefeller. "I looked down at his arm, he has a pistol in an unsheathed holster, and I decided from that point I couldn't dare take my eyes off that guy, because I had no idea what he was going to do," Bailey recalls.

His colleague John Deardourff is reminded of a German Bund meeting in the 1930s. To Happy Rockefeller, a collector of stray cats, the crowd more nearly resembles untamed animals. Strangely subdued in the pitching sea of noise is Alabama's delegation of Goldwater loyalists. This is due to the presence of a tall, athletic black man standing in a nearby aisle and shouting, "That's right, Rocky. Hit 'em where they live." Baseball legend Jackie Robinson is a Rockefeller Republican. He may be a hero to millions of Americans, but not even Robinson can escape the fury directed at his candidate. At one point a 'bama delegate, enraged by Robinson's chant, leaps to his feet. He is about to commit physical assault on the star athlete until he is restrained by his wife.

"Turn him loose, lady, turn him lose," bellows Robinson.

At the podium, Rockefeller is openly taunting the crowd: "This is still a free country, ladies and gentlemen." In his trailer, Clif White realizes with sickening clarity—here is the incident that Goldwater's opponents have tried all week to provoke. It comes far too late to prevent the senator's nomination. But it pins the extremist label on Goldwater and his movement more effectively than Lyndon Johnson ever could. As the minutes crawl by, the Cow Palace becomes a political slaughterhouse, wherein any prospects for Republican victory in November are rapidly expiring before a stunned television audience. "All call! All call!" White barks into his console. "If there is any booing in your delegation, stop it immediately." White's deputies hasten into the galleries to try to quiet the hooting crowd.

Behind the lectern, Rockefeller taps his foot nervously. Mark Hatfield is reminded of a bull pawing the ground. *You don't have to nominate me,* is the unspoken message delivered to the bull baiters. *But you're going to have to listen to me.* It is one of those rare moments in history when a page is visibly being turned, a past noisily discarded. The drama of personal confrontation obscures much of what Barry Goldwater's party is rejecting: the polarizing governor of New York, to be sure, and with him the presumption of regional superiority, the stranglehold of eastern money, and the liberal consensus that, for most of the twentieth century, has offended fundamentalists of various schools. In politics as in art, it is Rockefeller's fate to be surrounded by primitives.

The booing escalates as he decries "anonymous midnight and early morning phone calls. That's right. . . ." A fresh wave of anger swamps the podium as Rockefeller lashes out at "smear and hate literature, strong-arm tactics, bomb threats, and bombings. Infiltration and takeover of established political organizations by Communist and Nazi methods!" His Aldrich jaw protruding like a ship's prow, Rockefeller half shouts into the din, "Some of you don't like to hear it, ladies and gentlemen, but it's the truth." More boos. Renewed cries of "We want Barry!" At the lectern, a glowering Morton wields his gavel as a weapon. "I'm going to finish this last line," Rockefeller insists. "I move the adoption of this resolution." At last, with a flippant wave, he turns to go, appearing "for all the world like he had been given a standing ovation," marvels Mark Hatfield. "He couldn't have had a happier look on his face." The next morning, hours after all three moderate motions went down in flames, Rockefeller encountered his communications director, Hugh Morrow. "You look like the wrath of God," he told Morrow, who blamed his appearance on the previous night's fiasco, described by *The New York Times* as "Bastille Day in Reverse," and his subsequent quest for alcoholic oblivion.

"I had the time of my life," said Rockefeller.

Elsewhere this same bleak Wednesday, Bill Scranton telephones Eisenhower to inform him of plans to withdraw from the race (something Ike has been urging on him for days). Out of the question, says Rockefeller. If Scranton gets out, then he will get back in. *Someone* has to carry the moderate banner. Too much is at stake to allow their actions to be governed by bruised feelings, bogus appeals to party unity, or the specter of public humiliation. His pep talk convinces the patrician governor of Pennsylvania, mocked by detractors as the

Hamlet of Harrisburg, to let the drama play itself out. And it illustrates the central paradox of Nelson Rockefeller, who is never more appealing than when fighting for his life, even if it is his own conduct that places him in that precarious condition.

7

THE PITCHED BATTLE of July 1964 fostered an enduring image. To admirers of his principled stand, no less than those who loathed his politics and personality, Nelson Rockefeller appeared, literally, monolithic. The truth was far more complex. At once a creature of instinct and a convener of task forces, to his lawyer and friend Oscar Ruebhausen Rockefeller was a protean puzzle— the most generous, and ruthless, man he ever met. By far the wealthiest American ever to seek public office to that time, the owner of five houses, as many boats, and sixteen thousand pieces of art was without irony on the subject of his privileged position. When press secretary Les Slote left the Rockefeller operation for a job with RCA, he justified the decision to the governor by mentioning that he had a child to educate. Rockefeller put his arm around Slote's shoulders. "Les, I know exactly how you feel," he told him. "I have a young son myself."

Rockefeller could lecture Albert Schweitzer on the dysentery-fighting properties of sulfasuxidine with the same brass-plated assurance that caused him to move furniture in strangers' houses and rearrange a sound system installed by the shah of Iran in one of his palaces. His personal flamboyance was an affront to Rockefeller family discretion. In dedicating the Vatican Pavilion at the 1964 New York World's Fair, Francis Cardinal Spellman credited his friend the governor for the pavilion's existence. Smelling a story, Rockefeller aide Arthur Massolo confirmed his employer's donation of $250,000 to the project.

"Nelson, let me tell our press people," said Massolo. "They can quietly place it."

"No, no, no," Rockefeller replied in the tone of one unaccustomed to repeating himself. "That's my gift."

Yet this same self-denying philanthropist was capable of financial joyriding on a jaw-dropping scale. Once, transported with enthusiasm at a Boys Club fund-raiser, Rockefeller blurted out an offer to match the total amount raised, only to find himself owing $500,000 he didn't have. Though exerting a Pied Piper effect around children, he was as reluctant to kiss babies as to autograph the blank checks thrust at him by opportunistic bystanders. Next to Lyndon Johnson the most tactile politician of his generation, Rockefeller himself recoiled from being touched. Advancemen were ordered to maintain a distance of ten to twelve feet—not too far to rescue their charge from bores or special pleaders, whose unwelcome presence was signified by two tugs on his ear. Riding a Wyoming buckboard or submitting to a hoary initiation rite making him an honorary caveman in Grants Pass, Oregon, he delighted in the crowd's notice. Yet he shunned presidential suites for their ostentation and silenced police sirens in motorcades lest they disturb elderly ladies.

The quintessential pragmatist, supportive of fallout shelters and foreign aid alike, Rockefeller was also the most unyielding of Cold Warriors. Though denounced as a party wrecker, he refused to switch political allegiances, even for the presidency. An emotionally guarded extrovert happiest in the world of artistic contemplation; a scion of the American Establishment who was most comfortable playing the renegade: All his life Rockefeller went against the grain. If no humanitarian in the conventional sense, he could be deeply moved by the plight of society's victims. In his youth, he had decried his family's oil company for distancing itself from the Latin Americans it employed and exploited. Much later, as governor of New York, he chanced one day to fly over the blasted landscape of the South Bronx in a helicopter. Looking down in dismay, he shook his head. "There's no excuse for people to have to live like that," he exclaimed in disbelief.

The Urban Development Corporation, rammed through a reluctant state legislature in the wake of Martin Luther King's assassination in April 1968—Rockefeller was in Atlanta at the time, attending the funeral largely organized and paid for by his operatives—was a typically headstrong attempt to blend compassion, social engineering, creative financing, and eye-catching architecture. When New York's financial house of cards began to topple in the mid-1970s, the UDC went first, symbolic of an era of financial excess and overreaching government. Long before then, Rockefeller's popular image as a leader hardened to the suffering of others had been copper-riveted by the violent retaking of Attica Correctional Facility following a prisoner revolt in September 1971.

That he was in fact haunted by the deaths of thirty-two inmates and eleven guards remained a secret. The day after state police and National Guardsmen bloodily reasserted control over Attica, a friend complimented the governor on his tie.

"Red," murmured Rockefeller. "The hangman's color."

His subsequent eclipse mirrors that of his Democratic contemporary Lyndon Johnson, whose Great Society was similarly immune to doubt. Still, Johnson is admired for his civil rights record and passionate commitment to the War on Poverty. Moreover, he had the foresight to bequeath thousands of hours of tape recordings attesting to his mastery of the political process. Rockefeller left no such record. Following a bittersweet turn as Gerald Ford's vice president, he withdrew from the public arena. The humiliating circumstances of his death in January 1979, which only confirmed a womanizing streak long withheld from the public, overshadowed the accomplishments of his life. In the age of Reagan, he became the Flying Dutchman of American politics, scorned by the Left for Attica and his punitive drug laws, denounced by the Right as a spendthrift with a Hamiltonian belief in the corporate state.

In his lifetime, few took the full measure of this backslapping, blintz-eating, tax-raising force of nature, as comfortable in a union hall as an East Side deli or SoHo art gallery, who never saw a vacant lot he didn't want to build on or a problem he couldn't resolve. In truth, he was less a politician who collected art than a frustrated artist for whom the exercise of power fulfilled his creative needs. Far from the monolith of July 1964, Nelson Rockefeller was a compound, at times unstable, of opposing dynastic traditions—torn between ambition and conviction, combining in his own words "a Democratic heart with a Republican head." Even his name was a hybrid, a fitting tribute to the achievements of two nineteenth-century giants who also happened to be, at the dawn of the twentieth century, the most hated men in America.

Part One
BORN TO LEAD
1908–1936

Once a small creature came into the world. He took the largest fortune in the world and decided to enjoy it.

—HAPPY ROCKEFELLER

One

THE HOUSE THAT SUGAR BUILT

I had a grandfather—don't jump to any conclusions; this was my mother's father. He was the collector of art. He also happened to be a politician, which is a rather unusual combination, to be frank.

—NELSON A. ROCKEFELLER

1

THE HEADLINES WERE predictable. CROESUS CAPTURED. BEAUTY TO WED WEALTH. SON OF RICHEST MAN IN THE WORLD GIVES UP CHURCH AND GOES IN FOR DANCING TO WIN MISS ALDRICH. Americans in the autumn of 1901 were both fascinated and repelled by the pending alliance between the world's greatest fortune and the country's dominant lawmaker. The site of the wedding was never in doubt. Although the bride expressed her preference for a modest ceremony in a small Warwick church, and the groom would have been perfectly happy to plight his troth before a handful of witnesses in New York's Little Church Around the Corner, the choice didn't rest with Abby Greene Aldrich or John D. Rockefeller, Jr. In the Aldrich household, senatorial privilege governed; unmitigated by senatorial courtesy, it reserved all questions of importance to the imperious figure popularly labeled "the General Manager of the United States."

Virtually forgotten today, for twenty years straddling the end of the nineteenth century, Nelson Wilmarth Aldrich pulled the nation's financial strings in tandem with Wall Street confederates like J. P. Morgan and Paul Warburg. "He was so much the man of power that he never thought about his power," wrote Aldrich's official biographer. "It was natural to him, like breathing air." Much the same would be said of the senator's grandson and namesake, who emulated his appetite for command, his chronic restlessness, and his unabashed delight in art at once spiritual and sensual. "Most people don't know what they want!" Aldrich grumbled. This was not a criticism frequently directed at the senior senator from Rhode Island. The recent assassination of President William McKinley, long a champion of economic protectionism, may have been grim news indeed for like-minded Republicans like Aldrich. Yet the death of a president, however untimely, could not be allowed to interfere with the wedding of Abby Aldrich four weeks later.

If anything, uncertainty about McKinley's swashbuckling successor, Theodore Roosevelt, lent a note of urgency to the invitations Aldrich dispatched to his Capitol Hill colleagues. "Come right to Warwick and stay," he told one. "We will have a committee [meeting] right away after. There are a number of things I want to talk to you about." The new president, precluded by the requirements of public mourning from attending the nuptials, was nonetheless careful to solicit senatorial counsel as he composed his first, defining message to Congress. Aldrich took such deference as his due. As a child he had come to see himself among the elect, a status reinforced by his mother's claims of descent from New England patriarchs John Winthrop and Roger Williams. While still a newcomer to the Providence City Council, Aldrich had resolved to build a great country seat on the west shore of Narragansett Bay at Warwick. Even now, architects were drawing plans for a seventy-room château, serviced by a two-hundred-yard private railroad laid down to muffle the clatter of tradesmen making deliveries. The parklike setting already boasted a large stone teahouse, in the elegant ballroom of which Abby and John would exchange their vows.

None of the several hundred invited guests who made their way there on the morning of October 9, 1901, by steamer or special streetcar could fail to be impressed by the waterfront estate Aldrich called Indian Oaks and muckraking journalists made notorious as the House That Sugar Built. Its owner, the son of a millworker from Foster, Rhode Island, had traveled an improbable road in his sixty years. Before his tenth birthday, Aldrich passed up a visiting circus and, with the money saved, purchased the self-improving volume A Tinker's Son, or, I'll Be Somebody Yet. At seventeen, he landed a job as a wholesale grocer's clerk in the state capital of Providence. Attending evening lectures at a local lyceum to compensate for a meager formal education, Aldrich paid special attention to the rules of debate and parliamentary procedure. The attack on Fort Sumter interrupted his bookkeeping labors, but only briefly; a bout of typhoid fever earned him a discharge from the Tenth Rhode Island Volunteers garrisoning wartime Washington.

Sickened by the possibility that he might remain one of the "dumb driven cattle" constituting the bulk of humanity, Aldrich returned to Providence in the autumn of 1862. He began courting Abby Pearce Chapman, a Mayflower descendant to whom he confided a fierce resolution to achieve, "willingly or forcibly wrested from a selfish world Success! Counted as the mass count it, by dollars and cents!" The ambitious clerk dreaded anonymity only slightly less than the soul-killing drudgery of the ledger book. Within a year of their 1866 marriage, Nelson and Abby welcomed a son, christened Nelson Jr. The boy's death at the age of four devastated his parents. But it was the father who fled to the Old World, leaving Abby to console herself as he applied the healing balm of art.*

At the Parthenon ("the most sublime of all temples or churches"), Aldrich was nearly overcome by the urge to prostrate himself on the marble pavement. Rejecting the stern theology of his New England fathers, Aldrich found inspiration in the parallel universe of artistic and literary expression. Denied creative talent, Aldrich was frustrated a second time when his hopes of becoming a great orator, a modern-day Cicero, went glimmering. Politics beckoned. Elected to the Providence City Council in 1869, Aldrich served simultaneously as president of the city's Board of Trade and the First National City Bank. After making his peace with the Republican boss of Rhode Island, General Charles Brayton, he won a seat in the state legislature. His subsequent ascent to the Speaker's chair foreshadowed two terms in the national House of Representatives and three decades as a senatorial powerhouse.

His reliance on government as an engine of democratic capitalism placed Aldrich in the nationalistic camp of Alexander Hamilton, a financial wizard rejected by the very people whose democratic experiment he capitalized. Hamilton believed that only by linking the interests of the state "in an intimate connection" with citizens of great wealth could the success of the young republic be assured. For Nelson Aldrich, the line demarking self-interest from the public good was indistinct, if not invisible. From an early age, Aldrich the self-made aristocrat entertained visions of grandeur centered on Warwick Neck. Lacking the cash to realize them, the freshman senator and his growing family made do with a suite of rooms in a Washington hotel, supplemented by rented houses in Providence. Eventually there would be eleven Aldrich children, eight of whom survived infancy. These included a daughter born in October 1874 and named for her mother. As the elder Abby faded under the strain of repeated pregnancies and the physical and emotional distance imposed by Nelson's political pursuits, the second Abby came to fill the void in her father's life. Belying his reactionary image, Nelson Aldrich was a thoroughgoing progressive when it came to educating women. Thus his daughter began her formal schooling with a Quaker governess, precursor to Miss Abbott's School for Young Ladies in Providence, at which modern languages, ancient history, and art lent ballast to the traditional curriculum of dancing, gymnastics, and edifying verse.

Young Abby became a voracious reader, with a versatility extending far be-

---

* Nearly a century later, Nelson Rockefeller would suffer the loss of his son Michael on an art-collecting expedition to New Guinea. In another twist of fate, Michael had chosen to write his Harvard undergraduate thesis on his much criticized ancestor Nelson W. Aldrich—much as Michael's father had devoted *his* Dartmouth thesis to a defense of John D. Rockefeller, Sr., and his role in Standard Oil.

yond the classroom. She enjoyed baseball as much as needlework. Tutored by
her father, who entered the Senate when she was seven years old, Abby became
proficient at poker, bridge, and games played for much higher stakes. She observed his quiet domination of the Philosophy Club, a powerful quartet of senators that convened on the front porch in Warwick to deal cards and determine
the national agenda. In modern parlance a workhorse, not a show horse, even
as chairman of the Senate Finance Committee Aldrich held no press conferences, published no manifestos, submitted to no interviews. Trained observers
like the painter Anders Zorn found him inscrutable. "Of all the sitters I ever
had Senator Aldrich is the most difficult because of the expression of his eyes,"
said Zorn. "It is so hard to get."

By his stubborn refusal to concede public accountability, as in his social
Darwinist preference for the strong over the weak, Aldrich mirrored his close-
mouthed counterpart in business John D. Rockefeller, Sr. (who famously declined to answer critics by muttering, "Let the world wag"). Each man had
escaped youthful poverty with the aid of a motivating mother and his own
towering ambition. Each invited caricature at odds with his complex motivations and personal magnetism. Certainly Aldrich, a muscular six-footer with
dark hunter's eyes and a florid mustache, cut an imposing figure in Capitol Hill
cloakrooms, where a brisk nod or sidelong glance could fix the fate of legislation. At home in the shadows, according to one lobbyist, "He made no noise . . .
but when we saw him moving about, and whispering to Senator Allison, and
just giving a wink to Senator Hale and Senator Platt of Connecticut, we knew
our cake was dough."

Aldrich's domestic table was less amply furnished, his official salary of
$5,000 being insufficient to maintain two residences and raise eight children.
Too proud to live off his wife's money, in 1892 the senator announced his retirement from politics. A group of Rhode Island businessmen, grateful for his help
in consolidating a tangle of rival street railway companies in Providence, offered to make him president of the United Traction and Electric Company.
This set off boardroom alarms in the American Sugar Refining Company, the
so-called Sugar Trust, whose economic interests had never been far from the
senator's heart. Now Big Sugar filled the Aldrich wallet, beginning with
$100,000 from chief lobbyist John E. Searles, Jr. As events would demonstrate,
this was a mere down payment on Aldrich's continued services. All thoughts of
resignation from the Senate were buried under $5 million of Searles's money,
used by Aldrich to capitalize the fledgling transit company. This, in turn, laid
the foundation for a personal fortune exceeding $15 million. His sudden pros-
perity enabled Aldrich to purchase a mansion in the elegant College Hill
neighborhood of Providence and to realize his boyish dream of possessing an

estate grand enough for the Philosophy Club, if less garish than the oceanside palaces of Newport.

Each summer, the Aldriches gathered at Warwick Neck to bask in nautical breezes and navigate the choppy currents of Narragansett Bay. Besides sailing lessons, the patriarch imparted to Abby his unconcealed joy in acquiring European masters, Persian rugs, and Chippendale chairs. (One of the senator's proudest legislative achievements was the elimination of import duties on art and antiquities, thereby accelerating the Yankee plunder of Old World collectibles.) By the time she made her social debut in the autumn of 1893, nineteen-year-old Abby Aldrich was a beguiling compound of majesty and mirth. Tall and bosomy, her Gibson girl figure topped by luxuriant chestnut hair, she was outgoing, free of prejudice, and exuberantly original, with a low, slightly nasal voice that erupted in frequent laughter. Her square jaw and thick blade of a nose marked Abby as a true Aldrich. If these rendered her appearance more vivid than beautiful, they did nothing to diminish the line of suitors who bestowed on her no fewer than fifty-two bouquets. Nor was it difficult to see why: boasting confidence to spare, Abby exuded the intuitive sympathy and warmth that make a man feel more of a man.

Denied access to power by a society that placed women on pedestals to avoid dealing with them as equals, Abby channeled her political energies into such respectable substitutes as the Providence Day Nursery and the Dorrance Home for Aged Colored Women. She enjoyed an active social life. No dinner of the period was complete without a Welsh rarebit; in her diary, each was "the best I have ever tasted in all my life." On foreign travels, everything was "marvelous . . . I simply can't understand it," Abby wrote of her less impressionable companions. "They just don't enjoy *anything* so much as I do." (An indiscriminate use of superlatives, topped by the all-purpose "Faa-bu-lous," would reappear in the speech of her son Nelson.)

One evening in November 1894, Abby went to a party at the home of a friend whose father was a trustee of Brown University. There she met a shy, socially awkward Brown sophomore who had never been to a "round dance" out of fear it might offend his deeply religious mother. Simply attending the party was, for John D. Rockefeller, Jr., an act of muffled rebellion. He did not ask Abby to dance, fearing that he might slip and fall on the highly polished dance floor. Miss Aldrich compensated for his timidity. Distilling the pattern of their lives together, John would recall, "She treated me as if I had all the savoir faire in the world, and her confidence did me a lot of good."

2

I F **ABBY ALDRICH** was her father's daughter, the youth Brown classmates
called Johnny Rock was emphatically his mother's son. All his life he insisted
that there could be but one John D. Rockefeller; to the end of his days he was
known as Junior, Mr. Junior to family retainers.* The struggle for self, intensified by spiritual perfectionism, left him physically vulnerable and emotionally
stunted. Such was the inheritance bequeathed her only son by Laura Spelman
Rockefeller, the deacon's daughter with the blood of New England abolitionists
in her veins. An early advocate of equal rights for black Americans, she was just
as outspoken in promoting education and votes for women. At Cleveland High
School, her valedictorian's address was entitled "I Can Paddle My Own Canoe."

After 1859, Laura taught school and let herself be courted by John D. Rockefeller, a stone-faced high school classmate staked to the commission merchant
business with $1,000 of personal savings and an equal amount advanced
him—at 10 percent interest—by his hedonistic father, William Avery Rockefeller. The elder Rockefeller had first appeared in the countryside around Rich-
ford, New York, in 1835, displaying a slate chalked with the statement "I am deaf
and dumb." Among those taken in by his act was red-haired Eliza Davison,
who in twenty-four unremarkable years had never done an imprudent deed—
until she defied her father and wed the charismatic peddler in February 1837.
Economic uncertainty, sexual fecklessness, and public humiliation were her
reward. Cayuga ("Land of Superior Cunning") County seemed tailor-made for
"Devil Bill" Rockefeller, a charming scoundrel and self-styled "botanic physician," whose phony cancer cures were less embarrassing to Eliza than his habit
of impregnating housemaids.

After installing a girlfriend named Nancy Brown as his "housekeeper," in
two years the con man fathered four children between his emotionally battered
wife and his mistress. In 1849, a hired girl in nearby Moravia accused him of
rape. The case never went to court. Instead, Rockefeller moved his legitimate
family to the village of Owego. Then he took to the road. Abandoned for
months at a time, Eliza and her youngsters lived precariously on credit extended by sympathetic merchants. Youthful insecurity bred in her second
child, John Davison, an adult need, bordering on compulsion, to control his
circumstances and environment. John's father, superfluously, instructed the
boy to "never trust anyone completely, even me." When trading with his three

---

* According to columnist Leonard Lyons, who had it confirmed by Junior himself, the younger
Rockefeller had protested the *Social Register*'s listing of him, after his father's death in 1937, as
John D. Rockefeller. He finally convinced the editors by sending them a check for the book,
signed without the "Junior." It bounced. *New York Post*, March 5, 1953.

sons, bragged the elder Rockefeller, "I . . . skin 'em and I just beat 'em every time I can. I want to make 'em sharp."

In this, Devil Bill succeeded beyond even his gaudy imagination. As a child, John sold turkeys to neighbors and candy to his siblings. By the age of twelve, he was profitably lending money to farmers in the hardscrabble region between Binghamton and Ithaca. His father promised him $5 if the boy read the Bible clear through. Religion supplied a different kind of solace to Eliza, who trained her children to be everything her irresponsible husband was not. According to John's biographer Ron Chernow, the disastrous mismatch "left both her and her eldest son with a lifelong suspicion of volatile people and rash actions." In the autumn of 1853, the Rockefellers departed western New York for Cleveland, where John attended high school for two years, excelling at mathematics and debate. He dropped out about the time his father entered into a clandestine marriage with a New York girl half his age.

Determined to atone for his parent's outrageous conduct, the sober, systematic youth completed a ten-week course at Folsom's Commercial College. Weeks of dogged pursuit led to employment as an assistant bookkeeper with the local firm of Hewitt & Tuttle. For the rest of his life, Rockefeller celebrated the September 26 anniversary of his hiring as Job Day. Distinguishing himself for honesty and precision, John earned rapid promotion to cashier and bookkeeper. Out of his monthly salary of $25, he squeezed contributions to a German Sunday school and a Catholic orphanage. On Sundays, he rang the bell and swept the floors of the little mission church where he had been baptized a year earlier. After two and a half years at Hewitt & Tuttle, John left to establish a commodities brokerage with Maurice B. Clark and his brother. The Civil War years were lucrative ones for commission merchants like Rockefeller and Clark. For $300, Rockefeller hired a substitute to fight for him, a practice emulated by J. P. Morgan and Grover Cleveland, among others. Profiting from the conflict he thus evaded, Rockefeller supplied Union armies with salt and mess pork, all the while drawing mental pictures of vastly greater wealth to be had in the embryonic oil industry.

Spurning the precarious existence of the wildcatter, he entered the refinery business with a transplanted English chemist named Samuel Andrews. In 1867, their partnership acquired a hard-nosed negotiator in Henry M. Flagler. Rockefeller and Flagler developed a playful code for telegraphic communications built around the word *AMELIA*—four syllables translated as "Everything is lovely and the goose hangs high." Soon the wires hummed with news of a secret deal committing their firm to ship at least sixty daily carloads of refined oil on Jay Gould's Erie Railroad, in return for a 75 percent rebate from the Erie. This cozy arrangement heralded the birth, in January 1870, of the Standard Oil Company, with an initial capitalization of $1 million. Henceforth Rockefeller and Flagler employed the law of the jungle to civilize a chaotic industry blind to the consequences of overproduction.

Anything but a free marketeer, Rockefeller blamed wild fluctuations in the price of oil on ruinous competition. Practicing vertical integration before the term was known, the Standard manufactured its own paint, built its own barrels, established its own depots, warehouses, and docks. Size equaled leverage, multiplied by efficiency and an infinite capacity for taking pains. By using thirty-nine drops of solder on kerosene tins instead of forty, Rockefeller calculated, he could save "a fortune." Such attention to detail paid off handsomely: the company's first dividend was a whopping 40 percent. As quickly as he established local dominance, Rockefeller invaded the Oil Region of neighboring Pennsylvania. Inevitably, this brought him into contact with Pennsylvania Railroad president Thomas Scott and his South Improvement Company, a cartel of railroads and refiners designed to insulate oil prices and freight charges from market uncertainties. The scheme promised substantial rebates for the Standard, coupled with crippling surcharges, or "drawbacks," levied on its competitors.

Rockefeller didn't initiate the South Improvement Company. But he was at the head of the wolf pack that stood to gain from it, and he bore the brunt of popular fury when Scott's plan became public knowledge. After the Pennsylvania legislature repealed the company charter in April 1872, Rockefeller organized in its place the Central Association of Refiners—"the Alliance"—to pursue consolidation with a vengeance. Where persuasion failed, Standard resorted to harsher tactics, underselling the competition, redirecting shipments to friendlier carriers, and exploiting its stranglehold over key storage tanks and pipelines. Once omnipotent railroads now cringed before customers they had recently, regularly, bilked. Few shed tears of sympathy. "Who can buy beef the cheaper?" Rockefeller demanded with relentless Darwinian logic. "The housewife for her family, the steward for a club or hotel, or the quartermaster or commissary for an army? Who is entitled to better rebates from a railroad, those who give it for transportation 5,000 barrels a day, or those who give 500 barrels—or 50 barrels?"

3

To THE PUBLIC he might appear a buccaneer compelled to sleep with a revolver next to his bed, but at home Rockefeller exemplified the domestic virtues flouted by his rakish father. By all accounts, his marriage to Laura Spelman was deeply satisfying. Four daughters preceded the birth of the couple's only son, John Jr., in January 1874. To the prayerful Laura, her children were "my precious jewels—loaned to me for a season to be handed back when the call comes." Fittingly, John Jr.'s first memory was of the Infant Department at the Cleveland Sunday school overseen by his parents. A picture of Junior, aged two, shows a wary, unsmiling child, clad in one of the hand-me-down dresses he wore until he was eight. At the time, the Rockefellers lived on Cleveland's Euclid Avenue, locally dubbed "Millionaires Row." They also owned Forest Hill, a rambling, extravagantly ugly piece of Victorian gingerbread originally built as a homeopathic sanatorium. Senior ran it as a sort of family hotel, with a dozen friends treated as paying guests and the children working in the vegetable garden. Junior chopped wood for fifteen cents an hour.

His pleasures were solitary ones: picking strawberries, tree planting, skating on frozen ponds. The housekeeper's son was his sole playmate. On broiling summer days, the youngsters found relief in a small lake on the estate, watching as their father swam a mile without removing the straw hat he comically donned for protection against the sun. "There were two avenues that led to whatever appreciation of beauty I have," the adult Junior acknowledged. "One was music and the other was nature." The former was another legacy from his mother, an accomplished singer and pianist. Indeed, music was to the Rockefellers what books were to the Aldriches. Junior began taking cello lessons when he was seven years old. In league with his siblings, he performed in a Sunday school orchestra, a brief hiatus from the rigid Calvinist doctrine pervading Forest Hill. Mornings brought pre-breakfast prayers, with latecomers fined a penny. Friday night prayer meetings afforded more public devotionals.

In a formal pledge signed before his tenth birthday, Junior forswore tobacco, profanity, and alcoholic beverages. He kept an account book inspired by his father's famous Ledger A, a meticulous rendering of personal expenditures that became a holy relic in the saga of Standard Oil. In its pages, Junior noted twenty-five cents spent to fix a fountain pen, five dollars sent to survivors of the Johnstown flood, and two cents earned for every fly he killed. His most frequent entries were for childish charities to the houses of worship he attended with his parents. Though their spiritual roots ran deep, the Rockefellers were otherwise nomads. Senior never traveled without two books—*Optimist's Good Morning* and *Optimist's Good Night*. His confidence was well-placed. By 1879, the Standard controlled 90 percent of American oil refining and fourteen thousand miles of pipeline. As it grew in size, it mutated in administrative structure. Thirty-nine allied companies pooled their resources to form the Standard Oil Trust, a concentration quickly dissolved by the Ohio Supreme Court and just as quickly reconstituted in the grafter's paradise of New Jersey, whose corporate statutes held more water than a railroad's fraudulent stock. Thereafter, dozens of seemingly autonomous units attained a unity of purpose as the first truly multinational corporation. By 1885, it has been estimated, 70 percent of Standard's business was being done abroad.

A year earlier, JDR had paid $600,000 for a chocolate-colored house and several lots on New York's West Fifty-fourth Street, a shaded thoroughfare just off cobblestoned Fifth Avenue. A few doors away lived his brother William, part of a Standard colony that regularly gathered for breakfast at 4 West Fifty-fourth. Appearing belatedly one morning, JDR asked what was on the menu.

"We have Baptist Fish, Mr. Rockefeller," replied John D. Archbold, the sharp-tongued minister's son whose alcoholic thirst did not prevent him from becoming Senior's handpicked successor.

"And what kind of fish is that?"

"That is the kind that doesn't stay good very long after it is taken out of the water."

Archbold's jest hinted at the contradictions of his employer, for whom bread and milk were preferable to steak and champagne and whose ruthlessness was on a par with his piety. Senator Robert La Follette branded JDR the greatest criminal of his age. To the painter John Singer Sargent, he more nearly resembled a medieval saint. Rockefeller's sometime golf partner William James was nearer the mark when he called the "strongly bad and strongly good" robber baron "a man 10 stories deep, and to me quite unfathomable." One of the richest men on the planet, Rockefeller bemoaned the $300 cost of a new racing sleigh. "Very extravagant, I know," he wired Junior early in 1888, "but the sleighing is so good could not resist the temptation to buy it and hope to get the worth of our money." The chief patron of modern medical research sought relief by smoking mullein leaves in a pipe. He also championed osteopathy, the manipulative treatment of the joints that was to be adopted, with bone-crushing enthusiasm, by his grandson Nelson. Rockefeller encircled his estate with barbed wire and wished to be known as "Neighbor John." A financial mainstay of the Anti-Saloon League, he nevertheless surrounded himself with tippling associates and inebriated butlers.

Pressed long afterward to justify his grandfather's methods, Nelson Rockefeller denied that he was a lawbreaker. "But a lot of laws were passed because of him," he added jauntily. This was true enough: the Interstate Commerce Act of 1887 (opposed by Senator Aldrich) prohibited railroad rebates, while the Sherman Antitrust Act, enacted three years later, outlawed combinations in restraint of trade. Both were in direct response to Senior's brand of monopoly capitalism. In 1889, Eliza Rockefeller died under her son's West Fifty-fourth Street roof. Conspicuously absent from her funeral was Devil Bill, then living with his polygamous second family under the pseudonym "Dr. Livingston." On the eve of the ceremony, Senior directed the presiding minister to portray his late mother as a widow. In years to come, this habit of embroidery, evasion, or outright fabrication would goad sensation-seeking writers into producing accounts that strayed even further from the truth yet gained wide acceptance in the face of Rockefeller's strangely passive attitude toward public opinion.

His Midas touch presented problems of another sort. Making a fortune proved less debilitating than the flood of financial appeals lapping Rockefeller's heels wherever he went. From childhood he had believed himself divinely sanctioned to earn as much as he could, as long as his gifts equaled his acquisitions. By the 1890s, both had grown beyond individual oversight. To preserve his sanity, and intelligently distribute "God's gold," Rockefeller employed yet another Baptist minister's son, Frederick T. Gates, whose insistence on "scientific giving" directed at education, health, and social research helped to remake popular attitudes toward the Rockefellers. But not even Gates could prevent the nervous collapse that felled Senior in the winter of 1891. Under the strain of overwork, aggravated by a steady drumbeat of legal and press attacks on the Standard, JDR's health gave way. His hair fell out; almost overnight the virile Rockefeller was transformed into the mummified wraith of his later years. At first he covered his baldness with a skullcap. This gave way to a collection of wigs customized for the golf course, the church pew, and the courtroom. He wore at least as many masks.*

4

AS HIS FATHER edged toward retirement, Junior reached adolescence keenly aware of public hostility toward his family and, by extension, himself. Mail addressed to 26 Broadway, the iconic address of Standard Oil popularly known by its initials as the SOB, brought a daily quota of crank letters. Some begged, others threatened. Senior took an odd satisfaction in reading them aloud to Laura and the children at the breakfast table. For JDR's namesake, a frail youngster who attended a succession of private schools, academic success was purchased at the cost of nervous exhaustion. Choosing a college touched off a fresh crisis of confidence in the boy. "I do not make friends readily," Junior conceded in the spring of 1893. Under the circumstances, Brown, smaller if less exclusive, seemed preferable to worldly Yale.

That fall, young Rockefeller arrived in Providence, a millionaire's son on an annual allowance of $1,200. His frugality became the stuff of legend, the new college man hemming dish towels as casually as he trimmed ragged shirt cuffs

---

* "I saw John D. Rockefeller but once," Henry Ford said. "But when I saw that face I knew what made Standard Oil." Thus did the pot call the kettle black.

with a pair of scissors. Young ladies in Providence were amused when the heir to the Standard fortune treated them to a soda, before carefully noting the cost of such hospitality in his ubiquitous ledger. Though his entertaining was limited to chocolate parties in his quarters at Slater Hall, to Laura it appeared that her son was leading a life "largely given over to pleasure." Rather than sulk, "Old Ice Wagon" took stock of his situation. "Somewhere during the middle of my sophomore year I made up my mind that I had to conquer my shyness," he said afterward. "I had to get a measure of social ease if I was going to obtain any satisfaction out of my college course."

Attending the party at which he met Abby Aldrich whetted his appetite for human contact. Junior pledged a fraternity, learned the art of ballroom dancing, and developed a passion for the theater. Without surrendering his ideals, he became more tolerant of dissenters. Elected class president, he professed delight over the traditional stag cruise to Newport, boasting afterward, "Only three men had to be helped aboard. About fifteen were jolly but not unmanageable . . . when we landed at 2 a.m., again headed by the band, we marched up the hill, every man on his own feet and without aid—a thing which has never been true of a Junior Celebration before." Increasingly, the name of Abby Aldrich figured in his correspondence. He recounted visits to Warwick, "a charming spot a few miles down the bay," its charms considerably enhanced by the presence of the senator's daughter. Together they attended church and the theater, explored the Rhode Island countryside on a tandem bicycle, and canoed the nearby Ten Mile River.

Junior's election to Phi Beta Kappa helped soothe the finality of graduation. The ceremonies concluded, he repaired to Warwick for a visit with Abby and her family. Putting aside thoughts of a world tour followed by law school, the freshly minted graduate instead answered a call from 26 Broadway, which his father had all but ceased to visit. No formal announcement of Senior's retirement was issued, however, an oversight with profound consequences for JDR's reputation and Junior's peace of mind. Rockefeller père was equally silent in providing guidance to a son embarking on a career for which he had scant aptitude and less training. Maintaining a brave front, Junior assured his mother, "I am not afraid to work or do whatever is required of me, and with God's help I will do my best."

5

AMONG THE GREETINGS tendered the newest recruit to 26 Broadway, none carried more weight than the cautionary words of Frederick Gates, Senior's philanthropic gatekeeper. "In this business you have to live the life of a recluse," the older man admonished Junior. "Never make friends. Don't join clubs. Avoid knowing people intimately. Never put yourself in a position where your judgment is swayed by unconscious motives." The practical effect of this advice was to extend Junior's innate wariness of strangers to include presumed friends. One day, a Brown classmate appeared in the drab ninth-floor suite Rockefeller shared with other "associates" answerable to Gates. After a few minutes of amiable chatter, Junior inquired sharply, "Tom, why did you come in to see me?" The friend replied that he had just dropped by to see how his fraternity brother liked his new responsibilities.

"Do you know," said a visibly relieved Junior, "you are the first man to come in here to see me in two months who hasn't had an axe to grind?"

His menial responsibilities offered Junior little in compensatory satisfaction. During his first weeks at the SOB, the apprentice filled inkwells, chose a tombstone for the family plot in Cleveland, and selected wallpaper for a pink sitting room. Eager to prove himself on his father's turf, in the autumn of 1899 Junior fell under the spell of a Wall Street scam artist named David Lamar. Before he was through, the greenhorn investor had squandered almost $1 million of Senior's money. "I would rather have had my right hand cut off than to have caused you this anxiety," a mortified Junior told his father. JDR quietly paid his son's debts, in the process obligating still greater emotional ones. Even as he entered, with halting step, into his inheritance, Junior experienced financial and emotional manipulation that would one day be revisited on his own children. To work off churning emotions, he regularly reduced twenty-foot logs to firewood with a cross-buck saw, before running several miles from his father's stable to the Rockefeller home on West Fifty-fourth Street.

Romantic complications added to his turmoil. Fearing solitude less than an unhappy marriage, the young man prayed over his feelings for Abby Aldrich every day for four years. According to Abby's biographer Bernice Kert, he sought more practical direction in the pages of such frankly modern volumes as *Sane Sex Life* and *What a Young Husband Ought to Know*. In the spring of 1901, he submitted to a six-month trial separation from the woman he loved. Refocusing his energies on work, Junior stared down J. P. Morgan and negotiated a $50 million profit on the sale of his father's iron ore holdings in Minnesota's Mesabi Range. Senior rejoiced in this unexpected victory over the lordly financier nicknamed Jupiter. "Great Caesar, but John is a trump!" he exclaimed. Laura took the occasion to remind her son that "control of self wins the battle, for it means control of others."

But what of the emotional battlefield? In a wrenching soliloquy beside the lake at Forest Hill, Junior all but begged his mother for release from his self-imposed isolation. "Of course you want Miss Aldrich," she responded. "Why don't you go and get her?" On August 21, 1901, he telegraphed a request to see Abby. Two days later came news of their betrothal, though not before Junior, oblivious to the humor of the situation, dutifully assured Senator Aldrich that he could provide for his daughter's financial security. "I can't believe that it is really true, that all this sacred joy, this holy trust is mine," an ecstatic Junior told Laura. Less elevated sentiments filled the nation's press. "Miss Abbie [sic] is not pretty, but she is bright, attractive, and fond of society," hissed *Town Topics*. The *New York Telegraph* wryly noted, "It is altogether probable that the young couple will have sufficient means to keep them from actual hunger even at first."

In the first week of October, an occupying force of the nation's social and political elite filled three floors of the Narragansett Hotel in Providence. Reporters described Junior's bachelor dinner, washed down with six different brands of water served at the teetotaling groom's behest, as the costliest in Rhode Island history. Wednesday, October 9, dawned warm and mellow. Shortly after ten o'clock, most of the three dozen guests invited to the private ceremony boarded the Aldrich yacht *Wild Duck*, shadowed by fifteen Pinkerton guards on Senior's payroll. Laura Spelman Rockefeller remained in her suite at the Narragansett, confined to her bed by colitis. On reaching the Aldrich dock, passengers strode past rows of trees dressed in their autumn livery of orange and crimson, from which Indian Oaks took its name. Scarcely less colorful were the rustling silks and glittering jewels assembled at this plutocratic gathering of the clans. Outside the estate gates, reporters for Joseph Pulitzer's *New York World* jostled with rubberneckers straining for a glimpse of the arriving guests.

Junior kept his eyes fixed on Abby, stunning in an ivory satin gown and veil trimmed with orange blossoms. Shortly before noon, John and Abby were married in a seven-minute ceremony performed by the same Congregational minister who had united Nelson and Abby Pearce Aldrich thirty-five years earlier to the day. Following the exchange of vows, the wedding party left the teahouse for a nearby marquee, where hundreds of guests waited beneath a suspended garden for a wedding breakfast catered by Louis Sherry. Plainclothes detectives mingled in the crowd, gawking at gold plates from the William Rockefellers, their brazen splendor rivaled by elegant china, cut glass, Empire mirrors, and valuable paintings and engravings lavished on the newlyweds. From the Henry Osborne Havemeyers—his American Sugar Refining Company controlled half the nation's supply—came a rare ostrich fan. Senior and Laura gave Abby a set of matched pearls. Junior presented his bride with $1,000, which she immediately turned over to the Providence YMCA.

That afternoon, John and Abby returned to New York City. They spent the first night of their married life at the Plaza before embarking on a four-week honeymoon at Pocantico Hills, a tiny hamlet thirty miles north of the city, whose scenic acreage Senior had been accumulating for several years. Spurred by the arrival of the New York City and Northern Railroad in 1881, the unincorporated village between the Saw Mill and Hudson rivers appealed to the elder Rockefeller as a place "where we can live simply and quietly." Lured by the promises of an aggressive land developer ("No ferries. No tunnels. No fogs. No swamps. No mosquitoes"), Rockefeller took for his summer home the Parsons-Wentworth House, a dowdy frame dwelling of three stories near the summit of Kykuit—Dutch for "lookout"—Hill. From his spacious porch, Senior could gaze at the Tappan Zee and the anchorage where Henry Hudson had moored his *Half Moon* in September 1609.

It was to this idyllic spot, high above the Hudson's broadest expanse, that Junior brought his bride. Alone except for Senior's servants, the couple passed a "sacred month," according to the bridegroom, notwithstanding Abby's declaration "out of a clear sky and on an unruffled sea of bliss, that if I should ever strike her, she would leave me." After a brief stay with Senior and Laura, the newlyweds moved into a three-story, bow-fronted limestone residence at 13 West Fifty-fourth Street. This was to be their home for the next decade. JDR paid the annual rent of $9,600, later raised to $12,000 (at a time when the rent bill for an average American couple was $144 a year). In 1906, he bought the place outright, then transferred it to Junior for $1 "and other valuable considerations." The new owner installed an Otis elevator and centralized vacuum-cleaning system. Later he added a fourth story to accommodate his growing family.

The woman of the house, as modern as her appliances, exhibited an independent turn of mind. Allergic to sacerdotal gloom, Abby laughingly fell back on genetics to explain her irregular habits of worship. "I don't think too much church agrees with the Aldrich family," she said, citing as evidence a sister who had sustained a spinal injury while kneeling in prayer. It was hard to imagine the new Mrs. Rockefeller on her knees to anyone. Her husband's casual proposal that she keep a ledger of weekly expenses met with a flat refusal. For Junior, comfortable habits proved even harder to break. Early in his marriage, he dropped by Tiffany's. "I suppose that I shall have occasion in my lifetime to buy a good deal of jewelry," he alerted the store manager. "I know nothing about jewelry, and I would appreciate it if you would assign somebody in your concern to talk to me about it." It was vintage Junior—the application of a dry, precise intelligence to impose system on impulse.

His unromantic course in precious stones contrasted sharply with the contemporaneous inquiry undertaken by the daughter of a Pennsylvania oilman for whom memories of the South Improvement Company still rankled. "The task confronting me is a monstrous one," wrote Ida Tarbell, managing editor of *McClure's Magazine,* as she contemplated the tangled history of John D. Rockefeller, Sr. "I dream of the octopus day and night and think of nothing else."

6

L IKE AN AGING author whose fame grows in inverse proportion to his literary output, Senior gained his greatest notoriety in retirement. For this dubious achievement, he had Senator Aldrich to thank. Nearing the zenith of his influence over the nation's finances, the Republican leader of the Senate was regularly castigated in print as J. P. Morgan's Washington floor broker, the snarling "Head of It All." Following a particularly virulent assault on his nominal ally, Theodore Roosevelt coined the derisive term *muckraker*—lifted from *Pilgrim's Progress*—to pillory Aldrich's assailants.* It was after reading a muckraking assault on Aldrich and the Sugar Trust that Ida Tarbell conceived *The History of the Standard Oil Company,* a nineteen-part series published by *McClure's Magazine* beginning in November 1902 and issued two years later as a 550-page book.

Understandably loath to accept this scandalous family portrait, Junior imagined instead a "long-suffering and charitable father" floating serenely above his critics. The truth was more complex. Amid the uproar provoked by Tarbell's book, the American Board of Commissioners for Foreign Missions returned as "tainted money" a $100,000 Rockefeller gift it had actively sought. Contemporaneously, Junior drafted a letter for his father's signature formally transferring a block of Standard stock to the General Education Board, a hugely ambitious charitable venture drawing on Junior's scientific humanism, Laura's passion for color-blind instruction, and Senior's exploding fortune to promote educational improvements "without the distinction of race, sex, or creed." As originally worded, Junior's letter included a passing statement relieving the GEB of responsibility for criticisms directed at its benefactor. This was too much for Senior, who administered a bitter tongue-lashing to the secretary whose services he shared with Junior, then resumed his rant a few days later, meeting Junior in a Jersey City railway station for what onlookers described as an unusually solemn discussion.

---

* "He is a kingpin in my game," TR told journalist Lincoln Steffens. "Sure. I bow to Aldrich . . . I respect him, as he does not respect me. I'm just a president, and he has seen lots of presidents." Such exposure had done little to make Aldrich sympathetic to the latest president's brand of reforming conservatism.

The incident sheds light on the treacherous ground Junior was forced to navigate. "I did not seek nor choose to be the recipient of great wealth," he once remarked. "It has not meant the greatest happiness." Coming from his unreflective father, such a claim would have been unthinkable. Junior, however, was cut from a different bolt of cloth. Many of the grinding self-demands he made, and the ill health they fostered, can be attributed to conflicting drives so intense as to amount to cognitive dissonance. Outwardly, he wanted nothing more than to please an idealized parent. As eager to black the old man's shoes as to advance his larger interests, over time Junior became *plus royaliste que le roi*, especially on the subject of money. Singling out for criticism a Forest Hill gardener whose passion for rosebushes exceeded his fiscal prudence, Junior tattled to his father, "He has not learned our ways. He seems to feel that because we have money, it is not necessary to economize and spend every dollar to the best advantage."

Beneath his crust of prim rectitude seethed emotions barely comprehended. At his fiftieth class reunion, Junior would declare that only in college had he enjoyed "a completely independent personality." Desperate to justify his father's love and generosity, he found it necessary to simultaneously defend the oil tycoon *and* redeem the Rockefeller name for, and through, his children. The incessant conflict between filial loyalty and a pure conscience left Junior divided and perpetually unsatisfied. Senior urged his son to delegate more ("You know I have shirked all my life"). This overlooked the younger man's eagerness to lose himself in minutiae. Just as JDR had elevated cheeseparing to the level of principle, so Junior would make a fetish out of details, telling his children and anyone else who would listen, "It's the last 5 percent that counts."

This perfectionist creed was applied to loved ones no less than to his professional interests. However many times Abby assured him of her devotion, for example, it was never enough. "He wanted her to be with him always—if not immediately by his side, then immediately available," recalled their son David. "He wanted to retreat with her into their own private circle of two." Junior found sanction for his possessiveness in a higher authority. "I'm sure the Lord made me with special needs which you alone can supply," he wrote Abby, "and I know that after living so many years without you He intended that when He gave you to me we should always live constantly together." The November 1903 birth of his daughter, Abby, known within the family as Babs, did nothing to diminish Junior's neediness. Adding to the strain of fatherhood was the first great construction project of a life in which building was a kind of mania. Where other men of his class might flash a Phi Beta Kappa key or diamond stickpin, Junior went nowhere without his folding four-foot rule. Years later, he startled a New York real estate developer by confiding, "You know, I envy you. Yes, I envy you. You have built great monuments to leave behind you."

After a fire destroyed his parents' country house in 1902, Junior and Abby hastily refurbished a nearby property as a temporary home. Just as rapidly, Junior began to imagine a far grander dwelling, one befitting his father's historical accomplishments, crowning the five-hundred-foot summit of Kykuit Hill. "Father had no conception of art or beauty," said the younger man in the closest he ever came to outright criticism. Privately, he dismissed his parents' houses as "excrescences." Now father and son commissioned rival firms to create the new Kykuit. Senior's preference for Queen Anne traditional, with its steeply pitched tile roofs and modest interiors, clashed with the design produced by Delano & Aldrich, Junior's architects of choice. When this proved too opulent for the old man's liking, there emerged a two-and-a-half-story hybrid, girdled with a broad wooden veranda, topped with dormers, and sheathed in fieldstone quarried on the estate.

Fresh differences followed the selection of celebrated landscape architect William Welles Bosworth to level the rocky hilltop and create a 250-acre park surrounding Kykuit. Initially budgeted for $20,000, Bosworth's neoclassical terraces and gardens eventually consumed $1.3 million of Senior's fortune. Under mounting pressure at work and on the work site, Junior's health gave way in the autumn of 1904. Accompanied by Abby and infant Babs, he spent six months recuperating in the south of France. For many months after his return, Rockefeller avoided office routine. Officially, his chronic insomnia and migraines were blamed on overwork. That he had, in fact, suffered a nervous breakdown remained a family secret for half a century. By the following summer, Junior's recovery appeared complete, but he never fully escaped the specter of invalidism or the periodic rest cures, sanatorium visits, and vigorous outdoor exercise prescribed for his brittle nerves.

In March 1906, Abby gave birth to the couple's first son, John 3rd. Newspapers welcoming "the Richest Baby in History" speculated on the size of his adult fortune. Yet even as Andrew Carnegie sent telegraphic congratulations ("Aldrich-Rockefeller combination should count"), a zealous army of process servers prevented the infant's paternal grandfather from visiting "Demi John." Inspired by Ida Tarbell, the Roosevelt administration had launched a wave of antitrust suits aimed at Standard Oil; in addition, half a dozen states were pursuing independent claims against the company. To be sure, there was in TR's outrage an element of political calculation: to light fires under a resistant Congress, the president deftly leaked word of Rockefeller opposition to his proposed Bureau of Corporations. Two months after TR asserted his intention to bring Standard Oil to justice, Junior sent his father-in-law the proposed charter of a $100 million foundation bearing the Rockefeller name, audaciously designed to "promote the well-being of mankind throughout the world." Senator Aldrich promised assistance in obtaining federal authorization for the massive philanthropy.

But Aldrich's power was on the wane. With his genius for making politically useful enemies, Roosevelt found the senator from Rhode Island a useful foil. In happier times, Roosevelt had paid a visit to Indian Oaks, where Aldrich and his cronies feigned camaraderie over meals at the boathouse. "The President telegraphed for the Senators and they all departed this morning," Abby wrote Junior from Warwick in August 1903. "They talk about him as if he were a spoiled child who needed constant watching." That Aldrich should flourish in the years before the Seventeenth Amendment vested election of United States senators in the electorate at large, rather than purchasable state legislatures, was no coincidence. Before relinquishing his Senate seat in 1910, he formulated a first draft of the Federal Reserve banking system. Less constructively, he rammed through Congress the Payne-Aldrich Tariff Act, a protectionist charter violating his own party's promises. Thus did Aldrich hasten the fatal Republican division of 1912, with consequences still being felt half a century later, when his grandson was to unfurl the banner of progressive Republicanism once raised by Theodore Roosevelt.

"He serves his party best," said TR, "who most helps to make it instantly responsive to every need of the people." Here, Americanized, was Disraeli's One Nation brand of property-owning democracy, a canny conservatism that courted the masses by righting injustices before they could spark revolution. Reform exacted a price, however, one from which not even reformers were immune. Amid the rapidly shifting political sands of the Progressive Era, securing a federal charter for the Rockefeller Foundation was a long shot at best. First the *New York World* ferreted out salacious new details of Devil Bill Rockefeller's double life. Then William Randolph Hearst, faithful to his scandalmongering instincts, used purloined letters to reveal Standard's crude purchase of Ohio senator Joseph Foraker and other politicians. The same press lord assailed both Aldrich and his son-in-law for their participation in a syndicate exploiting mineral and rubber concessions in the Belgian Congo. Embarrassed by his involvement in the scheme, promoted by missionary friends as a way of improving the spiritual and material lot of the African native, Junior unloaded his shares in the American Congo Company.

By 1908, he stood at a personal crossroads. The prospect of life as a lobbyist or businessman held no allure. "All the money in the world will not take the place of friends," he insisted. "Riches breed but sin." Fortunately, he had in Abby the ideal partner with whom to fashion an alternative design for living. For years she had urged him to abandon his weekly talks before the Men's Bible Class of the Fifth Avenue Baptist Church. "The leadership of the class is a great thing for John," Senior gibed mirthlessly, "but pretty hard on the boys." The opposite was more nearly true, as Junior lavished three nights a week on the preparation of homilies ridiculed by a hostile press. These included "How to Get On in the World" and "Opportunity," the latter illustrated by the five foolish virgins who failed to conserve their oil.

Whatever Junior's shortcomings, no one ever said he lacked courage. Public criticism only made the earnest lay preacher cling all the tighter to his ecclesiastic soapbox, at least until the latest unsavory revelations about Standard campaign contributions left him distraught and groping for new directions. His resignation from the Bible class marked a turning point as critical in the Rockefeller story as Job Day had been to JDR's career. It confirmed as well a subtle shift in family dynamics, as Junior came increasingly to rely on the judgment of his wife and to develop a grudging respect for her eclectic tastes in art, politics, and companions. Senior may have founded the family fortune, but it was Junior and Abby—together with their children—who would make the Rockefeller millions respectable.

Two

OIL AND WATER

I can think of nothing less pleasurable than a life devoted to pleasure.
—John D. Rockefeller, Jr.

If I had my way, I really think I should like to give a party every day.
—Abby Aldrich Rockefeller

1

AMID THE SMOKING ruins of her Pocantico home, Laura Rockefeller had found consolation in the example of her resourceful daughter-in-law. "A man is fortunate who has a brave and uncomplaining wife, one who can 'Bear up under her burdens,'" she advised Junior. "This helps the most hopeless of situations and I am not surprised that it has been true of Abby." A local doctor observing the newest Rockefeller's casual embrace of strangers offered a more colloquial assessment. "Pay attention to the filly," he said. "She's the one really worth watching."

Long-suffering or life-enhancing? Though both assessments have validity, the latter is closer to posterity's view of Abby Aldrich Rockefeller as a bubbling protofeminist synthesizing the nobler qualities of Margaret Sanger, Mabel Dodge, and Auntie Mame. Both fun and formidable, Abby frowned on flatterers and self-promoters, "chairs made for lounge lizards," *Time* magazine, and Gothic architecture "obviously out of keeping with time and place." Equally at home chairing the Good Fellowship Council of the Park Avenue Baptist Church or stringing spaghetti around her fork at the Italian Welfare Club, Abby was the kind of employer who could instruct her housekeeper over breakfast to "come in and laugh with me before we get started on this day. It's going to take some laughing to get through." No one in her adopted family had Mrs. Junior's fizzy exuberance, much less her sense of fashion as performance art. Her most flamboyant hats were chosen as stage props, Abby readily acknowledged, "to cheer people up." By the same token, she wore fussy daytime gowns from Worth or Patou so that her children, on returning home from school, "won't think their mother is slipping."

As Junior retreated into good works and the strict enforcement of rules governing his offspring, it fell to Abby to raise a family whose sense of duty did not smother its capacity for enjoyment. One evening, the Rockefellers attended the surreal Broadway comedy *Harvey,* the loopy protagonist of which conversed with a six-foot rabbit invisible to everyone else. As the curtain fell, the whimsically challenged Junior turned to his wife and asked what, if anything, the show proved. "I told him it proved the importance of having pleasant people in the world," Abby replied. "Though the principal character was a drunkard, he was so very delightful that you have the feeling all the time that perhaps to be pleasant and amusing might be more important than to be sober and disagreeable."

Like any successful marriage, Abby's was both a great love affair and a dependence of baffling oddness. However great the contrast between her freespirited ways and Junior's emotional constipation, their core convictions harmonized. Each was keenly attuned to natural and man-made beauty. Neither tolerated shoddiness or self-indulgence. The couple's strictures against racial or religious bigotry had historic repercussions, as did their unyielding opposition to divorce. "Marriage is an art and not an experiment," Abby maintained. For her, the rough was decidedly outweighed by the smooth. Even after twenty years, physical separation from Junior seemed "to take all of the color out of life. . . . Nothing is as interesting or as beautiful when not shared by you."

For all her joie de vivre, there was a puritan streak to Mrs. Junior, as evidenced one rainy day when a Pocantico estate worker encountered the squire's lady retracing her steps along the road leading to the village schoolhouse. She had left her umbrella in a classroom, explained Abby, and was going back to retrieve it.

The laborer offered to get it for her.

"No, thank you, Tom," Abby said with grim gaiety. "I must punish myself for forgetting!"

Perhaps it was this harsh introspection that inspired her mother-in-law's praise. Laura Spelman Rockefeller, herself a feminist in a man's world, understood that men derived strength from the women they married and that this endowed their wives with an element of command wielded most effectively from the shadows. By deploying classic weapons of wifely subservience, flattery, and eroticism, Abby made herself at once indispensable and irresistible. Married less than a year, she wrote Junior, "It was dear of you to telegraph me, sweetheart, I wanted to hear from you. When I woke up this morning I found that I had your picture in my hand and then I looked out and found the sun shining and you didn't seem quite as far away as I was afraid you would be." Later in the same letter, Abby described some elegant Mission-style furniture on which her heart was set. Indeed, she intended to ask the artist to create some for the Rockefeller home, "if it doesn't cost too much. Don't you think it would be attractive in the library?"

The discovery that Junior had deposited $900 in her bank account elicited fresh expressions of gratitude, mixed with guilt. "I am so ashamed," Abby wrote. "I feel like a defaulter." Her letter crossed with a wistful appeal from "a sleepy boy who is writing to you tonight on his way to his solitary bed." To most people, the austere John D. Rockefeller, Jr., appeared an unlikely lothario. Appearances were deceiving: racked by self-doubt in so many fields, the highly sexed Junior was not above pinching his wife's legs on a stairway. Because she released him from an imprisoning reserve, he loved Abby unreservedly. Riding a lonesome train in June 1908, Junior poured out his feelings. Putting aside a forty-page article on foreign missionaries, he turned to the far more absorbing occupation of "writing to the girl I love. . . . It grows harder rather than easier, for you see, I keep loving you more and more. But that is your fault; I can't help myself and yet I have to suffer as a result of it. . . ." The next day, Abby answered in kind. "To be with you, dear, gives me all that makes life worthwhile and nothing else takes its place, not even the children or all the luxury with which you surround me; it is all incomplete without you."

2

"HAVE YOU HEARD that we are to have a present in the shape of another member added to the family this July?" Abby wrote her sister, Lucy, early in 1908. "I'm rather hoping that it may be a boy. I am afraid that little John may be spoiled." John, like his sister, Babs, had begun life in a second-floor bedroom at 13 West Fifty-fourth Street. This time, however, Abby's confinement would take place far from the city's steaming alleys. At the prompting of her Manhattan doctor, who summered in the Maine community of Blue Hill, the Rockefellers decided to spend the hot-weather months in the nearby coastal resort of Bar Harbor, a popular watering hole since painter Frederic Church in the 1850s had caused a sensation with his *Fog off Mount Desert*.

No less than the Rockefeller marriage, the fifteen-mile-long island offered a study in contrasts. Here restless ocean and ancient mountains locked in scenic embrace. Eroded by time and prehistoric glaciers, looming humps of pink granite nurtured flowering shrubs and spruce pine, wild plum, and cherry trees. Dense stands of balsam fir perfumed the salt air, and orchids grew incongruously in brackish marshland. From the south side of the island, stony fingers reached into the Atlantic to enclose Northeast Harbor, Seal Harbor, and Otter

Cove. Summer southerlies made for a sailor's paradise, notwithstanding a mercurial climate and gauzy fogs obscuring the fifteen-hundred-foot summit of Cadillac Mountain. The advent of steamship service opened up the island's craggy isolation to rusticating educators like Harvard's Charles W. Eliot and wealthy summer residents pursuing what one called "the simple life on a grand scale." Wealth and eccentricity went hand in hand on Mount Desert. One summer resident, angered by local press coverage of his dinner parties, spent $1 million to create his own newspaper. A more established publisher, Joseph Pulitzer, being averse to noise of any kind, built a retreat locals dubbed the Tower of Silence to escape the mordant bleat of a foghorn on nearby Egg Island.

Fifteen years after his initial visit to Mount Desert, Junior was glad to return to a place that promised relative privacy without discomfort. For his wife, the island's pebbly beaches and fogbound seascapes revived memories of Narragansett Bay and joys soon to be shared with her own children. In the third week of June, a heavily pregnant Abby boarded a sleeping car of the *Bar Harbor Express* streaking north from Grand Central Terminal to Bangor, thence east to the Maine coastline, jagged as cut glass, and a bracing ride on the Maine Central Railroad steamer *Norumbega* across the chill blue waters of Frenchman Bay. At the dock, a horse-drawn buckboard waited to transport the Rockefellers to their rented quarters on Wayman Street, a roomy shingled dwelling built by a wealthy Boston merchant named J. Montgomery Sears.

As Abby endured the penultimate weeks of her pregnancy, Junior shuttled between Mount Desert, his New York office, and Kykuit, then in the final stages of construction. Early in July, expressing herself "very anxious to *see* the new baby," Abby asked her husband to obtain a copy of the recently published *On the Training of Parents.** Junior was present when, shortly after noon on a cool, misty Wednesday, July 8, Dr. Allen Thomas extracted a nine-and-a-quarter-pound male from Abby's womb. By prearrangement, the squalling infant was named Nelson Aldrich Rockefeller in honor of the senator whose namesake son had died forty years earlier. There was more to the gesture than a daughter's sentimental attachment. "I have done my duty by this family," Abby reputedly said at the time of Nelson's birth. "I have given you a John 3rd. This one is mine."

Thus marked from birth for high achievement, Abby's second son—and political surrogate—would occupy a unique place in her affections. This was far from the only ace he drew in life's lottery. "My mother said to me . . . you can

---

* Whose author asserted that "the only way of escape from disorder and confusion is not by adjusting the child's environment to him, but by adjusting him to his environment," a lesson manifestly lost on Abby Rockefeller's second son.

grow up to be president," an adult Rockefeller asserted. By coincidence to everyone but the newborn, who glimpsed the hand of destiny in the timing of his arrival, July 8 also happened to be Senior's sixty-ninth birthday. Both events found their way into the national press, though overshadowed by the Democratic convention in Denver that awarded William Jennings Bryan his third and final presidential nomination. True to his populist roots, the Great Commoner made an issue of corporate corruption, going so far as to demand the jailing of John D. Rockefeller, Sr. Only somewhat less punitive than Bryan, his Republican opponent, William Howard Taft, was equally vocal in opposing the Rockefeller Foundation charter ("the proposed act to incorporate John D. Rockefeller").

Dynastic thoughts of a different order consumed the occupants of Sears Cottage. After comparing pictures of his "very well and good baby," Junior allowed, "I think I did pretty well if that is the poorest." Truth be told, the birth of a son was something of a distraction from Junior's other act of creation that summer. As Abby read Trollope to the slap of ocean waves, the new father played clerk of the works at Kykuit. While she fretted over fluctuations in Nelson's weight, Junior obsessed about electric fixtures, Aunt Lute's rosebud wallpaper, and a pair of beds from Tiffany's. When Senior and Laura finally crossed the threshold of their new home for the first time in October 1908, it was as if roles had been reversed, with Junior the beaming parent proudly displaying his architectural offspring. Reacting much as anyone does when confronted by an ugly baby, the elder Rockefellers cooed convincingly, until they were out of the nursery. Built to placate everyone, Kykuit satisfied almost no one. Laura disliked the cramped third-floor guest rooms. JDR objected to smoking chimneys, noisy elevators, and the distracting racket of a service entrance two floors below his bedroom window. After living with its inadequacies for two years, the owners decided to reconstruct Kykuit along radically different lines.

3

AT EIGHTEEN MONTHS, Nelson impressed his aunt Lucy as "the flower of the family," an assessment Abby delighted in quoting. In the autumn of 1911, it was three-year-old Nelson whose words she repeated, telling the absent Junior that she, too, would like to "feel" him. After taking Nelson and his infant brother, Laurance, for a drive around the Pocantico estate, Abby reported that both had been very good, "particularly Nelson, he is so observant." He could hardly fail to notice the building crews that made his childhood a string of lavish construction sites. Bracketing his first five years was the reinvention of

Kykuit, as William Welles Bosworth and Ogden Codman transformed a Gallic–Georgian–Colonial Revival residence into a Beaux-Arts mansion of four stories and forty rooms. Finally completed in 1913, the new Kykuit looked as if Andrea Palladio had imagined a French château sitting atop an English garden.

When Junior's son, as governor of New York, gutted downtown Albany to construct a government complex derided as Brasilia on the Hudson, he was merely upholding family tradition. From his earliest years, Nelson had seen nature yield to human will and wealth. Next to golf, his Rockefeller grandfather's favorite pastime was improving on God's landscape, moving ninety-foot trees as casually as he relocated St. Joseph's College and the New York Central Railroad tracks whose sooty exhaust marred his time on the links. Nelson was barely out of his infancy when the imposing forecourt of Kykuit was expanded by five hundred feet, a feat of engineering made possible through twenty thousand cubic yards of fill held in place by a massive stone retaining wall.

With the birth of Laurance in 1910 and Winthrop in 1912, the Rockefellers outgrew their Manhattan townhouse at 13 West Fifty-fourth Street. Junior hired Bosworth to construct a nine-story replacement across the street. First occupied in the fall of 1913, the new residence contained a gymnasium, infirmary, rooftop squash court and playground, library, drawing room, and stately entrance hall furnished in English Chippendale and Louis Quinze antiques. The largest private home in New York City, 10 West Fifty-fourth easily accommodated eight Rockefellers, their domestic staff, and an unending parade of visiting royalty, church leaders, educational visionaries, and medical pioneers. Nelson remembered the place as an ongoing seminar in public responsibility, replete with table conversations about the Social Gospel movement championed by Junior and the crusade being waged by the Rockefeller Sanitary Commission to eradicate the southern hookworm. The Polish virtuoso Ignacy Paderewski played the piano in the second-floor music room. Of far greater entertainment value to a small boy was the appearance of former president Theodore Roosevelt, onetime scourge of Standard Oil and more recently a progressive-minded renegade from the GOP Right. Other children might have been intimidated by the blustery dervish whose voice and personality monopolized any space he invaded. Not Nelson. Perched on TR's lap, he demanded to know how the aging big-game hunter had transported giraffes from Africa to American shores. Roosevelt explained that a complicated set of pulleys and levers made it possible to lower the animal's long neck just enough to clear railroad tunnels.

Ten West Fifty-fourth was both a celebrity magnet and a museum to be lived in, its paneled halls supplying an elegant backdrop for Junior's Polonaise rugs and porcelains from the Ming and K'ang-hsi dynasties. Exacting in all things, he derived his greatest pleasure from artistic and architectural detail. "I can see him now sitting on the floor with a magnifying glass," Nelson recalled late in life. Finding cracks in the porcelain that had been painted over, Junior scraped out the paint with a knife before returning the flawed treasure, along with his demand for a refund, to the dealer from whom it had been purchased. "And he had a very good eye if anything was an inch off center," boasted Nelson, who exhibited this same obsessional trait as he strode through Kykuit's rooms, frequently pausing to right a painting or move an ashtray a fraction of an inch. In time, an adjoining house on West Fifty-fourth was purchased and converted into display space for the Gobelins and French Gothic tapestries favored by Junior. Abby, more catholic in her tastes, began collecting Japanese prints. She went on to assemble primitive art, Far Eastern sculpture, American works both primitive and contemporary, "and then the whole modern European period, from the post-Impressionists," said Nelson. "She had a gallery in the house [with] changing shows. And so I grew up in this atmosphere—and it is a very exciting atmosphere in which to grow up."

From West Fifty-fourth Street, the family shuttled each spring and fall to Abeyton Lodge, a sprawling residence in the shadow of Senior's manor house at Pocantico. Summers meant Mount Desert. After renting for two years in Bar Harbor, Junior spent $26,000 to purchase the Eyrie, a mock Tudor cottage near the village of Seal Harbor. Nelson was seven when his father set to work enlarging the place, the remodeling of which continued, cathedral-like, for decades, until the house stretched 160 feet along the summit of Barr Hill, under a roof dressed with five railroad cars of slate. As a college student, Nelson watched in admiration as Abby juxtaposed Korean tomb figures and yellow tiles from Peking's Forbidden City in a walled garden of surpassing beauty. Asked by a reporter years later how long he had harbored presidential ambitions, Rockefeller replied, "Ever since I was a kid. After all, when you think of what I had, what else was there to aspire to?"

This should be weighed against a competing desire confided to his notebooks. "I would like to have the Sistine Madonna," Nelson scribbled before his eighth birthday. "I would hang it in my dining room. I would not sell it for all the money in the world. I would not give it to the Museum." Politics and art—even then they defined his world. While still a teenager, he looked on as John Singer Sargent painted his grandfather's portrait in a barn at Pocantico. By his own admission, his "first childhood love" was a marbled bodhisattva, or enlightened soul, from the Tang dynasty, displayed in the elegant reception hall of 10 West Fifty-fourth. Nelson asked Abby to leave it to him in her will. She readily complied.

4

ARTIFICE, NO LESS than art, shaped his formative years. Behind intricate wrought-iron gates patterned after Hampton Court, Nelson watched his parsimonious father turn off lights to avoid waste. At other times he availed himself of the grandest of all the Rockefeller "Playhouses," a $500,000 complex near Abeyton Lodge that resembled nothing so much as a French Norman farmhouse on steroids. Besides squash, basketball, and tennis courts, the Playhouse held a swimming pool, as well as billiard and card rooms. On its completion, the inhabitants of Pocantico Hills were treated to a party at which Nelson and his brothers set pins in the two-lane bowling alley customarily reserved for them and their friends. These semi-feudal surroundings supplied the backdrop for a game of financial "let's pretend." As an eight-year-old, Nelson received his first weekly allowance of twenty-five cents. Of this he was encouraged to save a third and deposit an equal share in the collection plate on Sunday. But even this pittance was conditional, subject to a thorough auditing of financial accounts every Saturday morning in Junior's study. Items unaccounted for resulted in five-cent penalties, while perfect accuracy in record keeping gained a nickel reward.

More intimidating still was Junior's unvarying query "What have you accomplished this week?" Every account of Rockefeller's youth repeats the escapade of a baseball lost through a manhole and Nelson's descent into the sewer, crowbar in hand, to retrieve it. "How else was I to get the baseball back?" he asked. "How could I know what was down there if I didn't climb down?" Cited as evidence of Nelson's insatiable curiosity, the story actually illustrates his chronic lack of funds. Having paid a quarter for the ball, he dreaded his father's lecture about the price of such carelessness. "I had a very sharp focus on making money," Nelson would remember. Together with his enterprising brother Laurance, he padded his income by catching mice, killing flies, pulling weeds, and shining shoes. The pair hit on the idea of marketing homebred rabbits to the Rockefeller Institute. Lacking capital, "we went to the Institute and we borrowed a mother rabbit that was about to have babies." The scheme went awry after the first reproductive group turned out to be males. The boys turned for assistance to a night watchman, "a very nice black gentleman," who differentiated the sexes for them. A subsequent attempt to sell pigeons fell short, said Nelson, "there being less enthusiasm for squabs." Even the rabbit trade was abruptly curtailed one winter morning after a murderous fox leapt a low fence and Nelson found the half-eaten carcasses of baby rabbits frozen in the snow.

Gardening was less traumatic. Nelson and Laurance hawked homegrown pumpkins, at thirty-five cents apiece, to local grocers. As an adolescent, the older boy earned date money by picking Kykuit's rose gardens clean of beetles.

Fittingly, one of his earliest letters was a promissory note cosigned by his mother promising $1 if he didn't miss a single day of school that year. Not to be outdone in mercenary perfectionism, Junior dangled the promise of $2,500 to any of his children who refrained from smoking until reaching the age of twenty-five (a reward claimed by Nelson and David). The same Pavlovian incentives were applied to long tramps through the woods at Pocantico or along the Maine shoreline, with Junior withholding lumps of maple sugar or chocolate until the hiking party reached its destination. Pocantico afforded Junior a measure of compensation for a life otherwise beyond his control. Here and at Seal Harbor, he insisted on filling his children's days with tightly scheduled activities, rather like a summer camp. "Deviations from the plan were not greeted with plea-sure," wrote David Rockefeller. "I remember his saying, when someone pro-posed a new activity, 'But we *planned* something else.' For him that was reason enough not to do it." A corollary to this uncompromising attitude was a horror of idleness. If he thought his progeny insufficiently busy, Junior clapped his hands in wordless reprimand.

Like most parents, he reproduced what seemed the best of his childhood. Long after declaring war on narrow sectarianism, the public face of the Inter-church World Movement enforced under his own roof the cheerless religiosity of his youth. Each morning at seven forty-five, male members of the family gath-ered in Junior's study for prayers and Bible verses, the latter printed on note cards helpfully supplied by Abby (who remained heathenishly in bed). Grace preceded every meal. The Sabbath was rigorously enforced; not until his children were fully grown did their father permit them to play tennis on the Lord's day. And no Sunday evening was complete without "a sing" in the music room, where govern-esses and tutors joined their employers in performing favorite hymns.*

A poem by eight-year-old Nelson shines a light on this training in virtue:

> *If I want to be happy*
> *And quick on my toes,*
> *I must bit my food slowly*
> *And breathe through my nose.*

And so it goes, through seven stanzas of childish self-improvement, conclud-ing:

> *Yes, if I could be healthy,*
> *And free from all cares,*

---

* The flip side of this spiritual fervor: According to longtime estate workers at Pocantico, profan-ity was a firing offense.

I must do all I've told you
And mean all my prayers.

Not always so compliant, he perverted the Sunday evening ritual by deliberately singing off-key and shattered the reverential mood of morning prayers by firing rubber bands at his kneeling brothers. "He surely is a little devil for getting into mischief, but in spite of it all is a likeable kid," concluded Wallace Worthley, a recent University of Chicago graduate hired as a companion and tutor to the Rockefeller boys. In church one morning, Worthley stared in amusement as Nelson passed notes, camouflaged in a hymnbook, to his sister during prayers. An Episcopal service was more to the boy's liking, its elaborate rituals and colorful priestly attire "just like a circus." Until old enough to appreciate serious conversation, the Rockefeller children ate most meals with their caretakers, one of whom denied Nelson dessert after he emptied a powder box over his three-year-old brother, Winthrop. Reporting this to Abby, a governess remarked blandly that Nelson had accepted punishment "in his usual philosophical way." He was a stoic as well as a clown.

Acknowledging that "we really didn't do children's things with our parents," Nelson relied for companionship on surrogate mothers like Florence Scales, the governess who monitored his health and fashioned a Marco Polo costume—brown tights, green tunic, and blue cape—of Nelson's own design for a school play. It was Miss Scales who reported to Abby that the ten-year-old boy had received an honorable mention for his drumming with the Knickerbocker Grays drill team. Greater still was the impact of Miss Scales's successor, a former lady-in-waiting to the czarina of Russia who had narrowly escaped the revolutionary pogrom. Her name was Regina de Parment Halberstadt, and for six of the most formative years of his life, this exotic creature was to have profound influence over Nelson's development.* More than half a century later, he marveled at her versatility and cultivation. "She was beautiful. She spoke perfect French. She sang. She served. She cooked. She played the piano." With a temperament as mercurial as the climate of her homeland, Mademoiselle alternated between periods of Muscovite gloom and almost giddy exhilaration. "I learned to adapt to her sensitivities," said Nelson, foreshadowing his appreciation of the volatile Latin temperament and of scarcely less mercurial politicians and legislators. As a bonus, the boy learned French by repeating what he heard from his governess.

Even as a small boy, Nelson worked hard at being fearless. Night after night,

---

* "I always figured he was raised by the help," remarked one of the more observant Rockefeller retainers to the author. The same source theorized that in these relationships were planted the seeds of his later intimacies with female co-workers.

he heard sounds that convinced him a rattlesnake was lurking outside his room. "And then I finally got my courage to look out and the watchman was walking by . . . he had corduroy pants on and as he walked . . . you could hear this strange sort of sound from the corduroy rubbing together." To correct his childish thumb sucking, Nelson's closed fist was encased in a ball of aluminum. Using his left hand at the dinner table sparked a generational test of wills, an unequal struggle involving physical restraint instead of maple sugar bribes. Junior's subsequent victory may have been pyrrhic; it surely was poignant. "I asked somebody which is my left hand," Nelson remembered long afterward, "and they told me and I said I had hoped so much it was the other one . . . because you're supposed to eat with your right hand."

As governor, Rockefeller caught sight of his then press secretary, Ron Maiorana, switching a dinner fork from one hand to the other. Maiorana explained that although he was naturally left-handed, as a boy his father had tied that hand to a chair to discourage its use. A startled Rockefeller related similar treatment by *his* father and wondered what, if any, long-term effects Maiorana had experienced. He was more or less ambidextrous, said Maiorana, able to write and throw with either hand. He regarded his left hand as strong and his right hand as smart.

"I should be so lucky," said Rockefeller.

The adult Nelson had no valet. He didn't need one, having learned to pack a creaseless suit from Junior, who also transmitted his boyish proficiency at sewing, a skill Nelson would put to good use on the campaign trail when his trousers split. At times, his resourcefulness bordered on the bizarre. While vice president of the United States, Rockefeller attended an elaborate function in Detroit's Cobo Hall wearing an ancient tuxedo whose lapels were approximately the width of Sixth Avenue. After ducking into the bathroom of Air Force Two, he emerged a few moments later, pointing to the crisply folded pocket handkerchief complementing his boiled shirt.

"Toilet paper," he informed an astonished aide.

Another paternal legacy was the inclination to study a problem, or solution, to death. In fairness, this was part of Junior's inheritance from JDR. When it came to realizing their philanthropic goals, said the old man, "we have the money. What we lack is the men." Junior was even more dependent on the best minds, a secular faith Abby warmly embraced. Repeatedly she urged her children to surround themselves with "people who are smarter than you." In Nelson's case, the advice took with a vengeance. "If there's a phrase that sums him up," according to one member of Rockefeller's Albany team, "it's the question I must have heard a thousand times: 'Who's the expert?'"

"He had great instincts, and his favorite question was, 'What does your gut tell you?'" Ron Maiorana says of his boss. "But he battled against trusting his instincts too much." Determined to avoid becoming the prisoner of his subordinates, Rockefeller played staff like so many pawns on a chessboard, all the while keeping his own counsel. "Never show more surface than necessary," he quoted Junior. It was the ultimate compliment to one whom he resembled more than he knew.

5

IN JANUARY 1910, after a tortured "race with my own conscience," Junior resigned from the board of Standard Oil. A year later, the United States Supreme Court voted to disband the Standard Oil Trust, an act that did more to expand the Rockefeller fortune than anything undertaken in the corporate boardroom. John D. Rockefeller may have pushed back from the table, but no one thought to inform the chef. The numbers said it all: From 800 in 1898, the ranks of American automobile owners grew to 618,000 by 1911. The motorist's unslakable thirst for gasoline multiplied at the same dizzying rate. By trading his shares in the dissolved trust for stock in thirty-four companies spun off from the leviathan, Senior graduated to the title long held by Andrew Carnegie— richest man on earth. On a single day in September 1916, calculated *The New York Times*, his assets grew by $8 million. That same year, he began transferring huge sums to his son, a reward for Junior's handling of an unexpected crisis. This was ironic, given that it was the younger Rockefeller's uncharacteristic neglect of "the last 5 percent" that had helped bring on the calamity in the first place.

The nominal culprit was the Colorado Fuel and Iron Company, on whose board Junior had continued to serve even after severing his ties to the Standard. In September 1913, eight thousand miners in southern Colorado, many of them immigrants ruthlessly exploited by paternalistic employers, went on strike against CFI and other operators. Junior, summoned to testify before Congress, gave unequivocal support to his managers on the scene. He rejected arbitration by the Labor Department and declared the mines off-limits to union organizers. Senior, delighted with his son's performance, awarded him ten thousand shares of CFI stock. His congratulations were premature. On April 20, 1914, two weeks after Junior's testimony, a deadly battle erupted between strikers and National Guardsmen assigned to keep order near the small Colorado town of Ludlow. Before it ended, soldiers torched the miners' tent city, causing the deaths of two women and eleven children and setting off a national chain reaction of organized fury.

Mass meetings of New Yorkers enraged by "the Ludlow Massacre" howled for Junior's blood. Socialist writer Upton Sinclair addressed picketers outside 10 West Fifty-fourth Street, while Emma Goldman and militants from the Industrial Workers of the World charged the locked gates of Pocantico. Four of the IWW "Wobblies" died when a bomb intended for Junior exploded prematurely. Confronting the severest test of his life, Junior turned to Ivy Ledbetter Lee, a Georgia minister's son who had worked as a New York City newspaperman before hiring out his promotional genius to business clients at $1,000 a month. Dispatched to Colorado as his new employer's eyes and ears, Lee uncovered the use of strikebreakers and other deceptions by CFI management. Armed with this information, a dismayed Junior made the rising Canadian politician William Lyon Mackenzie King his unofficial minister of labor.

Together, King and Rockefeller visited the troubled region for themselves in September 1915. For two weeks, the Standard Oil heir talked to miners in their (company) homes, danced with their wives, donned denim work clothes, and descended into the Stygian underground. "I don't mind it a bit," Junior replied when asked to have his picture taken alongside reporters, "but are you sure they care to risk their reputations by posing with me?" The favorable publicity generated by the trip came as a tonic to Abby, still in mourning over the recent deaths of Nelson Aldrich and Laura Rockefeller. "I told the children this afternoon what fine brave things their father was doing," she proudly notified Junior. In place of the hard line urged on him by CFI managers, Rockefeller promised miners improved pay and hours, as well as the freedom to meet, shop, and live where they chose. Encouraged by King, he offered a plan for employee representation, instantly labeled "the Colorado idea," that stopped well short of full unionization. The proposal won overwhelming approval anyway.

Overnight, the bloodstained wretch of Ludlow was reincarnated as a progressive force in industrial relations. President Wilson invited Junior to participate in a Washington conference on the subject; there he befriended Mother Jones and, still more improbably, Ida Tarbell. During the summer of 1920, his eldest sons accompanied Junior on a western swing that included the Colorado mines. A case of mumps prevented Nelson from visiting the scene of his father's cathartic triumph. Yet the stigma of Ludlow lodged in his boyish memory.

6

A MAN OF MANY precepts, Junior divided the world into two classes of people: "leaners and holders-up." Fearing his children would be spoiled by money, he devised a system of rewards wherein cash was doled out to the most charitable or dutiful of his offspring. Inevitably, this penalized rebellious natures like his daughter, Babs. As their eldest child, she paid the price for Junior's rigidity, her parents' inexperience, and her mother's frank preference for boisterous males. She retaliated as best she could by neglecting schoolwork, smoking cigarettes at fifteen, and enjoying fast cars and the fast set. Rejecting Junior's financial incentives for good behavior, Babs turned up her nose at minor chores, insisting, "I can always get a dollar from Grandpa." In Maine, she avoided the Eyrie in favor of the neighboring Milton household, whose son David became the first of her three husbands. Making their estrangement all the more poignant, father and daughter had overlapping interests. Both loved music and the theater. Her disdain for money snobbery—she pointedly distanced herself from girls at a summer camp who lived in bigger homes with more maids and lorded it over less fortunate tent mates—did her parents proud. Yet true intimacy with them seemed always just out of reach. Sadly, the adult Babs became as persnickety as Junior and as easily undone by trifles. Though she enjoyed travel, her youngest brother remembers, the slightest inconveniences—bathwater a shade too cool or a meal delayed—could blacken her mood. Simultaneously liberated by, and punished for, her early defiance, Babs drifted in and out of the Rockefeller orbit.

No such option existed for her brother John 3rd. Of all his children, Junior most trusted his namesake to handle money wisely. But the youth in whom he reposed this confidence had little of his own. Convinced that his angular right jaw was somehow deformed, as a boy Johnny rarely smiled, relaxed, or questioned the accepted wisdom of his father. Hypersensitivity over his status and appearance fed smoldering resentments. While still a Princeton undergraduate, Johnny reflected sourly on the cost of conformity. "During the last few years," he wrote in his diary, "I haven't uttered a swear word, touched a drop of alcohol (ever), smoked a cigarette (ever), studied on Sunday, played tennis (except at Seal and Pocantico with the family) or cards on Sunday, done anything I shouldn't with the girls, or done anything I didn't think the family wouldn't want me to do." What did he gain by such adherence to his father's code? "I am not popular, or especially well or strong, as lots of fellows who do all of the above mentioned things!!!!"

John's relationship with his dynamic younger brother was complex, an occasionally toxic stew of admiration, envy, and self-reproach. ("Nelson dances very well, I am rotten.") A 1921 family photograph taken outside the Eyrie says it all: in his long pants, immaculate jacket, and tie, Johnny smiles self-consciously for the camera. His siblings emulate his pose—all except Nelson, whose laugh-creased face carries an unmistakable glint of devilry. His sun-bleached hair is in need of combing, his coat is unbuttoned, his collar is untended. Though relegated to the sidelines, it is the second son who commands attention. He always would.

As a teenager, Nelson played pickup baseball games with boys from Pocantico, who laughingly boasted of their "million-dollar outfield." Watching from a distance, seemingly detached yet missing nothing on the field, was his brother Laurance. "Sister and I were very close friends," Nelson remembered, but "the focus of my life growing up was really Laurance." Two years younger than his childhood accomplice and lifelong alter ego, Laurance—the unusual spelling reflecting his parents' wish to honor Laura Spelman Rockefeller—bore a surface resemblance to John 3rd. Owlish and introspective, Laurance, too, was subject to bouts of ill health. His mother voiced concern that Nelson was "a bit too strenuous" a companion for his more delicate brother. Yet Laurance possessed inner resources, versatility, and a loner's assurance denied the firstborn son. Laurance's slightly dreamy demeanor veiled a wit sharp enough to puncture even Nelson's balloon. These qualities enabled him, while honoring Rockefeller family tradition, to be very much his own person.

From the beginning, Nelson and Laurance were inseparable. Sharing rooms in each Rockefeller home, they took turns occupying the bed nearest the door, thereby alternating spankings when the sounds of their late night high jinks roused a disciplining nurse. Given the frequency of their assaults upon established order, this was sound strategy. Tinkerers both, the boys wired a bedroom trunk to an electric lightbulb and made hot chocolate after the rest of the household was asleep. Readily conceding "we were difficult for the nurse," Nelson and his younger brother staged nighttime potty races on the Eyrie's sleeping porch. "In the bath tub when we would play she would come in and slap us and we learned the technique of just going underwater as soon as she would hit and she would get wet."

One day, on finding the German nurse—replaced by a French-speaking substitute as soon as World War I broke out—giving Laurance a hard time, Nelson promptly pulled the rug out from under the unfortunate woman, sending her sprawling on the floor. "We never took those people very seriously," he later acknowledged. At an early age, the brothers decided their Christian names were insufficiently manly. So they rechristened themselves: Laurance became Bill ("Just a good regular guy name," said Nelson, who borrowed it from Zane Grey), the title by which his older brother addressed him for the rest of his life, to the mystification of those not in on the joke. Nelson was to be Dick, but this early attempt at reinvention failed to catch on. To his siblings, he remained Nel or Nellie.

On Christmas morning, it was Nelson and Laurance who woke their parents by singing carols outside the bedroom door at half-past six. At meals, Nelson wasn't allowed to sit next to Babs or his brother Winthrop "because I could get both of them going very easily" through a repertoire of table tricks that made their plates jump or snapped bread out of his sister's hand. "He loved to throw food at the table," Laurance remembered, "a baked potato or maybe a butter-ball." Adding to the enjoyment for small boys, this breach of etiquette was daringly conducted under the noses of their formally dressed parents. Otherwise, remarked Laurance, "the only advantage of being rich was that if something was left over from lunch, at least we didn't get it for supper." More appetizing were campfire breakfasts cooked on the shores of Mount Desert's Bubble Pond, under the supervision of Wallace Worthley. The young tutor and his charges picked blueberries, for which Abby paid them twenty-four cents a quart. Once they hiked five miles in the rain, returning to the Eyrie happily soaked to the skin.

Junior's passion for horses became a family affair, the boys joining him for rides through the forested interior of the island. At Anemone Cave, known locally as the Devil's Oven, Nelson collected sea urchins and starfish. He watched, fascinated, as crews of workmen employed by Junior cut trees and blasted hillsides prior to building a network of scenic carriage roads servicing Acadia National Park. Junior occasionally joined in the heavy labor of road building, with whose construction crews he was known to trade sandwiches. This was not, as some thought, a becoming gesture of solidarity with the workers. "The truth was that he really wanted a corned beef sandwich and was damned tired of watercress," remembers one longtime island resident. On their own, Nelson and Laurance teamed up to construct a cedar log cabin with working fireplace in the fragrant pine woods behind the Eyrie. Rainy days found them bowling in the Playhouse or attending dances with neighboring children. At one of these impromptu affairs, according to Worthley, "Mr. R. behaved himself just like a kid, dancing and cutting up all sorts of capers."*

In emulation of his grandfathers, Nelson never entered a contest except to win. Not even Laurance, an expert chess player, could escape a challenge from his fiercely competitive older brother. Goaded into greater concentration by repeated losses, Nelson made up his mind "to think hard and move slowly . . . that was the thing I needed." Through self-discipline, he was able to win as many chess games as he lost. But if Laurance brought out the best in Nelson, their brother Winthrop consistently evoked the worst. One of life's vulnerables,

---

* His uncharacteristic friskiness extended beyond the dance floor. After Junior died in 1960, the Eyrie was demolished, leaving only Abby's garden to mark the family's presence. Nelson had occasion to escort Ashton Hawkins, a Harvard classmate of his son Michael's, around the grounds. The tour included the former site of the big house, Playhouse, tennis courts, and other landmarks familiar from his childhood. One of these was the Rest House, a modest bungalow in the woods to which his parents regularly retired after lunch. "No one, literally no one, was to disturb them during the hours of three and five in the afternoon," says Hawkins. "Nelson told me they liked to have sex during that period." Ashton Hawkins, AI.

Winthrop had a sweetness of character that endeared him to many. At prep school during the Depression, he offered free haircuts to forty boys who couldn't afford the local barber and would have sheared more had the headmaster not put a stop to his charity.

Placid, trusting, and oversize, Winthrop presented an irresistible target. Nelson bestowed on the boy, five years his junior, the hated nickname Wissy-Wissy. He inflicted repeated humiliations by pulling chairs out from under Winthrop, tying him to a tree, or luring the gullible child onto a seesaw before leaping off the other end, sending his brother crashing to the ground in impotent fury. ("It was not a very nice thing to do," an adult Nelson conceded, "but it was ingenious.") Maddened by abuse, one day Winthrop seized a pitchfork and sank it into his brother's leg. "It was a Sunday morning so father said that after church we would come to his dressing room and that we would both have to get a spanking," said Nelson. "I remember poor Winnie was in tears all during church and I couldn't understand why because spankings didn't really hurt very much. Father would send you into the closet to get a slipper and you would have to take your pants down. Then he would say that it hurt him more than it hurt you. I never understood that. But it never hurt me very much. I thought it was part of life, so I just accepted it."

Born three years after Winthrop, as the baby of the family David Rockefeller escaped the harshest parental discipline. Asked once by a schoolchild whether there was anything in his life that made him feel bad, David replied, "Yes, there is something. I was a fat little kid and I wasn't very good at sports." He immersed himself instead in books and bugs, the latter hobby born in the swamps of Mount Desert. The kind of child older people dote on, David impressed elders through a precocious knowledge of plants, flowers, butterflies, and beetles. "I am so thankful we are not rich—that we haven't got as much money as the Fords," young David remarked to his aunt Lucy, "because those children have to have a guardian all the time and can't go around by themselves, and I should hate that." To his brothers he was an object of derision. One day Nelson and Winthrop, the latter undoubtedly grateful for a diversionary quarry, hosed seven-year-old David with a sprinkler. A gardener watching the unprovoked attack asked the older boys why they engaged in such cruelty. "Because he's fat and lazy," they replied gleefully. "We want to keep him moving!" Phlegmatic by nature, David took his fraternal harassment in stride, telling his mother he was merely waiting until he was big enough to lick them on his own.

7

ANOTHER KIND OF education was gained through everyday contacts with carpenters, painters, and electricians around the Pocantico estate. As boys, Nelson and Laurance fantasized themselves a plumber and mechanic, respectively. Nelson in particular was drawn to the lathe and tools. Encouraging his creativity was his extroverted mother, whose relationship with her children resembled that of co-conspirator. On Saturday mornings, fresh from their weekly financial accounting to Father, they trooped to Abby's room to roast and eat chestnuts. Rather than contradict her husband openly, Abby relied on subtle contrivance, a lesson not lost on her favorite child. Unlike Junior, a latter-day Gradgrind who sermonized to his children as if they were the Fifth Avenue Bible class, Abby made a game out of learning and a production out of life. Her empathy and unbridled enthusiasm stamped her as a natural instructor, imparting to her children the mysteries of auction bridge, Five Hundred, and Senior's favorite, Numerica.

Abby saw her children off to school in the morning and welcomed them home when they returned from playing in Central Park. At five each afternoon, they gathered in the second-floor library of 10 West Fifty-fourth as she read aloud or invited childish confidences. Supervising postdinner homework, Abby set aside extra time to hear Nelson recite his multiplication tables. In church one Sunday, she looked the other way as he concealed a trio of tiny rabbits in her muff. On another occasion, animal tragedy produced shared grief. The mysterious death of a mother rabbit prompted Abby to speculate, "Perhaps it was eating your shoestrings that killed her." When Junior was away on one of his frequent trips, it was a treat for Nelson to sleep in his bed in the room his parents shared. Sixty years later, he could describe the French clock with the visible works that sat atop the little table between the beds. Just as vivid were memories of Abby's dressing room, where he liked to talk things over with his mother as she dressed for dinner, surrounded by chromium furniture and satin wood paneling.

In later years, Abby remarked how glad she was to have given her father's name to her second son—they were so much alike. One Aldrich attribute passed on to Nelson was a frankly sensual pleasure in beautiful things, displayed every time she ran her fingers over Rockefeller china, silver, or pieces of folk art. "It is great fun changing pictures, rearranging furniture, and putting in more lamps in certain places," Abby told Nelson during his freshman year at Dartmouth. This was preaching to the converted. "He couldn't sit five minutes in a room without doing something," his brother Laurance would remember, "and often it was to get up and rehang the pictures, rearrange the furniture, straighten up the desk. His eye!"

A classic life enhancer, the cosmopolitan Mrs. Junior gained strength from meeting people, another quality she bequeathed to Nelson. Her legacy included the zestful embrace of strangers, untested ideas, and original forms of artistic expression. To be sure, modernism had its limits. Her religion of good works could be every bit as stringent as the more orthodox piety enforced by Junior. "I long to have our family stand firmly for what is best and highest in life," announced Abby. "It isn't always easy, but it is worthwhile." The practical application of this ideal could prove, literally, backbreaking. Late one afternoon at Pocantico, Tom Pyle came upon Nelson weeding a flower garden. Asked why he was working so late, the boy explained that he had neglected the job earlier in the day and must complete it before he could go to dinner. Pyle offered to lend a hand. "No, you'd better not," Nelson replied. "Mother will probably come along to check." She did, a few minutes later.*

In November 1916, Nelson took the occasion to gently upbraid his mother, then visiting Colorado with Junior. "I am sorry that you were not here on Abby's birthday," he wrote, adding that Winthrop was getting "very fat" and that "the baby sends his love." The immature scrawl cannot conceal a precocious assumption of authority. In a strictly governed household, Nelson made his own rules. While John 3rd habitually saved most of his allowance, his younger brother routinely exhausted his in a shop on Sixth Avenue where he lay on the floor on his stomach, devouring Tootsie Rolls and the funny pages. With a calculating charm worthy of a Tammany boss, Nelson entreated his mother to let him quit a music class "because it would be much better for me to go out in the park than to sit in a hot stuffy house when I have a chance to go with the boys."

This appeal fell on deaf ears, but practice makes perfect, and Nelson honed his techniques of persuasion as other boys his age worked on their pitching game. Possessing boundless energy, he resembled a top that can maintain its equilibrium only by spinning ever faster. Fearless, experimental, and headstrong, he accepted little at face value. Even as a child, he recalled, "I'm not sure how much I was fooled by this Santa Claus stuff." At the age of twelve, he sent Abby "a little sachet that I made this morgning with <u>out</u> the help of anyone." Whether he was charging a hornet's nest, mangling the alphabet, or prematurely planting a garden in disregard of adult counsel, what mattered about Nelson's mistakes, no less than his triumphs, was that they were *his*. Nothing, it seemed, could curb his appetite for the next adventure or his delight in fresh

---

* Breathing vitality into Junior's religious formalism, Abby encouraged her children to take up the cudgels against racial or religious discrimination. "What I would like you always to do is what I try humbly to do myself," she urged her sons. "That is, never say or do anything that would wound the feelings or the self respect of any human being, and to give special consideration to all who are in any way repressed."

discoveries. "I blue up the *fut ball* two months ago and have been playing with it ever since," he bragged to Johnny. "I can punt two miles hight and I can dope kick 6 miles." One summer at Seal Harbor, he learned the rudiments of photography from Wallace Worthley; it was the start of a lifelong passion, one he shared with Laurance. ("Father used to pay us for the good ones," said Laurance of the resulting images.)

A fresh enthusiasm seized Nelson in the spring of 1917, when America entered World War I on the side of the Allied powers to which his family and other Anglophile New Yorkers had long since committed themselves emotionally. The Rockefellers enlisted for the duration, rationing bacon to two helpings a week and forgoing sugar on their breakfast cereal. Wallace Worthley reported to his family that he hadn't tasted beef since his arrival. "Only twice since I've been here have I seen white bread." At Pocantico, Nelson and his brothers planted Victory Gardens, while in the city they rolled bandages under the auspices of the Red Cross and enjoyed a display of tanks and military tableau at the Coliseum. "I saw General Joffer yesterday evening," Nelson wrote his mother in May 1917. The hero of the Marne was easily surpassed as an object of public interest by Fifth Avenue lampposts bedecked with Allied flags, and a galaxy of red, white, and blue lights splashed across the front of the Savoy Hotel. "I hope you will be here to see the decorations before they are taken away," Nelson concluded a bit wistfully.

By August, Abby was back at the Eyrie after a rest cure ordered by her doctors. Savoring a brief lull in "the usually exciting, strenuous life that we lead," she found the remote shores of Mount Desert infected by martial fever. On the Ocean Road, Nelson glimpsed a government wireless station manned by two hundred sailors who handled twenty thousand messages a day between Washington and the American Expeditionary Forces in Europe. The fall of 1918 brought a victory parade in which Nelson marched down Fifth Avenue beating his snare drum. Outside St. Patrick's Cathedral, he watched as New Yorkers hung Kaiser Wilhelm in effigy. The war had a terrifying sequel. At his mother's New York home on East Sixty-fifth Street, Assistant Secretary of the Navy Franklin D. Roosevelt tossed in his bed, struck down by the Spanish influenza then raging unchecked through the world's depleted armies and brutalized civilian populations. At that, FDR could count his blessings: 12,562 other New Yorkers succumbed to the plague. "We have gotten through the epidemic very well indeed," Abby noted in the third week of November. Of the Rockefeller household, only John and Nelson had been affected, with John's case a mild one. Unfortunately, she went on, "Nelson had it very energetically, as it seems his nature to do everything strenuously."

8

MANY YEARS LATER, with his parents long dead and his own family inhabiting Kykuit, Nelson acknowledged, "I know people can't give me gifts like I can give them. All I ask is that they say thank you. You'd be surprised how many don't." Uttered in a slightly world-weary tone, the comment spoke volumes about flattery and ingratitude, the yin and yang of Frederick Gates's "business of benevolence." On July 4, 1919, a family celebration of Independence Day was enlivened by gallows humor about a Bolshevik bomb being hurled at Kykuit—this in response to more than a dozen mail bombs addressed to Junior and other establishment figures in politics and business. Three days later, Nelson celebrated his eleventh birthday in tandem with Senior's eightieth. At a lunch in Abeyton Lodge, the oil king gave each guest a $5 gold piece. Nelson received a check for $100. Afterward, a New York orchestra played dance music and tea was served on a terrace overlooking the Hudson. That night, there was a dinner inside the big house and a towering cake illuminated by eighty candles. "The old man joked all the time," said one onlooker.

This would have come as no surprise to his grandsons, each of whom he addressed as "Brother." To them the patriarch was a genial, even playful, companion, not above juggling plates or balancing crackers on the edge of his nose to earn a laugh. Each morning, his Swiss valet supplied JDR with a daily quota of dimes for distribution to passengers on the Tarrytown–Nyack ferry or other public venues. Rockefeller in his later years handed out an estimated thirty thousand dimes, plus an unknown number of horse chestnuts he slipped into the hands of covetous petitioners, allegedly as a cure for rheumatism. To Nelson, he appeared as comfortable around the king of Belgium as the local parish priest with whom he played golf. In the mazelike hallways of Abeyton Lodge, Senior initiated the boys in a favorite game, sometimes pausing in the middle to declaim, "Life is like a game of blind man's bluff."

As if hoping to disprove his own maxim, Senior cheated time by controlling his diet as thoroughly as his environment. On Sundays, Nelson donned an Eton collar and striped trousers and joined his siblings for short prayers and long dinners around his grandfather's Kykuit table. Between admonitions to chew each bite twenty-seven times, milk included, the wizened host enlivened meals with a repertoire of stories that would be recycled forty years later before Rockefeller campaign crowds. These included the oft told tale of a town drunk who, one starless night, fell into a water trough. Thrashing about like a drowning man, a performance its narrator enthusiastically reenacted by waving his arms in mock distress, the sot generously instructed local police, "I'm all right; save the women and children first."

As a rule, JDR's anecdotage steered clear of personal history. A surprisingly contemporary figure, he kept only what he found useful of the past, an attitude shared by his grandson. Voters gushing their desire to live like a Rockefeller received a blunt rejoinder. "You should have had my grandfather for your grandfather," Nelson told them. Behind the bravado lurked glimmers of vulnerability. "Nelson didn't drink," says Kershaw Burbank, for many years a mainstay of the Rockefeller family office. "He seemed to fear it. He said that he had a sweet tooth; he was afraid he would indulge himself with alcohol in the same way if he had the chance. He seemed haunted by his great-grandfather." Maybe so, but others recall Rockefeller chuckling indulgently over the roguish ancestor he dubbed "the snake oil salesman." He could afford to harbor contradictory feelings about the scalawag whose outré conduct had inadvertently laid the groundwork for the world's greatest fortune.

About this, at least, Nelson's attitude was unambiguous. Intoxicated over his latest building project or art acquisition, he exclaimed, "Wasn't it wonderful of Grandfather to make all this lovely money?" His smile faded abruptly when asked to assess the muckrakers and their depiction of Rockefeller family history. "I lived it," Nelson replied a bit testily. "Why should I read about it?" This was a curiously incurious response coming from the boy who chased baseballs into New York sewers and interrogated former presidents about their big-game-hunting exploits. In fact, Rockefeller's stock response masked a condition misdiagnosed and misunderstood, not least of all by himself. Concealed for most of his life from the public, it goes a long way toward explaining the unquestioning optimist who rarely ventured into the political arena without his intellectual security blanket.

Three

"WHAT ARE WE GOING TO LEARN TODAY THAT'S *NEW*?"

I did not learn from somebody telling me you get burned if you touch a hot stove. I had to touch it.

—NELSON A. ROCKEFELLER

1

WALLACE WORTHLEY WAS baffled. "I had known for a long time that Nelson is very deficient in reading," his tutor acknowledged in August 1920, "but that he reads much better in books of his own choosing, if they are not too difficult. . . . Nelson's difficulty is a peculiar one; he seems to be able to master, to a large extent, long and difficult words, yet mispronounces and miscalls very simple and elementary ones. He frequently reads on as no, as as was, the as of, and as the, etc., and does not seem to realize that he has entirely altered the meaning of the sentence. I have known him to read one sentence five times and yet make the same mistake each time."

Worthley was describing the classic symptoms of dyslexia, the genetic disorder frequently mistaken—then and later—for intellectual impairment. Unlike speech, an automatic response grounded in fifty thousand to one hundred thousand years of human development, reading is an acquired skill, an evolutionary latecomer no older than the written word. Rising to the challenge, the human brain converts words on a page into sound units called "phonemes," the building blocks of pronunciation. Most children attain reading proficiency by the age of seven. But because their brains are wired differently, dyslexics have trouble with the first step in the conversion process. Relying on auditory rather than visual memories to form words, they operate at an even greater disadvantage in English, a language that has more than eleven hundred different ways to spell its forty phonemes.*

---

* It bears noting that Rockefeller could speak fluent French, which he learned by ear as a child, without being able to conjugate Gallic verbs. Likewise, he flunked early exams in Spanish, only to master the language as an adult by enrolling in the Berlitz school.

Characterized by poor reading, writing, and spelling skills, the misuse of words, and the transposition of numbers, dyslexia was first observed in nineteenth-century victims of brain injury. Later cases of so-called word-blindness were ascribed to cerebral damage at birth. Rockefeller himself never heard the word *dyslexia* (which he pronounced "die-lexia") until he was in his fifties. Revealingly, he blamed his "reverse reading" on the clumsy attempt by his father to undo a boy's natural left-handedness. It was all the more ironic, then, that Worthley's prescription for dealing with the mysterious handicap should reflect Junior's firm belief that an untrained mind was a disorderly mind. Commencing that summer in Maine, twelve-year-old Nelson was to be drilled two hours a day in reading, writing, spelling, and arithmetic. "For his composition work I have suggested that he rewrite his diary which he kept throughout his trip to the west with his family, adding whatever of interest he happens to remember," Worthley noted. "He has fallen in with my scheme and intends to illustrate the diary with pictures that he took on the trip. . . ."

Worthley may have regarded the boy's mangled language with amusement, but to Nelson it was an enduring source of shame, buried fathoms deep. Only near the end of his life was he persuaded that by going public with his disability, he might offer encouragement to youngsters who were similarly afflicted. Even then, however, he shied away from any bid for personal sympathy. "No long sob story," Rockefeller instructed his communications director, Hugh Morrow, ghostwriter of a 1975 article on the subject for *TV Guide*. Looking "like something out of Easter Island," recalled Morrow, his employer clearly would have preferred to discuss anything else. "You have no idea how humiliating it is," Rockefeller finally blurted out, "for an eight-year-old boy to stand there in front of the entire family at Vespers and not be able to read the 23rd Psalm." In print, the then vice president of the United States delivered a bristling message recalling the frustrations he had known as a child. "Don't accept anyone's verdict that you are lazy, stupid, or retarded," he exhorted them, "you may very well be smarter than most other children your age." Acknowledging dyslexia to be "a hell of a handicap," Rockefeller displayed little sympathy for those inclined to blame the condition for their lack of success. To the contrary: adversity was merely opportunity disguised.

With the invention of magnetic resonance imaging and sophisticated brain-scanning techniques, dyslexia has yielded most of its secrets to modern science. Today, three million American children are enrolled in special education classes, while millions more benefit from computer games, books on tape, and voice recognition software. None of these advances were available to Nelson Rockefeller, whose undiagnosed condition caused him to read and write numbers backward. "So I had a hard time balancing my accounts," he once explained. "I felt badly, but I just seemed to make mistakes and didn't know why."

His scrambled words and apparent inability to memorize fed doubts, not about his brain, but about his brainpower. These were seemingly confirmed by the Stanford-Binet test, a primitive form of IQ examination administered to the boy in the autumn of 1917, soon after his enrollment in the third grade of the Lincoln School. An offshoot of the Teachers College of Columbia University, Lincoln was founded to promote the child-centered theories of John Dewey, as interpreted by Abraham Flexner, a Kentucky schoolmaster more recently employed as secretary to the Rockefeller-financed General Education Board. Flexner's seminal article "A Modern School" in the *American Review of Reviews* supplied a blueprint for a radically different kind of secondary education. Divorced from the classics and hostile to rote learning, it was as unorthodox as Abby Aldrich Rockefeller's nonrepresentational art or Junior's nonsectarian Protestantism.

Thus the Lincoln curriculum replaced traditional subjects with interdisciplinary units drawn from real-life situations and selected, in part, by the students themselves. More than learning by doing, the school emphasized intellectual cross-pollination. A second-grade class drew maps while studying how food travels from farm to city. For third graders, an intense focus on boats opened multiple doors to geography, literature, and other disciplines. Or a creative music class might examine mambo making within the context of colonial history. Stressing individual initiative and social relevance, Lincoln exercised a powerful allure for a father seeking to expose his children to what passed for the real world. The school's racial and class diversity fell short of later, idealized portrayals; David Rockefeller was not alone in his inability to recall a single black face among his classmates. But by the standards of the time, it was a bold venture in classroom leveling.

Originally located opposite the Seventh Regiment Armory on Park Avenue, not far from the Rockefeller townhouse on West Fifty-fourth Street, Lincoln boasted significant representation from New York's German Jewish aristocracy, plus a sprinkling of middle- and lower-middle-class students. After the coeducational school moved to a new, seven-story building in Morningside Park at 123rd Street, its enrollment broadened to include the offspring of Columbia's professoriat, for whom it proved a potent recruitment tool. More than one hundred students were taught by twenty-three instructors, each vetted for his commitment to "the whole person." In contrast with other hotbeds of educational innovation, Lincoln did not allow its teachers to be addressed by their first names. Little else of classroom convention survived. "I never took an exam until I got into college," Nelson would recall. Grades didn't make their appearance until his senior year.

Work and play were interchangeable at Lincoln. Conventional scholastics took a backseat to youthful interrogation. "What are we going to learn today that's *new?*" Nelson breathlessly asked of one instructor. Free to follow his instincts, he gravitated to power. He spearheaded a fifth-grade constitution, under which students elected a chairman, sworn to an oath he provided, who in turn appointed class committees and enforced proscriptions reminiscent of Junior's admonitory discipline: "Don't scribble on blackboard," "Don't throw things around the room," and, most important, "Obey the class chairman." For these and other infractions, Nelson proposed punishments ranging from five-cent fines to expulsion from office, the latter extremity reserved for a defaulting treasurer or higher officer if he played hooky "or says anything against God or his country."

Encouraged to go as far as fast as interest and aptitude would permit, Nelson excelled at mathematics, notwithstanding his habit of reversing numbers. Placed in a small advanced class, he completed the physics and calculus required of a college freshman. Preferring carpentry and candle making to history and literature, Nelson remembered, "I was very good at sewing. I threaded the sewing machines for the girls. We made paper. We made soap . . . we made cement window boxes." Nelson waged a halfhearted battle to conquer the cello, winning release from public recitals only after a succession of strings broke, accidentally or on purpose. Science classes evoked much greater enthusiasm, biology being a particular favorite. He delivered a youthful lecture, frank to a fault, on the reproductive habits of rabbits. "I explained all about rabbits right through the mating and what happened to the father rabbit after he mated. He would lie down and take a rest. . . . The teacher was a little upset and some of the class giggled, but I was very interested."

Much of Lincoln's flavorsome menu was served up outside the schoolhouse, with New York City itself an extended classroom. After a visit to the Museum of Natural History, Nelson reproduced an Eskimo sleigh displayed there. Such excursions enriched the curriculum. They also bred informal contacts among students in wildly varying environments. Visiting the modest apartments of his classmates, Nelson could be found washing dishes in the kitchen after a meal. "Even as a kid he always knew how to ingratiate himself," one student reflected. "When you'd run into him, he'd always draw you out about your activities, never talk about himself unless asked. At any gathering, he'd go out of his way to speak to everybody. It was almost a compulsion." The future Linda Jamieson Storrow, then a first-year student, never forgot the handsome, charismatic upperclassman who borrowed money from female classmates outside the girls' locker room and who complimented her stage performance in a Spanish-language production. "He was always sort of bouncing around the way he did later," said Storrow.

His unaffected ways contributed to his popularity, as did the zeal with which he pitched into any activity that caught his fancy, from arm wrestling to student theatricals. In a sixth-grade operetta, he excelled as "an obstreperous frog." This may have been typecasting. With the help of a purloined master key, Nelson broke into another boy's locker, where he stuffed onions into his classmate's hatband and coat pockets. A more serious altercation had near tragic consequences. Nelson got into a fight with a Cuban boy, in the course of which, he remarked archly, "somehow one of his teeth had come through his lip and he took it personally." The aggrieved party pulled a knife from his pocket and chased Nelson up and down the building's fire stairs. Young Rockefeller escaped, narrowly, and switchblades were henceforth banned from the hallways of Lincoln.

His friends, an eclectic lot, included Sheldon Stark, a lawyer's son from the Hasidic Brooklyn neighborhood of Borough Park. Invited to 10 West Fifty-fourth Street for dinner, Stark found the place deserted except for some servants. "Come on," said Nelson, "I want to show you something." They climbed an imposing staircase, pausing at a landing where Nelson pressed against a section of the wall, which slid open to reveal one of Junior's treasured medieval tapestries. The boys stared in silence into the refrigerated hideaway for a few moments before retracing their steps to the hotel-like foyer. Other classmates sampled the rustic luxury of Seal Harbor. William Alton, perhaps his best friend at Lincoln, was hired by Nelson's parents to provide companionship for young Winthrop Rockefeller, in which role Alton also broke bread with Henry Ford and played water polo with Charles Lindbergh. In later years, Alton worked in Nelson's Latin American enterprises, eventually being given free office space in Rockefeller Center from which to pursue his ministry of Christian Science healing.

There was more to such gestures than noblesse oblige. In youth, Nelson was less guarded than he would ever be again. It was no accident that first at Lincoln and later at Dartmouth, he established lifelong relationships marked by uncomplicated loyalty and mutual trust. Yet even here lurked an element of calculation. From an early age, Nelson sensed that he could have it both ways, impressing the Starks and Altons with the trappings of wealth *and* his seeming indifference to what, in point of fact, he regarded as his birthright. More than any other Rockefeller, he appeared comfortable in his skin, eager for the tang and clatter of life as experienced by less privileged classmates. Unfortunately, his name kept getting in the way. "They weren't *treated* any differently," said classmate Pauline Faulk, "but everybody knew who they were. How could you not?" Abby, keeping a low profile, restricted herself to faithful participation in PTA meetings. Not so Junior. Replicating the challenge posed to his children, he launched an aggressive antismoking crusade that included an original student musical comedy, *Nix on Nicotine*. After the show, an elaborate dinner celebrated the smokeless paradise about to dawn. "I was seated between John

D., Jr., and Old Dean Russell of Teachers College," Faulk recalled. The latter had a luxuriant beard and mustache, their snowy expanse fouled by tobacco stains.

2

WALKING TO SCHOOL was preferable to being driven, Abby Aldrich Rockefeller maintained, as it improved both circulation and appetite. When they got older, Nelson and Laurance often made a trek of forty blocks uptown on roller skates, before boarding the Fifth Avenue bus through Harlem. In the afternoon, the route was reversed. One day, having reached Ninety-second Street on skate power and finding no chauffeur to transport him the rest of the way, Nelson skated through Central Park, where he was stopped by a policeman, to whom he explained his predicament. If only he would wait, said Nelson, the cop could hear his story confirmed straight from the chauffeur's mouth. "He was a very nice policeman so we talked until the car came. I said I wouldn't do it again."

Though Lincoln frowned on overt competition, not even John Dewey could repeal a thirteen-year-old's compulsion to cross a finish line before anyone else. Small for his age, standing just five feet tall and weighing ninety-eight pounds, Nelson flourished in the shot put and track events. "It was so funny about your getting stuck up the rope," he wrote his brother Johnny. "The very afternoon I got your letter I beat the school rope climb record by 1/5 sec, making it in 4 3/5 sec. Hum! Hum!" Shrewdly, Lincoln headmaster Otis Caldwell guessed that Nelson's appetite for attention might be harnessed to his need to excel. To counter the disquieting results of his IQ test, Caldwell assured Nelson that no one used his brain to its full capacity. Through extra effort and concentration, he could overcome his intellectual deficiencies. This was by no means a sure thing. Many dyslexic youngsters, constantly pressed to try harder, feel as if they are being set up to fail. Some withdraw into themselves. Others play the class clown or adopt a self-consciously superior attitude toward those who would make them feel otherwise.

Nelson's early antics hint at this path. With adolescent omniscience, he informed a recent addition to the Lincoln faculty, "You're new here. I've been around for quite a while now. If you need any help, let me know." His swaggering presumption may have been a cover for intellectual insecurity or a mask for resentment of his globe-trotting parents. In light of the duties imposed upon him, said a rueful Junior, he wished he could work sixteen hours a day. The Rockefeller children might be excused for believing that he did. Their father's multiplying commitments to the Interchurch World Movement, various building projects in New York, and restoration efforts at Versailles and Colonial Williamsburg added to his remoteness. So did his uncertain health. Abby battled her own ailments, chiefly hypertension. Yet they did little to slow her frenetic pace. On a single day in December 1926, she made a flying trip to Philadelphia for an exhibit of Persian art, followed by a dash home for tea with Commander Richard Byrd and the arrival of houseguests scheduled for a three-day visit. The next night, she hosted a lecture for one hundred invitees. Reverend Harry Emerson Fosdick and his wife were booked for dinner on Wednesday. "On Thursday we are giving a big dinner. And on Friday you come home," Abby reminded Nelson, adding, "We probably will not meet you because the Sunday School have the celebration that afternoon and evening."

In place of their Russian governess, Abby employed the first in a series of students from the Union Theological Seminary to look after Nelson and Laurance when they returned from their Lincoln School day. At a summer camp in upstate New York, Nelson declared a twelve-mile canoe trip with portages— enlivened by the discovery of a dead pig en route—"great fun . . . I paddled all the way in the bow and carried one end of the 80 lb canoe on the carries." He drew a plan of his tent, promised to show Abby twenty-eight pictures he had snapped, and reassured Junior that his accounts had been kept faithfully. "You can telefone from New York," Nelson hinted to his mother, affording the barest glimpse of boyish homesickness. On his fourteenth birthday, he monopolized Abby, who read to him for hours as he recuperated in New York's Presbyterian Hospital after shooting himself in the knee with an air rifle. To suggest that the injury was anything but accidental would be pure speculation. Nevertheless, it touched off predictable hand-wringing by Junior, who anxiously scanned the Maine horizon in search of his mate. Word of their pending departure from New York was joyously received, he told Abby, which only deepened his disappointment after doctors postponed Nelson's discharge from the hospital. Two days later, she received a plaintive message from her husband, vowing, "Home is not the same without the head of the family." Exactly whom, Abby was entitled to ask, was she mothering?

Nelson had reached a difficult age. Recalcitrant one moment, obsequious the next, he never wavered in his desire to be first. When Junior presented his sons with a thirty-six-foot sloop, the *Jack Tar*, Nelson took to the coastal waters of Maine as though he had webbed feet. A photo taken on the Seal Harbor dock shows a gangling, tousled-haired youth in white duck pants and herringbone jacket. His head cocked to one side, a rakish smile convulsing his features, he is the personification of adolescent high spirits. Besides sailing and tennis, Nelson cut a wide swath through the dance lessons staged for the children of summer residents in the Eyrie's Playhouse. He had been to two small dances, Abby told her sister, Lucy, in September 1922, and greatly enjoyed them.

His active social life shadowed his academic performance. "We got our marks the other day," he alerted Johnny, "mine weren't much but I beat Laurance all to pieces." Writing her sister, Lucy, Abby dropped her guard. "Nelson has been the family problem this winter. He hasn't looked very well and he has felt rather restless. But he is settling down now. They have put him up a grade in school so that he has to work much harder and he thinks he can get into college sooner— He wants to go to boarding school, but as he has a desire to seek the toughest gang he can find, I hope we can have him at home until he passes through this stage of his existence and the good in him gets the upper hand."

Nelson continued to chafe his less popular siblings, telling Johnny in February 1923, "What a coincidence! The very day that I got your letter in which you mentioned that most beautiful and docile creature Lydia Garrison, I also received a letter from the forsaid, heaven-sent person. And to tell you the truth it was not the first one eather." But when "Dear Lydia" failed to maintain the correspondence, Nelson embarked upon his first schoolboy romance with a Lincoln classmate named Geraldine Chittolini. The daughter of a violin maker who lived near Carnegie Hall, Gerry impressed one classmate as having "ash blond hair and an ash blonde psyche." At her instigation, Nelson joined the staff of *The Lincolnian* as photographic editor. Four days a week the pair rode downtown after school; at night they ran up phone bills that caught Junior's disapproving eye.

Yet even then, Nelson had eyes for more than one attractive female. Miffed that a girl on whom he had set his sights had instead invited his elder brother to a house party, the fifteen-year-old man of the world offered Johnny a dour assessment of the opposite sex: "Women are tratoures creatures and never trust one unless you have to!! That's that!!!"

3

IN THE SUMMER of 1924, the Rockefellers went their separate ways. Abby and Babs journeyed to Europe for culture and clothes, while Junior took his three eldest sons on an extended tour of western parks. Between games of medicine ball in their private railcar, Nelson and Laurance fashioned slingshots out of forked sticks and pieces of rubber inner tube, the perfect weapon with which to target rats on railroad sidings. As they were descending Pike's Peak, the cog railway on which they were traveling lost traction and their car began hurtling down the mountain. Disaster was only narrowly averted, thanks to the timely intervention of a red-faced conductor applying the hand brake. Though the Rockefellers returned to the base safely on foot, those few minutes of terror would haunt Nelson's dreams for years, returning every time he rode the rails.

At Yellowstone National Park, the appearance of grizzly bears scampering up tree branches to escape the tourist onslaught evoked laughter among the eastern tenderfoots. Another day they watched in horror as a man and his wife backed their Ford over the rim of a canyon and fell hundreds of feet to their death. From Yellowstone, it was but a short ride to Jackson Hole. Junior, transfixed by the beauty of the rugged Grand Tetons, set in motion a typically exhaustive review process, culminating in his purchase of the valley floor—the heart of Grand Teton National Park. His time out west marked a turning point in Nelson's development. He "seems suddenly to have become a man," concluded Abby, "and except for his childish actions at moments, you would think he was very grown up." By the autumn of 1924, sixteen-year-old Nelson hoped to follow his brother to Princeton. There was a glitch, however: In a spelling exam of one hundred words, he lamented, "I only got 37 wright." His latest grades in French, math, botany, and English, were "like hell . . . ," he told Johnny. "You can imagine what Father had to say."

It was at this worst possible moment that a fresh distraction made irresistible claims. "My Ford comes next week," Nelson exulted in May 1925, "I can hardly wait." On his seventeenth birthday that July, repairs and embellishments to his Model T caused him to miss a joint celebration for him and his grandfather. Upon setting off the next morning for Mount Desert, he discovered the hard way that a newly installed "Cadilack muffler" was of little help when flames began spewing through the floorboard. His engine problem was soon fixed, but speeding along a country road at forty or better, "I was just about to pass a man when all of a sudden he put out his hand and turned across the road. It was the worst feeling I ever had in all my life . . . well the crash came and I felt kind of funny. But we were going so fast that we went on for about 15 yard before we stopped." Nelson handed the other driver $5—"his car was only an old Buick"—and the two parted friends.

At Seal Harbor, his social life blossomed anew with a "peach Deb from Philadelphia" who had agreed to go sailing with him. Mary Todhunter Clark, Tod to her friends, was the daughter of Percy and Elizabeth Clark. Descendants from early Pennsylvania Quaker stock, the Clarks had grown quietly rich on railroads and investment banking. Sharing a house with six brothers, Tod became something of a tomboy, climbing trees and riding horses around Willoughby, the Clark estate in the leafy Main Line village of Cynwyd. Highly competitive on the tennis court and the ocean racecourse, Tod was an avid hiker and practical joker who excelled at Junior League theatricals and did a mean Charleston. Her sharp tongue and tall, angular form might have served as a prototype for Katharine Hepburn's Tracy Lord. Tod's Foxcroft School manners and Sorbonne-taught French were just as refined, her old-money rectitude likewise marbled with suppressed laughter.

Nelson, her junior by a year, had known Tod casually from adolescent dance classes. Now he saw her, as it were, for the first time, a young woman whose preference for social work over society trumped her parents' ambition for her to attend Wellesley, the fashionable college for women of her pedigree. No conventional, highly buffed product of an exclusive finishing school, Miss Clark possessed an independent mind and strong convictions. She was a collector of rare plants and an amateur ornithologist who later maintained bird-watching stations on two continents. By the middle of August 1925, Nelson was spending considerable time at Seal Cove with the Clarks. He was going out almost every evening, Abby reported, "although we have had to restrain him to two dances a week."

4

NELSON BEGAN HIS senior year at Lincoln inauspiciously enough, scoring a D on his latest Spanish exam. To his brother John, he confided the ache of desire. "If you only knew how good I've been," Nelson moaned. "I haven't looked at a girl during schooltime and I have used all my study periods for study." He and Gerry had a serious talk. Though she was "just as dear as ever," the demands of preparing for college narrowed his social options. Miss Chittolini was written off like a bad check. "I guess the affair between Gerry and I is about over," Nelson alerted Junior and Abby. His friend had changed "a powerful lot since last year, and to my mind it was not for the better. Of course there is realy nothing bad about her, it is just her general attitude." For the record, he attributed their breakup to the mounting academic pressures of senior year.*

But if he was working hard, Nelson was playing even harder. In the same letter revealing the end of his relationship with Gerry, he confessed to nine invitations from as many young ladies over the upcoming Christmas vacation. "I have accepted nearly all of them so far." He hoped to convert several of his childhood fur coats into a single stylish garment. "If I can only get a durby now

---

* For his parents, he shared some revealing fantasies of life outside the Rockefeller cocoon. Threading Manhattan's heavy traffic, he pretended that he was a taxi driver—"a great time. But of course I am very careful so it is perfectly safe." On another occasion, he planned on motoring to a friend's house at the far end of Long Island "and do all our own cooking and everything."

and a cane. Say! Won't I be the snaps." Amid the social whirlwind, his preference for Princeton wavered. Dartmouth now caught his fancy. "I really think that is a better all around college and that I could get more out of it," Nelson informed his parents. Two weeks later, the decision was made for him. Forced to "a rather radical step," Nelson dropped Spanish altogether in order to manage his heavy course load. "This means that I will not be able to go to Princeton but I think it is for the best," he concluded breezily. Ignoring clouds in favor of silver linings was becoming a habit.

Several factors influenced his choice of a college, Nelson himself claiming that he selected Dartmouth for its fancied resemblance to Lincoln. "I heard it was a place which let a person learn by his own experiences," he said. Advantages of another sort moved Nelson's father to write, "The president at Dartmouth is an extraordinarily fine man and the spirit of the institution progressive and modern." Ernest Martin Hopkins was Junior's idea of a scholar. Prior to assuming the college presidency in 1916, Hopkins had spent several years in private business. Even now he exhibited a preference for character development over the PhD, cheerfully confessing that on opening his morning paper, he turned first to the sports pages and next to *Little Orphan Annie*.

That fall, Nelson received a conditional acceptance from the New Hampshire school, assuming that his year-end grades were C or better. Faithful to the Lincoln credo of learning what he liked, he taught himself to type, practicing every morning. In later years, Rockefeller lost no opportunity to proclaim his debt to progressive education. By exposing him to a much wider range of human contacts than the typical prep school, Lincoln undoubtedly did broaden his sympathies. Moreover, its emphasis on self-directed pragmatism dovetailed perfectly with his practical intelligence. "I enjoy problems," said the adult Rockefeller. "The greatest game is to try and solve them." On another occasion, he denied ever being bored. "Leave me alone for fifteen minutes and I'll find something to do and I'll be able to throw myself into it."

In the final analysis, Lincoln encouraged Nelson to be himself. For that reason alone, he entertained more than the usual old boy's nostalgia for the place. He established the Emily Ann Barnes Fund, named for a favorite teacher, to financially assist Lincoln faculty members down on their luck. (The school's advanced ways did not extend to providing staff pensions or other benefits, leaving Nelson to pay funeral expenses for at least one man and his wife.) He retroactively credited Lincoln and its headmaster with helping him to develop the focused intensity required to battle dyslexia. Other men of destiny believe in their star. Nelson, pressed for the secret of his success, pointed to a homelier source. "I can go for hours with sustained concentration," he asserted. As proof, he once conducted a press conference in the throes of excruciating pain from kidney stones. No reporter present ever guessed at his discomfort.

In at least one critical respect, however, his Lincoln years instilled the very opposite of concentration. Far from the obsessive presidential aspirant of popular memory, Rockefeller told the truth when he said, "I never had a long-term plan." Lincoln was all about living in the moment. It intensified experience, to be sure, and celebrated originality, while imparting little of the critical thinking that can distinguish between useful innovation and novelty for novelty's sake. Ultimately, the combination of Lincoln and dyslexia made Rockefeller both more and less dependent on the superior minds he collected at the behest of his mother and in response to his father's example. His regard for expertise left him vulnerable to the latest guru or academic for hire—disdainfully labeled "earpissers" by nominal insiders who failed to see how, for example, Edward Teller's skills in building a hydrogen bomb qualified him to give advice on the sanitation woes of New York City.

Dyslexia might have crushed a less robust spirit than Nelson Rockefeller. His lifelong struggle with the written word testified to his resourcefulness and stoicism. But it also left this self-professed "puzzle child" feeling equally reliant and resentful, balanced precariously between intellectual deference and cocky self-assertion.

5

DARTMOUTH WAS NELSON Rockefeller's kind of college, hearty in its fellowship, moderate in its scholarly demands, a sociable sequel to the freewheeling creativity of Lincoln. Whereas the New York school gloried in its novelty, however, Dartmouth had lived—some would say languished—nearly two centuries in the shadow of Ivy League powerhouses like Harvard and Yale. Founded in 1769 by a Connecticut minister zealous to educate and Christianize Native American youth, the institution subsequently severed its shallow roots and migrated north to the village of Hanover, on the right bank of the Connecticut River that separates New Hampshire from Vermont. Granite State lawmakers eager to revoke the school's erstwhile royal charter touched off a schism, with rival Dartmouths staking claims to legitimacy until Daniel Webster, class of 1801, argued the case for a private college before the United States Supreme Court.

His appeal stressed the sanctity of contracts, but it was Webster's emotional invocation of alma mater ("It is . . . a small college. And yet *there are those who love it!*") that won him legal immortality. Like Dartmouth's second most famous graduate, the godlike Daniel spent a lifetime running after the presidency and, between elections, behaving in ways that put the White House effectively beyond his grasp. A century later, Webster's ghost would not have felt out of place among the white-brick structures of Dartmouth Row bordering the Green, a former cattle pasture fenced off by Victorian-era undergraduates. The first week of college is a gauntlet line of alien faces, behavioral novelties, and instant traditions. For Nelson Rockefeller, the most disagreeable of trials were embraced like a pretty girl. At the start of October 1926, he told his brother John that he hadn't enjoyed a moment's rest between running errands and carrying trunks for sophomores eager to expunge memories of their own slavish treatment the previous year. Characteristically, Nelson didn't wait for anyone to assign him the task, but hustled to clean the first upperclassman's room he found. Its occupant became an early friend and mentor.

In return for beating carpets ("and to beat a carpet is no joke"), Nelson received a vigorous paddling of his hindquarters. To this perpetual optimist, even ritualized humiliation had its positive aspect, as "of course we met lots of nice fellows and it brought all the fellows in our class closer together right away for protection." Class spirit provided scant defense when cries of "Thirty up" echoed through Hitchcock Hall, the newest occupants of which passed one Saturday clad in baby bonnets, their underclothes, and nothing else. "Luckily it was warm," Nelson reported. Less fortunate classmates contracted pneumonia while standing naked atop the porch of a Dartmouth frat house, counting out the time every five minutes. Deposited one night in unfamiliar country and ordered to find his way back to campus, a resourceful Nelson stashed a Boy Scout knife inside a rolled-up sock as protection against farmhouse dogs in the lonely countryside. On another occasion, he took his chances inside a stone tower whose spiral staircase became an obstacle course for blindfolded youths, uncertain whether anyone would catch them before a nasty fall.

Forced to make ends meet on an annual allowance of $1,500 (raised to $2,100 at the start of his junior year), nothing did more to establish his everyman image, and subsequent popularity on campus, than Nelson's habit of mooching change wherever it could be had. Undergraduate Victor Borella was talking to a classmate one evening when an unknown student appeared out of the darkness to cadge a quarter for a picture show. On learning his identity, Borella was incredulous. "I thought it was a joke," he said later. "I knew there was a Rockefeller in college, but I couldn't imagine why he'd be borrowing money." A professor encountering Nelson on the street invited him to dinner "sometime."

"How about tonight?" replied Nelson, whose pockets held twelve cents at the time.

It was at Dartmouth that Nelson began to run with the hares and hunt with the hounds, moving comfortably between President Hopkins's dining room and the rowdy back porch of Ma Smalley's boardinghouse. From the Eyrie came Chinese rugs and comfortable chairs with which to furnish his three-room corner suite on the top floor of Hitchcock. Nelson slept on a $6 mattress, stretched across a pair of skis to support his back. (Muscle cramps and chronic lower back pain were to plague him for the rest of his life.) During his first semester, he shared these quarters with his Lincoln classmate Sheldon Stark. At midyear, Nelson switched roommates. His new companion was an introverted prep school grad named John French, whose mother served with Abby on the national board of the YWCA. Reputedly blessed with the highest IQ in the class, French could read Charles Austin Beard's *Rise of American Civilization* the night before a history exam and ace the test. Nelson, by contrast, rose at five o'clock each morning to memorize dates, only to pull a B minus on the same test.

"This is where I became very competitive because I had four years of trying . . . to keep up with him," Rockefeller said of French. "I really carried him socially and he carried me intellectually." French detected in his new friend a surprising naïveté to match his lack of pretense. In the spring of their freshman year, the pair cosigned a letter to *The Dartmouth* protesting the time and effort diverted from academic labors by the rituals of fraternity rushing. Nelson was appalled to find his words reproduced on the front page of the next day's *New York Herald Tribune*; the last thing he wanted was to call attention to himself. In the fall of 1927, the White and Connecticut rivers rushed over their banks, burying the town of White River Junction in mud. Nelson was in the vanguard of Dartmouth students who rushed to the scene to offer assistance. His sole request was to be sent to a remote stretch of riverfront. For the same reason, he ducked out of sight when his soccer teammates arrived at West Point for a much publicized game with Army. "If we get our picture in the paper," Nelson revealed to his mystified coach, "Father cuts our allowances."*

6

WEDGED AMONG THE foothills of the White Mountains, closer to Montreal than to Boston, Dartmouth was defined by its isolation. Now, as in Daniel Webster's time, physical exertion competed for student attention with

---

* On another occasion, President Hopkins himself received a dressing-down from the pilot of a Ford trimotor plane in which the president had enjoyed a demonstration ride, accompanied by Nelson and several other students. Never mind the president's safety; if it ever got back to Detroit that Rockefeller had risked his life by leaning out a plane window to take pictures, the pilot told Hopkins, he could lose his job.

mental calisthenics. Winter treks through the nearby Presidential Range substituted for urban fleshpots. Cynics taunted Ernest Hopkins's school for having the largest gymnasium and the smallest library in the East. ("That burned me up," said Hopkins, who persuaded financier George F. Baker to donate $1 million for the library that bears his name, constructed in the president's favorite Oxbridge style, mocked by architectural modernists as "boxcar Georgian.") Nelson, reasonably well acquainted with each, found time nonetheless to join the Dartmouth Outing Club and its offshoot, Cabin and Trail. A sprained ankle ruled out football, but not soccer, in which he earned a varsity "D" for his aggressive, down-the-middle approach to the game. He also took up skiing, skimming the icy crust on cross-country excursions, wrapping his skis in sealskins before ascending the slopes in that pre–tow lift era.

With few outlets for student aggression besides snowball fights, Rockefeller organized freshman forces in a wild scrimmage with sophomores. He inserted fire hoses through the mail slots in dorm rooms and, one night, broke a window by hurling oranges across Hitchcock's courtyard. Yet he was no rebel. By his own recollection, "I didn't drink. I didn't smoke. I didn't like dirty stories." Answering to the nickname Rocky, Nelson was on a first-name basis with virtually everyone he encountered. Especially the faculty. "My idea has been to get to know the teachers as soon as possible," he wrote home during his first semester. "I felt I could get more out of the courses if there was more of a personal relationship between the teacher and I."

His sunny demeanor disguised a budding grind. Before major exams, Nelson often disappeared from campus, holing up in nearby Woodstock, where fewer distractions threatened his marathon study sessions. "Time is pretty valuable at college," he advised his brother Laurance, "and you'll find that the boys who sit around in other fellows' rooms all the time and spill a lot of hot air usually don't get very far. . . ." Less conscientious students dropping by 18 Hitchcock found Nelson reluctant to join in late night bull sessions. When he did take part, said one contemporary, he "always seemed to have minority people— the downtrodden—on his mind." His parents had trained him well. Alerted to a pair of classmates spending their Christmas holiday in a cheap New York hotel, Nelson invited them for dinner at 10 West Fifty-fourth, after which Abby conducted a tour of her Japanese print collection and took the young visitors to the theater.

"Well, I got my first exams, and am sill in college," Nelson announced in the spring of his freshman year. "To tell you the truth, when it came right down to taking the exams, I really enjoyed it. It is sort of like a challenge or a game, when you see how many questions you can answer." Most days he got in a few hours' study before a breakfast of cold cereal, after which he made his bed and cleaned his mother's carpets. Classes occupied him from midmorning until midafternoon. Soccer practice or photography assignments preceded a sober New England supper, followed by more studying until nine o'clock. Then he and John French put away their textbooks to patronize a student vendor selling "toast sides" and milk outside their dorm. Thus fortified, the boys settled back to ponder subjects of perennial fascination to college males: the future and girls.

At the moment, Nelson entertained only vague thoughts of working in the family enterprises. Assessing his romantic prospects, he oscillated between delight over the latest correspondence from Tod and gloom occasioned by her seeming neglect. Apologizing for her infrequent letters, when she did write Tod offered self-deprecating jabs at the mildewed traditions of her social set. Of a particularly dull tea party, she declared, "No one could be a bigger failure than I am. I just manage to get out of sight when Mother comes dashing over and says, 'Come dear. I want you to meet so and so who knew your Aunt's daughter's sister's cousin.' I then stand on one foot and another to try to think of something to say and succeed in being most unattractive. . . . Pray for me as I'm scared to death. I don't seem to be able to do anything but act crazy at a dance here just as I do at N[ortheast] H[arbor]. (How I miss it!) Most of the older people think I have a screw loose and I know I have."

More seriously, she praised Nelson for passing his exams and urged him not to abandon his soccer game. Nelson reciprocated by sending her an etching and a gold sailboat for her charm bracelet. In January 1927, Tod endured the final ball of the debutante season. Off the dance floor, she enrolled in a Junior League program that exposed her to slums and took her into Philadelphia-area hospitals. Rather like the young Eleanor Roosevelt, another ugly duckling who despaired of becoming a swan, Tod reproached herself in advance. "I am no success with the sick," she complained, "they all suffer relapses when I come along, those that are partly blind lose their sight at once . . . and the poor people commit suicide the instant they see my pretty face." Meanwhile, Nelson began making the 110-mile trip to Northampton, Massachusetts, where he courted a Smith College student named Alida Milliken, about whom he felt "really quite crazy." His rapture was short-lived. He was in "a bad way," Nelson lamented, "because I can't fall in love with anyone and Tod won't give me any time. I do wish I really liked some girl a lot. It makes life much more interesting."

Sorely missing "the sensitivity of the family and a co-educational school," beginning in April 1927 he taught a Sunday school class for little girls at Hanover's White Church on Wentworth Street, successor to an earlier chapel demolished in a long-ago student riot. It took courage to saunter by the Freshman Commons after his class let out, holding hands and chatting animatedly with half a dozen nine-year-olds. One Sabbath, taunted beyond endurance, the sensitive pugilist knocked down one of his tormentors, then resumed his stroll. He plunged into a campaign to beautify the Dartmouth campus by installing flower boxes outside his rooms. The conventional Johnny French, fearing for their social prospects, pleaded with his roommate to avoid a fresh round of derision.*

Nelson was immovable. With the advent of the spring planting season, he received a package of English daisy seeds from the head gardener at Pocantico. To French's amazement, other boys began to emulate his roommate's example. Looking back, Rockefeller recounted the episode for its moral, rather than aesthetic, significance. "Do what you think is right in this world," he insisted. "Others will follow."

7

THE SOLICITUDE OF his mother remained a constant, if occasionally cloying, part of Nelson's life. "I have a feeling as if your eyes had just been opened to the possibilities of the world, both spiritually and socially," Abby rejoiced in the spring of his freshman year. She had ordered him a suit for an upcoming European trip. "Shall I get you golf stockings and a cravat for it or will you do that? I do hope you like it. I thought it nice and smart and sporty." His personal interest in clothes remained negligible. In an era when Dartmouth men attending the Harvard weekend packed white tie and tails, he thought nothing of turning up at a house formal in his usual dirty corduroys. That he appeared at all was something of a concession. Resenting the hours stolen from his classwork, he dragged himself to a series of open houses and tolerated emissaries from half a dozen fraternities.

After a period of indecision, he finally settled on Psi Upsilon, the self-imagined gentlemen's fraternity. Displaying a rare touch of inferiority complex, Nelson likened his new crowd to the sorts of fellows his brother John might encounter at a Princeton club or Yale fraternity. "Not backwoodsmen," he added pointedly. In the end, neither he nor John French ever lived in the frat house, preferring to remain in Hitchcock until the start of their senior year, when both moved to Casque and Gauntlet, an elite senior society whose unheated top floor—"the wind tunnel" to its shivering occupants—afforded

---

* His classroom venture may have been inspired by Tod. In the same letter in which she pronounced herself "mad with jealousy" over Nelson's frequent allusions to a girl named Elly Moss, she revealed her own plans to teach Sunday school. "They'll all probably grow up to be Mohammedan or something as soon as I get thru with them." MTC–NAR, "Dear Nelson," Saturday, 1927 [otherwise undated], RAC.

barracks-style sleeping accommodations. On winter nights, when the indoor thermometer registered eighteen below zero, Nelson wore an old raccoon coat to bed. "It was a lot of fun," he insisted.

At Psi Upsilon he befriended Edwin Toothacher, a Denver boy recruited to play football by a group of alumni who had promised to pay his tuition. Toothacher lost his place on the team after being placed on academic probation. His would-be financial backers simultaneously lost their interest in him. In despair, the young man trudged to the telegraph office to wire his father for a ticket home. There he encountered Nelson, from whom he received a pep talk, followed by a loan from his scanty reserves. By the end of the year, Toothacher was off probation and on his way toward handsome grades, a scholarship, and a letter in football. After graduation, Nelson quietly pulled strings to land him a job with the Colorado Fuel and Iron Company.

For his postfreshman summer, Nelson planned a European holiday with his brother John. In Geneva, they dined with officials from the League of Nations interested in advancing world peace through Rockefeller philanthropy. Venturing into Weimar Germany, blind to hyperinflation and flaring political unrest, Nelson purchased a pair of ornate beer steins "to drink milk in." His nineteenth birthday found the brothers in Berlin. There Nelson received a message from Junior, absolving him of some earlier financial carelessness, "and what a treat it turned out to be! It was great and I just couldn't wait until tomorrow to answer it, so I got up and here I am." Apologizing profusely for some unpaid bills in Hanover, Nelson also convicted himself of "cowerdness. I've been trying to fight that in myself for quite a time now, but every once and a while just when I get in a tight place I do the easy thing like a coward instead of being a man." If anything, he continued, Junior had been unduly lenient with him. His contrition was real enough, but so was the artfulness with which he inextricably wove sincerity and pose.

"You know I really don't think I deserve any creadit for my change in attitude tward my work during the last two years," said Nelson, exhibiting a cheeky mixture of self-congratulation and self-flagellation. "I think rather I should be condemd for not coming round to a sensable viewpoint sooner and having wasted so much of my time and your energy and money in bringing me to the right way of thinking." Anyone doubting his inheritance of the Aldrich political genes should consider the manipulative talents Nelson deployed in the fall of 1927. Until now, his studious roommate, John French, had been credited with sparking the dramatic surge in Nelson's grades during his sophomore year. Rockefeller himself was explicit on this point, insisting that he would be "damned" if he let French outperform him. In time, both boys secured election to Phi Beta Kappa, causing French to grumble, "It doesn't mean anything if Nelson Rockefeller can be a Phi Beta," and reportedly threatened to discard his key.*

Deserved or not, Nelson's pursuit of scholarly recognition had less to do with academic than automotive glory and a cunning plan to get a new car out of his tightfisted father. Freshmen at Dartmouth were prohibited from possessing automobiles. Returning for his sophomore year, Nelson realized that his chances of trading in an all-too-conspicuous bicycle for the Buick of his fantasies equaled those of the lowliest scholarship student. It galled him to see other boys driving around in elaborately customized vehicles. He *had* to have a car to entertain girls, Nelson told his brother John: "If . . . you want to go anywhere—say Smith—to see one, you need a car to get there." At a recent Vassar weekend, made possible by John French's 1924 Cadillac, his future sister-in-law Mary French had introduced Nelson to "heaps of nice people," among them yet another future family member, Blanchette Hooker. Dancing ensued. "Being cut in on by the girls was lots of fun," said Nelson, well aware of his desirability.

This was not an argument likely to move his traditionalist parent. Nelson had a brainstorm. If he could somehow raise his grade average to Phi Beta Kappa levels, his bargaining position with Junior would be greatly strengthened. "I have already won Ma over," he confided to John, "and I don't see why Pa wouldn't buy into the plan." Securing Abby's support would not have been difficult under any circumstances, but Nelson took no chances. He gave her one of two fraternity pins he had received on joining Psi Upsilon. "I don't expect you will be able to wear it much," he remarked, "but keep it as a symbol of the love that comes with it." Over the Christmas break, mother and son visited several Manhattan art galleries. He felt as if he were being introduced to a new world of beauty, Nelson wrote afterward, "and for the first time I think I have really been able to appreciate and understand pictures." Indeed, once he returned to New York permanently, he hoped to "maybe do a tiny bit of collecting myself."

At present, Nelson told Abby, he saw no girl he loved enough to spend his life with. "I suppose I'll meet one someday. Mum, if only you were a girl that would solve the problem. But then, of course, I'd be without the best mother in the world." Comforted by this fulsome tribute, Abby presented Nelson with an

---

* Their competition did not preclude the roommates from cutting a deal whereby Nelson ran successfully for sophomore class vice president, a warm-up for his election as president of the junior class. In return, Nelson agreed to support French for the same office during their senior year. In the event, Nelson split the presidential vote with another fraternity man, opening the way for a football player named Al Blumgarten to take the prize. To show there were no hard feelings, he helped write Blumgarten's inaugural address.

"amusing" Daumier lithograph bought in Paris for his rooms. Looking to the future, she wrote, "It would be a great joy to me if you did find that you had a real love for and interest in beautiful things. We could have such good times going about together and if you start to cultivate your taste and eye so young, you ought to be good at it by the time you can afford to collect much." The same week he informed his mother that their gallery explorations constituted "the outstanding event of my vacation," Nelson opened a second front in the car wars. After reconsidering the matter, Nelson let it be known, he had come to accept the paternal view that having his own car on campus might not be a healthy influence on the other men.

This was a mere flanking maneuver. The main thrust came in February 1928, when he reported three B's and two A's, "which gives me an average a little better than Phi Beta." Word of their son's latest accomplishments, communicated personally by President Hopkins, evoked differing parental reactions. Junior rushed to share the news with educators at the Lincoln School. Abby was more measured in her response. Never doubting the quality of his mind, she had feared "a little" Nelson's willingness to discipline his intelligence through hard study. "Dear boy," she wrote, "your life, if it is to be really useful, consecrated and successful will need all the brains, all the courage, all the wisdom and all the patience that you have in you. . . . I am sure that you have the power, but it must be harnessed to steadiness and a desire for perfection."

From his father, he expected more tangible rewards. Lauding Junior's "desire to do the right thing" where his automotive interests were concerned, Nelson shrewdly gave ground on the secondary issue of a new car for campus use. He was perfectly willing to settle for a rental car in Hanover, he concluded, if supplemented by the vehicle of his choice at home, "which of course would belong to you as the other cars have." The Buick mentioned by his father was "ideal . . . it is exactly what I had been thinking of." As evidence of this, he had thoroughly researched the virtues of a sporty roadster versus a five-passenger touring car. While the latter might, at first blush, appear more practical, the truth was that he hardly ever used a backseat except for baggage. Upon careful consideration, wrote Nelson, "I would really rather have the roadster—that is, if you don't object." He would be all the more grateful if the vehicle could be delivered by mid-June, so it might be broken in before he embarked on another European summer.

His father's resistance melted. Nelson had made the entire family proud by his classroom accomplishments. He had shown good faith in agreeing to the use of rental cars around college (though allowing Junior to reimburse him for their cost). In return for these achievements and this concession, Junior duly ordered a black six-wheel Buick deluxe roadster, customized with red stripe and spokes and deliverable within ten days. He was "happy beyond expression," Junior informed his son, "to feel that we can always all of us talk over any matter with open minds, in the confident assurance that each one wants only what is best and that the decision reached ultimately will be mutually satisfactory and wise." Thus Nelson got his car, and his father got taken for a ride.

Four

"THE LUCKIEST PERSON IN THE WORLD"

*Of course we read in the paper that you had gotten a black eye in the
Sophomore–Freshman scrimmage. I hope that this was only rumor. . . . I
was sorry to see that the Freshmen got the better of you. One doesn't mind
a black eye if he is on the winning side.*

—ABBY ALDRICH ROCKEFELLER, to Nelson, April 1928

*I always liked girls. I found them very good company and much more
sensitive than men.*

—NELSON A. ROCKEFELLER

1

FOR A MONTH in the summer of 1928, Nelson resided with a doctor's family
in Le Mont-Dore, a sulfur-scented spa resort in the Dordogne region of
France. Accompanied by a Union Theological seminarian, the young American worked on his tennis game and explored the wooded countryside by car.
Lessons of another sort were imparted by the woman of the house. One night
she entered Nelson's room and locked the door behind her. "I was 18. She was
about 35." He finally persuaded her to leave. "This was getting too complicated," he told himself. He quickly pulled up stakes and headed for the Amsterdam Olympics. A different fate befell Nelson's seminarian-tutor. He chose to
stay behind and was named corespondent in a divorce case involving the doctor
and his faithless wife.

Nelson did not lack for feminine company. In Paris, he dallied with a Belgian princess and escorted an American girl to Montmartre for Bastille Day
festivities. With his brother John working in the information section of the
League of Nations, Nelson let the world come to him in the form of "8 or 10
rather nice girls" of various nationalities, none of whom generated much interest. Tod remained the only serious contender for Nelson's affections, yet that
did not prevent him from visiting Alida Milliken or other potential flames. In-

tellectually, too, he hedged his bets by joining the Dartmouth honors group in economics, where a course on business organization let him dispute a visiting lecturer's claim that wealth and intellectual achievement were incompatible. Each student in the class was invited to survey a particular enterprise before applying its lessons to the economic principles extolled by the professor. "Of course I have chosen the Standard Oil Co. for my study," Nelson wrote home. Typically, he went to the source, asking his father to persuade Senior to share stories of his business career. When the old man declined, Nelson fell back on an unpublished company history and some extensive interviews of Senior conducted by a friendly scholar.

In prefacing "The Standard Oil Company and Its Monopolistic Tendencies," Nelson said it would be easy for him to make a defense of the industrial giant assailed by turn-of-the-century muckrakers—which is pretty much what he did for the next fifty-one pages. No firm had been coerced into joining the nascent monopoly, Nelson maintained. Rather, meritocracy had exerted its relentless logic. "They could not hope to compete with us," he quoted JDR. "We had the best machinery, the best methods and the best minds in the oil business." In the courts and, even more, in the court of public opinion, Standard had been punished for conspicuous success accruing from "good business practices"—hard work, brains, thrift, "and the most elaborate accounting system."

Apparently, the protagonist of this heroic narrative never read his grandson's brief. In his final years, determined to live to one hundred, Senior avoided controversies and conserved his energies. It was another John D. Rockefeller for whom Nelson's thesis was written. He didn't know when anything had interested him more, Nelson told his father in February 1929. "For the first time I felt that I really knew Grandfather a little—got a glimpse into the power and grandeur of his life." He had tried to put these feelings on paper and share them with the old man, but, "speechless" over Senior's influence for good, he gave up after several feeble attempts. "Among other things [his paper] brought out the importance and value of money. And I was able to see as never before the reason and true significance of keeping accounts as you have always asked us to do . . . it dawned upon me that I have up to now merely been obeying the letter of the law, as it were, and not the spirit, and that I have been missing the whole point."

Under the circumstances, Nelson concluded, it would be wrong to accept his father's hundred-dollar bonus for keeping orderly accounts in 1928. Therefore, "with many thanks," he was returning the gift. For his thesis, Nelson received an A minus. His reward for so publicly honoring Rockefeller family values was incalculable. Junior excerpted his son's most honeyed words and sent them, confidentially, to Senior, with compliments of his own for "a marvelous heritage in achievement, in constructive and creative power," bequeathed by the old man.

2

"THE MORE I know of life and the more I read history the more I realize the importance of Wives and Mothers," Abby informed Nelson. "Brains, breeding, character and charm are essential." Here were the Four Horsemen of suitable courtship and successful marriage.* Early in 1929, Nelson told his parents of a distant cousin in Cleveland, whom he had visited five days in a row. "Now I suppose you think I'm forgetting Tod and have fallen for Helen. Well, I have fallen for Helen in a sense, but it doesn't effect my love for Tod in the least bit. I think I'm too young to only know and like one girl, so I periodically fall for someone—about once a year—but always giving them to understand how I feel about Tod."

That spring, Nelson put his emotional cards on the table, describing the tall brunette whose vitality and sense of fun made him think of his mother. "Tod has almost everything—as far as I can see," he confided to Abby. "Intelligence; a wonderful sense of humor; a good sense of balance, and of values; the ability to manage people and things and at all times to keep her head; she is never dull or uninteresting. . . . And for no other girl or woman could I say this except my mother, who has always been my standard and a mighty high one." He was franker still in weighing the negatives of his potential bride. "The only trouble with Tod is that she is slightly taller than I am when she has on high heels, that she isn't terribly good looking and that she is a little over a year older than I am."

This antiseptic estimate was of a piece with Nelson's resolve to marry at twenty-one. "I wanted to get on with the business," he explained later. That his parents counseled patience was hardly surprising given their own protracted courtship. But they also entertained reservations, it appeared, about the woman Nelson had settled on. Late in 1928, Junior accepted an invitation to tour Egypt's Nile Valley, where he was lauded as a generous benefactor of the Oriental Institute and its archaeological work in Luxor. Thirty-six hours before their departure, the Rockefellers added Mary Todhunter Clark to their guest

---

* Flouting the rules egregiously, Nelson bet his roommate that he could persuade a couple of showgirls pictured in the *Herald Tribune*'s Sunday "Rotogravure" to go out with them. He neglected to tell French that both young ladies had been among his Lincoln School classmates. "I had them to the house and I remember the family was horrified," Nelson chortled. NROH, July 19, 1977, 47–48.

list. At first all went well. "Mary is the life of the party," reported Junior in January 1929, "she is running true to form in every way. She is always ready to do whatever is suggested, never is the slightest bit of trouble or responsibility and adds very greatly to the pleasure of us all." Abby agreed, describing Tod as "so sensible and amusing that all of the men in the party like to talk with her and she is always nice to them but never silly."

Tod felt less sure of herself. "I've never seen so many prime ministers and things in all my life," she told Nelson, "and am speechless with fright in front of them." She hoped that his family didn't regret including her in their party. "It certainly was a wild thing to do and I'm doing my best to keep them from fully realizing how hopeless I am in so many ways." She was right to be apprehensive. Somewhere among the nightly slide lectures, the examination of antiquities in the ramshackle Cairo Museum, and the dinners with Lord Allenby and Lady Colfax, Junior had developed second thoughts about his possible daughter-in-law. Acknowledging Tod to be "always pleasant and agreeable and liked by everyone," he had also come to regard her as "self-contained and inexpressive. I never know what she is thinking," he informed Nelson, "nor do I feel that Mama and I know her any better now than when we sailed."

3

AS A COMPOSITE of Rockefeller piety and Aldrich urbanity, Nelson the Dartmouth undergrad resembled a circus rider attempting to maintain his balance astride two mounts. Conflating his twin interests of business and art, he launched *Intercollegiate Pictorial*, a journal that quickly fell victim to the deepening hard times. *Five Lively Arts*, a glossy magazine Nelson contemplated in tandem with his classmate Walter Chrysler, never got off the drawing board. Then a course in landscape gardening moved him to reconsider his academic priorities. "Sometimes I wish I had majored in Art," Nelson notified Abby, "but I guess the economics will be of more value. I do love some of these other things, though. . . ." Eventually he decided to do them all: writing the paper on Standard Oil to gratify his curiosity about Rockefeller family history, while sampling the dizzying freedom of self-expression celebrated by his mother and her artistic circle.

Sixteen years after the revolutionary Armory Show of 1913 had jolted the art establishment, her annual art allowance from Junior doubled to $50,000, Abby Aldrich Rockefeller struck out in directions testing even his uncritical adoration. In the course of their Egyptian tour, Abby had run into Lillie P. Bliss, a gifted pianist and art patron who, out of respect for the more traditional sensibilities of her aged mother, hid her accumulated treasures in the basement of the family townhouse on East Thirty-seventh Street. On the return voyage, Abby met another adventuresome collector, Mary Quinn Sullivan, a onetime Indiana farm girl married to a prominent New York attorney. In May 1929, the three ladies lunched at 10 West Fifty-fourth Street with A. Conger Goodyear, a military man whose brush cut and gruff manner gave no hint of his passion for the sinuous nudes of Aristide Maillol and the gauzy mindscapes of Renoir and Gauguin. The martinet, it turned out, was also a modernist. As president of Buffalo's Albright Gallery, Goodyear had spent $5,000 to purchase Picasso's *La Toilette*, an action that led horrified trustees to evict him from office.

Moving to the more adventurous precincts of New York City, Goodyear needed less than twenty-four hours to accept Abby's invitation to become president of a museum devoted to modernism in the visual arts. Her mind was full of ideas for a new Museum of Modern Art, Abby wrote Nelson excitedly. "Wouldn't it be splendid! It will be ready for you to be interested in when you get back to N.Y. to live." At Dartmouth, Nelson found his own cultural tutor in Churchill Lathrop, a self-confessed maverick from Princeton recruited by President Hopkins to develop an outstanding art library. Under Lathrop's guidance, Nelson immersed himself in texts extolling cubism, surrealism, and other modernist schools. He enrolled in drawing and sculpture classes, tried his hand at the etching press, experimented in clay. He also took painting lessons from visiting masters like Thomas Hart Benton and Charles Woodbury. That he had more interest than ability became glaringly apparent. Decades later, learning of a staff member in Albany who doubled as an abstract painter, Rockefeller asked the man how he came by his talent. Told that it welled up from inside, from a self-expression demanding release, Nelson responded dejectedly, "That's how I felt, but I could never do anything about it." Lathrop salved his disappointment by stressing the vital role of the art collector and patron. In April 1929, Nelson finished among the top scorers in a nationwide art appreciation test. "I think perhaps I'm beginning to acquire some of your good taste," he notified his mother.

Elsewhere that spring, Nelson picked up Tod in Philadelphia and drove her to Princeton for his brother John's graduation. In the course of the trip, some kind of emotional crisis occurred, prompting Tod to question the depth of Nelson's attachment. "Don't you think that you want to fall in love with me more than you actually are?" she wrote plaintively. "Don't force yourself into it." As for her own feelings, "All I know is that I miss you dreadfully and ten times a day I wish you were here. At such moments I decide I love you and that is all there is to it. The next second I go to a tennis party and in swimming with a crowd of people and decide I don't love anybody and couldn't think of attaching myself to one person." Of one thing she was certain. She didn't want to be hurt. "For heaven's sake get all that flirtatiousness out of your system before you and I get married if we ever do. If we should be married about a year and you came to me with a love confession about falling in love with some charming woman—well—it would break my heart that's all."

By the time this cri de coeur reached him, Nelson was thousands of miles away, dodging ice floes off the Canadian Maritimes with his brother Laurance. They were part of a crew commanded by Sir Wilfred T. Grenfell, a Schweitzer of the ice caps, whose medicine and missionary work did for the inhabitants of Labrador what his German counterpart was to do for the natives of Lambaréné. July 8, 1929, marked Nelson's twenty-first birthday. He spent it on board Grenfell's ship, the *Maravel*, washing dishes and pondering the ninety years being observed that same day by his grandfather. He felt like a little sapling in the shadow of a mighty fir. "But, the sapling still has time to grow and develop, and someday it might itself turn into a tree of some merit." To Abby, he took the occasion to reiterate his love for Tod—"whatever being in love means"—before adding, "She is the only girl that I know who measures up anywhere nearly to the standards set by you." Promising to do nothing in haste, he assured his parents that at least a year would elapse before the couple could even become engaged.

"You have become a man and must 'put away childish things,'" Tod advised him, "but I'm wondering if that is at all possible." Nelson had sent her a copy of Walter Lippmann's *A Preface to Morals*, which he recommended for its selective embrace of modernity (birth control), its frank repudiation of an anthropomorphic God, and its heretical refusal to equate popular government with good government. Lippmann's "disinterested man" was defined by stoic detachment. "When men can no longer be theists," he wrote, "they must, if they are civilized, become humanists." Equally rigorous was the author's view of present-day marriage. "Love and nothing else very soon is nothing else," Lippmann asserted. Compatibility trumped passion. Tod was perplexed. "You worry me with all your careful thought out philosophy," she told Nelson. What could Lippmann possibly know of moonlight sails when she donned her lover's sweaters and he wrapped himself in a spinnaker as protection against the cold salt air? Or Seal Cove picnics or the sunset over Mount Desert? "Don't think about marriage so cold-bloodedly," Tod pleaded. "To tell you the honest truth I never have tried to philosophize on love before. I've always thought I'd want to find out a little more about it." Adding to her worries, she and Nelson communicated better in letters than when they were together. "We write things we never get a chance to say and I have a feeling that it is rather dangerous."

Nelson got a chance to display Lippmann's self-reliant heroics when the *Maravel* became fogbound on its return trip and Laurance was laid low by appendicitis. Grenfell wanted to operate on the eighteen-year-old with a sterilized knife. Nelson refused. Insistent on getting his brother back to a mainland hospital, he steered for the Bay of Islands and a train that ran but twice a week. "The Captain said he couldn't take us back because the fog was too heavy. I said I'd take responsibility for the ship. There was a cliff that I had seen coming out, where I could take a compass course from the mouth of the harbor, straight to the cliff, and from the cliff the reflected sound gave us another compass course which directed us into the harbor. Fortunately, we caught the train." At the Eyrie, Junior and Abby were left to ponder another of their son's birthday declarations. He didn't relish the idea of going into someone else's business, said Nelson, "making a few minor changes here and there," only to finally gain control "for a few years" in his sixties. "No, that isn't my idea of having a real life . . . unless I have some definite goal I'm afraid I'll just repeat my career at college over on a larger scale—that is, go into a lot of different things, do a little in each, but not really make a success of any of them." He had been giving serious thought to becoming an architect, Nelson concluded, "but we'll have to discuss things when I get back." With another year of college staring him in the face, there was no rush to decide.

4

IN THE FALL of 1929, Nelson returned to Hanover for his senior year. In mid-September, he and Tod enjoyed a brief, highly charged reunion. "Your letter came this morning and I've been reading it over and over all day," she told Nelson following his departure. "For one whole month I hadn't thought of another thing but you, then suddenly you were gone again and there I was trying to pick up my life where it left off but utterly unable to since in that one month I had completely changed inside and out." Nelson's transformation was hardly less dramatic. Telling his parents he was "really and truly despritly in love," he counted the days until the October weekend when he and Tod could be together again, this time at Pocantico. The anticipation only aggravated Tod's self-doubt. "The more I get to know myself the more I realize how queer I am . . . lately I've been peculiar beyond words and so this is a letter to warn you that within six days you will see me face to face so you better decide between now and then whether or not you can resign yourself to having a queer wife."

Her anxieties evaporated in the flamboyantly colored Pocantico Hills, which she explored with Nelson on horseback and by automobile. Their four days together banished any lingering reserve, Nelson notified his parents on October 23. Only one incident marred the couple's joy. Of *Radiant Motherhood* and other sexually explicit titles recommended to Nelson and his Dartmouth roommate by birth control pioneer Margaret Sanger, an embarrassed Tod wrote, "Don't you dare tell Johnnie French you gave me those books, because I never would be able to look him in the eyes again." Nelson shared news of his engagement with his brothers John and Laurance before telling his father, who objected to the headstrong manner in which Nelson had rushed into the match with minimal family consultation. "I'm afraid I cause you much more trouble and worry than your business problems," Nelson wrote Junior in response. "Some day I'll learn to think more before I act. . . . I know I've bungled things pretty badly to date in connection with Tod—but Pa . . . I mean to do the right thing."

For thirteen pages, he chipped away at paternal resistance. He would begin by apologizing to Mr. Clark. The wedding would take place after Nelson's June graduation. Setting aside his reservations about climbing the corporate or charitable ladders, he promised to take his place in the family office no later than December 1, 1930. He and Tod planned on taking a small apartment in the city but would otherwise reside at Pocantico. Finally Nelson appealed to his father, "as a connoisseur on diamonds," for guidance in choosing an engagement ring for his fiancée. Hearing what he wanted to, Junior charged off his son's impulsiveness as a trait common to youth. "Because you are in that respect more like Mama," he wrote Nelson, "it is easier for her to understand you and more rightly to evaluate your thought and action. But that does not for a moment mean that you and I cannot see eye to eye completely and wholly. It only means"—and here came the sting in the tail—"that I will try to take less seriously things which you say and plans which you propose until I know they represent a real conviction . . . while you in turn will perhaps grow to earmark for my benefit opinions and plans which are tentative and subject to change."

This veiled rebuke scarcely prepared Nelson for what followed. His father advised an early announcement of wedding plans and the shortest possible engagement. He offered Nelson and Tod use of the Eyrie between their wedding day and the start of their global honeymoon (singling out for praise as an "adorable place for quiet times together" the Rest House he and Abby favored for afternoon trysts). He also dangled before the couple a Revolutionary-era house on the Pocantico estate as an appropriate country residence. Junior spent $120,000 on a necklace of pink pearls for his daughter-in-law-to-be. For Nelson, he set aside $25,000 in stock, augmented by the rent of a ten-room penthouse apartment just off Park Avenue and the repair, furnishing, and maintenance of the Pocantico farmhouse.

Nelson thrilled over "Pa's wonderful letter," he told Abby on November 23, 1929, "but Mum, I shall always feel that if it wasn't for you things wouldn't be the way they are now." Tod was "such an adorable person—but one of the reasons I love her so is because she is more like you than any girl I have ever met."

He considered himself "the luckiest person in the world. To have you and Pa for parents, and Tod for fiancé, combined with all the wonderful breaks that I have had, is really more than one person deserves. But I guess the thing for me to do is to see if I can't make myself worthy of them all." Asked much later to identify the criteria on which he had based his decision to marry, Nelson adopted a matter-of-fact tone. "Somebody you loved," he responded crisply. "Somebody you were compatible to be with. Somebody who could cope with the kind of life that I wanted to live, which was being involved in national and international affairs, moving around meeting people. She had the capacity. She was very poised socially."

That fall, in anticipation of the public career he imagined for himself, Nelson accepted several speaking engagements in and around Hanover. Envisioning for her second son a more conventional life, Abby turned to her brother Winthrop, then president of the Chase National Bank. "Nelson is so young that we are very anxious that he should have a little more contact with the world before he goes downtown," she wrote. "Being a fond and proud mother I perhaps foolishly think that he is really quite unusual in his ability and charm, but he does need a little toning down." This, said Abby, would come from contact "with people of culture and character." Accordingly, she solicited banker Aldrich for the names of admirable influences in China, Japan, or India, countries that figured prominently in Nelson's honeymoon itinerary.

That his ideas about life after college might diverge from family expectations became even clearer as he contemplated Junior's offer of a house at Pocantico. DeLap Cottage was a snug Dutch Colonial under whose weathered roof George Washington was reputed to have slept at the time of the Battle of White Plains. If he was going to live in an Early American house, Nelson wanted to fill it with period pieces. Too expensive, said Junior. Not necessarily, replied Nelson. Armed with a set of blueprints and a copy of the seventh edition of antiquarian Wallace Nutting's furniture catalog, he carefully identified all the items needed to make DeLap Cottage livable, then totaled the estimated bill for reproductions. "Here is the plan," he told his father. "Here is the layout. Here is the cost. Now, if I can buy antiques within this total figure and furnish the house with antiques, would you be willing?" Warily, Junior nodded his assent. Henceforth, Nelson, sometimes accompanied by Tod, spent autumn weekends scouring the New England countryside in his Buick roadster, traipsing through cobwebbed attics and sagging barns in search of spindle chairs and curly maple highboys to be restored by a French Canadian carpenter in the nearby New Hampshire village of Lebanon. As a result, DeLap Cottage, rechristened Hawes House, was at least as historically authentic as anything to be seen at Colonial Williamsburg.

Meanwhile, he still had a final semester of college to complete. As one of

Dartmouth's inaugural group of senior fellows, Nelson could have his cake and eat it, too. Technically, he remained an economics major, bowing to Junior's expectation that he would one day join the family firm. In practical terms, the program allowed him to indulge his artistic interests. Thus vocation was trumped by avocation, and the mother-son alliance strengthened. In a course popularly known as Universe I, a professor displayed two images: the first, a sunset scene with church towers by French painter Jean-François Millet; the second, *Three Red Horses* by the German artist Franz Marc. Invited to choose between them, Nelson selected the less representational work, the only member of the class to do so. His teacher nodded in approval, explaining that the emotions generated by Millet's pious art were as obvious as they were powerful. With repeated viewing, the painting took second place to the *thought* in the picture. *Three Red Horses*, by contrast, was anything but predictable in the responses it generated. In art, if not in politics, instinct would always be Nelson's guide.*

Only a son of Abby's would drop economics for Monet and Artemus Packard's seminar "The Meaning of Art." Only a son of Junior's would have made a science out of leisure, as Nelson did in an article in the June 1930 issue of *Dartmouth Alumni Magazine*. By the time it appeared, the economic firestorm engulfing the United States was singeing the ivy-covered walls of Dartmouth. With a tin ear, he chose the onset of the Great Depression to advise his countrymen on "how to most profitably and enjoyably spend their leisure." Acknowledging the popularity of movies, cards, golf, and gossip, Nelson warned that, carried to an extreme, "they have a decidedly narrowing influence on the individual." In the third week of June, his family turned up in Hanover for commencement. In a talk before graduating seniors, Junior bluntly urged the all-male gathering to "live your lives [so] that you can look any damn man in the face and tell him to go to hell."

No one in his audience would heed this counsel more enthusiastically than his twenty-one-year-old son, a cum laude graduate in the class so fiercely exhorted. Dartmouth branded Nelson Rockefeller for life. In the 1930s, he became one of the youngest trustees in school history and a bulwark of the Hopkins administration. In the 1940s, he was the driving force behind the selection of Hopkins's successor, John Sloan Dickey. In the 1950s, he donated $1 million to help finance the Daniel Webster Scholarships. Another $500,000

---

* His senior year was made notable for his leadership of the Arts, a student organization fallen into disrepute—"come into the hands of a group of light-footed tea drinkers," as he archly phrased it—that staged a vigorous revival under his management. A student poetry competition elicited more than four hundred entries. Bertrand Russell inaugurated a lecture series that showcased Thornton Wilder, Sinclair Lewis, Carl Sandburg, and a very thirsty Edna St. Vincent Millay. Nelson played host to, and introduced, them all.

went to establish a professorship. Together with his father, Nelson bankrolled the modernistic Hopkins Center for the Arts, dedicated in 1962. Rockefeller became only the second recipient, after Robert Frost, of multiple honorary degrees from the college. Tipped off to the presence of Dartmouth alumni in a campaign crowd, Nelson could spontaneously break out in a chant of "Wa-hoo-wa," much to the puzzlement of the uninitiated.

Sentimental ties aside, Rockefeller created around him something of a Dartmouth Mafia, paralleling John F. Kennedy's Irish Bostonians and the sun-bronzed Californians who surrounded Ronald Reagan. Victor Borella, the college dropout who witnessed Nelson scrounging for funds, became the first director of industrial relations for Rockefeller Center, where he helped his classmate forge lasting bonds with George Meany and other powerful labor chieftains. In 1958, Pat Weaver, the television pioneer responsible for both *Today* and *The Tonight Show*, neutralized Rockefeller's dyslexia by crafting campaign spots emphasizing the candidate's warmth and sincerity. Elected "Most Likely to Succeed" by the class of 1930, Bob Bottome also beat out Nelson for the title "Most Versatile." He wound up managing a Venezuelan ranch owned by his friend and classmate. Bob McClory served multiple terms in Congress, where he juggled his convictions as a Rockefeller Republican against the more conservative leanings of his rural Illinois district. As one of the first Republicans in the House to support Richard Nixon's impeachment, McClory helped elevate Gerald Ford to the presidency and Rockefeller to the nation's second highest office. Meade Alcorn was one of five former chairmen of the Republican National Committee to endorse Rockefeller's 1968 bid for the White House. Sprinkle in the usual quota of railroad executives, university presidents, advertising directors, and brokerage house officials, and it should surprise no one that the class of 1930 regarded itself as one of the most accomplished in Dartmouth history.

5

I T IS NOT easy to reconcile the formidable, upright, occasionally waspish figure of the mature Tod Rockefeller with the moonstruck young woman who lowered her emotional guard in the months preceding her June 1930 wedding. Her letters to Nelson that spring sound alternating notes of romantic conviction and the distant dog's bark of abandonment. "It doesn't seem possible but every time I see you my love grows," she told him. "You're the most precious, most thoughtful, the most understanding, the most delightful, most lovable person I know. . . . To think that it took me three years to discover it makes me very ashamed. But we're both still only babes and have our lives ahead of us so I will try to make amends. My only fear now is that I shall go to the other extreme and love you too much and thereby cause you to tire of me as they do in books."

Tod entertained other doubts, feebly disguised even at moments of greatest anticipation. "Of course our life shall be one long romance, especially if we establish that total mutual understanding which is in the process of developing now. There is romance in everything in life if you only know how to find it. It's only the cold, prosaic, matter of fact people that can't find it and I don't think either of us belong to that type. If either of us ever feels that they have to go elsewhere to find romance and beauty, then that is the proof that there is something terribly wrong between us and I pray to God that this never happens." Tod flirted with modernity, while beating her wings against the gilded cage of Main Line decorum. She thanked Nelson for obtaining birth control devices for use on their honeymoon. "I don't know how I'd have managed it—probably had a child or two in India."

Capable of solemn deference one moment, she could be humorously irreverent the next. If Nelson persisted in addressing her as Toady, Tod would call him Nelly Jelly. At other times, her casual self-mockery was the opposite of amusing. "Our children (when we have them) must be cute and precious for I won't love them if they're not," Tod warned her fiancé. If they met these standards, on the other hand, "I shall be a very good mother to them and have one a year for 10 years. . . . If they are like you all well and good, but if they are like me I'll be thoroughly disgusted. I won't have any lanky, spindly spooks around my house." Disturbed by the intensity of her feelings, Tod told Nelson, "You have become so much the light of my life and I admire you so increasingly that I find I'm shaping all my ideas and points of view as yours. I must stop this for fear of completely losing any individuality. We do make a rare pair tho I'm sure and when we are together I get a terrific superiority complex and feel there is nothing we can't do."

The wedding took place in a small church in Bala Cynwyd on the afternoon of June 23, 1930. John 3rd was his brother's best man. The bride thoughtfully wore flat ballet slippers to mask the discrepancy in height between her and her groom. That night, the newlyweds took a nine o'clock train to New York. For the next two weeks, oblivious to two dozen servants at their beck and call, they honeymooned in Seal Harbor. On July 16, the couple boarded the *Broadway Limited* for a transcontinental passage to San Francisco, from which they set sail on the first leg of their global transit. Long days at sea encouraged both intimacy and reflection. "Tod certainly makes an ideal wife," Nelson told his brother John. He amplified this in a letter written aboard the SS *President John-son* as it churned the waters between Shanghai and Hong Kong. "Married life is a great success," declared the husband of six months. "We couldn't be happier, and we get along better every day. Tod really is a wonderful person and I know you're all going to like having her in the family."

Adopting his worldliest tone, Nelson played big brother to his big brother. "Any time *any* of you fellows . . . want *any* information of any kind I'll be only too glad to give it to you and when you get engaged Tod can and will be glad to have a little talk (if desired) with the prospective. I believe in being very frank about all the matters of sex. Its nowhere as complicated or as mysterious as people like to make it out to be. I'll get some copies of some good books Johnny French had, when we get to England." He had found these to be "*very*" helpful," said Nelson. There were as yet no signs of children, he concluded.

Only a Rockefeller would turn a honeymoon into ten months of self-improving visits to Hawaiian leper colonies, experimental clinics, and libraries made possible by family largesse. Guided by emissaries from Standard Oil and the Chase National Bank, Nelson and Tod careened between official entertainments, rides atop Indonesian elephants, museum excursions, and haggling over native art in steaming outdoor markets. (Recalling his honeymoon for a young friend long afterward, Rockefeller pointed to a knife handle in the shape of a shrunken head he had bought in Sumatra. "Not a very good omen," he observed sardonically.) At the time, however, he rejoiced in his good fortune, writing home that married life was "ideal, but I should imagine it would be quite the opposite unless you had the right person." Fortunately, no such worries attached themselves to Tod—"there is never a time but that I'm proud of her."

Accustomed since childhood to rubbing shoulders with foreign students at Rockefeller-sponsored International Houses, Nelson adapted easily to the most exotic surroundings. "Everything is terribly interesting and we really couldn't be *more thrilled*," he wrote John in October 1930. His unmodulated enthusiasms included Angkor Wat, the Yangtze River, a Japanese jazz band, and a Tibetan monastery at Lhasa that provided inspiration, three decades later, for the reconstruction of Albany. During this period, Nelson kept accounts in thirteen different currencies and proudly shared them all with his father. Standard Oil representatives nearly smothered the couple with their hospitality. "For over a month now we haven't had a meal by ourselves. On the boat we always get put at the captain's table. They sent a man to Bali with us (He was a young fellow and pretty wet)," complained twenty-two-year-old Nelson. Attempts to break free only offended their fawning hosts. "Perhaps you might speak to Mr. Cole again so that he could warn the men in India that we appreciate, but don't need so very much care," Nelson told John. Besides, "we have the letters to the governors there." The letters in question had been penned, at Junior's request, by British prime minister Ramsay MacDonald.

On the morning of March 4, 1931, Nelson and Tod were treated to a *tour d'horizon* from Mohandas K. Gandhi, whose Congress Party was dedicated to an early end of British rule. Gandhi had enjoyed less than an hour's sleep following late night discussions that cleared the way for renewed talks in London, but he beckoned the young Americans to accompany him and Jawaharlal Nehru on their daily stroll around an old Moghul fort on the outskirts of Delhi. "For more than an hour we walked up and down the rampart together, as he told us of his conversations during the night with the Viceroy," Rockefeller recalled. Against a melodramatic backdrop of distant thunder, the ascetic revolutionary traced his disillusionment with British rule to his days as a lawyer representing his countrymen in racist South Africa. The spiritual force Gandhi radiated was in no way diminished by his political sophistication. "He is a remarkable man—terribly nice, too," said Nelson.

The rest of the trip was, inevitably, somewhat anticlimactic. Junior expressed mild envy over the couple's visit to the biblical Ur of the Chaldees, in newly created Iraq, where Nelson traced successive layers of bygone civilization by descending to the bottom of a forty-five-foot archaeological shaft. Abby's thoughts ran to the more contemporary. "I wish that I might transport myself to Paris," she wrote at the start of April 1931. "What fun we could have shopping." During their absence, she had busied herself debating paint colors for their Pocantico farmhouse and scouting suitable furnishings for their Manhattan apartment on East Sixty-seventh Street. The Museum of Modern Art, her latest passion, had opened its doors in November 1929 with an exhibition of loaned works by Cézanne, Gauguin, Van Gogh, and Seurat. A brilliant twenty-seven-year-old art historian, Alfred H. Barr, Jr., had been hired away from Wellesley College to serve as the museum's first director.

In Abby's exhibit gallery at 10 West Fifty-fourth Street, Barr conducted a postgraduate course for Lincoln Kirstein, George Gershwin, Philip Johnson, and other members of the museum's Junior Advisory Committee. "Wait 'til Nelson gets back," his mother told Johnson more than once that spring. She had reasons other than MoMA for hastening his return, reasons grounded in a family venture testing Nelson's ability to cross-pollinate the severe perfectionism of his father with his mother's warmhearted embrace of novelty. "Unfortunately the architects and contractors showed the models and designs of the new radio center to the reporters and to the public," Abby reported to her son, "and there has been a terrible howl about their being done in the modern style. Of course, it seems to me perfectly ridiculous to think of doing them any other way but there has been a great furor about it and I am glad you are coming home to hold the fort for the modern."*

6

S HAKING OFF THE dust of ancient places, Nelson and Tod returned in the third week of April 1931 to a civilization in crisis. Nearing the trough of the Great Depression, at least a million New Yorkers were unemployed. One-third of the city's factories were closed or on the verge of shutting down. Suicides reached record levels; so did reported cases of starvation. On a single frigid day in January, eighty-five thousand inhabitants of the world's greatest city scrounged for subsistence in eighty-two breadlines. Thousands more, tossed from their homes, slept in subways, under bridges, and in shanty towns, the largest of which sprouted in the middle of Central Park. Groucho Marx cracked that he knew things were bad there when "the pigeons started feeding the people." From the pulpit of Riverside Church, Harry Emerson Fosdick, Junior's favorite pastor, preached a funeral sermon for the profit motive. "Individualism in the modern world is insanity," he thundered. Capitalism must adjust itself to the needs of the present age by embracing social planning and other controls, Fosdick continued, or else cede power to radical elements.

At the White House, President Herbert Hoover clung doggedly to the voluntary relief measures he had once employed to feed occupied Belgium and sustain the Allies in World War I. But the economic holocaust of the 1930s dwarfed any humanitarian challenge to date. The Rockefellers did not escape the meltdown of modern capitalism. From its peak of $57.6 million, Junior's annual income fell to $16 million in 1934. Less elastic was his tax bill. In 1930, he paid nearly $7 million to the federal government and an additional $1.3 million to New York State. Upkeep and real estate taxes on the Pocantico, Seal Harbor, and New York homes devoured many times the $40,000 the properties generated. Already precarious, Rockefeller's financial situation could only deteriorate as he became mired in a vast midtown construction project.

Metropolitan Square was a cultural and commercial development slated for twelve fraying acres of midtown Manhattan stretching for three blocks north of

---

* "Never can such universal condemnation have been visited upon a great artistic project as that which has been the lot of the suggested buildings for Radio City," sniffed *The New York Times*. Other critics likened an elliptical structure on the site of today's skating rink to a pillbox or gashouse. Junior reassured his architects, who feared they might join the lengthening lines of the unemployed. He had avoided reading potentially painful news stories, he told them, ever since the Ludlow Massacre.

Forty-eighth Street between Fifth and Sixth avenues. The project's success hinged on two imponderables—a profitable sale of the existing Metropolitan Opera House ("the Yellow Brewery") at Thirty-ninth Street and Broadway; and a complex set of transactions involving the Met, Junior, and Columbia University. The neighborhood had a colorful history. Successively owned by the Dutch and British crowns, the area was lavishly developed after the Revolution as the Elgin Botanic Garden by Dr. David Hosack, who bankrupted himself in the process. In 1814, the twenty-acre parcel was transferred to Columbia College, which designated it the Upper Estate (as distinguished from its downtown campus, or Lower Estate). By the early years of the twentieth century, the college had become a university, abandoning its Park Place address for a new home on Morningside Heights. In need of construction funds, Columbia trustees sold off a block of the Upper Estate.

It was the remaining parcel that the Metropolitan Opera coveted as a potential building site. Inspired by the Paris Opera, architect Benjamin Wistar Morris drew plans for an elegant auditorium, flanked by an office tower and a plaza with extensive gardens and dancing fountains. Not only would Metropolitan Square restore Fifth Avenue to its former splendor; according to company chairman Otto Kahn, it would simultaneously raise the floor beneath Junior's extensive real estate holdings in the area. Encouraged by family publicist Ivy Lee, Junior at the start of 1929 signed a twenty-one-year lease committing himself to pay Columbia $3.3 million annually (a third of the university's Depression-era income). For this princely sum, Rockefeller gained the leasehold to 228 decaying brownstones, struggling small businesses, speakeasies, and houses of ill repute. All told, they generated scarcely $300,000 in annual revenue. But this was the 1920s, when limits were unacceptable, or at least un-American. With the opera house as its anchor, plans went forward for the largest urban mixed-use project in the nation's history.

To manage the construction and operation of this city within a city, Junior turned to the engineering firm of Todd, Robertson, and Todd, whose autocratic chief, John R. Todd, demanded $450,000 a year for six years, plus one-third of net profits for the life of the lease. Soon three separate architectural firms were engaged to design Metropolitan Square, while a committee of academics and museum professionals counseled Junior on its artistic embellishment. Almost immediately the project got a new name, for the worst of reasons. With the onset of the Depression, Met trustees, unable to sell their existing hall, announced that in addition to donating the site for a new opera house, they expected Junior to cover at least half the $8 million construction bill. His reaction can be imagined. The Met withdrew from the venture, to be replaced by David Sarnoff's National Broadcasting Company and its parent firm, the Radio Corporation of America. In league with filmmaker RKO, RCA signed a $4.25 million lease for a million square feet of space. The deal envisioned multiple theaters, only two of which were actually built, including the sixty-two-hundred-seat Music Hall in what was quickly renamed Radio City.

"Opera was the great old art, radio the new," Nelson rationalized in the first of many messages drafted for him by Radio City's PR professionals. His glossy tribute to "the newest miracle of this scientific era" offered scant consolation to Junior, who was left holding the bag in a grossly overbuilt New York real estate climate. His doctors ordered him to spend the winter of 1930–1931 in Arizona. On returning east, he was laid low by a crippling attack of stress-related shingles. "I don't sleep so well," he muttered to a young architect working on the erstwhile Metropolitan Square. "I walk the floor nights, wondering where I'm going to get the money to build these buildings." It was an act of faith, or folly, little appreciated at the time. More representative of the zeitgeist was novelist F. Scott Fitzgerald, who had an epiphany while perched atop the Empire State, gaudiest of all the city's towers, in the autumn of 1931. "Full of vaunting pride the New Yorker had climbed here and seen with dismay what he had never suspected, that the city was not the endless succession of canyons that he had supposed, but that it had limits," Fitzgerald wrote. "And with the awful realization that New York was a city after all and not a universe, the whole shining edifice that he had reared in his imagination came crashing to the ground."

The Rockefellers conceded nothing of the kind. While still on his honeymoon, a somewhat dubious Nelson had been reassured of the enticing future awaiting him in Fitzgerald's canyons. "Life in New York is enormously interesting and the opportunities seem endless," Abby insisted. "Downtown . . . is an embarrassment of riches." On May 1, 1931, her son appeared for the first time at 26 Broadway. Three weeks later, Nelson and Tod paid a visit to Colonial Williamsburg. Floor plans of the long vanished Governor's Palace had recently turned up in an English library. Nelson, with his perfectionist's eye, couldn't help observing that the main stairway of the palace, slightly off center, might be architecturally improved. "We are doing a restoration, not our own creations," Junior reproached him. Nelson willingly relinquished his seat on Williamsburg's executive board to his brother John. "I did not want to go on any boards I was not interested in and sit and listen to other people talk about what they were going to do," he reasoned. "I wanted to do my own thing."*

Junior had other plans. Loath to share his sons, he effectively blackballed

---

* Williamsburg became Junior's favorite retreat. Their unassuming conduct would endear the Rockefellers to their Virginia neighbors. The story is still told of a costumed hostess who spied Abby sitting on a bench in the courtyard of the restored Governor's Palace. On being invited inside, Mrs. Rockefeller replied, "I have no money and I'm waiting for John to bring me fifty cents." Later, the elderly couple joined the shuffling ticket line like everyone else. *Bassett Hall*, Colonial Williamsburg Foundation, 1984, 11.

Nelson's candidacy to become a trustee of the Metropolitan Museum of Art. Sandwiched among droning discussions about the proposed merger of Standard components Socony and Vacuum, Nelson greeted the king and queen of Siam, lunched with Charles Lindbergh, and understudied his father's creation of the Cloisters, a stunning museum of medieval art in Manhattan's Fort Tryon Park. On a drizzly autumn afternoon in 1932, he scouted the great basalt cliffs overlooking the Hudson River known as the Palisades, soon to be rescued from commercial development through Junior's generosity. At a Pocantico school opening, it was Nelson who spoke for his family. Along with his father and eldest brother, he reviewed architectural plans for Metropolitan Square. He was part of the conversation, spearheaded by Ivy Lee, at which the development was renamed Rockefeller Center.

After getting his real estate license, Nelson took charge of the family's Cleveland properties. Soon he was able to report the sale of one house and the lease of eleven others on the former Forest Hills estate. His renovation of the Pocantico farmhouse given him by Junior delighted everyone, Tod most of all. "I think she really loves it there," wrote Abby, "and shows no signs of being bored and very little inclination to dash down to Philadelphia." She had even less reason to absent herself after learning, in the autumn of 1931, that she was pregnant. On the brink of fatherhood, Nelson drew closer than ever to the family patriarch. Twice that fall he played golf with Senior in Florida, where the old man and his acolyte enjoyed "floods of orange juice" while reading psalms to each other.

In January 1932, flush with the donation of Senior's old desk from 26 Broadway, Nelson partnered with two friends in Turck and Company, a brokerage office whose vaguely worded prospectus scarcely hid the respectable influence peddling at its core. Company president Fenton B. Turck proposed to monetize new and existing connections between Rockefeller Center and prospective tenants. As Nelson explained Turck's business model, "If you had a connection with a company, let's say Standard Plumbing, and you were buying a lot from them and then you looked up and saw who was on their board of directors . . . you can go to the president of the company and say that we are doing all of this buying and you have so and so on your board and we would like an introduction to this company. We want to talk to him about space." Rockefeller admired his friend's ingenuity, but he took his inspiration from a higher power. "Father always had a very simple admonition," said Nelson. "If there is any doubt as to whether you might cross the line of what should be done or shouldn't, stand way back of the line . . . I wanted to get back of the line."*

---

* It may well have been his experience at Turck and Company that prompted Rockefeller's later exclamation that he had never wanted to be vice president of anything. After employing a jobless

Within a year, both Turck and secretary Webster Todd agreed to sell him their modest stakes in the business. Reinvented as Special Work, Inc., the firm exploited Nelson's deal-making abilities to the fullest. Under one arrangement, Rockefeller Center contracted for one hundred thousand tons from the Consolidated Coal Company, in return for which Consolidated agreed to lease seventeen thousand square feet in the RCA Building. Westinghouse supplied elevators to the center in exchange for three floors in the same structure. The Chase Bank's reward for sharing useful information with Special Work clients was $1 million in new deposits. Another intervention by Nelson secured International Paper's oil business in the Northeast and Canada, a transaction worth $80,000 a year to Socony-Vacuum. His approach to marketing Rockefeller Center was refreshingly direct. "I was able to get in to talk to people who wouldn't have seen most men my age," he observed with rare understatement.

By the spring of 1934, Special Work claimed credit for twenty-one leases, amounting to 110,000 square feet in the RCA and RKO buildings. Rivals were quick to take note. Realtor August Heckscher, livid over the migration of tenants from his building at 730 Fifth Avenue, sued the trustees of Rockefeller Center for $10 million. Heckscher charged Nelson in particular with making threats, offering financial inducements, and assuming unexpired leases to seduce clients away from their present landlords. In short, with crossing Junior's bright ethical line. None of his actions were illegal under existing law, Nelson retorted. The case dragged on for several years, until rendered moot by Heckscher's death at ninety-two. In the interim, and perhaps beyond, it fostered a reputation for ruthlessness unusual even by the standards of the Manhattan real estate crowd. Long afterward, Rockefeller would attribute a lack of enthusiasm for his presidential campaigns in New York's financial establishment to resentment over his early real estate raids.

Earning less than $5,000 in profits on 1933 income of $30,883.71, Special Work offered too small a stage to gratify Nelson's craving for independent accomplishment. Acknowledging that he was "continually in a state of flux as far as my ideas and theories are concerned," he notified Junior that he was "back in the fold again" and eager to assume a larger role in the family office. This was a tacit concession that he was not the Rockefeller in Rockefeller Center. Already the move of Special Work into the RCA Building had been delayed because Junior's office, a Jacobean fantasy equipped with the skyscraper's only working fireplace, was not ready for occupancy. Once installed on the fifty-

---

Dartmouth classmate, Nelson looked on helplessly as his friend suffered a nervous breakdown and became persuaded that the Rockefellers had tapped his phone and were keeping him under surveillance. Rejecting an appeal from the man's wife to have her husband legally apprehended, Nelson instead extended his classmate's salary for a year and offered to pay for his hospitalization. NAR–Thomas Debevoise, June 29, 1934, Friends and Family, Box 4, Folder 47, RAC.

sixth floor, Nelson objected to sharing a secretary with his brother John. Nelson's college friend Bill Alton, attuned to his classmate's wandering eye, helpfully announced that he had found the perfect replacement: "She weighs close to 200, has red hair, and is a niggir. . . . Safety first."

Nelson launched an effort to restructure the family organization, soon to be known by its nominal address in the RCA Building, Room 5600. His proposed Family Council foundered on a too-obvious concentration of authority in the hands of a single son, to the detriment of his four brothers. Less concerned about Rockefeller Center's commercial prospects than its artistic possibilities, Nelson inquired: Why not make the center itself a work of art, a classroom for popular taste, and a grand showcase for the modernism hatched in MoMA's incubator? Needless to say, these views were not shared by Junior's Art Advisory Committee. Its inoffensive theme, "New Frontiers and the March of Civilization," set the tone for a program suffused with earnestness and technical virtuosity. Lee Lawrie's bronze *Atlas* outside the International Building became one of the most photographed works of the era, second only to Paul Manship's gold-plated *Prometheus* riding the fountains in the famous plaza. Watching over the sixty-foot-high grand foyer of the Music Hall was Ezra Winter's incomprehensible mural *Fountain of Youth*.

Even as these commissions were being handed out, both Nelson and his mother schemed to secure their share for more adventurous artists. Mother and son welcomed architect Wallace Harrison as their newest ally in the battle to rescue Rockefeller Center from cloying sentiment and stale grandiosity. As the official Art Advisory Committee wallowed in the mundane, MoMA championed the radical alternative. Early in 1932, the museum moved from cramped quarters on the twelfth floor of the Heckscher Building to a temporary space in Rockefeller Center. Yielding to the grim realities of the era, trustees imposed a 10 percent staff salary reduction. At the same time, they undertook to raise $1 million to secure a collection of postimpressionist paintings, conditionally willed to MoMA the previous year on the death of Lillie Bliss. Nelson's contribution to the effort was necessarily modest, since he received no earnings beyond his $10,500 allowance from Junior. Most of his $1,000 pledge was supplied by Abby, to whom he promised to do more as soon as his income allowed.

7

For Nelson Rockefeller, the art of politics was inseparable from the politics of art. MoMA was his smoke-filled room. Denied real money, he began assembling real power as chairman of the Junior Advisory Committee.

Among those he recruited was Lillie Bliss's pretty young niece Eliza. "He would always say . . . 'We've got to put on a show,'" she later recalled. "And somebody would say, 'But we haven't got any money to put on a show.' And he'd say, 'Well, put it on anyway, we'll get the money afterwards.'" Nelson's charisma and boundless energy contrasted sharply with the painstaking scholarship and bouts of indecision afflicting Alfred Barr, Jr. Yet this odd couple shared a common vision of MoMA as global tastemaker. Disproving Gertrude Stein's witticism that "you can be a museum or you can be modern, but you cannot be both," in less than two years the upstart institution had introduced Americans to the work of Picasso and Matisse, while popularizing the International Style of Walter Gropius, J.J.P. Oud, and Le Corbusier. Throngs flocked to a one-man show by the Mexican muralist Diego Rivera. Eleanor Roosevelt made two visits to a blockbuster Van Gogh exhibition and returned again to see the iconic *Whistler's Mother* on loan from the Louvre. By displaying a motley assortment of Abby's aged weather vanes, carved roosters, and primitive portraits, the museum helped make folk art respectable.

So it should have surprised no one that Barr, regarding photography much as Abby did her chalkware and cigar store Indians, should welcome the initiative of the Junior Advisory Committee in mounting *Murals by American Painters and Photographers*. The exhibit was curated by twenty-four-year-old Lincoln Kirstein, whose predilection for such left-wing artists as Ben Shahn and William Gropper confirmed Junior's worst suspicions about the institution he called "Abby's Folly." His dismay was shared by museum trustees unattuned to the class struggle as espoused by social expressionists like Hugo Gellert, whose *Us Fellas Gotta Stick Together* had all the subtlety of a *New Masses* editorial. Gellert depicted J. P. Morgan with a glass of champagne in his hand and a curvaceous chorus girl in his lap. Rounding out the canvas, wielding machine guns while taking cover behind a rampart of money bags, were President Hoover, John D. Rockefeller, Sr., Henry Ford, and Al Capone.

A generational war erupted. Kirstein, pressed to be reasonable, dug in his heels. Nelson supported his friend's refusal to evict Gellert and other artists so offensive to graybeards on the board. On April 24, less than three weeks before the scheduled opening of *Murals*, Nelson became a father. "We tried to christen him Nelson," said Junior of his first grandson, "but were sternly informed that his name was not to be Nelson but Rodman." Every inch the proud parent, Nelson and a Dartmouth classmate made book on how large their respective sons were likely to be at age twenty. "If it had not been for the fact that I have a brother-in-law as well as a brother over 6'4" I should have demanded odds," he joked.*

---

* Each of the five Rockefeller children, revealingly, would be given the middle name of Clark, in recognition of their mother's Philadelphia roots.

Welcome as it was, Rodman's birth offered only a momentary respite from the turmoil at MoMA. Angry trustees wanted Kirstein sacked, his provocative exhibit scaled back, and Barr's accompanying catalog canceled. Nelson rejected all such demands. "If we threw it out it would be front page of the *Times* and other papers," he reasoned. Hoping to avoid such negative publicity, he went to see Morgan in his Wall Street lair. "Don't give it another thought," the financier told him. "Of course you ought to have it. This is life." In the end, the harshest comments about the show came from art critics, one of whom expressed mock terror "of what may happen to our public buildings if all the young experimentalists were given free rein."

Actually, private buildings were just as vulnerable. Prodded by Abby's favorite art dealer, Edith Halpert, Rockefeller Center employed a decorating genius named Donald Deskey to work his magic on the interior of the cavernous Music Hall, scheduled to open before the end of 1932. By eliminating most of the nominal budget for furniture and fixtures, Deskey was able to commission artists familiar to any visitor to *Murals*. From sculptor William Zorach came *The Spirit of the Dance*, a larger-than-life kneeling figure, unclothed, cast in aluminum. Unfortunately, no one had thought to clear the work in advance with Samuel Lionel "Roxy" Rothafel, the bombastic showman whose namesake movie palace at Seventh Avenue and Fiftieth Street was a mere curtain-raiser to Radio City. Hired by the Rockefellers at $150,000 a year to program the Music Hall as a London Palladium–like vaudeville house, Roxy communicated his aesthetic sensibilities in the two-word instructions he gave to Deskey: "Portuguese Rococo."

As offended by nudity as MoMA trustees were by agitprop, Roxy banished *The Spirit of the Dance* to the basement. This ignited another fracas, with Nelson firing off an angry telegram demanding reinstatement of the work. Roxy backed down, though he enjoyed a modicum of revenge by relegating the sculpture to a spot between the men's lounge and the ladies' powder room. Naked maidens were the least of his problems on December 27, 1932, when the oversize curtain of the Music Hall rose for the first time. Nelson was in the audience, along with Amelia Earhart, Gene Tunney, Walter Lippmann, Noel Coward, Rose Kennedy, and Leopold Stokowski, for a five-and-a-half-hour pageant of excess that threatened to close the vast theater before it ever opened. "The show was an absolute bust," recorded Nelson, who remained in his box until two thirty in the morning and the concluding projection of a gigantic American flag against a rising—or setting—sun. Afterward he withdrew to Roxy's art deco apartment atop the hall, where he sat through "one of the grimmest, most depressing meetings I have ever attended." Besides its theater leases, RKO was obligated to pay more than $1 million in entertainment and other contracts authorized by the free-spending Rothafel.

With customers hard to come by at prices of seventy-five cents and two dollars, Roxy's twice daily vaudeville extravaganzas were terminated after just eighteen days. Within a month RKO declared bankruptcy, forcing the Rockefellers to step in and program both the Music Hall and the nearby Center Theatre. For Nelson, the catastrophic premiere was made worse by a seemingly innocuous act of self-promotion. In contrast with his father, who had shielded his face with a top hat while hurrying past photographers at the corner of Sixth Avenue and Fiftieth Street, the younger Rockefeller readily assented to having his picture taken, a fact duly reported in the next day's *Herald Tribune.* When Lincoln Kirstein shortly thereafter proposed a magazine profile of his friend, Nelson rejected the idea out of hand. "During the last two or three months it happens that I have had an unfortunate amount of publicity due, naturally, to my family name," he told Kirstein. This was "decidedly undesirable. The best thing I can do is to remain as inconspicuous as possible for the next six months at least."

Five

THE ART OF THE POSSIBLE

You give me too much credit when you say you don't think that I really am hard and unfeeling. I'm sorry to say that I am both of these, not naturally, but by schooling myself to be. That sounds strange, but I think it is true. It is the result of my overpowering ambition. If one is going to get very far in this world one must be impersonal and not waste one's emotional strength on irrelevant things. The result has been that I take a pretty cold attitude about most things. . . .

P.S. I bought a swell blue hippopotamus by Carl Walters from Mrs. Halpert. Wait until you see it!

—NELSON A. ROCKEFELLER to his mother, March 1933

1

"NELSON NEEDS ART more than any man I know," claimed Alfred Barr, Jr. At once relaxing and stimulating, spiritual and materialistic, art supplied a powerful antidote to the frustrations, obligations, and compromises of everyday life. Rockefeller himself attributed his love of painting, sculpture, and photography to the escape they offered from "the conformity surrounding us on all sides . . . you can have any concept, or have any kind of world you want. The freedom is absolute." Freedom, one might reasonably speculate, to disregard restrictive rules of scale and conduct imposed by family traditions. Freedom, too, to lessen the emotional constraints of life as a Rockefeller, to indulge sexual appetites outside marriage, and to inhabit, however fleetingly, a nonconformist land of the imagination.

Art permitted Nelson the luxury of a second self, as intensely lived as and yet different from his fiercely ambitious public persona. It replaced competition with contemplation. And it was of the moment. "I'm interested in art that relates to life in our own day, that expresses the spirit of the time," he remarked, "art that isn't cloistered and set apart, art that includes the house and the motor car . . . as well as painting and sculpture." Pointedly reminding the uninitiated that "art is not a picture," when he did hang a canvas, said Rockefeller, "I'm not so much interested in its historical value. I'm more interested in the pleasure it gives—the contribution it makes to the room and the house." His first preference was for sculpture, "because to me plastic art has greater strength and vitality." And while he might not initially comprehend so-called primitive art, Nelson acknowledged, it never seemed strange to him. "I felt its power, its directness of expression and its beauty."*

For the dyslexic, art offered a language of the emotions in place of conventional, often treacherous, patterns of speech. The artist communicated wordlessly, without theorizing or academic heavy lifting. "The more intellectual you get about art the less esthetic you become," argued Rockefeller. "I like strong, simple painting without a message." He rejected surrealism and Dada for the same reason he disdained Junior's cultural sermonizing and the play-it-safe symbolism favored by the Art Advisory Committee of Rockefeller Center. In November 1931, he contacted his former Dartmouth instructor Artemus Packard with a proposition. From his mother, Nelson said, he had learned of a campaign to install frescoes in Carpenter Hall, home to the college's Fine Arts Department. Was Packard aware that Diego Rivera at that very moment was creating a special set of frescoes mounted on a light steel frame for exhibition at MoMA? Perhaps these could be done on panels transferable to the Dartmouth campus. "In this way the College could probably get the work more reasonably," Nelson hinted broadly, "and at the same time save the Museum some." Packard leapt at the idea, but Rivera begged off on financial grounds, asserting that such an arrangement would put him at a disadvantage with institutional clients.[†]

In retrospect, the outlines of *l'affaire* Rivera, otherwise known as the Battle of Rockefeller Center, were foreshadowed in Nelson's first tentative approach to Artemus Packard. Propelled on the whitewater of his enthusiasm for an artist

---

* As if to vouch for this, Laurance Rockefeller described his brother's visceral response to an unfinished canvas he spotted on an African tour. "Don't spoil it, let me have it just as it is," Nelson told the young artist before reaching over and lifting the painting from its easel.

"He saw something, he felt it, he experienced it," said Laurance of his sibling. "It was emotional." Laurance Rockefeller, HMI, 8.

† The commission, and a much larger one to cover the walls of Dartmouth's Baker Library, went to José Clemente Orozco, who formed, with Rivera and David Alfaro Siqueiros, the triumvirate responsible for the interwar "Mexican Renaissance." Orozco's socialist politics, no less than his nationality and modernism, roused a storm of protest from conservative alumni and xenophobes on the National Commission to Advance American Art. Out of his personal fondness for President Hopkins, Orozco offered to make changes in one panel that depicted skeletons in academic robes worshipping dead knowledge. Hopkins would not hear of it. When he invited a man to Dartmouth, said the president, "it was to represent himself and not to become a propaganda agency for some theory of our own." All the same, years later he had but a single piece of advice to impart to his successor, John Sloan Dickey: "Never have anything to do with murals."

his mother greatly admired, Rockefeller had attempted what he did every day through Special Work, Inc.—to broker a deal. And why not? The benefits to Abby, her museum, and his esteemed alma mater were indisputable. Rivera was another matter. In his pragmatic zeal, Nelson had overlooked the pride, and the pocketbook, of an artist who refused to let anyone deal for him. The clash of cultures that would rivet Depression-era Americans had its roots in a 1928 visit by Abby Aldrich Rockefeller to an art exhibition organized by a young Texan named Frances Flynn Paine. With $15,000 from the Rockefeller Foundation, Miss Paine made herself into an expert on Mexican folk art, which she then marketed to collectors like Abby. The two women formed the Mexican Arts Association to foster enhanced understanding between the United States and its uneasy neighbor to the south.

Among their early successes was the MoMA retrospective—the same exhibition Nelson described to Artemus Packard—containing 150 Rivera oils, drawings, watercolors, and frescoes. Crowds were still flocking to the show in January 1932 when Abby and Nelson welcomed the artist to lunch at 10 West Fifty-fourth Street. Forty years before Tom Wolfe coined the phrase, the Rockefellers were practicing radical chic. Their guest of honor was a forty-five-year-old frog-eyed fabulist, six feet four inches tall and weighing nearly three hundred pounds. A committed Marxist who chafed under party discipline, Rivera the artist had successively reinvented himself as a landscape painter, a cubist, and an ardent disciple of Picasso, Cézanne, and Renoir. Though he was best known for his identification with pre-Columbian Mexico, it was Rivera's portraits of Babs Rockefeller and her children that led to a much grander commission, at the crossroads of American capitalism.

In his imagination, Nelson visualized the main lobby of the RCA Building as a permanent showplace for Rivera and those other modernist giants Matisse and Picasso. To realize this unlikely trifecta, he must win over risk-averse members of his father's Art Advisory Committee. The strategy he devised flattered their egos while steering them firmly toward his desired outcome. "Gentlemen, we seem to have reached an impasse in the judgment and the time is getting late," Nelson told the group. "If you select the work of the well known artist and it turns out badly, then it is his fault. If, on the other hand, you chose the work of the unknown artist and it turns out badly, then it is your fault." Junior was persuaded by the most practical of arguments. "Although I do not personally care for much of his work," Mr. Rockefeller informed his managing agents, "Rivera seems to have become very popular just now and will probably be a good drawing card."

Presumably, Matisse and Picasso would have drawn as well, had their courtship not been entrusted to the ham-handed duo of John Todd and architect Raymond Hood. Matisse politely rejected any idea of a competition, as well as the monochromatic scheme demanded by the agents, who never got in to see Picasso. Chosen in their place were two lesser lights, the Catalonian Josep Maria Sert, best known for some murals painted on silver in the Waldorf-Astoria Hotel, and Great Britain's Frank Brangwyn, a competent illustrator favored by Todd. Rivera was on the verge of being scratched from consideration altogether when Nelson intervened, promising the artist that there would be no competition. He persuaded the managers to yield a second time, on the issue of color versus black and white. He came to Rivera's support in Detroit, where the artist had undertaken to interpret modern industrial life in twenty-seven hotly debated panels around the inner courtyard of the city's Institute of Arts.

His patron in the auto capital was Nelson's friend and future MoMA trustee Edsel Ford. After the fact, Ford's staunch defense of artistic freedom would be favorably contrasted with Nelson's craven surrender to political and economic pressure. But the RCA Building was not a museum. It was a commercial and, still more, a family enterprise struggling to gain a foothold in the depths of the Great Depression. Moreover, it stood across Fifth Avenue from St. Patrick's Cathedral. Neither God nor mammon, it appeared, welcomed the artistically adventurous. At the start of November 1932, Rivera submitted for Junior's consideration a preliminary sketch reflective of the didactic theme chosen by the managing agents: *Man at the Crossroads Looking with Hope and High Vision to the Choosing of a New and Better Future.* Later, much was to be made of this windy prospectus and of the fact that nowhere in his early drawings did Rivera portray Lenin. Yet no one aware of his past history should have been surprised by the Worker's Paradise about to occupy a thousand square feet above the information desk in the RCA Building.

Bracketed by Brangwyn's "ethical evolution" of humankind and Sert's hymn to technocracy, Rivera offered an idealized portrayal of the oppressed laborer. At the Frontier of Material Development, said the artist, "the Worker gives his right hand to the Peasant who questions him, and with his left hand takes the hand of the sick and wounded Soldier, the victim of War, leading him to the New Road." To his Rockefeller patrons, this turgid word portrait mattered less than a friendship explicitly reaffirmed when Rivera begged Abby for permission to paint in fresco rather than "the hateful lined canvas." Verbally tugging his forelock, the artist promised "to do for Rockefeller Center, and especially for you, Madame, the best of all the work I have done up to this time." Describing Rivera as "a terribly good sport," Nelson signaled approval of the artist's vision. Rivera also got his way on the fresco technique. His $21,000 fee was sufficient to employ half a dozen assistants and speed completion of the mural in time for the building's scheduled opening on May 1, 1933.

In January 1933, Raymond Hood signed off on a second, more refined sketch of the project. Two months later, Diego left Detroit for New York accompanied by his third wife, creative peer, and political conscience, Frida Kahlo. Having crash-dieted away more than one hundred pounds, the painter was scarcely recognizable to old friends. His physical metamorphosis was mirrored in a world undergoing violent change. At the White House, the discredited Hoover had given way to Franklin D. Roosevelt and his New Deal. Rivera commenced work on his mural days after the German Reichstag was bludgeoned into granting Hitler absolute power. Man might well be at the Crossroads, but his New, Better Future seemed more elusive than ever.

2

WHAT HAPPENED NEXT has been described many times, but never satisfactorily explained. Traditional accounts pit a brilliant man-child against the callow, if not spineless, scion of wealth. Seen in isolation, stressing conflict over context, Rockefeller vs. Rivera is as theatrically obvious as the ill-fated mural that collapsed under the weight of competing expectations long before it was physically chipped from the walls of the RCA Building. The facts are sufficiently dramatic without embroidery. To begin with, Nelson was never a free agent. Besides Todd, Robertson, and Todd, there was his father, a stickler for detail and a public prude, already offended by some allegorical nudes cavorting above the entrances to NBC's studios. "Since I shall not be able with complete satisfaction and pleasure to enter my new office building by either the north or south entrance because of the [Leo] Friedlander sculpture," Junior primly informed the managing agents, "I am the more anxious to be able to come in at the west entrance with a sense of unalloyed pleasure in all that strikes my eye."

These instructions were issued several months after Rivera's ouster, but the attitude they conveyed had been entrenched long before that particular tempest. The message was unmistakable: *My name is on this building, and I dictate what will, or will not, adorn its walls.* Thus the bar was raised—and responsibility divided between Nelson and the watchful agents—long before Rivera applied his first coat to the lime plaster stacked five layers deep as protection against a nearby elevator shaft. To meet the aesthetic demands of his father while gratifying the imaginative and political freedom of the artist was akin to squaring the circle. Complicating matters, the mural was far from Nelson's only, or even his chief, priority in the first weeks of 1933. Repeating his Dartmouth experience, Rockefeller was scattering his energies—consolidating his position at MoMA, swapping *Elmer Gantry* with his brother Laurance for José Ortega y Gasset's ode to pessimism *The Revolt of the Masses*, and dabbling in politics. "I'm a liberal to the nth degree in theory," he told Laurance. "As for personal practice I have come to no conclusions."

Nelson met with local power brokers to promote a consolidation of the two Tarrytowns. He briefly contemplated running for justice of the peace in the nearby town of Mount Pleasant. Instead, at the behest of Billy Ward, the county's Republican boss, Rockefeller accepted appointment to the newly formed board of the Westchester County Health District. By the time he left the board twenty years later to assume rank as undersecretary of the U.S. Department of Health, Education, and Welfare, Westchester had been purged of deadly ailments such as diphtheria, whooping cough, measles, scarlet fever, and typhoid. Vaccination clinics were established and nutritional education introduced, along with more enlightened treatment of mental health issues. A new emphasis on prenatal care halved infant mortality and stillbirth rates.

For Rockefeller, the Westchester County Board of Health opened a window on the gritty realities of government: how to craft budgets and how to settle jurisdictional disputes (did the commissioner of health have statutory authority to declare mosquito-breeding places in the city of White Plains a public hazard?). It introduced him as well to the small human dramas and petty rivalries embedded in public policy. Nelson underwrote production of annual reports enlivened with the graphic and pictorial material he favored over the printed word. For him, public education and public relations were inseparable. The Battle of Rockefeller Center would illustrate the limits of each. Despite, or perhaps because of, his multiplying responsibilities, Nelson that spring was in an uncharacteristic funk. Lincoln Kirstein discovered this for himself in pleading for Nelson's help in establishing a ballet company as part of a larger arts complex within Rockefeller Center.

But he had nowhere near the clout his friend assumed, Nelson protested. "My God," he exclaimed, "I have to spend my whole life being nice to people." "Except to me," Tod said, smiling.

Her husband's allowance had been raised to $13,500 a year, yet it remained an *allowance*, not a salary. A married man with an infant son, Nelson relied on Junior to pay his monthly rent, heat, and water bills. The same oracle decided whether a Pocantico handyman could wash his son's car ("an extra not contemplated in our arrangement," ruled Junior, and "therefore not something to count on"). Much later in life, Nelson would describe a pattern of incessant activity, seemingly for its own sake. "I was doing anywhere from four to six or eight things at the same time. I don't know why but I always did a lot of different things." Was his ferocious commitment to *doing* a protest against the continuing dependence enforced by a domineering parent, or did it point to an emptiness resistant to introspection?

"You can't be any more worried about me than I am myself," Nelson confessed to Abby in March 1933. He found life "as perplexing and pointless" as Laurance, "only as I have a driving force in me, and a happy-go-lucky nature, I keep on going." Nelson rejected his mother's advice to focus more on his own activities. "Talking about one's self is man's greatest weakness, and a sign of conceit," he wrote. "Lord knows I have enough trouble fighting down conceit." Using the words that form the epigraph of this chapter, Nelson insisted that he was indeed hard and unfeeling, "not naturally, but by schooling myself to be . . . to take a cold impersonal point of view about life is very important to sound impartial judgment, and it certainly saves one from a lot of useless worrying." Among his worst habits was a "strong tendency towards a very contemptuous attitude—contemptuous of certain people as well as of certain social institutions."

Nelson offered no excuses. "Probably if I were a little more humble it would solve a good many questions. . . . If I saw the point to it all it would be somewhat simpler. But who knows, I may someday. Don't worry, Mum, we'll all stick together anyway." As penetrating a diagnosis of his malaise as he ever offered, the letter was signed, "Your devoted bad boy Nelson." On Thursday, April 6, Nelson lunched at the Recess Club with Junior and John, whose diary tersely noted, "Nel suggested to Father that he have as his major interest the various oil companies. Father was sympathetic to the idea." His sympathy was about to be put to the test, for even as Nelson groped for a viable purpose, uptown Rivera was affixing his futuristic vision to the walls of the RCA Building, thirty square feet at a time. Curious New Yorkers bought tickets to watch the artist on his scaffold, toiling through the softening spring nights, oblivious to the hot meals Frida brought him. In the basement, his assistants blew off steam by learning Bulgarian folk dances.

On April 19, Rivera assistant Lucienne Bloch recorded a visit to the work site by Nelson, who was said to be "crazy" (in the positive sense) about the unfinished fresco. Competing for his attention: an incipient coup at MoMA, where friction between Conger Goodyear and Alfred Barr threatened the young institution's survival. For several days, Nelson had furtively discussed with museum staffers a change at the top. All agreed with him that while Barr could not last much longer under Goodyear, he would thrive if Abby became president. With his mother traveling in Europe, Nelson dispensed with formalities, such as obtaining her permission in advance. Instead he brashly assured her, "I'll have you in the chair before you come back." In the same letter, he unveiled plans to raise a badly needed endowment, beginning with a $300,000 gift from Abby herself. Other trustees would pledge additional amounts, Nelson explained, until the million-dollar goal was attained. The promised sums were to be collectible over twenty-five years, with each donor paying 5 percent annual interest on his outstanding balance.

His presumption startled even Abby. "This is so sudden! . . . Do you think it proper for a son to go around campaigning for his mother's promotion in office. It seems to me it might be thought a little strange." In the event, none of Nelson's changes were realized, the putative takeover falling victim to his impetuosity (and, one may surmise, to the adamant opposition of his father). Always it came back to Junior's wishes and needs and a continuing subservience symbolized by Nelson's paltry $15,000 pledge to the museum endowment campaign. At lunch on April 24, Nelson took his brother John into his confidence. He had crafted a letter, to be signed by all six Rockefeller children, raising the delicate subject of financial independence. The issue would be broached, paradoxically, in the name of family unity. "As we get older, natural forces will tend to pull us apart unless we are on guard," the draft asserted. Lamenting the routine, vexatious concerns that intruded on their time together—"the detail of a trip abroad, the relative merits of one apartment as against another, or the desirability of buying a Chrysler instead of a Buick"—the authors contended that family frictions would be avoided "if our allowances were to completely cover not only those things at present included, but also such items as apartment rent, hospital expenses at childbirth, moderately priced cars, summer vacation expenses, including trips abroad—in short, all those things which you would be paying for us anyway."

With legalistic precision, Nelson reeled off the advantages of such a policy. First, it would relieve Junior of "an infinite amount of detail." Second, it would free the children when in their father's presence to discuss more important questions, "as well as to hear of your many interesting doings." Third, it would make the younger generation more competent to deal with future challenges. Fourth, it would instill appreciation of their financial legacy "by requiring greater thought and care on our part in the planning of our major responsibilities."

In response to this unsubtle appeal, Junior increased Nelson's annual allowance to $18,000.* Even this modest raise seemed generous given the banner headlines coinciding with the brothers' April 24 lunch meeting. That morning's *New York World-Telegram* said it all: RIVERA PERPETUATES SCENES OF COMMUNIST ACTIVITY FOR R.C.A. WALLS—AND ROCKEFELLER FOOTS BILL. By the time reporter Peter Lilly finished describing red flags, red headdresses, and "waves of red in a victorious onsweep," the overseers of Rockefeller Center were undoubtedly seeing the same color. Making matters worse, the voluble artist had obliged Lilly with juicy quotes affirming his solidarity with the worker class for whom he did his painting. In his autobiography, Rivera would go fur-

---

* Before the year ended, Junior would make his two eldest sons financially independent, an action he may well have been contemplating at the time of Nelson's family letter.

ther, conflating events to suggest that he had already inserted the deal-breaking portrait of Lenin by the time he spoke with Lilly.

Actually, this alteration came in response to Lilly's April 25 follow-up story, in which the artist's erstwhile comrades on the left castigated Rivera, in their eyes a painter for millionaires, as a political turncoat. Stung by the criticism, Rivera scrapped his planned image of a vaguely conceptualized Worker-Leader and asked his assistants to find him a good photo of Lenin. His Marxist credentials in doubt, he would demonstrate his loyalty on this most public of soapboxes. And he would make the archcapitalists pay for their own humiliation.

3

THE PACE OF work accelerated. Presently, well-muscled female gymnasts were leaping hurdles in socialist joy. Germs of poverty and sexually diseased microbes thrived on the Fascist side of the wall, otherwise occupied by a cocktail party infested with rich exploiters and brainless players of bridge. On May 3, Nelson returned to the RCA Building. While viewing the progress of "your thrilling mural," he wrote Rivera the next day, "I noticed that in the most recent portion of the painting you had included a portrait of Lenin. The piece is beautiful but it seems to me that his portrait appearing in the mural might very seriously offend a great many people. If it were a private house it would be one thing, but this mural is in a public building and the situation is therefore quite different. As much as I dislike to do so, I am afraid we must ask you to substitute the face of some unknown man where Lenin's face now appears."

In other words, to return to the artist's original conception.

This was not the first revision urged on Rivera. According to his assistant and later biographer, Bertram Wolfe, Frances Paine had repeatedly passed on hints from the managing agents to make the mural—figuratively *and* literally—less colorful. Nelson's letter upped the ante. Wolfe advised Rivera to haul down the red flag of Leninism, in order to preserve the rest of the painting. Not so fast, said Ben Shahn and other assistants, who threatened to strike should the artist surrender to his wealthy patrons. Then there was Frida Kahlo. "Frida was peeking in and out of the door to keep check on developments," recalled Nelson. "And the result was that when I went out, she came in." Perhaps, in his eagerness to consummate a deal, Nelson retroactively believed that there had been negotiations. If so, his recollections conflict with every other version of what happened following Rivera's May 6 response (drafted by Ben Shahn).

While offering to balance the Lenin portrait with a likeness of Lincoln, "surrounded by John Brown, Nat Turner, William Lloyd Garrison, or Wendell

Phillips and Harriet Beecher Stowe," the artist refused to "mutilate" his fresco by painting over the father of Soviet Communism. "I should prefer the physical destruction of the conception in its entirety," said a defiant Rivera. Late on the afternoon of Tuesday, May 9, Hugh Robertson of Todd, Robertson, and Todd led a phalanx of guards and workmen into the lobby. He ordered Rivera down from his scaffolding, paid him the balance of his commission, and terminated the project. Rivera was still in the building when angry demonstrators threw up a picket line outside. Their cries were echoed, from a distance, by Lewis Mumford, Van Wyck Brooks, Alfred Stieglitz, and New Deal economist Stuart Chase. The John Reed Club of Boston likened the action to Nazi book burning, an analogy Rivera repeated the next day at a Columbia University rally calling for the overthrow of the school's autocratic president, Nicholas Murray Butler. "They have no right, this little group of commercially minded people, to assassinate my work," he told reporters. Glorying in his notoriety, the artist claimed that the Rockefellers had known all along of his intention to place the figure of a "leader" in his mural. Why the big fuss? Lenin, he pointed out, was "the most modern leader in the world."

The Rockefellers had their defenders. "An apotheosis of Lenin on the walls of Rockefeller Center is about as appropriate as a frieze of swastikas over the doors of a synagogue," argued *The New York Times*. Using somewhat homelier language, humorist Will Rogers declared that the builders of Rockefeller Center had ordered a plain ham sandwich, only to have Rivera put some onions on it. Acknowledging Rivera's artistic primacy, Rogers concluded, "You should never try to fool a Rockefeller in oils." In a "Memo for Mr. Nelson from his Father," dated May 12, Junior directed that any complaints about the Rivera matter be referred to the managing directors of Rockefeller Center. Though hardly a ringing vote of confidence, this at least removed Nelson from the direct line of fire. Ironically, by winning the right to paint on fresco rather than canvas, Rivera had made it impossible for the work to be preserved in another setting. This didn't keep Nelson from devising a complex scenario whereby MoMA would ask for the mural and promise to assume any costs incurred in its removal from the RCA Building. To MoMA staff, he simultaneously expressed confidence that Rockefeller Center would advance necessary funds for the museum to do just that. To recoup the investment, Nelson intended to exhibit the controversial work to throngs of the curious at a dollar per head.

Regrettably, no one knew how to slice the plaster from the lobby walls intact. On February 9, 1934, Rivera's mural was ripped apart, then carted off, ignominiously, in fifty-gallon oil drums. Denouncing this act of "cultural vandalism," art groups briefly threatened to boycott Mayor La Guardia's Municipal Art Show scheduled for later that month in the Rockefeller Center Forum. Nearly as disturbing were xenophobic letters of praise sent to Nelson from the National

Association of Manufacturers and the United Scenic Artists of America. Seventy-five years later, John Todd's granddaughter Christie Todd Whitman confirmed that it was Junior who ordered the murals covered and later torn from the lobby wall (in a none-too-subtle reference to paternal displeasure, Nelson acknowledged that both he and his mother had "lost ground" in the dispute). By a twist of fate, the elder Rockefeller happened to visit Dartmouth days after Rivera was ushered out of the RCA Building. While on campus, he viewed the Baker Library murals of "the other Mexican painter—Oresco or some such. All I can say is that I am glad they are not on the walls of Rockefeller Center."

It took eight years, but eventually Rivera and Rockefeller resumed speaking. Even Frida came around in time. True to the "happy go lucky" nature he analyzed for his mother, Nelson bounced back from the mural fiasco with astonishing speed. Beneath the surface, however, the affair left ineradicable scars. In later years, he grew visibly annoyed when reporters pressed him to interpret the headless torsos and abstract forms that filled his houses and cluttered his lawns. "You writers are all the same," Rockefeller muttered. "You want to know what something means. You're trained to be word people." What *really* mattered, he insisted, was "how does that make you *feel*." And feelings were bound to vary depending on one's mood or outlook.

Ultimately, it was not the artist who defined his work, but its owner. Estate manager Joe Canzeri recalled the arrival at Pocantico of a large red sculpture, immediately repainted black per orders of his employer. To an angry curator who disputed his right to tamper with the creator's vision, Rockefeller had a ready response.

"Hey," he told Canzeri, "if he wanted me to keep it that color, why the hell did he sell it to me?"

4

ON THE OCCASION of his twenty-fifth birthday in July 1933, Nelson orchestrated the family photographs, including a memorable picture of him clutching fourteen-month-old Roddy and flanked by Senior, who turned ninety-four that day. The implication was clear: Forget accidents of chronology or claims of primogeniture—here was the true line of dynastic renewal. What seemed obvious to Nelson, however, was less evident to Junior, who persisted in treating all five of his boys as boys, with sometimes ludicrous results. Discovering that Nelson had given his brother David $100 to help defray the cost of a visit to their grandfather in Florida, Junior insisted the money be returned. In the future, he would appreciate it if Nelson, "before taking action that was at variance with what I was trying to do," might discuss such matters openly with his father, "so that we might not be working at cross purposes."

In the third week of July 1933, Nelson and Tod sailed from New York to Veracruz. "We carefully avoided all the other passengers and had lots of fun by ourselves," he wrote home. The couple made obligatory calls at the U.S. embassy and Chase Bank, then "started right in on Rivera's frescos. As far as I'm concerned his work down here is far superior to what he has done in the United States." Mexico cast a permanent spell over Rockefeller. Tutored by Frances Paine, an erudite guide whose unrivaled contacts opened doors to some of the world's finest collections of Olmec, Toltec, and Aztec art, the visitor from New York was captivated by the country's lavishly decorated churches, more than a hundred in the city of Pueblo alone. With childlike glee, Nelson waded into outdoor markets, scooping up artistic spoils that quickly filled two dozen packing crates. Having purchased virtually the entire output of an elderly Indian woman who wove brilliantly colored serapes, Nelson bought several stone and wood carvings from sculptor Mardonio Magaña. The next day, he went with the artist to a nearby school where Magaña taught classes in sculpture for teenage children. Nelson carted off twenty-two pieces at $10 each, most destined for the walls of his Pocantico garden, to which he returned by the end of August.

That fall, Junior toiled for days on a radio address cautiously endorsing FDR's National Recovery Administration, under which Uncle Sam was empowered to suspend antitrust laws and promote a complex web of industrial codes regulating wages, hours, and production levels. ("All the companies that John is connected with have signed the agreement," Abby told her sister, Lucy, early in September. Both Kykuit and the Eyrie were operating according to NRA rules. "Fortunately they do not ask to have domestic service put under this system," she added with palpable relief.) Like many a mogul of the era, Junior did not object to paternalism as long as he was clearly acknowledged the founder of the feast. To his children and their families encamped around the Pocantico compound, he supplied fuel, dairy products, watchmen for security, and transportation for maids. All new construction or landscaping must have his approval—he didn't hesitate to veto a child's tree house—as Pocantico more than ever became his refuge from a world in flux. Public comments notwithstanding, Junior harbored grave doubts about Roosevelt and his New Deal. These found expression when his son David and a Harvard classmate decided to abandon Cambridge one autumn weekend for a visit to the Eyrie. "Evidently the students of our great universities have gone NRA also," Junior observed sourly.

Nelson shared his father's Republican loyalties, though he was markedly less hostile to the administration in Washington. One day in September 1933, he convened a meeting in his office to determine how large a contribution the family would make to Fiorello H. La Guardia, a maverick Republican congressman and Roosevelt sympathizer, then leading a fusion ticket against Tammany rule of city hall. It was decided to give La Guardia neither more nor less than previous reform candidates. After his upset victory in November, La Guardia was to prove a useful, if erratic, ally. Later that week, Nelson was awakened in the middle of the night by excruciating pains. An ambulance transported him to Presbyterian Hospital in the city for an emergency appendectomy. "It seemed very silly to have my appendix out," he wrote a friend, "but at three in the morning one hardly knows what is going on and before I knew it they had me on the table."

A more restless convalescent could hardly be imagined. Though Tod promised her in-laws she wouldn't let him overexert himself, Abby worried anyway. "Nelson is full of nervous energy and has all sorts of theories about it not being necessary for anyone of his age to rest or to consider his health," she told her son's doctor. If only he could learn to conserve his strength, "I believe it would add very much to the length of his life." In the meantime, she took consolation from his apparent outgrowth of a slight heart tremor diagnosed when he was a small boy. It was Abby's health that concerned Junior. Much as he resented the demands made on her depleted vitality by MoMA, he believed an even greater toll was exacted by her children and grandchildren. Fearing the worst, Junior pressed Nelson and his siblings to forgo family meals and shut down one or more of their satellite homes on the Pocantico estate. Nelson in turn pleaded with his mother to dismiss MoMA and its financial problems from her mind—he would oversee the current endowment campaign himself. He telephoned her daily, pretending to a postoperative jauntiness he did not feel lest Abby's concern over his health endanger her own.

Junior's expression of appreciation was not long in coming. On more than one occasion, he had worried aloud to his sons that they would one day have too much money rather than too little. Needless to say, this was not an anxiety shared by Nelson and his siblings, who remained embarrassingly dependent on paternal largesse well into their adult years. All this began to change on December 20, 1933, when Junior presented John and Nelson with $3.2 million apiece of Socony-Vacuum stock. The windfall came wrapped in cautionary advice, Junior urging his sons to limit increases in their regular expenditures to five "or at the outside ten" thousand dollars annually.

Nelson's immediate response was to pledge, anonymously, $100,000 to the stalled drive for a MoMA endowment.* He also purchased, for $55,000, a

---

* "Ever since you were a very little boy we seemed to love the same things," Abby told Nelson on learning of his donation. That he should give so generously to her most cherished cause, without

fourteen-room duplex apartment at 810 Fifth Avenue, just across Sixty-second Street from the Knickerbocker Club. With a second child due in May 1934, a growing family required additional living space at Pocantico as well. Nelson and Tod let Junior pay for a new wing and other improvements to Hawes House. The older man concluded with satisfaction that "while the construction work has exceeded by $6,398.62 the rough figure of $15,000 which you and I had in mind at the outset, I note that the furnishings has run under our rough estimate by $28.81."

5

JUNIOR TURNED SIXTY in January 1934. Contemplating his increasingly frequent absences from the office, he designated his Brown classmate and lawyer, Thomas Debevoise, to be his surrogate. The special relationship between their father and Debevoise, who was referred to around Room 5600 as "the Prime Minister," could only complicate any succession plans made by Nelson and John 3rd. During a Pocantico weekend that spring, Junior reminded both that his own father had never formalized a transition of authority, leaving it to his namesake to gradually assume responsibility. The hint was not lost on Nelson. On May 13, 1934, Tod Rockefeller gave birth to her second child, a daughter named Ann. "A most adorable person," concluded her grandmother; Roddy, however, remained her favorite. "Nelson gave me a long lecture the other day as to how I was to treat him, which amused me tremendously and which I took very meekly," said Abby.

Her son exerted far less control outside the home, a deficiency he was eager to correct. "My chief desire is that we as a family should ultimately develop into a closely knit, effective group," Nelson told his mother. He refused, however, to become a captive of the family office. On his own initiative, he began spending mornings in the Utilities Department of the Chase Bank, where instructors guided him through a maze of federal regulation. The next chapter in his financial education was inspired by Dartmouth's president Ernest Hopkins, whose criticism of "the provincial Wall Street attitude" prompted Nelson and a group of Chase officials to commandeer a private railcar and embark on a cross-country tour. For a month, the eastern moneymen interviewed their

waiting for her to die, and with the first riches that were his to command, filled her heart "with a joy and gratitude she had never before experienced. Dear boy, it was you who put the museum on its feet and made it permanent, without that hundred thousand it would have failed." "Serendipity at the Rockefeller Archive Center": Abby Aldrich Rockefeller letter to Nelson A. Rockefeller, May 1934, *Rockefeller Archive Center Newsletter*, Spring 2002, 7.

counterparts in William Jennings Bryan country. In Hollywood, they were photographed beside Shirley Temple as the pint-sized superstar stood atop a table. Amon Carter, Texas oil baron and publisher of the *Fort Worth Star-Telegram*, welcomed Nelson to the Lone Star State with the gift of a white hat and polo coat. Carter's sprawling ranch house, its bar and elevator cab transplanted from the old Ritz Hotel in New York, was easily surpassed in appeal by "a very attractive girl" Nelson chanced to meet in Dallas.

Nearly as memorable were his encounters with mill hands, lumbermen, cotton merchants, citrus growers, and grain dealers Nelson sought out for informal conversations along his route. Together, concluded Rockefeller, they opened his eyes to "a saner, more balanced point of view" than he was accustomed to hearing in Manhattan. Upon his return home, Nelson busied himself as chairman of the Roof and Exhibitions Committee of Rockefeller Center, organizing displays of artwork by high school students and corporate trade shows in the forty-five-thousand-square-foot Forum. More to his taste was the Rainbow Room, a spectacular art deco restaurant–cum–floating cabaret on the sixty-fifth floor of the RCA Building. Here men in white tie and Ginger Rogers wannabes admired the night-lights of Manhattan, while eight hundred feet below, grim scenes of hardship testified to the persistence of mass unemployment. Diverting though it was, the Roof and Exhibitions Committee absorbed only a fraction of Nelson's creative energy. In the summer of 1934, he launched a fresh assault on Rockefeller Center management, enlisting John 3rd in a radical reorganization aimed at replacing John R. Todd.

Junior initially voiced no objection to the plan, leaving its review and implementation to others. On September 2, 1934, their father revealed to John and Nelson his intent to establish substantial new trust funds, dwarfing his earlier gift of Socony-Vacuum stock, for them, their siblings, and their mother. Three days later, Nelson's friend and ally Bart Turnbull was named treasurer of Rockefeller Center, and his proposed Executive Committee was formally ratified. He had won a great victory, or so it appeared—until what the official history of Rockefeller Center describes, with unofficial candor, as "an upheaval in the relations with the Managing Agents." Influenced by Tom Debevoise, Junior executed an abrupt volte-face. Instead of being demoted, Todd, Robertson, and Todd were given a ringing vote of confidence, their position enhanced by equal representation on most of the committees reconstituted in place of Nelson's short-lived management structure.

Yet time was on his side. By securing for himself an exclusive liaison role, and keeping Todd off the critical Executive and Finance committees, Nelson had created a springboard to future control. Even Debevoise, until now a staunch ally of the managing agents, might come around if properly cultivated. After all, it wasn't Todd Center over which they were arguing. Any disappointment Nelson might feel was assuaged by the $12 million trust fund to which his father had alluded a few months earlier. "As you are still comparatively young," said Junior, "it might have been more prudent to have waited a few years." Overcoming his innate caution was a steep rise in federal gift taxes, the unwelcome price for FDR's recent lunge to the left to avoid being outflanked by latter-day Robin Hoods Huey P. Long and radio priest Father Charles Coughlin.*

And even as he transferred vast wealth to his eldest sons, Junior congratulated himself on selecting as their trustees men "of matured judgment and in sympathy with our family policies." With the 1934 Trusts, as they became known, Nelson was financially born again. From $142,000 in 1934, his income soared to $499,000 a year later, reaching nearly $750,000 in 1936. At twenty-six, Nelson was at last free to pursue his multiple interests, the more successfully as he learned from past errors. Far from resenting Tom Debevoise for torpedoing his attempted takeover of Rockefeller Center, Nelson set out to recruit a Debevoise of his own. His timing was fortuitous. Just when his need for a sympathetic lieutenant was greatest, Rockefeller happened upon a self-made architect from Worcester, Massachusetts, named Wallace Harrison. Although his senior in years, in every other respect Nelson's latest acquaintance filled the role of junior partner. Long afterward, still shaking his head at the audacity of the thing, Wally Harrison remarked, "Sometimes you'd think he was the architect and I was something else."

* Forty million Americans tuned in each week to hear Father Coughlin, who had once declared the New Deal to be Christ's Deal, take an increasingly venomous approach to the Roosevelt revolution. Long of Louisiana signed up seven million adherents for his Share Our Wealth campaign that promised every family a home of its own, free schooling from kindergarten through college, and "reasonable comforts of life" up to $6,000 a year. The former lard salesman from Winn Parish puckishly offered to make John D. Rockefeller, Jr., the first chairman of his populist crusade.

Six

PROMETHEUS

It was always an interesting relationship between Nelson and his father, because hardly ever did his father ask Nelson to do something. Nelson would walk in and see something to be done. He'd take it up and he'd work at it . . . and if his father didn't say anything, he'd keep working at it. That was the way they transferred their responsibilities. Nelson just sort of took them until he . . . well, until he became president of Rockefeller Center.

—WALLACE K. HARRISON

1

NELSON ROCKEFELLER AND Wally Harrison couldn't agree on when they first met. Harrison remembered a bustling, deferential young man, suddenly appearing in a boardroom of the Graybar Building one morning in 1931. It was nine o'clock, and a clutch of architects had already been toiling for hours, assembling their latest blueprints for Junior's review. "Can I be of any help in pinning up the drawings?" Nelson asked. To Harrison, he appeared "a man who could get a job done. He radiated youth and confidence, but there was no side to him." Rockefeller's memory of the encounter differed revealingly. He recalled a meeting of Junior and several architects who were pondering the slablike RCA Building. "Father was accustomed to buildings that had fluted columns or Gothic arches marching up their sides," said Nelson, sounding very much as Junior had in condescending to the alleged philistinism of *his* father. The men around him listened respectfully as Junior outlined his traditionalist preferences.

All but one.

"Goddammit, Mr. Rockefeller, you can't do that," Harrison exploded. "You'll ruin the building if you cover up its lines with that classical gingerbread."

His roar of protest foreshadowed half a century as Nelson's closest collaborator, sometime conscience, alter ego, and occasional foil. As described by his friend and fellow architect Harmon Goldstone, Harrison "jumps from one thing to another in a series of brilliant intuitive flashes . . . he never knows how he'll react to the next moment of life." To his partner, Max Abramovitz, Harrison was "a perpetual progressive" with a horror of the status quo. "Whatever you do, you can't stand still," Harrison once told a writer for *The New Yorker*. "My father was a hell of a good guy. He lost out because he thought everything was perfect—Worcester, the Elks, the foundry that he worked in and that was set up along the old lines, as if the workers were craftsmen. I saw it as a kid. And I saw him rolled over by the modern factory. No matter what the cost is, you've got to move forward."

To Nelson Rockefeller, this was holy writ. He seemed to have grasped by instinct the essential duality of this Park Avenue bohemian whose experimental outlook was tempered by ingrained pragmatism. Born in the central Massachusetts city of Worcester in 1895, Harrison was fourteen when his mother died, and he quit school to work as an office boy for a local contractor. Six years later, having saved $35 for the adventure, Harrison moved to New York City. From a room on Twenty-third Street, he applied for a position at McKim, Mead & White, then the nation's premier design firm. Told there were no openings for draftsmen, Harrison offered his services free of charge. Within two weeks he was hired, at $20 a week, to prepare a book of hospital drawings.

His new employers introduced Harrison to Harvey Wiley Corbett, a California architect who used his workshops to decry, among other aesthetic offenses, the Renaissance conservatism of McKim, Mead & White. In October 1919, Harrison passed the grueling twelve-hour entrance exam of the famed École des Beaux-Arts in Paris. Sustained by bean soup and café argumentation, he came to admire the sleek functionalism of youthful rebels like Walter Gropius and Ludwig Mies van der Rohe. In 1926, Harrison came within the Rockefeller orbit. That year, he wed Ellen Milton, whose brother David was married to Babs Rockefeller. After brief stints with the New York City Board of Education and the Columbia School of Architecture, Harrison became a junior partner in the firm of Helmle & Corbett. "I finally knew for sure that I wanted to be a *modern* architect," he reflected. "I don't mean I was a purist. That isn't in me. But while I was hacking away at the Board of Education, it became absolutely clear to me that the only sound approach to architecture is to think in terms of the people who will be using the building—that the function of architecture is to take care of human beings in a pleasant way."

In a field crowded with self-dramatizing tyrants like Frank Lloyd Wright and Le Corbusier, Harrison stood out for his modesty and collegial approach. "Do you know what an architect is?" he asked with a wry smile. "When all is said and done, an architect is a designer with a client." By the late twenties, Harrison had connections at the National Broadcasting Company, linchpin of the Rockefellers' proposed Radio City. As a junior member of the design team, he argued, unsuccessfully, against architect Raymond Hood's setbacks on the seventy-story RCA Building. Harrison lost a second time when Junior demanded an ornate metal railing to adorn the skyscraper's bare rooftop. It was his forceful denunciation of any further Gothic decoration, coupled with a suggestion that the money thus saved should be allocated to contemporary art, that introduced Harrison to Nelson as a kindred spirit.

In truth, each filled the other's needs. Erich Fromm might have had Nelson Rockefeller in mind when defining the necessary conditions for human creativity: "to be puzzled; to concentrate; to accept conflict and tension; to be born every day; to feel a sense of self." What an artist imagines, an architect implements. Rockefeller did both. As a Dartmouth student trying his hand at painting and sculpture, he had been dismayed to learn that no amount of desire could supplant talent. His failure left a vacancy that he would fill as artistic patron and public builder. Long afterward, in a rare lament over the course his life had taken, Rockefeller said that he would have liked to be an architect but couldn't justify "a personal whim" in view of his family responsibilities. Harrison was more explicit. "His mother wouldn't let him," he claimed. "She said, 'You just have too important a job to do in life.'"

Harrison admitted Rockefeller to a creative partnership, enabling him to vicariously indulge ambitions blocked by his family. For Harrison, the benefits of the relationship were even more seductive. The son of an alcoholic Worcester foundry man embraced the role of court builder for the chance "to work with great people and do beautiful buildings. . . ." Late in life, Harrison conceded, "I've always taken money too seriously." Rockefeller projects sustained the young firm of Harrison & Fouilhoux during the fallow thirties, when Harrison gave his staff the imaginary task of redesigning Central Park. By the start of 1933, Harrison was allied with Special Work, Inc., receiving one-quarter the regular brokerage commission on any client he delivered. An annual retainer of $4,000 from Nelson fed his appetite for modern art.

Beyond price was the gift of Nelson's intimacy. "He was a lot of fun," said Harrison of his new friend, a natural extrovert who was "crazy" about jazz, loved to dance, held his own on the tennis court and golf links, and relished driving the latest-model cars at the highest possible speeds. Each winter, the Rockefellers and Harrisons vacationed together in the Vermont ski country. On long train rides north from Grand Central, the husbands dreamed up ways to smuggle their kind of art into Rockefeller Center. Both men were disappointed by the rejection of Carl Milles's towering glass Indians in favor of Paul Manship's totemic *Prometheus* (to sniggering critics, "the Daring Young Man on the

Flying Trapeze"). They were reminded of this defeat every time they entered the sunken plaza, as yet without its famed ice rink or outdoor café. With increasing frequency, Harrison could expect a cheery midmorning phone call.

"Do you want to have a cup of coffee?"

This was the signal to repair to a small restaurant just behind *Prometheus*, from which they could look out on the largely deserted plaza. As Rockefeller breakfasted on sandwiches of buttered toast, marmalade, and bacon, a delicacy for which Harrison rapidly developed a taste, the two men pondered how to increase foot traffic in the unfinished complex. One scheme envisioned a large rail station boosting the flow of commuters, many from New Jersey train lines not then serviced by any New York terminal. That idea fizzled, as did the notion of creating an underground mall stretching from Grand Central Terminal to Rockefeller Center. Opposition from within the family nearly scuttled Nelson's next brainstorm, a 120-unit apartment house on West Fifty-fourth Street, which his brother John deemed unnecessarily risky at a time when the family was already overcommitted in the real estate field.

Why not sell the property to be developed by others? he argued. Why let outsiders reap the rewards that should more properly be theirs? retorted Nelson. He stressed other benefits before the public, portraying the Rockefeller Apartments as a catalyst for the rejuvenation of midtown Manhattan, where no significant residential construction had occurred since 1930. Nelson won the argument; Harrison won the contract. Aided by Max Abramovitz and a young Frank Lloyd Wright disciple named Edward Durrell Stone, Harrison put yesterday to work for tomorrow. Drawing on youthful memories of Massachusetts bay windows, the architect adapted these quaint features to modernist use by creating much deeper bays, ideal for dining, with cantilevered windows to break the monotony of the building's brick façade. Critic Lewis Mumford declared the Rockefeller Apartments, bolstered by amenities such as woodburning fireplaces and a private interior garden, "the most brilliant and most successful example of modern architecture in the city."*

Hunched over their marmalade-and-bacon sandwiches, Rockefeller and Harrison envisaged a "cinematic mural," the joint creation of French cubist painter Fernand Léger and Walt Disney, to be projected on a white marble wall above a bank of escalators in the lobby of Rockefeller Center's International Building. When this inspiration fell victim to the bean counters, its promoters

---

* Regrettably, such praise did not pay the bills, of which there were more than enough to validate the doubts about profitability expressed by John 3rd. Nine years after they opened, the Rockefeller Apartments were sold at a loss to Junior of more than $600,000. Still resolved to jump-start development in the area, Nelson urged construction of a tony department store on Fifth Avenue. Eventually the site he had in mind was assigned to MoMA, an institution infinitely closer to his heart and his checkbook.

each took satisfaction in commissioning a Léger mural for their homes. Throughout the 1930s, Nelson's 810 Fifth Avenue apartment served as a laboratory for ideas too outré or expensive to win a committee's approval. Disdaining mere reproductions, for $25,000 Rockefeller obtained the services of Paris designer Jean-Michel Frank. Soon a convoy of oceangoing vessels began disgorging their treasures: customized sofas covered in yellow handwoven silk; low green sharkskin tables; green leather armchairs by Hermès; and carved consoles, metal lamps, and andirons crafted by Alberto and Diego Giacometti.

Wally Harrison tailored a cache of eighteenth-century French parquet flooring to fit smaller rooms and created a circular dining room by turning corner spaces into storage areas. The same room featured an onyx black table surrounded by two dozen tapestry chairs. Should conversation flag, guests could enjoy music piped throughout the apartment via the Stromberg-Carlson Telek-tor, an elaborate system of hidden consoles and speakers engineered to be echo-free. Egyptian-style lighting fixtures added to the eclectic look of the place. No detail of construction or aesthetics escaped Nelson's attention. The blue in one bedroom, he decreed, must be more "ultramarine." A stairway leading to the rooftop penthouse (soon converted into a playroom for Roddy, Ann, and a third child, Steven, born in 1936) required a Lucite railing, precisely 1.5 inches in diameter. The entrance to his glass brick bathroom should be moved south by one brick.

The result was not to everyone's liking. Abby objected vigorously to a living room mantel by the sculptor Gaston Lachaise, best known for his voluptuous female nudes. Tod Rockefeller agreed with her mother-in-law. But it was only when the redoubtable Lucy Aldrich joined the chorus of dissatisfaction that Nelson yielded, replacing Lachaise with a venerable wooden mantel extracted from one of the English country houses he and Tod visited in the summer of 1935. Within a year of occupying their quarters, Nelson was negotiating to purchase, for $50,000, the floor immediately below. "What with our growing family we really had to do something," he explained to its owner, "and this will make a perfect arrangement. Our only regret is that we will no longer have you for our neighbor. I am afraid we have incurred the ill will of all the other tenants," concluded Nelson, "because everyone feels very badly at the thought of your departure."

A squib in the *New York Sun* predicted it would cost him $10,000 to integrate old and new. In fact, the project devoured more than $80,000—a fraction of the $260,000, not counting fees paid to Wally Harrison and his firm, that Rockefeller lavished on the entire twenty-four-room apartment. To connect the twelfth and thirteenth floors of 810 Fifth Avenue, he had Harrison unspool a twisting staircase. Nelson watched, mesmerized, as Fernand Léger extended his artistry down the side of the stairwell, improvising around the unexpected play of light and shadows. (Not to be outdone, Harrison invited Léger to create a mural on the floor of his swimming pool.) Rockefeller also commissioned Henri Matisse to paint a female quartet framing the fireplace in the twenty-eight-by-eighteen-foot living room whose indirectly lit walls were sheathed in cork. *La Poésie* (*Poetry*) was fashioned in the artist's Paris studio, then shipped to New York for installation. "I am afraid that he might be doing something crazy," Nelson confided to Abby. When next in Paris, could she please drop in on her old friend and casually review the work in progress? In the end, both mother and son were delighted with the mural's oxblood reds, sunny yellows, and aubergine the color of eggplant—inspired, said the artist, by some K'ang-hsi porcelains he had glimpsed a decade earlier while dining with Junior and Abby.

In his bedroom overlooking Fifth Avenue, Nelson hung a small Matisse canvas given him by his mother when he joined the MoMA board. Where other men might deposit spare change in a bureau drawer, Nelson kept cherished samples of indigenous art close enough to gratify tactile urges. Elsewhere in the room, a Wei dynasty carving complemented *The Golfer,* a witty, wiry caricature of Senior from the hand of Alexander Calder. The old man had routinely moved hills to improve on nature; denied a Central Park view by the balustrade outside his study, Nelson again turned to Wally Harrison, who solved the problem by constructing a platform, reached by steps, on which Nelson's desk, a sofa, and some chairs were positioned to afford their users unobstructed vistas of the park.

Nearby zebra-wood cabinets offered a dazzling array of pre-Columbian stone figures and African necklaces. Emulating their owner, none of these objects remained in one place for long. "I like moving things around in these cases just the way I like to re-hang my pictures every so often," Nelson acknowledged. His favorite weekend recreation was to grab a hammer, stuff his pockets with nails, and rearrange canvases signed by Picasso, Miró, Hopper, Gris, and other giants of twentieth-century painting. Relaxation was pursued with the same frenzied intensity that characterized his working life. If Nelson had any fault, said Harrison, "it is that he works you too hard—he doesn't know how to stop himself and drives others." This view was seconded by Gus Eyssell, assistant manager of Radio City Music Hall. "If you wanted to reach him at 8:30 in the morning he was at the office," said Eyssell, "if you needed to reach him late at night he was always available. He was there to talk about any problem that came up and always would come up with a productive idea on how it should be worked out."

Only much later, illusions burned away, did Wally Harrison conclude that his relationship with Nelson had been primarily a working friendship, "never relaxed for more than ten minutes." With an old man's candor, he confessed, "I was tough enough to be a part of the group that he used to get things done."

2

H AVING POLITELY REBUFFED the Boy Scouts of America, the Lenox Hill Neighborhood Association, American Express, the Society for the Improvement of the Condition of the Poor, and International Paper and Power, early in 1935 Nelson revealed where his true interests lay. "Some day I should like to be on the board of the Chase National Bank," he informed Junior. This explained his continuing education in the bank's Utilities Department, including a nine-month stint in the Foreign Department captained by Joseph Rovensky, the self-made son of Czech immigrants to whom Junior entrusted the extracurricular schooling of his sons. "For the first time in my life I have really become 'world conscious,'" Nelson told Rovensky in June 1935. A few days later, he deposited Roddy and Ann with their grandparents on Mount Desert and sailed with Tod for Europe, where brief tours of duty had been arranged in the London and Paris branches of Chase.

More than one writer has portrayed the trip as a strategic retreat from the wreckage of his aborted coup against John R. Todd. This not only overlooks the January 1934 starting date of his Chase tutorial and its eighteen-month duration, but underestimates Nelson's growing geopolitical interests and his role in the concurrent restructuring of RKO. To be sure, his responsibilities on the trip were not onerous. Each morning Nelson attended a ten o'clock staff meeting, reserving the balance of the day for departmental visits, lunches, and informal discussions with Chase competitors, insurance firms, and brokerage houses. This left plenty of time to accommodate country house parties, Standard Oil dinners, and shopping sprees arranged by Aunt Lucy Aldrich. Along with Tod, Nelson joined MPs in the dining room of the House of Commons, from whose galleries the visiting Americans listened as Winston Churchill and Foreign Minister Sir Samuel Hoare debated the Anglo-German Naval Agreement and a youthful Anthony Eden briefed the Commons on diplomatic efforts to forestall Mussolini from invading Abyssinia.*

Upon his return to New York at the start of September, Nelson hastened to assure Senior that his six-week Chase interlude had been "most profitable." Grandfather and grandson enjoyed frequent skull sessions beneath the vaulted, Raphael-inspired ceiling of Kykuit's opulent teahouse. Reclining in a Morris chair, rug around his shoulders, JDR pumped his young admirer for the latest gossip of Rockefeller Center. Administering regular doses of statistical reality to quell Nelson's ardent visions of new business ventures, the old man demanded,

---

* Per Junior's directive, the cost of the trip, $7,130.39, was paid by Room 5600 as an office charge. The same accounting methods would spare Nelson and Tod from picking up the tab for Idaho ski trips and journeys through Latin America.

"What do the figures show? It's the figures that count." In return, Nelson gently ribbed his grandfather, sending him a German newspaper clipping in which the aged widower featured prominently "with a very lovely looking young lady who, if I am not mistaken, is none other than the beautiful movie star, Marlene Dietrich." Not being conversant in German, Nelson continued, he was uncertain what the picture meant. But he had a hunch. "Evidently Father did not tell us all" after visiting Senior at his Florida retreat in Ormond Beach.

What might have been a shocking breach of propriety coming from anyone else became a sly dig in the ribs from one man of the world to another. Backseat pinching aside, Senior's declining health left him little energy for activities amorous or otherwise. Even in this semitropical setting he rarely ventured out before donning a neck scarf and tweed cap with earflaps. Fearful of Communism and worried about his greatly diminished fortune, the tycoon handed out nickels instead of his iconic dimes. Eventually these, too, dried up. By the third year of Franklin Roosevelt's presidency, it was becoming harder for any Rockefeller to maintain a sense of humor, let alone a sense of proportion, where the man in the White House was concerned. Nelson couldn't resist passing along Aunt Lucy Aldrich's tongue-in-cheek strategy to keep some much loved stone Chinese figures in the family, unburdened by New Deal inheritance taxes. Unorthodox as ever, Miss Aldrich urged Junior and Abby to build themselves a mausoleum with the statues incorporated into its design, although "she was a little afraid," Nelson observed impishly, "Father might not like having pagan figures on top of his grave."

Abby's fears were of a different order. "When I think of the way the people's money is being wasted it makes me weep," she moaned to her youngest son. "Your father will do so much more good with money than the United States will ever do, that it is a crime to let it change hands." Her own hands were far from spotless. Learning of $77 million in federal funds earmarked for New York City, Abby put aside her scruples, explaining to Nelson, "It seemed a perfect shame to me that the Modern Museum shouldn't get some." Thus encouraged, Nelson imagined a new building to be located in Bryant Park and housing not only the fabled music collections of the adjacent public library, but gallery space, auditoriums, and other facilities to serve MoMA. Nothing came of the idea, as Washington took a pass and Mayor La Guardia scaled back his plans for a municipal cultural complex.

For Nelson, long accustomed to pursuing multiple interests at the same time, the 1930s were a time of explosive creativity. Besides MoMA and Rockefeller Center, he overcame his father's objections and joined the board of the Metropolitan Museum of Art, where he befriended Alan Priest, director of the Met's Far Eastern Division. "He used to go to China every year to buy for the Museum and I would give him a small amount of money and he bought objects for me," recalled Rockefeller, who returned the favor when Priest came under fire from an avenging board chairman named George Blumenthal. Some Met trustees were not above blackmail in their determination to remove Priest, whom they accused of being homosexual. "I thought he was a great guy," said Nelson. Threatening to go public with the shameful tactics employed by Priest's enemies, "I made it embarrassing enough . . . that they had to keep him. The whole thing was a disgrace, but I learned a lot."

3

N ELSON WASN'T THE only one thriving in a hostile climate. MoMA itself was enjoying rapid growth, notwithstanding the economic holocaust that made cities like New York dependent on federal largesse. The original concept of an American Luxembourg, a showplace for living artists, for masterpieces in the making, had evolved along more populist lines. The fledgling museum boasted departments of publications and industrial art, as well as a pioneering film library preserving Mack Sennett's custard pies and a smoldering Rudolph Valentino in *Monsieur Beaucaire*. A radio art program emanated from MoMA, as did traveling exhibits that carried the modernist banner to ninety-eight cities. By apotheosizing propeller blades and ball bearings, shows like Philip Johnson's 1934 *Machine Art* constantly pushed the envelope. So did a surrealism exhibit made notable, or notorious, by Marcel Duchamp's *Why Not Sneeze, Rose Sélavy?*, archly described by *The New Yorker* as "a birdcage containing a postage stamp, some lumps of sugar, and a thermometer."

At the center of it all was Alfred Barr, Jr., the ascetic museum director likened by members of the nearby University Club to a defrocked Spanish priest. Less biased observers detected in Barr a curious mixture of moral intensity and personal detachment. As advanced in his social views as in his artistic vision, Barr was careful to sit in the section of a Washington–New York train reserved for blacks only. He refused to move even when ordered to do so by a conductor. No one around MoMA doubted Barr's taste, scholarship, or lapidary prose. What furnished ammunition to detractors was his slapdash management style, neglect of would-be donors, and positive genius for upsetting trustees, a significant number of them frustrated museum directors. His quarrels with the irascible Conger Goodyear, dubbed "Toughie" by MoMA staff, extended to other board members nearly as influential.

Barr's relationship with Nelson Rockefeller boxed the compass. Nelson never lost sight of the immense contributions made by the man he called "the high priest of modern art." But Nelson's need to put his own stamp upon

MoMA touched off a contest of wills as unequal as it was unavoidable. Within its short existence, the museum had outgrown a series of temporary homes. Languishing in storage was a small but expanding permanent collection ("the stuff downstairs," Nelson called it, much to the dismay of curatorial staff). That MoMA required a permanent address befitting its self-assumed position of leadership was a view shared by Nelson, Barr, and Conger Goodyear. The board of trustees concurred. There the consensus ended. While Nelson envisioned a MoMA presence at the upcoming New York World's Fair, Barr emphasized a new, permanent museum structure in midtown Manhattan, designed in the International Style by a prestigious European architect like Mies van der Rohe or J.P.P. Oud.

The presumptive chairman of the Building Committee, Abby Aldrich Rockefeller, resigned before the first meeting, though not before advising both Nelson and Goodyear to read the museum's constitution and bylaws. Nelson invited architect Philip Goodwin, himself a board member, to draft provisional plans for a forty-thousand-square-foot structure. Within three days of receiving Goodwin's initial draft, Rockefeller responded with some "random thoughts" of his own. For starters, he wondered if "we would not be making a mistake in putting the Museum gallery space on the third and fourth floors. Would it not be possible to drop the auditorium floor into the basement, running a wide staircase down from the lobby to the auditorium, which would bring the suggested mezzanine floor down to the first floor? Then the second and third floors could be devoted entirely to gallery space and the fourth floor to library and office space."

Privately he harbored even yeastier ambitions. Encouraged by Wally Harrison, Rockefeller Center had been surreptitiously acquiring parcels of land between the existing development and family properties on Fifty-fourth Street. Nelson contemplated a Venetian plaza stretching at least three blocks to the north. On one side of this grand pedestrian thoroughfare, a marble-clad opera house and symphony hall would rise cheek by jowl with Solomon Guggenheim's Museum of Non-Objective Painting. Across the street, land was to be set aside for the Columbia Broadcasting System, a potential project underwriter. The new MoMA, as yet undesigned, would serve as the plaza's northern terminus and architectural centerpiece. The identity of its designer fueled speculative intrigue throughout the gossipy art world. On February 21, 1936, a week after submitting rough drawings, Philip Goodwin sent Nelson names of a dozen potential candidates. Heading the American contingent were Frank Lloyd Wright, Eero Saarinen, and Wally Harrison. Foreign possibilities included Le Corbusier and Walter Gropius, plus Barr's personal favorites, J.P.P. Oud and Mies Van der Rohe. He had purposely left out anyone associated with the search committee, Goodwin wrote delicately, "because it may not seem desirable, although the matter is an open one."

Early in March, Nelson took the hint and formally asked Goodwin to assume lead responsibilities on the museum project. Conceding that Goodwin was "extremely conscientious," Barr made no attempt to hide his anxieties. "Please don't decide not to have a really great architect until we talk with Oud," he beseeched Nelson. About to depart for Europe to organize a major surrealist show, Barr volunteered to personally interview both Oud and Mies. But while he was abroad, his hopes were dashed by a letter from Conger Goodyear confirming the board's selection of Goodwin, to be assisted by Edward Durrell Stone, the Wally Harrison protégé whose work on the Rockefeller Apartments had so impressed Nelson. An incredulous Barr tracked Abby Rockefeller and her son David to the Crillon Hotel in Paris. The museum's credibility was on the line, he argued. Nothing less than an architect of worldwide stature would suffice. On July 2, Barr wired Nelson in New York. Would he take a transatlantic phone call from his mother? A flurry of sharply worded cables ensued. Abby requested a delay until she and Barr returned to the States, "if collaborating architect not actually engaged." She also declared her support for Mies van der Rohe ("Everyone agrees he is best possible man"). Barr dispatched an urgent missive of his own, describing the German architect as "deeply interested" and insisting that MoMA "cannot afford possibly mediocre architecture."

In New York, both Rockefeller and Goodyear expressed satisfaction with Goodwin's preliminary design plans. Barr would have none of it. Reminding Nelson, "You yourself suggested Mies first choice," he wired his resignation from the Building Committee, accompanied by a final blast ("Fear museum losing position of leadership") at its chairman. Nelson, unperturbed, took advantage of the director's withdrawal to reconstitute the committee to his own specifications. The new roster contained just three names—Conger Goodyear, trustee Stephen Clark, and Nelson Rockefeller. It seemed desirable to keep the group small, Nelson informed Clark, "in order that the work may be expedited with the least amount of confusion."

That such assertiveness could mask even a trace of diffidence would have astonished most people in Nelson's circle. Abby knew better. Writing from a New Hampshire ski slope in the winter of 1936, Nelson assured his mother that he was getting the rest she had urged, "and a chance to think! First I had to get calmed down enough so that I could. That took the first week and now I'm going to make a general mental survey. Heavens knows what I'll find—probably nothing, but who knows." For Nelson, self-effacement was a strategy, not an instinct, one that served him well in remaking MoMA. A quarter of the estimated $1 million construction budget came from Abby's purse. Nelson himself contributed $85,000. On a scale with his project fund-raising was an unflagging enthusiasm that salved bruised egos and restored minds gone stale. "I don't know of any job where there have been as many diversified interests represented or where there was less precedent," he consoled Phil Goodwin in August 1937. "However, I am convinced that what you are doing is going to be a very real contribution in the development of architecture in this country."

This turned out to be prophetic. With its austere, unornamented surfaces, milky-white marble skin, and translucent Thermolux panels, Goodwin's MoMA smashed the elitist notion of the art museum as palace. A piano-shaped canopy on West Fifty-third Street became an instant icon, as did the Bauhaus stair, with its black terrazzo treads and stainless-steel handrails, leading to the second-floor galleries. Critics praised its spaciousness, yet the museum was actually quite intimate: white-on-white, low-ceilinged rooms laid out in harmony with Barr's sequential canon of artistic evolution from Cézanne to Matisse. Characterized as America's first "functional" museum, the new MoMA was augmented by an elegant outdoor sculpture garden on the site of the West Fifty-fourth Street homes formerly occupied by Senior and his son.[*]

By employing equal parts ardor, diplomacy, doggedness, and guile, Nelson had succeeded in raising a striking temple of modernism and a lasting memorial to his mother. His triumph was only slightly diminished by the demise of his proposed midtown arts plaza, as the owners of the 21 Club flatly refused to relocate their establishment from West Fifty-second Street. Hyperbolic by nature, Nelson did not exaggerate in describing MoMA as his political classroom. Indeed, even as the new building went up, skills honed in outmaneuvering Alfred Barr were being applied to a larger canvas, against an adversary far wilier and more entrenched.

4

JOHN R. TODD often gave the impression that Rockefeller Center was his in all but name. In the autumn of 1936, he made the mistake of doing so in print. Two years after he had denied a New Yorker request to profile him, Todd alerted Nelson and John 3rd to a forthcoming piece in the magazine that was unlikely to please any of them. Frantic attempts to rewrite the article by Geoffrey T. Hellman only made matters worse. When "The Man Behind Prometheus" appeared (in two installments) in November 1936, it downgraded

---

[*] From 10 West Fifty-fourth, Junior and Abby moved to a twenty-thousand-square-foot triplex apartment of forty rooms at 740 Park Avenue.

Junior to the status of largely silent partner, skewered Todd's inflated ego, and dredged up August Heckscher's lawsuit with all its claims about Nelson's sharp elbows. Henceforth, decreed Nelson, anything related to Rockefeller Center publicity was to be referred either to him or to Merle Crowell, the promotional genius responsible for many of the stunts and stories that kept the center constantly before the public.*

For Todd, the self-inflicted damage couldn't have come at a worse time. His presumed champion Tom Debevoise entertained growing doubts over Todd's handling of long stalled negotiations involving Rockefeller Center and the bankrupt film studio RKO. For the Rockefellers, scarcely recovered from the calamitous opening night, and morning, of Radio City Music Hall, this latest corporate default was a body blow. Dumping Roxy Rothafel's costly pageantry in favor of family movies and the tasteful display of skin à la the Rockettes brought the vast auditorium back from the brink. But it didn't resolve the financial problems that eventually led to demolition of the nearby Center Theatre. It didn't begin to satisfy Rockefeller Center's legal claims against RKO for unpaid rent. A court-appointed master ruled that these amounted to $9.1 million. The beleaguered filmmaker proposed settling for $3.5 million. Todd thought $5 million a reasonable figure. Demanding more risked foreclosure, he argued, in which case the Rockefellers might have no alternative but to purchase outright the husk of RKO. Did his staid employers really wish to become embroiled in the uncongenial business of moviemaking?

A newly emboldened Executive Committee responded with a fusillade of criticism directed at Rockefeller Center's top-heavy management structure. Agreeing there was something "fundamentally wrong" with their current approach to RKO, Tom Debevoise faulted Todd for not coordinating negotiating strategy with his employers. As early as May 1936, Debevoise and John 3rd were advising Junior to replace the managing agents and install Nelson as president of Rockefeller Center. Though unprepared to go that far, his father raised no objection to having Nelson fill the void once the Todd-RKO negotiations broke

---

* The most famous of these was entirely Nelson's doing. After a gawking Junior was unceremoniously shooed away from the construction site by an overzealous security guard, Nelson invented the Sidewalk Superintendents' Club. This was a loafers' parliament awarded prime viewing space on an elevated platform eighty feet long, with holes thoughtfully cut in the wall to afford the best possible views of the work site. Intended for "spectators with inquiring minds," the idea struck an instant chord with the media. Within a week, the club boasted twenty thousand members. Junior himself was made Member Number One by the Office and Lift Superintendents Union Local 164. Soon Nelson was distributing membership cards inscribed with an alleged old Dutch motto translated as "The best pilots stand on the shore." Six-year-old Rodman Rockefeller received a copy of the hastily published A Steam Shovel for Me. Back on the front line, meanwhile, a uniformed attendant circulated among the kibitzers, handing out cards that declared, "Nobody can work here who isn't a union member."

down. Not yet twenty-eight years old, Nelson spent much of that summer and fall sitting across a table from David Sarnoff, the father of RCA, and Floyd Odlum, the venture capitalist whose Atlas Corporation was even then in the process of devouring RKO. Ironically, he benefited from low expectations. Sarnoff and Odlum expected "a pushover," Nelson would reflect. "But I was not operating on the basis of personality or age. I was operating on the basis of facts . . . I had projections made at various levels of earnings for the next ten to twenty years," he continued, "showing the return to Rockefeller Center based on the different combinations of RKO securities that might result from a settlement."

"Don't go into something unless you are fully familiar with all the facts [and] you know where you want to come out. . . ." This was the lesson Nelson took away from the RKO dispute, augmented by his mother's oft heard refrain that success required him to associate with his intellectual superiors. True to form, Nelson borrowed from the Chase Bank a young accounting wizard named Harold Bruckner, who helped him devise a negotiating strategy built around common stock. This approach, as cautious as it was coldly analytical, recalled the exhaustive preparation and hired expertise that JDR had relied on to power his takeover of the American oil industry. But it was one thing to eliminate the element of chance in business, quite another to make politics risk-free. An element of insecurity lurked behind Nelson's bravado. "I am imaginative. I am not bright," he confessed shortly before his death. "I am creative and I can solve problems," he maintained, if able to call upon the Harold Bruckners and their political counterparts to compensate for his own shortcomings. Meanwhile, the lessons learned in negotiating with RKO would be employed—for better and worse—throughout his subsequent careers in Washington and Albany.

A sharp economic downturn in the fall of 1937 cast a shadow over RKO's fragile recovery. Floyd Odlum wanted to merge the studio with United Artists. Nelson proposed an alternative strategy: stealing away UA's highly regarded vice president and general manager, George J. Schaefer. Rockefeller prevailed, but at a price. Schaefer spent lavishly in pursuit of quality films and the creative talent to match. To secure the services of Orson Welles, the temperamental prodigy behind radio's *Mercury Theatre on the Air*, Schaefer offered Welles a writing/directing/producing/acting contract that was to land the Rockefellers in unsought controversy even as it produced arguably the greatest film ever made on American soil. By then, having displayed a patience for which he was rarely credited, Nelson had forged a settlement that guaranteed Rockefeller Center five hundred thousand shares of common stock in a company free of debt and boasting vigorous, even visionary, front-office leadership. The reorganization plan that enabled RKO to emerge from receivership in January 1940 bore his fingerprints. He was lucky, too: thanks to the wartime appetite for moviegoing, RKO-owned theaters were able to subsidize the film studio, until company profits reached $7 million in 1943.

In the end, it wasn't his mishandling of a bankrupt movie studio that sealed John Todd's fate, but disputes over the pace of construction at Rockefeller Center. Todd's predicted completion date of 1940 struck Nelson and his experts as unrealistic. "There were about eighty engineers on the job, and what with the Depression and all they weren't in any hurry," Nelson would later assert. "They kept telling us we couldn't rent the place anyway. Wally [Harrison] and I had to knock a couple of heads together before they got the idea that we'd take our chances on the renting and weren't in the mood for a stretch-out." A seemingly minor incident dramatized Todd's marginalization. In April 1937, he informed Nelson, then embarked on a ten-nation tour of South America, that a replacement had at last been identified for the despoiled Rivera mural in the lobby of the RCA Building. Conceding "nobody is very enthusiastic," the managing agent described a second submission by José Maria Sert, even less distinguished in its historical flag-waving than his original contribution to the building.*

Todd didn't know it, but Nelson had already learned about the Sert proposal from his brother Laurance, who doubtless spoke for many in declaring himself heartily sick of "the wailing wall." Nothing remained but to formalize the changing of the guard. Nelson was still out of the country when he was made executive vice president of Rockefeller Center, with Junior's blessing. In recognition of past services, Todd was encouraged to craft a credible outside offer; he was also given a three-year severance package worth $105,000. Similar deals were meted out to the other managing agents—all except Hugh Robertson, whose loyalty to Nelson during the Rivera fracas, and again as a key ally in the RKO negotiations, earned him a place on the Rockefeller Center board, along with Wally Harrison. Robertson also gained a new title—executive manager—reporting directly to President Nelson Rockefeller.

---

* In fairness to the artist, Sert was only adhering to instructions from Junior, who specified that the world's workers should be depicted "in a very happy way. He also hopes that the figures of Poetry, Art, and Music will look so cheerful that casual observers will see at a glance that they are happy." John R. Todd–J. M. Sert, April 23, 1937, Rockefeller Business Interests, Series 2C, Box 94, Folder 709, RAC.

Part Two
FULL THROTTLE
1937–1955

I'm optimistic about South America. But you'll have to qualify that by saying I'm optimistic about everything.

—Nelson A. Rockefeller

Seven

A LATIN FROM MANHATTAN

Throughout the world today the rights of the individual or corporation to possess property are being challenged . . . if we wish to continue our present system of individual initiative and private ownership, management must conduct its affairs with a sense of moral and social responsibility in such a way as to contribute to the general welfare of society.

—NELSON A. ROCKEFELLER, remarks to the 1937 annual meeting,
Standard Oil of New Jersey

1

A RT AND OIL. Pleasure and profit. Aldrich and Rockefeller. For Nelson, his 1937 foray to South America was pivotal in forging a coherent identity out of his family's conflicting traditions and temperaments. For two months that spring, he pursued a synergy of his mother's artistic interests, his father's hardheaded philanthropy, and his grandfather's eye for opportunities where least expected. Long before returning to New York, he had distilled these into a new and consuming passion for Latin America. The ostensible purpose of his journey was to inspect the Lake Maracaibo oil fields in northwestern Venezuela. This sensational find had been developed in large measure by Creole Petroleum, a subsidiary of Standard Oil of New Jersey, on whose board Nelson sat as a major investor.

One country not on his itinerary was Bolivia; its government had nationalized Standard Oil property a month before Nelson and Tod left New York. In any responsible boardroom, this warning shot ought to have caused shudders. Certainly Nelson was aware of the dangers it heralded. His primary interest, however, was in digging for treasures other than oil. Prompted by stories in the *London Illustrated News*, he teamed with Bill Harkness, another trustee of the Metropolitan Museum of Art, to propose a joint archaeological mission with New York's Museum of Natural History. Their reasoning escaped Metropolitan director Herbert Winlock, an Egyptologist jealously guarding his funding sources. The two men had already clashed over the proposed gift to the museum of a Rodin sculpture, with Winlock regarding the nude figures of an embracing man and woman as being in questionable taste. Such prudery left Nelson incredulous. His South American initiative roused no more enthusiasm in the director's office. Spurned by the Met, Rockefeller went on to assemble under his own auspices one of the world's preeminent collections of indigenous art.

Enlisting help wherever it could be found, on arriving in the Peruvian capital of Lima, Nelson was introduced to Julio César Tello, an archaeologist famed for his work in the high desert country around Paracas, formerly inhabited by the sun-worshipping Nazca Indians. The scholarly Dr. Tello had made the mistake of entering politics, going so far as to win a seat in the Peruvian Senate. When the government changed hands, a not infrequent occurrence in Peru, Tello forfeited his job as director of the National Museum of Archaeology. Worse, he saw the work of a lifetime imperiled, since the regime of President Óscar Benavides, contemptuous of Indian culture, refused to fund preservation of three dozen Paracas mummies left to wilt in the humid climate around Lima.

Nelson paid a courtesy call on Benavides, to whom he portrayed the endangered mummies as an international treasure. He offered to bankroll the preservation work himself. To assure that his money would not be siphoned off by a greedy Ministry of Education, Rockefeller deposited funds at the U.S. embassy, to be doled out as needed to Tello and no one else. Before leaving the country, he added a pair of mummies to his growing stash of textiles, ceramics, and native handicrafts. He also bought a clutch of reputedly unlucky Peruvian opals. Their reputation was tested on May 1, when Nelson and his traveling companions strapped themselves into a twin-engine plane for the long haul from Lima to Santiago, Chile. Unable to climb above the looming Andean peaks, the overloaded aircraft was forced to thread its way via rugged mountain valleys.

While the others dozed, Nelson scratched out his impressions of a beguiling continent. Unfortunately, he observed, the goodwill generated by the Rockefeller Foundation and its efforts to eradicate yellow fever had been largely squandered by American businessmen quick to distance themselves from despised "natives." As on their honeymoon, "much to the amazement of the Standard Oil people," Nelson and Tod had gone out of their way to mix casually with important locals. Suddenly overcome by airsickness, Nelson put down his pen and retreated to the back of the plane, where he spied a window fouled by an oil leak. Moments later, one of the engines began sputtering. Fearing the imminent loss of its twin, the pilot turned back toward Lima. As the aircraft shook violently, passengers wondered if they would reach their destination. They did, but only after the plane skidded off a runway and through an adobe wall, finally coming to rest in a plowed field.*

Nelson and his traveling party pushed on to Venezuela, a continent in itself. No country better dramatized Latin polarities, its breathtaking displays of natural beauty juxtaposed with crass human exploitation and squalor. A seemingly unbridgeable chasm separated the barbed-wire compounds set aside for Creole employees, few of whom spoke Spanish, from the pestilential shacks of the local population. Appalled by what he saw, Nelson vowed to do something about the gross disparity in living conditions. But he couldn't linger—a ninety-foot Standard Oil yacht was waiting to transport him down the broad Orinoco River, from whose banks chattering birds and shrieking tree monkeys serenaded the Rockefellers. Nelson's thoughts strayed to politics. One night he and Tod dined with President Eleazar López Contreras, his wife, and two of his cabinet officers. The president's February Program represented a sort of Latin New Deal, complete with public works and agricultural assistance sustained through a policy of *sembrar el petróleo,* or sowing the oil. Two weeks of Berlitz lessons helped Nelson to compensate for awkward silences between North and South. "This country is as sound and conservative politically and economically as any in the world today!" he enthused to his brother Laurance. "As for the oil, there seems to be no limit." With estimates of hidden reserves constantly being raised, Nelson asked Laurance to purchase an additional five thousand shares of Creole Petroleum for his portfolio.

He had just arrived in Panama and was anticipating a restful cruise home with Tod when he learned of Senior's death in the predawn hours of Sunday, May 23. The night before, JDR had appeared somewhat weaker than normal, but it hadn't prevented him from chatting and joking with his household staff. Around four in the morning, he slipped painlessly away. "Really it was a wonderful ending," said Abby. On receiving the news, Nelson chartered a Pan American plane for the arduous flight to New York. The next day, he took his place in the somber welcoming party at the Tarrytown train station, gamely

---

* For Nelson, it was a week of narrow escapes. The perilous approach to Lima was actually less unnerving than a short journey he had made in October 1936 aboard the German dirigible *Hindenburg.* The massive airship, pride of the Nazi regime in Berlin, was on a goodwill circuit around New York, and Nelson had gone aloft with flying ace Eddie Rickenbacker. In examining the cotton-skinned space above the passenger quarters, Rickenbacker had detected the presence of highly flammable hydrogen.

"My God, Nelson, let's get out of here!" he shouted.

Rockefeller later called it one of the most frightening experiences in his life. His ingrained fatalism was strengthened on May 6, 1937. Less than a week after his emergency landing in Lima, thirty-five people died when the *Hindenburg* exploded while trying to land at Lakehurst, New Jersey.

submitting to the exploding flashbulbs of press photographers and the gawking curiosity of several hundred onlookers awaiting the private car carrying Senior's body.

Shortly before noon on May 26, family members and business associates crowded into the big house inhabited by the man whose casket rested before a massive picture window overlooking the Hudson. Instead of eulogies, the half-hour service featured some of JDR's favorite hymns, performed by the organist from Riverside Church. At its conclusion, estate workmen were admitted to file past the open casket. That evening, Nelson joined his father and brothers for the trip to Cleveland, where John D. Rockefeller was buried in the family plot at Lake View Cemetery beneath an awning of spring foliage, as a single motion picture cameraman recorded the event from a nearby hill. The mourners remained long enough for the grave to be filled in. Then, amid a heavy downpour, the Rockefeller men left to inspect the nearby Forest Hill estate then being converted by Nelson into an upscale housing development.

The death of his grandfather, no less than the South American trip it interrupted, marked his true coming of age. But it also presented a singular challenge. Outsiders found it hard to imagine a third-generation Rockefeller having something to prove. They failed to reckon with *this* Rockefeller, for whom the status of paternal agent could never gratify a consuming need for independent accomplishment. Seeking a purpose, Nelson had chanced upon South America. The neglected continent invited big ideas, a trailblazing mind-set, and the useful merger of individual compassion with the profit motive. In pursuing his separate course, however, Nelson never forgot the economic revolutionary who had been so fabulously rewarded for his audacity.*

He began, ironically, with an earnest lay sermon before the annual meeting of Standard's overseas operating heads. His topic: the social responsibility of the modern corporation. No doubt the blood pressure of many in his audience rose as young Rockefeller congratulated the Roosevelt White House for undertaking reforms that private industry ought to have promoted out of self-interest, if no other motive. Under attack at home and abroad, Nelson continued, capitalist wealth must be justified before it could be multiplied. Oilmen stayed ahead of the competition by adapting to changed circumstances. Unless their economic and social policies were similarly reshaped, he warned, future profits and ownership itself might be imperiled. Those who buried their head in the sand risked losing it altogether.

---

* Years later, in a closet of his Washington residence, Rockefeller hoarded a shoebox filled with letters from JDR, signed "With tenderest affection." Yet even familial loyalty was tinged with competitive urges. His grandfather had lived to ninety-seven, Nelson remarked in his later years. He intended to make it to a hundred. Elizabeth Skerritt memoir.

His counsel for would-be executives venturing into foreign lands was equally stern. They must learn to speak the native tongue and develop an understanding of local customs and psychology, Rockefeller told his listeners. Those who couldn't, or wouldn't, meet these basic requirements should forget about employment or promotion at the company founded by his grandfather. Nelson sat down to tepid applause, the presiding officer whispering in his ear, "I didn't know we had a Communist in our midst."

2

FOR ITS NOVEMBER 1937 meeting, the New York Building Congress wished to hear the story of Rockefeller Center. Ideally, they wished to hear it from a Rockefeller. Tom Debevoise advised Junior to send Nelson in his place. Like the understudy trumping an indisposed star, Nelson made the most of the occasion. Writing to Junior afterward, journalist Herbert Bayard Swope praised the pinch hitter for his "extraordinarily effective" speech. Increasingly, people were taking notice of Nelson, many of them drawn by his frank, disarming manner and insatiable curiosity. "He was a very attractive, very nice, intelligent guy," recalled Wally Harrison's architectural partner, Max Abramovitz. "He wanted to know all about you. At times he asked too many questions. But he was bubbly and full of ideas." Tourists in the lobby of the RCA Building were amazed to find themselves chatted up by an authentic Rockefeller, but no more so than the Broadway booking agent who went there to inspect potential office space. After being shown a number of rooms, the agent nudged his polite, businesslike guide and cracked, "If I move in here, d'ya think I'll get a chance to look at some Rockefellers?"

"If it'll please you," replied his host, "my name is Nelson Rockefeller."

Early in 1938, Nelson's doctor prescribed a month in Arizona for a painful sinus condition. On the porch of his cottage, Nelson, whose musical tastes ran to Benny Goodman, Count Basie, and Ella Fitzgerald, set up a Victrola and played jazz records. Accompanied by Wally Harrison, he rode twenty-six miles on horseback through the parched mountains around Tucson. At other times, he scoured the region for Indian baskets and related crafts. One day he flew off to Palm Springs for a final round of negotiations with RKO's Floyd Odlum. "Everything went well and I got what we wanted in connection with the reorganization plan," Nelson reassured his father. Less happily, he apologized to Junior for failing to clear in advance the expansion of his Pocantico garage. "You see with the addition which we are expecting to our family this spring we will have to use our only guest room," wrote the contrite father of three.

Together with Harrison, he had developed plans for a two-room guesthouse. "I'll talk that all over with you as soon as I get back," he promised Junior. Nelson returned to New York a month before the birth, on May 18, 1938, of Michael and Mary, his fourth and fifth children, christened "the Gold Dust Twins" by the *Daily Mirror*. "The Nelson Rockefellers apparently are no believers in birth control," opined an Indiana newspaper. The neat, two-year intervals between Tod's pregnancies hinted otherwise, as did an apartment floor plan explicitly designed to accommodate four children. Adhering to family tradition, Junior dispatched checks of $100 to each of the newborns on their arrival in "this strange, weird world." Publicly, the new father declared himself thrilled by the latest additions to the family. The subsequent appearance of the first child born to Laurance and Mary French Rockefeller evoked a wry addendum. "That brings the grandchildren up to an even dozen," wrote Nelson. "From now on as far as I am concerned Winny and Dave are going to have to carry the major burden."

Behind this gentle self-mockery lurked strains in a marriage entering a perilous phase. Rockefeller family correspondence is peppered with complaints about Tod's frequent trips to Philadelphia, with or without her husband. In one harsh passage that Junior edited out of her published correspondence, Abby chastised a very pregnant Tod for her sense of fashion. "This time she has gotten clothes that are most appropriate and she is very presentable," remarked the older woman. Whether Tod could have been more stylish on her $500-a-month allowance is beside the point; as her own woman, with her own politics and priorities—among them a lifelong interest in the nursing profession—she was reluctant to surrender her identity as a Clark if that was the price of becoming a Rockefeller.*

By all accounts a devoted mother with five small children to nurture, Tod appeared more matronly than her age. Nelson, by contrast, remained incorrigibly boyish, emotionally restless, and physically unsated. A one-man force field of celebrity, charm, and undisguised virility, he had little difficulty sweeping a woman off her feet. "We knew he liked women," reminisced Max Abramovitz not long before his death in 2004. "He always had secretaries working around him. He paid a lot of attention to them. He'd move them from where they were, nearer his office. Later on, they got a little closer." A pattern of romancing female co-workers was established. "He was always doing something, and he'd

---

* Her formal allowance is a poor measure of Nelson's financial generosity toward his wife. In a four-year period beginning in 1934, he placed in trust for Tod nearly $250,000, even as he made charitable donations exceeding 15 percent annually, going into the red in the process. He also began the habit of making loans to friends—$30,000 to an associate starting a business, $10,000 to newspaperman David Lawrence, $8,900 to a sculptor's widow—a practice that would land him in hot water when applied to political colleagues.

get them involved as well," said Abramovitz. The waspish Philip Johnson offered his own explanation for Rockefeller's infidelities. Without citing his source, Johnson claimed that Nelson was less sexually potent than he appeared, a condition he battled as intensely as his dyslexia and with even more to prove to himself.

Under the circumstances, Rockefeller's decision to commission a Harrison-designed guesthouse for a wooded hillside behind Hawes House took on added significance. From the outset, the two pavilions were built with a single occupant in mind. Dressed in fieldstone, with a Léger-inspired opening cut in the connecting passage and electrically operated floor-to-ceiling windows opening to an outdoor swimming pool, this became Nelson's alternative home once it was completed in 1939. Henceforth he took meals with the family but slept elsewhere, a permanent guest in his own guesthouse. Faithful to the conventions of their class, Nelson and Tod would maintain appearances for another twenty years. But their sexual union ended with the birth of Mary and Michael. Inevitably, most of the responsibility for child rearing fell on Tod. "I made all my mistakes with my first family," Nelson confessed in later years.

Rockefeller acknowledged something else as well: that there were very few people who could reach him emotionally. Pressed late in life for a definition of love, he recalled a campaign motorcade through a nameless city and the memory of some strangers on the second floor of a wooden building. "I caught their eye and waved to them. It wasn't a big city. It was close so I could see that their faces lit up," said Nelson of the fleeting encounter. "I know those people felt a warmth and love just in that response and that that was a very important thing to them. And I could feel it. That is love."

3

H E WOULD ALWAYS prefer the company of women, and not just in the bedroom. Beginning with his mother, Nelson had learned to value the opposite sex for its superior intelligence, sensitivity, and trustworthiness. Anna Rosenberg confirmed his judgment. A petite, dark-eyed sparrow of a woman who retained a trace of her native Hungarian accent, Anna resolved her first labor dispute as a teenager attending a Bronx high school whose male students had walked out of classes to protest compulsory military training. Shortly thereafter, her feminist outlook and organizational talents caught the eye of Governor Alfred E. Smith's legendary policy adviser Belle Moskowitz. In retrospect, New York under Smith can be seen as a dress rehearsal for the New Deal, as state government entered the lists on behalf of the economically distressed, and as a steward of resources hitherto plundered by unregulated profiteers. Defying postwar complacency, the Empire State enacted laws to shorten hours and improve working conditions for women and children; institute workers' compensation; promote old age pensions; reorganize a cobwebbed bureaucracy; and create new parks and public works on an unprecedented scale.

Having cut her teeth in this laboratory of urban liberalism, Anna Rosenberg passed on what she had learned to young Nelson Rockefeller. It was Rosenberg who first detected the makings of a beautiful friendship between the conservative radical then dominating American politics like no figure since his swashbuckling cousin Teddy and the young renegade from the House of Standard Oil. For $6,000 a year, Anna became, with Wally Harrison, the first of many experts for hire, opening doors in Washington, counseling Rockefeller Center on how to attract World's Fair visitors, and serving as Nelson's Sherpa on the treacherous slopes of organized labor.*

Nothing so exposed the limits of John D. Rockefeller, Jr.'s paternalistic liberalism as his disdain for union organizers. His attitude nearly produced an open breach with John 3rd, who couldn't reconcile his father's public philanthropy with his adamant refusal to pay overtime to Pocantico estate workers. Long after the New Deal transformed relations between labor and capital, Junior clung to the compliant company union calling itself the Independent Association of Rockefeller Center Employees. In March 1938, he reported to Nelson, then in Arizona, that all was quiet on the labor front. "Your brain trusters, supplementing us common garden variety of mortals, approved the form of contract yesterday which our lawyers have approved and which Mr. Robertson is very hopeful will be accepted," Junior wrote.

His confidence, like his condescension, was misplaced: within six weeks of issuing this smug forecast, Junior faced mutiny in the ranks. The aging philanthropist's opposition to the closed shop was a given. But the National Labor Relations Act (better known as the Wagner Act) had reshuffled the deck, elevating to positions of power a new kind of union chieftain, personified by a gruff Bronx plumber named George Meany. In a single year as president of the New York State Federation of Labor, Meany secured, with the vital assistance of Governor Herbert Lehman, enactment of seventy-two laws sympathetic to la-

* Life on the public payroll didn't prevent Rosenberg from pocketing lucrative retainers from Studebaker, Macy's department store, and Marshall Field. This habit of working both sides of the street, coupled with her privileged entrée and rampant ego, made her a controversial figure in New Deal circles. Expressing a view widely held around Washington, White House appointments secretary Marvin McIntyre muttered, "Of course she's a chiseling bitch, but she's our bitch." McIntyre's resentment was understandable, since it was his job to throw a protective cordon around the Oval Office, which in Mrs. Rosenberg's case was demonstrably porous. Jonathan Daniels, *White House Witness, 1942–1945* (Garden City, NY: Doubleday, 1975), 38.

bor's cause. Sharing his expansionist agenda was Thomas A. Murray, Meany's successor at the New York Building and Construction Trades Council. Both men were eager to best their rivals in the left-wing Congress of Industrial Organizations by signing up the janitors, elevator operators, and scrubwomen who maintained Rockefeller Center.

In Nelson they had a prospective ally, while in the überlobbyist Anna Rosenberg they had a direct pipeline to the sympathetic state officials. The original multitasker, Mrs. Rosenberg could frequently be seen clutching two separate telephone receivers, purring flattery into one, barking abuse into the other. Employing her verbal magic, with a few calls to Albany Mrs. R saw to it that the Building Maintenance Craftsman, an AFL union, was certified as bargaining agent for thousands of Rockefeller Center employees, without recourse to the usual public hearings. Overnight the company unions were dissolved, solidifying Nelson's budding reputation as a liberal and forestalling recruitment efforts by the more militant CIO. The action helped to establish a personal rapport with Meany that was to pay handsome dividends down the road.

Late in 1938, Nelson's Dartmouth classmate Victor Borella received a lunch invitation from his old friend. How would Borella like to come to work for him at Rockefeller Center? asked Nelson. "I just signed a contract with a labor union and I think they're here to stay."

4

NELSON SPUN OFF new ventures with dervishlike intensity. In the early thirties, he befriended Bob and Helen Kleberg, whose cactus-studded principality, the celebrated King Ranch, sprawled over a million acres of South Texas. At the same time, he was introduced to the playboy congressman Dick Kleberg and his hyperkinetic administrative assistant, Lyndon Johnson. The Klebergs' Kingsville home served as base camp for annual slaughters of deer, quail, and ducks flushed from the savannahs and wild oaks of this otherworldly landscape. After a few visits, Nelson decided that he, too, wanted to be a cattle rancher. Facing owners reluctant to sell and a father unwilling to advance the necessary funds, he was forced to wait nearly forty years before realizing his dream of a Lone Star Xanadu.

He struck out a second time trying to persuade Junior and the Rockefeller Foundation to invest in educational films, a cause that united Nelson with Robert Hutchins, the cage-rattling prodigy who presided over the University of Chicago before his thirtieth birthday. Another unconventional academic snagged in the Rockefeller net was economist and statistician Beardsley Ruml.

"B" to his friends, Ruml was in many ways the prototypical Rockefeller idea man. Lured away from the Carnegie Corporation to oversee the $80 million Laura Spelman Rockefeller Memorial Fund, Ruml championed grants to improve race relations and professionalize government service. In 1934, this intellectual jack-of-all-trades swapped a job as dean of social sciences at Hutchins's University of Chicago for an annual salary of $70,000 from R. H. Macy & Co. His sole formal responsibility, according to the store's chairman, was "to challenge our thinking."*

Unsuccessful in recruiting Nelson for the Macy's board, Ruml himself was enlisted as creative spark plug behind the Junta, a private brain trust formed by Nelson in response to a surge of economic nationalism in Latin America. Initially the group met at Ruml's Greenwich Village townhouse, though later it adjourned to the Rockefeller apartment on Fifth Avenue. At Nelson's request, Ruml and Anna Rosenberg launched a pincer movement on the White House. Secretary of the Treasury Henry Morgenthau, Jr., urged the president to appoint Rockefeller to a junior position in the administration, only to have FDR bat the idea away like a bothersome insect. A personal meeting between Nelson and kitchen cabinet members Benjamin Cohen and Tommy Corcoran also failed to elicit the desired White House invitation.

In the first week of March 1939, gossip columnist Walter Winchell reported that Nelson was being considered for a job at Harry Hopkins's Commerce Department. Actually, Winchell had it backward: it was *Nelson* who hoped to cultivate Hopkins through emissaries like Ruml and Rosenberg. The commerce that interested him was to be found not in a federal bureaucracy, but in the shrinking markets of South America, a victim of high tariff barriers and falling commodity prices. Yankee arrogance of the sort embodied in Creole's armed camps, coupled with sour memories of gunboat diplomacy and U.S. Marine occupiers, had opened South American doors to German and Italian entrepreneurs. By 1936, Brazil was importing more automobiles from the Third Reich than from Great Britain. Chile relied on Berlin for a quarter of its foreign goods. Even Mexico, whose populist president Lázaro Cárdenas had infuriated Standard and other American oil companies by nationalizing their properties, did a thriving business with Nazi Germany.

Against this backdrop, Nelson left New York on March 16, 1939, for his second Venezuelan tour. En route to Caracas, he stopped in Washington, where his long-sought appointment with Roosevelt had finally been arranged by

---

* Ruml exerted a powerful backstairs influence on the Roosevelt White House: his historical scenario of government aid to nineteenth-century railroads and high protective tariffs was cited by FDR to justify anti-recessionary deficit spending. Still later, B would invent income tax withholding, sold to a reluctant Congress as a means of financing the staggering cost of World War II.

Harry Hopkins. In the course of their meeting, FDR asked Rockefeller to convey his regards to President López Contreras. The visitor had a favor of his own to request. Would the president be willing to participate in a national radio broadcast commemorating the opening of the new MoMA on May 10? Roosevelt agreed to speak on condition that event organizers got him a prepared text in advance. Eight years had passed since Nelson's sole previous encounter with the Roosevelts, an excruciatingly dull evening in a Metropolitan Opera box occupied by the president's mother, Sarah. No doubt FDR cared as little about the melting watches of Salvador Dalí as Nelson had for Wagnerian arias. But the master charmer was himself charmed by the energetic young man who likely evoked memories of his callow self in the years before polio had attacked his body. Moreover, the two men shared a common determination to ward off the Nazi threat by promoting hemispheric solidarity.

This would not be easy. In Venezuela, Nelson again encountered his countrymen as colonizers. Visiting a boys' reformatory, he inquired about a youngster whose blond hair made him stand out. "He's the biggest problem we have here," said the director. "He's an absolute terror." Closer inspection revealed the youth to be the illegitimate son of an American worker.

What had the father done about him? asked Nelson.

"He doesn't even know he's here. He went back years ago."

"What has the American community done?"

"As a matter of fact, you are the first American who has ever come out here."

Challenging stereotypes of Yankee indifference, Rockefeller began appearing unannounced in newspaper offices, thrusting out his hand and proclaiming, "I'm Nelson Rockefeller and I'd like to meet your editor." That is how he eventually befriended Rómulo Betancourt, a future Venezuelan president deeply suspicious of the wealthy *norteamericano* and his motives. Writing in the pages of *Ahora* after Nelson's trip, Betancourt pictured Rockefeller returning to his warm home and grand office, heedless of half a million unschooled Venezuelan children and a workforce deprived of adequate food or shelter. The editor was in for a surprise. Once back on American soil, Rockefeller dispatched a dozen Berlitz instructors to Venezuela, his down payment on making every Creole executive fluent in Spanish. Under Nelson's not-so-gentle prodding, Creole undertook public improvements more commonly associated with a government than an oil company. As outlined by Darlene Rivas in her authoritative *Missionary Capitalist,* schools were built, along with extensive worker housing and a seventy-five-bed hospital in Caripito. Hookworm, malaria, and other tropical diseases were targeted for elimination, while foreign experts promoted crop research and cattle-breeding experiments.

Outside the compound gates, independent water systems and power grids were developed. Eventually, Venezuelans marketed these essentials to the oil companies, instead of the other way around. Drilling and maintenance operations were entrusted to local workers, as were laundry and food services. A Rockefeller-commissioned survey confirmed the dominance of oil to the detriment of agriculture, leaving millions dependent on food imports. Reversing the capital imbalance was, by rights, the responsibility of Venezuela's sovereign government. Yet it, too, operated on the narrow margins of an oil-based economy. A catalyst was required, preferably one as disinterested as possible, to harness foreign resources to a homegrown agenda for economic diversification. To fill the vacuum and put back into local circulation some of the petrodollars flowing from Lake Maracaibo and other fields, Nelson created the Compañía de Fomento Venezolano (Venezuelan Basic Economy Corporation, or VBEC).

Management of the new business was delegated to his Dartmouth classmate Bob Bottome, a second Dartmouth prodigy named Carl Spaeth, and Edward "Hutch" Robbins, a cousin to President Roosevelt. Robbins's wife, Louise, herself the granddaughter of Woodrow Wilson's legendary counselor Colonel House, captured the missionary fervor behind Rockefeller's latest crusade. "Nelson would ask us up to his apartment to talk over his plans," she recalled. "We all sat around in a circle while he gave us a solemn indoctrination in the philosophy of hands across the sea, the need to learn Spanish, and the great challenge to the private sector of the United States." Not altogether sure what this meant, Louise was infected anyway with Rockefeller's enthusiasm; it was only a question of time before she and others were off to Venezuela "to save the country single-handedly."

VBEC weighed the stimulative merits of flour mills, supermarkets, pharmaceutical plants, and road building, before settling on a hotel to leave its mark on the land of Simón Bolívar. Rockefeller listened attentively as President López Contreras described his vision of a first-class hostelry for Caracas, then a sleepy town of two-story buildings with more burros than tourists. The sole existing accommodation, the misnamed Majestic, was a Victorian rat hole, whose guests were compelled each morning to turn over their shoes and shake out the scorpions. The capital's only decent restaurant boasted a French chef reputedly sprung from Devil's Island. Foreign developers were reluctant even to consider the hotel project unless it was attached to a gambling casino, an option López Contreras just as staunchly opposed.

Rockefeller assured the president that alternative financing could be obtained through a public stock offering, something new to Venezuela. In practice, most of the million-dollar cost fell on VBEC and the oil companies. Accompanied by Wally Harrison and Hutch Robbins, Nelson scoped out several possible locations, finally settling on an old sugarcane plantation at the foot of a mountain in the Los Cabos district. Designed for three hundred guests, the Hotel Avila was a hacienda in the International Style, with reinforced concrete walls replacing the usual masonry as protection against earthquakes. The stuccoed exterior, dyed in the national colors of red, yellow, and blue, was broken by windows resembling ocean liner portholes. Large grilles covered with orchids adorned the façade. Inside, plentiful screens and high ceilings invited cooling breezes, without resort to mechanical air conditioners (a rare instance of modern ingenuity that Nelson detested). The onset of war slowed construction work, as every bathroom fixture had to be supplied from New York. Yet the hotel was a success from its opening day. In the 1950s, Caracas began a period of explosive growth, and the Avila became a magnet for international travelers.

5

W HEN HE RETURNED to New York in April 1939, Rockefeller learned that Harry Hopkins had reserved the subject of South America for his personal attention. Nelson did not lack for activities to occupy his time while waiting for the White House to act. May promised the triumphant opening of MoMA and a simultaneous changing of the guard as Conger Goodyear yielded the museum presidency he had filled for almost a decade. The prospect of Nelson as his successor bred doubts among insiders. These were reinforced at a trustees dinner on May 8, at which Rockefeller presented the retiring president with a trompe l'oeil painting entitled *Playbill and Dollar Bill*, in maladroit recognition of Goodyear's unsalaried service.

Two nights later, a national radio audience heard announcer Lowell Thomas introduce Edsel Ford, Robert Hutchins, and Walt Disney, before cutting away to the White House and the unmistakably cultured voice of the president of the United States. Using a text adapted from catalog copy for the museum's blockbuster opening exhibition, *Art in Our Time*, Roosevelt paid eloquent tribute to artistic freedom in a world convulsed by tyranny. Praising MoMA as "a citadel of civilization," FDR lauded its tastemaking potential through traveling exhibits broadening the popular definition of art to include contemporary industrial design, architecture, and housing, as well as photography, commercial advertisements, the theater, and moving pictures. Nelson was effusive in his thanks. The presidential speech had prompted CBS to offer MoMA a twenty-eight-part series, he informed Roosevelt. Rival NBC was also talking collaboration.

For Rockefeller, as for so many others, the summer of 1939 was a restless interlude. MoMA was opened, a source of pride but hardly a full-time occupation. Work on the final buildings at Rockefeller Center was winding down. Still waiting for a summons from Washington, Nelson jumped at the chance to practice some freelance diplomacy in the wake of Mexico's expropriation of

U.S. oil and other interests. Negotiations between the government of President Lázaro Cárdenas and several American oil companies were deadlocked. Hoping to break the impasse was Walter Douglas, a former section manager for the Southern Pacific Railroad in a part of Mexico where Cárdenas had begun his career as local caudillo. Professing admiration for Nelson's ability to get things done, Douglas proposed a friendly meeting between him, the Mexican president, and the young scion of Rockefeller wealth.

Junior didn't think much of the idea. What if John R. Todd were to independently negotiate with Rockefeller Center unions, he asked his son, "without first coming to you. . . . I think you will agree that you would feel considerably affronted." Why should Standard Oil be any more willing to cede its vital interests to an unaccredited outsider? Junior's qualms were no match for Nelson's blithe self-assertion. As it happened, securing paternal assent was child's play compared with bargaining with Mexico's Great Commoner. Boarding a train bound for the president's ancestral home in the village of Jiquilpan de Juárez, Nelson was still haggling with the owner of a $35 rug stretched between them as the cars pulled out of the station. It might have been a dress rehearsal for his negotiations with Cárdenas.

The Rockefellers arrived at the presidential residence late on a Saturday afternoon. The women adjourned for a house tour, leaving their husbands on the patio. A large, handsome, powerfully built man, much loved by downtrodden Mexicans for his willingness to confront traditional power brokers—during six years in office, he redistributed twice as much land as all his predecessors since the 1910 revolution—Cárdenas impressed Nelson by his simplicity and lack of hovering aides. Setting aside the divisive subject of oil, the visitor led off with the plight of some young Mexican doctors enrolled in public health courses thanks to Rockefeller Foundation fellowships. Strict union rules in their homeland precluded these promising trainees from putting their skills to work. Some had no alternative but to sweep streets. As a result, the foundation was considering pulling the plug on the program. Cárdenas acknowledged the absurdity of the situation and promised to take corrective action.

Only then was the oil controversy broached. Nelson claimed, more than a bit disingenuously, that he had no official credentials. Cárdenas nodded, before expressing regret over State Department propaganda directed against his regime, the attempt by foreign companies to embargo Mexican oil, and his subsequent decision to trade with Fascist powers. Rockefeller agilely switched topics, describing for his host an immense MoMA exhibition in the making that would cover twenty centuries of Mexican art. Cárdenas agreed to split the $40,000 cost of the show, even offering special cars and free transportation on the national railroad. Dinner followed, capped by an invitation to stay the night. The next morning, Nelson rose early. Walking in the garden, he encountered the president. Their conversation resumed.

Though quick to cite his own liberalizing experiences in Venezuela, Rockefeller had failed to anticipate the negative lessons imparted by North American wealth and arrogance. Cárdenas set him straight, recounting a litany of humiliations: the loss of Texas in 1836, the later cession of New Mexico and California, and the cross-border chase after Pancho Villa by General John J. Pershing. To these historical grievances he added the continuing mistreatment of Mexicans in the United States. The discussion turned personal; for twenty years, Cárdenas remarked bitterly, he had owned a locker in a golf club adjoining that of British Petroleum's chairman. Not once had the Englishman so much as acknowledged his Mexican neighbor.

Personal slights fed national resentments. Cárdenas cast his nationalization of oil as the key to Mexico's spiritual and economic liberation. But his country lacked the technicians to extract or process the oil beneath their feet, Nelson protested. The president was unmoved by this, as by his visitor's claim that expropriation might actually lower Mexican standards of living. "Look," said Cárdenas, "I would rather leave this oil in the ground. I would rather lose all of the economic advantages which may accrue to our country and preserve the self-respect and the legacy of the people of Mexico which has been achieved by this act." Rockefeller hinted at grave repercussions; the Mexican president called his bluff, expressing doubt that an administration in Washington eager to cultivate Latin trade and unity would allow vengeance to jeopardize its geopolitical agenda.

Nelson asked if there was any possibility of accommodation. Cárdenas was surprisingly flexible, offering to return 49 percent of the stock to the oil companies, along with managerial responsibilities. Not ungrateful, Rockefeller pointed out that no company could accept a minority position in its own house. Cárdenas stood his ground. Nearly four hours of conversation produced agreement on the division of earnings, change of management, and company obligations to the broader community. But consensus on who would control the decisive 51 percent remained elusive. The historical and psychological gulf could not be bridged in a single encounter. Yet it could be narrowed, substantially. The encounter taught Nelson to appreciate what he called "the human element" in diplomacy. "Human dignity, respect, is far more important than a lot of economic prerequisites," he concluded. Having reaffirmed his belief that the ownership of property, foreign or domestic, depends ultimately on the wisdom of its owners, the young American put away his thirteen-point program and thanked the president for his candor. As they shook hands, Cárdenas assured Nelson that he would always have a warm friend in Mexico.

6

O N NOVEMBER 1, JUNIOR drove the symbolic last rivet in the United States Rubber Company Building on Sixth Avenue, marking the completion of Rockefeller Center. The world beyond Manhattan barely took notice, its attention focused on ominous headlines from abroad. Nazi Germany had overrun Poland, which it just as quickly divided with Soviet Russia in an act of breathtaking cynicism. Though Hitler's armies had temporarily halted their advance, the tottering Western democracies braced themselves for renewed assaults in the spring of 1940. The fighting had profound consequences for the global economy, nowhere more than in Latin America, since any British blockade of Hitler's Fortress Europe would throttle the flow of goods between South America and its former customers on the enslaved continent. Closer to home, the crisis turned a spotlight on the White House, whose well-seasoned occupant was tempted to challenge the long-standing tradition limiting presidents to two terms. Navigating the shoals of entrenched isolationism in Congress, and the growing Nazi menace in his own backyard, FDR moved with crablike indirection toward coalition government.

"I got the job the way I get all my jobs," Rockefeller said later of his appointment as coordinator of inter-American affairs. "I thought up something that had to be done and somebody"—in this instance, the president of the United States—"said, 'O.K. it's your idea. Now let's see you make it work.'" As a comprehensive explanation, this was analogous to Captain Ahab acknowledging a passing interest in white whales. Nelson exhibited greater self-knowledge in describing himself as "sort of a catalyst. When I see a problem I get people together to talk about it and we make studies. When we've got all the facts, I usually can put my finger on what's to be done and how to do it."

By the spring of 1940, his experts in the Junta had identified multiple problems poisoning hemispheric relations. To those proverbially south of the border, the only thing more offensive than Yankee high-handedness was neglect by the colossus of the North. For much of their history, Americans had been nearly as dismissive of Europe, regarding the Atlantic and Pacific as sheltering moats divinely placed for their protection against corrupting foreigners. But as the Nazi juggernaut rolled over France and chased the British Expeditionary Force from European soil, indifference became an unaffordable luxury. The world was shrinking at an alarming rate. Were North Africa to fall before the German military machine, for example, it required scant imagination to picture Hitler's forces leapfrogging the South Atlantic at its narrowest expanse (from Dakar to the eastern bulge of Brazil was a mere five-hour trip for modern offensive aircraft).

Already Nazi influence was making itself felt throughout the region in commercial aviation, motion pictures, and radio news services. In most Latin countries, German radio broadcasts outnumbered English ones ten to one. A heavy infusion of German marks subsidized local newspapers through advertising revenue. From Carl Spaeth, his trusted man in Caracas, Nelson learned that the democratic sympathies of Venezuela's business community might not survive the economic stranglehold of a Nazi-dominated Europe. And Brazil, scene of a failed 1938 coup led by the Fascist Integralista movement, was by no means the only Latin nation to send its top military personnel to Germany for training.

In Washington, Roosevelt sounded the alarm about a United States strategically isolated from the Old World and threatened to the south by a continent in economic vassalage to Berlin. That spring, the Roosevelt White House retired Dr. New Deal in favor of Dr. Win the War. But in formulating a coherent response to the German menace, Roosevelt was hamstrung by tensions between Cordell Hull's State Department, which worshipped at the altar of free trade gained through reciprocal tariff reductions; Agriculture, where Henry Wallace championed the agrarian Left; Treasury under Henry Morgenthau, Jr., who wanted the focus kept on Europe, and Hitler defeated before he could massacre even more Jews; and Commerce, the hub of foreign economic policy making, whose nominal leader, Harry Hopkins, had moved into the White House as a virtual deputy president.

Amid the uncertainties, one fact stood out: Before Roosevelt could fulfill his pledge to make the United States the arsenal of democracy, he must first mend his tattered relations with private business. To fill one of six newly created administrative assistant positions, he turned to James Forrestal, president of the Wall Street firm Dillon, Read & Co. Not for the first time, the right hand of the Roosevelt White House didn't know, or particularly care, what its left hand was doing. As Forrestal struggled to make sense of the administration's fragmented South American policy, Harry Hopkins from his sickbed on the second floor of the White House had several confidential exchanges with Nelson. The situation was rich in irony. Like ships passing in the night, a government all but paralyzed by turf battles now sought guidance from a private study group unable to marshal support in the business community.

At the request of Hopkins, Nelson produced a thousand-word memo, largely the work of Beardsley Ruml and aptly described by one writer as "a typical Rockefeller presentation: broad in the statement of the goals; emphatic about their necessity; optimistic about the prospects; and on the skimpy side on details." Nothing less than the international position of the United States hung in the balance, the memo's authors asserted. Immediate steps ought to be taken enabling the United States to absorb agricultural and mineral surpluses piling up on South American docks. Tariffs should be reduced or eliminated, with corporate interests compensated for their losses. Nor should government officials hesitate to offer subsidies if no other means existed to bolster shipping and communications facilities. The same policy makers might consider converting existing debts into obligations payable in local currencies, thereby swelling the pool of investment capital.

Memories of drunken ambassadors and politically insensitive hacks underscored Rockefeller's demand for more and better diplomats to represent American interests throughout Central and South America. The integration of private interests, no less than the coordination of government activities, required a "common policy, program, and timing." To realize this goal, the Junta proposed a presidential committee, advisory in nature yet enjoying direct entrée to the Oval Office. A second committee, its membership drawn from the relevant departments of government, would share in the design and implementation of hemispheric policy. A brief concluding paragraph emphasized the need for a vigorous campaign of cultural, scientific, and educational outreach, with government funds employed where private agencies proved unable or unwilling to act.

On June 14, a triumphant Nazi army marched into Paris. That evening, Nelson, accompanied by Beardsley Ruml, strode into the White House and the room once used as Lincoln's study. There Harry Hopkins asked Rockefeller to read aloud the memo in his briefcase. As he listened, the enfeebled Hopkins became visibly energized. A barrage of questions extended the meeting late into the night. Before it ended, the presidential adviser promised to share the document with Roosevelt. The next day, FDR dispatched copies of the Rockefeller memo to his cabinet officers. On June 28, Roosevelt made James Forrestal's appointment official, thereby implementing the Junta's call for an administrative assistant wholly devoted to South American concerns. Almost as quickly, Forrestal concluded that the State Department, racked by personal animosity between Secretary Hull and Undersecretary Sumner Welles, willful men who agreed on little besides the need to reserve Latin American policy to themselves, was poorly equipped to think or act strategically.

Aided by Paul Nitze, another graduate of Dillon, Read, Forrestal devised plans for an entirely new agency—the Office for Coordination of Commercial and Cultural Relations Between the Americas. (In truth, most of the coordinating would involve the fractious Departments of State, Agriculture, Treasury, and Commerce.) On July 9, one day after his thirty-second birthday, Nelson joined Forrestal and Nitze in the garden of Washington's F Street Club. Told that the president had discussed his memo in cabinet, Rockefeller responded with a volley of ideas. "I talked with all the enthusiasm and conviction of one who sees clearly the possible solutions of a problem," he remembered, "but is not inhibited by the necessity of working out the details of its execution."

Harry Hopkins wasn't the only Roosevelt intimate arguing Nelson's case with the president. In response to a similar appeal from Anna Rosenberg, FDR asked plaintively, "Oh, Anna. Haven't I got enough Republicans on my hands?" Also singing Nelson's praises was Sidney Hillman, organizational mastermind behind the Congress of Industrial Organizations. Eager to foster unity on the eve of war, Hillman urged Roosevelt to convene a conference of high-level delegates from labor, agriculture, government, and industry. Furthermore, were he, Hillman, speaking for the business community, he would be reaching out to the likes of Nelson Rockefeller and Wendell Willkie, the latter a Jeffersonian Democrat and utilities executive, originally from small-town Indiana, then enjoying modest celebrity as one of the more thoughtful critics of the New Deal.*

Hillman was more prescient than he knew. By the summer evening four months later when Nelson and Forrestal had their dinner on F Street, Willkie had snatched the Republican presidential nomination from party conservatives through an unorthodox campaign funded largely by the GOP Eastern Establishment. As one of Willkie's biggest financial angels, John D. Rockefeller, Jr., wasn't keen on having his son join hands with the Roosevelt White House. "Nelson has talked with his Uncle Winthrop [Aldrich]," Junior informed Tom Debevoise on July 22. The powerful banker strongly opposed any cooperation with the Roosevelt administration, fearing that it might lessen Willkie's chances of election. Junior was inclined to agree with his brother-in-law, "if the war threat is not imminent and if delay in establishing satisfactory cooperative defense plans with the other Americas is not a real jeopardy to this country."

On July 23, Nelson secretly flew to Salt Lake City to meet the candidate himself. His brief encounter with the rumpled, charismatic Willkie left no room for doubt in either man. "If I were President in a period of crisis such as we face now," Willkie roared, "and I asked somebody to undertake what I considered was an important assignment in the national interest and that person turned it down for political considerations, I would lose my respect for him totally." Of course Nelson should take the job. Hearing what he had come for, Rockefeller changed his travel plans. He canceled a meeting with Debevoise in New York and returned instead to the nation's capital. On Friday, July 26, Forrestal showed him the latest draft of what had been renamed the Commission for Pan American Affairs. The president had approved the idea in principle, said Forrestal. Better yet, he had suggested that Nelson be made the group's

* According to Henry Wallace, who replaced Vice President John Nance Garner as Roosevelt's running mate that summer, FDR didn't think much of the political amateur dubbed "the Barefoot Boy of Wall Street." During an August 1940 visit to Hyde Park, Wallace found the president cradling a Scottish terrier pup he proposed to name Wendell Willkie, "because it wasn't housebroken yet." On second thought, Roosevelt opted for a less partisan name—Fala.

chairman. "Now look, I'm going to give him the job," was how Roosevelt put it to Anna Rosenberg, "but when he's in trouble, he's your boy. You get him out of it."

Roosevelt confirmed the appointment in a White House meeting with Rockefeller later that afternoon. Waving aside his visitor's connections to Standard Oil, FDR declared, "As far as I am concerned, your name is connected with the Rockefeller Foundation." In any case, "That's my decision, not yours." Assured a free hand in choosing his subordinates, for specifics of administration policy Rockefeller was referred to Forrestal. Inquiries about his prospective budget produced another classic Rooseveltian rejoinder. "What do I have in mind for a budget?" repeated the president. "Look, I didn't suggest this. You did. Go on, make up a program and budget and give it to my people."

Another neophyte, condemned to sink or swim in Washington's shark-infested waters, would have prudently withdrawn. Nelson charged forward. "I feel a great opportunity for service lies ahead of us," he wrote Forrestal at the end of a long, transforming day. Their formal partnership was to be short-lived. Dismayed by the internecine warfare ravaging the executive branch, on August 5 Forrestal accepted appointment as undersecretary of the navy. Still, it was largely his blueprint that established the coordinator's office by executive order rather than congressional authorization. This gave Rockefeller an identity separate from the State Department, which would have much preferred to keep him on a short leash. Thanks to Forrestal, Nelson was to be an active participant in the regular Thursday afternoon meetings involving FDR and his Council of National Defense.

On August 16, Roosevelt formally inaugurated the Office for Coordination of Commercial and Cultural Relations Between the American Republics—soon, thankfully, shortened to the Coordinator of Inter-American Affairs (CIAA). On paper, Nelson's new assignment was worthy of Rube Goldberg. To begin with, the coordinator was a liaison among departments. But he was also empowered to "review existing laws, coordinate research by the several Federal agencies, and recommend . . . such new legislation as may be deemed essential to the effective realization of the basic objectives of the Government's program." Although charged with formulation of policies in cooperation with the State Department, the same official was to "be responsible directly to the President, to whom he shall submit reports and recommendations with respect to the activities of his office."

Transcending the muddy language, one fact stood out: Status in Washington was measured by proximity to power, executive power above all else. In the political minefield bequeathed him by Jim Forrestal, nothing would determine Nelson's fate so much as his relationship with the man in the Oval Office.

Eight

AT WAR

Nelson Rockefeller's definition of a "co-ordinator" is a man who can keep all the balls in the air without losing his own.

—VICE PRESIDENT HENRY WALLACE
to President Franklin Roosevelt, December 1942

1

I N AUGUST 1940, bankrolled with $3.4 million from the president's emergency fund, Rockefeller began his Washington career as coordinator of inter-American affairs. Four other people shared his ornate, high-ceilinged office, once the domain of Gilded Age secretaries of war, in the rococo State, War, and Navy Building next door to the White House. They weren't there long. At Nelson's request, Roosevelt issued an executive order directing the Patent Office to vacate its space in the fortresslike Commerce Department on Fourteenth Street. An architect from Wally Harrison's office designed working quarters for the fledgling CIAA, the coordinator himself footing the bill. Within weeks he was supervising seventy-five employees, nucleus of a workforce that eventually topped fourteen hundred.

Everything about his new job was provisional. What became known in Washington shorthand as "the Rockefeller Office" was a classic Rooseveltian expedient, born of frustration over the diplomatic establishment and its blinkered refusal to think, plan, or act unconventionally. "It was always going to louse somebody up," acknowledged Nelson's legal counsel, John Lockwood, for the simple reason that "it . . . cuts across the activities of every department of the government." Beyond a never-ending struggle to survive, the history of the CIAA might be divided into two chapters, of equal intensity and unequal length. The first, from its inception to America's formal entry into the war in December 1941, was a largely improvised effort to counter Axis influence in South America, which had long harbored colonies of German- or Italian-speaking expatriates. During this period, economic warfare was supplemented by cultural activities designed to bolster the Roosevelt Good Neighbor policy.

The second phase of CIAA operations, instituted in the weeks after Pearl Harbor, was marked by an audacious attempt to raise living standards throughout the Southern Hemisphere. Though ostensibly aimed at the continuing Nazi menace, Rockefeller's Basic Economy Program was, in truth, directed at a more shadowy foe. Foreseeing a postwar contest with the Soviet Union for the hearts and minds of 130 million Latinos, Rockefeller hoped to demonstrate the superiority of democratic capitalism in bettering their health, education, and economic prospects. In the process, he branded himself as both New Deal liberal and early Cold Warrior.

Rockefeller brought to his new position skills honed in the New York real estate wars. His battery of secretaries maintained an elaborate card file holding the names of every visitor to the office, their reason for calling, any striking apparel they might have worn—even the weather coinciding with their visit. Such trivia, reconstituted in advance of a second encounter, helped the neophyte ingratiate himself with official Washington. Fueled by his boundless energy and unhindered (for the most part) by civil service or political considerations, the CIAA attracted high-octane talents. Emblematic of these was Paul Kramer, a short, sharp-eyed Rhodes Scholar from Cincinnati. Encountering Rockefeller for the first time, Kramer sized up his new boss as a brashly charismatic salesman, possessing a keen eye for talent and the female form. Of Nelson's three secretaries, each a polished product of Katharine Gibbs, Kramer was instantly drawn to a dark-eyed beauty named Imogene Spencer. He considered asking her out but held back, figuring the odds hopelessly stacked against him. This was a good guess, since Nelson had already bought the young woman a car to spare her the inconvenience of riding a late night bus home. His generosity backfired, and bureaucratic suspicion was aroused when the coordinator bestowed several raises on the undeniably efficient Miss Spencer. A civil service investigator dispatched to Room 3989B of the Commerce Department fell head over heels for the ravishing secretary, who fully returned his feelings.

Like many a newcomer to the town, Nelson learned more from his mistakes than his successes. Following an early White House meeting at which he presented several thorny subjects for executive review, appointments secretary Edwin "Pa" Watson took him aside. He should never raise problems with the president, Watson told Rockefeller, unless he came with a proposed solution in hand, "or you will not see the president very much more." He did not have to be told twice. On September 27, 1940, citing materials prepared for him by the coordinator, Roosevelt offered a bleak assessment of the Latin American economy, which had lost nearly half its export business because of the European conflict. That same week, Congress increased funding and lending authority for the federal Export-Import Bank from $200 million to $700 million. Tipped off to large-scale purchases by Japanese agents, subsequently shipped through Soviet Russia to their German allies, Rockefeller argued successfully for preclusive buying of industrial diamonds, rubber, lead, and other strategic commodities to keep them out of Nazi hands. Joining forces with J. Edgar Hoover, he probed Nazi connections to U.S. commercial interests in eighteen South American countries.

Early in January 1941, the coordinator went public with the results of his commercial investigation. They were predictably disturbing. According to Rockefeller, Uncle Sam's interests in Latin America were frequently entrusted to fifth columnists, who relayed sensitive trade data to the enemy. With the approval of Assistant Secretary of State Adolf Berle, Jr., plans were developed targeting a dozen prominent industrialists from firms such as DuPont, John Deere, and the Standard spin-off Socony-Vacuum. Heading the list was General Motors and its reactionary chairman, Alfred P. Sloan, Jr., unsurprising given that the top GM executive in Europe had received from Hitler's own hands the Order of the Golden Eagle, the highest Nazi honor bestowable on foreigners. At a tense State Department meeting, Undersecretary of State Sumner Welles argued his case with a GM vice president. Seeing Welles getting nowhere with appeals to duty, Rockefeller pulled the man aside. "This is stupid for American industry," he declared. With war looming and national security on the line, did GM really want to thumb its nose at Washington? The evidence of Nazi collusion was irrefutable. If the company persisted in its mulish attitude, Rockefeller said he would release the incriminating information—"tomorrow"—and let the public judge.

GM replaced its offending agents. Other companies followed suit. During the first half of 1941, U.S. firms in Latin America severed ties with more than a thousand individuals identified as Nazi sympathizers by the Rockefeller Office. What was originally a voluntary blacklist became mandatory at the end of May 1941, when the White House announced a national state of emergency. One consequence of the commercial boycott was the ouster of German and Italian management from several Latin American airlines. Chief beneficiary of the purge, funded with $8 million from Roosevelt's emergency purse, was Juan Trippe's Pan American. In return for government contracts to build military airfields, Pan Am employees supplied the War Department with useful information gleaned in Brazil and other countries honeycombed with Axis collaborators.

The same project brought Rockefeller into close contact with General George C. Marshall, U.S. Army chief of staff, for whom he conceived an admiration second only to his grandfather and FDR. Marshall reciprocated, as much as his famously reserved personality allowed. Shortly after Winthrop Rockefeller enlisted in the army, Nelson went to the War Department, where he found the general at his desk, signing a batch of orders. At length, Marshall put down his pen.

"What can I do for you?"

He had come to talk about Winthrop, said Nelson—more specifically, about his present assignment to a desk job. Marshall's face hardened.

"My brother has tried every way to get out from under the general and get sent to active duty," Nelson continued. "You are the only way he can get it."

"It is done," said Marshall. "I was afraid that you were coming in like everyone else to get him special treatment." He extended his hand, sealing an alliance that would have profound consequences for Rockefeller's Washington career.

2

To his associates outside government, Nelson appeared to be tilting at windmills. Even within the Eurocentric State Department, Latin America had traditionally invited neglect or, worse, ridicule as a continental opéra bouffe performed by chronically unstable juntas and bloated oligarchs undeserving of the Monroe Doctrine and Uncle Sam's protective embrace. Rockefeller rejected this caricature, though it must be said that his attraction to the region had less to do with history than chemistry. "He was something of a Latino himself," recalls John Camp, who served Rockefeller in Paraguay during the war and later cobbled together a quartet of Venezuelan coffee plantations to create for his employer a mountaintop estate, larger than Manhattan, called Monte Sacro ("Sacred Mountain"). "He loved at his ranch to go out and ride horseback with local cowboys." Chatting up campesinos or plunging into open-air *mercados*, Rockefeller indulged his natural exuberance and curiosity about people.

He also previewed his later campaign style. "The Latins love and will follow a strong man with a kind heart," explained this Fifth Avenue caudillo with more than a little machismo. His appreciation of Latin culture enabled the Rockefeller Office to diversify its agenda far beyond commercial shadowboxing. Early in 1941, three hundred oil and watercolor paintings by contemporary American artists were sent to major South American cities, though not before the coordinator debated their selection with Capitol Hill philistines. "The purpose of this show is to explain ourselves to the people of . . . the other American republics," Rockefeller told one skeptical lawmaker. "They feel that we are a people whose sole interest is in money and power." The art on display might not be to the congressman's liking, Nelson acknowledged, or to his own, for that matter. "But this is what the directors of the five greatest museums in the United States say is the best contemporary form of cultural expression. And this is what we are sending down."

The Yale Glee Club stirred no such controversy as it performed twenty-five concerts before appreciative Latin audiences. Neither did *Man and the Land*, an exhibition incorporating photographs from Ansel Adams and the Farm Security Administration. The American Ballet Caravan undertook a six-month tour, organized by Nelson's friend Lincoln Kirstein. The CIAA also spearheaded creation of an Inter-American Music Center; brought Latin American journalists and labor leaders to the United States; scheduled reciprocal visits by Chilean skiers and American swimmers; encouraged the teaching of Spanish in U.S. classrooms; and underwrote campus conferences and workshops on Latin history and culture. Closest to Rockefeller's heart was a series of taxpayer-funded archaeological expeditions.*

To direct his cultural programs, Rockefeller turned to Wally Harrison, someone more attuned to Rockefeller's obsessive work style. "Nelson ran an office that started at half past seven or eight in the morning," said Harrison, "and ended around eleven o'clock at night." Saturday was no different. "Sundays he gave us an extra hour of sleep." Rockefeller led by example. Up at six each morning, he rarely returned home before dinner and a second workday spent entertaining members of Congress or the diplomatic corps. Everyone around the CIAA knew their boss received no salary. At the same time, his personal generosity helped to make up for the impossible hours. Busloads of stenographers were sent to Colonial Williamsburg for a weekend at the coordinator's expense. Employees on the verge of burnout recovered their enthusiasm amid the splendors of Kykuit. One young woman, stricken with infantile paralysis, received treatment at Johns Hopkins and an iron lung courtesy of the Rockefeller Foundation. Profligate with praise, Nelson alerted staff to impending visits from military brass or civilian bigwigs. A brief outline of subjects relevant to their guest was chased by a verbal slap on the back: "Okay, kids. Go run with it."

Though the FBI rejected his proposed joint Institute of Public Opinion, Rockefeller did not lack for sources of sensitive information. Contacts in the newly built Pentagon identified areas of Latin America deemed most vulnerable to Nazi attack. Civilian agencies funneled confidential data linking the continent's worst living conditions and its most strategic military targets, a connection reinforced at daily staff meetings. These were held in a second-floor

---

* An incomparable source for this and other aspects of CIAA history is the 1967 dissertation of Claude C. Erb, a student at Clark University in Worcester. Grounded in exhaustive research, it remains, more than forty years later, the most authoritative account of the agency.

briefing and chart room, complete with built-in movie projectors, that Nelson reached by private stairway. Most days brought a fresh infusion of graphics measuring the readership of a glossy magazine called *En Guardia*; the size of audiences reached by CIAA shortwave radio broadcasts; or the latest export figures for Uruguayan wool.

Offsetting feverish discussions of the Argentine peso and presidential politics in Mexico was the absurdist humor of real life. Reports that the llamas of Ecuador had abruptly stopped reproducing sent scientists scrambling for a solution. The Rockefeller Office claimed credit for introducing artificial insemination to the country. Less successful was the cultural brainstorm of a thirtyish club woman who appeared one day to pitch her idea of an inter-American rumba contest "to promote better feeling between the Americas."

3

THE CIAA WAS originally divided into two departments—one for economic affairs and another dealing with cultural and information matters. The latter functions were soon separated, and an Office of Public Information established under Francis A. "Frankie" Jamieson, a slender, gray-haired, charmingly profane newshound straight out of *The Front Page*. As an Associated Press reporter covering the Lindbergh kidnapping trial, Jamieson had won a Pulitzer Prize before his thirtieth birthday. Though his formal schooling was scanty—he claimed to have matriculated at the International Correspondence School—the new man had much to teach his employer, especially on politics, a subject Jamieson had mastered on the gritty streets of Jersey City. Having stood up to the bruising machine of boss Frank Hague, Jamieson was tapped to manage the successful 1940 gubernatorial campaign of Charles Edison. Rejecting a job offer from the governor-elect, Jamieson went to work instead for Nelson Rockefeller and the CIAA. This wasn't his first exposure to the Rockefellers; prior to the Edison campaign, the savvy reporter had been employed by Winthrop Rockefeller and the Greater New York Fund. As long as Junior ruled Room 5600, successful public relations was defined as keeping the family name out of print. This applied with special force to Winthrop, with his postcollegiate fondness for showgirls and the bibulous surroundings of El Morocco.

Nelson, unsurprisingly, took a more proactive view of press agentry. It was only a question of time before he appropriated Jamieson for his own purposes. One of a handful of associates to address the coordinator by his first name, Jamieson didn't hesitate to question Rockefeller's more quixotic inspirations or accept the ensuing period of disfavor, during which Nelson addressed him as

"Frank" rather than the conspiratorial "Frankie." Much more common was the sight of the rumpled, slouching Jamieson, feet splayed on a tabletop, cigarette dangling from his mouth, offering unvarnished counsel from an unabashed New Deal Democrat. "What does Frankie think?" opened many a conversation in the Rockefeller shop and closed many a debate. A recovering alcoholic, Jamieson limited his consumption of spirits to a single glass of New Year's champagne, shared with his abstemious boss. Next to his brother Laurance, Frank Jamieson was probably the closest thing Nelson ever had to a true friend, someone valued as much for the sheer pleasure of his company as for his professional acumen. "It was like a marriage," explained Jamieson's widow, Linda. "A marriage with continual battles."

Almost as close to the coordinator was John Lockwood, a mordant Harvard Law School graduate trained by Justice Oliver Wendell Holmes and Tom Debevoise. Lockwood impressed Rockefeller from the moment they met during a hopeless campaign to preserve the financially troubled Lincoln School as an independent institution. Disregarding the wishes of its founders, Columbia University proposed a merger of Lincoln and the nearby Horace Mann School. In the resulting controversy, Nelson became the focus of intense media scrutiny, wedged uncomfortably between a cheeseparing administration and angry Lincoln alumni and parents, including some he suspected of Communist sympathies. In later years, Rockefeller would credit this unlikely academic dustup for his passionate aversion to Communism. John Lockwood was just as willing to attribute Nelson's hard-line views on the Marxist menace to Arthur Packard, a Room 5600 functionary to whom Junior delegated much of his charitable giving. "This guy is full of beans," Lockwood concluded of the younger Rockefeller, "but he's vulnerable. So I tried to keep him from making charges or getting involved in something for which he could be sued for libel." By extricating his client, as gracefully as possible, from the tempest engulfing Lincoln, Lockwood won the lasting gratitude of more than one Rockefeller. His title of general counsel to the CIAA inadequately conveyed the versatility of "Johnny Lock" or the scope of his troubleshooting on Nelson's behalf.

Early in 1941, feeling the weight of his new position, Rockefeller resigned the presidency of MoMA, though not before anonymously establishing a $25,000 fund to purchase works by Latin American artists. He contracted with the museum to produce for the Latin market films with titles like *Highway to Friendship* and *Der Fuehrer's Face*. Notably less successful was a film purporting to show Mexico entering the war against Fascism. It was a phenomenal hit with Latin moviegoers, and only later did the CIAA creative team discover that Mexican audiences cheering themselves hoarse thought their country was invading the United States. Seeking a Spanish-language alternative to Nazi propaganda coming out of Spain and Argentina, Rockefeller established Prencinradio to help jump-start the Mexican film industry. In exchange for equipment and expertise supplied by Hollywood—RKO helped construct several sound stages—Mexican producers agreed to make movies advancing Roosevelt's Good Neighbor policy. Little came of the effort. Far more successful was a Spanish edition of the *March of Time* newsreel.

Ironically, it is a movie that never got made for which Rockefeller is most harshly remembered. Even while negotiating a settlement of their claims against RKO, Nelson and his family retained a substantial financial interest in the studio. At the end of January 1941, Nelson learned of a film said to be patterned on the life of media tycoon William Randolph Hearst. *Citizen Kane*, starring and directed by Orson Welles, represented half of a generous two-picture deal with Welles that Rockefeller himself had promoted. So claimed Pauline Kael in *Raising Kane*, her much debated version of the ultimate conflict between Hollywood art and avarice. Nelson shared a different set of memories with speechwriter Joseph Persico, who incorporated them in his memoir *The Imperial Rockefeller*: "They told me this fellow just had to see me about making a movie. He came in, a big, good looking guy. He started carrying on about how important his movie was. Very emotional. He was practically on his knees. I thought he was going to kiss my hand. He made me terribly uncomfortable. The thought passing through my mind was, How do I get him out of here? So I agreed to give him some money. Mostly to get it over with."

A week before its scheduled world premiere at Radio City on February 14, 1941, Rockefeller learned that *Citizen Kane* was being delayed while studio executives reviewed possible cuts to the film. This was a cover story; acting on behalf of an industry fearing reprisals from the lord of San Simeon, MGM boss Louis B. Mayer had offered $800,000 to his RKO counterpart, George Schaefer, in an attempt to buy, and destroy, the unreleased *Kane*. Schaefer courageously spurned the Mayer proposal. The Radio City Music Hall was less venturesome. It passed on showing the film, after Hearst gossip columnist Louella Parsons telephoned Nelson in Washington with an unsubtle message: "How would you like to have *American Weekly* magazine section run a double-page spread on John D. Rockefeller?"

Kane, of course, went on to make cinematic history. (Rockefeller himself never set eyes on the movie against which all American films are judged.) The idea of making a South American film—*Pan America*, later retitled *It's All True*—to promote better understanding on both sides of the equator originated in an October 1941 conversation between John Hay "Jock" Whitney, head of the the CIAA's motion picture division, and Lourival Fontes, Brazil's minister of propaganda and popular culture. After the fact, Welles claimed to have accepted the project under duress. This overlooked his long-standing interest in Latin America; a hedonistic streak that welcomed the chance to participate in

Rio's bacchanalian Carnaval; and the lavish financial terms outlined by the Rockefeller Office that came as manna from heaven to the chronically strapped filmmaker. That the South American project might conflict with editing work on *The Magnificent Ambersons*, his adaptation of Booth Tarkington's small-town novel of family hubris and decline, didn't faze the polymath Welles. After three exhausting days in the cutting room, the director entrusted the incomplete film to his young assistant Robert Wise.

In the first week of February 1942, Welles left for Rio de Janeiro. But instead of a picture postcard or live-action Disney travelogue, Welles bit the hand that financed him by training his lens on Rio's *favelas*, or shanty towns. His absence could not have come at a worse time. Already put off by unfavorable audience previews of *Ambersons*, studio brass proceeded to butcher Welles's masterpiece. At the same time, they voiced objections to the director's South America project. ("A lot of jigaboos jumping up and down," Welles quoted one RKO executive sourly dismissing his footage of voodoo rituals and street debauchery.) For George Schaefer and his commitment to quality pictures, this was the perfect storm. By June 1942, Floyd Odlum owned 47 percent of RKO stock, more than enough to force Schaefer's ouster as studio president and the eviction of Welles and his Mercury Production unit from the RKO lot to make room for an upcoming Tarzan picture.

For the rest of his life, Welles blamed everyone but himself for the ruined *Ambersons* and aborted *It's All True*. He saved his harshest criticism for Rockefeller, whose financial guarantees to the filmmaker did not survive the changes in RKO management. "Nobody was ever more cowardly than Nelson, you know," Welles told his sympathetic biographer, Barbara Leaming. The director exacted his revenge in *The Lady from Shanghai*, a 1948 tour de force centered around the amoral figure of George Grisby, a cackling psychopath plotting to stage his own murder and double-cross everyone else. Broadway actor Glenn Anders played Grisby in semi-demented fashion as a takeoff on Nelson Rockefeller, down to the crassly insincere "fellas" sprinkling his speech. In this, he merely took direction from Welles.

4

IN JANUARY 1941, Nelson and Tod were invited to a presidential birthday dinner and benefit performance aiding the March of Dimes. More invitations would follow, the Rockefellers joining the Roosevelts and half a dozen other guests for Sunday evening suppers of scrambled eggs prepared by the First Lady, while the president mixed drinks in the Green Room. Overnight

Roosevelt established himself as Nelson's political father figure, a glamorous, protean role model. Politics is theater, and few leaders were as comfortable under the spotlight. Roosevelt once described Orson Welles, to his face, as the second best actor in America. He meant it as a compliment. Gifted with rare timing and near perfect pitch, FDR held the reins of power, writes James MacGregor Burns, "by deliberately fostering among his aides a sense of competition and a clash of wills that led to disarray, heartbreak, and anger but also set off pulses of executive energy and sparks of creativity."

Dispensing with his initial businessman's skepticism, Rockefeller came to admire the president's circuitous methods, behind which lay a brutal simplicity. Those unable to adapt to changed conditions, as FDR did intuitively, found themselves marooned in bureaucratic isolation. Few were fired, but many were disillusioned. These included Secretary of State Cordell Hull, the silver-haired Tennessean whose courtly manner was belied by the foulest mouth in Washington and a lisp ("Jesus Cwist!") that invited presidential mockery. Along with the Japanese—"them goddamn pissants"—Secretary Hull reserved his choicest epithets for Undersecretary Sumner Welles, declaring, "I'm not going to get into a public pissing contest with a polecat." That Welles enjoyed a long-standing friendship with Roosevelt, in whose 1904 wedding he had served as a page, did nothing to ease Hull's resentment. To Nelson, Welles appeared "a brilliant, austere, somewhat pompous but greatly respected man who really hated my guts."

More to Rockefeller's liking was Henry Wallace, the Iowa agronomist and secretary of agriculture who became vice president in January 1941. Dubbed "the corn-fed proletarian" for his left-wing sympathies and dreamy idealism, Wallace personified the maverick, fertile in thought, bold in action, to whom Nelson naturally gravitated. United in their fascination with Latin America, the two men became fast friends. The vice president's daughter, Jean, found temporary employment with the Rockefeller Office. At cabinet meetings, Wallace invariably defended the rapidly growing CIAA against charges of bureaucratic poaching. Rockefeller showed his gratitude by steering funds to Wallace priorities such as the Inter-American Institute of Tropical Agriculture in Costa Rica and deferring to the vice president on the tennis court. On Sunday nights, Wallace and other guests assembled under Nelson's roof for dinner and Spanish-language films, after which the group joined in a surreal sing-along—the vice president of the United States and the grandson of John D. Rockefeller leading them in choruses celebrating the expropriation of U.S. oil assets by the government of Mexico. "They put on a record," remembered Linda Jamieson Storrow. "Everyone put his glasses on and in the most formal un-Spanish way, we went through these Spanish songs. It was deadly."

Irony was never to be Rockefeller's style. In this, as in his lethal charm and unquestioning optimism, Nelson emulated his mentor in the Oval Office. "No job ever seemed too big or too impossible for Nelson to tackle," recalled one wartime associate. With food shipments to Latin America falling prey to German U-boats in the South Atlantic, someone in the coordinator's office proposed building a canal to link the Amazon and Orinoco rivers. "Nelson didn't stop to talk about it," the perplexed co-worker remembered, "he just had a survey made and the survey showed that it was engineeringly possible to do it. The trouble was that it would have been something like digging half a dozen Panama Canals. . . . God knows what would have happened if the Navy hadn't suddenly begun knocking off Nazi submarines at a highly satisfactory rate."

Something else bonded FDR and the coordinator: To observers, Nelson seemed to have no discernible ideology. As congenial and remote as Ronald Reagan half a century later, Roosevelt counted millions of admirers and practically no intimates. Nelson was a case in point. Having grown close to FDR, or what passed for closeness, he made the cardinal error of forgetting that others had been closer for longer. Sumner Welles, for example. A respected Latin American specialist in his own right, the older man understandably resented the wealthy amateur meddling in affairs best left to trained diplomats. Confident that Rockefeller sooner or later would betray his inexperience, Welles bided his time. His patience was rewarded in the spring of 1941, when the CIAA launched an elaborate advertising campaign designed to attract South American tourists and replenish the empty coffers of media outlets throughout the continent. It was bad enough that the ads, whipped up by Madison Avenue, displayed a cultural tin ear for Latin sensibilities (running Spanish copy, to cite but one snafu, in Portuguese-speaking Brazil). More embarrassing still was the expenditure of Yankee dollars in publications singled out for their supposed pro-Axis leanings by the coordinator himself. The ad blitz loosed a flood of complaints from the diplomatic corps, many registered in decidedly undiplomatic language.

Welles saw his opportunity and seized it. On April 22, working off a draft provided by the undersecretary, FDR administered a stern reprimand to Nelson. The tactful language of his letter did not conceal the genuine annoyance of its author. Henceforth, said Roosevelt, Rockefeller must keep State apprised of all his activities. "You've just got to get along with them," the president told Nelson when they next met, "because if it ever comes to a showdown between your office and the Department," he would have no alternative but to back the professionals "and Mr. Welles." Owning up to his shortcomings, Nelson vowed to do better. For help in repairing the breach with State, he turned to Welles's deputy Laurence Duggan. The offending ad agencies gave way to grassroots committees comprising prominent U.S. citizens living abroad, their membership decided in tandem by CIAA and State.

Outwardly answerable to local embassies, these "coordinating committees" were in practice independent operators, jamming shortwave broadcasts to fifth columnists in Brazil, sponsoring a daily radio program in Chile, and channeling CIAA press material to sympathetic newspapers throughout the region. The committees were only part of Nelson's campaign to regain White House favor. Following a casual suggestion from Roosevelt to Hutch Robbins, the presidential cousin who had earned his spurs in Rockefeller's Venezuelan operations, Nelson promised an investigation into air travel between Australia, New Zealand, Cape Colony, and South America. When FDR speculated about changing the name of the Caribbean to the American Sea, the coordinator took the idea seriously, or pretended to. He personally advanced an islands tour by Eleanor Roosevelt, later presenting the First Lady with a handsomely bound album of favorable stories generated by the trip.

From all outward appearances, Nelson had weathered the storm caused by his maladroit ad campaign. But the near death experience left its mark. A sunny exterior concealed feelings of intense stress and intuitive suspicion. "I would wake up at three or four in the morning with that fluttering feeling in my stomach," he said later, "and I would know like that . . . where somebody was knifing me. . . . Then I would really work. The reason I was able to survive was because I worked harder and longer and moved around town faster than the opposition." During his first months in Washington, Nelson lived with his original sponsor, Jim Forrestal, and his wife, Jo, in their home on Woodley Road. Not knowing how long his present job might last, and eager to be reunited with his family, Nelson was delighted to learn about an estate for lease in a verdant part of northwest Washington. Baker's Acres, so named for its current owner, contained a Revolutionary War–era farmhouse flanked by tennis courts and extensive grounds. It took one visit to 2500 Foxhall Road to convince Nelson that the secluded property would make an excellent home away from home. Four years later, exercising an option to buy, he expanded the house to thirty rooms and his landholdings to twenty-six acres.

Known simply as Foxhall Road, the latest Rockefeller dwelling combined the informality of summer camp with the earnestness of a public policy seminar. Not content to polish his tennis game and Spanish accent on the premises, Vice President Wallace practiced his boomerang in Nelson's backyard. Beside the long driveway that curled up to the house, the new occupant posted a sign reading, "Careful, Children at Play." One day it mysteriously disappeared, only to resurface in the midst of a heated intellectual bull session. The youngsters thus protected grew up surrounded by foreign tongues and cultures. (Education was reciprocal, with young Steven Rockefeller coming to his father's aid when asked how to spell "yours" at the bottom of a letter.) Hosting an outdoor cocktail party one evening, Nelson did a double take at the flapping jodhpurs on Paraguay's elaborately dressed army chief of staff. Closer inspection revealed Steven's irrepressible younger brother, Michael, grinningly manipulating the general's trousers from behind.

Alone among his siblings, Michael appeared more Rockefeller than Clark, a comparison not lost on his grandfather. "I have never seen a child more companionable or interesting to talk with," said Junior of his grandson. "He is certainly full of original ideas." One morning at the breakfast table, Michael glanced at a mustachioed South American dignitary and asked, "Why do you have grass growing above your mouth?" To another visitor, the boy proudly exhibited a handful of pennies he'd been given. Picking them up one by one, he announced, "This is for my piggy bank. This one I give away. This one is for fish food. And this one is for me!" For Michael's parents, Washington protocol involved a steep learning curve. Tod Rockefeller is recalled by one of her husband's co-workers as "a tall, slender woman, totally honest, and totally unprepared for life in Washington." Admirably free of airs and graces, Tod insisted on riding a bus to her volunteer work in order to save gasoline for the war effort. Lacking Nelson's pneumatic drive, she caused others to speculate on how she coped. "I sometimes wonder," Junior wrote his son, "if you realize what it means to manage the details of the lives of five children, to say nothing of the amount of time, strength and thought that she must give to her social life." Outsiders could only imagine the toll exacted by living on terms set by others. At Pocantico, for example, her father-in-law thought nothing of ordering his grandchildren out of a wading pool. Taking their cue from the squire, his agents made an issue of Mrs. Nelson's casual request to borrow a riding horse from the Kykuit stable.

More personal humiliations, as yet unsuspected, would in time resuscitate fears expressed during her courtship. In a conversation on the subject of spousal fidelity with Drew Pearson's wife, Luvie, a close friend, Tod sounded a confident note. "I don't have to worry about Nelson," she insisted. "Whenever he gets those urges, he just goes outside and moves some great tree around." Her belief in the restraining force of landscape architecture was not universally shared. According to Cary Reich, the coordinator had an affair with Janet Barnes of his staff, a woman Jock Whitney jokingly dubbed Cerberus. One day in the spring of 1943, the guard dog abruptly disappeared from her post. Enter Libby Shemwell, a twenty-three-year-old Kentuckian, part of the vanguard of working women for whom World War II amounted to a second American Revolution. Moving to Washington shortly after Pearl Harbor, Libby submitted multiple job applications. These produced an immediate offer of secretarial work at the CIAA, less government bureau than personal fiefdom. (Her immediate supervisor had, until recently, been employed as manager of Rockefeller Center's Rainbow Room.)

One morning, she literally bumped into "a very young, rather handsome man, obviously full of energy and impatience," as he bounded out of an elevator before its doors were fully open, trailing apologies in his wake. This was Libby's introduction to the man called NAR (pronounced like "WAR") by the secretarial pool. Her mailroom duties included drafting replies for the coordinator, to be collected in a file for signing when Rockefeller had a few spare moments. His dyslexia redefined the secretarial function, for Nelson neither read incoming letters nor dictated answers. Instead, he depended on people such as Libby to brief him on the contents of each missive and to translate his verbal instructions into serviceable prose. "This kept him from having to spend time deciphering the written word," she explained. "His forte was solving problems with big ideas, which absolutely gushed from his brain."

One day Libby arrived at the mailroom to find her desk missing. From two other employees she learned that it had been moved to the front office and that she had been advanced to the position of personal secretary to the coordinator. Knowing nothing of the Janet Barnes affair, in later years she seriously doubted whether Rockefeller had either the time or the opportunity to conduct office romances. Of her own sudden promotion, she reflected, "It was so outrageous that only NAR would have done it that way. He regarded me as one of his tools, and he chose to use me this way. There was never any explanation, not even a welcome. I sat down at my desk and the day continued as if I had been there for years." No raise accompanied the new assignment and its all-consuming demands. "NAR worked a 24 hour day, and we secretaries did the same." This was only a slight exaggeration. Each evening, Rockefeller left the Commerce Department clutching a briefcase or two packed for him by Libby and Susan Cable, an even younger, Spanish-speaking co-worker from Santa Fe, New Mexico. The next morning, the two women emptied the overstuffed cases, carefully noting personalized comments scrawled by their employer late at night or in predawn sessions under a sun lamp (an unsuccessful attempt to colorize his pale Aldrich skin). Libby learned to keep $50 in her purse for emergencies. These occurred with the frequency of mealtimes, since NAR never carried money. "He got tired of always being expected to pick up the check."

Occasionally, the coordinator would interrupt an office meeting to declare himself in need of rest. Since he appeared constitutionally incapable of being alone, Libby was asked to go with him to Foxhall Road. "After he had put on pajamas and gotten into bed, we continued working as if he were at the office," she recalled. In midafternoon, an elegant tea tray appeared, laden with cinnamon toast and a clutter of intricate utensils. Libby was expected to preside over this civilized ritual. Sundays offered scant respite from the punishing routine. A driver was sent to fetch her from the Chastleton Apartments, under whose roof her co-worker René d'Harnoncourt, a future director of MoMA, made friends with cockroaches he named Sonia, Zelda, Jean, and Robert. When they finished working, Rockefeller took Libby home in a Lincoln Continental convertible he clearly loved to drive. From behind the wheel, he brought her up-to-date on office activities and how they related to the global conflict. His thoughtfulness impressed the young woman, who didn't realize until later how greatly she had been stretched by her sleepless, sink-or-swim existence at the right hand of Nelson Rockefeller.

5

BY 1941, FRUSTRATION over the lack of cooperation between the FBI and military intelligence agencies made Roosevelt receptive to British spymaster William Stephenson's call for an American version of British Security Coordination. Moreover, Stephenson had just the candidate in mind to oversee such an agency: his friend Colonel William Donovan. The fifty-nine-year-old native of Buffalo, New York, was known as "Wild Bill," a moniker variously attributed to his performance as a Columbia University quarterback or his heroic service with the famous "Fighting Irish" 165th Infantry Regiment in World War I, for which he had received the Medal of Honor. Donovan attended Columbia Law School at the same time as FDR; he enjoyed greater success in the courtroom than on the campaign trail, losing a 1922 race for lieutenant governor of New York and being swamped a decade later by Roosevelt's Albany successor, Herbert Lehman.

In his affinity for untested ideas and his disregard for formal lines of authority, Donovan bore more than a passing resemblance to Nelson Rockefeller. The two men were bound to clash, their overlapping responsibilities mirrored in their conflicting egos. Rockefeller's hope to block the Donovan appointment fell through when Sumner Welles spurned his offer of a preemptive alliance. In unveiling the latest of 136 emergency agencies created by his administration, Roosevelt awarded with his left hand what his right hand withheld. Colonel Donovan as head of the Office of the Coordinator of Information (COI) would collect data bearing on national security, said FDR, but not at the expense of existing intelligence services, the FBI, or other agencies. This mandate for chaos was quickly put to the test. Countering Anna Rosenberg's claim that Rockefeller was already handling Latin America to Roosevelt's satisfaction, Donovan asserted his own control, promising to inform Nelson only "whenever he thought additional work was needed."

On July 16, the two men met over dinner at Foxhall Road. Before the dessert course, they reached a gentleman's agreement reserving the Western Hemisphere for the CIAA. So, at least, thought Rockefeller. In a follow-up "Dear Bill" letter, Nelson described his propaganda efforts to date. Admittedly, these had gotten off to a slow start, hampered by the paucity of shortwave radio stations in the United States at the time—a mere twelve money-losing outlets, plagued by poor reception and few Spanish- or Portuguese-speaking employees. Rockefeller convinced both NBC and CBS to expand their Latin American outreach, CBS chairman Bill Paley's network contracting with the government to broadcast fifteen-minute newscasts by radio telephone. Using $200,000 of public funds, the coordinator also took over WRUL, a failing, noncommercial station in Boston. His promise to subsidize increased Latin American coverage brought him into conflict with Donovan, who insisted that *nothing* go out over the airwaves without his approval.

From his earlier run-in with the State Department, Nelson had learned never to fight a bureaucratic war without reserves. On the same day he hosted Donovan for dinner at Foxhall Road, he struck a deal with Welles deputy Laurence Duggan that committed State to the continuation of CIAA as a separate hemispheric operation. "Until I am quite sure which person from our office can best serve you in this capacity," Rockefeller told Donovan, he was designating himself to represent the CIAA on Wild Bill's policy committee. Here matters stood in August 1941, when Rockefeller left the capital for a rejuvenating hunting trip in Alaska. He almost didn't return. An Indian guide saved his life by finishing off a fast-charging Kodiak bear that Nelson had wounded but failed to bring down. A few days later, Rockefeller chased some mountain goats onto a narrow mountain ledge, only to freeze in terror as he peered over a four-hundred-foot cliff. Five minutes went by until, paralyzed with vertigo, he could be coaxed from the ledge.

Official Washington afforded only marginally surer footing. Fortunately for Nelson, Donovan had made a host of enemies, many agreeing on nothing but their disdain for Donovan. Neither Attorney General Francis Biddle nor J. Edgar Hoover, who already counted 150 secret agents in Latin America, was in any mood to turn them over to the COI. Members of Congress likened Donovan's fast-growing agency to the Gestapo. The U.S. Navy resented his raids on its supersecret K Organization, while the Bureau of the Budget wailed in distress over the exploding payroll and shapeless flow chart of the Donovan operation. In so charged an atmosphere, petty controversies rapidly escalated into heated confrontations. Claiming that his office was not yet sufficiently organized to commit to any particular procedure for pooling information, Donovan denied Rockefeller reports from the critical Russian front. Hiring a disaffected CIAA employee with inside knowledge of Rockefeller's radio operations reinforced the perception of Donovan as a bureaucratic predator. At a State Department meeting called to coordinate the coordinators, Donovan crudely turned to Larry Duggan.

"Whom do I deal with on Latin American problems? I guess I deal with you, don't I?"

"No," replied Duggan. "I think you deal both with us and the Co-ordinator's office."

As Rockefeller and Donovan pawed the ground in mutual distrust, rumors flew that FDR had furnished Donovan with one of his patented confidential notes: specifically, dividing propaganda responsibilities between Wild Bill and Fiorello La Guardia, the volatile New Yorker whose lackluster performance as head of the Office of Civilian Defense supplied one of the few points of consensus in an otherwise fractious administration. A presidential directive wasn't the only thing Donovan had in his pocket. To further ingratiate himself with the White House, he had employed the services of Captain James Roosevelt, who in turn promised unparalleled access to his father. Add to this a twenty-year advantage in navigating the back alleys of official Washington, and it is easy to understand the confidence with which Donovan on the morning of October 11 had an ultimatum hand-delivered to his upstart rival at the Commerce Department building.

As a practical matter, it stated, "only one agency can deal with the broadcasting companies . . . in the transmission of news and in the matter of program schedules, direction of beams, and all the mechanical matters pertaining to transmission and retransmission. . . . This is no mere jurisdictional question," Donovan continued. "It is a matter of major policy. I accept your statement that you are acting for the State Department in South America and that your plan of independent operation has met with the approval of the President." However, no such Oval Office directive had been sent to Donovan. Until it was, "I must continue to meet my obligation in the manner he has directed." Rockefeller appealed to Anna Rosenberg. "The most dangerous thing of all would be to have a good neighbor policy conducted by State and ourselves with Donovan operating independently on an intensive campaign of psychological warfare . . . completely unrelated to the President's basic concept of our Hemisphere relations," he told her.

Disputes over radio frequencies and news dissemination masked the real issue at stake: CIAA autonomy and, with it, an approach to Latin America that recognized what was unique about the region and its historically troubled relationship with Uncle Sam. Over the weekend, Rockefeller tried his hand at drafting an agreement to which both men could sign their names. This effort was broken off abruptly on Monday, October 13, once he learned that Jimmy Roosevelt had shared Donovan's confrontational letter with the White House.

At a tense encounter that afternoon, Donovan claimed presidential approval for his consolidation plan and notified Nelson of a pending transfer of information programs "from your office to our office . . . Jimmy will tell you about it." Not so fast, said Rockefeller. "I want to get this clear on policy. Is Jimmy here as his father's son or is he working for you—because if he's working for you, I'd rather not deal with the office boy." Rockefeller showed Jimmy a copy of his most recent letter to Donovan. Knowing the answer in advance, he asked, "When you talked to your father did you tell him this side?"

At the end of ninety fruitless minutes, Rockefeller proposed that he and Donovan pay a joint visit to the Oval Office. "Father's too busy to be bothered with this sort of thing," Jimmy protested. In his stead, the president's son recommended as arbitrator Judge Sam Rosenman, an original New Dealer and trusted Roosevelt speechwriter. Donovan said there was nothing further to discuss. "Bill, I think you're wrong," Rockefeller responded. "You'd better lay off this. But if you insist on trying to take this function away from me, okay it's war and we'll go to bat on it." From the Donovan office, Rockefeller went straight to the State Department. After shoring up his position with Sumner Welles, he obtained renewed promises of support from Harry Hopkins and the Budget Bureau. Henry Wallace offered something better than sympathy. "You know what you ought to do is use the same technique Welles has used on both you and me with the president," Wallace advised. "Give him something that's ready to be signed."

"You mean like this," said Rockefeller, pulling from his pocket a document prepared for just such a contingency. Five paragraphs long, it reserved to the CIAA responsibility for all "information, news and inspirational matter going to the other American republics" and enjoined the warring agencies to negotiate in good faith with radio companies over the use of their facilities. Once more, Rockefeller asked Anna Rosenberg to work her magic. On October 15, she placed his draft on the president's desk, along with assurances that both Budget and Welles were in sympathy with her patron. "You don't have to tell me about Welles," said FDR, chuckling. "After all the trouble I've had with Nelson and Welles, now Welles is his strongest advocate in Washington!" Roosevelt made minor revisions to the memorandum, then signed his name to it.*

Now it was Donovan's turn to erupt in fury, taking out his anger on the hapless Jimmy. An exasperated president directed Mrs. Rosenberg to get together with the Budget Bureau and "fix it up." Nelson beat her to the punch. A second meeting with Jimmy Roosevelt produced a meticulously detailed, albeit cumbersome, plan of operations, with joint committees and weekly meetings to

---

* Small wonder, then, that Nelson should tell a friend in 1945, "Everything I feel I've achieved here in Washington, I owe to Anna Rosenberg." William Benton, CCOHC, 124.

determine future operations. The world, it turned out, was just large enough for Nelson Rockefeller and Wild Bill Donovan.

6

ROCKEFELLER AND DONOVAN did not speak to each other for a year and a half. Yet Wild Bill was never far from Nelson's thoughts. He teamed up with Attorney General Biddle and J. Edgar Hoover—"an unlikely three-some," Rockefeller laughingly acknowledged—to thwart Donovan before he could plant agents in South America. "Bill had offered jobs to friends of mine, whom he didn't know were friends of mine, to work in Latin American intelligence," said Nelson. One of these was Lincoln Kirstein, who came to Rockefeller seeking advice. J. Edgar Hoover had his own methods of dealing with Donovan. "Hoover was working closely with local police and had a couple of Bill's men thrown in jail in Latin America and left there," Rockefeller claimed. "Bill couldn't say anything because he didn't want to admit they were his men."

After Pearl Harbor, establishment of the Board of Economic Warfare under Vice President Wallace opened yet another jurisdictional can of worms. As Rockefeller and Wallace debated their respective roles in the new setup, Rockefeller heard whisperings that his deputy Carl Spaeth was plotting a separate agency reporting to himself and Paul Nitze, another alumnus of the Rockefeller Office who currently worked for Milo Perkins, Wallace's handpicked director at the BEW. To the alleged conspirators, this was a logical attempt to keep their mutual employers from drowning in operational minutiae. To Rockefeller, it was rank disloyalty. "Nelson doesn't expect you to be a yes-man," explained one aide. "But he does expect you to be a Rockefeller man—first, last, and always." Hastening to see Perkins, Rockefeller came straight to the point. "Look, Milo, I am going to fire Carl Spaeth and you fire Nitze." Perkins didn't argue.

It was far from Nelson's finest hour, but it wasn't simple paranoia either. His ruined friendship with Spaeth taught Rockefeller a fateful lesson. "Never, but never, have all your eggs in one basket," he concluded. Henceforth, he was careful to distribute responsibilities among a small cadre of the trusted, and even then his confidence was of the provisional kind. This dilution of authority was to have a serious impact on his national political career, sacrificing strategic coherence to the babble of competing voices. As an aspiring president, unwilling to wholly trust either a Jim Farley–style *supremo* or his own gut instincts, Rockefeller would pay dearly for the memory of Carl Spaeth's freelancing.

7

T HE JAPANESE ZEROS that ravaged the U.S. Pacific Fleet in December 1941 may have caught military planners unprepared, but not the CIAA. It gave him "personal satisfaction," Rockefeller told his staff four days after Pearl Harbor, that "we are working on something positive for the future and that we are not just consecrating our lives to destruction." What he was working on was a plan to improve health and sanitary conditions in Brazil, to which military planners envisioned sending U.S. troops as protection against Nazi invasion. As the danger of foreign aggression receded, it was replaced by the threat of internal subversion—the consequence, Rockefeller believed, of a democracy deficit he blamed on rampant poverty, illiteracy, and sickness throughout the region.

By December 1941, his vision had expanded into a veritable New Deal for the Americas. Moreover, he had enlisted an improbable ally in Jesse H. Jones. "Uncle Jesse" to his friends, "the Emperor Jones" to everyone else, this poker-playing, deal-cutting wizard of finance became Nelson's tutor in the black arts of official Washington. Every Wednesday afternoon at five, the younger man hurried to Jones's Commerce Department office. What he learned there would shape his later service as a subcabinet officer and hyperactive governor of New York. "He was the one who told me that the only way to operate in Washington effectively was to get the right to set up corporations," a grateful Rockefeller remembered. "Then you could get out of the bureaucratic red tape and out of all the entangling agencies and . . . be able to make contracts for more than one year."

Exploiting the climate created by Pearl Harbor, Rockefeller went straight to the top to sell what became known as his Basic Economy Program. A few days after Christmas, he entered the White House clutching an album densely illustrated with his trademark graphs and overlays. Clearly impressed by what he saw, Harry Hopkins rose from his bed, donned slippers, and shuffled into the president's room next door. Fifteen minutes later, he emerged.

"You can start the program with $25 million."*

Sensitive to the pride of his Latin friends, Nelson shunned a unilateral approach to foreign aid, the very success of which risked embarrassing the recipient, but whose failure reserved all blame to the donor. In its place he offered a

---

* According to George Dudley, the album's creator, the only reason it took fifteen minutes was that the president wished to share the book with his houseguest, Winston Churchill. In a 1977 oral history, Rockefeller praised Roosevelt's decisiveness. "This is my idea of the way a great leader in a time of crisis should operate," he said. In fact, the scheme made less impression on FDR than he thought. At a May 15, 1942, cabinet meeting, the president expressed surprise that he had ever awarded Rockefeller $25 million with which to tackle the health problems of Latin America. George Dudley, AI.

partnership, or *servicio*, under which the newly chartered Institute of Inter-American Affairs would supply U.S. technical and managerial assistance through appropriate local government agencies. Adopting another Rockefeller Foundation innovation, the IIAA devised multiyear contracts on a sliding financial scale, with Uncle Sam paying 80 percent or more of program costs during the first year, a figure that declined in proportion to the rise in grassroots support for the activity in question. At the end of a fixed period—say, three or five years—the decision to continue rested with local authorities, who by then were expected to assume all operating expenses. Scholarships facilitated the training of homegrown replacements for American managers (some fifteen hundred public health officials alone).*

Rockefeller formally unveiled the Basic Economy Program in March 1942. He got an immediate boost when George Marshall agreed to the transfer of General George Dunham, a public health expert with intimate knowledge of tropical medicine. Within months the Rockefeller initiative was introducing crop diversification, staging livestock demonstrations, and distributing thousands of baby chicks and pigs in ten Latin American countries. A massive public health effort took shape in the rubber-producing Amazon Valley basin, after the fall of Malaysia and Singapore early in 1942 more critical than ever to the Allied war effort. Filtered water plants eliminated bacterial pollution, the cause of widespread amoebic dysentery. Counting only two hundred professional nurses to care for forty-five million people, Brazil welcomed thousands of *visitadoras* trained by Rockefeller agents to assist expectant mothers and other patients at clinics in outlying areas.

Rockefeller *servicios* built a leprosarium in the Paraguayan capital of Asuncio to combat the disfiguring ailment, a teaching hospital in Guatemala City, and a sewage system for Quito. Even Walt Disney entered the fight against insect-carried disease, the Seven Dwarfs leading a campaign to destroy mosquito larvae. On a visit to Haiti, Rockefeller was deeply moved as he cradled infants suffering from yaws, the national scourge. Penicillin imported from the United States brought the disease under control. Elsewhere, the Institute of Inter-American Affairs battled bubonic plague in Ecuadorian villages. Parts of the same country, ravaged in a border war with Peru, were rebuilt by the same division that supplied highway construction jobs for Hondurans left destitute after a lack of shipping crippled banana exports.

In four years, Rockefeller agents trained more than ten thousand in-service

---

* Rockefeller developed additional safeguards, as much to protect his bureaucratic flanks as to combat malaria or introduce contour plowing to steep Andean hillsides. None of the IIAA's two thousand projects could proceed until vetted by the State Department for budget, duration, and staffing requirements.

workers, nurses, doctors, midwives, sanitary engineers, and home demonstration agents. With the end of the war, much of this work was handed off to local agencies or entrusted to private groups. Long after propaganda broadcasts and Disney cartoons faded from memory, Latin Americans benefited from the brief but intense involvement of the United States with their continent. As a result, Rockefeller enjoyed a popularity among Latinos second only to Franklin Roosevelt. This mystified U.S. diplomat Spruille Braden, a frequent antagonist of the dollar-a-year man whom he succeeded in 1946 as assistant secretary of state for Latin American affairs. Yet even Braden grudgingly acknowledged the value of Rockefeller's *servicios*, pronouncing them "the only really good thing that," he recalled, "Nelson Rockefeller—did during the war." Nelson, predictably, took a more assertive line. "We haven't had decent relations with the Latin Americans since," he grumbled long afterward.

Nine

UNITED NATIONS

For sweet Christ's sake! Who is making the foreign policy around here anyway?

—Undersecretary of State Sumner Welles, July 1942

1

FRANKLIN ROOSEVELT WAS at his most disarming as he welcomed Rockefeller for an Oval Office *tour d'horizon* on May 19, 1943. Mention of the coordinator's recent travels to Brazil and Mexico sparked a flight of presidential fancy. Anticipating a peacetime surge in tourism south of the Rio Grande, FDR envisioned a host of smart new tourist hotels constructed with American tax dollars. Taking the hint, Rockefeller promised to return soon with a program. The conversation then pivoted to the Soviet Union and its postwar agenda. As long as Stalin ruled in the Kremlin, Roosevelt predicted, international Communism would be muted in its aggressiveness. Repeating the formula attributed to Maxim Litvinov, Soviet ambassador to the United States, the president told Rockefeller, "Communism has gone 20% of the way towards capitalism, and would go a total of 40%." As for the United States, since 1933 it had moved 20 percent toward Communism. Roosevelt expected it would go another 20 percent. "This would bring us in the 40–60 relationship," he concluded, "close enough so that we could have a working understanding between the two nations."

Yet even as Roosevelt assumed convergence of U.S. and Soviet interests, his protégé at the CIAA was girding for a different kind of combat. Where "liberal leadership" of the Americas was concerned, Rockefeller told the president, every country outside the hemisphere must take a backseat to the United States, "whether it was Russia or anyone else." This attitude would shape his course throughout the war, complicating efforts by Secretary of State Cordell Hull and Roosevelt himself to extend the U.S.-USSR alliance through a global peacekeeping organization, the contours and authority of which had yet to be defined. Sensitized to the issue of Communist subversion by his failed attempt to maintain an independent Lincoln School, Rockefeller began distributing copies of *Das Kapital* to co-workers. The threat was genuine, he concluded, and as proximate as the Rio Grande.

A decade had passed since Nelson's first trip to Mexico sparked a lifelong attachment to the country and its culture. When Roosevelt returned from his April 1943 cross-border summit with President Manuel Ávila Camacho, he appointed Nelson to a new Mexican-American Commission for Economic Cooperation. By the start of 1944, Rockefeller had twenty-two projects ready to proceed, with an additional $400 million in the pipeline. This put Mexico in the forefront of postwar economic planning, a process Rockefeller hoped to repeat in Brazil and other Latin nations. His vision was not widely shared. On Capitol Hill, Congressman Sol Bloom of New York complained that the coordinator was making a mess of things, thanks to "a lot of half-baked publicity men running around Latin America." Others questioned the military value of training two hundred meteorologists at a CIAA institute in Medellín, Colombia, or leasing the windswept Galápagos Islands, six hundred miles off the Ecuadorian coast. The latter Rockefeller brainstorm was shot down by the U.S. Air Force, which declared the islands worthless as a frontline defense for the Panama Canal.

It was Nelson's salvation that the person who mattered most emulated his expansive thinking. "That Basic Economy report is extraordinarily interesting and I hope that you can get some good Mexican stories written about it," FDR told him in June 1943. "I do want to get across the idea that the economic and social welfare of Jesus Fernandez in Brazil does affect the economy and social welfare of John Jones in Terre Haute, Indiana." Thus encouraged, Rockefeller submitted a ten-year, $3.5 billion blueprint for Latin American development. In the run-up to D-Day, however, the climate for social engineering was cooling. Moreover, by the summer of 1943 many of his strongest allies in the administration had either left their posts or were locked in fierce combat with bureaucratic rivals. That August, he sustained a major loss with the abrupt departure of Sumner Welles. For three years, Welles's enemies had assiduously circulated rumors shockingly at odds with his patrician façade. These concerned drunken advances the diplomat had allegedly made to Negro porters on board a presidential train returning from the September 1940 funeral of House Speaker William Bankhead.

FDR did his best to suppress the lurid story, but he was powerless to keep calculating men from gauging their chances should Welles be driven from office.* For Rockefeller, Welles's resignation removed a known, if prickly, quan-

---

* Fanning the controversy was William C. Bullitt, a born intriguer—and yet another Groton alumnus—whose undistinguished turns as U.S. ambassador in Moscow and Paris had done noth-

tity, someone with whom he had been able to do business. Far less flexible was Cordell Hull, whose passionate belief in an international peacekeeping organization made him unsympathetic toward Latin Americans and their regional loyalties. Argentina in particular remained a bone of contention, as the government of Ramon Castillo sheltered Nazi spies and welcomed German investment in shipping lines, banking, and pharmaceuticals. Stymied in its attempt to organize a neutral bloc with Chile, Paraguay, and Peru, Buenos Aires showed no inclination to honor even its modest promises made to the Allies at the 1942 Rio Conference. Eight months after a June 1943 army coup toppled Castillo, a second putsch installed the figurehead of General Edelmiro Farrell. Henceforth, real power was concentrated in the hands of Colonel Juan Domingo Perón, a fiery nationalist who filled dual roles as Argentine minister of war and vice president. Peronist truculence caused Hull to dig in his heels, even as it frustrated Rockefeller's pursuit of hemispheric unity. By the end of 1943, the secretary and the coordinator were on a collision course.

2

A N IRON LAW governed Nelson's wartime activities. "If you were close to the president, you were in," he remembered. "If you weren't, forget it, and I stayed close to the president for five years." Proximity was not to be confused with influence, a truth that eluded him as late as October 1944, when the Rockefellers joined Supreme Court justice William O. Douglas and his wife for a restful, if perplexing, weekend with Roosevelt at his Shangri-la retreat in the hills of western Maryland. Writing to his father, Nelson described a scene of pine-scented domesticity—the president reading his mail, Douglas listening to a football game on the radio, Tod and Mrs. Douglas in a leisurely perusal of the Sunday papers. "It's been very informal and pleasant," Rockefeller concluded, "but to tell you the truth I can't exactly see what's back of it as there has been no talk of anything specific."

Rockefeller, allergic to inactivity, could not imagine that an overworked chief executive might find temporary solace in a change of scene or a change of pace. His own workload remained formidable, even for a thirty-five-year-old

---

ing to diminish his appetite for Welles's job. His thinly veiled blackmail over Welles's sexual risk taking infuriated the president. So when Hull, his co-conspirator, approached Roosevelt about a fresh diplomatic posting for Bullitt, FDR rocked back in his chair and stared blankly at the Oval Office ceiling.

"That's right, Cordell," he said. "What about Liberia? I hear that's available." Benjamin Welles, *Sumner Welles: FDR's Global Strategist* (New York: St. Martin's Press, 1997), 27.

with a full tank of confidence. Prior to any appearance on Capitol Hill, Rockefeller was careful to memorize photos and biographies of every committee member before whom he testified. His dyslexia shaped his preparation in other ways as well. "He was a bear for figures," said John Lockwood. "He could never understand words. From numbers he understood." Beyond this, Nelson relied on charm to plane the rough edges of disagreement. When Senator Kenneth McKellar dismissed his talk of postwar challenges as premature, Rockefeller disarmed the irascible Tennessean with some bantering remarks. In time, McKellar became a valued ally. So did Harry Truman, chairman of the war production oversight committee that bore his name, who agreed to film a brief appeal for Pan American Week.

No one was more impressed by Nelson's deft handling of congressional showboaters than his father. "I could not have begun to do as well," Junior confessed. This did not prevent the old man from exercising an oversight, where his children's finances were concerned, as exacting as that of any committee chairman. Before 1944 ended, Nelson duly reported that his spending over the previous six years had exceeded his income by approximately $600,000. The establishment of trust funds for Tod and their children accounted for much of the shortfall. Setting him back another $150,000 was his latest architectural collaboration with Wally Harrison, a stunning twenty-one-room oceanfront home of concrete, wood, and glass (from the master bedroom, a ship's ladder ran down to a heated saltwater pool) at Seal Harbor on Mount Desert Island. Nearly as much went for art purchases and improvements to his Fifth Avenue apartment. Finally, Nelson revealed, he had donated 20 percent of his income to charitable causes and political candidates.

In response, a surprisingly mellow Junior wrote off the cumulative deficit as money "well invested, although the return from it is in health, pleasure and enjoyment of yourself and your family rather than in dollars and cents." Mindful perhaps of his own absence from the ranks in World War I, Junior acknowledged to Nelson "that again and again you have felt that you ought to be with your brothers in the armed forces and that your remaining where you are might be misunderstood." This was a sensitive subject. Twice the coordinator had gone to FDR offering to resign and enter active military service, only to be reminded that the president of the United States had selected him for his current post and would determine the best use of his talents. Roosevelt himself had been thwarted in a similar attempt to enlist during World War I, he told Nelson, with Woodrow Wilson insisting that his assistant secretary of the navy was more valuable behind a desk than in a foreign trench.*

---

* In trying to dissuade his CIAA colleague Jock Whitney from joining up, Nelson employed arguments he no doubt applied to himself. "Selective service means what it says—every man and

Junior provided reassurances of a different character, subscribing to $3 million of war bonds in Nelson's name. Other paternal concerns were addressed obliquely, if at all. On being designated Man of the Year by the Junior Chamber of Commerce, Nelson received a cautionary message from a parent whose pride rarely clouded his perspective. "The higher a man rises in public service," his father admonished him, "the more broadly his fellow men acclaim and honor him, the more essential it is that in both his public and private life his character be unimpeachable. May God give you the determination and the strength to be worthy of the confidence and esteem which is being accorded you in ever-increasing measure!" Was this a veiled reprimand for Nelson's marital faithlessness? It was not a subject either man could comfortably discuss.

In the first week of January 1944, George Marshall publicly urged Rockefeller's appointment as assistant secretary of state for Latin American affairs. With Welles out of the picture and Hull in declining health, the department appeared rudderless and adrift. Replacing Welles was Edward R. Stettinius, Jr., a former chairman of United States Steel who had emerged from one of Roosevelt's wartime reshuffles as Lend-Lease administrator. Forty-four years old, Stettinius was a natural conciliator. He had charm, good intentions, and, thanks to the steadily advancing Allied forces, a winning hand in the diplomatic poker games. With his bland features and prematurely white hair, he looked the part of diplomat, much as Warren Harding had looked like a president. To many he seemed likewise out of his depth.

As a fading Cordell Hull raced the clock to establish a universal peacekeeping organization, Rockefeller struggled to keep postwar Latin America from receding into irrelevance. His recipe for U.S. diplomacy after the war had a distinctly Latin flavor. The CIAA should be made permanent, he told Stettinius, with one person held to account for integrating all departmental activities, political and economic, pertaining to Latin America. Anything less would validate Nazi claims that the Good Neighbor policy was a mere wartime expedient. Stettinius bucked the memo to Laurence Duggan, a Welles holdover whose days at State were accordingly numbered. Ominously, the undersecretary did notify Rockefeller that his South American coordinating committees were to be mustered out of service.

Nelson had reason to be grateful to Stettinius for one thing, at least. W. Kenneth Riland was a native New Yorker and graduate of the Philadelphia College

---

woman at work in the job for which he is best fitted to perform in the common cause," he wrote. Whitney might disagree, "but I honestly think that one test of a man's courage is whether, having come to a clear and objective analysis of where his talents and experience can be most useful in this war, and having found an opportunity to use them he is able to resist the appeal of conventional glamour whether in the form of honors, display or conspicuous bravery." NAR–John Hay Whitney, May 1, 1942, NAR Personal Projects, Box 263, Folder 27, RAC.

of Osteopathic Medicine. After a brief period in private practice, Riland had gone to work for United States Steel. There he met, and manipulated, Stettinius, applying healing hands to reduce muscular tension and work-related ailments. The original osteopath, Dr. Andrew Taylor Still, had claimed that he could "shake a child and stop scarlet fever, croup, diphtheria, and cure whooping cough in three days by a wring of its neck." Only slightly less assertive about the benefits of osteopathy, Kenny Riland used manual therapies to achieve a "reaction" and bring about harmony between skeletal alignment and knotted muscles. When they first met, Rockefeller was suffering from acute lower back pain and a chronic sinus condition, both of which yielded to the osteopath's touch.

"He and I just hit it off like gangbusters," recalled Riland, who became, along with his portable table, an indispensable part of the coordinator's entourage. Several times a week, the man with the magic hands ministered to a patient whose continuing headaches and insomnia testified to his stressful existence. He didn't stop there. In an attempt to control Nelson's diet, Riland issued stern warnings, fiercely resisted by his patient, against mayonnaise, orange juice, and macadamia nuts. None of this affected their growing intimacy. From a distance, the two men could pass for twins; on more than one occasion, Riland was pressed into service as a Rockefeller stand-in, waving to happily deceived crowds. Though he refused to leave U.S. Steel for a full-time position on Nelson's payroll—realizing, even in the earliest stages of their relationship, that to do so would compromise his independence—Riland quickly established himself as a healer, sidekick, sounding board, and court jester. "I always treated him like one of the boys," said Riland of his new friend, "and he treated me like one of the boys."

3

ON THE AFTERNOON of June 5, 1944, Rockefeller was summoned to an emergency meeting at the War Department. His office was alerted not to expect the coordinator back that day. The next morning, he turned up rumpled and unshaven, but in buoyant spirits, having passed the night locked away with other officials to prevent compromising leaks as Allied forces stormed the beaches of Normandy. Heartening news from Europe was shadowed, however, by developments in Argentina. Hitler's fate might be sealed, but the colonels in Buenos Aires remained defiant. Indeed, four days after D-Day, Perón publicly called for mobilization of his country's armed forces to combat what he called Yankee imperialism. To Secretary Hull, this was tantamount to a declaration of war. He responded by recalling Ambassador Norman Armour and freezing Argentine gold reserves in the United States. The junta pronounced a retaliatory ban on American ships in Argentine ports.

Two days before the United States, Soviet Union, and Great Britain met at Washington's Dumbarton Oaks to draft an operational plan for the embryonic United Nations, Rockefeller again raised with Hull the vexing question of Argentina. Insisting that he shared the secretary's disdain for Perón, Nelson reminded the secretary that the United States each year bought Argentine products worth $300 million. It supplied millions more in Lend-Lease funds to Great Britain, which recycled them to import beef from the Argentine pampas. Hull's verbal thunderbolts aimed at the colonels in Buenos Aires would carry much greater moral force, Rockefeller argued, if Uncle Sam stopped doing business with them. Hull was unpersuaded. Suppose Rockefeller had his way and the flow of Argentine beef to British consumers was cut off; compensatory reductions in American diets would be unavoidable—starting with a one-quarter cut in already modest domestic meat rations. For U.S. politicians staring down the barrel of elections that fall, said Hull, the idea was laughable.

A resentful Nelson spent two weeks writing and rewriting a for-the-record letter to the secretary in which he detailed the department's alleged obstructionism. Before dispatching it on September 5, he was careful to get a presidential green light from Harry Hopkins. Two days later, Rockefeller sent Hull a second, unsigned letter, specifically decrying the stalemate over Argentina. Nelson resurrected his old fantasy of quitting a dead-end job and enlisting in the army as a private soldier. At the end of November 1944, ravaged by disease and embittered by the knowledge that he had been used as a prop in Roosevelt's hard-fought campaign for a fourth term against New York governor Thomas E. Dewey, Cordell Hull saved him the trouble by tendering his own resignation. The new secretary was Ed Stettinius. The day he was appointed, Stettinius phoned Rockefeller, then on a swing around the Caribbean, and asked him to return immediately to Washington. There he offered him the position of assistant secretary for Latin American affairs. (According to White House insiders, this was actually the president's doing, implemented over stiff objections from Stettinius.)

On December 4, Rockefeller's name was submitted to the Senate, part of a sweeping reorganization that made the old China hand Joseph C. Grew undersecretary, backed by six assistant secretaries—Dean Acheson, Will Clayton, James C. Dunn, General Julius C. Holmes, and Archibald MacLeish in addition to Nelson. Together with the underwhelming Stettinius, the new team was instantly, if unjustly, dubbed "Snow White and the Seven Dwarfs." There was audible disappointment on the left. Eleanor Roosevelt thought Tom Dewey might as well be president. Rockefeller, remembers one colleague, was "ecstatic" about the latest turn of events. With Wally Harrison stepping into his cast-off shoes as coordinator of inter-American affairs, Nelson saw an end to the intramural rivalries that had entangled Latin American policy making for years.*

Following his confirmation on December 20, he occupied a large corner office on the third floor of the same Victorian pile in which the CIAA had taken shape four years earlier. To mask the drabness of government-issue furniture and file cabinets, Nelson paid for a magnificent chandelier and desk and hung Venezuelan landscapes commissioned from artist Rainey Bennett. His elegant oval conference table became the talk of the building. Presidential assistant Jonathan Daniels heard about the makeover from a wide-eyed elevator operator. "You should have seen Mr. Rockefeller's dining room furniture," she told Daniels, who questioned what need an assistant secretary of state had for such furnishings.

"Oh, he's going to have a private dining room."

And what of the five other assistant secretaries? Daniels persisted.

"I reckon that if they know he is, they will."

Rockefeller controlled little outside his immediate environment. His wages being set by act of Congress, he couldn't even redirect his $9,000 salary to help defray the cost of official entertaining. Domestic politics and personal foibles imposed more serious restrictions. "He was never able to establish himself in the State Department as a mature, capable officer who saw the whole picture," according to Libby Shemwell. "His eyes were always on what he wanted to accomplish regardless of how it fit into the overall picture." Still clinging to the idea of economic sanctions on Argentina, Rockefeller calculated that by rationing soap and paint, the United States and its allies could forgo four hundred thousand tons of Argentine fats and oils. Out of the question, he was told. Before meeting with Lord Halifax, the British ambassador Nelson and Tod had first encountered a decade earlier on their honeymoon, he was admonished against raising the issue of an Argentine beef boycott.

Impatient with the status quo, Nelson began to practice his own brand of diplomacy, outside the fusty precincts of State. On December 21, he invited Latin American representatives to a strategic planning session over lunch at Foxhall Road. There his guests debated a call from Mexican foreign minister Ezequiel Padilla for a hemispheric conference in Mexico City to discuss post-

---

* On assuming his new position, Rockefeller made an appointment to see Wild Bill Donovan, by then a two-star general. "General," he said, "it seems to me that it's time we buried the hatchet. We're all working for the same war and the same country."

"I guess that's right," replied Donovan. The two men shook hands.

"We've been good friends ever since," said Rockefeller, a claim confirmed to the author by Donovan's postwar assistant William J. vanden Heuvel. NRI, CCOHC, 295.

war needs and whether Argentina should be asked to take part. Nelson took down in Spanish a conference agenda dictated by Chilean Marcial Mora; it practically duplicated an earlier draft he had prepared himself and kept in his pocket for just such an occasion. The issue of Argentine participation was finessed by limiting invitations to nations actively engaged in the war against Fascism.

On January 3, Rockefeller obtained FDR's blessing for the Mexico City gathering and for a secret mission to Buenos Aires testing Perón's protestations of good faith. His chosen emissary was Costa Rica's Rafael Oreamuno, chairman of the Inter-American Development Commission. Traveling to the Argentine capital on the pretext of commission business, Oreamuno was to offer Perón U.S. recognition if he transferred his powers to the Argentine Supreme Court, which would then oversee free and fair elections. In addition, Perón must declare war on the Axis, arrest Nazi agents in his country, and enforce the blacklist of firms sympathetic to the enemy. In retrospect, the scheme sounds naïve, reckless, or both. Even then it represented a high-stakes gamble by Rockefeller and the administration, the premature leak of which would have left both open to cries of appeasement.*

Yet the very boldness of the mission, Rockefeller wagered, would appeal to the president's love of covert operations. He bet correctly. A few days later, he returned to the Oval Office with a guest, former Colombian president Eduardo Santos. Concerned by the region's fragile balance of power and latest saber rattling, Santos dusted off an old Wilsonian proposal, first made in 1915, to guarantee national borders in a hemispheric treaty of nonaggression. Would the United States be willing to promote the idea at the forthcoming Mexico City conference? Roosevelt endorsed the concept on the spot, adding shrewdly that Santos's initiative would carry more weight if presented by Colombia rather than the United States. For a few minutes, the ailing president seemed revitalized by a discussion over the precise meaning of aggression. "How would you define attacked?" he mused, before answering his own question. "Well, I guess the simplest thing is if a man with a gun crosses the border."

Events would demonstrate that where the idea of a regional security pact was concerned, nothing was simple. Though Cordell Hull might be gone, his

---

* Nelson had already urged a joint State-FBI investigation of departmental leakers, only to be decisively outvoted by his colleagues. According to Rockefeller, his sole ally in the anti-leak campaign was Will Clayton. Acheson and MacLeish, he claimed, viewed the FBI as "a fascist organization." He couldn't help contrasting the differences between him and Clayton, alleged reactionaries, and department liberals such as Acheson and MacLeish. Of the latter he wrote, "They were strong believers in the people, but it seemed to be a theoretical interest . . . they both talked about the people with great facility and Archie wrote about them beautifully, but neither of them seemed to want to have actual contact with them. . . ." NRI, CCOHC, 434.

State Department heirs remained staunchly opposed to anything detracting from the police powers of the proposed United Nations, as exercised by an omnipotent Security Council. These included Leo Pasvolsky, a Russian-born émigré who headed the department's international division, and Alger Hiss, a well-connected lawyer-diplomat ensconced as the same division's executive secretary. Neither Pasvolsky nor Hiss welcomed Rockefeller's inter-American conference in Mexico City. They viewed it, rightly, as a platform from which to champion regional over global peacekeeping and as a vehicle enabling Perón's Argentina to escape retribution for its heavy flirtation with the Axis. Personal acrimony widened the gulf opened by professional disagreement. Rockefeller's easy access to the president grated on department veterans, as did his exclusionary approach to conference preparations. "These are the items we want on the agenda," he crisply informed John Lockwood. Nelson had no intention of ceding control of the Mexico City parley to the Hisses or Pasvolskys.

On January 20, 1945, the same day he was sworn into office for a fourth term, FDR approved a conference blueprint that balanced support for Dumbarton Oaks, with discussion of regional security, the joint guarantee of national boundaries, and U.S. assistance to smooth Latin America's postwar transition. Argentina alone remained beyond the pale. On February 14, Rockefeller agent Rafael Oreamuno sat down with Colonel Perón in his office at the Argentine Ministry of War. Beyond the mere fact of their meeting, the encounter produced no surprises. Declaring, "I can't turn the government over to a corpse," Perón rejected any notion of stepping aside in favor of ailing Supreme Court president Nicolás Repetto. Instead, said the colonel, he would submit to the freest, most honest elections in Argentine history, just as soon as the voting census and electoral code were completed.

A coded account of Oreamuno's talks reached Washington as Nelson was departing for Mexico City. "It is going to be an interesting but hectic three weeks," Rockefeller wrote his father, "and we have a great opportunity."

4

O N FEBRUARY 20, DELEGATES from twenty nations assembled at Chapultepec Castle, formerly home to Montezuma II and the upstart emperor Maximilian. Here, in September 1847 Mexican troops had made a last stand against American invaders commanded by General Winfield Scott. The symbolism was not lost on conference planners eager to put the past behind them. "It is sound diplomatic practice not to hold a conference unless you think you can reach an agreement," Rockefeller noted archly. "A conference for the purpose of quarreling is of very little use." For Nelson, Chapultepec was to be an exercise in confidence building, a task made all the more urgent by the snubbing of Latin America at Dumbarton Oaks. His personal agenda was simple: first, to secure enactment of the mutual security pact endorsed by FDR six weeks earlier; and second, to prevent anything, Argentina included, from interfering with the first.

Over the next two weeks, Rockefeller divided his time between the American delegation, with whom he nominally resided, and a second home at La Reforma, the hotel favored by Latin delegates. From FBI sources, he learned that the presidential suite reserved in his name was bugged, microphones having been planted in its walls during the hotel's construction. With a conspiratorial flourish, Nelson invited a group of Latin diplomats to join him on the terrace of La Reforma. There he revealed the presence of listening devices inside and the consequent need to install jamming equipment before they could engage in any substantive discussions. Nearby restaurants were similarly equipped for official eavesdropping. Wherever they dined, Rockefeller advised his guests, they should avoid tables or booths suggested by the maître d'hôtel.

He failed to mention a much larger surveillance effort being masterminded by J. Edgar Hoover, whose operatives were ensconced in the Mexico City telephone department and other strategic locations around town. As Nelson recalled it, they "did a damn good job," supplying him with daily briefings informed by delegate gossip as well as more official communications. Even before arriving in Mexico City, Rockefeller had picked up disquieting signals about the foreign minister of Colombia, a charismatic former journalist named Alberto Lleras Camargo. By questioning the blatant disregard of Latin America at Dumbarton Oaks, Lleras Camargo offered a potential rallying point for those resentful of U.S. dominance or the concentration of power enshrined in the putative Security Council.

Conspicuous by its absence from Mexico City, Argentina was very much on delegates' minds. Scarcely were his bags unpacked before Rockefeller convened a group of diplomats to review the issue. Unaware of the furtive U.S.-sponsored mission that had already ended in failure, Lleras Camargo called for a direct, Latin-generated approach to Perón. Even as he did so, however, he expressed doubts the Americans would go along. "I am not so sure," Rockefeller told him airily. "Why don't I cable President Roosevelt and ask him?" Armed with Oreamuno's report of his secret meetings with Perón, Nelson had nothing to lose, and much to gain, from any Latin initiative that deferred the contentious issue of Argentina. Pleasantly surprised by the cooperative attitude of his American counterpart, Lleras Camargo removed his suit coat and seated himself at a typewriter to compose a list of conditions. These turned out to be a virtual carbon copy of the terms already offered Perón on Nelson's behalf and rejected by the Argentine strongman. A Peruvian delegate volunteered to transmit the document to Buenos Aires.

Rockefeller could not have scripted a better opening to the conference had he written it himself, which, in a way, he had. For with Argentina relegated to the back burner, delegates were free to concentrate on his preferred issue of regional security. His contentment was not universally shared. Flying into Mexico City from Yalta, an overworked Ed Stettinius criticized his deputy's latest backdoor approach to the Roosevelt White House. But when FDR endorsed the Rockefeller ploy, Stettinius had no choice but to go along. Other members of the U.S. delegation took issue with Rockefeller's unrelenting advocacy of Latin interests. Internationalists like Pasvolsky and Hiss feared that the cause of global peacekeeping advanced at Dumbarton Oaks might be sacrificed to purely regional loyalties. Nelson argued just the opposite. By fostering a sense of security within their own backyard, he insisted, a hemispheric nonaggression pact could actually make it easier for Latin nations to accept a world body dominated by a handful of larger powers.

By the morning of February 27, weary delegates had hammered out a draft of what would become known as the Act of Chapultepec, proclaiming an attack on any nation in the hemisphere to be an attack on all. A Cuban diplomat, riding a wave of festivity, moved the immediate adoption of the compromise document. Before the train could leave the station, however, its brakes were applied by Senator Warren Austin, a liberal Republican from Vermont, whose internationalism was well seasoned by Yankee practicality. With Nelson out of the room, Austin requested a twenty-four-hour postponement to allow for translation of the agreement into English. His senatorial colleague, Democrat Tom Connally of Texas, had been delayed in reaching Mexico City, and the deferral would give Connally time to familiarize himself with the document. This was a stall, pure and simple, by a lawmaker who grasped instinctively the dangers lurking in the Act of Chapultepec and its putative guarantee of national boundaries. Under the U.S. Constitution, only Congress could authorize military action involving American forces. And members of Congress, even relatively enlightened ones like Austin and Connally, were loath to cede power to the White House, let alone a world parliament. Indeed, it was on these same treacherous rocks that Wilson's peacekeeping league had foundered a quarter century before.

February 28 witnessed the stormiest session yet within the American delegation, as Pasvolsky and other globalists were vigorously rebutted by regionalists, Rockefeller among them. To Nelson it was an open-and-shut case. By the logic of his opponents, the United States could not legally repel an attack on the Panama Canal without first obtaining Security Council approval. Echoing his views were military representatives, led by General Stanley Embick of the Joint

Chiefs of Staff, for whom the principle of hemispheric self-defense was insepa-rable from the Monroe Doctrine. Emotions boiled over as a red-faced Pasvolsky demanded that Nelson return to Washington and obtain formal authorization for his regional security pact. But he already possessed the only sanction that counted, said Rockefeller, waving the document carrying the initials *FDR*. Turning the tables, he threatened Hiss and Pasvolsky with ejection unless they muted their opposition. "You have got your own conference in San Francisco," Nelson muttered, referring to the upcoming gathering of nations to formally inaugurate the UN. Chapultepec was *his* show.

It was at this juncture that a tired and cranky Tom Connally finally reached Mexico City, and Rockefeller almost outsmarted himself. All his life, he har-bored a child's delight in secrets. Like a child, he derived such pleasure from whispered confidences that he couldn't resist whispering them to others. His background press conferences for sixty-five American reporters, few of them conversant in Spanish, were credited for the largely positive coverage Chapulte-pec received back home. Now, anxious to lock in a deal on his regional alli-ance, Nelson had Frank Jamieson leak the story to James ("Scotty") Reston of *The New York Times*. Rockefeller was careful to note that nothing could be fi-nalized until Senator Connally gave his imprimatur. This proved more elusive than anticipated. He would be "goddamned," a surly Connally told Nelson, if he was going to transact any business until the next day. Belatedly alerted to his peril, Rockefeller appealed to Reston to hold the story for twenty-four hours. "I'm afraid I can't," said Reston. "I thought this was in the bag. I may have been a little ahead of myself, but I wanted to get it up there and I'm sure it's too late to stop it." The next morning, his scoop took pride of place on the front page of the *Times*.

For Nelson, the ensuing twelve hours were among the longest of his life, requiring frantic efforts to keep the paper out of Connally's hands, at least until the chairman of the Senate Foreign Relations Committee could be won over to the position implicitly endorsed in Reston's lead. Ultimately, it was compromise language offered by Senator Austin that soothed congressional objections with-out offending Latin sensibilities. With Solomon-like dexterity, Austin split the Act of Chapultepec into two parts, the first formalizing a wartime alliance—which had the added desirability of spotlighting noncompliance by Argentina—and the second pledging signatories after the war to enact a security treaty consistent with any international peacekeeping organization to emerge from San Francisco.

In reality, Austin did not buy time so much as he borrowed it. In kicking the ball down the field, he afforded Pasvolsky and Hiss a second chance, at the upcoming UN conference in San Francisco, to scuttle Nelson's regional ar-rangements. On Argentina, too, a diplomatic straddle merely postponed the unpleasant. For the better part of two weeks, delegates had been pestering their Peruvian colleague for any news from Buenos Aires. Now, as the conference entered its final weekend, he had some astonishing intelligence to impart: Perón had rejected the olive branch extended by his Latin neighbors. A fresh resolution treated Argentina as a wayward family member,. whose misguided leaders might yet be compelled by popular pressure to make war on the crumbling Axis. Senator Austin was less accommodating. Merely hoping Perón would join the Allied war effort was not a policy Austin could support. The onus of proof lay squarely with Buenos Aires. At a concluding press conference Rockefeller fudged the issue, his evasions in line with the deliberately ambiguous language of the resolution itself.

5

ON MARCH 9, NELSON left Mexico City for Washington with Stettinius. Almost immediately he entertained second thoughts about what had been done—and left undone—at Chapultepec. Together with his Brazilian counterpart, Rockefeller hastily convened an informal Latin summit on March 14. Fifteen nations meeting at Washington's Blair House renewed their invitation for Argentina to sign the Act of Chapultepec. In return for joining the war effort, the Perón regime would be accorded formal recognition. Of equal importance, the United States would recommend that Argentina be permitted to add its name to the United Nations Declaration. This formula won quick endorsement by the Pan American Union and a State Department staff committee.

On March 16, it was ratified by FDR. That morning, Rockefeller entered the Roosevelt Oval Office for the final time. He found the president sadly diminished. "For the first time I saw him momentarily without a spark or glimmer of life," said Nelson. Still, the old enthusiasm about the Americas flared, along with the urbane pleasure in subterfuge as Rockefeller described the twists and turns of conference politics. Based on what he had seen at Yalta, Roosevelt expressed confidence that future global leadership would rest with the New World. The following evening, Nelson was back at the White House. Along with Tod, he joined a small group invited to celebrate the Roosevelts' fortieth wedding anniversary. For a few hours concerns of state evaporated, and a desperate gaiety filled the room. Over dinner, Tod, a passionate gardener, engaged Supreme Court justice Robert Jackson in spirited debate about the fertilizing virtues of hen versus horse manure. FDR beamed.

As the war in Europe entered its final days, Rockefeller's persistent courtship of Argentina seemed validated. In the last week of March, the colonels in Buenos Aires declared war on the Axis and moved to freeze the assets of German and Japanese firms doing business in their country. In response, the United States and its sister American republics joined Great Britain and France in formally recognizing the Peronist regime. On April 10, Rockefeller left the capital for a series of speaking engagements. Thus he was out of town two days later, when Roosevelt died at Warm Springs, Georgia. The city to which he returned throbbed with conflicting emotions, anticipation of imminent victory on the European front muffled by sorrow over the death of its warlord. The grief was genuine—Nelson himself was overcome as he stood on the north lawn of the White House, watching Franklin Roosevelt's final departure—but so was the uncertainty caused by the sudden disappearance of the president, Moses-like, at the entrance to a promised land whose boundaries appeared hazier than ever.

One thing seemed certain to Rockefeller: Without FDR, Ed Stettinius appeared lost. As for the new president, said Nelson, "he knew even less than Ed did." (Truman once greeted a Bolivian diplomat to the Oval Office by remarking, "I remember you; you are the man who plays a piano and whose country needs an outlet to the sea.") At a department meeting on April 14, Rockefeller claimed Roosevelt's support for admitting the Perón government to the United Nations. Assistant Secretary Jimmy Dunn asked to see the Blair House agreement initialed by FDR. It didn't take him long to find the loophole he sought. There was no time commitment spelled out in the Rockefeller memorandum, said Dunn. Considering the long history of Argentine duplicity, he urged postponement of any invitation until Buenos Aires supplied convincing evidence of its good faith. Acheson and MacLeish strongly seconded this view.

But American honor was at stake, Rockefeller argued, no less than American interests. The specter of broken promises would surely complicate hemispheric relations, without dissuading Argentina's embittered neighbors from raising the membership issue on their own at San Francisco. The exchange grew heated. Stettinius counseled delay. British foreign secretary Anthony Eden was coming to Washington in a matter of days, he said. Why not revisit the question then? On April 18, determined to vindicate his forecast of Argentine cooperation, Rockefeller dispatched Avra Warren, a gruff former envoy to Panama and the Dominican Republic, to Buenos Aires. Over the course of three days, Warren obtained renewed assurances that the Chapultepec commitments would be honored, interspersed with fierce complaints about U.S. support of anti-Perón elements. Never was the Janus face of Peronism so brazenly displayed. After informing Warren of recent conversations with Soviet representatives in Montevideo, Perón requested American trucks, merchant ships, and fuel, along with the diversion of Brazilian rubber to his own use. The Warren mission did nothing to bolster Nelson's tenuous position at State.

Equally disheartening was his encounter with Stettinius and British foreign secretary Anthony Eden. "Here are these two frightened and mousey guys, they don't know what to do, and they had just won the war!" he marveled. Adding to their fears, real or imagined, was the presence in Washington of Soviet foreign minister Vyacheslav Molotov, who had come to press his country's claims on behalf of the puppet Lublin government of Poland. At Yalta, Stalin had given his blessing to a deliberately vague formula promising free elections in the new Poland, where a regime beholden to Moscow was committed to incorporating representatives of the London-based government-in-exile. Any likelihood of enforcing the pledge expired with Roosevelt. Now, as Rockefeller's eyes widened in disbelief, Stettinius asked Eden if he would raise the Argentine question with Molotov. The British foreign secretary replied that he saw no reason why he should.* Nelson interrupted the *Alphonse and Gaston* act long enough to inject some hard numbers, reminding Eden and Stettinius that Latin America represented almost half of the fifty nations attending the conference. "You are not going to be able to do anything without their support," he pointed out. Why not let the Soviets be the ones to reject Argentina, isolating themselves while strengthening hemispheric unity? His plea fell on deaf ears.

Informed that he would not be part of the U.S. delegation to the upcoming conference, Nelson resolved to go anyway, if necessary as one of several hundred accredited observers and "correspondents" (among them his old sparring partner Orson Welles, actress Lana Turner, and a politically ambitious young war hero named John F. Kennedy). In the end, his threat evaporated, as Stettinius, in need of allies to resist escalating Soviet demands, surrendered to the arithmetic of Us versus Them. Whatever baggage Nelson carried, concluded the secretary, it was more than outweighed by the votes he could deliver. Such, at least, was the Rockefeller version of how he came to be in San Francisco the last week of April 1945. Actually, his belated inclusion in the American delegation owed more to a talent for infighting than it did to any last minute conversion by Stettinius. On discovering that General Stanley Embick, his Pentagon ally at Mexico City, had likewise been excluded from San Francisco, Nelson went "quietly but directly" to the War Department. Whatever happened in the city by the bay was bound to affect American national security, he reminded Embick. By keeping the generals in the dark, the globalists had overplayed their hand. Thus Stettinius came under pressure to include Embick just as

---

* Here memories differed. Stettinius reported discussing the issue of Argentine membership in the UN with his British counterpart on April 17, at which time Eden agreed to raise the subject with both the Soviet and the Chinese foreign ministers.

Molotov turned up the heat to win recognition for his Polish clients. Not for the last time, the blustery Soviet diplomat proved to be his own worst enemy. Both Embick and Rockefeller were added to the U.S. roster.

6

O**N APRIL 21, NELSON** boarded another chartered plane crowded with Latin diplomats and flew to the West Coast. He might be excused a sense of déjà vu, for in many respects the UN conference offered a reprise of issues, personalities, and tactics first glimpsed at Chapultepec, even if the expanded cast of players was contending for immeasurably greater stakes.

- THE SOVIET UNION: Harboring meager expectations for the world body, Stalin at the last minute sent Foreign Minister Molotov to San Francisco out of respect for FDR's memory. If they were going to participate at all, the Soviets wanted voting privileges for multiple members of their confederation. If they could at the same time legitimize their Polish client state, nucleus of an Eastern European empire in the making, so much the better.
- THE UNITED STATES: American ambitions were fragmented, with congressional representatives on guard against any dilution of U.S. sovereignty, a position backed by Pentagon representatives—and just as fervently disputed by State Department globalists.
- LATIN AMERICA: United in opposition to the veto power reserved for Security Council kingpins, the Latin bloc was equally determined to include in the UN Charter the regional security arrangements set forth in the Act of Chapultepec.
- ARGENTINA: Like the opportunistic cuttlefish that attaches itself to a larger predator, the Peronist regime hoped to exploit emerging rivalries among the wartime Allies, gaining a place in the world body, and the respectability it implied, on the cheap.

This by no means exhausted the list of those jockeying for advantage against the purple-and-gold splendor of San Francisco's Opera House. Among the emerging nations resolved to play an independent role in the drama ostensibly scripted by the victorious Big Three was an Arab bloc, as well as imperial spin-offs such as Australia. As he had in Mexico City, Rockefeller shuttled between his own country's delegation at the Fairmount and Latin American representatives housed at the St. Francis Hotel. He received the same early morning briefings from FBI agents, who one day offered startling evidence that Alger Hiss, the conference secretary-general, was "working hand in glove with the Soviets."*

For the next two months, Nelson alternated nonstop politicking with lavish entertainments. One evening he rented the St. Francis Yacht Club for an elaborate dinner featuring Carmen Miranda, the fruit-bedecked entertainer who took it upon herself to rearrange place cards at the last minute. Afterward there was dancing until three in the morning. At daily meetings of his Latin American caucus, Rockefeller left the hustling for votes to others. "Every time Pedro [Baltrán, of Peru] took a position that was the position. If he said anything we had twenty votes just like that," he said afterward. Should a dispute arise, "I had it worked out with the Latins. We never would . . . ask for their votes unless it was necessary, and anybody who had a problem at home politically, they could forget it." Rockefeller shared Latin suspicions of the proposed Security Council and the veto power accorded its permanent members. His reasoning amounted to an early draft of the domino theory. Imagine even one South American nation falling victim to Communist subversion—what was to prevent the Soviet Union from vetoing UN assistance to anti-Communist forces in its suddenly vulnerable neighbors?

With equal fervor, the internationalists at State labored to prevent San Francisco from becoming the graveyard of the Grand Alliance already strained at Yalta. Their work was cut out for them, especially where congressional members of the U.S. delegation were concerned. Reprising his role at Mexico City, Tom Connally was on hand to guard against a repeat of Woodrow Wilson's League of Nations. This time, Connally was joined by an equally powerful Republican lawmaker, armed with an astonishing admission from the dying FDR. Shut out of the proceedings at Chapultepec, Arthur Vandenberg had agreed to participate in the San Francisco gathering at the personal request of the late president, who had taken with him to Yalta fifty copies of the senator's recent address setting aside his earlier isolationism. Rockefeller quickly established a relationship with the owlish senator from Michigan, close enough for Vandenberg to confide details of a White House meeting at which the president acknowledged having miscalculated his ability to handle Stalin. Alarmed by the possible consequences of Soviet intransigence at San Francisco, Roosevelt had asked the self-regarding Vandenberg to join the American contingent there as "the only person whom they [the Soviets] feared." The exchange,

---

* "I didn't dare tell anybody," Nelson said afterward, his hard-line deputy Avra Warren excepted. "They already thought I was too tough anyhow and because of my relations with Argentina they suspected that I was a fascist." As for Hiss, "We never got along," Rockefeller acknowledged. "I didn't like him and he didn't like me, but I could have said that about a lot of people in State." Eventually he did pass the explosive information on to John Foster Dulles, by then Hiss's employer at the Carnegie Endowment for International Peace. Dulles rejected the story out of hand.

if it ever took place, reveals as much about senatorial vanity as presidential modesty. It effectively dispels the view that Roosevelt at twilight had forfeited his matchless ability to manipulate men to carry out his bidding and think it their own.

In reality, no one did more to maintain the fragile unity of the U.S. delegation than the abrasive foreign minister of the Soviet Union. From the outset, Molotov appeared determined to make himself, and his government, as noxious as possible. He stonily demanded admission of the Communist-backed World Federation of Trade Unions. When this was rejected, he switched gears, bringing up Allied pledges at Yalta to award voting rights to the Soviet republics of Byelorussia and Ukraine, which he compared with India and the Philippines, two client states granted voting privileges at the request of Great Britain and the United States. With the possibility of a Soviet walkout judged real, neither Stettinius nor Eden was in a mood to resist. Molotov found the South Americans made of sterner stuff. At an April 28 meeting called to discuss Argentina, the Soviet diplomat offered representatives of Mexico, Brazil, and Chile a deal.

"I will support the admission of Argentina," he told them, "if you will support the admission of the Lublin government."

This classic bait and switch found no takers. Molotov, his hopes of splitting the hemispheric alliance dashed, launched into a fiery denunciation of Argentina and its wartime perfidy. The meeting broke up inconclusively. Two days later, the United States tabled an Executive Committee motion to admit the two Russian states as requested by Molotov. It passed without dissent. Ezequiel Padilla then moved to invite Argentina. Molotov, according to Rockefeller, "went through his prescribed song and dance" on Poland, before losing on a vote of 8 to 3. Receiving reporters at his hotel, Molotov was the picture of calm moderation. He said he desired nothing more than a few days in which members could ponder the Argentine issue. Before the General Assembly, however, he reverted to form, quoting back Hull's anathemas on the regime in Buenos Aires while the Americans squirmed in embarrassment.

Rockefeller pressed Stettinius to play his ace card. "Get up and tell them the deal that he offered. . . . All you have to say is that they told us they would agree to it if we would let the Lublin government in." Stettinius would do nothing of the sort. Instead, when his turn came, he stressed the pledges made by his government at Mexico City and subsequently endorsed by Roosevelt. The sheer weight of numbers ensured a lopsided roll call in favor of the U.S. position. By a margin of 31 to 4, Argentina was admitted to the United Nations. That same evening, Nelson left San Francisco for a quick trip to Washington and a previously scheduled appearance before the House Appropriations Committee. Leaked versions of his testimony included the impolitic boast that by securing

UN membership for Argentina, the United States had solidified a hemispheric bloc with which to oppose any further encroachments by the Soviets.*

This was not a view held by his superiors back in San Francisco. The Soviets wanted permission to form military alliances with neighboring countries, part of a larger security system aimed at Germany as a "former enemy state." A similar proviso would authorize the Soviet Union and China to link arms in resistance to a resurgent Japan. In the days leading up to his Washington trip, Rockefeller had seen in these demands an opening tailor-made for his Latin American regional pact. "Look, this is easy," he counseled Stettinius. "We can make a trade. . . . You get a clause that permits us in the Western Hemisphere to act and then you can agree to the Soviets' position and we can trade the two off."

Upon returning to San Francisco on May 5, Rockefeller was dismayed to learn that Stettinius had given ground to the Soviets without exacting similar concessions on Chapultepec. He tried to see the secretary, who, pleading exhaustion, fobbed him off on Jimmy Dunn or Leo Pasvolsky. Recognizing this as tantamount to surrender, Nelson invited Senator Vandenberg to dinner at the St. Francis. There he recounted for his friend the origins of the regional security alliance adopted at Mexico City and its significance to the Latins as a bulwark against Communist subversion. The restive republics were up in arms, Rockefeller confided to the senator. He didn't forget to mention the Monroe Doctrine.

"Have you got a secretary I can dictate to?" asked Vandenberg.

Rockefeller staffer Susan Cable, her recently deceased father among the senator's closest friends, was on hand for just such a contingency. So while she fought back tears caused by Vandenberg's cigar smoke and the paternal memories it evoked, the Michigan lawmaker reverted to his nationalist self in a letter that carried the unmistakable threat of congressional repudiation unless the UN charter was amended to reflect the Act of Chapultepec. The conference had made an exception for European and Asian alliances directed at former Axis powers. Now Vandenberg demanded similar treatment for the Western Hemisphere. Alberto Lleras Camargo pronounced the Vandenberg draft "beautiful." Other characterizations suggested themselves to John Foster Dulles, the heavily credentialed secretary of state in waiting, who had emerged from Tom Dewey's 1944 campaign as a leading advocate of bipartisan foreign policy. The mere sight of Rockefeller unleashed a stream of invective surprising in a Presbyterian churchman of his standing. He had been sent to San Fran-

---

* Perhaps to counter the negative press growing out of his very public campaign to welcome Buenos Aires into the fold, Rockefeller supported a Mexican initiative to exclude the Fascist regime of Spain's Francisco Franco from the United Nations.

cisco, Dulles shouted, expressly "to keep Senator Vandenberg from doing some goddamned thing." Now Rockefeller's backstage meddling threatened to undermine nothing less than "the whole future security of the world." It was the last occasion for ten days that Dulles spoke to him.

Hardly more forthcoming was Vandenberg's prospective rival for the 1948 Republican presidential nod, Harold Stassen. Not yet the chronic campaigner of later years, ridiculed for his quadrennial seizures of self-delusion, Stassen was understandably reluctant to get into the same hot water as Vandenberg. Rockefeller appealed to his vanity, telling the former boy wonder of Minnesota politics, "You are the only one that is bright enough in this delegation to figure out how to solve this problem." Finally, Stassen agreed to have dinner with him.

"I was so mad by that time," Nelson later recalled. "So I started out, 'Harold, how did it happen you got into politics?'" By the dessert course, Stassen was asking, "Don't you want to talk about this problem on mutual security?"

Well, yes, allowed Rockefeller, he'd be happy to if that was what his guest wanted.

It just so happened that Stassen had been giving thought to the knotty issue, his ruminations coalescing around the right of self-defense, as ancient as Roman law. Under the Stassen formula, nothing in the proposed UN charter should abrogate the inherent right of nations to defend themselves, at least until the Security Council chose to act.

"Harold, you have got it."

In time, a mollified Dulles came forward with language of his own to help bridge Dumbarton Oaks and the Act of Chapultepec. Although this satisfied the American contingent, others remained steadfast in opposing any mention of Chapultepec in the UN Charter. "Either we have a world organization or we don't," maintained Anthony Eden. Even Vandenberg, at a raucous meeting of the U.S. delegation, declared himself sick of the Latin Americans "pushing us around." At this inopportune moment, a dustup over intelligence rekindled memories of Nelson's near disastrous leak to *The New York Times* at Mexico City. "You have had it. You are going to be sent back," Jimmy Dunn casually informed his rival one morning. Pressed for details, Dunn claimed that Stettinius was livid over the intercept of some anti-Soviet remarks made by Nelson to his Latin caucus. Rockefeller wasted no time in dispatching his trusted agent Avra Warren to the code-breaking room, where FBI agents read delegates' incoming and outgoing messages. On his own he tracked down Stettinius, who denied seeing the offending cable in question but upbraided Nelson anyway for his undiplomatic language.

For three weeks at San Francisco, the Latins had given invaluable support to their American hosts, putting aside grave doubts about the veto and Security Council. In return for this, the draft UN charter contained no explicit recognition of Chapultepec, only the right of self-defense clause found in the Rocke-feller/Stassen-inspired Article 51. On May 15, at an emotional confrontation in Stettinius's suite at the Fairmount, restless members of the Latin bloc called in their chits. Their demands included a fixed time and place for the promised regional conference, along with guarantees of a treaty implementing the Act of Chapultepec. Not satisfied with endorsements from the U.S. delegation, they sought the imprimatur of President Truman as well. Absenting himself from the ongoing discussion, Stettinius motioned for Nelson to join him in his bed-room.

"Will you come and talk to Truman because I don't really understand all this stuff?"

The presidential blessing was quickly obtained. The next day, Stettinius, ratifying a deal negotiated between Rockefeller and Brazil's foreign minister, pledged himself and his government to attend a meeting in Rio no later than August 1945. When even this concession proved insufficient to quiet Latin res-ervations about the veto, it prompted fresh outbursts in the U.S. delegation. Again Rockefeller sided with Latin America against his State Department col-leagues. Only after the veto was grudgingly approved in the closing days of the conference did he realize he had gone too far. For weeks, Leo Pasvolsky had made it his daily practice to telephone the ailing Cordell Hull at Bethesda Naval Hospital and pour into his ear the latest betrayal carried out by "Little Rockefeller." Now, anxious to repair the breach, Nelson asked a friend to ar-range a hospital visit with Hull. A preliminary phone call was duly placed and the receiver held out so that the assistant secretary could hear the old man's response: "You can tell the young whippersnapper to go to Hell."*

7

IF STETTINIUS HAD appeared distracted in San Francisco, he had good rea-son. Rumors of his pending replacement by Truman favorite Jimmy Byrnes

---

* This pretty much summed up the attitude of the diplomatic establishment with which Rocke-feller had so often crossed swords. Dean Acheson never acknowledged Article 51 as the founda-tion on which he and Harry Truman, powerfully backed by Vandenberg and other internationalist Republicans, erected the Truman Doctrine, NATO, and other Cold War expedi-ents to keep the Russian bear at bay. John Foster Dulles, who would succeed Acheson as secretary of state in 1953, was more generous. Finding himself at a New York dinner seated beside his onetime adversary, Dulles said he owed him an apology.

"What for?" asked Nelson.

"Well . . . if it hadn't been for you there would have been no NATO, no SEATO, no Rio Pact."

had rattled throughout the conference. These were gracelessly confirmed on June 27, when a presidential emissary conveyed the grim news to the returning secretary, as Rockefeller looked on, at Washington's National Airport. Nelson had no intention of falling victim to what he called "the usual Washington firing." To be sure, he had submitted his resignation, as courtesy dictated, on the death of Franklin Roosevelt. But that was a mere formality. Americans might be eager to demobilize and Congress anxious to eliminate wartime agencies like the Office of Inter-American Affairs. But Rockefeller was too emotionally invested in Latin America, had too many schemes to finish, repair, or justify, to walk the plank after six stormy months as assistant secretary.

In Buenos Aires, the faithless Perón was waving the bloody shirt of foreign intervention in the run-up to national elections set for February 1946. Rockefeller proposed a series of speeches to explain his actions toward Argentina and, hopefully, rally other nations in the hemisphere to exert continued pressure on the Perón regime. Undersecretary Joseph Grew, to whom he first broached the idea, advised caution pending the return of Secretary Byrnes from the Potsdam Conference, at which Truman, Stalin, and Churchill discussed the future of Europe and a climactic assault on imperial Japan. No fan of Byrnes ("a reconciler rather than a taker of positions"), Rockefeller repeatedly sought a meeting with the secretary, whose attention, unsurprisingly, was focused elsewhere. Hard on the heels of Potsdam came the atomic explosions at Hiroshima and Nagasaki, forerunner to Japanese surrender on August 14.

Heedless of these demands, Nelson sent Byrnes the text of a major address he was to deliver to the Pan American Society of Massachusetts and Northern New England. On August 23, the day before his scheduled appearance in Boston, he got his appointment. Byrnes complimented Rockefeller on his text. Unfortunately, he went on, it was so much wasted effort, given the president's knowledge of his wish to be relieved.

"You know that is not true," replied Nelson. "I don't want to be relieved."

His wishes didn't really matter, said the secretary. "The president is accepting your resignation."

Rockefeller's face hardened. "Fine," he told Byrnes. In that case he would make an address as a private citizen. "I will tell the truth about what has happened since you took office. I don't think it will be a speech you will be crazy about. Or I will make this speech which I am planning to make as assistant secretary." Byrnes beat a strategic retreat. Nelson could deliver his speech; the announcement of his resignation would be held until the next day. With this parting blast, Latin America's most outspoken champion in the State Department burned his bridges in order to make his point. It was getting to be a habit. If not exactly a loose cannon, Nelson cannot be said to have been a team player—unless, of course, the team was his own. When he returned to Washington, he saw Truman, whose attitude toward Rockefeller may well have been colored by an incident reflecting little credit on either man.

At once a farsighted statesman and a by-product of Missouri's notorious Pendergast machine, Truman had asked Nelson to find a job for Tom Pendergast's nephew. In reply, Rockefeller said that John Lockwood of his staff would gladly meet with the younger Pendergast to determine his qualifications for State Department employment. The sequel to this wary exchange should have come as no surprise to anyone, least of all Nelson. "He wrote back one of the typical Truman letters saying he wouldn't recommend somebody who didn't have qualifications." Later that same week, the Pendergast file disappeared from his office—"stolen out of our file cabinet," Rockefeller claimed. Now, alone with Truman in the Oval Office, Nelson made a halfhearted plea to keep his job, reassuring the president that he respected him no less than his predecessor. A visibly uncomfortable Truman sat at his desk, "tearing up little pieces of paper like a schoolboy caught with his hand in the cookie jar." Rockefeller got up and left.

The next morning, Libby Shemwell delivered a White House letter to the disconsolate group assembled in Nelson's office. "Well, gentlemen, here it is," she blurted out, then fled the room in tears. Within a week, the Rockefeller suite, occupied barely eight months, was stripped of furniture, chandelier, and paintings. Personal files filling fourteen packing cases were prepared for shipment to New York. For the moment, Nelson was unemployed and without plans for the future. None who knew him expected either condition to last very long. From Beardsley Ruml came a mischievous invitation to "resume the conspiracy where we left off." Nelson responded in character, describing his Washington interlude as a great adventure and concluding, "I am all set to start the next conspiracy!"

Ten

TOO MUCH, TOO SOON

Capitalism is a very useful tool to achieve objectives; but the objectives are people.

—NELSON A. ROCKEFELLER

1

IN THE WAKE of his firing, no message supplied more healing balm than one dispatched from 740 Park Avenue the night of August 25, 1945. "No soldier at the front, however brave, has rendered a greater service to his country than you have in your war work now so creditably concluded," it read. "You have added new luster to the family name. We are very proud and very humble. . . . Your position as President of the Center is waiting for you. Your return to the office will be a happy day for me. I need you and have untold confidence in you. . . . With a heart full of love, Father."

To resume oversight of Rockefeller Center might be thought a distinct comedown after the heady atmosphere of the Roosevelt White House or a seat at the table with architects of the postwar world. Nelson, however, refused to consider himself demoted. On the contrary, the city to which he returned in September 1945 glittered with possibilities. "New York City in 1945 was the most successful place on earth," according to Daniel Patrick Moynihan, "and in terms of its size and population, the most successful place in history." A generation had passed since H. L. Mencken likened New York to "the icing on the pie called Christian civilization" and voters had repudiated Al Smith, the raspy-voiced personification of a city they judged too alien to send one of its own to the White House.

In 1945, one out of every nine Americans lived in the Empire State; one in seventeen called the five boroughs of New York City home. The island of Manhattan sent more representatives to Congress than did Florida. Certainly Mencken's boast would have met with little dissent from the 1.3 million factory workers (twice the number employed in service industries) who made New York a global hub of manufacturing. The nation's unquestioned media capital, headquarters for forty-one of its hundred largest industrial companies, the Big Apple chalked up one-fifth of America's wholesale trade. It welcomed more oceangoing vessels, published more books, conducted more financial transactions, and influenced more policy makers than any city but London at its imperial zenith.

Nelson Rockefeller returned to a town, already fabled, that looked to the future with more than its customary swagger. "You ain't heard or seen nothing yet," cackled Fiorello La Guardia. Ironically, the Little Flower had exhausted himself, and his welcome, in a metropolis grown weary of his histrionics. Even as he passed from the scene, a gaudy assumption of superiority masked the genesis of decline. Proud and provincial, New Yorkers turned a blind eye to demographic shifts already under way as wartime government contracts were diverted to shipyards and munitions plants in the South and West. By 1950, thousands of factory jobs would disappear, while a quickening migration to the suburbs left the city poorer and more racially polarized. All that, however, was over the horizon. In her charming valentine *Manhattan '45*, Jan Morris reports two million air passengers flew into Gotham that year, a small fraction of the seventy million who arrived by train.

Twice each month, GIs disembarking from the *Queen Mary* flowed six blocks east to Rockefeller Center, before fanning out into the theater district. Here the survivors of Anzio and Omaha Beach could enjoy performances of *Oklahoma!*, *On the Town*, or *The Glass Menagerie*. For many, Tin Pan Alley took second place to Swing Street, under the harsh glare of the noonday sun an unglamorous block of West Fifty-second between Fifth and Sixth avenues, but by moonlight a jazz nirvana dispensing the bebop of Dizzy Gillespie and the musical melancholy of Billie Holiday. Drama of a different sort unfolded nightly at the city's nine hundred nightclubs, in whose smoky precincts Winchell, Sullivan, Cholly Knickerbocker, and Toots Shor generated enough gossip to sell ten daily newspapers. A hundred tongues and a thousand traditions jostled for attention on the overcrowded island and its polyglot satellites. As a boy raised in blue-collar Brownsville, wrote Norman Podhoretz, he never thought of himself "as an American. I came from Brooklyn, and in Brooklyn there were no Americans; there were Jews and Negroes and Italians and Poles and Irishmen."

An impending exodus of Puerto Ricans from their Caribbean island would soon add yet another accent to the dizzying babble of neighborhoods and politics. A quarter of all New Yorkers in 1945 were Jewish, yet they were hardly monolithic. Until the cause of Israel bonded them in these anxious years, Yiddish-speaking merchants on Hester Street had little in common with German-descended assimilationists flocking to Temple Emanu-El on Park Avenue. Five years had passed since Father Divine's departure for Philadelphia, but the Harlem he abandoned remained the undisputed capital of black America. To be sure, the Harlem Renaissance of the twenties was a distant memory, a cultural sunburst eclipsed by wartime riots and mounting tensions between local residents and absentee landlords. But the neighborhood retained its pulsing vitality, along with such celebrated residents as Ella Fitzgerald and Thurgood Marshall, Bill "Bojangles" Robinson, the Reverend—soon to be Congressman—Adam Clayton Powell, Jr., James Baldwin, and Langston Hughes.

In 1945, Marlon Brando, Tennessee Williams, John Cheever, and Leonard Bernstein were at the dawn of their New York careers, while Toscanini, Babe Ruth, and Damon Runyon were in the twilight of theirs. On Sunday, inhabitants of Sin City could think positively with Norman Vincent Peale, bask in the enlightened liberalism of Harry Emerson Fosdick at the Rockefellers' Riverside Church, or genuflect to ruddy, rotund Francis Cardinal Spellman, "the American Pope," at St. Patrick's Cathedral. Cyril Connolly, writing in *Horizon* magazine, paid homage to "what a city ought to be: that is, continuously insistent and alive, a place where one can buy a book or meet a friend at any hour of the day or night, where every language is spoken and xenophobia almost unknown, where every purse and appetite is catered for. . . . If Paris is the setting for romance," concluded Connolly, "New York is the perfect city in which to get over one, to get over anything."

His advice applied to Nelson Rockefeller as much as to anyone. It was no accident that within days of his return, Nelson agreed to chair both the Victory Clothing Committee of New York and the United Jewish Appeal to aid one and a half million displaced Jews in Europe. In doing so, he endowed these causes with a visibility, even glamour, that no other patron could bestow. Friends, aware of his longing for a Washington sequel, thought he was killing time. They underestimated his capacity to juggle multiple ambitions. For Abby Aldrich Rockefeller's son, there could be no greater joy than to see New York supplant Paris as art capital of the world. Symbolic of the trailblazing artists chased out of Europe by repressive regimes was his friend Fernand Léger, whom Nelson engaged for $5,000 to decorate the sloping walls of the United Nations General Assembly. (Harry Truman compared the finished murals to a fried egg and a rabbit emerging from a hat.) A few blocks away, Picasso's iconic *Guernica* occupied a place of honorable exile at MoMA, from which it balefully condemned the Franco government for usurping Spanish democracy. Adding immeasurably to the excitement of the era was the emergence of the New York school of abstract expressionist painters, their names on the cusp of international fame: Robert Motherwell, Franz Kline, Jackson Pollock, Mark Rothko, Paul Klee, Helen Frankenthaler, and Willem de Kooning. Nelson would patronize, and promote, them all.

If anything was more foreign, and therefore suspect, to Americans west of the Hudson than the United Nations, it was the colorful chaos of Pollock's action painting, wherein meaninglessness took on a meaning all its own. But it was de Kooning, a Dutch-born stowaway who had first entered the United States on a British freighter in 1926, who put into words the cultural fault lines that long predated Al Smith's doomed campaign for the White House. "It's not so much that I'm an American," said de Kooning. "I'm a New Yorker." Nelson Rockefeller recognized no such distinction. Others would, however, to the lasting detriment of his political aspirations. For the moment, riding the crest of postwar possibility, he was more than content to reinsert himself in the management of Rockefeller Center as if he had never been away. Barely settled into his office on the northeast corner of Room 5600, Nelson began scouring the complex for unused space with which to increase earnings. He defused a potential crisis when NBC threatened to leave New York for the West Coast, an environment better adapted than an urban skyscraper to the space requirements of television production. Turning to the versatile Wally Harrison for a solution, Rockefeller welcomed the floor-sized stages, movable via immense elevators, that his friend created for the RCA Building. NBC decided to stay put.

The first of five Rockefeller brothers to report home from wartime service, Nelson stood out for the sheer energy, magnetism, and imagination he brought to the family enterprise. Few disputed that he was *the* Rockefeller of the coming generation, least of all at the Brothers Meetings that followed Christmas lunch at Pocantico, one of several planning sessions held each year in the estate's sprawling Playhouse. No staff penetrated these hermetically sealed conferences; as the junior member present, David kept the minutes. With his degrees from Harvard, the University of Chicago, and the London School of Economics, the youngest Rockefeller was the family scholar, just as Winthrop filled the thankless role of playboy and Laurance played the venture capitalist who had daringly bankrolled Eastern Airlines after Nelson turned down an appeal from their mutual friend Eddie Rickenbacker. Until he carved out a separate identity in the 1950s through the Asia Society, Lincoln Center, and the Population Council, John 3rd remained typecast as the decent, earnest heir denied his rightful place by a charismatic younger brother.

Any feelings of sibling rivalry this might have stirred were considerably diluted by Nelson's willingness to stand up to Junior. Even before the war, he had been instrumental in establishing the Rockefeller Brothers Fund, inspired in part by the plight of Bill Harkness, a fellow trustee of the Metropolitan Museum of Art, whose wealthy father had left his estate in the hands of lawyers. "A ward of the state," in Nelson's words, Harkness periodically received a check but had no voice in determining his family's affairs. "I wasn't going to let that happen in our family," he insisted. True to form, when Junior talked of bequeathing his stock in Rockefeller Center to the Rockefeller Institute, it was Nelson who forcefully urged him to reconsider. His persistence was rewarded in 1948, at which time Junior sold Rockefeller Center to his sons for pennies on the dollar.

For most men, running Rockefeller Center would constitute a career. For Nelson, it was but one of several priorities clamoring for his attention. Latin America exercised an unrelenting hold over his imagination. "I hope to be able to pull together in private hands a good many of the things which we started in government with regard to the other American republics and which are now in the process of being eliminated," he confided to his wartime associate Chester Bowles. "It would be a shame to lose all the ties which have been made with cultural, liberal and labor groups, to say nothing of those in the area of trade and commerce." Almost a year elapsed before this vague intention was to be made real. In the meantime, Nelson didn't lack for other enthusiasms. Repeating his Rockefeller Center experience, he slipped back into the MoMA presidency as he might a comfortable pair of slippers. A generous benefactor himself, Nelson was at ease recruiting donors like Peggy Guggenheim or Tom Watson of IBM. He promoted radio and television broadcasts to raise the museum's profile and broaden its membership base and supplied General Dwight Eisenhower with expert advice on how to display his collection of ceremonial swords.

During the war, forty masterpieces, identified as such by Alfred Barr, had been secreted away at Pocantico for protection against enemy air raids.* Their preservation constituted the latest debt that MoMA owed to its curatorial genius. Unfortunately, Barr's administrative shortcomings remained as glaring as ever. Resorting to a familiar stratagem, Nelson created a management committee, with his CIAA protégé René d'Harnoncourt serving as secretary. An imposing six and a half feet tall, the courtly Austrian brought to his duties a confident taste and generous encouragement of other people's ideas, rare in the museum world, that sparked enthusiasm without envy. D'Harnoncourt rapidly gained the confidence of museum trustees and staff, exactly as his sponsor had hoped. In 1949, he was named director, a position he filled with distinction for nineteen years.

---

* After Hiroshima, and with the onset of the Cold War, Junior addressed the prospect of thermonuclear conflict as he did most things in his life: he appointed a study committee. Its members decided that duplicate copies should be made of every document in Room 5600, "the destruction of which would be seriously embarrassing in its consequences." David Rockefeller helpfully volunteered the facilities of the Chase Bank to expedite the project. Stephen Clark, meanwhile, wryly observed that if atomic warfare did come to Manhattan, MoMA would be more liable to lose its customers than its collections. JDR, Jr.–Thomas M. Debevoise, August 21, 1950, Series 4L, Box 13, RAC.

2

ROCKEFELLER CENTER AND MoMA were not the only institutions to be jolted by Nelson's return. His arrival at Room 5600 had all the subtlety of a brass band at halftime. Before long, the exile from Washington had succeeded in replacing his father's aging coterie with his own set of advisers. Nelson commissioned Wally Harrison to redo the suite of offices earmarked for the returning brothers. ("I felt badly to walk out on you, leaving that job in your hands," confessed John 3rd, who would opt for a more traditional look in his work space.) The result, all curving walls, minimalist furniture, and Noguchi sculptures, confirmed Mr. Junior in his preference for Jacobean paneling and red carpets. That the patriarch was more impressed than he let on may be inferred from another gift he made to his second son, a property steeped in Rockefeller family history. In the spring of 1946, Nelson took title to 13 West Fifty-fourth Street, the townhouse where Junior and Abby had begun their married life nearly half a century earlier. More recently, the place had served as an upscale apartment building, complete with maid and valet service. Eviction of tenants began almost immediately, but five years passed before Nelson was able to finish remodeling the stout limestone structure to his liking. Reborn as the Clubhouse, it afforded an admirable setting for power lunches and free-wheeling discussions by the Junta, the prewar brain trust now reconstituted to advance its patron's political and policy interests.

More than a convenient pied-à-terre, the Clubhouse served Rockefeller as think tank, trysting place, mess hall, and art storage facility. Its owner glided easily between his formal surroundings and the workaday existence of facilitators such as Libby Shemwell, the wartime secretary who had accepted Nelson's invitation to become part of his growing New York staff. On her first day in Room 5600, Libby was assigned an office on the west side of the RCA Building, overlooking the Hudson River. Catching sight of the *Queen Mary*, reborn as the world's most luxurious troop carrier, as it nosed into Pier 90, she called out to her employer; his excitement surpassed her own. Still disarmingly boyish at thirty-seven, Nelson had inherited his mother's gift for finding magic in the mundane. Like Abby, he could invest the most routine occurrence—ordering an over-the-counter tuna-fish sandwich or monitoring the progress of a floating monarch and her tugboat courtiers—with a breathless delight that infected those around him. "Everything was equally exciting," recalled Linda Jamieson Storrow. "I mean an Oreo cookie was just as great as caviar."

His uncritical enthusiasm made Nelson stand out from the modulated voices and hushed deference of Room 5600. An elderly factotum steeped in Rockefeller family values instructed Libby: "One *never* talked about what went on in the office. One *never* discussed the family, even within the office." If she encountered the senior Mr. Rockefeller in the hallways, a pleasant "Good morning" would suffice. Should problems arise pertaining to personnel or accounting, one went to the appropriate office and spoke in a low voice to the appropriate individual. Though laid down in understated tones, these rules were ruthlessly enforced. One day, a year or so after her initiation there, Libby noticed the absence of a friendly face, a woman who had spent twenty-three years in the employ of Mr. Junior. Was she ill? It was worse than that, came the whispered reply. She had been indiscreet.*

Working for a Rockefeller required ingenuity as well as restraint. In New York as in Washington, no one ever discussed Libby's salary requirements, but when she stepped off a train at Tarrytown for a Saturday work session, Nelson met her behind the wheel of his familiar Lincoln convertible. "I imagine you need money for a hotel," he said, and handed over a check for $500. The eighteenth-century decor of Hawes House didn't prepare the visitor for the startlingly modern wall of glass that, on closer inspection, revealed itself as a floor-to-ceiling fish tank. Libby repaired with Nelson to a large shade tree beneath whose canopy they worked, interrupted by a lunch of sandwiches, pickles, potato chips, and iced tea served picnic style. It was a far cry from the window table and Baked Alaska specially prepared by a Rainbow Room chef or the white-gloved ambience of Room 5600, where time stood still and fashion was defined by Junior's high-buttoned shoes.

Nelson readily conceded that he wore people out. With both Susan Cable and the regular receptionist absent, Libby one morning found herself balancing a constantly ringing phone against multiple queries from the file room and a letter-signing session with her boss. The telephone rang once too often, sending her to the ladies' room in tears. At length she heard a knock on the door, trailed by the beckoning voice of an elderly black messenger. He was standing outside with a wheelchair, waiting to take Libby to a taxi.

"Mr. Nelson says you are to go home, and you are to take a week off. Perhaps you would like to visit your mother?"

Libby returned after a short rest to find a dramatically altered workplace. First Rockefeller asked her to welcome Vera Goeller, a fixture of the La Guardia city hall, who had been recruited to assist with Nelson's unfocused political ambitions. Might Libby do the same for a former CIAA treasurer, recently added to the staff for purposes as yet unspecified? Gradually, it dawned on her: Just as she had overnight, and without explanation, supplanted Janet Barnes in

---

* Another young woman, summoned to Junior's office after she submitted an invoice for under $1,000, found herself reviewing the bill item by item with Mr. Rockefeller. "You will be well advised, young lady," said the old man, "that we in this office are not as loose with our money as the young generation is." Martha Dalrymple recollections, Alvin Moscow Papers, RAC.

the Office of the Coordinator of Inter-American Affairs, so others were now replacing her in the magic circle. A public display of vulnerability had caused her to be eased out, discreetly, by a culture both paternalistic and Darwinian. Of all the new hires, none was more influential than Louise Auchincloss Robbins, widow of Rockefeller's CIAA compatriot Hutch Robbins. Before enlisting in the Army Air Corps, Robbins had been assured that in the event of his death, Louise would be taken care of. After his friend was killed in the summer of 1944, Nelson more than kept his promise.

The stylish widow was initially employed by the CIAA motion picture office. Later she worked on the Rockefeller-led drive to collect three million pounds of clothing for war victims. In reward for her crisp competence and unwavering loyalty, she was given oversight of Nelson's ragged schedule. As Louise Boyer—the name by which she was known following her 1947 marriage to Laurance's right-hand man, Allston Boyer—she quietly established herself as the most capable of the many women to whom Rockefeller entrusted significant responsibilities. If Boyer was the soul of discretion, her vivacious assistant, Joan Ridley, was an emotional billboard. When, much later, as the Washington socialite, public relations executive, and television personality Joan Braden, she penned an aptly named memoir, *Just Enough Rope*, it confirmed what many in Room 5600 had long suspected: whether Ridley or Braden, Joan craved nothing so much as attention.

A downscale Pamela Harriman, with aspirations to become her generation's Alice Roosevelt Longworth, Joan rarely let marriage vows get in the way of a liaison with richer or more powerful men.* Introduced to Libby Shemwell, Joan began quizzing her about where she worked. On hearing the name Nelson Rockefeller, she became more animated than usual. Before the evening ended, she announced that she, too, wanted to work for the Rockefeller office. Shortly thereafter, Joan placed a telephone call to "Rockefellers, Offices of the Messrs."; soon she was riding the world's fastest elevators (two floors per second) to Room 5600. Spurning the offer of a file clerk's position—"After all, I had a degree in economics," she reasoned, "I spoke Spanish. I had worked with campesinos"—Joan went home to East Seventieth Street, where she resumed looking out the window. Her trance was broken by an unexpected call from Mr. Nelson, as he was addressed by the soft-spoken retainers on the family

* Her coy, name-dropping portrait of an "open marriage" to journalist Tom Braden—a former CIA operative best known for the seventies television series *Eight Is Enough*—might be said to have pioneered an entirely new genre in confessional literature: the don't-kiss-but-tell-all. One chapter title—"Start with Snuggling"—admirably conveys the exhibitionism of a woman who, according to Arthur Schlesinger, Jr., himself a startled recipient of her late night calls, liked to telephone friends from her bed at times when it was being used for purposes ordinarily kept private. Arthur Schlesinger, Jr., AI.

payroll. Claiming to remember her from their sole previous meeting at the inauguration of Mexican president Miguel Alemán, Rockefeller mentioned the fourteen crates of State Department papers, as yet unorganized. He dangled the prospect of unspecified, though less menial, assignments down the road.

Joan swallowed her pride and began work as a card clerk reporting to Vera Goeller. She quickly graduated to a desk beside Louise Robbins. When the older woman got married and took a month's vacation, twenty-five-year-old Joan filled in. An associate recalls her as "a fresh-faced young woman with short curly hair and freckles sprinkled across her nose and cheeks" and a wholesomeness that was skin-deep. "She exuded IT (shades of Clara Bow)." Both men and women were attracted to her, men especially. The women in the office soon learned to be wary of her—"not that she threw her weight around, but she was a very disturbing presence." A male co-worker is harsher in his estimate, insisting that "people in Room 5600 hated her" for the way she flaunted her intimacy with Mr. Nelson. Drawn to Joan's Indiana background and seeming lack of sophistication, Rockefeller made a habit each morning of ruffling her hair, then laughing at the feigned annoyance this produced. They began racing each other to work, getting up earlier and earlier until the day a confident Joan strode into Room 5600 shortly after seven o'clock, only to encounter Nelson beside her desk.

"What would you say," he asked, "if I met you outside your apartment at a respectable hour every morning and we walked to work together?" So commenced her (apparent) seduction at the hands of "the most enthusiastic, life-loving, ebullient, and intuitive" man ever to enter her life. Awed by his sense of beauty, Joan was no less impressed by his instinctive grasp of where to plant a tree, hang a picture, or place a sculpture to harmonize with its outdoor setting. His conviction that any problem could be mastered, if only one assembled the right people and plans, was put to the test after a passing discussion of the challenges faced by New York City commuters. These were frustrations no Rockefeller need ever concern himself with. But Nelson was different. "Joannie," he announced one day, "I don't know enough about railroads, so let's have a meeting and find out about them." Experts were duly convened and questions fired for as long as it took to erase Nelson's ignorance and, equally important, to establish a bond with those who made railroads their business.

Joan detected in Rockefeller a vulnerability hidden from others. "What Nelson wanted, more than anything else in life, was to succeed despite his name," Joan maintained. "Everything he did, his mannerisms, his style, his countenance, was intended to make people forget his name and to look upon him as himself. That's where 'hiya fella' came from and his insistence on sitting in the front seat with the chauffeur, when he had to have a chauffeur. That's why he always stopped in the kitchen when visiting a friend's house to thank the person who had prepared the meal. That's why he shook hands with the elevator operator; that's why he usually carried only ten dollars in his pocket and frequently borrowed change from startled companions. It was all intended to show the world that he was not just a very rich man, but a good joe, a nice guy, intelligent and able, a doer in the practical world who yet respected the intellectual world, and whose name happened to be Rockefeller."

There was considerable truth in Joan's diagnosis. But it seems just as probable that the compliments and handshakes, the exaggerated gestures of ordinariness, were meant to impart a flashbulb's worth of the intense charm and reflected celebrity that all but overwhelmed Joan Ridley. One day at work Nelson crossed a line, blurting out a mutual understanding between Tod and himself. "We will never get divorced but will live our separate lives," he informed Joan. He justified sharing such intimacies by explaining that "we're working together, and I think working together and sleeping together are the same thing." Joan professed shock, though not enough to change anything about her routine—not even after the night she and Nelson worked late at the Rockefeller townhouse and Joan, having accepted a party invitation, asked if she could take a shower. Nelson pointed the way. A few minutes later he returned, uninvited, and climbed into the shower wearing nothing more than a grin.

Flustered and angry, Joan jumped out and seized a towel. Not until much later, in the pages of her memoir, did she concede that her behavior might have struck a red-blooded male as suggestive. An erotic Janus, alternatively channeling June Allyson and Kim Novak, she dispensed psychological insights like Halloween candy. Only a woman, she decided, could know, *really* know, Rockefeller. "Because Nelson was not suspicious of women. He was totally himself with women. Whereas he was very suspicious and not totally himself with men." Joan Ridley had her own wandering eye, which led her to Tom Braden. Yet another Dartmouth alumnus, class of 1940, Braden was thirty-one years old in the spring of 1948, when he was recommended to Nelson by Vic Borella. To Rockefeller, Tom Braden looked every inch an executive vice president, perhaps more, for MoMA. Joan Ridley saw him in a different light. In her book, she described a heated confrontation in which a jealous Nelson threatened to send her lover abroad or, worse, ensure that he would never get another job.

Others regarded the December 1948 Braden nuptials, attended by Nelson, as the prototypical marrying off of friends, some more intimate than others. In the years that followed, Rockefeller served as godfather to the Bradens' first child and to Tom's career as a newspaperman. For as long as he lived, neither of the Bradens escaped Nelson's gravitational field or the rumors fed by their friend's hospital room visits, sometimes in advance of the proud father, that coincided with the birth of Joan's children.

3

D URING THE WAR, Nelson had boasted that he could get anyone in Washington to take his phone call, then proved his claim by reaching, without delay, General Marshall. Those days were long past. The Office of the Coordinator of Inter-American Affairs officially went out of business in the spring of 1946. A handful of projects initiated by Nelson's Basic Economy Program lingered on, ghostly reminders of an alliance written off by his Washington successors. Cancellation of the Rio Conference, promised to Latin delegates in San Francisco a year earlier, reinforced a continental sense of abandonment.* As noted by Claude Erb, in the five years after the war Belgium and Luxembourg each received more direct assistance from the United States than did all of Latin America. To Rockefeller this was intolerable, but no more so than his inability to influence events as Europe became the chief field of contention in an escalating Cold War.

As coordinator he had been a maverick, creating public corporations that functioned much like private businesses, with a minimum of red tape or congressional oversight. Now, having returned to the private sector, Rockefeller asked himself and his assembled experts: Could one reverse the process and establish businesses that resembled charities? For John Lockwood, the question answered itself. The profit motive was incompatible with the philanthropic impulse, said the family lawyer, at least so far as the U.S. tax code was concerned. Rockefeller listened grimly, set his jaw, and continued planning his international development foundation—or was it a trade and development corporation? "He never could quite understand why you couldn't have a charitable outfit and a business outfit all in one corporation," said Lockwood, "like the Coordinator's Office, all seeking one basic purpose, do good for the Latin Americans or for the poor. It was a governmental, not a private, conception."

Aided by Dartmouth economist Stacy May, to whom he had become close during the war, Rockefeller embarked on a search for what Lockwood called "a better capitalism." Forgoing the usual entrepreneurial practice "of looking around and seeing where some money can be made by meeting a need in the marketplace," Nelson advanced a markedly different strategy. "The theory being that if there was a social need," Lockwood explained, "the capitalistic system should meet it." During the first half of 1946, there evolved the idea of a hybrid organization, part business, part philanthropic, that would earn enough through private entrepreneurship to underwrite the export of technical knowl-

* The conference was eventually rescheduled for 1947, by which time Washington was eager to establish the Rio Pact, an anti-Soviet alliance that anticipated such other Cold War groupings as NATO and SEATO in Europe and Southeast Asia, respectively.

edge, modern equipment, and managerial training to Latin America. In essence, it was an updated version of Rockefeller's wartime Basic Economy Program, though with one critical difference: This time he must depend entirely on private resources instead of government funds.

On July 1, 1946, Rockefeller incorporated the American International Association for Economic and Social Development (AIA), whose lofty mission statement proclaimed the faith of its founder "in the inherent dignity and worth of the individual and in the capacity and desire for self-improvement of human beings of whatever nationality, race, creed or color." The best way to strengthen democratic free enterprise in its ongoing contest with aggressive Marxism, Rockefeller believed, was to demonstrate to impoverished Latinos that capitalism had a conscience. Not satisfied to tackle Latin American health, education, and agriculture, he also imagined a full-scale assault on illiteracy in China.

That there were limits to what he and his victorious countrymen could do to remake the world was painfully illustrated by a visiting Indian who sought Nelson's help on a vast land reclamation project. To his amazement, Rockefeller discovered that a U.S. economy beset by postwar shortages could not produce the needed machinery. Even if it could, a successful scheme would feed only one year's explosive growth of the Indian population. Momentarily chastened, Rockefeller decided to limit AIA, at least initially, to Venezuela, where his prewar contacts and personal stake in the oil industry established his bona fides; and to Brazil, the underperforming giant in transition from the New Deal–ish statism of the deposed Getúlio Vargas to the more conservative economics of President Eurico Dutra.

"We have to get Nelson to visit Brazil," Dutra told friends. His timing was providential. Within weeks of establishing AIA, Nelson was rushing veterinarians and vaccines to assist Brazilians combating an epidemic of hog cholera. For less than $9,000, he and his agents were able to rescue an industry on the brink of extinction. During the second half of 1946, Rockefeller undertook a series of fact-finding trips to Brazil. On the hilly outskirts of Rio and São Paulo, he repeatedly asked his traveling companions, "What do you think could have been the cause of these shanty towns?" The mystery was easily solved: farmers and others in rural Brazil were flocking to the cities in search of jobs. AIA thus evolved as a rural assistance and credit program, offering as initiatives to stay on the land mobile health clinics and home demonstration programs designed to raise standards of nutrition, sanitation, and child care. An agricultural extension service promoted soil conservation and taught dairy farmers to increase milk production by spraying their cattle for parasites. Thousands of 4-S Clubs, patterned after the 4-H movement in the United States, tutored the next generation of Brazilian farmers in how to produce greater yields without exhausting the land.

Admirable as these programs were, they didn't pay for themselves. They weren't supposed to, not as long as AIA's for-profit division lived up to its name. That it did not only vindicated John Lockwood's counsel to split the AIA baby and establish what he called "a Sunday company and a weekday company." Under this scenario, AIA would continue as a nonprofit concern; in order to make his Sabbath charity possible, Nelson would establish a profit-making spin-off, the International Basic Economy Corporation (IBEC). As of January 1, 1947, he had two companies, each with its own mission, each in need of capitalization. U.S. tax laws made it difficult to approach outside funding sources, while many a prospective investor regarded the Rockefeller name as more hindrance than help. "You know what that man is thinking now?" remarked a grinning Nelson after an unsuccessful call on a Coca-Cola executive. "He's thinking to himself, I'm not going to put my money into something that's going to prove that Nelson Rockefeller is a worldwide philanthropist."

So he became his own angel, supplying 70 percent of IBEC's initial capitalization of $2 million and eventually pouring $7 million into the two concerns. His enthusiasm lit a fire among his brothers, with David Rockefeller invading his trust to invest $1 million in IBEC and the rest pledging smaller amounts. "I have had no trouble in getting capital up to date," Nelson told his sister, Babs, whose desire to support the new venture on the same basis as her male siblings touched him deeply. So did Junior's purchase of $4 million of IBEC stock. To supplement family resources, Nelson tapped Creole, Shell, and other oil companies then doing business in Venezuela, where President Rómulo Betancourt had slapped a 50 percent tax on their profits. If only to avoid worse, Rockefeller implied, the oilmen should join his economic development effort. In June 1947, Nelson called on Betancourt, a genial socialist whose criticism of Rockefeller's prewar Venezuelan operations had not prevented him from working in the press section of the coordinator's Caracas office during the war.*

Now, as fifteen-year-old Rodman Rockefeller looked on, the two men engaged in a spirited debate over the nature of modern capitalism. Nelson stressed the connection between human dignity and the efficient production of goods and services on an affordable scale. "You will be exploiting the people," retorted Betancourt, who demanded a 6 percent limit on earnings by IBEC's local subsidiary, the Venezuelan Basic Economy Corporation (VBEC). Not at all, said Rockefeller, before delivering a lecture on the benefits of private versus state-run enterprise. "If we produce goods and services cheaper than you and

---

* As founder of Acción Democrática, Betancourt helped spearhead the 1945 October Revolution ushering in the *trienio*, a three-year period of political and economic reform, culminating in the election of Rómulo Gallegos, an eminent writer strongly backed by Betancourt's party, to the Venezuelan presidency.

make a profit because we do sell them cheaper in competition, we are doing something for your people, creating capital which can then be reinvested. If you limit the profits the incentive is gone," he told Betancourt.

Fearful that Yankee investors would engorge themselves at the expense of his countrymen, Betancourt demanded the right for his government to purchase $4.5 million, roughly half, of VBEC's preferred stock. At the end of ten years—less if management realized its declared objectives—a majority of voting shares would be offered to private Venezuelan investors. Convinced of his mission and deaf to advice that he should begin modestly, Nelson accepted the president's terms, overlooking the political consequences if expected profits failed to materialize. To be fair, Rockefeller wasn't the only one in a hurry. With oil-dependent Venezuelans importing roughly 40 percent of their food, the government and the oil companies were both anxious to do something about rampant inflation and empty store shelves.

VBEC's response was to launch an ambitious quartet of ventures in farming, fishing, food distribution, and the dairy industry. Over time, VBEC doubled the number of cattle per acre. Tomatoes and potatoes, which had degenerated to the size of peanuts because of poor farming practices, were restored to their original dimensions. Unfortunately, a lack of planning caused the first vegetable crop at Monte Sacro, once home to Simón Bolívar, to rot on the ground. Another large ranch generated enough sugarcane to sustain a profitable rum-making business, which was judged inappropriate as a Rockefeller family venture and promptly shut down. A boatload of Australian butter spoiled before it could be distributed to a population that didn't eat butter. Heavy rains left tractors stranded in fathomless mud. As the fields dried, corn was planted, only to have weeds outgrow the unharvested stalks in the rainy season. "We couldn't get anybody to harvest because they were afraid of the snakes," Rockefeller recalled. "So we had to knock it down with harrows and pick it up by hand."

VBEC's fishing venture, capitalized at $1.5 million, was equally jinxed. The richest fishing grounds lay beyond the reach of Venezuelan sailboats. "So we put motors in the sailboats," explained Nelson, the crews of which showed a distinct preference for the Dutch East Indies and its lucrative smuggling trade. Once boatloads of red snapper and Spanish mackerel finally began arriving in port, a new challenge arose. In Rockefeller's words, "How do you get the fish up into the interior, in the tropics?" This was a long-standing dilemma, serious enough to cause the Catholic Church to ease its ban on Friday meat eating. In preference to grouper, some Venezuelans dined on *chigüires*, likened by Nelson to "a big woodchuck or a rodent which lives in water."

An $800,000 refrigeration plant helped, yet few Venezuelan housewives possessed the means to buy fresh fish had they wanted to. Rockefeller had an epiphany. Why not teach villagers to raise chickens, the sale of which could pay for whatever his fleet of fishing boats harvested from the Caribbean? Thousands of broiler chicks were installed in newly built housing, and thousands succumbed overnight to Newcastle disease.

A mood of disbelief settled over his Venezuelan partners.

"But you're a Rockefeller," said one coinvestor. "How can you lose money? How can we lose money with you?"

"I just showed you how," Nelson replied.

He took consolation in small victories. Traditionally, Venezuelans drank raw milk, much of it sold door-to-door and delivered by burro. A VBEC dairy company supplied the country's first pasteurized milk in sanitary paraffin containers. The same concern marketed vast quantities of ice cream, cottage cheese, and chocolate milk. "Everybody said that you couldn't have supermarkets in Latin America," Rockefeller would reflect. Customers much preferred to shop in small, family-owned bodegas. Hoping to disprove conventional wisdom, in 1949 VBEC opened a neon-lighted, air-conditioned facility in Maracaibo, which was soon serving two thousand customers daily. Within five years, a chain of stores was operating successfully, with a third of the stock and a majority of the workforce supplied locally. No one benefited more from the resulting competition than Venezuelan consumers.

In its first five years, AIA burned through $5 million. That was to be expected. Indeed, it was supposed to be covered by profits from IBEC. Only there weren't any profits. With red ink as far as he could see, Nelson had no choice but to pull the plug on several of his start-up companies. His list of reasons why was longer than the rainy season at Monte Sacro, the mountainous Venezuelan ranch to which he took title in 1954 as IBEC liquidated much of its corporate farming operations. A three-hour drive from Caracas, Monte Sacro commanded heart-stopping views of the verdant Andes. The red-tile-roofed hacienda, festooned with purple and red bougainvillea, was built around a circular swimming pool, replenished out of a font once used in Aztec sacrifices. Having constructed a school for the children of his farmworkers, Rockefeller personally interviewed teaching candidates. He exercised less dominion over bad weather, postwar scarcities, and resistance to technological change, all of which contributed to IBEC's rocky launch.

But so did Rockefeller's eagerness to solve every problem at once. A more accurate name for his crash campaign to improve Latin living standards might have been lifted from his popular Venezuelan supermarket chain: Todos, Spanish for Everything. "It was a case of too much, too soon, rather than too little, too late," Nelson told the *Christian Science Monitor* in 1952. A decade after its founding, IBEC reported an annual profit of $1.2 million, insufficient to support its philanthropic twin, AIA, yet substantial enough to fuel criticism from economic nationalists and Marxists alike. Sixty years later, the gospel of rural development appears less uplifting and the Rockefeller vision of progress as threatening to the Amazon basin, and the native people inhabiting its shrinking rain forests, as Senior's economies of scale were to nineteenth-century individualism and the beatitudes he worshipped every Sunday.

Ironically, what made the whole enterprise truly original—the synergy of private entrepreneurship with a miniature Marshall Plan for Latin America—moved latter-day critics to allege blatant self-interest. By the time AIA was disbanded in 1968, management of IBEC had been entrusted to Nelson's oldest son, Rodman, whose first job was in a Caracas supermarket. With ventures in two dozen countries, IBEC attained a place on the Fortune 500. Working off designs by Wally Harrison, its housing division built ten thousand prefabricated dwellings in Puerto Rico alone, with thousands more planted in Central America and the Middle East. Yet subsequent events showed IBEC to be too feeble in corporate structure to attract needed capital and at the same time too visible a symbol of outside exploitation to escape left-wing violence, government expropriation, or both.

4

NELSON SPENT THE first week of December 1946 relaxing at the King Ranch in Texas. On Sunday, December 8, he received a call from Frank Jamieson, passing on a hot tip from Scotty Reston of the *Times:* The committee entrusted with finding a permanent home for the United Nations was primed to reveal its choice—and it wasn't New York. What happened next has often been portrayed as a bolt from the blue, with a cliff-hanging finale that turned on Junior's unexpected intervention. Actually, it represented the latest twist in a long-running competition pitting the Rockefellers, Wally Harrison, and allied power brokers such as Abby's brother Winthrop Aldrich of the Chase Bank against dozens of outlying communities—from Boston and San Francisco to the remote Black Hills of South Dakota and the Choctaw Nation seat of Tuskahoma, Oklahoma—all vying for the vanity title "capital of the world."

In hindsight, the UN was the last thing New York needed to formalize its postwar hegemony. Even at the time, more than a few New Yorkers argued that re-creating the human family on the teeming East Side of Manhattan was bringing coals, in the form of suffocating traffic jams, to Newcastle. But for Nelson, securing the UN represented more than an expression of hometown pride; success would affirm his status as a man who got things done on a global scale. Named to Mayor William O'Dwyer's United Nations Committee for the City of New York, he threw himself into the project with an urgency that had lain dormant since his forced departure from Washington, financing architectural plans and a one-reel film promoting Flushing Meadows, the former Queens municipal dump transformed by parks commissioner Robert Moses into a shimmering backdrop for the 1939–1940 World's Fair.

By the fall of 1946, San Francisco, Boston, and Westchester County had been eliminated from the competition. So had the Connecticut suburbs, where a scouting party of UN officials was met by stone-throwing residents. All eyes turned to Philadelphia, which offered the diplomats a large swath of scenic Fairmount Park. This prospect did not sit well with UN secretary-general Trygvie Lie. Not bothering to conceal his pro–New York leanings, the Norwegian diplomat asked Wally Harrison early in December, "Where is Nelson?" Informed that he was in Texas, Lie said he must come home at once. "Otherwise, you have lost your last chance to get the UN into New York City."*

It was around five on the afternoon of December 9 when Rockefeller landed at LaGuardia Airport, to be met by Harrison, Frank Jamieson, and Clark Eichelberger of the UN Association of the United States of America. The quartet headed straight for Lake Success, the world body's nearby interim home, to make a renewed pitch for Flushing Meadows. In reality, only one person, Robert Moses, was enthusiastic about the old fairgrounds. Most delegates felt that if the UN was going to be in New York, *it should be in New York*—that is, Manhattan.

This was the moment Wally Harrison had been waiting for. Fresh from liquidating the Office of Inter-American Affairs that spring, Harrison was in the market for new challenges. "Give me a job sometime when you're working on something in the UN," he remarked to Nelson. As a rule, he didn't have to ask. Before resigning as a trustee of the Metropolitan Museum of Art, Rockefeller had made certain that Harrison took his place. He also put the family architect in charge of IBEC Technical Services, an international consulting firm, at $20,000 a year plus $5,000 in expenses. IBEC footed the tab for Harrison's two-bedroom apartment at 834 Fifth Avenue, a posh address whose top three floors were occupied by Laurance and Mary French Rockefeller. Meanwhile, his Rockefeller connections earned Harrison high-profile commissions like a new U.S. embassy in Rio, dubbed "the Ray-Ban Building" for its twenty-seven thousand square feet of green glare-proof Solex glass.

No Harrison project, however, approached the UN for prestige or visibility, not to mention the grinding frustration of overseeing a room full of the world's most celebrated, and quarrelsome, architects. Of course, all this depended on

---

* Lie's daughter was just one of the children of establishment figures—among them New York developer William Zeckendorf and CIA director Allen Dulles—who found employment with IBEC.

finding a site acceptable to the selection committee chaired by Colombia's Eduardo Zuleta Ángel. As it happened, Harrison had a ready candidate in Turtle Bay, an East River abattoir christened "Blood Alley" on account of its foul-smelling confluence of cattle pens and slaughterhouses. For several months, Harrison and his associate George Dudley had been toiling in strict secrecy to realize the improbable vision of William Zeckendorf, a flamboyant real estate magnate said to know the value of every property on Manhattan Island. With a gambler's instinct and Trump-like flair for self-promotion, Zeckendorf had graduated from a boyhood job selling *The Saturday Evening Post* to owning most of the Hoboken waterfront before he was forty.

Like many a later empire builder, Zeckendorf inhabited a house of cards, his debt load the only thing bigger than his dreams. Now, defying the odds yet again, he proposed to do the Rockefellers one better by creating his own $200 million city within a city. Operating out of the Monte Carlo, a Madison Avenue nightclub he owned in tandem with his partners in the real estate firm of Webb & Knapp, Zeckendorf stealthily assembled options on seventeen acres between Forty-second and Forty-ninth streets, the nucleus of what he called X City. Financing for the mammoth development proved elusive, however, with the result that less than six weeks after unveiling his plans, Bill Zeckendorf was entertaining second thoughts. Early in December 1946, he telephoned Mayor O'Dwyer and offered the city, and the UN, his East River property. "Nelson was aware of this going on," according to George Dudley. Yet Rockefeller remained skeptical about the developer's willingness to abandon his signature project without pocketing a hefty fee.

Seeking an alternative, on December 10 Nelson convened a meeting attended by his brother Laurance, John Lockwood, Wally Harrison, and Frank Jamieson. The latter rehashed his phone conversation with the *Times'* James Reston. Perhaps, said Jamieson, the selection committee might be willing to reconsider Westchester. Nelson sat up.

"Do you mean our place?"

Within minutes, maps of the four-thousand-acre Rockefeller estate and its environs carpeted the office floor. Nelson hastily scheduled a lunch with his father, and an overflight of Pocantico for Le Corbusier and other committee members (the Soviet representative seemed most curious about the cost of the private plane supplied by the Rockefellers). Laurance offered to donate his home if that would help close the deal. John 3rd followed suit. A compromise was discussed, under which Kykuit and a park of several hundred acres might be preserved for Junior's lifetime use. To offset this loss, Nelson and his real estate agents began to secure options on property adjoining the Pocantico estate. Their frenzied activities masked the real action transpiring that Tuesday afternoon, as Wally Harrison zeroed in on Zeckendorf's Turtle Bay property, exploring what, if any, additional land might be needed to accommodate the international organization and gauging the attitude of UN power brokers toward the East River site. Hovering in the wings was Robert Moses, an un-elected government of one, who alone could guarantee the prerequisite street closings and municipal funding for site improvements.

As darkness fell, Harrison voiced the opinion that Zeckendorf would be will-ing to sell his holdings to the UN for something around $8 million. By then the Pocantico option was also on the table. Holding two birds in his hand, Nelson called Warren Austin, the former Vermont senator who had replaced Ed Stet-tinius as permanent American representative to the UN. Austin stated a clear preference for the East River site. This was relayed by telephone to Junior, who had but one question: How much?*

Nelson told his father that Zeckendorf's property could be had for $8.5 mil-lion. He paused to let the news sink in. Suddenly his eyebrows arched in de-light.

"Why, Pa!" he exclaimed into the receiver. "That's most generous."

"He wants to give them the New York City property," Nelson mouthed si-lently to Harrison, Jamieson, and the others gathered in his office. The little group raised a cheer. Then they went back to work. A deal had to be formal-ized, a conversation turned into a covenant. By nine o'clock, Harrison had tracked Zeckendorf to a back room of the Monte Carlo, scene of a well-lubricated birthday party. In one hand, the architect clutched a map of Man-hattan, on which a full block of the proposed UN site had been cunningly eliminated. By giving Zeckendorf a slice of the development action, Harrison hoped to obtain his confirming signature—fast.

Shortly before midnight, Harrison placed a call to Room 5600 from a pay phone in the St. Regis Hotel.

"Did you get it?" Nelson asked him.

"Yes, I have it in my pocket."

"Wonderful, buy a bottle of champagne and come back to the office."

Here was one Rockefeller directive not even Harrison could execute. Besides the signed map granting the UN a thirty-day option on the Turtle Bay site, his pockets held just twenty-five cents. The champagne order was placed with a

---

* The elder Rockefeller attached a condition to his gift—that he avoid the penalty incurred a decade earlier, when a federal gift tax had been levied on his contribution of a library to the ill-fated League of Nations. Junior subsequently gave conflicting versions of what happened that night. Writing Nelson in February 1947, he said, "Had it not been for the indefatigable and dauntless efforts of you and your associates the United Nations would have voted to accept the Philadelphia site the morning following our telephone talk." In a contemporary letter to his sister-in-law Blanchette, Nelson himself credited an unselfish offer from John 3rd of his own Pocantico home as "the thing that really moved Father to do what he did." NAR–Mrs. John D. Rockefel-ler 3rd, December 14, 1946, Family and Friends, Box 46, RAC.

nearby club. Less than a bottle was actually consumed: too much unfinished work remained for Nelson and his team to party. Governor Dewey must be notified, along with Mayor O'Dwyer and Robert Moses. Once John Lockwood vouched for the legality of Zeckendorf's unorthodox document of transfer, Nelson alerted Senator Austin to the deal. Arrangements were made for Secretary of State Byrnes to give it his imprimatur. The next morning, refreshed by a few hours' sleep, Nelson appeared at his parents' 740 Park Avenue address. "We've been up all night patching up the details, but it's going to work," he told Bill Zeckendorf, whose feelings must have been bittersweet. Credit for securing a Manhattan home for the United Nations would go to the Rockefellers, who managed in the bargain to nail shut the coffin containing X City. No rival would threaten Rockefeller Center just as the older complex was turning its first profits.

The necessary paperwork signed, Nelson, accompanied by Wally Harrison, paid a quick visit to Senator Austin, who conditioned congressional funding for the new United Nations on its meeting his architectural specifications. ("For a while Wally had to hold his hand on getting something in the form of a dome," conceded one Harrison associate. The required feature was eventually tacked on to the General Assembly Building, otherwise all sweeping curves, like a cake that has fallen in the oven.) A few minutes after ten, their business completed, Rockefeller and Harrison climbed into a taxi. They had traveled only a few blocks when Nelson spied an antiques store on Third Avenue, in whose window five carousel figures were displayed. He motioned for the driver to stop.

"Wally, we've got to celebrate."

Nelson disappeared inside the store. Moments later he emerged grinning, clutching his latest purchase, his acquisitive lust momentarily sated.

5

OBTAINING THE UN for New York marked a turning point for the Rockefellers, as for the city they called home. By 1946, Junior and Abby were well into their seventies; cherishing their dwindling moments together, the couple gladly entrusted civic obligations to the next generation. At 740 Park Avenue, the war years had offered the same mix of pride, anxiety, and self-denial that defined millions of other American homes. Abby's scruples, only slightly less rigid than the sugar rations then in effect, forbade homemade ice cream. To the annoyance of her husband, for whom the radio was an unwelcome intruder, she sometimes crept from bed in the middle of the night to catch the latest frontline reports while perched on the edge of a bathtub. Sunday mornings, she passed up worship services to write long, chatty letters to sons in remote locations. When not fretting over her distant children, Abby opened her arms to their surrogates, welcoming a dozen enlisted men to a Williamsburg Thanksgiving dinner and frequently stopping to offer rides to startled GIs.

On V-J Day, as Nelson weighed his chances for survival in Harry Truman's Washington, his parents heard the pealing of Mount Desert's church bells from their cherished Rest House. For once, even Junior was grateful for the radio. That night, the couple dined on blueberries, bread, and butter. Tempering their joy was Abby's failing health. After the war, determined to shield her from family stress, Junior took his wife away each winter to the Arizona inn where, a decade earlier, Nelson had cured his sinusitis in the southwestern sun. In February 1947, a wistful letter postmarked Tucson arrived at 810 Fifth Avenue. "I think Papa and I would feel very shut off from the world if it were not for all the things that you and your sister and brothers are doing," Abby wrote. "So if I get to feeling very lonely for you and your family don't be too surprised if I call you up."

Junior claimed that his wife was made hoarse by her excessive, and costly, use of the long-distance telephone. Abby went on calling, picking up the receiver to decry Nelson's habit of wearing striped shirts with white collars. They made him look like a schoolboy, she complained. Reverting to earlier habits, the family matriarch urged her son to get a haircut and, for heaven's sake, some new clothes. She was equally blunt in advising MoMA, her other "child." She was "deeply grieved," wrote Abby, to learn of the pending exhibition of a painting entitled *Figure of Erotic Torture*. Indeed, the news had caused her to lose faith in the judgment, taste, and integrity of the museum staff. Revised procedures were quickly put in place and a new director of painting and sculpture designated. The storm passed. But the incident hinted at a flintiness hidden from outsiders. Near the end of his life, Nelson observed that his mother, who typically flooded any room she entered with an incandescent warmth, could, as with the flip of a light switch, recoil from emotional contact. "She had a very strong personality, and if the current was on you could feel it," he said. For a while, he conceded, "there really wasn't any current between us."*

Much the same would be said of Nelson by his children. "If Father was in favor of what you were doing," remembers his son Steven, "you were buoyed and supported by this tremendous energy and enthusiasm. You were fantastic. You were marvelous. You were the greatest." Seriously contradict him, however, and the light went out. "It was almost a physical thing. Father just withdrew his

---

* "After I got married she withdrew much to my disappointment and irritation," Nelson said of his mother, "although I guess from my wife's point of view it probably was appreciated." NROH, July 12, 1977, 54.

emotional embrace, and he became cold, silent, and indifferent. . . . As long as you were dependent on that emotional support he had you." Like mother, like son. For Christmas 1947, Abby gave Nelson and Tod some Etruscan vases once owned by her father. A week later, she presented her son with a carved lizard Senator Aldrich had kept on his desk. Were these spontaneous gestures or the acts of a woman putting her own house in order? In February 1948, Abby asked Nelson to take responsibility for her obituary notices. Having little enthusiasm for Junior's agent, "if . . . you and Mr. Jamieson would take it over, without hurting your father's feelings, I would really be very much relieved."

At the beginning of April, Junior and Abby returned to New York from Arizona. On Saturday morning, April 3, Nelson drove his mother to Pocantico. "It was like the old days," he would remember. "We had a marvelous time." As the early spring sunshine washed over Kykuit, Abby rejoiced in her gardens, cradled her grandchildren, and savored long conversations with Nelson and his siblings. On Sunday evening, David and his wife, Peggy, drove Abby back to the city, where she happily relived the family gathering over the phone with her sister, Lucy. The next morning, April 5, she awoke feeling unwell. Junior summoned a doctor, and it was while she was describing her symptoms to the physician that Abby's tired heart stopped beating. An anguished Junior called Nelson, who raced over to 740 Park Avenue to find his father near collapse. "Take this blow away," cried Junior, unable even to look at the lifeless form of the woman he had adored for half a century. At his insistence, Abby was cremated the same day.

Nearly as devastated, Nelson had lost the most important person in his life, in the estimation of his son Steven "probably the only woman to whom he was totally devoted." He clung to her memory in ways both predictable and surprising. At his instigation, Henri Matisse accepted a commission, his last, to design a memorial window for the little chapel just outside the gates of the family estate. Pictures of Abby occupied places of honor in Nelson's bedroom and study. More tangible souvenirs were displayed elsewhere. Two months elapsed before Junior consented to bury his wife's ashes in the ground designated by the couple a decade earlier as a family cemetery. Before the urn containing the cremated remains was sealed, Nelson reached in and cupped a handful of gray, powdery dust. He put it in his pocket. The gesture defined him, for both its childlike impulsiveness and its brazen sense of entitlement. When in due course he claimed Kykuit for himself, he housed the precious substance in an antique funerary urn in the ivory-and-gold drawing room, known as Mother's Room, just off the barrel-vaulted entrance. On a nearby wall he hung portraits of mother and son, their profiles so alike as to be almost indistinguishable.

Eleven

THE GENERAL MANAGER

A very kind man who liked people and liked to be liked.
—NELSON A. ROCKEFELLER on Dwight D. Eisenhower

1

IN COMMON WITH most Republicans, Rockefeller anticipated a change of administration in Washington come January 1949. A month before Election Day, the Council on Foreign Relations approached him about developing a Latin American program "available to Mr. Dewey and Mr. Dulles when they come in." On Tuesday, November 2, the American electorate rendered this assignment moot by choosing Harry Truman over his heavily favored Republican opponent, denounced by one foot soldier in the GOP Old Guard as "that snooty little governor of New York." The surprising defeat of Tom Dewey represented the first crack in the phalanx of eastern media, financial, and legal interests that had nominated Wendell Willkie in 1940 and twice since entrusted its fortunes to the former "Gangbuster" whose electoral success in polyglot New York had done little to endear him to conservatives elsewhere.

The same election elevated Democrats with whom Nelson was on friendly terms. Early in January 1949, he wrote a "Dear Lyn" letter praising freshman senator Lyndon Johnson for his action in securing a burial plot at Arlington National Cemetery for a Mexican American soldier denied the rites accorded his white compatriots in tiny, bigoted Three Rivers, Texas. It was reassuring to know, replied Johnson, "that you, with your great understanding of the Latin American people, believe I did the right thing."

Elsewhere in the nation's capital, events were transpiring that would afford Nelson a fresh chance to burnish his hemispheric credentials. Within days of Truman's reelection, a State Department speechwriter named Ben Hardy, Jr., sent his boss in the Office of Public Affairs a memorandum on foreign aid. Inspired by Hardy's earlier work with the Office of the Coordinator of Inter-American Affairs, the proposal was summarily rejected by Acting Secretary Robert Lovett. A second Hardy draft met the same fate.

On his third try, the speechwriter took his ideas directly to a young White House staffer named George Elsey. Soon presidential adviser Clark Clifford got wind of the initiative, which Truman, in search of a punchy headline for his January 20, 1949, inaugural address, immortalized as Point Four—"a bold new program for making the benefits of our scientific advances and industrial progress available for the improvement and growth of underdeveloped areas." No one welcomed the proposal more heartily than Rockefeller. Unfortunately, his enthusiasm for Point Four wasn't shared by the Truman State Department. Besides the usual bureaucratic fear of the unknown, few in the administration grasped the role of free enterprise in fostering economic development. ("They took their hat off to it as they went by," gibed Nelson.) From his own Latin American experience, Rockefeller had learned that technical assistance without long-term capital investment was a recipe for frustration among donors and recipients alike.

On visits to Washington that spring and summer, Rockefeller buttonholed lawmakers directly, making the case for an agency outside the State Department that would handle foreign aid and economic development. In practical terms, it mattered little who administered the program, since the $45 million voted by Congress—later slashed by $10 million at the insistence of isolationists like Robert Taft—bordered on insult. By its first anniversary, Point Four appeared fated to join the ranks of other inaugural headlines scuttled by inertia and turf wars.

Then fate intervened a second time, as Rockefeller's financial problems in Latin America came to a head against a backdrop of rising global tensions. By some estimates, his Venezuelan operations alone were bleeding $9 million in red ink. The combined effects of IBEC's financial hemorrhaging and Cold War rivalries made a return to government service more tantalizing than ever. "Things were too serious in the world," Rockefeller concluded, "to just spend my time trying to get a whole bunch of little companies on a profitable basis, while Rome burnt." The flames spread in June 1950, after Communist North Korea invaded its southern neighbor, brutally challenging both the United Nations and Truman's policies of containment in the atomic age. Nelson asked for a meeting with the president; Truman conditioned any interview on his first seeing Secretary of State Dean Acheson. Turned down by the imperious secretary, Rockefeller went back to the White House, which noted his effort and granted his request. Outside the Oval Office, Nelson encountered a suave Acheson, who purred, "Do come and see me." When they were alone, Rockefeller urged Truman to publicly acknowledge the support his Korean policies were receiving throughout the hemisphere.

"You know," said Truman, "I'm just as enthusiastic about Latin America as you, if not more so!"

"Wonderful, Mr. President. I just kind of put a few thoughts together for you in case it might be helpful."

"You take it up with Acheson. I think we ought to do this. I'll make any speech he sends over. What occasion could I use?"

Retracing his steps to the State Department, Rockefeller found Acheson outwardly gracious but wary of any commitment. Nelson next sought out Averell Harriman, "the one bright spot to me in the Washington scene" and a casual friend since the 1930s, when the two men skied the slopes of Harriman's Sun Valley, Idaho, resort. In the intervening years, the politically ambitious Harriman had become a New Deal troubleshooter, representing FDR at Stalin's court, earning the title "Expediter" for his work on Lend-Lease, and winning fresh plaudits for his implementation of the Marshall Plan through the Economic Cooperation Administration. Early in October 1950, Harriman approached Nelson about chairing the International Development Advisory Board, established by Truman to carry out Point Four. His responsibilities needn't interfere with the ongoing work of AIA and IBEC, Harriman assured him. A presidential promise of unfettered access to the Oval Office sealed the deal.

In announcing his appointment on November 2, 1950, Truman characterized Nelson as the group's managing director. "The whole foreign economic picture in Washington is in a state of flux," Rockefeller wrote his cousin Richard Aldrich. His new assignment "may give us a real chance to help get things cleared up a bit." For the next five months he worked harmoniously with a dozen members drawn from the ranks of business, labor, agriculture, and the academy; their headquarters was the West Fifty-fourth Street townhouse recently deeded to Nelson by his father. For help with his latest project, Nelson turned to Oscar Ruebhausen, a thirty-eight-year-old Manhattan attorney recommended to him by David Rockefeller after it became clear that IBEC and its continuing struggle for survival would monopolize John Lockwood. "A gentle, soft-voiced intellectual," says one colleague of Ruebhausen's, "with a great sense of ethics and propriety . . . a counselor in the best sense of the word." Ruebhausen's credentials as a liberal Democrat were at least as attractive to Nelson as his legal acumen. A good lawyer can master any subject in two weeks, Ruebhausen claimed. "Now that I like," replied Rockefeller, because "with the help of any good lawyer I can do the same."

Thus began a thirty-year relationship, professional and personal, wherein Ruebhausen functioned as adviser without portfolio. "He would just call up and I'd come over with no idea what would be involved or who would be present," Ruebhausen recalled. The topic at hand might be a Manhattan real estate deal, the expansion of Social Security in the Eisenhower years, or a Cold War crusade to build fallout shelters for every New Yorker. Beginning late in 1950,

Ruebhausen shared work space at 13 West Fifty-fourth with John French, the Dartmouth roommate whom Nelson had designated executive secretary to the International Development Advisory Board. Half a century earlier, their office had served as a bedroom for Junior and Abby. An adjoining dressing room housed secretarial staff, with board stationery stashed in Junior's former shirt drawers.

Ruebhausen's new friend could intuitively read other people better than anyone the lawyer had ever known. "Many times I've been with him, a new person came on, and within seconds of their first meeting they were buddies," he observed. "It used to be said that no one ever came into Nelson's office who didn't go out floating on Cloud Nine." Yet Rockefeller's sunny outlook did not blind him to individual shortcomings. "People have strengths and weaknesses," he told Ruebhausen. "You use their strengths, you play to their strengths, and if the weaknesses overwhelm the strengths . . . you have to drop them." Until then, the pragmatic Rockefeller resolved to think, and extract, the best of his professional colleagues. At meetings of the development board—wryly christened by Ruebhausen "the Commission to Decide What Point Four Was Supposed to Be Doing"—Nelson kept people talking. More than a good listener, he played the egos around his committee table like rare instruments. Inevitably after some tedious intervention, Rockefeller turned to staff members lining the perimeter of the room. "Make a note," he instructed them, "make sure that that point is covered in our report," recalled Ruebhausen. "The speaker would feel ten feet tall."*

Conceding the group dynamics thus generated, Ruebhausen remained mystified by Nelson's emphasis on atmospherics. Then pollster Samuel Lubell introduced his preliminary findings, sparking a lively debate between publisher Henry Luce and labor leader Jacob Potofsky. Others joined the clash of ideas, until it seemed everyone around the table was demanding to be heard. Rockefeller complimented his colleagues for a useful session, then suggested they adjourn for the balance of the afternoon. As chairs were pushed back and committee members filed out onto Sixth Avenue, the chairman beckoned to Mr. Lubell—could he possibly stay behind for a minute? The door closed behind them. "Sam," said Nelson, his face setting like concrete, "in the space of two minutes you destroyed what I've tried to do for six months, which is to bring this group together."

He paused, to let the sting of his words sink in.

"All you need to do is tell me what you want," said a nonplussed Lubell, "and I'll find the words that you'll like."

---

* Invited to name Rockefeller's closest friends, Ruebhausen replied unhesitatingly, "Whoever he's working with at the moment." Oscar Ruebhausen, AI.

But Rockefeller had already moved on. "We cannot have a divided committee. We have to reach consensus."

In that moment, the scales fell from Oscar Ruebhausen's eyes. All the months seemingly wasted indulging dubious proposals or taking questionable detours were part of a plan, shrewdly drawn and meticulously executed, by a man who knew precisely where he wanted to lead his colleagues. Rockefeller's tactics paid off at the beginning of March 1951, when committee members unanimously approved *Partners in Progress*, a sweeping blueprint for change anticipating by thirty years the global debate over North–South inequities and free trade linked to worker protections. The report urged creation of an Overseas Economic Administration, capitalized with $500 million to spend on improved public health, job training, and education in underserved parts of the globe. A second agency, the International Development Authority, would fund infrastructure, transport, and irrigation works.

While the IDA aided needy countries, a new International Finance Corporation would assist needy companies by employing less restrictive loan-making criteria than the World Bank. Rockefeller wanted U.S. tax laws amended to encourage overseas investment. Finally, long before NAFTA and other free trade agreements, *Partners in Progress* advocated liberalized trade policies through the negotiation of mutually beneficial commercial treaties. Chairman Rockefeller had reason to be pleased with his handiwork. Therein, by the tortured logic of official Washington, lay the problem. His success set off alarms throughout the bureaucracy. Officials in the Budget Bureau opposed a new superagency outside of State. So, unsurprisingly, did members of the Truman cabinet. The unkindest cut of all came from Nelson's friend Averell Harriman. "Like a little boy with an apple," Rockefeller went to see Harriman, whom he belatedly realized had no intention of surrendering the control he exercised through the Economic Cooperation Administration. Pulling rank, Harriman withheld permission for Nelson to personally present *Partners in Progress* to the president. Worse, he dropped hints the report would never see the light of publication.

To this, Nelson responded with a muffled threat of his own.

"You know how it is," he told Harriman. What with *The New York Times* snooping around town, he had reason to believe that the paper might have obtained a copy of the report (which it had, courtesy of Frank Jamieson). It would be "unfortunate" were such a leak to appear in print before the president had a chance to review his own committee's product.

"All right," said Harriman. "I guess we had better let it out."

That this was a pyrrhic victory became evident when Truman presented his foreign aid package to Congress on May 24, 1951. The president asked for an additional $400 million in economic assistance for the underdeveloped world.

Otherwise he gave no evidence of having even read the Rockefeller report. A bit forlornly, Nelson informed his aunt Lucy early in June, "I've been wandering around the country making speeches, trying to arouse some public interest in this question of international development and its importance to our own economy as well as our security." With $4 million of Ford Foundation money, Nelson told its president, Paul Hoffman, he could break the back of Indian famine. His request anticipated that country's green revolution. But the challenge, and glory, of converting the world's largest democracy into agricultural self-sufficiency would fall to others.

In October 1951, Truman announced that Averell Harriman was to direct the newly established Mutual Security Agency, with Acheson's State Department retaining control of all technical assistance efforts. By then it was painfully obvious to Rockefeller that Point Four would never amount to anything more than assistance "along extension service lines." Before tendering his resignation, he shared what he had learned with U.S. ambassador to India Chester Bowles. If India's crushing needs were to be addressed seriously, local enterprise must be supplemented by international investment "both governmental and private." And the only way to mobilize such resources, he told Bowles, was through "a joint commission under the leadership of outstanding men."*

Once a Rockefeller, always a Rockefeller.

His second departure from Truman's Washington was amicable enough, the president expressing regret that he couldn't appoint Nelson to another post in his aging administration. He also urged Rockefeller to become a Democrat. In later years, much would be made of Nelson's failure to heed the presidential counsel. This overlooked one crucial factor, quite apart from familial loyalties: At the start of 1952, with the Korean War in bloody stalemate and China overrun by Mao Tse-tung's Red armies, Truman and his Democratic brethren were widely discredited. Adding to public angst, Soviet spies had shattered the West's nuclear monopoly. Fears of domestic Communist subversion were on the rise. Petty White House scandals added to a pervasive sense, after twenty years in power, that Truman's party was out of touch. In the twilight of his presidency, Truman enjoyed the lowest approval ratings since the dawn of modern opinion polling.

Under the circumstances it defied logic for Nelson, nearing the end of a long, often frustrating voyage under Democratic captains, to lash himself to the mast on the eve of a Republican restoration. Moreover, by 1952 the GOP's

---

* Putting his money where his mouth was, in 1950 Nelson invested $100,000 in the Amun-Israel Housing Corporation, a joint venture by the International Ladies' Garment Workers' Union and the Amalgamated Clothing Workers to construct low-income housing in Israel. Sixteen years later, the bonds were paid off, with interest.

Eastern Establishment, long synonymous with the Rockefeller family, felt confident that its brand of progressive conservatism, shorn of isolationist barnacles and broadly accommodating to the welfare state bequeathed by FDR, might at last command a majority of restive voters. Especially if the face of Republican realignment wore a grin as wide as the Kansas prairie.

2

THE SMILE IN question concealed manipulative talents of a rare order. Like his boyhood hero George Washington, Dwight Eisenhower was a gifted conjurer, whose greatest trick was to present himself as a political innocent. "I don't like this business; these politicians are terrible," Eisenhower complained to a visitor during the 1952 presidential campaign. To reinforce his point, the reluctant candidate lifted up a corner of the carpet on which he stood. "You see them crawling out from under there," Eisenhower fumed. Not until he was several years out of office, his presidency dismissed by academic historians as a gray-suited interregnum between the stirring forties and liberating sixties, did more discerning observers detect in the simple old soldier both guile and ruthlessness. In 1967, Nelson agreed to an interview on the Eisenhower administration for the Columbia University Oral History Collection (after stipulating the transcript was to be sealed for thirty years or his own death, whichever came later). Then in his third term as governor of New York, Rockefeller chose his words carefully. Even so, he could barely conceal his disdain for the 1950s as a time of missed opportunities and the Eisenhower presidency itself as "an acceptance of the status quo, which, in terms of the moment, was perfectly adequate."

Faint praise indeed. Rockefeller was tone-deaf to the popular desire for what Warren Harding had memorably, if ungrammatically, called normalcy. Yet that is precisely what most Americans craved following a tumultuous quarter century scarred by economic hardship, incessant warfare, and a precarious, nuclear-tipped peace. A decade later, out of office and with Ike in his grave, Rockefeller offered a more candid, if even less charitable, assessment. By then scholars had begun to recast Eisenhower as a shrewd and steady hand in times of global uncertainty. Rockefeller disagreed. To him the Eisenhower presidency represented "a slow retreat" before the advancing Soviet Union and the death rattle of European colonialism.

In reality, Ike's greatest shortcoming lay for Nelson in the fact that he wasn't Franklin Roosevelt. A treasured photograph of the late president, boldly inscribed, "To my old friend Nelson Rockefeller," occupied a prominent place in the West Fifty-fourth Street Clubhouse. "Everything about Roosevelt Rockefeller just adored," says Richard Allison, who worked in Rockefeller's vice presidential office. "He felt Roosevelt saved the country from Communism. . . . 'If you don't give people something to hope for,'" Allison quoted Nelson, "'eventually they're going to take it away from you.'" Roosevelt the pragmatist had not lost any sleep over deficit spending as an alternative to mass unemployment. Moreover, as Theodore Roosevelt's temperamental heir, he had gloried in his self-proclaimed status of "preacher president." Not so Eisenhower, whose stern fiscal orthodoxy gave birth to the "New Look" defense policy emphasizing nuclear deterrence in place of more costly conventional weapons and whose suspicions of the rhetorical presidency made him uncomfortable in the bully pulpit. "The job is to convince, not publicize," Ike maintained. In less guarded moments he went further, contending that if a president's words were the measure of his leadership, the American people could elect Ernest Hemingway.

In contrast with his immediate predecessors, politicians and publicists to their fingertips, Eisenhower appeared to Nelson a prisoner of the army hierarchy, wherein the man at the top took responsibility for decisions crafted by underlings and endorsed by his chief of staff. A life in uniform had left Eisenhower not merely apolitical, claimed Rockefeller, but ignorant of most issues with which a modern chief executive must deal. This made him all the more dependent on subordinates, most notably his dour, tough-talking secretary of state, John Foster Dulles. Nelson had sung a markedly different tune in the spring of 1952. Then he had been quick to congratulate Dulles, chairman of the Rockefeller Foundation board, for his part in negotiating a permanent peace treaty between the United States and Japan. Moreover, he professed delight that Dulles was joining the campaign to draft Eisenhower for the GOP presidential nomination.

Rockefeller, hoping for an entrée into the next administration, bankrolled a series of government reorganization studies carried out by Temple University and building on the efforts of a landmark commission chaired by former president Herbert Hoover. Within days of Eisenhower's election, the Temple surveys in his pocket, Rockefeller urged the president-elect to exploit the "negative veto" invented by Congress in a spasm of demobilizing fervor. Goaded by the original Hoover Commission, lawmakers had passed the initiative to the executive: any restructuring plan he introduced would be automatically implemented unless rejected by both houses of Congress within sixty days. Taking advantage of the power shift, Nelson advised Ike to create his own reorganization panel, chaired by future CIA director John McCone.

Eisenhower accepted the idea, albeit with a twist. On January 27, 1953, he issued the first executive order of his presidency, establishing the President's Advisory Committee on Government Organization, to be led not by McCone, but by Nelson Rockefeller. Rounding out the three-member board were educator Arthur Flemming, who also doubled as head of the Office of Defense Mobilization, and the president's brother Milton, whose service under four presidents gave him an unparalleled knowledge of the federal government and its workings. The inclusion of Milton Eisenhower on PACGO confirmed the committee's special status, even as it placed discreet limits upon Nelson's mandate as chairman.

For the third time in a dozen years, Rockefeller moved into a hastily prepared suite of offices in the former State, War, and Navy Building next door to the White House. To supplement a small staff borrowed from the Office of Defense Mobilization, Nelson raided the Civil Service Commission and the Bureau of the Budget. He also laid on a sprinkling of experts from Room 5600, paying them out of his own pocket. The lights in the garish old structure burned late as the ad hoc group rushed to take advantage of the new president's political honeymoon. During their first weeks in office, Rockefeller went out of his way to consult Secretary Dulles, whose desire to concentrate his energies on policy formulation dovetailed neatly with Nelson's long-standing wish to divorce the State Department from foreign aid and economic development. Dulles consequently raised no objection when Rockefeller and his committee recommended creation of the Foreign Operations Administration—an initiative recycled from the ill-fated *Partners in Progress* report—and a separate United States Information Agency.

Not all Rockefeller's plans won such ready acceptance. His call for a federal Department of Transportation found little favor among Detroit automakers, who blocked its implementation until 1967. Likewise, the notion of a single, all-powerful councillor replacing the Council of Economic Advisers never left the gate. Only in his famed farewell address did Eisenhower endorse Rockefeller's proposed first secretary of the cabinet, a sort of deputy president for foreign policy. Of much more immediate interest was a Pentagon overhaul, designed to strengthen civilian oversight and curtail interservice rivalries. Besides eliminating five hundred positions in the defense secretary's office, Ike wanted to abolish the Munitions Board, the Research and Development Board, and the Defense Supply Management Agency. This guaranteed stiff opposition from friends of the status quo. Appearing before the relevant congressional committees, Rockefeller convinced enough skeptics to secure final passage of a watered-down proposal.

In time, PACGO advanced thirteen restructuring packages, ten of which were implemented. Contrary to its original mandate, the committee did not fold up in 1953 but stayed in business throughout the Eisenhower years, thereby confirming the old saw that nothing in Washington is so lasting as a temporary government agency. Grateful for the direct pipeline to the Oval Office, Rockefeller remained on the board until his election as governor of New York in 1958. Eisenhower welcomed his input, to a point. "He has one hundred ideas," the president told his personal secretary, Ann Whitman. "One of them may be brilliant . . . it's worthwhile to have him around because that one idea is worth the ninety-nine that aren't."* One such line of thinking is hinted at in an April 1953 exchange between Nelson and Vannevar Bush, president of the Carnegie Institution of Washington and godfather to the wartime mobilization of American scientists that culminated in the atomic bomb. "Our little chat about the utilization of solar energy has prompted me to get to work on it," Bush informed Rockefeller. "You jarred me out of my quiescence."

He was happy to hear it, replied the grandson of John D. Rockefeller. As for the possibility of converting sunlight into a substitute for fossil fuels, Nelson concluded, "I could not be more interested."

3

DURING THE FIRST week of March 1953, Rockefeller reported to his son Rod the completion of five reorganization plans, singling out for mention a patchwork quilt of existing agencies, bureaus, and offices loosely arrayed around the New Deal–era Federal Security Agency. "We have been negotiating with the various medical and educational groups, all of whom are anxious to have separate departments for their own activities," wrote Nelson. It was all "terribly interesting," and it was only a matter of time before leaders in Congress gave their assent to the emerging department. Did Rockefeller envision a place at the cabinet table for himself? As it happened, Eisenhower already had a candidate to oversee the departmental hybrid called Health, Education, and Welfare. Oveta Culp Hobby was the modish publisher of the *Houston Post*, which she owned jointly with her husband, former Texas governor Will Hobby. A conservative Democrat, Mrs. Hobby had been instrumental in carrying the Lone Star State for Eisenhower, who reciprocated by naming her director of the FSA, with an implied promotion to secretary should the agency be elevated to cabinet status.†

---

* A much more favorable estimate of Rockefeller's contributions to the Eisenhower administration came from General—then Colonel—Andrew Goodpaster, who served as White House staff secretary. Informed in 2001 of Whitman's remark, Goodpaster told the author, "I would put the ratio [of good ideas] closer to fifty–fifty."

† Nelson's unsubtle methods of ingratiation with the heroic figure in the Oval Office may have hurt his cabinet prospects more than they helped. Early in the administration, Rockefeller installed a one-hole golf course at his Foxhall Road estate. He paid for trees and more than two

A month after Eisenhower submitted Reorganization Plan #1 to Congress, its author was offered the job of HEW undersecretary as a consolation prize. For Rockefeller to accept a second-tier appointment was shrewd, if surprising. A stint as Hobby's deputy would broaden his knowledge of the domestic scene; equally important, it would establish him as a team player among Republicans suspicious of his previous service in Democratic administrations. By succeeding at HEW, Nelson could help Eisenhower succeed as the first Republican president since Herbert Hoover, dispelling the GOP's Depression-era stigma as the party of the boardroom and the country club. Ironically, in doing Ike's bidding to broaden Republican appeal, Rockefeller made more enemies than friends among fiscal conservatives within the administration, to say nothing of an emerging coterie of rightward-thinking opinion makers, academics, and polemicists.

Openly critical of Senator Joseph McCarthy and his increasingly reckless charges of Communist subversion, at PACGO Nelson argued in vain for creation of an executive branch investigatory body to steal McCarthy's thunder. One Saturday morning, the phone rang in the Washington hotel room of Charles Metzner, a Republican lawyer from New York then serving as an assistant to Attorney General Herbert Brownell.

"This is Nelson Rockefeller calling, and I need some help." With Brownell out of town, the newly installed HEW undersecretary was reaching out to Metzner in his place. "I've got a subpoena here that is from McCarthy and he just asked for all our files. What shall I tell him to do?"

"Tell him to go to hell," said Metzner. He went on to explain that owing to the volume of identical requests from other agencies and government officials, the Justice Department had drafted a form letter with which to respond to the senator's documentary fishing expeditions. Now, as the Red scare crested in the early fifties, Rockefeller wrote letters of his own extolling the loyalty of Lincoln School classmates and of wartime co-workers tainted by their New Deal associations. He engaged in lobbying of a different sort with the American Medical Association, whose objections to HEW must be overcome before the new department could be formalized. With that hurdle cleared, in the second week of April 1953 Nelson accepted Hobby's job offer.

"*E pluribus unum*," joked Nelson of HEW, a disjointed behemoth of ten

---

thousand tulip bulbs at Eisenhower's Gettysburg farm, gifted the president with a sketch map of the Gettysburg battlefield endorsed by Union victor General George Meade, and, a decade after D-Day, presented Ike with the chairs and table used in planning the Allied invasion. The course went unplayed, the historic furniture found a home at the Dwight D. Eisenhower Library in Abilene, Kansas. And a Rockefeller subsequently embittered by his own failure to reach the White House would privately lambast the recipient of these presents as "the biggest freeloader around." Stuart Spencer, AI.

separate operating units and three federal corporations, whose thirty-five thousand employees administered an annual budget of $6 billion, two-thirds of it earmarked for Social Security recipients. The most unlikely of bureaucrats, "he never ambled into a room," recalled one bemused co-worker. "He came in like a bullet or a bolt of lightning, on time and expecting everybody else to be on time. He wouldn't sit down but would jitterbug around until he'd finished talking." Rockefeller ordered up "the Chart Room" for HEW, reminiscent of the wartime setting in which he had promoted his agenda as coordinator of the CIAA. "In the beginning he used the Chart Room as the vehicle to knock heads together," one colleague would remember. Weekly staff meetings became daily ones, as the Children's Bureau was introduced to the Food and Drug Administration, and the Office of Vocational Rehabilitation learned what the surgeon general was thinking.

The Chart Room was a metaphor for Rockefeller's HEW: bustling, informal, full of surprises, and subject to congressional scrutiny for its alleged extravagance. Charts had another advantage—they limited verbosity. Even so, it took three months to get everyone talking around the same table, the prerequisite to developing a common legislative agenda. When the Public Health Service, already resentful of its forced cohabitation with Social Security and various welfare agencies, attempted a budgetary end run before the House Appropriations Committee in 1954, Rockefeller was on hand to deliver a scathing public rebuttal to the "technician" it had dispatched to engage in "empire building." Citing his own two decades with the Westchester Board of Health, he stressed the desirability of a local, community-based approach over federal domination. Rockefeller took a special interest in Howard University, the historically black college in the nation's capital, for which he secured $6 million in federal construction funds, while substantially modernizing the Freedmen's Hospital.

Switching from Mr. Inside to Mr. Outside, Rockefeller hosted a parade of congressmen, each treated to a chart presentation and a heavy dose of undersecretarial salesmanship. One early visitor was freshman senator Barry Goldwater, an ardent conservative from Arizona, whose antipathy to government programs made him suspicious of Eisenhower as an appeaser of the New Deal. Goldwater had nevertheless agreed to attend a departmental briefing and pitch on behalf of expanded vocational rehabilitation, promoted by Nelson as a cost-effective means of freeing individuals from government dependency. Since Rockefeller didn't like to use an easel, this entailed scaling stepladders to hang the appropriate graphics, each designed to be read from fifty feet away, like so much washing on a line. Assisting in the process was a young woman unable to reach the needed height herself, who sought help from someone she took to be head of the graphics department.

A few minutes later, Rockefeller walked through the door. Visibly annoyed, he asked if someone could please call Senator Goldwater's office to learn his whereabouts.

"I'm up here," said Goldwater from atop the ladder as he finished hanging the last of Nelson's charts.

Rockefeller was just as likely to turn up where least expected. Offsetting the gray facelessness of bureaucracy, Nelson remembered birthdays. Sick co-workers were astonished to find the undersecretary ringing their doorbell, clutching the one-man apothecary that earned him the nickname "Dr. Rocke-feller." Facing a Government Printing Office deadline for a departmental booklet, he stayed until five in the morning, cheering on his troops. Most days lunch was a hurried snack at his desk between meetings. "There's no question but that the federal government has just gotten too big and hard to manage," he wrote his aunt Lucy Aldrich in May 1954, "but I don't know what can be done about it!"—a curious observation coming from the chairman of PACGO.

His zeal and intellectual energy made Rockefeller de facto leader of HEW. Yet he was careful to walk two paces behind Secretary Hobby, an accomplished woman in her own right and a mother of two who resented Nelson's habit of peering into her appointment book for the telltale words *beauty parlor*. One sultry Washington evening she got to upstage her deputy, literally, in his own backyard as the Rockefellers threw a party for the entire cabinet at Foxhall Road. Spurning a proffered glass of wine, Hobby asked for Scotch, bourbon, gin, vodka, and rye. "I want it for everybody and I want it right now," she muttered through clenched teeth, pointing out that Secretary of Defense Charles Wilson was about to die. Nelson disappeared into the house. Shortly afterward he returned, with Tod, who said that dinner was ready to be served. It could wait, Hobby directed. "Hold it until everybody has had a drink and don't serve it until the secretary of defense has had two." Their meal remained uneaten as dusk fell and Charlie Wilson rose to perform, at Mrs. Hobby's request, a well-lubricated rendition of "The Face on the Barroom Floor."

4

THE SLIGHTLY FLUSTERED young woman who had mistaken Barry Gold-water for the head of the graphics department was a pretty extrovert of twenty-five, transplanted to Washington from Cashiers, North Carolina. In the spring of 1953, her politics were undoubtedly closer to those of the Arizona senator than to those of her new boss. Like many women of her generation, Nancy Hanks was to be a quiet revolutionary, one for whom the struggle to reconcile tradition and trailblazing exacted a high price. The successful job application letter she mailed to Charles E. Wilson,* chairman of Harry Truman's Office of Defense Mobilization, was in fact written by her father, a Wilson friend. With the changing of the political guard early in 1953, her curiosity was piqued by the incessant activity unfolding at the other end of the corridor in the Old Executive Office Building, where Nelson Rockefeller and his PACGO crew were burning the midnight oil.

Nancy volunteered her services, putting in twelve-hour workdays and burying her nose in briefing books when away from the office. Rockefeller's hunch about her professional potential was fully vindicated. Long after carving out a distinguished career of her own, culminating in the chairmanship of the National Endowment for the Arts—a federal program itself sprung from the head of Rockefeller's New York State Council on the Arts—Nancy Hanks in turn credited Nelson for showing her how to work to exhaustion; to win over recalcitrant lawmakers by thinking like them ("He says if you want to win a discussion . . . you start talking from the other person's point of view, not your own"); even how to distill twenty pages of turgid government prose into one-page "Nancy memos" in recognition of his dyslexia.

She learned as well to emulate his perfectionism. Ordinarily the soul of courtesy, Nelson could turn petulant if his beloved charts were out of order. Other than this, Nancy could recall only a single instance in which he lost his temper in her presence. An unkept promise triggered the outburst. From everyone around the HEW conference table, Rockefeller had obtained assurances that a vital objective could be realized. Events proved otherwise, causing him, most uncharacteristically, to vent his anger in public. "He really didn't care that it was impossible to do," said Hanks. "He cared that no one told him it was impossible when he could have done something about it."

With her slim figure, shy smile, and Carolina drawl, Nancy offered a captivating cross between Becky Thatcher and the Gibson Girl. Appreciated for her fresh-faced, unmolded quality, she exuded a sensuality all the more potent for its freckled innocence. (Her closest approach to profanity: a ladylike "By gum!") Inevitably, Nancy became part of Nelson's life away from the office. Colleagues noticed her slipping off to Foxhall Road for marathon work sessions with the boss. In letters to her parents, she described their "comradeship" in terms suspiciously domestic. She fixed Nelson's socks and accompanied him on excursions to the museum and gardens at Dumbarton Oaks. When Rockefeller mentioned a rekindled interest in the Bible, Nancy presented him with a revised edition.

---

* Not to be confused with *Ike's* Charles Wilson, the former auto executive whose political ineptitude at the Pentagon was to severely test Eisenhower's patience.

His gifts to her were considerably more elaborate. They included Picasso drawings and a stock portfolio worth $200,000.

Co-workers thought the relationship close but not clandestine. "Nancy once brought him around to my house," recalled Nadia Williams of Nelson's HEW staff. "She felt he needed to brush up against regular people." In August 1954, Nelson paid his first visit to Nancy's parents in western North Carolina. He later sent them a $5,000 check, enabling her father, Bryan, to dam a mountain stream on his property and thereby create "Rock Lake." Nelson invited himself back to Cashiers for a post-Christmas look. "I can just imagine Bryan's mountain, with maybe a light snow on the ground," he wrote in advance of his trip. "Wouldn't it be wonderful to have a picnic lunch by a big fire there on the ledge looking out over the valley and the mountains. Then maybe we could walk down to Rock Lake by the little cabin in the woods. I did so like the story you told me about it." Between the recent off-year elections and budget preparations, Rockefeller continued, life in Washington was hectic as ever. "Nancy as always has been a tower of strength. Her good judgment and quiet ability to deal with all problems mean more to me than I can say. . . . But you know what a wonderful person she is," Nelson enthused, "and very much like her parents."

5

IN HIS 1977 oral histories, recorded in anticipation of a memoir that was never written, Rockefeller expounded one of his more curious theories about Dwight Eisenhower, whose alleged insecurities he blamed on an unhappy marriage. How different things might have been, Nelson maintained, if only Ike had permitted himself the sustaining emotional support of his devoted secretary, Ann Whitman, or even Mrs. Hobby. Instead, he contended, the president was harassed by a jealous wife unable to let go of Eisenhower's wartime relationship with his driver-aide, Kay Summersby. One can only speculate whether Rockefeller was projecting onto Eisenhower his own marital inadequacies. Certainly the hours he spent with Nancy Hanks represented time subtracted from Tod and their children. During the war, the Rockefellers had lived together at Foxhall Road. Now they were separated by geographic distance, Nelson's middle-aged restlessness, and the unavoidable splintering of a family with college-age youngsters. "It leaves the house very empty," Nelson told Lucy Aldrich in October 1952, "and Mary (Tod) particularly has missed them tremendously."

Rarely seen in Washington, Tod Rockefeller divided her days between 810

Fifth Avenue, now grown to thirty-two rooms, and Hawes House on the Pocantico estate. Well past her childbearing years, she remained rail thin and high-minded. A younger visitor to the Fifth Avenue triplex described the woman of the house as "pure Main Line," hastening to add, "The best of the Main Line." By this he meant a starchy integrity that didn't conceal her basic kindness. On one occasion, Tod found herself penniless on the Fifth Avenue bus. "Oh, dear driver, I have forgotten to bring any money," she informed the man behind the wheel. "But I am Mrs. Nelson Rockefeller, and if you will give me your address, I will send you money." The driver ordered her to the back of the vehicle.

Young Johnny Apple, then serving his journalistic apprenticeship with *The Wall Street Journal*, briefly dated Mary, the younger Rockefeller daughter. Visiting 810 Fifth Avenue one afternoon, Apple saw Tod pick up a persistently ringing phone.

"Yes, yes. I see. . . . No, Mrs. Rockefeller is not here. But I'll be certain to pass on the message. What is the name again? . . . Christini."

Tod hung up. Turning to her guest, she said, deadpan, "They'd be horrified if they thought I answered my own phone."

It was Tod who pushed her husband into changing restrictive rules that prevented Jews from joining the Seal Harbor Club. Once a year she welcomed her bridesmaids for a raucous reunion at which they kicked up their heels and performed the Charleston with undiminished glee. The tomboy of her youth lingered still in the middle-aged matriarch who shunned makeup and cheerfully climbed into cherry trees, seeking fruit for a pie. Gardening remained a passion. So did ocean racing off the Maine coast in the *Nirvana*, a seventy-foot ketch that Nelson gave her one Christmas; and roughing it in a rustic camp on Shingle Island, an hour's sail from Seal Harbor.

His prolonged absences left a special vacancy in the lives of Nelson's children. Compensation came in the form of extended family trips to Europe, Africa, and South America, Thanksgiving in Bermuda, and long car journeys to Choate, Exeter, or Wellesley. Visiting Spain in the spring of 1952, Nelson informed his aunt Lucy, "Six of us traveled in a station wagon with a chauffeur! We had to stop every hour because those riding in the back seat showed serious signs of wear." His head was spinning yet with cathedrals, mosques, and El Greco canvases. Another spring he took the twins, Mary and Michael, to pick up their sister, Ann, at her Swiss school; they then repaired to Paris for a "heavenly" few days.

When in New York, it was Nelson's custom to wake the youngsters each morning for a vigorous round of push-ups and sit-ups in his dressing room, after which he led them in prayers and a short Bible reading. Reenacting another childhood ritual, Nelson insisted on account keeping and the obligatory character-building allowance, minus 10 percent to be saved and an equal amount set aside for charity. When called for, he administered discipline with a hairbrush. His return at the end of a strenuous day in the city was an event. Clutching his father's briefcase, Steven marched up the hill to the guesthouse, whose construction, more than a decade earlier, symbolized the unspoken marital pact by which his parents maintained appearances. An invigorating dip in the pool was followed by quiet moments of father-son interaction. After Steven gave him an Indian figure he had carved from wood, a delighted Nelson began calling him Chief or Chiefie, terms of endearment that were soon applied to his youngest son, Michael, as well. The boys reciprocated in the private language with which families communicate, baffling those not born to the blood.

Chiefie was not a name easily applied to the fastidious Rodman Rockefeller. When asked what he wanted for his ninth birthday, the eldest Rockefeller son answered neckties. Such decorum, reinforced by his lean, angular features and public diffidence, denoted the Clark in his makeup. From his father, Rodman derived a lifelong interest in the visual arts. Together with his sister Ann, he attended the Lincoln School until it shut its doors permanently in 1948. From there the boy went on to the Deerfield Academy and, inevitably, to Dartmouth College. Summer jobs as an oil company laborer and a Venezuelan farmhand preceded a two-year stint in the army and graduate work at the Columbia Business School. In one respect, at least, the firstborn beat his father to the punch. In 1953, a full year before his Dartmouth commencement, Rodman wed Barbara Olsen, with whom he would raise four children. That same year, he received from his father a New Year's check for $2,000 in recognition, said Nelson, of his understanding of the value of money.

Unusual for his generation, Rodman relished his patrimony. "I can honestly say that being a Rockefeller has never been a burden," he told authors Peter Collier and David Horowitz. "It's one thing I have no doubts about." His siblings were more ambivalent. By his own account, Steven spent his happiest summer far from New York, working on his grandfather's JY Ranch in Wyoming, where he ate meals with the foreman and his wife in their small kitchen. As for his sisters, Nelson consulted J. Edgar Hoover over their security, and Louis Armstrong performed at their coming-out parties, yet on a trip to Versailles Ann Rockefeller was embarrassed to discover the role her grandfather had played in its restoration. Within the family, Ann's adventurous outlook evoked comparisons with her grandmother Abby. She spent the summer of 1953 as a social worker in London's East End, living in a $10-a-week youth hostel. There she met Robert L. Pierson, an Episcopal seminarian she married in 1955, a year after his ordination. Following their wedding, the Piersons moved to Evanston, Illinois, where Robert promoted campus ministries and Ann seemingly found contentment as a suburban mother.

Ann's sister, Mary, studied clinical psychology at Vassar. "They are crazy about Mary," Nelson informed Rod in November 1952. "Her marks were all B- or better. You seem to have set a standard which everyone is trying to live up to. Stevie has only one mark below 90." Yet while Rodman accepted without question the advantages that went with his name, Mary was eager to sample life beyond the Rockefeller orbit. At the urging of her twin brother, Michael, she found solace in the anonymity of an Arizona Navajo reservation. "We lived in a trailer and ate out of cans and lived among people who had never heard of a Rockefeller," she said long afterward, still cherishing the memory. Back in New York, Mary was courted by journalist Johnny Apple. One afternoon, the couple pulled out a record player and danced to the popular standard "On the Sunny Side of the Street." As the vocalist crooned about being rich as Rockefeller, Mary visibly winced.

"I hate to be called rich," she confided to her partner. "Father always brought us up not to think about money."*

Michael Rockefeller remained something of a family pet, accompanying his father on Saturday afternoon visits to New York art galleries, much as Nelson had been indoctrinated into modern art by his mother. Nelson sent the boy's passport photo, aged eleven, to Lucy Aldrich. "I wish your mother could see it, she was so fond of him," the old lady replied. In February 1954, his parents brought young Michael along when visiting Aunt Lucy at the Aldrich mansion in Providence. "It was such fun to see you and to share with Tod and Michael the wealth of beautiful things in your house," Nelson told his aunt afterward. "Michael was simply enchanted with the visit and everything he saw."

At Pocantico there appeared little, at least at the outset of the fifties, to distinguish the generation known as "the cousins" from "the brothers" before them. Nelson's children were taught how to drive in a 1949 Crossley Hotshot, doorless successor to the Red Bug Flyer their father and his siblings had used for the same purpose. On weekends, the vast Playhouse beckoned to anyone interested in a swim, a game of tennis, or bowling, though the place struck Ann Rockefeller as dark and ominous, the perfect setting for games like Murder in the Dark and Sardines. Only slightly more cheerful was Sunday dinner with Grandfather, their arrival at the big house timed precisely for one o'clock in deference to his unvarying routine. This hardly set them apart; even now Junior's children saw their father by appointment. Increasingly he lived in the past, traversing his principality at ten miles per hour in an electric coupé that

---

* This was no isolated incident. On a visit to the island of Marguerite off the Venezuelan coast, Ann Rockefeller spotted some beautiful pearls retrieved from nearby waters. "Gee, I wish I were rich," she remarked, an observation that sparked considerable mirth among the locals. Clifford Wharton, AI.

had a steering stick instead of a wheel. "I really belong in Williamsburg," acknowledged the patriarch, clinging to habits that formed a bulwark against the frenetic, unmannerly culture lapping at his gates.

After 1951, even the gates were no longer his own. Confronting his mortality meant taking steps to head off potentially crushing estate taxes. According to David Rockefeller, it was Nelson who first approached his father with the idea of selling Pocantico to his sons. Junior's less than enthusiastic response led Nelson to issue an ultimatum of sorts ("stretching the truth by quite a bit," in David's telling): Failure to sell would likely prompt him, John, Laurance, and David to follow in the footsteps of their sensationally divorced brother, Winthrop, who was soon to abandon New York for a fresh start in Arkansas. Backed into a corner, Junior created the Hills Realty Company, to which he transferred formal ownership of the estate early in 1951. A year and a half later, he sold his shares, for $152,059 apiece, to his five sons. Their eagerness to take title to the property did not extend to paying for its upkeep as long as their father was alive.

In the interim, Junior exacted a revenge of sorts. Three years after Abby's abrupt death, he remained inconsolable. To his supportive daughters-in-law, he talked of the dead woman constantly. Hungry for companionship, on August 15, 1951, the lonely widower married Martha Baird Allen, the fifty-six-year-old widow of a Brown University classmate. Nelson alone went out of his way to welcome "Aunt Martha" into the family, an act of kindness for which he would be lavishly rewarded. Any coolness resulting from his remarriage did not prevent Junior in 1952 from making a gift of $58 million to the Rockefeller Brothers Fund or settling an additional $42 million in trusts for the benefit of his grandchildren, whose birthdays were invariably marked with a check, accompanied by words of exhortation and spiritual uplift. "Money is a useful thing to have," Junior had reminded Steven on the boy's tenth birthday. "You can buy candy with it, and tops, and marbles and boats and many other things you might like to have. . . . You will enjoy the tops and the marbles much more when you have given something he needs to the boy who has less than you."

6

A FTER A YEAR in office, Dwight Eisenhower felt like a political orphan. "The Republican party must be known as a progressive organization or it is sunk," an unhappy president confided to his White House diary. Rockefeller shared Eisenhower's frustration with congressional naysayers unaccustomed to having one of their own party in the Oval Office. His efforts at HEW to expand Social Security, finance school construction to accommodate the first wave of baby boomers, and increase the number of Americans covered by private health insurance formed the nexus of Eisenhower's first-term domestic agenda. At a July 1953 cabinet meeting, the president railed against Republicans in the House of Representatives who wanted to slash funding for the new department's Office of Education. "If any of those fools were running for reelection right now," he stormed, "they'd lose the vote of every liberal in the country— and that includes me."

Ike's liberalism was of the nineteenth-century variety. Left to his own devices, he would outdo Bob Taft in extricating Uncle Sam from activities best left to the private sector. Of the Tennessee Valley Authority, for example, he told his cabinet, "I'd like to sell the whole thing, but I suppose we can't go that far." Intent on recasting the Republican Party as both "forward thinking" and fiscally responsible, Eisenhower rejected Budget Director Joseph Dodge's appeal for a 25 percent cut in HEW spending, but only after Nelson and Mrs. Hobby warned that such drastic reductions would shred administration credibility. By August 1953, when Secretary Hobby and her energetic deputy saw him at the summer White House in Denver, Ike had on his desk the recommendations of a presidential commission on Social Security reform. These envisioned adding nearly ten million workers to the system, while simultaneously increasing monthly benefits.

From his first day at HEW, Rockefeller had made broadening Social Security coverage his top priority. This all but guaranteed a clash with Republican congressman Carl Curtis of Nebraska, a prototypical rugged individualist. Curtis proposed to abolish not Social Security, but its burgeoning Trust Fund, to his jaundiced eye a potentially bottomless well from which to irrigate future growth of the welfare state. Instead of relying on employer-employee contributions, Curtis would fund the program out of general revenues. Rockefeller was hardly alone in fearing the consequences of making Social Security compete for scarce dollars with other government programs at the same time. Mindful of the suspicions he roused, Rockefeller pushed back, hard, when lobbied by medical research advocates like Mary Lasker. Employing techniques pioneered by her husband, advertising mogul Albert Lasker, "Mary and her little lambs" had convinced lawmakers to establish the National Institutes of Health (NIH). A trustee of the Museum of Modern Art, recruited for the board by Nelson personally, Lasker welcomed his appointment to HEW. She confidently assumed that his involvement with the Rockefeller Foundation and Rockefeller Institute would sensitize him to the need for additional federal funds to combat cancer and heart disease.

A meeting was scheduled for August 4, 1953. It did not go well. Lasker's pitch for increased research dollars touched a raw nerve.

"These discoveries aren't made with money!" Rockefeller told her with obvious irritation.

"I know of no one who has made any discoveries recently who wasn't paid," retorted Lasker.

A querulous Rockefeller complained of "pressure" applied by Lasker and her supporters. His visitor left feeling despondent. One can imagine her surprise, several weeks later, on hearing from a well-placed source that Nelson had cited her visit, and the potent forces she could allegedly summon, in arguing against large cuts in research funding. Confirmation of this came in January 1954, when Eisenhower publicly called for a strengthening of cancer and heart research programs, though his NIH budget contained $10 million less than what Harry Truman had recommended in his final spending plan. Even Mary Lasker would praise Rockefeller's next brainstorm, a complex scheme of government-backed guarantees intended to lure private companies and non-profit organizations into covering many of the sixty-three million Americans without health insurance.

The challenge, as Rockefeller defined it, was to promote experimentation on the part of timid private insurers. In the summer of 1953, he approached doctors affiliated with the Rockefeller Foundation. Out of their conversations emerged his "reinsurance" plan, under which the federal government would insure the insurers—offsetting at least part of any losses sustained by private firms that agreed to expand their coverage. Hobby and Rockefeller created a task force, and several weeks of discussion in an HEW conference room produced a modest breakthrough, with the administration agreeing to establish a $25 million revolving fund to indemnify insurers. Even this trifling amount stirred a hornets' nest of opposition from the United States Chamber of Commerce and the American Medical Association. Just as eager to hold Washington at bay were insurers accustomed to the cozy regimen of regulation at the state level. When members of his own party let the reinsurance bill die of neglect in July 1954, Eisenhower railed against the AMA. "As far as I'm concerned, the American Medical Association is just plain stupid," the president snapped. "This plan of ours would have shown the people how we could improve their health and stay out of socialized medicine."

Nothing better illustrated the perils associated with traveling the middle of the road. While small-government advocates were fervently opposed to the reinsurance plan, so were New Deal liberals who dreamed of national health insurance as proposed by Harry Truman in his populist 1948 campaign. After Democrats recaptured both houses of Congress in the 1954 elections, Rockefeller repackaged his scheme to fit the more generous spending preferences of the new majority. His $25 million pilot program became a $100 million grab bag of incentives for catastrophic illness coverage and private industry innovation, with special emphasis accorded low-income and farm families. It didn't matter. Ingenuity was no match for inertia, much less the organized fury of opposing interest groups, a lesson relearned multiple times across the next half century whenever the subject of national health insurance resurfaced.

Equally disappointing to Rockefeller was Washington's reluctance to invest in education. Eisenhower was loath to intrude on state and local prerogatives or to launch any new initiatives that might undercut his drive for a balanced budget. In the event, constitutional niceties were overwhelmed by the postwar baby boom. Already the nation had a deficit of at least 140,000 classrooms. Looking ahead to 1965, said Rockefeller, Americans could expect a 40 percent increase in demand for professional and technically trained personnel. To create a countervailing groundswell for reform, he organized an elaborate White House Conference on Education, with hundreds of smaller meetings at the grass roots.

He also commissioned one of his trademark studies. Inspired by his work with PACGO, in April 1953 Rockefeller had announced formation of the New York–based Government Affairs Foundation, "to advance and improve the science of government and the administration of public affairs." As with any Rockefeller enterprise, its charter anticipated the future (above all its founder's political future). A full decade before the urban crisis of the 1960s, Nelson and his experts were exploring ways in which regional governments might ward off municipal bankruptcy. The same group took up the cause—visionary in 1954 and for a long time to come—of converting federal welfare programs into block grants to the states. To oversee his private think tank, Nelson recruited Frank Moore, a former New York State comptroller currently serving as Tom Dewey's lieutenant governor. Tasked with examining federal aid to education, Moore in turn sounded out John Mitchell, a brainy young Wall Street bond lawyer whose fiscal inventiveness had attracted Rockefeller's notice. Mitchell outlined a convoluted process by which semiautonomous state agencies might issue bonds to finance school construction, then lease the buildings back to local school districts, paying off the bonds with the revenue thus generated. In the unlikely event that revenues failed to cover costs, the shortfall would be covered from a reserve fund established for the purpose.

Rockefeller saw broader applications for the scheme, dubbed "moral obligation bonding" because participating states were not legally required to make good on any defaulting bonds. In the short term, Mitchell's plan enabled Eisenhower to propose seeding up to $6 billion in school construction nationwide. Yet not even the popular president could avoid a repetition of Nelson's reinsurance debacle. Denouncing the program as too clever by half, the teachers' lobby demanded direct federal support, no strings attached. Conservatives, on the other hand, angrily protested the latest Rockefeller ploy mimicking the New Deal at the expense of sound actuarial principle. On Capitol Hill, Mitchell's fiscal sleight of hand was dead on arrival. Nelson filed away the audacious concept for future reference.

The news wasn't all bad. By the summer of 1954, Rockefeller and the rest of the so-called Hobby Lobby had neutralized Carl Curtis and passed the administration's Social Security expansion plan. Under the new law, a widow and two children under eighteen would receive up to $200 in monthly benefits—"the equivalent," Rockefeller pointed out, "of $60,000 in savings invested at 4 percent." He did a lot of explaining that fall. "Frankly I don't think the Republicans have done a very good job in telling of the really great accomplishments of the last two years," he confided to his son Rod on the eve of the 1954 midterm elections. He had just returned himself from a round of supposedly nonpolitical speeches "made during a very political time. My personal opinion is that there were very few votes changed as a result!"

Having struck out on his health and education initiatives, Rockefeller was growing disenchanted with a job too small for his aspirations. Publicly, his relationship with Mrs. Hobby was that of the loyal subordinate. In private, says one HEW associate, "there were plenty of times when Nelson was frustrated by her and her indecisiveness. She wasn't the most insightful person in the room." Adding to the strain was Hobby's limited clout on Capitol Hill. With her blessing, Rockefeller pressed the White House to establish a national council on the arts. Eisenhower embraced the idea, and legislation drafted with the help of Nelson's friend and cultural guru Lincoln Kirstein was duly sent to Congress. Unfortunately, the lawmaker to whom the measure was entrusted jokingly dubbed it "the free piano lessons bill," a label from which it never recovered. Rockefeller was left to ponder his options. A year earlier, Adolf Berle and other reformers had urged him to run for mayor of New York, where the line of succession from Fiorello La Guardia to Bill O'Dwyer to Vincent Impellitteri did little to bolster the case for either democracy or Darwinian evolution. Rockefeller said he would do nothing without the blessing of Governor Dewey, who made it clear he didn't think much of the idea. "Tom Dewey doesn't want to pick anybody who will have a chance," an embittered Frank Moore told Nelson.

This theory was put to the test a second time early in 1954, when a retiring Dewey and his allies in the New York GOP quashed a Rockefeller-for-Governor boomlet. Anointed in his place was U.S. senator Irving Ives, an unabashed liberal who, it was hoped, might emulate Dewey's crossover appeal to normally Democratic voters. In practice, Ives proved an indifferent campaigner with a serious drinking problem. Nelson agreed to appear with Ives in Harlem, where the Rockefeller family name was magic and even a slight uptick in the Republican vote could spell the difference in a tight contest against Democrat Averell Harriman.

Unfortunately, by the time the candidate finally showed up at Smalls' Paradise for his rally, he was himself tight. The ensuing event was a shambles. On Election Day, a freak blizzard hampered Republican get-out-the-vote efforts north of the state's dividing line, where the Bronx meets leafy Westchester County. In the closest gubernatorial race in New York history, Ives lost to Harriman by eleven thousand votes. Ten days later, Nelson Rockefeller submitted his resignation as undersecretary of HEW.

Twelve

BRAINSTORMING

You just can't have two Secretaries of State.

—John Foster Dulles to Dwight Eisenhower

1

ONLY SOMEONE OF Nelson Rockefeller's unflagging optimism would trade the sinecure of HEW for a White House staff position with a mandate as vague as it was visionary. A pay cut—from $17,500 to $15,000—was the least of Rockefeller's problems. More important, it appeared that no one could agree on his new title or responsibilities. In his memoirs, Eisenhower referred to Nelson as his special assistant for Cold War strategy, yet at the time of his appointment Rockefeller himself thanked the president for entrusting him with "development of increased understanding and co-operation among all peoples." His nebulous job description reflected the zigzag track of Ike's Cold War policies, on which bursts of diplomatic outreach and high-flown rhetoric alternated with CIA-engineered coups and casual talk about the "liberation" of Soviet satellites.

The resulting intellectual whiplash had led Rockefeller's predecessor, a senior editor at *Time* and sometime Eisenhower speechwriter named C. D. Jackson, to bail out after little more than a year on the job. But that was different, Nelson consoled himself; Jackson's portfolio had been narrowly defined as psychological warfare, public relations for the atomic age. His own agenda encompassed a much broader field. "The whole idea was that maybe Nelson could put some new ideas into the White House," insisted Nadia Williams. "That's what we were there for, to try out new ideas." White House staff secretary Colonel Andrew Goodpaster agreed. Ike, claimed Goodpaster, wanted Rockefeller "to tell the story of America, to explain its values" to an increasingly skeptical world. Success would free Eisenhower to pursue, in a favorite presidential phrase, "our enlightened national interests."

As of the first week of January 1955, Rockefeller commanded a splendid corner office in the Executive Office Building, previously assigned to Secretaries Hull, Stettinius, and Byrnes. Each of those worthies had left the premises feeling disillusioned, if not betrayed. Their somber history alone should have been enough to instill caution in the suite's latest occupant. Testing the parameters of his new position, Rockefeller took up Eisenhower's invitation to attend meetings of the cabinet and National Security Council. He explored ways to revive the president's moribund Atoms for Peace initiative, under which the world's nuclear powers would contribute fissionable materials for use in medicine, agriculture, and energy production. Pollster Lloyd Free of the Gallup organization was hired to conduct surveys gauging world opinion toward the United States and its Cold War adversaries.

Sensitive as ever to his physical surroundings, Rockefeller tapped George Dudley, the mastermind behind his wartime chart room, to replace standard government green walls with Williamsburg yellow. The color scheme quickly spread to other offices throughout the bureaucracy. Tipped off that Ike's chief of staff, Sherman Adams, wished to demolish the Executive Office Building, with its Victorian mansard roof and wedding cake façade, and replace it with a modern, soulless office building, Rockefeller argued the architectural merits of the Second Empire relic with the contrarian former governor of New Hampshire. Finding Adams unresponsive, he went behind his back and appealed directly to the president, who saved the structure from the wrecking ball; today, it bears his name.*

Rockefeller found his closest White House ally in Eisenhower's executive secretary, Ann Whitman. The two entered into a conspiracy of paperwork. "He was a great one for ordering memorandums and public opinion surveys," Whitman recalled. "He wanted the president to see them, but was afraid they would never reach him if they were sent through Goodpaster or Adams. So he would give them to me to give to the president at my discretion, and I did." Often a small gift accompanied these transactions. Occasionally, Nelson invited Ann for dinner in the library at his Foxhall Road estate, after which he drove her home. Employing different tactics, he enjoyed similar success in his courtship of Admiral Arthur Radford, chairman of the Joint Chiefs of Staff, and the avuncular, pipe-smoking CIA director, Allen Dulles. Capitol Hill was not overlooked. On the job less than two weeks, Nelson received a note of thanks from Massachusetts senator John F. Kennedy, then recuperating from a serious back

---

* As governor it had been Adams's custom to carry his lunch pail to work every day. Appealing as this might be to frugal Granite Staters, to Rockefeller it hardly constituted the necessary training for a position Adams was to fill until 1958, when it was revealed that he had accepted gifts from a shady New England industrialist and Ike's hidden hand showed him the door.

operation. "Hospitals are gloomy places, I'm afraid," wrote JFK, "and it makes a tremendous difference to be remembered." The exchange inaugurated a relationship marked on both sides by wary respect and competing ambitions.

In another category altogether were his dealings with Allen Dulles's brother. John Foster Dulles was the namesake grandson of one secretary of state and nephew of another. Ponderous and remote, though unquestionably able, Dulles had reputedly been studying for his current position since he was five years old. It wasn't Dulles's exhaustive preparation that concerned Rockefeller, but his continuing education. "He had the world in his head and he had it all laid out," Nelson contended. "If what actually went on didn't fit what was in his head he either thought it was wrong or he didn't recognize it." Dulles's refusal at an international summit to shake hands with Chinese premier Chou En-lai typified a willful disregard for whatever offended his moral sensibilities. ("If I so much as took into account what people in other countries are thinking or feeling," Dulles once confessed, "I would be derelict in my duty as Secretary of State.")*

Dulles was a dangerous man to cross. So was his undersecretary, Herbert Hoover, Jr. Inheriting his father's phlegmatic obstinacy and seemingly none of his pawky humor, Hoover took an instant dislike to the "starry-eyed" enthusiast who presumed to encroach on his turf, which included oversight of covert operations for the National Security Council. State Department professionals were left to grind their teeth as the Rockefeller portfolio expanded to include, in no particular order: American defenses against biological warfare; Communist laborers in U.S.-owned plants in Italy; rural economic development in the Philippines; an administration initiative to boost Caribbean prosperity; adapting newsman Lowell Thomas's Cinerama filmmaking technique to U.S. trade fairs abroad; and preparations to launch a forty-pound "bird," or earth-orbiting satellite, in conjunction with the upcoming International Geophysical Year (the CIA offered to underwrite a quarter of the project's $28.5 million budget).

Rockefeller's attitude toward global Communism remained as unyielding as ever. He opposed the initiative of Secretary of Agriculture Ezra Taft Benson, ordinarily the flintiest of cabinet conservatives, to sell surplus wheat to the Soviet people. "Agricultural shortages promise to create internal dissatisfaction," Rockefeller reasoned, "which may be to our advantage to promote rather than to diminish." He was no more enthusiastic about dispatching a production of

---

* To Rockefeller, the snub was needlessly rude; worse, it was self-defeating. Recalling his personal diplomacy with Mexican president Lázaro Cárdenas before the war, he faulted Dulles for deliberately ignoring the Communist Chinese as an "anti-Christian people" at a time when dozens of newly independent nations in Asia and Africa were shedding their colonial allegiances— a process dramatized by the April 1955 Bandung Conference of nonaligned countries—and entertaining rival bids from the United States and USSR.

the Gershwins' *Porgy and Bess* to Moscow, though he did look with favor on sending "topflight jazz orchestras" and exhibitions featuring modern artists like Marc Chagall and other Russian exiles. Even as he settled into his new job, an unsought assignment reminded him of what he had left behind at HEW, where a botched polio vaccination program had landed Secretary Hobby in controversy and the White House turned to her former deputy in hopes of averting a public relations meltdown. Within days, Eisenhower announced a reversal in his hands-off approach to vaccine supplies judged insufficient or, worse, tainted. Shortly thereafter, Hobby let it be known that she would be returning to Texas to care for her ailing husband. And Nelson was put in charge of a campaign to distribute the Salk vaccine globally.

Secretary of Defense Charlie Wilson, weary of political infighting and journalistic ridicule, envied Mrs. Hobby her retirement. Quietly, he sounded Nelson out about becoming his deputy secretary and all but certain successor. The president raised no objection; neither did Sherman Adams. Treasury Secretary George Humphrey was another story. "If you put that spendthrift in I am quitting right now," Rockefeller quoted his chief critic in the cabinet. The job offer was hastily withdrawn. Humphrey was not alone in questioning Nelson's devotion to fiscal restraint. As a staunch advocate of foreign developmental assistance, Rockefeller had argued the case for a $130 million low-interest loan from the Export-Import Bank to assist the Indian steelmaker Tata. Frowning on the neutralist policies of India's Jawaharlal Nehru, Dulles nixed the loan, notwithstanding warnings from U.S. diplomats that this could drive the Indians into the Soviet camp.[*]

With Soviet acquisition of the hydrogen bomb, 750 times more lethal than the device that incinerated Hiroshima, and stockpiles of doomsday weaponry growing on both sides of the Iron Curtain, Eisenhower spoke for humanity when he proclaimed, late in 1954, that "there is no longer any alternative to peace." Stalin's death the previous year had opened the door to "competitive coexistence," the newly heard mantra coming out of Moscow, where Premier Nikolai Bulganin and Communist Party first secretary Nikita Khrushchev shared power in an uneasy troika with Foreign Affairs Minister Vyacheslav Molotov. Their motives might be suspect, but diplomatic momentum was clearly with the Soviets. By withdrawing their occupation forces from Austria, acquiescing in a Korean armistice, and tabling broad disarmament proposals in May

---

[*] Money was as sensitive a subject with Nelson as with his bureaucratic rivals, though for different reasons. According to one associate, the surest way to provoke the normally affable Rockefeller was to respond to one of his many initiatives by saying, "Gee, Nelson, if you believe in it so much, why don't you just write out a check for it?" On one occasion, Rockefeller got up from the table in silent fury and walked out of the room. "Capital Circus," *New York Daily News*, June 2, 1959.

1955, Stalin's successors made it all but impossible for the United States to avoid a summit conference in Geneva that summer.

That the times called for a strategic reappraisal was acknowledged by Washington's European partners long before Dulles's State Department. Ten years had elapsed since Yalta poisoned the well of major power summitry. Shameful memories of that meeting, and of Munich before it, weighed heavily on the American secretary of state. So did fears the West might be compelled, through skillfully manipulated public opinion, to surrender hard-won strategic and military advantages. Unable to prevent the summit, Dulles strongly discouraged Eisenhower from offering any substantive new proposals when the United States, USSR, Great Britain, and France met on the shores of Lake Geneva in July. Rather, said Dulles, leaders of the Big Four should content themselves with identifying the most pressing issues confronting their nations, leaving actual negotiations to their foreign ministers. Moreover, Ike should avoid socializing with or even smiling at his Soviet counterparts, lest his personal warmth be mistaken for a thaw in Western resolve.

Recognizing that this scenario, in Andrew Goodpaster's words, held "zero appeal" for the White House, Rockefeller saw his opening. For years, friends and family had accustomed themselves to his relentless grilling of guest "experts" at dinner and cocktail parties, firing questions while tapping his glasses against the visitor's lapels. Now Nelson organized an intellectual cocktail party, an ad hoc gathering of academic heavyweights in advance of Geneva and literally beyond Dulles's reach—at the U.S. Marine Corps Officer Candidates School in Quantico, Virginia, a spartan facility fifty miles south of Washington. To this impromptu brain trust, Rockefeller gave the anodyne name the Vulnerabilities Panel, conjuring up images of thumb-sucking PhDs engaged in faculty lounge debates over the Soviet bomber fleet.

As speculation about his intentions mounted, Nelson informed Ike on June 3 that his pre-summit summit had no objective beyond examining "the current international relations situation," with particular emphasis on the psychological factors involved. Of course, he was quick to add, any findings of relevance would be made available to the president and others "for their consideration in policy and operations planning." Two days later, the veil dropped. On the evening of Sunday, June 5, Rockefeller met for the first time with his assembled experts, eleven in all, as carefully chosen as the country house protagonists in an Agatha Christie mystery. As he looked on, participants jousted over the future of NATO, emerging strains in the Sino-Soviet alliance, and the reconstruction of Japan. What emerged from the week-long conclave reflected the contradictions of its organizer, an unconventional Cold Warrior whose suspicions of the enemy were on a par with his congenital optimism and instinct for deal making.

The latter traits found expression in calls for expanded trade, relaxed travel restrictions, and a freer exchange of ideas and information—steps intended to establish a climate of trust *before* diplomats took up the vastly more difficult issues of disarmament and the future of a democratic Germany. One participant likened the process to the slow untying of a knot. A final report, drafted at Nelson's request by Walt Rostow of MIT's Center of International Studies, credited Washington with a "significant but transitory" military advantage over the Soviet bloc. Practically speaking, the United States and its allies had at best two or three years in which to redraw the map of Europe and pursue arms control from a position of undoubted superiority. After that, the U.S. monopoly on long-range bombers capable of striking the Soviet Union from NATO bases in Europe would be rendered obsolete by Soviet bomber development or, worse, the creation of intercontinental ballistic missiles whose existence would drastically recalibrate the balance of terror.

Half a century later, debate still swirls around the document known as Quantico I. It extends to the most significant legacy of the Quantico seminar, a bold disarmament package incorporating the exchange of military blueprints, on-site inspections, and unrestricted overflights by unarmed planes to monitor each side's compliance.* Eisenhower himself sounded dubious on first hearing the concept he made famous at Geneva as Open Skies. "I doubt they will agree to it," he said of his Soviet counterparts, "because secrecy means so much to them. They see secrecy as a great strength." Buried elsewhere within the Quantico findings was yet another Rockefeller recommendation, much closer in spirit to the special assistant's job as originally conceived. Stressing the need for accelerated economic growth in underdeveloped parts of the free world, Rockefeller urged foreign investment in Japan, South Asia, and Indochina. (One draft went even further, envisioning "a worldwide plan" by which East and West might cooperate in fostering growth.) Here, barely concealed, was the latest extension of Nelson's long-running campaign, launched as wartime coordinator of inter-American affairs and more recently advanced through Point Four, AIA, and IBEC, to win the battle of ideas by improving living standards in the developing world.

For Rockefeller, Quantico was to have repercussions that went far beyond Geneva. For several days in June 1955, he had applied to public policy the same organized expertise that Junior tapped for his philanthropies and that Senior had once summoned to gain advantage in a brutally competitive business

---

* A series of erudite papers buttressed the main report. Only recently declassified, these make for chilling reading, a bleak syllabus of superpower mistrust and worst-case assumptions at a time when nuclear weapons were still a novelty, and by no means did everyone around him share Eisenhower's view of atomic conflict as unthinkable.

world. In the process, Nelson exposed the intellectual timidity of the State Department in dealing with adversaries who claimed to have time, if not morality, on their side. The success of this initial brainstorming exercise foreshadowed his later reliance, as governor of New York and would-be president, on a dizzying array of study groups, commissions, and grand planners. "If somebody said two words to label Nelson Rockefeller as a politician," observed journalist Johnny Apple, "I would use task force. He loved task forces—'I've brought together the best minds in the state, the best minds in the country, the best minds in the hemisphere, to study this very difficult problem.'" No intellectual himself, Rockefeller had a gift for distilling ideas from those who were; in the words of pollster Lloyd Free, "to extract the real 14 carat nuggets from their often prolix advice" and then devise practical means for their accomplishment.

Something else distinguished Rockefeller from the typical policy wonk, said Free. "Once decided that an idea is good, all hell cannot stop him from forcing it through." Yet even Nelson knew better than to launch a frontal assault on John Foster Dulles. Instead he relied on surrogates to convince the secretary that the Quantico report was something other than "a one-shot, off-the-top-of-the-head effort by some ad hoc enthusiasts." In response, Dulles routinely acknowledged the "many worthwhile ideas" in Rockefeller's white paper. He was scarcely more receptive on the afternoon of July 6, when informed that Ike himself was on the line. "Nelson is here and he has got a tremendous idea," Eisenhower told his secretary of state. Cringing over the president's direct linkage of his name to the aerial inspection proposal, Rockefeller wasn't surprised by Dulles's perfunctory dismissal of the latter idea as a public relations stunt.

He was more concerned, at a preconference planning session the next day, to hear both the president and secretary reiterate a minimalist agenda in the face of the Soviet peace offensive. Unable to keep silent, at length he muscled his way into the conversation. "Mr. President," he said heatedly, "I don't think you can do this psychologically. The world is looking to you as the leader for peace. You can't go there and simply identify the areas of trouble and then say we will leave it to the secretaries. . . . To begin with, the Russians will come up with some proposal, and, if they don't, the British and the French are certainly going to come up with something. They've got to for home consumption." Citing his latest polling of European public opinion—a factor Eisenhower himself had raised at a recent press conference—Rockefeller reminded the president that in many quarters the United States was viewed as "a warmonger with an atomic bomb." Geneva presented a rare opportunity to set the record straight and to regain the initiative against the Soviets and their seductive refrain of Ban the Bomb.

"We don't want to make this meeting a propaganda battlefield," Dulles snorted. Eisenhower nodded his approval. But Rockefeller wouldn't be put off. Twice he returned to the forbidden subject.

"God damn it, Nelson. I have told you we are not going to do that," Ike snapped. "We are going to do what Foster recommends."*

The display of presidential temper may have been spontaneous, or it may have been staged for Dulles's benefit. "Eisenhower never showed all his cards," notes Andrew Goodpaster. "Anyone who thought otherwise was deluding himself." Whatever the truth behind this momentary loss of composure, it didn't deter Rockefeller from his self-appointed mission. Besides commissioning an opening address for Eisenhower's use in Geneva, he had position papers drafted on a dozen subjects, including the aerial inspection plan explicitly ruled out by Dulles. His instincts were validated in the days leading up to the summit, as Eisenhower, always more sensitive to public opinion than his secretary of state, began to waver. However remote the chances for meaningful progress, particularly on the vexed issue of Germany, no one wanted to pronounce the conference a failure before it started. The higher public expectations rose, the greater the appeal of Open Skies.

On July 11, still hedging his bets, Eisenhower directed Rockefeller to fly to Paris, there to await further instruction. Making the trip with him were Special Assistant for Disarmament Harold Stassen, Deputy Secretary of Defense Robert Anderson, his Pentagon colleague Gordon Gray, and Admiral Arthur Radford of the Joint Chiefs of Staff. On his own, Rockefeller brought along Nancy Hanks and several other members of his White House staff. Within hours of touching down on French soil, Rockefeller dragooned his weary fellow travelers, none of them in the mood for weighty talk about nuclear weaponry, into a full-scale briefing session. First pollster Lloyd Free made a presentation testifying to the growing doubts in Europe regarding the United States and its peaceful intentions. Then Nelson took the floor and launched into a hard sell on behalf of Open Skies. His audience remained skeptical. An hour passed. A groggy Bob Anderson reminded everyone of the prior agreement forestalling policy innovations at the summit. What Rockefeller had in mind bordered on mutiny.

* Harold Stassen's biographers, Alex Kirby, David Dalin, and John F. Rothman, contend that it was Stassen, Ike's special assistant for disarmament, who anticipated Rockefeller's Quantico retreat by convening his own staff at the same marine base in mid-April. Stassen in turn credited the legendary Jimmy Doolittle with the idea of mutually sanctioned "flyovers" to ease fears of surprise attack. On May 26, Stassen submitted his findings to the president. These included establishment of an International Armaments Commission, "with the right to inspect by land, sea, or air." In contrast with Rockefeller, Stassen depicted Eisenhower firmly rebuking Dulles over the proposed superpower summit in Geneva. This, of course, was the exact opposite of the treatment accorded Rockefeller when he argued for a more proactive approach at the forthcoming conference.

2

S EVERAL HUNDRED MILES away, diplomats from both sides of the Iron Curtain were assembling in the valley of the Rhine. Public interest centered on the Soviets, for whom Geneva represented something of a diplomatic coming-out party (except for the Tehran Conference in November 1943, Stalin had never left Russian soil during the war). Drawing special attention was round, raucous Nikita Khrushchev, a coal miner's son from Ukraine whose earthy mix of insecurity and belligerence may have been exacerbated by the contrast between his delegation's two-engine Ilyushin Il-14 and the sleek four-engine aircraft carrying his Western adversaries to Geneva. Quick to accept a British invitation to visit London, the Soviets were much less forthcoming on the subject of German reunification, Bulganin telling Prime Minister Anthony Eden, "Stalin would never have done that."

On Monday morning, July 18, negotiators took their places in the steeply tiered council chamber of the Palais des Nations, a sprawling white marble complex built in the 1920s to house the League of Nations. In his opening remarks, Eisenhower adhered closely to the Dulles script, decrying the forced division of Germany and the subversive actions of international Communism. Without offering specifics, he urged both sides to enter into serious talks to reduce the nuclear menace. After he finished, Eden floated the idea of a demilitarized zone between East and West. Then Bulganin swung for the fences by proposing strict limits on the armed forces of each major power, a necessary prerequisite to the dissolution of both NATO and the Warsaw Pact. His call for an outright ban on the manufacture or use of atomic weapons left little doubt as to the winner of the opening round. That evening, Eisenhower hosted an informal dinner for the Soviet delegation at his lakefront château. Filipino waiters from the White House mess served the Russian guests vodka in large wineglasses, a single piece of ice floating in the fiery liquid.

As it happened, July 18 coincided with the birthday of Deputy Foreign Minister Andrei Gromyko. Eisenhower tried to make an occasion of it, but the hatchet-faced Gromyko kept his distance. A discussion of nuclear inspection methods went nowhere, the Soviets arguing for the placement of observer parties at fixed locations, a concept already tried and found wanting in Korea. Eisenhower recognized a stalemate in the making. Anticipating as much, Rockefeller in Paris continued pounding away on his plan for aerial inspections. The first of the little group of exiles at the Hôtel de Crillon to crack was Admiral Radford. "Maybe you've got something here, after all," he said wearily. "The Russians know all about our military dispositions and we know very little about theirs. Maybe this scheme of yours could really pay off."

Before long, Anderson and Gray climbed down from the fence. On July 19,

Radford and Anderson cabled Dulles, urging him to take a second look at Open Skies. Rockefeller made sure a duplicate of their message reached the president through his Geneva co-conspirator Andrew Goodpaster. Within hours, the expected summons arrived: accompanied by Stassen, Nelson was to fly to Geneva and meet with the president on Wednesday morning, July 20. Once he was in the air, his mind flashed back ten years, to the thorny confrontation with Dulles at San Francisco and the right of national self-defense written into the UN Charter with Stassen's assistance. Now here they were, again struggling to reconcile differences under the international spotlight. Wagging his head in bemusement, Rockefeller told Stassen, "Harold, with your brains and my intuition, it's just a shame we can't work together on these problems."

Upon arriving at their destination, the two men were ushered into the library of Eisenhower's villa for a forty-five-minute meeting. He had decided to use Open Skies, the president told his visitors. He requested their aid in developing a speech for use the next day. Intent on retaining the element of surprise, Eisenhower reserved to himself the most critical editorial revisions. Shortly after lunch on July 21, he picked up a black grease pencil and scribbled a few notes on the back of one page. "If I were to say this," he calculated, "right about here . . ." Storm clouds darkened Lake Geneva as the presidential party left for the Palais des Nations. In a rare sign of favor, Eisenhower asked Rockefeller to accompany him in his car and to sit directly behind him at the conference hall. After briefly summarizing earlier arms control proposals, and explaining why each had been judged unworkable, Eisenhower paused in his remarks. Removing his glasses, he sat back in his chair, his features contorted in thought.

When he resumed speaking, it was with all the earnestness he could muster. Addressing himself directly to the Soviet delegation, he acknowledged the reciprocal fears and dangers of a rogue attack that could destroy civilization. Such a calamity was too dreadful to contemplate and too menacing to ignore. "I propose, therefore, that we take a practical step," said Eisenhower, "that we begin an arrangement, very quickly, as between ourselves—immediately." All eyes were riveted on the American president as he unfurled the details of his plan, with its exchange of military blueprints and the establishment of airfields from which inspection flights could take off and land (each plane to include in its crew one or more representatives of the nation under inspection). Just as he concluded his presentation, nature unleashed an exclamatory bolt of its own, a sudden, deafening clap of thunder that rattled the building and plunged the room into darkness.

"I didn't know I would put the lights out with that speech," Eisenhower jested. The Soviets joined in the nervous laughter around the table. By the time power was restored, positions were reversed. That the British and French should praise Open Skies was to be expected. But when Premier Bulganin pronounced the plan worthy of serious consideration, Eisenhower—and Rockefeller—knew they had scored a triumph. It was short-lived. Leaving the conference room, Nelson stayed close to Ike as he strode briskly into an adjoining lounge for the daily cocktail hour. On the other side of the president, struggling to keep pace with his vigorous gait, Khrushchev blurted out his disagreement with Bulganin. Open Skies, charged Khrushchev, was nothing but a license for Western espionage directed at the Soviet Union. "You are trying to look into our bedrooms."

The outburst proved helpful in one respect. "Now I know who's in charge of the Russian delegation," Eisenhower commented out of earshot. In a holiday mood, the president ordered an open car and made sure Rockefeller sat beside him during the ride back to his villa. Cheering crowds lined Geneva's streets, offering dramatic evidence of how deeply the presidential initiative had stirred popular imagination. That night, Rockefeller treated his staff to dinner and dancing at a posh restaurant in Lausanne. Few in the State Department shared his celebratory mood. If anything, Ike's all-too-evident favor made Nelson a renewed target of professional resentment. At a subsequent social gathering, Rockefeller, who bore a striking physical resemblance to Russian diplomat Jacob Malik, was teasing Khrushchev about how often the two men were confused for each other and how damaging this must be to the Soviets.

"Foster came over absolutely like a storm cloud to chase me away," Nelson recalled later. "Nobody should be joking with a Soviet." The ultimate joke was on Dulles. As the party wound down, the secretary of state watched the rest of his delegation climb into cars designated to carry them home. He was still cooling his heels when over his shoulder he heard the unmistakable voice of his Russian nemesis.

"Why, Mr. Dulles, your chauffeur must have gone," Khrushchev said, chuckling, fully aware that his comrades had gotten the American driver drunk. "We would be glad to send you back in the Soviet car." Outwardly polite, a livid Dulles finally accepted Rockefeller's offer of a ride.*

3

MUCH BALLYHOOED AT the time, the Spirit of Geneva proved ephemeral. Conceding that the summit had lessened the chances of war, Dulles nev-

---

* Ann Whitman recounted a more serious tale of behind-the-scenes frustration. On July 23, the formal conference ended. As the Americans were packing their bags prior to departure, Eisenhower suddenly announced, "I am going to make one more effort. I am going to call on the Russians." But by the time he reached their nearby château, they were gone. Ann Whitman, HMI, 12–13.

ertheless stuck to his hard line. "We are having a moratorium," he told Nelson on August 11, though on precisely what remained vague. "But if the changes"—German reunification and freedom for the vassal states of Eastern Europe—"don't take place as a result . . . then it can't be." The Soviets matched his intransigence *nyet* for *nyet*. An autumn meeting of foreign ministers, staged in the same Palais des Nations, accomplished nothing. Open Skies was quietly shelved. The secretary of state observed no such time-out in his running feud with Rockefeller. His unrelenting complaints about Nelson's cloudy mandate and ever-expanding staff left Eisenhower little choice but to elicit from his special assistant a promise of deference reminiscent of the pledge extracted by FDR in the spring of 1941. The sting of rebuke was magnified by Rockefeller's realization that after fifteen years spent battling the mandarins at State, he was recycling the petty controversies of his youth.

But it was a second confrontation, this one involving Eisenhower directly, that completed his growing disillusionment with the administration. Attending a top-secret briefing on military preparedness, part of the regular process by which U.S. and Soviet strength was projected ten years into the future, Rockefeller heard disturbing evidence that Moscow was narrowing the gap in both firepower and delivery systems. Rumors of atomic-powered, bottle-shaped planes glimpsed in the skies above a remote, mountainous region near the Soviet border with Afghanistan had already found their way into print. Now it appeared the Soviets were on the verge of possessing intercontinental ballistic missiles. If true, the development would render obsolete all previous assumptions about U.S. security. Leaving the briefing, Rockefeller reminded Eisenhower of his obligation to go on television and radio and sound the alarm. Only the president, said Nelson, employing the bully pulpit and his enormous personal prestige, could educate Americans to the dangers and sacrifices that would be their lot for years to come.

"Why should I always have to be the one to bring the bad news to the people?" replied Eisenhower. To this there was no answer other than the obvious, and impolitic, "You ran for the office." For once Rockefeller bit his tongue.*

No compensating joy in his personal life offset these professional disappointments. Later it would be claimed that Nelson gave serious thought around this time to divorcing Tod so that he could marry Nancy Hanks. Little supporting evidence for this can be teased out of his sole surviving love letter to Nancy, if that is what it was, preserved in her papers at Duke University. Written from Seal Harbor in the aftermath of the Geneva Conference, the six-page missive contains lyrical descriptions of the natural environment and of Rockefeller's

---

* Rockefeller hinted at this pivotal encounter in his 1967 Columbia oral history, but he waited a decade before providing details in interviews conducted for a planned autobiography.

attempts to catch it with his $2.95 Brownie Holiday camera. "I feel very close to you—sitting here looking out over the dark blue water," he wrote. "So often I've thought of you on this trip—in the early morning as the first long rays of the sun came slanting through the trees to make long shadows across [the] beach and bright green spots in the water—during quiet walks on the beach looking for shells and coral . . . and always at the end of the day when saying prayers."

There was nothing more beautiful, Nelson went on, "than our love or the understanding, the strength and the completeness that it brings." He would guard "as a precious treasure" memories of the past year, especially the difficult prologue to Geneva. "You have brought to 'us' your penetration and perception, your sensitivity and depth of understanding, your dedication to service and your determination to see things through. . . ." Taking advantage of the perspective afforded by "this peaceful island," Nelson recognized that "we were brought together and . . . we jointly have before us an opportunity to serve Him and to do His work in a way that one could hardly have dared pray for."

Beyond this intense spiritual bond, Rockefeller defined their personal relationship as a call to service (whatever that meant). "In this light the problems of the past weeks seem small and unimportant—to be dealt with love and understanding." The words tantalize; is their author referring to the public challenges so deftly overcome at Geneva or to more intimate matters as Rockefeller weighed his post-Washington options, including an entry into New York politics that would almost certainly preclude their being together? His language conveys professional need rather than romantic ardor. Indeed, the entire letter suggests a delicate distancing, a middle-aged man's emotional transition from lover to friend. That fall, Nancy complained of Rockefeller's detachment. He felt "numb," said Nancy, and so did she.

Human relations were subject to a tidal ebb and flow, but art never failed to work its magic on Nelson. Journalist Johnny Apple experienced this for himself the first time he visited the Rockefeller apartment at 810 Fifth Avenue. "I got off the elevator, and the first thing I see is the *Bird in Flight* of Brâncuşi, right there, and he says, 'How are you? Do you like art?' I said, 'Oh yeah. Yes, I do. Very much.' Without a word to Mary"—the younger Rockefeller daughter and the ostensible reason for Apple's visit—"he went down . . . and then took a right and there was a full room with the kinds of things they have in study collections—those big sliding walls on rollers. You pull one out and there are eight or ten pictures on it. And they were amazing things. I said, 'These things just sit in here unless somebody comes and you roll them out?' He said, 'Out of walls.'"

Apple couldn't restrain himself. "Four or five houses and you're out of walls?"

"I've been out of walls for years."

At his Maine summer house, Nelson spent many an hour arranging stone Buddhas and Japanese lanterns amid a forest of stunted pine trees. He remodeled a wharfside coal shed into a picture gallery, its thirteen-foot ceilings well adapted to display outsized canvases by Franz Kline and Grace Hartigan. Less successful was Wally Harrison's outdoor swimming pool (complete with poolside ice-cream bar to gratify Nelson's cravings) intended for the Playhouse at Pocantico. A cubist painting in three dimensions, it boasted bright colors and iceberglike water slides that proved too jarring for Junior's tastes. Wherever Rockefeller was able to control his environment, Picasso was almost sure to be present, in his prints and drawings, his sculpted owls, and his paintings, such as the iconic *Girl with a Mandolin,* for which Nelson paid $98,000—at the time a record price for a cubist work. As costs escalated beyond even his means, he hit on an ingenious substitute. Upon learning that the artist's antiwar masterpiece *Guernica* had been reproduced as a tapestry, Rockefeller promptly bought it. "Then I got the idea of picking Picasso's paintings which I really was crazy about" but that reposed, regrettably, out of his reach, mostly in museums. Securing permission from their owners, he bargained with the artist to reproduce in yarns and wools *Night Fishing at Antibes,* a 1915 *Harlequin,* and sixteen other Picasso favorites.

Rockefeller had always embraced the primitive as well as the modern; indeed, he saw them as inescapably linked. In June 1955, he marked his twenty-fifth Dartmouth class reunion by presenting the college with a seven-foot-tall wooden Indian, rescued from a nineteenth-century tobacco warehouse. More than once during the contentious Eisenhower years, a jaded Rockefeller picked up the phone and cajoled MoMA director René d'Harnoncourt into flying down to Washington with a suitcase full of Peruvian gold work or pre-Columbian figures. The mere sight of these objects restored Nelson's spirits. With help from d'Harnoncourt, Rockefeller converted his personal collection of indigenous art into the Museum of Primitive Art, located in a brownstone at 15 West Fifty-fourth Street, next door to his Clubhouse. Opened in 1957, the museum broke ground as a showcase for ancient and tribal handicrafts.

"I think I inherit my weakness for shopping from the Aldrich family," Nelson confided to Aunt Lucy. "There's nothing in the world I'd rather do." Henry Moore's *Seated Family,* in later years visible from the dining room at Kykuit, was purchased in London as emotional compensation for a "run in with John Foster Dulles." Picking up where they left off, Rockefeller and Dulles clashed over Egypt's Gamal Abdel Nasser, a zealous Arab nationalist. Having seized power with the assistance of his nation's armed forces, Nasser had since applied to Washington in hopes of securing military hardware for his sponsors. If turned down, said the colonel, he wouldn't hesitate to approach the Soviet bloc. Dulles took a predictably dim view of the Egyptian leader and his pressure tactics. Nelson, on the other hand, preferred the carrot to the stick. The surest way to drive Nasser into Moscow's embrace, he maintained, was for the United States and its allies to withhold funding for the Aswan High Dam, a vast development project that, by harnessing the mercurial waters of the Nile, promised a boost to Egyptian pride and productivity.*

Rockefeller had exhibited a similar pragmatism at Quantico II, the academic follow-up to Geneva that he staged during the closing days of September 1955. Much of the cast was new, for reasons testifying to his continuing icy relations with Herbert Hoover, Jr. By withholding a necessary security clearance, Hoover prevented Walt Rostow from reprising his chairmanship. Replacements included a brooding thirty-two-year-old German émigré and Harvard University instructor named Henry Kissinger. No stranger to Rockefeller largesse, Kissinger had received a $26,000 grant from the Rockefeller Brothers Fund to underwrite a short-lived foreign policy quarterly called *Confluence*. More recently, he had stirred discussion with an April 1955 *Foreign Affairs* article advocating "limited nuclear wars" as a counter to Dulles's strategy of massive retaliation.

Rockefeller chief of staff Ted Parker had first learned of Kissinger from Fritz Kraemer, another political expatriate from Hitler's Germany and the first of several mentors to the solemn young infantryman he had transferred during the penultimate months of World War II to Eighty-fourth Division Intelligence. (Dismissing Kissinger's heavily accented English, Rockefeller would remark, "Why should I worry about an accent, living in New York?") Half a century later, Kissinger described their introduction as if it had occurred that morning. "He came into the room with a broad smile on his face, slapping backs and calling everyone by his first name," said Kissinger. "Or what he thought was their first name. I thought, My God, just what we need—another politician." Planting himself at the front of the room, Rockefeller listened politely to a hail of suggestions, most relating to tactics and presentation rather than policy substance. His campaigner's smile vanished. "Don't tell me how to operate in Washington," he remarked. "Tell me what is right."

Building on Quantico I, Rockefeller and his strategic planners presented a

---

* A preliminary deal announced in December 1955 committed Western aid for at least the initial phase of the dam's construction. Six months later, angered by Nasser's recognition of Red China and his continuing flirtation with the Soviet satellites of Eastern Europe, Dulles revoked the agreement. His action occasioned a wave of anti-Western protest, culminating in a decision by Nasser to nationalize the Suez Canal—and the disastrous intervention of British, French, and Israeli forces that would ultimately drive Anthony Eden from office and prompt demands for Dulles's resignation.

surprisingly nuanced view of the forces driving newly independent or impoverished nations in Asia and the Middle East toward Swiss-style neutralism. Their forty-one-page final report, *Psychological Aspects of United States Strategy*, offered a six-year action plan to strengthen the American military, bolster economic assistance to underdeveloped nations, and intensify the propaganda wars through the United States Information Agency. Its $18 billion price tag was sure to enrage the administration's budget hawks, but only if they could get their hands on the document. Rockefeller chose to withhold the report until he could present it to Eisenhower in person.

Unfortunately, that wouldn't be anytime soon. In the predawn hours of September 24, while vacationing in Denver, Ike suffered a heart attack that sent official Washington into panic. No one was in a more delicate position than Vice President Richard Nixon, Nelson's near contemporary and frequent ally in budget and policy disputes. At meetings of the cabinet, according to Rockefeller, Nixon "had his feet cut right off" by Ike's inner circle. Their shared frustrations brought the two men, not yet rivals for Republican affections, closer together. As the president rallied, "one's spirits seem to come back," Nelson told Milton Eisenhower on September 30. Simultaneously, he notified Sherman Adams of his intention to resign at the end of the year and return to New York. On October 10, Adams duly passed the news on to a recuperating Eisenhower, whose sympathy for his beleaguered special assistant was insufficient to talk him into staying.

There is reason to believe Rockefeller hoped for such an appeal. Certainly he gave no hint of his pending departure in a Thanksgiving message to Bryan and Virginia Hanks. Although acknowledging that "things have been a bit difficult in Washington," Nelson sounded enthusiastic about discussing his Quantico II findings with the president. "It should be very interesting—and quite exciting to see what decisions are going to be made." A week later, he shared with Nixon his latest sampling of American public opinion, confirming his belief that U.S. taxpayers were willing to pay for increased defense measures. On December 5, shadowed by the omnipresent Adams, Rockefeller traveled to Ike's Gettysburg farm, where he found the president cordial but unconvinced of the need to implement the Quantico II recommendations. Any lingering desire Rockefeller might have had to remain in Washington expired in the presidential study.

So ended what Sherman Adams would call "the Rockefeller experiment." The exchange of letters formalizing his departure from government contained the usual expressions of mutual regret and esteem. Ike went a step further, however. As a parting gift, he presented Rockefeller with one of his own paintings, a graceful gesture tinged, perhaps, with a remorse he could not otherwise communicate.

4

I⊤ WAS ANOTHER present, a Christmas remembrance from his friend Percy Douglas, for which Nelson gave effusive thanks two weeks after his return to Room 5600. "I can't wait for you to see me in my new red shirt," he told Douglas. "Frankly, it is the gayest thing I have had in a long time and fits right into my mood of being back in New York." Any resentments he might harbor were subsumed in a typically strenuous round of activities, themeless but for Rockefeller's lifelong conviction that it was good to have "four or five things going simultaneously . . . one of them is bound to work." He wrote a check enabling MoMA to photograph hundreds of Shaker buildings and furnishings. Under the auspices of IBEC, he had economists study investment possibilities in Brazilian papermaking and European supermarkets. He wrote an article for *The New York Times Magazine* promoting foreign economic development; discussed New York politics with the familiar trio of Jamieson, Lockwood, and Harrison ("We're a group that can think together," Nelson explained. "It saves time"); and kept his hand in government reorganization through PACGO. Three months after departing the White House, Rockefeller returned as Eisenhower's guest for a stag dinner.

To keep the Time-Life media empire in Manhattan, Rockefeller offered Henry Luce a choice building site on Sixth Avenue (renamed the Avenue of the Americas after Nelson convinced Mayor La Guardia it would be a fitting tribute to "our friends in Latin America"). Soon a sleek procession of new office towers, several bearing Wally Harrison's vaguely Internationalist stamp, marched up the avenue in tandem with the existing structures of Rockefeller Center. Inferior as architecture, the center extension was a financial ten-strike for the Rockefellers. Instead of being held hostage by a third party—Columbia University, which owned the land on which they built—the family was able to enter into more conventional partnerships with Time Inc., Exxon, Sperry Rand, and other corporate giants putting up nearly half the required funding.

At times, the grueling pace of his life caught up with Rockefeller. A frequent consumer of tranquilizers like Miltown and Transentine, he once confessed to Nancy Hanks's parents, "It doesn't make any sense to work the way we have been—it leaves no time for living." The alternative was worse, as Frank Jamieson's wife, Linda, could attest. "I'm sure he wasn't doing nothing, because that never happened in his life," she said of Rockefeller around this period, "but he wasn't doing anything that was satisfying him. He wasn't in the limelight particularly . . . it was at some dinner, some public dinner, and we were at the same table, and he was nasty to the waiters, for instance—he was petty. I could see what it would be like if he wasn't doing something that was fulfilling." His first summer back in New York, outracing boredom, Nelson took Tod and three of their children on a marathon journey of discovery through fourteen African countries in the twilight of colonial rule. "I don't think he ever stopped to rest," remembered one of the younger Rockefellers. "He wanted to see everything and talk to everybody from the top government officials to the people working in the fields." The whirlwind tour left lasting impressions—above all, visual impressions—and it classified Rockefeller among the rare Western leaders with a genuine interest in Africa and its people.

As the range of his activities spilled beyond the confines of Room 5600, Nelson spent more than $400,000 for a pair of slightly tattered brownstones on West Fifty-fifth Street, one block north of his Clubhouse at 13 West Fifty-fourth, and the adjoining structure, destined to house his growing collection of primitive art. A two-story annex linking the buildings was abandoned in favor of a corrugated-tin-roofed walkway that ended at the back door of 13 West Fifty-fourth, to which the new owner alone had the keys. Inside, a few flights of stairs led to an elegant red velvet dining room and sitting area overlooking busy Fifty-fourth Street. Asked why he didn't go out more often to sample Manhattan's pulsing nightlife, Rockefeller replied, "I don't need to go out. I've got my own nightclub."

His purchase of the paired structures at 20 and 22 West Fifty-fifth called into question Nelson's claim that he had left Washington because of family responsibilities. Visiting the Oscar Ruebhausens at their Mount Kisco weekend retreat, he blurted out the truth: "Oscar, I'm forty-eight, I've held all kinds of appointive offices, and you can't get . . . power in appointive office." Tired of bureaucratic infighting, Rockefeller hungered for the legitimacy uniquely bestowed by the ballot box. In a favorite phrase of his Latin counterparts, he wanted to become an authentic representative of the people. There was more to it than that, of course. By succeeding in elective politics, demonstrating a popular appeal unimaginable to anyone familiar with Ida Tarbell or the Ludlow Massacre, he would polish the Rockefeller legacy like fine silver. "Nelson had this . . . belief in his star," said John Lockwood. "That he was the guy to do all these things for the world." Inspired by the example of FDR, Rockefeller realized that he could never fulfill his destiny, or gain the power he sought, through the private sector. "Therefore, he had to get it politically," Lockwood contended.

About this time, a Room 5600 co-worker, taking note of proliferating rumors concerning Nelson's political plans, asked Frank Jamieson, "Do you really think he'll run for governor?"

"He really wants to run for President," Jamieson replied. His wife, Linda, sharing in the general curiosity, inquired of another Rockefeller associate, "What do you think Nelson really wants to be?" Her colleague hesitated, but only for a moment, before blurting out, "Pope!"

Ego gratification aside, Rockefeller wished to be seen as an *homme sérieux*, enamored of ideas rather than ideology, someone for whom the substance of governing outweighed the tribal rituals and backstairs gossip of Washington. He hoped to continue his policy studies, Nelson told Virginia and Bryan Hanks, "either for the President or for publication and general public information." But in what form? During his first weeks back in New York, he toyed with several possibilities—establishing a Council for Bipartisanship in Foreign Policy or a citizens' committee devoted to the same subject. Nelson's White House colleague Bill Kintner, a former army colonel and planner of covert operations for the CIA, outlined a modern-day Committee of Correspondence "to convince the people everywhere that the Free World, not the Communist Bloc, will inherit the 20th Century." Blaming recent Soviet advances on U.S. passivity and confusion among the West's leadership class, Kintner reached a chilling conclusion: that "co-existence and atomic stalemate may facilitate an ultimate Communist victory."

It was hard to read his diagnosis as anything but criticism of a president hoarding his popularity, the mere implication of which carried immense political risks at the start of 1956, when Eisenhower stood poised for a second electoral drubbing of his 1952 opponent, Adlai Stevenson. Rockefeller seemed oddly unaware of the danger. Still another project under discussion in Room 5600 that spring entailed an elaborate study of Republican Party policies, until Nancy Hanks observed, with a detachment missing in her employer, that any campaign to whip up support for "dynamic, long-range economic and international programs" under the GOP banner would inevitably be seen as an indictment of the Eisenhower White House. At Nelson's request, Hanks telephoned Walt Rostow with an invitation: Would the former Quantico chairman be willing to outline the defining issues likely to confront the United States in the next twenty years? Rostow's positive response supplied the genesis of what came to be known as the Special Studies Project, a sweeping examination of America and the world at midcentury, enlisting the talents and reputations of more than one hundred prominent citizens.

In defining a national sense of purpose, Rockefeller would fashion one for himself. He had long believed that his country, like his family, must justify its riches through good works and the sharing of wealth. The Special Studies Project would not be inexpensive. But to the new president of the Rockefeller Brothers Fund—with $60 million in assets the nation's tenth largest foundation—money posed no obstacle. The only place big enough for a May 1955 organizational meeting was a Radio City rehearsal hall, complete with mirrored wall and dancers' barre, ordinarily reserved for the Rockettes. Music Hall set makers built a vast conference table, "covered with miles of green felt," in Nancy Hanks's recollection, while a round-the-clock mimeographing operation was entrusted to a Radio City usher in white gloves and black-and-gold vest.

For once, Nelson's timing was perfect. The 1950s were an age of anxiety as well as affluence, notable for an emerging consensus among the country's elites that democracy itself was on trial, with internal complacency posing as grave a danger as Soviet missiles to the American way of life. A vastly endowed civilization felt, to many, adrift in banal materialism. A generation that had overcome the Great Depression and banished Fascism from the planet had every reason to believe in its future. But only a Rockefeller report—specifically, one initiated and carried out by Nelson—could rhapsodize, "There is more than enough excitement in the problems it faces to keep American democracy occupied for some time."

True to form, Rockefeller began by assembling the bluest of blue ribbon commissions. More than a few of its members and, consequently, its ideas were recycled from his earlier brainstorming efforts in the Truman and Eisenhower administrations. This explained the presence of such New Deal stalwarts as Adolf Berle, Jr., Chester Bowles, and Anna Rosenberg. Representing the business community were David Sarnoff, Charles Percy (the youthful president of Bell & Howell), and Thomas B. McCabe of Scott Paper. Media titans Henry Luce and John Cowles agreed to serve, alongside Edward Teller, father of the hydrogen bomb, and former Atomic Energy Commission chairman Gordon Dean. John W. Gardner of the Carnegie Corporation signed on, as did Harvard sociologist David Riesman and Notre Dame president Theodore Hesburgh. For the woman's viewpoint, Nelson turned to Oveta Culp Hobby and Margaret Hickey, public affairs editor of the *Ladies' Home Journal*.

If the group was elitist, it was also eclectic. Thus conservative economist Arthur Burns rubbed shoulders with Jacob Potofsky of the Amalgamated Clothing Workers of America, while General Lucius Clay, fresh off his leadership role in the postwar occupation of Germany, sat across from Lester Granger, executive director of the National Urban League. A lonely voice for the emerging Sun Belt was California's Justin Dart, founder of Rexall and, much later, a member of Ronald Reagan's kitchen cabinet. Nelson himself chaired the "Overall Panel," which coordinated the work of half a dozen smaller groups formed to examine U.S. foreign policy, the global economy, national security, domestic economic and social concerns, education, and the democratic idea itself.

To direct the massive research project, Rockefeller casually observed, "I got Henry down from Harvard." Sitting in front of the Matisse fireplace at 810 Fifth Avenue, the two men discussed a six-month venture fitting neatly into Kissinger's planned sabbatical from Cambridge (in reality, the project would require

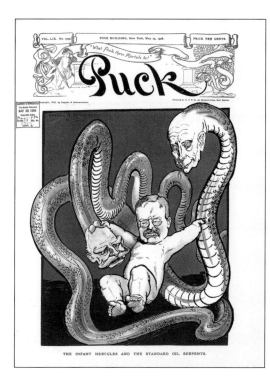

THE INFANT HERCULES AND THE STANDARD OIL SERPENTS.

Puck magazine cast Theodore Roosevelt as young Hercules battling the forces of monopoly personified by Rhode Island senator Nelson W. Aldrich and his business counterpart John D. Rockefeller, whose name was synonymous with the Standard Oil Trust. (LIBRARY OF CONGRESS)

The Aldrich-Rockefeller alliance was sealed at the October 1901 wedding of Senator Aldrich's daughter Abby to John D's namesake son.

"This one's mine," declared Abby Aldrich Rockefeller on the birth of her second son, shown here as an infant perched on his father's lap and flanked by his mother, brother John 3rd, and sister Abby, known within the family as "Babs."

Nelson's boyhood home, adjoining that of his grandfather on West Fifty-fourth Street, was Manhattan's largest private residence.

Thirty miles to the north, Nelson and his family enjoyed weekends at Abeyton Lodge, part of a four-thousand-acre estate overlooking the scenic Hudson River.

Nelson (middle, looking into camera) and his siblings walked or roller-skated to the experimental Lincoln School, where his poor reading skills fed suspicions about his I.Q. His undiagnosed dyslexia caused the boy acute embarrassment. It also led the adult Rockefeller to heed his mother's advice to surround himself with people "smarter than you."

This is to be Nelson's costume.
drawn by himself.

Marco Polo. Play
Nelson in Lincoln School.
april 18th 1919.

Nelson was ten years old when he designed this costume for a school play. Frustrated in his creative desires, he became a lifelong patron and promoter of the arts. His Albany press secretary was not alone in questioning whether American voters were prepared to elect a president who collected Picasso.

"I did not learn from somebody telling me you get burned if you touch a hot stove," Nelson acknowledged. "I had to touch it." On his fourteenth birthday he enjoyed his mother's undivided attention after shooting himself in the knee with an air rifle.

At Dartmouth Nelson impressed classmates with his lack of pretense. A true Aldrich, he honed his political skills to obtain from his tightfisted father the car of his dreams.

Born to a wealthy Main Line family, Mary Todhunter Clark was an independent-minded woman ill-prepared for the campaign trail. Nelson fell in love with "Tod's" character, humor, and intelligence, even while conceding that "she isn't terribly good looking."

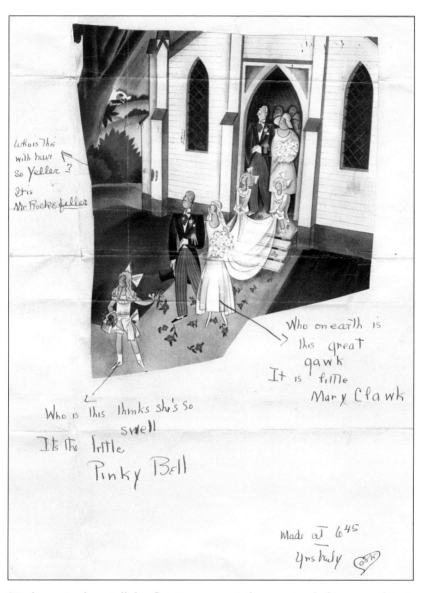

"For heaven's sake get all that flirtatiousness out of your system before you and I get married if we ever do," Tod warned her future husband. Her insecurities gave rise to this self-mocking depiction of their June 1930 wedding.

The newlyweds on their ten-month, round-the-world honeymoon. In India they visited New Delhi as the Viceroy's guests and heard Gandhi describe his expanding campaign for Indian nationhood.

Tod and her first child, Rodman, held here by his doting grandmother Abby. The two most important women in Nelson's life were not always so friendly.

Nelson meets Shirley Temple, the nation's reigning box-office attraction, during a 1934 excursion exposing Chase Bank executives to "the other America" west of the Hudson River.

A passionate photographer, Nelson aims his lens at the family's Pocantico Hills estate while riding in the ill-fated German dirigible *Hindenburg*. Tipped off to the dangers of flammable hydrogen by air ace Eddie Rickenbacker, Rockefeller later called the trip one of the most frightening experiences of his life.

President of Rockefeller Center before his thirtieth birthday, Nelson felt as comfortable socializing with construction workers as with New York mayor Fiorello La Guardia and RCA kingpin David Sarnoff.

Having assisted his father in the creation and promotion of Rockefeller Center, Nelson spearheaded construction of this 1939 showcase for the trendsetting Museum of Modern Art—"Mother's museum."

In August 1940 Nelson was appointed Co-ordinator of Inter-American Affairs by Franklin D. Roosevelt, whose pragmatic liberalism and personal charm made an indelible impression on young Rockefeller. Here FDR welcomes Rockefeller and other members of his National Advisory Commission to the Oval Office.

The nerve center of Rockefeller's wartime operation was the daily staff meeting, which was called to review the Co-ordinator's latest cultural offering, propaganda campaign, or health initiative designed to combat Nazi influence—and anticipate Soviet competition—in Latin America.

Pulitzer Prize–winning journalist Frank Jamieson (left) was a rare Rockefeller adviser willing to say no to his employer. His premature death in 1960 was a body blow to Nelson's presidential ambitions. More compliant than Jamieson, Wallace Harrison doubled as Nelson's architectural collaborator on such projects as Rockefeller Center, the United Nations, and Albany's South Mall.

The Anchorage. Harrison took orders from Nelson in designing this oceanfront retreat, complete with a saltwater pool and an interior loft for drying sails.

Unsolicited ideas received by the Co-ordinator's office included a rumba contest "to promote better feeling between the Americas." Here Rockefeller conducts his own brand of diplomacy.

Promoted to assistant secretary of state for Latin America, Rockefeller clashed with Alger Hiss and other departmental globalists over his support for regional alliances (like NATO) to combat the spread of Communism. At the organizing conference of the United Nations in April 1945, he argues his case with Secretary of State Edward R. Stettinius, Jr., and Senator Arthur Vandenberg.

Pursuing his postwar quest for "a better capitalism," Rockefeller established the International Basic Economy Corporation as a hybrid of entrepreneurship and social conscience. Profits were elusive. After thousands of chicks succumbed to disease, Venezuelan investors demanded to know how a Rockefeller could lose money. "I just showed you how," replied Nelson.

THE OUTDOORSMAN:

South American
cattleman

Texas hunter

Down East
sailor, with
sons Rodman
and Steven

Five years after firing him, Harry Truman invited Rockefeller back into government to help promote his Point Four initiative, forerunner of JFK's Peace Corps and Alliance for Progress. Like FDR before him, Truman urged Rockefeller (shown here with Everett Clinchy of the National Council of Christians and Jews) to become a Democrat.

With Ike at HEW. From left to right: NAR, his son Michael, daughter-in-law Barbara, daughters Mary and Ann Rockefeller, Joan Braden, President Eisenhower, Tod Rockefeller. Seated: HEW secretary Oveta Culp Hobby.

As a first-time political candidate in 1958, Rockefeller quickly ingratiated himself with New York State Republicans.

Traveling the state without an entourage, accompanied only by his son Steven (left) and Westchester County Assemblyman Malcolm Wilson—later his running mate—Rockefeller turned on the charm in a grassroots campaign that downplayed his wealth as it exploited his celebrity.

Rockefeller's uphill effort to dislodge incumbent Averell Harriman was dubbed "The Battle of the Millionaires." In a Democratic year few gave him much of a chance. (NEW YORK STATE ARCHIVES)

Nelson's inability to remember names led to an all-purpose greeting—"Hiya, fella"—that barely hinted at his talent for connecting with people outside his milieu. Whether upstate farmers . . .

or the polyglot inhabitants of Manhattan's Lower East Side. Here Attorney General Louis Lefkowitz escorts him on the famous "blintz tour" of neighborhood eateries, October 1, 1958. (ASSOCIATED PRESS)

On Election Day, Rockefeller won in a rout, establishing himself overnight as a Republican presidential prospect. Come January 1959, he and Tod, virtually estranged for much of their marriage, would share Albany's ramshackle Executive Mansion.

Beginning with Samuel J. Tilden in 1875, the house Theodore Roosevelt's children likened to a railroad station had sheltered three American presidents and four presidential nominees. (NEW YORK STATE ARCHIVES)

more than three years to complete). As for the methodology to be followed, explained Nelson, "We had two papers for each panel. We would have an oral presentation, and then we would have a discussion on the papers which was based on the presentation." Rockefeller the catalyst approached intellectual wallflowers and identified policy linkages eluding the specialists around him. He made Nancy Hanks executive secretary, in which role she functioned as academic den mother and traffic cop, assuring the timely production of nearly one hundred, admittedly uneven, papers while ministering to the eggshell sensitivities of as many self-styled best minds.

No one demanded more (or toiled harder) than Kissinger himself, whose gift for synthesizing complex subjects fully validated his description by *Newsweek* as a scholarly firecracker. Besides objecting loudly to anyone who tampered with his prose—he dismissed one secretarial editor as the highest-paid proofreader in the country—the moody political scientist had a habit of resigning on a whim. This occurred with sufficient frequency to test even Hanks's prodigious capacity for reassurance. Behind Nelson's back, Kissinger sometimes mocked his patron for failing to do his homework. Within earshot, he was deferential to the point of sycophancy, lavishly complimenting Rockefeller's contributions to the panel discussions.

"You have often deprecated your role in conversations with me by saying that you have only been asking questions," Kissinger told Nelson six months into the project. "This is not quite accurate but even if it were, it would not matter. I have heard too many clever answers to be impressed by easy solutions. Questions determine the level of discussion and the conceptual framework of any discourse." As proof, Kissinger cited Nelson's inquiries about the spiritual basis of economics. In coupling individual freedom and human dignity with more widely dispersed prosperity, number crunchers on the foreign economic panel merely reiterated what Nelson had been asserting since his earliest forays to Latin America. A heavy emphasis on parental and church involvement in the report dealing with education and manpower issues was traceable to the same source.

Kissinger, more worldly in his outlook, let pass few opportunities to remind Rockefeller of his own growing stature. He shared some complimentary references from Eisenhower about the professor's influential *Nuclear Weapons and Foreign Policy*—unaware that a staffer in Room 5600 had already reduced the complex volume, then and later a sourcebook for American policy makers, to a single-page summary at Nelson's request. "The best way to read a book is to get the author to tell you about it," Rockefeller maintained. "I'm a great believer in sitting down with a group on a subject." This theory was put to the test throughout the Special Studies Project. "We'd have authors in at the panel discussion.

They disciplined themselves to tell us about their books in fifteen minutes and that way we got the essence." Left unmentioned was Nelson's dyslexia, the spur to his learning by listening.

After the two men became friends and Kissinger was transformed into an academic and media superstar, various theories were advanced about their relationship. "Each one helped to make the other," concluded Laurance Rockefeller. Most assumed that Nelson took Kissinger at face value, even when the practiced courtier wore more than one face. It would be closer to the truth to say that Rockefeller valued Kissinger's brilliance enough to put up with his bluster. He had, after all, spent most of his life making excuses for extravagantly talented people; in this regard, the academic temperament differed little from the artistic one. "I think Henry Kissinger is one of the real comers in this country," Rockefeller told William Benton of the *Encyclopædia Britannica* in August 1957, "and I can't speak highly enough of him."

That did not mean his patience was unlimited. Even as he sang Kissinger's praises to Benton, tempers were fraying on the Special Studies panels entrusted with military and diplomatic policy. Openly scornful of disarmament schemes, Edward Teller enlivened one discussion by removing his wristwatch and hurling it at the unreconstructed liberal Adolf Berle. Amid such tensions, Kissinger's latest threat of resignation failed to elicit the usual response. To all outward appearances, Rockefeller oozed sympathy. He thanked his executive director profusely for his contributions to the project. Of course he understood Kissinger's desire to leave. "I told him I had no feeling but one of gratitude and that he shouldn't give it another thought. It is totally understood."

Several weeks later, Nelson received a phone call from Cambridge. Kissinger had changed his mind and wished to complete what he had started. Rockefeller, just as predictably, was "thrilled" to reclaim the professor's services. As a rule, his appreciation of staff ran in more utilitarian channels. One Christmas holiday season, Rockefeller expressed satisfaction that Nancy Hanks was at last enjoying an overdue rest with her family. After the first of the year, he told her, things would hopefully fall into more of a routine at the Special Studies Project, so "you will be able to give more time to the Fund's work and Gov[ernment] Research. They both need it and so do I!"

5

THROUGHOUT THE 1956 presidential campaign, Rockefeller enthusiastically identified himself as an Eisenhower Republican. He attended the GOP convention in San Francisco and donated substantially to the party war chest. On the morning of November 7, the Eisenhower-Nixon ticket having swept New York and all but seven other states, Nelson scribbled a congratulatory note to the vice president. "Under you and the President," he told Nixon, "the Republican Party is now emerging, at home and abroad, as the great and liberal party of the future." This was not as far-fetched an assessment as later events would indicate. Eisenhower had rolled up the largest popular vote ever recorded, and the second largest plurality, behind only FDR's 1936 tidal wave. Saddled with a no longer solid, but stubbornly racist, South, Democrats had yet to embrace an unequivocal position in favor of civil rights. Ike ran unusually well in northern urban areas, capturing nearly 40 percent of the black vote and winning an outright majority among Catholics, both mainstays of the old New Deal coalition.

In victory he reached out to Rockefeller, identifying him among the leaders of his generation who would shape the Republican future. More immediately, Eisenhower appealed for Nelson's help in promoting the administration's forthcoming budget. In light of their subsequent rift over defense spending, the request carried an ironic twist. But the issue of military preparedness involved organization as much as money—and here Dwight Eisenhower had every reason to consider Rockefeller his staunch ally in remaking the Pentagon. It will be recalled that as chairman of the President's Advisory Committee on Government Organization, Nelson had spearheaded a 1953 reshuffle of the defense establishment. In the years since, rival services had sullenly accepted Eisenhower's New Look defense policy, with its emphasis on cheaper nuclear deterrence at the expense of conventional forces.

Behind the scenes, however, Ike confronted a low-grade rebellion over strategic doctrine and fears generated by Soviet advances in both conventional and nuclear weaponry. During his tenure as secretary, the hapless Charlie Wilson was targeted by tattling generals and alarmist members of Congress for allegedly permitting a "bomber gap" to develop between the superpowers. A reluctant Eisenhower agreed to accelerate production of the B-52 bomber. He also began to ponder changes at the Pentagon far more radical than the modest reforms engineered four years earlier by Nelson Rockefeller and PACGO. Rockefeller, who might have been in Wilson's place himself but for the unyielding opposition of George Humphrey, shared Ike's concerns. But while Eisenhower viewed unification of the services as the surest way to hold the line on overall defense spending, Nelson's inflated estimates of the Soviet threat placed him closer to Vice President Nixon than to the old soldier in the Oval Office. "This issue has driven an unfortunate wedge within our own party," Rockefeller complained to Nixon in April 1957, "and has resulted in placing the President somewhat on the defensive in areas where it is natural for him to take a strong positive position." Under the circumstances, said Nelson, he wished he could advance publication of the Special Studies reports to influence the current session of Congress, "because we are working on some ten- to fifteen-year projections . . . both in relation to growing needs and the capacity of our economy to meet them."

He did the next best thing. Rushed to completion in the closing weeks of 1957, *International Security: The Military Aspect* was timed to coincide with Ike's 1958 State of the Union message. For Eisenhower, the first Rockefeller report was a canary in the coal mine of Pentagon reform. In reality, each man was using the other to advance his agenda. So while Ike chose to ignore parts of the report that implied criticism of his tightfisted stewardship, Rockefeller reserved the right to speak independently through the Special Studies Project. It was the hidden hand versus the pointed finger. Both men were responding to the crisis atmosphere engendered by the Soviet Union's recent ballistic missile test, followed two months later, on October 4, 1957, by Moscow's successful launch of *Sputnik*, the first satellite to be placed in earth orbit. Overnight, Eisenhower's countrymen lost both their sense of security and their sense of proportion.

If the post-*Sputnik* hysteria had a silver lining, reasoned the president, it led straight to military reform. Within days of appointing Procter & Gamble chairman Neil McElroy to replace Charlie Wilson at the Pentagon, Ike pointedly urged McElroy to tap Rockefeller's expertise on the subject. When McElroy hesitated, fearful of alienating the very services Eisenhower wanted tamed, Nelson filled the vacuum with a nineteen-page manifesto decrying Pentagon waste, duplication, and inefficiency. He offered a radical set of solutions, beginning with a truly unified military force. Transcending the historic categories of land, sea, and air, Rockefeller would create "strategic forces" drawn from each service to wage conventional war, along with a second, "tactical command" designed for the post-Korea, pre-Vietnam limited war or Communist-fueled insurgency.

By the autumn of 1957, Rockefeller was coordinating his ideas with Eisenhower and his latest budget director, Percy Brundage. Frustrated with the pace of McElroy's reorganization committee, Nelson urged the president to attend one of the group's meetings, where his unsubtle prodding convinced everyone but the sluggish McElroy. At one point, the secretary's foot-dragging provoked what historian Gerard Clarfield called a "nasty confrontation" between McElroy and Rockefeller—who further turned the screws at the start of 1958 by publishing the first of the eponymous reports meant to inventory America's most pressing challenges. *International Security: The Military Aspect* projected a drastically simplified chain of command, with the secretary of defense converted into nothing less than "deputy commander-in-chief" and given vastly increased authority over research, development, and weapons procurement.

The chairman of the Joint Chiefs of Staff, meanwhile, would become principal military adviser to the president.

No longer the chairman's equal—or competitor for scarce resources—the other service chiefs would busy themselves with logistics, training, and procurement. Existing military departments ought to be removed from operational command, the report contended, the first step toward dissolving service loyalties altogether. If Rockefeller had his way, all officers above the rank of brigadier general would receive their permanent promotions not from an individual service, but from the Department of Defense. Each, in turn, would be designated an officer of the United States Armed Forces. By encouraging strategic thinking over parochial loyalties, streamlining lines of authority, and eliminating organizational roadblocks, Rockefeller hoped to forge an American military capable of the swift and cohesive response demanded by modern warfare.

Appearing on NBC's *Today*, he promised a free copy to anyone who wrote in to request one. A quarter million viewers availed themselves of his offer. At the White House, Eisenhower passed over, for the moment, Rockefeller's plea to spend an additional $3 billion a year into the next decade. Publicly, he chose to emphasize the positive—above all, the report's clarion call for sweeping changes to a wasteful, anarchic defense establishment—while downplaying criticism of his administration's nuclear readiness. For the president, the Rockefeller report had served its purpose. Before lawmakers left town that fall for the campaign hustings, he compromised on legislation recognizing the separate organization of each service *and* declaring that each operated under the "direction, authority, and control" of the secretary of defense. The same bill strengthened the secretary in his oversight of newly unified commands.

The 1958 Defense Reorganization Act may have fallen short of what Eisenhower—and Rockefeller—wanted. But Ike, at least, was prepared to declare victory. For Nelson, by contrast, half a loaf was woefully inadequate when the survival of freedom hung in the balance. In apocalyptic language eerily reminiscent of his Quantico I findings, *International Security: The Military Aspect* declared there was no time to lose. "Our position a year or two hence depends on decisions that must be taken immediately." It was bad enough that Soviet conventional forces dwarfed those of the West; by sacrificing its civilian economy, the USSR had caught up with and, in some areas, surpassed the United States qualitatively as well.

Accepting intelligence forecasts of an overwhelming Soviet missile advantage by the early sixties, the Rockefeller panel saw oceans teeming with hostile submarines, each equipped with missiles capable of reaching forty-three of the fifty largest American cities; skies blackened by the world's largest air force; and a Soviet civil defense system far superior to that of its Cold War rivals. "Unless present trends are reversed, the world balance of power will shift in favor of the Soviet bloc," the report asserted. "If that should happen, we are not likely to be given another chance to remedy our failings." Might the tipping point already have been reached? Emphatically not, concluded Rockefeller and his fellow panelists, "if we are prepared to make the big effort now and in the years ahead."

Already legislation had been introduced in Congress to establish a cabinet-level Department of Civil Defense and to authorize construction of bomb shelters sufficient to protect 170 million Americans from nuclear holocaust. This panicky prescription was heartily endorsed by the Rockefeller report, which valued such "passive defense measures" no less than a retaliatory force capable of withstanding surprise nuclear attack and of delivering a crushing counterblow. Nor did Rockefeller and Kissinger shy away from the unthinkable. "In resisting aggression we cannot in advance forego weapons that technology makes available to all who seek them," they intoned. "The willingness to engage in nuclear war, when necessary, is part of the price of our freedom."

Probably no other document did more than the first Rockefeller report to instill national paranoia about a nonexistent missile gap. As a candidate for the presidency in 1960, John F. Kennedy invariably responded to foreign policy inquiries by instructing press secretary Pierre Salinger, "Hey, Pierre, get the Rockefeller Brothers Studies. It's all there." Once elected, Kennedy recruited no fewer than ten Rockefeller panelists to join his New Frontier, among them Rockefeller Foundation president Dean Rusk as secretary of state and Roswell Gilpatric, who assisted Robert McNamara in the cause of Pentagon reform. By raising overall defense spending and scrapping Dulles's theories of massive retaliation in favor of a more flexible response to proxy wars such as Vietnam, the Kennedy White House faithfully implemented much of the Rockefeller agenda, while adopting a markedly more hopeful view of arms negotiations.*

In a life littered with might-have-beens, Rockefeller's alienation of Dwight Eisenhower appears as fated as it was politically self-destructive. Long after both men were dead, their efforts at military restructuring were revived during the presidency of Ronald Reagan. Costly procurement scandals and operational embarrassments in the Iranian desert, a U.S. Marines barracks in Lebanon, and the tiny Caribbean island of Grenada created conditions ripe for reform. Legislation passed in 1985 made the secretary of defense at last undis-

---

* The influence of the Special Studies Project reached far beyond the Pentagon. Borrowing extensively from the Rockefeller reports, Kennedy and Johnson policy makers employed tax cuts, increased public works spending, and accelerated write-offs on capital improvements to prime the economic pump; pursued reciprocal trade agreements and lowered protectionist barriers to increase the flow of goods; established a federal Department of Transportation; and initiated greatly expanded programs of education and manpower training.

puted master in his own house. The same bill empowered the chairman of the Joint Chiefs of Staff along lines first drawn by Rockefeller three decades earlier. A year later, the Goldwater-Nichols Act bolstered the unified commands, linked officer promotions to joint duty experience, and required the services to cooperate in a variety of missions. "Our separate ground, sea, and air warfare by individual services is gone forever," declared the bill's leading sponsor, Senator Barry Goldwater. Once Rockefeller's ideological nemesis, in the evening of his Senate career Goldwater became the unlikely executor of his military policy will.

Part Three
AN AUTHENTIC REPRESENTATIVE OF THE PEOPLE
1956–1964

I'm a great believer in power.

—NELSON A. ROCKEFELLER

Thirteen
ROLLIN' WITH ROCK

I'd like to give Averell Harriman a run for his money.

—Nelson A. Rockefeller

1

"I HOPE YOU ARE not going to let them persuade you to run for Mayor," Mrs. Russell Davenport pleaded with Nelson early in 1957. "You have much more important things to do!" Together with her late husband, a writer and editor at Henry Luce's *Life*, Mrs. Davenport had been instrumental in the 1940 campaign to place that most irregular Republican Wendell Willkie in the White House. Now, anxious to see Rockefeller succeed where Willkie had fallen short, Davenport begged her friend not to become the latest GOP sacrificial lamb slaughtered by the city's Democratic machine.*

Her fears were groundless. Having spurned earlier appeals to run for city hall and for the United States Senate seat snared by Jacob Javits in 1956 ("All they do there is talk," said a contemptuous Rockefeller of the World's Greatest Deliberative Body), Nelson had his sights set on another position altogether. For almost a century, the governorship of New York had been viewed as both training ground for and springboard to the presidency. Grover Cleveland and the two Roosevelts had apprenticed in Albany; so, less successfully, had Charles Evans Hughes, Al Smith, and Tom Dewey. Ironically, Nelson had been handed the perfect vehicle with which to advance his ambitions by the present holder of the job. Like Rockefeller, W. Averell Harriman was an extravagantly wealthy president-in-waiting, with a robber baron in his past; a complex marital history; consuming interests in foreign affairs and art; and four homes (five including

---

* A distinction reserved for one Robert Christenberry, a Manhattan hotel manager whose charges that incumbent Robert Wagner was soft on crime lost much of their sting after police raided an illegal casino in the basement of Christenberry's hotel. In November, the Republican challenger secured 29 percent of the vote against Wagner.

the barnlike Executive Mansion on Albany's Eagle Street) in which to display his Renoirs and Rousseaus.*

If credentials alone could elect a president, then this "troubleshooter in a troubled world" would be in the forefront of Democrats hoping to succeed Harry Truman in the Oval Office. Unfortunately for Harriman, delegates to their party's July 1952 convention chose among candidates, not résumés. His dour persistence and grasp of detail were the skills of the negotiator; they stirred little popular enthusiasm. Though Harriman presented himself as an uncompromising liberal in the New Deal–Fair Deal tradition ("a Park Avenue Truman," snorted Dwight Eisenhower), his plodding style proved no match for the urbane governor of Illinois, Adlai Stevenson. Only a handful of delegates picked up the "I Crave Ave" buttons designed by Harriman's wife, Marie, to advertise her husband's forlorn candidacy. Among those offering consolation to his fellow New Yorker was Nelson Rockefeller. "You did an extraordinary job in your whirlwind campaign," Nelson wrote Harriman, to whom he had earlier deferred over the lease of a United Airlines executive aircraft for use in corralling delegates.

Two years later, Harriman was to enjoy greater success in his own backyard. Belatedly entering the contest for his party's gubernatorial nomination, the patrician candidate relied on gamy Tammany Hall and its undisputed boss, Carmine De Sapio, for his margin of victory over Congressman Franklin D. Roosevelt, Jr. That fall, Harriman parlayed a desire for change, strong organization backing, and the shortcomings of his Republican opponent into the narrowest of election victories. In his inaugural address, the new governor promised New Yorkers a "bold, adventurous administration." This did not reckon with an obstructionist legislature, much less Harriman's pedantic style and reflexive horror of debt (he routinely referred to constituents as "shareholders"). His small-bore approach to governing reflected the squirearchy of Arden, not Albany in the heroic age of Smith, Roosevelt, and Lehman. Per his orders, Harriman was notified within twenty-four hours of every traffic fatality on New York roads. Thereafter, asphalt replaced macadam surfaces, and potentially dangerous roadside shoulders were filled in. Admirers applauded the

---

* When Harriman in the 1930s established the Sun Valley resort in Idaho to promote rail travel and popularize downhill skiing, he made sure to include among the charter members of his private ski club his Fifth Avenue neighbor Nelson Rockefeller. Away from the slopes, Harriman's fiercest competitive skills were reserved for the croquet lawn at Arden, his family's hundred-room manor house crowning a twenty-thousand-acre reserve fifty miles north of Times Square. Harriman played with the same dogged intensity that had earned him Jazz Age distinction as the nation's fourth-ranking polo player, not to mention a personal fortune conservatively estimated at $75 million. Appropriately, it was over a hard-fought game of croquet that Harriman was recruited by Harry Hopkins to join the New Deal, several years before the same presidential talent scout brought Nelson into the Roosevelt circle.

governor for his attention to detail; foes derided him as Honest Ave, the Hair-splitter.*

The Harriman years were not without accomplishment. The cause of con-sumer protection became a gubernatorial priority. So did a more enlightened approach toward the mentally ill, with an emphasis on research and treatment over the warehousing of patients. Other innovations languished because of cost. Harriman vetoed tax deductions directed toward working mothers and the elderly, as well as a politically popular measure to license station wagons at the same rate as regular passenger cars. Stymied in his national ambitions, Harri-man sought reform on the cheap, by ending the system of legislative apportion-ment that made New York, in Al Smith's words, "constitutionally Republican." This result was achieved by the time-honored practice of awarding undue weight to rural, upstate counties at the expense of heavily Democratic New York City. Fortunately for Harriman, the state constitution contained a mecha-nism for its periodic revision, though nothing about the process was simple. Before voters in November 1957 could decide whether or not to hold a constitu-tional convention, a temporary commission had to be established to compile information for potential delegates and provide elected officials with such rec-ommendations as deemed useful by its members. Selection of the fifteen com-missioners was apportioned equally among Governor Harriman and his harshest critics in the legislature: state senate president Walter J. Mahoney of Buffalo, a gregarious Irishman with a cigar permanently clenched between his teeth; and assembly Speaker Oswald "Ozzie" Heck, a Schenectady Republican who had ruled the lower house since 1937. Neither man made any secret of his desire to replace Harriman in the Executive Mansion.

Somehow these scorpions in a bottle had to agree on a chairman acceptable to all. After the fact, Harriman would be mocked for creating in Nelson Rocke-feller a political Frankenstein's monster that turned on him in the 1958 guber-

---

* Journalist Jack Germond, then working Albany for the Gannett newspaper chain, never forgot a late night flight from Buffalo to New York in the governor's lumbering old National Guard plane. Together with *New York Times* correspondent Warren Weaver, the only other reporter on board, Germond had taken the precaution of obtaining alcoholic refreshment to ease the rigors of travel without steward or food service.

To the surprise of both men, Harriman had simultaneously directed his press secretary to pick up a fifth of Dewar's Scotch. For the next few hours, the airborne quartet traded the bottle back and forth as Germond and Weaver killed time by playing gin rummy. Upon landing in New York—the journalists having still to fly on to Albany—Harriman reached for his briefcase. "Have I got everything?" he asked his press aide.

"I think so."

"Have I got *everything*?"

Dutifully, Weaver handed over the bottle of Dewar's, a third full. Harriman carefully packed it away before bidding his traveling companions good night. Jack W. Germond, *Fat Man in the Middle Seat: Forty Years of Covering Politics* (New York: Random House, 2002), 29.

natorial contest. In fact, the naïveté was bipartisan. It extended to the governor's far more seasoned Republican adversaries in both houses of the legislature. Simply put, in the summer of 1956 neither Harriman, Mahoney, nor Heck regarded Nelson as a threat to his conflicting ambitions. Rockefellers were philanthropists, not politicians. The thought of one running for office seemed outlandish. If anyone was playing a double game, it was Republican state chairman L. Judson Morhouse, an ambitious forty-two-year-old lawyer-lobbyist who first met Rockefeller in 1955, following a gathering of major party donors in New York City. He appears to have concluded on the spot that the charismatic millionaire represented the best hope for a Republican restoration in the Empire State—and for himself to remain chairman.

He launched a campaign of ingratiation, writing Nelson in January 1956, "It looks like an interesting year—in many ways," and volunteering his assistance in any plans Rockefeller might entertain. On learning that these did not include the Senate seat being vacated by Herbert Lehman, Morhouse began promoting Nelson for chairman of the Temporary State Commission on the Constitutional Convention. Most around Rockefeller were cool to the idea, for reasons spelled out by Frank Jamieson. Suppose Nelson as chairman wound up endorsing a convention. In that case, he would in effect align himself with the Democrats on legislative reapportionment and just as surely alienate GOP activists whose support he needed for a gubernatorial nomination. Embracing the status quo, on the other hand, risked offending independents in the fast-growing suburbs of Long Island, as well as persuadable Democratic voters in the five boroughs—the latter bloc identified by Jamieson as the key to victory in 1958.

Reapportionment wasn't the only hot-button issue likely to confront commissioners. A gathering movement for racial integration in housing and the workplace demanded more than Brotherhood Week symbolism. "While this could have positive advantages," Jamieson concluded, "it also must be recognized that it would be very difficult, as racial tension increases, to satisfy the emotional demands of the Negro." Outweighing these dangers was the opportunity to gain statewide recognition, the prerequisite to running for office, and to cultivate the state's political elite. By the middle of June 1956, Jud Morhouse was authorized to raise Nelson's name with Walter Mahoney. For Mahoney, an upstate conservative and devout Catholic, it was smart politics to broker a deal with the governor's office by promoting a born-and-bred Manhattanite with a reputation for bipartisan service under three presidents.

More puzzling was Harriman's response. He and Nelson had worked together in New Deal Washington, each holding the title "Special Assistant to the President." They appeared to have few ideological differences. Just as Harriman had once been a Republican, so Nelson's GOP loyalties hadn't prevented him from donating $1,000 to young FDR's 1950 congressional campaign, party labels be damned. "Harriman wasn't a weak governor. He was a passive governor," asserts William J. Ronan, the savvy academic destined to become Nelson Rockefeller's closest deputy in Albany. Relying largely on subordinates, the governor may have thought it unnecessary or ungentlemanly to condition Rockefeller's selection on his explicit support for holding a convention. This initial miscalculation paved the way for a second, with even graver consequences. "Harriman felt that a Rockefeller would never expose himself to public office," claimed Nelson's friend and lawyer Oscar Ruebhausen. "He saw Rockefeller . . . as interested in art, very light, unsubstantial . . . a Boy Scout."

The appointment was announced on July 8, 1956, Rockefeller's forty-eighth birthday. Carmine De Sapio told Harriman he had placed a dagger in the hand of someone who wouldn't hesitate to thrust it into the governor's back. "My dear Mr. Secretary of State," sniffed Harriman. "Nelson and I are friends, and he would never do that to me." Questions over their mandate dogged commission members from the start. Their role was to "hear and report," declared Rockefeller, whose neutrality could not have pleased his gubernatorial sponsor. "I am having fun," an exhilarated Rockefeller told Oscar Ruebhausen's wife, Zelia, after an early meeting, "and when I get through with this deal I think I'll run for some kind of public office—if I knew what ticket!"

2

ASSEMBLING A STAFF amounted to a casting call for a Rockefeller governorship. For his executive director, Nelson tapped Bill Ronan, a forty-four-year-old PhD and dean of New York University's graduate school of public administration and social science. Until recently a deputy mayor in Bob Wagner's city hall, Ronan had burst onto the state government scene a few years earlier as director of studies for New York State's so-called Little Hoover Commission. One product of its labors was a yellow-covered volume detailing the perils associated with public authorities—autonomous agencies that issued bonds backed by revenues such as tolls. Exempt from taxes and lawsuits alike, their very lack of accountability made them attractive to überbuilder Robert Moses, who welcomed any means of funding large-scale public projects without recourse to a fickle electorate or resistant legislature.

That Professor Ronan should criticize, even implicitly, the legendary Moses at the zenith of his power and prestige was characteristic of this occasionally abrasive academic in his London-made bespoke suits. Intimidating in height, manner, and intellect, Ronan exuded an armor-plated self-assurance in keeping with Rockefeller's frankly stated affinity for "aggressive people." Skeptics might question how many of the shiny new ideas emerging from what came to be known as the Wholly Ronan Empire actually originated with its namesake. Yet no one disputed Ronan's versatility, his nose for talent, or his sure-footed ability to cut through red tape. Displaying an aptitude for political theater more often associated with the smoke-filled room than the ivory tower, Ronan orchestrated a series of well-reported public hearings at which individual New Yorkers and interest groups could sound off before the constitutional commission. Tapping his connections in the academic world, he recruited nearly seventy expert consultants to conduct policy reviews, with Rockefeller his star pupil.

Exhibiting more of the courtier's tact than Frank Jamieson—known in heated moments to upbraid Nelson, "You can't do that—don't be an idiot"—Ronan nevertheless reserved the right to challenge his boss. Within limits. "We had an understanding from the beginning," he says. "I could disagree with Nelson twice. The third time he had his way." Inevitably, the Ronan portfolio grew in proportion to his employer's multiplying interests and surging ambitions. That their collaboration, ending only with Rockefeller's death, revolved almost entirely around work made it all the more durable. In later years, Ronan professed astonishment to hear Martha Baird Rockefeller identify him as one of her stepson's few close friends. ("He has a lot of acquaintances," she told Ronan, "and very few friends.")

To balance his executive director from New York City, Frank Jamieson reminded Nelson, he must look upstate for a commission counsel. Sources at Milbank, Tweed tipped him off to George Hinman, a quietly impressive fifty-one-year-old partner in his family's Binghamton law firm and a quintessential establishment figure in the southern tier region straddling the Pennsylvania border. The antithesis of the stereotypical New Yorker, "Hinman had a very easy manner about him," recalled Oregon governor and senator Mark Hatfield. "You had to almost strain to hear him speak. He was low voiced, low keyed—everything was low about him in terms of his profile." To his peers on the Republican National Committee, Hinman was affectionately known as "Uncle George." His thin, serious face and owlish glasses gave him a vaguely scholarly appearance, which masked a fierce temper. Hinman and Ronan, the operative and the operator, harmonized dueling aspects of their employer in their approach to governing as in their individual characters. Hinman supplied a cautious detachment with which potentially risky actions were pondered, sometimes to the point of indecision. His bent toward conciliation offset Rockefeller's driving intensity. By contrast, Ronan, a broadly conceptual thinker, played to the brashly confrontational side of Nelson's character, while reflecting his disdain for bean counters and naysayers.

Useful as each man was, neither enjoyed the authority of Frank Jamieson. Frankie remained sui generis, the closest thing to a Louis Howe in the Rockefeller entourage. Yet even he couldn't persuade Nelson that 1958, the sixth year of an aging and increasingly out of touch administration in Washington, promised electoral disaster for Rockefeller and other Republican candidates caught in the undertow. Dismissing early polls and the conventional wisdom they fed, Nelson said he would take his chances. Nearing fifty, he was too old to wait for a favorable turn in the political climate. At the March 1957 Legislative Correspondents Association dinner in Albany, he got an unlikely boost from the maladroit Harriman, who lightheartedly tagged Nelson as a Republican prospect in the coming election. ("You could have knocked me over with a feather," an astonished Rockefeller said of the unexpected recognition.) Three months later, the governor welcomed members of the constitutional commission to the Executive Mansion for lunch. After loftily inviting his guests to partake of "the New York grape" in their wineglasses, Harriman turned to his handpicked chairman and assembled legislative leaders. "A lot of you are contenders for the governorship," he told them. "The lease is up next year. Why don't you look around the mansion and see if you might like it."

Devising a plan to put Nelson there permanently fell to Jamieson. "Most politicians have to build themselves up," he reminded Rockefeller. "You've got to bring yourself down." FDR had famously managed the trick; so, to a lesser degree, had his swashbuckling cousin Teddy. Harriman was trying as hard as he could, and it showed. "Jamieson said to Nelson, 'You know the art world, this world, that world,'" remembered Oscar Ruebhausen. "'You're going to get identified with the people. . . . Walter O'Malley is going to take the Brooklyn Dodgers to Los Angeles. Why don't you get involved and make an offer to keep the Dodgers here?'" To loyal fans of the Bums, the thought of their heroes decamping for the West Coast seemed nothing short of treachery. Over the previous decade, the fabled team had won six pennants, drawing more than a million fans a year to Ebbets Field, a 1913 relic emblematic of the city's neglect. Closer examination, however, revealed O'Malley's juggernaut to be running on fumes. Jackie Robinson had played his last game in Dodgers blue. Franchise players such as Duke Snider, Pee Wee Reese, and Don Newcombe were all past their prime.

So, feared O'Malley, was Brooklyn itself. "He always knew he was going" to Los Angeles, maintained Ruebhausen, Nelson's representative at the ensuing talks. Believing that he could possess three hundred acres of prime California real estate without any up-front investment, O'Malley looked askance at New York's somewhat grudging counteroffer. Then Rockefeller stepped in, volunteering to purchase a twelve-acre site on Atlantic Avenue for $2 million and let O'Malley and the Dodgers use it rent-free. As the phantom negotiations sputtered to their preordained conclusion, New York surrendered its second major league baseball team to the West Coast in a few months (the Giants, egged on by O'Malley, had already decided to abandon the decrepit Polo Grounds for a sleek new facility in San Francisco). Yet Rockefeller's eleventh-hour rescue attempt had caught the public fancy, precisely as Jamieson intended. Amid a flurry of favorable press coverage earned by his prospective rival, a comment by Governor Harriman went largely unnoticed. Graciously adding his own praise for the Rockefeller intervention, the frugal chief executive made it clear he had other uses for the Harriman millions.

3

SEPTEMBER 1957 MARKED a significant escalation of Rockefeller's stealth campaign for the governorship. Acting on George Hinman's counsel, Nelson broke bread with William H. Hill, octogenarian publisher of the *Binghamton Sun*, whose title of Broome County Republican chairman scarcely conveyed his political clout among GOP county leaders, the group most skeptical of a Rockefeller candidacy. By all accounts, Nelson made a positive impression. According to one guest present, "You went away knowing you had met a very dominant, affirmative type of guy who was going to go someplace." A second, private dinner two months later confirmed the Rockefeller-Hill alliance. Among organization types generally, Nelson inspired more curiosity than commitment. There were doubts about his toughness, conveyed in Walter Mahoney's harsh strictures against a "pussyfooting" campaign that blurred philosophical differences between the parties. Rockefeller's ability to connect with ordinary voters was called into question, as was his soporific speaking style and wonkish reliance on eye-glazing statistics to buttress his arguments. Even his New York City base was suspect, reinforcing as it did the aura of New Deal liberalism.

Among his chief competitors for the nomination were Mahoney, a Buffalo conservative virtually unknown in New York City and its rapidly expanding suburbs; and bald, burly congressman and former Republican National Committee chairman Len Hall, the son of Teddy Roosevelt's coachman, dubbed "the Pearl of Oyster Bay" by his political brethren. (Speaker Heck, potentially a formidable rival, was sidelined by a serious diabetic condition.) Pollster Sam Lubell neatly summarized the challenge facing Rockefeller: "It is how to keep the asset of coming to politics with clean hands and the assurance of an honest administration, but not seen like someone who is so inexperienced in state politics as to cause voters to demand, 'what's he got to fit him to be governor besides his money?'" Here the commission on constitutional reform proved a godsend. In the third week of September, Rockefeller presented an interim report containing almost three hundred specific proposals for change. On the divisive issue of whether or not to hold a convention, however, he refused to take a stand. His reticence was not emulated by New York's famously combative politicians, parties, or regional interests. Before dubious suburban audiences, Governor Harriman denied that constitutional reform was a smokescreen behind which Tammany-bossed Democrats in New York City could annex Nassau County. Robert Moses, as eager to join the fray as Nelson was to avoid it, urged voters to reject the convention outright "unless you like controversy, oratory, and vaudeville."

Two weeks before the election, under increasing pressure to tip his hand, Rockefeller released a statement clarifying the commission's role and restating its neutrality. His cautious approach was vindicated on Tuesday, November 5, when upstate voters strangled the convention in its cradle. Surprised and angered by the result, Harriman lashed out at Rockefeller for his hands-off stance. The governor enjoyed a measure of revenge by killing GOP legislation that would advance each party's nominating convention from August to June 1958. Besides shortening the fall campaign against him, Harriman's action was seen by many as a body blow to Rockefeller's undeclared candidacy. As the jockeying for advantage swirled around him, Rockefeller turned down a request from Billy Hill to address a forthcoming Lincoln Day dinner. "Your appearance at such a dinner would possibly be interpreted as indicating active candidacy," cautioned George Hinman. This pose of studied indifference, justified at the time by Rockefeller's continuing work on the Special Studies Project, as well as his concurrent efforts to promote Pentagon reform for Ike, hearkened back to an earlier, quasi-aristocratic culture, wherein the office sought the candidate. Hinman was to recommend a similar strategy in more than one presidential campaign, with results ranging from disappointing to disastrous.

For now, a political novice deferring to the pros around him, Nelson stuck to their script. He appeared on *Meet the Press* to promote his Cold War agenda but skipped a series of candidate forums sponsored by the National Republican Club. A *New York Post* reporter had no greater luck in eliciting the failings of the Harriman administration. "That's bringing the situation too close to home," Nelson told him. "I prefer not to discuss New York." For the annual dinner of Westchester County Republicans in January 1958, he made an exception. Sharing the dais in the Commodore Hotel atop Grand Central Terminal was Assemblyman Malcolm Wilson, a widely respected legislative workhorse then in his tenth term representing the Hudson River town of Yonkers. Some lawmakers can empty the chamber in which they serve merely by standing up to speak; Wilson had the opposite effect. As New York's toastmaster, he magnetized colleagues with his ornate, spread-eagle oratory, making skillful use of an Irish wit and the occasional Latin phrase sprinkled like holy water across his Fordham University erudition.

Wilson's command of the governing process was matched by an encyclopedic knowledge of the Empire State gained from twenty years of visits to county fairs, Knights of Columbus gatherings, and VFW halls. Nursing gubernatorial ambitions of his own, Wilson at forty-four was young enough to wait for a more favorable environment. Instead of pursuing voters, he found himself among the most eagerly pursued. His endorsement held particular value for Rockefeller. Like Billy Hill, Malcolm Wilson enjoyed a credibility among GOP conservatives that was priceless—if it could be transferred. It should have come as no surprise, then, that the day after the Commodore Hotel dinner, Wilson received a phone call from Westchester County party chairman Herb Gerlach. Could the assemblyman drop by Gerlach's office the following Sunday for a chat with Nelson Rockefeller? At the appointed hour, Nelson launched into an appeal for the support of his home county, whose party apparatus had benefited greatly over the years from Rockefeller largesse. In point of fact, Gerlach replied, Wilson's long service gave him first claim as Westchester's favorite son. But he wasn't running, said Wilson. Personally, he thought Rockefeller entitled to Westchester's endorsement. Besides, he added slyly, he knew how to get Nelson nominated.

And there matters stood, awkwardly, for the next two months as Rockefeller weighed his chances and Jud Morhouse, increasingly possessive of his hot political commodity, told Nelson to avoid both Wilson and Tom Dewey until Jud himself prepared the ground. Again Rockefeller did as he was advised. Which explains why the phone in Malcolm Wilson's White Plains law office did not ring until the first week of April 1958. "Remember when we had our meeting with Herb?" said the caller. Appearing later that day in Wilson's doorway, Nelson posed another, equally direct inquiry: What had Wilson meant in saying he knew how to get Rockefeller the Republican nomination for governor? The plan Wilson outlined in response was at once simple and brilliantly counterintuitive. Anticipating by four decades Hillary Clinton's pre-senatorial "listening tour" of New York, he would exploit Rockefeller's celebrity while demonstrating his common touch. Let other aspirants pursue the traditional route to nomination by appealing on bended knee to county leaders; Rockefeller would burrow under the GOP establishment, winning over grassroots Republicans through a direct and unrelenting courtship.

Not for the first time, Nelson the outsider prepared to take on his party's hierarchy. It didn't hurt that Billy Hill in the first week of May gave him a robust endorsement in the pages of his newspaper. Within days, a survey in the *Syracuse Post-Standard* revealed surprising Rockefeller strength outside of New

York's five boroughs. This, too, was part of an emerging game plan to promote Nelson as the *upstate* favorite, in counterpoint to the label of Manhattan liberal pinned on him by conservatives, who professed to see in Rockefeller the second coming of Wendell Willkie. Enough Republicans shared these suspicions, reported *The New York Times* on June 23, to relegate Nelson to third place in the delegate count behind Mahoney and Hall. Shrugging off the attacks, Rockefeller described a three-way stalemate to his cousin Richard Aldrich. "This I hope to break after I declare!" he added.

Politicians no less than generals are prone to refight yesterday's battles. That the old rules might no longer apply in 1958, arguably the first New York election in which television undermined traditional party allegiances, was grasped by only a few, among them Jud Morhouse. One day after his party's annual $100-a-plate fund-raising dinner on June 5, Morhouse convened a group of GOP insiders to review his latest polling data. No one else came close to Nelson's popularity, contended the state chairman. Dropping any pretense of neutrality, Morhouse launched a statewide "shirtsleeves tour" in advance of Rockefeller's formal entry into the contest. For Nelson, winning an election was a means to an end, and the end would always be governing. For months leading up to his entry into the race, a heavyweight policy group had been meeting in Roxy Rothafel's art deco suite at Radio City Music Hall to vet program ideas. Led by Roswell "Rod" Perkins, a pivotal member of the HEW team responsible for Social Security's expansion, the operation meshed old hands such as John Lockwood, Nancy Hanks, and economist Stacy May with recent recruits Bill Ronan, Malcolm Wilson, and George Hinman.

Also present, earning $40 a week in her first paid job as a note taker, was thirty-two-year-old Margaretta Fitler "Happy" Murphy, a Rockefeller neighbor at Pocantico and Seal Harbor. The nickname first bestowed in childhood seemed customized for this friendly, unpretentious woman, whose impact on Rockefeller's career was to surpass that of anyone in the room. A formal declaration of candidacy was scheduled for June 30 in Room 5600. At its conclusion, Wilson would drive Rockefeller to the Hudson Valley town of Kinderhook for a dinner meeting with the Columbia County Republican Committee. Since Nelson refused to go before the committee empty-handed, the issues group worked later than usual the night before his announcement. "We came up with the idea of urban state parks at about three fifteen in the morning," says Bill Ronan.

Waiting for the candidate at the Dutch Inn restaurant was Myrtie Tinklepaugh, the group's improbably named chairwoman. Still grateful for Nelson's appearance several years earlier at a local high school debate, Mrs. Tinklepaugh now returned the favor by arguing for his electability that fall. The committee agreed, unanimously awarding him their five delegates.

Though this represented only a tiny fraction of the 586 votes needed to win the nomination, the carefully timed endorsement generated disproportionate media coverage. Nelson was no pushover, Eleanor Roosevelt told readers of her "My Day" column. Moreover, wrote the former First Lady, in words that ought to have tempered Democratic complacency, if the fall contest was indeed Rockefeller versus Harriman, "we can at least feel confident in the integrity of both candidates."

4

S O BEGAN THE headiest learning experience since Rockefeller's early days in New Deal Washington. For six frenetic weeks that July and August, he was introduced to whitewashed hamlets and fraying industrial centers such as Utica and Schenectady; had his first glimpse of the scenic Finger Lakes and Chautauqua regions; discussed the price of apples and the plight of dairy farmers in places so remote, their only apparent link with civilization was the television aerials sprouting from widely dispersed roofs. The region's ingrained conservatism—only two upstate counties had a Democratic sheriff—made Rockefeller all the more dependent on Malcolm Wilson. "Nelson was his own best salesman," a modest Wilson said later. "He was the merchandise. I was the door opener." Wilson, in fact, acted as scheduler, tour guide, interpreter, and coach. "In the car he would brief and prepare Father before each stop," remembers Steven Rockefeller, then twenty-two, who was behind the wheel for the entire trip. "One day . . . we saw a farmer with a load of manure going down one of those highways in upstate New York. Len Hall had just leveled a bitter attack against Father, and Malcolm Wilson's comment was, 'There goes Len Hall with his platform.'"

Rural Cortland County, just north of Binghamton, was Ozzie Heck country. It was also emblematic of Rockefeller's pre-convention odyssey through fifty-three of the state's sixty-two counties. With assistance from the area's assemblyman, an old friend, Wilson arranged a luncheon at an American Legion post. Well in advance of the advertised time, a large crowd assembled outside, eager for a glimpse of American royalty. Several policemen had been detailed to clear curb space for the expected Rockefeller entourage. As it happened, their services would not be required. Shortly before noon, Wilson's green Buick pulled into town, a grinning Nelson in the front passenger seat. That a Rockefeller should visit their easily bypassed community caused more than a ripple of civic pride. That he should appear without advancemen or personal retinue, requiring but a single parking space to accommodate his traveling party, conveyed a modesty at odds with popular expectation.

The image of Nelson carrying his own luggage into charmless hotels, often past knots of gaping spectators, lingered in memory long after people forgot what he had said to them over lunch. His basic stump speech quoted "my son Steven, who is traveling with me" and his disturbing inquiry, "Gee, Dad, isn't politics a dirty business?" Sometimes the candidate said nothing more than, "Hello, I'm Nelson Rockefeller. I'm running for governor. It's a real pleasure to say hello to you." In small-town diners, by contrast, over poached eggs and morning coffee, reported *Time*, he "chomped and chatted like a traveling salesman in women's ready-to-wear." Patting voters on the back, signing countless autographs, Rockefeller repeatedly stopped to talk with children, much to the dismay of his campaign schedulers. "If we could get the voting age down to six, I'd be in," Nelson claimed. "If we could get it down to two, it'd be a landslide." As for the adult electorate, "They come out to see whether he's for real," one mystified upstate pol observed. "I don't know what's doing it, that grin or the winks he throws around or just that he looks so goddamn regular they believe in him. I guess he surprises them. Whatever it is, it's dynamite."

At this stage of the campaign, Rockefeller was very much a work in progress. Expressions of support elicited the phrase "Thanks a thousand," a rich man's tin-eared attempt to divert attention from his wealth. Trained from childhood to initiate conversation as a way of putting others at ease, Nelson had yet to learn how to end the dialogue lest bores and special pleaders take his listening tour altogether too seriously. "We went with him to a potato festival in Savannah," recalls Jack Germond. "There was a farmer there complaining about a new state law requiring taillights on all farm equipment that went on state roads. . . . And Nelson stood and talked to this guy for like fifteen minutes." Accompanying reporters contrasted his substantive discussions with "the new record for free-style handshaking" established by Governor Harriman during his visit to the same agricultural fair. Both men were notoriously poor at remembering names. But the colorless, soft-spoken Harriman's all-purpose greeting of "Hello, stranger" rarely led to anything more and, in any event, was rendered far less convincingly than Nelson's ebullient "Hiya, fella!"

Nelson perfected his techniques of mass seduction at a reception and buffet dinner for delegates from Oneida, Madison, and Herkimer counties. "I am glad to be here," he told the assembled guests. "I understand that your counties have endorsed Walter Mahoney, who's a great Republican and a great friend of mine, and all we are interested in is getting responsibility back to Albany." For the balance of the evening, he mingled informally with the crowd, asking as many questions as he answered. Within a week, all three counties defected to the

Rockefeller camp. Still, personal charisma could carry him only so far. To prevail at the nominating convention in August, he would have to persuade suspicious upstaters—as he had already convinced Malcolm Wilson—that he wasn't the reflexive liberal of caricature. Before a Junior Chamber of Commerce dinner in Rochester, Nelson endorsed tax cuts over a public works program as "a sounder method of dealing with a mild recession." He voiced alarm at the flight of private capital and cited numbers showing the Empire State falling behind its neighbors in job creation. Rockefeller hinted darkly that Harriman was soft on crime, though he clearly preferred talking about what an invigorated state government could do to combat juvenile delinquency.

Behind closed doors, he repeated to county leaders the anodyne pledge he had given Wilson: In the event of his election, "anytime you have a problem with my program, you and I will talk it over. If we have differences of opinion, we'll resolve them." After twelve years of Tom Dewey's dictation to the pliant body he called "my legislature," and four more in the political wilderness under Harriman, even Old Guard Republicans welcomed the prospect of negotiating across a table with Nelson Rockefeller. In Syracuse, making a pledge that bore Jud Morhouse's fingerprints, he endorsed the patronage system as an inescapable part of New York government. When Morhouse subsequently was embroiled in scandal and it became politically advantageous to downplay his contributions to the 1958 campaign, a revised narrative emerged, neatly summed up by one biographer as "Travels with Malcolm." Truthfully, there was more than enough credit to go around. Practicing a strategic coordination notably lacking in Rockefeller's national campaigns, Wilson and Morhouse functioned like grindstones wearing down opposition in what amounted to a (mostly) friendly takeover of the New York Republican Party.

Morhouse was especially vigilant in guarding against arrogance, the slightest appearance of which could be lethal to a Rockefeller. So when an independent group calling itself People for Rockefeller derided Hall's "insignificant" delegate support, Morhouse administered a firm rap on the knuckles. It was bad form for a front-runner to belittle a failing competitor, he reminded those around the candidate, "especially a competitor whom you eventually want to have on your side." Nor was Morhouse shy about opposing Nelson's plan to take two weeks off for a Maine vacation. Such an action smacked of overconfidence, he said. Rockefeller cut his Seal Harbor respite to four days.* By mid-July, fresh

---

* There was nothing self-indulgent about Rockefeller's desire for some downtime. "He would campaign very hard all day long, and he'd be exuding all this enthusiasm and energy," recalls Steven Rockefeller. "When he'd get back to his hotel room around 11:30 p.m. or midnight, and the door on the outside world closed, his whole face would just collapse. He would get his clothes off and fall into bed, and boom, he was out cold. Then in the morning Kenny Riland would arrive and give him a treatment, and off he'd go again." Steven Rockefeller, HMI, 8.

reports of upstate conversions emboldened campaign strategists to pull back the curtain on previously concealed strength in New York City. On July 10, Morhouse notified the candidate that he could expect all sixty-one delegates from the Bronx. The next day, Paul Williams, the U.S. attorney thought to be Tom Dewey's favorite, relinquished his claim to Manhattan's eighty-one votes.

Len Hall fought back as best he could, challenging his adversary to a series of Lincoln/Douglas-style debates. Rockefeller parried the thrust by saying he had no intention of fighting a fellow Republican. Disgruntled rivals attributed his progress to money, not magnetism. Publicly, Rockefeller sought to downplay his financial advantage. Confronted by rumors he was prepared to spend $3 million to win the governorship, he shot back, "I understand Harriman spent $27,000 in '54 and won." Not that he engaged in unilateral disarmament; rather, consistent with family tradition, Rockefeller found more subtle ways to exploit his wealth. He replaced the honey locust trees in front of St. Patrick's Cathedral for his friend Francis Cardinal Spellman. On learning that Joe Carlino, Republican leader in the state assembly, was planning a family vacation, he made sure that a cottage was reserved for him at the Rockefeller-owned Caneel Bay resort in the Virgin Islands. Bill Pfeiffer, a Buffalo congressman who had doubled as Jud Morhouse's predecessor at the Republican state committee, let it be known that he might quit one or both jobs for financial reasons. Pfeiffer received a call from Nelson Rockefeller. "I've talked to Bill Zeckendorf and don't be surprised if you hear from him," Nelson said somewhat cryptically. In due course, a plainly reluctant Zeckendorf notified the GOP chairman that at the request of the Rockefeller family, he was sending Pfeiffer a check for $40,000—half the commission on the last piece of land the developer had assembled for the United Nations. A grateful Pfeiffer was invited to lunch with Nelson; their two-hour conversation was an important chapter in Rockefeller's political education.

Early in the campaign, Jud Morhouse forcibly denied that his law firm was on a $3,000 monthly retainer from the Rockefellers. He neglected to mention that Nelson *had* introduced him to family counsel John Lockwood for what both men assumed was their mutual benefit. Rockefeller attempted something similar with Malcolm Wilson. Noting that any extended absence from his law firm was sure to depress Wilson's income, he murmured elliptically, "I don't know how you handle those things around here." But if he expected Wilson to ask for some business to be sent his way, Nelson was in for a surprise. "I always dealt with him as if he were on welfare," Wilson insisted. This meant refusing the hospitality of any Rockefeller family resort property. More immediately, it foreclosed Rockefeller donations that spring to the Westchester County Republican Committee, the sponsoring organization from which Wilson drew reimbursement for his expenses incurred in the pre-convention road show.

Certainly it wasn't the prospect of financial gain that prompted Wilson to make the ultimate sacrifice after Nelson, for whom travel by automobile was torture ("He would fly from Tarrytown to North Tarrytown"), suggested they fly over the Adirondacks to attend a scheduled luncheon the next day in Massena, close to the Canadian border. He'd simply call the family office, Rockefeller told Wilson, and have a plane meet them in Utica. Malcolm confessed that he had never been aloft. "It's great," Nelson assured him. "Nothing like it." That night, Wilson telephoned the Republican vice chair of Oneida County to learn if the church nearest his hotel had a seven o'clock Mass. The next morning, she accompanied him to St. John's Catholic Church, where the reluctant air traveler consigned his soul to its Maker. Prayers of another kind were answered on August 17, when Len Hall quit the race, telling a friendly journalist, "Who can compete with that kind of money? Besides, he'll lose in November." Three days later, Walter Mahoney followed suit. Carmine De Sapio professed joy at the prospect of running against a Rockefeller. Max Lerner of the *New York Post* offered Harriman a tongue-in-cheek slogan on which to seek reelection: "Don't swap multimillionaires in midstream." The governor himself reasserted his claim to have chosen Nelson as his fall opponent. Keynoting his party's convention in Buffalo on August 25, Democratic state chairman Michael Prendergast had a different explanation for Rockefeller's success, crediting his nomination to "the self-perpetuating clique of power-drunk bosses who dominate the Republican party's machinery."

Rockefeller didn't look bossed to Republicans simultaneously assembling for their convention in Rochester. At his insistence, a platform plank calling for a one-year residency requirement for welfare recipients was dropped. Discarding the ancient customs mandating geographic, religious, and ethnic balance on the ticket, Rockefeller prevailed on Wilson, his Westchester County neighbor, to run for lieutenant governor. For attorney general, the convention confirmed incumbent Louis Lefkowitz, a street-smart product of Lower East Side settlement houses and political clubs. The nod for state comptroller, a likely payoff to secure the pivotal delegation from Queens, went to former borough president James Lundy. That Monday evening, Rockefeller himself was nominated by acclamation, after a display of orchestrated spontaneity that had delegates snake-dancing through the shabby War Memorial Auditorium to the sounds of Lionel Hampton's jazz band. Fueling the demonstration was eight tons of noisemakers, fancy hats, placards, ticker tape, and balloons, all stockpiled weeks in advance by efficient Rockefeller planners.

In his acceptance speech, rewritten by John Lockwood to arraign the "vacillation and veto" of Averell Harriman's Albany, Nelson flailed the incumbent ("He vetoed . . . he has dragged his feet . . . he has undermined . . . he has allowed the economy of the state to drift") for his alleged lack of leadership. At its conclusion, Tom Dewey approached the nominee and, with barely concealed astonishment, said to him, "You know, I have to tell you I think you have a good chance of winning." George Hinman agreed. "The job you have done in gaining the nomination, with nobody bloody and nobody mad, is the greatest I have ever seen," he wrote Nelson. "Watch your health and Steve's driving and we'll see you in Albany on New Year's Day."

Like Harriman in Buffalo, Rockefeller went into his convention without a candidate for United States senator. Dewey refused a draft. Joe Carlino preferred to remain in the assembly, where he was poised to succeed a mortally ill Ozzie Heck as Speaker. Attention turned to Kenneth Keating, a small, vain, pink-faced congressman from Rochester who washed his snowy-white hair every day with an egg. Keating was understandably reluctant to surrender the House seat he had occupied since 1947. It required the better part of two days, the browbeating intervention of Dewey, Jud Morhouse, Jacob Javits, and Rockefeller himself; a telephone call from Vice President Nixon; and the reported promise of a federal judgeship if, as expected, he lost in November. Only then did Keating agree to run. At fifty-eight, he was the oldest member of a ticket that exuded vitality.

In Buffalo, by contrast, warring Democrats made Harriman appear subservient to Carmine De Sapio and his Tammany allies, who insisted their party endorse Manhattan district attorney Frank Hogan for the Senate. Hogan was an Irish Catholic of unblemished integrity and demonstrated voter appeal, but no foreign policy credentials. To Eleanor Roosevelt and other reform Democrats, Hogan's parochialism was less offensive than his ties to De Sapio. The ensuing contest inevitably became a test of gubernatorial backbone. By accepting renomination before settling the Senate fight to his liking, Harriman sacrificed any leverage he might have over the bosses. And with no obvious candidate of his own once Mayor Wagner refused to run, the governor became a spectator to his own humiliation. Making matters worse, to guarantee its victory Tammany cut a deal with Erie County boss Peter Crotty, in return for which Crotty was nominated for attorney general over a list of three candidates submitted by Harriman. The governor's wife, Marie, offered a perceptive, if earthy, analysis when she declared, "They gave old Ave a real Philadelphia rat fucking."

More to the point, they gave Rockefeller a club with which to beat the incumbent over his surrender to the machine. "That's it," said Frank Jamieson as he watched the postmidnight shambles unfolding in Buffalo on a flickering screen in the Rockefeller hotel suite. "That's our campaign issue." Malcolm Wilson and others in the room shook their heads wearily. Republican denunciations of Tammany were an election year ritual, of questionable impact even among those living virtuously north of the Bronx. But Jamieson had grasped an elemental truth hidden from the jaded professionals around him. Thanks to television, Tammany was no mere abstraction, the predictable object of editorial scorn or partisan applause lines. After Buffalo, and the clash of cultures vividly enacted before millions of viewers, the machine had a face and an equally distinctive personality behind it. With his camel-hair coats and trademark dark glasses—worn because of iritis, a chronic inflammation of the cornea—the slight hint of a lisp, and an ornate speaking style reminiscent of Nicely-Nicely and other Runyonesque hoods, Carmine De Sapio was the Boss from Central Casting. Through his mishandling of the Senate nomination, Averell Harriman did for his Republican opponents what they couldn't do for themselves.

5

THE DAY AFTER his convention triumph, accompanied only by his son Steven, Rockefeller motored through the verdant farm country of western New York. At one point he signaled for Steve to stop the car, then got out of the vehicle, strode into a field, and introduced himself to a farmer atop a tractor. In short order he was invited indoors, where the conversation continued around the kitchen table. One-on-one: This was Nelson's métier, the possibility with each fleeting encounter to forge enduring loyalties. Jackie Robinson, in later years part of the Rockefeller administration, was in 1958 a Harriman supporter. In his autobiography, *I Never Had It Made*, Robinson analyzed Rockefeller's appeal. "It is almost impossible not to like the man," he concluded. "He gives two distinct impressions: that he is sincere in whatever he is saying and that in spite of his frantic schedule, power, and influence—at that specific moment of your contact—he has shut everything else out and is focusing his complete and concentrated attention on you."

But there were nearly seven million residents of the Empire State registered to vote in the fall of 1958 and barely ten weeks until Election Day. Not even Rockefeller could make that many personal connections. He did his best, traveling eighty-five hundred miles, shaking an estimated one hundred thousand hands, making at least 135 formal speeches. In one of the first, delivered less than a week after his nomination, Rockefeller casually suggested that Harriman might consider dropping out of the race in favor of De Sapio, who was already "sort of running the state as it is." This could be dismissed as a cheap shot, but a lack of enthusiasm on the part of their Liberal Party allies made Democrats justifiably nervous. Adding to their jitters was a Rockefeller organization sprawling over three separate buildings in midtown Manhattan and just as lavishly stocked with political talent. Jud Morhouse had the title of campaign manager, with Bill Ronan in charge of research and speeches. Functioning as adviser without portfolio was George Hinman, whose suggested campaign slogan—"Get Rollin' with Rock"—was gently passed over.

From their main command post on the seventh floor of the Roosevelt Hotel, Rockefeller promoters crafted individualized appeals targeted at writers, actors, artists, athletes, lawyers, doctors, women, veterans, college students, and farmers. Similar messages were directed to New Yorkers of French, Irish, Hungarian, Greek, Spanish, Scandinavian, Chinese, Czech, Polish, Puerto Rican, and Ashekenazi Jewish ancestry. To counter arguments of inexperience, a lavish thirty-page booklet, *Meet Nelson Rockefeller,* extolled the candidate's efforts at HEW to extend Social Security benefits and channel federal aid to school construction. Newspaper readers were encouraged to call designated phone numbers and hear Rockefeller expound on the issues in prerecorded messages (forerunner to the dreaded computer-generated robocalls of our own time). As the first punishing winds of autumn scoured the Adirondacks, conventional political roles went topsy-turvy, with an aggressive Republican challenger accusing a Democratic incumbent of betraying the state's liberal traditions of innovation and generosity. Harriman's veto of increased workers' compensation and unemployment benefits came in for criticism, as did his loyalty to a party whose southern governors formed the vanguard of opposition to civil rights.

Depicting his rival as custodian of the status quo, Rockefeller decried the Harriman years as a period of "do nothing and drift." The alternative he set forth included more affordable housing and a significant expansion of the state university established ten years earlier under the Dewey administration. Nelson proposed greater funding of local education as well, along with higher salaries for state employees; development of a basic water resources policy; a reforestation program double the current level; and early construction of the Northway, Empire Stateway, and Southern Tier expressways. He called for an Office of Transportation to promote mass transit and revive dying rail traffic; extension of the St. Lawrence Seaway through new channels opening Albany and Troy to oceangoing commerce; a boost in state support for agricultural research; and expansion of the state attorney general's investigatory powers in order to release the New York waterfront from the grip of racketeers.

Running against the less agile incumbent from both Left and Right, Rockefeller opposed right-to-work laws as an infringement on collective bargaining. Yet in his next breath he pummeled those in power for living beyond their means. Harriman, he declared, had presided over a 50 percent increase in state expenditures, without a single major new program to show for it. By 1958, the state was being run with borrowed dollars, its creaky administrative structure crying out for modernization. In place of a governing ideology, Rockefeller prescribed a dynamic growth economy, the same cure he had been promoting to Latin Americans for twenty years as the surest route to individual prosperity and social justice. He blamed Harriman's lack of vision, inadequate planning, and inconsistent tax policy for fostering a climate hostile to business. To combat economic stagnation and bolster New York's competitiveness, Rockefeller vowed a return to the "pay as you go" fiscal policies of the Dewey years.

Left unaddressed was the question of who would pay what in order to realize his sweeping agenda. Repeatedly pressed about the possibility of new taxes, Rockefeller surprised reporters expecting the usual evasions. Lunching with a conservative newspaper publisher, the candidate appeared to have forgotten his earlier call for stimulative tax cuts. As a matter of fact, said Rockefeller, the next governor would be lucky if he didn't have to *raise* taxes. "We're going to need a hundred and fifty or two hundred million just to keep up." To admirers, such candor confirmed Nelson's status as a political original, entirely his own man. "He was for many of us a knight in shining armor then," reflected Steven Rockefeller. "I mean, he was saying what *he* thought he should, and his hands were not tied in any way. It was a great time."*

Every campaign breeds its own mythology. Rockefeller's first run for office is remembered less for the ideas he espoused than the blintzes he ate and the star quality that led to his mobbing by a crowd of three hundred thousand beach-goers at Coney Island. In fact, Rockefeller kept a relentless focus on public policy. "Mr. Rockefeller is trying a new campaign technique," wrote James Reston in *The New York Times*. "He is using facts and, on occasion, even ideas. . . . He knows precisely how New York stands with ports such as, say, Milwaukee, in percentages of trade, manufacturing, and runs batted in over the last few years." As well he should: thanks to the Radio City research team, Rockefeller carried with him several thick volumes, indexed and cross-referenced, detailing some two dozen major issues and incorporating the most extensive economic surveys ever made of the Empire State. His command of the issues and, still more, his exuberant habit of plunging into crowds in neighborhoods rarely, if ever, visited by a Republican established Rockefeller as a campaign natural.

The impression didn't survive exposure to his stilted speech making. Nothing so worried his campaign strategists that fall as the candidate's oratorical deficiencies. With considerable courage, George Hinman showed Nelson unflattering field reports about his halting delivery and drab monotone. He pleaded for additional rehearsal time in advance of critical television broadcasts. Finally, he volunteered what Rockefeller disdained as "Hinman down to

---

* One man's independence is another's imperiousness. Over lunch with a dozen leading members of the Knights of Columbus, Rockefeller was harangued about what he must do as governor for Italian Americans. Nelson thanked the group's chairman for his input. The men around the table needed to get one thing clear, he said in an icy tone. No one would tell him what he should think, say, or do. Steven Rockefeller, HMI, 5.

earth stuff" in place of densely worded paragraphs telling voters more than they cared to know about equalization rates and milk production. Rockefeller was better on camera than in his platform appearances, but only by comparison with Harriman's ducal manner and prep school accent. As for the real problem, his dyslexia, "he saw it as a weakness," says one associate from Room 5600, "and he could not stand to be weak on anything." A solution was devised by Nelson's Dartmouth classmate Sylvester "Pat" Weaver. Dispensing with scripts and teleprompters alike, Weaver filmed a series of person-to-person encounters at gas stations, supermarkets, suburban schools—anywhere Rockefeller could be showcased at his conversational best. The contrast with his formal speeches was dramatic. Although he would never spellbind, Nelson improved steadily with practice. "For a beginner it was quite a professional job," declared Jack Gould in *The New York Times* following the candidate's late September television debut.

By his own admission, Harriman ran a lackluster campaign. He muddied his message, first castigating Rockefeller for promising more than the state could afford, then undercutting the argument by predicting that Nelson, if elected, would be taken over by his party's Old Guard, "just like Eisenhower was in Washington." His refusal to promise to serve out a full four-year term did nothing to advance the governor's cause. Harriman campaigned like a man who wanted to be president, said the *New York Daily News,* unlike his challenger, who confined his appeal to state issues. There was good reason for this, given Harriman's strenuous efforts to make the contest a referendum on the Eisenhower administration. The more he sought to nationalize—and internationalize—the race by linking Nelson to the Eisenhower recession, the more he reinforced his own image as a leader indifferent to state and local concerns. Battling a bronchial throat condition and feeling all of his sixty-six years, the overscheduled incumbent scarcely hid his displeasure with the demands of electioneering. Visiting a Rochester meatpacking plant one day, Harriman wryly observed, "I ought to join a union. I'm working a sixteen hour day."

6

ANOTHER MYTH ABOUT the 1958 campaign is that of a nail-biting affair down to the wire. On September 30, Rockefeller informed Oveta Culp Hobby that he had "a good fighting chance, with the polls running just about neck and neck." That same week, he showed up at Yankee Stadium to root for the home team in game one of their World Series contest with Milwaukee. Attracting nearly as much attention as the players, he told reporters that the victorious Yanks' performance—"you know, coming from behind, a good strategic position"—paralleled his own uphill effort. More detached observers concluded that he was, if anything, understating his prospects. Reporter Warren Weaver of *The New York Times* and Gannett's Jack Germond each won a handsome windfall by betting on a Rockefeller victory. The novice, they concluded, was a natural, hitting his stride as a campaigner just as most voters began to pay attention to the race. His comic timing wasn't bad either—stooping to pick up a dime on a Bronx sidewalk, Rockefeller exclaimed, "This is like carrying coals to Newcastle."

Dropping in on an upstate bar whose patrons were watching the World Series on television, Rockefeller knew better than to interrupt the game. After treating everyone to a round of beers, he prudently withdrew. The most indelible images of the campaign stemmed from a Louis Lefkowitz brainstorm. Proposing "something different" to combat lingering impressions of a rich man's insularity, Lefkowitz suggested a walking—and eating—tour of the Lower East Side, the colorful, culturally hostile Jewish neighborhood in which Lefkowitz, the son of an immigrant vest maker, had his roots. Rockefeller readily agreed. A light rain was falling shortly before noon on Wednesday, October 1. It didn't prevent a battalion of reporters and cameramen from recording Nelson's gustatory adventures as he wolfed down cheese blintzes and sour cream before two hundred astonished patrons at Ratner's kosher dairy restaurant, while simultaneously shaking every hand within reach. "Terrific," he declared between mouthfuls, "absolutely delicious." Autographing waiters' checks and paper napkins, Rockefeller said he had no idea whether he was winning votes, "but I'm having a lot of fun."

Next stop: Weitzman's Delicatessen on Delancey Street. Here Nelson impetuously ordered herring and potato soup. ("I was worried he would be sick all night," Lefkowitz said later.) After donning an apron, he posed for pictures with a counterman named Ben, munched on a corned-beef sandwich, and haggled with the proprietor over the gift of a five-pound salami. "Take it, your credit is good," the owner assured Rockefeller, who compromised by paying wholesale— three dollars instead of five. Making his way through excited street crowds, the candidate sampled the pizza and hot dogs at Jack Levy's Famous, where he paused to chat in Spanish with some Puerto Rican customers at the counter. The refusal of one old man to shake his hand left the visitor momentarily nonplussed.

"I just wanted to say hello to you," Nelson persisted.

"Can I put hello in the bank?"

As reporters scribbled furiously to capture every exchange in this increasingly surreal incursion, an elderly Jewish woman approached Nelson with a request of her own. "Mr. Rockefeller, I need an apartment," she said. More specifically, she required suitable housing at a rent she could afford. "That is a very serious problem," he acknowledged, proceeding to explain in detail a pair of housing-related bond issues on the November ballot and the manifest improvements sure to follow their passage. His petitioner stared blankly. "I should live so long," she remarked. (Rockefeller subsequently located a place for her to live.) It lasted barely an hour, but the "blintz tour," as it came to be known, received front-page treatment by *The New York Times* and other papers. Its very incongruity helped to establish Rockefeller as the most electrifying street campaigner since Fiorello La Guardia, maybe since FDR. By contrast, when Averell Harriman a week later dropped by a heavily Jewish Brooklyn neighborhood to sample gefilte fish with horseradish, the story was relegated to page thirty-four of the *Times*.

Rockefeller enjoyed a second triumph when he invaded the garment district, a Liberal Party stronghold, where he was mobbed by workers hoping some of his millions might rub off in a handshake. Elsewhere, thousands of Harlem residents turned out to hear Count Basie and, coincidentally, the Republican candidate for governor. An even larger crowd in Spanish Harlem raised Nelson to their shoulders after he addressed them in Spanish wearing an outsized sombrero. In Greenwich Village, Rockefeller answered questions from the back of a truck, scoring points with a strong endorsement of government funding for the arts. Behind the scenes, he offered reassurances to organized labor, telling union leaders, "I know you're obligated but, however this turns out, we're friends." By the third week of October, even the cautious George Hinman thought it was time to take the formerly tongue-tied candidate out of wraps. In the closing days of the race, discarding the formal texts supplied by headquarters, Rockefeller spoke from notes or off-the-cuff. He had found his voice, even as he lost six pounds to the rigors of the campaign trail.

Members of his family lent varying degrees of support. "John 3rd was upset by Nelson going into politics," says Kershaw Burbank of Room 5600. "He felt the family shouldn't be in politics—they had too much power already." These reservations didn't prevent Nelson's older brother from contributing $18,000 to the campaign, the amount John Lockwood had identified as appropriate to each of the candidate's siblings. A tangle of separate committees and support groups allowed them and other wealthy donors to multiply their gifts, resulting in such anomalies as Junior's $3,000 check made out to "Democrats for Rockefeller." In addition to his son Steven, twins Mary and Michael Rockefeller both worked on their father's campaign before returning to college in the fall. Even Tod set aside her ingrained distaste for publicity to attend "Coffee and Cake with Rockefeller" events, where she mingled with strangers while her husband held forth on the issues. Making her own foray into the Lower East Side, she also visited two public schools (one chosen because it was "well integrated") and a pair of housing projects in Harlem.

Appearing game, if somewhat out of her element, Tod accompanied Nelson on several trips around the state. At an event in Rochester, she recognized the familiar face of Libby Shemwell, her husband's former assistant, now married and a mother. After embracing Libby like a long-lost friend, Tod took her aside for a lengthy chat about their respective children. Politics went unmentioned. Never had Libby felt closer to the vulnerable woman struggling to balance the ambitions of her spouse against her own values and innate desire for privacy.

7

E NTERING THE HOMESTRETCH, the Harriman camp exuded optimism. Belying his public confidence, the incumbent took to the airwaves to warn that a Republican governor in Albany would terminate rent controls affecting nearly two million units of housing, most in New York City. Designed to scare wavering Democrats back into the fold, the eleventh-hour broadside, augmented by a million pamphlets threatening higher gas and electric rates in the event of a Rockefeller win, frightened Nelson most of all. An extensive ad campaign was mounted to defuse the rent control issue in the five boroughs.* In the end, aided by $800,000 in short-term bank loans, Rockefeller outspent Harriman $1.8 million to $1.1 million. Of this sum, roughly 40 percent was invested in radio and television buys. That it was money well spent became clear only later. At the time, Rockefeller pollster Sam Lubell was flummoxed. He couldn't reconcile the verbal anger directed by New York voters at the Eisenhower administration with their stated intentions to vote for Rockefeller. Doubting his own findings, in the closing days of the campaign Lubell went back into the field. Nationally, he found growing support for Democrats everywhere, except in New York. There his surveys showed Rockefeller stronger than ever.

Such a divergence was unprecedented in his considerable experience. Lubell began to speak of a rout in the making, one with historic implications for the future of American politics. "In '52 and '56, I didn't have anybody tell me they shifted their vote because of what they saw on TV," the pollster said afterward.

---

* This was ironic, as Rockefeller privately made no bones about his opposition to rent control— at least until Frank Jamieson persuaded him it was political suicide. On the Friday before Election Day, Charles Metzner rented sixty-five loudspeakers, from each of which blared hastily drafted reassurances on the subject, recorded at the last minute by the Republican candidate for governor. Charles Metzner, HMI, 16–17.

"In '58 I ran into quite a number of people who did tell me they were changing their votes because they saw Rockefeller. Harriman was tired, Rockefeller was eager." The power of personality, Lubell decided, had trumped party identification. All this was in retrospect. A mid-October poll conducted by his campaign that showed Nelson leading by two points was greeted with skepticism. For all his strengths, Rockefeller was still a Republican in a Democratic year, swimming against the tide of the harshest economic downturn since the 1930s. Visiting a steel mill near Buffalo, he confronted a picket line of workers with signs reading, "Sorry we can't all be here to greet you Nelson. We've been laid off due to the Republican recession." Unfazed, Rockefeller planted himself in front of the factory gates and pumped hands vigorously. "Stay away from Eisenhower and Nixon," one worker advised him. "They aren't going to do you any good."

It was a conclusion he had long since reached on his own. Already he had disavowed Eisenhower's more partisan language, including a presidential call to "fumigate" corrupt labor unions. He had kept his distance from the president during an Eisenhower visit to New York on Columbus Day. Then, on October 22, Vice President Nixon arrived for a thirty-six-hour campaign swing through the state. For Rockefeller, whose electoral hopes rested on the votes of independents and disaffected Democrats, Nixon's presence entailed more risk than reward. An upstate storm kept him away as the vice president attended a pair of fund-raising luncheons in the city. Eventually the skies cleared, no doubt to his regret. Upon his return to Manhattan on the afternoon of October 23, Nelson discussed the thorny situation with Frank Jamieson. Concluding that "the only decent thing is to go see him," Rockefeller phoned the Waldorf Towers, only to be told that Nixon was busy preparing a statewide television address on behalf of Republican candidates. That evening, while Nixon rallied the GOP faithful behind Ken Keating and the rest of the ticket at a Garden City event honoring the memory of Theodore Roosevelt, Nelson attended a reception at the Hotel St. Moritz, barely twenty-five miles away.

To curious reporters, Rockefeller explained that Nixon was supporting senatorial and congressional candidates, whereas "I am running for Governor, and I've said all I want to do is discuss state issues." This failed to quell speculation about a possible snub directed at the vice president and whether the onetime Washington allies might already be competitors for their party's 1960 presidential nomination. Another flurry of calls ensued, with Rockefeller finally reaching Nixon around midnight. They agreed to meet over breakfast in the visitor's hotel suite. Harriman seized on the resulting headlines to plant doubts about Rockefeller's vaunted independence. What secret arrangements had the two men reached over their coffee? Had they consummated a ticket for 1960? Rockefeller returned the volley, telling reporters, "The governor is so accustomed to running for the presidency that he naturally suspects that whenever two people get together, they are making some kind of deal involving the presidency. My only ambition," he reiterated, "is to be governor."

His chances improved with every day. Betting odds, once three to one in Harriman's favor, had shifted on the eve of voting to nine to five Rockefeller. Most of the remaining suspense involved the Hogan-Keating race for the Senate, with handicappers giving the nod to the Democrat. Jud Morhouse's prophecy of a Rockefeller sweep by 550,000 votes was universally written off as a campaign manager's hyperbole. It was a little after nine o'clock on Tuesday morning, November 4, when Nelson, Tod, and Steven Rockefeller voted at a Pocantico Hills firehouse. Election Day for any candidate is an interminable stretch of uncertainty, punctuated by rumors and sobered by second guesses. Would Rockefeller pay a price at the polls for not including an Italian American on his ticket? And what of the weather, that perennial subject of turnout speculation? As an early season snowstorm around Syracuse gave way to clear skies, Republicans breathed an audible sigh of relief. They were counting on upstate voters to neutralize the usual Democratic advantage coming out of New York City. This led to the biggest imponderable of all. Could Rockefeller attract 35 percent of the city electorate, the minimum required if he was to have any hope of winning statewide?

By late afternoon, a visibly nervous candidate was ensconced in his suite at the Roosevelt Hotel. Early returns, mostly from urban areas, showed a modest Harriman lead. It didn't last long. Shortly after ten p.m., Jud Morhouse appeared in the ballroom of the Roosevelt to claim victory by "upwards of 300,000." Even this grossly understated the dimensions of a political earthquake with national ramifications. A reporter encountering Tom Dewey in the happy throng asked the former governor what explained the Rockefeller sweep. "Rockefeller!" said Dewey. That it was indeed a personal triumph became glaringly apparent as the hours ticked by. Nationally, the GOP suffered its worst showing since 1936, losing thirteen Senate seats and forty-eight House districts.*

Yet no one could dispute Rockefeller's mandate. The electorate had turned out nearly six million strong. Defying expectations, Nelson won a third of the black vote and a similar share among Jewish voters. In New York City, which registered three Democrats for every Republican, he slashed Harriman's 1954 margin of 700,000 to barely 300,000. In the process, he carried both Queens and Staten Island. His Pocantico Hills neighbors voted for him 224 to 24. The rest of the upstate numbers weren't that lopsided, but they were sufficiently robust to swell Rockefeller's final margin to 573,034 votes—surpassing even Jud

---

* One bright spot: the come-from-behind victory of thirty-five-year-old John V. Lindsay in the "Silk Stocking" Seventeenth Congressional District on Manhattan's East Side.

Morhouse's heady preelection forecast. Comptroller Arthur Levitt was the only member of the Harriman ticket to survive the wreckage, and his slender victory wasn't confirmed until daybreak, several hours after Averell Harriman had stepped before the cameras to acknowledge the end of his political career.

At the Roosevelt, three thousand cheering Republicans set up the chant "We want Rockefeller!" Still Nelson held back, waiting to see if Ken Keating could ride his coattails to an upset over Hogan. At eleven thirty, satisfied that Keating had done exactly that, the governor-elect and his family descended to the noisy, overcrowded ballroom. Joining hands, they threaded their way toward the stage behind a protective wedge of police. With Tod at his side, looking regal in a pale blue dress, corsage, and pearls, Nelson thanked everyone he could think of, then promised New Yorkers, "We'll give it everything we've got." Offstage he shook hands with Frank Jamieson. Neither man spoke; words were superfluous. At a subsequent press conference, someone asked Rockefeller if his father had given him any advice. "He's been giving advice for fifty years," said Nelson in a response perhaps more revealing than intended.

Privately, he expressed gratitude to his son Steven, who had negotiated the campaign "side by side with me as a partner, the greatest experience of my life. Together we met the ultimate challenge of going before the people." Meeting with reporters, Nelson repeatedly denied any interest in the White House. He also dropped the clearest hint yet that a tax increase might be necessary to address a prospective budget shortfall. Prior to leaving for ten days at his Venezuela ranch, Rockefeller welcomed Republican legislative leaders to 810 Fifth Avenue for a review of the state's deteriorating finances. Somehow, between discussions of rent control and the fifteen-cent subway fare, he found time to resolve another fiscal emergency, this one threatening the Museum of Modern Art, where a recent fire and subsequent closing had more than doubled a projected $180,000 deficit. Some departments faced extinction, warned director René d'Harnoncourt. An entire floor of exhibit space was likely to be mothballed.

Nelson took a decidedly less grim view of the situation. "You have mixed emergency capital expenditures with current operating budget," he admonished d'Harnoncourt. As a result, "the whole picture has been thrown out of kilter." Previewing his style as governor, Rockefeller advised d'Harnoncourt to delete a $100,000 revenue loss and other costs associated with the fire and reconstruction. He was confident these could be handled by a separate fundraising drive. Alternatively, said Nelson, the museum could dip into its capital, raise the admission fee to ninety-five cents, and institute a "slight" increase in membership charges, "which are certainly justified in view of the increased costs with which we are confronted." A few expedients, some creative accounting, and a robust faith in untapped revenue streams: It wasn't so hard to balance a budget.

Fourteen
PAY AS YOU GO

We are the greatest state in the greatest nation in the most exciting period in the history of the world, and yet we find ourselves bogged down with frustrations and harassed by problems and uncertainties when we should be concentrating our attention with enthusiasm and excitement on shaping the forces of the future.

—NELSON A. ROCKEFELLER, November 1959

1

NELSON ROCKEFELLER'S FIRST twenty-four hours as governor—hyperactive, physically transforming, dismissive of musty precedent—set the pattern for 5,460 days to follow. Because the incumbent's term ends with the last chime of the midnight clock on New Year's Eve, the Empire State requires not one, but two oath takings to guard against any lapse in gubernatorial authority. Which explains why, on the final night of 1958, fifty friends and Rockefeller family members crowded into the Yellow Parlor of Albany's gloomy Executive Mansion. They were there to watch Nelson, in a rare bow to tradition, take the oath of office upon a Bible that had belonged to his grandmother Laura Spelman Rockefeller. Earlier in the day, keen to personalize the grimly Victorian structure, home to New York governors since Samuel J. Tilden, Rockefeller had busied himself hanging some of his favorite abstract paintings in public rooms and shadowy hallways. Impatient with the pace set by the workmen summoned for the task, he called for a hammer and stepladder, doffed his jacket, and drove nails into the paneled walls himself.

Even as Rockefeller arranged his Pollocks and Picassos, an elaborate stereo system was being installed in the drawing room by Dr. James Slater "Robin" Murphy, whose wife, Happy, had recently graduated from her campaign note-taking job to a desk just outside the governor's New York City office on West Fifty-fifth Street. The Murphys were present for that evening's dinner and private swearing-in. The next day, they joined nine hundred invited guests who filled every seat in the ornate state assembly chamber—normally home to 150 members and sixty-seven spittoons—an hour before the start of the public ceremony. Only the most venerable could recall another January inaugural, six decades in the past, when a furiously energetic agent of change had charged the seventy-seven steps of the hulking French château that serves New York State as a capitol. By the time Theodore Roosevelt occupied the second-floor executive suite, construction work on the building patterned after Paris's Hôtel de Ville had consumed thirty-two years, longer than it took to raise Cheops's Pyramid. Once in office, Roosevelt turned his righteous wrath upon urban sweatshops, unscrupulous landlords, and tax-evading street railways and utilities. GOP bosses, horrified by the governor's reformist tendencies, were nearly as quick to promote him to the comfortable obscurity of the vice presidency.

TR would no doubt have recognized many of the rituals with which Albany's changing of the guard is to be formalized on this first day of January 1959. The thermometer registers fourteen degrees Fahrenheit as the Rockefellers arrive at St. Peter's Episcopal Church, where both Tom Dewey and Averell Harriman had been vestrymen. Dispensing with the customary morning coat and striped trousers, Nelson wears a double-breasted business suit of dark blue. After the service, he hosts an inaugural luncheon for his predecessors in the dreary official residence likened to a railway terminal by the Roosevelt children. Lunch consumed, the Rockefellers and their guests retrace the five blocks to the Capitol. At one thirty, the doors to the assembly chamber swing open, signaling the arrival of the new governor, accompanied by a misty-eyed Averell Harriman. In another break with custom, the honor of introducing Chief Judge Albert Conway of the New York Court of Appeals falls to Caroline Simon, the first woman appointed to the secretary of state's job.*

For the second time in sixteen hours, Judge Conway administers the gubernatorial oath to Rockefeller, who bows stiffly in acknowledgment of the crowd's applause. Barely pausing to savor the moment, Nelson launches into his fourteen-minute inaugural address. Its central theme, familiar to any reader of the Rockefeller reports, is "the ordeal of freedom" in the treacherous middle years—"this fatal testing time"—of the twentieth century. Deferring any mention of the Empire State until the fourth page of his text, Rockefeller is careful to link New York's future to events beyond its borders. "Our neighborhood is the world," he declares. "The speed of the rocket and the force of an atom bomb, the strength of America and the strength of her enemies: such things

---

* This was no accident. Tradition dictated that a party official, usually the state chairman, occupy the position. Rockefeller had other ideas. He rejected appeals on behalf of Jud Morhouse, including the anguished plea of one prominent New York City Republican who warned the governor-elect that his scheme to appoint someone else, "especially a woman," would set a dangerous precedent.

"That's exactly what I want to do," replied Rockefeller. Norman Hurd, HMI, 67–68.

mean that every state of our Union, every community of our state, every citizen in each community—all face a common challenge and share a common cause." Humanity in turn looks to the United States for morally consistent leadership. Reminding his audience, "We can serve—and save—freedom elsewhere only as we practice it in our own lives," Rockefeller is openly scornful of southern states that prefer closing their public schools to integrating them. "We cannot speak of the equality of men and nations," he contends, "unless we hold high the banner of social equality in our own communities."

Promising an administration with a heart as well as a head, Rockefeller presents himself as a latter-day TR, intent on expanding social and health insurance, encouraging private investment in middle-class housing, modernizing an antiquated court system, improving programs for the aged, and promoting the state's cultural resources. Above all else, he seeks to broaden educational opportunities for his fellow New Yorkers, "for what we do not teach, we cannot save—and this is true of freedom itself." Renewing his campaign pledge to put the state's fiscal house in order, he leaves specifics to a later budget message. For now, he attempts with words to inoculate himself against hostile and limiting labels. "We shall be conservative," Rockefeller asserts, "for we know the measureless value that is our heritage. . . . We shall be liberal—for we are vastly more interested in the opportunities of tomorrow than the problems of yesterday. We shall be progressive—for the opportunities and the challenges are of such size and scope that we can never halt and say: our labor is done."*

From the assembly chamber Nelson sprints to the second-floor Red Room, whose vast dimensions and chilly formality had led Al Smith to observe that he might as well work in Macy's window. It offers a suitably imposing stage on which to install other elective officials, as well as key members of the team Rockefeller has recruited to help him govern the nation's largest state. His congratulations are hearty but brisk; the new governor is expected at the Executive Mansion for the annual New Year's open house. For ninety minutes, hundreds of the curious are admitted to tour first-floor rooms where William McKinley was entertained the night before his Buffalo assassination and from which FDR had delivered monthly radio reports to his fellow New Yorkers. Nelson and Tod warmly greet their new neighbors in front of a fourteen-foot Christmas tree. Yet it is eye-catching works by Matisse, Klee, and Dufy that capture the popular fancy. "They look like they're all scribbled up," offers one nine-year-old art critic.

---

* "A state paper touched with eloquence, perhaps with greatness." So pronounced *The New York Times* of Rockefeller's inaugural address. A more skeptical *New York Daily News* called it the first speech of the 1960 presidential campaign. "Cloud Nine stuff," said an indiscreet Rockefeller aide. "All the stuff we wouldn't let him say during the campaign." *Time*, January 12, 1959.

The feeble light of a winter's afternoon is extinguished before the final caller is ushered out onto Eagle Street. Still, the ceremonial changing of the guard isn't over, as Albany dresses up for its first inaugural ball in a dozen years. A light snow is falling as the Rockefellers enter the Washington Street Armory, to be cheered by eight thousand celebrants, many of them veterans of the recent campaign. Along with the obligatory local fife-and-drum corps, and forty-five thousand cookies washed down with New York sauterne punch, the jubilant crowd is treated to a preview of their new governor's cosmopolitan tastes. Cab Calloway sings and struts. The New York City Ballet, led by Nelson's friend Lincoln Kirstein, performs George Balanchine's *Stars and Stripes.* Eventually Rockefeller himself takes to the dance floor, whirling a succession of partners around the cavernous hall to the strains of Meyer Davis & His Orchestra. None of those in attendance pays a dime for admission, except the guest of honor, who picks up the full tab for the daylong extravaganza. At $40,000, it represents four-fifths of his gubernatorial salary. As Rockefeller frequently observes, he has more money than time.

2

WHAT NELSON ROCKEFELLER did not have was an in-box mind. "He loved big challenges, the bigger the better," recalled Rockefeller staffer Isabelle Savell. "'We created these problems,' he would say, 'and we can solve them if we put our minds to it.'" His new job was custom-tailored for a leader of Rockefeller's temperament. For almost two centuries, New York governors had enjoyed a combination of statutory authority and accumulated prestige unique among American executives. Long before the practice caught on elsewhere, post-Revolutionary New York elected its governors by popular ballot. In an era suspicious of centralized power, the same state imposed no limit on how many terms its chief executive could serve, enabling the legendary George Clinton to cling to office for twenty-one years, before stepping down to the vice presidency under both Jefferson and Madison. That the state itself could be an engine of economic development was heroically demonstrated by Clinton's nephew DeWitt, whose visionary Erie Canal, the ultimate public works project, made New York in fact as well as name the Empire State.

By the late nineteenth century, New York had become at once a magnet for the world's oppressed and a hothouse for the most wretched excesses of unregulated capitalism. As immigrants, many of them Jews from Eastern Europe, took the lead in unionizing workers in the garment and other industries, so did Progressive Era reformers like Charles Evans Hughes use the governorship to champion public over private interests. "I am here under a retainer," said Hughes. "I am here retained by the people of New York." In the 1920s, the patrician Hughes lent his credibility to constitutional reforms championed by his social opposite Al Smith. A superb administrator, Smith consolidated state agencies to make them more accountable to the governor, whose term was extended from two to four years. To underwrite an embryonic welfare state, he engineered New York's first income and gasoline taxes. Perhaps Smith's greatest legacy was the executive budget system, ratified by voters in November 1927. Heretofore, each agency and division of state government had submitted its own budget request directly to the legislature for review, without regard to overall expenditures or gubernatorial priorities. The new system made the governor master in his own house. Legislators were free to reduce or delete individual items in his spending blueprint, but they could not increase them without his approval.

The executive budget was but one weapon in a formidable arsenal at Rockefeller's disposal. With his annual message, the governor set Albany's agenda. During the session, each bill must be on members' desks at least three days before it could be enacted. The governor could override this requirement by issuing a "message of necessity," taking precedence over anything else under consideration and requiring action within twenty-four hours. By withholding his most important recommendations, contained in "program bills," until the frenetic concluding days of the session, when exhaustion set in and logrolling was most blatant, the executive greatly increased their chances of passage. (Of nearly 1,200 bills enacted during the 1959 legislative session, 508 were approved in the last three days.) In addition to the line item veto, Rockefeller had history on his side—Ulysses Grant was in the White House the last time a New York governor saw his veto overridden. Rockefeller had sole discretion to call legislators back to Albany for a special session, whose agenda he alone dictated. Ready access to Manhattan-based television and radio broadcasts magnified his voice and gave him a national audience. That both political parties a priori regarded any governor of New York as presidential timber imparted to the office an aura no constitution could bestow.

On top of everything else, the man in the Red Room had a generous supply of carrots and sticks on which to draw. In 1959, approximately eight thousand state jobs were exempt from civil service. Simply by withholding a much-sought-after appointment to the New York State Liquor Authority or Court of Claims, Rockefeller could entice a reluctant legislator into supporting his program or punish a renegade for his apostasy. His personal dominance of the state Republican Party, liberally greased with campaign contributions from the governor and his family, endowed Rockefeller with a measure of control rooted equally in gratitude and fear. Certainly Nelson brought to Albany resources dwarfing those of any of his predecessors.* As one of its first acts, the new administration announced a ban on all outside gifts to the governor and members of his administrative team. It went so far as to publicize the return of a dime, attached to a congratulatory letter, from a Long Island high school student council. The same press office was understandably silent about gifts *from* the governor to those on the public payroll, commencing with a $75,000 check made out to Bill Ronan days before he was confirmed as secretary to the governor—in effect, the second most powerful man in Albany. Ronan may have been the biggest beneficiary of gubernatorial largesse, but he was hardly alone. G. Russell Clark, an official with the American Bankers Association, was Rockefeller's choice for superintendent of banks. A New Jersey resident at the time, Clark pocketed a $25,000 sweetener from the governor for "relocation expenses." Not everyone succumbed to Nelson's blandishments. On a postelection visit to Pocantico, Malcolm Wilson and his wife, Katherine, received separate offers from Nelson and Tod of a house on the Rockefeller estate. Politely but firmly, the Wilsons demurred; they would stay put in Yonkers, thank you.

Rockefeller had no intention of abandoning his lieutenant governor, whose knowledge of Albany's legislative culture made him an invaluable asset, to his White Plains law office. Come January 1959, Wilson joined the bureaucratic family inhabiting a pair of imperfectly connected Manhattan townhouses at 20 and 22 West Fifty-fifth Street. The first-floor press office, remembers one who worked there, contained a single window overlooking a "filthy, dirty courtyard." One flight up was the threadbare room in which Rockefeller served coffee and doughnuts to visitors, pausing to stir his cup with the heavy stem of his glasses. Because his office was in one townhouse and Bill Ronan's was next door, the two men were forever running up or down stairs to communicate with each other. The alternative was an ancient and unresponsive cage elevator, whose dilatory ways earned it frequent kicks from an impatient landlord. Speechwriter Joseph Persico, working out of a converted fifth-floor bedroom, was frankly mystified as to why someone of Rockefeller's resources and taste should willingly ensconce himself in such an environment. "The floors were covered in indoor-outdoor carpeting," recalled Persico with a shudder, its color a nauseating bile green.

From these unprepossessing quarters, Rockefeller governed the state when not in Albany. "It was a rabbit warren," concedes Bob MacCrate, initially hired

---

* On the eve of his inauguration, Rockefeller purchased a $15,000 custom-built Chrysler limousine appropriate to his new station and applied for New York State license plate #1. On learning that no private vehicle could be so designated, Rockefeller donated the Lincoln to the state, which duly granted him its most distinctive license plate.

as an assistant counsel in February 1959. "I think this was part of his aspiration for the common touch. No one was put off coming into that place." (Neither were taxpayers assessed for the cost of midtown Manhattan office space.) That Rockefeller's workdays sometimes began in an even more unlikely setting did not escape the notice of Harry Albright, a young Albany attorney who subsequently joined the administration as a deputy secretary to the governor. During his first week on the job, Albright observed the big black Chrysler parked outside the Fifty-fifth Street townhouses, its motor running. Inside, scribbling away in the right-hand passenger seat, was the governor of New York. Several times as Albright watched, Rockefeller repeated this morning ritual, delaying his entry into the building by half an hour or more. In due course, Albright learned the reason why: As a young man, Nelson had been admonished by his father to complete each day's labor, no matter how long it took, before embarking on the next. The habit carried over to his governorship, which explained the front-seat paper shuffling following a late night of multiple dinners or event drop-ins that prevented Rockefeller from reading every memo in the overstuffed red document folders he routinely carried home.

Seedy as it appeared, Fifty-fifth Street had nothing on New York's official capital. In the 350 years since Henry Hudson dropped anchor in the brackish river that would bear his name, there had been no lack of stirring events or colorful personalities to distinguish the outpost dubbed Fort Orange by the Dutch West India Company. Here Alexander Hamilton married the daughter of General Philip Schuyler; Martin Van Buren, Boss Tweed, and ugly, honest Grover Cleveland ("We love him for the enemies he has made") perfected their political arts; and Susan B. Anthony narrowly escaped mob violence while addressing a convention of abolitionists. Thomas Edison had breakfasted at Keeler's, a popular State Street eatery whose proprietor first advised Al Smith to get himself a trademark brown derby. A generation later, Mrs. Thomas Dewey surprised Executive Mansion guests by remarking as she gazed out the window, "How I love it here when it snows." Asked why, she replied, "Because it covers up Albany."

The raffish riverfront town of 130,000 seemed an unlikely incubator of presidents, yet for most of the twentieth century it was a mecca for national political correspondents and columnists. For those assigned there permanently, it was considered hardship duty. "Other than eating, drinking, and politics, Albany had not one goddamned thing to do," recalls Betty Bixby, a Fifty-fifth Street press aide who was part of the weekly migration north that coincided with the legislative calendar. "The legislature convened on Monday night at eight thirty p.m. to start the week's session," says Ilene Slater, Rockefeller's personal secretary at the time. "You didn't know whether they were going to recess at nine o'clock or one o'clock in the morning. So we'd work through the day on Monday, go out to dinner, then come back at eight thirty." Finding a decent meal could be problematic. As downtown emptied out to the suburbs, what passed for social life revolved around the (Republican) Ten Eyck and (Democratic) DeWitt Clinton hotels, their smoke-filled bars and restaurants teeming with politicians, lobbyists, and reporters, many pursuing alcoholic respite from the prolonged Hudson Valley winter.

In discussions about joining the young administration, Bill Ronan had made it clear that he had no intention of living in Albany. "Neither do I," Rockefeller assured him. Unknown to the public, in the days following his election, the governor-elect had furtively scouted out a handsome red-brick dwelling on State Street, close to the Capitol, as a possible alternative to the depressing Executive Mansion. Ultimately, the house on Eagle Street was one Albany tradition even Rockefeller respected. But he didn't hesitate to remake it, or the city around it, in his own image. In the sloping backyard, he installed a tennis court and brick terrace where Al Smith had maintained a private zoo stocked with creatures sent by admirers, among them a 350-pound bear that once escaped and caused havoc in a neighboring orphanage. FDR's swimming pool gave way to a modern replacement, complete with lavish pool house. On being presented with an old Civil War cannon, Rockefeller decided it belonged on the mansion's front lawn—as long as the barrel wasn't pointed at the adjoining property holder, the Cathedral of the Immaculate Conception.

Struck by the barren appearance of the route he traveled each day to work, Rockefeller called Mayor Erastus Corning, his boyhood friend from Mount Desert, and proposed that the state and city split the cost of planting trees along Eagle Street. Corning said he would have to check with his political godfather, "Uncle Dan" O'Connell, the crusty boss whose Democratic machine had controlled the town for half a century. A week later, the mayor called back. "I have talked with Dan," said Corning, "and we will buy three trees." And so they did, leaving it to the state to supply the rest. In his first months there, the sheer joy of operating the levers of power made it easy for Rockefeller to overlook Albany's aesthetic shortcomings. Most days he rose around seven, then scanned half a dozen newspapers before breakfasting with Tod. At nine o'clock he was driven to the Capitol, the short trip affording a jump start on the day's most pressing patronage and legislative concerns. At the State Street entrance, Rockefeller rode a private elevator, originally installed for Franklin Roosevelt, to the second floor, where he supplied marching orders to staff. Some preferences were communicated nonverbally, as newly hired assistant press secretary Jacob Underhill discovered to his chagrin. A former *Newsweek* correspondent eager to hand Rockefeller some AP wire copy he'd requested, Underhill made the mistake of shadowing Nelson one morning as he addressed their colleagues. His reward was an unmistakable look of gubernatorial annoyance.

"You're hovering," whispered a fellow staffer. A perplexed Underhill looked in her direction.

"You're hovering," she repeated. "He doesn't like hovering. Sit down." Underhill threw himself into the closest seat he could find.

Others wished they could vacate theirs. "The governor loved meetings," said Ann Whitman, Eisenhower's hugely competent secretary who would in time replace Ilene Slater at Rockefeller's side. Often these sessions took on marathon dimensions. "Try sitting in the same chair for five hours," Whitman groaned. Whatever their length, these discussions were heavily influenced by Rockefeller's experiences in the Roosevelt White House, where Oval Office supplicants were expected to propose solutions and not simply add to the president's ample supply of difficulties. "Nelson would never tolerate . . . anyone in the discussion saying, 'Well, I think it is bad,'" according to Malcolm Wilson. "He wanted them to go on and suggest alternatives. . . . You recognize that there is a problem," was how Wilson described the Rockefeller approach. "I have proposed what I feel is the solution. If you disagree with what I say, that's fine, but tell me why you disagree and then tell me what you propose as an alternative."

Few resorted openly to the dreaded n-word (for "no"), though Bill Ronan perfected the art of strategic delay, staffing out the more dubious Rockefeller enthusiasms in the hope they might, over time, evaporate. One man around the table stood out for the license with which he spoke his mind. "In our staff meetings, Frank Jamieson always sat next to Nelson," recalled Bob MacCrate, "and he always spoke last, I noticed." Though a frequent visitor to Albany, Jamieson was glad to leave the daily care of the press to Richard Amper, an intense, forty-four-year-old *New York Times* reporter hired during the 1958 campaign. Jamieson didn't have to be on the state payroll to retain Nelson's ear. Privately, he urged Rockefeller to forgo the 1960 presidential race. It was too soon following his election, he argued. Moreover, Richard Nixon had a hammerlock on the party organization. In keeping with Nelson's demand for positive alternatives, Jamieson offered a simple strategy to advance his White House ambitions. "Be the best governor of New York you can be," Frankie told him. "They'll come to you."

That Rockefeller might reject such counsel, as he had earlier disregarded Jamieson's advice to pass up the race against Harriman, caused Dick Amper's phone to ring constantly in the first months of 1959. Newspaper and magazine writers beat a path to Albany, eager to judge for themselves if the newest Republican star could govern as well as he made reports. Journalists recorded Rockefeller's bubbling delight in his job, his breathless description of a routine budget meeting as "wonderfully exciting," and the frequent exclamations of "Isn't this fun?" sprinkled throughout his conversation. They couldn't miss the breezy informality of a governor who got down on the floor of the Red Room to chat with a visiting group of children or interrupted a cabinet meeting to greet a Girl Scout troop he chanced to see through an open door.

"Hiya, kids. How are you?"

Moments later, surrounded by green uniforms and outstretched autograph books, Nelson introduced the Scouts to Commissioner of Education James Allen, Jr. They should write Allen if they had any problems at school, said the governor. "On second thought," he reflected, "I hear some of you children want a four day week."

Rockefeller revealed another side of himself when, striding briskly into the Red Room for a swearing-in ceremony, he was dismayed to learn that no one had thought to secure a Bible. "Whose show is this? Who is the producer here?" he asked sharply. Receiving no answer, Rockefeller arched his expressive eyebrows in the gesture of silent displeasure dreaded by associates. "Well, come on now," he muttered, "let's do things right, shall we?" Moments later, scurrying aides returned clutching no fewer than three Bibles.

Around labor leaders, Rockefeller could approximate the earthy discourse of the work site or locker room. His secretaries occasionally heard a "goddamn" escape his lips. A particularly objectionable idea was "for the birds," while the worst that could be said of an opponent was a dismissive "He's a lightweight." Rockefeller's pet peeves included cigarette smoke—it bothered his sinuses—fat people (obesity he viewed as a sign of weakness), and classical music ("Doesn't it put you to sleep?"). Food was one of the few things to which he was indifferent. Besides a leg of lamb and anything chocolate, says Robert Bennett, who managed the Executive Mansion for four governors, "he loved a good hamburger." Visitors to the mansion were routinely offered Nelson's favorite hors d'oeuvre—peanut butter and bacon. At the Capitol, someone from his staff was dispatched to the first-floor cafeteria each day at one thirty to pick up a sandwich. Rockefeller never specified what kind; only once did he complain about what he got. Black coffee and a fruit cup completed his meager lunch, eaten at his desk.

Afternoons were occupied with more paperwork: a flurry of legislative messages as the session neared its climax, interspersed with proclamations declaring Polish Constitution Day, New York Egg Month, and Baseball Week ("There is no new argument in favor of playing ball—baseball is its own argument"). Some days Rockefeller might review patronage concerns with George Hinman, a one-man employment agency for deserving Republicans; engage in bantering games of cat and mouse ("Oh no, you don't!") with the Albany press corps; charm a visiting delegation of Methodist churchwomen; or listen with a deadpan expression as Comptroller Arthur Levitt extolled the virtues of the New York State Employees Pension Fund. "I'm aware," said Levitt, "that you have some independent resources, but you can never tell what might happen."

Rockefeller signed up on the spot. Once a week, he was handed the Friday Report, a ten-page digest of the most pressing issues and initiatives throughout state government. Drafted by Bill Ronan for Rockefeller's review each weekend at Pocantico, it was an important tool in policy, and political, oversight.

The Capitol's floor plan neatly reflected an undisputed separation of powers. "The second floor" was shorthand for the state's highest officeholder. Never in memory had an occupant of the Red Room left his gilded fiefdom, climbed a flight of stairs, and wandered into the offices of opposition leaders for a friendly chat. Rarely had one invaded the sacred precincts of his own party's legislative hierarchy. But on the eve of the 1959 legislative session, Rockefeller appeared without warning in the reception room of senate minority leader Joseph Zaretzki. "I'm Nelson Rockefeller," he told a stunned receptionist. "I'd like to talk to Senator Zaretzki." He was hastily ushered into the senator's private office, where he spent thirty minutes gossiping and swapping stories with Zaretzki, before repeating the performance with Anthony Travia, the Democratic leader of the assembly. "You feel at ease in his presence," an awed Zaretzki confided to a reporter later. "You feel you can talk to him."

Rockefeller typically left the Capitol around six thirty, in time for dinner at the mansion with Tod. Often he brought guests (fourteen at one meal), severely testing the kitchen staff's ingenuity and temper. Sometimes legislators and their wives were invited over on the spur of the moment for an evening of dancing, the governor himself helping to roll up the carpets. Occasionally the Rockefellers ventured out to sample Albany's cultural life. One night they attended the opening of an exhibit of Israeli arts and crafts at a local museum, where Nelson took the occasion to laud Jewish contributions to the West. After returning to his office in the Capitol for meetings running late into the night, he might drop by a State Street diner, whose recipe for crisp bacon he passed along to Minna, the mansion cook. Rarest of all were quiet evenings spent rearranging his artworks or simply lounging in an easy chair with some paperwork while listening to Dave Brubeck or Errol Garner. Another favorite was trombonist Urbie Green, whose latest album, joked writer Gay Talese—*Let's Face the Music and Dance*—might sum up the state's looming fiscal dilemma.

3

THAT ROCKEFELLER INTENDED to be a different kind of governor became evident in his first message to the legislature. Harry O'Donnell, a legendary Republican operative whose unceasing attacks had driven Averell Harriman to distraction, cautioned him against any mention of tax increases. Otherwise, said O'Donnell, the resulting media frenzy would only obscure the affirmative programs he hoped to implement. Rockefeller was defiant. "I don't know how they used to do things around here, Harry"—an obvious dig at O'Donnell's mentor, Tom Dewey—"but I intend to be honest with the people." Delivered on January 8, his initial message was largely a restatement of campaign promises, albeit with a twist. Long critical of what he saw as Eisenhower's crisis management, Nelson was determined to practice crisis prevention. It wasn't enough to meet contemporary needs, he insisted. Government must anticipate and prepare for future contingencies as well. "That's difficult politically," he acknowledged on another occasion, "because the public lives in the present, even some in the past, and to try and take action that is going to be meaningful five years or ten years from now, but is going to cost money today, is not a popular thing to do—particularly if it involves tax increases."

Even had he been less naturally proactive, demographic trends left Rockefeller little choice. The postwar baby boom, in tandem with explosive suburban growth, exerted enormous pressure on schools at all levels. An accelerating influx of poor, often unskilled workers into New York's urban centers fed a rising demand for state services. To maintain its competitive edge in the 1960s and beyond, the Empire State had need of additional roads and more reliable mass transit. Throughout his campaign against Harriman, Rockefeller had done little to hide his belief that fresh revenue sources must be found. Now, in a stunning break with convention, the rookie governor moved to get them even before he formally submitted a budget for legislative review. Two weeks into his term, Rockefeller launched a political blitzkrieg aimed at securing an increase of two cents in the state's gasoline tax and three cents in the levy on diesel fuel, before industry lobbyists could catch their breath or mobilize grassroots opposition.

The bold move put to rest any doubts about the cooperation between Rockefeller and his party's legislative leadership. Over the years, New York's quasi democracy has been distilled into an evocative phrase—"three men in a room." That is because, second only to the governor, power is centralized in the assembly Speaker and senate majority leader. Each in his own chamber is an uncrowned monarch, historically designating the membership, and leadership, of every standing committee; controlling the allocation of committee staff and campaign funds; and distributing lulus—"allowances in lieu of expenses"— with which meager legislative salaries are padded. In the assembly, Ozzie Heck's viselike grip on power allowed him at the beginning of each session to know the ultimate fate of legislation yet to be introduced. By the start of 1959, however, complications from diabetes made it increasingly difficult for Heck to get around. Rockefeller flattered the ailing lawmaker by moving strategy sessions to the Speaker's third-floor office. On one occasion, the governor flew through a snowstorm to visit an ailing Heck in his Boston hospital room. While Heck's loyalty was never in doubt, his illness and subsequent absence inevitably weakened his hold over the ninety-two part-time lawmakers who constituted the Republican caucus.

Members were paid $7,500 for a session that rarely went past Easter. Crammed into makeshift work spaces, half a dozen to a dingy room, and deprived of adequate staff or independent research capacity, few had the time or curiosity to read more than a handful of the eight thousand bills drafted during the session's opening weeks. February was dominated by the governor's budget message, which set the stage for various committees to work their will through the appropriations process. In March, the legislative pace quickened, with hundreds of bills, the most pressing tied in a gubernatorial message of necessity, tossed into the hopper at the last minute. During the final hours of the session, it was not unusual for clocks to be turned back or tempers to fray as the Speaker broke more than one gavel in attempting to maintain order among his weary flock. Responsibility exacted its own price on legislative chieftains, never more so than when the demands of party loyalty clashed with personal conviction. Rockefeller's tax program posed such a test for Walter Mahoney. A decade earlier, Mahoney had made his reputation by leading an antitax revolt against the omnipotent Tom Dewey. More recently, both houses had flung back into Averell Harriman's patrician face his appeal for a one-cent gas tax increase. Should Mahoney, the son of a Buffalo fireman, be nursing any grudge over his defeat by the wealthy rookie now inhabiting the Executive Mansion, he could always plead ideological consistency in opposing Rockefeller's taxes.

He did nothing of the sort. Instead the majority leader, whose inexhaustible attention to the needs and foibles of individual senators earned him comparison with Lyndon Johnson, took to the senate floor to commend the governor's courage in relying on honest tax dollars instead of bonded debt. Democrats to a man opposed Rockefeller's gas tax, but they made no effort to force a debate. On January 20, the governor stayed up late so that he could sign the bill within minutes of its passage. "If my grandfather could only see me now," he observed mordantly, pen in hand. February 1 was Budget Day. Traditionally, an emissary from the second-floor hand-carried the governor's message and accompanying legislation to the two houses. Well aware that his request for $277 million in new revenues would win him scant applause, Rockefeller overruled the counsel of Malcolm Wilson and others and presented his budget—the state's first to exceed $2 billion—in person. At the end of formal remarks received in stony silence, Rockefeller issued an unscripted challenge. Of the proposed spending increases, he told lawmakers, 81 percent were mandated by law, a none-too-subtle reminder that they couldn't have it both ways. Those unwilling to support his tax program should have the fortitude to slash aid to localities, highway construction, and other politically attractive programs.

The math was unyielding. Between them, the gas tax and a two-cent hike in cigarette taxes would produce about a third of the revenue needed to balance the budget. To obtain the rest, Rockefeller proposed automatically withholding state taxes from workers' paychecks, a practice initiated by the federal government in 1943. In a stroke, half a million tax cheats would be snared, while honest taxpayers need no longer borrow to meet their annual or quarterly assessments. Rockefeller's second stab at tax conformity exacted a heavier toll, financially and politically. In 1959, Uncle Sam granted a uniform exemption of $600 per person, far less than the $1,000 New York awarded single taxpayers or the $2,500 state exemption for married couples. Adopting the federal standard, as urged by Rockefeller, meant anyone earning more than $6,000 a year could expect a substantial increase in tax liability. To spread the pain, the governor wanted to add three new brackets to the top of the tax schedule, culminating in a 10 percent levy on incomes over $15,000.

The specter of the multimillionaire Rockefeller reaching into working-class pockets evoked Democratic cries of "soak the poor." More worrisome were charges of betrayal from upstate Republicans, self-proclaimed "apple knockers" as complicit as their nominal opponents in approving more government than they were willing to pay for. The hub of the incipient rebellion was Syracuse, where Senator John Hughes, strongly supported by that city's influential newspapers, the *Herald-Journal* and the *Post-Standard*, demanded $80 million in budget cuts as the minimal price of his support. Hughes was destined to be a thorn in Rockefeller's side for as long as both men were in Albany. A torrent of mail, much of it ginned up by local radio stations and running one hundred to one against the plan, swamped legislative desks. On finding two lonely letters endorsing his stand, Rockefeller said he would frame them.

One decidedly ambiguous missive reached him from the White House. "You seem to have quickly become a controversial figure in the financial thinking of New York State," wrote Eisenhower, who went on to relate complaints from Oval Office visitors distressed by the new governor's failure to reduce state services. Not having read his full budgetary message, said Ike, he had contented himself with anodyne reminders "that we must, at all echelons of government, live within our means." Under the circumstances, this passed for encouragement. Opening a sports show in New York's Coliseum, Rockefeller was loudly booed for five minutes as he tried to speak. He made a joke out of his plunging popularity, telling upstate audiences, "Look, I know how you feel. Someone told me my grandfather had spent the last part of his life giving away dimes—and here I am, trying to get them back again, all at once." Yet enactment of the Rockefeller program would at least put New York on the path to fiscal integrity. The governor himself vowed that by the end of his first term, "pay as you go" would bring revenues into line with expenditures, thereby eliminating costly borrowing and setting the stage for renewed economic growth.

His thoughts, characteristically, were focused on the long haul. He had no intention of scraping by for four years, a Harriman-like caretaker sustained by budgetary sleight of hand. By acting boldly at the outset of his administration, he would ensure the resources to implement an innovative program of humane, socially conscious government. At the same time, mindful of the economic orthodoxies embraced by GOP convention delegates, he would establish his conservative credentials by reversing the state's slide toward insolvency. "Every man in public life is constantly faced with the choice of telling people the comforting half-truths they would like to hear," Rockefeller told a Lincoln Day dinner attended by the Republican faithful, "or the hard facts they need to know in order to shape their future intelligently."

Lobbying legislators, Rockefeller preferred charm to the lash. In a series of face-to-face meetings with lawmakers, dubbed "Operation Butter Up," he applied his formidable powers of persuasion. The Boy Scout in him truly believed, according to Budget Director Norman Hurd, that the insurgents would come around to his way of thinking if only they understood the fiscal gravity of the situation. Hurd, far more experienced in the mercenary habits of Albany, had his doubts. These were confirmed as he watched dazed rebels emerging from the governor's office, shaking their heads and exclaiming in wonder, "He didn't promise anything" (as in thruway exits or plum appointments). Less naïve than he appeared, Rockefeller was perfectly willing to play good cop to Malcolm Wilson's and Jud Morhouse's bad. Wavering assemblymen were told to forget about their most cherished local bills. Visions of choice jobs, as yet unfilled, were dangled before patronage-hungry county leaders. Assemblyman Charles Schoeneck of Syracuse, a potential leader of the rebellion, had a change of heart after his name was floated for majority leader in the event the incumbent, Joe Carlino, became Speaker.*

Rockefeller's Washington experience had taught him that the road to executive success contained multiple lanes. On the inside track, his wooing of lawmakers was reinforced by a massive shake-up of the state's Republican organization, its stated goal that of attracting younger and urban voters. Sinecures were found for the longtime secretary and vice chair of the New York Republican State Committee. When George Hinman replaced Dewey loyalist Dean Taylor as Republican national committeeman from New York, Rockefel-

---

* As Carlino did following Ozzie Heck's death in May 1959. Schoeneck was duly elected to fill Carlino's shoes, an act of treachery for which voters retired him in 1960. Rockefeller later made him state Republican chairman.

ler's party makeover was complete. Its thoroughness could not have been lost on GOP county leaders or on legislators flirting with rebellion. At the end of February, Rockefeller went into full salesman mode, appearing on statewide television five times in less than a week. Employing his trademark charts and graphs, he deconstructed the budget in language any viewer could understand. The bulk of state expenditures was in the form of aid to local government, he explained—most of it for schools—without which local property taxes would go through the roof. He documented extensive cuts made to Harriman's final budget and accused his predecessor of shading the truth about a looming $400 million budget gap. This became a mantra, repeated so often, cracked Bill Ronan, "that even Harriman believed it."

Rockefeller intensified his courtship of opinion leaders. Over dinner at the Executive Mansion, he pleaded his case with legislators, union leaders, educators, businessmen, and representatives from civic and religious organizations. He got a break in the first week of March when Ozzie Heck left his sickbed and returned to Albany, vowing to restore discipline in his ranks. In the end, however, not the governor's persuasiveness but his pragmatism carried the day—specifically his willingness to cut a deal with Walter Mahoney. Behind closed doors, the two men negotiated spending cuts of $40 million, much of it hacked from a New York City supplemental aid package Nelson had promised Mayor Wagner. Rockefeller reassured Republican holdouts there would be no further tax increases in 1960. On March 11, the senate approved the amended budget by a vote of 31 to 25. Later that day, it cleared the assembly with two votes to spare. A jubilant Rockefeller told an aide, "We can go ahead with our program now. This should give us what we need to work on."

Outsiders were duly impressed, with *BusinessWeek* declaring Rockefeller "the Wunderkind of American politics." To columnist Joseph Alsop, New York's governor had inherited the mantle of progressive conservatism that had slipped from Eisenhower's shoulders. Such an assessment may startle those who view Rockefeller retroactively through the lens of the mid-1960s, when he created at the state level a government whose soaring aspirations rivaled Lyndon Johnson's Great Society. A different atmosphere prevailed around Albany in 1959. More observant of limits than in the "all things are possible" sixties, Rockefeller in his first term regarded government chiefly as a catalyst for change, a spur to private investment. His response to New York's transit woes illustrates the point. A dramatic increase in automobiles and superhighways, and a corresponding drop in usage of commuter railroads and bus lines, had set off a vicious cycle of diminished revenues, deteriorating service, and ever more congested roads.

Reluctant to have the state assume operational responsibilities, Rockefeller instead offered $16.5 million in tax relief for three railroad lines—New York

Central; New York, New Haven, & Hartford; and Long Island—with state government assuming half of any financial loss sustained by local communities. In return, the suburban carriers must improve service to meet newly established standards. To help them do so, the Port of New York Authority, using $20 million from Albany, would purchase four hundred new, air-conditioned coaches for lease to the commuter lines.* Rockefeller again turned to the private sector to combat an acute shortage of middle-income housing. His scheme, adopted in the closing hours of the legislative session, would leverage a $100 million bond issue into twice as much in private financing; the resulting public-private partnership would generate twenty-one thousand new units of affordable housing.

End-of-session assessments bore out Rockefeller's disdain for ideological labels. Legislation to check racketeering in labor unions won praise from the right, while liberals applauded a two-year extension of residential rent control and the expansion of workers' compensation to include previously uncovered workers. Reformers generally welcomed his plans to modernize the state's court system, as well as the creation of new state offices dedicated to transportation, local government, and atomic energy. Hanging in the front hall of the Executive Mansion, where its formless splotches of color mystified many a visitor, Richard Lytle's *Composition* was said to be Nelson's favorite canvas. "It's a completely abstract painting," Tod Rockefeller explained to the uninitiated. "It means something different to each person."

That her husband's political character might be as susceptible to differing interpretation was indicated by two small yet revealing actions he took during the rush to legislative adjournment. Attending a party at Albany's Fort Orange Club, his friendly recognition of lobbyist Victor Condello in front of some important clients demonstrated anew Rockefeller's talent for putting others in his debt. Condello, it transpired, had brought along a guest that evening, a professional colleague on the payroll of the Petroleum Institute. After a few drinks, the oil lobbyist decided to give the governor a piece of his mind. "He starts mouthing off about Nelson's taxes," recalled Condello. "He goes up to Nelson and starts putting his finger in his chest. Well, the next day I call the guy, and nobody knows where he is. That's the last anyone ever heard from him."

Then there was Walter Mahoney, whose deal-making skills had proved so critical to final passage of the Rockefeller budget. "Is there anything I can do to help you?" Nelson asked Mahoney during the final hours of the legislative session. The question answered itself soon enough, as a top Mahoney aide was

---

* The third leg of Rockefeller's program would eliminate featherbedding practices that drained millions each year from railroad coffers. Pro-union legislators in both parties forced him to settle for a study of the problem by the state's Public Service Commission.

appointed to the Public Service Commission, one of the most coveted positions in state government. Additionally, the governor cleared the way for a $5.9 million loan for port development in Mahoney's home city of Buffalo, which also received $1 million to create a nuclear research center at the University of Buffalo.

"Dear Nelson," wrote the senate majority leader to his erstwhile rival on the second floor. "We certainly have them confounded."

"We certainly have!" replied Rockefeller. "And will increasingly as time goes by!"

4

THE END OF a legislative session is for any governor of New York a mixed blessing. With the final crack of the Speaker's gavel, the clock starts ticking on the thirty-day period and a constitutionally mandated review of every bill not already acted upon by the executive. In the spring of 1959, this meant almost a thousand pieces of legislation demanding Rockefeller's close attention. Swelling his workload was a campaign promise to issue a written justification for every veto, a gesture to open government deemed unnecessary by his predecessors. Since Rockefeller rejected nearly a third of the bills that reached his desk—a ratio in keeping with tradition—this generated immense pressure on counsel Rod Perkins and his half dozen assistants, not to mention a dyslexic governor. Foreshadowing his later hard line on the subject, Rockefeller vetoed legislation abolishing mandatory minimum penalties for the sale, attempted sale, or possession with intent to sell narcotic drugs. By contrast, in rejecting a measure authorizing public school teachers to spank unruly students, he contended that discipline begins at home.

Early in May, Rockefeller cheerfully exchanged the thirty-day period for two weeks at his Venezuela ranch. There he relaxed, strenuously, climbing mountains and covering a hundred miles a day by jeep or on horseback while checking up on his hybrid cattle. When an unusual-looking plant or flower caught his eye, Nelson, hatless and bare-chested in the tropical heat, clambered down a steep hillside or ravine to pluck the blossom for transplantation far from its native habitat. In June, he returned to Washington for a meeting with the New York congressional delegation and a thirty-minute courtesy call to the Oval Office. Avoiding talk of presidential politics, Nelson told a Capitol Hill stag dinner that evening, "I'm going to stay in Albany. Life's a lot simpler there." Few accepted his dismissal at face value. Journalists noted Rockefeller's purchase of an elaborately refitted Convair CV-240 in place of the five-seat Beechcraft for-

merly used for official state travel. The new plane was a flying lounge, of sufficient size and comfort to accommodate a presidential candidate and his
entourage.

From California came word of a grassroots effort by a group of young professionals calling themselves "Cal-Rocks" to put Rockefeller's name on that state's
Republican primary ballot. The news barely ruffled his chief adversary, Richard Nixon. On the heels of his July 1959 visit to Moscow, where his celebrated
"Kitchen debate" with Nikita Khrushchev had generated reams of favorable
coverage back home, George Gallup reported that 61 percent of Republicans
wanted the vice president to head their party's ticket in 1960. More ominous to
Rockefeller supporters was the trend line of opinion: for while Nixon had
gained ten points since the GOP rout of November 1958, Rockefeller had lost
even more—plummeting from 31 percent to just 18 percent after six months in
Albany. Not for the last time, his ambitious agenda for New York risked alienating conservative voters west of the Hudson. The right-wing publication *Human
Events* spoke for many in warning of the GOP's "emasculation" should the
party turn to "High-Tax, Big-Spend Nelson Rockefeller."

Of more immediate concern to the Rockefeller for President drive was the
serious illness that sidelined Frank Jamieson for much of 1959. In September,
Jamieson underwent surgery for lung cancer. As soon as he could, he returned
to Room 5600. But his prospects for recovery were bleak. At a critical moment
in his career, Rockefeller was deprived of the adviser he most trusted to counter
his own inexperience and occasional tin ear. "One of the toughest things about
Nelson is he had poor judgment at times," says Cynthia Lefferts, another staff
assistant who divided her time between Albany and Fifty-fifth Street. With
Frankie's voice at least temporarily silenced, Rockefeller relied on a team that
included Bill Ronan, George Hinman, Henry Kissinger, and other policy
gurus. Conscripted for a Rockefeller speech before an advertising group meeting at the Waldorf, Kissinger produced a text that addressed, in eye-glazing
detail, the technical capabilities of the U.S. submarine fleet. A protracted group
discussion took place at Fifty-fifth Street, with Rockefeller polling members of
his inner circle for their reaction. At length, he turned to Lefferts.

"We haven't heard from you."

"I think your audience has been to at least two cocktail parties, and they
don't want to hear this kind of thing from Nelson Rockefeller," Lefferts replied.
The ensuing silence spoke volumes. So did Rockefeller, when he stepped before a restive ballroom full of Madison Avenue types to deliver the speech.
"The evening was a total catastrophe," Lefferts recalls. "Nobody talked about it
the next day. I remember Mrs. Boyer said to me, 'Don't bring it up.'" None of
this came as a surprise to Nancy Hanks. Early in his governorship, Rockefeller

commissioned a report to justify his proposed tax increases. Frank Jamieson took one look at the bulky document and said no one would read it. Maybe so, replied Nancy, but Nelson wanted the facts—all the facts—on the record.

On seeing the edited version for himself, Rockefeller was indignant. "That mind could be photographic when it wanted to be," Hanks would remember.

"Put it back," said Rockefeller of the eliminated material.

"The presses are rolling."

"Stop the presses."

That evening, after working a party at the Executive Mansion, Nancy in her gold lamé dress was picked up at ten thirty p.m. and driven across the river to a printing plant in Troy, where she spent much of the night proofing the governor's restored message line by line. Nor was that the worst of it. After hearing from Jamieson that her presence was sparking politically harmful gossip, Rockefeller packed Hanks off to New York to work on the remaining Special Studies reports entrusted by Nelson to his brother Laurance. Her banishment said less about newfound caution on the governor's part than his transference of affections elsewhere.*

Professionally, too, there was no shortage of replacements for Hanks. By the fall of 1959, the Rockefeller townhouses on Fifty-fifth Street strained to accommodate a staff of seventy, the majority employed in presidential politics. The phantom campaign was divided into six sections; tellingly, there was no finance division. For any other candidate, the quest for delegates would dictate hiring and the allocation of resources. Rockefeller, noted Henry Kissinger, ran for the presidency "as if the competition was for some academic prize." In his first year as governor, Rockefeller convened more than forty study groups—not to deflect problems, as is customary, but to attack them with the assistance of the best minds in their field. There were task forces to increase milk consumption and combat juvenile delinquency; examine catastrophic health insurance and plan airport development and pilot safety; chart middle-income housing needs through 1975; and anticipate the state's long-term electric power requirements.

Of all his expert panels, none held more urgent appeal for Rockefeller than the Special Task Force on Protection from Radioactive Fallout, chaired by his

---

* Rockefeller was dismissive of Nancy's October 1959 proposal for a direct telephone line (a "survival" or "peace" line, she called it) to the Soviet Union. She couldn't know it at the time, but in proposing this doomsday alternative—portrayed by Hanks as a logical sequel to Open Skies—she was anticipating the Washington–Moscow hotline that would be put to historic use during the 1962 Cuban missile crisis. Rockefeller rejected the concept, citing arguments by his pollsters Lloyd Free and Hadley Cantril that the Senate would "have a fit," with U.S. allies likewise objecting to such a bilateral arrangement. "Memorandum for Mr. Nelson," NAR response, October 13, 1959, Series 4f, Box 7, RAC.

close friend and former scientific adviser to Congress Oscar Ruebhausen. Simulated nuclear attacks on New York had produced grim estimates that half the state's population would die, the overwhelming majority from blast fallout and the delayed effects of radiation sickness. Rockefeller had long believed that with stringent civil defense measures in place, many of these casualties could be avoided. His view was echoed, unsurprisingly, by an advisory group stacked with his commissioners of health, mental hygiene, and taxation. In the light of history, their crusade to stockpile biscuits and bottle openers for the survivors of Armageddon has come to be seen as laughable, if not more than a little weird, the bureaucratic equivalent of duck-and-cover maneuvers practiced in numberless American schoolhouses during the Cold War.

It didn't feel that way in 1959. The existing national plan placed responsibility on individual citizens to survive the first two weeks after a nuclear holocaust. Believing his fellow New Yorkers "completely unprepared" for this scenario, Rockefeller swung into action. In addition to public education about the dangers of fallout and possible defenses against it, he wanted building codes and architectural design standards revised to minimize the threat; protective "shielding" incorporated into all new construction; and forward planning to include fallout shelters equipped with food and water, eating utensils, battery-powered radios, soap, candles, first-aid kits, and bedding. Rockefeller insisted that his was a message of hope, not fear. Nuclear war was survivable. Moreover, a fully prepared civilian population might act as a deterrent to conflict, a safeguard against atomic blackmail.

His aggressive response earned praise from the White House. "You certainly have met the threat in your state forthrightly," Eisenhower told him at the end of July. A more equivocal response came from Rockefeller's gubernatorial brethren at their meeting in San Juan, Puerto Rico, a few days later. Although most endorsed his New York initiative in principle, only a handful were eager to replicate the program in their own states. Rockefeller's political coming-out party in San Juan included a lavish reception for six hundred guests and a news conference at which he deftly parried reporters' questions. But he stumbled badly during a lengthy background session with a second group of journalists, to whom he stressed the importance of public opinion polls in determining his course for 1960. Inevitably the story leaked, casting doubt on Rockefeller's political instincts and commitment to principle. It was a textbook illustration of what a healthy Frank Jamieson might have averted. So was the governor's denial, on returning to Albany, that he said what he had said in San Juan. Reinforcing the appearance of calculation was a Joe Alsop column hinting that the forthcoming marriage of Steven Rockefeller to Anne-Marie Rasmussen, daughter of a Norwegian fish canner and, until recently, a Rockefeller housemaid, was a publicity stunt to advance the White House aspirations of Steven's father.

The truth was both darker and more poignant, a tale of two young people whose social and cultural disparities were surpassed by a common desire to escape their origins. Anne-Marie was an emotionally fragile woman of twenty-one, who had fled a fishing village on the southern coast of Norway in search of her own American dream. An unlikely sequence of events led to her employment at 810 Fifth Avenue, where she polished her English by reading the *Daily News* and was scandalized by the nudes she dusted along with other Rockefeller art treasures. The family treated Anne-Marie kindly, even if Nelson complained that her raucous laugh disturbed him in the morning and Tod upbraided her for wearing sweaters that were too tight and failing to prepare dinner as scheduled ("I had to take my husband to Hamburger Heaven on Madison Avenue!"). At Christmas, the newcomer received from her employers an envelope containing $10. If she stayed another year, a co-worker thoughtfully informed her, the amount would be doubled.

Increasingly, Anne-Marie was drawn to Steven Rockefeller, recently graduated from Princeton, who returned her interest, if not necessarily her feelings. Class distinctions aside, the developing romance held echoes of the ambivalent courtship a generation earlier involving Steven's parents. From the start, the young man made it plain he did not love Anne-Marie, though perhaps, he allowed, with time, he could learn to do so. Juggling sexual passion and Rockefeller probity, Steven seemed more attracted to the *idea* of marrying his social opposite, a decorous act of rebellion, than to surrendering his tightly guarded emotions to her. "I almost feel pity for him," Anne-Marie wrote her parents in August 1957. "He is a young person who is desperately looking for a meaning and purpose in life." As their relationship became public knowledge, the press exploited the latter-day Cinderella story shamelessly. Traveling to Norway in the summer of 1959 for his wedding to Anne-Marie, however, Steven thought only of putting such fairy tales to rest.

He hadn't reckoned with more than a hundred reporters and photographers who descended on the coastal village of Søgne late in August or five thousand rubberneckers outside the small Lutheran church in which Steven and Anne-Marie said their vows. Still larger numbers lined the route to nearby Kristiansand, hoping for a glimpse of the newlyweds or, better yet, of the celebrated father of the groom. For their honeymoon, the couple decamped to Steve's beloved JY Ranch in Wyoming and a rustic cabin that satisfied his craving for simplicity, even as it reminded Anne-Marie of all that she had deliberately left behind. Back in New York, her husband accepted a position in the rental office of Rockefeller Center. "I was conscious of the previous career of Nelson Rockefeller," he later reflected. "I felt somehow that it was my responsibility to go and do likewise."

5

S TEVEN'S FATHER MIGHT be forgiven for wishing the road to the White House began in Norway, not New Hampshire. With no Iowa caucuses in 1960 to dilute the impact of its first-in-the-nation primary, the Granite State exerted a disproportionate influence on the nominating process. No one appreciated this more than Richard Nixon, the beneficiary of a 1956 grassroots campaign that had produced more than twenty-two thousand write-in votes, effectively blocking any movement to drop him from that year's GOP ticket. In the years since, Nixon had only solidified his grip on the party establishment led by United States senators Styles Bridges and Norris Cotton. Of more equivocal value was the support of New Hampshire's polarizing governor, Wesley Powell, and his journalistic ally the *Manchester Union Leader*, whose fiercely combative publisher William Loeb delighted in abusing "Dopey Dwight," also known to Loeb's readers as "that stinking hypocrite in the White House."

Officially, Rockefeller was in the exploratory phase of his campaign when, late in September, he returned to Hanover for the Dartmouth–Holy Cross football game. The torchlight parade accorded him on his arrival didn't prepare the visitor for a news conference arranged by the local GOP, at which party workers preempted the working press in asking hostile questions. His alma mater extended a much warmer welcome, though it paled beside the crowds that showed up a week later to greet Nixon at a nearby flood control ground-breaking ceremony. Among rank-and-file Republicans, Rockefeller trailed Nixon badly, one poll measuring his support at just 15 percent. Yet no one counted him out, Nixon least of all, because no one disputed his ability, given the chance, to connect with ordinary voters. A two-day visit to Chicago in October showcased both Rockefeller's people skills and his distance from the GOP hierarchy. "Nice guy," remarked the doorman at the Hilton. "Anybody who'd let his son marry the maid is okay in my book." An elevator girl at the same establishment couldn't get over the visitor's manners. "He thanked me three times," she said, adding, "I sure would like to meet one of his sons."

Nelson's easy interaction with a group of midwestern editors impressed many in the group. So did the capacity audience of five hundred that turned up for a reception in his honor hosted by the Cook County Young Republicans. Markedly cooler was the greeting of Governor William Stratton and the state's Republican establishment. Downright frigid was the atmosphere in the tony Chicago Club, where a group of prominent businessmen sat on their hands— and wallets. Rockefeller's testing of the waters bore a marked resemblance to the pre-convention phase of his 1958 campaign (even down to Len Hall's vigorous opposition, this time as Nixon's campaign manager). Once again Jud Morhouse hit the road, taking soundings and urging uncommitted Republicans to remain neutral pending Nelson's entry into the race. As they had in introducing him to rural New Yorkers two years before, Rockefeller planners willingly entrusted organization and logistics to local party leaders. But with no Malcolm Wilson to call in chits—indeed, with no chits to call in—his enemies were able to present Rockefeller in the most unflattering light possible. When new polls showed the vice president heavily favored among GOP voters, Rockefeller was hard-pressed to establish his own appeal. "What do you do," he snapped at one point in frustration, "take an applause meter along with you?"

As JFK would soon demonstrate, commencing outside the factory gates of New Hampshire, that is what primaries were for. Ever after, it would be an article of faith within the Rockefeller high command that 1960 represented his best shot at the White House. "It always bugged him," said George Hinman of Nelson's conviction that the presidency lay within his grasp that year, "if he had just been nominated." That the Kennedys themselves subsequently endorsed this view only betrayed their ignorance of the GOP culture as the party prepared to face life after Eisenhower. For a Democrat to promise to get the country moving again after the allegedly somnolent fifties was a surefire applause line; for one of Ike's Republican brethren to campaign on such a platform, as Rockefeller implicitly did, ranked somewhere between base ingratitude and outright treachery.

Rockefeller's October 22 address before the annual dinner of the Alfred E. Smith Foundation could have been delivered by the Democratic senator from Massachusetts: "We live in an age of revolution and explosion. Exploding bombs, exploding population, revolutionary wars, revolutionary wants . . . in such an age . . . we shall learn to be the masters of circumstance, or we shall be its victims." Ensuring that his message reached far beyond a New York ballroom, Henry Luce's *Life* published three articles on Rockefeller in six weeks. *Reader's Digest* ran separate profiles of the governor by Stewart Alsop and William Manchester. "Nelson Rockefeller: A Republican FDR?" asked *The Progressive*. The extensive coverage did nothing to lower expectations. "If Jesus Christ came down off the cross today," said *New York Times* reporter Warren Weaver following the governor's successful legislative session, "he couldn't beat Nelson Rockefeller."

Few observations were as revealing of the Manhattan mind-set that characterized Rockefeller's fifteen years on the national political stage. In the last weeks of 1959, he embarked on a pair of exploratory trips designed to gauge his prospects outside his backyard. Arriving at Los Angeles International Airport on the morning of November 12, he was greeted by Republican national committeeman Ed Shattuck—wearing a Nixon button. That evening, Rockefeller addressed the Western Republican Leadership Conference while standing beneath a huge portrait of the vice president. Prior to this indignity, the eastern visitor, unescorted by his hosts, had entered a crowded reception at the wrong end of the hall. From there he was forced to make his way against a surging tide of unfriendly faces.

"Here we are again," joked Nelson, "bucking the tide."

His wry comment neatly captured the spotty reception he received on the West Coast and on a second, six-day swing from Minneapolis to Miami. At the University of Oregon in Eugene, political observers professed astonishment over the crowd of seventy-five hundred drawn to a campus gymnasium on a sleepy Saturday morning. Thousands more filled the lobby of a St. Louis hotel, where Nelson vowed to stay as long as it took to shake every hand. That night he experienced another side to the Show Me State, converting a hostile business crowd by improvising a narrative of the budget crisis he had inherited in Albany and the pay-as-you-go measures that were eliminating the state's debt.

By the time he finished, Rockefeller had his skeptical audience on its feet.

GOP officials did their best to squelch any Rockefeller insurgency. In Wisconsin, 1,500 people had requested tickets to a Milwaukee luncheon with Nelson. In the event, only 225 guests were admitted, each one handpicked by the state organization. Again he put aside his text, winning compliments from the traveling press corps, if not the stone-faced regulars before him. Wherever he went, Rockefeller drew throngs of female admirers. In Oklahoma City, otherwise notable for the number of references he made to Abraham Lincoln in that stronghold of segregation, the tipsy wife of a local dignitary tried to gain entry to Nelson's suite. As Rockefeller and Ken Riland hid out in the bathroom, political aide Carl Spad made the mistake of opening the suite door. "She forced her way in and had a case of whiskey and all the New York State champagne and was all set for an evening," Riland wrote in his diary. "Carl managed to get her out once, and then she got back in again. In the meantime, Nelson and I had looked in the bedroom and there was [a] note from her on the bed. A note to him"—its contents too suggestive for Riland's pen.

Rockefeller's appearance the next day before the Dallas World Affairs Council stirred no such fervor. Indeed, the warmest greeting he got in the Big D came from Sam Rayburn, the legendary Democratic Speaker of the House, who drove thirty miles in order to show Nelson "that he has friends in Texas." Most of them, it appeared, belonged to the wrong party.* The incident was nevertheless revealing of a top-down mentality driving the Rockefeller campaign to pursue Republican kingmakers, many of them barely able to stomach Theodore, much less Franklin, Roosevelt. At the time, his chilly reception was attributed to inferior organization and hardball tactics employed by Len Hall

---

* It did not aid his cause when Adlai Stevenson said of Rockefeller that he appeared to be "a thoughtful and sincere liberal."

and other Nixon strategists. This overlooked something much larger, a mutation occurring within Republican ranks, as the party's center of gravity shifted right and the polarizing emotions of the sixties evicted Eisenhower-style moderation.

6

BASED ON COMMENTS from those closest to Rockefeller, Warren Weaver alerted *Times* readers to expect a formal declaration of candidacy within days. Seconding this view was Bob Novak, whose reporting convinced him that Nixon's grip on the party apparatus was more tenuous than it appeared. Were Rockefeller to upset the vice president in even one primary, insiders told Novak, the GOP establishment would have no choice but to take a fresh look at the upstart. Christmas came and went. Nelson spent much of December 26 working at 20 West Fifty-fifth Street before boarding a late afternoon train to join Tod and her Philadelphia relations for a holiday gathering. In Albany, press secretary Dick Amper alerted the capital press corps to expect a major announcement at one o'clock. The decision even then being mimeographed in the governor's press office had been finalized two days earlier, at a meeting attended by Frank Jamieson, George Hinman, John Lockwood, and Emmet J. Hughes—"Eminent John Hughes" to his bemused former colleagues at Time-Life—a disenchanted Eisenhower speechwriter whose mere presence in the Rockefeller circle was taken by Ike as a personal affront.

Also present was Happy Murphy. "He had the meeting in what we call the Harrison House down the hill [from Kykuit]," she recalls. "Bill Ronan told him this was the only time that he would ever have a chance to become president. Nelson went around asking for their opinions. George Hinman made an impassioned talk about how he'd just been elected governor of New York; he would be abdicating his responsibilities to the voters of New York." Ronan confirms the exchange, though he remembers it taking place at the Albany airport rather than Pocantico. "Nelson turns to me and said, 'What do you think?' I said, 'I think you ought to go.'" Countering Frank Jamieson's argument that Rockefeller had yet to establish himself as governor, Ronan points to the opposition. "Against Kennedy, I think you could win. What executive experience has he had?" It was a fair question, though unintentionally revealing in its emphasis on successful governing over what it would take to win a Republican nomination. Long afterward, Ronan attributed Rockefeller's decision to forgo the contest to George Hinman's caution and to more pervasive doubts entertained by Jamieson.

"I think Jamieson was always a little concerned about Nelson in public life," Ronan says.

Defying expectations, Nelson in his December 26 statement backed away from a fight to which "the great majority of those who will control the Republican convention stand opposed." To join the fray was to neglect his obligations as governor. He reiterated in Shermanesque language his disinterest in the vice presidency. And though he made a routine nod in the direction of GOP unity ("I expect to support the nominees, as well as the program, of the Party in 1960"), he passed up the opportunity to say anything remotely generous about Richard M. Nixon. To the contrary, Rockefeller reserved the right to speak out on issues of concern as part of the "profound and continuous act of self-examination" he prescribed for his countrymen. Reaction was swift. In Washington, Nixon thought reporters were joking when they first related his rival's announcement. Eisenhower, visiting his grandchildren in Gettysburg, declined public comment, though he had expressed regret when Nelson communicated his decision by phone. Remarking, "You never know what will happen to Dick in the meantime," the president had urged Rockefeller to attend the Chicago convention as New York's favorite son.

A thousand telegrams, most urging him to reconsider, crossed the governor's desk in Albany. Reaching new levels of sycophancy, Henry Kissinger acknowledged feelings of despair, "not for you but for the country and the cause of freedom in the world. . . . In an age dominated by little men with strong wills you have permitted us a vision of greatness. In a period of clever, petty calculation, you have shown the possibilities of conviction." Lincoln Kirstein praised Nelson for his "absolutely wonderful decision. All of us who love you and will follow you, only pray the SOBs who denied you your due now, will not prevail upon you later, through your innate loyalty" to do anything—like accepting second spot on Nixon's ticket—that might deprive the nation "of a great president in 1964." A dying Frank Jamieson promised to quit if Nelson went back on his word about the vice presidency.

On December 28, feeling somewhat deflated by the latest turn of events, Nixon telephoned Rockefeller. The vice president and his strategists had come to see the advantages of a spirited contest, confident as they were of victory and eager to demonstrate strength among independent voters. In their conversation, Rockefeller emphasized the need for Nixon to talk issues in the coming campaign. The vice president replied that he had been too busy making speeches to give thought to the issues. Second-guessing columnists, meanwhile, had a field day unearthing hidden motives for Rockefeller's early exit. Joe Alsop came closest to the truth when he claimed that the governor had indeed considered entering the primaries, not because he expected to defeat Nixon at the polls, but "to make a record and to stake a claim." More specifically, wrote

Alsop, Rockefeller wished to record the inadequacies of American foreign and defense policies, backed by a Churchillian call to preparedness in the face of official laxity. Inevitably, this would bring him into pitched conflict with Dwight Eisenhower. Such a contest, hopelessly one-sided yet mutually destructive, had, for now, been averted. But for how long?

After the fact, Rockefeller attributed his withdrawal to the negative consensus within his political family. "I'd been in politics what, about a year I guess, and here I was with everybody against me. Everyone I talked to told me I didn't have a chance and that I could only ruin everything." A decade later, he was more explicit in his finger-pointing, telling Walter Cronkite in 1973 that his chief political operatives—easily identified as George Hinman and Jud Morhouse—both lacking national experience, "came to me and said, look, we can't handle this, we're quitting. Now not being a politician myself and having that situation on my hands, I just was not in a position to cope with that problem and continue the responsibilities I was trying to handle as governor."

Hinman's recollections differed. "The party was locked up," said Hinman, "and Nelson was locked out." Returning from his December 1959 road trip, Rockefeller himself had had no illusions about his prospects. To continue his quest was to court humiliation. Reinforcing this advice were key New Hampshire supporters led by Dudley Orr of Concord, a moderate Republican who had graduated from Dartmouth a year ahead of Rockefeller. "They wanted out," according to Hinman. "They couldn't hack it." Reiterating, "We didn't run out on him," Hinman conceded that he and Morhouse might, "to underline to him the desperateness of the situation, have said something like, 'It's impossible—at least we can't do it. We'd have to get out rather than take you down this road.'"

"The national party and Nelson were never really meant for each other," Hinman asserted in a 1979 oral history. "His vision was so much broader than theirs." Ultimately, Hinman's counsel mattered less than something Rockefeller himself said not long before his death: "When I became insecure because of events getting out of control and beyond my capacity I always pulled back to a base which was controllable." *Out of control. Beyond my capacity.* His comments help to explain much that is otherwise baffling about his mercurial pursuit of the presidency. At the end of 1959, moreover, Rockefeller's feelings of political insecurity were magnified by domestic stresses. "No man can run for the White House," he told Oscar Ruebhausen, "if his own house isn't in order."

Fifteen
IN AND OUT

Nelson's mistake in 1960 was not in getting out but in getting back in.
—George Hinman

1

FRANK JAMIESON'S LIFE ended in a New York hospital on January 30, 1960. He was fifty-five. Having long despaired of his friend's recovery, Nelson had, near the end, written the dying man a tender letter of reminiscence and gratitude (it would be delivered, unopened, to Jamieson's widow, Linda). Expected though it was, the loss of Jamieson hit Rockefeller hard, tearing away the stoic's mask firmly in place since the death of his mother a dozen years earlier. Typical of the condolences he received was a message from Max Ascoli of *The Reporter*. "I know there are many people who are devoted to you," wrote Ascoli, "for you have a rare gift for inspiring devotion. But you will never find another Frankie, and I haven't the slightest doubt in my mind that you know it."*

As if to confirm this forecast, two weeks later press secretary Dick Amper succumbed to a massive heart attack. Rockefeller's relationship with Amper, a Jamieson protégé whose chaotic press office he likened to a Marx Brothers movie, had been strictly professional. But the shock of his premature death was felt all the same. To fill his shoes, Nelson turned to Bob McManus, an experienced Albany hand who had performed the same function for Averell Harriman. The obvious candidate to succeed Jamieson as head of the family's public relations was his longtime assistant in Room 5600, Martha Dalrymple. Obvious, that is, to everyone but Nelson. Without bothering to consult his brothers, and even as Frankie lay in a hospital bed recuperating from lung surgery, he had already settled on his replacement.

---

* Calling on Jamieson's widow after the funeral, Rockefeller vowed not to forget Frankie and his family—a pledge he honored by underwriting, among other things, the education of Jamieson's daughters, Margo and Frannie. He also commissioned Wally Harrison to design a tombstone for his friend.

"I am happy with the time we spent together yesterday," Emmet Hughes wrote Nelson on October 18, 1959. "I am happy with all you are doing. I am happy—and proud—to be helping in every manner. And I hope this help can grow and grow." Assuming Rockefeller could meet his personal and financial requirements, Hughes looked forward to providing not just words for speeches, but what he called "disciplined and reflective strategic planning." Thirty-nine years old, black-haired and rakishly handsome in a style vaguely reminiscent of Edward R. Murrow, Hughes was equally adept at self-dramatization. "I remember him in a black cape," says Happy Rockefeller, "never getting up early in the morning and coming in sort of like Batman." As *Time*'s senior foreign correspondent, Hughes straddled the line between facility and brilliance. Colleagues marveled at his whiskey-fueled ability to bang out in one sitting a cover story on the death of a pope or the rising winds of third world nationalism. This same gift for rapid assimilation, plus a florid, neo-Churchillian style, enabled Hughes, who had never been to Albany in his life, to craft Rockefeller's January 1959 inaugural address.

In retrospect, Hughes would characterize Nelson's on-again, off-again candidacy in 1960 as "an explosion of temperament without rational political basis." Much the same might be said of Hughes, a moody and combative Irishman who loved to flash his engraved card reading "Office of the Mssr. Rockefeller" and whose political judgment was secondary to his wordsmith's feel for language. Being a liberal Democrat in an administration of gray flannel suits hadn't kept Hughes from authoring some of Ike's most memorable phrases. At the same time, he had exploited his privileged status to write down seemingly every unguarded comment made by the president and his intimates. This foreshadowed a pair of highly critical books: *America the Vincible*, published in 1959, and, four years later, a venomous kiss-and-tell memoir (*The Ordeal of Power*) that set the seal on Eisenhower's feelings of betrayal.

With all the baggage trailing Hughes, the question naturally arises: Why hire him in the first place? The simplest answer is that Hughes supplied a vital element missing from Rockefeller's skill set. For years, those around Nelson had accepted his idiosyncratic spelling, ascertaining that the Benat Surf with whom he had made dinner reservations was, in fact, the New York publisher Bennett Cerf, and later transmitting personal messages from Rockefeller to Mr. Joe N. Lie of the People's Republic of China. Accustomed to his patchy vocabulary, associates didn't bat an eye when the governor praised a colleague for doing his job "horrendously." Speechwriters endured brain-numbing sessions prolonged by the search for a perfect word or phrase.*

---

* Years later, press secretary Ron Maiorana was summoned one morning by an angry governor to hear the latest outrage committed by New York City mayor John Lindsay. "Can you believe he

To a dyslexic suspicious of the written word, Hughes offered, in suitably presidential language, the means to communicate Rockefeller's vision. "He expected Emmet to do for him what he had done for Eisenhower," maintains Jim Cannon, a journalistic colleague who subsequently joined the Rockefeller staff himself. In the meantime, Rockefeller's dyslexia remained hidden from the public. A 1959 campaign biography attributed his "remarkable inability to spell" to "peculiar vision." Later authorized accounts supplemented this fiction by alluding to tutorial inadequacies and Junior's determination to convert his southpaw son into a right-hander. Try as he might, Rockefeller never wholly escaped his disability. Inadequate preparation or physical exhaustion left him vulnerable to public embarrassment. Appearing on the state university campus in New Paltz, he expressed delight to find himself in New Platz. Making the case for an ambitious state-run health insurance program, the governor invited listeners to imagine a typical family of four earning $100,000 a year. Cited afterward as proof of Rockefeller's remoteness from the average New Yorker, the malaprop said less about his insensitivity than it did about his habit of transposing numbers—in this instance, $10,000 into $100,000—through an act of dyslexic treachery. Rockefeller tried to make light of his handicap, telling friends, "If not for that, I might have amounted to something."

And if Emmet Hughes hadn't existed, Rockefeller would no doubt have found someone like him to whom he could outsource his public voice; someone whose alarmist outlook and lofty contempt for what Hughes labeled "the petty conflict of the moment" matched his own. Tellingly, the two men shared bleak memories of Eisenhower's Washington and of repeated clashes with Dulles's State Department. That wasn't all Rockefeller had in common with Hughes, a seductive charmer who conducted his private affairs as recklessly as his political battles. Gannett newspaperman Bill Ringle, himself a newcomer to Albany, asked Arthur Massolo of the *New York Post* his opinion of the new governor. Rockefeller had but one weakness, said Massolo: "He can't keep his pecker in his pants." In the prevailing locker-room culture of a macho, and largely protective, press corps, Rockefeller at times appeared almost boastful of his sexual prowess. Attending the dedication of a women's dormitory at an upstate college in May 1959, the governor was handed a ceremonial key. "You better give the key back to the girls," he told Frank Moore, his appointee to chair the New York State Board of Regents. "I'm surprised you gave it to me in the first place."

A Freudian slip, perhaps, but Dan Rostenkowski, upon his election to the

---

said that?" vented Rockefeller, waving a *New York Times* story reporting that Lindsay had "chided" his Albany nemesis. As Rockefeller raged on about the mayor's foul language, it dawned on Maiorana: his boss didn't know the meaning of the word *chide*. Ron Maiorana, AI.

House of Representatives in 1958 the youngest member of Congress, vividly recalls encountering "old Nelse" on several occasions in the Town & Country lounge of Washington's Mayflower Hotel. Each time, he was accompanied by a fetching blonde. "It wasn't that he used women," explains one member of Rockefeller's traveling entourage as governor, "it was more that he liked them. You'd be out with him for a day, and fifty women would try to grab . . . I mean it was just constant. He was like Joe Namath." Unsurprisingly, the strains of the Rockefeller marriage were exacerbated by the demands of being "Governor and Mrs. Governor—or whatever I am," as Tod remarked to a group of reporters invading 810 Fifth Avenue within days of her husband's election. To a photographer asking her to pose for "half a minute," she replied tartly, "I hope your idea and my idea of 'half a minute' is the same."

Tutored by Frank Jamieson, she gradually overcame her diffidence, if not her distrust of the fourth estate. "I am learning how to fend off embarrassing questions," she notified Jamieson after her first out-of-state trip in April 1959. Admirers noticed how deftly Tod compensated for her husband's chronic inability to remember names. "I liked being with her," reflected John Gardner, who had first made Tod's acquaintance through his involvement with the Special Studies Project. "There was a kind of sophisticated and humorous view of life that came through in her conversation." Her lack of pretense moved Ken Riland, an unsparing diarist, to conclude during their November 1959 West Coast travels that Tod was a major political asset. Other observers remarked on her intelligent take on issues. "I always suspected she was smarter than Nelson," contended Jack Germond, who once observed Tod pick apart the Sunday papers on a flight from Dartmouth to Albany. Malcolm Wilson agreed. "Nelson never realized how sagacious Mary Todhunter Clark Rockefeller was," said Wilson. "He never really realized that much of what he did and many of the things he said had come from her."

Still others, guessing at her plight, felt sympathy for the tall, cranelike woman playing a part for which she was clearly miscast. "I think the Albany setting was a pain in the ass to her," said Al Marshall, who succeeded Bill Ronan as secretary to the governor. "She was a lady, never anything but, but you could just sense, God, she'd rather be doing something else than shaking hands" with a roomful of "slobbering assemblymen and senators." Occasionally, resentment of her lot pierced the thick armor of self-possession. "Nelson abhorred smoking . . . and she would smoke in the car," remembers Henry Diamond, a former CBS journalist who subsequently worked for both Laurance and Nelson. "I think she didn't give as good as she got, but she gave some." On another occasion, Tod refused to greet supporters from around the country who had assembled at 810 Fifth Avenue to discuss Nelson's prospects for 1960.

Kershaw Burbank of Room 5600 thought he knew why. "She was terribly embittered by his philandering," according to Burbank, from whom Tod once borrowed a secretary to help cope with the demands of a daughter's forthcoming wedding. The woman returned to the family office after a few days. "She couldn't take it anymore," said Burbank. "Tod was so imperious, so nasty." Mark Hatfield conceded an unfortunate first impression of Main Line hauteur and "New England lockjaw. They can talk without ever moving their jaw. But underneath it all," Hatfield continued, "when you really got close to her, she was a very warm person. But she was totally ill-fitted for politics and, as many people came to think, with Nelson. They just didn't look paired."

Only a handful of intimates knew how close Nelson had come, on the eve of his 1958 campaign, to walking away from his marriage of nearly thirty years. Unable to convince Rockefeller to forgo a race against the heavily favored Averell Harriman, Frank Jamieson had more success in persuading Nelson that a divorce would scuttle his political career before it began. "Jamieson was like a guard on the basketball court," claimed Al Marshall. "His job was to protect Nelson Rockefeller." With Jamieson gone, there was no one to offer such protection.

2

L ESS THAN THREE months into his governorship, Rockefeller revealed plans for a "weekend office" to be built on his Pocantico estate. Described as a "simple, rustic guesthouse" (it ultimately cost $130,000), the glass-and-concrete structure resembled a toadstool growing out of the densely carpeted woods in a secluded corner of the vast property. Yet another Wally Harrison project, the Lodge was to be Nelson's hideaway from his earlier hideaway, the Harrison-designed guesthouse into which he had moved in the late 1930s. His newest retreat featured a small lake, stocked with bass, and an islet occupied by Jacques Lipchitz's Song of the Vowels. A bubbling brook flowed pleasantly close to the bedroom windows. Although a number of work-related meetings took place there, the Lodge was built with nonpolitical pursuits in mind. By the time Rockefeller occupied the saucerlike structure, his relationship with Tod had reached an impasse. "What had become an empty marriage long before," wrote Theodore H. White, "bound only by love of children, became slowly a prison."

Hard choices, painful for all concerned, intruded on Nelson's forested retreat. Americans in 1960 had never elected a divorced man to the nation's highest office. Glimpsed narrowly through the lens of political ambition, Rockefeller's divorce and subsequent remarriage were seen as acts of breathtaking folly. So focused were his competitors then, and historians since, on the price exacted by his extramarital passion for Happy Murphy that few have ever paused to consider its possible emotional compensations. Bill Scranton was an exception to the rule. "I knew both Tod and Happy well," says the former Pennsylvania governor, whose Main Line connections afforded him unusual insight into the world the two women inhabited. "Tod was very bright, and I liked her. But I never thought she was Nelson's type. More than most men, Nelson was someone who needed warmth. It's not the same thing as sex," Scranton cautions. "And Happy is a very warm person. She could give him what Tod couldn't."*

In pondering what was missing from his marriage to Tod, Nelson didn't have far to go for a contrasting example of emotional support. Not once, but twice, he married women who embodied different aspects of his idealized mother. Heavily influenced by her example, Nelson had always relied on women to bolster his place at the center of the universe. Within a week of graduating from Dartmouth, he wed Tod, whose modern outlook and Aldrich-like commingling of high purpose with cutup humor reminded her suitor of free-spirited Abby Aldrich Rockefeller. On this point he was explicit, glossing over the fact that neither woman was a conventional beauty. Barely out of adolescence, Nelson fell in love, or convinced himself that he had, with Tod's *character*, with her adventurous spirit and resourcefulness and integrity, attributes his mother possessed in abundance.

But this did not exhaust Abby's womanly appeal—far from it. From childhood, Nelson had observed the humanizing effect of her uncritical adoration on his brittle and increasingly withdrawn father. That she still excited her husband's erotic imagination, long after most couples had settled into a passionless twilight, did not go unnoticed. Both qualities were reproduced in Happy Murphy. On the surface, both of Nelson's wives were mildly rebellious products of insular Philadelphia, eager to leave behind their stratified surroundings. There the similarities end. For Mary Todhunter Clark grew up in a loving, cohesive family, imbued with the verities of her class, social and moral guideposts that became ever more sustaining as her marriage withered. By contrast, her younger rival and eventual successor was raised largely by surrogates in a household scarred by emotional conflict and from which an early marriage promised escape.

Margaretta Large Fitler was born in June 1926, an infant whose sunny dispo-

---

* The point was reinforced by Rockefeller osteopath and confidant Ken Riland. Never close to the second Mrs. Rockefeller, Riland put aside their differences one evening when Happy, in the midst of a personal health crisis, asked why he thought Nelson had married her. Riland replied that with her appearance on the scene, love had entered the Rockefeller home for the first time. KRD, November 20, 1974.

sition earned her the lifelong nickname "Happy." Though her father, William Wonderly Fitler, Jr., inherited $8 million from the family rope-making business, it wasn't enough to prevent Happy's mother, also named Margaretta, from mocking her husband's family for being in trade. A self-absorbed beauty with a predisposition to ancestor worship, Mrs. Fitler boasted of her connections to General George Meade, the victorious Union commander at Gettysburg, and to a railroad builder employed by Czar Alexander II of Russia. "I had this aunt who claimed that her husband was related to Benjamin Franklin," says a bemused Happy. "I said, 'Which one of the illegitimate children?'" That her parents were sadly mismatched didn't ease the strain of their divorce in 1936. Henceforth, ten-year-old Happy was discouraged from seeing her alcoholic father. Responsibility for her upbringing passed to the child's formidable grandmother, yet another Margaretta.

A childhood friend remembered Happy as "a very pretty, sweet thing, always smiling—but there was a quiet sadness too." A natural athlete, at the exclusive Shipley School she excelled at basketball, tennis, and other sports. Never a clotheshorse, she much preferred jeans and sneakers to her crisp school uniform. In another rebellion against the stifling decorum of her grandmother's regimen, Happy took to riding her bicycle down a steep hill, hands in the air, a most unladylike posture. Still she made the Shipley honor roll, impressing classmates with her "bright smile and perpetual good humor." According to the 1944 class yearbook, her pet expression was a noncommittal "Mmm—could be. Besetting sin—eating. Pet hate—hay fever. Suppressed desire—to fly. Destiny—Navy wedding."

As she grew to maturity, Happy Fitler left the daredevil behind. Tall—about five feet seven inches—with honey-blond hair and a dazzling smile, she had a figure that drew appreciative glances from men. Male admirers used words like "wholesome" and "voluptuous," often in the same sentence, to convey Happy's well-scrubbed sensuality. Large, luminous brown eyes hinted at intimacy, while adding to her air of wistfulness. In later years, people often commented on a vulnerability that made them want to take care of her. Happy passed up college for the American Women's Voluntary Services. "If you want to know how sheltered my upbringing was," she told Cary Reich in 1988, "when I was at the [Philadelphia] Naval Hospital there were a lot of burn casualties from ships that had been torpedoed, and one of the first casualties was a black man who had third-degree burns all over his body. And I was shocked to realize, when I looked at him, that he was black all over—that black people weren't like Al Jolson."

In 1946, she met James Slater "Robin" Murphy, a U.S. Army Medical Corps captain six years her senior. In addition to degrees from Princeton and Johns Hopkins School of Medicine, tall, debonair Robin Murphy had sufficient blue blood coursing through his veins to satisfy even a Main Line dowager. On his mother's side, he could trace a line of descent to the Rhode Island textile pioneer Samuel Slater. His father, a renowned cancer specialist at the Rockefeller Institute for Medical Research, had served as a Rockefeller family physician, accompanying Nelson and his siblings on their summer travels. (It was the senior Dr. Murphy who sparked Junior's interest in the new Memorial Hospital— later Memorial Sloan-Kettering—and its war on cancer.) Apart from their rarefied antecedents, Robin Murphy shared a family stigma with Happy Fitler. For he, too, was a child of divorce, a fact later blamed for a character variously described as austere and emotionally withholding. But all that came later. At their December 1948 wedding in Philadelphia's Holy Trinity Episcopal Church, onlookers saw only a glamorous young couple, brilliantly launched on lives full of promise.

Thereafter, home was a twenty-five-room townhouse at East Sixty-fourth Street and Park Avenue, inherited from Robin's father. A boy, whom they called Jamie, was born in 1951. Three daughters followed: Margaretta, known as Wendy, in 1953; Carol two years later; and Malinda in 1960. For part of the fifties the Murphys lived on the West Coast, where Robin assisted a Nobel laureate in his Berkeley lab. Their subsequent return to New York was engineered at least in part by David Rockefeller. So was Robin's appointment to a position at the Rockefeller Institute. The youngest Rockefeller brother and his wife, Peggy, lived next door to the Murphys in midtown Manhattan. In the summer, both families retreated to Mount Desert Island. Their friendship blossomed in the waters off Northeast Harbor—also known as "Philadelphia on the rocks"— where Robin crewed for David on the nautical racecourse and Happy joined them for coastal cruises aboard the Rockefeller sloop *Jack Tar.*

In August 1953, the Murphys attended a friend's wedding in Portland, Maine. Elizabeth Shemwell, once employed by Nelson in Room 5600, has vivid recollections of the occasion. "At the reception following the wedding, Happy got me off [in] a corner and said, 'I want to talk to you about Nelson Rockefeller.'" This seemed odd at first, until Elizabeth remembered that the Murphys had inherited Miradero, a summer cottage close to Nelson's Seal Harbor estate, the Anchorage. "I thought perhaps she was worried about living next door to NAR," according to Shemwell, "but that didn't fit, for she came from Philadelphia's Main Line and had a background very much like Tod Rockefeller's. She wanted to know what he was like; what was it like to work for him."

Happy was no stranger to the Rockefellers. A decade earlier, she had chanced to run into Junior in the woods of Mount Desert. They chatted briefly and parted, without the mannerly stranger ever identifying himself. Their next encounter occurred three years later, in the summer of 1948. "His wife had died in April, and in June he was terribly lonely, and when he walked into the club which he had given to the community, everybody pulled back, away from him," recalls Happy, "and you know how that makes you feel. And because I was so dumb, grew up in Philadelphia, I didn't know what a Rockefeller was. And so I ran forward to him to say hello, and he never forgot it." Junior took both Murphys under his wing, assisting Robin to land jobs at Berkeley and the Rockefeller Institute. In a virtually unprecedented gesture, he sold the couple a thirteen-acre parcel of prime Pocantico real estate on which to build a weekend retreat. David Rockefeller was instrumental in this unusual transaction. At least he thought he was. "Later on I learned that Nelson had played an important role in encouraging Father to make the sale," he revealed in his 2002 memoirs.

Nelson's interest didn't end with the signing of deeds. Enlisting the services of his architect friend George Dudley, he threw himself into designing a contemporary house for the Murphys. "They were so delighted with the plans that they gave them to their architect in Philadelphia, who hasn't been heard from since!" Rockefeller wrote Dudley in December 1956. Ultimately, convention won out. This should not have surprised anyone; to all appearances, the Murphys personified success as measured by their class. Carefully airbrushed out of smiling pictures were Happy's first stirrings of dissatisfaction with her *Social Register* existence. As tensions multiplied in the Murphy household, the dedicated microbiologist struggled to comprehend a classic 1950s wife who scarcely understood her own groping for something beyond the inbred gentility of her surroundings. Increasingly restless, Happy began seeing a prominent New York psychologist and marriage counselor. As portrayed by Theodore White, who was careful to reflect the views of his friend Nelson Rockefeller, Robin Murphy was a controlling husband, whose suspicions about his wife caused "frightening scenes" in their household.

Oddly, his jealousy never seemed to be directed at Nelson, even though Happy's professional responsibilities in the Rockefeller campaign appeared as vague as her relationship to the candidate. "I first met her in 1958 at the Time-Life Building," recalls Kershaw Burbank. "I thought she was a friend of Laurance and Mary [Rockefeller]." That fall, Happy eased Nelson through his early television appearances by standing next to the teleprompter, a reassuring surrogate for the unseen audience. Reporting to Bill Ronan, with whom she forged an unspoken alliance against the traditionalists of Room 5600, as of January 1959 Mrs. Murphy sat in on gubernatorial meetings as Nelson's confidential secretary, the position once filled by Nancy Hanks. "Rockefeller didn't want to record anything," explains Joe Boyd, who later performed similar duties. "Basically that staff person's job was to keep track of what he committed to his visitor to do, and then implement that into the bureaucracy of state government, and report back to him weekly whether it had been accomplished or not." If it hadn't, Boyd notes, "he'd pick up the phone and say, 'I understand you're blocking this. Why?'"

Precisely when Nelson and Happy began their affair remains elusive. As long as John D. Rockefeller, Jr., lived, they practiced discretion. Claims by other journalists to have ferreted out the relationship are dismissed as "garbage" by Jack Germond. "The people who say they knew, didn't know," he insists. Confirming evidence of this is Ken Riland's ignorance of Happy Murphy as late as the July 1960 Republican convention in Chicago. Only in hindsight did Nelson's conduct during this period fit neatly into a story line that could have but one conclusion. A month after the new governor danced with Happy Murphy at his inaugural ball, he appointed her husband to the New York State Mental Hygiene Council. Before the year was out, Robin Murphy became chairman of the group. His appreciation mingled with surprise, Murphy told friends he had no idea Nelson admired him so much. The true object of Nelson's admiration eluded Murphy, as it did others, throughout Rockefeller's aborted campaign for the White House, terminated in December 1959, as he cryptically noted, because of turmoil in his own house.*

3

A NEWCOMER TO THE governor's office asked speechwriter Hugh Morrow how the place was organized. Morrow picked up a pencil and piece of paper, on whose surface he placed a dot, around which he drew a circle. "The dot is Nelson," he explained. This failed to take into account Rockefeller's reliance on Bill Ronan. "I can get from him in five or ten minutes the essence of the problem," said Nelson, a priceless asset for one who valued time over money. "He felt more comfortable with strong people than weak people," adds Happy Rockefeller. "Bill measured up to his strength." A Ronan penchant for secrecy dovetailed neatly with Junior's admonition to his son to "never show more surface than necessary." Consequently, most of their communications were verbal. "He always insisted I have a phone connected to him," says Ronan. "You won't find great memos I wrote in the archives because I burned them."

"Nelson had a weakness," according to Harry O'Donnell. "He felt that if a PhD were good at one thing, he was good at everything." As for Ronan, "I think

---

* Nelson's old habit of mixing work and romance made virtually any woman on his payroll liable to prurient speculation. "People have kidded me all my life about that," says one former female staff member. "I only came close twice and I stopped it. I knew it was coming and I stopped it. It was in the backseat of the car. . . . Apparently it always began in the backseat of the car." Confidential source.

he made enemies for Nelson faster than Nelson could make friends. I remember Walter [Mahoney] stopped me one day in the hall and said, 'What's going on down there on the second floor? I can't get to see Rockefeller. Ronan doesn't even return my calls.'" Sensitive as he was to the feelings of his chief deputy, Rockefeller wasn't blind to his limitations. After Ronan's bulldozing style alienated many in the state's higher education establishment, the governor made legal counsel Bob MacCrate his emissary to the professoriate. "A couple of times I would say to him, 'You know, if I were you, I'd fire me,'" says Ronan. "That'd be too good for you," replied Rockefeller. In truth, Ronan was at a loss to understand why his total loyalty was not returned. "I saw him angry several times," recalls Cynthia Lefferts. Invariably, he raised the same question. "Why did he do that without consulting me?"*

By the end of 1959, Ronan had assembled a parallel government built around an elite group of "program associates," five or six generalists, fertile in thought, aggressive in outlook, whose commission was to goad a sluggish bureaucracy into action. Besides channeling the work product of Rockefeller's forty-plus task forces, the same troubleshooters found themselves in the awkward but heady position of dictating to much older and more experienced commissioners. Long-term planning was another Rockefeller fetish. Prompted by a similar effort in Hawaii, in 1960 he established the Office for Regional Development (later renamed the Office of Planning Services) to encourage zoning on a state-wide basis. With New York divided into ten regions, experts in each identified an ideal mix of parks and recreational areas, agricultural tracts, and urban neighborhoods ripe for entrepreneurship.

No less an authority than Lewis Mumford praised Rockefeller for promoting intelligent land use planning on a scale not attempted in the United States since the Tennessee Valley Authority was created in the 1930s. But the potent combination of grassroots inertia and suspicion of bureaucratic outsiders riding roughshod over the wishes of local property owners proved impossible to overcome, even for Rockefeller. Moreover, sometimes the future stubbornly refused to be planned for. To direct his first-in-the-nation State Atomic and Space Development Authority, Rockefeller hired Oliver Townsend away from the Atomic Energy Commission in Washington. Townsend imagined fleets of nuclear-powered civilian ships reinvigorating the docks of New York harbor. His vision

---

* Only slightly less annoying were visitors who, overstaying their welcome in Rockefeller's office, were shunted off to see the governor's secretary. "I used to get furious with him," concedes Ronan. "So one day a group of ladies from Westchester waited upon him for something, I forgot what the hell it was. They were all important Westchester people socially. And he had spent about a half hour with them and he'd had it, so he sent them to my office. I finally got rid of them, and I went up to him. I said, 'Nelson.' And he said, 'Wait a minute. What do you think of the Junior League thirty years later? I couldn't stand any more.'" William J. Ronan, AI.

might have been realized had such vessels ever been built on the scale predicted. A second initiative involving an atomic waste disposal area in the salt mines of Cattaraugus County was plagued by leaks. As for the utilization of heat from spent atomic fuel, regarded by some experts as a potentially inexhaustible source of industrial energy, the technology never caught up with the hype.

In 1959, one poll showed nearly seven out of ten Americans believed nuclear war to be imminent. A federal report concluded that two hydrogen bombs dropped near the Brooklyn Bridge would result in the deaths of six million people. Moving to capitalize on public fears, Rockefeller appointed Henry Luce, David Sarnoff, Thurgood Marshall, and other luminaries to a revitalized New York State Defense Council, the opening act in his campaign to convince New Yorkers that the threat of Soviet attack was real and best met by constructing fallout shelters in every home, school, and public building in the state. Legislation to this effect was introduced early in the 1960 session. To promote it, Rockefeller went on television, demonstrating for viewers of the *Today* show the comforts of life in a mock-up shelter complete with bunk beds and "fallout crackers," as his favorite post-holocaust snack became known.[*]

In Albany, Rockefeller equipped a thirty-foot-square coal bunker under the Executive Mansion garage with fans, portable sanitary facilities, and double-decker cots. A $4 million shelter, linked to NORAD and its early warning system, took shape beneath the state campus, a cluster of buildings housing government workers on the outskirts of town (he startled Sol Corbin of his counsel's office by declaring that should doomsday come, there wouldn't be room underground for staff wives). Additional shelters were established at Rockefeller homes in Maine, at Pocantico, and at 810 Fifth Avenue. Rockefeller harangued visiting Indian prime minister Jawaharlal Nehru on the subject. Governor Rockefeller was a very strange man, Nehru concluded after their meeting in March 1960. "He talked to me about nothing but bomb shelters." Lawmakers balked at imposing the estimated $400-per-shelter cost on constituents. They remained opposed, even after Rockefeller scrapped the mandatory elements of his program in favor of tax incentives for individual homeowners. Still he persisted, confident that events would vindicate his obsession.

He was just as adamant in promoting the first state arts council in the country. Thwarted by legislative philistines during his first year in office, early in 1960 Rockefeller threatened to withhold committee funds unless lawmakers

---

[*] In March 2006, municipal workers conducting a routine inspection of the Brooklyn Bridge's masonry foundations stumbled upon a horde of long forgotten provisions stockpiled against a nuclear attack. The trove included medical supplies, drugs used to treat shock, water drums, and an estimated 352,000 Civil Defense All-Purpose Survival Crackers. *New York Times*, March 21, 2006.

gave him what he wanted. Forced to settle for a mere survey, budgeted at $50,000, of the state's cultural resources, he did secure authorization for the embryonic council to "make recommendations for encouragement of the fine and performing arts." Even this was enough to touch off a raucous display in the state senate, where the idea of taxpayer-funded toe dancing came in for ridicule. "It was disgraceful," said Bill Ronan of the ensuing spectacle, in which the red-faced senate Democratic leader, Joe Zaretzki, dismissed administration promises of consideration for the outmaneuvered minority. So the arts council wouldn't be shoved down their throats, bellowed Zaretzki. Big deal. "They'll shove it up our ass instead." Ronan offered a more nuanced explanation of the outcome. "We traded judges for ballet dancers," he said.*

4

T HE SHEER AMOUNT of legislation demanded by the second floor irritated legislators accustomed under Rockefeller's predecessors to dealing with a single major initiative a year. Many who welcomed the product objected to the process, since the mere existence of Ronan's program associates called into question the relevance of legislative committees. The governor's habit of submitting "pre-session memorandums" effectively preempted the normal flow of legislative business. At the same time, his withdrawal from the 1960 presidential race released lawmakers in his own party from any obligation to make Rockefeller look good. Facing a potentially hostile political climate that fall, upstate Republicans in particular were eager to show their independence of the free-spending, tax-raising executive whose latest encroachments on individual choice included mandatory fallout shelters and civil rights legislation forbidding discrimination in the sale or rental of private real estate.

And this time they had a leader. For Walter Mahoney, the 1960 legislative session represented payback. Within days of Rockefeller's pullout, and in brazen defiance of Jud Morhouse and his state party apparatus, Mahoney publicly endorsed Nixon for president. Factors of personal resentment and institutional prerogative came into play, bolstered by a cold-blooded estimate of what was necessary to preserve Mahoney's senate majority and his grip on power. Aware of Rockefeller's desire to implement his vow of pay-as-you-go government a year

---

* As intended, this was the camel's nose finding a way into the tent. Within a decade, the New York State Council on the Arts was providing more than $20 million a year to underwrite seven thousand separate events and keeping some six hundred nonprofit cultural organizations afloat. In 1965, New York's program inspired creation of the National Endowment for the Arts, a Great Society initiative that, under Nixon and Ford, was administered by Nancy Hanks.

ahead of schedule, Mahoney proposed a tax cut instead. A retroactive tax cut. The tax program enacted a year before with Mahoney's last minute assistance had produced, literally, an embarrassment of riches. "Withholding was the greatest bonanza the state could have asked for," acknowledged tax commissioner Joseph Murphy. "Norm, what are you doing to me," Rockefeller told his budget director in mock horror, "here's another twenty million dollars revenue that we got that you didn't estimate."

Such largesse could not be hidden indefinitely. As a result, much of the 1960 legislative session involved a tug-of-war over the meaning of the word *surplus*. Even innocuous measures came under fire. Resentful assembly members objected to a series of highway safety measures introduced by the administration. Both houses voted to deny welfare benefits to anyone residing in the state less than a year. Conceding the move's popularity, Bob MacCrate pleaded with Rockefeller to reject the new law. "My basic pitch was, my grandfather was on welfare when he came to America, where he got a job," says MacCrate. "He responded to that." On March 22, 1960, citing New York's long immigrant tradition, Rockefeller vetoed the measure. The responsibility of preventing abuses lay with the Board of Public Welfare, said the governor. "Shortcomings in the administration of our laws must not be mistaken for shortcomings in the principles upon which our laws are based."

Eight days later, on the final night of the legislative session, Walter Mahoney got his revenge by killing legislation that would outlaw racial or religious discrimination in multiple dwellings and developments of ten or more houses. The bill didn't go as far as Rockefeller would have liked. But the very notion of the state telling private homeowners how they could and couldn't dispose of their property enraged many. Only an eleventh-hour appeal from the governor to Speaker Carlino led to the bill's passage in the assembly. The senate was a different story. Having promised his fellow lawmakers to entomb the offending statute in committee unless a majority of Republicans signified their support, Mahoney now thumbed his nose at the second floor. Rockefeller was quick to exact punishment. Judgeships are the mother's milk of politics, their desirability a rare instance of bipartisan agreement. A deal struck at the tag end of the session promised a dozen new judges for Manhattan and Brooklyn, with two Democrats joining the bench for every Republican.

A last minute display of pique by Mahoney put this cozy arrangement at risk. "Fuck the governor," muttered the senate Republican leader. "I'm the majority leader of this house. No one talked to me about this bill." Mahoney's outburst actually had less to do with violations of legislative protocol than the dismissive treatment accorded his candidate for a judicial opening. Lawmakers could assuage his fury by authorizing a thirteenth judgeship. But with time running out, a gubernatorial message of necessity was required to bring the matter to the floor before adjournment. It was almost three in the morning when counsels for the legislative majority notified Rockefeller of the unexpected snag in the senate and formally requested his assistance.

"Fuck Walter Mahoney," he told them.

Failure to obtain his civil rights legislation or the fallout shelter program cast something of a pall over Rockefeller's sophomore session in Albany. But it couldn't obscure an impressive list of administration priorities that did become law. The governor's $2 billion–plus state budget was passed virtually intact. Beyond this, Rockefeller won approval of the arts council, an acceleration in state highway construction, and creation of a Housing Finance Agency to spur investment in middle-income housing. As he prepared to face the grueling thirty-day period, Rockefeller could also take satisfaction in the state's first minimum wage law, enacted despite conservative objections to guaranteeing workers a dollar an hour. Small business gained modest tax relief, and the prospect of a general tax cut was floated, however tentatively. A conservation work camp program, part of a larger administration effort to combat juvenile delinquency, was expanded. Workers' compensation and unemployment insurance were increased. Yet another Rockefeller program offered workers displaced by automation the option of enrolling in vocational retraining courses, without sacrificing their jobless benefits.

Most satisfying was the announcement, withheld until legislators were about to leave town, that the Empire State had achieved pay-as-you-go financing in the current fiscal year. "Rigid economies" had produced $40 million in budget savings, claimed Rockefeller, almost as much as increased tax collections brought in. The rest of the state's revenue growth was attributed to an economic recovery spurred by more than $2.5 billion in private investment since Rockefeller had taken office. The improved financial picture enabled him to address another long-standing headache. Like every New York mayor before and since, Robert Wagner bitterly resented the city's status as a ward of the state, unable to set its own property, sales, or cigarette taxes without obtaining Albany's permission. During his first year in office, Rockefeller had launched a probe into city finances. Most New Yorkers yawned at the revelations of the Seymour Commission, an ostentatious probe of city finances that they wrote off as an amateurish attempt by Republicans to mine political gold from city hall malfeasance.

A more tangible example of state intrusion into municipal affairs came on March 23, 1960. Hours after Rockefeller signed a law increasing by 5 percent the state's contribution to its employee pension benefits, he marched with Wagner at the head of a Loyalty Day parade. As recounted by Ken Auletta in *The Streets Were Paved with Gold*, no one was more vocal in their approval of the governor's action than New York City police and firemen. "Atta boy, Rocky!" they shouted as their new hero strode briskly up Fifth Avenue. Wagner, anticipating the pressure on city hall by municipal unions demanding similar largesse, turned to Rockefeller and said—in his no doubt sanitized recollection— "You son of a gun, taking all the credit."

With his dumpy physique and phlegmatic bouts of uncertainty, Robert Ferdinand Wagner, Jr., was easy to underestimate. He might be mayor of New York, jeered Dick Schaap of the *Herald Tribune*, but Wagner belonged in Newark. His desire to please led Brooklyn GOP boss Johnny Crews to quip, "He's so light he could tap dance on top of a Charlotte Russe." Tom Dewey dubbed him "Solemn Bob," while Dewey's henchman Harry O'Donnell mocked Wagner for his "dynamic indecision." In truth, as each of Rockefeller's most recent predecessors could attest, Bob Wagner was not to be crossed lightly. Wagner's twelve years in office were notable for his pioneering employment of blacks and Hispanics, as well as the practice of charging municipal operating expenses, funded out of tax revenues, against capital budgets financed through the sale of bonds. Besides charting the rise of Democratic reformers and the concurrent decline of the Tammany Hall crowd, the same era produced a growing gulf between working-class New Yorkers, many pursuing their version of the American dream in the outer boroughs, and a new breed of Manhattan liberal, warmly sympathetic to the civil rights movement and its cultural offshoots.

Wagner's bobbing and weaving, his low profile and lunch bucket liberalism, made him the natural leader for a city in the throes of economic and ethnic transition. By the start of the sixties, the exodus of white middle-class New Yorkers from the city to the suburbs, the continuing migration of Puerto Ricans from their island home, and a postwar baby boom that had yet to peak left the city more dependent than ever on outside sources of revenue. It could not have been pleasant for the mayor, possessor of a storied political name in his own right, to go hat in hand to Albany. Soon he and Rockefeller were trading insults in the press. This didn't prevent them from deal making when it served their interests. According to Warren Moscow, a veteran *New York Times* journalist then working in city hall as a mayoral assistant, backdoor discussions early in 1960 produced an agreement whereby Wagner would provide sufficient Democratic support in the legislature to pass a Rockefeller-favored banking bill stymied in the previous year's session. In return, the Seymour Commission would quietly fold its tent.

In the event, enough Democrats switched their votes to enact the legislation sought by Chase and other big banks. Amid recriminations over the commission's continued existence, Moscow received an angry phone call from the governor. Rockefeller wished to straighten him out regarding a $75 million bond issue to expand state parklands. Mayor Wagner, echoing his senatorial father's trademark advice—"When in doubt, don't"—had withheld an endorsement of the measure, pending agreement on the city's share. Moscow told Rockefeller he should be talking to the mayor. "Don't horseshit me," said Nelson. "I know who's making the policy and what's more, I'll tell you, fella, if you get in my way, I'll ride you down."

Moscow reported the conversation to his boss. "Is that the first time you've had the treatment?" Wagner replied. "An arrogant son of a bitch." Wagner was not without weapons of his own. After he convinced local newspapers that the city was indeed getting the short end of the financial stick, articles documenting this injustice began to appear, accompanied by a coupon readers could cut out and mail to Governor Rockefeller in protest. It did not take long for the message to penetrate the granite walls of Albany's Capitol. On March 26, two days before he proclaimed New York's fiscal integrity restored, Rockefeller appeared with Wagner to announce a last minute settlement boosting the city's share of state funding by $40 million.*

5

H IS ATTENTION MONOPOLIZED by a balky legislature, Rockefeller had stayed close to home since his "definite and final" withdrawal statement the day after Christmas. If anything, party elders found Rockefeller *too* quiet. Twice that spring, hoping to secure an endorsement of Nixon, Eisenhower reached out to the governor by phone. Each time Rockefeller put him off, contending that such a gesture would carry more weight the closer it came to the convention. Not that the vice president had much to worry about. Fewer than three thousand New Hampshire Republicans had troubled themselves to write in the name of Nelson Rockefeller on their primary ballot. In neighboring Massachusetts, a bastion of liberal Republicanism, Nixon write-ins outnumbered those for Rockefeller twelve to one. Ironically, Nixon's string of uncontested victories earned him less favorable press coverage than Jack Kennedy received for his impressive wins over Hubert Humphrey in Wisconsin and West Virginia (the latter triumph particularly significant as it dispelled fears of Kennedy's Catholicism). On the first of May, staring at fresh polls that showed him falling

---

* Rockefeller again came to Wagner's assistance by quietly ceding to the mayor control over the revision of New York City's governing charter. This resulted in more power flowing to city hall, at the expense of the Board of Estimate and borough presidents. Among other reforms contained in the new charter, approved by voters in November 1961, was a provision giving the mayor sole power to estimate city revenues. It would come back to haunt Wagner and his fiscally profligate successors. Earlier that same year, Rockefeller overruled his own education commissioner's call for a state takeover of the city's scandal-tinged school system. As Margaret Thatcher would later observe of Mikhail Gorbachev, Rockefeller found in Wagner a man with whom he could do business.

behind Kennedy, Nixon in an off-the-record session with Washington reporters floated Rockefeller's name for vice president. Three days later he went public, noting "tremendous support" for the New Yorker to have a place on the ticket.

"Did he say what place?" Nelson shot back. His wisecrack arose out of a genuine fear that he might be drafted against his will, like Theodore Roosevelt in 1900, for a mostly ceremonial job reminiscent of his frustrating stints in appointive positions. "I am not a legislator," Rockefeller pointedly reminded the press, "and I am used to actively being responsible for administration and policy decisions." Explicit as to what he did not want, Rockefeller was less forthcoming in spelling out his objectives. Early in March, Nixon chief of staff Robert Finch approached Burdell Bixby, the veteran Dewey hand now working for Rockefeller as secretary of the New York Republican State Committee. What could his boss do to improve relations with the governor? inquired Finch. Would Rockefeller like to chair the forthcoming convention in Chicago? Perhaps he might prefer to deliver the keynote address? He certainly ought to take a prominent part in crafting the party platform. Any of these roles would put him in the limelight, said Finch.

Bixby recommended that Nixon call Rockefeller as a prelude to getting together with the governor for a private chat. The counsel went unheeded—for now—as outside events intervened to revive Rockefeller's flagging hopes. On May 1, even as Nixon turned up the heat on the vice presidency, surface-to-air missiles blasted an American U-2 spy plane piloted by Francis Gary Powers out of the sky over Sverdlovsk, twelve hundred miles inside the Soviet Union. As the ensuing crisis wrecked a long scheduled diplomatic conference in Paris and plunged superpower relations back into the deep freeze, Rockefeller seized on the incident to question the fundamental direction of U.S. foreign policy. His political advisers urged restraint, and not just in his handling of the U-2 affair. On May 12, George Hinman told Rockefeller that Nixon's strong showing in the primaries had increased his stranglehold—Hinman's word—on the Republican nomination. Criticism of Nelson's churlish attitude toward the presumptive nominee was being heard in his own backyard. Under the circumstances, claimed Hinman, refusal to accept an offer from Republican National Committee chairman Thruston Morton to address or preside over the convention "could badly aggravate the image of poor sportsmanship." (Rockefeller had suggested he might stay away from Chicago altogether, if that was the only way to avoid a vice presidential stampede.)

Sensitive to his friend's wishes, Hinman couldn't bring himself to slam the door altogether. It was just possible, he conceded, that global events, combined with Kennedy's sudden rise in the polls, might jar Republicans out of their complacency. But it was "extremely unlikely." At this point, Nelson's attention was diverted by a family crisis. On May 11, his father died in a Tucson, Arizona, hospital. At his bedside, Nelson and Laurance joined Martha Baird Rockefeller, who by isolating the old man in his final years had validated the worst suspicions of his loved ones. In keeping with tradition, Junior's cremated remains were buried next to Abby's in the family cemetery at Pocantico. His children prepared to face the future without the distant, often difficult parent whose efforts had radically transformed popular attitudes toward all Rockefellers. On the day of Junior's memorial service, as the Rockefeller men were escorted before the cameras outside Riverside Church for the obligatory group photo, Nelson reflexively stepped forward to arrange the shot and to reserve the most prominent place in the lineup for himself. "In view of the many beautiful editorials that have been written about Father," he wrote his brother John, "it would be nice if someone wrote the editors on behalf of the family expressing our appreciation." It seemed only fitting that Junior's namesake should undertake this task. No doubt Room 5600 could provide John with appropriate drafts.

6

T HE PASSING OF John D. Rockefeller, Jr., less than four months after Frank Jamieson's premature death effectively removed any restraints on Nelson's personal and political conduct. So it would be asserted after the fact, as if to explain what by conventional logic was inexplicable—his self-defeating pursuit of a nomination long since locked up by Nixon; the mortal offense given Dwight Eisenhower in the process; and the deliberate snubbing of conservative activists already preparing to fill the post-Eisenhower vacuum. More than once that spring, his Dartmouth roommate and lifelong friend, John French, thought to himself, "If Frank Jamieson were only still around, this sort of thing wouldn't have happened."

In point of fact, Nelson's aggressiveness mirrored his vulnerability. For months, a shadowy contest had been under way for control of the New York GOP. A replay of the 1958 scrimmage involving Rockefeller, Walter Mahoney, and Len Hall, it pitted restive upstate conservatives against the governor whose charm and electability had proven unexpectedly seductive. With Nixon planning to visit Mahoney's Buffalo and other upstate cities in mid-May, George Hinman sensed a revolt in the making. "There is a real and imminent danger that Mahoney will capitalize on the present situation," he warned Rockefeller. "It is made to order for him." Convinced the senate majority leader was angling for the vice presidential nomination spurned by Rockefeller, Hinman feared that Mahoney might lead thirty or more delegates into Nixon's corner. Such a mass defection would cripple Rockefeller's hold over the state party and almost certainly destroy any national ambitions he might harbor.

Recognizing something had to be done, fast, to freeze the New York delegation in place, Jud Morhouse convened an emergency meeting of all county chairmen in Albany. Rockefeller broadly hinted at his newfound openness to a draft. Moreover, said the governor, he had decided to attend the convention after all—at the head of an uncommitted delegation. Simultaneously, Hinman met with Ken Keating in Washington, where he played on the freshman senator's vanity by proposing him as New York's candidate for the vice presidency. Keating, "overjoyed" at the thought, promised to stick with Rockefeller "1000 percent. . . . He volunteered he'd be with us even if we wanted Goldwater!" Hinman wrote afterward. The rebellion was suppressed, though for how long no one could say. Hinman, his sights fixed on future possibilities, urged Rockefeller to take a conciliatory stance. "By frankness, realism and magnanimity," he asserted on May 20, "I believe you can win understanding and sympathy for the tough position we have been staking out and in doing so help yourself with the delegates—in fact open the door again for really sympathetic consideration." To this memo Hinman attached two and a half pages of talking points, heaping praise on Nixon's performance as vice president and downplaying Rockefeller's chances for the nomination as "a standby possibility only."

Rockefeller had other ideas. Over the Memorial Day weekend, he retreated to Pocantico with Emmet Hughes. Even Hughes, the putative bomb thrower who yielded to no one in his contempt for Richard Nixon, was stunned by what he heard. Nelson wanted a statement of "quite explicit challenge" to Nixon on a wide range of issues, to be followed by a trio of major policy addresses covering defense, foreign affairs, and domestic issues. Like Hinman, his temperamental opposite, Hughes pressed Nelson to consider "the 1964 argument." This presumed Nixon's defeat in the fall, Rockefeller's rapid emergence thereafter as party leader, and "a much more conservative line of conduct than we are now contemplating." Unable to shake his doubts, Hughes advised the governor to get a second opinion from the prudent Hinman. On reading the inflammatory document prepared by Hughes, Hinman told Rockefeller that the party would never forgive him.

"That's irrelevant," said Nelson. June 8 was set as the release date for his declaration of conscience.

Rockefeller spent that morning at the White House. Over breakfast with the president, he limited himself to a broad reiteration of concerns as old as the Rockefeller reports. Consequently Eisenhower was as surprised as anyone, and angrier than most, when Nelson later in the day unleashed his twenty-seven-hundred-word jeremiad. "We have come to a time that calls for plain talk," it began. What followed more than lived up to this premise. Rockefeller accused the Democratic opposition, bitterly divided over civil rights, of offering voters nothing better than "worn answers from the past." This made all the greater his own party's obligation to raise the nation's sights as well as its standard of living.

"I cannot pretend to believe that the Republican Party has fully met this duty," said Rockefeller. He faulted "the leading Republican candidate for the Presidential nomination" for not spelling out his program in advance of the convention, insisting, "We cannot, as a nation or as a party . . . march to meet the future with a banner aloft whose emblem is a question mark." Seemingly oblivious to the feelings of the old soldier in the White House, Rockefeller asserted that "our position in the world is dramatically weaker today than fifteen years ago, at the end of World War II." He called for an immediate $3 billion increase in defense spending, $500 million for a crash program of civil defense, and the total reorganization of a complacent military establishment. His saber rattling reflected a growing unease among Americans, who believed by a 47 to 33 percent margin that their country trailed the Soviet Union in nuclear missiles. Rockefeller questioned the administration's preparations for disarmament talks in Geneva.

He didn't limit his criticism to national security. On the domestic front, he decried foot-dragging on the enforcement of the Supreme Court's school desegregation rulings. The justices had spoken of "all deliberate speed," Rockefeller noted. "The deliberateness must not be sabotage." Washington should be more aggressive in funding school construction and providing special educational assistance to needy areas. It should treat medical care for the elderly as a national priority, financed through the existing Social Security system and not the cumbersome, fiscally unsound subsidies proposed by the White House. In all these areas, implied Rockefeller, Nixon had failed to articulate a distinctive course for the sixties. "The path of great leadership does not lie along the top of a fence," he proclaimed in a final burst of Hughesian fireworks. "It climbs heights. It speaks truths."

Disbelieving allies scratched their heads. To the New York Herald Tribune, flagship of the Eastern Establishment, Rockefeller's "buckshot indictment" of Nixon was "quite indefensible." Henceforth, contended Fletcher Knebel in the New York Journal-American, the letters GOP should stand for Grand Old Patricide. Clearly Emmet Hughes had outdone himself, his sledgehammer rhetoric sure to be exploited by Democrats all the way to November. Yet however soaring his phrases, the logic behind them was flawed. For where else had Rockefeller been the past five months but atop a fence, calculating his chances for a nomination that, even now, he refused to pursue openly? On June 8, he tossed into the ring his ideas, but not his hat. As Hughes predicted, Nixon smoothly evaded any public confrontation. Professing mild astonishment that his long public record could be seen as anything but an open book, the vice president offered to submit to a televised grilling from Rockefeller if that would clarify things (away from the cameras, Nixon was less measured, remarking that Rockefeller deserved "a good swift kick"). Eisenhower's reaction was nearly as caustic. "I see the fine hand of Emmet in this," he muttered.

On June 9, Rockefeller telephoned the White House with a surreal request of the president whose accomplishments he had trashed a day earlier. He wanted Eisenhower's opinion, said Nelson. Should he become an active candidate? Ike waited two days to return the call. Dryly noting that the governor had gone considerably further in his public statement than in their Oval Office conversation, Eisenhower acknowledged Rockefeller's strong feelings on the subject of national defense. He also encouraged him to couch any future comments on the subject in "positive, realistic terms rather than in terms of personal criticism." As for openly contesting the nomination, the president feared that his entry into the fray now would subject Rockefeller to derision as "off again, on again, gone again, Finnegan." While no one could object to having Nelson's name placed before the convention, Ike considered his prospects of victory "very remote." Warming to the subject, Eisenhower warned Nelson against getting "too much at cross purposes with the President" and thereby damaging his political future. Were Nixon to lose in the fall, Rockefeller would surely be a leading prospect for 1964. All the more reason, then, for him to avoid the status of "a lone wolfer—à La Follette." There was nothing wrong with cultivating independent voters, said Ike, but not at the expense of the party he hoped to lead.

One other thing, Eisenhower interjected.

"Don't let anyone else write your speeches."

Long after this exchange, the target of Eisenhower's wrath attempted to put Rockefeller's quixotic behavior into perspective. "Nelson felt he could be the conscience of the Republican Party," contended Emmet Hughes. "It was not an effort to get the nomination by the back door, or destroy Nixon. It was more in the context of the guy presiding over the Rockefeller panel reports . . . the critic . . . the admonisher . . . a neo-Churchillian role, warning the party and the country that things were not as rosy as they seemed." In line with this reasoning, Rockefeller over the next six weeks unleashed a string of position papers, in Teddy White's estimation "one of the most remarkable collections of political documents in American campaign history." As detailed as they were comprehensive, these endorsed government-funded health care for the aged; economic stimulus through targeted tax cuts, accelerated depreciation, and an end to featherbedding in the workplace; federal aid to education, including scholarships for the ablest undergraduate students, to be funded on a matching basis by Washington and the states; government reorganization; and a strong commitment to civil and voting rights for every American, regardless of color.

In the single most radical proposal made by any candidate that year, Rockefeller contended that the nation-state was becoming obsolete. In its place, and as a counter to the Soviet bloc, he advocated a North Atlantic Confederation, with a common market, joint defense, and coordinated programs of assistance to underdeveloped parts of the globe. Rockefeller would establish a similar fraternity of nations in the Western Hemisphere to promote agrarian reform, encourage industrialization, lower trade barriers—even inaugurate "an inter-American kind of FHA for low cost housing." Estimating his chances of being nominated at one in ten, Rockefeller left it to others to improve those odds. On June 16, George Hinman met in New York with Bill Brinton, a young San Francisco lawyer and organizer of California's first Citizens for Rockefeller chapter. His candidate's withdrawal in December had done nothing to dull Brinton's commitment, and he was far from alone in his enthusiasm; amid the renewed interest generated by Rockefeller's quasi campaign, draft committees sprang to life in at least twenty states. They shared a common strategy: to convince Republican delegates that Nixon couldn't win in November and that Nelson Rockefeller could. Since Rockefeller had skipped the primaries, his advocates had no recourse but to the polls—specifically, a clutch of Rockefeller-financed surveys that showed Nixon losing to Kennedy in five of the nation's largest swing states (by a 49 to 28 percent margin in New York alone).

Technically, it wasn't Rockefeller money that paid for Brinton's newspaper ad blitz in twenty-one states or an elaborate command post in Chicago's Conrad Hilton Hotel. The funds were obtained from a list of names provided to Brinton by George Hinman. With a start-up loan from the Bank of San Francisco, also secured through Rockefeller contacts, the National Citizens Committee for Rockefeller was in business. In three days Brinton's print ads generated forty thousand replies, a response far outstripping expectations. Television time was purchased for a nationwide appeal on the eve of the convention. Rockefeller supporters, their numbers swelled by journalists spoiling for a fight, fantasized a repeat of Wendell Willkie's 1940 convention—a Frank Capra–esque uprising in which wildly cheering galleries combined with leading media outlets to produce the nomination of a rank outsider. But whereas Willkie may have been the unlikeliest of candidates, at least he *was* a candidate. It is hard to fathom precisely what Rockefeller had in mind, other than waiting, like Mr. Micawber, for something to turn up.

"I have to get my hands on the decision-making apparatus," Nelson told Teddy White early in July. "I knew there would never be a draft," he later acknowledged, "but I had to do something to make them listen to me." Attention shifted to the Republican platform committee chaired by Illinois's Charles Percy, another colleague from the Special Studies Project. On July 7, Percy flew to New York, where he spent three hours with Rockefeller in a line-by-line review of the draft platform. Two days later, Rockefeller dispatched a lengthy memorandum to Percy, taking issue with his committee's handiwork on foreign policy, defense, arms control, education, health care, and civil rights. On Monday, July 18, the governor shared his concerns with the 103 members of the platform committee in Chicago. His polite reception was in stark contrast with the whistling, chanting, table-pounding ardor the group showed Arizona's Barry Goldwater and his message of undiluted conservatism.

Next door to the hotel where committee members met, the marquee of the Blackstone Theatre proclaimed: "Pick a Winner—Draft Rockefeller." Few believed the claims of Bill Brinton and his youthful insurgents to have 275 first-ballot votes for the New York governor. Even as Rockefeller remained in Albany, an advance guard of New York operatives took over an entire wing of Chicago's Sheraton Towers Hotel. Malcolm Wilson and Joe Carlino looked out for Rockefeller interests on the platform committee, while back at the Sheraton, Wilson periodically joined George Hinman, Bill Ronan, Rod Perkins, and other loyalists in greeting a thin but steady stream of political leaders visiting their penthouse suite. According to Wilson, nearly all mouthed some variation of the same lament: "My God, isn't it awful. We'd like to vote for Nelson Rockefeller, but we have given a commitment." Many bemoaned, with varying degrees of conviction, the governor's withdrawal from the race seven months earlier.

Nonsense, concluded George Hinman. There may have been some delegates who adhered to the Wilson scenario. "But there weren't many. And I've always wondered where they were when we were looking for them in '59, before the convention. You couldn't find them with a search warrant."

7

A S THE WEEK unfolded, with no evidence the platform committee was moving his way—especially on the signature issues of national defense and civil rights—Rockefeller became ensnared in a web of his own making. Combative as ever, on the morning of Friday, July 22, he lobbed yet another shell from his Albany redoubt. His threat of a floor fight brought an immediate response, not from the platform writers but from the man expecting to run on their handiwork. "I'm always willing to take a chance," Richard Nixon once remarked. "I think that has been the hallmark of my career." This reliance on intuition, as opposed to the clinical empiricism of Rockefeller's experts and pollsters, made Nixon more of a risk taker than his rival. Nothing better illustrated their temperamental differences than the phone call Nixon placed that Friday afternoon to former attorney general Herb Brownell, in which he suggested a meeting between him and Rockefeller on the neutral ground of Brownell's Manhattan home. Brownell immediately passed the request to Rockefeller, who delayed any response until he could discuss the Nixon overture with his advisers. Emmet Hughes in particular raised objections, resulting in terms of engagement that were almost humiliatingly one-sided. The vice president must personally solicit any meeting with Rockefeller, in whose Fifth Avenue apartment the encounter would take place. In addition, the timing and content of any news release describing what transpired between the two men was reserved for the Rockefeller press office.

"Tell Dick to call me," Rockefeller informed Brownell.

Moments later, the phone rang in the governor's office at Fifty-fifth Street. "Nelson," said the familiar voice on the other end of the line, "I want to go all the way with you on defense and foreign policy. You've got me off the hook." Presumably this was Nixon's way of threading the needle between unquestioning adherence to the Eisenhower record and the independence required of any vice president hoping to establish his own identity. Tactics aside, Nixon's deference to his once and future rival owed as much to personal instinct as to political calculation. "Nixon feared Rockefeller's power," claims John Sears, who would oversee Nixon's 1968 bid for his party's nomination. "In 1960, remember, it was still a fairly liberal party seemingly ruled by the Eastern Establishment. Nixon wasn't part of the establishment . . . of which Rockefeller was the embodiment."

Nixon didn't know his own strength. Without informing his staff, accompanied only by military aide Don Hughes and a Secret Service agent, the vice president of the United States boarded a late afternoon Eastern Airlines flight for New York. Nixon arrived at Rockefeller's residence a few minutes after seven thirty p.m. For the next hour or so, he and Nelson reminisced about their Washington experiences over lamb chops, corn on the cob, and canned peas. Following dinner, Nixon brought up the vice presidency, his argument bolstered by the recent nomination of Texas senator Lyndon Johnson to run with Kennedy. By diminishing GOP prospects in the South, Johnson's selection increased the pressure on Nixon to win northern industrial states such as New York, Pennsylvania, Michigan, and Ohio. Campaign polling data showed that Rockefeller's inclusion on the Republican ticket added two points, a potentially critical margin in a contest everyone expected to go down to the wire. (Nelson, more than slightly miffed, remembered it as three points.)

According to Henry Kissinger, who presumably got it directly from Rockefeller, Nixon sweetened his offer by promising Nelson control over foreign policy

as well as all New York State patronage in the event of their election.* Rockefeller turned him down anyway, telling Nixon that he wasn't designed to be
standby equipment—a position the current vice president of all people might
find crassly insensitive. Around ten o'clock the two men took up the platform,
deconstructing Rockefeller's ideas as committed to paper by his favorite wordsmith. Emmet Hughes, dictating over an open telephone line from Chicago,
could barely restrain himself. "We are sitting here with a pair of 3's," he gloated,
"and acting like we had three aces." Whether, as some believed, Nixon hoped
to entice Rockefeller to change his mind on the vice presidency by yielding to
him as much of the platform as he did will probably never be known. For the
most part, the two men found their differences easily reconciled. Nixon accepted Rockefeller's regional confederations, while Nelson settled for imprecise language on the rate of economic growth and the best approach to funding
a federal program of medical care for elderly Americans. Nixon voiced no objection to Rockefeller's tough civil rights plank, with its explicit praise for young
demonstrators whose sit-ins at southern lunch counters reserved exclusively for
whites formed the vanguard of a growing movement to desegregate the region.

The only real snag of the evening involved the defense budget. According to
Rockefeller, "Dick gagged . . . on that one." Small wonder. The vice president
knew better than anyone how close he was sailing to the wind of presidential
repudiation. In *Six Crises*, Nixon would make a lawyerly distinction between
advocating "new or stepped-up programs for the future" and the slightest criticism of existing administration policies. After prolonged discussion, Rockefeller offered to drop the specific figure of $3.5 billion, or 9 percent, for which he
had argued strenuously all year. In compensation, Rockefeller/Hughes defined
the preparedness issue in words sure to infuriate Dwight Eisenhower. "There
must be no ceiling on America's security," thundered the final communi-
qué—as if Ike in his tireless pursuit of a balanced budget had neglected the
looming Soviet menace.

At midnight, a call went out from 810 Fifth Avenue to Charles Percy in his
Chicago hotel room. For the next three hours, interrupted around one o'clock
when a Chicago switchboard operator abruptly went home, the chairman of a
suddenly irrelevant platform committee was part of a four-way conversation
involving Nixon, Rockefeller, and Emmet Hughes. By the time it ended, fourteen points of agreement had been hammered out, half of them dealing with
national defense. At three thirty a.m., eight hours after he stepped off the eleva-

---

* The Kissinger account is valuable chiefly as evidence of Nelson's tendency to hear what he
wanted to. It strains credulity to think Nixon, with his consuming interest in foreign affairs,
would cede the subject to his vice president. More believable is Kissinger's characterization of
Rockefeller's feeling toward the Republican nominee for president: "He *loathes* Nixon." Arthur
M. Schlesinger, Jr., *Journals: 1952–2000* (New York: Penguin Press, 2007), 84.

tor and into Rockefeller's apartment, a bleary-eyed Nixon left for the airport and a flight back to Washington. He was still in the air when Bob McManus put out a predawn press release announcing what journalists instantly dubbed "the Treaty of Fifth Avenue." Vice presidential press secretary Herb Klein learned about the meeting from columnist James Reston, to whom Rockefeller had slipped advance word—early enough to make the morning edition that greeted a vacationing Eisenhower in Newport, Rhode Island.

Publicly, Ike maintained an ominous silence. In private, he accused Rockefeller of "personal treachery." At his direction, Jim Hagerty called the hapless Percy in Chicago and informed him that the revised defense plank was unacceptable to the White House. PACT OPENS WAY FOR PARTY AMITY, headlined *The New York Times* for July 23. Rarely had instant analysis been so wide of the mark. The *Chicago Tribune* more nearly captured the mood among delegates with an editorial entitled, "Grant Surrenders to Lee." Members of the platform committee wept on learning of what Barry Goldwater denounced as "the Munich of the Republican Party," dictated by "a spokesman for the ultra-liberals." Five states refused to make their allotted contributions to the party's finance committee. While Goldwater talked of floor fights, hard-shell conservatives talked about nominating Goldwater from the floor of the International Amphitheater. Calling the Treaty of Fifth Avenue "a damned sellout," Texas delegation chairman Thad Hutcheson invited his fellow southerners to join in resistance to the proposed civil rights plank.

Not all reaction was so harshly negative. Kentucky senator John Sherman Cooper, chairman of the platform subcommittee on foreign relations, pronounced the Nixon-Rockefeller agreement the best thing that could have happened to the Republican Party. Tom Dewey said it would be helpful to the party's prospects in November. *Time* praised Nixon's "brilliant timing and tactics" in using the Rockefeller challenge to position himself as a candidate of change. But these voices were scarcely audible above the cries of betrayal heard wherever disbelieving Republican delegates gathered that Saturday morning. By the time an ebullient Rockefeller flew into town, to be met by Al Peters and his Windy City Marching Band, along with 250 cheering partisans—most, it was noted, too young to vote—he was the target of growing anger and resentment. What had seemed, just hours earlier, a stroke of tactical genius, extricating him from an untenable position in his own backyard, was beginning to look like a strategic disaster, branding Rockefeller as a spoilsport who refused to play the game by any rules but his own.

"Both Nelson and I were quite shortsighted at the time," Emmet Hughes conceded in a 1980 interview. "A lot of the national press was astonished that Nelson Rockefeller had the leverage to force the fourteen points. But if he needed to do anything to alienate the right wing, that was it. It was a momentary triumph for which he paid a high price." It was worse than that. Had Rockefeller only waited a day, he could have had a defense plank to his liking. According to columnist Joseph Alsop, who related the story in his memoir, *"I've Seen the Best of It,"* both Secretary of State Christian Herter and Defense Secretary Thomas Gates had tracked Eisenhower to the Newport Country Club and convinced a reluctant president that a $4 billion increase in defense spending was needed to correct any Soviet misapprehensions about American resolve. Rather than announce this on the spot, Herter, to his lasting regret, asked for a few days to staff it out. Eisenhower agreed. Then came the Treaty of Fifth Avenue and Nixon's seeming repudiation of his military stewardship. Livid, Ike declared the deal was off. Any call for increased defense spending now would be seen as a surrender to Rockefeller. And Dwight Eisenhower wasn't in the habit of surrendering to anyone.*

Taking a cue from Ike, on Saturday night the platform committee reaffirmed its sovereignty by publishing its original draft and rejecting the Rockefeller-Nixon civil rights plank calling for "aggressive action" to eliminate discrimination in voting, housing, education, and jobs. The next day, Rockefeller carried the fight to the Liberty Baptist Church on Chicago's South Side, where he was introduced by NAACP executive secretary Roy Wilkins as the man "who made a backbone plank out of a spaghetti plank." Nearly six thousand onlookers, their numbers spilling out onto the sidewalks, heard Rockefeller say he welcomed a fight over "the great and burning issue" of their times. Thirty-three times the crowd interrupted him with applause. A few miles away, Bill Brinton and his student brigades circulated broadsides demanding a convention, not a coronation, and warning that Nixon's nomination would drag down Republican candidates across the board.

Their pleas did not go entirely unheard. A televised appeal over the weekend touched a raw nerve among many independent voters, as well as Republicans eager for their own New Frontier. Within twenty-four hours, more than a quarter million pieces of pro-Rockefeller mail flooded Chicago hotels. Switchboards became clogged with incoming calls. By midweek, more than a million letters and telegrams had arrived, most from outsiders earnestly pleading with insiders to defy expectations and choose in 1960 a Republican nominee as unorthodox as the one their fathers had raised up in 1940. Journalists eager for a story seized on this alternative to an otherwise cut-and-dried narrative. But it was never more than a sideshow to the main action, as Nixon moved with considerable skill to establish his mastery over the party and its platform. Staring down bitter opposition from conservatives, the vice president got the civil rights plank he

---

* "If that increase had gone through, we would have another president of the United States." So President-elect John F. Kennedy told Alsop following his narrow victory that fall.

wanted, though not before cashing in what one aide frankly acknowledged was "every political IOU we held in the country." Though disappointed that it failed to mention the lunch counter sit-ins, Rockefeller recognized the revised plank for what it was—the strongest on the subject ever adopted by a Republican convention.

Even more sensitive was the defense plank. In the end, Republicans duly pledged themselves to a military posture "superior to all foes." By changing two words in the Rockefeller-Nixon formulation, they turned admonishment to boast, announcing, "There *is* no price ceiling on America's security." Also given short shrift: Nelson's hemispheric confederations, which were judged entirely too radical to pass muster with the ideological descendants of Robert Taft and John Bricker. From his Hyannis Port summer home, happy to exploit GOP divisions, Jack Kennedy complimented Rockefeller for getting a majority of Republicans to adopt his views. "Progress is not their business," said JFK. "He is moving them ahead." With the platform at last settled, Rockefeller formally endorsed Nixon before a closed-door session of the New York delegation on Tuesday, July 26. He almost missed his big moment, as a million Chicagoans turned out to cheer Dwight Eisenhower's victory lap from Meigs Field to the Sheraton Blackstone. Tons of confetti darkened the skies, burying the Loop in an out-of-season blizzard.*

At the Sheraton Towers, meanwhile, Ken Riland was doing a slow burn. Nelson, closeted in his suite with a female staffer, appeared in no hurry to emerge. Only Riland in his immediate entourage had the nerve to pound his fist on the door and announce in a loud voice that they had exactly thirty seconds to get moving "or we're going to get caught in the Eisenhower parade." Moments later, the door opened; Rockefeller and his companion made a dash for the governor's car. The offending stranger wound up sitting in Riland's lap. "Look," he snapped, "if this ever happens again I'm going to see you're shipped the hell home. I don't give a damn who you are."

Thus was Ken Riland introduced to Happy Murphy.

---

* Not every member of the Rockefeller family was happy with the belated endorsement. "Nelson has just come into the room wearing a big Nixon button," Tod informed a friend, "and I could throw up." Drew Pearson diary, July 25, 1960.

Sixteen
LOSS AND RENEWAL

A sweet boy. He was a very sweet boy.

—NELSON A. ROCKEFELLER on his missing son, Michael, November 1961

1

VISITING SEAL HARBOR during the third week of August 1960, Henry Kissinger found his patron in uncharacteristically low spirits. A month after the convention that paired Nixon and UN ambassador Henry Cabot Lodge, Jr., culminating in Nelson's famously maladroit introduction of Richard E. Nixon, Rockefeller had yet to shake his disappointment. This did not prevent him from delivering more than two hundred speeches in the ensuing campaign or visiting eight states at the behest of the national party. With local polls predicting a Kennedy sweep of New York by a million votes, Rockefeller devoted much of October to a rescue mission for endangered Republican legislators upstate and in the New York City suburbs. His biggest applause lines had little to do with the national ticket. Addressing one Wall Street rally, the governor evoked roars of approval by revealing that he was contemplating a 10 percent rebate on state taxes. (Later that day, Rockefeller was approached, unsuccessfully, by a panhandler at Herald Square. "That's funny," the man said afterward. "I asked him for a handout, and you know what he promised me? A tax cut.")

Privately, Rockefeller was quick to blame Nixon for losing the election before the first ballots were cast. In an off-the-record conversation with reporter Bob Novak, he faulted the vice president for chasing unattainable southern electoral votes at the expense of northern industrial states that might yet be won by reaching out to urban and African American voters. (Barry Goldwater voiced similar frustration in drawing exactly the opposite conclusion, complaining to Novak that Nixon wasted his time in courting irredeemably Democratic black voters instead of the conservative—read:

segregationist—South.)* Tenuous at best, Republican unity barely survived the excruciatingly long night of November 8 that ended in a Kennedy victory by the slimmest of margins. Nelson let a week pass before conveying his regrets to the defeated candidate. "I honestly thought that the upsurge of the final weeks would carry New York into the victory column," he told Nixon. Whether he believed this is debatable. Meanwhile, the very closeness of the contest encouraged a search for scapegoats, with *The Wall Street Journal* and *New York Daily News* pointing the finger of blame at Rockefeller. Their criticism quickly hardened into a conservative article of faith: his attention fixed on 1964, Nelson had lent the Nixon-Lodge ticket only perfunctory support. Even his success in staving off a Democratic takeover of the New York State Legislature was perversely cited as evidence of what Rockefeller might have achieved through more vigorous barnstorming on Nixon's behalf.

His efforts to mediate a strike by New York City tugboat operators prevented Rockefeller from attending the Kennedy inauguration on January 20, 1961. In his message of support to the new president, he singled out for praise Kennedy's eloquent—and militant—inaugural address. JFK responded three days later. "I need hardly tell you that I shall always welcome your advice and criticism as we attempt to reach our common objectives in foreign affairs," he told Nelson. Rockefeller was to interpret this invitation liberally. Indeed, it was only with considerable difficulty that his advisers had dissuaded Nelson from turning a postelection note of congratulations to the president-elect into a full-scale pitch for his latest scheme to provide health insurance to the elderly. Inevitably, the subject found its way into Rockefeller's January 4 address to the New York Legislature. By pumping an additional $40 million into the (pre-Medicare) system designed for the "medically indigent," Rockefeller more than doubled the number of elderly poor receiving medical care. At the same time, he shrewdly appealed to middle-class New Yorkers by relaxing the despised means test that forced some applicants for assistance to assign their property over to the state in case of prolonged illness.

His rhetoric about a "pioneer state" and history's judgment on their deliberations was as lofty as ever, but it was Rockefeller's talk of "partnership government" that signified a major course correction by a politician whose attention was focused squarely on reelection. Chastened by events of the previous year,

---

* While Rockefeller lamented Nixon's highly symbolic appearance at South Carolina's statehouse, a shrine for unreconstructed segregationists, Goldwater took offense at vice presidential candidate Lodge's vow to include a Negro cabinet member in any Nixon administration. Nixon drew some of his largest, most frenzied crowds of the campaign in southern cities—85,000 in Memphis, 150,000 in Atlanta. Although an unreliable harbinger of his showing in November, the throngs supplied a powerful incentive to deemphasize the liberal civil rights plank in the Republican platform.

he delayed any renewed push for fallout shelters until the Kennedy administration signaled its civil defense intentions. He adopted an incremental approach to government reorganization in place of a sweeping—and, some thought, punitive—overhaul crafted earlier by Bill Ronan. Rockefeller became notably more accessible to individual legislators and the press. That he hadn't lost his appetite for programming on a grand scale was evidenced by a $1 billion highway construction program, accelerating work on the 175-mile Albany–Canada Northway and on the Long Island Expressway snaking eighty miles east from Queens.

Lawmakers of both parties welcomed a 10 percent rebate on state income taxes. When combined with the abolition of taxes on cigars and other tobacco products, and a series of tax breaks designed to lower the cost of doing business in New York, the gesture took much of the sting out of Rockefeller's earlier tax increases. Enough of these remained in effect to support a record budget and underwrite fresh initiatives such as the Job Development Authority, a $100 million public investment bank that made loans to nearly seventy local nonprofit development corporations in economically depressed parts of the state. Simultaneously, the governor's Office for Regional Development, working off a previously identified stockpile of building projects, targeted capital construction funds to areas of persistent joblessness.

Rockefeller Republicanism stressed compassion as well as competence. Here the governor's belated truce with Walter Mahoney paid off in ways that made both men look good. In exchange for tightening administrative enforcement, Rockefeller avoided any formal residency requirement for welfare recipients. Likewise, by accepting some minor modifications demanded by Mahoney and his caucus, Rockefeller secured passage of the Metcalf-Baker Law, banning discrimination in most private housing and commercial space and prohibiting discriminatory practices by real estate brokers and lending institutions. Having outlawed racial and religious bias, as of July 1961 the Rockefeller administration broadened protections for workers discriminated against on account of age. Three decades before Congress enacted the Americans with Disabilities Act, Rockefeller's New York mandated handicapped accessibility in all state buildings.

By his third year in office, Rockefeller had learned to accept half a legislative loaf, secure in the knowledge that programs, once established, took on a life of their own. This was especially true of those, such as the New York State Council on the Arts, that paid unexpected electoral dividends to their sponsors. Originally authorized as a mere survey of New York's cultural offerings, the council rapidly grew into a thriving grant-making entity under the chairmanship of Buffalo banker and world-class art collector Seymour "Shorty" Knox. The appointment of Knox, like those of his celebrity cohorts Helen Hayes, Richard

Rodgers, and publisher Cass Canfield, was no accident. His upstate residence and hardheaded fiscal reputation were intended to reassure skeptics. ("If Shorty Knox says it's OK," explained one of his successors, "it must be OK.") The artists did the rest, as the New York City Ballet performed in Utica and eighteen other venues; residents of the sleepy Hudson Valley community of Troy turned out en masse for Leonard Bernstein and his New York Philharmonic; and thousands of first-time theatergoers were introduced to Shakespeare and Shaw.

Rockefeller planted other seeds in 1961, some requiring years to bear fruit. Among the thirteen hundred pieces of legislation that awaited his signature that spring was a thorough review of the state's criminal code, precursor to repeal of the death penalty. In the predawn of environmentalism, he pushed through stringent restrictions on landscape-defacing billboards. A Temporary State Commission on the Capital City, chaired by Lieutenant Governor Malcolm Wilson, was sold to lawmakers as a comprehensive review of Albany's housing, parking, and employment needs. That it might lead to the total reconstruction of downtown, displacing more than three thousand households in the process, was unimaginable anywhere but the second floor of the Capitol. By his own acknowledgment, few things gave Rockefeller more pleasure than "to see the dirt fly." Rare indeed was the occasion when he let jurisdictional boundaries get in the way of his urge to build. Take Lincoln Center for the Performing Arts, the vast cultural complex then rising atop the rubble of a Manhattan neighborhood featured in the film version of *West Side Story*. His brother John spearheaded the project, in which old friends like Lincoln Kirstein and Philip Johnson were also heavily engaged.

"Kirstein came and had lunch with him one day in the very early sixties," recalls Edward Kresky, a program associate and former deputy to Bill Ronan in the constitutional revision effort. "The World's Fair was in the news and he made a commitment to them about the state's contribution to the World's Fair." Creatively interpreted, this meant that New York taxpayers were on the hook to the tune of $15 million for a theater, designed by Philip Johnson for George Balanchine and his New York City Ballet, as part of Lincoln Center.

Kresky was perplexed. "Governor," he said, "the World's Fair is in Queens, and this here is on the West Side."

"I know where Queens is," Rockefeller replied with hooded eyes. "I know where the World's Fair is, and I know where this theater is going. Just write it up."

He wasn't through with the fair. Johnson received a second commission from his friend in Albany, this one for a New York State Pavilion showcasing the works of Andy Warhol and other contemporary artists. Rockefeller made a single stipulation to Johnson: New York's trio of towers soaring high above Flushing Meadows must be taller than any other structure on the site.

2

REPORTERS BEGAN FILING stories on "the New Rocky," a political realist converted by harsh experience to the art of compromise. Nowhere did this newfound flexibility have more profound consequences than on the college campus. Influenced by his own struggles in the classroom, Rockefeller the dyslexic revered education as a blind man does sight. As a candidate for governor, he vowed renewed support for the State University of New York (SUNY)—in truth hardly a university at all, but an undistinguished jumble of twenty-nine teachers colleges, agricultural schools, technical institutes, and medical schools, the entire underfunded system serving thirty-nine thousand students. Only one institution of the lot, Binghamton's Harpur College, bestowed a liberal arts degree.

Such tokens of academic legitimacy were reserved for New York's 138 private colleges, as mandated by the Board of Regents. When Congress in 1862 passed the Morrill Land-Grant Act, it played midwife to state universities throughout the North and West. A notable exception was New York, whose legislators allocated their portion of Morrill funding to a newly chartered private institution named for state senator Ezra Cornell. By the mid–twentieth century, the Empire State, a trailblazer in so many fields, ranked forty-seventh out of forty-eight states in its support of higher education. In the spring of 1948, persuaded that his state's private colleges did not always welcome black, Jewish, or Catholic students into their ranks, Governor Thomas Dewey chartered SUNY despite opposition from the Board of Regents. Dewey salted the wound by insisting that the new university have its own board of trustees, answerable to him and his successors. Simultaneously, the state initiated a modest program of financial aid to New York City's municipal colleges, long a bastion of educational opportunity for ambitious, if impoverished, immigrants and their offspring.

There things stood for the next decade, as SUNY offered mostly old wine in hastily relabeled bottles. A state university with minimal state involvement, lacking a flagship campus or influential alumni, SUNY was ill-equipped to challenge the existing private school hammerlock, much less grow out of its officially enforced mediocrity. Rockefeller's election in 1958 raised hopes that the poor sister might yet become Cinderella, with the new governor the prince of her dreams. It certainly didn't hurt that Frank Moore, Nelson's original tutor in state government, chaired the Board of Regents. In his inaugural address, Rockefeller made passing reference to a rapidly growing college population but otherwise withheld substantive comment on a recently passed $250 million bond issue earmarked for SUNY's enhancement. In his first budget, the governor did include funding for eleven gymnasiums across the system. "And the legislature, in a desire to show they were economy minded, knocked out ten," he later reflected. The sole survivor was located in the district of the senate finance committee chairman. The message was not lost on Rockefeller.

In December 1959, he made his move. Mindful of skyrocketing enrollment figures, and fearing a brain drain to other states, Rockefeller launched a comprehensive examination of higher education in New York, part of a consensus-building effort radically unlike his damn-the-torpedoes campaign to require fallout shelters of every New Yorker. Hoping to defuse private school opposition before it could gain traction, Rockefeller enlisted the regents as partners in the review, which was chaired by Ford Foundation president Henry Heald. In their report, Heald and his colleagues predicted the state's current college enrollment of four hundred thousand would double by 1970 and likely triple by 1985. Were every private school in New York to realize its expansionary goals, it would still leave a shortfall of at least eighty-six thousand places by the end of the decade. Hewing closely to Heald's recommendations, in a special message to the legislature at the end of January 1961 Rockefeller called for two new graduate centers, one on Long Island and the other upstate; a broadened liberal arts curriculum in the existing colleges of education; a clutch of new two-year community colleges; and establishment of a consolidated City University of New York (CUNY). Equally important, he proposed to give SUNY trustees unprecedented latitude over tuition and other administrative issues.

Opening the door to tuition charges caused the governor to be hung in effigy on some campuses—CUNY would remain tuition-free until New York City's fiscal meltdown in 1976—but Rockefeller insisted that such revenues were needed to help service the cost of a massive building program. Even as he put finishing touches on his legislative package, Rockefeller was busy orchestrating the rollout of SUNY's expansion plans for maximum political advantage. Days before his speech to lawmakers, residents of Rochester, Syracuse, and several upstate counties learned of new community colleges in their future. Within the shadow of the Capitol itself, the Rockefeller administration laid claim to the Albany Country Club, its verdant acreage destined for reuse as a strikingly modernistic campus complex designed by Edward Durrell Stone. Rockefeller and his staff devoted the first weeks of January 1961 to crafting a scholarship and loan program generous enough to buy off the state's private colleges and universities while evading New York's ban on aid to religious or denominational academies.

Rockefeller entrusted the task to his chief counsel, Bob MacCrate. The resulting Scholar Incentive Program promised every full-time undergraduate student up to $200 toward annual tuition costs of $500 or more. For advanced degree candidates, the state would provide as much as $800. Since no SUNY facility in 1961 charged anywhere near these fees, the practical effect was to pump an immediate $6 million into private school coffers, an infusion of state

aid sure to grow as the program became fully operational. In addition, Rockefeller would guarantee taxpayer support for the top 10 percent of each year's
high school graduates by doubling the existing number of Regents Scholarships. Finally, he embraced a generous student loan program introduced by
assembly Speaker Joe Carlino. Under its terms, participants could borrow up to
$1,500 a year—more if they were studying to teach or practice medicine—with
the state covering interest payments as long as they remained in school.

The Scholar Incentive Program was warmly received by much of the educational establishment. But it incensed *The New York Times* and civil libertarians
for whom the idea of *any* tax dollars going to Catholic or other denominational
schools was anathema. Reporter Jack Germond spoke for many New Yorkers
when he protested to the governor, "It says right here in the Constitution, 'No
direct or indirect aid to religious institutions.' So how can you do this?"

"It's necessary," replied Rockefeller.

It might have been the motto of his fifteen years in Albany.*

With his education agenda mired in a debate over the separation of church
and state, Rockefeller again turned to Bob MacCrate for some creative lawyer-
ing. Together with his legal whiz kids, MacCrate converted the Scholar Incentive Program from one of *institutional* assistance to one of *individual* aid,
funneling state money directly to some 120,000 students rather than the schools
they attended. Academic and economic criteria were stiffened, though even
then recipients of state aid were required merely to "give promise of satisfactory
completion" of the degree program in which they were enrolled. By mid-
March, both houses of the legislature had given their assent. Nineteen sixty-
one marked the beginning of New York's revolution in higher education. By the
time Rockefeller left office in 1973, SUNY was the world's largest university
system, with a quarter million students attending classes on sixty-four campuses. For years, an argument would rage over whether the university was overbuilt, an unavoidable consequence of political logrolling. Such complaints
were rarely heard from a student population newly exposed to eminent instructors in eye-catching surroundings.

"Only Nelson Rockefeller could have pulled it off," says Clifton Wharton,
himself a later SUNY chancellor, whose familiarity with Nelson's methods of
persuasion dated to his youthful work for the postwar AIA in Latin America. By
adroit use of the trial balloon and the blue ribbon panel, and through exhaus-

---

* Germond looked more favorably on another Rockefeller initiative, even more unorthodox and
therefore doomed from inception. At a time of rising concern over welfare costs, experts identified a stream of Florida migrant workers who had settled outside Rochester, where they drew
benefits triple those available in the Sunshine State. Using state funds, Rockefeller wanted to
underwrite low-cost loans to develop agricultural jobs in Florida. "A brilliant idea," says Germond. "It didn't work, because they couldn't get people to do it." Jack Germond, AI.

tive consultation, well-timed flexibility, and a willingness to court (and, on occasion, co-opt) his detractors, the self-professed education governor demonstrated just how much he had learned on the job.

3

IN THE MONTHS following John Kennedy's election, Washington informants echoed the advice earlier imparted by Frank Jamieson and now reiterated by George Hinman: Rockefeller should stick to Albany for the present, concentrating his energies on winning reelection in 1962 by a sufficiently impressive margin—Hinman set the number at 750,000—as to all but guarantee his nomination for president two years later. At the White House, JFK readily acknowledged Rockefeller as his likeliest opponent in 1964. For now, the two men remained studiously cordial. Within days of the inauguration, newspaperman Charlie Bartlett sought permission for the new president, desirous of escaping the executive bubble, to stroll the superbly landscaped grounds of Rockefeller's Foxhall Road estate in northwest Washington. Nelson professed himself "delighted" to have the property used in this way.

Soon after this, Rockefeller friend and *Today* show host Dave Garroway related a presidential promise to expect "something of importance" in the civil defense field. Nelson showed his appreciation following the disastrous April 1961 Bay of Pigs invasion, in which Cuban rebels trained by the CIA were crushed by forces loyal to Fidel Castro. After meeting with the embattled president in the Oval Office, Rockefeller urged public support for JFK "in whatever action he considers necessary to defend freedom." His subsequent endorsement of Kennedy requests for additional foreign aid spending and tariff reduction ruffled feathers among congressional Republicans. This, in turn, complicated life for George Hinman, whose assignment was to travel the country making friends for Rockefeller among GOP regulars, for whom memories of his 1960 challenge to party orthodoxy remained hot to the touch.

"Hinman understood people very well," according to his protégé, later secretary to the governor, Robert Douglass, whose WASPy boyishness made people address him as "Bobby" well into old age. "Hinman adored the governor. He thought that if you meet Nelson and listen to him, you'll be won over." In the spring of 1961, there was considerable evidence to support this view. Senator Styles Bridges, a crusty conservative from New Hampshire, all but publicly endorsed Rockefeller for 1964. In neighboring Maine, Senator Margaret Chase Smith pledged her support. Longtime Nixon backers in Wisconsin and North

Dakota indicated friendship, as did congressional newcomers such as Arch Moore in West Virginia and Tennessee's Howard Baker, Sr. Even Eisenhower sounded a reassuring note after Rockefeller called on him in Gettysburg. Gratified by the progress he was making, Hinman pressed Rockefeller to deemphasize "giveaway" programs in promotional materials distributed by the New York State GOP. "The temper of the Republican party is very different than it was in the 40's and early 50's," warned Hinman. "Emphasis on ultra-liberalism and ultra-liberality is not the way to the nomination in 1964."

Yielding to Hinman's battle plan required Rockefeller to put party loyalty above personal consistency and, sometimes, coherence. Scrambling to repair the damage he had done in urging adoption of Kennedy's foreign aid program, Rockefeller in August 1961 criticized JFK's proposal to establish a cabinet-level Department of Urban Affairs. Speaking before a sympathetic audience of county officials in Chicago, he said it would be "a tragedy" if state and local governments abdicated their responsibilities to Washington. Assailing Kennedy for playing racial politics—specifically, for broadly hinting that he would appoint a Negro, Robert Weaver, to oversee the new department—Rockefeller looked craven and sounded opportunistic. Far more credible were his objections to a nuclear test ban treaty with the Soviets, whom he insisted would never agree to any system of inspection that didn't advance their interests.

His hard-line views on the Cold War proved useful in another respect: cautioned that Nixon might try to play him off against Barry Goldwater, Rockefeller went out of his way to cultivate the Arizona senator, with whom he shared a reflexive distrust of Moscow. The two men met regularly over breakfast at Foxhall Road, Goldwater arriving in a sporty red Corvette he drove himself. He left persuaded, as he told skeptical allies on the right, that "he's really not such a bad fellow. He's more conservative than you would imagine." Rockefeller reciprocated, in his way. Earlier that year, Nelson had leaned hard on Jacob Javits to drop his challenge to Goldwater's position as chairman of the National Republican Senatorial Campaign Committee. When conservatives on the Republican National Committee selected Buffalo congressman William E. Miller to replace Thruston Morton as national party chairman, Rockefeller voiced no objection.*

---

* A fascinating instance of what might have been: In February 1961, Republican wunderkind F. Clifton White, the Karl Rove of his day, approached Rockefeller operatives seeking their support for the GOP national chairmanship, or, if that was out of reach, a job as the party's executive director. White, a New Yorker who had cut his organizational teeth working for Tom Dewey, offered assurances that he was not then, nor would he be, "tied with Goldwater." Hinman let the matter drop—and White went on to mastermind the Goldwater takeover of the GOP. George Hinman–NAR, February 25, 1961, Series JH.2, Box 91, RAC.

Clearly the post-Eisenhower GOP was in the throes of change. That spring, New York's Manhattan Center hosted the first national rally of Young Americans for Freedom. Chants of "We want Barry!" greeted the senator as he addressed the overflow crowd of college students lured to the heart of enemy territory from 115 campuses across the nation. Of Goldwater himself, mused a disapproving Jacob Javits, "He's made it respectable to be a conservative again."

4

I T WAS SHORTLY before eleven o'clock on the evening of March 2, 1961, when head butler Robert Bennett opened the door of Albany's Executive Mansion to welcome Nelson and Tod back from a dinner engagement. As soon as they retired for the night, Bennett went to his room on the third floor, where Theodore Roosevelt had once rigged up a boxing ring in which to teach his sons the manly sport. Bennett had just switched off the television news and climbed into bed when he heard Tod's voice crying out to him to rouse two elderly cooks whose quarters were down the hall from his own. Awakened by the smell of smoke, Tod had emerged from her bedroom to find the central stairwell engulfed in flames. She pounded on the door of Nelson's room. He, too, had detected the acrid odor, which he at first attributed to a nearby commercial blaze reported on the late news. After throwing some clothes over his pajamas, he helped Tod through a second-floor window and out onto the porch roof. He was preparing to make the fifteen-foot leap to some bushes below when the Albany Fire Department arrived and a rescue ladder was extended to the governor and his wife.

Having determined that everyone was safely out of the house, Rockefeller raced back into the burning structure to salvage a portrait of his father, as well as drawings by Picasso and Van Gogh. The fire, blamed on faulty electrical wiring, was quickly brought under control, but not before it destroyed seventy pictures and sculptures, including works by Matisse, Braque, Klee, and Picasso. Also lost to the flames were canvases by Early American masters Gilbert Stuart and Thomas Sully that had been left in the residence by Averell Harriman. For a while, it appeared the smoking ruin of a building would be abandoned. Rockefeller decreed otherwise. Professing affection for the old house and its neighborhood, a feeling shared by Tod, Nelson contributed handsomely toward the mansion's renovation and refurbishment. In the meantime, the Rockefellers relocated to the presidential suite of the nearby Ten Eyck Hotel.

Outwardly, things continued as before. Two weeks after the fire, Tod presided over the wedding of her younger daughter, Mary, to navy ensign William Strawbridge. But she didn't return to Eagle Street. Neither did she accompany Nelson on a Caribbean vacation or to a June governors' conference in Honolulu, where New York's chief executive, appearing unusually detached, glumly accepted a watered-down civil rights resolution ("A fight wouldn't have changed anything") in the face of southern resistance. A speculative buzz developed, fed by pictures of the Rockefellers escaping the burning mansion—from separate rooms. That Averell and Marie Harriman, like the Roosevelts before them, had enjoyed similar domestic arrangements remained hidden from the public.* Later, one New York newspaper would claim that Happy Murphy had also been in the house the night of the fire. The report was false, but it gained currency after Mrs. Murphy two months later quietly left her position as confidential secretary to the governor.

About this time, a cryptic Rockefeller threw cold water on the plans of Jim Desmond, the *Daily News'* man in Albany, to write a campaign biography in advance of the 1964 presidential contest. "Something may happen to take me out of the picture," Nelson told Desmond. The reporter's resulting confusion testifies to the cloak of secrecy surrounding the crumbling Rockefeller marriage. Robert Bennett, who moved to the Ten Eyck Hotel with the Rockefellers following the mansion fire, saw nothing then or later to suggest a marriage in crisis. Emmet Hughes knew better. Sometime that summer, Rockefeller summoned Hughes and handed him a piece of paper with a single sentence announcing the governor's separation from his wife of more than thirty years. He wanted the statement released that day. Hughes protested. It made no sense, he told his employer, to put out a story that raised more questions than it answered. When Rockefeller insisted on immediate publication, Hughes drafted a letter of resignation to Laurance Rockefeller. On the fourth day, Nelson and Hughes resumed their argument over breakfast at 810 Fifth Avenue and again as they were driven the few blocks to work. Outside 22 West Fifty-fifth Street, an exasperated Rockefeller leaned into the car and demanded, "Are you *sure* you are right?" The announcement was postponed, much to the surprise of Tod Rockefeller, who later told Hughes that Nelson had been pressuring her for six months to accept the end of their marriage.

His path to marital freedom blocked at least temporarily, Rockefeller looked for alternate fields on which to demonstrate his control. Nineteen sixty-one was

---

* The plainspoken Mrs. Harriman, a night owl in contrast with her early-rising husband, liked nothing better than chatting with a state trooper while downing two bottles of beer—preferably English Whitebread—left out for her enjoyment by the mansion staff. Once forced to make do with a locally brewed product, the manufacturer of which had a job in the state conservation department, she likened its taste to "cow piss." Robert Bennett, AI.

an election year in New York City. In a town where registered Democrats outnumbered them three to one, it was a rare Republican who thought city hall a prize worth contesting. Rockefeller, ever the optimist, saw the mayor's race as a dress rehearsal for his upcoming reelection bid. His preferred candidate, John Hay Whitney, was too emotionally committed to his dying newspaper, the *Herald Tribune*, to join the fray. Acting a familiar part, Senator Jacob Javits toyed with the idea of running just long enough to elicit flattering testaments to his electability, before slamming the door on would-be supporters.

This left Attorney General Louis Lefkowitz, not yet the electorally unassailable figure of later years, whose chances were further diminished by his status as a Rockefeller stalking horse. Lefkowitz invoked the ghost of Fiorello La Guardia, but it was at best a feeble imitation of the Little Flower and his long-ago fusion tickets offered by the AG and his ethnically inclusive slate. Indeed, the most vivid thing about the Lefkowitz campaign was the multicultural jingle emanating from ubiquitous sound trucks made possible by Nelson Rockefeller's checkbook:*

> *You'll be safe in the park*
> *Anytime after dark*
> *With Lefkowitz, Gilhooley and Fino.*

Reinvented as a reformer, Robert Wagner easily won renomination over his onetime machine sponsors. Brushing aside GOP charges of one-party rule and fiscal mismanagement, the mayor shrewdly aimed his fire at Republicans in Albany for perpetuating fiscal crimes against a chronically shortchanged city. On Election Day, Wagner swept past Lefkowitz by four hundred thousand votes. Yet Rockefeller registered no complaint, as Lefkowitz bettered Nixon's 1960 performance in the city, and a Rockefeller-brokered deal with Liberal Party leaders Alex Rose and David Dubinsky produced the first Republican borough president in the Bronx since 1913.

---

* Rockefeller enjoyed Lefkowitz's company so much that he had him move into the Executive Mansion, where he didn't hesitate to wake him in the middle of the night for a legal opinion or, more likely, political advice. Lefkowitz was to be his tutor in other respects: "What's a nose job, Louis?" Nelson once asked him. Lefkowitz prided himself on knowing the name of every newsstand vendor in New York. Rockefeller wasn't the only one to perfect his political techniques by watching "the People's Lawyer" in action. Jack McGrath, a Lefkowitz advanceman who subsequently went to work for Rockefeller, got an important lesson in ethnic campaigning. Lefkowitz told him to schedule any Irish-themed event—"You know, the Knights of Shamrock or the Irish fireman's association"—at seven p.m. rather than nine or ten. When asked why, Lefkowitz replied, "Jack, they drink. They are big, I'm little; they're heavy, they lean on me." Jack McGrath, AI.

5

A T THE HEIGHT of the campaign, Blanchette Rockefeller thanked her brother-in-law for some birthday flowers. She appreciated them all the more, "Hookie" told Nelson, "as I know how many worries and problems are besetting you just now." His disintegrating marriage left Rockefeller increasingly alienated from his children. Unhappy over their mother's treatment, the younger Rockefellers abstained from group pictures advancing their father's political interests. Early in September, alerted to the domestic crisis threatening his family, Michael Rockefeller cut short an art-collecting foray to the trackless jungles of southwest New Guinea, an area referred to by its seventeen thousand Asmat ("the true people") inhabitants as "the land of lapping death." Hastening back to New York, Michael just as quickly concluded that he could do nothing to prevent his parents from divorcing. After a week on Fifth Avenue, he returned to New Guinea by way of Cambridge. There he confided to Robert Gardner, the charismatic, thirty-five-year-old director of Harvard's Film Study Center of the Peabody Museum, his ambition to make a career of anthropology.

From the time Michael was a boy, his father had envisioned him one day at the helm of MoMA. Inheriting Nelson's restlessness and love of speed, Michael could be reckless on the ski slopes and behind the steering wheel (with the traffic citations to prove it). That he might crave more exotic adventures became evident in the spring of his senior year at Harvard. Through his Eliot House roommate Sam Putnam, Michael learned of Bob Gardner's prospective trip to the remote Baliem River Valley in Dutch New Guinea. Peabody Museum director J. O. Brew put the expedition in context. With aboriginal cultures in the region rapidly disappearing, wrote Brew, "it is essential to get records on film before they are nothing but a memory." The very obscurity of the Dani people they hoped to chronicle in New Guinea promised "an extra break" for Gardner and his team. It made the Dani "more fun to work with." Michael was easily persuaded. A few weeks before their June 1960 commencement, he and Putnam volunteered their services. Avidly pursued by Brew, Michael also agreed to underwrite expedition fieldwork, and related film production costs, up to $50,000.

After fulfilling a six-month commitment to the army reserve, the twenty-three-year-old Rockefeller arrived in the Baliem River Valley in the first week of April 1961, a pair of 35mm Nikon cameras dangling from his neck. As group photographer, he was to snap more than four thousand images, many of lasting value. Doubling as a sound technician, Michael captured on tape the strange molar music of the Dani tribes, whose war dances unfolded to the synchronized grinding of combatants' teeth. Leaving the irrigation of potato gardens to their women, Dani warriors adorned in soot and pig grease waged unending battle with bows, arrows, and fifteen-foot-long spears. Michael was mesmerized. His frequently heard exclamation, "It's *unbelievable!*" quickly became an expedition catchphrase. By all accounts he worked tirelessly, never pulling rank or complaining about the primitive conditions or meager diet. "Even though the existence here is utterly different from anything I have known before, it is no longer strange," he wrote his uncle John in July 1961. "Indeed, there is a beauty in the simplicity and something compulsive in the way the Ndavi [*sic*] have a grip on life. . . . I can think of nothing better for Americans than to be placed at the foot of Ndavi culture for six months."

In the same letter, Michael mentioned a recent visit to the Asmat country, an alluvial rain forest veined with countless inlets emptying into the Arafura Sea, which separates New Guinea from Australia. Innocent alike of clothing, Western missionaries, and colonial oversight, until recently the Asmat had routinely practiced head-hunting and cannibalism. Even now, they made art out of shrunken heads and drew beauty from vengeance. As befitting a society without pottery or stone, the tribes relied on wood for fuel, transportation, and food. They accorded special status to the sago tree, whose pitch was converted into an edible starch; warriors stuffed their mouths with Capricorn beetle grubs filched from its trunk. "The key to my fascination with the Asmat is the wood-carving," Michael acknowledged. "The sculpture which the people here produce is some of the most extraordinary work in the primitive world." On excursions to Asmat villages, Michael bartered steel hatchets and tobacco for hand-carved wooden bowls, shields, spears, drums, paddles, and a handful of human skulls. He reserved his greatest excitement for the towering *bis*, or ancestor, poles fashioned from the sacred mangrove tree and planted in the ground outside the local *yeu*, or ceremonial lodge. Each intricately patterned totem, some of them thirty feet high, was believed to contain the spirit of an Asmat warrior killed in battle.

They were less tombstones, however, than tokens of retaliatory violence to come. Sensing a tragedy in the making, Michael lamented the corrupting influence of modernity. "For many of the villages have reached that point where they are beginning to doubt the worth of their own culture and crave things Western." Left unaddressed was the part unwittingly played by outsiders like him in hastening the loss of identity. Thrilled by his discoveries, Michael made plans to return to the Asmat country for two months of additional collecting in the fall of 1961. If all went well, he'd be back in New York for Christmas. Writing to his father, he floated the idea of "a mammoth exhibition which would do justice to the art of these people" under the auspices of Nelson's Museum of Primitive Art. "You can imagine what fun I am having dreaming these wild dreams and creating earth shattering hypothesis about the nature of Asmat art," enthused Michael, sounding very much Nelson Rockefeller's son.

6

O N THE OTHER side of the world, his parents played out their marital drama. At least two of Nelson's brothers advised Tod to refuse his demands for a divorce. Laurance alone held out, mildly remarking on the "incredible self-confidence" of "those Philadelphians" and his sister-in-law's tendency to "throw her weight around." External events provided no lift to Nelson's spirits, even if they appeared to vindicate his militant stance toward the Soviet Union. Coming off the Bay of Pigs fiasco, a confrontational Vienna summit with Nikita Khrushchev, and construction of the Berlin Wall permanently dividing the city, JFK privately estimated the chances of nuclear war at one in five. The president went on television in July 1961 and told a jittery nation, "We do not want to fight, but we have fought before." In the same speech, Kennedy called for a $3.2 billion increase in military spending and an additional $207 million for a crash civil defense program.

Suddenly, fallout shelters were back on page one. For reasons obvious to everyone but Rockefeller, Kennedy was reluctant to meet with him in his capacity as chairman of the Civil Defense Committee of the Conference of Governors. Relying on the counsel of Edward Teller, Herman Kahn, and other hard-liners, Rockefeller estimated the cost of an adequate national shelter program at $20 billion, one hundred times the amount Kennedy had in mind. As cooler heads within the administration began questioning the practical value and even the morality of backyard shelters, JFK deftly shifted his emphasis to communal protection in existing facilities, such as school basements and municipal buildings. To Rockefeller, this was Armageddon on the cheap. Exercising his gubernatorial prerogatives, he called a special two-day session of the legislature for mid-November to consider his proposal to reimburse schools for half the cost of retrofitting themselves as nuclear hideouts. Lawmakers, given only a few hurried hours in which to digest and debate what many considered a $100 million boondoggle, passed the Rockefeller plan anyway. Its substantial majority reflected popular fears that were to culminate a year later in the Cuban missile crisis.*

Twisting legislative arms was preferable to what lay ahead. One evening in November, Nelson invited Malcolm Wilson to dine with him at Albany's Ten Eyck Hotel. At the same hour, Tod Rockefeller by prearrangement broke bread at her Pocantico home with Wilson's wife, Katherine. Before dessert was served, each of the Wilsons learned what was embargoed from the general public until

---

* Rockefeller could browbeat the legislature into passing his program, but he couldn't persuade its supposed beneficiaries to share his sense of urgency. Over the next five years, barely $2 million of the $100 million set aside for shelter construction was actually spent.

the evening of Friday, November 17—that the governor and his wife were separating after more than thirty years of marriage. The fervently Catholic lieutenant governor begged Nelson to reconsider. Even in a nation where a quarter of all marriages ended in divorce, for a Rockefeller to walk away from the mother of his five children was political suicide. Certainly he could forget any White House aspirations, said Wilson.

But love took priority over politics, Nelson replied. To another friend who tried to change his mind, Rockefeller claimed the moral high ground, insisting that he could no longer justify the hypocrisy of a sham marriage. If anything, Nelson and Tod had been too adept at maintaining appearances; the public, oblivious to the pair's long-ago emotional parting, had difficulty fathoming their physical separation now. This didn't prevent the Rockefeller PR operation from going into overdrive. At the stroke of six p.m. on November 17, messengers from Room 5600 hand-delivered a tersely worded announcement to all seven of New York's newspapers, plus the two wire services. Couched in the most decorous language, the statement confirmed a property settlement (reportedly $10 million to $14 million) and indicated that the governor would be temporarily residing with his brother Laurance. It was notably silent as to which party had initiated the divorce proceedings.

George Hinman was in Atlanta on the night of November 17, wooing southern Republicans at a two-day regional conference. Incredibly, Rockefeller had kept his chief delegate hunter out of the loop. A reporter who spoke with Hinman after dinner found him badly shaken. He wasn't alone. Feelings of "shock and dismay" were universal, Hinman told Rockefeller afterward. On hearing the news, Alabama state party chairman Claude Vardaman, a rare island of support in a hostile region, lost his appetite. Virginia national committeewoman Hazel Barger threw up her hands in frustration, wondering out loud to whom she could transfer her allegiance. North Carolina Republicans postponed a fund-raising dinner at which Nelson was to be the chief draw. The dust had yet to settle ten days later at a gathering of midwestern Republicans. Employing the euphemistic language of the courtier, Hinman nevertheless lobbed a warning at his employer. "Everyone we talked to asked the question as to whether there was another interest," he informed Nelson. "When we assured them there was not, they expressed relief." That said, it was made abundantly clear "that if there were anything like that in the picture, it would mean the end."

Not everyone rushed to pronounce Rockefeller's political eulogy. Barry Goldwater said that his putative rival's "family troubles" shouldn't influence voters in 1964. Drawing on personal experience, the divorced Adlai Stevenson reported that he had received more angry letters on account of his Unitarian faith. Many assumed that Tod, fed up with political life, had requested the separation. In a snidely amusing commentary, the *Syracuse Herald-Journal* weighed possible motives behind her complaint. Might it have stemmed from nonsupport? The prospect of living in a bomb shelter? Perhaps Mrs. Rockefeller had fallen victim to claustrophobia from being cooped up in a Fifth Avenue apartment or five other homes from Maine to Venezuela?

Gossipy speculation reached as far as the Kremlin, where Nikita Khrushchev drew a torturous link between the presence of U.S. troops in West Berlin and the bombshell report emanating from Room 5600. JFK refused to take the bait, though privately he expressed astonishment after one of Tod's brothers unmasked Nelson as the instigator of the divorce. "I don't believe it," the president told Kay Graham. "No man would ever love love more than he loves politics."

7

I T WAS SUNDAY, November 19, less than forty-eight hours after their stunning announcement, and the estranged couple had retreated to separate corners of the Pocantico estate. While this enabled them to evade the press, the same tactic made it that much harder for anyone else to reach them, even in an emergency. Consequently, several hours elapsed before the call from the Dutch ambassador to the United States could be put through to Nelson, who was lunching with his brother David and sister-in-law Peggy at their Hudson Pines home. Michael Rockefeller was missing, and feared lost, in the turbulent waters of the Arafura Sea. Few additional details were immediately available. The envoy's message cut through Nelson like a freshly sharpened knife.

Over the next few hours, a sketchy scenario emerged. Accompanied by a thirty-four-year-old Dutch ethnologist named René Wassing and two Papuan guides in loincloths, Michael had embarked on a journey to retrieve some undelivered *bis* poles thirty-five miles from the Dutch administrative outpost of Agats. Rather than waste days, possibly weeks, navigating the watery back alleys of southern New Guinea, Michael had determined on a shortcut across the estuary of the Eilanden River, whose muddy shoreline was remade with every high tide. On Saturday morning, November 18, the quartet departed from Agats on a forty-foot catamaran improvised from two dugout canoes lashed together and powered by a single eighteen-horsepower motor. Overloaded with supplies and gear, the fragile vessel and its crew made the downriver passage without incident. But when they reached the open sea their luck ran out, as a rogue wave swamped the rickety craft, silencing its motor and leaving the four men on board drifting helplessly a mile or more from the mouth of the Eilanden. The native guides swam to shore, from which they could see Rockefeller and Wassing clinging to the tin roof of the makeshift catamaran. Moments later, it went into a slow capsize. The guides walked eleven miles to Agats. From there, word of Michael's plight traveled by shortwave radio to the colonial capital of Hollandia and, eventually, to David Rockefeller's country house overlooking the gray and chilly Hudson.

Absorbing the news, Nelson decided on the spot to fly halfway around the world and take personal charge of the search operation. He shouldn't expect too much, the ambassador warned him—the Dutch navy had already tested two good swimmers against the current and held out little hope for Michael's survival. Mary, Michael's twin, insisted on accompanying her father. It was nearly midnight when their commercial jet left New York on the first leg of a ten-thousand-mile journey. From the first, Nelson understood the odds he confronted. "But if you are a father you can't accept that there is no chance, so you go out." After reviewing options with his staff, a pale, haggard-looking Rockefeller sat beside Mary until she dozed off. Eventually he fell into a seat next to James Desmond of the *Daily News*, one of a dozen reporters making the trip. "I pride myself on being a realist," Nelson told Desmond. "I don't think we've got a chance, not any kind of a chance, of finding him."

Nothing he heard while changing planes at San Francisco and Honolulu altered his fatalistic outlook. To be sure, René Wassing, still attached to the capsized vessel, had been rescued after being spotted by a Dutch flying boat twenty-two miles from shore. Had Michael been more patient, he too might have been saved. But passive acceptance was not in his nature, any more than in his father's. During his first twenty-four hours on New Guinea, Nelson reconnoitered 150 miles of indistinct shoreline from a chartered DC-3 aircraft. Swooping down to within 250 feet of the spongy terrain and endless green canopy, he trained his binoculars on the grim landscape. No sign of human life greeted him. After four hours in the air, Rockefeller returned to Merauke, a malarial backwater without a decent hotel or other creature comforts. There he debriefed René Wassing, who described the final moments before Michael, unwilling to take his chances on a long-shot rescue, had abandoned their overturned vessel in a desperate attempt to reach shore.

"I warned him about the crocodiles," Wassing told Michael's father and sister. "I told him I could take no responsibility for him." Naturally headstrong and confident in his athletic abilities, Michael had stripped to his underwear, strapped on a pair of bright red, five-gallon gasoline cans to help keep him buoyant, and slipped into the inky water. "I think I can make it," he told Wassing, then disappeared over the horizon, his progress slowed by a powerful tide propelling mile after mile of choppy waters teaming with sharks and box jellyfish and dotted with mud banks and energy-sapping eel grass.

Like Michael before him, Nelson now heard what he chose to hear. "Reasonable chance Michael reached shore," he wired Room 5600 after speaking to Wassing. "Intensive search requires helicopter support because of extremely shallow coastal waters and mud shoal coast." Louise Boyer was instructed to contact Deputy Defense Secretary Roswell Gilpatric, a longtime friend, for assistance in securing choppers from Dutch and Australian military units in the area. "Also, Shell Oil has two helicopters on the island that might be chartered." Rockefeller turned down the offer of an aircraft carrier from the U.S. Seventh Fleet to aid in the search. He fixed his hopes instead on a local flotilla—more than a thousand tribal canoes manned by Asmat villagers promised 250 sticks of tobacco, a small fortune in native currency—for evidence of Michael's whereabouts.

He was leaving the search to the experts, Rockefeller told reporters at one of his daily press briefings. "They know what to look for, I would only take up space in the plane." This didn't prevent him from undertaking a second flight, to the jungle outpost of Pirimapoen, where he made inquiries among the Dutch missionaries and, through them, the local inhabitants. His tightly coiled emotions betrayed him when one scribe tactlessly asked if he had any idea what the hunt for Michael was costing. "No. Have you?" Rockefeller retorted. Regaining his composure, he murmured, "It's almost over. Things look bad."* Rockefeller took comfort in late night phone conversations with Happy Murphy—adding to the growing distance and sense of betrayal felt by his daughter Mary. On his fourth day at Merauke, the governor learned of a Dutch seaman who had survived more than a week in the treacherous region where Michael would have landed, had he reached shore. Hopes fluttered. His son might be in some remote part of the island, Rockefeller theorized, cut off from communications. Then a Dutch naval vessel plucked from the sea a red gasoline can, thought to be one of the pair to which Michael had strapped himself. But the discovery led nowhere.

Conceding that it would take a miracle to find his son alive, Nelson waited one more day, then left New Guinea for the thirty-hour flight to New York. Greeting him at Idlewild Airport on the evening of November 29 were several family members, backed by a contingent of state officials and two hundred newsmen. *New York Times* reporter Russell Porter conveyed the sympathy of the press corps to an exhausted and grieving parent. Rockefeller responded with an impromptu tribute to Michael, poignantly phrased in the present tense: "Ever since he was little, he has been very aware of people, their feelings, their thoughts. He is a person who has always loved people and has always been

---

* He nearly came to blows with an Australian journalist who suggested that the entire trip was a cynical distraction from Rockefeller's marital troubles.

loved by people. He has a tremendous enthusiasm and drive, love of life. He has always loved beauty in people, beauty in nature and beauty in art, whether it is in painting or sculpture, and has been quite an artist himself. I think it is fair to say that he was never happier than he has been out there for some seven or eight months."

With that, Rockefeller concluded, it was time "to go out in the country and see Mrs. Rockefeller." Were there any questions? No one intruded on the moment. Journalists stood in silence as the Rockefellers left for Pocantico. Tod greeted him in the living room of Hawes House.

"Hello, Nels," she said.

"Hello, Tod. I am sorry to bring such tragic news back to you."

On the floor, he spread out a large map of New Guinea, around which the family group huddled on their knees as Nelson described the forbidding landscape and treacherous currents of the Asmat region. Finally, he rolled up the map, kissed Tod on the cheek, and left for Kykuit, the manor house into which he had moved following their separation. He had still to relate the story of his failed mission to Happy Murphy, to whom he offered a benediction of sorts for his favorite child.

"I hope Michael meets Mother in Heaven."

The disappearance of his son led to speculation that Nelson and Tod might be reunited. This overlooked the unique place Michael had occupied in his father's dynastic hopes. If anything, losing him intensified a middle-aged man's sense of urgency about realizing a second chance at marriage and parenting. His commemoration of Michael's life was discreet yet pervasive. "The only picture he had on his desk was of Michael," recalled Rockefeller press secretary Les Slote. Nelson asked Wally Harrison to design a modernistic stone cross in his son's memory. Located a short walk from Kykuit, it served for the rest of Nelson's life as a spiritual retreat and place for reflection. Before settling Michael's $660,000 estate, Nelson appropriated nearly seventy works of art executed by the youth whose creative talent had clearly surpassed his own. One of Michael's paintings occupied a prominent place in the Foxhall Road house. A large photograph of him sitting in a boat hung over the entrance to Nelson's underground art gallery at Kykuit.

In September 1962, a temporary structure took shape in the MoMA garden named for Michael's grandmother Abby Aldrich Rockefeller. Inside the ad hoc exhibit gallery, hundreds of Asmat items assembled by Michael were supplemented by some of his most evocative photographs. Dominating the collection were the towering *bis* poles, some with figure-eight configurations representative of the tangled roots of the banyan tree, others carved to resemble a crocodile or praying mantis. Among the first visitors to the show was Bob Gardner, whose admiration for its "reticent drama" didn't keep him from reminding the governor of Michael's unfulfilled financial pledge. Rockefeller promptly turned over to Harvard $20,000 of Standard Oil of New Jersey stock. In the end, Rockefeller money accounted for more than two-thirds of the expedition budget, the balance being supplied by the government of the Netherlands.

For years, Rockefeller avoided discussion of his son's fate—in part, it was said, to protect Tod from grisly speculation. Even so, her mail had to be sifted to forestall appeals from bogus visionaries, professed spiritualists, and others promising, for a price, the secret of Michael's whereabouts. "I don't think anybody will ever know the truth of what happened to him," says Happy Rockefeller. "I think they preferred to think he drowned." On this score, Nelson harbored no doubts. His son "gambled and lost." That the alternatives were too horrible to ponder didn't inhibit self-promoting writers and journalists from offering a variety of gruesome scenarios. Defying all odds, it was said that Michael had somehow made it to shore, only to be killed and devoured by Otsjanep warriors in revenge for the murder of four tribesmen at the hands of a Dutch patrol officer. An alternative theory had him falling victim to tribal warfare touched off by the Gardner expedition in a foolhardy attempt to heighten its cinematic drama—a notion conveniently overlooking the vast distance separating the Baliem River Valley from Asmat country. Weirdest of all was the claim that Michael had survived to join the Asmat, living out his repudiation of Western ways, even as the tribe itself was absorbed into the newly independent nation of Indonesia.

In January 1964, a Westchester County judge granted Nelson's request that his son be declared legally dead. Four years later, the Museum of Primitive Art published an elaborate volume incorporating Michael's Asmat photographs and excerpts from his field journals. "He was one of those intuitive people," Nelson told Deirdre Carmody of *The New York Times*. "There are a lot of sensitive people in this world, but some of them are overwhelmed by their own sensitivity. . . . He had that joy of life that is so rare today. Maybe he was too lacking in fear. But there's no use in speculating . . . he wanted to do it."

There's no use in speculating. Did his own sensitivity lead Nelson, sitting by Michael's empty grave at Kykuit, to ponder the loss of a child whose relentless pursuit of art, inspired by a father's passion and underwritten by the family fortune, had sealed his doom? The cost of introspection was prohibitive. Better to pronounce the case closed, cauterizing the hurt by affirming that Michael had suffered the least terrible of fates in a selfless attempt to reach shore. Other members of his family exhibited more curiosity. Within days of Nelson's death in January 1979, Tod Rockefeller reportedly enlisted the services of Australia's leading detective agency to conduct a final investigation into Michael's disappearance. If the story is true, neither the Monte Security Company of Sydney nor the Rockefellers have ever shared the results of their probe.

8

R OCKEFELLER'S RETURN TO New York coincided with unsourced press reports that he wouldn't seek reelection in 1962; the *Daily News* claimed he was on the brink of resignation. Backing his instant denial with actions, Rockefeller took a more prominent part than usual in Albany's holiday rituals, presiding over several legislative dinners and personally hosting the general public for the annual New Year's open house at the restored Executive Mansion. He attributed the withdrawal rumors to Mayor Wagner, widely seen at the time as his most formidable prospective challenger. In reality, the chief threat to Rockefeller's continued dominance wouldn't come from New York's fragmented and leaderless Democrats, but out of his own party's ranks. Even before the state's fledgling Conservative Party mailed out its first fund-raising appeal in February 1962, mounting fury on the right nationally had prompted President Kennedy, in a Los Angeles visit coinciding with Rockefeller's heartbreaking trip to New Guinea, to decry "those on the fringes of our society who have sought to escape their own responsibility by finding a simple solution, an appealing slogan, or a convenient scapegoat."

JFK's speech was carefully timed. Meeting in Dallas that same week, eighteen hundred delegates to the National Indignation Convention cheered film star Ronald Reagan's denunciation of the progressive income tax as an idea "spawned by Karl Marx a hundred years ago." The concluding speaker mocked a predecessor for his alleged moderation. "All he wants to do is impeach [Chief Justice Earl] Warren—I'm for hanging him," he announced to appreciative laughter. The NIC had plenty of company in channeling right-wing anger. A grassroots militia calling itself the Minutemen claimed to have twenty-five thousand patriots armed and ready to resist a Soviet invasion of U.S. soil. In Birmingham, Alabama, Dr. Fred Schwarz, whose Christian Anti-Communism Crusade enjoyed the support of John Wayne, James Stewart, and other Hollywood luminaries, castigated the visiting Bolshoi Ballet as a Soviet fifth column. Simultaneously, a Long Island housewife revealed the menacing presence of Russian peat moss in local nurseries. "Remember to ask where your peat moss comes from," Mrs. Raymond Terwilliger admonished her complacent neighbors.

Most prominent of the rightist groups was the John Birch Society, founded by a retired Massachusetts candy maker named Robert Welch, Jr. Besides opposing the fluoridation of water and federal registration of firearms, Welch proclaimed Dwight Eisenhower—like John Foster Dulles before him—to be "a dedicated and conscious agent of the Communist conspiracy." Such roundhouse swings won frenzied approval from Welch's estimated sixty thousand followers. But they massively complicated the efforts of intellectuals such as

William F. Buckley, Jr., and politicians like Barry Goldwater to plant the flag of renascent conservatism. In Goldwater's Phoenix, an activist group calling itself Stay American nominated a slate of municipal candidates pledged to abolish government by city manager, which it decried as a Communist innovation. This overlooked Goldwater's leadership a decade earlier in promoting the cause of city management. Not for the last time, the senator had to disentangle himself from the movement he inspired.

In the autumn of 1961, both appeared headed for bigger things. Goldwater's ghostwritten manifesto, *The Conscience of a Conservative*, had sold more than seven hundred thousand copies, and its author was the subject of flattering profiles in many of the nation's largest publications. By the end of the year, F. Clifton White (ironically an alumnus of Tom Dewey's New York Republican organization), operating out of three rooms in the shadow of Grand Central Terminal, was spearheading a grassroots movement to draft Goldwater for president. Dubious about Republican chances against Kennedy in 1964, Goldwater was quick to deny White House ambitions to anyone who would listen. His putative rivalry with Rockefeller might have remained in murky equilibrium a while longer, but for an issue that caused even George Hinman to discard his normal caution. Acknowledging that until now he had been recommending "a passive course" regarding Goldwater, Hinman sang a different tune in the weeks leading up to Christmas 1961. The party of Lincoln, he warned, was in danger of subversion by southern racists.

In sounding the alarm, Hinman felt confident where his employer's sympathies lay. On the eve of Martin Luther King, Jr.'s June 1961 visit to Albany, Rockefeller staffers had debated a suitable response. Someone observed that sharing a stage with King, though it might be the right thing to do morally, posed an undeniable political risk. "If it's morally the right thing," Rockefeller countered, "it's the politically right thing." In the event, Rockefeller not only introduced the civil rights leader at a public rally, he supplied King with a private plane, treated him to dinner at the Executive Mansion, and hired a film crew to capture King's speech for posterity—part of a larger effort, explained Rockefeller, "to interest the television networks in doing a thoughtful study of your work."

Well aware of the historic role played by the Rockefeller family in advancing Negro rights, Hinman hardly needed to spell out what was at risk if national GOP chairman Bill Miller and organizers of the RNC's Project Dixie had their way. "The theory is that by becoming more reactionary than even the Southern Democratic Party," wrote Hinman, Republicans in the region might rebuild their party around renegade Democrats "and by consolidating them with the conservative strength in the Middle West and Far West" finally prevail in their long-running contest with northeastern liberals. Strategic considerations buttressed his moral outrage. Rockefeller had raised other issues before the American public, Hinman acknowledged, "but none of them have had much emotional impact, much sex appeal." This was different. "What you need at the present moment is a role of aggressive leadership in a great national issue which will submerge the family issue. . . . We've got a great thing here. The American people will never go with the ultras on this."*

As a first step, Hinman offered to draft Rockefeller's forthcoming Lincoln Day speech scheduled for Niagara Falls. As delivered on February 15, 1962, it combined praise for past Republican leadership on civil rights with a damning indictment of the Kennedy administration's unkept promises. During the 1960 campaign, JFK had vowed "by the stroke of the president's pen" to end any vestige of discrimination by the federal government. In office for more than a year, Rockefeller lamented, "Mr. Kennedy has never been able to find the pen." The only legislation passed by the New Frontier to date was a two-year extension of Dwight Eisenhower's Civil Rights Commission. No action had been taken to eliminate southern poll taxes, outlaw lynching, or establish a permanent Fair Employment Practices Commission.

Sandwiched between his historical credit taking and his contemporary fault-finding, Rockefeller all but read out of the GOP those who would "speak softly on civil rights to whisper an appeal for southern votes." Declaring a party without a conscience to be a party without an identity, he insisted that Republicans everywhere reject "preachers of racism or extremists of reaction." On returning to Albany, Rockefeller submitted a legislative package prohibiting racial discrimination in all apprenticeships and other training programs; adding motels, swimming pools, trailer camps, retail stores, and public transport to the list of public accommodations where discrimination was outlawed; and changing the name of the 1945 State Commission Against Discrimination to the more affirmative State Commission for Human Rights. Working in tandem with commission chairman George Fowler, Rockefeller injected himself into a dispute involving the NAACP and Hilton Hotels. After a black guest was turned away from the Atlanta Hilton, the civil rights organization called for a boycott of all Hilton facilities in New York, beginning with the chain's flagship, the Waldorf-Astoria. Rockefeller summoned representatives of both organizations to his Fifty-fifth Street offices, where he brokered a deal committing Hilton to abandon its "local custom" in Atlanta and the NAACP rescinded its boycott.

---

* The same day he penned his fervent appeal to Rockefeller, Hinman took chairman Miller to task for addressing a GOP dinner in Mississippi from which Negro James Edwards had been unceremoniously barred on account of his race. To Hinman, such actions were as incompatible with Republican traditions as they were destructive of Republican prospects.

Rockefeller had less success converting his fellow governors, many of them Southern Democrats. Meeting in Hershey, Pennsylvania, in July 1962, the group rejected his resolution committing them to equal opportunity in housing, employment, public accommodations, and education and promising universal voting rights. During a foray to the West Coast and Rocky Mountain states, the heart of Goldwater country, Rockefeller didn't back off from his civil rights advocacy, but he didn't emphasize it, either. Before a gathering of Colorado Republican women, the eastern visitor stressed his Cold War credentials. Rockefeller credited atomic weapons with ensuring the survival of democracy and countering the limitless manpower of China, "which otherwise would have given the balance of power to the Soviet bloc. Let us not fear to use this reserve force of power if necessary," he concluded to loud cheers from his partisan audience.

While western Republicans applauded Rockefeller's tough talk about the Soviets, some conservative-minded New Yorkers questioned his stance on urban crime, an issue just beginning to polarize the electorate along racial and ethnic lines. Several times during his first term, Rockefeller had not hesitated to commute a jury's death sentence to life imprisonment. None of these cases, however, touched a raw nerve like the iconic story of Salvador Agron, aka the Capeman. Sixteen years old, alternately abused and neglected by his divorced parents, Agron was shuttled between his native Puerto Rico, where one day he chanced to discover the body of his suicidal stepmother dangling from the ceiling, and the combative alleys of Brooklyn's Fort Greene neighborhood. The youth joined a street gang called the Vampires, his trademark black cape with red lining lending flamboyance to his thuggery.

On a misty August night in 1959, Agron and other gangbangers planned a rumble with the Norsemen, an Irish-Italian gang from Hell's Kitchen, in an unlit basketball court on West Forty-fifth Street. Two blocks from the Broadway theater in which Riff and Bernardo nightly reenacted their blood feud to the music of Leonard Bernstein's *West Side Story*, Agron fatally stabbed a pair of sixteen-year-old bystanders with a twelve-inch dagger. By morning's light they were shown to be victims of mistaken identity—the Norsemen never showed—but Agron was unrepentant. Arrested two days later, he said he had committed murder for the simplest of reasons: "Because I felt like it." The prospect of being tried as an adult held no fear. "I don't care if I burn," Agron told reporters. "My mother could watch me."

The senselessness of his crime was matched by the sensationalism with which it was exploited by newspapers and television. The charismatic Agron became the smirking face of random urban violence. To many, he personified evil imported from an alien culture. Others, pointing to his hellish upbringing and severe mental deficiencies, raised objections to his pending execution. Eleanor Roosevelt petitioned Rockefeller for clemency. So did the father of one of Agron's victims. The ensuing hearing in the Capitol's Red Room was packed with advocates from both sides, the mayor of San Juan prominent among those seeking mercy for the youngest New Yorker ever sentenced to die in the electric chair. Going into the hearing, gubernatorial counsel Bob Mac-Crate had no idea how his boss was leaning. Following dueling appeals from the district attorney and Agron's lawyer, MacCrate listened spellbound to "perhaps the most eloquent presentation I ever heard," as Rockefeller, switching effortlessly between English and Spanish, deconstructed Agron's short life through a series of bluntly worded queries. "Where were you then?" he asked the young man's advocates. "What were you doing in your community? How does a life like this come about?" At length Rockefeller turned to MacCrate. "Come on, Bob, let's go," he said. On February 7, 1962, citing Agron's age, his mental impairment, and the wretched conditions of his early life and upbringing, Rockefeller commuted the Capeman's death sentence to life imprisonment.*

9

H IS ACTION IN the Agron case might have raised conservative hackles, but it was nothing compared with the anger stirred by Rockefeller's fiscal policies, in particular his growing reliance on so-called public benefit corporations. Before taking office, he had been harshly critical of Robert Moses and his shadow government, likened by Rockefeller to the lawless corporations of the Gilded Age. In April 1961, he signed legislation mandating greater transparency in public authority budgeting. A second bill made authority officials more accountable for their professional conduct. Yet even as he took these modest steps, Rockefeller served as midwife to the New York State Housing Finance Agency (HFA), first in a series of bureaucratic enablers that allowed him to evade constitutional limits on state spending and debt.

Where public borrowing was concerned, these were unambiguously restrictive. Debt in the form of general obligation bonds, backed by the full faith and

---

* In prison, Agron became a born again Christian. He earned his high school equivalency diploma and a degree in sociology from SUNY at New Paltz, wrote poetry, and established a fund to compensate his victims' families with money he received for a television movie based on his life. Released from jail in 1979, Agron died in 1986 at the age of forty-two. His story inspired Paul Simon's 1998 Broadway musical, *The Capeman*.

credit of the state, required the approval of voters in a referendum. Elections were tricky things. Voters in November 1961 narrowly rejected Rockefeller's $500 million bond issue earmarked for a vastly expanded SUNY. The governor, having no intention of abandoning his program, repackaged it as a test of his "creative capitalism." Working in league with John Mitchell, Wall Street's reigning bond lawyer, Commissioner of Housing and Community Renewal James Gaynor fashioned an independent housing authority whose tax-free bonds would carry interest rates roughly comparable to what New York paid to service its "constitutional" debt—but without the state's full faith and credit in back of them or the popular approval this required. HFA bonds were secured by revenue from the projects they made possible. To reassure skittish investors, a reserve fund was established, augmented by language directing the governor to obtain a legislative appropriation in the unexpected event that project income failed to cover outstanding debts. Since there was nothing compelling lawmakers to accede to the executive's request for emergency funding, these moral obligation bonds rested on a promise with no enforcement mechanism.

Mitchell's scheme was a direct descendant of his earlier attempt to stimulate federal school-building efforts during Rockefeller's stint at HEW. Nelson had even greater incentive as governor to embrace the concept. Not only did moral obligation bonds afford a way around the electorate's racially tinged opposition to public housing; because public authorities were off budget, Rockefeller could extol his dramatic expansion of middle-class housing (or the state university or mental health facilities or other capital investment programs) without adding a nickel to the state's legal debt or a penny to individual tax rates. Running for reelection, he could boast of *lowering* state indebtedness by $85 million and reassert his faith in pay as you go. Bemoaning the small-mindedness of Arthur Levitt and other fiscal traditionalists who accused him of backdoor financing, Nelson insisted the bonds were perfectly lawful. "It is just using some imagination. Everybody has accepted the idea that bridges were paid for out of tolls. People want to cross a bridge so they pay the toll. Nobody quarreled about that. The whole idea was to extend that concept to housing and the state university and the others."

Levitt found the idea repugnant. "I always thought, well, when punch [sic] comes to shove, who the hell is going to buy these moral commitments?" he subsequently confessed. "Bearing only the hope that the legislature will validate this by an appropriation. That's all there is. Who would buy it? But what happened was amazing. What happened was the banks went at this with a vengeance. They underwrote it in the first place, eagerly . . . and they put it in their portfolios, and they sold it to their customers. And they drew into the underwriting group banks from all over the country, and *they* sold it to *their* customers. And the interest rates were high, much higher than those of the pro-faith and credit obligations."

Equally useful was the HFA's versatility. Operating outside the state budget process, the agency and its offshoots escaped legislative oversight. This effectively reserved to Nelson Rockefeller all decisions concerning the location and design of SUNY facilities. Had New York voters rejected his $500 million construction program? Very well—on March 31, 1962, Rockefeller put his name to legislation establishing the State University Construction Fund, its bonds to be marketed through the HFA and its debt serviced by student tuition and other fees. Few voices were raised in protest. Prospective students might not like paying tuition, but they applauded the governor for cutting in half the university's construction schedule. Over the next twenty years, $2.6 billion in academic building was funded through the HFA. None of the projects defaulted. Small wonder that Rockefeller celebrated moral obligation bonding as "the greatest system ever invented."

10

U NDER NEW YORK'S divorce laws, unchanged since the eighteenth century, the only justification for dissolving a marital union was adultery. This compelled Tod Rockefeller to assert her claim of extreme mental cruelty in that bastion of moral relativism, Reno, Nevada. First, however, she must establish legal residence in the Silver State by spending at least six weeks there. A reservation in the name of Mrs. Clark was duly made at the Donner Trail Guest Ranch, in the foothills of the Sierra Nevada near Lake Tahoe. "I have been busy every waking hour getting business problems settled, removing all my affairs from office and learning about taxes, insurance, safe deposit boxes, etc., etc.," Tod wrote Blanchette Rockefeller on the eve of her February 1 departure. "There is no news on other fronts. Gossips still prattling, Nelson is busy with his hands full in Albany and the other two are together with their children as far as I know."

Unable to bring herself to pronounce the names of Robin and Happy Murphy, Tod may have nevertheless been an unwitting source for columnist Drew Pearson, whose wife, Luvie, she counted among her closest friends. According to Pearson, the Murphys had just returned from a cruise to Bermuda with their children, a trip carrying an unmistakable hint of reconciliation. So where did this leave Nelson? Walter Winchell, Hedda Hopper, and other gullible scribes linked him romantically to the fading screen actress Joan Crawford, whose postscreen career as Pepsi's chief saleswoman made her the beneficiary—and likely instigator—of such publicity. "I just don't know what to do to stop this nonsensical hullabaloo," an unconvincing Miss Crawford wrote Nelson. His response amounted to a polite brush-off.*

In Reno, Tod was accompanied by her daughter Mary, whose resentment of Nelson's conduct found ironic expression in a local church. Having astonished herself by harvesting a cascade of silver dollars the first time she slotted a coin in a machine, Mary hauled her winnings to Sunday services, where she dumped them into the offering plate, whispering, "Here are your thirty pieces of silver, Father." On March 16, 1962, her head bowed and fighting back tears, Tod Rockefeller entered a Reno district courthouse on the arms of her sons Rodman and Steven. It took seven minutes to dissolve her marriage of nearly thirty-one years. "This is a great break for Reno," the presiding judge tipped off a reporter. "It may mean Alabama-bound divorce seekers will come here again." When Tod returned to 810 Fifth Avenue a few days later, it bore scant resemblance to the art-filled triplex in which she had lived for a quarter century. Having no need for thirty-plus rooms, she relinquished to Nelson the twelfth floor, which everyone assumed he would sell before relocating to an address that carried less emotional baggage.

He did nothing of the kind. After removing the Léger-painted stairway connecting the two floors, he purchased a floor roughly corresponding to his own in the newly constructed building next door. Once he'd punched through the intervening wall, he began to transform the twelve thousand square feet to accommodate his needs. Some concessions were made to his former wife's sensitivities. A written agreement stipulated which day of the week was set aside for each household to make use of common laundry facilities. Nelson and his guests also consented to come and go through a different entrance (a change reflected in his new address of 812 Fifth Avenue). At Pocantico, roles were reversed, as Tod vacated Hawes House for a Westchester County estate to which she gave the name Sardana. Those inquiring as to its meaning were told it was a secret.

---

* More accurate than her American counterparts was Lady Jeanne Campbell of the *London Evening Standard*. Writing five days before Christmas 1961, she identified Happy Murphy by name. "She is young, in her early 30s, and a country loving girl. Already people are comparing her to the Duchess of Windsor when she was plain Mrs. Simpson." At the time of his separation from Tod, Nelson had moved in with his brother Laurance at 834 Fifth Avenue. He showed his appreciation by presenting his younger sibling with a 1963 Ferrari 400 Superamerica Coupe.

11

THE ELECTORAL RAMIFICATIONS of the Rockefeller divorce injected a note of uncertainty into New York politics. Early in 1962, Bob Wagner raised what, until recently, had seemed a rhetorical question. "Can Rocky be licked for reelection this year?" inquired the mayor. City hall consultant Warren Moscow thought he could—"by a Lehman type Jew," shorthand for former governor Herbert Lehman, a high-minded, good-government New Dealer manqué. Moreover, Moscow had a specific candidate in mind, a sixty-two-year-old state appellate judge named Bernard Botein. The Kennedy White House was less convinced. Keeping a close watch on the man he still regarded as his most likely opponent in 1964, JFK had some advice for his friend Ben Bradlee, whose *Newsweek* was having trouble getting access to the governor for an upcoming cover story. "You ought to cut Rocky's ass open a little this week," Kennedy told Bradlee. A good place to begin was his war record.

"Where was old Nels when you and I were dodging bullets in the Solomon Islands?" pressed Kennedy. "How old was he? He must have been thirty-one or thirty-two. Why don't you look into that?"

Not waiting for the press to do its job, the Kennedy administration conducted its own probe of Rockefeller vulnerabilities, if key Albany staffers are to be believed. "I got a call from the IRS," recalls Bill Ronan. "Would I come down to 100 Church Street?" On his arrival, two agents asked the secretary to the governor if he had brought his attorney. "I said, 'What the hell, do I need a lawyer?' They said, 'Well, this is an investigation.' I said, 'What do you mean, an investigation?' They said, 'This is not an audit, this is an investigation.'" Ronan answered some of their questions, deflected others. "They said, 'Now Mr. Ronan, what do have in your apartment?' I said, 'I have a dog and I have my wife, and from time to time, my younger daughter.' They said, 'No, we mean furnishings.' I said, 'None of your goddamn business.'" The agents persisted. Did his wife own a mink coat?

"Get a subpoena and look in the closet and see if you find one."

The government sleuths did the next most intrusive thing, unleashing a stream of calls from Bonwit Teller, Saks, and other stores where Mrs. Ronan had a charge account. Sporadically, the same agents would direct a fresh round of questioning at Ronan directly, only to be told—literally—where they could go. A similar experience was reported by Sol Corbin, who succeeded Bob MacCrate as Rockefeller's counsel in the summer of 1962. Coincidence? Ronan doubted it. His suspicions were confirmed one day when a mysterious Mr. Solomon of the IRS called him to impart rather than solicit sensitive information. "They finally told me it came from on high," says Ronan of his harassment. "They said they weren't supposed to tell me . . . they didn't identify him, but they said from on high, which I took to mean Bobby Kennedy."*

To White House pollster Lou Harris's prediction of a New York governor's race going down to the wire, JFK snorted, "Old Lou is full of shit on this one." Dismissive as he was, Kennedy still hoped to find a Democratic contender who would cut into Rockefeller's 1958 victory margin, thereby complicating his rival's path to the GOP nomination. In May, Mayor Wagner, hoping for another shot at the Senate in 1964, removed himself from contention. Trial balloons were floated for Jim Farley, the legendary New Deal politico, and Franklin D. Roosevelt, Jr. At seventy-four, Farley was too old, while in the minds of many the younger FDR had yet to grow up. In mid-August, Lou Harris returned to the Oval Office with his candidate. Robert M. Morgenthau, forty-three, was U.S. attorney for New York's Southern District, a position to which he had been appointed a year earlier by JFK. Happily married, a much decorated veteran of World War II, Morgenthau, like Herbert Lehman before him, belonged to an eminent German Jewish family. His father, Henry, was FDR's Hyde Park neighbor and, for an eventful decade, his secretary of the Treasury. (It had fallen to young Bob, during a wartime visit to the Morgenthau farm by Roosevelt and Winston Churchill, to hand each man a mint julep.)

All this, it was believed, would bolster Morgenthau's appeal among older, New Deal Democrats, many of them Jewish, who had deserted their party in 1958 to support Rockefeller. A Harris poll, commissioned at the president's behest, duly confirmed Morgenthau as the strongest Democratic prospect to take on Rockefeller. Mayor Wagner rallied enthusiastically to his cause, but neither city hall nor the White House could avert a bloody slugfest at the Democratic convention in Syracuse. To their considerable embarrassment, both Wagner and Morgenthau required the help of Bronx County leader Charles Buckley, one of the stereotypical bosses against whom Wagner had campaigned for reelection a year earlier. A near riot ensued, with raucous cries of "Down with the bosses!" drowning out the band music that was supposed to drown them out. It was four in the morning when Morgenthau finally clinched his nomination on the second ballot.†

---

* In *The Other Side of the Sixties* (New Brunswick, NJ: Rutgers University Press, 1997), John A. Andrew 3rd documents an IRS audit of twenty-two right-wing groups by the Kennedy administration. The Ideological Organizations Project, launched late in 1961, grew out of a memorandum ("The Radical Right in America Today") prepared for the White House by the Reuther brothers, Walter and Victor, along with Joseph L. Rauh, Jr., of Americans for Democratic Action. Inevitably, the probe of tax-exempt organizations graduated to include audits of their major contributors.

† To oppose Senator Jacob Javits, a mission reminiscent of the wartime kamikaze attacks Morgenthau had experienced in the South Pacific, the convention chose James B. Donovan, a New York City lawyer and political newcomer best known for negotiating the release of U-2 pilot

Morgenthau's acceptance speech was punctuated by the sound of delegates leaving the half-empty hall. At that moment, it dawned on those who had seen him as a latter-day Herbert Lehman—Lehman's oratorical shortcomings had mattered little in the pre-television era, when a lack of charisma was taken for proof of integrity. Under the merciless glare of the TV camera, however, Morgenthau simply came off as dull. "He had never run for anything," marvels William vanden Heuvel, then a rising star among New York Democrats, who was particularly close to Bobby Kennedy. "Harriman was stiff. Morgenthau was stiffer. He maybe was the worst single candidate that ever ran for public office." Tall and owlish, a physical cross between Ichabod Crane and Wally Cox's Mr. Peepers, the Democratic nominee for governor was an introspective figure, "the kind of guy who," griped one Democratic partisan, "when you say hello, is lost for an answer." He exhibited no compensating skill at raising money. From the outset, his stance toward Rockefeller resembled the long-suffering schoolmaster saddled with an incorrigibly exhibitionistic child. In public, Morgenthau questioned Rockefeller's truthfulness and financial management of the state. Privately, he called him "a prick."*

On September 19, Republicans meeting in Buffalo renominated Rockefeller by acclamation. Reprising his 1958 attack on Democratic kingpins—this time roosting in New York City Hall and the White House rather than Tammany Hall—Rockefeller drew a line between those "bossed in Buffalo" four years earlier and their successors "stifled in Syracuse." Prospects appeared bright for a record GOP margin in November. Yet even as Rockefeller claimed his prize in Buffalo, an upstart group of dissidents was preparing an assault on the liberal consensus that held both major parties in its grip. The idea of starting a Conservative Party in New York predated the Rockefeller governorship. It was first raised during a January 1957 discussion attended by Bill Buckley, Jr., philanthropist Jeremiah Milbank, Jr., and others dissatisfied with the political status quo in the cradle of the New Deal. Taking advantage of New York's quirky election law, the insurgents showed less interest in electing a separate slate of candidates than in moving the GOP several notches to the right, much as the Liberal Party had long exerted its gravitational pull over New York Democrats.

Francis Gary Powers from Soviet captivity. The same convention made history by selecting Manhattan Borough president Edward R. Dudley to oppose Louis Lefkowitz for state attorney general. Dudley was the first African American to be nominated for statewide office in New York.

* Morgenthau would go on to earn legendary status, not in elective politics, but as New York's district attorney for life (in fact, thirty-four years), serving as inspiration for *Law & Order*'s irascible DA Adam Schiff and prosecuting everyone from John Lennon's killer and "Subway Vigilante" Bernie Goetz to white-collar criminals like Dennis Kozlowski of Tyco fame. Along the way, too, he mentored the likes of Andrew Cuomo, Eliot Spitzer, Sonia Sotomayor, and John F. Kennedy, Jr.

No serious organizational efforts were made, however, until the days immediately following John Kennedy's election, when a pair of young Wall Street lawyers, J. Daniel Mahoney and Kieran O'Doherty, sat down to lunch with others as dismayed as themselves over Nelson Rockefeller's alleged indifference toward the Nixon campaign. Soon thereafter, Mahoney and O'Doherty were introduced to Buckley, who welcomed their aid in the escalating war on Me Too Republicanism. *National Review* senior editor Frank S. Meyer drafted a Declaration of Principles emphasizing smaller government, lower taxes, and an unswerving commitment to the anti-Communist cause. An initial fund-raising appeal produced sufficient response to open a midtown headquarters.

By the summer of 1962, the anti-Rockefeller forces were girding themselves for an obstacle course designed by, and for, the state's major parties. To qualify as a third party on the November ballot, the Conservatives would have to secure at least fifty signatures in each of the state's sixty-two counties and twelve thousand statewide. Every voter's signature must precisely duplicate the one on file with the Board of Elections; forsaking a middle initial or including a professional title rendered the name invalid. The Conservatives nevertheless accumulated more than forty-four thousand signatures, enough to provoke a scorched-earth response from the Republican establishment. In some neighborhoods, Jud Morhouse's agents went door-to-door encouraging signatories to recant. The new party didn't wait until it was assured of a place on the ballot before settling on a candidate to oppose Rockefeller: a forty-four-year-old Syracuse businessman named David Jaquith. President of a local steel-fabricating company, the bald, bespectacled Jaquith was to prove a more convincing prosecutor of the Rockefeller record than the professional Morgenthau. To run against Javits for the Senate, the Conservative state committee designated party cofounder and chairman, Kieran O'Doherty. In his first stump speech, O'Doherty demanded that the United States sever diplomatic relations with the Soviet Union and "all other Communist dominated nations." He also blasted the Supreme Court's recent decision banning prayer in the public classroom.

That Rockefeller was the only governor at a recent meeting of state chief executives to refrain from court bashing didn't sit well with voters for whom cultural issues were beginning to supplant economic ones as matters of concern. Whether Morhouse and his allies could have short-circuited the Conservative challenge will never be known. At the eleventh hour, the Republican power structure threw in the towel, with Rockefeller reportedly overruling his state party chairman. The incumbent felt less threatened by his critics on the right than by the voter apathy. "There's an election going on, but I think a lot of people haven't found out about it yet," he quipped.

12

THIS WAS NOT due to any lack of effort on his part. A year in advance of the election, Rockefeller approached William Pfeiffer to manage his campaign. A profane, tough-as-nails former congressman from Buffalo, Pfeiffer turned down the offer, saying he couldn't afford it. Rockefeller offered to pay him more than his current income of $75,000. "Understand this now," said Nelson, "whatever figure we agree on is coming from me and not as governor." Pfeiffer would not be on the state payroll, nor would he draw a penny from the Republican state committee, "because they haven't got it." Pfeiffer was persuaded. The ensuing campaign was a model of organization, with two hundred paid workers, among them a small battery of women cutting out newspaper articles and other research material so that Emmet Hughes and other speechwriters could customize every Rockefeller text to reflect the interests of whatever audience he happened to be addressing.

Once again the candidate made a point of visiting every county in the state, alternating between his private two-engine Convair plane, the *Wayfarer*, and a campaign bus whose driving time between stops was carefully pre-clocked by advanceman Joe Boyd. In dairy country, Rockefeller blamed Bob Wagner's Department of Health for circulating literature discouraging people from drinking milk "because of cholesterol and other things." Throughout the upstate region, he contrasted the $40 million the state paid each year in debt service with the more than $400 million in debt charges levied on the sadly misgoverned inhabitants of New York City. On street corners in the Bronx, by contrast, Rockefeller offered voters a fifteen-point program to make "all the people well housed, well clothed, well fed, well educated and well protected from adversity."

Morgenthau attacked Rockefeller from the left, alleging a secret plan to increase taxes after the election. The charge met with an immediate and heated denial but lost much of its potency when Morgenthau's running mate Arthur Levitt refused to give it his stamp of approval. Jaquith and the Conservatives enjoyed more success excoriating the incumbent for an ever-expanding financial waistline. Rockefeller's budget was dishonestly balanced, they insisted, reliant on gimmicks such as accelerated tax collections and bond issues. Even *The New York Times* questioned Rocky's arithmetic. "Maybe," the paper editorialized, "prospering business will carry New York through the 1963 calendar year without tax revision upward. Maybe." Stung by the allegations, Rockefeller assured voters that pay as you go was here to stay. "We're not going to raise taxes again," he declared wherever he went. Morgenthau's attacks on the Rockefeller economic record ran afoul of the most basic statistics—unemployment, 7.7 percent in 1958, had dropped to 4.5 percent four years later. At Bill Ronan's instigation, the Rockefeller campaign began publishing a Morgenthau Mistake of the Day, a practice halted late in the contest amid fears it might inadvertently generate sympathy for the Democratic nominee.*

With the race for governor seemingly becalmed, attention veered to a far more gripping confrontation. By mid-October, U-2 flights over Cuba had confirmed the presence of Soviet intermediate nuclear missiles less than a hundred miles from U.S. soil. As fearsome rumors began to circulate, MoMA sent a hundred canvases for safekeeping in the Coach Barn vault at Pocantico, and Kennedy scheduled a prime-time television address for the night of October 22. That afternoon, Bill Ronan got a panicky phone call from press secretary Bob McManus, traveling with the governor. Rockefeller was about to make a statement of his own, prepared by Emmet Hughes, that was harshly critical of JFK.

"Don't put it out," Ronan replied. "I want to talk to him." He was equally blunt with the candidate. "Nelson, if you put out that statement, forget it. You cannot do that."

"Well, this thing's come out," Rockefeller protested, referring to the offensive weaponry even then being assembled on Castro's Cuba. Ronan had an alternate plan. People craving reassurance would likely punish anyone exploiting the crisis for selfish gain. Rockefeller should convene the New York State Defense Council, conspicuously halting his campaign in the bargain. It was good advice, and Nelson followed it. Arriving two hours late for a Republican women's meeting, the governor apologized for his tardiness. He had been delayed, said Rockefeller, because he was putting the state on "maximum readiness alert." Following Kennedy's televised confirmation of the Soviet thrust, Rockefeller contented himself with a brief statement acknowledging the danger and urging all Americans to rally around the president. The next day, he had his symbolic meeting with the State Defense Council. On Saturday, October 27, as the crisis neared its climax, Rockefeller and nine other governors met with Kennedy at the White House. Rockefeller restated his support for the administration, while telling reporter Martin Agronsky that "we have to be ready to face whatever eventuality that may be necessary in the defense of freedom."

Khrushchev's subsequent agreement to remove his offensive missiles from Cuba sent JFK's stock soaring. Democrats everywhere took heart as Election

---

* Even a Rockefeller had to keep a watchful eye on campaign expenditures. "Every Thursday, we would have to go up to Pocantico Hills to see the old lady, the stepmother," explained Bill Pfeiffer. "Lived in the big house and we had to be there promptly at 3 o'clock because all she did was listen to the television all day long. Except she didn't like a certain program at 3 to 4 on Thursday afternoons." Accompanying Pfeiffer on these regular visits was John Lockwood. "John would have a note for a million dollars or whatever the amount was," recalled Pfeiffer, to whom Junior's widow invariably turned for the latest campaign assessment. "I don't think Nelson knows himself," Aunt Martha said, "because he doesn't tell me anything but good things. But he was always saying it's getting more expensive." William Pfeiffer, HMI, 21–22.

Day, November 6, approached. Morgenthau redoubled his efforts to cast the campaign as Rockefeller versus Kennedy. For weeks he had taunted Rockefeller for his refusal to debate him. When the two men—and three minor party candidates—finally met on the Sunday before the election, Morgenthau was primed to deliver a slashing attack on Rockefeller's fiscal policies and personal credibility. (Though he didn't go as far in head gaming his rival as urged by New York City Council president Paul Screvane, who wanted Morgenthau, just before the start of the debate, to go up to Rockefeller and say, "You know, I'm fucking your first wife.") For much of the program, the prosecutor had his opponent on the defensive. Afterward, Morgenthau refused the customary handshake with his rival, a graceless act that distracted attention from an otherwise strong performance.

Democratic officials, citing his energetic debate performance, predicted a Morgenthau win by three hundred thousand. Nonsense, scoffed Bill Pfeiffer, who as late as eight p.m. on election night was forecasting a record victory for Rockefeller. Early returns showed Morgenthau bettering Harriman's upstate showing of four years earlier. In addition, Jaquith and the Conservatives were cutting into Rockefeller support, most notably in and around the antitax hotbed of Syracuse. Originally scheduled for nine thirty p.m., Rockefeller's victory speech slipped two hours. The news wasn't all bad: Rockefeller came within two hundred thousand votes of taking New York City. If the divorce hurt him at all, it was among Protestant voters upstate, not Catholics in the five boroughs. Yet even this accomplishment was overshadowed by Jacob Javits's million-vote landslide at the expense of his Democratic rival.

At a subsequent press conference, Rockefeller sparred with reporters over the size of his win—his final margin of victory was 529,000—and Republican prospects to take back the White House in 1964. Jaquith and the Conservatives had polled 141,000 votes, the vast majority cast in protest of Rockefeller's spending and taxation. Nationally, Democrats benefited from the missile crisis and a surge in presidential popularity. Defying tradition, JFK's party actually picked up three seats in the Senate. The same effect dulled the sharp edge of Republican redistricting. Far from gaining nine seats in the New York congressional delegation, as had been hoped, the GOP was lucky to pick up one. The outcome, disappointing if measured against inflated expectations, was actually quite respectable in light of Rockefeller's tax increases; his divorce and the public sympathy generated by Tod's Nevada sojourn; the bubbling dissatisfaction on the right; and a powerful anti-incumbent trend that sent several Republican governors in the East packing. If Rockefeller entered 1963 with a less robust mandate than he might have hoped, it was as nothing compared with the annus horribilis that lay in store.

Seventeen
SECOND CHANCES

There are two things you must remember. One, he is the Governor of the State of New York. And the other is that he is a Rockefeller.

—HUGH MORROW

1

IN THE POSTMIDNIGHT haze of electoral humiliation, an obscure Rochester judge and political neophyte named John Lomenzo was unprepared for the contrast between his overcrowded headquarters at the Roosevelt Hotel before the polls closed and the late night shambles of empty glasses and cigarette butts that certified his lopsided loss to state comptroller Arthur Levitt. Greater still was his surprise when, at quarter to one on the morning of November 7, the door to his suite opened to reveal Nelson Rockefeller, tie askew, returning to the Roosevelt from a private victory celebration at 812 Fifth Avenue. "He put his arms around Dorothy and me and insisted we wake up the children," Lomenzo remembered. "He sat at the edge of the bed and told the children what a great guy I was." After thanking the defeated candidate profusely for his contributions to the campaign ("You never made a speech anywhere without mentioning me and the others"), Rockefeller urged him to get some rest. "And after two weeks I want you to call me."

This was the first step in a process leading, in August 1963, to Lomenzo's appointment as New York secretary of state, a position he was to occupy for more than a decade. It was also vintage Rockefeller. As the doorman at 812 Fifth Avenue relied on Nelson to help pay his daughter's hospital bills, so Hugh Morrow used a $100,000 Rockefeller "loan" to defray the cost of his teenage son's cancer treatment. Throughout the boy's illness, the governor instructed Morrow not to worry about work, but to spend as much time as possible with his dying son, a grim bonding denied Nelson and Michael Rockefeller. Morrow's second wife, Carol, also afflicted with the disease, received a Christmas check for $25,000, "to help with the fight," Rockefeller wrote in a companion note.*

For every such act of altruism, another testified to Nelson's arrogance. Executive assistant Cynthia Lefferts once singled out for praise a painting displayed in the Executive Mansion. "You admire it," said Rockefeller. "I got it." Lefferts exploded in nervous laughter. "You have it," she conceded. At the end of a long workday in the capital, Hugh Morrow was anxious to avail himself of a ride to New York City offered by a fellow staffer. "You better stay," Nelson interrupted. "You've got nothing better to do." On Christmas Eve, sitting in the big conference room at 22 West Fifty-fifth Street, the clock drawing near to six, Rockefeller had to be reminded that some of those around the table had families in Albany. Such was the forgetfulness of one who had never had to worry about how he was going to get from one place to another.

"Nelson wanted to be a man of the people. But he wasn't a man of the people," contends John Goldman, a *Los Angeles Times* reporter once invited, along with his national editor, Ed Guthman, for breakfast at 812 Fifth Avenue. "The grapefruit were as big as my head and Ed wore his PT-109 tie pin. He was very close to Bobby Kennedy and the Kennedy White House. Nelson looked at him and asked, 'Were you in the submarine service?' and he wasn't kidding. . . . He just didn't know that PT-109 was a Kennedy symbol." A staff colleague asked Ann Whitman to explain the governor's seeming detachment from reality. "It's deliberate," she answered, "to keep you off balance." As a social animal, Nelson appeared infinitely self-assured, his vast wealth "an asset in a way. People expect you to be stuck-up, or a snob, and when you turn out to be like anybody else . . ." The sentence finished itself. Yet there was much it left out. Louis Lefkowitz, a more or less permanent houseguest at the Executive Mansion during the year between Rockefeller's divorce and remarriage, learned to expect a knock on the door of his second-floor room, followed by Nelson's inquiry, "Did you have dinner? Do you mind if I have dinner with you?"

Magnifying his isolation were issues of trust. After hearing political aide Carl Spad recite some youthful challenges he had confronted as a polio victim, Rockefeller momentarily relaxed his guard. He understood Spad's lament, "but imagine going through life never knowing who your friends really are," he blurted out. On this point Ann Whitman was explicit. "The thing about Nelson is that he had no friends," claimed Whitman, who repeatedly urged Rockefeller to emulate in Albany the convivial White House stag dinners staged by

---

* Rockefeller spent $200,000 a year in personal funds to operate and staff the office complex on West Fifty-fifth Street. His gubernatorial salary of $50,000—raised to $85,000 in 1971—was held as a reserve to be tapped for political and other expenses. Rockefeller speechwriter Joe Persico called it his "mad money."

General Eisenhower. From personal experience, Whitman could rattle off the names of two dozen corporate cronies for whom Ike would gladly host an impromptu meal. "Not Nelson," she observed. "Nobody called him unless they wanted something." Osteopath Ken Riland brashly claimed for himself the title of best friend, unaware that behind his back Rockefeller said he had spent thirty-four years trying to convince Riland that "he's my doctor, not my friend."

He might discourage intimacy, yet Rockefeller remained a classic extrovert, for whom meeting people, in the well-chosen words of Nelson Rockefeller, Jr., "filled up his sponge." Late at night, gray with fatigue, all he needed to hear was that there were strangers somewhere, still waiting to shake his hand. "And this pallid, exhausted man suddenly would enter that ballroom," says one eyewitness, "and everything came alive. The adrenaline started to flow and he became warm and alert again. The same way you knew that in a campaign stop hotel, if somebody had a five-year-old kid, [and] the kid hung around the governor's door, he was going to get a big greeting from Nelson." Not everyone was satisfied with a grip and grin. Tax commissioner Joseph Murphy, standing in the lobby of Albany's Ten Eyck Hotel at the end of a typically strenuous day, watched as a sullen young man in military uniform rebuffed the governor's aggressive handshaking. Nearing the exit, Rockefeller looked back over his shoulder. "I wonder what the hell's the matter with that soldier?" As Murphy looked on, Nelson retraced his steps.

"Next thing I knew, I saw the guy smiling, shaking his hand," Murphy related. What had brought about the transformation? he asked Rockefeller once they were outside.

"Well, he was a little drunk and he said he was broke," Nelson explained. "And he was going to miss his train back and he didn't have any money to buy a ticket." So Rockefeller handed him $50.*

Rockefeller told the truth when he said that he liked people. He also knew that a spontaneous act of kindness on his part had a multiplier effect. Staff members were showered with paintings and prints, silver cigarette boxes and Steuben glass paperweights. Rockefeller established a trust fund for his lawyer-adviser Oscar Ruebhausen without telling him. Another Rockefeller fund underwrote the care of Wally Harrison's institutionalized daughter. For her sixty-fifth birthday, Ann Whitman received two thousand shares of Eastern Airlines stock worth over $19,000. When the stock declined in value over the

---

* The extraordinary thing about the encounter is not that Rockefeller bought a train ticket for the young soldier, but that he was carrying sufficient money to pay for it. Other, less spontaneous gifts were clearly made to advance his political interests. Three months after his election as Republican National Committee chairman, William E. Miller was the beneficiary of a $30,000 loan from Laurance Rockefeller, arranged by Nelson in a transparent, if unreported, effort to curry favor with the conservative congressman from Buffalo.

next six months, Rockefeller made up the difference. Joe Murphy saw to what lengths Nelson would go to avoid hurting the feelings of others. Following a working breakfast at the Executive Mansion, Murphy joined several staffers accompanying the governor for the short ride to the Capitol. As the big black Chrysler Imperial pulled up to the curb, Rockefeller alighted from his usual place on the right side of the backseat. Moments later Murphy heard a sharp intake of breath, followed by an exaggeratedly polite request in the familiar sandpaper voice: "Would you mind opening the door, please? My finger is caught." It was, in fact, badly broken. Hastening to absolve the horrified guard who had slammed the door on his finger, Nelson claimed responsibility. "I wasn't paying any attention," he insisted.*

He showed similar forbearance when a reporter's tape recorder malfunctioned and an interview had to be repeated. But he was not always so considerate. On a campaign plane, Rockefeller was perfectly capable of turning to Johnny Apple of *The New York Times*, whom he had met a hundred times, and inquiring, "What do you do for a living?" Once, addressing an upstate audience, the dyslexic governor was distracted from his text by a reporter talking in a low tone at the back of the hall. Stopping in midsentence, Rockefeller asked the offending journalist by name, "Am I going to make this speech or are you?"

As a near perfect composite of presumption and leniency, it would be tough to beat one hastily arranged Sunday night meeting of his inner circle at Rockefeller's Fifth Avenue apartment. Outside, a fierce snowstorm raged, making travel hazardous. "Aren't the trains running?" Nelson inquired in all innocence. Somehow the brain trust managed to cover the 150 miles from Albany to New York by rail. After dinner, the group assembled before the Matisse fireplace in the living room. Joe Murphy took what he thought was an ashtray and put it down beside his chair. "The wind was blowing very heavily," recalled Murphy, strong enough to scatter some ashes out of the fireplace and onto the floor. "The butler came in to sweep up the ashes with a broom. The Governor thought he was going to put the broom handle through the Matisse. And he started on a dead run for the butler to stop him and he stepped in the ashtray. . . . Apparently it was a piece of Ming china." Rockefeller knelt down to sweep up the shattered pieces. "I think we ought to make ashtrays available around here," he said in the voice of throttled rage Murphy had heard once before, when his finger got smashed in the car door.

A staff newcomer basked in gubernatorial praise. "Look at that memoran-

---

* At the Executive Mansion, Nelson frequently visited the kitchen to compliment the cook on dinner—after first giving her time to change her apron. He repeated the gesture in hotel dining rooms and restaurants on the road. He never failed to thank a police escort or elevator operator, or set foot in Binghamton without visiting the nursing home where Billy Hill, his original political sponsor in 1958, lived out his final days.

dum," he said. "It says excellent on the bottom." The reality was soon explained to him. "He'd write at the bottom, 'Fantastic,'" recalls one insider, "but if you got anything less, it was considered you hadn't made your point." So extravagant in his verbal encouragement, Rockefeller conveyed displeasure through a pair of raised eyebrows. Like his hero FDR, he rarely fired anyone, preferring instead to move offenders somewhere they couldn't do any harm. A notable exception came in the summer of 1963, when he parted company—temporarily, as it turned out—with Emmet Hughes after his chief wordsmith published a blistering account of life in the Eisenhower White House. Self-assertion of a different sort cost state conservation commissioner Harold Wilm his job. Wilm was part of the airborne entourage accompanying Rockefeller to a speaking engagement in Rochester. As their F-27 turboprop flew north along the Hudson, Nelson realized it had failed to make the necessary turn to the west. Upon directing inquiries to the cockpit, he learned that Commissioner Wilm had ordered a change of course.

"Governor," said Wilm, "I want you to look down and see what they're doing to the Adirondack forest, my forest." Gazing out the window, Rockefeller spied the concrete ribbon of the Northway, a major traffic artery then under construction between Albany and the Canadian border.

"Yeah, I see," said Nelson. Failing to disclose his own role in selecting the offending route, Rockefeller directed the pilots to resume course for Rochester. "Two weeks later," says a fellow passenger, "we put out a press release announcing that the governor had 'reluctantly' accepted the commissioner's resignation."

2

THE ROUGHEST PATCH of Rockefeller's governorship, surpassed only by the 1971 Attica prison uprising and its aftermath, began with an act of fraternal promotion. Specifically, Nelson wished to elevate his brother Laurance, a lifelong conservationist and, more recently, one of the architects of the state's $100 million park expansion program, to the chairmanship of New York's State Council of Parks. There was just one problem with this scenario. The position was occupied, as it had been for thirty-eight years, by Robert Moses, who showed no inclination to vacate it anytime soon. On November 27, 1962, three weeks before Moses's seventy-fourth birthday, Rockefeller invited the legendary urban planner to Fifty-fifth Street. As Moses described the encounter, Nelson dangled before him a one-year extension of his charge as president of the Long Island State Park Commission—one of three regional park jobs Moses filled, in addition to controlling positions at the State Parks Council, the New York State Power Authority, the Triborough Bridge and Tunnel Authority, and the forthcoming New York World's Fair. In return, Rockefeller asked Moses if the time hadn't come for Laurance to assume the state parks chairmanship.

Moses responded in the only way he knew. He flew into a rage—"threw a fit," in the words of onlooker Bill Ronan. "Bob, why are you sore?" said the governor with a grin. "You picked him—I didn't," he observed of Laurance's appointment to the council. This attempt at levity did nothing to ease tensions. When Rockefeller persisted, emphasizing the need for a smooth transition and orderly planning for the expansion program approved by voters in two referenda, Moses veered to the other extreme, declaring with an old man's petulance his intention to resign *all* his park jobs and, while he was at it, the State Power Authority chairmanship as well. It was the impulsive act of someone long accustomed to having his way with mere governors. Disregarding Rockefeller's offer to sign extensions for all his jobs *but* the State Parks Council, Moses angrily called for his hat and coat, then stalked out of the brownstone.*

That same afternoon, a confident Moses turned the screws on Fifty-fifth Street by reiterating his threat in writing. Within twenty-four hours, he had his answer. Rockefeller accepted his resignations. The master of intrigue had outsmarted himself. Desperate to put his own spin on the news before Rockefeller could reveal it, Moses rushed out a statement accusing the governor of nepotism and ingratitude. "It is regrettable," Nelson declared with icy restraint, "that, in his letter of resignation to the press, Mr. Moses has made an invidious reference to my brother Laurance," whose association with the state park system dated to his 1939 appointment by Governor Lehman to the Palisades Interstate Park Commission. This was an offense far greater than mere rudeness to the state's chief executive.

Moses sought to undo the damage in his wake, even as he drummed his fingers in anticipation of the journalistic cavalry that never came. He sent his trusted deputy Sid Shapiro to feel out Bill Ronan. "He came to me and he said, 'You know, the old man feels very badly about it, and he'd like to mend fences,' and so on. I said, 'Sid, forget it.' When he resigned, and the governor accepted his resignation, I advised him to just shut up and take it," says Ronan. "If there's one thing I know about my man, when he makes a decision like that, it ain't going to be changed very easily." By forcing a public confrontation with the governor, Moses had destroyed the myth of his own indispensability.

If Moses's self-inflicted humiliation contained elements of farce, a second, contemporaneous fall from power bordered on tragedy. It also posed far greater

---

* As he went out, Oscar Ruebhausen came in. He found Rockefeller unruffled and in good spirits, contrary to the agitated figure described by Moses himself. Oscar Ruebhausen, AI.

danger to Rockefeller's political ambitions. Two days after Christmas 1962, Jud Morhouse resigned as state GOP chairman rather than be fired by the governor over his refusal to waive immunity in a mushrooming scandal involving the New York State Liquor Authority. Rockefeller had already terminated SLA chairman Martin Epstein for stonewalling investigators led by Manhattan district attorney Frank Hogan. Pleading ill health—he'd just lost a leg to cancer—Epstein fled to Florida, where he was photographed basking in the sun. His wife was no more talkative when pressed by Hogan's agents to explain the source of $45,000 she had recently invested in Canada. An SLA investigator charged with conspiracy and bribe taking avoided trial by hurling himself in front of an IND subway train at rush hour.

Three long years would elapse before Morhouse was formally charged with conspiracy and bribery—specifically, accepting an $18,000 payoff disguised as "publicity" and "legal services" to help secure a liquor license for Hugh Hefner's Playboy Club on Fifth Avenue. His subsequent conviction marked the worst scandal of Rockefeller's governorship. In fact, official graft was nothing new; but rarely had it been practiced so openly as under Martin Epstein—"my boy Marty" to Johnny Crews, the Republican boss of Brooklyn who served as Epstein's political sponsor. With Rockefeller's victory in 1958, Crews insisted his boyhood friend Epstein be appointed to the SLA. Legislators from both parties competed in praise of the nominee. They changed their tune after District Attorney Hogan, tipped off to corruption within the agency, placed Epstein under surveillance. Soon Hogan had on tape Epstein's own narrative of how he helped himself to an undeserved share of New York's billion-dollar liquor business. On paper it cost a restaurant owner $1,200 a year for the privilege, and profit, of serving thirsty New Yorkers. Epstein levied much higher fees: $2,500 in Brooklyn, $7,500 in Greenwich Village, $12,000 and up in Harlem. Licenses, once obtained, were not portable. Restaurant or liquor store owners compelled to move to another location—a not uncommon event given New York's incessant remaking of itself—were forced to reach into their pockets a second time to satisfy SLA greed. Dishonest cops shared in the loot by "discovering" prostitutes or homosexuals on the premises of uncooperative establishments.

The system reeked of impropriety, yet Albany seemed impervious to its stench. As for Jud Morhouse's influence peddling, "I heard some rumors that he had been making some deals here and there," says Bill Ronan. "But I was surprised at the extent of it." So was Rockefeller. On first hearing of Morhouse's attempted shakedown, he reportedly asked, "Why didn't he ask me if he needed $18,000?" As it happened, Nelson had already taken steps to ease the financial strain on his unsalaried party chairman. In December 1959, he arranged a $49,000 loan from his brother Laurance that enabled Morhouse to purchase stock in two companies, one of which he sold back to Laurance less than two years later for nearly $80,000. In September 1960, Nelson himself loaned Morhouse $100,000 to help him buy some Long Island real estate where the New York Telephone Company housed its trucks.

Reaction to the Morhouse exposé broke along predictable lines. Senate Republican leader Walter Mahoney accused the Kennedy White House of trying to smear Rockefeller, its harshest critic. More constructively, Rockefeller chose a well-regarded former FBI agent named Donald Hostetter to replace Epstein at the SLA. He left the criminal investigation to Frank Hogan and his chief associate, Alfred J. Scotti, both graduates of Tom Dewey's gangbusting operation in the 1930s. Another Dewey assistant, former New York State housing commissioner Herman Stichman, was tasked by Rockefeller with a probe of state agencies to ferret out any Epsteins who might be lurking in the bureaucracy. Finally, acting under the state's Moreland Act, which empowered the governor to undertake investigations in the public interest, Rockefeller enlisted still another Dewey alumnus, retired judge Lawrence E. Walsh (widely known for his later work as an independent counsel in the Reagan-era Iran-Contra probe), to review and recommend needed changes in the state's antiquated liquor laws.

Although no one accused Rockefeller of personal wrongdoing, one could hardly toss an empty beer bottle around Albany without hitting a prominent Republican linked to the SLA mess. Journalists tabbed Louis Lefkowitz's law partner, Hyman Siegel, as the most influential liquor lawyer in New York City. The law firms of both senate president Walter Mahoney and Speaker Joe Carlino exercised suspicious clout with the tainted agency. Long before Hef and his scantily clad bunnies appeared on the scene, Manhattan Republican chairman Bernard Newman had convinced Epstein and the SLA to restore a liquor license to the Gaslight Club, a members-only establishment notorious for its red wallpaper and busty waitresses. Regrettably for the club's owners, Newman's $20,000 fee purchased only temporary protection. By the time they were compelled to repeat the entire charade, Newman was in no position to help his former clients even had he wanted to. The politically connected lawyer had ascended to the bench, courtesy of Governor Rockefeller.

3

ROCKEFELLER'S SECOND TERM began much like his first, with a New Year's Eve dinner for family members and close associates in the Executive Mansion, after which celebrants gathered in the drawing room to await the stroke of midnight. Their host had other plans. No night owl, Nelson bade his guests good night at ten thirty before disappearing to his room. For those living in the Albany area, the abruptly curtailed evening was merely inconvenient. Out-of-towners were forced to improvise. State banking commissioner Oren Root and former attorney general Herbert Brownell, together with their wives, drank in 1963 at the bar of the DeWitt Clinton Hotel. A far greater act of political discourtesy touched off a full-scale legislative revolt. Two months after winning reelection on an ironclad promise of no new taxes, Rockefeller submitted a record state budget balanced through increases in the price of liquor licenses and auto registrations. Embarrassing enough was his failure to consult Republican legislative leaders in advance; worse was Rockefeller's stubborn insistence that he hadn't broken his word to the electorate. The new charges he called for weren't taxes at all, claimed Nelson, but fees. The cost of registering a motor vehicle in New York hadn't gone up since 1923. Liquor taxes hadn't been raised since 1934. What could be more reasonable?

Adding a touch of the surreal, Rockefeller faulted the Kennedy White House for his tax—or, rather, fee—increases. Since the president had failed to deliver on promised economic growth, the governor of New York could hardly be blamed for seeking new revenue sources with which to balance the state's budget. "Promises in politics are nothing new," scoffed the *Dallas Morning News*. "But when a Republican repudiates his promises because a Democrat's promise doesn't materialize, that's news." Republicans already spooked over their 1964 prospects were left to wonder: Which Rockefeller was running for president? The tax cutter of the mashed-potato circuit or the tax raiser of Albany? Already Rockefeller collected 85 percent more revenue than his predecessor. If this was inadequate to enforce a pledge of no new taxes, then GOP lawmakers wouldn't hesitate to slash the proposed budget, killing the auto registration tax/fee and scaling back the liquor license increases. The latter action, welcome as it was, didn't prevent bars across the state from advertising the Rockefeller Cocktail: "Same old ingredients, just add 15% to the price."

"When I make a mistake, it's a big one," Rockefeller conceded. More important than the amounts involved, which were relatively modest, was the changing definition of fiscal responsibility itself. In 1959, Rockefeller had won praise for his courage in raising taxes rather than rely on borrowed money to plug the gap between what New Yorkers demanded of their government and what they were willing to pay for. By 1963, he was far more likely to be criticized for the unchecked growth in state expenditures—up 61 percent from Averell Harriman's final budget—and corresponding holes in the increasingly tattered fabric of pay as you go. In one of his few memorable lines from the 1962 campaign, Bob Morgenthau had recast the governor's cherished formula to mean "we pay"—as in the New York taxpayer—"and you go—to Washington." Rockefeller's sophomore slump, its severity muffled by an ongoing newspaper strike in the Big Apple, had yet to diminish his front-runner's status in the GOP presidential race. A poll of Republican voters in February 1963 gave him a whopping 49 to 17 percent advantage over Barry Goldwater.

That such numbers might be misleading was confirmed by a *Congressional Quarterly* survey of delegates to the 1960 Republican national convention. While nearly two-thirds expected Rockefeller to be their nominee in 1964, when asked to identify their *personal* preference, 46 percent said Goldwater, and only 34 percent named his rival from New York. Murray Kempton, writing in the *New Republic*, neatly assessed the situation in an article entitled "He Has It If He Wants It, and He Does." While Kempton conceded Rockefeller the Republican nomination, the same author described him as "a receiver in bankruptcy" and listed JFK as a prohibitive favorite to win reelection. It's not hard to see why. By the spring of 1963, John F. Kennedy had skillfully preempted the middle of the road. Although a late convert to the cause of black Americans, and as yet only a measured advocate of nuclear disarmament, he was politically well positioned on both issues.

Kennedy's opponents were called on to exhibit a corresponding nimbleness. On economics and Cold War concerns, Rockefeller ran at JFK from the right. His position on civil rights was just as clearly to the president's left. Only a few months after the Cuban missile crisis ended in what was widely viewed as an American triumph, Rockefeller accused the administration of scuttling the Monroe Doctrine by allowing Soviet troops to remain on Cuban soil. Kennedy's refusal to support fresh military action by anti-Castro Cuban exiles, à la Bay of Pigs, left the governor scratching his head. His use of the emotionally charged word *appeasement* earned Rockefeller a rebuke from *New York Times* columnist James Reston.

In April 1963, Rockefeller took his conservative act on the road. Addressing what was billed as the largest political dinner in Kansas history, he was interrupted by applause more than thirty times as he railed against "domination from Washington." Before an even bigger crowd in Omaha, he contrasted a sluggish economy and 5.6 percent unemployment with JFK's 1960 campaign promise to get the country moving again. Rockefeller promised to create twenty million new jobs over the next five years by boosting the annual rate of economic growth. Taking issue with Kennedy's proposed $8.7 billion tax cut spread over thirty months, the New Yorker demanded an immediate cut of $10 billion in personal and corporate taxes. In the short run, he acknowledged, this was sure to increase the federal deficit. But the spurt in economic activity generated by his tax cuts would produce a surplus within two or three years. A generation before Ronald Reagan instituted similar policies, Rockefeller offered the nation a preview of supply-side economics. Midwestern audiences ate it up.

Republican members of Congress pronounced themselves equally impressed following a closed-door question-and-answer session with the out-of-town visitor (though even here Rockefeller needlessly diminished his triumph by failing while in the capital to call on New York senators Javits and Keating, as protocol demanded). Wherever he went that spring and summer, the governor balanced traditional Republican passwords such as "individual initiative" and "private enterprise" with Lincolnesque tributes to "equal opportunity" and "the worth and dignity of every individual." Asked if his stance on racial justice might not harm Republican prospects in the South, Rockefeller stood his ground. "We have certain responsibilities that transcend political advantages," he responded, "and one of them is certainly in the field of civil rights." The issue received priority treatment in Rockefeller's 1963 legislative program in New York. Building on previous initiatives, he expanded fair housing laws to include 95 percent of all dwellings in the Empire State and strengthened minority access to state contracts and construction projects.

His support for the social revolution reaching its moral crescendo in Birmingham during the first week of May 1963 made Rockefeller anathema to the Conservative Society of America, a right-wing splinter group whose national chairman doubled as leader of the Louisiana chapter of the John Birch Society. To the CSA, Rockefeller was a dangerous northern agitator bankrolling Dr. King and other troublemakers. It was right about the bankrolling part, at least. After hundreds of Birmingham youngsters, responding to King's appeal, were jailed for taking part in the so-called Children's March on May 2, King lawyer Clarence Jones was summoned to the vault of the Chase Manhattan Bank. There he was handed a briefcase full of Rockefeller cash. Officially described as a loan, the money helped pay bail costs for the movement's youngest foot soldiers. On his return to Birmingham, Jones found in his mail an unsigned receipt, informing him that his "loan" had been fully repaid.

4

THE EXECUTIVE MANSION was ablaze with light, its fanciful contours starkly outlined against a smudged winter sky late in January 1963. The sound of massed feet crunching on snow gave way to animated chatter as Governor Rockefeller greeted his guests at the door. For once he knew the names of those crossing his threshold. It was a gathering such as Albany had never witnessed: sixty of the nation's premier architects, each of whom the governor led on a tour through the old house with its extensive display of museum-quality art from his private collection. Rockefeller was in his element. "That's not modern," he assured one guest who professed bewilderment over a particularly challenging canvas. "Picasso painted that fifty years ago."

Between cocktails and hors d'oeuvres, Rockefeller made a pitch for the State University Construction Fund, established on his own initiative after voters turned down his bond issue underwriting the rapid expansion of SUNY. In the past, responsibility for public design and building had rested with the state's Department of Public Works. The resulting buildings, produced at a glacial pace by engineers rather than artists, inspired no one. Not content to expedite the process, Rockefeller wanted instead to blow it up. His solution was to consolidate responsibility—empowering a single designer and general contractor to think, and build, outside the box—while minimizing interference by bureaucratic middlemen. "We have devised a scheme for tapping the best talent in the country," he enthused. At the same time, he decentralized overall planning. So while the Board of Regents decided what was taught in SUNY classrooms, the physical appearance and character of each campus in the system reflected local input.

As Rockefeller made good on his promise to slash red tape, world-class architects put aside their doubts and accepted his invitation to work for the state. By the fall of 1963, the State University Construction Fund had committed more than $70 million to twenty-two separate campus designs, many the fruit of Nelson's personal recruitment efforts. In tiny Fredonia, working in vineyards formerly devoted to the making of Welch's grape juice, I. M. Pei created a stunning array of circular buildings linked by elevated walkways. Ulrich Franzen's laboratory building at Cornell University won numerous awards for design excellence. For a new, arts-oriented college at Purchase in Westchester County, Rockefeller gave his blessing to an all-star creative team that included Edward Larrabee Barnes (a theater complex), Philip Johnson and John Burgee (an art museum), Venturi and Rauch (social sciences building), and Gwathmey, Henderson and Siegel (dormitories).*

Given his passion for building, it was only a question of time before Rockefeller turned his sights on New York's capital, whose proud past served only to accentuate its current decay. Suffering the same exodus of people and businesses that afflicted much of urban America at the threshold of the 1960s, Albany was unmistakably a city in decline. Said one close Rockefeller associate, "It makes Tobacco Road look like Park Avenue south of 72nd Street." The September 1959 visit of Princess Beatrix of the Netherlands presented the governor with a severe logistical challenge. Having Her Royal Highness arrive by boat

---

* The State University Construction Fund soon had a twin using the same off-budget financing mechanisms to build hospitals and other facilities serving New Yorkers with various mental illnesses.

limited her exposure to the blighted environs around the Executive Mansion. A year later, the king and queen of Denmark flew into town, and short of blindfolding the eminent visitors, there was no way to hide the shabby face of the old Dutch trading post. Both visits would later be cited as catalysts for Rockefeller's defining building project.

In truth, a more prosaic reality governed Rockefeller's actions. "We needed space for state office buildings," says Bill Ronan. Beyond this stark fact, "Nelson was very interested in doing something downtown because downtown was dying," he claims. Rockefeller hadn't forgotten some advice, delivered at the start of his governorship, by Tom Dewey's protégé Burdell Bixby. "Start building a monument to yourself," Bixby had counseled him. Confirming evidence of this came in 1964, when the former governor's name was formally affixed to the 562-mile New York State Thruway constructed on his watch. Within weeks of taking office, Rockefeller had ordered the grimy old Capitol scrubbed and its western façade floodlit at night. Neglected lawns were replanted, dotted with beds of roses, the state flower. A fountain appeared in a park hitherto given up to derelicts. Inside the massive structure, Rockefeller streamlined the executive work space. He transformed a dusty Civil War museum through the addition of modern lighting, exhibits, and professionally trained guides.

All this was merely prelude to the main event. From the governor's second-floor office, the view south toward the Executive Mansion encompassed some forty blocks, whose six thousand inhabitants had proven themselves reliable supporters of Dan O'Connell and his Democratic machine (on occasion reporting more votes than census-counted voters). The area went by multiple names. To historic preservationists, whether of buildings or political majorities, it was the Pastures, a deep-rooted, lower-middle-class neighborhood of Italian row houses and Jewish-owned shops, descended from a seventeenth-century common grazing space. To Rockefeller, it was the Gut, a sinner's paradise notable for the 1931 murder of gangster Legs Diamond and for more recent commercial establishments with names such as French Emma's, Big Charley's, and the Red Onion. In the years prior to World War I, the area had supported an estimated twelve hundred prostitutes, from dollar-a-trick streetwalkers to bunny-hugging hostesses whose refinements earned them $25 an evening.

For a brief time in the 1940s, Tom Dewey had menaced the O'Connell machine by launching a series of highly publicized investigations into municipal and county government. The former Gangbuster called off the dogs only after O'Connell threatened to identify prominent Republican patrons of some of the Gut's seamier establishments. By the time Rockefeller took up residence, the neighborhood featured as many vacant lots as rooming houses. Rockefeller considered this an affront to every New Yorker. "There is nothing in the laws of nature or the nature of men," he declared, "to require that a state which is big and vital and productive must also be mundane, dirty, and ugly." In April 1961, he established his blue ribbon Temporary State Commission on the Capital City in defiance of Mayor Erastus Corning. First elected in 1943, the product of a dynasty grounded in Martin Van Buren's Albany Regency, Corning had no intention of surrendering control of his city to some (Republican) outsider intent on using it as a springboard to the White House. Especially *this* outsider.

The two men had a history. In the 1920s, the Cornings, enriched by their stake in the Albany Iron Works and a healthy share of government contracts during World War I, had established a summer residence on Maine's Mount Desert Island. Young Erastus and Nelson Rockefeller, his senior by fifteen months, had competed against each other on the tennis courts of the Northeast Harbor Club and in the tricky waters off Mount Desert. Now the boyhood antagonists battled for supremacy before a national audience. Whether they had, in fact, grown up was open to dispute, never more so than when Nelson ordered sycamore trees planted within sight of Corning's city hall, confident it would offend the mayor's aesthetic sensibilities. Nor was it accidental that Rockefeller's intervention on behalf of a more beautiful Albany should occur six months after the mayor took the wraps off his own downtown improvement effort. Corning accused Rockefeller of trampling on home rule.*

But these were mere skirmishes compared with the mortal combat joined early in 1962. By then the Wilson Commission, entrusted with site selection for a state government complex, had considered five different locations, most too remote from Albany's downtown core to boost the local economy. That Rockefeller had his own ideas on the subject was confirmed one Saturday afternoon when he appeared with Wally Harrison in the office of counsel Bob MacCrate. "Bob," said Rockefeller, "do you mind if Wally and I sit on the table behind your desk? It's the only place on the second floor of the Capitol where we can look all the way over to Lincoln Park." For the next two hours, as MacCrate organized the coming week's business, his visitors mapped out the future South Mall (in Nelson's spelling, the South Maul). They took pains to conceal their intentions from their counterparts across State Street in Albany City Hall. For the state to surrender the element of surprise was to invite an orgy of land speculation and semiofficial extortion.

On a Sunday evening in January 1962, Rockefeller assembled key staff members in the Executive Mansion. Budget Director Norm Hurd presented a list of projects and programs where overspending had occurred, all relevant to the state's deficiency budget.

---

* It didn't escape popular notice that Corning's demand for an extra $6 million in state aid dovetailed neatly with Rockefeller's discovery of $9 million in unpaid Albany property taxes.

"Does anybody have any other things to add or discuss?" Rockefeller asked those in attendance.

Ronan took his cue. "Why don't we put in $33 million to take the property downtown?"

"Great idea," said Rockefeller.

"Governor," Hurd interjected, "this is a deficiency appropriation."

"Well, this is a deficiency. We want the land, and this"—figuratively calling their attention to the seedy landscape surrounding the mansion—"is a deficiency." Ronan supplied the legislative rationale, declaring, "If you put this up as an individual item, you will never pass it . . . if you put it in right up front, you'll know whether you can go with it or not." Rockefeller was well pleased. In the event, lawmakers swallowed hard and approved the full sum. In March 1962, surveyors appeared on downtown street corners, instruments of their trade in hand, trying to look inconspicuous. Should questions be raised by citizens or probing journalists, the surveyors were to identify themselves as students (some, admittedly, a bit long in the tooth) from nearby Rensselaer Polytechnic Institute, engaged in a class project. On March 27, a Rockefeller aide strode into the county clerk's office clutching a newly drawn map of downtown Albany. Malcolm Wilson, who maintained close ties to the state's Catholic hierarchy, had managed to save the massive Cathedral of the Immaculate Conception from the wrecking ball. Not so with 1,150 other structures on 98.5 acres, among them 4 churches, 29 saloons, a new high school, and a police station. Once the transfer was officialized, Bill Ronan notified Rockefeller that he was now landlord of seven whorehouses.

"You don't say," Nelson replied.

Erastus Corning wasted no time in denouncing the process from which he had been deliberately excluded. Decrying the "sterile monument" Rockefeller would impose on the rubble of a vibrant urban neighborhood, Corning filed suit to block the state's "ruthless takeover." The lawsuit achieved its immediate objective, by demonstrating to constituents that Corning had no intention of rolling over for the Republican governor and his bulldozers. His outrage eased perceptibly once Rockefeller offered assurances that no one would be evicted in time to affect existing voting rolls or, presumably, the usual crushing Democratic majorities in that fall's elections. Confident of his legal position, on May 24 Rockefeller announced that Wally Harrison had accepted his invitation to take the lead in developing an overall plan for the South Mall. ("I had a lot to do with everything Nelson didn't do," was how Harrison subsequently described his contributions to the project.) Flying up from Washington one day, Rockefeller had taken him into his confidence. "He drew on the back of an envelope a sketch plan—and asked me what I thought of it," Harrison said later. "I said I didn't know but it looked pretty good to me."

He would live to regret those words. Half a mile long by a quarter mile wide, the vast tract spanned a deep ravine christened Rat Creek by early Dutch settlers. In the nineteenth century, six hundred thousand yards of gelatinous blue clay had been dumped into the streambed to provide building sites for a growing city. Rat Creek itself was converted into a sewer, emptying into the nearby Hudson River. It was Rockefeller's idea, "because he wanted the feeling of separation," to bridge the creek with a great wall, in fact a multitiered platform. He had seen such an arrangement in the Tibetan capital of Lhasa on his first honeymoon. Thus did the soaring palace of the Dalai Lama lend inspiration for the new Albany. Atop this structure, with its six floors of parking, mechanical systems, and a twenty-five-hundred-seat convention center tucked away for good measure, Rockefeller envisioned a quintet of marble-clad office buildings, one taller than the rest, a uniquely shaped ovoid performing arts center, a pair of reflecting pools, each the size of a football field, and a 336-foot-tall Arch of Freedom to contain within its base draft copies in the president's hand of Lincoln's Emancipation Proclamation and Washington's Farewell Address.

On June 30, 1962, an appeals court reversed the injunction earlier granted to the city. Rockefeller celebrated by ordering the demolition of sixty-six abandoned buildings. Mayor Corning vowed to fight on but soon changed his mind. His suit had been brought, the mayor explained, to gain time for the city "to find out just what this Mall meant." While reiterating his warning of a $600,000 loss in tax revenues, Corning nevertheless praised the governor for his sympathetic understanding. His Damascene conversion was complete. What happened next has long been enshrouded in Albany legend. According to Samuel Bleecker, who studied the matter exhaustively for his Rockefeller book, *The Politics of Architecture*, Corning telephoned bond lawyer Joseph McGovern, a trusted friend, and described a stalemate in which the heart of Albany was hollowed out, yet Rockefeller was unable to secure a bond issue to pay for "Brasilia."

"Joe," Corning concluded, "is there any way the city or county can do it for them?"

There was, just as Erastus Corning knew all along. The state would turn the property over to the city (later Albany County) before leasing it back. Albany County would in turn finance construction of the South Mall by selling a series of forty-year bonds, their proceeds to be funneled back to the state as the county's agent. When the outstanding loan was paid off in 2004, the completed mall would revert to state ownership. Corning's initial explanation of his scheme elicited no response from the governor. A month later, Corning repeated his performance. "Oh, is that what you meant?" said Rockefeller. Corning, quick to assume credit for cutting the fiscal Gordian knot, claimed that Nelson "went after the scheme like a trout for a fly."*

On April 16, 1963, the legislature overwhelmingly approved the deal with Albany County. Casual estimates pegged the cost of the South Mall at $250 million. Much depended on when ground was broken. Although negotiations with property owners proceeded more smoothly than expected—less than 1 percent of transactions ended up in court—the same talks dragged on for eighteen months. Corning's stall tactics, interspersed with public charges of misrepresentation and bad faith, would delay major construction until 1968. When, a generation later, he was asked on his deathbed to identify his greatest satisfaction in a political career spanning almost fifty years, Corning replied unhesitatingly, "I had Nelson by the balls." This missed a larger point: for while Corning indulged an ancient grudge, his city had been permanently remade by the adversary whose signed photo the mayor hung over his commode. There is little doubt which man had the last laugh.

5

ADOPTING HIS FAVORITE guise of disinterested problem solver, Rockefeller liked to say he was interested not in politics, but in government. "He had an almost pathetic belief in the power of an idea," confessed his first state budget director, Norm Hurd. At one point during the 1962 reelection campaign, Henry Kissinger had chanced to mention the fragility of global water supplies and touted the conversion of seawater as a possible solution. Within days Rockefeller confided to campaign manager Bill Pfeiffer, "I have someone working on this." Now, in anticipation of the approaching presidential race, Nelson undertook an elaborate graduate course in public policy, reminiscent of Quantico and the Special Studies Project. For instruction he relied on the enigmatically named DNA Group, a private think tank that operated out of Rockefeller Center. Kissinger headed the section dealing with foreign affairs, while domestic concerns were entrusted to Rod Perkins and his youthful deputy John Deardourff. The latter explained how the latest Rockefeller brain trust worked.

---

* Corning's solution was less radical than it appeared. Private industry had long relied on lease-purchase arrangements to acquire needed work space. Averell Harriman had resorted to similar tactics in the 1950s, when expanding his predecessor's state office campus on the outskirts of town. Rockefeller, however, enlarged the concept to unimagined dimensions, and not just in Albany. The same formula would be used to finance construction of new state office buildings in Binghamton, Buffalo, and Utica, among other cities.

"He liked to get fairly detailed position papers, with a lot of information about the pros and cons; who thought what, who was on which side of what issues," said Deardourff. "If it was some labor issues, or some business–labor conflict, where was George Meany on this, where was the New York transit workers, where was the U.S. Chamber of Commerce?" The next step was to assemble a group of leading experts and specialists. "Sometimes they would want to be paid," according to Deardourff, "sometimes . . . they thought being paid was compromising." Two or three hours would be blocked out on Rockefeller's schedule and a set of questions prepared to ensure the time was put to good use. "He would get them in that room together, and he would make very flattering opening remarks about how they were the best there were, and he knew they didn't always agree on everything, but maybe there was some common ground that we could talk about. Maybe there wasn't. But he wanted to hear what they thought."

Each of these sessions was taped and transcribed, Deardourff continued, after which "we would do a synopsis of what was said and get those back to him." Any campaign organization has its share of internal rivalries and competition for the candidate's time and favor. Around Rockefeller, no one battled more incessantly than Henry Kissinger and Bill Ronan. Kissinger deputy Doug Bailey remembers drafting an early speech on Vietnam, which his boss thoroughly rewrote before submitting it for group vetting at Fifty-fifth Street. "There were about ten people who sat around the table," recalls Bailey. Rockefeller was at the head, flanked on either side by Kissinger and Ronan. Everyone was given a chance to review the draft and to offer comments, though "generally you didn't argue much with Henry Kissinger." Ronan was the exception. "Henry, this is just superb," he declared of the Vietnam text. Indeed, there were only two changes he would suggest for the governor's consideration.

"Here on page one, where it says yes, why don't we say no. And then on the last page, when it says none, why doesn't it say all?"

Kissinger made ready to leave. "When you go to Spain and you buy a Picasso," he told Rockefeller over his shoulder, "and you bring it back and hang it in the Governor's Mansion, you don't hire a housepainter to touch it up."

Paradoxically, the DNA Group might have benefited from more, not less, infighting. For while it produced no shortage of promotable ideas—among them an early version of Richard Nixon's federal revenue–sharing scheme—an aura of groupthink clung like mothballs to the organization's earnest white papers and recycled scholarship. For all its good intentions, DNA did little to advance Rockefeller's chances in a party, and a process, where empirical analysis was increasingly trumped by ideological fervor. DNA contributed to the appearance of a candidate with more ideas than convictions, an impression strengthened by the contrast between his activist agenda in New York and his strident criticism of the Kennedy presidency before Republican audiences.

6

THE ROCKEFELLERS WERE like any family in their capacity for turning the disposition of an estate into a surrogate battle over rank and long simmering resentments. Martha Baird Rockefeller, though reluctant to move into Kykuit following Junior's death, had no doubt who should take her place. It would give her much pleasure, she told Nelson, "with the developments in your personal life and your tremendous official obligations," if he would make Kykuit his home. As an added incentive, she offered to continue paying the costs of upkeep, not excluding servants' food bills. David Rockefeller tells a somewhat different story. No one disputed that the big house built for his grandfather lent itself to Nelson's gubernatorial duties. But it *belonged* jointly to him and his siblings, John, Nelson, and Laurance. As for the irreplaceable contents of Kykuit, David proposed to replicate the lottery system most recently used to apportion furnishings and artwork from the Eyrie, the vast cliff-top dwelling on Mount Desert that was demolished in January 1963 (thereby saving the family $10,000 annually in state and local taxes). At this Nelson became, in David's words, "absolutely livid, angrier than I had ever seen him." He needed the house, said Nelson, treasures intact, for entertaining. His public service was in the family's interest; for that reason alone, nothing in the place should be disturbed.

David, already dismayed over his brother's divorce and continuing relationship with Happy Murphy, was in no mood to surrender the canary-yellow De La Courtille porcelain dessert service (1773–1800). Not only was Junior's will explicit on the subject; David had the law on his side. His bluff called, Nelson backed down. Of course, everyone should take what they wanted, he declared, without resort to a lottery or other formal selection process. "Typically, once he had lost the battle," wrote David, "Nelson accepted the decision. He never carried a grudge." Actually, he had something far grander in mind. Viewing Kykuit as a prospective monument to his family, Nelson began readying this national treasure for the distant tramp of visiting tour groups. Predicting that "one day it will really soften the house," he planted wisteria vines that half a century later envelop his grandfather's hilltop castle. In his artistic tastes as in his politics, Rockefeller combined opposites with astonishing facility. Kykuit's eighteenth-century music room, stripped of JDR's Aeolian pipe organ, became a medley of the traditional and contemporary. A stern-faced portrait of Nelson Aldrich took up watch opposite the colorful chaos of Joan Miró's *Hirondelle Amour*. Both pictures blended harmoniously with Chinese ceramics, Persian carpets, and a bronze chandelier. Underneath the house, Philip Johnson reworked Senior's service tunnels into gallery space for Nelson's Picasso tapestries, which shared wall space with works by Robert Motherwell, Grace Hartigan, and Fritz Glarner.

Outdoors, the changes were even more dramatic. In place of his grandfather's classical figures in formal gardens, Rockefeller sited Claes Oldenburg's *Homage to Mickey Mouse*, Louise Nevelson's *Atmosphere*, and a larger-than-life nude modeled by Lincoln Kirstein. Helicopters were employed to install Henry Moore's monumental *Knife Edge*, much to the annoyance of David and some important Chase Manhattan Bank clients he had invited to play golf on Senior's nine-hole course. Enlisting the services of landscape architect David Harris Engel, Nelson planted a double row of clipped hornbeam trees leading to Moore's abstract bronze piece. He worked closely with Engel to fashion a Japanese garden, complete with rustling bamboo grove and twelve-foot waterfall. At his client's urging, Engel dispensed with new granite cubes as pavers. Instead he went to Albany's municipal dump, where he found thousands of worn cobblestones still bearing the marks of nineteenth-century carriage wheels. It was yet another of Nelson's eureka moments; he had seen in these casually discarded stones a beauty that eluded other eyes.*

Nelson in full curatorial mode presented a memorable sight, as John Deardourff witnessed for himself one Sunday morning, ostensibly set aside by the Rockefeller high command for an earnest discussion of policy and politics. Arriving late, Nelson told the assembled group that he would join them as soon as he attended to some pressing business.

"And it turns out the something that he has to do is to help uncrate and site a very large piece of sculpture, which has just arrived at about the same time we did, on this big van. And that is going to have precedence," recalls Deardourff. From the sidelines, he watched as a burly quartet of movers unloaded their host's latest acquisition. "They get this thing off the truck and they sit it upright. It's crated, and it takes a while, it's not like the UPS man has arrived. And we're all sitting there, the time was nine or nine thirty, and they get the crate undone, and the piece emerges, and it's a Brâncuşi sculpture. Then the fun begins, because it's clear that Nelson has an idea of where he wants it. . . . And it has to do with the angle of the sun from the room where he can see it in the morning. And it's back and forth, he has to go up and look, and then he has to come back

---

* Just as he secured a large pair of planters atop the old Ten Eyck Hotel in Albany before its demolition. Happy Rockefeller, AI.

down, and moves it an inch this way, that. And this goes on until almost eleven in the morning. And then the meeting. And it wasn't until that was done, and he was satisfied that it was exactly the right place, that we could continue."

Martha's offer to vacate Kykuit reflected an understanding, as yet limited to the immediate family and a handful of advisers: Nelson had no intention of living there alone. She may have left her job as confidential assistant to the governor in the spring of 1961, but Happy Murphy was still very much part of the Rockefeller entourage. Al Marshall, then deputy budget director, thought she was "some kind of a consultant on 'the woman's viewpoint.'" At a staff conference, Rockefeller counsel Sol Corbin was about to object to something said by a woman he didn't recognize. "Suddenly I felt this grip on my thigh"— Malcolm Wilson's way of admonishing Corbin to silence. Corbin's ignorance was matched by the condescension of other Rockefeller staffers, who blithely pigeonholed Mrs. Murphy as the latest in a procession of gubernatorial dalliances. "She seemed typical of her class for the time," says one co-worker. "A time when women from her background were discouraged from attending college." Though she lacked a degree, Happy read voraciously, especially history and literature. Revealingly, she identified with the world-beaten heroines of Edith Wharton.

It wasn't her taste in fiction that captivated Nelson. "She was a gorgeous woman, lush in femininity, and Nelson was almost like a schoolboy in love," remembers journalist John Goldman. "She was just dazzling in those days," adds George Gilder, briefly employed as a Rockefeller speechwriter. "She had a way of glowing at you, and her glow made you feel you were the most brilliant man in the world." Gilder comes as close as anyone to putting into words the utter intensity of focus, light-years beyond mere charm, flattery, or, for that matter, sex appeal as conventionally defined, that ignited in Nelson a need bordering on obsession. "He was the pursuer," Happy asserts. "And I never knew whether it was because if he couldn't get what he wanted, he went after it harder." Well aware of the raised eyebrows in Room 5600, she contends, "I didn't want to control him. As a matter of fact, I wanted to be controlled by him." The potential impact of their romance upon his presidential prospects was never discussed. Indeed, over time Happy came to question his desire to be president. "Because every time he came close," she observes with laughing eyes, "he went and did something stupid—like marry me!"*

Defying the popular view that Nelson waited until his father's death to go

---

* In conversation with the author in 2000, Oscar Ruebhausen testified to the feverish nature of Nelson's courtship of Happy Murphy, so unlike his scattershot pursuit of the presidency. "There are thousands of pages of handwritten love letters," he revealed, all in Rockefeller's hand, and none likely to see the light of day.

public with their courtship, Happy maintains that Junior was aware of the developing relationship and raised no objection. Again inverting conventional wisdom, she attributes to Junior a compassion more often associated with his wife. "The mother would not consider divorce," she notes. "Abby would not condone divorce. I think more of her sons would have"—here she paused—"because they were too young when they got married." As for Tod and Nelson, "They knew that they were mismatched." She and Nelson were a different story. "We were cut out of the same piece of cloth. . . . Nelson said, 'Happy, you make me strong,' and I told him, 'Nelson, you make me strong.'"

Cynthia Lefferts saw another side of the evolving relationship. "Happy added a wonderful kind of exuberance and a lightheartedness to his life," says Lefferts, qualities long suppressed in his marital cold war with Tod. "Did that man ever need to be loved," agrees Evelyn Cunningham, a pioneering African American journalist who joined the Rockefeller staff after an interview that turned into a two-hour monologue about the loss of Michael Rockefeller and other emotional deprivations in Nelson's life. Away from the office, Nelson and Happy did little to cover their tracks. "Discretion wasn't in him," says Bob Pyle, later a member of the Seal Harbor police force, but then one of the teenagers in the Maine costal community who conducted their backseat gropings—in local jargon, "watching the submarine races"—in a suitably romantic oceanfront overlook. More than once, they were joined by a gold-colored Avanti whose official license plate instantly identified its middle-aged occupants. "He could not have possibly believed that he was getting away with anything," Pyle marvels. "Everybody knew it was going on." Everybody, it appeared, but Robin Murphy. "Who's going to tell him?" asks Pyle.

That Rockefeller might exercise less command than he or Happy presumed became embarrassingly clear as their relationship came under scrutiny. Early in 1962, *Time* magazine picked up on rumors of an impending Rockefeller marriage to the mysterious Mrs. Murphy. In April, a much fuller account of the Rockefeller-Murphy romance appeared in *Confidential*, a furtively read scandal sheet with a profitable addiction to thinly sourced tales of interracial sex, Hollywood abortions, "lavender lads," and "baritone babes." Left out of *Confidential*'s account was the private anguish of a family disintegrating under the hot lights of the modern media. A full year passed, during which the Murphys unsuccessfully attempted a reconciliation. Robin Murphy, hounded by intrusive reporters and held up to ridicule by a sensationalist press, did not lack for weapons in the unfolding emotional combat. Unable to prevent Nelson Rockefeller from expropriating his wife, Dr. Murphy had no intention of surrendering his four children in the bargain. For Happy, the price of a divorce was nothing less than custody of the Murphy children. Afterward, the lack of a specific plan for visitation rights enabled her to claim that the issue of custody remained unsettled. But that is not how most people interpreted the outcome, with disastrous consequences for Rockefeller's presidential hopes.

Speculation about her marital plans, subdued for much of 1962, was rekindled in April 1963 when Happy secured her own out-of-state divorce in Idaho on grounds of irreconcilable differences. Thereafter, the journalistic frenzy approached levels associated with Hollywood's most notorious adulterers, Richard Burton and Elizabeth Taylor, whose highly publicized affair on the set of their ill-fated epic, *Cleopatra*, had riveted the public for months.* Through it all, Rockefeller kept his counsel. "He won't tell us and I know it's no use asking him," George Hinman confessed to a curious GOP official. "One of these days he'll call a meeting and tell us his decision without any preliminaries and without asking our advice." In the end, it fell to *BusinessWeek* to say out loud what Republican strategists were beginning to whisper in confidence. "If he marries Mrs. Murphy," the magazine quoted one party source, "he might as well take the gaspipe."

This discouraging prophecy had just hit the newsstands on Saturday, May 4, when fifty-four-year-old Nelson Rockefeller wed thirty-six-year-old Happy Murphy in a brief ceremony moved at the last minute from Hawes House—redolent of Tod Rockefeller's thirty-year residence—to the nearby home of Laurance Rockefeller.† Happy's children stayed away, but one of her brothers attended, as did a cousin, also named Margaretta. Conspicuously absent from Laurance's living room were the groom's other siblings and two of his four surviving children, who with their spouses chose this sunny afternoon in May to stroll the estate's expansive grounds. After the exchange of vows and a celebratory lunch, Nelson called Barry Goldwater to apologize for missing an upcoming dinner at which he was scheduled to pay tribute to the senator. "Rockefeller just got married," a nonplussed Goldwater informed his wife, Peggy. "Bully for him!" she replied.

"You have so needed a partner who could share your trials as well as your successes," wrote Nelson's Lincoln School classmate Bill Alton. This was a distinctly minority view. More representative of the raw emotions sweeping many an American household that convulsive weekend was a Bill Mauldin cartoon

---

* When the film finally opened in New York a month after Nelson wed Happy, ten thousand delirious fans showed up to see, cheer, and bask in the reflected notoriety of Liz and Dick. Clearly, fornicating politicians were held to a different standard from that of their movie counterparts.

† The night before, Laurance called Happy and asked whether she had the help of experienced public relations and legal personnel. When she replied in the negative, Nelson's brother offered to dispatch such assistance early the next morning. "Your marriage to Nelson is going to be national news, and I do not want you to be hurt." It was an act of kindness she never forgot. Bruce Sundlun, "How Happy Rockefeller Changed My Life," *Providence Sunday Journal*, July 25, 2004.

in which a perplexed Rockefeller sits in his doctor's office, describing his latest symptoms. "I keep hearing bells," says the distinguished patient. "First they peal, and then they toll." *National Review* publisher William Rusher had no doubt for whom the bells tolled. Acknowledging the controversy surrounding custody of the Murphy youngsters, a mordant Rusher cracked, "Rockefeller is the only candidate who has turned motherhood into a liability." Journalist Fletcher Knebel suggested that a university bestow on Rockefeller the title Doctor of Romance Languages. Barber Conable, a future Republican congressman and World Bank president then serving his first term in the New York Senate, chuckled approvingly when his wife renamed their amorous tomcat Nelson.

Some of the harshest criticism emanated from the least expected places. Liberal theologian Reinhold Niebuhr, citing feelings of outrage expressed by his cleaning woman, rapped the governor on moral grounds. The *New Republic*'s TRB columnist, a Greek chorus of the responsible Left, didn't mince words ("He is through") in questioning Rockefeller's capacity to provide the country with ethical leadership. The newlyweds were still honeymooning at Nelson's Venezuela ranch when the Pulitzer Prize board, offended by the play's frank depiction of adultery, overrode a recommendated award for Edward Albee's *Who's Afraid of Virginia Woolf?* Connecticut senator Prescott Bush, father and grandfather to American presidents, delivered the most stinging rebuke, rhetorically asking an audience of graduating prep school students, "Have we come to the point in our life as a nation where the governor of a great state can desert a good wife, mother of his grown children, divorce her, then persuade a young mother of youngsters to abandon her husband and children and marry the governor?"*

Rockefeller pollsters offered reassurances that the storm would blow over in a matter of months. Publicly, George Hinman wore his bravest face. "With love sweeping the country," Hinman told reporters a few days after the wedding, "I've decided to take a few weeks off and take my wife to Europe." Before leaving, Hinman and other Rockefeller strategists reached out by phone to a hundred of their staunchest supporters around the country. One recipient characterized the call as "friendly, inquisitive, and a bit anxious." Hinman aggressively marketed the new Mrs. Rockefeller as "political dynamite. She's an-

---

* Rockefeller might be forgiven for questioning the double standard applied to his romance, which after all culminated in a second marriage, compared with the sexual recklessness routinely practiced by the incumbent president of the United States—a situation well-known to reporters, who didn't dream of confiding their secrets to print. As early as the 1960 Wisconsin primary, journalists aboard the Kennedy campaign bus had devised a private slogan for the charismatic candidate: "Let's Shack with Jack." Hal Bruno, AI.

other Jackie Kennedy, a real campaign asset." It was a claim unsustained by the Gallup poll. Prior to his May 4 nuptials, Rockefeller had enjoyed a commanding 43 to 26 percent lead over Goldwater among Republican voters. At the end of May, as the newlyweds returned by way of the Virgin Islands from their honeymoon at Nelson's Venezuelan ranch, Goldwater was ahead 35 to 30 percent. Nearly as ominous was a surge of support for Michigan's first-term governor, George Romney, a political moderate whose Mormon faith infused his public moralism. The shift of independent voters away from Rockefeller was even more pronounced.

Upon returning to New York at the end of their seventeen-day honeymoon, the Rockefellers embarked on a whirlwind of political fence mending. There was the annual Waldorf dinner benefiting the state GOP; a tea for Happy sponsored by Republican women of the Hudson Valley; and a series of "backyard cookouts" around the Empire State, staged so that New York Republicans could reconnect with their governor and meet the state's new First Lady. It was to please Nelson that Happy conquered her shyness, overcame her indifference to designer clothes and lavish jewels, and charmed strangers come to see what the scandal was all about. Her first tentative campaign outings left him beaming with pride. Her personal enjoyment of these rituals was less evident. Indeed, in her preference for home and hearth, the new Mrs. Rockefeller resembled no one more than Tod, unless it was Jackie Kennedy. Reinforcing her feelings were some ugly incidents that would have traumatized a far more experienced public performer. At one early reception in the Executive Mansion, Happy extended a gloved hand in greeting, only to have the woman before her spit on the floor. Out of earshot, waspish Albany cave dwellers rechristened the old house the Woman's Exchange.

A classic man's woman, Happy had few close female friends. She developed a surprising affinity for the working press; reporters in turn appreciated her unspoiled ways. Many sympathized over the plight of a woman precluded by law and circumstance from exercising her obvious maternal instincts. As for Nelson, attaining his marital object had done nothing to diminish his sense of entitlement, much less his cheerful disregard for any obstacles in his path. Under the circumstances, even those sympathetic to his politics, or concerned for his happiness, came to regard his divorce and remarriage as symptomatic of deeply flawed judgment.*

---

* Just as Winston Churchill, royalist to the core, had belatedly concluded that statues should be erected to Wallis Simpson in gratitude for her role in aborting the reign of Edward VIII, so many a Republican offended by Nelson Rockefeller's personal and political weaknesses might recognize the woman he loved to the point of infatuation.

7

WHEN THE REPUBLICAN National Committee convened in Denver for its summer meeting on June 22, George Hinman had a new partner in his advocacy of Rockefeller interests. Joining him in the elegant confines of the Brown Palace Hotel was the short, gnomish figure of Freddy Young (real name Fred Capobianco), the governor's handpicked replacement for Jud Morhouse as GOP state chairman. Addicted to profanity and garish ties—which it was his habit to whip off before presenting them to surprised recipients—Freddy outdid himself in Denver. Table-hopping at a committee luncheon meeting, the New Yorker approached his patrician counterpart from Alabama and brightly inquired, "When are you going to stop jerking off with Goldwater?"

"I beg your pardon, suh," said the disbelieving son of Dixie.

Young repeated his challenge. Violence was threatened. "Ten minutes later, however, they were pals," said one onlooker. "They left arm in arm . . . the blue and the gray together, with Freddy as the force." Sectional harmony was harder to come by when the conversation turned to a winning strategy for 1964, and especially to issues of race. For southern Republicans, many of them lifelong Democrats with the paint still wet, Birmingham had been as galvanizing as it was to progressives who shared Rockefeller's allegiance to the party of Lincoln. Encouraged by their showing in the 1962 elections, still more by a decline in Kennedy support among white southerners as the administration became identified with Negro protesters, a new breed of southern Republicans rallied under the banner of states' rights. For many in both parties, this was a code word for segregation. The Denver conclave heard the boisterous southern chairman talk openly of "niggers" and "nigger lovers." "There's an insanity in the air around here," muttered George Hinman.

That their electoral votes, no less than their moral convictions, were deemed expendable by the emerging Goldwater majority came as a profound shock to Republicans in the industrial Northeast and Midwest. Their surprise turned to horror a week later, as they observed the strong-arm tactics and slashed telephone lines that characterized a two-day meeting of Young Republicans in San Francisco. Columnist Robert Novak wasn't the only observer to conclude that California's pivotal delegation was "infested" by members of the John Birch Society. Tactics of delay and disruption were employed, as one meaningless roll call after another exhausted the less ideologically fervent. It was shortly after five o'clock in the morning when the insurgents secured the victory, by two votes, of their candidate for YR chairman, one Donald "Buz" Lukens, a Capitol Hill staff member whose platform called for abolition of the income tax and exalted the free right of association—that is, opposition to federally mandated desegregation.

The outcome might have been different had George Hinman granted the request of Bruce Chapman, a Harvard undergraduate and cofounder of *Advance*, a magazine promoting the cause of progressive Republicanism. Early in 1963, Chapman pleaded with the Rockefeller organization for $50,000 to prevent the Young Republicans from falling under Birchite control. Since this ran counter to Hinman's strategy of making no enemies that could be avoided, Chapman went away empty-handed. There is no evidence that his appeal was ever communicated to Rockefeller personally. The breakfasts with Goldwater at Foxhall Road; the darting forays into conservative strongholds and subsequent blurring of ideological distinctions; the studied neglect of natural allies such as Bruce Chapman: All this reflected Rockefeller's reliance on sinuous charm and tactical flattery to realize his objectives.

Writing in the *New York Herald Tribune*, Roscoe Drummond predicted more of the same. "Mr. Rockefeller intends to work diligently to promote unity in Republican ranks," said Drummond. "It is his conviction that for either Republican conservatives or Republican liberals to 'go fishing' because the GOP nominee might not be to their liking at every point would be self-punishment of the worst sort. *This is why Mr. Rockefeller does not plan to campaign against any Republican competitor* (emphasis added). His campaign will be for himself and for national policies that he believes will promote a strong economy and a better stance in the cold war." But that was before the Young Republicans rumble triggered Rockefeller's confrontational side. "Had he been born poor," says one who helped him man more than one barricade, "he would have been the best barroom street fighter on the Lower East Side."

No small part of Rockefeller's deficiencies as a presidential candidate can be traced to these warring selves and to the resulting oscillation between the patience required for prolonged courtship and the thrusting ambition to bulldoze one's way to victory. A one-man House Divided, suspended between backroom maneuver and frontal assault, throughout his political career Rockefeller was careful to surround himself with advocates for each of his dueling identities. Initially, the disarming Frank Jamieson had been paired off against the more combative Bill Ronan. More recently, Nelson had wavered between the urbane diplomacy of George Hinman and the slashing tactics of Emmet Hughes. In the summer of 1963, the familiar debate again roiled the Rockefeller camp. Encouraging Nelson to draw a line in the sand against their party's right wing was California senator Thomas Kuchel, a moderate Republican in the Earl Warren tradition. In a state where Birchers already held sway over the California State Assembly, Kuchel had defied warnings from Goldwater and others to mute his public criticism of extremist groups. Remaining true to his convictions, the outspoken senator had won a second term in the fall of 1962 by three-quarters of a million votes. For Kuchel, the Young Republicans convention represented a point of no return. The identity and even the existence of his party hung in the balance.

From Washington, Jacob Javits echoed Kuchel's preemptive challenge. Indeed, Javits would have Rockefeller issue his declaration of principle on national television, hugely magnifying its audience and impact. Objections to this were raised by Fred Young and others who feared a repeat of the governor's disastrous June 1960 jeremiad assailing Nixon on the eve of the Republican convention. Characteristically, Rockefeller went his own way. Genuinely dismayed by the brutish conduct exhibited in Denver and San Francisco, he could scarcely believe that the heirs to Lincoln, TR, and Ike might now recast themselves as the White Man's Party. Another, more personal motive drove Rockefeller to unload on his right-wing tormentors. Fairly or not, he had convinced himself, as he told Goldwater, "You conservatives are picking on me for marrying Happy."*

On Saturday, July 13, Rockefeller alerted Goldwater to expect within twenty-four hours a statement of "common interest." This hardly prepared the senator for the broadside to come, starting with its premise that "the Republican Party is in real danger of subversion by a radical, well-financed and highly disciplined minority." For proof, Rockefeller pointed to the recent Young Republican convention in San Francisco. Boring from within, "vociferous and well-drilled extremist elements" had pursued "the tactics of totalitarianism" in order to seize control of the YRs. Now, flush with success, "Birchers and others of the radical right lunatic fringe" were hell-bent on capturing the rest of the party. In the process, they proposed to write off black and other minority voters, ignore the industrial states of the North—"representing nearly 50 percent of the country's population"—and turn their backs on the urban electorate, in favor of an electoral strategy built on the South and West.

"The transparent purpose behind this plan," said Rockefeller, "is to erect political power on the outlawed and immoral base of segregation." Such a program would not merely defeat Republicans in 1964; by putting states' rights ahead of individual rights, it risked destroying the only truly national party in America. "Political success cannot be divorced from political morality," Rockefeller thundered. His concern was authentic. But he exaggerated the grassroots appeal of his argument and his own credibility in making it. Goldwater, furious over what he regarded as a rank betrayal, crisply informed his staff, "There'll be no more breakfasts. None at all." Predictably, the most biting denunciation came from Bill Buckley's *National Review*. Criticizing Nelson's rule-or-ruin

---

* "Not this conservative, Nelson," Goldwater replied. "I've never said a word." There is every reason to believe him.

tactics, the editors concluded, "Let Mr. Rockefeller preach his ideas of the principled life to his various families, and spare the nation his cynical moralizing."

This was to be expected. Of more immediate worry to the Rockefeller camp was the lack of enthusiasm his call to arms generated among fellow moderates such as Hatfield, Scranton, Romney, and Nixon. The most deafening of silences enveloped Gettysburg, where Dwight Eisenhower showed no appetite for joining the fight, especially if it meant aligning himself with his frequent critic in Albany. On August 5, Rockefeller made things worse by refusing to pledge his support for Goldwater as a Republican presidential nominee "if he were a captive of the radical right." So much for Roscoe Drummond's forecast of a positive, unity-minded Rockefeller campaign. By Labor Day, the entire Rockefeller effort was teetering on the brink of irrelevance. Visits by the candidate to Illinois and Virginia were notable for the local Republican luminaries who contrived to have scheduling conflicts that prevented them from sharing a platform with the former front-runner. Rockefeller chose Roanoke, Virginia, no hotbed of pro–civil rights agitation, as a platform from which to criticize the Kennedy administration for appointing federal judges unsympathetic to the Negro cause. Arch Gillies, the young advanceman who organized his visit to southwest Virginia, sensed the candidate's discomfiture. "New York was his dukedom," says Gillies. "He was never easy on the road where I saw him in '63 to '64. He was outside of his barony." One-on-one, Rockefeller remained a fabulous campaigner. "But he didn't move around, he didn't really have the instincts for national politics."

Foreign policy remained his first love. In the third week of September, Rockefeller crossed the Atlantic for a two-week, six-nation European tour. More comfortable in Rome than Roanoke, he chatted in French with Charles de Gaulle at the Élysée Palace and received a warm greeting from Konrad Adenauer in Bonn. In divided Berlin, Rockefeller made the obligatory Cold War pilgrimage to the Wall (he couldn't resist waving to an East German border guard, who smiled back). At the Vatican, the visitor defused an awkward situation by leaving Happy behind when he called on newly elected Pope Paul VI. A more urbane atmosphere pervaded Chequers, the country residence of British prime minister Harold Macmillan. Ahead of the Rockefeller visit, Macmillan notified Edward Heath, his Lord Privy Seal and future successor, where his true interests lay. "I really want to meet Happy," the PM told Heath. He was in for a disappointment. As the Rockefeller car pulled up to the front door, Nelson popped out and began a vigorous pumping of Macmillan's hand.

"Where is your wife?" said Macmillan.

"Oh, she decided to go shopping in Bond Street. But I have brought my adviser, Henry Kissinger, with me."

Macmillan got even over lunch, impishly diverting the flow of conversation whenever it veered close to Rockefeller's objective, which was to extract from the PM a confidential exposition of his views and policies. Instead Macmillan, son of a great publishing family, played verbal games, urging his visitor to write a book describing his current European tour. Finally the wily host escorted his mystified American guests to the door.

"And don't forget to write the book," he called out in parting. Turning to Heath, Macmillan let down his guard. "After all," said the old fox, "he ought to have known that I am Jack Kennedy's man."

Rockefeller enjoyed no greater success on his native soil. One rain-swept autumn evening in Manhattan, Alfred Barr delegated to a MoMA subordinate named Rona Roob the regular delivery to 812 Fifth Avenue of a packet containing art catalogs and color transparencies for Rockefeller's review. Roob's evident displeasure with the assignment led Barr to admonish her. "Rona, I want to tell you that Nelson Rockefeller was the best president this museum ever had," he said. "And it's our job to keep him really interested in all the new things that are going on, because he's never going to be president of anything else. And when all this is finished"—presumably a reference to Rockefeller's foray into politics—"I hope he'll come back here and take up his role."

Nothing better illustrated Rockefeller's frustrations than his embarrassingly prolonged quest for a national campaign director. With Herb Brownell having long since ruled himself out of contention through his opposition to the governor's divorce, Rockefeller humbled himself sufficiently to court his former rival Len Hall. When Hall said no, Nelson appealed on bended knee to his Dartmouth classmate—and Hall's predecessor as Republican national chairman—Meade Alcorn. Again he struck out. In near desperation, Rockefeller finally turned to Jack Wells, a savvy graduate of the Dewey political organization and William P. Rogers's law partner. A white-haired Buddha whose cheap cigars and man-of-the-street persona masked his Rhodes Scholarship and establishment connections, Wells had no shortage of experience. Most recently, he had managed Louis Lefkowitz's 1961 campaign for mayor and Jacob Javits's reelection effort the following year. But he was the first to concede that he lacked the national contacts and credibility of a Hall or Brownell.

By the time Rockefeller made his formal declaration of candidacy on November 7 on NBC's *Today* show, many had written him off. These included the man he hoped to replace in the Oval Office. Once, JFK had expressed fear that Rockefeller might switch parties and take him on as a Democrat. "I can beat Goldwater," Kennedy told author Gore Vidal, "but Nelson's something else." But that was before Nelson's divorce and remarriage. On November 13, 1963,

John Kennedy spent three and a half hours in preliminary planning for an expected campaign against Goldwater, a personal friend and political foil, whose likely strength in the South would be more than offset in urban and industrial regions where Eisenhower had built his landslides. When talk turned briefly to Rockefeller, the president was dismissive. His nomination "would be too good to be true," mused JFK, "but he doesn't have a chance."

Eighteen
THE ROAD TO SAN FRANCISCO

Rockefeller's wife ain't going to let him get off the ground.

—Lyndon B. Johnson, February 1964

1

No one privy to his schedule for November 22, 1963, could doubt Nelson Rockefeller's commitment to an admittedly uphill campaign. At his Fifty-fifth Street office complex, he juggled work on the upcoming state budget with final preparations for a weekend trip to New Hampshire, site of the nation's first presidential primary. Unusual for a Republican, Rockefeller's New Hampshire itinerary included meetings with local labor leaders as well as a dinner allowing the governor to work his charm on radio, TV, and newspaper executives from across the Granite State. It was a safe bet no representative from the *Manchester Union Leader* would be present. Four months had passed since the state's paper of record had briskly declared that "the people will not accept a wife swapper as President." This was one of the milder jabs directed at Rockefeller by the *Union Leader* and its famously abusive publisher, William Loeb. A striking resemblance to Daddy Warbucks was the least of Loeb's cartoonish qualities. "I believe that there is a publisher who has less regard for the truth than William Loeb," John F. Kennedy had once observed, "but I can't think of his name."

The *Union Leader*'s clout could not be so readily dismissed. Even among readers repelled by Loeb's personal attacks, many sympathized with his disdain for "saltwater bastards" on both coasts who presumed to set the cultural and political bars for their countrymen. This made Nelson Rockefeller, no less than the city he called home, a perfect foil for Loeb and his editorial writers. For evidence of New York's exaggerated sway in political, media, and financial circles, one need only follow a random sampling of Republican power players navigating its glass canyons on this last Friday before Thanksgiving: former president Dwight Eisenhower (of Abilene, Kansas) is ensconced in a suite of the Waldorf Towers, a dozen floors above the last Republican president, Herbert Hoover (West Branch, Iowa), who abandoned his California refuge twenty years ago in order to be closer to the nexus of American politics and communications. Last night, Ike was honored by Columbia University, over which he briefly presided after World War II. Today he is scheduled to attend a luncheon promoting the United Nations, another Rockefeller family institution dismissed by critics on the right as a verbose token of One World futility.

Eisenhower's vice president, Richard Nixon (Yorba Linda, California), is in the air this morning, bound for New York aboard an American Airlines flight that left Dallas less than three hours before President Kennedy was to motorcade through the streets of Big D. Like countless New Yorkers before and since, Nixon is a transplant from the Other America, drawn to the Big Apple by meritocratic ambition and a low threshold for boredom. A year after losing the California governorship to Pat Brown, Nixon is settling into a new life at the Wall Street law firm he shares with John Mitchell (Detroit, Michigan), the dour-faced bond lawyer and architect of Nelson Rockefeller's creative approach to government finance. In one of those "only in New York" coincidences, Nixon and Rockefeller are neighbors at 812 Fifth Avenue, the co-op building into which Rockefeller had expanded following his 1962 divorce from Tod.

For today's lunch, Rockefeller has penciled in the name of Thomas E. Dewey (Owosso, Michigan), godfather to Nixon's national career and personification of the GOP's once mighty Eastern Establishment. The two men, king-maker and dauphin, are to meet at Rockefeller's Fifty-fourth Street Clubhouse for a discussion of the upcoming contest for Republican supremacy. Dewey's support of Rockefeller has less to do with individual loyalty—he is personally closer to Nixon—than with professional calculation (the Dewey law firm having no wish to incur Rockefeller displeasure on their shared turf). As the two men talk politics, a few blocks east of 13 West Fifty-fourth, Eisenhower at the Hotel Chatham is listening earnestly to a presentation by UN secretary-general U Thant.

The diplomat has yet to finish his remarks when, shortly after one o'clock, Richard Nixon settles into the backseat of a cab parked outside Idlewild Airport. The taxi threads its way through residential Queens, halting momentarily near the Queensboro Bridge, where an agitated pedestrian approaches the car to ask whether the driver has his radio on. The same man says he has heard reports of shots being fired at the presidential motorcade in Dallas. On West Fifty-fourth Street, the news is confirmed all too quickly, a black maid tearfully interrupting the Rockefeller-Dewey lunch with word that JFK has been mortally wounded. As Dewey slips out of the brownstone, and Eisenhower makes his excuses at the Chatham, Rockefeller telephones each of his children to relate what he knows and offer reassurance about the country and its future. After arriving home to be greeted by an emotionally distraught doorman, Nixon places a call of his own to FBI director J. Edgar Hoover. "What happened," inquires the former vice president, "was it one of the right wing nuts?"

It is a thought that occurs to many. In the few brief hours before Dallas police announce the arrest of a pro-Castro Marxist named Lee Harvey Oswald, a barrage of death threats forces the national Draft Goldwater headquarters on Washington's Connecticut Avenue to temporarily lock its doors. From New York, Rockefeller issues a statement conveying his shock and grief. He suspends all political activity for thirty days, then drives home to Pocantico to be with his wife of six months. Inevitably their conversation turns to the new president, Lyndon Johnson, a Rockefeller acquaintance since the 1930s. Nelson recalls a recent governors' conference at which his courtesy call on the vice president had prompted a Johnson diatribe over the frustrations of a meaningless job. Tossing aside a prepared speech text, LBJ snorted his disagreement with its contents. The White House had insisted that he deliver it unchanged. It was typical of his treatment, complained Johnson, who felt isolated and ridiculed by those around the president.

Now this volatile, brooding Texan, his talents on a par with his self-doubts, is to occupy the Oval Office coveted by Rockefeller. Nelson, unsurprisingly, foresees problems. "Oh, Happy," he tells the woman beside him, "Lyndon thinks it's going to be like chasing the deer off the Pedernales." They join the vast audience of dazed Americans who, amid the unfolding tragedy, turn to the three television networks for help in distinguishing fact from speculation. At one point, CBS anchorman Walter Cronkite mistakenly reports that a previously scheduled political function will prevent Barry Goldwater from attending the late president's funeral. In fact, Goldwater is in Muncie, Indiana, this Friday afternoon, overseeing preparations for his mother-in-law's funeral. He has already dispatched a note of condolence to Jacqueline Kennedy. Cronkite's on-air apology does little to dispel the belief, fervently held by Goldwater loyalists, that what a later generation would label "the mainstream media," physically and emotionally grounded in Manhattan, are profoundly biased against the Other Americans living west of the Hudson River.

Truth be told, Goldwater was badly shaken by Kennedy's death. Although polar opposites in style and outlook, the two men had genuinely enjoyed each other's company. Lately they had fantasized about waging an unconventional contest of ideas in 1964, a modern-day equivalent of the Lincoln-Douglas debates, in which the opposing candidates might even share a plane as they traveled from one venue to the next. It was not a campaign Goldwater expected or even hoped to win, except intellectually. Little about the modern presidency appealed to the senator from Arizona, a reserved, often cantankerous man, openly scornful of Rockefeller's backslapping, blintz-eating approach to the campaign trail. Privately, Goldwater harbored doubts about his own intellectual capacity for the job. Still, he reasoned, if he could score even 45 percent of the national vote against the charismatic Kennedy, it would represent a moral victory for his brand of unapologetic conservatism. And it would massively advance the goal he cherished far more than the White House—wrenching control of his party from the grip of "New Deal Republicans" such as Nelson Rockefeller.

Early polls in pivotal New Hampshire gave Goldwater a three-to-one advantage over Rockefeller, a head start underscored by the organization of the late senator Styles Bridges and the fervent support of Bill Loeb's *Manchester Union Leader*. The same surveys showed far more voters praising Goldwater's forthright sincerity than criticizing his support by the radical Right. More respondents thought Rockefeller was prone to making irresponsible statements than his Arizona rival. Goldwater thus began the New Hampshire campaign as an idealized version of himself. But Rockefeller believed that what Granite Staters didn't know about his opponent's libertarian distrust of government might yet trump what they thought they knew about the free-spending (and free-loving) governor of New York.* November 22 strengthened him in his hunch, even as it sparked a reassessment of Goldwater's prospects by pundits and party officials alike. A recent Gallup poll had shown the senator leading JFK by ten points in the South. With Kennedy gone, and his successor claiming deep roots in the Lone Star State, the region seemed likely to revert to its traditional Democratic loyalties.

At the same time, the substitution of Johnson for Kennedy restored to competition a number of industrial states in the Northeast and Midwest. "They say Nelson is too much like Kennedy was," explained a hopeful Rockefeller aide. "Well, if Kennedy had that appeal in the North, so will Nelson." Should Rockefeller fail to exploit the opening, there was no shortage of moderate alternatives, as Goldwater freely acknowledged. With the frankness that was at once his most appealing and most self-destructive attribute, the Arizonan told reporters that if he fell short of the necessary majority at his party's San Francisco convention, he would flip a coin between Dick Nixon and Pennsylvania governor William Scranton. Toward the new president, he harbored less generous feelings. Away from the cameras, he railed against LBJ as a treacherous wheeler-dealer who would "slap you on the back today and stab you in the back tomorrow." Depressed and withdrawn, Goldwater told his wife, Peggy, that he wasn't running.

---

* For example, a third of Goldwater's New Hampshire supporters took issue with their candidate's vote against the recent treaty to bar nuclear testing; two-thirds challenged his belief that the United States should withdraw from the United Nations if Red China gained admission to the world body.

On December 8, a small group of friends and advisers hoping to change his mind assembled in Goldwater's Washington apartment. Like it or not, they told him, he had become Mr. Conservative, a title whose obligations transcended individual desires. New Hampshire senator Norris Cotton likened his colleague's historical mission to Charles de Gaulle's wartime rescue of French honor. Len Hall took a less lofty approach. "For God's sake," he boomed, Goldwater had to make the race if Republicans were to choose "somebody besides Rockefeller." Hall's logic was not lost on the reluctant candidate. "If I'd said no, it would probably have meant Rockefeller's taking over, and I could never sit still for that," Goldwater conceded long afterward. On January 3, promising the electorate "a choice, not an echo," he made it official. Three days later, as Goldwater flew east to launch his New Hampshire campaign, the *Union Leader* summed up the flailing Rockefeller candidacy in three words: Deception, Deceit, and Divorce.

2

L ESS BUCOLIC, OR monolithic, than its Currier & Ives caricature, New Hampshire was a state in flux. The supposed Yankee bastion was in fact 40 percent Catholic, home to substantial voting blocs of French Canadian, Polish, Irish, and Greek descent. That said, Granite State politics were less diverse than its population. Notwithstanding a Democratic governor and United States senator, the result of internecine squabbling over which Republican would fill the Senate seat left vacant by Styles Bridges's death in November 1961, New Hampshire was essentially a one-party state, wherein the politics of factionalism proved pettier and more bitterly personal than clashes over ideology. One consequence of this was a Goldwater bandwagon crowded with officeholders—and office seekers—who despised one another more than they admired Goldwater. In a party of one was former governor Wesley Powell, evicted from office in 1962 after he alienated both the *Manchester Union Leader* and Bridges's equally conservative widow, Doloris, whose plan to succeed her husband in the Senate had not survived a rough-and-tumble GOP primary. A vengeful Powell nourished his own White House ambitions, though he would gladly settle for a place on a ticket headed by Richard Nixon.

These were just some of the rapids Rockefeller would have to negotiate in advance of the March 10 primary. So treacherous a course required the services of a pilot experienced in the state's shifting allegiances and enmities. Someone very much like Hugh Gregg. Elected to the State House in the Eisenhower sweep of 1952, Gregg at thirty-four had been the youngest governor in the state's history. A decade later, he was as desirous of getting his old job back as Mrs. Bridges was of going to the Senate. A tightfisted administrator even by New Hampshire standards, Gregg would appear an unlikely advocate for Nelson Rockefeller—which helps explain why George Hinman was so ardent in his pursuit of the former governor throughout the first half of 1963. In August, Gregg and his wife, Kay, were invited to Pocantico, where Rockefeller stressed his budget balancing in New York and an approach to foreign policy firmly rooted in the postwar bipartisan tradition.

The encounter opened Gregg's eyes to a Rockefeller more conservative than his public image. To the former governor, Nelson's down-to-earth personality was tailor-made for the retail politics of New Hampshire. The 1964 primary, open to independents as well as registered Republicans, was expected to attract one hundred thousand or so voters, an electorate ideally sized to Rocky's one-on-one salesmanship. Ten days after this initial meeting, Hinman returned Gregg's visit. He didn't leave the Gregg household until he had his agreement to manage the Rockefeller campaign in the Granite State. Reinforcing their outreach to the Right, Rockefeller and Hinman also hired Gregg's youthful protégé Bert Teague, formerly statewide director of Young Americans for Freedom. For Nelson it was 1958 all over again, with Gregg and Teague filling the role of Malcolm Wilson in vouching for the candidate's conservative credentials. Gregg's strategy was to showcase Rockefeller in informal settings where no question was off-limits, no subject taboo. Scheduling "coffee hours" in motels and other public facilities exposed hundreds at a time to the governor's charisma and fluent command of the issues. It also meant dispensing with the usual Rockefeller entourage, a condition of Gregg's employment that he found increasingly difficult to enforce as primary day drew nearer.

For twenty-eight days, Rockefeller bounced across the state in a bus. Overcoming his aversion to early morning events, he actually seemed to gain energy from the grueling routine of street tours and VFW halls, high school assemblies and Chamber of Commerce lunches. Visiting a hockey arena near the Canadian border, he stood on the ice between game periods and addressed the crowd in French. Kelly's Drugstore in Newport exhausted its supply of ice cream after Nelson promised to buy cones for all the youngsters in the crowd. Between stops, Rockefeller took pains to schmooze, not with the national reporters he had long cultivated, but with the editor of the *Coos County Democrat* and other local opinion makers. Gregg insisted on it. Nelson hadn't entirely outgrown his old suspicion of entrusting a subordinate with excessive authority. This included Hugh Gregg. One day Gregg, mindful of a slipping schedule, attempted to pull Rockefeller away from a loquacious factory tour. The candidate responded by seeking out a worker at the opposite end of the building and chatting with him for fifteen minutes. The message to would-be handlers was hard to miss.

As ever, events exercised a control beyond any organization's planning. A few days after Christmas 1963, the governor's office announced that a pregnant Happy Rockefeller expected to give birth around June 1. Three weeks later, the Rockefeller campaign taped a potentially game-changing broadcast assailing Happy's sometime tormentor Bill Loeb as a figure to be pitied, only to shelve the program out of fear it would reopen the divorce issue. As long as the contest was about Rockefeller—his marriage, his morality, his activist record in Albany—the New Yorker was at a disadvantage. Somehow he had to alter the dynamic of the race, enlisting Yankee caution on his side, promoting himself as the Responsible Republican while convincing a critical mass of voters that Goldwater was no Bob Taft conservative, but a trigger-happy zealot whose views were dangerously outside the mainstream. He got a lucky break in the first week of January, when Goldwater's arrival in the state was followed by a string of politically maladroit comments that had the senator's supporters scratching their heads.

At his first press conference in Concord, Goldwater declared that Social Security could be improved by making it voluntary. He also endorsed a renewed invasion of Cuba by Cuban exiles trained in the United States. This was just the beginning of Goldwater's ordeal by candor. In the next few days, the senator startled the Pentagon by calling America's nuclear missile deterrent "undependable"; offended labor by blaming a lack of worker skills on low intelligence and lack of ambition; and neutralized his personal record of promoting desegregation by arguing against civil rights legislation then bottled up in the Senate. Singling out for constitutional censure the bill's section on public accommodations, Goldwater rasped, "I don't believe for a moment that laws are going to solve this." When Fidel Castro turned off water supplies to the American base at Guantánamo, Goldwater vowed to send in the U.S. Marines to turn them back on. Such pronouncements led New York Times columnist James Reston to describe the Goldwater platform as a witches' brew of "rugged individualism, jungle economics, and gun boating diplomacy."

Quick to pounce on his opponent's gaffes, Rockefeller told a Manchester audience on January 9 that leaving Social Security to individual choice would wreck the system (only two states skewed older in their population than New Hampshire). He contrasted his record of support for education with Goldwater's opposition to federal involvement in the nation's classrooms. At a January 24 dinner in Concord attended by thirteen hundred supporters, Rockefeller went further than ever before in pinning the extremist label on his opponent. He singled out for criticism Goldwater's opposition to the graduated income tax and his "half-baked" proposal for the United States to withdraw from the UN should Red China be admitted to the organization. To eliminate the progressive tax system, as the senator advocated in his book (a copy of which was conveniently stashed in Happy's handbag), and replace it with a flat tax would mean higher taxes for nine out of ten Granite Staters.*

There was more to the Rockefeller campaign in New Hampshire than fear-mongering about Goldwater. Whenever he had a chance, the governor reverted to his favorite fall campaign topics—a lagging economic growth rate, the weakening of U.S. alliances abroad, and Washington's alleged failure to understand Communist objectives and methods. With conditions in Vietnam "visibly deteriorating," the new administration oscillated between expanding the war and honoring JFK's October 1963 pledge to withdraw a thousand U.S. military personnel before year's end. Rockefeller began talking of a "leadership gap" under Johnson, whose murky policies in Southeast Asia were already subsumed in White House news management.

3

SOONER OR LATER, however, he returned to Goldwater bashing. His rival made it hard not to. Before an intimate gathering, drinking coffee in a rural living room, the visitor from Arizona could charm Yankee voters as he thanked them for the opportunity "to find out what's on your mind and you to find out whether I have one." But he tired easily, hobbling around the state on crutches following an operation to remove a calcium spur on his right heel (he had one foot in a cast, wags said, and the other in his mouth). Some days the oversched-uled candidate marched grimly past assembly lines without shaking a hand in sight. Inevitably, grassroots dissatisfaction with the leading contenders coaxed others into the field. An extensive write-in effort to promote Richard Nixon was launched with his tacit approval. Senator Margaret Chase Smith from neighboring Maine became the first serious female contender for the presidency.

---

* The worst damage to the Goldwater campaign was self-inflicted, much of it caused by loose-lipped surrogates such as Doloris Bridges. In a single, jarringly quotable day, Mrs. Bridges heaped praise on the senator for "penetrating the Social Security fraud," vowing an end to the popular Tennessee Valley Authority, and cracking wise about lobbing a bomb into the men's room of the Kremlin. Confronted at a morning staff meeting with these and other verbal missteps by the Widow Bridges, Norris Cotton produced from under his desk a bottle of Old Crow. With grave expression, he placed it before Richard Kleindienst, a young member of the so-called Arizona Mafia who surrounded Goldwater.

"Richard," said Cotton, "you must go fuck Doloris." William F. Buckley, Jr., *Flying High: Remembering Barry Goldwater* (New York: Basic Books, 2008), 109–10.

When the *Manchester Union Leader* wrote her off as "Moscow Maggie," it merely confirmed Mrs. Smith's place to the left of Goldwater and the right of Rockefeller. Spending less than $300 on the campaign, driving herself in her 1961 sedan over a thousand miles of country roads, Smith won more admiration than votes.

Of far greater concern to Rockefeller forces was the phantom candidacy of the man they came to label "Henry Sabotage." It was the brainchild of four Bostonians, political entrepreneurs in search of an entertaining sequel to young George Lodge's valiant 1962 campaign against Ted Kennedy to reclaim the Massachusetts Senate seat once held by his father and great-grandfather. The most unlikely candidacy of 1964 was born of Rockefeller neglect and the promotional skills of a forty-three-year-old journalist, PR man, direct mail specialist, purveyor of scientific instruments, and former CIA operative named Paul Grindle. Given the brush-off after volunteering for the Rockefeller campaign, Grindle joined Boston lawyer David Goldberg and an exceptionally attractive pair of local debutantes, Sally Saltonstall and Caroline Williams, in posing a theory pregnant with meaning for the future of American politics. From their work on behalf of George Lodge, Grindle and Associates had concluded that the weakest part of any political campaign was usually the candidate. What if they could identify, or manufacture, the "perfect candidate"—that is, a contender who said and did nothing to interfere with the persuasive efforts of his promoters?

Enter Henry Cabot Lodge, Jr., an urbane Boston Brahmin and former senator—he'd lost to JFK in 1952—who hadn't, in fact, won an election in seventeen years. Lodge's deficiencies as a campaigner were painfully demonstrated in 1960 when Richard Nixon, unable to lure Rockefeller onto his ticket, turned to Ike's Cold War ambassador to the United Nations in an effort to placate his party's Eastern Establishment. It had proved a disastrous choice. Keenly aware of his father's death at an early age, Lodge had made it his custom to don silk pajamas for a two-hour afternoon nap, preceded by his favorite snack of skinned Portuguese sardines. The habit did not endear him to professional politicians. But they wouldn't be voting in New Hampshire on March 10, 1964. A majority of Granite Staters lived within fifty miles of Boston; many regarded the former senator as one of their own. That Lodge was in fact ten thousand miles away, serving the Kennedy White House as its ambassador to war-torn South Vietnam, was an even greater plus, and not just because his diplomatic status enforced silence where domestic politics were concerned.

The last thing in the world Grindle wanted was to have Lodge come home prematurely and actively campaign for the nomination. As he put it, "The minute Cabot Lodge made his first ten speeches across the United States, it would have all been over." Using lists developed from George Lodge's unsuccessful

Senate campaign, Grindle raised enough in small donations to pay for a series of mailings to ninety-five thousand Republican voters. The first generated more than eight thousand cards pledging support for Lodge—an astonishing rate of return in a state the size of New Hampshire. For $750, Grindle skillfully edited some old footage from a 1960 campaign broadcast, airbrushing Nixon out of the picture and inserting a well-timed blast of trumpets over an Eisenhower tribute to that year's *vice* presidential nominee, leaving a distinct impression that Henry Cabot Lodge was Ike's preferred candidate in 1964.

Well aware that Lodge could shut down their operation at any time, his self-appointed advocates approached Bill Treat, the state's GOP national committeeman. At their behest, Treat journeyed to Saigon with a simple message for the ambassador: "For Christ's sake, if this is going to really piss you off, let us know." Treat returned with an appropriately diplomatic response: "The ambassador sees no reason to get pissed off." Lodge's attitude was not shared by Nelson Rockefeller. Following his marriage to Happy, he had been strongly encouraged by Lodge to enter the presidential race. At least, he believed he had. Even now, the ambassador offered an explicit pledge to do nothing that might undercut Rockefeller's campaign against Goldwater. Yet by siphoning off moderate Republican votes that would otherwise go, however reluctantly, to the New York governor, that was the inevitable result of Lodge's noncommittal stance toward Paul Grindle and his merry band.

Polls were notoriously imprecise in measuring support for a write-in candidate. Still, Rockefeller was sufficiently concerned to write a friendly letter to Saigon, reminding Lodge of his earlier promise. This failing to produce the desired withdrawal, several attempts were made to reach the ambassador by phone from Rockefeller's Concord hotel. None succeeded. When a long-distance connection finally was established, Lodge flatly refused to disavow the draft effort. Two days later, Rockefeller placed a second call to the South Vietnamese capital. The plan went awry when, on the evening of February 22, a loudspeaker at Franconia College bellowed, to the astonishment of accompanying reporters, "Governor Rockefeller, your call to Saigon is ready." Lodge, nursing dreams of an Eisenhower-like draft, remained intransigent. Making matters worse, Rockefeller misrepresented his outreach, saying he merely wanted to clarify some negative comments about Lodge's performance in Saigon. The snafu dominated press coverage for days, affording Goldwater a rare breathing spell and making Lodge appear more statesmanlike than ever. Declaring, "I've got it made," Goldwater left the state three days ahead of the primary, but not before forecasting victory with at least 35 percent of the vote.

He was in for a surprise, as New Hampshire voters, undeterred by a foot or more of fresh snow in the southern half of the state, turned out in record numbers to reward the one candidate who hadn't set foot in the state. In the "beauty contest," or popularity poll, it was Lodge who won 35 percent of the vote. Goldwater trailed far behind with 22 percent. Rockefeller took 21 percent, while 16 percent wrote in the name of Richard Nixon. In the separate race for the state's fourteen convention delegates, Lodge's slate of unknowns overwhelmed establishment figures Norris Cotton and Hugh Gregg. Having come from nowhere to nearly tie Goldwater, Rockefeller took cold comfort in what he called "a victory for moderation." Speaking to supporters gathered at his Manhattan headquarters, he vowed that the New Hampshire results would make him fight all the harder for a nomination that most now believed beyond his grasp. True to his word, at seven o'clock on Wednesday morning, Rockefeller boarded a family-owned plane and flew to California.*

4

THE NEW HAMPSHIRE debacle, predictably, generated more free advice than claims of responsibility. Charlie Moore, a retired Ford Motor Company executive valued for his PR skills, urged Nelson to be more aggressive in his attacks on Goldwater and Lodge, while avoiding wonkish "twenty minute tirades" on, say, Uncle Sam's betrayal of the Oregon sugar-beet industry. "Our candidate's image is not coming through," lamented Bill Pfeiffer, the brass-knuckled manager of Rockefeller's 1962 reelection campaign. "There is surprising lack of knowledge of what his position is on important issues." (This was code talk, frequently heard that year, for combating Rockefeller's reputation as a big-spending liberal.) Needless to say, it hadn't been difficult generating a headquarters crowd to hear Nelson's defiant post–New Hampshire pledge to press on—not with three hundred persons on his campaign payroll (among them baseball great Jackie Robinson as "deputy director of special committees" and wordsmith William Safire as a PR consultant). That, according to Lodge strategist David Goldberg, was part of the problem. "You don't win too many

---

* With all eyes focused on the drama playing itself out in New Hampshire, scant attention was paid to a pair of convention states, Oklahoma and North Carolina, whose forty-eight combined votes would be in Goldwater's corner if he finished behind Margaret Chase Smith and Harold Stassen in the Granite State. Such reservoirs of strength in nonprimary states went largely unreported, an oversight that helped explain the April 6 prediction by U.S. News & World Report that it would take Republicans in San Francisco up to six ballots to choose their nominee for president. On the other hand, Goldwater showed weakness in virtually every primary state he contested—above all in those states where he was effectively unopposed. In Illinois, Mrs. Smith won a quarter of Republican primary voters; more embarrassing still, Harold Stassen secured a similar share of Hoosier Republicans, while a Nixon write-in held Goldwater below 50 percent in Nebraska.

wars if you can afford to have too many field marshals," claimed Goldberg. Based on his observations of the muscle-bound Rockefeller effort in New Hampshire and elsewhere, Goldberg decided, "there were too goddamn many very smart, very important people exercising power. And no leader that I could tell."

Nor did unlimited funds, the vast majority supplied by Nelson and other Rockefellers, offer any guarantee of the best campaign organization money could buy. Quite the opposite: Rockefeller, said Paul Grindle, was a "victim of his resources. He felt an obligation to believe things he'd spent so much money to acquire." Especially polling. "The polling, horseshit," Grindle barked. "What's it *feel* like?" The divorce and remarriage didn't destroy Rockefeller, he maintained. "What destroyed him, over and over, was his reliance on staff, on experts," to the detriment of his own instincts. And yet—it was Rockefeller himself whose impulse was to risk not one but two long-shot appeals to Lodge, only to have them explode in his face.

If his repeated attempts to gain the White House appeared amateurish in contrast with his campaigns in New York, the explanation may lie in Rockefeller's fundamental misunderstanding of the presidential nominating process— more specifically, his tendency to treat it as an unwanted distraction from the main event. His harsh criticism of Goldwater should be seen in this light. "The focus on Goldwater was temporary," insisted delegate counter John Deardourff. "What Rockefeller was really pointing toward was the general election. You come out of the convention and then turn your attention to the national audience, which was largely Democratic. You're going to have to bring all these independents and Democrats who were for Kennedy, but he wasn't there anymore. Now you're running against Johnson, and you're going to isolate him as a hick from Texas. You're going to show people that you are so goddamn smart and you've got so many ideas for improving this country, and that you are not a typical Republican—you're a progressive-thinking guy."

Such a strategy may have made sense in the 1940s and early 1950s, when Republican pragmatists acclimated to the New Deal sought to reassure skeptical voters by distancing themselves from their party's Old Guard. By 1964, however, roles were reversed in a GOP increasingly determined to free itself of eastern domination. The dynamic of change went beyond mere geography, to the displacement of established conservatives by less polished, though more ideologically reliable, Goldwater partisans. The purge began with the party's upper echelon. "They were all alike," remembers one campaign insider of the Republican National Committee. "I can remember the day when I walked into this room and fifty national committeewomen were there and fifty national committeemen were there, and two hundred other people. And I could pick them out—the ladies all had the blue hair; they all looked alike."

This was George Hinman's constituency. "The popular joke on the Republican National Committee was, 'Let's run George Hinman for president,'" according to Rockefeller delegate hunter Arch Gillies. More than a month before New Hampshire, Hinman unveiled a committee of over one hundred prominent Californians pledged to Rockefeller in the state's June 2 primary. Backed by such power brokers as Jack Warner and Leonard Firestone, Justin Dart, ex-governor Goodwin Knight, and former San Francisco mayor George Christopher, crowed Hinman, "Nelson is going to take this state hands down." Nothing better illustrated the Rockefeller campaign's outmoded approach toward winning Republican minds, let alone hearts. In many a boardroom and country club, 1964 boiled down to an unequal contest between Goldwater passion and Rockefeller prestige. So while Hinman cultivated his peers in the GOP hierarchy, below the radar, in precinct meetings and district conventions, an entirely new Republican electorate swarmed the barricades. It wasn't the Eastern Establishment alone targeted for elimination by Clif White's army; it was the *Republican* Establishment personified by all those lawyers and bankers and oil barons whose loyalty to their class, and to the social and cultural status quo, rendered them ideologically suspect to the emerging conservative movement.

5

H IS BACK TO the wall, a few days after New Hampshire Rockefeller appeared unannounced in the Fifth Avenue law offices of Republican city councilman Ted Kupferman and Robert Price. Abrasive and street-smart—literally, for he was said to have memorized every intersection in the five boroughs—Bob Price was the fast-talking son of Eastern European immigrants who operated a grocery store in the Washington Heights section of Manhattan. While still a student at New York University, Price had earned the notice of John Lindsay, a Yale-trained lawyer a decade his senior. Having cut his political teeth on Youth for Eisenhower and the New York City Young Republicans, Lindsay undertook a three-year stint as executive assistant to Attorney General Herbert Brownell. In 1958, he decided to run for Congress, with Brownell's blessing, in the legendary Seventeenth, or "Silk Stocking," District incorporating Manhattan's East Side and Greenwich Village.

After losing his original campaign manager, Charles Metzner, to Rockefeller in that year's gubernatorial contest, Lindsay had turned to young Bob Price. "Okay, John, but let's have one thing straight," Price replied with typical chutzpah. "I run the campaign, and I have 51 percent of the vote. When you're elected, I don't tell you how to vote on issues, and you don't tell me what color to make the brochures." The partnership of opposites clicked, with the resourceful Price stretching his campaign budget by taking advantage of confusion over the names of candidates Lindsay and state comptroller nominee James Lundy; by his own acknowledgment, Price charged $50,000 worth of campaign mailings to the Rockefeller mailroom. Perhaps it was this willingness to cut corners, together with his unmodulated intensity and talent for intrigue, that made the Rockefeller inner circle uncomfortable on the subject of Bob Price. But it didn't prevent Brownell and Tom Dewey as Price's sponsors from wangling an invitation to dinner at 812 Fifth Avenue one night late in 1963. The conversation around the Rockefeller table focused on the approaching campaign against Lyndon Johnson. Accustomed to speaking his mind, Price called Johnson a formidable foe. He had his weaknesses, George Hinman countered. "If the election were today," said Hinman, "I think Nelson could beat Johnson." If the election were today, Brownell jested, "it would be illegal."

In the event, Price was passed over by the Rockefeller high command— allegedly, it was whispered, on account of his Jewish faith.* The New Hampshire results rendered such considerations moot. Now Rockefeller himself came calling at Price's law office, asking him to take charge of a do-or-die primary campaign in distant Oregon. Who, asked Price, was currently in charge there? Rockefeller didn't know. Who would? The governor mentioned Jack Wells. A call was placed to Wells. "Can you tell me who's managing the campaign in Oregon?" Pause. "How long will it take for you to find out?" Rockefeller replaced the phone in its cradle. "Wells has to ask George Hinman." The suspicions thus aroused were fanned on April 5 when Price flew cross-country to Portland by way of Seattle. What he found was an organization in name only. "There wasn't anything happening. There was no headquarters"—aside from a nine-to-five storefront in Portland and two dormant facilities in Eugene and Coos Bay, the latter home to Rockefeller's nominal state chairman, a retired state senator who could not make time in his schedule to see the eastern emissary. "There were no posters, no workers, nothing." Half the $300,000 primary budget had been earmarked for television, which Price thought largely wasted.

"What we need now are firemen and surgeons," he concluded, "we don't have time for architects." On April 11, he walked into a conference room at 521 Fifth Avenue to present his findings.

"Read from your notes," Rockefeller told him.

Price was reluctant, and for good reason. What he had written to himself while in Oregon amounted to a multicount indictment of eastern neglect and

---

* Price took pains to absolve Rockefeller himself of any religious bias.

condescension. Sensing this, Jack Wells diplomatically recommended that he make a copy of his jottings for their review.

"Bob," said Rockefeller, "I want you to read every word on that sheet."

There ensued a scathing litany of failure in the making, dramatized by a series of unreturned phone calls. Before the meeting ended, everyone was more than willing to entrust Oregon to the brash outsider. Price held off giving a formal commitment until he could discuss the situation with his wife and with John Lindsay. Why Lindsay? multiple voices demanded. Because he was a loyal friend and campaign manager, said Price, and because his reelection in November was important to him.

"Is it more important than Nelson winning Oregon?" asked Hinman. Price shied away from a direct answer. "That was a very unfair question," Rockefeller interjected. It took Price two hours to secure the necessary releases from a grudging Lindsay. Before he could even present his terms, Rockefeller cut him off. "No," the governor said crisply, "first I want to know how much can I pay you?" Price reiterated his earlier refusal to be on the Rockefeller payroll. "I don't want to get paid because I want to be able to say to you, 'Governor, fuck off, I'm quitting.'"

"I can afford it," said Rockefeller. Four years out of law school, Price agreed to let Nelson pick up the tab for his hotel, travel, and other expenses. "You ought to stay at the Hotel Benson in Portland," Rockefeller advised him. "It's the best place to stay."

"I'd like you to write letters and come out whenever I ask you to," Price told Rockefeller. "'And nobody else comes. If any of your people criticize what I'm doing out there, because they're eavesdropping on me, I don't want to hear about it.' He said, 'Done. Can my car take you out to the airport?' I said, 'Sure, it'll save you a taxi bill.'" The tab for Price's recently concluded visit to the state provoked another dispute, with the obstinate young attorney insisting that his law firm would take care of it. "Money was his tool," Price said of Rockefeller. "He was a wonderful guy, but he couldn't conceive of people not wanting him for money."*

To assist him, Price requested the services of John Deardourff, with whom he had previously worked in New Hampshire. "He and I moved out there, took two rooms in the Benson Hotel. It was the craziest thing in some ways," Deardourff later marveled. "Price is very quick. He said, 'I want you to get the best list we can get of Oregon voters. We're going to mail them and ask them for help.' We must have sent out four hundred thousand pieces of mail almost

---

* Later, as John Lindsay's deputy mayor, Price was a frequent visitor to 13 West Fifty-fourth Street. Over lunch one day, Rockefeller handed Price a piece of Ming dynasty china. "Please take it . . . come on, it cost me $2,000." Price politely rejected the offer. Robert Price, AI.

overnight." Back came three thousand favorable replies, which Price inflated in whispered press confidences to ten thousand. In their Portland hotel suite, related Deardourff, "the two of us sat there and organized the cards by county." Eventually he reached for the phone, both to thank respondents—a personalized letter from Rockefeller would shortly be in the mail—and to solicit input regarding the best location in their community for a Rockefeller campaign headquarters. Perhaps, said Deardourff, Mr. Price from New York could continue the conversation in person the next day.

This was the signal for Price to go into action, aided by his secret weapon, "an American Express card that said 'Robert Price,' and the company was 'Nelson A. Rockefeller.' You'd be surprised what that does at airports." After meeting the prospective volunteer wherever his plane touched down, Price proposed a drive down Main Street in search of a vacant storefront. On spotting a promising location, he asked, "Do you think we can rent that? That will be our headquarters." (Carrying several thousand dollars of Rockefeller cash on his person expedited on-the-spot decision making.) If the building in question was unavailable, Price entrusted the quest for a substitute to his newly designated local chairman. A quick coffee break with a handful of area Rockefeller enthusiasts, and it was back to the airport and several additional stops before, and after, sundown.

Within two weeks, all thirty-six counties in the state were organized, at least on paper. Money being no object, Price purchased three copies of the Republican voter list for Multnomah County (Portland), half the number in existence, just to deny them to the opposition. In rural parts of the state, he cultivated small-town editors by running multiple ads costing $30 or $35 apiece—manna from heaven for precariously financed weekly publications. A glossy twenty-page booklet, *The Nelson Rockefeller Story*, was sent to nearly two hundred thousand Oregon households. Separate mailings targeted women, senior citizens, conservationists, and hunters. In time stolen from his frenzied travels, Price drafted a script to be used by telephone volunteers to identify Rockefeller voters, the essential first step toward a successful turnout effort on primary day. Hoping to put twenty telephones in each county, Price was dismayed to learn that Pacific Telephone's lines did not reach every corner of the vast state. He placed a call to David Rockefeller in New York. "David, do you know anybody at Pac Tel?"

As Price recalled, "He said, 'Where are you?' And I gave him the number." (In the pre–cellular phone era, a considerable amount of political business was transacted in phone booths at rural airports.) It wasn't long before the younger Rockefeller called back. The company chairman would be in touch shortly, David told Price, to learn precisely where he wanted the phones installed.

6

L ONG A WESTERN outpost of the progressive movement codified at the start of the twentieth century by Hiram Johnson in California and the La Follettes of Wisconsin, Oregon conducted a primary unlike any other. Its secretary of state placed on the ballot the name of every candidate, declared or otherwise. Only by filing a special request could those so identified remove themselves from contention. This meant that both Lodge and Nixon would be formally listed for the consideration of Oregon voters (among the dark horses, only George Romney of Michigan took his name off the ballot). Spooked by his previous experience, Barry Goldwater did the next closest thing, effectively pulling out of the state after a single trip there. His name remained on the ballot, but Goldwater had no taste for more New Hampshire–style barnstorming. Abandoning Oregon allowed him to husband his resources for its gigantic neighbor to the south, while hopefully diluting the impact accorded the winner in a shrunken primary field.

An early April poll had Lodge lapping the field, with Nixon a distant second and both Goldwater and Rockefeller trailing the former vice president. Equally important, Lodge enjoyed near universal acceptability among Beaver State Republicans, a third of whom said they couldn't vote for Goldwater in November (27 percent said as much of Rockefeller). It wasn't hard to see why. Boasting a political culture as pristine as its mountain streams, Oregon was the League of Women Voters with fir trees. Twice as large as New York State, it combined dazzling geographic variety with a seemingly homogenized population of 1.8 million. Overwhelmingly Protestant and Caucasian—African Americans accounted for just 2 percent of the state's inhabitants—with a heavy concentration of white-collar professionals, an unemployment rate more than a point below the national average, and a habit of electing mavericks such as Senator Wayne Morse and young Mark Hatfield, Oregon appeared primed for Lodge much as New Hampshire had been branded Goldwater country.

Yet the same state had one of the highest divorce rates in the nation. Would its supposed tolerance translate into votes for the divorced governor of New York? Bob Price feared not. Price pleaded with his East Coast bosses to address Rockefeller's marital history, either in a separate television broadcast or as the dramatic conclusion to a half-hour discussion of campaign issues "with a substantially conservative twist." He submitted a draft script, in which the candidate would speak of the differences that can grow up between people as tiny cracks become emotional chasms. To Price it all came down to acknowledging the obvious. "He can admit his first marriage was a mistake."

But it wasn't that simple. Until now, the Rockefellers had studiously avoided recriminations over their breakup. Did Nelson want to risk such civility by violating his family's code of privacy? Could he be certain that Tod, or her aggrieved representatives, would remain silent in the face of such provocations? On the explosive issue of Happy Rockefeller's children from her first marriage, he appealed for media restraint. "They are working together . . . Mrs. Rockefeller and Dr. Murphy . . . in the best interest of the children and to preserve the love and affection of the children." Beyond this meager reflection, Rockefeller was immovable; there would be no televised soul baring in the style of Richard Nixon's famed Checkers speech of 1952 or John F. Kennedy's confrontation eight years later with a roomful of Catholic-baiting Houston clergymen. Instead Rockefeller would confine himself to subjects of more direct relevance to Oregonians.

Asked how his stand on Vietnam differed from that of Ambassador Lodge, he replied, "It is difficult to know Lodge's stand as he has not been here to take a stand." As for himself, he promised to return as often as possible prior to the May 15 primary. "I want to know what *you* think about the problems we face, and I think you have a right to know exactly where I stand on these issues." Here was the genesis for the canny slogan conceived by John Deardourff: "He Cares Enough to Come." Filling the vacuum left by Goldwater's withdrawal, Lodge's detachment, and Nixon's studied pose of noncandidacy, Rockefeller made half a dozen trips to the state. "He'd go to tank towns where they grew berries and nothing else," recalls Albany program associate Ed Kresky, whose speechwriting skills were frequently pressed into service that spring.

The pace was bruising. A typical day featured an early morning airport rally, followed by a Masonic Lodge reception and a couple of factory visits, a shopping mall appearance, and the official opening of his Beaverton headquarters—all before lunch. Wherever he went, Nelson seasoned his pitch with content prepared to order by Deardourff. He assailed Johnsonian foreign policy in the university town of Eugene. Within sight of Mount Hood, he addressed the future of federal forest lands. At Grants Pass, he returned to the subject of Vietnam, calling for the hot pursuit of Vietcong guerrillas by South Vietnamese forces into Cambodian or Laotian sanctuaries. Just as Tom Dewey in 1948 had thawed his frosty image by submitting to local customs along the Oregon Trail, so Rockefeller at a Rotary luncheon in Coos Bay allowed a group of costumed pirates to prick his forefinger and sign his name in blood. When fog forced Rockefeller to reroute his plane to Portland, he rented a limousine and napped in the front seat as the driver navigated dismal weather and rugged terrain to reach his original destination at four in the morning. Three hours later Nelson appeared at a breakfast event, his eyes practically swollen shut but his enthusiasm unimpaired.

Oregonians took notice. His repeated visits established the New Yorker as a fighter deserving of sympathy and, just maybe, support. Polls in late April detected movement in his direction, though he remained a distant second to Lodge. Adding to the physical toll of the campaign, Rockefeller insisted on returning home each weekend to be with Happy, then in the final weeks of her pregnancy. Yet even now, the combined demands of a national campaign, governing New York, and impending fatherhood were insufficient to monopolize his imagination. Late one Friday night, Nelson retreated to the tail of the F-27 prop plane, which had been reconfigured to include a bed for its owner.

"So we're on our way back from Portland," recalled John Deardourff, "it's probably one a.m. eastern time, and just about everybody else is asleep. But I'm not. . . . So I'm sitting with my little reading light on.

"'Johnny.'

"I look around, and he's sitting like a potentate with his legs crossed and he's got his bathrobe on and he's in the back of the plane.

"'Come back here.'

"He's got something spread out in front of him. I go back and I get on the bed with him, and he's got the plans for the Albany mall. And he proceeds to spend two hours telling me about what this is going to look like, and how important this is going to be to the architecture world, and how this is going to give Albany a kind of class that it never has had. It's going to be the most important capital in the world . . . and he goes on and on and on. I'm twenty or twenty-five thousand feet in the air, we're chugging along in this thing, and here I am at age thirty-one, I'm sitting with Nelson Rockefeller in his bathrobe in his airplane. And he gives me the whole story of what this Albany mall is gong to look like when he gets the legislature to approve the money. And it's clearly as important to him as the trip we were just completing.

"And I don't know that he even saw it as a monument to himself. I don't think he did . . . it was almost like a fallback position. . . . It was something he could have loved no matter what." That it could hardly love him back was immaterial.

7

I F ON OCCASION he appeared dead tired, Oregon wasn't the only reason. Rockefeller was still governor of New York. "This is my primary responsibility," he told reporters ten days after New Hampshire. "Whatever happens elsewhere—well, it's just part of the game." If ever tempted to forget his day job, Rockefeller had only to glance over his shoulder at demonstrators trailing him through Yankee villages in protest of the proposed World Trade Center to be built in lower Manhattan under the auspices of the Port of New York Authority.

Also competing for his attention was the latest chapter in the slow-motion bankruptcy of the New Haven and other commuter railroads; the April 22 opening of the New York World's Fair; and a bitter dispute over state aid to local schools in which Rockefeller, uncharacteristically, threatened to veto any tax increases to meet the demands of fast-growing Nassau County and other suburban districts. Foreshadowing a more conservative approach to the issue of crime, Nelson braved the wrath of civil libertarians opposed to his "no knock" and "stop and frisk" bills expanding police powers to execute a search warrant without advance notice and detain and search persons "reasonably" suspected of committing a serious offense.

Nothing, however, generated more resentment than his attempt to legislate an end to the State Liquor Authority scandal that had already cost him the services of Jud Morhouse. The powerful liquor lobby threw its full weight against a package of reforms endorsed by Judge Lawrence Walsh and his investigative brethren and subsequently embraced by Rockefeller. These would outlaw retail price fixing, which added an estimated $150 million a year to New Yorkers' bar tabs; repeal current laws mandating a distance of at least fifteen hundred feet between liquor stores in New York City (seven hundred feet in the rest of the state); and abolish the widely flaunted requirement that taverns serve food. Once again conventional roles were reversed, as Rockefeller argued for a free market solution and his critics conjured a New York, in the words of conservative Republican lawmaker John Marchi of Staten Island, deregulated into "a wide-open market, a dumping ground for cheap liquor, a paradise for the conniver and the loss-leader advocate."

Since anything that made distilled spirits cheaper or easier to obtain was likely to offend guardians of traditional morality—in this case the New York State Council of Churches, backed by countless individual congregations—the Rockefeller initiative united in passionate opposition the strangest of bedfellows. It wasn't only the makers and marketers of alcoholic beverages who denounced the governor; so did social conservatives, especially rural Republicans like Barber Conable, then a state senator from the Rochester area. Heavily influenced by the Baptist Church, Conable's constituents linked possible sales of liquor in supermarkets or drugstores to a growing teenage drinking problem. "Rocky accused me of being a tool of the liquor lobby," Conable would remember. "I got thirteen bills through the legislature, and he vetoed nine of them—six with phony veto messages."

Rockefeller didn't help his cause among legislators by demanding a tough new code of ethics that would prevent sitting lawmakers, many of them lawyers, from arguing before state courts or agencies. The recommended changes struck many as a crudely timed attempt by the governor to restore his own reputation, tarnished by the Jud Morehouse scandal, at the legislature's expense. No doubt Rockefeller *was* glad to change the subject from his lax oversight of the State Liquor Authority; yet he also had compelling, and highly personal, motives for coupling reform of the liquor laws with a legislative code of ethics. Hidden from the public was a recent confrontation between the governor and a youthful petitioner, described by Teddy White as the "scion of a great whiskey—and spirits—empire." It was, in fact, Edgar M. Bronfman, Sr. Failing to persuade Rockefeller to reduce state taxes on his family's product, Bronfman declared, "I've never seen a legislature I couldn't buy."

Rockefeller, pale with suppressed fury, rose from behind his desk.

"Now I must ask you to leave this room," he told his visitor.

Brazen as he appeared, Rockefeller's caller knew his trade. On the last night of the 1964 legislative session, Barber Conable joined a bipartisan majority that handed the governor a stinging defeat. In the assembly, his measure to end price fixing mustered only thirty-nine of the seventy-six votes needed for enactment. (The senate didn't even extend Rockefeller the courtesy of a roll call vote.) With national attention focused on Albany, he couldn't afford to suffer the fate of George Romney, whose presidential trial balloon had crashed and burned after Michigan legislators rejected a tax reform package on which the governor had staked his prestige. On April 7, Rockefeller took to the airwaves to rally the public against industry price fixing that fleeced consumers while lining the pockets of a privileged few. He summoned lawmakers back to the capital for a two-day special session the following week. Splitting the opposition, he set tavern and bar owners, who were only too glad to eliminate costs associated with providing meals few of their patrons ever ordered, against package store proprietors fearful of price wars and the "economic chaos" of true competition. At the same time, Rockefeller accepted modifications in his program to soften church opposition. By the time a sullen legislature reconvened on April 14, intense lobbying by the governor and his allies in the leadership had produced seventy-three Republican votes in the assembly and twenty-nine in the senate— just short of the necessary majority.

What followed showed Rockefeller the horse trader at his most adroit. It was no secret that Bronx Democratic boss Charles Buckley badly wanted revisions in election law that would assure top ballot position to the organization fielding the largest number of candidates in a contested primary—in other words, to the Organization answerable to Buckley himself. In return for this presumed advantage over their reformist challengers, enough machine regulars in both houses voted with the Republican governor on his liquor reforms to avenge his earlier loss and demonstrate yet again that it was a mistake to count Rockefeller out before the final votes were tallied. He could only hope that the same lesson applied to West Coast Republicans.

8

O REGON STOOD OUT, wrote Theodore White, as one of the two venues where Rockefeller stirred genuine emotion in the 1964 campaign (the other being his stormy confrontation with Republicans at the party's San Francisco convention). Filling the unaccustomed role of underdog, the candidate whose name was synonymous with wealth and power displayed a Trumanesque grit and determination. "If you're behind in the polls, and running on principle," Rockefeller told a luncheon gathering in the Oregon capital of Salem on May 7, "you don't run for cover. You just fight a little harder. That's what I'm doing." He took to calling himself "the Lone Ranger," and the name stuck. For once he was defined by his resolve, not his resources, as his backslapping joviality gave way to a deeper, more attractive humanity. In a word, Rockefeller was vulnerable.

He was also unavoidable. In the four days leading up to May 15, Rockefeller delivered twenty-four speeches in nine Oregon communities. Though his right hand was swollen and callused, he seized every outstretched palm in sight, drumming home the message equally flattering to himself and his audience—He Cared Enough to Come. "What do the absent advocate?" Rockefeller demanded of a University of Portland audience. "Where do the silent stand?" Some days his voice was little more than a croak, but it didn't preclude his scrambling atop a truck and exhorting a rain-swept knot of listeners, "If you vote Friday, remember my name. It's Nelson Rockefeller. Thanks, folks." At the end, he even unbent a little on his divorce and remarriage, telling one questioner, "I think that in life more people have problems in their own lives than others realize. And what we have to have the courage to do, is to face those problems honestly inside of ourselves." It was hardly a full-throated mea culpa, but to the mannerly electorate of Oregon, the fact that the issue had been addressed at all allowed Nelson to score points for a sensitivity rarely glimpsed in public.

It didn't hurt that his eldest children, Rodman and Ann, were by their father's side during the closing stretch. Moreover, his presence in the state had become entwined with a cause larger than mere personal ambition. For Oregonians, the fight over political extremism was no abstraction. A year had passed since right-wing elements hostile to Governor Hatfield had seized control of the Multnomah County GOP organization. Rockefeller and his campaign supplied a rallying point for moderate Republicans hoping to recapture their party. By the second week of May, Lodge's lead was melting faster than the snowpack in the Cascade Range. Pollster Elmo Roper spoke of an upset in the making. On Friday morning, May 15, an exhausted Rockefeller attended a final breakfast meeting before flying home to New York. That he planned on watching the returns alone with Happy at Kykuit suggested limits even to his optimism. At 11:03 eastern time, NBC pronounced him back from the dead, having come from fourth place to defeat Lodge, ninety-three thousand votes to seventy-eight thousand; Nixon edged Goldwater for third place. So unexpected was the Rockefeller triumph that a Saturday morning press conference in New York had to be delayed more than an hour while a suitable victory statement was prepared. "We retired with CBS at midnight," explained the victorious candidate.

Oregon reshuffled the Republican deck, without narrowing the field significantly. To be sure, the Lodge boomlet collapsed for good. Barry Goldwater dismissed the results as "a victory for the radical left. . . . If I drop dead today, he [Rockefeller] still couldn't get the nomination." Spot checks in Washington State, Colorado, and Illinois indicated Goldwater delegate strength holding firm. Not until Saturday afternoon, twenty hours after the polls closed in the Beaver State, was Rockefeller able to connect with his Oregon campaign manager. At the Benson Hotel, the house detective let himself into Bob Price's hotel suite, the incessant jangle of phones having failed to wake the battle-weary Price.

"Where the hell have you been?" asked Rockefeller.

"Sleeping."

"You didn't tell me."

"I assume you have a television set," Price said. "I tried to call you, but I didn't know where you were."

"I love you," said Rockefeller. "Will you go to California?"

One can only speculate as to the course history might have taken had John Lindsay released Price to work the Golden State—less for the potential impact on California Republicans than on the turbulent relationship that was to cast a shadow over Lindsay's star-crossed mayoralty. That Rockefeller resented Lindsay for not extending the loan of Price's services was demonstrated two months later, on the disorderly Tuesday night in San Francisco when Nelson was roundly booed by Goldwater partisans at their party's nominating convention. Off the floor, Price ran into the governor, mad as a hornet—not at the delegates and guests who had tried to shout him down, but at Price (and, by implication, Lindsay). "If you had gone from Oregon to California, I would have won California," Rockefeller spat out, "and this would not have happened tonight."

9

ROCKEFELLER ALREADY HAD a California management team in place, one strongly recommended to him by Tom Kuchel, who had entrusted the same hired guns with the Southern California portion of his successful 1962 reelection effort. The eponymous firm of Spencer-Roberts combined under one roof the functions of strategic planning, survey research, media production and placement, and press relations. Its principals included thirty-seven-year-old Stuart Spencer, impish and disheveled, a former parks and recreation director for the city of Alhambra, California; and Bill Roberts, thirty-nine, a portly, smooth-talking onetime television salesman and funeral director. Each man brought a distinctive temperament and skill set to the business of campaigning. "Bill is very good at taking an established candidate, a front-runner, and holding the lead," explained Spencer. "I'm better at taking somebody that's behind and blitzing the thing." Neither was ideologically driven. As Spencer put it, "I don't care about the issues. I care about the votes." Both would have their work cut out for them in the Rockefeller campaign. Only after accepting the first installment of their $50,000 retainer did the partners chance to see a January 1964 in-house poll that showed Goldwater leading among California Republicans 58 to 27 percent. The lopsided margin, reflective of a continuing antipathy toward Rockefeller on the part of many voters, dictated their go-for-broke strategy.

"We said, you know, we had to bring Barry back down to us," Spencer reflected. "There was no way we were going to catch him in a straight-out, heads-on, positive campaign. We had to attack him, bring him down to our level, and then rebuild ourselves into something that was feasible as a presidential candidate. So we attacked . . . I mean we attacked everything. Some of it was valid. Some of it was borderline." Spencer acknowledged another, more personal reason to concentrate their fire on Goldwater. "We were trying to confuse the issue," he conceded, by making voters forget about Nelson's divorce and remarriage. Was Rockefeller bothered by the harshly negative tone? "Nah," says Spencer. "Nelson was as tough as any person I've ever worked with. . . . Street tough." Indeed, he seemed to relish the coming battle, telling reporters even before Oregon that "I've got him by myself now. I will attack his extremist stands. It's going to get rough."*

California had just passed New York as the nation's most populous state, and its dynamic growth, no less than its storied climate, set it apart from its eastern

---

* Spencer, in a 2000 interview with the author, also described Rockefeller as "the toughest anti-Communist I ever saw. Much more than Reagan, much more than Barry. I said to him, 'Why?' He said, 'If you were a Rockefeller, wouldn't you be?'"

rival. On closer examination, however, the two coastal giants had more in common than many supposed. Exactly reversing New York's political and demographic alignment, California had a liberal north anchored by San Francisco, and a conservative south dominated by Los Angeles. Together with its rightward-leaning neighbors, Orange and San Diego counties, Los Angeles accounted for 60 percent of the state's eighteen million inhabitants (triple the population three decades earlier). Mobility defined the Golden State, the end of the road for millions escaping northern cold and southern poverty. Amid the freeways and sun-baked housing tracts, waves of newcomers, rootless and starstruck, represented the future in ways they could scarcely appreciate.

Yet this was hardly the full story of California, for the simple reason that there was no such thing as the representative Californian. As befitting the state that had incubated such progressive icons as Hiram Johnson, Upton Sinclair, Earl Warren, and Tom Kuchel, more than two-thirds of California Republicans in 1964 classified themselves for pollsters as moderates or liberals. To win, concluded Rockefeller, he had "to get that 70% stirred up." He and Kuchel began by preparing a list of twenty-five programs endorsed in the 1960 Republican platform and subsequently supported by virtually every GOP senator—except Barry Goldwater. The Rockefeller campaign mailed out two million copies of a brochure contrasting Goldwater ("This Man Stands Alone") with Rockefeller and his moderate brethren Nixon, Lodge, Romney, and Scranton. "Which Do You Want, a Leader? Or a Loner?" the Rockefeller literature demanded. ("A Leader, Not a Lover," retorted Goldwaterites.)

Addressing the California Newspaper Publishers Association at the end of April, Rockefeller presented himself as a constructive alternative to the Johnson administration *and* a dogmatic, militant minority within his own party, "mesmerized by a mythical yesterday and devoid of program for today's and tomorrow's problems." He reminded listeners of such past Republican initiatives as the Morrill Land-Grant Act, signed by Lincoln in 1862 and the genesis of the University of California; and the 1957 Civil Rights Act promoted by Eisenhower and gutted by Lyndon Johnson, James Eastland—and, by implication, Barry Goldwater. The next day in Los Angeles, Rockefeller kept up the attack, using words such as "preposterous" and "extremist folly" to describe Goldwater's approach to foreign policy. To the surprise of many, his reception in this conservative stronghold matched the enthusiasm displayed twenty-four hours before in the more congenial north.

In nearby Pasadena, nearly three thousand admirers stood in line to shake his hand, the first of many such crowds turned out by Spencer-Roberts. Faithful to their non-ideological roots, the firm shamelessly exploited California's infatuation with celebrity. "We used the Rockefeller magic," according to Spencer. "So we would put together one big event where we'd send out twenty thousand invitations, and they thought they would have dinner with Rockefeller or something. Two or three thousand would show up, and he'd shake every goddamn hand in the place." In San Jose, eight thousand people waited up to six hours to meet him. San Diegans turned out in similar numbers.* Supplementing these personal appearances, the campaign relied on direct mail, telephone banks, radio, billboards, and television to convey its message of moderation. To the chagrin of his promoters, Rockefeller the policy wonk much preferred broadcasting a five-minute mini-speech to the sixty- and thirty-second spots designed for a viewer's abbreviated attention span. For prospects requiring more than a hearty handshake accompanied by a robust "Hiya, fella!" Nelson came better prepared than most candidates. For several weeks, Spencer had tried to arrange a meeting with Dorothy "Buffy" Chandler, the formidable doyenne of Southern California's most prominent newspaper family and a dominant figure in the cultural life of Los Angeles.

"The Chandlers weren't wild about Rockefeller," Spencer readily acknowledges. "Of course, they cared even less for Goldwater." Eventually, a mutually convenient time was found. "Nelson shows up first, and he's got a $25,000 Picasso etching under his arm," says Spencer. "Then Buffy appears. I escorted her into the room with Nelson, closed the door, and waited outside in the hall." As the minutes ticked by, Spencer began to fret. Well aware of his candidate's reputation where women were concerned, he imagined the worst, then banished the thought from his mind. Mostly. When at last the door opened and Mrs. Chandler took her leave, the tart-tongued Spencer couldn't suppress either his curiosity or his puckish sense of humor.

"I hope that painting is all you gave her," he told Nelson. Rockefeller exploded in laughter.

"I think the Picasso will do the trick," he said, grinning.

Whatever the incentive, within days of the Oregon primary the *Los Angeles Times* gave Rockefeller a timely boost as the candidate representing "the broader spectrum of Republican philosophy." The paper was not alone in its change of heart. As the shock waves from his Oregon win made themselves felt across California, Lou Harris showed Rockefeller surging into an eleven-point lead. Much of his newfound support was necessarily soft. An unusually large portion of the electorate—Harris pegged the number at 17 percent—remained undecided. Many Californians wished they could vote for someone not on the ballot, a feeling that only intensified as the two sides waged all-out war. "The Goldwater people were really so god-awful," according to Paul Grindle, who, hoping to assist the sole moderate left in the race, had taken up temporary res-

---

* In their excitement, noted Spencer, some voters held out blank checks for the candidate to autograph. "It really pissed him off." Stuart Spencer, AI.

idence in Los Angeles. Youthful Goldwater partisans outside Rockefeller rallies distributed pamphlets entitled *The Socialist Views of Nelson Rockefeller.* Telephone receptionists in several Rockefeller offices around Los Angeles were greeted with derisive messages of "Nigger lover!" and a brisk hang-up.

Shadowing Goldwater appearances were Rockefeller pickets carrying swastika-bearing placards proclaiming, "Goldwater: The Fascist Gun in the West." While Stu Spencer complained that Goldwater himself was being kept under wraps—holding no press conferences, limiting appearances to friendly audiences, and muting his rhetoric to avoid any New Hampshire–like snafus— the senator's supporters were everywhere. By noon of the first day of eligibility, an estimated forty thousand Goldwater volunteers had secured nearly four times the required signatures to put their hero's name on the California primary ballot. By contrast, Rockefeller's paid staff required a full month to qualify. "We didn't have any troops," Spencer acknowledged. "We had all the money in the world." Of the roughly $2 million Spencer admits to spending on the race—other estimates have the number as high as $3.5 million—at least 90 percent was attributed to the Rockefeller family. Much of this was donated by Nelson's stepmother, the same "Aunt Martha" whose gifts to his various campaigns, both state and national, would ultimately top $10 million. "Periodically we would need money," Spencer reflects; then the message would be relayed through George Hinman, their chief conduit to New York, that it was time "for Nelson to bring the family together."

Perhaps a few hundred thousand dollars—Spencer has provided varying estimates over the years—went to reregister black voters, normally Democratic in their sympathies, so they could support Nelson in the GOP primary. It was an unexpected break for a campaign unable to rouse passionate support elsewhere. A "little breakfast" with some black leaders in Los Angeles, expected to attract 25 or 30 supporters, generated a crowd of 250. Many were graduates of Spelman College or patrons of the United Negro College Fund. "They loved him," Spencer says. "So we went back, and I said, 'We got to redesign this campaign,'" with the result that roughly fifty-five thousand African American voters, most in and around Los Angeles, switched their party registration. On Election Day, generous supplies of "walking-around money" were distributed to neighborhood leaders, pastors, and others who, backed by a fleet of loudspeaker trucks, did their best to turn out the vote. "An interesting phenomenon," Spencer muses. "Never saw it before, or since."

That there might in fact be too much Rockefeller money sloshing around the state came home dramatically to Paul Grindle. Traveling in style, the erstwhile Lodge promoter occupied Clark Gable's former bungalow at the swank Beverly Hills Hotel. On his first full day there, and for several days thereafter, he received a brown envelope containing $5,000 in hundred-dollar bills, his own walking-around money. Anxious to rid himself of the unsought windfall, Grindle communicated his unease to the Rockefeller camp. In response he was instructed to fly to Denver, where an unnamed stranger waited for him in a bookstore at the Brown Palace Hotel. Ten minutes after hearing this mysterious figure mutter, "Eleven oh seven," Grindle knocked on the hotel door bearing that number. Inside, a prominent Rockefeller family retainer (almost certainly George Hinman, though Grindle only chuckled when interviewers tried to pin him down) wordlessly accepted the bag containing tens of thousands of dollars, distributed without instructions and never formally accounted for. His business transacted, Grindle returned to the sybaritic comforts of Beverly Hills.

By his own admission, what remained of the Lodge campaign was never integrated into the Rockefeller effort in California. Grindle did encounter Rockefeller several weeks later, by which time they had both pledged themselves to Bill Scranton's quixotic Stop Goldwater candidacy. They met at Margate, the Scranton estate outside the Pennsylvania mill town to which the family had given its name. Amid these baronial surroundings, reminiscent of Pocantico, Rockefeller relaxed sufficiently to ask Grindle what it would have taken to bring about his withdrawal from New Hampshire.

"A bribe," Grindle said, deadpan.

"How much?" asked Rockefeller.

"For ten thousand dollars, you would have seen the back of me."

"Oh, my Christ," sputtered Rockefeller. "And I spent three million."

<h2 style="text-align:center">10</h2>

ROCKEFELLER GOT A break on May 24, when Goldwater told Howard K. Smith on ABC's *Issues and Answers* that North Vietnamese supply lines in neighboring Laos might be defoliated through the strategic use of "low-yield atomic weapons." (The senator had prefaced his comment by saying this was one of several policy options, adding, "I don't think we would use any of them." But his qualifying words were left out of wire service reports, feeding the impression of nuclear recklessness.) The next day, Eisenhower weighed in with a ghosted appraisal of the ideal Republican nominee in the *New York Herald Tribune*. Effusive in its praise of the party's 1960 platform, his article pointedly endorsed civil rights, the UN, and other emblems of "responsible" Republicanism. Eisenhower's "Personal Statement" was widely read as a condemnation of Goldwater, if not quite an outright endorsement of Rockefeller. The impact of Ike's intervention was blunted, however, if not reversed, when George Humphrey, his former Treasury secretary and a fervent Goldwater backer, called the former president and reproached him for deviating from his stated neutrality. Not for the last time that spring, Eisenhower executed a strategic retreat, telling reporters that he had no intention of reading Goldwater out of their party. Simultaneously, Nixon, Scranton, and Romney—each of whom secretly hoped to exploit a Rockefeller win in California to advance his own cause—publicly repudiated the use of their names or likenesses in a Rockefeller brochure contrasting Goldwater with his moderate brethren.

Reporters heaped praise on the finely tuned Rockefeller organizations. They mistook logistical proficiency for unity of purpose. They also overlooked growing divisions within the campaign over strategy, message, and the looming birth of a Rockefeller child. "You got to remember this," Stu Spencer summarizes the situation forty years after the fact. "There was the New York crowd, and then there was us. . . ." To his dismay, the full Rockefeller entourage descended on California in the campaign's closing days. "Twenty-seven of them around the pool of the Ambassador Hotel in Los Angeles," Spencer says of the last minute influx. "Second-guessing us." The same hotel housed an alternative speechwriting operation answerable not to Spencer-Roberts, but to Rockefeller's chief operative in governing New York, Bill Ronan. "He wrote speeches, and we ash-canned them," claims Spencer, who scorned Ronan as an outsider lacking any feel for California sensibilities.

Unfortunately for the nominal campaign management team, Ronan retained the trust, as well as the ear, of a candidate torn between his naturally aggressive instincts and those around him who argued that an ostentatious display of Rockefeller wealth would backfire. So even as the Goldwater forces prepared a final weekend blitz of the state's television and newspaper outlets, Rockefeller eased off on his media purchases. That he was conflicted over the newly cautious approach was demonstrated by a late inquiry from New York to Bill Roberts, asking how the campaign might usefully employ a $200,000 infusion of Rockefeller money. Roberts, an honorable man, replied that in his belief they had done all that money could do to reach and motivate California Republicans. That didn't mean he agreed with the "don't rock the boat" strategy. Spencer-Roberts had a simple philosophy: Never remove your foot once you have it on an opponent's neck. Attacking Goldwater had brought them from thirty points behind to a shaky lead in the polls. Why go soft now?

In fact, the belated restraint was a reaction to the campaign's latest mail blitz—an incendiary brochure sent to every registered Republican in the state that inquired, none too subtly, "Who Do You Want in the Room with the H Bomb?" On Wednesday, May 27, Rockefeller campaign offices in Los Angeles reported 140 bomb threats fueled by conservative outrage over this broadside. Security around the candidate was tightened. That same day, James Francis Cardinal McIntyre dropped a bomb of his own, canceling a Rockefeller speaking invitation at Catholic Loyola University. A staunch traditionalist, Cardinal McIntyre said he didn't wish to convey a false impression of church support for one whose sinful divorce had been made worse by his subsequent remarriage. Across town, the Rockefeller high command was engaged in a bruising debate over *The Extremists*, a half-hour program—introduced by Rockefeller and hosted by Dave Garroway—set to air the following evening. The show's title said it all. To the menacing, hypnotic beat of a snare drum, *The Extremists* showcased Robert Welch of the John Birch Society and other right-wing zealots. Among the "witnesses" summoned to give evidence on camera were a minister whose house had been bombed; a corporate executive whose attempts to foster improved race relations had been disrupted by members of the John Birch Society; and a Republican loyalist from Oakland who testified to the undemocratic methods by which a Birchite minority had taken over her local GOP organization.

On the morning of May 28, barely ten hours before its scheduled statewide broadcast, the final cut of *The Extremists* was shown to Rockefeller and a small army of advisers assembled in a Warner Bros. studio set. At the end, hearty applause was followed by anguished reappraisal, as Rockefeller sought the opinion of each person in attendance. The film was shrill and counterproductive, said Bill Ronan, sure to cost Nelson a hundred thousand votes on primary day. Charlie Moore argued just as strenuously to the contrary. The latest polls, though encouraging, provided no grounds for complacency. They couldn't risk surrendering the initiative to Goldwater. John Deardourff likewise feared a last minute opposition ad barrage, contrasting the two candidates and their family values. "People kept saying that the Goldwater people were somehow going to raise that specter at the end. Some nasty mailings or phoning or whatever, and that it was going to take something—even if it was controversial—to kind of refocus people."

The patrician Leonard Firestone reminded everyone that as chairman of the Los Angeles United Way, he couldn't afford to alienate prospective donors. Stu Spencer, excluded from any part in the film's conception, agreed that it was over-the-top, though he later criticized the New York crowd for canceling several other negative spots he wanted to run that weekend to keep Goldwater on the defensive. In the end, *The Extremists* fell victim to the campaign's eleventh-hour prudence. "I killed it," boasts Bill Ronan. The other side was quick to exploit the opening. Later that Thursday, a group of sixteen Protestant evangelical ministers denounced Rockefeller for undermining the sacred institution of marriage and called on him to quit the race. Together with the heavily publicized cancellation of his Loyola appearance just six hours before he was to speak on campus, the ministerial intervention could only redirect public attention to the divorce and remarriage. Rockefeller left the Golden State that Friday and flew home to be with Happy, who was believed to be hours away from giving birth. "I have a show opening on both sides of the continent the same weekend," Nelson cracked unhelpfully.

Spencer-Roberts couldn't say they weren't warned. "Hinman had come to us a week out, and he posed the question in this way," says Stu Spencer. "Would it have any political effect if this child is born before Tuesday's election? And Bill and I climbed the wall." In another recollection of that heart-pumping exchange, Spencer asked Hinman, "'Is it going to happen?' He said, 'We don't know, it could happen.' I said, 'Do something. Hide it. You're a Rockefeller, you can do something.'" Roberts, characteristically, employed milder language to convey a similar panic. "My suggestion would be that it would be nice to have the baby on Wednesday"—the day after the primary. Not for a long time did Rockefeller's California managers learn of the political calculation surrounding the blessed event. As described by Spencer, "The New York people thought that this was going to be a plus—that he become a father and the whole thing."

Even now, it is hard to believe anyone giving, or crediting, such counsel. That it was reportedly decided at the "highest level" of the campaign to induce labor, if that is what it took to ensure the birth of Nelson Rockefeller, Jr., over the weekend, is confirmed by a Rockefeller staffer who accompanied the governor to the former Lying-In Hospital on East Seventieth Street, where Happy gave birth to a baby boy at four fifteen p.m. on Saturday, May 30. Rockefeller was at his wife's bedside throughout the day. Happy, he told reporters, was "doing wonderfully." The same could not be said for the Rockefeller campaign in California. That weekend, a barrage of Goldwater ads, including no fewer than four and a half pages of paid promotion in the Sunday *Los Angeles Times*, deluged the Republican electorate. Images of the proud new father in New York competed with full-page portraits of Barry Goldwater, his sensibly middle-aged wife, and their photogenic, *adult* children. Voters, women in particular, were once more reminded of what Spencer-Roberts had spent $2 million to obscure—"that he was a wife-stealer," lamented Bill Roberts, "and that she was a home wrecker."

Not everyone blamed the baby's birth for what happened on primary day. "On Friday he had won," insists Rockefeller aide Joe Boyd. "Stu Spencer and Bill Roberts took off for the weekend. And that's when they found out that Goldwater planted all these ads. And, of course, nobody could find them. Then he came back on Monday, after Nelson was born, for a fly-around of the state. And the whole atmosphere changed completely." Jack Germond remembers things somewhat differently. On the Sunday before the primary, while skeleton crews manned Rockefeller offices across the state, Spencer expressed doubts grounded in the decision to forgo a heavy media buy at the eleventh hour.

"I think we've blown it," Spencer told Germond. "Barry is everywhere [on TV]."

Interestingly, Clif White gave credit to his volunteers, tens of thousands of whom rang doorbells in the six southern counties that provided an electoral cushion sufficient to overcome Rockefeller pluralities elsewhere. On the Friday before the primary, White predicted a fifty-thousand-vote margin for Goldwater. The final tally gave the senator from Arizona 1,089,133 votes (51.3 percent) to Rockefeller's 1,030,180 (48.7 percent), close enough to generate plenty of alternate scenarios in the losing camp. Network computers called the race before polls had closed in the pro-Rockefeller north. Had their rush to be first cost Rockefeller votes? Some were inclined to relitigate the cancellation of *The Extremists*, their arguments bolstered by a last minute poll showing a big drop, from 47 percent to 33 percent, in the number of Californians for whom political extremism was an important issue. Reporters pressing Rockefeller for an explanation of his defeat were told simply, "I listened to the wrong people." It was getting to be a habit.*

---

* It bears noting that Stu Spencer, outspoken in attributing the California loss to the birth of Nelson Jr., was quick to assert that the infant's father could not have won that year's Republican presidential nomination even had he carried the Golden State. "Goldwater had the votes," says Stuart, an attitude Rockefeller himself adopted in retrospect. Reflecting on his tumultuous appearance in the Cow Palace on the second night of the GOP convention, Rockefeller imagined an even messier scene had he somehow prevailed in California and arrived in San Francisco a viable alternative to the Goldwater juggernaut.

Part Four
THE LIMITS OF POWER
1965–1971

There is no problem that cannot be solved.

—Nelson A. Rockefeller

Nineteen
CHANGE OF COURSE

He'd have solutions going around looking for problems.

—AL MARSHALL

1

THE LAST TIME Republicans met in San Francisco, in August 1956, it was to renominate Dwight Eisenhower for a second term. Reflecting GOP confidence about that fall's rematch with Adlai Stevenson, party chairman Len Hall had opened the proceedings with the jaunty inquiry "Is everybody happy?" This was not a question likely to be put to convention delegates assembled in the same city just eight years later. Among rank-and-file Republicans, pre-convention polls showed a marked preference for the presidential candidacy of Pennsylvania governor William Scranton, a last minute entrant backed by Rockefeller and other moderates. Inside the Cow Palace, however, these numbers were reversed, and then some, as newly empowered conservative forces loyal to Barry Goldwater steamrollered all opposition.

In a seismic break with the past, GOP platform writers made scant mention of Eisenhower, though they found space to criticize the hotline established between Washington and Moscow in hopes of avoiding thermonuclear war through superpower misunderstanding. The limits of such technology were demonstrated on Wednesday night, July 15; less than twenty-four hours after Goldwater supporters tried to shout down his nationally televised appeal for political moderation, Rockefeller telephoned the victorious nominee to offer his congratulations.

"Hell," rasped Goldwater, "I don't want to talk to that son of a bitch."

Angered by attacks portraying him as reckless, racist, and an unstable war-monger, the senator skipped the ritualistic consultation with party elders over the second spot on his ticket. His selection of New Yorker William Miller, a little-known congressman ("How many lawyers from Niagara Falls get to run for Vice President?" Miller acknowledged) and fiercely partisan Republican national chairman, was a poke in the eye to Rockefeller and other party moderates. With his uncompromising acceptance speech, Goldwater spit in the other eye. Decrying the moral and spiritual decay attending the loss of frontier values, Goldwater warned against a Republicanism "made fuzzy and futile by unthinking and stupid labels." After virtually reading out of the party "those who do not care for our cause," he spoke the two sentences that sealed his electoral fate and his place in the conservative pantheon: "I would remind you that extremism in the defense of liberty is no vice. And let me remind you also, that moderation in the pursuit of justice is no virtue!"

Ken Keating had heard enough. Already facing a tough reelection fight against Robert Kennedy, the freshman senator from New York stalked out of the Cow Palace, trailed by several dozen members of his delegation. Rockefeller missed the speech, but not the opportunity to assail Goldwater for his "dangerous, irresponsible, and frightening" words. The Albany mailbag held balm for the defeated candidate's spirits. "Your courageous presentation at the convention—for which I have heard countless hurrahs," wrote Bill Scranton, "was but frosting on the cake of a great American." To another Pennsylvanian, Senator Hugh Scott, Rockefeller expressed gratitude for Scott's loyalty "in a cause that was hopeless but very much worthwhile." The record they had made in San Francisco would prove useful as they set about "returning our Party to sanity along the road of its heritage and tradition."

This would not be easy. A century after Lincoln's fiery trial, six decades since Theodore Roosevelt's zealous trust-busting, Republican moderation had come to be defined by the blandly utilitarian standard "Does it work?" Crusading for competence, valuing expertise over doctrine, Rockefeller—and Scranton, too—lost, according to journalist Robert Novak, "because they had nothing to offer the people but themselves." This overlooked the moral dimension of Rockefeller's strong support for civil rights, a position that made him anathema to many of the newest converts to Republicanism. But it correctly diagnosed a coming sea change in public attitudes, as the 1950s Cold War consensus began to fray, racial divisions fostered political realignment, and social upheaval splintered the old New Deal coalition. With governing elites increasingly discredited, Rockefeller-style pragmatism generated diminishing enthusiasm among Republicans for whom government was fast becoming an object of mistrust, if not outright hostility.

A more opportunistic leader would have adopted the post-convention counsel of Lieutenant Governor Malcolm Wilson. "There were those of us around him who urged him to support Goldwater, even though it was a lost cause, and especially because it was a lost cause," recalled Wilson. "'Be out there with the boys so that you will be remembered in 1968 as someone who worked for Goldwater.'" Rockefeller would never be one of the boys. Neither, however, could he bring himself to emulate the clean break declared by Ken Keating and Congressman John Lindsay, among other prominent Republicans for whom the Goldwater campaign asked too much in the name of party loyalty. So he engaged in an ungainly straddle, signaling support for the entire GOP slate while refusing to say how he would vote for president on November 3. He ruled out a fusion ticket with the New York Conservative Party (which ran dozens of its own against Republican legislators and other officeholders, Keating included).

Carrying New York for the Goldwater-Miller ticket was a hopeless cause in any event. Rockefeller conceded as much in designating Michael Scelsi, a second-tier state party operative, to oversee the fall campaign effort in the Empire State. Did he fear retribution for a humiliating defeat? To the contrary, said Scelsi long afterward, chuckling. "I think I would have been punished had we won." On September 25, a plainly uncomfortable Goldwater and Rockefeller appeared together at a rally on the state Capitol steps in Albany. Both men were glad their schedules ruled out lunch at the Executive Mansion—or any other contacts for the duration of the campaign. The timing of Goldwater's brief visit added to its awkwardness; away from the crowd, Rockefeller's attention was focused on contests at once more personal and, theoretically, more winnable.*

2

O N JULY 17, ONE day after Republicans concluded their San Francisco convention, Happy Rockefeller petitioned the New York State Supreme Court to regain custody of the children she had relinquished as the price of her Idaho divorce. As justification, her lawyers cited the remarriage of Robin Murphy a month earlier to Chapin School teacher Victoria Thompson. While Robin and his bride honeymooned for three weeks in Hawaii, the Murphy youngsters had stayed with their mother at Kykuit. The three oldest—James, thirteen; Margaretta, known as Wendy, eleven; and Carol, eight—rejoined their father and new stepmother once the couple returned to New York. Happy's refusal to turn over four-year-old Malinda at the same time foreshadowed her subsequent attempt to reverse the original agreement trading custody for liberal visitation rights.

New York State Supreme Court justice Joseph F. Gagliardi, a Rockefeller appointee whose offer to recuse himself from the case was spurned by both parties, set a September 2 hearing date. Much of the pretrial publicity swirled

---

* Scelsi's New York office housed an elaborate teletype device linking him with Goldwater headquarters in Washington. Acknowledging a stream of complaints from Goldwater managers unable to reach him, Scelsi observed, "Of course they couldn't. I always had the goddamnned thing turned off." Michael Scelsi, AI.

around young Malinda, with Murphy attorney Vincent J. Malone vowing to introduce unspecified medical testimony. "We've got plenty to talk about," Malone blustered, "and we're not going to be pushed aside." In response, Rockefeller lawyer Edward S. Greenbaum denounced "a father coming into court wanting to air all these facts," a cryptic rebuttal that only fueled public curiosity. Putting off any separate decision regarding Malinda, Judge Gagliardi closed his courtroom to reporters and the public alike. Spectators were reduced to watching Happy's daily arrival at the White Plains courthouse. Without Nelson at her side, Happy appeared a rather forlorn figure. Her testimony, buttressed by that of her cousin Margaretta Iselin, as well as a longtime Murphy nursemaid and the family pediatrician, filled six and a half hours over two days.

The judge spent two weeks pondering a thousand pages of testimony. In the end, he deferred to expert opinion and to his own narrow reading of precedent. "This court has not been called upon to decide the initial question of custody," Gagliardi began his five-page decision, issued on October 1. That had been previously determined, by both parties, in favor of Robin Murphy. The issue at stake was simple: Were the best interests of the "infants" realized under the present arrangement? Though both parents were qualified by character, education, and material resources to have custody, nothing about the status quo endangered the youngsters' health or welfare. Malinda was another story. "The evidence overwhelmingly established that all four children should be kept together as a unit," Gagliardi wrote. "This is where their great strength lies, and it would be a mistake of the first magnitude to separate any one of them from the others." Gagliardi gave Happy until October 15 to return her youngest child to her former husband.

When the warring parents failed to agree on visitation rights, the judge imposed a settlement more generous to the Rockefellers than one might have expected from his original ruling. Under its terms, the newly designed children's floor at 812 Fifth Avenue, complete with playroom, nurse's quarters, and library, would not, after all, be left permanently empty. Her children were to join Happy and Nelson on alternate weekends during the school year, as well as two months in the summer, half the Christmas and Easter vacations, and on certain other holidays. The deadline for an appeal came and went. Before the case faded from the headlines, enterprising journalists mined at least one shiny nugget from the opposing lawyers. Negotiations over custody of the children, they discovered, had started in the spring of 1961—six months before Nelson and Tod announced their separation and fully two years before the Murphy divorce was finalized.

The new information did nothing to quiet whispered speculation about Malinda's position at the heart of the dispute. Then and later, members of the Rockefeller inner circle discerned a startling visual resemblance between the little girl and her new stepfather. In his diary, Rockefeller intimate Ken Riland adopted a tone of knowing irony when discussing Malinda, being careful to put the word *stepfather* in quotes. Wally Harrison's wife, Ellen, was even less discreet, claiming that Malinda's parentage was an open secret among Rockefeller associates. In later years, when Malinda traveled extensively with Happy and Nelson, an unmistakable closeness bonded her to the man she referred to as her father, though it's unclear whether she used the term merely out of gratitude for Nelson's generosity and acceptance. Rockefeller in his will made special provision for Malinda—a gesture matching that accorded his two sons by Happy, Nelson Jr. and Mark. In a 1988 conversation with Cary Reich, Happy categorically denied that Nelson was Malinda's father. By then the youngest Murphy child was married to Francis "Chip" Menotti, adopted son of composer Gian Carlo Menotti. The couple welcomed two children into the Scottish castle they called home. Tragically, Malinda did not live to see her boys grow up. Her premature death in 2005 followed a life scarred by the Fitler family curse of alcohol and addiction.*

3

O N NOVEMBER 3, 1964, Lyndon Johnson swept to victory with 61 percent of the popular vote, and forty-four of fifty states in his electoral column. Come January 1965, Democrats would enjoy veto-proof margins in both houses of Congress, their largest since 1937. "I doubt that there has ever been so many people seeing so many things alike on decision day," an ebullient LBJ told cheering supporters in Austin's Civic Center. For New York Republicans, the carnage was especially grim, as the president crushed Goldwater by a record two and a half million votes, carrying every one of the state's sixty-two counties— another first—and besting the Goldwater-Miller slate by a two-to-one margin in Miller's own House district. Though Ken Keating outdistanced his party's doomed ticket by more than a million votes, he still lost to Robert Kennedy. New York Democrats picked up eight House seats despite artful Republican gerrymandering.

---

* Gossip about Happy's youngest daughter reached unlikely places. Early in 1965, faced with growing tensions between his own Southern Christian Leadership Conference and the younger-skewing, more militant Student Nonviolent Coordinating Committee, Martin Luther King, Jr., said that any divorce would have to be initiated by SNCC. "And if they do," he chortled, "I'll be just like Rockefeller's wife when she discovered Happy was pregnant. I'll not say a word." Taylor Branch, *At Canaan's Edge: America in the King Years, 1965–68* (New York: Simon & Schuster, 2007), 130.

The same wave inundated the state legislature, giving Democrats control of both houses for the first time in thirty years and decimating GOP leadership ranks in the process. Walter Mahoney, the longest-serving senate majority leader on record, was tossed from office by Buffalo voters; on suburban Long Island, a similar fate befell assembly Speaker Joseph Carlino. The emphatic result not only dispelled claims of "a great silent latent majority" of conservative-minded voters, wrote Walter Lippmann; it reaffirmed that in America one could govern only from the center. For those more disposed to look beyond the obvious, the repudiation of Goldwater did not mean the annihilation of his movement. A Gallup poll taken one week after the election showed a virtual tie between self-identified liberals and conservatives. In California, the same electorate that gave Johnson a thumping 59 percent of their votes rejected by an even greater margin the open housing initiative endorsed earlier in the year by Rockefeller. On election night itself, Johnson's feelings of triumph were muted by forebodings about issues beyond his control. "I'm afraid of Vietnam," the president confided to his aide Bill Moyers.

No one was more keenly attuned to the possibilities this presented than Richard Nixon. Votes were still being counted when Nixon leveled a finger of blame at "spoilsport" Rockefeller, whose failure to support the Goldwater-Miller ticket stood in contrast with Nixon's vigorous campaigning in thirty-six states that fall. "It's a rule of life," added the former vice president, "that when you fail to pitch in and fight in a tough battle, you cannot lead in the next battle." Rockefeller wrote off Nixon's "peevish postelection utterance" as "neither factual nor constructive." At his own postelection press conference, a reporter quoted back to him Goldwater's assertion that the conservative cause was not lost.

"Well," Rockefeller shot back, "you would hardly say it was won."

A two-week vacation in Spain allowed time to contemplate the novel prospect of power sharing with a Democratic legislature. His first six years in Albany had been shaped—some might say distorted—by a severe case of presidential fever. Under its disfiguring influence, Rockefeller had made pay-as-you-go budgeting the centerpiece of a campaign to persuade conservative Republicans of his fiscal orthodoxy. Then came 1964 and the transformation of a party resolved to put as much distance as possible between itself and the fading Eastern Establishment. Repudiated at San Francisco, Rockefeller returned home less embarrassed by his defeat than liberated. Henceforth he needn't tailor his actions to appease Wyoming cowboys, southern bigots, or tax-hating legislators from Syracuse. The American presidency having eluded him, he would find compensation in being president of New York, a virtual nation long accustomed to showing the way for less venturesome members of the Union.

The Empire State would have its own Great Society, even broader in scope than its Washington namesake. This seemed only appropriate: next to Lyndon Johnson, no one better than Rockefeller personified the era's muscular confidence in American know-how, the purity of American motives, and the capacity of the world's richest nation to eliminate poverty by making opportunity color-blind and education universal. Free to act on his instincts, beginning in 1965 Rockefeller worried less about balancing receipts and expenditures than he did about achieving a shadowy equilibrium between economic growth and "pressing social needs." An early casualty was pay-as-you-go financing. "It isn't the end of a policy," he protested, even as he tapped unspent bond issues for $120 million, "it's an exception to a policy. Let's put it that way."

On January 20, 1965, Nelson and Happy drew cheers and cries of "Next time, Rocky!" as they rode in LBJ's inaugural parade. That evening, Nelson stole the spotlight at a reception honoring the nation's governors. His relationship with Johnson blossomed, watered by a stream of verbal flattery, state dinner invitations, and advice seeking from the accomplished seducer in the Oval Office. His support for Johnson's Vietnam policy earned Rockefeller the president's gratitude, visibly expressed in his appointment to the Advisory Commission on Intergovernmental Relations. Rockefeller used this as a platform from which to advance federal revenue sharing and more flexible grants-in-aid from Washington to the states. He thus anticipated Richard Nixon's New Federalism, even as he emulated LBJ's Great Society.*

Nineteen sixty-five represented the apogee of twentieth-century liberalism. Before it ended, Medicare and Medicaid had been written into law, along with federal aid to elementary and secondary schools and a sweeping overhaul of the nation's immigration policies. The Department of Housing and Urban Development was established that year, as were the National Endowments for the Arts and Humanities. Rockefeller approved of it all, but he reserved his warmest support for the landmark Voting Rights Act passed in the wake of Bloody Sunday, March 7, when Alabama state troopers clubbed and beat several hundred demonstrators of both races at the start of their planned march from Selma to Montgomery. Rockefeller had strongly endorsed the Freedom March, designating his cousin Alexander Aldrich and George Fowler, chairman of the New York State Commission for Human Rights, to be his personal representatives on the scene. Later in the year, he packed Martin Luther King's Ebenezer

* The president took a particular shine to Happy Rockefeller. During the crippling electrical blackout that struck the northeast United States and parts of Canada on November 9, 1965, one of the first outside calls to reach the Rockefellers in their candlelit Fifth Avenue duplex was from the White House. "How's my girlfriend?" barked LBJ, whose sense of urgency about restoring power had nothing to do with seeing Nelson in the light. Happy, chortled Johnson, was another matter altogether. (Transcript of telephone conversation between LBJ and NAR, November 9, 1965, 9:15 p.m., Recordings and Transcripts of Coversations and Meetings, LBJ.)

Baptist Church in Atlanta for a Men's Day sermon, a gesture of solidarity reinforced by a $25,000 contribution to King's newly founded Gandhi Society for
Human Rights. (He had already imported Italian craftsmen to restore the sanc-
tuary's stained-glass windows.)

On a visit to New York, the King men, father and son, pastors both, huddled
with Rockefeller in the living room of his Fifth Avenue apartment, while elsewhere in the sprawling duplex Coretta King confided to Happy Rockefeller
fears for her husband's life. Where his Baptist faith buttressed the Rockefeller
credo of racial equality, Nelson's civic religion was practical, energetic, ahead
of the curve. Too busy *doing* to entertain doubt, "he believed New York State,
and for that matter, the nation, could not stand still," says Bill Ronan. "And *he*
certainly couldn't. Either you went forward or you went back. You had to go
ahead to meet your problems, before they became crises and overwhelmed
you." Rockefeller had scant patience with the commissioner of mental hygiene
who, pressed for ways the Empire State might usefully spend proceeds of a
$500 million bond issue, mentioned a leaky roof on the Hudson River State
Hospital and another facility in need of a paint job. More to the governor's taste
were maverick thinkers such as Hudson Institute director Herman Kahn, a
frequent visitor to 20 West Fifty-fifth Street. One day Rockefeller asked Bobby
Douglass of his staff to sit in on an impromptu Kahn seminar. "He's always
entertaining," said Rockefeller, "and he's always got great ideas." Kahn's opening gambit left Douglass believing his boss half-right.

"Nelson," said Kahn. "Great bridges of the world."

"Golden Gate."

"Good."

"Brooklyn Bridge."

"Very good. Any others?"

"George Washington Bridge," Nelson replied.

Kahn tossed out the Italian city of Florence. Rockefeller mentioned the
Ponte Vecchio. More compliments from his interlocutor. "But what's different
about the Ponte Vecchio?" It crossed the Arno, said Rockefeller. "And there are
shops on both sides."

"Very good, Nelson. Now you're getting to the point." Pause for effect.
"Manhattan—Forty-second Street," said Kahn. "Roosevelt Island. Queens."

A dawn of recognition spread across Nelson's face. "Why didn't I think of
that? Herman, it's brilliant!" For Douglass, the visual shorthand took slightly
longer to decipher. "They were going to take Forty-second Street," he reflects
three decades later, shaking his head at the audacity of the thing, "bridge it on
the tip of Roosevelt [formerly Welfare] Island, and run it over to Queens."

"God," Rockefeller reiterated, "it's a great idea."

There was only one flaw in the plan, said Kahn. While Manhattan at Forty-second Street was comfortably above the East River at high tide, Queens breasted the waterway by only a few feet. "That's not *too* bad," Rockefeller replied. Think again, Kahn told him. The 1899 Rivers and Harbors Act required a sixty-five-foot clearance for warships. "Don't worry, Herman," Rockefeller said dismissively. "I'll go down to Washington. I'll get it changed. We don't need the East River for warships." Kahn wished him luck, adding that no one had been able to revise the law since its passage. "I'm gonna do it," Rockefeller vowed. "And he went after it," confirms Douglass, with a tenacious lobbying effort that finally crashed on the rocks of bureaucratic inertia. Exhibiting the same disregard for limits, Rockefeller used the eight weeks between his party's rout at the polls in November 1964 and the start of a new legislative session in January to float a series of legislative trial balloons. "I've got the program," he told Democratic legislators privately. "You've got the power. Together we can do business."

On January 5, 1965, he made good on his boast, unveiling the state's first $3 billion budget, replete with new and expanded efforts to protect the environment and combat racial discrimination; fight juvenile delinquency; raise workers' compensation and disability benefits; extend rent control; and dramatically increase state aid to education. In the same message, Rockefeller proposed a concerted attack on drug abuse—the second of his governorship. He urged stricter traffic safety laws, a six-month probation period for new drivers, and mandatory state inspection of all automobiles, including those fresh off the assembly line. This by no means exhausted the gubernatorial wish list. It included subsidies for low-income families living in private middle-income housing; a statewide UHF educational television network; and supplementary, unspecified help for cash-starved New York City, whose current budget exceeded the state's by a third of a billion dollars. Rockefeller recommended additional recreational facilities to serve a rapidly growing population; training and guidance centers for women entering the workforce; an extra $90 million to cover burgeoning welfare costs; and a strengthened ethics code for legislators and state employees. The fact that voters the previous November had rejected a $165 million bond issue to underwrite low-income public housing did not preclude him from asking for a still larger replacement.

ROCKEFELLER WANTS MORE OF EVERYTHING, headlined the *New York World-Telegram*. The sheer scope of his agenda, and the resulting speculation over which taxes—or fees—would have to rise in order to pay for its enactment, masked the extent of his fiscal U-turn. When pressed, Rockefeller blamed the end of pay as you go on the new majority in Albany. Left to themselves, he argued, Democratic lawmakers would outspend him on education, health, and welfare. They also had fewer reservations about deficit financing. Ironically, this made them a useful foil for a governor whose agility in playing off one party against another anticipated Bill Clinton's successful triangulation strategy of the 1990s. In proposing the state's first sales tax—2 percent—plus a doubling of cigarette taxes and auto registration fees to bring his budget into balance, Rockefeller sounded a note of contrition, telling reporters, "I feel worse about this than anything since I've been in office." Unconsulted were the feelings of working-class New Yorkers taxed every time they bought a can of beer, made a telephone call, had a suit dry-cleaned or a TV set repaired. Yet rare was the Democrat prepared to vote against programs long championed by his party.*

Having co-opted much of the opposition program, Rockefeller presented himself to Republican skeptics as a brake on Democratic excess. Claiming it was bad for business, he vetoed an increase in the state's minimum wage from $1.25 to $1.50, though allowing he would be willing to reconsider the matter if and when the federal government adopted the same figure (as it did in 1966). Of course there was criticism. The Conservative Party railed at his extravagance and redoubled its efforts to prevent a third Rockefeller term. Individual lawmakers mocked the governor's failure to tax the very air they breathed. Yet Democratic opposition to the sales tax as an unjust burden on those least able to afford it was oddly muted. For nothing about 1965 was ordinary, beginning with the one-year legislative term mandated as part of a court-ordered reapportionment in line with the Supreme Court's one-man, one-vote edict. Eager to demonstrate their capacity to govern, Democrats instead spent six critical weeks knifing one another over the choice of a senate president and assembly Speaker. Had tradition prevailed, senate minority leader Joe Zaretzki and his assembly counterpart, Brooklyn's Anthony Travia, would have been routinely promoted to the leadership positions. That they were not was attributable to backstairs plotting worthy of the Borgias, plus the nebulous intervention of the state's newest Democratic power broker.

4

CONSIDERING THE SOURCE, the story is almost too good to investigate. Yet documentary evidence confirms Joan Braden's claim to have written simultaneous, though by no means identical, letters to Nelson Rockefeller and

---

* Norman Hurd had vivid memories of Rockefeller's 1965 annual message and of the post-speech meeting in the Executive Mansion at which Democratic legislators, "feeling their oats" over their newfound majorities, included one party spokesman who pointed his finger at the governor and declared, "We are going to use those bond issues. You aren't throwing out pay as you go, we are." Norman Hurd, HMI, 15.

Robert Kennedy. These she proceeded to place in the wrong envelopes, accidentally or otherwise, with the result that each man received a missive meant for the other. Summoned from the golf course to take Kennedy's call, Braden was told, "I have a letter which begins 'Dear Nelson.' Do you want me to read it?"

"I know perfectly well that you already have," said Braden.

Two days later, a Rockefeller assistant rang her up concerning a letter misdirected to the governor. Would Mrs. Braden like it returned? When in due course Joan mailed the original to its intended recipient, she made sure to include a cover note rebuking Bobby Kennedy. "This is the way a gentleman behaves when a lady makes a mistake," she wrote.

They may have played by different rules of etiquette, but Rockefeller and Kennedy were both accustomed to getting what they wanted, heedless of cost. Each man had the word *ruthless* attached to his name as if it were a Homeric epithet. During the 1964 campaign for Ken Keating's Senate seat, Rockefeller had castigated Kennedy the carpetbagger as "a boss-picked outsider who can't even vote in New York State, and whose unbridled ambitions and arrogance have led him into outrageous campaign excesses." A victorious Kennedy used the occasion of his maiden Senate floor speech to mock Rockefeller's poverty-fighting credentials. Specifically, Kennedy wanted to redirect federal assistance to Appalachia, a region synonymous with economic despair, to include thirteen counties in south-central New York. Rockefeller responded that the senator might better serve the state's interests by a more vigorous pursuit of federal highway dollars.

Three days before Christmas 1964, Democratic legislators convened at Albany's DeWitt Clinton Hotel to designate candidates for Speaker and senate majority leader. The chief antagonists were what Nelson called the two Roberts—Kennedy and Wagner—one a rising, the other a setting, sun in the chaotic universe of the New York Democratic Party. Poised to seize command, with Kennedy's tacit support, were mutineers led by Brooklyn's Stanley Steingut, son of the state's last Democratic Speaker in the 1930s. The result wasn't even close, as Steingut's regulars amassed fifty-three votes to Tony Travia's thirty-five. Once it was announced, custom dictated that the nomination be made unanimous. For a few hours, the Kennedy takeover appeared complete.*

Now it was Wagner's turn to startle his foes. Disregarding the caucus results,

* Party unity proved more elusive on the senate side. There Julian Erway, a former Albany County district attorney chosen as a sop to Dan O'Connell, met with scorn from liberal members because of his past opposition to civil rights legislation. Erway did not advance his cause by producing a Christmas card signed "With love" from his African American maid. Failing to muster the needed thirty votes, Erway was eventually replaced by the more substantive Jack Bronston of Queens.

the mayor's allies in the assembly belatedly rallied around Travia in numbers sufficient to deny Steingut his expected majority. Ballot after ballot revealed the same intractable division, with Democrats hopelessly split into pro- and anti-Wagner factions. Republican senator Earl Brydges of Niagara Falls, a hard-drinking, Swinburne-quoting Rockefeller ally, satirized the Democrats' plight in light verse: "When the aunt of the vicar has never touched liquor, beware when she tastes champagne." Whether Rockefeller joined in the laughter may be doubted. It was his habit to carry about with him a piece of paper, its contents jealously guarded from associates, on which he listed each session's legislative priorities. Sometimes these were scrawled across the back of a plain envelope. Not necessarily confined to the "program bills" that constituted his public agenda, "this was a list of what he really wanted," remembered gubernatorial aide Harry Albright. From time to time during the session, Rockefeller could be seen glancing at its contents, mentally tabulating his box score before returning the document to a pocket of his suit coat.

Pondering the list during the first weeks of 1965 was an exercise in frustration. With no presiding officers in place, there could be no legislative committee assignments, no public hearings, no floor debate, and no action on the governor's checklist. By Rockefeller's own count, at least two hundred bills were stacked up, with more than sixty appointments awaiting confirmation by the senate. Mayor Wagner, on the other hand, had no problem dealing with legislative paralysis. Brinkmanship was his forte. Five weeks into the crisis, he received a call from the governor. "It's time that we settle this," said Rockefeller, who wasn't taking any chances. As he spoke, GOP state chairman Carl Spad and his immediate predecessor, Fred Young, were exercising their powers of persuasion on Republican lawmakers in a room just around the corner from the office of GOP assembly leader George Ingalls. On the morning of February 3, to the astonishment of everyone not in on the plan, Republican senator John Hughes began the twenty-sixth ballot for president pro tempore of the upper chamber by nominating Democrat Zaretzki, who went on to break the deadlock with the votes of twenty-five Republicans and fifteen Democrats. The next day, Wagner Democrats joined forty-six Republicans in the assembly to make Tony Travia Speaker.

Charges of corrupt deal making flooded the Capitol. Democratic state chairman William McKeon denounced the election of Travia as a "down payment on a Rockefeller-Wagner sellout of the people"—that is, passage of the governor's sales tax. Wagner lieutenant J. Raymond Jones, the first African American Democratic Party boss in Manhattan, attributed the settlement to a larger Stop Kennedy drive orchestrated by Rockefeller. Gene Spagnoli, who reported on Albany for the *New York Daily News*, stressed more personal factors, including the chemistry between Rockefeller and the winning Democrats.

"Zaretzki was a good friend of his. Even Tony Travia," said Spagnoli. "Tony would bluster and holler and bellow, but Rocky would talk to Travia and . . . although he gave quid pro quo, he usually got more quid than quo." A master of deference, at one pivotal meeting with the leadership Rockefeller made a show of yielding his seat to the Speaker. Travia preened before his colleagues.*

In the senate, Nelson enjoyed an even closer relationship with the resolutely uncharismatic Joe Zaretzki. The new majority leader enjoyed needling Rockefeller, whose Executive Mansion artwork reminded him of something that should be referred to the Select Committee on Pornography. ("Governor, I know that one," said Zaretzki, planting himself before a Joan Miró painting, "it's that Assembly district we gerrymandered in Brooklyn.") Nelson was always ready to do Zaretzki a favor, whether it was loaning the senate majority leader a Rockefeller family aircraft so he could make a political dinner on schedule or sidelining a formidable Zaretzki primary opponent by naming him to a lucrative state job. Such interventions gave credence to the Albany witticism that Rockefeller owned one party and leased the other.

The rent was not exorbitant. "What am I going to get for my city?" was a favorite Zaretzki refrain. Most of the concessions he extracted—social services, hospital funding, education aid—were the meat and potatoes of constituent politics. In return, Rockefeller enjoyed a level of bipartisan cooperation unimaginable in today's fiercely polarized climate. He installed telephone "hotlines" connecting his office with those occupied by Zaretzki and Travia, a courtesy not extended to their Republican predecessors. By contrast with the GOP leadership, said Rockefeller, deadpan, "I never have trouble with the Democrats." This included the controversial sales tax. "We made a swap with the city," is Bill Ronan's succinct explanation of what happened. Over lunch at the Algonquin Hotel with Morton Baum, the financial maestro behind the City Center of Music and Drama, the conversation turned to the state's revenue needs. "We had a real problem," says Ronan, "because the city had a sales tax and the state didn't. And if you put in a state sales tax, what were you going to do for the city?"

The answer was obvious, said Baum. Give Wagner the proceeds of a stock transfer tax, in return for which "he'll cut back on his city tax, and you collect it for him." A grateful Wagner subsequently deployed his influence with Dem-

* On another occasion, a toothache sharpened Travia's resistance during a tough budget negotiation. Rockefeller aide Harry Albright asked the governor if he had any whiskey on the premises. Rockefeller said no—what did he expect of a faithful Baptist? Excusing himself, the resourceful Albright slipped away to a first-floor hangout patronized by state drivers. Presently he returned with a brown paper bag containing a bottle of Old Bushman's for a grateful Travia, whose assessment of Rockefeller's budget priorities grew markedly more favorable as a result. Albright, *Portrait*, 102–03.

ocratic legislators to enact the sales tax and other levies sought by Rockefeller. "Can't you Democrats see what you are doing?" protested one outvoted regular on the floor of the senate. "Rockefeller still wants to be president, and we are helping him when we pass his program." This argument gave way before another kind of logic. Buried in the avalanche of legislation from which Rockefeller had thirty days to dig himself out was a pair of bills greatly easing the financial pressures then gripping New York City. One enabled Wagner to borrow $46 million to balance his current municipal budget. The other expanded this authority to $256 million in 1965–1966.

"A bad loan is better than a good tax," Wagner liked to say. Now, with the fiscal holes in his leaky government plugged for another year, the stolid mayor could reiterate his commitment to "the war on crime, the war on poverty, the war on narcotics addiction, the war on slums, the war on disease, and the war on civil ugliness."

5

I N HIS 1962 Godkin Lectures at Harvard on the future of federalism, Rockefeller had heaped scorn on "a timidity of leadership that rarely glimpses the dawn of any new concept—but passively awaits the high noon of crisis." His eagerness to resolve problems at the state level sometimes landed Rockefeller in a bidding war with the Johnson White House. Case in point: In May 1965, two days after the president and Lady Bird Johnson entertained industrialist Joseph Hirshhorn over lunch, Rockefeller paid a visit to Hirshhorn's Greenwich, Connecticut, estate. He left confident of what he had come for—Hirshhorn's pledge to donate his vast collection of modern art to the SUNY campus at scenic Purchase, New York. A press release announcing this cultural coup was drafted, only to be rendered moot by LBJ's last minute promise of a choice spot on the National Mall, plus $15 million to build a museum and sculpture garden bearing the Hirshhorn name. The sting of losing Hirshhorn was short-lived: Rockefeller had a backup candidate in Roy Neuberger, a longtime MoMA trustee and personal friend, who gifted more than seven hundred objects and substantial financial support to underwrite a building designed by Philip Johnson and John Burgee.

The tug-of-war over Hirshhorn's collection did, however, illustrate an important truth: For all his cordiality toward the president, Rockefeller remained a political competitor. "He was impatient with the federal government, even before the Great Society," recalled Al Marshall, then preparing to succeed Bill Ronan as secretary to the governor. "He'd say, 'Goddamn it, that's a problem.

Let's do something about it.' You might say, 'Yeah, but that's a federal problem, of a magnitude or a nature that the state can't take it on.' That was not a very compelling argument with him." The Rockefeller brand of states' rights included a war on drugs far surpassing anything contemplated by Washington. New York City in the mid-1960s, it was estimated, was home to half the nation's addicts; they in turn accounted for 50 percent of the city's spiraling crime rate. Along with a drastic revision of federal narcotics laws, Rockefeller wanted a cost-sharing formula under which Uncle Sam would assume the lion's share of program expenses, including construction of a major treatment center in New York.

More was at stake than federal dollars. Rockefeller sought Uncle Sam's blessing for a get-tough approach to the seemingly intractable drug problem, a social cancer afflicting countless families—"the split-level home as well as the cold-water tenement"—turning playgrounds into markets of addiction while fattening organized crime. Under his first antidrug program, encapsulated in the 1962 Metcalf-Volker Act, addiction was branded a disease rather than a crime. Addicts accused of certain felonies had the option of committing themselves to a three-year course of treatment and rehabilitation. The program was short-circuited by an overcrowded court system, which reduced 60 percent of all felony charges to misdemeanors, touching off a cycle of short sentences and repeated arrests.

Four years later, entering another election year, Rockefeller was primed to try something more radical. Inspired by a California statute that authorized compulsory treatment for addicts, he would employ the powers of the state to physically separate drug consumers from their source of supply. Supporters likened it to quarantining tuberculosis patients. Others questioned the emphasis on institutionalization. It was one thing to mete out stiffer sentences to pushers, they contended, quite another to segregate users in state-operated facilities against their will. "We used to joke about putting barbwire around the Adirondack Mountains and then just dump them all in there," conceded Al Marshall. Foreshadowing the punitive outlook behind the so-called Rockefeller drug laws of the 1970s, the governor arranged a meeting with HEW undersecretary Wilbur Cohen, a friend from their department building days a decade earlier. On the appointed day, Cohen had his experts lined up, with the United States surgeon general in reserve. "And his crew in their politest terms shot him down," according to Marshall. Better to treat the causes of addiction, they told Rockefeller, addressing the craving at its source, than to isolate its victims as virtual criminals.

It was not a message he wished to hear. Flying back to New York, Rockefeller nursed his Dubonnet, and a sense of grievance, as he sat across the aisle from Marshall, muttering, "Damn you, you won." Marshall certainly didn't feel victorious. Rockefeller remained committed to compulsory treatment, a process triggered by anyone "acting in good faith" who applied for an order certifying a user to a hospital or other treatment facility. Up to three years of intensive rehabilitation followed, much of it as a closely supervised outpatient, with vocational training offered as it was improvised. "We didn't know how to approach the rehabilitation, readjustment area," confessed Marshall. "So we funded damn near anything that came along. Somebody would say, 'Christ, painting is good,' so we'd set up a class in painting. We did oboe lessons on the theory that playing the goddamned oboe was going to help you break the drug habit."

Success was maddeningly elusive; this and would lead to a third, vastly harsher drug war in Rockefeller's final term. It wasn't easy to reconcile the antidrug crusader with the humane reformer who set aside his doubts and in July 1965 approved legislation making New York the twelfth state to essentially eliminate the death penalty (the only exceptions: cop killers and life prisoners who murdered guards or other inmates while in jail or trying to escape—a distinction that was to have a critical difference at the time of the 1971 Attica prison uprising). At the same time, Rockefeller commuted to life imprisonment the capital sentences of seventeen out of twenty convicted prisoners awaiting execution in the electric chair, first employed as an instrument of public justice in 1890.

He signed the death penalty bill without ceremony or comment, unlike another liberal initiative aimed at leveling the playing field by providing free legal services for needy defendants. Calling the right to counsel "as indispensable as the right to fair trial," Rockefeller noted that New York had always been a leader in protecting the rights of its citizens. "These bills represent a new high in the defense of liberty." They also strengthened his brief for a vigorous federalism in which assertive states functioned as laboratories of innovation. When LBJ unveiled a plan to subsidize rents for low-income families in middle-income housing, Rockefeller recognized the flattery of imitation. "They picked it up 100 percent," he said of federal policy makers. "It's our program."

Rockefeller again beat Uncle Sam to the punch with his Pure Waters initiative, a $1.7 billion crash program to end water pollution in five years. Early in his tenure as governor, he had reorganized state agencies and boards entrusted with water policy. In 1962, he asked his Office for Local Government to examine the problem of pollution, hitherto left to individual communities, few of which had the financial resources to build needed sewage treatment plants. During his 1964 California primary campaign, Rockefeller contrasted the water needs of the nation's two largest states. Whereas the Golden State relied on irrigation to correct a natural imbalance of supply between north and south, New York suffered the consequences of toxic chemicals and unfiltered effluvia dumped into the state's rivers, streams, and harbors. New York City discharged millions of tons of raw sewage into its harbor every day. On Long Island, waste from duck farms threatened supplies of drinking water. Liquid filth had extinguished the crab population and closed shellfish beds in the Hudson.

"Our problem [in New York] is not that we have too little water," Rockefeller concluded, "but that it is dirty." Again he turned to Bill Ronan, who enlisted program associates Richard Wiebe and Ed Van Ness to craft what became known as Pure Waters—"first in the nation, first in the world, still the largest of its kind on earth," Rockefeller bragged in 1970. Aided by a billion-dollar bond issue, Albany would defray 30 percent of the cost of local sewage treatment plants. In addition, Rockefeller offered to "pre-finance" another 30 percent representing Washington's share—a remarkable gesture, considering the ceiling on federal assistance at the time was $625,000 per project. Adopted unanimously by the legislature, overwhelmingly endorsed by voters in referendum, Pure Waters spawned more than 350 new treatment facilities and a rigorous upgrade of state-enforced pollution standards.

It didn't come close to eliminating the problem, as inflation made sewage plants costlier to build and Washington failed to honor its fiscal promises, but Pure Waters set a model for others to emulate. Moreover, its incentive-driven approach led many private industries to partner with municipalities in developing antipollution plans and treatment facilities. And it goaded Washington into doing more. "His example triggered Lyndon Johnson," claimed Laurance Rockefeller, a presidential intimate who chaired the 1965 White House Conference on Natural Beauty. ("Where's Lady Bird?" her husband asked with increasing frequency. "Is she out planting flowers with Laurance Rockefeller?") Specifically, the popularity of New York's Pure Waters program prompted the White House to establish the Land and Water Conservation Fund to facilitate environmental cleanup efforts around the country.

Laurance remained his brother's closest friend and most ardent defender. Often described as the most spiritual Rockefeller, with a gift for distilling opposing cultures and traditions, he forged a highly personal blend of traditional Christianity and Zen Buddhism. An incremental idealist, the man Lady Bird Johnson dubbed "Mr. Conservation" eschewed membership in what he called "the wilderness boys." Valuing the natural world as a source of profit no less than perspective, Laurance promoted ecotourism before it had a name. "No ordinary dudes," reported Newsweek on the wilderness adventures of the Rockefeller brothers in the fall of 1965. Steering a column of seventeen riders on a test run of some new bridle trails in the Adirondacks, Laurance and Nelson invited comment for their elegant approach to roughing it. At one clearing their group dismounted, to be met by a white-clad waiter serving sandwiches, doughnuts, apples, and coffee. That night's cabin grub included inch-thick steaks and strawberry shortcake.

The comforts of home against the glorious backdrop of God's creation: This was the spark behind Laurance's celebrated RockResorts, a chain of stylish retreats situated amid Hawaiian volcanoes, New England ski slopes, and palm-fringed Caribbean islands. Blessed with an aesthete's sensibility, a Rockefeller's resources, and the driving originality of a venture capitalist, Laurance became an enthusiastic advocate of "compatible development." Inevitably, this brought him into conflict with emerging schools of environmental thought. Published in 1962, Rachel Carson's *Silent Spring* acted as an alarm clock, rudely rousing millions of Americans to the dangers posed by modern science and mindless commercialism. That same year, Consolidated Edison unveiled a Buck Rogers scheme to gratify New York City's voracious appetite for electric power by dis-emboweling Storm King Mountain, a majestic granite sugarloaf in the scenic Hudson Highlands region an hour's drive north of Manhattan. A paradigm of sixties hubris, the Storm King project would convert the interior of the mountain into a pump storage hydroelectric plant. At night, water from the Hudson would be cycled through tunnels leading to an eight-billion-gallon storage reservoir atop the summit. In periods of peak demand, the same water was to reverse course, turning turbines and generating electricity for New Yorkers increasingly vulnerable to brownouts and shortages, with all their harmful consequences for the regional economy.

Nelson Rockefeller thought the plan "an imaginative large-scale attempt to relieve the power shortage." He welcomed the utility's agreement, under pressure from Laurance and the venerable Hudson River Conservation Society, to bury unsightly transmission lines underground—a prelude to relocating the bulk of the plant where it couldn't be seen. Con Ed's revised proposal offered a welcome alternative to urban smokestacks and steam-powered generators. This made it attractive to Nelson, who in 1964 instituted a first-in-the-nation air-zoning system, to identify and punish commercial and industrial offenders. A pioneering Clean Air program followed two years later, balancing tax incentives for industries that installed pollution control equipment, with legislative mandates requiring such devices on motor vehicle exhaust systems.

By then, the $150 million Storm King project was ensnared in a web of scientific, political, and legal controversies that neither Rockefeller brother could evade. The battle of Storm King Mountain was waged across two decades in courtrooms and living rooms, on editorial pages, and in bureaucratic fiefdoms. The clash of interests traced the incipient conflict between economic growth and the claims of nature. To the citizens of Cornwall, the river hamlet in which the mountain was located, Storm King meant jobs—perhaps even a permanent tax holiday. To New York's governor, it represented a daring yet realizable alternative to doing nothing. The environmental minefield tested one of Rockefeller's basic theories of governance. "The world needs visionaries, but not in leadership positions," he told his Albany counsel Michael Whiteman. A visionary, as defined by Rockefeller, was apt to get so far out in front of his troops that they lost sight of him. The leader, by contrast, was someone blessed with a vision, who most assuredly knew where he wanted to go but was only a step or a step and a half ahead of his constituency. "He's not way out there on the horizon."

FDR couldn't have said it better. Where he could strike a balance between environmental and economic concerns, Rockefeller offered his services as honest broker.* Yet Storm King stubbornly defied all efforts at mediation. When an unrelated accident at the nearby Indian Point nuclear power plant resulted in a massive fish kill, it confirmed the worst fears of environmental activists. State conservation commissioner Harold Wilm foolishly labeled the ecological disaster an act of God; Attorney General Louis Lefkowitz, with a far surer grip on public opinion as well as Old Testament theology, put the blame squarely on Con Ed. Lefkowitz sued the utility for $5 million. He also insisted on closing Indian Point until corrective measures were taken. None of this deterred Con Ed in March 1965 from obtaining a license from the Federal Power Commission. Storm King opponents now turned to Laurance Rockefeller, hoping to enlist Mr. Conservation in a public challenge to the FPC ruling. Laurance rebuffed their overtures, telling one supplicant, "I don't see any point in going through a useless gesture." (It's impossible to gauge how much this represented his true feelings in the matter and how much reflected a brother's desire to avoid still more controversy harmful to Nelson.)

A U.S. Court of Appeals showed more assertiveness in December 1965. Voicing harsh criticism of the agency's decision-making process, the court overruled the FPC. In a precedent-making action, it directed Con Ed to fully examine and publicly report on the environmental consequences of Storm King to striped bass, shad, sturgeon, and other species that supported a thriving commercial fishing industry said to be worth $20 million annually. The court-ordered review took three years to complete. Long before then, both Rockefellers had backed away from their original support of the project, Laurance telling reporters, "We hope they will not have to build this monster." His biographer Robin Winks credits the Storm King controversy with converting Laur-

---

* Informed that Georgia-Pacific wished to build a wallboard factory at the foot of scenic Mount Taurus in the same Hudson Highlands, he contacted the company's president. "Look, we'd love to have you in New York State," Rockefeller told the executive, "but not *there*." It was his intention as governor, he confided, to set aside the area in question as a scenic and recreational enclave. That said, Rockefeller gladly lent a hand to the search for an acceptable alternative. In the end, Georgia-Pacific got its new plant, New York got an infusion of jobs and tax revenues, and Rockefeller in 1967 got to dedicate the twenty-five-hundred-acre Hudson Highlands State Park. Nelson A. Rockefeller, *Our Environment Can Be Saved* (New York: Doubleday, 1970), 99–101.

ance the conservationist into an environmentalist painfully sensitive to the limits of compatible development (an undoubted factor in this was Laurance's son Larry, a prominent member of the environmentalist group Scenic Hudson). Litigation dragged on until 1980, a year after Nelson's death, when the Storm King plant was accorded a decent burial of its own, in return for which Con Ed won a ten-year reprieve on the construction of cooling towers that would reduce its intake of water from the Hudson.*

In his 1970 book, *Our Environment Can Be Saved*, Nelson Rockefeller minimized his support of Storm King. He airbrushed out of the picture entirely another environmentally sensitive project, one more directly associated with his family. This was the Hudson River Expressway, conceived as a six-lane, forty-seven-mile answer to traffic congestion on Route 9, the main north–south route through the crowded Hudson River Valley. Late in May 1965, the legislature took up bills vaguely authorizing both the expressway and a 3.5-mile connecting road—dubbed "the Rockefeller Spur"—slicing through the heart of Sleepy Hollow country immortalized by Washington Irving. Rather than a spectral stallion, warned detractors, the modern Headless Horseman rode a bulldozer. While Governor Rockefeller emphasized the benefits to tourism, local activists pictured heavy truck traffic barreling through their backyards at sixty miles an hour. The handful of sign-carrying protesters who paraded outside the New York Hilton, site of Rockefeller's February 1966 Conference on Natural Beauty, were but the vanguard of swelling hostility to both highway projects. Facing a tough reelection battle, Nelson reduced the expressway to a ten-mile stretch from Beacon to Tarrytown.

Opponents turned to the courts. In a final irony, they based their appeal on the same 1899 legislation that had stymied Nelson's plan to extend Forty-second Street across the East River to Queens. Under its terms, congressional approval was required before any dike or other potentially hazardous obstacle could be built in navigable waters. Since the proposed expressway rested partially on landfill, the ancient statute was deemed applicable. Still Rockefeller persisted, his state transportation department producing no fewer than five alternate routes for consideration. None met with popular approval. Not until voters in November 1971 rejected a $3.5 billion transportation bond issue did Rockefeller finally concede defeat. "People's priorities are changing," he acknowledged.

---

* Determined to prevent future Storm Kings, in his last term as governor Rockefeller established the New York State Board on Electric Generation Siting to fill the regulatory and procedural vacuum. An honest attempt to balance environmental and economic priorities, the initiative had little practical effect. As pointed out by Robert H. Connery and Gerald Benjamin in their authoritative study of the Rockefeller governorship, only one of seven power plant applications was approved in the 1970s, resulting in a "de facto moratorium" on new sources of electrical generation.

6

S UCCESS WITH THE 1965 legislature, especially as measured in new taxes, did little for Rockefeller's popularity. By May, in-house polls showed just 17 percent of New Yorkers credited him with doing a good or excellent job; 78 percent ranked his performance fair or poor. In test matchups with Democrats like Queens district attorney Frank O'Connor, Franklin Roosevelt, Jr., and Mayor Wagner, Rockefeller trailed each by thirty points or more. Worse, a consensus had formed within his own party that he should retire from the field so that Republicans could nominate Jacob Javits in his place. In office since 1947, Javits expected a deference accorded the state's senior Republican. Yet Rockefeller persistently held him at arm's length, an unavoidable, if insensitive, tactic given the governor's national aspirations. In moments of pique, Rockefeller called the militantly liberal Javits a Communist. Beyond the complications arising from a pair of outsized egos in conflict, there was Nelson's attitude, bordering on contempt, for the legislative function. "Look at Javits," he remarked. "He's never passed a bill with his name on it, yet he has a bigger plurality than anyone who runs." Both men worked at hiding their true feelings, as state GOP chairman Richard Rosenbaum discovered after taking Rockefeller to task for some extravagant puffery he had lavished on Javits at a Waldorf tribute-cum-fund-raiser.

"That double-crossing S.O.B.," Rockefeller groused when the two men were alone. "I hope I get a chance to get even with him."

In the winter of 1964–1965, it was Javits whose long simmering resentment of Rockefeller's dominance boiled over into print. Deep into his latest flirtation with a mayoral campaign, Javits wanted the GOP to designate its candidate by March 1 at the latest. In common with Congressman John Lindsay, another prospective contender, Javits counted on an early start to help offset the advantages enjoyed by Wagner or any other Democratic nominee. Rockefeller worked from a different set of calculations. Dependent as he was on votes from Wagner Democrats to enact his legislative program, the governor insisted there was no hurry in settling on a Republican challenger. At a Washington breakfast meeting with the state's congressional delegation on February 25, Javits lost his temper. Reminded yet again that Wagner's support was vital to passing the Rockefeller agenda in Albany, the senator snapped, "All right then, why don't *you* run for Mayor?" Rockefeller returned the volley, challenging both Javits and Lindsay to declare their intentions on the spot.

Javits, predictably, opted out of the race. The next day, declaring that his congressional responsibilities took precedence, Lindsay followed suit. At least he thought he had. This did not reckon with the wire-pulling wizardry of Robert Price, the Lindsay campaign manager in search of a campaign. Acclaimed as the mastermind behind Nelson Rockefeller's upset victory in Oregon, Price had convinced himself that Bob Wagner was sick. "And while I couldn't get any doctor at New York Hospital to confirm it," says Price, "nobody was denying it." Price saw a rare opportunity to promote Lindsay as a different kind of Republican, one whose entry into the race would scramble traditional loyalties and encourage anti-Goldwater forces out to reclaim the GOP nationally. That his prospects for victory in the heavily Democratic city appeared minimal hardly bothered Bob Price. "John, the question wasn't, Are you interested in *being* mayor?" Price told a reluctant Lindsay. "The question was, Would you like to *run* for mayor?" To Price it was a no-lose proposition. "You're a congressman for two years, you get a lot of publicity, and in the event Rockefeller vacates the governorship, you have a nomination."

While Lindsay consulted with supporters, Price approached George Hinman to gauge Rockefeller's attitude toward a Lindsay candidacy. Hinman, after calling the governor from a nearby phone booth, assured Price, "Nelson would love it." Lindsay remained fixated on the cost of running, estimated at $3 million to $5 million. Events assumed a breakneck pace as Price moved to close the deal. On Monday, May 11, he conspired to have Lindsay return from Washington for some ritualistic lobbying over dinner at the Executive Mansion in Albany, while he converted the august *New York Times* into a platform from which to launch the Lindsay campaign. Like most Price guarantees, the offer of a *Times* exclusive came with strings attached. "You can't ask anybody else," he told *Times* deputy managing editor Abe Rosenthal. "You have to run the story . . . on the front page, above the fold, last three columns."

As soon as he hung up, Price called Rockefeller in Albany. Be at the Butler Aviation terminal at six o'clock, the governor told Price; a plane would be waiting to transport him and Lindsay to the capital. Only then did Price dial his boss in Washington. "John, I've never asked you, but I'd like you to take the four o'clock shuttle and meet me at LaGuardia at five." Was he sick? No, Price told Lindsay, he wasn't sick. Mystified, the congressman reluctantly agreed to skip an important vote on foreign aid and rendezvous with Price at the designated time and place.

"Where are we going?" Lindsay inquired when they finally met.

"Albany," said Price, taking care to sign false names in the plane's manifest. "We're going to have dinner."

Once on board, he handed Lindsay an announcement speech for his review. At the Executive Mansion, Rockefeller went through the motions of asking Lindsay to run. The congressman said he was flattered. "Nelson," interjected Price, "can we count on you for half a million dollars?"

"An hour after he announces, you have half a million dollars." (Closer to

$800,000 by the time Nelson and other family members paid gift taxes on their contributions to the Lindsay campaign.)

Price called Abe Rosenthal at the *Times*. "Abe, run the story." Half an hour later, Lindsay and Price were back on the governor's plane, "with Lindsay understanding that Rockefeller would not say anything the next day. Later on we told Rockefeller he wasn't to say anything at any time." Price wanted the money. But he also wanted to keep his distance from an unpopular governor.* No doubt other actors in the drama would put their own spin on events. Lindsay staunchly maintained that his decision to run had been finalized the weekend before his hastily arranged pilgrimage to Albany. Rockefeller's chief memory of May 11 involved an awkward encounter at the mansion in which Lindsay, too proud or too timid to solicit the $500,000 himself, spent most of his time talking to Happy. Whether Price's narrative is accurate in every detail is beside the point, for it illustrates the staff-driven animosities that were to poison relations between Rockefeller and Lindsay. Al Marshall, whose subsequent attempts to bridge the gap won him scorn in the Rockefeller camp as a "Lindsay lover," put much of the blame on the mishandled campaign gift. "There was a danger when he 'lent' you money," said Marshall, himself the beneficiary of more than $300,000 in Rockefeller largesse. "He always felt that Lindsay was an ungrateful son of a bitch."

Feeling under siege, Rockefeller didn't reserve his anger exclusively for Lindsay, whose Kennedyesque aura and street-corner charisma were already generating talk of a future presidential bid. His differences with Jacob Javits boiled over when Javits leaked to the press a letter from Syracuse senator John Hughes predicting "nothing but disaster" should Rockefeller pursue reelection in 1966. "The fact is we are totally lacking in leadership," claimed Hughes, "and the Governor cannot lead since there are very few who will follow. He has no right to take the party, the Legislature and many local officials down with him." But it was his closing appeal, all but inviting Javits to elbow the governor aside and take his place, that caused an uproar when the letter became public knowledge. Publicly, Nelson put a brave face on rumors of a revolt by county leaders. "Where are they going to go?" he asked. "They need patronage, don't they?"

Rather than linger over incipient treachery, Rockefeller invited Javits to chair his upcoming campaign, the uphill nature of which was dramatized a

---

* As justification for his duplicity, Price insisted that keeping Rockefeller away from the Lindsay campaign was the only way to prevent the Kennedys or LBJ from intervening and perhaps tipping the scales for Abe Beame in November. It's a feeble rationale, delivered with more bravado than conviction.

few weeks later, when the governor joined in celebrating the tercentenary of the Long Island community of Smithtown. Exactly a week had passed since the state's new sales tax took effect; paradegoers reserved their loudest applause for a unit from the Suffolk County Democratic Committee and a little girl whose cardboard sign read, "Penny Collection for Rockefeller's Sales Tax." Not content to boo their governor, the citizenry of Smithtown pelted him with dimes as he marched at the head of the procession. "Dimes hurt," recalls assistant press secretary Jake Underhill, "especially when they hit a bald head like mine." Eventually, the big black gubernatorial Chrysler was backed down a side street, and Rockefeller escaped to the relative safety of Manhattan.

Lindsay remained distant, if not defiant, throughout the fall campaign. Pitted against the colorless comptroller Abe Beame and acid-tongued Conservative nominee, William F. Buckley, Jr., the congressman stressed his credentials as a La Guardia–type fusion candidate. Questioned about 1966, Lindsay said he expected to be far too busy governing New York to campaign for Rockefeller's reelection. Nelson was in no position to complain, having snubbed both Eisenhower and Nixon as a candidate for governor. This did not prevent him, two days before the election, from telling reporters that a successful Mayor Lindsay would in all likelihood seek the White House—in the process validating Beame's claim that the ambitious reformer had no intention of serving out a four-year term in city hall.

On election night, November 3, the governor was conspicuously uninvited to Lindsay headquarters at the Roosevelt Hotel. He showed up anyway, practically forcing his way into the ballroom and onto the stage, where Lindsay and his supporters were celebrating their come-from-behind victory. The winning candidate winced visibly as Rockefeller enthused, "We did it." In his own remarks, Lindsay reserved his thanks for Senator Javits. The next day's *Times* quoted unnamed aides to the mayor-elect expressing dissatisfaction over Rockefeller's role in the campaign. Outwardly, Nelson struck a cheerful note. "I get buried so often I'm used to it," he told Murray Kempton. "I just stay underground a little and then I get up. I use it as a rest period." He would do everything in his power to work with the new mayor. "But it will be a lot easier—and I hope it will happen—if there's some evidence that he wants to work with me."

7

AS A PROMISING newcomer to Washington, already being groomed for higher office by political handicappers, John Lindsay had introduced legislation to repeal the 10 percent federal tax on theater tickets. At the time, he was moonlighting as the narrator in an off-Broadway revival of Stephen Vincent Benét's *John Brown's Body*. "I am the greatest ham in the world," Lindsay acknowledged. "If the voters throw me out in November, I know where I'm going—on stage." Voter dissatisfaction was the last thing he had to worry about: in November 1964, he took 71 percent of the vote, bettering even Lyndon Johnson's showing in the Seventeenth. That Lindsay had refused to support Barry Goldwater against LBJ was characteristic of the maverick whose freshman term in Congress had been notable for his lonely, though well-publicized, dissent from a bill empowering the postmaster general to impound allegedly obscene mail "in the public interest." (For this, *The Village Voice* dubbed Lindsay "the Congressman from the Constitution.")

Lindsay's popularity in the district grew in inverse proportion to his regularity in the House Republican caucus. His passionate advocacy of civil rights, and of the liberal Warren Court, reinforced the image of one driven by conviction against the tide. With the faintest note of envy, Rockefeller himself acknowledged the congressman's bipartisan appeal. "One of the most important things I've learned in politics is that voters react to you intuitively," Nelson told journalist Nat Hentoff. "After a while, they can tell pretty accurately what kind of man you are, even if they've never looked at your voting record. And that's the important thing John has going for him—they can *feel* his independence."[*] At heart a loner, for whom a career battling windmills in a party veering ever further to the right held limited appeal, Lindsay had few avenues of political promotion open to him. With the governorship and both Senate seats filled, city hall offered both escape and a possible springboard to higher office.

For a critical mass of New Yorkers in November 1965, Lindsay's patrician conscience was reason enough to entrust him with the future of their decaying city. Anticipating a change at city hall, they cast the mayor-elect as JFK to Robert Wagner's Ike. Except that Lindsay had his Bay of Pigs even before he took office. His nemesis was Michael J. Quill, "Red Mike" to the thirty-five thousand members of the Transport Workers Union of America, a blustery Irish Republican with a mouth full of invective and a union undergoing rapid demographic change. "John Lindsay looked at Mike Quill and he saw the past," wrote columnist Jimmy Breslin. "And Mike Quill looked at John Lindsay and

---

[*] Six feet four inches in height and Arrow collar handsome, with his boyish cowlick and Ivy League patina, Lindsay was catnip to women. Bill O'Shaughnessy, president of Whitney Radio and the longtime editorial voice of Westchester stations WVOX and WRTN, captured the essence of Lindsay's appeal. "He was the WASP Jack Kennedy," O'Shaughnessy explains. "Before John Lindsay every Republican looked like Herbert Hoover, or Herbert Brownell." Lindsay's own attraction to his city's celebrity culture found intimate expression in an affair with stage and television actress Florence Henderson, whose 2012 memoir revealed the relationship and its most tangible legacy, a sexually transmitted case of pubic lice, inelegantly referred to as crabs.

he saw the Church of England." It was worse than that—as a Yale history major, Lindsay had written his thesis on Oliver Cromwell.

With contract negotiations deadlocked, Quill and his men vowed to walk off the job at midnight on New Year's Eve, just as responsibility formally passed into Lindsay's hands. Les Slote, Wagner's press secretary at the time, explained how the process was supposed to work. "Wagner had a deal with Quill. Before the negotiations started, the mayor would secretly call Quill and say, 'Mike, I've got $3 million to give you and that's it.' Okay. They made a deal. Then Quill could go out to the unions and say, 'If that bum Wagner thinks he's going to get the transit workers, he's out of his mind. . . .' He'd rant and rave. And then we'd meet at the Hotel Vanderbilt and Ted Kheel would be there, and the negotiations would go on. They'd stop the clock at midnight, then at two a.m. there'd be a settlement, which had been worked out. Every other year, I'd tell my wife, 'Goodbye, see you on New Year's Eve.' It was all preset. But Lindsay was too dumb. . . . The first thing he's mayor, we have a subway strike."

Reading disdain as well as weakness in his adversary's eyes, Quill called Lindsay a pipsqueak and a liar. He tore up a court order prohibiting his workers from walking off the job. As the strike took hold and Quill martyred himself in jail, Lindsay's soaring inaugural rhetoric about the Proud City was overtaken by crisis management. The new mayor appealed to Washington without success. Rockefeller, too, held back from any involvement. "Mr. Lindsay is Mayor," he reminded those petitioning him to call out the National Guard. No less than Lindsay, Rockefeller was engaged in a high-wire act of his own. Too large a rescue package would reward Mike Quill for his intransigence and spur demands for assistance from other financially strapped cities. This, in turn, would play havoc with his newest state budget, an election year document containing a healthy increase in local school aid and an 8 percent raise for state workers, but no new taxes. The situation was further complicated by Deputy Mayor Bob Price, who conducted freelance negotiations in Quill's hospital room after the union leader suffered a heart attack in his jail cell. According to Lindsay biographer Vincent J. Cannato, Price further undercut his boss by advising Rockefeller, "Lindsay's attention span is only two or three minutes, so you had better deal with me."

Rockefeller waited until the twelve-day walkout was settled, at a cost the White House denounced for its inflationary consequences, before promising the city a onetime windfall of $100 million. Only half of this was new money; the rest was an acceleration of funding owed New Yorkers in future budget years. Moreover, legislative approval would be required before a penny of the emergency funds, ostensibly earmarked to preserve the fifteen-cent transit fare, was released. Lindsay's gratitude was muted. "John is not interested in what I did for him already," Rockefeller acknowledged before a Lincoln Day dinner audience as the mayor looked on stonily. "He's interested in what I'm going to do for him tomorrow." Their relationship went downhill from there. Resentful of the governor's stranglehold over the state party, Lindsay took to calling his Fifth Avenue apartment Berchtesgaden. Practicing snobbery in reverse, the faithful vestryman of St. James Episcopal Church even questioned Nelson's Protestant credentials. "Rockefeller wouldn't drink," recalls Bob Price, "and Lindsay always said that is a Baptist trait, they're afraid of getting drunk."

That Lindsay held Rockefeller in minimal high regard is confirmed by former GOP committeeman Bill Kent. "He thought he was a schmuck," says Kent. Employing language only slightly more diplomatic, mayoral aides complained that Rockefeller was accustomed to having his way. Lindsay had never learned the art of compromise, retorted the governor's camp. Bill Ronan spoke for his employer when he characterized Lindsay as "a musical comedy mayor," uninterested in the substantive details of governing and consequently dependent on Bob Price and other subordinates pursuing their own agendas. Having by now examined the books left him by the Wagner administration—"Hell, he even bought *pencils* on credit"—Lindsay was in the position of the successful candidate shocked to realize that things are even worse than he claimed they were in order to get elected. Declaring himself "a receiver in bankruptcy," the mayor submitted to Rockefeller a breathtaking request for nearly $600 million in new state aid and taxing authority, including the city's first income tax and an equally controversial levy on commuters.

In his response, Rockefeller pointed out that New York City already received a quarter of the state's budget. Were he to accede to the mayor's wishes, opening the floodgates to similar requests from other municipalities, state income taxes would have to rise by 75 percent. Lindsay dug in his heels, denouncing unnamed "power brokers" who held his city financial hostage. Lindsay's ill-considered vow to campaign against legislators opposed to his tax package caused bipartisan resentment, with suburban Republicans practically begging the mayor to make good on his threat. Rockefeller, clearly miffed, rammed through the legislature a bill retroactively legalizing the wage settlement negotiated with the transit workers, who had threatened a wildcat strike if their pay increase was tied up in the courts.* Lindsay learned about it in the press. He

---

* Rockefeller himself had been reluctant to endorse such a statute, until the matter was referred to AFL-CIO boss George Meany and Central Labor Council president Harry Van Arsdale, Jr. Not only did Rockefeller change his mind; according to labor columnist Victor Riesel, he agreed to sign an increase to $1.50 in the state minimum wage law. He also appointed a ten-member commission to come up with a replacement for the discredited Condon-Wadlin Act, which prohibited public employees from striking. In return, Meany, Van Arsdale, and their aligned organizations promised to support the governor's third-term aspirations. *New York Journal-American*, February 23, 1966.

was again caught off guard when Rockefeller proposed to open branches of SUNY in each of New York's boroughs.

"That was quite a bombshell, wasn't it?" remarked the mayor.

On April 15, Lindsay formally presented his $4.6 billion budget—19 percent larger than Wagner's final spending request—to the New York City Council. Two days later, he explicitly challenged Rockefeller, saying the governor had an "obligation" to endorse his tax package and warning of massive reductions in city services if he didn't. Rockefeller, professing concern about New York's business climate, criticized the Lindsay plan for its failure to duplicate state tax deductions. He also questioned the city's capacity to go on supplying public services free or well below cost. In the last days of May, hoping to reach an acceptable compromise, Bob Price flew to Albany. He found Rockefeller surprisingly receptive. In place of Lindsay's 5 percent income tax on residents and commuters alike, the governor pitched a smaller payroll tax on commuters, plus a graduated tax on New Yorkers earning over $3,000 a year. A settlement along these lines was quickly arranged, giving the mayor most of what he wanted.

Not for the last time, Lindsay reneged on a deal negotiated in his name. Acting on objections from his Liberal Party ally Alex Rose, who thought the package too generous to commuters at the expense of his working-class constituents, Lindsay disowned the work of his deputy mayor. On June 8, Rockefeller blasted as "misinformed and totally irresponsible" a mayor who couldn't take yes for an answer. "He's interesting," Nelson said of Lindsay to Murray Kempton. "He has a brand new political style. You might call it The Cantankerous." Still hoping to function as an honest broker, in early June Rockefeller offered the Executive Mansion as neutral ground for three grueling days of budget negotiations. The governor began by asking each of the guests arranged around his dining room table to state his position; leading off was Frank O'Connor, his likely Democratic opponent in the fall elections. (During a break in the talks, Lindsay noticed O'Connor staring wide-eyed at the ubiquitous Rockefeller art collection. "Frank, the paintings don't come with the house," he cracked.) Any nervous laughter this generated was quickly dissolved in the mounting tension of stalemate. "I've never been involved in anything like this," Lindsay told aides. By comparison, the transit strike seemed like child's play. Rockefeller agreed. "These are the toughest negotiations I've ever been in," he confided to reporters on his lawn.

By the afternoon of June 15, the budget hung in the balance and with it the success of the young Lindsay administration. At one point late in the day, Lindsay got up from the table and made ready to go. Rockefeller followed him to the men's room, where he convinced Lindsay not to leave on an empty stomach. Slowly the antagonists repaired to the buffet line. "Eventually the mayor joined the others at the table," recalled Robert Bennett, whose roast beef and York-shire pudding may have saved the negotiations. After dinner, the talks resumed in a businesslike atmosphere. At ten minutes past four in the morning, Rocke-feller, to the amazement of Lindsay press aide Woody Klein, "still fresh in a light blue unwrinkled shirt," was able to announce a deal to reporters camped out on his front steps. Lindsay had his income tax, but little more; indeed, he emerged from the Executive Mansion with considerably less than Bob Price had secretly extracted during his talks with the man who lived there.

To Murray Kempton, there was only one winner in the affair. "The Great Swinger is on his feet again," wrote Kempton. "If you really want him taken," Kempton addressed an imagined Bobby Kennedy, "you got to go in and do it yourself. John Lindsay can't. The Democrats in Albany and at City Hall don't even want to." No shortage of Rockefeller adversaries were eager to put Kemp-ton's thesis to the test. Certainly Lindsay looked forward to a rematch on more favorable turf. Something more than the usual competition for higher office, or favorable press coverage, separated the wily pragmatist in Albany from the ear-nest reformer turned ringmaster of Fun City. Were he truly objective, Rockefel-ler might have glimpsed in Lindsay spectral evidence of his own promise as an untested governor resolved to do right, whatever the political toll exacted. In the meantime, there was always the "old bull versus young bull" theory. Leav-ing the Plaza hotel one evening following a charitable event addressed by both men, Rockefeller rhetorically asked an accompanying aide, "Why do you think he hates me so?"

Without pausing to identify the subject of this inquiry, the assistant replied that it was really quite simple.

"You get laid more often than he does."

"Naw . . . ," gushed Rockefeller, feigning shock at this display of lèse-majesté. "Do you really think so?" The grin on his face said it all.

Twenty
ROCK BOTTOM

I tell you, they were not going to make me walk out. They could throw me out. But I wasn't going to walk out. . . .

—NELSON A. ROCKEFELLER, November 8, 1966

1

FEW CANDIDATES FOR office have embarked on a campaign saddled with the personal and political baggage that Nelson Rockefeller carried in the spring of 1966. Traditionalists viewed his divorce and remarriage as symptoms of a culture in decline. Fiscal conservatives objected to his record budgets and his embrace of costly new social welfare programs such as Medicaid. Rockefeller's attempt to minimize the impact of "one man, one vote" legislative reapportionment angered urban liberals, though no more so than his coercive treatment of drug addicts or his efforts to channel state aid to parochial schools. His repeated, unsuccessful lunges for the presidency aggravated a widespread impression of gubernatorial negligence. And virtually everyone grumbled about his sales tax and other levies enacted in flagrant violation of previous campaign promises. Members of his family warned Nelson that he was courting humiliation at the polls. Even George Hinman, the ultimate loyalist, said he wouldn't give two cents for his friend's chances in November.

Bill Ronan disagreed. "One of the problems is that you've done so damn much for the state that people don't know what you've done," said Ronan, who had numbers to back up his assessment. An early poll showed that only one in four voters associated Rockefeller with any specific accomplishment as governor. Put another way, while everyone was aware their taxes had gone up, few had any idea what they were going for. Ronan told his boss what he wanted to hear. Withdrawal might be taken for cowardice—worse, as confirmation that his marriage to Happy had destroyed his political career. Moreover, with two terms under his belt, Rockefeller had a substantial legacy to protect. "I know what's going to happen if I lose," he remarked in private. "They're going right after the State University." Even more vulnerable in his estimation was the

South Mall. Determined to place both projects beyond the reach of his ene-mies, Rockefeller accelerated the pace of construction contracts (and election year ground breakings).

Disregarding traditional constraints of the calendar, beginning in Novem-ber 1965 Rockefeller undertook twenty-two one-day trips around the state. His talent for ingratiation undiminished by familiarity, he appeared for all the world as if there were nowhere he'd rather be than dropping in unannounced on a lunch meeting of the Elmira Lions Club. A typical foray included fence-mending sessions with area businessmen, labor leaders, educators, and com-munity activists, capped by an hour-long "town meeting" invariably prefaced by the same high-risk invitation: "Tell us what we're doing wrong, or what we're not doing that we ought to be." The unscripted format was a comfortable one for Rockefeller, who had employed it throughout his 1964 presidential cam-paign. Now he adapted it to publicize his administration's achievements, with special emphasis on local economic development. When a questioner in Corn-ing expressed concern over the loss of industry in the state, Rockefeller asked where he came from. "Rochester," said the man, who was promptly reminded that his hometown's unemployment rate of 1.8 percent was well below the na-tional average.

Rockefeller's wit was as quick as his statistical recall. He was about to ad-journ one meeting when someone in the back of the hall identified himself as a fireman. "I will always take a question from a fireman," said Nelson. His in-quisitor launched into an unexpected pitch for zero population growth, con-cluding with a bluntly worded demand to know where the governor stood on limiting a family to two children.

"I was the third child," Rockefeller replied.

Sometimes he was *too* quick on the draw, fatigue dulling his instincts as it sharpened his tongue. At one town meeting in Queens, a bone-weary cam-paigner was confronted by a heavyset black youth who disputed his empathy for the oppressed. "You've never had to go hungry," the young man charged. Un-thinkingly, Nelson fired back, "You know, you don't look like you've missed too many meals." Such gaffes were rare in a campaign entrusted to the fiercely competent Bill Pfeiffer. Dividing the state into six sections, Pfeiffer paid special attention to New York City, where Rockefeller agents recruited four workers for each of the city's 5,185 election districts. Dozens of storefront headquarters were supplemented by mobile units, directed to neighborhoods that showed the greatest promise or most worrisome slippage. A paid campaign staff unprece-dented in size served as a metaphor for the relentless expansion of state govern-ment under Rockefeller. To get back in the race, he must somehow rebrand his image as a serial tax raiser. More to the point, voters unhappy over the escalat-ing costs of Rockefeller's administration must be persuaded that his taxes were the justifiable price of better schools, safer streets, improved transport, and greater access to quality health care. Government itself must be redeemed.

Just when his situation appeared most desperate, Washington unveiled a program demonstrating beyond the dry irrefutability of any Rockefeller briefing book what a compassionate government could do to enhance the quality and duration of life in the Great Society. More than a bend in the river, 1966 can be seen as an ideological estuary, wherein the rising stream of liberal aspirations originating with the New Deal was first diluted by a conservative countercurrent, destined over the next half century to reach flood tide. Just as the Social Security Act of 1935 had defined FDR's largely improvised welfare state, so did the Title XIX amendments to Social Security, adopted thirty years later and repeatedly amended as their staggering cost came into focus, represent the high-water mark of federal beneficence. Initially something of an afterthought, Medicaid was piggybacked onto the landmark Medicare legislation that committed Uncle Sam to pay 80 percent of health costs for America's elderly.

For Nelson Rockefeller, an unpopular governor basing his slender reelection hopes on voting groups ordinarily hostile to his party, the timing of the new program was providential. Not that it was perfect—as a collaborative venture of federal, state, and local governments, Medicaid was designed to supplement—not subsidize—existing state efforts to provide needy Americans with access to quality health care. In relative terms, this punished innovators such as New York, which since 1929 had recognized an obligation to assist the medically indigent—defined by Rockefeller as "individuals of modest means, hardworking and self-supporting, who probably did not qualify for help with medical bills in the past—but who certainly are not so well-heeled that doctor bills are no problem." By 1965, New York's Medical Assistance Program was serving nearly one and a half million of the state's citizens, at an annual cost to taxpayers of $450 million.

At the time, New York mandated an income ceiling of $5,200 a year for a participating family of four. Rockefeller proposed a modest hike in the eligibility level to $5,700. Democrats led by Speaker Travia wanted the bar set much higher, at $6,900. The resulting legislative impasse—Republicans had regained control of the state senate in a special November 1965 election—jeopardized federal reimbursement checks, lending a sense of urgency to a process that could have greatly benefited from thoughtful deliberation. With the clock ticking toward his self-imposed April 30 deadline, Rockefeller turned to his chief negotiator, Al Marshall. A bearlike Irishman of irreverent charm and a great white mane that inspired his nickname, "the Silver Fox," Marshall had few peers when it came to assembling a legislative majority. Lawmakers invited to his second-floor office in the Capitol were encouraged to identify their district's most pressing needs. Unless the request was too outlandish, they rarely left empty-handed.

"There were lots of things that could be traded for votes," recalled Rockefeller counsel Michael Whiteman. "You would find a job for somebody, advance a highway project or a building someone wanted." In the event such enticements failed to convince a wavering legislator, Rockefeller could bring pressure to bear through the state GOP and its county leaders, via personal friends, major donors, and business interests. Equally important was his negative influence, which extended deep into opposition ranks. More often than not, the fear was self-imagined, a faint scent of unexercised power, as opponents conjured up what Rockefeller could do—above all, what he *might* spend to eliminate a personal or political irritant. As a rule, he was happy to leave the arm-twisting to Al Marshall. "I could find half a dozen things functioning in your district that meant an awful lot to you, and I could cut them off like that," explained Marshall. "Highway projects. It might have been some lake cleanup. Weeds in Lake Fredonia. There may have been some economic development or grant for a Pepsi-Cola plant. It might have been a local college—a health program that affected their hospitals. Maybe the hospital wouldn't get a CAT scan. The health-planning commission might have just come to the conclusion, 'No, we've got enough CAT scans. We don't need one there. People in Ithaca can go over to Utica and get their CAT scan.'"*

In the last days of April 1966, Marshall became a hovering presence around the Speaker's rostrum, for the simple reason that Tony Travia had stopped taking his calls from the second floor. Postponing a final vote on Medicaid for twenty-four hours, Travia secured a last minute settlement in which Rockefeller conceded far more than he gained. With the eligibility benchmark set at $6,000 a year for a family of four, and the state promising to cover services from eyeglasses to surgery, New York was effectively offering free medical care to one in three of its residents. Politicians in both parties basked in self-congratulation. No one was quicker to claim credit than Rockefeller, who chose the Queens meeting hall of the International Brotherhood of Electrical Workers in which to sign what he termed the most significant piece of social legislation in thirty years.

The festive atmosphere darkened before the ink on the governor's signature

---

* Marshall's gruff exterior and faux cynicism—one of his favorite mock maxims was "There are times one must rise above principle"—masked the tender parent of a developmentally disabled son; a reformed two-fisted drinker who wasn't reluctant to engage in shouting matches with his employer; and a sophisticated schemer, never more dangerous than when he slipped into the guise of good ol' farm boy from Fenton, Michigan. "He could hand you a budget cut or a lemon of an employee," remembers one co-worker, "and never break that friendly smile." *Remembering Al Marshall, 1921–2008* (Albany, NY: Nelson A. Rockefeller Institute of Government, 2009).

was dry, as conservative editorial writers lent their voices to a chorus of outrage from medical associations and local officials worried about the new law's impact on precariously balanced budgets. Cries of socialized medicine were raised, with the *Syracuse Post-Standard* railing against Medicaid as "insane, fiscally irresponsible . . . New York's Gigantic Giveaway." Backtracking legislators fell over themselves drafting amendments to the law they had so recently acclaimed. Rockefeller went on television to plead for a one-year test of the new program, which he justified as Washington's belated support for New York in its pacesetting efforts to treat medical care as a right—indeed, as a moral obligation. "If you don't have good education and good health," he asserted, "then I feel society has let you down." Dismissing predictions that medical offices would be swamped by hypochondriacs demanding free hearing aids and hangnail treatments, Rockefeller estimated additional program costs to the state at $200 million (New York City, he insisted, would likely save money). Against this, Albany was preparing a $217 million invoice for federal reimbursement.

"My God, Nelson, at the rate you're going," Jacob Javits upbraided him, "New York State will use up all the Medicaid money that Congress appropriated for the whole country." Javits didn't exaggerate; on the same day in June 1966 that Rockefeller flew to the capital, hoping to quell a revolt in the state's congressional delegation, HEW administrators revealed that $155 million had been allocated to cover Medicaid payments to the fifty states. Feelings of buyer's remorse permeated the governor's meeting with New York lawmakers. "If I had known what was in this legislation," griped one upstate House member, "I never would have voted for it."

"Great, Congressman," said Rockefeller, his voice dripping contempt. "Go back to your constituents and tell them just that. They will have tremendous confidence in your representation." A hasty salvage operation was mounted in Washington and Albany. At Javits's initiative, the United States Senate adopted a series of amendments designed to trim Medicaid rolls, as did the New York State Legislature. Provisions were written into the law to combat fraud and curtail local financial exposure. These changes didn't prevent more than three million New Yorkers from signing up for the program, with predictable consequences. "God, the first year was $1.3 billion," gasped Al Marshall, more than double his original cost estimate. Adding to the problem: Inflation, a by-product of Vietnam War spending and the seemingly unlimited demand for a limited product (health care), set in like gangrene. By some estimates, graft, double billing, and other abuses devoured a quarter of Medicaid expenditures.*

---

* One unintended consequence was Rockefeller's introduction, early in 1967, of a statewide plan, to be financed through payroll taxes, that would require employers to offer private health insurance for workers and their families. Critics across the ideological spectrum denounced the

By 1968, the inexorable growth of Medicaid spending led to a second, more drastic round of cuts in which the basic threshold for participation was slashed from $6,000 to $5,300. Coverage was eliminated for virtually everyone in the twenty-one to sixty-four age group. And preventive care, a principal justification of the original program, all but disappeared. Still, cost containment remained elusive; population growth, medical advances, and lax oversight saw to that. As late as 1979, the year of Rockefeller's death, New York's shriveled version of Medicaid lapped the field when compared with benefits available elsewhere. A state accounting for less than 9 percent of the national population spent 23 percent of all federal funds earmarked for the iconic program that tested the limits of official compassion.

2

R OCKEFELLER FORMALIZED HIS candidacy for a third term on April 8, 1966. That he chose Harlem as the setting for his announcement reflected a campaign as unconventionally imagined as it was lavishly financed. By the start of April, a preliminary budget of $4.7 million had been approved, allowing for the lease of two floors of the New York Hilton and two hundred paid staff. For $125 a day, advanceman Jack McGrath made sure there were at least two working microphones at every venue and a Coca-Cola box to mount in case the podium was too high. More important, McGrath was charged with remembering names and arranging political suitors to reflect the candidate's pronounced views. In a reception line, women and children were preferable to petitioners of his own sex, regardless of party. Rockefeller's enjoyment of children was as evident as his appreciation of attractive women, whose presence in a crowd rarely escaped comment. This became a game of sorts, a harmless, if juvenile, traveling salesman's distraction at the end of a long day spent knocking on doors. Occasionally, Rockefeller forgot whom he was with. "I know what you're doing," an exasperated Happy Rockefeller told her husband one night after a watchful McGrath poked him in the ribs to signal the proximity of a generously endowed female.*

---

scheme as a bald-faced attempt to shift exploding Medicaid costs onto the private sector. For five years running, Rockefeller tried without success to sell his concept of state-mandated health insurance to an increasingly skeptical electorate.

* Sometimes it was other urges that caused him to trash a meticulously drawn schedule. "We didn't always have a phone in the car in those days," McGrath recalls. "He'd all of a sudden stop the car, get out, and go in somewhere and phone to buy a piece of art. Right in the middle of a day of work. Just amazing." Jack McGrath, AI.

McGrath discovered surprising vulnerabilities lurking behind Rockefeller's iron man persona. "When it got late at night, he always wanted the cameras on the other side—he had that one eye that drooped." Hidden from all but a handful of traveling companions was the backseat cooler with its false bottom concealing a supply of cold beer. ("Somehow I was left with the impression that his father didn't like it. He wasn't to drink beer in public.") Rockefeller the campaigner made few concessions to his advancing age. At the end of a punishing day, gray-green with fatigue, he was not above exploiting his reputation for tardiness to avoid shaking every hand in an overcrowded room. "He's always in a hurry to leave, otherwise you'd never get out of the place," McGrath was to recall. "You got another appointment. He'd say, 'We're late for the next stop.' The next stop was home. But you'd say 'the next stop.' He wouldn't let you lie."

Bob Armao, a young protégé of Rockefeller's labor chieftain Vic Borella, observed firsthand this legalistic approach to the truth. As Armao looked on, Rockefeller picked up a sealed envelope, gave it a quick once-over, then replaced it in the pile of correspondence before him. Armao asked what he was doing. "A good Baptist never lies," Rockefeller explained. "When you see the return address of someone you really don't want to hear from, you don't open the envelope. You just put it up there and say, 'I've looked it over. Thanks for writing.' That was a favorite trick of my grandfather."

Politics is a dynamic profession, and 1966 produced more than its share of innovations. Forty percent of Bill Pfeiffer's campaign budget was earmarked for television advertising, a substantial increase over 1958 and 1962. Rockefeller strategists entrusted their ad account to Jack Tinker & Partners, the edgy firm best known for restoring Alka-Seltzer's fizz (actually "Plop Plop, Fizz Fizz"). Mary Wells Lawrence, at the dawn of her legendary career on Madison Avenue, made the firm's pitch in a meeting room overlooking the Museum of Modern Art. Taking an unorthodox approach to this most egocentric of trades, Tinker/Wells would create Rockefeller ads without Rockefeller.

On this point, Wells was emphatic. For most New Yorkers by 1966, merely to glimpse the overexposed face of their governor was to be reminded of his divorce and remarriage, his taxes, fees, and erratic performance on the national stage. Wells began by complimenting Rockefeller on his previous television successes. He was undoubtedly the most accomplished governor in the nation. Yet most New Yorkers knew more about his divorce than his achievements while in office. His record over the past seven years was Albany's best-kept—perhaps its only—secret. Wells and her colleagues intended to correct that, through an admittedly unconventional campaign, one in which the candidate absented himself from his own ads. When they finished, Rockefeller rose from his seat and applauded. What an operator. Two days later, Wells resigned to start her own agency. But the Tinker game plan, summarized by the memorable slogan "Governor Rockefeller for Governor," was to provide a stunning demonstration of how political advertising, entertaining as it educates, can melt the ice cap of popular resistance. Viewers sat up and took notice of the talking fish who personalized the virtues of the governor's Pure Waters program; the grinning janitor enamored of his new minimum wage law; and the endless highway shot from above to the unmistakable sounds of Hawaiian music, as a sober narrator reminded viewers that Governor Rockefeller had built twelve thousand miles of roads, enough to reach Honolulu and back.*

No spot did more to humanize Nelson than a sixty-second portrait, jarringly shot in negative, of a child at play. At the end, a few quiet words from Rockefeller described his program to enlarge and modernize facilities for the state's mentally retarded. Visually persuasive in a different context was the hand briskly laying out a spoon, hypodermic needle, brass knuckles, knife, and gun—implements used by drug addicts to support their habit. The process was reversed as the voice-over related efforts by Rockefeller to combat addiction. The impact of such advertising was magnified by its ubiquity. Interrupting the usual summer doldrums, an initial wave of commercials stressing Rockefeller's achievements ran at least seven hundred times *before* his renomination was formalized at the GOP convention in Rochester. The volume was turned up considerably as Election Day neared, until the average television viewer could expect each week to see at least nine Rockefeller spots of ten, twenty, or sixty seconds' duration.

The same campaign flooded the Empire State with an estimated twenty-seven million pieces of Rockefeller literature. Brochures customized to the state's various regions reminded voters of all the new health, recreational, cultural, and transport facilities transforming the area's quality of life; recently established colleges and scholarships; funding for secondary schooling; and a community-by-community listing of increased state aid since 1958—and of the tax increases necessary to compensate for its elimination. Heavily outspent Democrats claimed that Rockefeller had options on every billboard in the state and five million blue-and-white shopping bags to distribute for promotional purposes. Opposition estimates of Rockefeller's overall spending ran as high as $20 million. "I don't think it cost that much," says John Deardourff in retrospect, "but it cost more than they claimed ($5.2 million). There were ways to hide expenses. You simply didn't claim that it was part of the campaign. It was something else."

---

* "I got calls from county chairmen all over the state," says Bill Ronan. "'Ronan, you always were an idiot, but now you've really done it. Where's the candidate? Highways to Hawaii—what the hell does that have to do with the campaign?'

"I said, 'What do you remember about the ad?' He said, 'Highways.' I said, 'Who built them?' He said, 'Well, Rockefeller.' I said, 'That's all we want to know.'" William J. Ronan, AI.

Deardourff ought to know: although the candidate at one point was forced to solicit his stepmother for a $500,000 infusion to his coffers, there was more than enough cash on hand to hire field organizers in each of the state's forty-three congressional districts, their sole assignment to promote Rockefeller among young voters of both parties. According to Deardourff, the plan's author, this campaign sideshow alone cost more than $1 million—double what Democratic nominee Frank O'Connor spent on his entire election effort.

3

O'CONNOR WAS A fifty-six-year-old former state senator and Queens district attorney, a clubhouse Democrat whose legislative career had included support, long since withdrawn, of a one-year residency requirement for welfare recipients and a McCarthy-era loyalty oath for schoolteachers. More New Deal than New Frontier, O'Connor liked to make speeches on brotherhood before the Elks and the Knights of Columbus. His strongest epithet was "Cripes." Even those critical of his association with organization types such as Charles Buckley and Stanley Steingut acknowledged O'Connor's personal integrity. Admirers likened him, somewhat extravagantly, to Al Smith, another son of Irish immigrants and a Tammany Hall product who had broadened his sympathies while remaining true to his personal and political faith. "I've had to struggle to become a liberal," O'Connor conceded. "I used to be indifferent to Negroes. Then, in service, I saw how Negroes were treated, and it revolted me. . . . I'm proud I've changed. And I know I have more to learn. I want to learn, and if more change is called for it will come." True to his word, in the spring of 1965, eschewing personal publicity, O'Connor slipped off to Alabama to take part in the Selma-to-Montgomery voting rights march.

In that same year, O'Connor had made a long-shot bid for mayor, quitting the race after his own borough's organization declared for a rival contender. For this act of party loyalty, he was rewarded with the nomination for city council president on Abe Beame's ticket. In November, to the surprise of no one more than his clubhouse sponsors, O'Connor outpolled the lackluster Beame by three hundred thousand votes. It was in return for playing the good soldier then, claimed Franklin D. Roosevelt, Jr., on the eve of a Democratic convention stacked against him, that O'Connor now reaped the support of bosses Steingut, Buckley, and Harlem's Adam Clayton Powell, Jr. If willing to take orders in the mayor's race, said Roosevelt, what made anyone think O'Connor capable of withstanding machine pressure once in Albany? It was a question that had already occurred to Alex Rose. Since its formation in 1944, no Democrat had been elected governor (or president, save LBJ) without the support of the state's Liberal Party, whose aging founders, Rose and David Dubinsky, preferred honorable defeat to victory with Frank O'Connor. Rose entertained suspicions, confirmed in later years, that the Queens Democratic organization was susceptible to Mob influence, a baleful subject in the garment district, where idealistic young union organizers like Alex Rose had risked life and limb to keep out the racketeers.

O'Connor wasn't alone in believing Roosevelt's third party candidacy the result of a deal between Rockefeller and Rose. Others attributed it to FDR's ego, pure and simple. That Roosevelt harbored a personal animus toward O'Connor and his organization sponsors was as plain as the desire of Conservative nominee Paul Adams, a Rochester academic, to run Rockefeller out of the GOP. Whatever drove him to make the race, Roosevelt succeeded in dividing the opposition to Rockefeller, while lending credence to familiar Republican charges of machine rule. Post-convention polls showed O'Connor leading Rockefeller by at least half a million votes, with Roosevelt polling eight hundred thousand or more. In a contest of negatives, the incumbent's taxes generated far more resentment than another Irish DA with clubhouse connections.

Over the Labor Day weekend, Rockefeller plunged into boardwalk throngs at the Atlantic-facing beaches of Queens and Brooklyn. Acknowledging his 1962 pledge to hold the line on tax increases as "the big blooper I made in politics," Rockefeller said he had learned enough since to avoid a repetition. At the end of remarks before several thousand Bronx sun worshippers, Nelson announced, "Now let's all go for a swim." Borrowing a stranger's trunks, he ducked into a nearby bathhouse, from which he emerged to wave vigorously at poolside throngs. "He looks better than some of the lifeguards," squealed one teenage girl. His political prospects looked at least marginally better, too, as Rockefeller began to frame the tax issue to his advantage. His standard stump speech included a self-mocking encounter with a fervent education advocate frustrated in her attempts to bolster classroom instruction through higher taxes. "You raise taxes so well," she told Rockefeller, "why don't you just do it and give us the money?" In truth, as he never failed to remind audiences, 61 percent of the state's budget was already being returned to local government. Local tax savings, said Rockefeller, was "the untold story of this administration." Do the math, he urged: subtract current state aid, and a $200 school tax bill in Yonkers would cost $336, and be higher still in Islip, on Long Island.

O'Connor offered little coherent alternative. Blaming his opponent for "taxing too much and doing too little," the Democratic candidate spoke of tax cuts, but his failure to provide specifics undercut a credibility already stretched by claims that Rockefeller was a do-nothing governor where housing and higher education were concerned. His vagueness allowed Rockefeller to present himself as the principled defender of vital government services. "Ask them which highways they are going to curtail," he challenged a group of newspaper editors that September. "Ask them which mental institutions are going to operate shorthanded. Ask them which schools they will shortchange. Ask them whose scholarships get cut."

The race was an organizational mismatch. "It was like running against a ghost," asserts Jack McGrath. As Rockefeller traversed the state in his F-27 turboprop or silver-and-red campaign bus, O'Connor stumbled through upstate appearances marked by small crowds and logistical snafus. Things were scarcely better in New York City, where O'Connor conducted an awkward courtship of voters whose language he didn't speak. At the Puerto Rican Day parade, Rockefeller couldn't deny himself the pleasure of addressing milling spectators in Spanish. He knew they were Democraticos, said Nelson. Then he introduced a visibly uncomfortable Judge O'Connor as their candidate in November.

"¡Viva O'Connor!" shouted Nelson.

"¡Viva O'Connor!" answered the crowd.*

Rockefeller set a blistering campaign pace, scaling construction ladders and cherry pickers, riding elephants, donkeys, sanitation trucks, and the IRT. A reporter visiting campaign headquarters five weeks before Election Day was shown neatly stacked transcripts of Rockefeller statements, one for each day remaining in the race. These were designed to make policy as well as headlines, enabling the winner to claim not just a victory, but a mandate. At the height of the campaign, Rockefeller appointed a study commission, chaired by McGeorge Bundy, to develop new state assistance programs for private colleges and universities. He entered into negotiations with New York City to buy the historic Croton Aqueduct for conversion into a thirty-two-mile trailway for hikers, bikers, and equestrians. Stealing a march on the White House, Nelson unveiled a state-funded pollution study of Erie County, three days before President Johnson was to visit Buffalo for a firsthand look at a dying Lake Erie. (He let his silence speak for itself when LBJ came to Manhattan in the first week of October but couldn't find time to meet with his party's candidate for governor.)

The flurry of promises escalated in the campaign's closing weeks. Rockefeller vowed to bring the 1976 Olympic Games to New York City and to make New York State preeminent in oceanography. For small business there was an antipaperwork initiative. Residents of the Mid-Hudson Valley got a 50 percent reduction in tolls on the Newburgh–Beacon Bridge. Education advocates were

---

* Nor was this an isolated incident. "I can remember going with Frank down Second Avenue in East Harlem in a big truck," says Herman Badillo, then the first borough president of Puerto Rican descent. "We were waving to the crowds, and he says, 'Herman, I didn't realize the slums were so bad. If I get elected, I'm going to really do something about this.'" Herman Badillo, AI.

offered the use of nineteen state armories and naval facilities to alleviate over-crowding in New York City kindergartens and a state Teacher Reserve of former instructors lured back into the classroom. Rockefeller proposed a network of hostels to house mentally retarded youngsters requiring only moderate supervision and a new office in the state Department of Health dedicated to the fight against birth defects. State resources were pledged to combat arthritis, alcoholism, and heart disease. Harlem was promised a new, $20 million state office building. Relaxing his earlier opposition, Rockefeller said that he would sign "reasonable" legislation to establish a state lottery. In the Hudson Valley, he dropped broad hints that Con Ed might, with equal dexterity, be willing to re-consider its controversial Storm King generator project.

4

B Y COLUMBUS DAY, the odds had shifted perceptibly in favor of the incumbent. A mid-October Oliver Quayle poll for NBC showed Rockefeller ahead of O'Connor by thirteen points. Yet the race remained volatile. On October 21, the *New York Daily News* straw poll, fabled for its accuracy, showed O'Connor edging out front, sending a fresh jolt of anxiety through Republican ranks. Had the Rockefeller onslaught peaked? Might the saturation advertising be generating voter fatigue or, worse, sympathy for the underfunded O'Connor? Warning against panic, George Hinman called the poll a great motivator, contrasting it with an eleventh-hour Lou Harris survey during the 1964 California primary contest that had encouraged a fatal complacency. "You have been the greatest inspiration to all of us," Hinman assured Rockefeller at this critical moment. "You've brought it up from the depths of hopelessness to a dead heat. It's your finest hour." Swallowing his pride, Nelson let it be known through back channels that he would welcome a public endorsement from Richard Nixon, though he balked at Nixon's demand for Rockefeller money with which to finance a Nixon telecast in Iowa. "Iowa!" Rockefeller grunted. In the end, the former vice president lowered his price and extended his support.

Attention swiveled to the so-called fringe candidates for governor. In a weird reversal of form, FDR, Jr., was polling better upstate than in the city, while Conservative nominee Paul Adams did the opposite. Only one thing could explain the inversion. That summer, as Rockefeller trolled for votes at Coney Island and other pleasure centers, Mayor Lindsay was testing his conciliatory skills in East New York, where gangs of white, black, and Puerto Rican youths were rehearsing for a full-scale race war. Hoping to avert riots like those that had already racked Los Angeles, Chicago, and Cleveland, the patrician mayor spent several nights walking tense streets, hoping through his presence to defuse racial and ethnic antagonisms. Although he was lifted on the shoulders of black residents, Lindsay got a very different reception in an adjoining Italian neighborhood, where one onlooker shouted, "Go back to Africa, Lindsay, and take your niggers with you." Lindsay's gutsy intervention contained the violence, but not the ugly emotions behind it.

Against this menacing backdrop, New Yorkers divided over the mayor's Civilian Complaint Review Board, an initiative spurred by persistent complaints of police insensitivity, or worse, in black and other minority neighborhoods. While the city's liberal establishment lined up in support of the board, the Conservative Party and the Patrolmen's Benevolent Association forced a referendum on the CCRB to coincide with the November 1966 general election. The ensuing contest, a milestone in the history of American political realignment, quickly came to overshadow the gubernatorial race. Though Rockefeller had at one point expressed "complete agreement" with Lindsay's efforts to foster greater trust between the police and those under their protection, he repudiated an explicit claim of support made on his behalf by Jacob Javits.

Confronted by reporters, he offered a profile in evasion. "Luckily," as Rockefeller described his response, "my immediate reaction was, first, that I hadn't discussed the issue with him; secondly I was running for governor, not for mayor; and third, I would not consider intervening in the internal affairs of a strictly local issue in the city. . . . This kept me out of the issue whereas Frank got in the middle of it." If this sounded more than a bit self-serving, especially given Rockefeller's past (and, still more, future) selectivity on issues of home rule, it was also politically shrewd. O'Connor, desperate to stanch the flow of liberal (with a small as well as a big L) voters to Roosevelt or Rockefeller, embraced the review board wholeheartedly. Nor was this the only hot-button issue the challenger handed Rockefeller in the campaign's closing days. His advocacy of liberalized drug laws led O'Connor to dismiss the governor's proposed Narcotic Addiction and Control Commission as "an election year stunt" to be abolished on his first day in Albany. Acknowledging that his own campaign had "crucified" the hapless O'Connor, Rockefeller reflected, "Politics is a rough business, but a lot of fun if you enjoy it."

Suddenly it felt as if the candidates had lost their scripts and were reading from those of their rivals. As O'Connor took to the streets of Manhattan with Bobby Kennedy, Rockefeller executed his own U-turn. Whatever his earlier motivations regarding the Roosevelt insurgency, Nelson now decided it was robbing him of upstate Republicans (dubious) and urban Jews (much more plausible). He began running TV spots equating a vote for Roosevelt with a vote for O'Connor. Gone was the soft sell of summer; in place of animated fish and grateful janitors was the familiar rasp of Nelson Rockefeller declaring ominously, "If you want to keep crime rates high, O'Connor is your man." Seizing on his rival's opposition to compulsory treatment of drug addicts, Rockefeller told reporters that O'Connor's election would give addicts license to roam urban streets, "to mug, to purse-snatch, to steal, and even to murder." O'Connor's casual observation to a Washington reporter that subways should be free led the Rockefeller campaign to distribute a million copies of the statement to upstate voters. In the city, meanwhile, more than a few construction sites featured signs that read, "Protect Your Job—Vote Rockefeller."*

As O'Connor clung to his narrow advantage in the *Daily News* poll, *The New York Times* forecast a cliff-hanger, possibly as close as Averell Harriman's eleven-thousand-vote squeaker in 1954. "Do you *really* think I'm going to win, Bill?" a jittery Nelson asked repeatedly of Ronan as the two men hopscotched around the state on Monday, November 7. He was still in doubt twenty-four hours later, awaiting returns in a ninth-floor suite of the New York Hilton. Around ten o'clock, with his statewide lead passing 120,000, Rockefeller took a call from the Arkansas capital of Little Rock, where his brother Winthrop had just been elected the state's first Republican governor since Reconstruction. "Win," said Nelson, "this is just the most exciting damn thing I've ever heard." In one corner of the room, Happy Rockefeller in a blue maternity dress nursed a glass of soda water. Someone congratulated her on the victory in the making. "One thing it does," added the well-wisher. "It finally takes all this personal stuff about you and shoves it out of the way for good." Happy's hand shot out. "You're a good guy," she told her admirer.

It was an evening full of surprises, none bigger than the third-place showing of the Conservative Party, as Paul Adams rode his opposition to the Civilian Complaint Review Board past young FDR and the Liberals for third place and the coveted Row C on the ballot. Key to Rockefeller's win were Jewish voters, who, overwhelmingly Democratic but put off by the prospect of an O'Connor win, abandoned Roosevelt to support Rockefeller. Their switch enabled the incumbent, against all odds, to carry Manhattan. He also won Staten Island and O'Connor's own borough of Queens, where the Civilian Complaint Review Board issue cut deep. As the board went down to a crushing defeat, Rockefeller's improbable coalition of silk-stocking Republicans, Jewish liberals, minorities, *and* blue-collar voters fearful of drug-related crime held O'Connor's citywide margin below seventy thousand votes.

---

* Although the state AFL-CIO remained officially neutral, that didn't prevent unions representing more than a third of the state's organized workforce from rallying behind the Rockefeller-Wilson ticket.

Midnight in the Hilton suite. The network computers had long since called the race. O'Connor's telegram of concession had been received and read, with Nelson himself serving up the celebratory champagne. Now, as he and Happy prepared to claim their prize in the ballroom below, a slightly tipsy Rockefeller partisan made a bold prediction. If the governor's final statewide margin topped four hundred thousand, he exclaimed, they had themselves a presidential candidate.

"Oh my God," said GOP chairman Carl Spad. "Not that again."*

5

A S A TEXTBOOK example of how personal grit, even more than money, message, organization, issues, and luck, can reverse the longest of political odds, Rockefeller's 1966 bid for reelection ranks with Harry Truman's historic 1948 upset. It had even greater implications for future campaigns. The victor's media-driven electioneering, often cited as a model of sophisticated persuasion, foreshadowed a politics in which ideas yielded to images and public education was reduced to emotional shorthand. What seemed at the time a triumph of substance over salesmanship in fact blurred the line between the two. Of more immediate significance was the profound impact on Rockefeller's approach to governing. Disproving the oddsmakers and political professionals, the doubters on his staff and in his family—none of this bred humility. He hadn't merely survived divorce and remarriage; he had been vindicated for his defiance of convention, personal as well as political.

Indulging his maverick streak, Rockefeller became more receptive than ever to outside gurus like Franz Winkler, a psychologist and author of such proto–New Age works as *Man: The Bridge Between Two Worlds*. First introduced to Nelson in the late fifties by Mrs. Russell Davenport, Winkler rapidly established himself as mystic on call and champion of the intuitive. (To the puzzlement of many in the audience, Winkler's antivivisectionist passion for "the little animals" found its way into Rockefeller's annual State of the State message.) Though Nelson said he had never known him to be wrong, Dr. Winkler— "Vinkler," in his Ruritanian accent—was not everybody's cup of tea. His gushing tributes to youth in revolt rarely survived Bill Ronan's blue pencil. Worse was his Age of Aquarius appeals for government to intervene on the side of love and

---

* In the end, the margin was 392,000 votes, the smallest of Rockefeller's four campaigns, yet more than any of the last minute polls, his own included, had forecast.

beauty. As soon as these sentiments crept into Rockefeller's speech texts, Ronan edited them out.

One day, a plainly annoyed Rockefeller demanded to know what Ronan found so offensive.

"I just don't think you should be lecturing the people of New York about love," said Ronan.*

"The governor liked unconventional approaches," says a junior member of the Albany team. The unending quest for intellectual silver bullets was bound to take him outside bureaucratic ranks. "'These are the loyal troops,'" another staffer imagines Nelson concluding of the familiar faces on his payroll. "'I just want an outside view . . . is there another stroke of color here, another idea, something I've missed, that all of us have missed?' This is part of learning by listening, a willing- ness to accept crazy ideas and take them in and stir them up and think about them." It was all very Rooseveltian, rewarding originality even as it complicated life for the professional administrators around him. "Mondays were always an adventure," conceded Al Marshall, recalling how he would brace himself for whatever his boss may have conjured over a Pocantico weekend. Like Rockefel- ler's abrupt declaration of intent to buy the retiring *Queen Mary.* "We're going to put it in a slip and we're going to make it a drug rehabilitation center."

"You can't have junkies running around the *Queen Mary,*" Marshall sput- tered. Having registered his protest for the record, the secretary to the governor telephoned the Office of General Services. "For God's sake, have we ever bought an international steamship before in the state of New York?" The ma- chinery of state government cranked into gear. Bureaucrats scrambled to iden- tify a London admiral with whom the subject might be raised. In due course, Marshall's phone again lit up. ("When that red button flashed, your secretary couldn't answer it," explains another member of the administration. "That's the governor wanting to talk to you and only you, and he didn't want to talk to the secretary.") This time, however, Rockefeller was as angry as Marshall had ever heard him. Employing words such as "insubordinate," "disloyal," and "in- competent," Marshall's boss said he couldn't understand why it took so long to buy a steamship. The true source of his fury was to be found in a front-page story in that day's *Times.* Where the *Queen Mary* was concerned, it appeared,

---

* None of this meant that Rockefeller had abandoned his faith in groupthink. Prior to a stag Legislative Correspondents Association dinner, he consulted at least twenty-one individuals on the propriety of quoting a news item from the unwitting *Lockport Journal and Sun.* Finally, Mal- colm Wilson cast the tiebreaking vote in favor of the risqué passage: "Governor and Mrs. Rocke- feller came to Lockport accompanied by District Attorney and Mrs. John A. Ball of Buffalo. Following the cocktail party in the afternoon, the Governor was taken back to Buffalo by the Balls." Almost fifty years later, it's still cited as the funniest thing Rockefeller ever said in Albany.

great minds thought alike. John Lindsay, the paper reported with a straight face, had decided to buy the majestic liner and convert it into a floating high school to help alleviate overcrowding in the city's classrooms.

Marshall should not have been surprised, either by Lindsay's grandstanding or by Rockefeller's sulfurous response. The difference between the two adversaries was that Rockefeller had been *serious*, even if no one else took his idea seriously. With him, public policy was a consuming interest. Rockefeller had scarcely come down from his election night high in November 1966 when he gathered his closest advisers in a room of his brother's Dorado Beach resort in Puerto Rico. "He had his yellow pad," recalls one who was there. "He was great with yellow pads. And he says, 'This is what we're going to do in the next four years.' He wanted to pass tough antidrug legislation. 'We're going to set the state university really rolling this time. I've got a couple of bond issues.' He laid out his whole program. And, by God, most of that stuff saw the light of day."

6

IN A POSTELECTION note to Rockefeller, George Hinman also looked to the future. "You now have a unique position of national leadership that justifies all the travail and all the disappointments and all the long, unbelievably courageous, struggle," Hinman wrote, tiptoeing around the presidency like a teenager creeping upstairs hours after curfew. More than a year had passed since Rockefeller publicly renounced any lingering White House ambitions. More recently, he had bought off Jacob Javits by promoting him as a logical running mate for Michigan's George Romney, whose landslide reelection established him as an early front-runner for 1968. Romney's triumph was part of a GOP resurgence that produced an additional forty-seven House seats, three senators, and eight governors. In California's Ronald Reagan, a million-vote winner over Governor Pat Brown, the Republican Right didn't know—yet—what a potent successor it had to Barry Goldwater. Meanwhile, an impressive array of pragmatic newcomers—Charles Percy, Howard Baker, Jr., Edward Brooke, and Mark Hatfield in the Senate, plus governors such as Pennsylvania's Raymond Shafer, Win Rockefeller, Dave Cargo in New Mexico, and Spiro Agnew, a suburban county executive who had defeated a crudely racist Democratic challenger to seize the Maryland State House—sparked hope among GOP moderates that 1964 was indeed an aberration.

Within days of their reelection, Rockefeller extended his Puerto Rico visit to strategize with Romney, the former auto executive and self-professed citizen politician whose strong civil rights record put him at odds with the elders of his own Mormon Church. The budding Romney organization inherited Rockefeller's delegate files and issues research, along with the speechwriting services of Hugh Morrow and the foreign policy expertise of Henry Kissinger. To many in the Lansing crowd, Kissinger was a Trojan horse, sent from the East to keep Romney on the straight-and-narrow road of support for LBJ's Vietnam policies. The increasingly unpopular war tugged at Romney's conscience. In anticipation of a major address on Vietnam in April 1967, he delegated Bill Seidman, a Grand Rapids businessman, to run its contents by Rockefeller at Pocantico Hills. Seeking an alternative to the status quo, Romney and his advisers had devised a "peace with amnesty" formula combining support for American troops with growing doubts about the U.S.-backed government in Saigon. "One of the things it said was that Vietnam had to change its economic and social policies. Two percent of the people own 90 percent of the land," Seidman remembers. "Rockefeller said, 'I don't want that in there . . . I'm not sure we don't own 80 percent of the land.'" Reviewing the text in Kykuit's music room with Henry Kissinger, Rockefeller changed it "from a down-the-middle-of-the-road to a bomb-'em-into-the-stone-age speech." In the event, Romney accepted perhaps half the suggested changes, telling Seidman, "I'm the candidate, he isn't."*

An honorable man whose uncertainties over Vietnam were shared by millions of patriotic Americans, Romney effectively destroyed his fading prospects by telling a Detroit radio host at the end of August, "Well, you know, when I came back from Vietnam, I just had the greatest brainwashing that anybody can get. . . ." The ensuing firestorm of criticism rekindled doubts as to whether Romney was ready for prime time. "The day that Romney made his brainwashed remark, Kissinger packed up and left and we never saw him again," says Bill Seidman. "He went out of there like a shot." Barely a week later, Romney's hometown newspaper, the *Detroit News*, demanded that he quit the race before he had formally entered it, so that Nelson Rockefeller could take his place. Oregon's Tom McCall spoke for a majority of GOP governors in withholding any formal endorsement of their Michigan colleague; by keeping the situation fluid, McCall argued, "we can shake the tree and Rockefeller will fall out." Many of the same party officials who had been most strident in their opposition to Nelson in 1960 and 1964 now discovered hidden virtues in the noncandidate whose experience was matched by his electability. A Gallup poll that fall showed a so-called dream ticket of Rockefeller-Reagan defeating Johnson-Humphrey 57 to 43 percent.

---

* At one point, young Nelson Rockefeller, Jr., insistent on playing with his father, dragged him from the room. Kissinger leaned closer to Seidman and remarked, sotto voce, "That's the reason he'll never be president." William Seidman, AI.

"He is a presence, not a Governor," one Rockefeller informant said of Reagan in May 1967. At an early meeting of state executives, Reagan didn't impress his vastly experienced New York counterpart by asking someone to define for him an ad valorem tax. ("Oh Christ, Ronnie. . . .") On the other hand, Nelson readily acknowledged Reagan's oratorical talents, even if his own deficiencies in this area lent a note of condescension to his praise. It was a mistake, said Rockefeller, to write off Reagan as a Goldwater clone. "When he gets engaged with the realities of being a governor, you'll find he is no extremist." Affirmation of this prediction came in the largest-ever tax increase—$933 million—to balance the biggest state budget on record. For his part, Reagan was careful to alert Rockefeller whenever he expected to be in New York. Seeking common ground, Nelson shared with the Californian a number of steps his administration was considering to slow the growth of Medicaid spending. Reagan would return the favor, with interest, on welfare reform.*

Little of this preliminary courtship escaped an observant press corps. As a result, by the time forty-two of the nation's governors set sail for the Virgin Islands aboard the SS *Independence* in October 1967, a flailing Romney pleaded with Rockefeller to publicly, explicitly, deny any interest in the White House. Nelson went along, though his disavowal sounded more wistful than Shermanesque. "One of the advantages of getting older," he told a reporter that same month, "is the loss of fear. I'm not even afraid of not getting what I want." Playing down the chances of a draft—"If you had stood in front of that convention in 1964, you wouldn't think you were going to be nominated this time either"—Rockefeller forcefully requested New Hampshire supporters to cease their efforts on his behalf. He sent Les Slote to Annapolis to dissuade Maryland's Governor Agnew from promoting a Rockefeller candidacy against his wishes. Agnew, conceding that he was "sort of out on the end of the ice floe," refused to back off.†

---

* Stu Spencer attended an early strategy session at which Clif White and other movement conservatives discussed what it would take to nominate Reagan in 1968. Reagan himself seemed only half-sold on the idea. "The office seeks the man," he claimed to Spencer. "That's bullshit," responded the political consultant. "If you want to be President of the United States, you've got . . . to fight for it." Stuart Spencer, AI.

† Contrary to the moderate image that had helped get him elected, Agnew nourished conservative views long before the April 1968 assassination of Dr. Martin Luther King, Jr., engendered violence, physical and verbal, to which the governor's subsequent shift to the right has been attributed. At Agnew's request, Rockefeller called Ford Foundation president McGeorge Bundy, who denied a charge first made in *Barron's* magazine that his foundation was aiding radical elements on the left. Agnew, unpersuaded, warned Rockefeller that Republicans must undertake their own review of these "subtle linkings, lest we inadvertently find ourselves in support of the near-anarchists." Spiro T. Agnew–NAR, November 24, 1967; NAR–Agnew, December 20, 1967, RAC.

Increasingly, Rockefeller partisans focused their hopes on Oregon, whose inclusive rules and place on the political calendar made it the one primary their favorite *might* contest were Romney to fall by the wayside in New Hampshire or three weeks later in Wisconsin. Well aware of this, Romney proposed a joint campaign swing through the state. George Hinman rejected the idea as a stunt sure to backfire by diverting attention from the announced candidate to the undeclared alternative. Hinman was a busy man during the latter part of 1967. At a Palm Beach golf weekend with members of Reagan's kitchen cabinet, Hinman was pressed to identify the strongest Republican ticket against Lyndon Johnson. Rockefeller-Reagan, he responded, adding that he saw no practical means of bringing about such a combination. New Hampshire's GOP state chairman, unimpressed by Romney and hostile toward Nixon, sought an appointment with Rockefeller. Hinman put him off. "It's a time to keep our feet on the ground," he reminded Nelson. While the odds against a genuine draft were twenty to one, Rockefeller could reasonably hope to influence the convention's outcome "if we can just maintain our present position of absolute, complete non-interest and non-involvement."

An October leak by Emmet Hughes that Rockefeller might be rethinking his staunch support of Johnson's Vietnam policies infuriated Hinman, emptying a long-dammed reservoir of bitterness toward the man he blamed for alienating Eisenhower and the Republican base. "His judgment is the last to be trusted either as to one's personal political interest or the security of the United States," Hinman said of Hughes. He went on to describe for Rockefeller a background press briefing in Washington at which John Lindsay, after praising Nelson for taking a first step toward opposing the war, endorsed Chuck Percy for president. To Rockefeller supporters, the leaked exchange confirmed Lindsay's desire for a place on his party's 1968 ticket. Being vice chairman of the Kerner Commission, created by the Johnson White House to probe causes of the spiraling urban crisis, afforded the mayor a national platform from which to see and be seen. This only fueled fresh suspicions as his "nonpolitical" travels took him deep into the Republican heartland.

City hall wasn't blind to the problem. Deputy Mayor Robert Sweet, a welcome replacement for the Machiavellian Bob Price, reached out to Al Marshall in an attempt to defuse tensions between their superiors. These neared the breaking point in October 1967, following a contentious meeting at Rockefeller's Fifth Avenue apartment (and preceding a three-day Lindsay swing through Southern California). A truce was arranged, but trust remained elusive. "Lindsay was absolutely intractable," said his 1969 running mate, Fioravante Perrotta. "Nothing Rockefeller could do, other than slitting his wrists, or leaving center stage, would please Lindsay. . . . I think Lindsay always thought of Rockefeller as being an immovable object placed directly in his path." Kennedy Democrat

Bill vanden Heuvel saw things differently. "Nelson knew how to co-opt everybody," he says. "And he didn't co-opt Lindsay." The mayor rejected Rockefeller's offer to fund the city university system, seeing it as a raid, not a rescue. He reminded Rockefeller regularly that his job as mayor dwarfed that of any governor "in power, complexity, and responsibility."

Rockefeller responded by questioning Lindsay's competence. "If New York City was dumb enough to become a state," he confided to future Clinton cabinet officer Donna Shalala, "it would go bankrupt." More cutting still was the observation of state education commissioner James Allen, repeated by Rockefeller, that if the charismatic Lindsay "wasn't so tall or good-looking, he would be pushing a broom someplace." Sometimes he mispronounced the mayor's name (Lindsley), much as he occasionally confused his brother Winthrop's Arkansas with Alabama. Mostly he patronized him. "I wish Lindsay would become an actor," Rockefeller told GOP state chairman Dick Rosenbaum, "and leave the governance to me." Within months of Lindsay's election, Rockefeller rushed a public announcement of Battery Park City, a vast residential and commercial development to be constructed on Hudson River landfill dredged from the nearby World Trade Center construction site (told that his authority to create such a new neighborhood within the city was nil, Rockefeller hit on the idea of building over the water). So eager was Nelson to beat city hall to the punch that he didn't bother to inform his brother David, president of the Downtown-Lower Manhattan Association, whose Chase Manhattan Plaza, completed five years earlier, had been instrumental in sparking redevelopment of the area south of Canal Street.*

David first learned of his sibling's latest building project by reading about it in *The New York Times*. Fraternal relations went in the deep freeze. But Nelson had his headlines and Lindsay his comeuppance (the project was to be delayed for more than twenty years, as Rockefeller and Lindsay feuded over the amount of low-income housing to include and the city went into a steep economic decline in the 1970s). A few months later, Lindsay returned the favor by giving a thumbs-down to Nelson's vision of a grand Central Park allée stretching from Fifth Avenue to Lincoln Center. Neither the YMCA nor the equally venerable

---

* Contrary to what some have claimed, Nelson had nothing to do with the decision to build the nearby Twin Towers as the world's tallest structures, though his consolidation of state agencies in the South Tower proved essential to the project's economic success. On being told by architect Minoru Yamasaki that the towers contained 110 stories, Rockefeller asked if that meant two buildings of 55 stories each. "Oh no," said Yamasaki, "110 stories apiece."

"My god," Nelson observed to aide Ed Kresky, "these towers will make David's building look like an outhouse!" Jameson W. Doig, *Empire on the Hudson: Entrepreneurial Vision and Political Power at the Port of New York Authority* (New York: Columbia University Press, 2001), 546, fn 27.

New York Society for Ethical Culture would surrender their properties so that Nelson Rockefeller could enjoy an unobstructed west view from his living room, and Lindsay had no intention of seizing them through eminent domain. Their aesthetic differences opened an entirely new field of contention for the two men. One evening, press secretary Harry O'Donnell received a call from the mayor, who said he had been invited to the Rockefeller apartment to talk politics. Several hours passed. Close to midnight, O'Donnell's phone again rang. "How did it go?" O'Donnell asked Lindsay. "Oh, we never got into politics," said the mayor. "We were discussing architecture and got in an argument."

7

L INDSAY WAS NEVER far from Rockefeller's thoughts in 1967. That the year began on a surprisingly benign note was due to O'Donnell, the savvy pressman who had transferred from the Rockefeller staff to city hall once Nelson secured his third term. Since the days of Fiorello La Guardia, New York mayors had favored governors with "the Christmas letter," a yuletide accounting of the city's financial needs submitted in advance of Albany's annual budget ritual. The tone of the document—at once pleading, truculent, and accusatory—was as grimly predictable as its appeal for ever larger sums with which to patch holes caused by exploding welfare and other costs linked to the urban poor. The original version of the 1967 letter was no exception, a sterile restatement of fiscal injustices heaped upon the city by an uncaring state. With Lindsay's approval, O'Donnell rewrote it to applaud Rockefeller's "courage and candor" in correcting many of these wrongs, while blaming past inequities for current shortfalls.

"So, four or five days later we're up to Albany for the Inauguration," O'Donnell remembered, "and there was a receiving line there in the Red Room and John went through and Nelson shook hands with him vigorously and told him it was a 'terrific letter' and they slobbered all over each other." When O'Donnell's turn came, a conspiratorial Rockefeller leaned in close and said, "I think I detected your fine Italian hand in that." Whatever its provenance, the rare note of deference struck by Lindsay produced a $126 million windfall for the city in a year of significant belt-tightening (legislators were especially hostile to the governor's Narcotic Addiction and Control Commission, which treated a mere thousand patients during its first four months of operation). The rest of Rockefeller's agenda for 1967, from the state constitutional convention whose delegates would have Albany assume all local welfare costs, to a rat extermination campaign directed at the bleakest ghetto neighborhoods, might have been crafted with Lindsay's New York in mind.*

Certainly this was true of the year's two biggest initiatives. The 1966 transit strike had renewed public demands for reform of the Condon-Wadlin Act governing state workers. Enacted in 1947, this statute had formalized the common-law prohibition against work stoppages by teachers, firefighters, transit workers, and other civil servants. Under its punitive terms, anyone engaged in an illegal strike could expect automatic dismissal. So the law read; harsh experience had demonstrated these draconian penalties to be unenforceable. Memories of the transit strike were still vivid when Rockefeller named a panel of five experts, with a combined 184 years of labor relations experience, to review the measure so widely flouted. Chairing the inquiry was Professor George Taylor of the University of Pennsylvania, himself an arbitrator and industrial relations adviser to five U.S. presidents. As impressive as the group's credentials was its work ethic: members took less than three months to present their findings.

Though received too late in the legislative calendar for any action to be taken in 1966, Rockefeller assured the committee it had not labored in vain. Enactment of the Taylor Law—so christened because no politician would put his name on it—became a top gubernatorial priority the following year. The legislation retained the ban on strikes by public employees, prompting some unions to dub it "the Slave Labor Act." But that was all of Condon-Wadlin that survived. Rather than discipline individual workers, the Taylor Law would impose heavy fines on unions engaged in illegal work stoppages. What made it truly revolutionary, however, was the law's full-throated endorsement of collective bargaining for civil servants. Henceforth the state was required to negotiate in good faith, with unresolved disputes entrusted to the Public Employment Relations Board. If mediation failed, the next step was appointment of a fact finder to make nonbinding recommendations. As a last resort, the law stipulated a public hearing and binding settlement by the appropriate legislative body. A separate, parallel Office of Collective Bargaining was established by New York City in September 1967.

Enacted with bipartisan support, the Taylor Law quickly became a model for other states to emulate. Once more New York was a trailblazer, though

---

* Rockefeller's wish list for the first year of his third term was heavily weighted toward fulfilling his 1966 campaign promises. Among the initiatives *not* incubated as electoral incentives, Rockefeller proposed a review of the state's stringent abortion laws; established the State Historic Trust to preserve such endangered treasures as Olana, the castlelike home of Hudson Valley artist Frederic Church; unveiled a massive Outdoor Recreation Plan for the state; and signed legislation authorizing a direct primary to choose candidates for statewide office. Though he gave a tepid endorsement to the new constitution submitted to the voters in November 1967, he shed no tears over its thumping rejection at the polls.

Rockefeller readily conceded his preference for innovation over management. "I like to get a thing started," he explained to Al Marshall. "Then I'm not interested in following details. I get people to run it for me. [I'm] not going to chase a decimal point through a bowl of fly shit." The Taylor Law ushered in a long period of relative labor peace in New York, though latter-day critics have blamed it for driving up public sector compensation *and* fueling the rapid growth of public employee unions.

Greater still was the impact of Rockefeller's Metropolitan Transportation Authority. In crucial respects, the MTA *was* his governorship in microcosm. It will be recalled that as a newcomer to Albany, Rockefeller had recoiled from any state takeover of failing commuter railroads. Faithful to his Republican roots, his answer to the problem was corporate tax relief, an end to labor featherbedding, and the lease of new railcars from the Port of New York Authority. When this proved insufficient to overcome decades of neglect, the Tri-State Transportation Committee was formed in 1961 to link New York, New Jersey, and Connecticut in the first regional planning effort of its kind.

Over the next few years, a series of transportation dominoes toppled. The 1962 bankruptcy of the Hudson and Manhattan Railroad set in motion a complex sequence of events that was to alter both the Manhattan skyline and commuter travel beneath the briny Hudson. Even as the Port Authority Trans-Hudson (PATH) commuter line emerged from the wreckage of the old Hudson and Manhattan, the financially depleted Pennsylvania Railroad was unloading its Long Island subsidiary on the state of New York, which in 1965 established the Metropolitan Commuter Transportation Authority (MCTA), forerunner of the MTA, to restore the battered line to health. The Long Island Rail Road offered a textbook example of private sector failure justifying state intervention. Virtually bankrupt, the creaking, 334-mile line carried an estimated 260,000 passengers a day. To move such numbers by automobile would require twenty-six lanes of limited-access highways, costing $2 billion to construct. Faced with this unpalatable choice, Rockefeller agreed to purchase the ailing line from its corporate parent for $65 million. This was but a down payment on new stations, rolling stock, and electrified track stretching all the way to Montauk on the island's eastern tip. The line's overhaul was abruptly accelerated when, early in 1966, Rockefeller made an election year vow, impetuous even by his standards, that within sixty days the LIRR would be reborn as the best commuter railroad in the nation.

Nineteen sixty-five also saw the impoverished New Haven Railroad threaten suspension of commuter services. Refusing to be pushed into another LIRR-style bailout, Rockefeller and Connecticut governor John Dempsey were able to cadge enough federal funding to stave off immediate collapse. But this was a stopgap solution at best. In rapid order followed the 1966 transit strike that dramatized the vulnerability of the city's economic lifeline, redoubling the need for a coherent, reliably funded, *regional* approach to transportation in and around the Big Apple, where three sovereign states, the municipality of New York, and the Port Authority divided responsibility and competed for resources with the New York City Transit Authority, the aforementioned MCTA, and the Triborough Bridge and Tunnel Authority. Only the latter, held in the unyielding grip of seventy-eight-year-old Robert Moses, was flush with cash, which naturally made it a target of opportunity for all the others.

The idea of tapping Triborough's reserves to subsidize a fifteen-cent subway fare was not a new one; it had first been vetted in the Wagner administration. In the wake of the transit strike that unhappily defined his first days in office, John Lindsay introduced legislation that would effectively combine Triborough with the Transit Authority. But Moses had the constitution on his side, at least that portion of Article I that protected Triborough bondholders against any attempt to override an existing state contract. Lindsay quickly backed off from his raid on the Triborough surplus, estimated in excess of $100 million, but not the proposed consolidation. He would teach "the old bastard" a lesson. In the event, it was Lindsay who experienced ritualistic humiliation in legislative hearings where witness after witness decried the mayor's presumption, his naïveté, and his reading of the law.

Now, a year later, it was clear that Lindsay wasn't the only distressed officeholder eager to reach his hand into the Triborough till or require suburban motorists to finance improved mass transit—making rubber pay for rail, as the formula came to be known. Unlike the mayor, however, Nelson Rockefeller had carefully prepared for this moment; indeed, with the vital assistance of Bill Ronan, he had spent seven years laying the groundwork. "Lots of governors have built highways," wrote Neal Peirce in his 1972 volume, *The Megastates of America.* "Rockefeller's uniqueness resides in the absolutely unprecedented way he has inserted a state government into the field of mass transit." The heart of his plan was a $2.5 billion bond issue, the largest ever floated by an American state and shrewdly apportioned among highway construction, mass transit, and airports in order to secure votes upstate and in the suburbs as well as from urban straphangers. By spreading the rewards as well as the costs, Rockefeller removed the political stigma of bailing out profligate New Yorkers.

Cleverer still was the unorthodox administrative structure devised for his proposed Metropolitan Transportation Authority, in effect a holding company that didn't formally merge anything but treated each of its components— whether New York subways, commuter lines in the Hudson Valley and Long Island, or Moses's no longer sacrosanct Triborough Bridge and Tunnel Authority—as *subsidiaries* whose existing trustees were to be thanked for their services and then dismissed by the newly constituted MTA board, chaired by William

J. Ronan. In the spring of 1967, three obstacles stood between Rockefeller and implementation of this audacious vision. Most unpredictable was Moses himself, who had no intention of surrendering his Triborough redoubt without a potentially bruising fight. For weeks, Moses hinted at media bombshells to come. Early in March 1967, he met with Rockefeller at 20 West Fifty-fifth Street, the scene of their stormy encounter five years earlier.

His threat-making potential diminished by intervening events, including the financially disastrous 1964–1965 World's Fair over which he had presided, Moses was still a formidable adversary. Each man had something the other wanted, badly, and each left the meeting convinced that he had achieved his objective. Two days later, Moses unreservedly endorsed Rockefeller's "bold approach" to the region's transportation needs and the immense bond issue required to pay for it. Publicly, he attributed his turnabout to unspecified protections for Triborough bondholders. According to Bill Ronan, there was a little more to it than that. "When we created the MTA and took it over, the question was, How is Bob going to behave?" Ronan would recall. "Well, Bob behaved . . . because we abolished the board . . . we just voted them out and put ourselves in. And then I hired him as a consultant, so that he would continue to get his pay."

No one who knew Moses imagined that he would go quietly for a $25,000 consultant's fee, a car, and a driver. That may be all he was explicitly promised, but Moses left 20 West Fifty-fifth believing a leadership position awaited him in the new MTA. Even Ronan concedes that his long-standing adversary was offered a "major role" in the planning and construction of a gigantic new bridge spanning Long Island Sound for 6.5 miles from Rye in Westchester County to Oyster Bay. Wishful thinking, broken promises, or something in between— whatever Rockefeller said to Moses, it was enough to convert the legendary builder to vigorous support of the bond issue. Less than two weeks after their meeting, Rockefeller signed legislation authorizing the Rye–Oyster Bay Bridge and a second crossing to the east. In November, voters by a substantial margin approved the bond issue, thereby eliminating the second obstacle to Rockefeller's control of the largest public transportation system in the Western Hemisphere.

The referendum behind him, Rockefeller unveiled a new Department of Transportation to coordinate policy and supervise a vast capital-spending program. That there was no place in either initiative for Robert Moses was confirmed in March 1968, when the Metropolitan Transportation Authority formally came into existence. Conspicuously absent from the MTA board he had expected to grace, and no doubt dominate, Moses retained, besides his meaningless consultancy, vague assurances of an ill-defined role on a bridge vulnerable to rapidly changing political and environmental mores. With Moses

at last relegated to the sidelines, Rockefeller moved to implement the full financial merger with Triborough that had eluded Lindsay. Negotiations dragged on
through the winter months, reaching critical stage in the first week of February
1968, when they were eclipsed by the latest installment of a blood feud ranking
second only to the mutual destruction pact of LBJ and Bobby Kennedy. Once
again striking government workers were defying the law, only this time it was
the Rockefeller-sponsored Taylor Law they trampled. The immediate dispute
centered around seventy thousand tons of uncollected garbage clogging New
York's streets, but how it was resolved would have repercussions as far as the
White House.

8

ON THE MORNING of Friday, February 2, 1968, John DeLury, nominally in
charge of the Uniformed Sanitationmen's Association (USA) of New York,
experienced for himself the anti-establishment impulse that was to define that
rebellious year, from the tank-filled streets of Prague to the student-filled bou-
levards of Paris. The eggs tossed at DeLury by disgruntled sanitation workers at
a raucous rally outside city hall missed their target. But they achieved their
goal, hastening the union leader's capitulation to his angry rank and file. At the
time, the average New York sanitation worker took home less than $8,000 a
year. The city had offered a wage increase of $400, part of it retroactive to the
previous July, plus enhanced contributions to employee pension funds. What
was good enough for John DeLury was summarily hooted down by his membership.

Mayor Lindsay, mindful of police, firemen, and other unions waiting to take
their cue from the USA, staunchly opposed union demands for a $600 raise.
The resulting strike was illegal under the Taylor Law, and Lindsay had no intention of rewarding civil servants who broke the law. Seizing the moral high
ground, keenly aware as always of audience reaction, Lindsay proved more
adept at the theater of confrontation than in negotiating with men he neither
trusted nor understood. His initial response to the strike was to approach his
ally Victor Gotbaum, head of the American Federation of State, County, and
Municipal Employees, and other union leaders about mobilizing workers in
unaffected departments to pick up New York's garbage.

Not surprisingly, this divide-and-conquer strategy was rejected as thinly
veiled strikebreaking. Amid escalating tensions the city obtained a court injunction, and USA president John DeLury was jailed for contempt, a self-
defeating gesture that hardened attitudes on both sides while doing much to

restore DeLury's tattered credibility among his membership. On Tuesday, February 6, sandwiched between highly visible walking tours of foul-smelling neighborhoods, Lindsay made his first appeal for assistance to the governor. In response, Rockefeller instructed his civil defense director, General Manuel J. Asensio, and state health commissioner, Hollis Ingraham, to work with their New York City counterparts. The next day, Lindsay traveled to Albany. At a meeting in Rockefeller's office, the mayor revealed plans for a televised ultimatum to the union to return to work by Thursday morning at seven o'clock. Failure to do so would necessitate the declaration of a health emergency and a formal request to the state for "whatever assistance may be available under law, including use of the organized militia, if necessary."

If necessary. Around those two conditional words, and the multitude of interpretations to which they lent themselves, was to swirl a personal and political melodrama that riveted New York and spilled over into 1968 presidential politics. Snubbed by DeLury's union, Lindsay withdrew his earlier offer of continuous negotiations by an impartial panel of fact finders. At eight forty-five on the morning of February 8, the mayor's letter confirming the state of emergency and formally requesting National Guard assistance was delivered to 20 West Fifty-fifth Street. In handing off this hand grenade to the governor, Lindsay scored political points with ordinary New Yorkers even as he turned up the heat on his fellow Republican. Rockefeller never doubted Lindsay's motives. "I think he hoped to see on the front page of every newspaper in the country," he told one visitor that week, "pictures of chaos in New York City because Governor Rockefeller called out the National Guard."

If Rockefeller gave serious consideration to calling out the Guard, there is no evidence of it. To the contrary, numerous eyewitnesses testify to the counterpressure exerted by union leaders who promised a general strike in response to any troop deployment. Al Marshall heard a Teamster boss tell Rockefeller that were he to enlist the National Guard as the mayor requested, "I'll shut this town down so tight even babies won't get milk." Quite apart from this grim prospect, Rockefeller concluded that the part-time soldiers of the National Guard were ill-equipped by training or physical ability to collect more than a fraction of the ten thousand tons of refuse generated daily. Injuries were unavoidable, leading to lawsuits down the road. Worse, in the racial tinderbox that New York City had become, Rockefeller feared that an influx of white Guardsmen in minority neighborhoods might touch off violence. Already black militants like H. Rap Brown were on TV vowing armed resistance to any such intervention. Rockefeller took the threat seriously enough to call the White House to determine whether President Johnson would be willing to send troops to assist civil authorities in the event of a general strike. (LBJ said he didn't have any soldiers to spare.)

Finally, and most poignant, there was the memory of Ludlow and the long-ago miners' strike suppressed by the National Guard at ruinous cost in human life and to the Rockefeller family name. At one point in the week's deliberations, an uncharacteristically emotional Rockefeller recalled his childhood memories of the Colorado massacre. Later he would express astonishment that so many liberals supported use of the National Guard to break the current impasse. "Don't they remember the Colorado Fuel and Iron strike?" he asked. On the morning of February 8, he summoned antagonists on both sides to Fifty-fifth Street. Rockefeller aide Evelyn Cunningham watched as "Lindsay and his posse" entered the building. "And he just yells over . . . 'Nelson! Are you going to do something about this garbage, or shall I do it?'" This was bravado. By the time Lindsay and his aides were installed in a fourth-floor conference room, the initiative had in fact passed out of the mayor's hands.

The public relations battle was a different matter altogether. Here the camera-friendly Lindsay held most of the cards, using frequent television appearances and well-publicized walking tours to present himself as a fearless defender of order and decency pitted against union bosses who didn't mind risking the public health if that was what it took to get what they had failed to secure through honest negotiation. If Rockefeller was caught in the crossfire . . . well, there was a principle to uphold, the *Times* editorial board to impress, and millions of onlookers weighing the conflict from a distance. On Fifty-fifth Street, a much smaller audience witnessed the unfolding drama that Thursday as Harry Van Arsdale, Jr., union lawyer Paul O'Dwyer, and other labor men convened in a second Rockefeller conference room, one floor up from the governor's office at Number 20. Soon they were joined by John DeLury, temporarily sprung from his jail cell at the governor's request and with Lindsay's acquiescence.

The real action that morning played out in a second-floor office where Al Marshall and Bob Sweet were haggling on behalf of their employers. Periodically Lindsay appeared in the doorway to check on their progress. Occasionally he dropped in on Rockefeller next door. Mostly, however, he waited, a leading man unhappily relegated to the wings while other players took center stage. Acknowledging Rockefeller's resentment at the mayor for putting him in such a tight spot—"He would have had to be Jesus Christ not to be sore at the guy who did that to him," claimed Ted Braun—Hugh Morrow, for one, felt his boss could have been more sensitive toward Lindsay, "a proud, touchy man" who had become a virtual hostage on his adversary's turf.

Before leaving at five to return to city hall, Lindsay agreed to the creation of a mediation panel, whose members would report their findings by midnight. On his way out, the mayor told Rockefeller that the city would reject any settlement of $450. Far from torpedoing the talks, Lindsay's preemptive statement left everyone believing that a smaller figure would be acceptable. The outlines of a deal could be glimpsed. At two a.m., the mediation panel came back with a proposed settlement of $425. This would add $250,000 to a municipal budget in excess of $5 billion. The work of the mediators was immediately accepted by DeLury and his shop stewards. Rockefeller endorsed it as well. In a phone conversation with the governor at two forty-five a.m., Lindsay rejected the deal as excessive. Reverting to his earlier stance, he declared it a violation of principle to negotiate with an illegally striking union (a position that raised doubts about Lindsay's motives in acceding to the mediation panel in the first place).

He wasn't through. Now, said the mayor, was the time to break the public employee unions once and for all. Stunned, Nelson asked Lindsay to repeat his statement while he jotted it down on a yellow legal pad. At three thirty, the governor departed Fifty-fifth Street, leaving behind a handful of aides to ponder their narrowing options. Upon his return at nine o'clock Friday morning, Rockefeller found the switchboard at Number 20 deluged with angry calls, most denouncing him for caving in to union power. A flood of critical telegrams reinforced the point. His first meeting of the day had nothing to do with the strike. It was a power broker summit called to finalize legal arrangements for absorption of the Triborough Bridge and Tunnel Authority into the embryonic MTA. Months of negotiations had come down to this: For an additional quarter-point interest on outstanding bonds, a concession to the Chase Manhattan Bank that cost the state $12 million, Rockefeller demolished the third and final barrier to his undisputed control of a transportation grid moving eight to nine million users a day. Over the next decade, an estimated $1.2 billion in Triborough revenues was diverted into MTA coffers. Suburban motorists heavily subsidized an expanded mass transit system whose users paid far less than they would have had there been no merger.

The garbage strike reclaimed Rockefeller's attention. Resolved to say nothing that might imperil delicate negotiations, he held his tongue, even after Les Slote warned him that he was losing the PR battle to city hall. When he finally went on the air at six o'clock Friday evening, Rockefeller had conciliatory words for the mayor. Afterward, Louis Lefkowitz said it was time for the two men to get together. With state health officials warning that a snowstorm or even a heavy rain might require every New Yorker to get a cholera shot, Rockefeller was in no mood to argue. His call to Lindsay, made around seven thirty, included a gubernatorial invitation to meet on neutral territory (the Roosevelt Hotel was suggested), with only their deputies Marshall and Sweet present.

A contemporaneous account maintained by Rockefeller staffer Harry Albright records "a long silence" finally broken by Rockefeller: "You mean that the Mayor of the City of New York won't meet with the Governor in this crisis?" Another lengthy pause. Acknowledging their past misunderstandings,

Rockefeller said this was no time to dwell on such differences. Lindsay professed to see "no solution" to the deadlock. Still, not wishing to be outflanked, he agreed to send Bob Sweet back to Fifty-fifth Street for renewed talks. "Will he have negotiating power?" The mayor said that he would, though quickly adding, "I can see no area for negotiation." What was left out of this semiofficial chronology, and of the journalistic narratives spawned by the strike, revealed more than what was included. "We got Lindsay on the phone, and Nelson was talking to him," recalls one who was in the room. "He said, 'Well, John, we've got to do something about this.' And Lindsay said, 'Fuck you.' That was the kiss of death. It was all over."

That night, Rockefeller remained holed up in his office, while elsewhere in the complex Sweet and Marshall spent hours in a good-faith pursuit of common ground. At one point, Marshall believed they had an agreement to settle the strike—until a red-faced deputy mayor, returning from one of his periodic trips to Gracie Mansion, announced, "They think I'm too tired to negotiate and the Mayor won't approve." By now Rockefeller had reached the end of his rope. He had already instructed his Albany counsel Bobby Douglass to draft legislation over the weekend that would authorize the state to assume control of the Sanitation Department. He announced this radical step on television Saturday evening, but not before securing a verbal agreement from DeLury and his men to return to work immediately, under the terms agreed to two days earlier by the mediation panel.

Rockefeller had ended the strike, without violence or epidemic. But the political shock waves from his unilateral assumption of authority had only begun to reverberate. On Sunday, February 11, Lindsay returned to the airwaves to decry Rockefeller's proposed takeover for endangering home rule "not in New York City alone, but in every city of the State and possibly the Nation." He voiced shock at the governor's failure to join him in standing up to the "extortionist demands" of the sanitation workers. While he, Lindsay, had been out on the streets defending the Taylor Law, the man most responsible for its passage was lobbying state legislators to violate the statute and defy a court order in the bargain. Legislators marinated in public outrage denied Rockefeller permission to address them in person. His request for emergency powers was scuttled before it could be voted on.

With polls showing Lindsay the clear beneficiary of popular anger, the two sides on February 17 finally agreed to an arbitration package devised by Vince McDonnell, chairman of the State Mediation Board. The sanitation workers got their $425 raise, and the city was assessed more than it would have paid under the terms hammered out by Marshall and Sweet. For Rockefeller, the strike added up to a political disaster, the timing of which could not have been more damaging. While mayoral aides calculated the damage done to Rockefeller's hopes for a GOP presidential nomination—"George Meany and Harry Van Arsdale can't help him there"—Lindsay savored a rare triumph over his Albany nemesis, whose patronizing runner had long grated on the mayor. "He didn't call me Johnny this time," bragged Lindsay after the strike was resolved. Few boasts rang more hollow.

Twenty-One
TOO MUCH, TOO LATE

I'll accept anyone making a mistake once. But the same mistake more than once is not acceptable.

—NELSON A. ROCKEFELLER

1

ACCEPTING AN INVITATION to lunch with Rockefeller in the immediate aftermath of the garbage strike, Arthur Schlesinger, Jr., had expected to find 13 West Fifty-fourth Street a castle under siege. Yet when the eminent historian presented himself at the Fifty-fifth Street offices on February 16, 1968, a characteristically buoyant Rockefeller, putting aside his recent mauling by the press, expressed confidence that his efforts to avert a public health crisis would eventually be recognized. Affecting a late-blooming composure, he claimed immunity to disappointment, extending even to the denial of his lifelong ambition to be president. This would have no doubt surprised supporters of George Romney. "His people think I am double-crossing him," Rockefeller confided to Schlesinger and his other lunch guest that Friday, Henry Kissinger. Not only did Nelson expect to outpoll Romney in the March 12 New Hampshire primary, a contest in which his name wasn't even on the ballot; he thought he might well carry May's pivotal Oregon primary on the strength of write-ins alone.

Both predictions ran counter to his professed detachment. So did his assertion that Richard Nixon could sweep the primaries and *still* lose the GOP nomination, if his national poll numbers indicated vulnerability in November. "There are eighteen Republican governors who want me," Rockefeller boasted to Schlesinger. "They want to win this time." On the subject of Vietnam he was considerably less forthcoming, though hints were dropped that he had come to doubt a purely military victory. (Privately, Rockefeller accepted the need for an exit strategy, observing that if the French couldn't prevail in Indochina, neither could Uncle Sam.) Mostly, however, he used the lunch to identify values he shared with the premier historian of the Roosevelt era. "You know, I have my roots in the New Deal," Rockefeller insisted.

This was not an argument likely to sway Republican delegates to his side. Ideological objections were but one of the negative factors weighing on Rockefeller as he contemplated a third run for the White House. Little more than a year had passed since the birth of Mark Rockefeller, the second child of his marriage to Happy, whose dedication to her young family matched her distaste for the campaign trail. Neither Rockefeller longed to repeat the bruising experience of 1964. A different set of obstacles was posed by the primary calendar. Just ten days separated the voting in New Hampshire, where polls were unanimous in forecasting a Nixon rout, from Oregon's March 22 filing deadline. Practically speaking, there was no way Rockefeller could enter the latter contest, as supporters around the country were urging him, without confirming suspicions that he had been using Romney all along as a stalking horse. As his options narrowed, a torrent of conflicting advice flowed Rockefeller's way. Bill Scranton, anxious to fill the vacuum left by Romney's weakness, volunteered to organize Republican governors on Nelson's behalf. Rockefeller was the only Republican, argued Jackie Robinson, who could attract blacks, labor, independents, and disgruntled Democrats in numbers sufficient to regain the White House for the party of Lincoln.

From George Hinman came opposing counsel, a course of passivity bordering on defeatism. "Your position of non-candidacy has put you where you are today," Hinman insisted early in 1968. "It has put you at the top of public esteem. It has avoided a confrontation within the party. It has put you in a position in respect to the nomination where we never dreamed we would be." Hinman quoted a local sage who contended that if Rockefeller couldn't get the nomination at the convention, "he can't get it at all, and at least he will come out of it with his integrity intact and as the biggest man in America." If this argument sounded familiar, there was good reason: in George Hinman's world it was still 1959, with Rockefeller's only chance a Willkie-style draft by party regulars for whom his electability trumped their cultural and ideological affinity for Richard Nixon. The strategy hadn't come close to working then; in retrospect, it borders on the bizarre that anyone believed it could succeed in 1968, when Rockefeller's own polls showed the country demonstrably moving to the right. Yet enough others shared Hinman's fantasy to fuel talk of such a draft.

Then came the New York City garbage strike. Five days after his lunch with Schlesinger, Rockefeller convened a gathering of political advisers at 812 Fifth Avenue to assess the damage. He turned to one of his latest hired guns: Ted Braun, a California PR man with the profile of a cigar store Indian and an intolerance of lesser minds reminiscent of Henry Kissinger or Bill Ronan. "Ted didn't believe in anything other than his own brainpower," recalled his professional partner Clifford Miller. This, and the insights into mass psychology grounded in his consulting work for the Eisenhower White House, made Braun a hot property to one such as Nelson, who was forever on the prowl for original thinking to augment his existing brain trust. Braun's grasp of New York politics was what one might expect of a professional pitchman for Kotex, Pepsodent, and Sunkist oranges. ("He didn't know the difference between *Newsday* and *Newsweek*," claims one insider.) This did not prevent Rockefeller from entrusting him with much of his pre-convention planning. Together the two men envisioned a series of major policy speeches commencing in May, after the legislature adjourned but before the Oregon primary on May 28. Even this "availability strategy" was questioned by Bill Ronan, who was convinced that Nixon had the nomination effectively sewed up. Rockefeller had no campaign organization in place, Ronan reminded him: no field team and no DNA-style issues group to bring him up to speed on the nation's most pressing concerns.

On the last day of February, hardly concealing his feelings of betrayal, George Romney threw in the towel. His withdrawal from the race days before the New Hampshire primary only intensified scrutiny on a deeply conflicted Rockefeller. The first half of March combined the dangerous exhilaration of a high-wire act with the graceless uncertainty of a tug-of-war. In his diary, Rockefeller osteopath Ken Riland recorded the daily fluctuations of a man wavering between active candidacy and openness to a draft that few viewed as a realistic prospect. Never, wrote Riland, had he seen his friend so indecisive. On March 9, Rockefeller told Riland he had no intention of entering the Oregon primary. His resolve lasted barely twenty-four hours. The next day seven governors, three U.S. senators, three former RNC chairmen, and a sprinkling of House members joined Mayor Lindsay and a dozen of the usual suspects for a marathon discussion in the living room at 812 Fifth Avenue. Curiously, the strongest case for Rockefeller's entry into the race was made by Lindsay. Imbued with a sense of urgency by his work on the Kerner Commission examining the urban crisis, Lindsay described a country coming unhinged, its inhabitants frightened of the present and morose about their future.

Others wanted Rockefeller to run, but for radically different reasons. Spiro Agnew urged him to direct his harshest attacks at the War on Poverty, not the war in Vietnam. Congressman Charles Goodell, a moderate conservative from western New York, advised Rockefeller to say nothing critical of Nixon. Bill Ronan questioned the emphasis on Oregon and any bandwagon effect set off by a victory there. It was decided to send John Deardourff on a personal reconnaissance of the state. "I went out there, and I worked my butt off for three or four days," said Deardourff. "I drove all over the place. I talked to everybody. I talked to all the people we had had with us in '64; there was not a single defection." Both Mark Hatfield and his popular successor, Tom McCall, promised support. With doubts rife about Nixon's electoral viability, "it was absolutely clear to me," Deardourff concluded, "that we were better positioned in '68 than we were in '64."[*]

After a frenzied all-night flight across the country, Deardourff walked into Hinman's office on the morning of Friday, March 15. "I don't know, John," Hinman greeted the younger man, "it may have been a wasted trip."

Deardourff refused to be put off. "We can win," he told Hinman.

"You really think that?"

A call was placed to Rockefeller. Having already changed his mind at least twice since the March 10 conclave, Nelson asked Deardourff for a memo in advance of yet another war council to be convened at his apartment the next day. On Saturday morning, Rockefeller went over a draft statement with Emmet Hughes and Ted Braun. Hughes objected to its ambiguous tone. Either Nelson was a candidate or he wasn't, and if he was, he had no choice but to go all out in Oregon. The discussion consumed most of the day, interrupted by a passionate presentation from Deardourff, who insisted that a solid, if sketchy, organization was already in place. He estimated the cost of a successful Oregon campaign at $600,000. They needn't take his word for it, said Deardourff; arrangements were made to fly in a delegation of Oregon supporters, approximately twenty in number, for brunch and a vigorous interrogation the next day.

For three hours that Sunday morning, the group delivered a mixed message (along with petitions bearing the signatures of fifty-one thousand Oregonians). Insisting that their state was winnable, the visitors told Rockefeller that he would have to commit to at least twelve days of personal campaigning there. Beyond this, one admittedly skeptical participant in the meeting recalls "an awful lot of vague promises and nothing solid." Still, it was enough for Hinman to pull Deardourff aside and tell him, "I think Nelson's going." He asked Deardourff and his campaign management partner, Doug Bailey, to put together a campaign blueprint starting in Oregon. After the group from the West Coast left, the debate resumed among Rockefeller's badly divided court. From the windows of 812, they could glimpse the passing battalions of the St. Patrick's Day parade, led by Bobby Kennedy, reaching out to as many hands on both sides of Fifth Avenue as he could grasp. On the heels of an unexpectedly strong showing by Minnesota senator Eugene McCarthy in New Hampshire, Ken-

---

[*] "If you get the wrong ten people in a room . . . the odds are they're going to make the wrong decisions," Deardourff remarked long afterward. "I believe that there were around Rockefeller people who really never wanted him to seek the presidency. . . . I would put Ronan in that category as a guy who was on top of the world . . . as long as Rockefeller was the governor, and who would have been a sideshow if Rockefeller had gotten into the White House." John Deardourff, AI.

nedy had reversed course and joined the Democratic fray. Though his action revived old cries of Kennedy ruthlessness, it was nothing that a few primary victories wouldn't cure. In the meantime, the New York senator appealed to many of the same elements sympathetic to a Rockefeller candidacy.

Hoping to expedite the decision-making process, Emmet Hughes composed a pair of statements, one entering the contest, the other pulling out. Nelson grabbed the positive announcement, claimed Hughes, and "went flying off like an airplane with one wing." As Sunday's meeting broke up, virtually everyone in the Rockefeller camp expected him to run. The next day, Nelson flew to Washington to sample opinions among Republican members of Congress. That evening, Thruston Morton left a Foxhall Road dinner convinced that he would be Rockefeller's national campaign chairman. Morton informally presided over a March 19 breakfast attended by the candidate-in-waiting and sixteen GOP senators. Coffee had hardly been poured when it became painfully clear that most in attendance wanted Rockefeller to run merely to bolster the impact of Nixon's expected primary victories. Now, he might well have asked himself, who was the stalking horse?

Taken aback by what he had heard, Rockefeller instructed Hughes and Braun to meet him at eleven thirty that morning at Fifty-fifth Street. There he experienced the day's second unwelcome surprise. Overnight Hughes, without benefit of the dispiriting Washington breakfast, had changed his mind about Oregon. Instead of a springboard to the nomination, it suddenly loomed as a trapdoor. Seeming confirmation of this view came in a call from George Hinman, alerting the little group to a new Oregon poll giving Nixon a commanding lead. By one o'clock, the decision was made. "It's a no-go," Rockefeller said to Ann Whitman as he emerged from his meeting with Braun and Hughes. "This is it," he mused over lunch, "I know it's right." (Explaining the protracted indecision of that spring in another context, he told a staff member, "If I'm not caught up in an enthusiasm I'm not any good.") Rockefeller had but one remaining reservation—in bowing out, he didn't want to leave the impression that he was running away from a fight (which of course he was). A news conference was called for two days hence. To guard against leaks, only Happy Rockefeller and George Hinman were let in on the secret.[*]

---

[*] Les Slote insisted that Rockefeller, the day before his press conference, alerted him and other staff members to his decision and asked them to relay the information to key supporters in the field—Spiro Agnew included. The man tasked with calling Agnew failed to carry out his mission. Slote, reluctant to "besmirch his name," wouldn't divulge his identity to the author. Cary Reich had better luck, eliciting George Hinman's name from a reluctant Slote. Seeming confirmation of this comes in Joe Persico's 1968 campaign diary, which recounts an initial organizational meeting at which Hinman conceded it had been a mistake to withhold advance notice of Nel-

Nelson's failure to notify key supporters of his pending withdrawal would prove as harmful to his presidential prospects as the March 21 announcement itself. Ted Braun, characterizing the Maryland governor as notoriously indiscreet, specifically excluded Spiro Agnew from any call list. Meanwhile Agnew, fully expecting Rockefeller to vindicate his own long-running draft effort, had invited friendly reporters from the *Baltimore Sun* and other journals into his Annapolis office to watch the campaign launch on national television. All that remained was for Nelson, speaking in the ballroom of the New York Hilton, to spring his surprise. "I have decided today to reiterate unequivocally that I am not a candidate campaigning directly or indirectly for the presidency of the United States." The shock waves reverberated far beyond the Eastern Establishment. Coming as it did hours before the Oregon filing deadline, Rockefeller's withdrawal precluded the emergence of any moderate alternative to Richard Nixon.

A handful of diehards thought the decision actually strengthened Nelson's chances to be nominated. Far more common was the response of Oregon's Tom McCall, who publicly declared himself "shocked and dismayed."* Ted Agnew never forgave Rockefeller for his public humiliation. His revenge was not long in coming. Nixon's chief delegate hunter, John Sears, telephoned his candidate with an urgent appeal to reach out to Agnew. By the time Sears returned home from a delegate-hunting foray to Alaska, Nixon had sufficiently overcome his distaste for the Maryland governor as a Rockefeller partisan to invite him to lunch. "Now he thought he was a great guy," Sears says, chuckling, "because all Agnew did at lunch was say what a bad guy Rockefeller was."

2

"IT WAS THE polls," Nixon told William Safire on March 23 in explaining Rockefeller's aborted candidacy. "He has the same figures we have for the Oregon primary. Back in February they were Nixon 35, Rocky 35, Reagan 8, and just last week they were Nixon 47, Rocky 26, Reagan 3. It's all over for him.

---

son's March 21 bombshell from friends and supporters. Rockefeller subsequently apologized to Agnew in a chance encounter at Baltimore's airport—"and Agnew was having none of it," said a reporter who observed the exchange. "He was determined to make Nelson Rockefeller crawl." John Goldman, AI.

* Away from the cameras, McCall reacted with trademark humor. Asked by reporter Jack Germond whether he felt he had been manipulated, McCall replied, "Manipulated? I was fondled." Jack Germond, AI.

The only one who can stop us is Reagan." Not everyone in his entourage emulated Nixon's clinical detachment. Pat Buchanan, then a young Nixon speechwriter aggressively guarding the candidate's right flank, hints at other factors that may have played a part in Rockefeller's last minute withdrawal. So, at the time, did *Newsweek.* Employing the oblique language of the period, the magazine speculated whether Nixon supporters "would make capital of rumors that periodically haunt Rocky's personal life." The day before his withdrawal, identifying members of the John Birch Society as the culprits, Rockefeller himself confided to Ken Riland that a smear campaign was being waged against him in Oregon, reminiscent of a similar effort prior to the 1964 California primary.

The subject was a familiar one. Where women were concerned, acknowledged Emmet Hughes, "Nelson was just compulsive." Professional gossips such as author Truman Capote dined out on rumors linking Rockefeller and Gloria Vanderbilt. Less famous names with whom he was allegedly involved ranged from a minor member of Italian royalty to several current or former members of his own staff. A well-regarded national political correspondent maintained his professional detachment in covering Rockefeller, notwithstanding the governor's evident interest in the reporter's wife. On the road, Nelson tested the patience of handlers by inquiring about a hotel's telephone security, a necessary precaution before making a "private call." Campaigning in East Harlem, asserts one intimately acquainted with the local culture, "he used to flirt with every woman. I saw him go up to very good-looking Latin women, clearly making passes at them. . . . He was lucky he didn't get a knife in him." (The whispering campaign went both ways, with Rockefeller telling friends he had long been the object of pursuit by *New York Post* publisher Dolly Schiff and Pamela Harriman.)

Some were disappointed when the rumors proved to be just that. Kitty Carlisle Hart, onetime opera singer and Hollywood starlet turned game show panelist and cultural maven, was delighted to accept appointment as vice chairman of the New York State Council on the Arts. In this capacity she once spent the night at Kykuit, prior to a council event the next day at nearby Purchase. Hart was met at the door by the governor himself, who carried her bags upstairs and showed her to her room. He checked out her closet. Satisfied that the light inside was in working order, Nelson led Hart across the room, to a balcony opening onto a majestic panorama stretching to the Hudson and beyond. One day, sadly, everything within sight would disappear, he remarked, "because there's not going to be enough money to keep it going."

And with that he withdrew, leaving a slightly mystified Hart to reflect on why he hadn't stolen a kiss.

By 1968, the protective shield long maintained by journalists, not a few of whom welcomed a presidential campaign as a temporary suspension of their own marital vows, was beginning to slip. Yet Rockefeller conducted himself as if the old rules were immutable. At the annual dinner of the Westchester County Republican organization, chaired by philanthropist Frederic Powers and staged at the Commodore Hotel, he was presented with a custom-made replica of King Arthur's great sword Excalibur. "It was a museum piece, gorgeous," remembers radio executive Bill O'Shaughnessy. "All of a sudden Nelson lost it. He started laughing, and nobody knew what the hell he was laughing at. . . . Finally, he said, 'Fred, Mr. Chairman—are you suggesting in front of my neighbors that I'm a great swordsman?' I think Grand Central shook from the laughter."

No one was laughing in the wake of the 1967 national governors' conference aboard the USS *Independence*, when fresh reports began circulating about Rockefeller's alleged involvement with a woman on his office staff. By early December, both Babe Paley and Joan Braden were telling anyone who would listen that Nelson "had another girl—his personal secretary." The claims were disputed by Henry Kissinger. Rockefeller, he explained, depended on women for "emotional support." While Joan Braden said that Happy should have known what she was getting into, Emmet Hughes pointed the finger of blame squarely at Nelson. "He made Happy go through the misery of a divorce, and two years later was fooling around with a new girl in the office," Hughes remarked. "In 1968 we were concerned all the time that the press might get on to this new involvement." As well they might be: the rumors held center stage at a pre-Christmas 1967 dinner party attended by Drew Pearson, Ben Bradlee, and columnist Joseph Kraft. Conceding that the affair was "well-known" in the press—"I heard several reporters discuss it"—John Sears nevertheless questions how much the shadowy relationship influenced Rockefeller's decision to forgo an uphill challenge to Nixon.

Ironically, some of the most vociferous tattlers had been guests at the spectacular dinner dance Nelson hosted at Pocantico for Happy's forty-first birthday the previous June. "Every other birthday Happy has been having a baby or we've been campaigning," Nelson told a reporter in between greeting guests on the terrace overlooking the Hudson. Even Truman Capote, fresh from his celebrated black-and-white ball (at which the Rockefellers were no-shows), acknowledged feelings of envy over a list of attendees that included the Robert Kennedys, Jacob Javitses, Joshua Logans, Whitney Youngs, Kirk Douglases, Jackie Robinsons, Gardner Cowleses, and Cornelius Vanderbilt Whitneys. Joining them beneath a great green-and-white-striped tent in Kykuit's softly lit gardens (illuminations designed by Philip Johnson) were Cardinals Spellman and Cushing, Jerome Robbins, Tom Dewey, Walter Cronkite, Katharine Graham, Arthur Sulzberger, Robert McNamara, Richard Rodgers, Brooke Astor, and the aforementioned Capote, clutching a French crystal paperweight for the guest of honor. CBS chairman William Paley shared a table with labor leader Harry Van Arsdale, Jr., legendary choreographer George Balanchine, Mrs. Robert F. Wagner, television personality Peter Lind Hayes, and Mrs. John Loeb.

"We just thought it would be a nice idea to have a party for our friends," said Happy, stunning in a chartreuse chiffon dress with white beaded bodice. As a rule, Kykuit's grandiosity repelled the latest, and last, Mrs. Rockefeller to live there. No valet or lady's maid fussed over Nelson or Happy. To be sure, the formal dining room, dominated by portraits of Senior and Junior, continued to host intimate dinners for the great and powerful, among them several American presidents and their wives, the shah of Iran, King Hussein of Jordan, Anwar Sadat, Jackie and Ari Onassis, and Lord Mountbatten—not to mention Frank Sinatra, Marc Chagall, and Andy Warhol. "Nelson could barely sit at the table throughout a meal without having to get up to do something, or the phone would ring," Happy recalls. "And having two formal meals in that dining room was more than I could stand."

The problem was neatly solved by enclosing and heating the west porch, which enabled the family to enjoy a buffet lunch year-round in less intimidating surroundings. For the first time, the hilltop mansion housed small children—Nelson basked in his status as both the youngest and the eldest member of his Dartmouth class to father a child—their swing set competing for space with Alexander Calder's *Large Spiny* and an abstract horse by Marino Marini. A classical stone teahouse was converted into an ice-cream parlor, complete with Formica tabletops. The sunken lawns of Senior's inner garden made way for a pair of swimming pools, one boasting a sand beach for the Rockefeller youngsters and the visiting children from Happy's first marriage. The formal north porch of the house was expanded to include a "flower porch," where she could arrange blossoms, and a snack kitchen more inviting to small boys than the ancient gloomy kitchen a floor below.

The informality that characterized post-1963 life at Kykuit did not end at the estate gates. Arriving at the 21 Club for a romantic private dinner upstairs, or meeting friends there on a night of pelting rain, Happy stood out for the practical raincoat she wore in contrast with the lush furs adorning her sisters-in-law. Credited with modernizing her husband's slightly stodgy wardrobe, she says simply, "I got Bill Blass to work on that." As the ties widened and colorful shirts replaced banker's white, Nelson's old double-breasted suits were consigned to the closets. Her influence made itself felt in more substantive ways as well. "Nelson Rockefeller thought Happy read people as well and as quick as anybody else he ever knew," noted *Newsweek*'s Jim Cannon, who joined the Rockefeller staff at the end of 1968. An unlikely feminist, her role in promoting reform of New York's restrictive abortion laws included soul-searching conversations with Senate Republican leader Earl Brydges.

Ken Riland's diary, unapologetically biased in favor of Tod Rockefeller, portrays her successor as warmly outgoing one day and frostily remote the next. More sympathetic observers traced Happy's insecurities to her experience growing up in a household where love was rationed and alcohol the painkiller of choice. "Happy liked to have a bourbon cocktail before dinner," Cynthia Lefferts remembers, "and I was told it was okay for staff, so I ordered wine or something. And as soon as I sat down she said to me, 'Nelson thinks I'm an alcoholic' . . . a drink of sherry to him was practically a sin." The noisily staged rituals of a political dinner or Elks Hall testimonial were not Happy's milieu, any more than it had been Tod's before her. "She'd be fine when talking to the governor of Ohio, but most of the time you're talking to the head of the Okayaka City Council, or his wife," reflects one Rockefeller aide. "It's not that they're boring, it's just that they're not in her world. She wasn't running for anything, and so it was just hard for her. To help Nelson, yes, she'd do it occasionally. She was always gracious."

Even these appearances diminished in frequency as her boys outgrew infancy and began to make their own mark on Kykuit. Visitors to the underground art gallery were hurried past the Warhol portraits of the governor and his wife (which, truth be told, neither much cared for) and shown instead a finger painting by Master Nelson Rockefeller or a display of old glass bottles dug up on the estate by the proprietor and his young sons. At the end of 1967, a photographer from *Good Housekeeping* was admitted to snap pictures of Big Nelson and Little Nelson raking leaves; of a beaming father carving pumpkins for flaxen-haired Nelson and his infant brother; and of the smiling couple cavorting with their youngsters amid huge sculptural abstractions or holding hands in the long shadow of a Calder stabile and the distant Catskills. Pocantico was Nelson's favorite place, said Happy, "and mine too. I love to ride horses in the wonderful roads and I never tire of looking down at the river from the top of the hill. Now, if we could only get rid of the telephones!"

3

IT WAS AT a dinner honoring the Cowles journalistic dynasty (their flagship: *Look* magazine) on April 4, 1968, where Nelson learned that Martin Luther King, Jr., in Memphis to show solidarity with striking sanitation workers, had been gunned down while standing on a motel balcony. In an eerie historical replay, he got the news while dining with Tom Dewey, his lunch partner on November 22, 1963. Rockefeller ordered state flags lowered to half-mast in respect for the slain civil rights leader. That night, as John Lindsay returned to the streets of Harlem—at least until Manhattan borough president Percy Sutton, fearing for his safety, pulled the mayor into his car—Rockefeller contemplated more substantive ways to perpetuate the King legacy. "The true memorial to Martin Luther King cannot be made of stone," he said in a formal statement of condolence. "It must be made of action."

By sheer happenstance, Rockefeller already possessed what he considered the perfect instrument with which to advance King's work. First, however, more personal considerations vied for his attention. Not content to express his grief verbally to King's widow, on Saturday, April 6, Rockefeller dispatched to Atlanta Joe Canzeri, Joe Boyd, and the Reverend Wyatt Tee Walker, formerly King's chief of staff in the Southern Christian Leadership Conference and an influential Harlem pastor with close ties to Nelson. Their organizational skills, backed by the Rockefeller checkbook, were offered without limit to the grieving family. Half an hour after his arrival in Atlanta, Canzeri would recall, "I'm sitting at the bedside of Coretta King, making plans for the funeral services." He rented the entire top floor of Atlanta's Marriott Hotel. Through a contact at AT&T, Canzeri rounded up the only four automobiles in the city equipped with car phones. "And we ran that whole operation from the top floor of the Marriott and those four cars."

In the days to come, Canzeri picked out the casket, located and repaired an ancient farm wagon for the procession to the cemetery, found mules to pull it—and took the King children to see their father lying in repose at the Spelman Chapel (named for the family of Nelson's grandmother Laura Spelman Rockefeller). When Ralph Abernathy, King's designated successor at the SCLC, conveyed Mrs. King's desire to return to Memphis and complete the march canceled on account of her husband's death, Canzeri checked into the cost of renting a plane. "I called Louise [Boyer], and said, 'It's a lot of money, what should I do?'"

"Do what you have to do to make it right," Boyer replied. After the Memphis march, Canzeri was swarmed by reporters who scented a story. He asked Rockefeller for guidance. "Joe, we don't want to make any political hay out of the misfortune of the family." Nelson's involvement would go unreported throughout the campaign; only the sketchiest details about his role in the King obsequies would emerge during his lifetime. On the day of the funeral, Canzeri, self-professed "highest-paid bellhop in America," persuaded a reluctant widow to allow a single television camera inside Ebenezer Baptist Church. Leading a delegation of sixty-two New Yorkers, including all of its African American state legislators, Rockefeller took note of the other presidential candidates in attendance. Bobby Kennedy appeared deeply distressed, he said afterward, Richard Nixon "out of it." Nelson and Happy were among an estimated fifty thousand mourners who made the three-hour march to South View Cemetery.

It was late afternoon by the time Rockefeller returned to the Atlanta airport. Before wheels up, he asked Bob Douglass to check on the progress of his living memorial to the martyred civil rights leader. The call was strictly routine, legislative leaders in both houses having assured Nelson that while he took two planes filled with King admirers to Atlanta, lawmakers in his absence would formally ratify his proposed Urban Development Corporation. Seen by many as a response to King's assassination, the UDC was in truth born of long-standing frustration. Fresh off his 1966 campaign, in the course of which he had been exposed to a depressing array of (mostly) upstate communities pock-marked by empty storefronts, crumbling main streets, and white flight, Rocke-feller resolved, as was his habit, to do something corrective—something big, dramatic, and innovative. The UDC had much in common with the Rockefel-ler drug laws of his third term: each was the radical response of a problem solver stymied by forces he *knew* were vulnerable to the right combination of talent, resources, and blatant disregard for the status quo.

In this case, the most pressing need was for low- and middle-income hous-ing. Under Rockefeller, New York's limited-profit housing program had ex-panded from twenty-three hundred apartments in 1959 to fifty thousand eight years later. Another Rockefeller initiative authorized the state to lease up to half these units, which it then offered to families otherwise shut out of such accom-modations. Still, it wasn't nearly enough to close the gap between need and availability. Previous attempts to promote or subsidize public housing had been blocked by voter resistance to housing bond issues, opposition tinged with un-mistakable racial and class overtones. (Rockefeller's Housing Finance Agency, however useful as a funding mechanism, was powerless to initiate or complete projects of its own design.)

Then David Rockefeller in a Washington speech proposed a housing pro-gram using $4 of private capital for every $1 invested by government. After reading a newspaper account of his brother's trial balloon, Nelson picked up the phone and told him, "David, I've got the twenty cents if you've got the eighty cents." For many builders, financial obstacles were the least of their problems. By the late sixties, a private developer in New York City required the approval of ten separate government departments or agencies before he could break ground. With such red tape, inflation, and rising interest rates, it wasn't unusual for a project to consume fifteen years from conception to completion. The Urban Development Corporation was intended to remedy this. The new superagency would be empowered to develop and finance housing, condemn existing property, aid economic development efforts, and build educational and cultural facilities. By leapfrogging local prejudice and politics, the UDC could do for housing what the recently formed Metropolitan Transportation Authority did for mass transit.

This was the statutory price exacted for the services of Edward J. Logue, visionary architect of the New Boston and, before that, redeveloper of New Haven in the 1950s. In January 1968, Logue, still smarting from an unsuccessful campaign for mayor of Boston, was surprised to receive a telephone call from the governor of New York. "And he gets me, and he just pours it on," Logue remembered. "So he tells me I'm the greatest thing since whatever. He said, 'Can you come to New York?' I said, 'Sure, when?' He said, 'Tomorrow.'" The next day, Logue and Rockefeller met at Fifty-fifth Street to review the latest draft of the UDC bill. "This is a great piece of legislation, but it won't work," Logue declared with characteristic bluntness. The new agency, Logue predicted, would be hamstrung by local officials, John Lindsay in particular.*

"What the hell do you mean?" Rockefeller asked.

"Well, under this bill UDC will have to get a building permit from the Building Commissioner of the City of New York. . . . You want to do innovative things with this legislation." Logue had said the magic word.

"That's right."

"If you're going to do innovative things, you've got to get past Lindsay's zoning and planning operation. You've got to do it his way."

"You're right," said Rockefeller. "Come on downstairs." The charm offensive resumed. Imagine pursuing urban development on the world's greatest stage, unfettered by bureaucratic interference. Logue mentioned unpaid campaign debts. He lamented the high cost of living in New York City. Rockefeller referred such matters to his appointments secretary, Harry Albright (ultimately Rockefeller himself paid off Logue's $31,389 political debt and loaned him $145,000 to defray the expense of a Manhattan cooperative apartment). But by far the biggest incentive was a UDC redrawn to Logue's exacting specifications. The most controversial change authorized the state to override local zoning ordinances and other codes. This blatant suspension of home rule stirred intense opposition from an unusual alliance of upstate conservatives, suburban moderates, and more than a few urban liberals. (Not for nothing was Logue dubbed "the poor man's Robert Moses.")[†]

Countering the opposition were the emotions spawned by Martin Luther

---

* A year earlier, Logue had been invited by John Lindsay to review New York City's approach to housing and redevelopment issues. Lindsay, fearing a Moses-like czar in the making, rejected Logue's request to combine the city's planning and development functions, a concession earlier granted him by authorities in New Haven and Boston. No doubt Lindsay's failure to land America's preeminent urban planner only increased Logue's appeal for Rockefeller.

† "Logue remembered every trick in the book that he'd run up against," recalls Bobby Douglass, "and we'd load that into the bill." By the time they were through, "it felt like we were presiding over local plumbing codes." Robert Douglass, AI.

King's death and the ensuing spasm of violence that engulfed more than a hundred American cities. It was no coincidence that Rockefeller chose Tuesday, April 9, the very day King was to be laid to rest, to entrust the fate of the UDC to the legislative bodies he had dominated for almost a decade. His confidence was well-placed, if past experience was any guide. Then Senate Republican leader Earl Brydges—said to have been promised an international airport in Buffalo in return for his support of the UDC—was hopelessly compromised by a thirst not easily quenched. "And Rocky would ply him with martinis, one after another, to get his way," claims a senatorial colleague.

Brydges's Republican counterpart in the assembly, Perry Duryea, cultivated a reputation for independence from the second floor. Tall, tanned, and silver-haired, Duryea looked like a central European foreign minister. But he was also considered something of a dilettante, who "could never go toe to toe with Rockefeller on the substantive side of things." Other factors contributed to the bad blood between Duryea and Rockefeller. Duryea's undisguised gubernatorial ambitions didn't sit well with Malcolm Wilson, now in his third term as Nelson's loyal lieutenant. ("I've been Number Two longer than Avis," joked Wilson.) Institutional jealousies were rivaled by individual ones. "Perry was an extremely proud guy," says Ron Maiorana, a former *New York Times* reporter who succeeded Les Slote as Rockefeller's press secretary at the start of 1969. "He was kind of a self-made man. His father started the business"—marketing lobsters and other Long Island seafood—"and Perry expanded it. He came from . . . a formidable family . . . and he was not going to stand still for a Rockefeller pushing him around. He said, 'Who the hell are the Rockefellers? I'm a Duryea.' That was his mind-set."

The two Republican leaders put aside their differences in the first week of April 1968. Then Bob Douglass in Atlanta placed his call seeking confirmation of the UDC's passage. He was in for a shock. Brydges and the senate had delivered as promised. Not so the assembly, where rebellious members had voted by a narrow margin to send the bill back to committee—in effect, killing the UDC and dealing a body blow to Rockefeller's prestige.

"I got bad news," Douglass told his boss.

"What! Put me through to Duryea."

The Speaker was patched in. Dispensing with amenities, Rockefeller ordered Duryea, whom he accused of a double cross, to schedule a second vote. "It better pass by the time my plane lands, or you'll never get anything for the rest of my administration." This was no idle threat. "I had never seen him so angry," said Harry Albright, who believed that after that night Rockefeller never again trusted Perry Duryea to keep his word. Fairly or not, many suspected the Speaker of encouraging venal lawmakers to exploit the situation for personal advantage. Rockefeller wanted the UDC badly. Who knew what he might trade in order to get it? Quite a bit, as it turned out, though it was also true that rather more sticks than carrots were to be applied that evening. At Rockefeller's direction, the state police launched a dragnet unseen since Tom Dewey's whip-cracking days. Legislators hoping to escape the long arm of the governor were tracked to theaters, restaurants, and other favorite haunts. "We called everybody that was walking and talking," says Bob Douglass. One by one, the dissidents were brought to the second-floor office, where Douglass served as Rockefeller's chief enforcer.

The legislative debate resumed, a wordy backdrop to coercive tactics worthy of Huey Long's bayou dictatorship. One county chairman pulled out of a movie theater ("He thought his mother had died or something") was coolly notified that his continued employment depended on the willingness of his assemblymen to change their votes against the UDC. "I know you don't like the bill," Douglass told a legislator from Rockland Country, "but you're on the list of guys who are going to vote for it." The alternative, warned Douglass, was to wake up one morning to find the runway of Stewart Air Force Base extended "right through your goddamn district" (other versions of the story specifically targeted the lawmaker's house). Entering into the spirit of the occasion, Rockefeller personally threatened one key committee chairman with a primary fight. More generally, he vowed a ban on "personal favors . . . signing bills and appointments. Now I don't like to take this position," he continued unconvincingly, "but I think one has to use whatever authority one has when something of major importance to the people comes before you."

A few minutes before midnight, the New York State Assembly reversed itself by the emphatic margin of 86 to 45. The next day, Rockefeller without comment approved a new pension plan allowing lawmakers and staff to retire at half pay after twenty years of public employment (no more than five of those years had to involve legislative service). Unmoved by popular outrage over this blatant trade-off, Rockefeller showed far more concern that John Lindsay would try to scuttle the UDC before it was fairly launched. He solicited Jackie Robinson's help in promoting the new agency in minority neighborhoods. He would have need of such assistance. Already Harlem residents were protesting a Rockefeller plan to construct, with minimal community input, a new state office building in their neighborhood. In the turbulent spring of 1968, 125th Street, it appeared, was as hostile to enlightened liberalism as the nearby campus of Columbia University. Increasingly, Rockefeller and the white, moneyed establishment his family personified were viewed not as benefactors, but as enemies of black self-determination.

4

O N MARCH 31, 1968, exactly ten days after Rockefeller withdrew his name from presidential consideration, Lyndon Johnson executed an even more stunning renunciation by ruling himself out of contention for another term. Rockefeller's initial response was to pretend nothing had changed. "I am a great believer in waiting and absorbing the impact of what is going on," he remarked blandly. In truth, he still nourished hopes for a draft, if only to avoid a frontal assault on his party's conservative strongholds. In their lively contemporary portrait, *"I Never Wanted to Be Vice President of Anything!,"* New York Times reporters Michael Kramer and Sam Roberts devote barely two pages to the 1968 Rockefeller campaign. One might with even greater concision summarize his third run for the presidency as everything his third run for the governorship was not.*

Unlike that textbook effort, Rockefeller's stop-and-go pursuit of the White House in 1968 was late in starting, confused in management, and thematically incoherent. Things might have been different had Rockefeller succeeded in persuading Bill Pfeiffer, his original choice, to accept the job of campaign manager. Instead, a revolving-door cast of campaign operatives exercised divided authority, with the candidate himself lurching from a low-key courtship of delegates, during which he essentially ignored Richard Nixon, to becoming Nixon's harshest critic and a self-proclaimed apostle of the New Politics following Bobby Kennedy's assassination in June 1968. Lavishly financed as always, the Rockefeller campaign offered a perfect illustration of what money—as much as $10 million, much of it spent on the first ever pre-convention television ad blitz—cannot do for a candidate with too many advisers and insufficient fire in the belly.

Where presidential politics were concerned, Nelson Rockefeller in the spring of 1968 was rusty. Lost in the political news blackout surrounding the King assassination was an announcement out of Fifty-fifth Street that both Emmet Hughes and Henry Kissinger were formally joining the Rockefeller staff. One week later, on April 11, Hughes and other key players were present as Rockefeller outlined his vision for the campaign. With state business at last out of the way, he was free to concentrate on organization, issues, and the message

---

* Coauthor Michael Kramer, then a freshly minted law school graduate, was one of many Rockefeller recruits who ventured into the field to ascertain whether the Republican nomination was winnable. His experience mirrored that of other such emissaries. "I'd go out to some small town and be told by the local Republicans of an earlier meeting attended by, say, forty people or so, and addressed by Dick Nixon." This was something Rockefeller never would have done, said Kramer. "It all went back to his sense of entitlement—that he deserved the presidency." Michael Kramer, AI.

"of confidence, creativity, and stability" that he hoped to project to the electorate. That Rockefeller should award questions of public policy priority over the grubby hunt for delegates surprised no one familiar with his previous campaigns. To newcomers such as Ted Braun, however, it came as something of a shock. "I finally came to realize that Nelson had at no time, going back to the early Sixties, late Fifties, realized the problem of delegates," Braun concluded. "He had no concept . . . of forty-nine or fifty different methods of selecting delegates to the two national conventions. When they started, how they were handled, and all the rest of it."

At one early strategy session, Rockefeller spelled out his candidacy in almost Stevensonian terms. He wanted to make four major speeches, said Nelson, addressing the economy, the plight of urban America, foreign policy in general, and Vietnam, where, he claimed, "we've outlived our usefulness." On April 18, Rockefeller appeared before the American Society of Newspaper Editors in Washington, armed with a turgid text on the urban crisis—"another Emmet Hughes peroration," John Lindsay muttered after reviewing an advance copy—that was too long and too predictable in its demand for $150 billion with which to rebuild America's cities, such funding to be raised through "the imaginative and responsible use of credit." Mindful of Republican sensitivities, Rockefeller acknowledged the painful reality that "we cannot wage our wars, educate our young, aid our needy, swell our armies, train our unskilled, rebuild our cities, cleanse our waters, and chastise our enemies—all at one frenzied moment." He balanced this concession with a spirited assault on popular complacency and the millions of his countrymen who had sought shelter "behind the senseless sign: Do Not Disturb. For them, the American dream became the American slumber."

Judging from immediate reaction, Rockefeller succeeded in putting much of his own audience to sleep. ROCKEFELLER SPEECH HEARD IN SILENCE, headlined *The Washington Post*. In-house reviews were equally scorching, Hugh Morrow declaring Rockefeller's maiden campaign address the biggest bomb since Hiroshima. One listener, at least, took heart from his Marshall Plan for the cities. On April 23, Nelson and Happy were smuggled into the White House for a private dinner with Lyndon Johnson, who strongly advised Rockefeller to abandon his coy stance and become an active candidate. "He told me he could not sleep at night if Nixon was president, and he wasn't all that sure about Hubert," claimed Nelson, who purportedly told LBJ in response that he wasn't the Rockefeller that needed convincing. "Let me talk to Happy," said Johnson, whose legendary powers of persuasion were not found wanting. (Happy herself downplayed any conversion in a 2001 interview.)

Her husband's bread-and-butter note to the president, dated April 25, speaks for itself. "The confidence implicit in your conversation with us marks, literally, a high point in my life," Rockefeller told Johnson. The next day, word was passed to the staff on Fifty-fifth Street that the decision had been made to abandon what Joe Persico called "the available but not active" posture of the previous month. On the morning of April 30, as a national television audience looked on, Rockefeller made his candidacy official. Before the day ended, he was celebrating an upset, write-in victory in the Massachusetts primary over favorite son Governor John Volpe, seen by many as a Nixon surrogate. His unexpected win brought Rockefeller thirty-four delegates out of the gate. It was also the last good news his supporters were to receive for a long time.

5

S O BEGAN A hundred-day sprint to Miami Beach, guided by an unorthodox strategy imposed upon Rockefeller by his earlier refusal to enter the primaries. "It was a non-primary campaign, against the favorite of the party," Emmet Hughes explained, "using the polls in lieu of the primaries, using the thesis that Nelson can win and Nixon cannot. There was only one flaw: while the prospect of Nelson being nominated was appalling to the Republican conservatives, it was even more appalling that he might be elected." Hughes's mordant observation suggests the futility of traveling sixty-five thousand miles and visiting forty-five states to woo a closed electorate of predominantly hostile delegates, one-third of whom had attended the 1964 convention that ratified Barry Goldwater's takeover of the party.

At the same time, it minimizes other errors of judgment, beginning with the inexplicable decision to assign significant—if variable—campaign responsibilities to Hughes himself. "That whole headquarters was such a mess," Hugh Morrow was to recall. "Emmet was chief of staff, then he was chief of substance, of speeches, then he was campaign manager—Emmet's title changed every time he talked to the guy in *The New York Times*. To tell you the [truth] . . . Emmet was drunk much of that period." During his first weeks as an official candidate, shut out of the remaining primaries, Rockefeller oscillated between college campus rallies and private sessions with delegates, the latter reminiscent of his patented town hall meetings. His failure to support Goldwater four years earlier was frequently raised, as was his more recent handling of the New York City garbage strike. More harmful than either was the image of vacillation created by his March 21 withdrawal. "In 1960 they say I dropped out too soon," Rockefeller jested. "In 1964 they said I stayed in too long. Well, this year I've done both." Audiences chuckled, but few minds were changed.

As the weeks passed, Rockefeller introduced a variety of policy initiatives, including block grants to the states in place of four hundred categorical programs wastefully operated by Uncle Sam and a first draft of federal revenue sharing. On the foreign policy front, he anticipated Richard Nixon's historic change of heart by speaking of "building bridges" to Communist China. (China had long occupied a premium spot on his list of unvisited but desirable destinations.) Students at the University of Iowa cheered his call for a one-year lottery in place of the current, much despised, military draft. Little if any of this translated into delegate support. Pining openly for the days of the smoke-filled room, Hinman reminded the candidate, "A man named Warren Harding . . . won with a front porch campaign." Rockefeller appeared to be running its modern equivalent. When bad weather scrubbed a speech at Penn State, he spent the day inside his Pittsburgh hotel, rejecting suggestions to venture outside and meet prospective voters.

Jackie Robinson took him to task for snubbing a contingent of the Poor People's Campaign en route to its Washington campgrounds. Though they were registered at the same hotel, Rockefeller passed up a chance to meet Dr. King's brother, A. D. King, and an activist priest from Milwaukee, Father James Groppi. Instead he attended a private dinner with financier and art collector Richard King Mellon. "To have visited the poor people's march," Hinman insisted, "where Dick Mellon, U.S. Steel and a bunch of conservative delegates . . . were our targets would have been madness." Robinson dissented. Rockefeller could never win, he maintained, by trying to "out Republican Nixon. . . . Governor Rockefeller has to be Governor Rockefeller. His personal approach, his personality which is infectious, must be projected."

It wasn't just the front-runner's tactics and pace that dismayed Rockefeller supporters. In his anxiety to avoid resuscitating the old label of party wrecker, Nelson was careful to mute his criticism of Nixon. Indeed, he shied away from saying anything that might make news. So devoid of substance was a Pittsburgh press conference that the local paper captioned its photograph of the candidate "Governor Rockefeller: No Direct Answers." Rockefeller strategists took heart from a CBS News Election Unit estimate awarding their candidate more than 400 of the 667 delegates needed to win in Miami Beach. Clif White, the architect of Goldwater's nomination in 1964 and now a Reagan man, swore that Nixon had no more than 550 solid first-ballot votes. With much of the former vice president's southern support believed soft, all eyes turned to Reagan. In office little more than a year, the Californian held special appeal for southern Republicans, staunch conservatives whose recent electoral gains were threatened by the third party candidacy of Alabama governor George Wallace. On a four-day swing through the region in May, Reagan did more than raise money for GOP coffers. He raised his own profile and the pulse of many as he vowed to "kick the devil" out of the North Vietnamese if they failed to engage in serious negotiations.

Conservatives, long accustomed to being subjects of ridicule, laughed heartily at Reagan's description of the New Left as the unwashed remnants of the Old Right. While retracting his earlier characterization of Rockefeller as "a divisive force" within the party, Reagan continued to insist on two things—he was not an avowed candidate, and he had no intention of being anyone's running mate. "Reagan was very careful," reflected his press secretary Lyn Nofziger. "He never wanted to make a fool of himself. He always wanted to be sure. So he always waited till the last minute to get in." If the grassroots excitement he generated was any measure of momentum, May belonged to Reagan, not Rockefeller. Primary voters in increasing numbers checked his name on ballots in Wisconsin, Nebraska, and Oregon.

The low point of the Rockefeller campaign came on the morning of May 20, when the New Yorker practically forced his way into Reagan's New Orleans hotel suite while the governor was dressing. Insisting that philosophically they were not that far apart, Rockefeller wouldn't accept Reagan's polite demurrals. When he explicitly pressed his Stop Nixon agenda, Reagan cut him off. Eight minutes after he arrived, Rockefeller was ushered out through a back door to avoid the reporters he had tipped off in advance. The stunt backfired when Reagan, angered at such exploitation, adopted a Shermanesque posture on the vice presidency, and reporters pressing Rockefeller extracted a somewhat reluctant admission that "we do not share a common position on many issues."

A week after his ill-fated meeting with Reagan, Rockefeller gave vent to his growing frustration. One couldn't make news without making waves, he told the campaign brain trust over lunch at 13 West Fifty-fourth Street. If that required a little gut fighting at the expense of the front-runner, Rockefeller had never shown excessive deference to Dick Nixon in the past; why should he begin now? Claims of superior statesmanship might carry weight with readers of *Foreign Affairs*; they were of doubtful potency among Republican convention delegates. Moreover, his electability argument needed sharpening. Rushed into print was *Votepower*, a glossy summary of Nixon's and Rockefeller's contrasting appeal to Democratic and independent voters. Organizational changes were implemented, reconsidered, and revisited. "Nelson kept changing his own leadership," said Hugh Morrow. "He stuck Bobby [Douglass] and Emmet out on the plane . . . put Malcolm in charge, then put Len Hall in charge, then put Bill Miller in charge." Henry Kissinger and Emmet Hughes continued to feud over foreign policy. George Hinman all but begged Rockefeller to dispense with the self-promoting Hughes. Al Marshall, already taxed to the limit running the state in Nelson's absence, was persuaded to "lend a hand" to the national campaign, a commitment he honored to the point of physical exhaustion.

Then, without warning, gunshots in a Los Angeles hotel kitchen brutally rewrote history.

6

ROCKEFELLER RECEIVED THE news of Bobby Kennedy's assassination at his Foxhall Road estate in Washington. Returning to New York, he was at LaGuardia Airport when Air Force One arrived carrying Kennedy's remains. Once again, he offered the services of Joe Canzeri and other Rockefeller advancemen to assist the Kennedy family and its emotionally battered staff in organizing a public wake at St. Patrick's Cathedral, followed by a rail cortege to Washington, with burial at Arlington National Cemetery beside JFK.

Campaigning was briefly suspended. In Rockefeller's case, it was also transformed. Identifying "a vast reservoir of uneasiness" in the days following Kennedy's death, Henry Kissinger urged Nelson to tap into the country's latent idealism: "The focus should be less on attempting to sway delegates directly than in gaining such widespread popular support that the delegates have to reconsider their commitments." Up to that point, Kissinger added, "the campaign has stressed that you can win. Henceforth it should emphasize why it is important for the country that you do so." On Tuesday, June 11, Rockefeller returned to the Washington Press Club, scene of his disastrous debut in mid-April. This time it was a different candidate who spoke, full of fervor, an agent of change who offered himself as the improbable heir to Kennedy's army of the young, the disaffected, and the marginalized.

The oldest of that year's major contenders repackaged himself as the staunchest foe of the status quo. Speaking of Vietnam, Rockefeller warned that the United States must never again find itself "with a commitment looking for a justification." He paid tribute to Kennedy as a champion of the New Politics, a phrase best defined by what it was not. "The men of the Old Politics do not understand change," Rockefeller told listeners still reeling from the events of the past week. "They do not comprehend the new realities of American life. They do not appreciate the significance of emerging forces. And they do not seem to care." By the time he left the Press Club, Rockefeller had done more than reboot his lagging campaign. He had moved to fill the leadership vacuum created by Robert Kennedy's death.*

Two days later he visited Los Angeles, making sure to include time for a walk through the Watts neighborhood, which still bore the scars of recent rioting. The day's highlight was an unscheduled stop at an inner-city high school a few miles from the scene of Kennedy's assassination. Here Rockefeller the teacher

---

* In the same speech, Rockefeller faulted Nixon for his harsh criticism of the Warren Court and strongly implied that his rival welcomed the support of southern segregationists. ("I have talked to our man in New Orleans, Newt Gingrich," said Rockefeller operative William Watts, "and he corroborates this report.") William Watts–Emmet Hughes, June 6, 1968, RAC.

hit his stride, bonding with youngsters whose cheers found echo in the large, friendly crowds that formed outside. Similar scenes would recur in African American enclaves in Cleveland and Wilmington and Chicago's South Side. Each day brought fresh support from Robert Kennedy's grieving ranks. Martin Luther King, Sr., endorsed Rockefeller. So did James Farmer, former head of the Congress of Racial Equality. Lieutenant General James Gavin, a World War II icon who had grown disenchanted with U.S. policy in Vietnam, was among the prominent Kennedy backers who lent his name to People for Rockefeller.

Joan Braden was another. "He came down to Washington the Monday after the funeral," Braden remembered. "I know how bad it is for you," Rockefeller told her, "but I'd like you to come to work for me." Reasoning that "as Bobby Kennedy cared, so Nelson Rockefeller cares," Braden signed on for the duration. Hardly more objective was Teddy White, the journalist-historian whose *Making of the President* books reinvented campaign reportage. White, too, was caught up in the Rockefeller surge. Having "repealed the laws of partisanship," he wrote, Nelson was generating Kennedy-like crowds with a Kennedy-like message. "The hunger for a hero was the same . . . the same young people followed Rockefeller as had followed Kennedy in throngs as he travelled; the same heavy admixture of Negroes who wanted a champion made his rallies come alive."

Rockefeller himself seemed liberated, emotionally connecting with black audiences as he replied, "That's right, man, that's right," to throaty chants of approval. His criticism of Nixon grew more pointed as he lashed out at the front-runner for going silent on Vietnam and unveiled his own blueprint for extricating U.S. troops from the Asian bog. Henry Kissinger's four-part plan, the most detailed offered by any candidate in 1968, included a military standdown and separation of warring forces, the latter to be implemented by a multinational force created for the purpose. Internationally supervised elections would precede negotiations over Vietnam's future. Nixon's dismissal of ambitious new programs to combat the urban crisis as "pie in the sky" earned Rockefeller's scorn. America's cities, he insisted, would never be saved "by men who read speeches about crime control—and say not a word about gun control." When someone in a crowd held aloft a hostile sign proclaiming, "Nixon's the One," Rockefeller sneered, "That's right, he's the one. He's the one who lost it for us in 1960."

Overnight, it seemed, he had found his rhythm and his rationale. He and Happy delighted a noonday crowd in Cincinnati with their impromptu dance to "The Sidewalks of New York." The same campaign reunited Nelson with his son Steven, then living at Pocantico and completing a doctoral dissertation program at Columbia. The day after Bobby Kennedy was shot, Nelson sat with

Steve in the Kykuit garden and described the coalition he hoped to lead, of the young and minorities and progressive business elements. Heartened by his father's commitment to end the war and address the festering inequities in American society, the younger Rockefeller agreed to join the campaign. Nelson enjoyed less success with the Republican rank and file. In Milwaukee, only three of Wisconsin's thirty delegates turned up at a Rockefeller event. The response was better in Illinois and Indiana, and even distrustful conservatives went away impressed by his vigorous defense of his New York record. Still, he made more friends than conversions.

Nixon mocked his lavish effort and huge television buys as "too much, too late." Al Marshall agreed: "We ran Nelson Rockefeller—his candidacy for the nomination—as though it were a general election . . . he was trying to get the guy on the street to vote for him, when it was not the guy on the street who was going to get him nominated in those days. Dick Nixon knew this; that's why he had us hog-tied in '68 before we ever went into it." Steve Rockefeller was not alone in questioning a strategy he found puzzling. "I sometimes wondered whether Father really wanted that nomination, or whether he just enjoyed campaigning." The escalating attacks on Nixon produced a seesaw effect in the polls. As Rockefeller's popularity rose among Democrats and independents, it declined among Republican voters. His prospects took a further hit in the first week of July, when Nixon gained well-timed endorsements from Texas senator John Tower and Massachusetts governor John Volpe, who entertained vice presidential hopes despite his embarrassing primary loss to his fellow governor.

Desperate to prevent Spiro Agnew from formally going over to the Nixon camp, the campaign had David Rockefeller call a prominent Maryland banker, reportedly a close friend and personal financial adviser to the governor. (According to John Sears, this was by no means the only attempt to reach delegates through traditionally potent financial interests.) On July 8, his sixtieth birthday, the largest campaign crowds to date welcomed Rockefeller to San Francisco. That same day, he received private assurances of a forthcoming endorsement from Colorado governor John Love. Reporters accompanying Rockefeller on a flight to St. Louis staged an airborne birthday party, with ABC's Lou Cioffi and Morton Dean of CBS standing in for the Huntley-Brinkley duo. The plane had been festooned with toilet paper; an improvised chorus rendered "Rocky's Lament" to the tune of "A Bicycle Built for Two" ("Rocky, Rocky, give us your answer true, / Is the White House really the place for you? . . ."). The festivities culminated in the presentation of an abstract painting created en masse by the fourth estate—"probably," wrote Teddy White with undisguised affection, "the first time in his life that anyone outside his immediate family had thought to give Nelson Rockefeller a birthday present simply because they liked him."

Emmet Hughes missed the party. He spent the holiday weekend indulging cloak-and-dagger fantasies by slipping off to visit the Pacific Palisades home of Ronald and Nancy Reagan. In the course of ninety minutes, the two men cut no deals, formalized no alliances. Still, Hughes heard what he had come to hear—that Reagan's ambitions went far beyond favorite son status; and that he planned on contesting the nomination to the last delegate. No birthday gift could have pleased Rockefeller more. Until now, propelled on a wave of inexhaustible energy, Rockefeller had always appeared younger than his age. Now, it seemed, the years had abruptly caught up with him, notching deep lines in his pale Aldrich complexion. Rockefeller told Ken Riland he couldn't maintain the grueling pace. Vocal cords worn ragged by nineteen-hour campaign days, Nelson refused to leave his suite in Atlanta's Regency-Hyatt Hotel to greet some Georgia Tech students in an old roadster who had come to give him a ride. Eventually he was lured downstairs by youthful cries of "We want Rocky!" rising twenty-seven stories from the hotel driveway.

Goaded by the protective Riland, Rockefeller watched what he ate on the campaign trail, losing ten pounds during one two-week stretch. If he was ever tempted to transgress his strict Baptist upbringing, there was the cautionary example of his brother Winthrop to enforce restraint. In mid-June 1968, Nelson and his siblings staged a long-distance intervention with Win, whose alcoholism threatened his second marriage as well as his reelection prospects. "We write you as a brother and friend because we love you and need you," they told him, "as do the people of Arkansas." Nelson found such weakness baffling. "Joe, why do people drink?" he one day inquired of Joe Canzeri. His own intake remained limited to Dubonnet and an occasional glass of wine.

Rockefeller's continuing inability to remember names was hardly evidence of diminished capacity. "He was always saying to me, 'Hiya, fella,'" recalled Al Marshall, "and I've been with him for years." In truth, Rockefeller at sixty resembled the aging athlete, who may have lost a little off his game, but whose competitive instincts remain razor sharp. At a July 1968 governors' conference, he and New Mexico's David Cargo accepted an invitation to sit at George Wallace's table for lunch. As they took their seats, Wallace produced from his pocket an enormous black cigar, which he promptly lit and began to puff on. Too polite to ask Wallace to put it out, Nelson looked over his shoulder and spotted a black aide, part of his traveling party. He motioned for the man to join them. Wallace said nothing, but he let the noxious cloud of cigar smoke speak for him.

At length dessert was served. Wallace extracted the still glowing stump of tobacco from his pouty mouth, then ground it into the custard just placed before him.

"You know, George," said Rockefeller, "there are many things in this life that can be forgiven, but that isn't one of them."

7

MIAMI BEACH IN August 1968 was a ten-mile strip of sand dotted with architectural follies, sun-washed piles of pink and pastel stucco and concrete and glass, their perfumed swimming pools heated to eighty-five degrees, and row on row of reclining chairs, backs turned to the untidy Atlantic. Tenuously linked to the mainland by half a dozen causeways, Miami Beach had always been a place of escape from urban anxieties on the other side of Biscayne Bay. Over the years, the sultry climate and relative isolation of these barrier islands had attracted northern snowbirds and Jewish retirees, many fleeing New York's punishing winters and equally harsh tax climate. A recent influx of Cuban refugees had injected their culture, language, and anti-Castro politics into this saltwater Vegas, creating an incongruous setting for the twenty-ninth convention of the Republican Party, neatly summed up by Joe Persico as "a Protestant church bazaar magnified one thousand times."

Decidedly more monochromatic than their art deco surroundings, the typical Republican delegate was white—of 1,333 names on the convention roll call, 26 were African American—Protestant, a Mason or Elk, Legionnaire, or Chamber of Commerce representative. Columnist Jimmy Breslin, returning from the convention floor to the Americana Hotel housing the New York delegation, expressed relief to be back among "real people." Frustrated in his attempts to connect with so many pleasant, wholesome, well-meaning middle Americans, Breslin finally gave up. What he really wanted to do, he said, was to holler at his complacent countrymen, "Haven't you dumb ____ ever read a newspaper?" It was to the fourteenth floor of the Americana that Nelson brought his extended family following a beachfront rally on Saturday, August 3. After installing Happy and his brothers Laurance and David in their quarters, he joined the cavalcade of candidates and their representatives making forays to state delegations up and down Collins Avenue. That night, Happy asked a radio reporter how things were going. "Well," she was told, "you might have a chance on the third ballot or the fourth or the fifth."

In fact, the air had gone out of the Rockefeller balloon several days before the convention, with release of a Gallup poll that showed Nixon outperforming Rockefeller against both Hubert Humphrey and Eugene McCarthy. It hardly mattered that a subsequent Harris poll reinstated Nelson's electoral advantage— the "polls as primary" strategy was effectively undone. "I knew a hell of a lot about counting delegates," recalled Jim Cannon, then national political correspondent for *Newsweek*. To Cannon it appeared no one in the Rockefeller operation besides Len Hall had a grip on numerical reality. George Hinman insisted that Rockefeller had hidden reserves of strength in the industrial Midwest. But to exploit them on subsequent ballots, they would need to stop Nixon on the first. To do that, Ray Shafer had to deliver at least fifty of his sixty-four Pennsylvanians, and a sympathetic Senator Clifford Case of New Jersey must hold intact his state's forty votes.

Equally important, Ronald Reagan must find the key to unlock Nixon's southern strongholds. This meant besting South Carolina senator Strom Thurmond, the Dixiecrat turned Goldwater Republican to whom Nixon had promised a sympathetic hearing on future Supreme Court nominations, court-ordered busing for racial balance, and anything pertaining to national defense. Who better to vouch for Nixon's political character among wavering southern-ers? "Strom would take delegates on board one of those delightful boats docked off Miami," says Howard "Bo" Callaway, a former Georgia congressman who was Nixon's southern coordinator. "He'd make his pitch one-on-one." Aided by Texas senator John Tower, Thurmond personally doused Reagan fires in sev-eral restive delegations, none more critical than Florida, where the unit rule promised all thirty-four votes to whoever could command a majority. Governor Claude Kirk, visions of the vice presidency dancing in his head, had improba-bly endorsed Rockefeller, even as Clif White amassed within the same delega-tion a dozen votes for Reagan. And there the anti-Nixon coalition was halted, close enough to taste victory, the convention in miniature.

Throughout the week, Rockefeller seemed impervious to the lengthening odds on his candidacy. Hugh Morrow labored on an acceptance speech. George Hinman orchestrated a vice presidential search (leading candidate: Charles Percy). "During the last days of the campaign, there was always to be some grand play by which the Governor would put it altogether," Harry Al-bright remembered. Night after night, amid the insufferable heat of south Flor-ida in August, shadowy agents promoted various game changers certain to halt the Nixon juggernaut. At midday on Wednesday, August 7, scarcely ten hours before the convention balloting was to start, Ken Riland left a meeting with New Jersey's tottering delegation to take a call from Bob Douglass. "He had found confirmation of Nixon's psychiatric treatments, and I guessed the psychi-atrist," Riland noted in his diary, "but I refused to suggest any use of the knowl-edge at this point and stated as a physician I could have no part of this." The information went unused.

That evening Nelson gathered his family around the dinner table. Later they assembled before a pair of television sets to watch Pennsylvania governor Ray Shafer place Nelson's name in nomination. Rocky's demonstration, led by a colorful contingent of Philadelphia mummers, was pronounced best of show by theater critic Clive Barnes. Unfortunately, a massive balloon drop degenerated into a veritable turkey shoot, the slaughter led by suburban Republican matrons waging battle with their high heels. Elia Kazan, reporting on the convention for *New York* magazine, unearthed John Bricker, the octogenarian Ohioan who had run unhappily for vice president with Tom Dewey in 1944. Unmoved by the manufactured enthusiasm of the moment, Bricker was asked whether anything had transpired in the convention's first three days to change anyone's vote.

"Not a single vote," said Bricker. "He didn't get a damned thing for his six million dollars."

Bricker's estimate was validated early on the roll call that began just after ten o'clock. The suspense in Rockefeller's suite lasted no longer than the orange *Rocky* balloons littering the convention floor, as the Rockefeller-Reagan alliance failed to keep Florida's thirty-four votes out of the Nixon column. A few minutes later New Jersey broke wide open, with eighteen delegates abandoning Senator Case. Pennsylvania salted the wound, giving Nixon twenty-two of its sixty-four votes. "What's the use?" asked a shell-shocked Jimmy Breslin of no one in particular. "Goldwater . . . now this." At the Americana, Happy Rockefeller put a protective arm around her husband. Several miles away, rioting erupted in North Miami. Looters smashed storefronts on Collins Avenue. Four deaths were recorded that night—a bloodied snapshot of Rockefeller's urban crisis or, alternatively, of Nixon's "law and order" mantra.

Wisconsin put Nixon over the top. Rockefeller called his rival to offer congratulations. At a late night press conference, a red-eyed Happy at his side, Rockefeller observed that at least little Nelson would be pleased. "Now, Daddy," he quoted his young son, "we can play more together." Invited to explain his repeated failures as a presidential candidate, Nelson answered the question with one of his own.

"Have you ever been to a Republican national convention?"

Stepping down from the podium, Rockefeller received a spontaneous round of applause from reporters. Speculation turned to the identity of Nixon's running mate.* The eventual announcement of Spiro Agnew's selection elicited gasps of disbelief in the Rockefeller suite. "It's just like Dick," Nelson remarked. "He always blows the big one." Happy Rockefeller, for whom Lindsay's veto by southern conservatives led by Strom Thurmond was the week's final indignity, wept openly. Around the hotel swimming pool, stunned Rockefeller staffers indulged in gallows humor. "It's God's will. He wants Humphrey to be President." "We know Nixon was a sore loser. Now we know he's a sore winner."

At this most inopportune moment, Ken Riland confided that he had been asked by Nixon to give him an osteopathic treatment that afternoon. "He must

---

* Gene Spagnoli of the *New York Daily News*, on encountering Pat Buchanan, put in a plug for Mark Hatfield or, better yet, John Lindsay. Out of the question, replied Buchanan. "If we had Nixon and Lindsay, it would be like following *Death of a Salesman* with *Guys and Dolls*." Gene Spagnoli, HMI, 22.

have meant you when he said he'd like to have several of the staff," Rockefeller replied. "You're not going, are you?" Riland said it depended on when they were leaving town. They would be gone by noon, said Nelson. An argument ensued, with Riland insisting that Rockefeller must act the part of good loser. "That's your corporate mind working," Nelson snapped. To hell with that, Riland persisted. It was common decency and nothing more than the public would expect of a Rockefeller. Eventually a call was placed to Congressman Gerald Ford, the convention's permanent chairman, and a brief appearance was arranged to coincide with the start of the evening's televised session.

Recovering his composure, Nelson appeared his old self the next day. Together with Happy, he skipped a limousine for the ride to the airport, making the trip in a staff bus instead. On the flight north, stewardesses made no effort to hold back tears as Rockefeller circulated up and down the aisle, apologizing for letting down supporters and taking full responsibility for the loss. At the Westchester airport emotions were raw as the candidate parted company with his cadre of Secret Service agents. The next day the Rockefellers flew to Maine for a delayed vacation at Seal Harbor. From there Nelson sent Ann Whitman a long letter in his own hand, in which he emotionally thanked Ann for all she had contributed to his now concluded political career.

"Lord, he must really feel sorry for himself," mused a colleague to whom she showed the letter. "He doesn't feel sorry for himself," Whitman said. "He feels sorry for the nation."

8

ANOTHER INTENSELY PERSONAL letter, this one directed to Nelson, never reached him. On the morning of Tuesday, August 13, a drunk driver in New Suffolk, Long Island, struck and killed René d'Harnoncourt, the recently retired director of MoMA, as he walked to the post office to send a missive of his own to his longtime friend and collaborator. Devastated by the news, Rockefeller showed more emotion over the loss of d'Harnoncourt than he had over his failure to become president. Two days later he fought back tears while delivering a graveside eulogy.* The distraction of grief may account for his tardy response to a political feeler from former Massachusetts governor Endicott Peabody, a summer neighbor and staunch Democrat, who wished to draft Rockefeller for vice president on Hubert Humphrey's ticket. Peabody wasn't acting alone; the same proposal was communicated by Teddy White to Rockefeller

---

* He also renewed his financial support, $6,000 a year, to the d'Harnoncourt family.

press secretary Les Slote and to Rockefeller personally by Humphrey friend and agribusiness tycoon Dwayne Andreas.

Nelson let a week pass without acknowledging Peabody's appeal. On August 20, just six days before the opening of the Democratic convention in Chicago, Peabody renewed his pitch for a grand alliance of Rockefeller, Romney, Kennedy, McCarthy, and Humphrey supporters to forestall the triumph of "a leadership outright opposed to your policies." Humphrey himself called to make the case for a coalition government. Was Rockefeller tempted? He gave no sign of it to Humphrey, pleading age and lifelong loyalties to the party that had rejected him three times. Left unsaid was his temperamental aversion to the backup job first offered him eight years before by the man Humphrey now hoped to keep out of the White House.

This wasn't the only decision gnawing at him. Bobby Kennedy's death had created a senatorial vacancy to fill and a choice Rockefeller had postponed for as long as possible. Had he prevailed in Miami, he'd intended to offer the Kennedy seat to Richard Nixon. With that option foreclosed, Rockefeller was free to pick a Kennedyesque replacement—Kennedy aides Roswell Gilpatric and Burke Marshall suggested each other—or a nonpolitical Wise Man such as John Gardner, former cabinet officer and founder of the citizens' lobby Common Cause. Emmet Hughes urged him to appoint Coretta Scott King. Alternatively, he could go with the most obvious candidate, John Lindsay. But first Lindsay would have to ask him for the job. The mayor confided to journalist Nat Hentoff his version of a discussion at Nelson's apartment less than two weeks after the Kennedy assassination.

"Tell me why I should appoint you to the Senate, John."

"Nelson, you're starting wrong. You're inviting job applications. I don't do business that way. The stakes are high; we're grown up, we're not children. Are you making me an offer?"

"I've told you that you're my first choice."

"Then that's an offer."

"No it isn't."

"Okay," said Lindsay. "That's the end of the conversation on this subject. We'll tell the press no offer has been made."*

Another account of what happened is supplied by Jack McGrath, whose wife worked in Lindsay's city hall, giving him access to both sides of the story. As McGrath tells it, Rockefeller called Harry O'Donnell, himself a neutral by dint

---

* Lindsay later told Hentoff, "Sure, I'd turn it down." Rockefeller feared that he might accept, according to the mayor. "He's afraid there might be a riot while he's running for President and he wants me in the city to cool it for him." Nat Hentoff, *A Political Life: The Education of John V. Lindsay* (New York: Alfred A. Knopf, 1969), 209–12.

of his having filled the job of press secretary for both men. "And he said something to the effect, 'Would you ask John Lindsay if he wants to be appointed senator from New York.'" The request was grounded not in personal or political affection, but in a cold-blooded assessment of senatorial seniority, something Ken Keating had surrendered in 1964 and an assassin stole with Robert Kennedy's death four years later. "If Lindsay went down there, he'd have the city and he'd carry upstate Republicans and he'd get seniority," Rockefeller contended. So he communicated his interest through O'Donnell—"he didn't say he was absolutely going to appoint him; he said, 'Ask him if he wants to be appointed. . . . And if he wants it, have him call me.'"

"If he wants to appoint me senator from New York," Lindsay replied, "tell him to call me."

In the end, neither man trusted the other to risk possible humiliation. On September 9, Rockefeller surprised New Yorkers with his choice of Charles Goodell, a forty-two-year-old Republican congressman from Jamestown, in the far southwestern corner of the Empire State. His selection riled Kennedy supporters, few of whom could imagine the ideological transformation that was to make Goodell a vocal critic of the Vietnam War, disowned by many in his own party. At the time of his appointment, Goodell's cautious style and mildly conservative record in the House offered the strongest evidence yet of Rockefeller's accommodation to the new order within the post–Miami Beach GOP. That fall, he made a vigorous campaign for the Nixon-Agnew ticket in New York, while drawing the line at any alliance with the state's Conservative Party. On October 28, the former rivals appeared together on the steps of the Capitol in Albany. A far cry from the awkward Rockefeller-Goldwater encounter four years earlier, Nixon took the occasion to praise his longtime adversary, saying that "no man in the country has worked harder for this ticket than Governor Rockefeller." For a while, Nixon appeared competitive among New Yorkers, but by Election Day enough antiwar Democrats had returned to the fold to give Humphrey a statewide victory by almost four hundred thousand votes. Bowing to the inevitable, that night Rockefeller humbled himself sufficiently to pay a congratulatory visit to Nixon at his Pierre Hotel headquarters, only to be told that the president-elect was seeing no one.

The cold shoulder treatment foreshadowed—how many?—years of awkward deference to his successful rival, a disquieting prospect made worse by nagging questions of what if. Had Rockefeller not dashed the hopes of his supporters in March; had he personally communicated his decision in advance to Spiro Agnew; had he directed his subsequent campaign fire at the Johnson administration rather than Nixon; had he devised a strategy for winning the nomination less dependent on the vagaries of public opinion polling and Reagan's southern appeal; had Reagan been more open about his ambitions, throwing his hat into the ring as soon as Johnson withdrew and the Democratic alternative came down to the war-scarred Humphrey and a polarizing Bobby Kennedy; had Clif White persuaded even a handful of additional southern delegates to follow their hearts—Bo Callaway, for one, is convinced that Mississippi would have migrated to Reagan on the second ballot, followed by a stampede of Nixon turncoats. It is harder to envision an outcome in which the Republican Party, four years after nominating Barry Goldwater, would turn to Nelson Rockefeller. "He was always in the wrong church," concluded Al Marshall. "He was always in the wrong pew."

By mid-November, speculation was rampant over Nelson's place in the new administration. Reporter Gene Spagnoli brashly reminded the president-elect that Rockefeller would make a good secretary of state. "Well now, don't go picking my Cabinet for me, Gene," replied Nixon. Many in the press expected Nelson to be named secretary of defense, a scenario complicated by the possibility of David Rockefeller becoming secretary of the Treasury. Nixon speechwriter William Safire acknowledged as much in an Air Force One conversation with his boss a few days after the election. On second thought, Safire corrected himself. "No, you can't have two Rockefellers in the Cabinet."

"Is there any law that says you have to have one?" Nixon replied.

On Friday, November 22, Rockefeller convened his advisers to discuss what his attitude should be toward a possible Nixon job offer. Henry Kissinger was making the case for Nelson as secretary of defense when he was called away by a phone call from Nixon appointments secretary Dwight Chapin. Could Kissinger meet with the president-elect the following Monday? In Nixon's Hotel Pierre suite, Kissinger told Nixon that he would be willing to serve on Rockefeller's staff should Nelson be invited into the cabinet. "In retrospect," Kissinger confessed in his memoirs, "it is clear that my comment killed whatever minimal prospects existed for a Rockefeller appointment." Confirmation of this came the next day in a call from Rockefeller himself, recounting his own session with the president-elect, at which it had been made clear that Rockefeller could render greater service to his country by remaining as governor of New York than joining the Nixon cabinet. On November 29, strongly encouraged by his patron, Kissinger accepted Nixon's offer to become his national security adviser.

As the sun set on the Great Society, Nelson and Happy accepted an invitation from the Johnsons to spend their last Camp David weekend together. On January 12, the men watched the televised Super Bowl between New York's upstart Jets and the heavily favored Baltimore Colts. When Jets quarterback Joe Namath led his team to an upset victory, Rockefeller had the satisfaction of sending a postgame telegram to Baltimore fan Spiro Agnew.

"Dear Ted," he wired the vice president elect. "You can't win them all."

Twenty-Two
LEANING RIGHT

Yes, I'm a liberal. Of course I'm a liberal. Wasn't that the reason for all my troubles with the Republican Party?

—NELSON A. ROCKEFELLER, July 1969

1

"OURS IS A turbulent world that evidences no return to normalcy; we need a steady and decisive hand to guide us. You can do the job superbly." So Nelson Rockefeller addressed himself to Richard Nixon in a handwritten message delivered to the new president on his inauguration day, January 20, 1969. The same occasion marked the third opportunity in eight years for Rockefeller to ride in a parade he might have led. "Do you realize there have been four Presidents since I've been Governor?" he asked onlookers with a wink. "I wear 'em out fast." On his first full day in the Oval Office, Nixon met with Galo Plaza, secretary-general of the Organization of American States, described by one Rockefeller associate as "an old tomcatting partner of his in South America." The new president told his visitor that he was thinking of dispatching a fact-finding mission to Latin America—hardly surprising given Nixon's campaign criticism of a "floundering" Alliance for Progress. Launched with considerable fanfare in the first months of John Kennedy's presidency, the Alliance had raised hopes before living standards. Eight years after its formation, less than half the children of Central and South America attended school. Fueled by the world's highest birth rate, population growth in the region outstripped decent housing and job opportunities. Annual income ranged from $950 in Venezuela to $65 in Haiti.

During the same period, $6 billion in U.S. assistance, most in the form of interest-bearing loans, had done little to advance the cause of regional democracy. The most immediate flash point was Peru, where a leftist junta in October 1968 had nationalized, without compensation, the American-owned International Petroleum Company, a subsidiary of Standard Oil of New Jersey. The same nation, insisting that its sovereignty extended two hundred miles into the

Pacific, did not hesitate to seize and/or levy fines on U.S. tuna boats. Similar provocations came from neighboring Ecuador and its fiercely anti-American leader ("Give me a balcony and I will become president"), José María Velasco Ibarra. Latin Americans resented U.S. influence even as they criticized Yankee neglect. Weary of being studied by outside experts, Plaza told Nixon, they would respond more favorably to a personal emissary, someone like Nelson Rockefeller, a friend and advocate of Latin interests for thirty years. Nixon placed a telephone call to Rockefeller on the spot, which is more or less where the presidential invitation placed Nelson.

Neither man entertained illusions about the other. "Nixon thought of Rockefeller as a selfish amateur who would wreck what he could not control," Henry Kissinger was to write, "a representative of the Establishment that had treated him with condescension throughout his public life. Rockefeller considered Nixon an opportunist without the vision and idealism needed to shape the destiny of our nation." Rockefeller offered a more nuanced assessment of his longtime adversary in an interview embargoed until long after both men were dead. "Nixon's basic problem was that he had no roots," he reflected, his "wonderful" mother failing to compensate for a "disaster" of a father. A hardscrabble youth had deprived Nixon of any sense of security, "except in his own astuteness or cunning." The result was a man "who lived by his wits, a barker in the circus." Clever but introverted, untrusting, and defensive, "life to him was constant scheming and planning and outwitting rather than being a leader and pulling people together."

All this, needless to say, was for private consumption. The successful politician never permits antipathy toward a rival to cloud his judgment or block the path of personal advancement. By 1969, it was manifestly in Nelson's interest to bury the past. Not everyone around Rockefeller was so inclined. Shortly after Nixon's election, press secretary Les Slote was summoned to the governor's office. "Les," said Rockefeller, "I just got a call from the chairman of the Republican National Committee. He says you've been bad-mouthing the president-elect." Slote conceded as much. He picks up the story: "He said, 'Well, okay.' And I left. I realized my days were finished with Rockefeller because I was now becoming an embarrassment to him and he still felt he had a chance someday of becoming president." That afternoon, Slote walked a few blocks to the RCA Building, where he accepted a London job offer from David Sarnoff.

His formal departure at the end of January 1969 relieved Rockefeller of a significant irritant in his developing relationship with the new administration in Washington. Gone, too, were the red phones installed in every gubernatorial office as a hotline to the Johnson White House, which Rockefeller suspected was an eavesdropping device enabling LBJ to monitor his conversations, to move to another room. Nixon found other means to communicate with his former adversary. Messages were channeled through third parties such as John Mitchell, the onetime bond lawyer whom Nixon made attorney general; and Ken Riland, the man with the magic hands, who accompanied Nixon on his first European trip and would be at his side in both China and the Soviet Union. "Nixon said to me one day, 'you are going to see Nelson this weekend,'" Riland recalled. "I said yes. He said, 'this is a very important situation; I need Nelson's opinion on it.' Nixon would never ask anybody to do anything, he'd always use an intermediate . . . for fear of being turned down."

Rockefeller worked hard to gain the new president's confidence. Rare was the televised Nixon address that didn't elicit fulsome praise from Albany, often in late night conversations initiated by the president, who had once said of himself and Rockefeller that "no party is big enough to hold us both." Setting aside the dovish stance he had adopted in the previous year's campaign, Nelson became a vocal supporter of the president's policies in Southeast Asia. He lobbied Republican senators in Washington for passage of Nixon's antiballistic missile program. At the same time, Rockefeller muted his criticism of Nixon's Family Assistance Plan, a welfare reform initiative that would federalize benefits while shortchanging traditionally generous states like New York.

Nixon reciprocated by appointing several New Yorkers to significant places in his administration. James Allen, Jr., the state's well-regarded commissioner of education, was put in charge of federal education policy. Nancy Hanks was named to oversee the National Endowment for the Arts, whose budget under Nixon nearly doubled. Rockefeller himself received a coveted spot on the President's Foreign Intelligence Advisory Board. Bestowing the ultimate compliment on his chief party rival, Nixon declared that there were only three men in America who understood the use of power. "I do. John Connally does. And I guess Nelson does." At a Brothers Meeting that fall held in Nelson's Fifth Avenue apartment, the fledgling administration in Washington was a chief topic of conversation. Afterward, John 3rd wrote of his younger brother, "He seems to feel quite close to the President and is trying to support him as he can."

The proposed Latin American mission should be seen in this light. Properly handled, it might establish Rockefeller as a potential secretary of state, while earning him Nixon's gratitude and, with it, valuable chits for dealing with fiscal problems on the home front. Much would be made of Rockefeller's rightward shift during his final years in office, a repositioning widely attributed to unrealized White House aspirations. Though undoubtedly a factor, his presidential ambitions were just one element in a complex reassessment of government's capacity to address human needs while sustaining the vigorous private economy that enabled states such as New York to pay for their progressive traditions.

As early as December 1967, Rockefeller had publicly argued the need "to strike a balance between what is desirable and what is do-able, what we would like to have and what we can afford." Now, a year later, with the decade-long economic expansion showing signs of exhaustion, New Yorkers confronted a financial reckoning. Mandated increases in spending, most earmarked for local governments and school districts, added more than $1 billion to the previous year's budget. Rockefeller's response was to submit a phantom budget from which he subtracted a theoretical 5 percent across the board, leaving it to Albany lawmakers to specify actual cuts (or, alternatively, enact additional taxes).

Employing language not heard for ten years or more, he said that his proposed spending blueprint "defines the limits of our own capabilities." In the resentful words of Democratic assembly leader Stanley Steingut, High Tax Rock had morphed overnight into Skinflint Rocky. What the maladroit Steingut meant as an insult contributed instead to the rebranding of Rockefeller as a budgetary hawk (admittedly a relative term). Meanwhile, conservative activists dubbing themselves the Syracuse Tea Party innundated the governor's office with three thousand teabags symbolic of popular opposition to a proposed sales tax increase.

Though little noticed at the time, Rockefeller had neatly staked out the middle ground, framing the spending debate in anticipation of his campaign for a fourth term in 1970. In truth he was playing an even bigger game, laying the groundwork for potentially historic changes in the relationship between Washington and the states—yet another compelling reason, where the Nixon White House was concerned, to let bygones be bygones. That his friendship might carry a price was spelled out in an appearance before the New York State Bar Association at the end of January 1969. Claiming that for every dollar New York sent Washington, it got five cents in return, Rockefeller called for a substantial boost in federal aid to education and a nationwide standard for welfare benefits to alleviate the disproportionate burdens carried by New York City and the state. "I don't like you," one audience member told Rockefeller afterward, "but that was a great speech."

Two weeks later, Rockefeller appeared before Nixon and his Urban Affairs Council to press the case for a complete federal assumption of welfare costs. Claiming a prior commitment with the National Security Council, the president begged off on a Rockefeller slide show promoting block grants to the states, the federalization of welfare, and a system of national health insurance to take the financial pressure off the ballooning Medicaid program. Even as Uncle Sam collected two-thirds of all taxes, said Rockefeller, federal spending on "human needs" trailed that of underfunded state and local governments. By retaining LBJ's 10 percent income tax surcharge, originally enacted to help pay for the Vietnam War, Washington could begin to redress the "serious imbalance" in federal–

state relations. This was the opening salvo in a three-year drive to win Nixon over to federal revenue sharing, a conservative idea with liberal implications.

On February 17, Rockefeller returned to the Oval Office to be formally invested as the president's Latin American emissary. Jim Cannon recalled, "Nixon himself got me aside, and he said . . . 'I want to find those sons of bitches who are ambassadors down there against us.'" Presidents never change, Rockefeller observed to Cannon as they were driven through the southwest gate of the White House. "The only way you can deal with them is to pick no more than two or three things you really want to get them to do, and then you can concentrate on those few things, and don't give up."

2

A S PUNDITS DEBATED the sincerity of his conversion from big spender to penny-pincher, Rockefeller denied that he was getting out front of a conservative parade before it passed him by. "I'm not adopting an ideology," he said, bristling. "I'm taking a pragmatic position out of necessity to preserve the well-being of the state and its growth." Any rise in taxes beyond what he was proposing would weaken New York's competitive position. At a series of town meetings, Rockefeller hoped to defuse some of the anger generated by his latest budget. At one event, an intense young man, identifying himself as a member of the Conservative Party, praised his like-minded brethren whose lonely vigil on behalf of the taxpayer had forced Rockefeller to adopt their platform.

"Yours was an excellent presentation in terms of the problems of the taxpayers," Nelson told the earnest youth. "I am sure only the lack of time kept you from expressing the Conservative party's concern for those in poverty who need good healthcare and a good education, because when they get all these and when they make money—they can join the Conservative party."

Such retorts could not obscure Rockefeller's own shift to the right. When New York City's welfare rolls, having grown more in the last two years than over the previous decade, topped one million for the first time, Rockefeller asked HEW and his own Department of Social Services to investigate. Campus unrest, crystallized in highly publicized student takeovers at Columbia and Cornell universities, sparked Rockefeller legislation to curb possession of campus firearms, increase penalties for criminal trespass, and require every college and university to adopt procedures for the "maintenance of public order." Rockefeller also urged legislators to strengthen existing laws against hard-core pornography and extend jail time for prostitution.

None of this meant he'd lost his taste for government activism. The year 1969 saw passage of New York's first minimum wage for farmworkers; expanded day care facilities for working mothers; and Food on the Table, a new initiative combining federal food stamps with surplus commodities to improve the diets of 1.5 million New Yorkers receiving welfare benefits. In place of the state's 1830 statute outlawing abortion except when a pregnancy endangered the life of a mother, Rockefeller would legalize the procedure in cases of rape, incest, and severe impairment to a woman's physical or mental health. Involving himself in negotiations for an affirmative action agreement with the Buffalo Building Trades Council, he endorsed a moratorium on construction work until the adoption of an acceptable program to train and hire minority workers. Elsewhere, Ed Logue's UDC announced agreements with eight cities to build seventeen thousand new housing units, one-fourth of them as part of a massive redevelopment of New York City's Welfare Island, rechristened Roosevelt Island in recognition of FDR. Even Rockefeller's anticrime agenda had a progressive tint, at least where guns were concerned. One new statute he promoted would increase punishment for anyone using a firearm in the course of a robbery or burglary.

After ten years in office, Rockefeller was reverting to the ideological shape-shifting of his first term. He had always been a pragmatist, an outlook now reflected in a budget compromise that replaced his original across-the-board cuts with more selective reductions favored by legislators. To secure his penny sales tax increase, Rockefeller agreed to roll back overall spending by $60 million. Even then, however, he might have fallen short of a majority in the closely divided assembly, were it not for the timely assistance of two Democratic members. Disowned by their party, one of the apostate Democrats, Charles F. Stockmeister of Rochester, received a part-time gubernatorial appointment to the Civil Service Commission worth $27,500 a year.

"It's a good example of Rockefeller's high-handedness," one Democrat complained. "It isn't that he's corrupt. He's just so used to authority, so convinced of his superior view of the public good, that he thinks his methods are fair game." Rockefeller ignored the criticism. Questioned on whether the Stockmeister appointment was in fact a reward for his sales tax vote, the governor smiled broadly. "Well, it didn't hurt."

3

THE ANNOUNCEMENT OF his Latin American mission drew largely positive reviews, Venezuela's *El Nacional* calling it "a shrewd move" and the *Christian Science Monitor* concluding that it "could well prove to be just the right step to get the new administration's relations with Latin America off to a good start." Rockefeller described the forthcoming mission—actually four separate journeys scheduled around his gubernatorial responsibilities—as a listening tour, a chance to solicit the views of leaders in twenty-three nations. He wouldn't lack for assistance. Confirming Bill Rogers's worst fears, Rockefeller assembled a traveling think tank of three dozen experts, their diverse talents and multiplication of force compensating for a whirlwind itinerary that allowed as little as two hours in a country. As Nelson sat down with heads of state and other ranking officials, additional specialists fanned out to interview economic planners, government ministries, church-based groups, culture mavens, academics, private businesses, and health care providers. Mission statisticians calculated that by the time they were through, Rockefeller and his corps of experts met with three thousand key players in the region.*

The result was a Quantico retreat in overdrive, a Rockefeller report squeezed into ten weeks. The breakneck pace came in for criticism, as did the legitimacy of many leaders to whom Rockefeller professed such eagerness to listen. On May 11, he embarked on the first leg of his journey, a week-long foray into Mexico and six Central American nations. En route to Mexico City, he stopped to visit with Nixon at his Key Biscayne retreat. Old habits die hard: during the first part of their meeting, Nelson addressed his host as Dick, before slipping into the more deferential "Mr. President." Much of their conversation revolved around domestic politics, in particular the difficulties each man had experienced at the hands of John Lindsay and Jacob Javits. Nixon gave his Latin American envoy considerable latitude, asking only that he refrain from making specific commitments and that he stress the administration's preference for private investment over taxpayer-funded assistance programs, a formula neatly encapsulated by Nixon as trade, not aid. Afterward, Rockefeller in private praised the president for sincerely wanting change. Nixon, he said, was "a man who did what he said he would do."

Rockefeller's visit to Mexico went off without incident. On May 13, he met with Guatemalan president Julio César Méndez Montenegro at his heavily guarded country house. Advised by the Secret Service against overnighting in the Guatemalan capital, the Rockefeller party spent just five hours there before embarking on the short flight to neighboring El Salvador. Student protests didn't interfere with a scheduled reception and lunch at the presidential palace in San Salvador or that evening's reciprocal entertainment hosted by Nelson at his hotel. The first signs of serious trouble appeared in Tegucigalpa, Honduras. Rockefeller was inside the Moorish fantasy of a presidential residence when a nearby demonstration turned violent. Appearing on the front steps, he was ap-

---

* Special advisers, advancemen, speechwriters, and general staff brought the total retinue to nearly eighty. By one estimate, the enterprise cost Rockefeller $750,000.

proached by Hugh Morrow, who conveyed the news that a student had been shot and killed by security forces. "Thank you very much," said Nelson, before plunging into the crowd to shake hands, as cops cursed his display of machismo geared to the Latin psychology. "I'm trying to get understanding going both ways," he explained later.

This was a tall order. That evening, a well-lubricated stenotypist with the mission hurled Coca-Cola bottles from his hotel window at some Honduran protesters burning an American flag. A potential riot was only narrowly averted. "So they burned the flag," said Rockefeller on learning of the incident. "So what?" He sent flowers and a message of sympathy to the parents of the dead student. On May 16, the Rockefeller mission left Honduras for Nicaragua, where student voices were again raised in protest, this time against both the American visitor and the regime of Anastasio Somoza that Rockefeller by his presence helped to legitimize. Riding in the presidential limousine, Rockefeller asked that its windows be rolled down. "You don't understand," the dictator told his guest. In his country, one did not travel with the windows open. "That's how we travel in mine," replied Nelson. Things proceeded more smoothly in Costa Rica and Panama. Rejecting strongly worded counsel from U.S. ambassador Chuck Adair to avoid the sensitive topic of the Panama Canal, Rockefeller likewise dismissed objections from his security agents, who feared the consequences if he took to the skies in the helicopter of strongman Omar Torrijos.

The second leg of his mission, launched on May 27, entailed more tangible risks. Though Colombia's government mobilized a security force of twenty thousand to keep order in Bogatá and other cities, it couldn't prevent student clashes with the police and army that left one dead and two hundred injured. An honorary degree ceremony had to be canceled. "We ought to call the whole thing 'Sneaking Down to Rio,'" griped one member of Rockefeller's advisory group. "It's so humiliating to have to come and go like thieves." On landing in the Ecuadorian capital of Quito, Rockefeller acknowledged the challenge before him. "I bring no new programs, no easy remedies or simple slogans," he told his official greeters. "Let us talk frankly about what is bad and what is good, of hard realities, not only of pleasant things." In the event, the talks had to be moved from the presidential palace to the visitor's hotel—in whose garden a bomb was uncovered and which he reached only after being driven through back streets, fifty army rangers in combat gear surrounding his car and a protective helicopter hovering overhead. Having set fire to the library of the United States–Ecuadorian cultural center, student militants rejected a Rockefeller offer to meet and discuss their grievances.*

---

* At one point, security forces mistook an oxygen dispenser carried by Ken Riland for an explosive device and evacuated Rockefeller's Quito hotel.

That much of the unrest was incidental to his mission was confirmed at the end of May, when the Nixon administration announced a suspension of arms sales to Peru in retaliation for its seizure of several American tuna boats. President Juan Velasco Alvarado promptly canceled Rockefeller's one-day visit to Lima. Bolivia cut the visitor's stay to three hours at the La Paz airport, ironically named for John F. Kennedy, a stopover punctuated by bombings at the U.S. embassy and Bolivian-American Center. The ultimate indignity was yet to come. Twenty-nine hours before he was to land at Caracas's Maiquetía Airport, familiar as LaGuardia to one who had long regarded Venezuela as a second home, the pro-American government of President Rafael Caldera closed its doors to Nixon's envoy. "I had to tell him the news that he would not be welcome," Jim Cannon would recall. "He didn't say much, but it was obvious that he was hurt."

Happy Rockefeller consoled her husband, leaning across a table in their silver-blue-and-white air force jet and taking his hand as the aircraft barely cleared the jungle at the end of an Amazonian runway. "Well, Nelson, you're a wonderful guy to hook up with," she told him. The Nixon White House was less convinced. Well-timed leaks sought to distance the administration from the entire enterprise, derided by some reporters as "Nixon's Revenge." On June 4, the same day Chile became the latest nation to disinvite Rockefeller, that country's foreign secretary, Gabriel Valdés, submitted for the president's consideration a six-thousand-word document hammered out by twenty-one Latin American countries and consequently known as the Consensus of Viña del Mar, for the Chilean resort town where the plan was devised. The document offered an implicit alternative to whatever report Rockefeller would write. More than that, it signified Latin America's desire to shape future policies through its own initiative and not as reflected in the hastily formed impressions of an American politician.

Even those sympathetic to Rockefeller's motives found much to question in his methods. "He's a qualified man," said Bogotá's *El Espectador.* "But he came through Latin America as though he were campaigning for office. . . . We didn't need a campaign. We needed quiet understanding." Publicly, Rockefeller blamed his rude reception on a combination of outside militants and frustration born of his own country's long-standing indifference. Continued neglect of the region would only make things worse. Ever the optimist, amid the tumult and tear gas he was able to discern at least one bit of good news, quoting an unnamed Latin host who had reassured him, "You've gotten us off the back pages and on to the front page in the United States."

4

HUMORIST ART BUCHWALD, reminding readers of the well-documented antipathy between Nixon and Rockefeller, imagined a Latin American diplomat lecturing his Yankee friend on the differences between North and South America. "In most of our countries we jail or exile our opponents," said the mythical Gonzalez. "But in your country, you send them on good will tours." No serious thought was given to canceling the second half of the mission, not even after the generals running Brazil shut down universities and jailed more than a thousand student leaders and faculty members in advance of Rockefeller's arrival on June 16. By going ahead with the visit despite such provocations, Rockefeller appeared to endorse official repression.

Once on the scene, however, he made several gestures, public and private, intended to show U.S. displeasure with the ruling junta. Sidestepping a military decoration ceremony, Rockefeller went on to Brasilia's shuttered congress building, where he spent an hour with opposition legislators deprived of their seats by the military. In his meeting with President Artur da Costa e Silva, Rockefeller raised issues of press censorship, student arrests, and political freedom, notwithstanding the president's efforts to steer the discussion back to crop yields and the balance of payments. Rockefeller's stay in the Paraguayan capital of Asunción was extended by a day after a dozen bombings, most aimed at U.S. interests in Uruguay, forced mission planners to abandon Montevideo and meet instead at the ocean resort of Punta del Este. Uruguayan air force jet fighters and a heavy complement of ground troops ensured Rockefeller's safety as he concluded the third leg of his hemispheric voyage.

The final trip, beginning on June 29, was notable for the "No Welcome" sign hung out in advance of his visit to Argentina, where thirteen firebombs tore through IBEC-owned Mini-Max supermarkets, prompting the embattled military government of Juan Carlos Onganía to order up the largest show of force yet. In an unfortunate bit of timing, the American visitors arrived on the third anniversary of the military coup that installed Onganía in the Casa Rosada made famous by Juan and Evita Perón. "You've got a lot of courage," President Onganía greeted Rockefeller. His guest demurred, telling Onganía, "This is your country, not mine. You've got more courage than I have. You've got to handle the situation." Their conversation was interrupted by the sound of nearby gunfire, as left-wing radicals machine-gunned Augusto Vandor, a moderate labor leader whose fatal error was to withhold support from an anti-American general strike.*

---

* "We got the hell out of there," recalls Jack McGrath. "We went downstairs and one of the other advancemen was there, Jerry Wolfgang. Jerry was about the size of the governor. . . . I had the

Paradoxically the warmest welcome of the entire mission, and its biggest diplomatic faux pas, occurred in François Duvalier's Haiti. Ten thousand Haitians lined the route of Rockefeller's motorcade from the airport to the gleaming white French Renaissance National Palace, where another thirty-five thousand people waited under a blistering sun for a glimpse of the American statesman and their own enfeebled dictator, the murderous Papa Doc, whose health was rumored to be in decline. After reading his visitor a lengthy account of U.S.-Haitian relations, and his own unrewarded efforts to prevent the spread of Communism from Castro's Cuba, Duvalier rose from his desk and began to maneuver Rockefeller out onto the balcony overlooking Independence Square. Anticipating such a gesture, the governor, who hoped to diminish the impact of any resulting images, interposed two members of his staff between him and his host. One of these, Ken Riland, was also enlisted to put his medical skills to use by observing Duvalier up close and noting anything that might gratify the curiosity of U.S. policy makers regarding the dictator's survival prospects. Raising Duvalier's arm above his head, Riland managed a surreptitious pulse taking. His diagnosis of advanced prostate cancer was undoubtedly useful to the CIA. (Duvalier would die less than six months later.) But it could hardly compensate for the picture of a grinning Rockefeller scanning the crowd, seemingly oblivious to the 40mm antiaircraft trained on the cheering thousands by Duvalier's troops, his arm linked with the decrepit tyrant who clung to power by keeping his destitute nation in a permanent state of terror.

Rockefeller took his lumps. "Listen," he told Gloria Steinem afterward, "I know this is no political bonanza for me." In the same interview, he explained how he managed to keep going physically, outpacing his Secret Service agents, smiling through official dinners and tedious meetings with mendacious strongmen.

"I'm only happy when I'm reacting to people," Rockefeller claimed. "I really like this kind of trip."

His forty-three-thousand-mile odyssey ended at JFK Airport, where two hundred demonstrators chanted, "Free Cuba, jail Rocky," and eighteen policemen were treated after being sprayed with chemicals by the protesters. The target of their wrath never saw the angry reception committee, its shouted obscenities drowned out by the helicopter that whisked him away on the eleven-minute flight to Pocantico Hills. Calling it "gallant but ill-starred," *The New York Times* led a chorus of press criticism directed at the mission. Rockefeller

---

governor's hat and coat, and I said, 'Jerry, come here.' And I put the hat on. I said, 'Put this on and go back to the hotel in the lead car.' And he jumped in and left. And we all got in another car and went another way. And then Jerry realized what I had done to him. He was never my friend again." Jack McGrath, AI.

vigorously disputed such claims. "Let's face it," he said to his detractors. "Where do you go that you don't see riots and campus problems, and so forth?" It was no accident that Rockefeller chose to title his report *The Quality of Life in the Western Hemisphere*. The final product, all 137 pages and eighty-three recommendations, was drafted with help from Jim Cannon and Hugh Morrow. "Hugh Morrow was a gift to Nelson Rockefeller," said Cannon. "He was intelligent, he was indefatigable, he was totally loyal. He was a good writer, and he could write like he knew how Nelson liked to talk." Morrow had another invaluable quality, according to Cannon—"infinite patience. The governor would sit down and worry over prepositions in a speech. It would drive me up the wall. . . . He was really meticulous about going over every word. He read very slowly and very carefully, and he would stop and say, 'Well, what about this? Maybe we ought to say it this way.' . . . Nobody else read as slowly as he did. And nobody remembered it as well as he did." Finally, after hours of grim wordplay, Rockefeller would conclude, "'Hugh, why don't you do the rest of it?' And Hugh would go work it out, have it typed, get it back to the governor that night, the next morning."

The Rockefeller report on the Americas showcased both Morrow's talents and Rockefeller's affinity for the neglected continent. In its objectives, the report hearkened back to Rockefeller's wartime service under FDR. His emphasis on enhanced nutrition and pre- and postnatal care replicated his efforts as coordinator of inter-American affairs to raise regional standards of living. Just as earlier he had practiced the black arts of propaganda on a continental scale, so Rockefeller now criticized his own government for being outspent six to one by the Soviet Union on "foreign information programming." On the economic front, he urged a generous refinancing of Latin debts. Echoing his 1951 *Partners in Progress* report, Rockefeller argued for a mix of private as well as public investment. This required not only the revision of corporate tax laws and the revival of the old Inter-American Development Commission, but a new sensitivity on the part of the United States and a shift of responsibility to Latins wary of outside exploitation.

By contrast with his sophisticated rethinking of the economic status quo, Rockefeller's military views were grounded in the hoariest of Cold War thought. "At the moment, there is one Castro among the twenty-six nations of the hemisphere," he wrote. "There can well be more in the future." Even one Marxist regime on the South American mainland, aided by the worldwide Communist bloc, could pose a grave danger to regional security. Only as "a cohesive unit of free men," Rockefeller argued, could the hemisphere fulfill its potential. In 1940, the military threat had been *to* Latin America from a Nazified Europe. Three decades later, it was *from* a continent in ferment, where capitalism was on trial and subversion fed on material deprivation. In many countries, the ancient alliance between the Cross and the Sword to provide stability at the cost of economic justice had yielded to a new type of military man: a redistributionist tribune, impatient with corruption and inefficiency, in place of the tinhorn dictator beholden to the prevailing oligarchy and the United Fruit Company. The most controversial of Rockefeller's recommendations would have Washington sell modern weaponry to governments that might employ it on their own people. He also wanted more generous funding for programs bringing indigenous military and police personnel to the United States and its training facilities in Panama. In his response, Nixon offered reassurances that, contrary to what Rockefeller may have heard, no cutoff of military training or arms sales was contemplated to *all* Latin countries, "based on the fact that some are authoritarian."

Thirty years had passed since a Washington neophyte was tasked by FDR with securing a continent's allegiance to democratic values. By 1969, he was repeating himself. Worse, in believing Richard Nixon might emulate Roosevelt's pursuit of hemispheric solidarity, he was deluding himself. Gloria Steinem, writing in *New York* magazine, dismissed Rockefeller as "a good man with a good heart. But he is one of that group of politicians—personified by Hubert Humphrey—who are now out of date. And they will never know why."*

5

ALONG WITH HUGH Morrow, Jim Cannon lent his literary skills to the composition of the Latin American report. Part of the job was done in Seal Harbor, in the converted boat shed dominated by a Jackson Pollock canvas that had partially melted in the Executive Mansion fire of 1961. The rest was completed at Pocantico, where Cannon and his family spent the summer of 1969 as guests, and observers, of the Rockefellers. "He couldn't have been more hospitable," said Cannon of his host, whose latest enthusiasm was a Japanese-style home envisioned for his retirement years (begun in 1969, what was expected to be a $650,000 project took six years and $5.5 million to complete). Behind Pocantico's gates Rockefeller appeared more reflective, less guarded,

---

* Nixon did not, as later alleged, ignore Rockefeller's findings altogether. He elevated the position of assistant secretary of state for the region and undertook a new round of talks aimed at lowering tariffs and thereby encouraging hemispheric prosperity. But he wasn't about to exhaust limited political capital fighting domestic protectionists. Rockefeller's mission had indeed focused attention on the neglected continent. But it was short-lived, perhaps inevitably so, given the urgent challenge posed by Southeast Asia and the visionary potential of China and U.S.–Soviet détente.

than in public. Ritualistic workplace compliments gave way to a semblance of intimacy, never more so than the day Nelson turned to Cannon and remarked, "I wish you could have known Mother."*

Happy Rockefeller matched her husband in the warmth of her greeting. She seemed very much at home to Cannon, who quickly settled into the "grandly informal" routines of estate life. "You were in a house by yourself," he recalled, "but you could enjoy the facilities, the Playhouse, the tennis courts, the pool." Most days a hamburger lunch preceded a trip to the old-fashioned ice-cream bar, where eight or ten flavors were supplemented by chocolate sauce and caramel and all the trimmings. While Nelson found serenity in the Japanese garden, the youngest Rockefellers splashed in the ornate fountains, hid in the underground grottoes, or camped out in the woods behind the Coach Barn. Dispensing with a chauffeur, thinking to disguise himself by pulling his hat down and his collar up, Nelson traversed the streets of the adjacent village in a black-and-yellow Phantom V Rolls-Royce. Weekends he played dollar-a-hole golf on Senior's course with his brother Laurance, the two men emptying bags of heavy silver coins kept for the purpose.

Holidays were observed in style. At Christmas, Kykuit was bedecked in seasonal flowers and greenery, a huge tree poking its starry head through the music room oculus. One year en route to his city office, Nelson stopped in a store promoting Polish crafts and impulsively purchased the entire inventory as gifts for his extended family. Not everything at Pocantico was so idyllic. Sibling rivalries simmered, with John 3rd questioning Nelson's eviction of family retainers from estate housing and disputing his placement of large-scale artworks too conspicuously modern for John's liking. On weekends Nelson liked to stroll the grounds with Joe Canzeri, the diminutive Italian American code-named Little Caesar who would take notes as the squire pondered where his latest sculpture might be located to advantage. The designation of Canzeri as estate manager, ratified on the plane returning from the Republican convention in Miami, was announced to the rest of the family without consultation. Canzeri wished that Nelson had raised the subject in advance with David and his wife, Peggy. "Look, Joe, I run Pocantico Hills," Rockefeller told the new president of Greenrock, Inc. "That is my job. They designated it to me, and . . . I don't have to take that up with anyone." He compounded the offense by directing Canzeri to remove some shrubs prized by Peggy Rockefeller, a warm, down-to-earth woman who raised beef cattle, drove a tractor, and made furniture in her wood-

---

* According to Hugh Morrow, the only time he ever saw Rockefeller become teary-eyed was when Morrow's wife, Carol, concluded a conversation with, "Your mother would have understood." James Cannon, HMI, 4.

working shop. Along with her husband, Peggy had found it hard to accept Nelson's divorce and remarriage, something her brother-in-law didn't forget.

Nelson's unequal treatment of his two families bred its own resentment. "I think there was a lot of bitterness," said Canzeri of the adult Rockefeller children. "It wasn't really a family relationship. I think it was as much their fault as it was his. Happy was there, and then Nelson and Mark, and 'they are cutting into my inheritance.' All those factors existed." In May 1970, little Nelson, five years old, had his tonsils out. His father accompanied him to the hospital, where he slept in the same room with the child. "If he'd only done a little bit of this with his children by Tod," Ken Riland couldn't resist observing, "they'd be better off." Little camaraderie bonded Rockefeller and his eldest son, Rodman, by then nearly forty, with four children of his own. "He'd fly down [from Albany] to have breakfast with Nelson and Mark," recalled Jim Cannon, but "he never flew down to have breakfast with Rodman."

Craving his father's affection, Rod labored to win his respect. Deeply committed, as were his siblings, to the cause of civil rights, Rod also shared Nelson's interest in art and Latin America. Temperamentally, however, they might be opposites, with Rodman reacting negatively to almost any idea not his own. Frugal to the point of self-caricature, preferring a subway in the rain to paying a cabbie's fare, he was not above proposing a trip to Connecticut to buy liquor for a party because it was cheaper than in New York. "He struggled to be a Rockefeller," Al Marshall contended of Nelson and Tod's first child. "Some of the other kids didn't want to be Rockefellers. But Rodman felt an obligation to be a Rockefeller and to let everybody know he was a Rockefeller." Except for Michael, each of Nelson's children by Tod would run the gauntlet of divorce and remarriage, some multiple times. As the sixties unfolded, much of the tension around Kykuit centered on Steven and Anne-Marie Rockefeller. Mia, as she was known to the family, suffered three nervous breakdowns before being diagnosed with a chemical imbalance, a condition successfully treated with lithium.

In her 1975 memoir, *There Was Once a Time*, she described her quest for purpose while mothering three children and weathering the emotional decay of a marriage that in some respects strongly resembled that of her in-laws. Once again, a dissatisfied Rockefeller husband traded the family home for refuge in a nearby retreat—in this case a one-room cabin Steven Rockefeller built with his own hands, more reminiscent of Thoreau's Walden than Wally Harrison's gadget-filled guesthouse first occupied by Steven's father in 1938. By then Steve had embarked on a professional path radically different from his father's early marketing of Rockefeller Center. Following his studies at Union Theological Seminary and later Columbia University, he joined the faculty of Vermont's Middlebury College, where he became a popular and respected professor of comparative religion. For her part Anne-Marie took guitar lessons, studied flower arrangement, wove scarves and neckties of spooled silk.

While Steve worked behind the scenes in the 1968 campaign, Mia and some friends launched Scandinavians for Rockefeller. "If the Kennedys can do it," she told her father-in-law, "so can the Rockefellers." Nelson was delighted with the idea, though his feelings were not universally shared. As related by Anne-Marie, her sister-in-law Ann confronted her at one high-visibility event with the blunt inquiry "Are you campaigning for Father or for yourself?" The cutting remark hinted at conflicts more personal than political and an atmosphere thick with sexual intrigue and lurking suspicion. By the spring of 1969, a despondent Anne-Marie had raised the possibility of divorce. That summer she made plans to return to Norway, to visit her ailing father. Before leaving, however, she became a familiar sight around the Pocantico estate to Jim Cannon and his family. Cannon hid messages from Nelson Rockefeller to his daughter-in-law under a rock designated for the purpose and retrieved her responses.

On the day in 1969 when she left for her homeland, Nelson presented Mia with a jade bracelet. On August 1 her father died; within twenty-four hours Anne-Marie received a letter from her estranged husband conceding their incompatibility. Two months passed before Steven moved out of their Pocantico home and into his cabin retreat. The Cinderella marriage was formally dissolved in June 1970. At about the same time, Ken Riland was surprised to encounter Anne-Marie outside the Playhouse in the company of a Wisconsin businessman destined to become her second husband. The gossipy Riland couldn't resist describing what he had seen to Steve, who was upset to learn that his former wife was even on the estate. Riland convinced himself that Anne-Marie had treated the Playhouse as her "extramarital playpen." She insisted that her husband's family wished her to stay on in her grace and favor house for as long as she wanted. She recounted a family dinner at which Brooke Astor asked what she intended to do with herself. "Live, Mrs. Astor. Live." At the same gathering Nelson supplied the toast, asserting with no discernible irony that "Anne-Marie has given more to the Rockefeller family than we have given to her."

Over time, Mia carved out a separate identity apart from the duty-burdened family she would never wholly escape. Although her second marriage quickly failed, she found release in art—yet another parallel with her former father-in-law. She decided to write a memoir of her years with the Rockefellers, though the version that appeared in 1975 almost certainly underwent some judicious editing. One day Nelson appeared in Hugh Morrow's office clutching a thick manuscript, as yet unread.

"Here, Hughie," said Rockefeller, thrusting the document at his most serviceable wordsmith. "Tell me how much this is going to cost us."

6

H IS LATIN AMERICAN forays had for Rockefeller at least one advantage: They kept him out of New York City during a fratricidal Republican primary for mayor. John Lindsay tried to make a joke of the parallels between him and the governor who was nominally supporting his reelection bid against Staten Island state senator John Marchi, a respected lawmaker whose charisma deficit didn't hurt him among conservative voters—especially in the outer boroughs, where Lindsay's sluggish response to a paralyzing snowstorm in February 1969 crystallized feelings of abandonment. No walking tour could placate Lindsay haters in places like Brooklyn's Bay Ridge neighborhood, where his reception moved the mayor to humorous comparisons with Rockefeller's South America mission. On June 17, Marchi won the GOP primary by 6,000 votes out of 220,000 cast. Forfeiting the Republican designation freed Lindsay of any remaining allegiance to the party of Richard Nixon, Spiro Agnew—whose vice presidential nomination he had seconded at the Miami convention ten months earlier—and Nelson Rockefeller. Assured of the Liberal Party nomination, Lindsay caught another break when Democratic primary voters rejected former mayor Robert Wagner and Bronx borough president Herman Badillo and settled instead on Comptroller Mario Procaccino, a law-and-order Democrat whose malaprop-riddled style invited caricature among those Procaccino stigmatized as "limousine liberals." (Visiting Harlem, Procaccino sought to ingratiate himself by assuring voters, "My heart is as black as yours.")

For Rockefeller, Lindsay's defeat provided the latest evidence that the party of Tom Dewey, Jock Whitney, and Jacob Javits was unlikely to survive an era polarized by Vietnam and the racial and sexual liberation movements of the 1960s. Nelson's postprimary endorsement of Marchi was strictly pro forma, and he refrained from campaigning with the GOP nominee. Blaming Albany for his city's financial woes, early in September Lindsay tried to hijack a special legislative session called by Rockefeller to consider congressional reapportionment. He forged a coalition of the state's largest cities, dubbed "the Big Six," to pressure lawmakers and the governor into restoring cuts in funding to local governments. His endorsement of Rockefeller in 1970, Lindsay made plain, depended on more money for the cities. Rockefeller, unmoved, insisted that "the cupboard is bare as far as new taxes are concerned." Political allies urged Rockefeller to combat a growing impression that his personal feud with the mayor was harming New Yorkers. Even Happy Rockefeller joined the chorus, declaring, "My generation is tired of confrontations." Heeding their counsel, Rockefeller voiced sympathy for Lindsay's fiscal predicament, which he insisted could be resolved only by additional aid from Washington. But he also lodged a vigorous defense of his stewardship during a period when state assistance to New York City quadrupled to nearly $1.8 billion a year.*

On Election Day, Lindsay won a second term with 42 percent of the vote. What at first appeared a striking reaffirmation of urban liberalism would in fact prove to be a last hurrah for the New Deal coalition under siege by Richard Nixon's "silent majority." Nelson Rockefeller, balancing his activist instincts against his political calculations, had a foot in each camp. Thus he erupted in anger on reading Al Marshall's first draft of the 1970 State of the State message, with its bluntly worded concession "We have made New York State uncompetitive." In the end, he settled for a mild acknowledgment that New York's combined state and local taxes were as high as those of any competitor—a condition he cited as justification for federal revenue sharing. The same message contained a typically sweeping Rockefeller commitment "to eliminate poverty and injustice and to make the opportunity for good education and good health a universal right." His legislative wish list included new laws to outlaw racial discrimination in union training programs and to make it easier for consumers to file class action suits against offending businesses. Two years after he first called for reform of the state's 1830 abortion law, Rockefeller embraced the findings of a citizens' committee he had appointed to examine the issue, led by retired court of appeals judge Charles W. Froessel.

Early in April 1970, he was as surprised as anyone by the unintended consequences of senate Republican leader Earl Brydges's parliamentary maneuvering. A strong opponent of abortion, Brydges nevertheless allowed his colleagues to vote on legislation—assumed to be far too radical to pass—that would have the effect of legalizing abortion on demand. "I have a deep, real, abiding conviction that this is the wrong way for the state to go," Brydges told his colleagues, "because we are a bellwether state, and many other states will follow our lead." To his dismay, senators approved the bill 31 to 26. The drama moved to the assembly, where a modified measure, sanctioning abortion during the first two trimesters of pregnancy, fell just short of enactment. A second roll call on April 9 produced a 74 to 74 tie. Moments before the official tally could be announced, George Michaels of Auburn, a Democrat representing a heavily Catholic district, took the floor to describe a recent conversation with his son, a rabbinical student, who had pleaded with him not to cast the vote that doomed abortion reform. Another Michaels son had called his father a whore for opposing the bill on an earlier roll call.

"I fully appreciate that this is the termination of my political career," said

---

* This represented almost a third of the city's budget (federal aid accounted for an additional 15 percent).

Michaels. "But Mr. Speaker, I must have some peace in my family." And then he changed his vote to the affirmative.* On April 11, disregarding a last minute appeal from Terence Cardinal Cooke, Rockefeller signed the legislation eliminating virtually all restrictions on abortion in New York. "The wives of the Senate and the Assembly put this bill through," he said. "New York State did it again!" enthused John 3rd, a leader in the population control movement. "Women everywhere will be in your debt." An intense backlash set in, embroiling New Yorkers in a debate that continues four decades later.

Nearly as divisive were the incessant financial demands of New York and other cities. Rockefeller reluctantly agreed to John Lindsay's proposal to initiate offtrack betting as part of a state aid program totaling nearly $500 million. On the politically explosive issue of rent control, by contrast, he and the mayor parted company. Arguing that the city's housing crisis left him no alternative, Rockefeller pushed through legislation allowing for "vacancy decontrol" of apartment rents, relaxing tightly controlled prices on units vacated by their present tenants. Lindsay charged that such a policy would drive middle-income families from the city. Rockefeller countered that only the prospect of higher rents would encourage landlords and builders to rehabilitate existing housing and build new stock.

In 1970, American politicians discovered the environment as a potent issue. Rockefeller, as usual, prided himself on being ahead of the curve. "What are phosphates?" he asked staff assistant Mary Kresky and others briefing him on legislation to restrict their presence in detergents and dishwashers. Personally, said Rockefeller, he favored a small mop when washing dishes. "Governor, you wash dishes?" Kresky exclaimed. He did indeed, replied Rockefeller. Whenever he and his young sons went to camp, "we each take turns washing dishes. It's part of teaching them self-reliance." Laughter swept the room. Rockefeller was dead serious, however, in staking his claim to environmental leadership. The state's newly chartered Department of Environmental Conservation served as prototype for Richard Nixon's Environmental Protection Agency (EPA). Under Commissioner Henry Diamond, a longtime associate of Laurance Rockefeller, the state enacted vehicle exhaust emission standards, curtailed sales of leaded gasoline, and promoted urban tree planting and the removal of abandoned cars from city streets. It banned DDT and other pesticides before federal regulators. And it slashed mercury discharges into New York's rivers and streams from more than seventy pounds a day to less than three.

The first Earth Day was observed on April 22, 1970. To mark the occasion,

---

* Michaels was prophetic. Renounced by his Democratic brethren, he ran unsuccessfully for reelection on the Liberal Party line.

Rockefeller visited Brooklyn's Prospect Park, where he climbed on a bike for the benefit of photographers and TV cameramen. Suddenly a youngster, maybe fifteen years of age, zoomed into view.

"Race you, Gov," he taunted.

"Damned if Rocky didn't start racing him and going like a bat out of hell," recalled journalist Gene Spagnoli. He crossed the finish line a few yards ahead of his young rival. "He said to me later, 'That kid didn't realize that I am much heavier than he is and I can have a lot more power on those pedals.'"

By 1970, the pedals of state government were more than ever under his control. Among those benefiting was Charles Rangel, a Korean War veteran a few years out of law school and a rising star in the generation of black politicians poised to supplant the legendary Adam Clayton Powell, Jr. "We wanted him out," Al Marshall said of Powell, long a thorn in Rockefeller's side, though a hero to many in the black community, his roguish appeal enhanced by the action of his House colleagues in expelling him from their ranks in 1967. Voters wasted no time in reelecting Powell the next year in absentia, even as he cavorted on the Bahamian island of Bimini.

"We couldn't have a white hand show in the whole thing, so we sent word to Percy Sutton and to some of the other black leaders," Marshall continued. "You pick the guy that you want to run against Adam Clayton Powell, and don't you worry about his financing." Summoned to the second-floor executive suite, Charlie Rangel found the Red Room teaming with men on their knees atop a huge map of New York State. Rockefeller had a birthday gift for him. "We're drawing the congressional lines," explained the governor, handing Rangel a grease pencil. "And you better not touch Manny Celler's district, either!"—a reference to the crusty Brooklyn lawmaker who had been in the House since the Coolidge administration.*

7

THAT ROCKEFELLER'S NAME would appear on the same 1970 ballot as Rangel's was never in doubt. "He loved the job," said Louis Lefkowitz. More to the point, "in the back of his head he had one other ambition." Rockefeller himself acknowledged as much, telling Perry Duryea the morning after

---

* Having invited Rangel to draw his own congressional district, Rockefeller saw to it that the candidate was amply funded by some of New York's more prominent Republican donors. Following his election that fall, Rangel received still more help from his friends, as both Lindsay and Rockefeller pulled strings to get him a place on the prestigious House Ways and Means Committee, whose chairman, Wilbur Mills, was pivotal to Nelson's campaign for federal revenue sharing.

Richard Nixon's election that only a final shot at the presidency would induce him to seek a fourth term in Albany. In other conversations, he cited the unfinished South Mall as his motivation for challenging the state's modern office-holding record. As was customary, Nelson started the race an underdog. After twelve years in office, Rockefeller fatigue was palpable. Pollster Lloyd Free warned that his recent moves to restrain state spending had only muddied public opinion. According to Free, urban voters preferred a governor who put human needs ahead of budget discipline—exactly the opposite of upstate voters, who were most suspicious of Rockefeller's belated retrenchment.

His strategy for electoral victory in 1970 envisioned a very different coalition from the left-of-center one cobbled together for Lindsay's reelection a few months earlier, not to mention his own come-from-behind victory in 1966. Running against Frank O'Connor, Rockefeller had disproved conventional wisdom by winning substantial support in the black and Jewish communities. Four years on, each group had good reason to revert to its traditional loyalties, given the two men heading the Democratic ticket. Jews were expected to rally around gubernatorial candidate Arthur Goldberg, a former United States Supreme Court justice and UN ambassador, while African Americans likewise supported one of their own, Harlem state senator Basil Paterson, who was slotted for lieutenant governor.

Goldberg cast a larger shadow than either Bob Morgenthau or Frank O'Connor, at least on paper. As the AFL-CIO's longtime counsel before he was JFK's secretary of labor, Goldberg, it was believed, could rely on organized labor to offset at least some of Rockefeller's financial advantage. Appointed by Kennedy to fill the Supreme Court vacancy left by Felix Frankfurter, Goldberg had established himself as a pragmatic liberal and mainstay of the Warren Court, influential in broadening privacy rights and encouraging opposition to the death penalty. Under heavy White House pressure to replace the late Adlai Stevenson as U.S. ambassador to the United Nations, Goldberg had believed Lyndon Johnson's flattery. "I had an exaggerated opinion of my capacities," he later wrote. "I thought I could persuade Johnson that we were fighting the wrong war in the wrong place [and] to get out." After resigning his post in 1968, Goldberg joined the prestigious Manhattan law firm Paul, Weiss, Rifkind, Wharton & Garrison and served as president of the American Jewish Committee.

After flirting with a run for the Senate seat precariously held by Charles Goodell, in March 1970 he announced his candidacy for governor. From there it was all downhill for the windy, self-regarding Goldberg. A frequently told joke had the candidate demanding of his wife, Dorothy, whether he really was as puffed up as everybody claimed. "Of course not, Mr. Justice Goldberg," she replied. (The same honorific graced his office door at the Paul, Weiss law firm.)

At the state Democratic convention, Goldberg declared his intention to campaign from one end of the state to the other, "from Buffalo to Montauk, from Syracuse to Pufkeepsie." Ed Koch, then a Democratic congressman representing John Lindsay's old Silk Stocking district, once asked Rockefeller when he first realized that in the owlish, pedantic Goldberg he confronted the very opposite of a mensch.

"Well, you know when Goldberg was nominated I really worried about it, because Goldberg is a lawyer and he's a good debater and he's good on his feet, and I'm not a lawyer," Rockefeller replied. "And then I got onto the platform on the first occasion with him, and he began to speak, and I knew there was nothing to worry about." This left out a singular bit of head fakery. On the eve of the Democratic primary, Goldberg accepted an invitation to dinner at Pocantico. There he heard six-year-old Nelson Jr. declare, "Mr. Goldberg, I hope you win. I want my daddy home." Nelson's father had a less noble, if equally pointed, message to convey. "By inviting him up there," authors Sam Roberts and Michael Kramer quote a Goldberg aide, "Rockefeller said to Goldberg, 'You're a nice little Jewish boy from Chicago and you've done well for yourself. But if you think someone with all this is going to let you take it away, you're over your head.'" Goldberg's unexpectedly narrow primary victory over Howard Samuels, a millionaire businessman and perennial candidate for governor, diminished the aura of inevitability with which power-hungry Democrats had clothed his candidacy. When the same primary produced a decidedly unbalanced slate of four Jews and one black (the aforementioned Basil Paterson, of whom crusty old Dan O'Connell said that he was the only white man on the ticket), Rockefeller began to speak derisively of "the Manhattan Monopoly." Before upstate voters he cracked, "The whole group of them could go to work in one taxi."

Still, Rockefeller's own polling showed him trailing Goldberg by eleven points. Al Marshall, promised the CEO's office at Rockefeller Center as his reward for a fourth Rockefeller triumph at the polls, issued a characteristically forceful call to battle before a conclave of state commissioners and other gubernatorial appointees. "You sons of bitches have had your asses in the butter too long," Marshall thundered. It was time to get out in the field and sell the man to whom they all owed their jobs. They were to have plenty of company. For sheer imbalance of resources and strategic execution, the 1970 campaign was one for the record books. At $7.2 million, the incumbent's campaign budget was even more lavish, his advantage of 380 paid staff to Goldberg's 35 more lopsided, than in 1966.* The incumbent again ruled the airwaves, having rejected a Goldberg proposal that each candidate limit his broadcast expendi-

* Among the young advancemen working for the Friends of the Rockefeller team "fetching Fresca and Oreos" was the state's future three-term Republican governor George Pataki, whose

tures to seven cents per voter—around $430,000 statewide—in line with pending campaign finance legislation in Congress. Rockefeller vowed to observe any such restrictions in the unlikely event of their passage; in the meantime, he allocated more than $3 million for television ads, double the entire Goldberg campaign budget.

The Rockefeller media efforts were reinforced by the most elaborate polling and direct mail operations in American political history to that point. The former enabled Rockefeller to develop carefully tested themes—his emphasis on family stability in an unstable society came straight from a Sam Lubell memo. His pollsters supplied Rockefeller with the necessary data to hug the electoral center, even as the state's political center of gravity crept to the right. A *New York Times* Daniel Yankelovich survey of New York voters found 37 percent described themselves as conservative, 33 percent as moderate, and 27 percent as liberal. And where on the spectrum of values did these same voters place Rockefeller? Thirty-six percent said he was a conservative, 35 percent called him a moderate, and 25 percent applied the liberal label to him. Clearly, he had found his ideological sweet spot.

With the vital assistance of a California firm, Decision Making Information, Rockefeller managers gleaned millions of names from commercial mailing lists, state records, and their own polling. Journalist Neal Peirce estimated as much as 75 percent of New York's voting population had been computerized, the prerequisite to customized appeals from Travel Agents for Rockefeller, Chiropractors for Rockefeller, and Osteopathic Physicians for the Rockefeller-Wilson Team. German American voters, one of more than thirty separate ethnic groups singled out for individual attention, received literature emphasizing their strong interest not only in law and order, but in parks and recreation—because, in the words of one campaign strategist, "the Germans are very athletic and enjoy the out-of-doors." Rockefeller's campaign slogan—"He's Done a Lot. He'll Do More"—reflected his activist instincts. But it clashed with the emerging mood of fiscal retrenchment and social conservatism. After all, 1970 was the year of Cambodia and Kent State, where the loss of four students shot to death by Ohio National Guardsmen led Mayor Lindsay to lower the American flag atop city hall, touching off a near riot by New York construction workers and others who made the hard hat the unlikely symbol of pro-war, pro-Nixon sentiment.

In pre-YouTube America, it was much easier for politicians to tailor their message to the immediate audience. Addressing an Ithaca College commencement, Rockefeller decried the "devastating" effects of Vietnam, "a war that no

---

proudest boast was to return the state's highest personal income tax rate to 7 percent, far below the 17 percent level at which it topped out under Rockefeller.

one wants, that no one really understands, and that everyone prays can be ended." Speaking before a less youthful crowd, however, he gave tacit approval to Nixon's invasion of Cambodia. Visiting the World Trade Center construction site, he promised a million man-years of state-sponsored building projects over the next five years. Then he paused to autograph hard hats, at one point awkwardly donning the iconic headwear thrust upon him by cheering construction workers. Rockefeller's pledge to increase prison sentences for college bombers might have earned denunciation from Goldberg as "the shabbiest kind of pandering to the voters' worst instincts," but it undeniably struck a chord among white ethnic voters who had supported Mario Procaccino or John Marchi in the recent mayoral campaign.

Shamelessly, Nelson ordered state law enforcement agencies to drop words such as "Mafia" and "Cosa Nostra" from their lexicon, as slurs on upstanding Americans of Italian ancestry. At the Feast of San Gennaro in Little Italy, a thoroughly briefed Rockefeller asked in passable Italian for a trademark sausage made with onions and peppers. The next day, Mr. Justice Goldberg made his own visit to the festival. In the nasal monotone ordinarily used to answer, at numbing length, questions from reporters, he announced, "I'd like a piece of that Italian hot dog." Out of his element as a street campaigner, the challenger was out of his league contesting Rockefeller's dominance of the headlines. When Goldberg vowed to legalize marijuana for adults if it was consistent with scientific findings, Rockefeller scheduled a Washington meeting with Attorney General John Mitchell to discuss the war on drugs. He proposed creation of a whole new class of courts to combat the growing drug menace, and together with Jackie Robinson, whose namesake son was battling the ravages of heroin addiction, he hosted a series of "drug forums" around the state at which his hard-line message won fervent applause.

Rockefeller declared August 24 Miss Universe Day, in recognition of Marisol Malaret, the first Puerto Rican contestant to win the title. Following a celebratory luncheon that set him back $15,000, the governor and the beauty queen embarked on a motorcade through Spanish-speaking neighborhoods to cries of "¡Viva Rocky!" After some rogue Goldberg supporters threatened violence to their opponents, the justice went out of his way to publicly apologize to Rockefeller—only to have Nelson, keenly aware of the TV cameras capturing the scene, dramatically spurn his rival's proffered handshake. Instead he carried on about Goldberg—"a justice of the Supreme Court"—sanctioning such bullying tactics. Away from the cameras, Rockefeller conceded that the entire incident was "silly." But if one intended to play the game at that level, he mused . . . before shrugging his shoulders in a gesture more eloquent than words.

Like Averell Harriman before him, Goldberg sought to nationalize the contest, making it a referendum on the Nixon presidency and Vietnam. In doing so, he only widened the split in organized labor, a division that burst into public view at a tumultuous AFL-CIO convention during the first week of September. Held at the Concord Hotel in the Catskills, the gathering pitted the dominant building trades, whose votes had already secured a Rockefeller endorsement from the union's executive committee, against Victor Gotbaum, his American Federation of State, County, and Municipal Employees, and traditionally left-leaning groups such as the National Maritime Union and the International Ladies' Garment Workers' Union.

"The governor desperately wanted the AFL-CIO endorsement," according to Bob Armao. With the certitude of youth, Armao guaranteed the nod that had eluded Nelson in three previous campaigns. He had solid grounds for confidence. "In those days we weren't afraid to use patronage. . . . A labor leader came in and said, 'My son has applied for medical school in an out-of-state facility. Would you recommend him?' They would take pains to interview him and try to help out on a friendship basis." For many among labor's highest echelons, the sense of obligation went much deeper. AFL-CIO president George Meany, after introducing Armao to his assembled colleagues as "Nelson's man," would invariably fall to reminiscing. "Let me tell you about Nelson Rockefeller. During the Depression my family had nothing to eat. There was nothing going on in New York, so you know what I did? Nelson Rockefeller gave me a job as a plumber. You can never forget somebody like that."

The AFL-CIO hierarchy, beginning with state president Ray Corbett, made no secret of its preference for a governor in love with the smell of concrete. Hoping to forestall a roll call vote, convention chairman Corbett withheld from Goldberg supporters a list of delegates and their voting strength, as determined by the number of members paying dues to the state organization. Rumors flew through the hall that Corbett was conspiring with Harry Van Arsdale, Jr., of the International Brotherhood of Electrical Workers and the state Central Labor Council to pack the meeting, a claim strengthened by the reported delivery of a box full of delegate badges to a suite occupied by Vic Borella. In an emotional appeal, Goldberg stood on the convention floor, remembers Bob Armao, "like an old prizefighter who had been outmaneuvered." He took off his wristwatch and read the inscription warmly acknowledging his lifelong commitment to the labor movement. "Do you forget those words?" Goldberg pleaded with the delegates. "How can you do this to me?"

Goldberg's demand for a roll call was put to a standing vote, which Corbett briskly decided in Rockefeller's favor. On the floor, Victor Gotbaum shouted himself hoarse insisting the roll be called. Corbett silenced his microphone. Recognizing a motion to adjourn, and without bothering to consult the delegates, the chairman declared it passed. The house lights were shut off, prompting fisticuffs in the dark. Chairs were smashed; ashtrays sailed through the air. "God, they were throwing each other in the fountain," says Armao. Confronting Van Arsdale amid the bedlam, Gotbaum employed what was left of his voice to bellow, "You stole it from us, Harry."

Rockefeller had a different reaction when Armao called him with the news. "How about that?" His youthful operator had made good on his boast.*

Goldberg soldiered on. He denounced the Rockefeller war on drugs from a debris-littered lot set aside for a treatment facility never built. He assailed the governor's antipollution program, the costs of which had more than doubled in five years. Some of his harshest criticism was directed at Rockefeller's South Mall, whose escalating cost and receding completion date inspired comparisons with the Vietnam War. What had initially been portrayed as a four-year, $250 million construction job had morphed into . . . no one knew exactly what. The futuristic towers and sweeping vistas designed by Wally Harrison had nothing in common with the modest Dutch fieldstone complex originally proposed by Rockefeller's splendidly named director of general services, Cortlandt Van Rensselaer Schuyler. (According to Bill Ronan, Rockefeller took one look at Schuyler's unsolicited model and "exploded.") A triumphal Arch of Freedom, envisioned as the project's focal point, had been replaced by an upside-down structure, narrower at the base than the top, housing the state museum and archives.

In February 1970, blaming inflation and rising interest rates, Rockefeller announced a $75 million increase in project costs, to $745 million. This was at best a guess. Because only the southern half of the vast, six-story platform supporting the mall's surface structures had been designed, the project's completion date had already been moved back five years, to 1976. In an effort to speed things up, it was decided to work simultaneously on both the platform and the buildings growing out of it. This guaranteed a fierce competition for materials and labor. Restricted access to the construction site fostered clashes among work crews; platform builders complained that rubbish was being dumped on them from the skeletal forty-four-story office tower on which had been painted in ten-foot-high letters, "Rocky's Pyramid." Another recurring problem was theft: $500,000 worth of steel rods vanished in a day.

Dangerously high water tables, combined with a surfeit of Albany's notorious blue clay, compelled Wally Harrison to install more than four thousand "steel backbones"—304 miles of H-beam piling resting on the glacial till below. These did not prevent a burst main from inundating the work site in two million gallons of water. At least sixty fires plagued the site, one of them blamed for

---

* Chastened by negative press coverage, the union's executive committee declared a month-long recess, until October 14, at which time the Rockefeller endorsement was reaffirmed.

$2.4 million in damages and more in resulting work delays. Rockefeller's decision to sheathe the complex in Georgia and Vermont marble reportedly caused a yearlong backup in supplies. Through it all, his enthusiasm for the venture—"the greatest thing to happen in this country in a hundred years"—never wavered. John Marchi remembers walking into the governor's office on the second floor of the Capitol and finding Rockefeller on his hands and knees, playing with a scale model of the complex like a kid on Christmas morning. "They used to laugh at my grandfather when he built Rockefeller Center," said Nelson. "They'll come to like this place."

Rockefeller enlisted the services of prominent art experts, personal friends all, in selecting contemporary paintings and sculpture to complement buildings that were themselves pieces of abstract art. The status of these consultants as highly credentialed window dressing was inadvertently confirmed by *Knickerbocker News* reporter Arvis Chalmers, who kept badgering the second floor for a look at more than eighty works by contemporary New York artists, all paid for by New York taxpayers. Repeatedly his requests were turned down, yet Chalmers persisted in asking. Finally, Al Marshall raised the subject with Rockefeller directly. Displaying a series of photographs for his review, the plainspoken Marshall muttered, "I can't show him pictures of this junk."

"Al," said Nelson, "I picked out the art."

Much of the technology built into the South Mall was obsolescent before its completion. Thanks to advances in computer design and capacity, the quarter-mile-long motor vehicles building was twice as large as it needed to be. On the other hand, even the mall's harshest detractors conceded its transformation of downtown Albany. For better *and* worse, the enormous project planted seeds of gentrification, leading to the restoration and revival of adjoining neighborhoods, "turning a slug of a town into a handsome and prancing dude."

In the autumn of 1970, Arthur Goldberg came to Albany to stand under Rockefeller's office window and pour scorn on what local wags had taken to calling "Rocky's Last Erection." It was simply too good a photo op to pass up, particularly for a campaign necessarily reliant on free media. Fresh off the chaotic AFL-CIO convention, they overlooked one thing. Everyone in the swarming hive of workers filling the hundred-acre vacancy in downtown Albany owed his job to Nelson Rockefeller. Which was why, the moment Mr. Justice Goldberg appeared on the fringes of the work site to express the collective outrage of taxpayers over what novelist and Albany historian William Kennedy branded "one of the most perfectly designed perpetual opportunity machines in the history of boondoggery," his words were lost amid the earsplitting rejoinder of jackhammers, concrete mixers, truck engines, and a steam whistle or two. Rarely was the activity unfolding between Eagle and Swan streets so coordinated.

8

THE YEAR 1970 would also be remembered for a Rockefeller dirty trick, a defamatory campaign biography of Goldberg from the pen of Victor Lasky, a former journalist and radio commentator who had earned notoriety, and a nice piece of change, from such right-wing polemics as *Seeds of Treason* and *J.F.K.: The Man & the Myth*. Lasky was a friend of Jack Wells, Rockefeller's 1964 campaign manager and an unofficial adviser ever since. Neither man had much use for Arthur Goldberg. From there it was a short leap to Wells pitching an instant book on the Democratic candidate. In practical terms the book was a dud, as dull as its subject. At the time, Rockefeller campaign manager Burdell Bixby, the unwitting recipient of twenty thousand copies, plaintively asked a colleague, "What the hell do I do with them?" As Bixby told it, most were dumped in the Hudson River. Craig Thorne, another Rockefeller campaign operative, remembers hiring a van and dropping off thousands of copies at *Democratic* headquarters upstate.

Rockefeller sought to minimize the book's impact at his 1974 vice presidential confirmation hearings. But a newly energized press, turbocharged by official mendacity and the abuses of power revealed through the Watergate scandal, refused to let the matter drop there. In *The Rockefellers*, Peter Collier and David Horowitz paint a damning picture of what Nelson knew about the Goldberg book, and when he knew it. Initially denying any personal involvement in the project, he fingered his brother Laurance, who had indeed invested $65,000 in the venture—as a favor to Nelson—and who appeared characteristically, if unhappily, willing to assume the role of fall guy. In time Nelson changed his story, accepting responsibility for the book, on which he claimed to have spent no more than fifteen or twenty minutes in a busy campaign. Left to operatives in Room 5600 was the establishment of a dummy corporation to handle the book's publication.

Those incredulous that Rockefeller would approve such a scheme overlooked a critical factor: For much of the 1970 campaign, he expected to lose. Outlining plans for a dozen or more debates with Goldberg, he vowed to one campaign operative, "I'm going to go down fighting." In public, Rockefeller exuded his trademark enthusiasm and vigor. Defusing a tense confrontation with striking firefighters in Rochester, he refused to cross a city hall picket line. Instead he climbed atop a car and within twenty-five minutes had the hostile crowd cheering him. One-on-one, he remained the best campaigner in the business. The mother of future United States senator Alfonse D'Amato had no use for Rockefeller the liberal—until they met by chance at an event, where Nelson flattered her by asking in disbelief, "*You* have a son who is graduating from law school?"

"She melted," says D'Amato.

Only a handful of intimates detected in the candidate signs of mental fatigue and physical exhaustion. Speaking before a men's group in Harlem,
Rockefeller wrote off the chances of GOP comptroller candidate Ned Regan of
Buffalo, declaring incumbent Arthur Levitt "in like Flynn." Afterward, there
were conflicting reports about his alcoholic intake that evening—whether he
had seven, or several, Dubonnets. "I only saw Nelson that one night get loaded,"
says advanceman Jack McGrath. "Nelson was my father's age," McGrath notes.
"I couldn't say, 'Stop drinking.'" In any event, the problem never recurred.
Meanwhile, Rockefeller recovered smartly, calling Regan to apologize. "Hello,
Ned," he told his aggrieved running mate. "This is Judas."

He stumbled a second time in accusing Goldberg of attempted bribery of
Mario Procaccino, the alleged payoff being a job with the Metropolitan Transportation Authority. "The wheels are beginning to slow down and he doesn't
really give a damn," Ken Riland wrote about his friend and patient late in the
campaign. "He just goes through the motions. He said for the first time in his
elective career he's fed up with news conferences, fed up with rallies, fed up
with the whole thing, but it's only 3 more days so he'll make it." By then the
chief cause of concern in the Rockefeller camp was not the flailing Arthur
Goldberg, but an intense three-way U.S. Senate race pitting Charles Goodell,
appointed by Rockefeller to fill Bobby Kennedy's seat, against Conservative
Party nominee James Buckley and Democratic congressman Richard Ottinger.
Buckley, fresh off his million-vote showing against Jacob Javits and antiwar
firebrand Paul O'Dwyer in 1968, shrewdly presented himself as a Republican
first and Conservative second.

His timing couldn't have been better. During his short Senate career, Goodell had first startled, and then enraged, rank-and-file Republicans who had
trouble imagining one of their own outflanking Jacob Javits on the left. By his
own admission, Rockefeller was tired of playing devil's advocate within the
GOP. Buckley's vigorous challenge of the political status quo ("Isn't It Time We
Had a Senator?") offered Rockefeller the quickest way to curry favor with the
Republican Right. He couldn't endorse Buckley, of course, but he could adopt
a stance of practical neutrality, looking the other way as grassroots Republicans
abandoned Goodell in droves. Convincing himself that he could have it both
ways was not difficult: hadn't Rockefeller publicly rebuked Goodell for introducing legislation that would cut off funding for the Vietnam War? There was
also the White House to consider. The first week in September, Rockefeller
took a call from Nixon's domestic policy czar John Ehrlichman regarding Stewart Air Force Base in Newburgh, which Nelson coveted as a possible fourth
airport serving metropolitan New York. Ehrlichman agreed to the swap of some
adjoining post office property in return for a New York State diplomatic license

for entertainer Pearl Bailey—dubbed by Nixon his "Ambassador of Love." Rockefeller promised to stamp out a license himself.

His relations with the administration were not always so friendly. Rockefeller was furious when Vice President Agnew declared open warfare on Goodell, crudely equating the senator's ideological conversion to the sex change operation that turned George into Christine Jorgensen. During a brief stopover at the Westchester County Airport, Nixon himself all but publicly endorsed Buckley. After Rockefeller appeared wearing a Goodell button at a New York City fund-raising dinner, John Mitchell told him he should forget any federal aid as long as he continued to support the embattled senator. Formally, he remained in Goodell's corner, making a personal donation of $45,000 to the campaign and ensuring that the state party put up $250,000 more. This was peanuts in an election cycle where Dick Ottinger spent nearly $2 million just to win a Democratic primary. And when William F. Buckley, Jr., visited the Fifty-fifth Street offices early in 1970 to dangle (unsuccessfully) a possible Conservative Party nomination before Rockefeller, Nelson didn't exactly go to bat for Goodell.

"I really am a conservative, you know," he remarked to Buckley. "I've got a lot to conserve."

Thereafter, Conservative gubernatorial candidate Paul Adams faded from sight. In the brimstone-stained pages of *National Review*, Bill Buckley communicated the unthinkable in verse:

> *And so, despite the trauma and the shock,*
> *November, I'll be voting for the Rock.*

On Saturday, October 3, Rockefeller's attention was abruptly diverted from the campaign to prison riots in the Tombs, an aged, badly overcrowded facility on Manhattan's Center Street. The violence quickly spread to other institutions in Brooklyn, Long Island City, and Queens. Prominent among the ringleaders were Black Panthers and other self-professed political prisoners who demanded to meet with outside sympathizers, including Adam Clayton Powell, Jr., and radical lawyer and activist William Kunstler. As Rockefeller took soundings with Congresswoman Shirley Chisholm and her colleague Herman Badillo, Mayor Lindsay issued an ultimatum to those in the Tombs who were holding hostages. Eventually the inmates gave in, and the mayor honored his pledge to meet with them and discuss the appalling conditions under which they were imprisoned. The state agreed to relocate hundreds of prisoners from the Tombs. Many were shipped to the Attica Correctional Facility in remote Wyoming County, an hour's drive east of Buffalo.

Rockefeller returned to the campaign trail. His polling told him to ignore

Goldberg's harshest attacks, which were having the opposite of their intended effect among core Democratic constituencies. The same surveys showed Rockefeller making inroads among Jewish voters, especially the conservative Hasidic community. He picked up some key black endorsements, even as he solidified his lead among white ethnics. By mid-October, his internal polls looked too good to be released lest they feed complacency about the result. They got even better after Lindsay endorsed Goldberg on October 19. ("The man who nominated Agnew talks about principle," Rockefeller muttered.) He shouldn't have complained—the mayor's action drove his own numbers skyward. Still, he refused to believe the election was in the bag. Five days before voters went to the polls, four hundred thousand upstate Republicans and independents received simulated telegrams declaring, "I need your help. Unless you vote this Tuesday the organized Democrat Party of New York City could take over your state government. . . . Governor Nelson A. Rockfeller."

On November 6, Rockefeller held his traditional Election Day policy review in anticipation of the new year's legislative session. A billion-dollar shortfall in the 1971–1972 budget wasn't the worst of his problems. Skyrocketing costs for education, welfare, and health care—especially Medicaid—called into question New York's ability to fund its generous instincts without ruining its delicate economic machinery. To be sure, the Nixon administration seemed open to block grants and some form of federal revenue sharing, though the amounts envisioned—$500 million nationally, rising to $5 billion nationally by 1976— were woefully inadequate to the present crisis. For Rockefeller, pay as you go had long since been replaced by tax increases, short- and long-term borrowing, postponements, stretch-outs, and freezes. Even while returning sixty-three cents of every dollar it collected to local governments, Albany failed to satisfy the ravenous appetites of mayors and county executives, schools and hospitals.

Rockefeller would have preferred to have Washington assume total responsibility for welfare expenditures. But when Congress defeated Nixon's Family Assistance Plan, and the inexorable rise in his own budget threatened to exhaust the state's taxing capacity, he welcomed new ideas. It was Malcolm Wilson, perhaps envisioning the reduced inheritance that might soon be his, who convinced Rockefeller and his team that federal revenue sharing was preferable to raising taxes. The concept was at least as old as Thomas Jefferson's 1805 call for "a just repartition" of funds to promote "canals, roads, arts, manufacturers, education, and other great objects within each state." Most recently, Lyndon Johnson had given serious consideration to a revenue-sharing plan, until Vietnam devoured the projected federal surplus and opposition from organized labor and civil rights groups scuttled the presidential initiative. Why should Washington surrender the leverage of the purse string? Wilbur Mills, the formidable chairman of the House Ways and Means Committee, spoke for a bipartisan consensus of lawmakers in declaring, "I am not going to be a tax collector for anyone but the federal government."

For Rockefeller to have any chance at reversing the flow of dollars to Capitol Hill, he must somehow persuade Mills and others that change, radical change, was in their interest, at least as much as it was in his. Commencing on Election Day, plans were developed for what proved to be Rockefeller's only successful national campaign. That evening, Nelson hosted a cocktail reception at 812 Fifth Avenue before joining Laurance and Mary Rockefeller at their nearby residence. As they dined, New Yorkers registered their verdict on Rockefeller's twelve-year stewardship and his more recent shift to the right. The result could hardly be more emphatic. His 730,000-vote margin, the largest of Rockefeller's four campaigns, matched FDR's 1930 reelection record. As for Goldberg, his strength among Jewish and black voters was barely sufficient to carry New York City (by 16,000 votes). In the Senate race, Buckley nosed out Ottinger by four percentage points; Goodell finished a distant third. The morning after, as paperboys hawked the *New York Post* with its headlined assertion, ROCKY'S TURN TO RIGHT DID IT, Nelson treated Happy to breakfast at the 21 Club.

The celebration was short-lived. Barely had the campaign signs come down when Rockefeller ordered a freeze on state hiring and imposed fresh economies on government departments. He pondered which tax increases would inflict the least pain on a suddenly wobbly economy. If he expected any help from New York City Hall, he was quickly disabused of the idea. Defeated, out of a job, and broke, Charlie Goodell invited both Lindsay and Rockefeller to a post-election fund-raiser at the St. Regis Hotel. Putting aside his resentment over past clashes, Rockefeller used the occasion to appeal for party unity and to praise Goodell for his lonely campaign. Then Lindsay took the podium. "One thing about the Republican Party that people have to understand," said the mayor, his eyes fixed on Rockefeller. "Old men with old ideas don't belong here anymore."

Albany lawmakers baffled by the Rockefeller art collection likened one canvas to a gerrymandered legislative district and threatened to refer others to the Select Committee on Pornography.

Thriving in his new job, Rockefeller addresses representatives of the Farm Bureau in the ceremonial Red Room, whose dimensions reminded Al Smith of Macy's front window.

Legislative adjournment ushered in the thirty-day period during which Rockefeller, here assisted by counsel Rod Perkins, had to decide the fate of a thousand or more bills.

"An arrogant son of a bitch." So concluded New York City Mayor Robert F. Wagner, Jr., after early clashes with the new governor. In time the two men became allies, validating the claim that in New York, Rockefeller owned one political party and rented the other.

Rockefeller with William J. Ronan, his chief Albany deputy. He showed his appreciation by "loaning" Ronan over $600,000. (NEW YORK STATE ARCHIVES)

Rockefeller flirted with a run against Vice President Nixon in 1960, finally confiding to a friend that no man could seek the White House unless his own house was in order.

March 2, 1961. A near-fatal fire
in the Executive Mansion
ignites gossip about the state
of the Rockefeller marriage.
(ALBANY *TIMES UNION*)

Nelson's subsequent divorce
astonished John F. Kennedy,
who told Katharine Graham,
"No man would ever love love
more than politics."

Days after announcing their separation, Tod and Nelson learned of the disappearance of their youngest son, Michael, on an art collecting expedition to remote parts of New Guinea. His unexplained loss and the horrific theories it spawned haunted his family for years.

"I hope Michael meets Mother in Heaven," Nelson told Margaretta "Happy" Murphy, the woman he had already resolved to marry, regardless of the effect on his presidential ambitions.

With his personal life in turmoil, Rockefeller faced scandal in the State Liquor Authority overseen by his appointee Martin Epstein, shown here. The same affair cost him the services of chief political adviser L. Judson Morhouse.

A tumultuous run for the 1964 GOP presidential nomination began in the snows of New Hampshire, where a pregnant Happy encountered friendly crowds as well as snide inquiries about her "abandoned" children.

Arizona Senator Barry Goldwater—"Mr. Conservative"—whose unvarnished comments about Social Security, the United Nations, and the far-right John Birch Society cost him victory in New Hampshire. Bypassing Oregon's primary, Goldwater set up a classic right-left confrontation with Rockefeller in neighboring California.
(SENATOR BARRY M. GOLDWATER PAPERS, ARIZONA STATE UNIVERSITY LIBRARIES)

Long lines of celebrity-conscious Californians turned out to greet Rockefeller before the June 2 GOP primary. More surprisingly, more than fifty thousand registered Democrats, mostly African Americans, switched parties to support him.

At the Republican convention that July, New Yorkers, led by Rockefeller and Senator Jacob Javits (second to the right of Nelson), offered last-ditch resistance to the new order. (Associated Press)

"Oh, Happy, Lyndon thinks it's going to be like chasing the deer off the Pedernales." Rockefeller's early prediction about the Johnson White House suggested the (mostly) friendly rivalry between the two men as each offered his own version of the Great Society. (Lyndon B. Johnson Presidential Library)

Rockefeller shares the pulpit of Atlanta's Ebenezer Baptist Church with the Reverend Martin Luther King, Jr., in October 1965. Two years earlier Nelson had supplied critical funding to sustain King's Birmingham crusade. Two and a half years later, Rockefeller agents would organize and help pay for the funeral of the slain civil rights leader.

A rare gathering of five Rockefeller brothers, at a 1967 award ceremony. From left: David, Winthrop, John 3rd, Nelson, and Laurance.

New York wasn't big enough to contain the ambitions, or egos, of Republican mayor John Lindsay and Republican governor Nelson Rockefeller. In February 1968 the two men sparred over a New York City sanitation strike that was to prove disastrous to Rockefeller's presidential prospects. (NEW YORK STATE ARCHIVES)

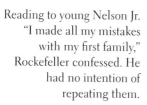

With Leonard Bernstein and Seymour "Shorty" Knox, chairman of Rockefeller's first-in-the-nation State Arts Council.

Reading to young Nelson Jr. "I made all my mistakes with my first family," Rockefeller confessed. He had no intention of repeating them.

Rockefeller settled early on Michigan Governor George Romney as the moderate alternative to Richard Nixon in 1968. Romney's subsequent failure bred feelings of betrayal and a late-starting Rockefeller campaign marked by internal confusion and conflicting messages.

After January 1969, Nixon and Rockefeller put their long-standing rivalry behind them. Nelson undertook a controversial Latin American mission for the White House. In return, Nixon supported federal revenue sharing and offered Rockefeller wiretapping and other assistance to investigate John Lindsay's city hall.

Moving to the right in his campaign for a fourth term, Rockefeller won support from William F. Buckley and pro-Nixon hard hats, the latter grateful for the governor's love affair with concrete that produced Manhattan's World Trade Center and Albany's South Mall.

In September 1971 a violent prison uprising at
the Attica Correctional Facility culminated
in the deaths of forty-three guards and
inmates. Rockefeller's refusal to visit Attica
was widely criticized, as was the state's
heavy-handed retaking of the prison.

Richard Nixon strongly advised
Rockefeller against becoming Gerald
Ford's vice president. Denouncing
his handpicked successor, Nixon
promised support for Nelson in 1976
if he kept his distance from Ford.

Their mutual personal
regard could not
obscure the conflict
between Rockefeller's
activist instincts and
Ford's fiscal restraint.

Sparing the president, Rockefeller reserved his criticism for White House Chief of Staff Donald Rumsfeld, shown here with Ford, Counselor Jack Marsh, and Secretary of State Henry Kissinger.

With two young sons to raise in New York, Happy Rockefeller largely avoided the nation's capital. In 1975 she made an exception for several housewarming parties in the newly decorated vice-presidential residence.

The smile is misleading. Rockefeller's swan song at his party's 1976 convention preceded a chest-thumping confrontation with his nemesis Dick Cheney.

Out of office, Rockefeller launched a scheme to recycle Arab petrodollars, entered the art reproduction business, and struggled to reassert his leadership of a family in the throes of generational change.

Among those assisting Rockefeller in his twilight years were his former Washington counsel Richard Parsons and Megan Marshack, a would-be journalist whose work on a series of art books did nothing to mask the growing intimacy between herself and her employer.

13 West Fifty-fourth Street. Inhabited by his parents early in their marriage, this townhouse became notorious as the site of Nelson's death in January 1979, amid circumstances that have never been fully explained.

"He was what he was," said Ann Rockefeller Roberts at her father's Riverside Church memorial service, "exuberant, energetic, extravagant." President and Mrs. Jimmy Carter offered the nation's condolences to Happy Rockefeller, pictured here with her sons Mark and Nelson Jr.

Twenty-Three

ATTICA

Spending money you don't have doesn't make you a liberal. It only makes you a damn fool.

—NELSON A. ROCKEFELLER, June 1971

1

ROCKEFELLER'S FOURTH INAUGURAL was a muted affair, as a New Year's Day snowstorm pummeled Albany, leaving him to take the now familiar oath before a half-empty assembly chamber. On the heels of his reelection, he had promised New Yorkers an administration "of change, of innovation, of creation to meet changing needs." Little could he conceive on this snowbound first of January how unlucky his thirteenth year in office was to be, or how much of the change it sired would be driven by events as uncontrollable as Albany's dismal weather. His inaugural address, replete with New Agish talk of spiritual impoverishment amid material wealth, was widely interpreted as a funeral oration for New York's proud, if costly, tradition of socially conscious government. On this point, *The New York Times* was explicit. "Governor Rockefeller buried a dream yesterday," the paper asserted in its January 2 edition. "It was the dream that state government, if it had but the will, could do almost anything to meet its own emerging needs."

Only a handful in his audience knew how wide a net Rockefeller had cast in seeking alternatives. Six weeks earlier he was at the White House, lobbying Richard Nixon for a federal revenue–sharing program large enough to address his state's looming budget shortfall. Though unwilling to be pinned down on numbers, Nixon, anxious to harness the nation's Republican governors in his bid for a second term, had shown himself surprisingly open to the concept. By the time of his January 22 State of the Union address, he was persuaded to make a $5 billion revenue-sharing initiative the cornerstone of his "New American Revolution." (Nixon was as immodest in packaging programs as Rockefeller was in conceiving them.) It wasn't the first time an American president had appropriated the Rockefeller agenda for his own purposes. "Perhaps this is my real role in politics," Nelson remarked of the parallels between his recent inaugural and Nixon's State of the Union appeal.

His personal lobbying efforts for revenue sharing were inseparable from the struggle to pass a "stopgap crisis" state budget of $8.45 billion. Since the former remained purely conjectural, the latter could be balanced only through a battery of increased taxes and user fees, the tapping of rainy day funds, and borrowing on a scale unimaginable in the palmy days of pay as you go. Readily acknowledging his contributions to the state's overextended position—"I'm a builder by nature"—Rockefeller nonetheless proclaimed as his highest priority for 1971 a $4 billion community development bond issue to subsidize private reconstruction of slum neighborhoods by Ed Logue's Urban Development Corporation. Within days of his budget presentation, Rockefeller took up the cudgels for revenue sharing with a speech to the National Press Club. February 22, otherwise observed as Washington's Birthday, was designated Revenue Sharing Day in the Empire State. Hoping to generate grassroots pressure on the state's congressional delegation, Nelson wrote every mayor in the state, spelling out the financial benefits to each if revenue sharing was enacted.

Concerned that Democratic lawmakers might be reluctant to endorse so prominent a Nixon administration initiative, he stocked a three-hundred-member citizens' committee with grandees of the opposition party such as Averell Harriman and Arthur Levitt. Before multiple congressional committees and a flurry of town meetings, he framed the debate in ideologically neutral language that everyone could understand. Revenue sharing was the essence of self-government, Rockefeller maintained; while two-thirds of the people's tax money was going to Washington, D.C., an even greater share of their most pressing problems cried out for resolution at the state and local levels. His aggressive campaign beyond New York's borders contrasted with his dwindling clout at home. He was sixty-two; few expected him to seek a fifth term in 1974. A lame duck governor, even one named Rockefeller, finds his ability to cajole, threaten, and reward greatly diminished. A growing number of Republican legislators, many owing their seats to the surging Conservative Party, took their cue from assembly Speaker Perry Duryea, whose eagerness to embark upon the post-Rockefeller era was Albany's worst-kept secret. Adding to his woes, Rockefeller confronted the state's most serious fiscal crisis since the Great Depression without benefit of his most experienced allies. A postelection changing of the guard made thirty-nine-year-old Bobby Douglass secretary to the governor in place of Al Marshall. Michael Whiteman, thirty-three, succeeded his mentor Douglass as counsel. Budget Director Norm Hurd got a new title as "Director of State Operations." Together they formed a highly capable team, but external events, culminating in the nation's deadliest prison uprising that fall, conspired to place them on the defensive from day one.

As austerity sapped the Rockefeller spirit, so personal trials magnified public affliction. The death of Martha Baird Rockefeller on January 21, 1971, snapped a last link to his parents' generation. Increasingly eccentric in her later years, the reclusive Aunt Martha never spent a night in the palatial residence, empty save for a pair of Rolls-Royces in the garage, built for her use when she turned Kykuit over to Nelson and Happy. Publicly, her death was attributed to a heart attack; to friends, Nelson suggested alcohol and drugs as contributing factors. An autopsy was considered but never performed, as Rockefeller discretion trumped disclosure, in an eerie foreshadowing of events surrounding Nelson's own death almost eight years later to the day. Truth be told, the passing of Junior's widow evoked few tears in a family that had never accepted Martha as a legitimate successor to Abby Aldrich Rockefeller. For Nelson, the loss of his stepmother was chiefly measured in financial terms. "I'm in a spot," he told his state budget director, Richard Dunham. "I had access to a billion dollars. Now I only have access to $500 million."

Martha's death ushered in a round of belt-tightening just slightly less demanding than what New Yorkers of more modest means faced at the start of Rockefeller's fourth term in Albany. On February 9, Perry Duryea declared his opposition to the governor's "bare-bones" budget, with its four thousand new jobs and 7.2 percent cost-of-living adjustment for welfare recipients. At a closed-door caucus of GOP members, the state's hemorrhaging welfare system came in for stinging criticism. Rockefeller took note. By mid-March, he was offering up at least $300 million in spending cuts. As the stalemate dragged on, exchanges between Rockefeller and his own party leaders grew more heated. Duryea recalled an executive "purple" with rage over the Speaker's unyielding insistence on $600 million or more in budget savings. When Duryea announced his intention to walk out of one particularly acrimonious meeting, a chastened Rockefeller practically begged him to return.

On March 27, insisting the time had come for a "complete reorganization, conceptually and structurally," of the state's welfare system, Rockefeller introduced a package of ten hurriedly crafted bills aimed at restraining costs, eliminating fraud, and incentivizing work. Reversing his politically risky stand of a decade earlier, Rockefeller now demanded a one-year residency requirement, notwithstanding the Supreme Court's 1969 ruling that such restrictions were unconstitutional. Seizing on a loophole in judicial logic authorizing residential requirements where a "compelling state interest" could be proven, he claimed that New York, already bearing the highest tax burden in the nation and further saddled with an acute housing shortage, met the test for legal exemption.*

---

* Rockefeller's shift on public assistance was less abrupt than it appeared. As early as 1964, he had appointed a Citizens' Committee on Welfare Costs to investigate a rapidly expanding case-

Rockefeller explained his U-turn to Deputy Secretary Harry Albright. On becoming governor, he had believed the Empire State capable of absorbing an influx of southern blacks and Puerto Rican immigrants attracted by its historic liberality. "Regrettably, I was simply wrong. The immigration of minorities from the South was overwhelming." Taking advantage of New York's generous welfare benefits, some communities provided their unemployed with free railroad tickets north. Over time, the wave of newcomers threatened to swamp the public finances, as one in ten New Yorkers drew on the state for subsistence. Adding to the problem, Rockefeller told Albright, most of those entering the United States from abroad had arrived with "formidable cultures, or traditional work ethics" that helped speed their integration. Not so domestic immigrants, "people who had not the remotest background of culture," many of them refugees from a racist South, said Rockefeller, with little or no legacy of self-support.

An aggressive probe of state and local welfare operations revealed a statewide ineligibility rate over 17 percent (in New York City, the figure approached 30 percent). Application procedures were overhauled, with would-be recipients of Aid to Families with Dependent Children required to submit an eleven-page form, accompanied by substantial documentation. The caseload dropped significantly. Welfare itself was redefined. More than a shield against want, it should be a bridge to work, said Rockefeller, not a substitute for work. Henceforth all adults, excepting the elderly, blind, and disabled and mothers regarded as unemployable, were candidates for public works jobs. Critics denounced the idea as punitive, though no more so than the 10 percent reduction in relief payments demanded by legislators. In addition, Rockefeller sought a waiver from the Department of Health, Education, and Welfare to let New York pursue what he called work relief.

Incentives for Independence, to give the program its more formal designation, was designed to be compatible with Nixon's unenacted Family Assistance Plan. Under the scheme, a national benefit floor of $2,400 for a family of four would be locally supplemented through financial incentives for socially responsible behavior—such as regular school attendance—up to the state's present ceiling of $3,756. Noting that New York City hospitals alone reported thirteen thousand job vacancies, Rockefeller sold the initiative as an opportunity to reestablish the work ethic while making a tangible contribution to the community. Detractors labeled it his "brownie point plan," a crude intrusion into family life reminiscent of the Dickensian workhouse.

Legislators moved quickly to enact the Rockefeller agenda, with mixed results. To classify mothers of children six or older as employable did not mean

load in a time of economic prosperity. Among the group's recommendations: a one-year residency requirement, an idea allowed to gather dust until the fiscal crisis of the early 1970s.

there was work available for them. Indeed, by June 1972 only about twenty-nine thousand welfare recipients had been placed in jobs. Rockefeller's one-year residency requirement fared even worse, as courts up to and including the U.S. Supreme Court reiterated their earlier findings of unconstitutionality. No one was more dismayed by Rockefeller's seeming abandonment of liberal principles than his longtime friend, and friendly critic, Jackie Robinson. In the last months of his life, blinded by diabetes and grieving over the loss of his son to heroin addiction, the legendary athlete took Rockefeller to task. "I cannot fight any longer, Governor," Robinson confessed in a May 1972 cri de coeur, "for I believe you have lost the sensitivity and understanding I felt was yours when I worked for you."

Times had changed, Rockefeller wrote in reply. "Putting on the brakes, retrenching, calling a halt—these are actions alien to my nature. But I have learned from bitter experience that liberalism ceases to work at some point if it is not controlled by realism. We have come face to face with the fact that state and local governments are running out of money, abuses have occurred, and an inevitable taxpayer reaction has set in. I am simply trying to bring things back into balance. . . . All I can say is that I am trying to do my best in a very difficult period and I hope we can sit down together and talk it over sometime soon. Just let me know if you want to."*

2

I T WAS ALMOST midnight on April 1, 1971, the legal deadline for a budget to be enacted, when Rockefeller and Earl Brydges dropped by the office of Senator John Hughes, the antitax crusader whose demand for an additional $100 million in cuts threatened a last minute revolt by New York City Republicans. Eleven hours of negotiation produced sufficient savings for Hughes to relent. The result validated Perry Duryea's claim that the legislature had become a coequal branch of government, as Rockefeller settled for less than half the tax revenues he had originally sought, and his adversaries crowed over $760 million in spending cuts.

His rebuff on the budget was only the most public of Rockefeller's defeats that spring. Persuaded it had no chance of passage in the current political climate,

---

* Whether such a conversation would have fostered reconciliation between the two men will never be known; any attempt was ruled out by Robinson's declining health. He died of a heart attack on October 24, 1972, aged fifty-three. Rockefeller, in Syracuse campaigning with Vice President Agnew, issued a statement of condolence before going on to address a Nixon-Agnew rally at the Oneida County Airport.

he withdrew his community development bond issue from the November ballot. His other announced priorities—no-fault auto insurance, comprehensive health insurance, gun control, and a reduction in legal penalties for possession of marijuana—never made it out of legislative committee. Acknowledging that the state's rehabilitative approach had yet to curtail drug addiction and that state-supplied methadone was merely a substitute fix for heroin addicts, Rockefeller appealed to the medical profession to develop a cure for the drug habit. This came dangerously close to throwing up his hands in despair. In fact, it was merely the preface to yet another, more radical attempt to combat the drug menace.

Another long-running source of frustration was New York City Hall, where John Lindsay was demanding $900 million in fresh state aid or taxing authority, at peril of discharging ninety thousand employees—a number, Rockefeller noted archly, that "would about bring the city back to where it was when he took over." Insisting there was "no data to back it up," Lindsay rejected a gubernatorial warning about the destructive impact of higher taxes on residents and commuters. The mayor had his hands more than usually full that spring. A renewed outbreak of strikes competed for attention with a spreading police corruption scandal and a rash of cop killings, many linked to political radicals such as Richard Moore, a Black Panther defendant who had skipped bail and soon thereafter opened fire on two policemen guarding the home of Manhattan district attorney Frank Hogan.

On May 26, the latest crimes against the NYPD provided a conversational opener between Richard Nixon and osteopath Ken Riland, who preserved the exchange in his diary. "What in the world are we going to be able to do about this, Kenny?" asked an agitated Nixon. "Mr. President," Riland replied, "the only way you're going to be able to solve these things, at least in New York, is to get rid of Lindsay. The guy's no good and if you federal people will put the pressure on, and some kind of a study like a Seabury investigation, or at least help Nelson do it, perhaps something can be done."*

"Well, will you tell Nelson he's got all the help in the world," said Nixon. "And what kind of a wiretap bill do you have in New York?" Riland said to his knowledge it was one of the best in the nation. "Well," the president continued, "if he needs any help from the FBI, or money, or anything else, you have him let me know." That night Riland relayed his White House conversation to Nelson in Albany. "All right," said Rockefeller. "Let's go for a Seabury type investi-

---

* Judge Samuel Seabury, a figure of legendary probity, had been tapped by Governor Franklin D. Roosevelt in 1930 to conduct an investigation of Tammany-sanctioned corruption in the New York City court system. A year later, the Republican legislature expanded his inquiry to include Mayor Jimmy Walker's administration. At the start of September 1932, Walker abruptly resigned his office. A week later, he just as abruptly sailed for Europe.

gation as soon as the session is over." On May 30, Nixon himself called his old adversary from Camp David to renew his offer of assistance. Attorney General John Mitchell rearranged his schedule to discuss the situation with Nelson over lunch on Friday, June 4. Nelson couldn't wait. Provoked by the mayor's repeated charges that he was locked out of crucial budget negotiations, Rockefeller joined Republican leaders in both houses of the legislature to decry the Lindsay administration as "inept and extravagant." Moreover, by accelerating the exodus of job-producing industries and businesses, the mayor's latest budget demands threatened to convert a "transitory crisis" into economic disaster.

Lindsay returned the fire, accusing state government of holding the five boroughs in a financial death grip. Targeting hostile elements in the legislature, he told a state conference of mayors that New York City had been "raped, but we're being charged with prostitution." This time Rockefeller didn't bother to feign sympathy. As for Lindsay, "He's not responsible for what he's saying. . . . The poor man has been under a lot of pressure." After the legislature settled on a $525 million tax package for the city, the governor vowed that it would be the last of its kind. He had already secured legislative approval to audit the city's finances. Now, with Nixon's words of encouragement fresh in his ears, Rockefeller announced formation of the Temporary State Commission to Make a Study of the Governmental Operation of the City of New York, better known as the Scott Commission for its chairman, New York State Bar Association president Stuart Nash Scott. Lindsay reciprocated by establishing his own City Commission on the State Government, with a mandate reaching beyond Albany's management and productivity, to include the possibility of statehood for New York City—an idea Rockefeller lampooned as "childish."

No doubt many of their constituents would apply the same adjective to New York's dueling executives. On August 9, Lindsay simplified matters by changing his party registration from Republican to Democrat. For once Rockefeller held his tongue, passing up a joke at the mayor's expense before a dinner of journalists. "It wasn't so much that the Republicans had lost a champion of the poor," Nelson was supposed to say of his nemesis in city hall, "but that the Democrats had gained a son of the rich."

"Too hot to use—by me!" Rockefeller told his would-be gag writer. He was to demonstrate more questionable judgment in a pending test, the severest of his Albany career and one with lasting consequences for his popular and historical reputation.*

---

* Rockefeller's inability to tell a joke created its own brand of humor. Suspicious of double entendres, and uncomfortable with cracks about his wealth, he frequently stepped on his own best lines. After the powerful trial lawyers lobby again shot down no-fault automobile insurance, Rockefeller accepted an invitation to receive their association's highest award. Reporter Gene Spagnoli offered him a one-liner to break the tension. "Governor, what you really ought to say in

3

I T SHOULD SURPRISE no one that Rockefeller's enthusiasm for new airports and island communities in the East River exceeded his interest in New York's prisons, most of them hulking throwbacks to an era when retribution trumped any claim to individual reform. Even in flush times, the state's penal system was something of a political orphan; in recent years, the share of New York's budget devoted to prisons and prisoners had slipped from 4.8 percent to 3 percent. Such numbers fail, however, to convey the whole story. In 1966, one year after agreeing to abolish the death penalty in New York (except for the murder of police or peace officers), Rockefeller created the Special Committee on Criminal Offenders to investigate how the state dealt with its lawbreakers. As he later explained the move, "I became increasingly concerned that while the parole program was moving along rehabilitative lines, correctional institutions were largely operated on a custodial basis."

These opposing schools of thought were well represented by the committee's co-chairs. Incumbent commissioner Paul McGinnis, the proverbial tough Irish cop, was to prisons what Bing Crosby was to movie priests. This had its advantages. "When I lay my head on the pillow at night," Rockefeller once observed, "the one department I don't have to worry about is Paul McGinnis and the Department of Corrections. He's got everything under control." More dynamic, if less predictable, was Russell Oswald, a fifty-eight-year-old reformer with a national reputation stemming from his leadership of prison systems in his native Wisconsin and Massachusetts. Early in the Rockefeller governorship, Oswald had raised over dinner the topic of parolees whose potential for success went unrecognized by the current system. The next morning, he was surprised to receive a follow-up call from his host. "Why don't you get going on this right away," Rockefeller exhorted him. "How much would it cost to institute the . . . the . . . gifted parolee program?" Thus was born the Gifted Parolee Unit, prototype of other special units for narcotics offenders, retarded youngsters, and those requiring psychiatric assistance. Rockefeller intervened with state departments, urging them to hire qualified parolees. He regularly checked with Oswald on the progress being made by his charges and was delighted to learn that only a handful had reverted to their former criminal habits.

In 1970, acting on the recommendations of the governor's special committee, the legislature agreed to consolidate the existing Department of Correc-

---

that speech is that Dr. Salk discovered the Salk vaccine that cured polio and no-fault insurance will cure whiplash." On the evening in question, Rockefeller told a mystified audience, "I want to tell you, that Dr. Salk cured polio and no-fault insurance will cure backlash." Gene Spagnoli, HMI, 27.

tions with the parole board. Oswald, the obvious choice to implement the merger, was reluctant to take the job. The timing couldn't be worse, given the state's fiscal condition and serious understaffing at the newly configured Department of Correctional Services. His immediate predecessor had warned of a "blood bath" without additional money for basic improvements throughout an aged and badly overcrowded system. No one knew better than Oswald that he was in a race against time. During the first week of November 1970, Auburn State Prison, a nineteenth-century fortress whose enforced silences had reminded Alexis de Tocqueville of "a desert solitude," erupted in violence after a small group of militant prisoners declared Black Solidarity Day. When protest organizers were subsequently confined to their cells, it sparked a full-scale uprising in which dozens of custodial officers and supervisory personnel were briefly taken hostage. Rampaging inmates trashed the mess hall, library, chapel, and other facilities. With the help of local, county, and state police, prison administrators regained control of the complex by the evening of November 4.

"This was not a classic prison riot," concluded the state's official investigative report. "It was, in truth, the breakthrough at Auburn of a volcano which is seething under virtually every prison in this state and nation." Prison overseers were equally confident they had identified the virus responsible for the contagion. "There is reason to believe that members of the Black Panthers . . . are intent upon violent revolution and that they foment it wherever they are transferred." One could as easily substitute for the Panthers the Young Lords, Black Muslims, Five Percenters, or Weathermen—slivers of the counterculture bonded in distrust of the white capitalist establishment. Forty years after the fact, it is impossible to isolate the events at Auburn or Attica from revolutionary currents unique to the era. Spontaneous combustion or organized uprising: Was Attica torn apart by self-labeled political prisoners, pushed beyond human limits by institutionalized racism and the hopelessness of captivity; or by *politicized* prisoners spouting a rhetoric of victimization to mask their crimes and exploit sympathies as specific to the era as Patty Hearst's beret and Leonard Bernstein's notorious 1970 fund-raising party for the Black Panthers?

With the perspective of time, one can see the uprising of September 1971 as confirmation of a revolution that had already occurred in the minds and hearts of profoundly alienated young men. In the words of the *Official Report of the New York State Special Commission on Attica*—hereafter referred to as the *McKay Report* for its chairman, New York University Law School dean Robert B. McKay—those prisoners displayed behind bars "enhanced self-esteem, racial pride, and political awareness." This was complemented by their refusal to accept the petty humiliations and racism that characterize prison life. Proponents of the commission found within prison walls the same explosive ingredients consuming Watts, Newark, Detroit, and other American cities in the turbulent 1960s. Critics detected in such reasoning a manifestation of white liberal guilt, a curdled idealism that came perilously close to excusing the rebellion at Attica as the inevitable consequence of racial inequity and societal neglect.

Ironically, on its opening in 1931, the Wyoming State Prison at Attica had been hailed as a "convict's paradise," complete with cafeteria, recreation rooms, sunlit cells, and spring mattresses. By 1971, the same institution had come to symbolize systemic failure and the unimaginative pursuit of security over rehabilitation. A thirty-foot wall, broken by fourteen gun towers, surrounded the prison's fifty-three acres. Its 2,243 inmates, a majority of them black, were housed in five cell blocks, overseen by a correctional staff of 398, all but one of whom was white. Meaningful work was as rare as the weekly showers granted prisoners. There were floors to mop, coal to unload, a laundry to operate. In the hot, dirty metal shop, otherwise known as the Black Hole of Calcutta, inmates assembled shelving and tables for daily wages of fifty cents or less. Some prisoners supplemented their income through drug sales, homosexual prostitution, or handcrafted pornography.*

No indoor athletic facility existed at Attica. Alone in their nine-by-six-foot cells for up to sixteen hours each day, inmates wore prison-made clothing, inadequate for seasonal extremes, and not a stitch of it blue—not even blue underwear—lest it breed confusion in any violent confrontation with guards. On discovering that the daily allocation of sixty-three cents to feed each inmate fell short of minimal federal guidelines, Oswald ordered dietary improvements (though prisoners continued to be entrusted with spoons only, and no eggs appeared at breakfast or any other meal). A growing Muslim contingent protested the frequency of pork, prohibited by their religious scruples, as a main course and in cooking fat. Again Oswald issued a corrective order. Corned beef was added to the list of acceptable items in holiday packages from the outside. In anticipation of the January 1971 departmental merger, New York renamed its six existing maximum security prisons "correctional facilities." Their wardens were rechristened "institutional superintendents." At Attica this position was filled by Vincent Mancusi, a thirty-five-year veteran of the state prison system, whose rewards included a handsome brick Georgian mansion, complete with putting green, located a stone's throw from the grim cell blocks housing some of the state's most hardened criminal offenders. The warden, no friend to re-

---

* A majority of the 15,468 offenders housed in New York State's fourteen correctional facilities and four youth camps were African American. Forty percent of the inmate population was under the age of thirty; only 20 percent had completed high school. In the autumn of 1971, approximately 2,500 inmates, some of whom were to play prominent roles in the Attica uprising, had been transferred into state custody out of the Tombs and other congested facilities in New York City.

form, reportedly used inmate labor to iron his shirts and wash his bed linens, for which he paid with a box of cigarettes at Christmas.

Forced by budget cutbacks to lay off four hundred employees—though none at Attica—Commissioner Oswald pursued cosmetic changes. With Rockefeller's approval, he expanded mail and visitation privileges, opened his facilities to visits by reporters, and broadened inmate access to books, newspapers, and magazines. There were plans afoot for improved libraries and a more relaxed furlough policy to alleviate the pervasive sexual tension behind bars. None of this addressed issues of chronic overcrowding, stunted educational and job opportunities, or a guard force deficient in professional training and racial sensitivity. (Officers who routinely assigned the best jobs to white inmates brandished clubs they called "nigger sticks.") Rockefeller's call for a guard training academy was held hostage to red ink, along with the summer education programs and expanded vocational offerings favored by Oswald. The commissioner encouraged prisoners, their families, and their attorneys to write him—and a growing backlog of unanswered mail mocked his good intentions. "The status quo is anathema to all," he wrote Rockefeller on May 10, 1971. In response, the governor authorized fifty additional corrections officers, a down payment on the force necessary to allow prisoners more time out of their cells.

A week later, Oswald communicated his fears in person, describing for Rockefeller a new breed of prisoner, militant in his politics, radical in his outlook, and bitterly distrustful of a government he considered illegitimate. Many blacks believed, with considerable confirming evidence, that the justice system from the bail bondsman to the parole board was rigged against them. On July 2, 1971, five inmates styling themselves the Attica Liberation Faction mailed a bristling manifesto to the commissioner, with a copy to the governor's office. Adapting language employed during the recent uprising at the Tombs in New York City, the authors decried "the fascist concentration camps of modern America," in which they were treated as slave labor. The rhetoric was more revolutionary than their demands for better food and clothing; improved medical care; recreational and job opportunities; a minimum wage; and, tellingly, "an end to the segregation of prisoners from the mainline population because of their political beliefs." Superintendent Mancusi wanted the five rebels transferred out of his institution. That was the traditional way of handling troublemakers. But Oswald overruled his superintendent, an act that won him the hostility of most corrections officers, without earning the trust of inmates hardened to official mendacity.

In his written response to the Attica Liberation Faction, Oswald outlined some of the improvements already made and pleaded for time to implement more basic reforms, not excluding the need to "re-attitudinize" guards as much as inmates. With tensions clearly on the rise, Oswald ordered each of his superintendents to submit riot control plans for review. A note of urgency infused his monthly report to the governor for August 1971: "I feel strongly that no other state agency holds the potential for disaster in terms of dollars and—more importantly—lives." Oswald's concerns were echoed down the ranks. Two weeks before he became the first fatality at Attica, twenty-eight-year-old corrections officer William Quinn, convinced that major trouble was brewing, insisted that his wife join him in reviewing their finances, in particular his life insurance policy. Other officers began leaving their wallets at home.

Events a continent away inflamed resentments. On August 21, George Jackson, a resistance hero in Black Panther ranks, was shot to death in a California prison escape attempt. The next day, hundreds of Attica inmates wearing black armbands paid tribute to the Soledad Brother by observing a self-imposed fast and period of silence. Oswald scheduled a visit to Attica for September 2. Unfortunately, his wife's illness caused the cancellation of a planned address by the commissioner to the full complement of prisoners. Before leaving, Oswald did hastily tape-record remarks to be played that evening over the prison radio. In language better suited to a conference of his correctional peers, he reiterated the modest changes implemented to date and described a futuristic vision of community treatment centers housing no more than four hundred inmates each. Yet he left untouched the existing monthly allotment of a single bar of soap and roll of toilet paper per inmate.

Oswald's request for patience produced the opposite of its intended effect. To many who heard it, his disembodied voice was worse than insulting; it was disrespectful. The commissioner, needless to say, held a different view of his motives. Oswald counted himself one of the good guys, an agent of liberal reform pitted against Attica's dehumanizing status quo, on the one hand, and, on the other, a simmering rage that sanctioned violence as a legitimate weapon to be turned against the system and its enforcers. At heart a modernizer, Russ Oswald would pay a heavy price for imputing rationality to others.

4

THURSDAY MORNING, SEPTEMBER 9, found Rockefeller hundreds of miles from Attica, cocooned in the quasi-presidential splendor of Washington's Old Executive Office Building. Thirty years after serving his apprenticeship there as Franklin Roosevelt's Latin American coordinator, he had returned to the former State, War, and Navy Building for a meeting of the President's Foreign Intelligence Advisory Board. Another appointive position, more prestigious than powerful, it nevertheless afforded Rockefeller an opportunity to keep his hand in official Washington while indulging his lifelong interest in foreign policy. Around ten thirty he was handed a note from Ann Whitman notifying him of trouble at the Attica prison complex. Details were sketchy, but it sounded serious, with an unknown number of hostages seized by rebellious inmates. Rockefeller waited until the current speaker finished, then slipped out of the room to place a call to Bobby Douglass and Mike Whiteman in Albany. His immediate concern, he later explained, was for the safety of the guards held captive and the restoration of order without further harm to anyone.

Subsequent reports fleshed out the initial bulletin. A scuffle in Attica's A Yard the previous day had caused Superintendent Mancusi to order the offending inmates segregated. Rumors circulated, later disproved, that the men removed from their cells were being beaten. Resentful prisoners in A Block, not content to vocalize their disapproval, threw whatever they could get their hands on between the bars of their cells. A responding officer was struck in the face by an unopened soup can. "We'll get you in the morning, motherfuckers!!" someone cried out to a departing officer. The first breakfast shift was served without incident. Then, some inmates implicated in the previous day's altercation—Company 5, in prison jargon—on their way to breakfast took advantage of a lockbox inadvertently left open to free inmate William Ortiz, the same offender accused of weaponizing a can of soup. Orders were given to divert the shuffling group of prisoners from their usual postbreakfast visit to A Yard and instead return them to their cell block until Ortiz could be recaptured.

Company 5 had other ideas. As the men passed through Times Square, so named because it formed the hub of Attica's four main cell blocks, Lieutenant Robert Curtiss, one of the officers involved in the previous day's fracas, was attacked and severely beaten. Two officers who went to his rescue barely escaped with their lives. It was a few minutes before nine o'clock. With explosive force, the balance of power flipped, as prisoners using purloined keys emptied whole cell blocks. Escaping inmates grabbed knives, pipes, baseball bats, and scissor blades secreted away or lying within reach. They set fires in the prison chapel, in classrooms, and in workshops. Nearing Times Square, they brutalized Officer William Quinn, leaving him unconscious in a pool of his own blood, his skull fractured in two places. Prison administrators, stymied by inadequate communications and their own failure to develop riot plans as requested by Oswald, watched immobilized as block after block fell to the rebels.

Around nine forty-five, inmates allowed Officer Quinn and several other injured hostages to be evacuated through the A Block gate. Quinn was rushed to a hospital in Rochester. His fate was to have profound repercussions for the nearly thirteen hundred prisoners swarming D Yard, together with their thirty-eight captives. A protective cordon of Black Muslims quickly formed around the blindfolded group, securing them against inmates shouting, "Kill the pigs!" and procuring them as potential bargaining chips. Almost none of this reached the state's chief executive in anything like real time. In his testimony before the McKay Commission, Rockefeller referenced "additional messages" that kept him apprised, however imperfectly, of unfolding events at the prison, followed at one thirty that afternoon by "a complete round up" from Norm Hurd. Commissioner Oswald was on his way to Attica, Hurd revealed. Efforts to retake the prison and free the hostages were on hold pending the arrival of sufficient state police to justify the attempt.

But, as would happen so often during those early hours of confusion and surmise, events had overtaken Hurd's reporting. Even as Oswald flew to Attica, a small force of state troopers, armed only with clubs and assisted by corrections officers, had recaptured three cell blocks, until they were repulsed by inmates who welded doors shut with equipment from the metal shop. No casualties and only a scattered few warning shots marred the operation. With supplies of disabling CS gas running low, however, and in the face of credible death threats to the remaining hostages, the counterattack stalled. A skeleton force was withdrawn from its forward position in B Block. Harry Albright, the Rockefeller staff member entrusted with crafting a detailed chronology of the Attica uprising, became convinced there might have been a different outcome had senior staff colleagues adopted a more aggressive stance in consulting the governor on fast-moving events, above all, on the "fatal decision"—Norm Hurd's own characterization—to halt the retaking of the prison.

In the 1920s, both Governor Franklin Roosevelt and his lieutenant governor, Herbert Lehman, acting in Roosevelt's absence, had refused to negotiate with rioting inmates at two of New York's prisons. Ringleaders of a December 1929 uprising at Auburn State Prison seized hostages and demanded safe passage beyond the jurisdiction of New York. Even after killing the prison's second in command, those responsible had insisted on amnesty for their actions. "Impossible," said Acting Governor Lehman. "As long as I am here there will be no compromise, no matter what the circumstances, or what the results might be." Eventually, Lehman ordered the prison retaken by the National Guard without additional loss of life, though several hostages were wounded. After the fact, Rockefeller would lament his failure to follow the Lehman precedent. Of the aborted action by state police that restored nearly a thousand inmates to administration control, he got only fragmentary reports throughout the afternoon of September 9. Not until six o'clock that evening, according to his testimony, did he receive a comprehensive briefing from Albany.

By then the die had been cast. Since arriving at Attica around two, Oswald had made a series of decisions dictated by circumstances and his confidence that he could negotiate a peaceful resolution and advance the cause of prison reform. (Years were to pass before a chastened Oswald confided to Hurd, "I just couldn't believe that I could ever get into a situation like this.") Preceding Oswald into D Yard, with his permission, were Arthur O. Eve, a state assemblyman from Buffalo who also published a weekly newspaper directed at that city's substantial black population; and Herman Schwartz, a member of the law faculty at the University of Buffalo active in the American Civil Liberties Union's National Prison Project. The two men had hastened to the prison as soon as they heard of the uprising. Once in D Yard, Eve and Schwartz were handed six "Immediate Demands" devised by an ad hoc negotiating committee. These included amnesty for any actions linked to the rebellion, a federal takeover of the state prison, which was to be reconstructed under inmate supervision, and transportation to a "non-imperialistic" country for anyone wishing to leave the United States.*

Oswald, well aware of the long-standing tradition that prison officials should never negotiate with a gun to their head, was no more predisposed to meet with rebel leaders on any but neutral ground. Yet his resolution crumbled quickly in the face of reality. Shortly before four o'clock, over the strenuous objections of Superintendent Mancusi, and with Eve and Schwartz in tow, Oswald ventured into an emotionally charged D Yard for the first of several visits. Additional concessions followed: removal of armed state troopers from surrounding rooftops; the admission of journalists to report on ensuing discussions (and, presumably, convey to the world the personal and political grievances of men long ignored by society); and a promise of no administrative reprisals against those who surrendered peacefully. A second trip to D Yard, and an expanded, more moderate list of prisoner demands, coupled with a continuing shortage of CS gas, strengthened Oswald's natural preference for negotiation over military force.

Rockefeller in Washington had little choice but to ratify the actions of his lieutenant on the scene. Any doubts he might have entertained were assuaged by state police officials who voiced support for the commissioner's strategy. By the time sufficient troops were assembled to resume the earlier offensive, Oswald had too much invested in negotiation to switch gears. The governor affirmed the decision to keep talking, though expressing concern that delay might foster an appearance of indecision. He inquired about cordoning off ap-

---

* One reason amnesty topped the list of inmate demands, according to Herman Badillo, was the unkept promise made to inmates involved in the most recent uprising at Auburn State Prison. Even though the incident had occurred prior to Oswald's installation, the memory of their betrayal rankled among Auburn ringleaders, some of whom showed up at the Attica negotiating table. Herman Badillo and Milton Haynes, *A Bill of No Rights: Attica and the American Prison System* (New York: Outerbridge & Lazard, 1972), 42.

proaches to the area and was assured that adequate controls were already in place. Rockefeller then asked Norm Hurd, who had worked closely with Oswald on his departmental reorganization, to go to Attica that same evening, accompanied by Major General A. C. "Buzz" O'Hara, a former commanding general in the state's National Guard. The choice of O'Hara was revealing, given his role in suppressing, with minimal bloodshed, a 1964 race riot in Rochester, after which Rockefeller had visited the city to see the damage with his own eyes and express his appreciation to the Guardsmen.

By midnight, Rockefeller's two emissaries were conferring with Oswald in the superintendent's office overlooking the prison entrance. They found a man visibly shaken by his third visit to the yard, in the course of which he had narrowly escaped being taken hostage. In what may have been the most pivotal conversation of the entire crisis, Oswald described his ordeal over the phone to Rockefeller, leaving a vivid impression of the dangers facing anyone who followed in his footsteps. Repeating the pattern established a year earlier at the Tombs, inmates had requested a group of outside representatives to negotiate on their behalf, among them the noted civil liberties lawyer and radical activist William Kunstler, Huey Newton of the Black Panther Party, Minister Louis Farrakhan from the Black Muslims, Clarence Jones, publisher of Harlem's *Amsterdam News*, and Tom Wicker of *The New York Times*. Again Oswald gave his assent.

Some names on the list defied expectation, though not logic. Perhaps the most popular, judging from the crowd response he generated, was John Dunne, a Republican state senator from Nassau County. The suburban lawmaker never forgot the experience, as a boy of nine, of sitting in Sing Sing's electric chair. As chairman of the joint legislative committee charged with prison oversight, Senator Dunne had led a series of prison tours for his committee brethren. He also organized an annual art exhibit of prisoner paintings, with prizes handed out by Governor and Mrs. Rockefeller. Inmates grateful for his interest now summoned him away from a judicial conference in bucolic Manchester, Vermont. Dunne wasn't the only conference participant to be drawn into the Attica vortex. To refute prisoner doubts about his guarantee of no administrative reprisals, Oswald agreed to seek a federal court order embodying his pledge. The same state plane that brought Hurd and O'Hara to Attica transported Herman Schwartz to Albany, from which he was driven through the night to Manchester's Equinox Hotel. There he roused Judge John T. Curtin of Buffalo, who immediately issued the desired document. At seven o'clock Friday morning, Schwartz was back in the superintendent's office, his mission accomplished.

Or so he thought. Oswald, more confident than ever that a peaceful solution to the crisis was at hand, had his hopes dashed by Thomas Soto, an outside observer representing the Prisoners' Solidarity League. From the outset Soto denied that he was part of any negotiating committee. His politics symbolized by the ring he wore, made from an American bomber shot down over Laos, Soto came to Attica for one reason only, to advocate for the oppressed brothers within. "No prison rebellion in U.S. history has ever been so politically conscious," he would later boast. Confronting Schwartz at the prison gate, Soto pronounced Judge Curtin's order subject to appeal and therefore meaningless. When Schwartz disputed this, Soto changed the subject, breathtakingly so: since any criminal actions attributed to Attica's inmate population were crimes of "survival," he contended, all prisoners should be set free. Picking up where Soto left off, inmates renounced Judge Curtin's court order as a hoax because it lacked a seal. By the time Schwartz managed to rectify this oversight, the atmosphere in D Yard did not allow for honest mistakes. Some in the crowd asked why the name of Governor Rockefeller appeared nowhere on the document. Jerry Rosenberg, a jailhouse lawyer whose death sentence for murdering two police detectives in Brooklyn had been commuted by the governor, seized the offending paper and tore it in half as inmates cheered and TV cameras beamed the proceedings to a mass audience.*

In Washington, Rockefeller had begun to entertain doubts about the outside observers, or "citizens' committee," whose members were even then making their way to Attica—for what? It was unclear, he said later, "what their function was, what their responsibilities were, who they were working for . . . how they were selected, how they were organized, who was their head." As observer ranks swelled past thirty—"It got out of hand," says John Dunne. "It was crazy. They didn't know how to handle it"—Rockefeller concluded that these freelancers represented Oswald's preferred method of negotiating at a safe distance from D Yard.

5

ROCKEFELLER RETURNED TO New York around five thirty Friday afternoon. From the airport, he contacted Douglass and Whiteman in Albany. Both men sounded discouraged, as continuing demands for amnesty reflected a hardening of inmate attitudes. It might even be necessary, the governor's men argued, to go in that night to rescue as many hostages as possible. The moment passed. Rockefeller spent the weekend at Pocantico, never more than a few steps from the telephone atop his eighteenth-century burl walnut desk in the

---

* Soto's intervention is reduced to a footnote in the *McKay Report*, while Oswald accords it extensive coverage in his memoir of those four days. This is typical of Attica reporting, which rivals the Hiss-Chambers spy scandal for sheer intensity of feeling and editorial polarization long after the fact.

first-floor office occupied by his father and grandfather before him. A portrait of Benjamin Franklin stared down from the east wall. A false bookcase concealed a television set, tuned in happier times to weekly favorites *Kojak* and *All in the Family*. From here Rockefeller monitored events and coordinated strategy with his agents in Albany and Attica.

By far the most influential of these was Bob Douglass. A native of Binghamton, New York, a Dartmouth graduate, and a protégé of George Hinman, Douglass was frequently described as the son Nelson Rockefeller wished he might have had. He was also a lawyer keenly sensitive to the moods and fancies of his employer. Deferential without being obsequious, Douglass knew when to tease the governor and how to make no sound like "maybe." In short, he had Rockefeller's number. So it came as no surprise that it was Douglass on Friday morning who reached out to Herman Badillo, the Bronx congressman whose efforts to defuse the recent uprising at the Tombs and other prisons on Long Island had earned him respect on both sides of the corrections debate. Badillo readily agreed to join the growing observer corps and to bring with him, as requested, another Puerto Rican leader from Buffalo, as well as "a younger and more radical type."

That afternoon, Badillo shared a state plane with newspaper publisher Clarence Jones and the Reverend Wyatt Tee Walker, a frequent consultant to Rockefeller on urban affairs. Within minutes of first entering D Yard, Badillo sensed divisions among the inmates assembled there and a more fractious atmosphere than at the Tombs. The search for consensus was to be complicated by inflammatory rhetoric from observers such as William Kunstler, who, even before he strode into D Yard late that Friday evening, declared criminal amnesty the defining issue in the standoff. Having proclaimed his solidarity with the rebellious inmates, Kunstler accepted an impromptu invitation to legally represent them. Tom Wicker questioned how Kunstler's commitment could be squared with his status as neutral observer. Wicker also noted how quickly his peers picked up the language of D Yard.

On hearing Kunstler declare amnesty the overriding question before them, Norm Hurd repeated Bobby Douglass's comment that it was not "a viable issue as we saw it." Wyoming County district attorney Louis James used less diplomatic language to say much the same thing when Russ Oswald asked him about it in a Friday night telephone call. James said he lacked the authority to grant amnesty. What's more, he wouldn't make such a concession had he the power to do so. His rejection fresh in their minds, the observers filed back into D Yard for five and a half hours of what Kunstler likened to Athenian democracy. It was not a comparison that suggested itself to John Dunne. Sympathetic though he was to prisoner complaints, Dunne had no illusions about the "negotiations" that began shortly before midnight. "Poor Russ went in there and got beat up real bad for the first twenty-four hours. And then when we went in . . . frankly most of us thought our lives were in jeopardy. That's why I refused to go in after two visits. But there was no way you could sit and negotiate across a table. The inmates were all making a bunch of speeches." Another complication was the factional mistrust diagnosed by Herman Badillo during his first minutes in D Yard. "If you expected agreement from the prison leaders," says Dunne, "they might wind up with a shiv in their back."

Amnesty aside, the most popular inmate requests involved dietary improvements and decent medical care. "They wanted to have more showers," recalls Badillo. "They wanted . . . freedom of religion, because many of them were Black Muslims. And they wanted the right to read the Black Panther newspaper. So we made a list—something like thirty-one or thirty-two demands." The exhausted observers spent much of Saturday negotiating with themselves. In the afternoon, Douglass and Whiteman, still in Albany, raised the issue of amnesty with Rockefeller. "They made the point to me legally I didn't have the power to give it," the governor told the McKay Commission. "From my point of view, we were now moving into a political area," an ominous development that rendered any form of criminal amnesty "totally impossible."*

"Seeing we were getting down to some pretty sensitive points in terms of legality," Rockefeller continued, he decided to send Douglass to Attica, accompanied by Mike Whiteman's deputy, Howard Shapiro. Their mandate was unclear, and Douglass in particular appeared to some observers standoffish. Some thought he had been sent to prevent any backsliding by Hurd and O'Hara. In fact, Douglass entered Attica knowing that Rockefeller had plans to retake the prison, "probably sometime tomorrow." (He had confided as much to Ken Riland after lunch that day.) A more hopeful atmosphere pervaded the superintendent's office at Attica, where Badillo and Oswald, lawyers both, reached agreement on what became known as "the 28 Points." Through recourse to basic constitutional protections, the two men resolved differences over freedom of religion and what constituted cruel and unusual punishment. No one disputed the inmates' right to additional showers and exercise. By the same token, only the most radical of observers expected the state to replace Superintendent Mancusi in response to prison demands. Amnesty remained a sticking point, but even here, the negotiators made progress. Civil amnesty for damage to the prison was easily granted, as was a guarantee of no physical reprisals against prisoners who returned to their cells.

---

* The state constitution is explicit on this point: "The governor shall have the power to grant reprieves, commutations and pardons after conviction, for all offenses except treason and cases of impeachment, upon such conditions and with such restrictions and limitations as he may think proper. . . ." William Kunstler thought there were constitutionally acceptable ways around this—for example, Rockefeller could promise clemency in advance of any legal proceedings.

"And then we got to the tough one, which was criminal amnesty," Badillo recalls. It was about to get a lot tougher. By five o'clock, just as Douglass and Shapiro appeared on the scene, Oswald had signaled his basic consent to the 28 Points. An hour later, Black Panther leader Bobby Seale arrived outside the prison. Douglass, fearing he might destabilize a situation on the verge of peaceful resolution, advised against admitting Seale to D Yard. Oswald, still very much in charge, and convinced by Kunstler and other militants that Seale might rally support for the 28 Points, decided to chance it. Then, suddenly, everything changed. The death of Officer William Quinn, confirmed early that evening, transformed a climate of possibility into one of dread. For an indeterminate number of prisoners, amnesty was no longer a philosophical debating point, but their sole protection against a possible murder charge, with a death sentence to follow.

Fearing for their safety, Rockefeller now insisted that every member of the observer group sign a waiver relieving New York State of culpability should they be taken hostage or harmed in a rescue attempt. Almost as an afterthought, the governor gave his blessing to the 28 Points. The inmates most emphatically did not. It was nine o'clock by the time the observers, accompanied by Bobby Seale, reentered the yard for the first time in sixteen hours. Seale's appearance proved something of an anticlimax, as he withheld comment on the 28 Points pending the approval of his party's central committee. Promising to return once he had authorization to do so, Seale left, trailed by a majority of observers, who felt the heat of inmate anger and disappointment in Seale's wake. Among those who remained, Clarence Jones was tasked with presenting the 28 Points for the prisoners' consideration. As he began to read a letter touching on criminal amnesty drafted earlier in the day by District Attorney Jones, jeers drowned out his voice. The publisher from Harlem, unintimidated and eloquent, reminded his listeners that politics was the art of the possible. It was one thing to echo Chairman Mao's observation that power comes from the barrel of a gun, quite another to be surrounded by other young men, infected with the "Kent State psychology" and only too willing to turn their loaded weapons on unarmed prisoners. Cries for amnesty echoed through D Yard.

Then it was Kunstler's turn to provoke gasps with his announcement of Officer Quinn's death. The 28 Points represented the best deal they could get at that time, he told the massed inmates, hastening to add, "You have a right to choose, a right to die like free men." There was no question where popular sentiment pointed. A powerful chorus of voices shouted disapproval of the 28 Points. One prisoner jumped onto the table from which Jones had addressed the inmates. Denouncing the proposed agreement as "trickery," he seized the 28 Points and ripped them to shreds.

6

THE McKAY COMMISSION aptly entitled its section on Sunday, September 12, "Clutching at Straws."* None of the observers was in a mood to concede failure, still less to accept the violence likely to ensue once their failure was formalized. Whatever may have divided them throughout the crisis was now subsumed in a unifying imperative: The state must at all costs be prevented from storming Attica. This meant a direct appeal to Governor Rockefeller. After three days on the sidelines, operating through emissaries and deferring to Oswald, Nelson was abruptly thrust stage center. "If the governor does not come," William Kunstler remonstrated with Bobby Douglass, "and if the prison is forcibly retaken, there will be uprisings all over the country." Douglass duly related the request to his employer.

"What am I coming for?" Rockefeller inquired of his most trusted adviser on the scene. "I said, 'You're coming for the two things that we can't deal with,'" Douglass would recall. Amnesty and the removal of Superintendent Mancusi as demanded by the more militant inmates. Think of the future consequences, Rockefeller responded. "If I go under these circumstances, anytime they want something, to bring the state to its knees, they just take hostages and demand that the governor or the president or the pope comes in. You can't run a country that way. You can't run a state that way. You can't operate under rule of law that way." Rockefeller instructed Douglass to draft a statement explaining his refusal to come to Attica. As pragmatism gave way to abstraction, more than physical distance separated Rockefeller in his Kykuit study from a disconsolate observer group, frantic to avoid bloodshed and hardly more willing to relinquish authority to Commissioner Oswald.

Rockefeller entertained no such doubts. "Russ had tried, this broadly representative group of citizens had tried, and they had been turned down," he reasoned. "And the group [of inmates] had hardened, according to reports that I got, and I just felt that in the face of this that the time had come when Russ was going to have to take this back in his own hands." Not that alternative means of bringing the rebellion to a nonviolent conclusion weren't discussed. At one point Happy Rockefeller asked whether it might be possible to drug the inmates' food or water supply—an idea her husband broached to Mike Whiteman shortly after noon on Sunday. It was quickly discarded as impractical and potentially counterproductive.

---

* At eight thirty that morning, Bobby Seale appeared at the prison entrance, only to be denied admittance to D Yard when he refused to reveal in advance what he planned to say to the rebels assembled there. (In the prison parking lot, Seale told Kunstler that the Panther central committee had voted to endorse the inmate demand for transport to a nonimperialist country and that he personally had no intention of endorsing the 28 Points.)

Press secretary Ron Maiorana unfurled a scheme of his own to defuse the crisis and save face all around. Maiorana, convinced that the inmates were looking for a way out, wanted Rockefeller at Attica to see and hear for himself the validity of their complaints. "Why don't you tell them, 'I'm in New York and you're up in Attica . . . I will get in my helicopter and I will fly one hundred miles. At the first stop . . . you will release a certain number of hostages as a show of good faith, because I'm coming up to talk to you.'" Rockefeller would fly another hundred miles, and so on, until he reached the prison, where he could meet inmates in a safe place. "I've seen you in worse situations than this," said Maiorana. "You can talk your way into anything." The issue at hand was simple, really: "They want you to meet with them."*

"You want me to walk into their yard by myself?"

He wouldn't be alone, said Maiorana. "I'll go with you." Why should he do that? Nelson inquired. What about Maiorana's family?

"You once told me that fate determines what's going to happen to us."

"When did I tell you that?"

"When we were in Oklahoma, and I could not get back on a plane because I was scared." Frozen in fear, unable to climb the stairs leading to the cabin of the aircraft, Maiorana had insisted on taking a train back to New York. And Rockefeller had talked him through his dread. Was Maiorana now implying an equivalence of terror? Rockefeller asked for time to think it over. As the governor pondered his options, Oswald banned further visitors to the yard, then relented as angry observers insisted it was too soon to stop talking. Outside the prison walls, relatives of the hostages kept vigil in a dismal rain. They watched with foreboding as fire hoses and gas masks were unloaded and carried inside.

By one o'clock, Tom Wicker had concluded that action to retake the prison by force was imminent. There was only one way to prevent a possible massacre, said Badillo. "We have to get Rocky to come here to give us some time and some credit with these guys in there." John Dunne pulled out his pocket address book. Wicker dialed the number and was immediately put through to the governor. For over an hour, Wicker, Badillo, Dunne, and Clarence Jones used every argument they could think of to win Rockefeller over to their viewpoint. Coming to Attica would demonstrate his concern for both inmates and hostages. By throwing his weight behind the 28 Points, he could increase the like-

---

* Maiorana's scheme was not as far-fetched as it may sound. "What Nelson should have done," Malcolm Wilson would contend, "and I think he had in mind doing it until he was dissuaded by others, was to go to a motel right nearby the prison and send word that nobody would negotiate under a gun but that, if the prisoners laid down their arms and released the hostages, he would meet with a committee of them to discuss their grievances." This overlooked the amnesty issue, inmate fears of guard reprisals, and the increasingly confrontational atmosphere pervading D Yard. Malcolm Wilson, HMI, 44.

lihood of their acceptance. Either way they would gain time for cooler heads to prevail. When his turn came to speak, Badillo didn't mince words. "Listen, Governor, if you storm the prison today, you are not only going to kill your own people . . . you're going to create a riot in the South Bronx and East Harlem and Bedford-Stuyvesant, because everybody is listening to what's going on, on radio and television, and if you kill a lot of people, there are going to be riots."

Having obtained Rockefeller's attention, Badillo offered a strategy to avoid mass bloodshed: "We want you to come to the prison, not to meet with the prisoners—we understand you can't—but to meet with us, because then you . . . can tell what's really going on." This was Badillo's euphemism for a growing dread he shared with Wicker and others as they encountered for themselves the racial and cultural antagonism of local residents, guards, and troopers alike. Fears were spreading that the forces of law and order, once unleashed to rescue their compatriots, might well exact murderous revenge on outgunned prisoners. Badillo reasoned that if Rockefeller met personally with the observers—some of whom had put their own lives on the line in response to his earlier appeal—"then we can go back and say you've shown good faith and I think we can settle it."

"I can't do that," said Rockefeller.

"Why not?"

"Because I'm getting a lot of telegrams from people saying that we cannot allow this to go on, that we have to take vigorous action, because prison riots cannot be permitted."[*]

"Governor," said an exasperated Badillo, "you got a prison riot, so you gotta deal with the reality of the problem."

The observers insisted they needed to buy time. From whom? Rockefeller asked Badillo. "Are you worried that the prisoners are going to move and kill the hostages, or are you worried the state is going to move?"

"No, we're worried about the state."

"Well, if it's more time you want, I can give you more time." The threat of urban violence had its desired effect. There would be no attempt to storm the prison Sunday afternoon. But Rockefeller, convinced that the Attica ringleaders wished nothing more than to prolong the revolutionary drama before the

---

* Jerry Danzig, a key media adviser, was left to ponder a conundrum of his own: "Several days into Attica I got a phone call from a very key man on our staff from Attica, who said to me, 'what are they saying about us? Are we being too tough, or are we being too soft?' And at the time, not knowing what was eventually going to happen—I thought, oh my God, politics are here again. We are now getting meter readings on something that is verging on human lives . . . it was not the kind of thing he would ask," said Danzig of Rockefeller. "It was something that a staff member might generate. But I have always wondered since how much this attitude measuring influenced the Governor's Attica decision." Jerry Danzig, HMI, 37.

largest audience they would ever command, had revealed to the observers his instruction to Oswald to "reopen the institution." Now, switching gears, he put a blunt question to his interlocutors: "Wouldn't you assume that if I got there the first thing they would do was say, we demand the Governor comes in the yard?" The observers—at least this quartet of relative moderates—agreed this was out of the question.

"I'm under great pressure to go to Attica," Rockefeller told Hugh Morrow as the television screen beamed images of hostages, filmed by their captors, begging for their lives. Morrow replied that as a matter of public relations if nothing else, he should give in. "John Lindsay would have been up there five days ago making speeches from the top of the wall." Lindsay's personal intervention in the Tombs riot, and the prisoner release it helped facilitate, was not a persuasive argument to make to Nelson Rockefeller. So Morrow settled for restating the obvious: "Your judgment has to be solely in terms of what's the best way to get those hostages out of there without getting them all killed."

The prospects for such an outcome dimmed with each passing hour. By Sunday afternoon, trenches had been dug in D Yard, barriers in corridors electrified, and Molotov cocktails stockpiled in readiness for a last stand. Morale on both sides was becoming ragged. Oswald fended off harsh criticism from observers angered by his latest ultimatum to the inmates ("Man, you and the Governor have just signed my death warrant," Arthur Eve told him). The committee, led by Herman Badillo, released its own statement warning of a pending "massacre" of prisoners and guards and imploring Rockefeller to come to Attica. Oswald permitted one more D Yard appearance by observers sympathetic to the prisoner cause. It was a disaster, at least from the state's view, with Eve demanding Rockefeller's immediate presence and Kunstler announcing, "There are four Third World and African country people across the street from this prison, prepared to provide asylum for everyone who wants to leave this country for this purpose"—a dubious claim he later justified because it would "make them feel better. . . . I thought if they were going to die, at least they should know that people were with them all over the world."*

During that same Sabbath, Vincent Mancusi had offered his resignation as superintendent in the hope that it might secure the hostages' release. Oswald rejected it on principle. Shortly after six p.m., inmates again ruled out negotiating anywhere but in D Yard. "I am now walking through the corridors of hell," Oswald moaned. "Join the crowd," replied an unsympathetic observer. At ten twenty, Wyatt Tee Walker phoned Norm Hurd with his own plea for guberna-

---

* For good measure, Kunstler used the occasion to reveal that Bobby Seale had been prevented from reentering the prison "because he could not bring himself, as a black man, to come in here and tell you what the Man wanted you to do."

torial intervention. Walker ascribed the intransigence of inmates to disbelief in the state's promises. Rockefeller's presence, in or out of the yard, could do much to convince them.

At ten thirty, the observers committee was formally dissolved. Minutes later, joined by "Buzz" O'Hara, the governor's original representative on the scene, Oswald placed another call to Rockefeller, asking him to change his mind. "Do you feel it will be productive?" said Rockefeller. "Will it save lives?" The bone-weary commissioner replied in the negative. Instead he repeated his earlier concerns over self-inflicted harm to the executive's image. Rockefeller dismissed his fears. ("Let the world wag," his grandfather had remarked in scorning public opinion.) Singling out the continuing demand for amnesty, Rockefeller saw no reason to change course. Oswald was not yet finished. Well after midnight, he made a final entreaty to Pocantico, trading the promise of gubernatorial action for a peaceful end to the uprising and the release of all hostages unharmed—only then, Oswald argued, should Rockefeller agree to discuss the 28 Points in person with a small group of inmates selected for the purpose. Even he must have recognized this was grasping at straws.

Nelson, meanwhile, remained fixated on the amnesty issue. "In life it's not easy to face a hard decision, particularly where human lives are involved," Rockefeller would later tell the McKay Commission. "It isn't for me, either, but I think that we have to look at these things not only in terms of the immediate, but in terms of the larger implications of what we are doing in our society." No doubt he believed this. Yet there were other factors shaping his behavior, motives of calculation as well as conviction. Hugh Morrow, unable to reconcile Rockefeller's present concern for his safety with the bravado he had displayed plunging into a Honduras mob moments after the violent death of a student demonstrator, developed his own rationale for the governor's refusal to go to Attica. "He got convinced that if he went there that next they would be demanding Nixon, and they would undoubtedly be holding him hostage as a counter." Herman Badillo blamed Rockefeller's unyielding stand on his courtship of the Nixon White House and Republican conservatives generally. Two other Rockefeller associates, both desiring anonymity, claim that the governor was on the phone to Attorney General John Mitchell and that this influenced his hard line. (Rockefeller told the McKay Commission that he did not speak to any outside officials.)

Still others attribute Rockefeller's stance to the counsel of surrogates such as Bill Ronan—except that Nelson repeatedly told Malcolm Wilson, then vacationing in Europe, that he wished Wilson had been there, "because he was surrounded by doves and he needed a hawk to support his views." He prayed over his decision; so he confided to Jim Cannon. "I think we got some bad advice from somebody on the scene who said, this is Mr. Law and Order," concluded Cannon, "and the responsibility of a governor is to preserve law and order, and, by God, if that's what it takes I'm going in there." Others traced historical parallels between Attica and the Ludlow Massacre early in the twentieth century, when the use of armed force and resulting deaths stained the Rockefeller escutcheon in ways that haunted the sensitive John D. Rockefeller, Jr., for the rest of his life. At the time, Junior took refuge in what lawyers call a "delegation of authority defense," remarkably similar to the tactics his son was to employ at Attica. "I have done what I regard as the very best thing in the interest of those employees and the larger investment I represent," the elder Rockefeller had told congressional investigators. "We have gotten the best men obtainable and are relying on their judgment." Was Nelson likewise trying to put as much distance between himself and the consequences of another massacre with his family's name on it?

His attitude mystified many who knew him as a relentlessly hands-on executive. "In every other crisis he was always in the middle of it," said Richard Dunham, who was at Rockefeller's side as the order was given to retake Attica by force. "He loved big problems to solve. He'd walk right into them. And I never understood why this was different. . . . I'm sure people told him, 'Don't go.' But my point is, it was so atypical, uncharacteristic." In 1964, Rockefeller had campaigned his heart out in Oregon, presenting himself to West Coast voters as the only candidate for president who cared enough to come and make his case in person. Now, seven years later, he refused to budge from his ancestral acres in Sleepy Hollow without solid evidence that doing so would advance a peaceful resolution to the crisis. His position had its defenders. Even the McKay Commission, though broadly critical of his decision not to go to Attica, conceded that the governor's presence there would likely have led to inmate demands for him to enter the yard—and that any refusal to comply would have been cited by rebels as evidence of bad faith, thereby worsening the situation.

But Dick Dunham had a point. Whether rebuilding Albany, promoting a bond issue, or encouraging Russ Oswald to recognize prisoners whose potential to succeed had eluded less creative administrators, Rockefeller, in Emily Dickinson's telling phrase, dwelled in possibility. The same dyslexic eye that conjured significance out of formless shapes on a canvas or shapeless forms in a public square was able to conceive and communicate with unbridled enthusiasm all the benefits sure to accrue from an unpassed law, unstaffed office, unbuilt tower. Nelson Rockefeller was defined by his imagination. At Attica it failed him—his moral imagination most of all.

There is yet another explanation for his refusal to go to Attica, one grounded less in crude ambition than in the fear of failure. For all the puzzlement generated by his action, there is a deeper, more painful consistency between the governor who kept his distance from D Yard and the would-be president who had twice before, in December 1959 and March 1968, entered the starting gate, only to back off before the starting pistol could be fired. Consider Rockefeller's testimony on the subject before his vice presidential confirmation hearings in September 1974, as reproduced by James Underwood and William Daniels in their masterful *Governor Rockefeller in New York*. After narrating the now familiar story of the 28 Points, the impasse over amnesty, and the unstated admission of defeat by the observers, Rockefeller summarized the final appeal directed his way in the predawn hours of Monday, September 13:

"If you came something might happen. Well, I am not a messiah. A miracle might happen, you see. This is great. What would happen would be that Nelson Rockefeller would be there and then if it did not succeed, he is there on the world television cameras, et cetera, as the man who failed in this thing, orders the troops in." Under the circumstances, one might argue that Rockefeller stayed away from Attica not because he wanted to be president, but because he didn't want it enough.

7

ROCKEFELLER LEFT POCANTICO for his New York apartment shortly before seven Monday morning. The scene at 812 Fifth Avenue bordered on the surreal: hoping to avoid the appearance of a state government paralyzed by events at Attica, he had scheduled a breakfast meeting to review his pending $2.5 billion transportation bond issue with Bill Ronan and other advisers. The ensuing discussion took place against the backdrop of a constantly ringing telephone, not twenty feet from the table.* On the other end of the line, Bobby Douglass provided updates from Oswald's command center at Attica. ("Bobby said it's not getting any better, but it's not getting any worse.") At seven forty-five, Oswald presented his final terms to the rebels, reiterating his desire for a peaceful settlement based on the 28 Points and immediate release of the hostages. Brother Richard Clark, the inmate leader to whom he addressed this appeal, told Oswald he would need to consult with the people's central committee. An hour later, the two men confronted each other again in the so-called DMZ, or demilitarized zone, near the A Yard gate. This time Brother Richard pretended ignorance of the 28 Points. Oswald produced a copy. Clark requested

---

* That same Monday morning, Rockefeller told both Wally Harrison and Ken Riland that a military-style operation to end the prison standoff would take place shortly—between nine and nine thirty, in Riland's recollection. The assault force was to include state troopers and National Guardsmen exclusively. "This will be a real bloody mess," concluded Riland. KRD, September 13, 1971.

additional time to discuss them "with the people." Oswald gave him twenty minutes.

Cries of "Prepare for war!" were heard from the yard. Eight hostages, blindfolded, their hands tied, were first led to the D Yard trench, to be incinerated with gasoline at the first shot fired by state forces. Since their value in forestalling an attack depended on their visibility, the hostages were subsequently removed to the catwalks flanking Times Square. This in turn increased the exposure of their potential "executioners" to the state's eighteen marksmen crouching on surrounding roofs and in sniper's nests. Douglass had already passed on Rockefeller's explicit instructions governing any assault: Minimal force was to be used, and then only to protect the lives of the hostages and their rescuers. Since General O'Hara's two-way radio inexplicably failed to work, the governor's order to exclude corrections officers from taking part in the assault went undelivered.

Afterward it was claimed inmates never thought the state would risk the lives of its own in taking back the prison. Of the state's arsenal of weaponry, Kunstler had at one point observed to Herman Badillo, "They're never going to use them." Badillo thought otherwise. The past four days had instilled lethal misunderstanding on both sides, with inmates questioning official resolve and the state only too convinced that inmates were poised to carry out their murderous threats.

The phone rang at 812 Fifth Avenue. "It's getting worse," said Rockefeller. "They're asking me to order the assault."

Ron Maiorana reminded him that he had options. "What about what we discussed?" he said, referring to his earlier proposal for a staggered release of hostages followed by a meeting between the governor and the prisoners.

"I don't think it will work," Rockefeller replied.

"But even if it doesn't work, you'll get credit for trying."

In D Yard, time seemed suspended. Success of the state's plan depended on CS gas, far more debilitating than ordinary tear gas, dropped on the prison yard by helicopter. Only then would an elite force of fewer than two hundred troopers commence the assault. An even smaller contingent, twenty-seven in all, was to snatch as many hostages as possible out of the jaws of death.

At 9:22 a.m., the voice of an inmate was broadcast via loudspeaker: "If you kill any inmates, we will kill the hostages. We want the Citizens' Committee in D Block Yard. There are hostages on the roof. It's up to you. Come in now with the Citizens' Committee and Oswald."

"Release the hostages now, and Commissioner Oswald and the Citizens' Committee will meet with you."

"Negative."

Rockefeller was told that the hostages were about to be killed. "You're the governor," someone reminded him. He had to be strong, "to show leadership." Maiorana objected. "You've got to show leadership by doing something about trying to solve the problem, not by ordering an assault." Oswald had run out of options. "Hang on a second," said Rockefeller, the phone to his ear. "I understand now that they're mutilating the prisoners. . . . I have to order the assault. Ron, I'm sorry."

Devastated, Maiorana didn't speak to Rockefeller for a week. Electricity was cut off to the prison at 9:42 a.m., four minutes before a pair of CH-34 Choctaw helicopters made a reconnaissance of D Yard and adjoining cell blocks. Some of the inmates, prematurely rejoicing that the copters passed over harmlessly, believed they were bringing Rockefeller to intervene. In a way, they were. On their next pass, the choppers sprayed the yard with CS gas. Popping sounds accompanied the dropping of gas canisters. Sharpshooters whose .270 rifles were equipped with telescopic sights took aim at the "executioners" who had promised speedy death to the hostages. As corrections officer Frank Kline felt the knife blade slash his throat, twice, inflicting wounds that would require fifty-two stitches to repair, gunfire erupted from all corners of the facility (more than two thousand rounds, by later count).

Amid the fusillade, a spearhead of troopers armed with twelve-gauge shotguns, pike poles, tear-gas grenades, and a two-and-a-half-inch fire hose emerged out of A Block. "The retaking of the prison was left in the hands of the state police," says Bobby Douglass, "because they were not corrections officers, they were well trained, and they really thought, and I thought"—this in reference to the rebellious inmates—"that they had a lot of gasoline and gas bombs and all kinds of stuff." The state's forces were under restraining orders, "which I gave," not to fire "unless it was to defend themselves, or to protect one of their fellow officers, or to save the hostages. But the inmates had dressed the hostages in prison garb, so it was pretty hard to tell who was who." Visibility was further hampered by the burgeoning gas cloud, a morning fog, and persistent drizzle. For six minutes, troopers and at least fifteen corrections officers emptied buckshot and dum-dum bullets outlawed by the Geneva Convention into D Yard.

"My God!" Rockefeller rasped as he was told of the first hostage brought to safety. His mood soared as Douglass ticked off each subsequent rescue. "I'll never forget the moment when the report was given that 14 guards had come out alive," Rockefeller told *Time* magazine's Roger Williams. "Now it's 15, now it's 16, now it's 18. And it went up to 21. I was just absolutely overwhelmed. I didn't see how it was possible, with 1,200 men in there armed, with electrified barriers, with trenches." Twenty-six inmates and nine of the thirty-eight hostages died on the spot; one more of the latter succumbed in the hospital to which he was taken. So did three inmates, on top of three more who had been killed by other prisoners during the uprising. An almost euphoric sense of achievement prompted a devastating misjudgment. As the first shards of information were collected in the hours following the assault, accuracy was sacrificed in the rush to own the story, confirm the official narrative, and justify a substantial death toll. Dick Dunham, for one, urged caution in any public comments. But stories were already beginning to circulate of atrocities committed by prisoners; of guards with throats slit and genitals stuffed in their mouths.*

Rockefeller contributed to the confusion, rushing out a statement conveying sympathy to the hostage families, while making no mention of the twenty-nine prisoners who lost their lives in the final assault. Instead he castigated "the highly organized, revolutionary tactics of militants who rejected all efforts at a peaceful settlement, forced a confrontation and carried out cold-blooded killings they had threatened from the outset." He lavished praise on the state police—and corrections officers—supported by the National Guard and sheriff's deputies, whose "restraint" had minimized casualties as three-fourths of the hostages were successfully plucked from their captors.

This mood of triumphalism was very much in evidence when President Nixon returned Rockefeller's phone call alerting the White House to the pending operation. In recordings discovered at the National Archives in 2004 by University of New Hampshire adjunct professor Theresa Lynch, Nixon expressed sympathy for "these poor fellows" shot in D Yard, while assuring Rockefeller that he backed his decision to use force "to the hilt." The president asked if the uprising was "basically a black thing"; Rockefeller replied in the affirmative. He emphasized the cautious tactics employed by the state's forces. Shots were fired "only when they were in the process of murdering the guards, or when they were attacking our people as they came in to get the guards."

"It really was a beautiful operation," Rockefeller told the president. In the same conversation, he played to Nixon's disdain for the press by decrying the emotionalism of Tom Wicker and "a motley crowd" of citizen observers who had pressured him to make the trip to Attica himself.

"Did you go?" asked Nixon.

"Of course not. I wouldn't go. . . . But I had to talk to those guys, Wicker and all those people, on the phone. You know. And I said, 'Look, I go up there. We can't give amnesty. The next thing is, "Well, we'll let them go, if you'll just come into the courtyard."'"

Over time, Rockefeller's refusal to go to Attica would become conflated with the state's heavy-handed—many would say botched—retaking of the prison

---

* John Dunne understood how such lurid reports got started. "After the takeover I was in the superintendent's office . . . I watched them carry those guys out on the stretchers, and I see a red bandage around their neck, and I would make the entry (in my diary)—throat slit, throat cut, because I'd heard these rumors. . . . It was totally wrong."

and the self-serving misinformation provided by state officials before they had all the facts. Even those who shared Rockefeller's doubts about the effect of his presence on the stalemated negotiations thought he had a responsibility, as the state's chief executive officer, to make his own appraisal of the situation before committing men to battle—if only to avert some of the operational deficiencies identified in the *McKay Report*. "If Governor Rockefeller had come to Attica," wrote Bryce Nelson in the *Los Angeles Times*, "he might have heard some of the comments made by State Police about 'When are we going coon hunting?' He might have heard some of the shouts of 'kill the niggers' which we heard on the streets of Attica on the night before the assault. He might have seen that his police were tired and testy. He might have realized that there was no overall commander of the assault, and that the police had not been given clear instructions about when to fire and no instructions about when to stop firing. He might have sensed that . . . the weapons used by many of the troopers—shotguns loaded with double-aught buckshot—were far too imprecise and damaging for the purpose."

An alert administrator, the reporter continued, would have taken measures to provide medical treatment for those injured in the final assault. In his conversation with Nixon, Rockefeller guessed that a pitched battle might have produced as many as three hundred casualties. Yet there were just two doctors and no surgeons, medics, or experienced litter bearers in the prison that morning; no anesthesia or blood bank; and no surgeries conducted until at least four hours after the shooting ceased. During this same period, more than three hundred inmates were physically abused by troopers and corrections officers. One inmate had his eyes shot out after his "fish kick" suggested he might somehow attack troopers who had already fired four bullets into his body. Half a dozen troopers went around D Yard firing blindly into holes. Hundreds of inmates, stripped naked, ran a gauntlet line of corrections officers with clubs swinging. These images of humiliation and reprisal added to the sense of something gone terribly wrong.

An errant Oswald gesture, a finger drawn melodramatically across his throat, was explicitly reinforced by his deputy, Walter Dunbar, who hastened to tell reporters of slashed throats and castrated guards. This was accepted as gruesome writ—until the next day, when Monroe County medical examiner Dr. John F. Edland, having examined eight of the dead hostages, announced that they all died from gunshot wounds. His findings, confirmed by two independent pathologists, were eventually accepted by Rockefeller, though he continued to insist there had been no "indiscriminate fire" and that prisoners killed in the hailstorm of bullets might be considered victims of justifiable homicide.

Public opinion turned on a dime, with one relative of a prisoner charging that his family member fell victim to "a bullet that had the name Rockefeller written on it." John Lindsay contrasted his personal involvement in recent prison uprisings, where "not a single firearm was used," with the callous disregard shown by the state's chief executive at Attica. Some of the most painful criticism came from black leaders. The Reverend Ralph Abernathy said that in sanctioning force, Rockefeller had made "a terrible and awful mistake." His sentiments were echoed by Roy Wilkins, Dr. Kenneth Clark, and Vernon Jordan. The White House, by contrast, voiced strong support for the governor. From California, Ronald Reagan decried those who would apply revolutionary doctrine to America's prisons. And the New York City Patrolmen's Benevolent Association called Rockefeller a hero for upholding government by law and accepting the consequences "with unflinching honor."

Within twenty-four hours, Rockefeller invited Chief Judge Stanley Fuld of the New York State Court of Appeals, along with the state's four presiding justices of the appellate division, to appoint a citizens' committee to probe events "leading up to—during—and following the riot." A year would pass before the investigatory commission chaired by Dean Robert B. McKay pronounced a measured judgment on individuals, and a much harsher one on institutions that, in Tom Wicker's words, "make men worse rather than better, cause crime rather than prevent it, endanger society rather than serve it." The McKay Commission said it could find no evidence that the uprising at Attica was planned. (That some sixty inmates identified by authorities as probable leaders in the original riot refused to cooperate with Dean McKay's investigators was barely mentioned.) A second panel, led by state supreme court justice Harry D. Goldman, was tasked with overseeing and reporting to the public on post-uprising changes at Attica. These were significant: not only was the inmate population cut in half, but the first minority guards were hired, and improvements were noted in food services, clothing allotment, and visiting restrictions. Rockefeller secured from the legislature a special appropriation of $12 million to fund systemwide reforms, on top of $5 million to repair the physical damage to Attica.

Finally, a separate, criminal probe entrusted to Deputy Attorney General Robert E. Fischer indicted sixty-two inmates and one trooper. Assistant prosecutor Malcolm Bell, frustrated in efforts to pursue additional troopers, complained that he was redirected by his superiors the very week that Rockefeller was nominated by Gerald Ford to be his vice president. Bell resigned in protest. Under Governor Hugh Carey, a blanket pardon absolved everyone charged by the state. This did not prevent inmates and their families from filing a class action suit accusing correctional officers and others in law enforcement of violating their civil rights during and after the prison retaking. Negotiations dragged on for years, until the state agreed in 2000 to pay some five hundred survivors of D Yard $8 million (with an additional $4 million for attorney fees and costs). Four years later, the state made a $12 million settlement (plus

$6.5 million in legal fees) with the families of the guards killed by its random gunfire.

Within days of the slaughter soon to enter the popular culture as a metaphor for excessive police force—thanks in part to Al Pacino's over-the-top chant of "Attica! Attica!" while holding a group of bank employees hostage in the film *Dog Day Afternoon*—Rockefeller conveyed his appreciation to Russ Oswald for saving twenty-eight lives. "You did what had to be done and you acted when you had to act. . . . I share the deep personal anguish you are suffering at the lives lost. . . . I remain convinced that by your actions, more lives were saved, bloodshed on a far greater scale was averted, the idea of social change through violence and coercion was rejected and the necessity for preserving a lawful society was upheld." Perhaps the most telling assessment of Rockefeller's part in the Attica tragedy comes from his secretary of state, John Lomenzo, whose brother-in-law was among the troopers who stormed the prison the foggy morning of September 13.

"I don't think Governor Rockefeller, if he had been there, would have ordered them to attack indiscriminately as they did and kill so many people," said Lomenzo. Recognizing that negotiations were stalemated, Lomenzo conceded, "It was anarchy, but the execution of the takeover of the prison was unbelievable." Rockefeller himself came to blame the resulting bloodbath, his private Ludlow, on Oswald's failure to press the early retaking of rebellious cell blocks. One fact seemed beyond debate: The more distance Rockefeller hoped to put between himself and Attica, the more indelible was their linkage in public estimation.

Part Five
OUT OF STEP
1972–1979

Never look back. Just keep on going.

—Nelson A. Rockefeller

Twenty-Four

THE BOSS OF NEW YORK

You have to understand me. I don't believe in working from the bottom up.
I believe in working from the top down.

—NELSON A. ROCKEFELLER

1

RICHARD NIXON COULD barely contain himself. "Rocky—this is his first crisis!" the president exclaimed in the wake of the Attica uprising. At Pocantico, the number of state troopers shielding the governor and his family was tripled. Ron Maiorana, the press secretary alienated by Rockefeller's refusal to go to Attica, suffered a heart attack one week after the prison was retaken. Though he recovered physically, his working relationship with Rockefeller never regained its former closeness. Summoned to the governor's office one day, Maiorana found him at his desk jacketless and with tie loosened.

"Sit down," said Nelson. "Ronnie, we have to have an understanding."

"About what?"

"About who is the Governor of New York State—you or me?"

Stunned by his greeting, Maiorana assured Rockefeller there wasn't the slightest bit of doubt on that score. "And if I have done something that makes you think otherwise, I apologize."

"It's just that you are always so sure of yourself with me and the staff. How did you get that way?" asked Rockefeller. Maiorana silently reviewed his past actions.

"Do you ever make a mistake?" Nelson pressed him. He had made plenty, answered Maiorana, "including whatever I've done to anger you. . . . Do you want me to resign?"

"No, not at all," said Rockefeller. "I just want you to back off."

The working press was less easily admonished. Claims that he might be contemplating resignation in the aftermath of Attica brought quick denials. Insisted one Albany associate, "Nelson Rockefeller wants one thing, to be President. He'll never quit and he'll never give up." Perhaps not, but in the long shadow cast by events of September 13, there was little to quiet the speculation. An impeachment motion filed by Assemblyman Arthur Eve went nowhere, but neither did administration efforts to delay public hearings by the McKay Commission until the completion of lengthy criminal proceedings. Popular disenchantment with the Rockefeller administration found a new outlet in November, when 61 percent of voting New Yorkers rejected the governor's latest bond issue, a $2.5 billion infusion of funds to complete Manhattan's Second Avenue subway line, improve commuter railroads, and, not least of all, close a $300 million gap in the state's current budget.

The same voters sounded a death knell for the Rye–Oyster Bay Bridge, though more than a year would pass before Rockefeller, having twice vetoed legislative restrictions on the project, conceded defeat. Nowhere was opposition more intense than in the tony Republican environs around Oyster Bay, which had secured Washington's protection by transferring to federal ownership large tracts of environmentally sensitive wetlands. Among the most prominent of bridge critics was the governor's publicity-shy sister, Babs, whose estate bordered the approaches to the span. Accustomed as he was to being picketed, after two hundred well-heeled protesters appeared outside the Capitol in April 1972, Nelson observed that this was the first time the demonstrators had worn mink.

Humor, like money, was in short supply around Albany that spring. In abandoning his earlier pay-as-you-go approach to budgeting, Rockefeller had allowed state-backed debt to more than triple during his time in office, reaching $3.3 billion by the end of 1971. Indirect debt, much of it generated by public authorities or lease-purchase agreements such as Albany's South Mall, had increased at an even faster rate. Defeat of the transportation bond issue, combined with Washington's continued foot-dragging on revenue sharing, made another fiscal crisis unavoidable. At the start of December 1971, Rockefeller announced two special legislative sessions, one to address a worsening budget situation, the other to draw lines for congressional and legislative seats in line with the 1970 census. The governor's call for $427 million in new taxes, coupled with what he creatively labeled "permanent postponements" in some forms of state assistance, did not go over well with the very lawmakers who had forced him during the regular session to accept substantial spending reductions. Upstate conservatives, their influence magnified in the narrowly divided assembly, felt confident they could beat back any Rockefeller attempt to repeal the historic cuts so recently adopted.

This overlooked Nelson's willingness to ally himself with supposed enemies if that was the price of victory. Enter Jerry Finkelstein, publisher of the *New York Law Journal* and, until recently, chairman of the New York City Democratic Committee. From his apartment at the Carlyle Hotel, Finkelstein pulled strings, raised funds, and dropped names on behalf of presidents, governors, and mayors of both parties. As eclectic in his friends as in his politics, Finkelstein was close to sometime Rockefeller campaign manager Bill Pfeiffer, who arranged for the Democratic power broker to meet the Republican governor. The two men formed an instant rapport, bonded by their love of intrigue and Finkelstein's access to Wilbur Mills, the congressional gatekeeper whose opposition to federal revenue sharing tested even Nelson's strategic gifts. Finkelstein also provided entrée to Meade Esposito, a brusquely charming, gravel-voiced, cigar-chomping former bail bondsman from Brooklyn's Canarsie neighborhood, for fourteen years undisputed sovereign of the nation's largest Democratic county organization.

Early in December 1971, Finkelstein brought Esposito to 812 Fifth Avenue for the first time. The Runyonesque pol ingratiated himself by taking one look around the sprawling premises and declaring Rockefeller's wealth to be "fucking obscene" (a remark he repeated at his host's insistence for Happy Rockefeller). Ice broken, the respective bosses got down to business. Describing the inevitable cuts to social services that would result from a strictly Republican budget, Rockefeller appealed to Esposito's conscience as much as his ego. "I don't know you except by reputation," said Nelson, "and I have a feeling that you have the same concern that I do for people and that this is something that neither you nor I want to see happen." Any new taxes, including a 5 percent surcharge on the existing state income tax, an additional penny on the sales tax, and increased levies on cigarettes, liquor, and other indulgences, could be enacted only with Esposito's help. "There is no one else in the state that can do it."

Convinced of Rockefeller's sincerity, and flattered by his attention, Esposito promised help in securing enough Democratic votes from Brooklyn and other organization strongholds to overcome opposition from rural Republicans. The talk turned to revenue sharing. Congressman Hugh Carey, a quick-witted black Irishman from the increasingly conservative Brooklyn neighborhood of Bay Ridge, was tracked down in the middle of his Christmas shopping and invited to join the conversation. No one had to remind Carey how useful Rockefeller's friendship might be in the upcoming lottery of redistricting. From the Fifth Avenue apartment a call was placed to Wilbur Mills a thousand miles away in his modest Arkansas bungalow.

"I'm here with the governor," said Carey, "and reapportionment is coming up."

"What does he want?"

"A letter from you saying you'll consider revenue sharing."

Mills was game. Rockefeller staffer Jim Cannon was dispatched to rustic Searcy, Arkansas (on Christmas Day, no less), to obtain in writing the chairman's forecast of a revenue-sharing program large enough to plug a $400 million hole in Rockefeller's upcoming budget. Entrusted with lobbying responsibilities for both redistricting and revenue sharing, Cannon got on well with the governor, save for the occasional instance when Rockefeller thought him "a little too soft" on members of Congress such as Senator Jim Buckley. "Governor, we have nothing to threaten him with," Cannon told his impatient employer. "We may get it by persuasion, but we're not going to get it by force or threats." A tactic more effective than either was bribery. By dangling the prospect of a $100 million loan from the state, Rockefeller won votes from urban legislators who feared a surge in New York City transit fares, and from their suburban counterparts concerned about the soaring cost of commuter rail travel.*

Joining urban Democrats and suburban Republicans in a fragile governing coalition carried a steep price. The Democratic minority exacted an increase in the amount of capital gains income subject to taxation and a top levy of 17 percent for the most affluent New Yorkers. They demanded and got exemptions to the spending freeze for school aid, welfare, mental health, narcotics control, and other social services. The result was solvency on paper, cinched by the promissory note from Mills and $407 million in new tax revenue made possible by Meade Esposito's compliant troops. For his efforts, Esposito famously was given a Picasso—only a print, he was quick to point out—a black-and-white rendering of an owl perched on a settee, accompanied by a note in Rockefeller's hand that read, "You are the wise old owl. The people of New York should know what you have done for them." Both Finkelstein and Esposito independently used the word *fun* to describe the experience of working with Rockefeller. The feeling was mutual. Around such operators, Nelson imagined himself a man of the streets. He laughed at their stories, showed them public deference, and took their advice about more than politics.

"You are a very rich man," Esposito remarked at one of their early meetings. "You look sloppy, your clothes are falling off you."

"I got no hips."

"I will get you my tailor."

In this as in every other transaction with Rockefeller to which he was a party, Esposito proved a man of his word.† The governor's wardrobe was updated, and

---

* Redistricting gave Rockefeller a forest of sticks, and carrots enough to sway members of both parties. Certainly GOP lawmakers stood to benefit from a legislative reapportionment plan favorable to the governor's nominal allies. Of course, Rockefeller told reporters, that bill hadn't been signed yet. Nor was it likely to be—not, at least, until he had wrung the last ounce of political advantage from the redrawn map. In the meantime, Wilbur Mills's Christmas pledge to make revenue sharing his top priority enabled Rockefeller to restore $95 million previously cut from the state's welfare budget. So much for his turn to the right.

† None of which helped Esposito in 1987, when he was convicted of bribing Bronx representative Mario Biaggi. Given a suspended two-year prison sentence and fined $500,000, the former boss

Nelson reciprocated by helping his friend's grandson get into medical school. In response Esposito told him, "Rocky, if ever you get gonorrhea, this boy will take care of you." Rockefeller found other ways to show his gratitude, at one point promising to make Esposito Republican state chairman if the boss from Brooklyn Heights renounced his Democratic loyalties. He telephoned Esposito's dying mother on her birthday. When he missed the old woman's funeral, Nelson made it up by giving Meade his choice of three candidates for a slot on the state racing commission. Relishing his time in the Rockefeller penumbra, Esposito took credit for converting Nelson into "a street guy. I taught him more four letter words than he ever knew in his life." The Brooklyn kingpin admired the way Rockefeller made everyone else feel important. (A rare exception to this rule was "sleazy" bankers or self-proclaimed masters of the universe as defined by Wall Street. Raised to consider money an unfit topic of conversation, Nelson had scant patience for those who talked of little else. At a party attended by some of the biggest names in the financial community, a bored Rockefeller turned to Jerry Finkelstein and said, "Let's get out of here. This is too stuffy.")

Following the conclusion of a particularly grueling legislative session, Finkelstein was surprised to receive a late night phone call from the governor. "I just told Happy, I didn't want to go to bed until I called you, and thanked you for all your help," said Rockefeller. The next day, a four-page handwritten letter embellishing these sentiments was delivered to the Finkelstein residence. More tangible expressions of appreciation included appointments to the boards of the Port Authority and Rockefeller Center. Such acts of generosity did not conceal a taste for political hardball. "If you ever crossed that man," said Meade Esposito, "you know what I say politically, don't get mad, get even. He would get even." Anyone doubting this might ask Republican assemblyman Clark Wemple of Schenectady. His habit of opposing the governor on the subject of taxes made Wemple an object lesson to others whose fierce antagonism toward government spending ended at their own district line.

Nineteen seventy-two was an election year, a good time to impress voters with showy infrastructure projects. As it happened, Schenectady contained an outworn bridge spanning the Mohawk River and badly in need of replacement. Naturally curious, reporters asked the governor if Wemple's constituents would be punished for his past transgressions. "There are certain legislators who make it very clear they don't want any expenditures in their communities," Rockefeller replied. "I just mention this with no feeling, of course." Presumably, he was equally disinterested in the fate of Herman Badillo, the former ally whose public denunciation of "official murder" condoned by the state at Attica perma-

---

was indicted a second time one year later, only to have bribery and tax fraud charges dismissed owing to age and ill health.

nently soured their relationship. Rockefeller recruited a popular young Democratic assemblyman, Manuel Ramos, to contest the new Twenty-first District; saw to it that the challenger did not lack for funds (à la Charlie Rangel versus Adam Clayton Powell, Jr.); and, when Badillo prevailed anyway, appointed Ramos to a judgeship on the court of claims.* When it was suggested, sotto voce, to the flamboyant liberal activist Bella Abzug that she might improve her redistricting prospects by signing a letter to Wilbur Mills urging quick action on revenue sharing, she did nothing of the kind. The woman for whom the word *chutzpah* might have been coined saw her district redistributed among four neighboring ones. She won a second term anyway.

Mills didn't need Abzug shouting in his ear to get the message. In June 1972, Rockefeller's hardball tactics paid off when the full House of Representatives agreed to consider revenue sharing under a closed rule. (Of the required eight votes in the Rules Committee to effect the restriction on amendments, Rockefeller or his agent, Jim Cannon, secured three. The rest were Republicans lobbied by Minority Leader Gerald Ford.) At the eleventh hour, Tennessee governor Winfield Dunn threatened to scuttle all these efforts by objecting to the House formula weighted in favor of urban, high-tax states such as New York. In response, Rockefeller offered a substitute combining state and local taxes in place of income taxation alone. Narrowing the funding discrepancy among states cost New York nearly half its projected windfall, but Dunn withdrew his blackball. Nixon signed the resulting legislation two weeks before the 1972 presidential election.

Nelson Rockefeller, so often a bridesmaid in national politics, could justifiably take much of the credit for this latest chapter in American federalism. Within days, he summoned Jim Cannon to his Fifty-fourth Street Clubhouse.

"Cash or stock," Rockefeller greeted him.

"Huh?"

"Cash or stock."

---

* Hugh Carey fared noticeably better than Badillo. Besides giving Carey a pass in the redistricting process, Rockefeller was not above sandbagging his own party's candidate for the Carey seat. In 1972, Republicans thought they had the perfect replacement for Carey in lawyer (and future city councilman) John Gangemi, who already had the GOP endorsement and, it was believed, that of the Conservative Party—until Brooklyn Conservative chairman Bill Wells purposefully left Gangemi's name out of the minutes at a crucial meeting and, in the words of party historian George B. Marlin, "somebody named Jones was put on the ballot at the last minute." This oversight was no accident; it was the result of complex maneuverings involving Rockefeller, his Republican chairman in Brooklyn, George Clark, and a reputed $10,000 payment from Carey to Wells. "I didn't get a dime," Wells would later insist. "Rockefeller and Carey got what they wanted and I just don't want to say any more." George J. Marlin, *Fighting the Good Fight: A History of the New York Conservative Party* (South Bend, IN: St. Augustine's Press, 2002), 214.

Ann Whitman interpreted the governor's cryptic utterance. He wished to reward Cannon, she explained, for his labors in enacting revenue sharing and securing a redistricted map to Rockefeller's liking.

Well, thought Cannon, in that case: "Cash."

A look of displeasure soured Rockefeller's face. "Nobody wants to hold shares in America anymore," he groused. Cannon subsequently received a check for $40,000, without elaboration other than a brief acknowledgment "to friendship and respect."*

2

AS A FORMER staff man himself, Rockefeller professed a special regard for those whose authority came directly from the voters. It was his custom to stand when elected officials entered the room—out of respect, he said, for the status uniquely conferred by popular election. Senate Republican leader Earl Brydges—more cooperative than his predecessor Walter Mahoney or his assembly counterpart Perry Duryea—was a particular favorite. Rockefeller would miss Brydges when the senator from Niagara Falls retired at the end of 1972. Asked what he would like for a going-away present, the senator mentioned how much his constituents would benefit from a performing arts facility. His wish was translated by Rockefeller into a multimillion-dollar theater and concert complex—the Earl Brydges Artpark—designed so patrons occupying a sloping lawn could simultaneously enjoy the onstage performance and refreshing breezes off the Niagara River.

A year earlier, Rockefeller had handed Brydges and his colleagues the ultimate gubernatorial carrot, a towering new Legislative Office Building, lavishly equipped with private offices for every member; conference rooms and hearing rooms with tiered theater seats; a grandiose atrium; even a gymnasium and sauna. The first of Rockefeller's South Mall structures to be completed, it was the only one whose occupants got to select the art adorning their workplace. This symbolized a turning point in the historically unequal relationship between New York's executive and its part-time legislature. Taking advantage of their newfound autonomy, legislators in 1972 alone filed nearly two dozen bills intended to curb gubernatorial powers. Some of these would subject the state's

---

* "It cost him $75,000 to give me $40,000," Cannon later explained, a consequence of IRS rules governing gift taxes. This might be remembered in considering Rockefeller's many other gifts and "loans."

highest office to term limits. Others would curtail the liberal use of gubernatorial "messages of necessity" preempting the legislative calendar. Objections were raised to the practice whereby controversial legislation, once passed, was deliberately held for weeks by GOP legislative leaders before going to the governor—thus effectively robbing opponents of time to negotiate changes or contest a last minute veto. None of the restraining measures came close to enactment, but they showed which way the wind was blowing.

That spring, the Capitol was overrun by trial lawyers working overtime to defeat Rockefeller's latest attempt to enact no-fault auto insurance. Their success, though temporary, gave evidence of a governor whose thoughts were focused elsewhere. Having vowed to carry New York in November for the Nixon-Agnew ticket, Rockefeller heaped praise on the president for his trips to China and the Soviet Union. Courting social conservatives within his party, he was not above issuing a proclamation recognizing Anti-Smut Day and the campaign for decency being waged by the Catholic War Veterans of the United States. At other times, however, Rockefeller fumbled his small-government lines like a rusty actor struggling to learn his part. Though sympathetic to the foes of busing schoolchildren to achieve racial balance, he vetoed a bill that would ban the practice, contending it was so broadly drawn as to impede virtually any attempt at classroom integration.

In May 1972, he went out of his way to recognize the founders of the crumbling New Deal coalition. Franklin Roosevelt's presidential library at Hyde Park had been reconfigured by the addition of two wings showcasing the contributions of his wife, and Rockefeller was determined to be part of the dedication ceremony. Getting there entailed a hair-raising trip by helicopter through some of the Hudson Valley's worst thunderstorms in memory. His pilot tracked the fog-shrouded river until conditions forced him to land at a field north of Hyde Park. Rockefeller arrived just in time to read a measured telegram of praise from the White House, before adding more effusive personal memories of "the best-known woman in the world. And I would not hesitate to add—the best-loved as well." His admiration for the Roosevelts found expression in words that belied his supposed turn to the right. "In this library," Rockefeller declared, "a young American will find a kindred spirit; a black American will find a constant friend; a poor American will find an open and generous heart."

On the same day that Mrs. Roosevelt's memory was being honored at Hyde Park, lawmakers in Albany gave final approval to a measure that would effectively kill a massive low-income housing project in the Forest Hills neighborhood of Queens. The racially inclusive complex had touched a raw nerve in the heavily Jewish enclave. To the surprise of many, Rockefeller vetoed the legislation, thereby paving the way for a smaller project to be built as cooperative housing.* As it happened, Forest Hills was but a warm-up to a still more divisive issue. Two years after New York eliminated most restrictions on abortion, an intensive campaign led by the Roman Catholic Church threatened to scuttle the new law. During the interim, Rockefeller had immersed himself in the moral complexities of the issue. Conversing with one staff member, a former Catholic priest, the governor referenced a recent newspaper editorial quoting the eminent theologian Thomas Aquinas. Did the staffer know him? If so, Rockefeller would very much like to arrange a meeting.

Informed that Saint Thomas Aquinas had died in the thirteenth century, Nelson laughed at his own ignorance. Then he asked for copies of the holy man's relevant writings. Ever the pragmatist, Rockefeller proposed to reduce from twenty-four to eighteen weeks the time frame in which a pregnancy could be legally terminated. He presented this as a compromise—the worst possible characterization to those on both sides of the issue who denied there might be more than one side. Enough legislators felt this way to revoke the 1970 law and reinstate in its place a near absolute ban on abortion. The bill's ultimate fate rested with the governor. An eleventh-hour intervention by the Nixon White House raised the stakes for Rockefeller while putting at risk his delicate rapprochement with the president. On May 7, Nixon, acting on the suggestion of speechwriter Pat Buchanan, wrote to New York's Terence Cardinal Cooke expressing his personal support for the church's position on repeal. His unexpected intercession upset Rockefeller, all the more so as it came just one day after Nixon rejected the findings of his own Commission on Population Growth, chaired by John D. Rockefeller 3rd.

In his message vetoing the legislative ban, Nelson made no reference to presidential displeasure. Instead he acknowledged the moral fervor guiding both sides of the abortion issue. Unfortunately, he wrote, "the very intensity of this debate has generated an emotional climate in which the truth about abortions and about the present state abortion law have become distorted almost beyond recognition. The truth is that this repeal of the 1970 reforms would not end abortion. It would only end abortions under safe and supervised medical conditions. The truth is that a safe abortion would remain the optional choice of the well-to-do woman, while the poor would again be seeking abortions at a grave risk to life in back-room abortion mills. . . . The bill is disapproved." His

---

* The Forest Hills dispute introduced millions of New Yorkers to Mario Cuomo, a Queens attorney whose efforts to broker a compromise over a proposed public housing venture in the tight-knit Italian American neighborhood of Corona led to his being invited to do as much for Forest Hills. Wading into the same controversy, more or less uninvited, a Manhattan congressman named Ed Koch settled old scores with Lindsay while moderating his own image as a Greenwich Village reform (that is, unabashedly liberal) Democrat.

reasoning would be upheld nine months later, when the United States Supreme Court legalized abortion in the landmark case of *Roe v. Wade*.

Politically, legally, and culturally, the abortion fight was a watershed in the Rockefeller governorship. Writing in *New York* magazine that same month, Richard Reeves traced just how far Nelson had traveled from the bored, distracted executive in the weeks after Attica to the domineering figure Reeves christened "the Boss of New York."

3

MEADE ESPOSITO HAD a simple explanation for Rockefeller's failure to achieve the presidency: "He was too liberal for the Republicans, and too conservative for the Democrats." Were he truly serious about shedding his liberal identity in the wake of Attica, Rockefeller would not have found time on his schedule for Steve Berger, a young Democratic activist who had made a reputation for himself managing campaigns for Richard Ottinger and Herman Badillo. Intrigued by the possibilities of municipal reform offered by the Scott Commission, established by the governor a year earlier to investigate New York City government, Berger had communicated his interest to commission staff. His reward was a barely civil brush-off.

Through Oscar Ruebhausen, he secured an invitation to Albany and a job interview unlike any other Berger had experienced. "We started talking Attica because the one common point we know about is Herman and Attica." Rockefeller asked about Badillo, described the congressman's role in the recent controversy, and listened intently as Berger addressed what he regarded as Rockefeller's mistakes. Expounding the case for delay originally made by Badillo, Berger expected this to bring the meeting to an early conclusion. "Instead, the Governor seriously and calmly laid out the reasons he made the decisions he did and we talked about it for almost an hour."

"Why don't we have dinner?" Nelson told Berger. That evening, their conversation resumed. Around ten thirty, his host said that Berger couldn't go home then. "You'll sleep here." Their long hello introduced Berger to something he was to glimpse rarely in his subsequent career chairing Hugh Carey's Emergency Financial Control Board, as New York's commissioner of social services, and as executive director of the Port Authority: an elected official talking candidly, constructively, with his adversaries while seeking common ground on which to advance. It was the same force of personality, Berger concluded, that enabled Rockefeller to reach "labor leaders, rural politicians, bankers, academics, intellectuals, and people across all political spectrums." For his part, Rockefeller had good reason to cultivate Berger, whose status as a reform Democrat lent needed credibility to the Scott Commission, already stocked by the governor with such heavyweights as Congresswoman Shirley Chisholm, General Lucius Clay, and Hudson Institute guru Herman Kahn.*

Rockefeller's hunch about Berger was validated as the commission's experts compiled a shelf full of volumes detailing the city's bloated spending, deficit-hiding gimmicks, and eroding economic base. Many of their recommendations, including long-range budgeting and productivity increases anathema to municipal worker unions, anticipated actions taken under duress during New York's later brush with bankruptcy. Berger derived less satisfaction from other Rockefeller assignments, including a brief stint leading Nelson's post-Albany Commission on Critical Choices. But each was to be a learning experience, as he watched Rockefeller reassert a degree of mastery thought to have vanished in the gunfire at Attica. In rediscovering the joys of hand-to-hand political combat, Rockefeller could invest even failure with style. When the state of New Jersey cut a deal to spirit the New York Giants out of their namesake home and into a new stadium in the windswept Meadowlands across the Hudson River, New York's governor had no intention of accepting the move without a fight.

As recalled by Berger, "I was sitting in the office when he called Ed Logue, who was chairman of the Urban Development Corporation, and told Ed that he wanted the UDC to announce that it would build a new Giants Stadium on the site of the Sunnyside yards in Queens." Though he couldn't hear the other end of the conversation, Berger had no difficulty imagining the multiple objections Logue might offer to this "truly nutty" idea. All the while, the smile never left Rockefeller's face. At length he hung up, transparently pleased with himself. Berger couldn't stifle his curiosity. Did Rockefeller believe there was still a chance of preventing the team's removal to New Jersey?

"Of course not," Nelson said, chuckling, "but we're not going to make it easy for them."†

---

* Acting on the advice of those investigating alleged corruption in the current justice system, Rockefeller in 1972 designated Maurice Nadjari, then counsel to the Scott Commission, as a sort of mega-prosecutor with the power to supersede existing district attorneys. A consensus soon formed that it was one of his worst appointments, as the self-promoting, overzealous Nadjari promised more than he delivered.

† An earlier incident, arising out of the first, and only, meeting of the Mid-Atlantic Governors Conference, suggests the limits of Rockefeller's commitment to regional cooperation. As chairman Bill Scranton welcomed those present and began to work his way through an ambitious agenda, he became aware of a muffled argument nearby. The voices grew louder, the language more heated, until finally the governor of New York, his patience exhausted, pushed his chair back from the table and exclaimed to his counterpart from across the Hudson River, "Damn it, by rights New Jersey shouldn't exist at all!" With that, Nelson Rockefeller disappeared, putting an end to the short life of the organization he had willed into existence. William Scranton, AI.

Well into his fourth term as governor, Rockefeller continued to seek outside advice, even if he seemed less inclined to act on it. For years his habit of ladling statistics into speeches, a self-defeating practice amid the shortened attention span of the television age, had been a source of frustration for his communications team. Convinced that Rockefeller would listen only to an outsider of undisputed stature, PR guru Ted Braun approached Walter Cronkite in hopes the legendary CBS News anchor might have more credibility with the governor than those already on the Rockefeller payroll. "Well," Cronkite allowed, "if Nelson, Happy, Betsy, and I sat down some night and we played a little poker, or we had a little dinner, it's possible along the way, we might talk about television audiences." Nothing professional, you understand, "but I might slip in a couple of licks." The dinner was scheduled. By all accounts it was a thoroughly enjoyable evening for everyone. And Rockefeller went right on burying his verbal appeals in fractions, percentages, and more zeros than most viewers could absorb.

His political career had spanned the rise of television and its more recent tendency to dramatize events in quest of sensation and ratings. No one personified the New Journalism better than Geraldo Rivera, a twenty-eight-year-old investigative reporter for WABC-TV in New York with a flair for putting himself at the center of any story he was covering. Rivera had turned his cameras on the Willowbrook State School on Staten Island, a dismal red-brick warehouse originally designed to house four thousand children with developmental disabilities. Six thousand called the place home in 1965, when Senator Robert Kennedy had described Willowbrook to reporters as "a snake pit" having more in common with a zoo than a modern treatment facility. After Kennedy's death, local newspapers picked up the cause, describing in graphic, often sickening detail the neglect of severely retarded children doubly abandoned, first by their families and then by foster care agencies or the state itself.

It was one thing to *read* of such callousness, quite another to *see* the gross overcrowding, filthy cells, and staff abuse captured surreptitiously by Rivera on film. As the story gained traction early in 1972, Rockefeller's initial response was to blame the messenger. Here was Attica all over again—a manifestation of radical politics as "revolutionary elements" akin to those roiling college campuses in recent years graduated and moved into other fields, including prisons and mental institutions. "These fellows smuggled in a cameraman who got pictures to show kids who were born tragically retarded," said Rockefeller. "Under the best of circumstances, for those who haven't seen this in life, it is shocking and horrifying. Under the less advantageous circumstances of a reduced budget, it's a horror story."

Ironically, Rockefeller had only recently restored funding for mental health programs ravaged by austerity. Sprawling, inhumane institutions such as Willowbrook began to give way to community-based, outpatient treatment centers ("hostels") that would reduce by more than half the number of patients in state-run facilities. Now, prodded by Rivera's keyhole journalism, Rockefeller invited an advisory council to conduct its own review of conditions at Willowbrook and to report back on necessary changes. He also approved revisions to the state's forty-five-year-old Mental Hygiene Law that would strengthen patients' rights and protect their property. None of this was sufficient to prevent a class action lawsuit filed in March 1972; the benighted school was finally closed in 1987.

4

LONG ACCUSTOMED TO command, Rockefeller became more arbitrary with age. On one occasion, as described for Cary Reich by Democratic assembly leader Stanley Steingut, an argument over the Rye–Oyster Bay Bridge escalated into physical assault, with Rockefeller striking Steingut in the chest—not once, but twice, as Perry Duryea and Bobby Douglass looked on.

"You little son of a bitch," Steingut cried, "I should really knock you on your ass." Instead he stalked from the room. Early the next morning he took a call from Duryea, who said the governor wanted to apologize. Shortly thereafter, a clearly embarrassed Rockefeller appeared in Steingut's office. Their subsequent handshake marked the beginning of a decent working relationship. That Rockefeller was thoroughly bipartisan in his treatment of dissenters was demonstrated by New York's Republican state chairman, Chuck Lanigan, during the 1971 fiscal crisis. Attending a budget review at Pocantico Hills, Lanigan argued against immunity for the State Council on the Arts.

"Chuck, I'm sorry, that's a closed subject with me," said the governor. Forty-five minutes later, Lanigan dared to again raise the topic. Rockefeller reiterated that his mind was made up. Thereafter Lanigan suffered in silence as education, the environment, and other popular programs each took a hit. Finally he broke his silence to offer a blunt warning of the electoral consequences if the State Council on the Arts was left unscathed.

Rockefeller, visibly angry, replied that he had heard such criticisms of the council before. "But let me ask you a question. What is government all about? What is life in this nation all about if it's not centered around our culture? You indicate that these issues of dance and the arts have nothing to say to us. But they are absolutely the essence that holds our culture together. . . . This isn't silliness. This is what we're all about." Cue Bill Ronan, whose responsibilities with the Metropolitan Transportation Authority hadn't precluded him from a continuing role as the governor's most trusted adviser without portfolio. Listening to Lanigan's feverish presentation, Ronan had come to exactly the opposite conclusion from the state party chief. Now, called on to offer his personal perspective, Ronan showed himself at least as creative as any artist looking to Albany for support. With eighteen-year-olds only recently given the vote, he contended, it was more important than ever for Rockefeller the progressive to demonstrate his commitment to free expression and public culture. Far from being reduced, the state arts budget should be *increased*, significantly.

Rockefeller leapt to his feet. "Bill, you're absolutely right. Absolutely right. Let's go in and have a Dubonnet and . . . some lunch."

Grateful as he was for additional federal revenues, and eager to discard his spoiler image within the GOP, Rockefeller made certain that Lanigan answered in the affirmative when White House operatives sought youthful volunteers for the 1972 New Hampshire primary, in which Nixon faced token challenges from both Right and Left. That August, he jumped at the opportunity to place Nixon's name in nomination before delegates to the Republican convention in Miami Beach. But on his home turf, at least, the campaign would be waged according to his rules. "We had committed to carrying the state for Nixon," explained Jim Cannon. "We didn't want his people in there . . . we were going to do it ourselves, our way." Specifically, this meant keeping the Committee for the Re-Election of the President (CREEP) at arm's length.

Long before Watergate entered the popular lexicon, Rockefeller believed, based on John Mitchell's own indiscretions, that dirty tricksters answering to Mitchell had bugged the Miami hotel suite occupied by the Rockefellers during the 1968 convention. Then came the arrest on June 17 of five men with ties to CREEP caught breaking into Democratic Party headquarters in Washington's Watergate complex. Two weeks later, Mitchell resigned his leadership position with the campaign. "We kept hearing this story," Cannon would recall. Initially they gave it little credence. "Like everybody else, we couldn't believe Nixon would do anything that dumb." When the rumors persisted, early in September Cannon flew to the nation's capital to consult Murray Chotiner, a key figure in Nixon's rise to prominence, and in Cannon's recollection "the most totally amoral person I ever met."*

"What the hell is this all about?" he asked Chotiner, who offered a crisp, if

---

* Old rivalries often persist at the staff level, and the Nixon-Rockefeller conflict was no exception. Henry Kissinger's birthday happened to coincide with the presidential visit to the Soviet Union in May 1972. At one point, the festivities were interrupted by the appearance of White House chief of staff H. R. Haldeman in jogging gear. The ultimate Nixon loyalist, Haldeman couldn't resist taunting Kissinger and Ken Riland, "The trouble with you two guys is you always back the wrong man," an unmistakable allusion to Nelson Rockefeller. Kissinger and Riland protested their loyalty to Nixon. Riland blamed Haldeman for his subsequent indictment on tax evasion charges, a rap he beat in federal court. W. Kenneth Riland, HMI, 93.

characteristically self-serving, response: "Number one, I had nothing to do with it. Number two, if I had something to do with it, we wouldn't have been caught. Number three, it'll blow over right after the election." Thus reassured, Cannon said nothing of the burgeoning scandal to his longtime friend Ben Bradlee at *The Washington Post.* "I went back and told the governor, 'I think we just disbelieve it.'" Nixon himself minimized "this distressing Watergate thing" in a September 14 White House meeting, at which Rockefeller said perhaps it was better if he didn't hear a fuller account from the president—that way, he could truthfully proclaim his own ignorance before the press. But he also sounded a sympathetic note, assuring Nixon that the public was far from shocked by claims of political espionage. "They know it's going on all the time."

Certainly nothing about the Watergate break-in appeared likely to derail a second Nixon term. With an ardor missing from earlier campaigns, Rockefeller went all out to ensure a sweep of the Empire State for his longtime adversary. On October 17, an appreciative Nixon thanked Nelson for his "magnificent support" to date. (He also recorded in his diary a strange dream in which he had been addressing a rally crowd at excessive length, only to have Rockefeller seize the microphone on an applause line and relegate Nixon to the sidelines.) Nixon approved Rockefeller plans for a presidential motorcade through Republican strongholds in suburban Long Island and Westchester County, followed by a dinner party and reception at Kykuit. Large and enthusiastic crowds along the route delayed the president's arrival at Pocantico by two hours. An unexpected sequel testified to the limits of the Nixon-Rockefeller rapprochement. "A couple months later we were having lunch at Pocantico," recalls one Rockefeller associate. "The usher comes in—there's a message from the president. He hands him a box, the governor opens it, and it's a plaque. 'Richard Nixon had lunch [sic] here on such and such a date.'

"'Oh, my God, he wants me to put that on the door.'" Somehow Rockefeller never found an appropriate spot to install the memorial to a rivalry that had done much to define the modern Republican Party.

On Election Day, Nixon carried New York State with 59 percent of the vote, his largest margin in any of the major industrial states he so coveted. Even before November 7, the two men were acting out a carefully choreographed drama, with Nixon inviting Rockefeller to undertake a postelection review of economic and social policy for the next ten years. Nelson's reply doubled as congratulations on the president's reelection and on his mandate to reshape the federal system by the time of the nation's bicentennial in 1976. "It is a task as important and historic as that of the founding fathers," Rockefeller gushed, restating his desire to assist Nixon in realizing his transforming agenda. Thus was born the last great Rockefeller study group. What he ultimately styled the National Commission on Critical Choices for Americans (and Albany wags dubbed the Commission to Save the World) closely resembled the Eisenhower-era Special Studies Project. That it was viewed as yet another Rockefeller-designed springboard to the White House was hardly a surprise.

Jim Cannon wasn't so sure. "This came about because, frankly, he had enough of being governor," said Cannon. "I don't think 'bored' was the word—he just had enough. . . . He was very loyal to Malcolm and he thought, Well, I'm not going to run again, so why don't I give Malcolm a break, give him a year in office." Initially conceived as an examination of the modern state in a changing federal system, by May 1973 Nixon, employing language drafted for him by the Rockefeller team, formally requested that the inquiry be broadened into a bipartisan examination of American prospects at the dawn of its third century.

Rockefeller's assembly of celebrity experts was even more eclectic than the Special Studies panels of the 1950s. It included historian Daniel J. Boorstin and agronomist Norman Borlaug; labor leader Lane Kirkland and ad executive Mary Wells Lawrence; Clare Boothe Luce and Daniel Patrick Moynihan; Bill Paley and Bess Myerson; plus the inevitable Edward Teller, Ed Logue, Bill Ronan, and Oscar Ruebausen: forty-two members in all, filling out six interdisciplinary panels addressing issues of energy and ecology; raw materials and world trade; food, health, and the quality of life. As if divining America's future course at the turn of the twenty-first century didn't offer sufficient challenge, in March 1973 Rockefeller accepted a second Nixon invitation, to chair a National Commission on Water Quality. His past involvement with Pure Waters and other pollution-fighting efforts in New York made Rockefeller a logical choice to wield the gavel. And although he had his differences with committee colleagues such as Maine's Edmund Muskie, he would devote far more time and energy to the project than anyone else around Nixon.

Embracing activity for its own sake, Rockefeller risked self-parody. Steve Berger would never forget walking down Fifty-fifth Street and running into the governor in his car, scribbling furiously on a yellow legal pad. Catching sight of the younger man, Rockefeller gestured for him to stop. His writing finished, he got out of the car and motioned Berger to join him in the doorway of Number 22. There he asked Berger to read from the pad, with its rough draft of testimony on the nation's energy shortfall that Rockefeller was to deliver before a congressional committee. Berger was dismayed by the well-intentioned boilerplate encapsulating the Rockefeller mantra of "Don't just stand there—do something." Gently he suggested to the governor that it was still early in the crisis. With so much unknown, might it not be better if he waited before testifying? "The notion that he shouldn't act *immediately* brought the most wonderful look of incredulity to the governor's face," said Berger. "At that moment he decided I was a Martian and had nothing to contribute to any serious discussion."

5

A N ILL-ADVISED ATTEMPT at kingmaking in the 1973 New York City mayor's race defined the limits of Rockefeller's power within his own party. The initial impetus came from Alex Rose, the seventy-four-year-old master strategist behind a Liberal Party in decline. With a third Lindsay term judged out of the question, a fearful Rose concluded that city hall was in imminent peril of returning to "the old days"—his euphemism for a conservative, outer borough product of the Democratic organization, or what remained of the post-Tammany party machinery. In a Democratic primary field crowded with liberals, it wasn't difficult to pick out the Un-Lindsay: Mario Biaggi, a twenty-three-year veteran of the New York City police, elected to Congress from the Bronx in 1968 as a Democrat with Conservative Party backing. The prospect of a Biaggi mayoralty was anathema to Rose, who had no trouble enlisting Rockefeller in a quixotic campaign to resurrect Bob Wagner on a Republican-Liberal fusion ticket to replace the Republican-Liberal champion elected in 1965 to clean up the mess bequeathed to New Yorkers by—Bob Wagner.

The former mayor, happily ensconced in a lucrative law practice following a turn as LBJ's ambassador to Franco's Spain, took some persuading. Eight years out of Gracie Mansion, Wagner insisted that New York City was governable, but the signals he sent regarding his own plans were decidedly mixed. His indecision over whether to enter the Democratic primary, or accept a Republican nomination, brought back unhappy memories. ("When in doubt, don't.") It also infected potential supporters. "Bob Price called me," remembered Ed Koch, then a Manhattan congressman financially priced out of that year's mayoral contest. Price, an old friend, told Koch that Rockefeller would like to see him at Fifty-fifth Street. Price told Rockefeller that Koch was willing to support a Wagner candidacy. Delighted by the news, the governor suggested to his visitor that they hold a press conference that very afternoon to make the endorsement public. Before Koch could respond, Rockefeller raised another question.

"Do you think he'll run?"

"Governor, you call me up here to endorse Wagner in the Democratic primary. Big deal. And you're asking me if *I* think he'll run?" There would be no press conference, pending clarification from Wagner himself. By March 12, Nelson claimed to have the necessary pledges of support from Republican county leaders for a ticket led by Wagner, with former Miss America Bess Myerson, fresh off her crowd-pleasing turn as the city's commissioner of consumer affairs, for city council president. His timing could not have been worse. Myerson, anxious to make some money after her years in municipal government, declined his invitation to run. An even greater shock awaited the man who had financially nurtured New York Republicans for more than a decade and whose family had sustained the party and its candidates far longer. Even as Wagner called a press conference to awkwardly declare his independence ("I've never been a puppet"), GOP borough chiefs exhibited theirs by turning on Rockefeller and Wagner. Bronx chairman John Calandra set the tone by calling the would-be fusion candidate "a moron." On March 26, Wagner, showing more conviction than he had in months, announced his withdrawal from the race, leaving Rockefeller without a candidate.*

Time was catching up to the children of Junior and Abby Aldrich Rockefeller. In Arkansas, Winthrop Rockefeller had withdrawn to his ranch on Petit Jean Mountain to brood upon his defeat for a third term as that state's governor. No Rockefeller family secret was more closely guarded than the remorse Nelson harbored over the youthful mistreatment of his younger brother. "I'm responsible for a lot of Winthrop's problems," he confessed to an associate. In the years since, he had tried to make amends, loaning Winthrop $2 million to help cover his first divorce settlement and encouraging him in the unlikely political career that made him Arkansas's first Republican governor since Reconstruction. Yet he was powerless to halt Winthrop's alcoholic binges or the gathering sense of futility around his postgubernatorial existence, culminating in a diagnosis of pancreatic cancer in September 1972.

Separated from his second wife, Jeannette, Winthrop grew a patriarchal beard and sought to repair the emotional damage inflicted upon his twenty-four-year-old son and namesake. The two had effected a reconciliation by the middle of February 1973, when the elder Winthrop flew to Palm Springs to escape the wintry chill of the Ozarks. And it was there, in the California desert, on Washington's Birthday, that he became the first Rockefeller of his generation to die. Nelson was tapped to deliver a eulogy at the March 4 funeral held in the antique auto museum on Petit Jean Mountain. "I'm never going to get through this," he fretted before the ceremony. In his verbal tribute, he was careful to drop the derogatory Winnie in favor of Win. He stressed Winthrop's lifelong sensitivity to race relations, something he credited their mother with implanting. Recalling his brother's response to the assassination of Martin Luther King, Jr., when he had stood with black mourners on the steps of the Capitol and sung "We Shall Overcome," Nelson quoted a particularly apt observation made at the time by Winthrop: "I am not my brother's keeper, I am my brother's brother." Listing Winthrop's accomplishments as governor, Nelson couldn't resist sounding an autobiographical note, refuting criticism of Win

---

* Ironically, the original rationale for a Wagner comeback evaporated in May when it was learned that Biaggi, the law-and-order candidate, had cited the Fifth Amendment sixteen times in grand jury testimony concerning his personal and campaign finances.

that he had "tried to move the State forward too fast in terms of raising the revenues to provide the essential services needed by the people."

6

YOU COULD SET your watch by it, the political equivalent of Old Faithful or San Juan de Capistrano and its punctual flocks. Every third year of Rockefeller's governorship was dotted with town meetings, freewheeling encounters at which the once and future candidate matched wits with representative New Yorkers, some too young to remember any other occupant of Albany's Executive Mansion. Since Attica, the tone of these gatherings had become more confrontational, the heckling more strident, the opportunities for Rockefeller to deploy his persuasive gifts undercut by protesters less interested in democratic debate than in prosecuting a war criminal. Eleven town meetings were scheduled for the fall of 1972. At one, a college newspaper editor appealed to the governor on behalf of a twenty-four-year-old student sentenced to seven to fifteen years in prison for selling marijuana to an undercover cop.

"All he wants to do is get out and do graduate work at Vassar," explained the campus journalist. "I respect the gentleman for wanting to go to Vassar," Rockefeller replied. A more substantive response awaited the Christmas season of 1972, when the offending student's name joined the list of six inmates whose sentences Nelson commuted. As governor, his charity was equaled by his perseverance, a trait that shaped his approach to the chief unfinished business of the Rockefeller governorship. "Jerry, do you know I wasted a billion dollars in the drug program," he observed to Jerry Finkelstein. Other men might be humbled, or embarrassed, by such an admission, but Rockefeller was taunted by failure to try yet again. No mere catchphrase, for him the war on drugs posed the ultimate test of his faith that no problem was beyond solution. Of course tactics and tools would change. In place of voluntary or coercive treatment, he would criminalize what had until recently been classed as a sickness. Many were shocked by his abrupt reversal. They shouldn't have been. Nelson Rockefeller was a serial alarmist. In earlier generations, he had warned with a town crier's fervor of the threat to American survival presented by Nazis and Communists. With equal conviction he had insisted that his countrymen pay attention to Latin America, that they build fallout shelters, support foreign aid and bigger defense budgets, renounce racism and the menace of extremist politics.

His approach to governing New York had likewise been tuned to the highest pitch. Housing shortages, water pollution, snarled transport, street crime, and the dry arcana of bond issues—each posed a crisis demanding immediate action. Fourteen years in office had done nothing to dull his sense of urgency, as demonstrated in the annual message delivered on January 3, 1973. Before legislators stunned into silence, Rockefeller escalated his war on narcotics to include the nuclear option, neatly summarized in a *Daily News* headline: ROCKY ASKS LIFE FOR PUSHERS. Promising an end to "the reign of fear" gripping many New Yorkers, Rockefeller frankly acknowledged that previous efforts to combat the drug trade had achieved "very little permanent rehabilitation—and no cure." Education and treatment having failed to reduce individual addiction, he now tacked in the opposite direction, decreeing life sentences without parole, probation, or plea bargaining for those using or trafficking in hard drugs. These he defined as heroin and other narcotics, LSD, amphetamines, and hashish. Rockefeller would impose similar terms for anyone who committed a violent crime under the influence of such drugs. Youthful offenders aged sixteen through nineteen had no special claim on his sympathy, though they could at least apply for parole after serving fifteen years of their sentence. Finally, Rockefeller wanted the state to offer $1,000 cash bounties for any New Yorker providing information leading to the apprehension and conviction of a known drug dealer.

Employing language as uncompromising as his proposed remedies, Rockefeller made no apology for his change of course. "The only way to deter this commerce in tragedy is by measures so strong, so effective, so fully enforced, that the hard drug pusher will no longer risk his own life and freedom by jeopardizing the lives of others." Rockefeller's speech met with predictable opposition from the American Civil Liberties Union, the Legal Aid Society, and the *New York Times* editorial board. Mayor Lindsay wrote off the governor's program as "impractical, unworkable, and vindictive." Veteran Manhattan district attorney Frank Hogan said it offended his sense of justice to make no distinction in punishing the addict selling a few bags to support his habit and the wholesaler dealing in kilo-sized lots. Judges complained that mandatory sentences would deprive them, and the judicial system, of any discretion in personalizing justice.

More surprising were objections raised by the Conservative Party, as well as police officials who pointed out that the proposed legislation would actually increase the risk to officers confronting suspects for whom the prospect of a mandated life sentence might loosen their trigger finger. Yet most New Yorkers sided with their governor. A February poll found his get-tough approach supported two to one. Fully 70 percent voiced approval of Rockefeller's $1,000 bounties. This didn't prevent questions from being raised about his motives. Frustration over past failure, genuine concern that drugs were corroding society and corrupting law enforcement in particular, response to public pressure, and rank political calculation were undoubtedly factors in his radical policy shift. Rockefeller himself credited Happy's children from her first marriage with influencing his outlook. Sitting around the dinner table, he had heard firsthand of the dangers associated with seemingly casual drug use, much of it the result of peer pressure. "I think it distorted his thinking," says counsel Michael Whiteman. "He attached so much weight to what those kids were saying. . . . He wanted to be the person who listened to them, wanted to be somebody they could talk to."

No one did more to shape Rockefeller's views than Bill Fine, president of Bonwit Teller, whose son had struggled with addiction. Fine and Rockefeller met at a party early in 1972, and out of their casual discussion of the drug menace came an invitation for the upscale retailer to visit Japan and determine why that insular nation boasted some of the lowest addiction rates in the world. Fine returned convinced that the secret to Japan's success was its law mandating life sentences for drug pushers. Mike Whiteman likened Fine to the blind man trying to describe what an elephant looks like. "He saw one feature and he brought that back, and the governor became enamored of it, without realizing . . . you couldn't take a piece of the culture out of the culture and expect it to work in a different culture."

Rockefeller had his panacea. "I've tried everything else," Whiteman imagines him saying. "Here's a bright new idea." Rockefeller first shared his thinking with key staff members assembled at Pocantico on Election Day 1972. Speechwriter Joe Persico could scarcely believe what he was hearing. Whiteman's principled objections evoked charges of disloyalty. Deeply hurt, the counsel went to Ron Maiorana. "What do I do? This is intolerable," he told him. Maiorana assured Whiteman that the only way to deal with Rockefeller was to take him head-on. "Because he respects people who stand up for themselves."

The next morning Whiteman, insisting, "I have only one client here," did exactly that. If Rockefeller accepted his motives, and had confidence in his professional judgment, fine. "And if not, I'll write out my resignation and be out of here by the end of the day. But you can't function, and I can't function, if you don't trust that." Whiteman's unvarnished words succeeded in clearing the air. "Let's shake hands on this," Rockefeller told his counsel, "and we'll put it behind us. . . . You do your job and we'll be fine." This did not mean he had any intention of revisiting the basic policy. "The governor was very open; he listened to a point," says Whiteman. "And when he had heard enough and had formulated his view, those hooded eyes started to come down, they glazed over, and if you watched the body language carefully, you knew to say, 'It's time to quit. I've either already won or I've already lost, but there's no point in going any further.'"

At the end of January, Rockefeller submitted to questioning by a joint legislative committee. Sparks flew when Assemblyman Arthur Eve arraigned the governor for his "ghetto genocide bill." He hadn't planned on interrogating Rockefeller, said Eve, because "I find it's an emotional thing talking to you at times."

"It's mutual," Rockefeller replied, before quoting a Harlem minister on the genocide presently inflicted on ghetto residents by drug pushers. Hewing to his tough line, he ruled out any exception for the suburban housewife giving diet pills to a neighbor—a scenario often cited in mockery of the proposed law's excesses—claiming that a four-month advertising campaign would educate both women as to the dangers, and penalties, associated with such behavior. When the New York State Bar Association questioned the state's readiness to handle an influx of new prisoners, Rockefeller countered with a $50 million expansion of the state court system, including the creation of a hundred or more politically appetizing supreme court judgeships, each one paying $43,316. Pressed on whether appointing these justices violated the state constitution, which mandated their popular election, Rockefeller had a ready response:

"It's only unconstitutional if you call them a Supreme Court judge. Call them something else, it's constitutional."

Assembly Democrats took to calling him "Lord Nelson." One member of the minority held out black coat hangers for Republican lawmakers to hang their judicial robes on. Even this redounded to Rockefeller's advantage, as he exploited the judicial shortage to ram through the legislature his long delayed no-fault auto insurance bill—one result of which, he argued, would be to free exactly 112 sitting judges from adjudicating cases brought by alleged accident victims. Not everyone, however, wanted to be a judge. With those immune to such blandishments, Rockefeller didn't shy away from playing hardball.

Assemblyman Dale Volker was a former cop, the son of a longtime representative from western New York who had lost his seat to redistricting after falling afoul of Rockefeller over taxes and Medicaid. First elected in 1972, the younger Volker was in the vanguard of opposition to the governor's proposed drug laws. In response, Rockefeller called Volker's father to complain, "Your son is giving me a really hard time. I really think you ought to talk to him." The elder Volker did as he was asked, but not in the vein urged by Rockefeller. "I don't know what you're doing," he told his son, "but you're doing something right." That evening, father, son, and a third individual were walking down State Street en route to the annual dinner of the legislature's Codes Committee at Jack's Restaurant. "I happen to notice this limousine coming down," says Volker. "It's Rockefeller. The guy pulls across, drives right up on the sidewalk, opens the window. Rockefeller looks at my father—'Well, Julie, I hope you've been able to talk to your son.' And my father says, 'He's a stubborn guy.'"

The conversation resumed upstairs at Jack's, without intermediaries. "Next thing I know, I'm walking around, and the governor was in my face. . . . 'This could be a disaster for the Republican Party.' Sort of, 'Who do you think you are?'" As Volker recalled the confrontation, "He eventually put his finger on my chest and pushes me against the wall," while very publicly chastising the uncooperative assemblyman, "You'll be making a big mistake." Volker pushed back, physically and verbally. Daring Rockefeller to run a candidate against him "because I'll beat the shit out of him" was an impolitic gesture, as Volker readily conceded; the withholding of a Conservative Party endorsement two years later assured Volker's early retirement (though Rockefeller couldn't prevent Volker from returning to Albany via a 1975 special state senate election).

The Volker-Rockefeller dispute did not end at Jack's. Days later, Volker detected suspicious sounds of static on his office phone line. He went to see Perry Duryea. "If mine is tapped," he remembers telling the Speaker, "I'll bet yours is tapped too. Then we find out that there's another Democrat, his line is tapped." Asked later if he was certain the tapping was related to the drug law, Volker replied, "Oh yes. There is no question. . . . I had a friend who worked for Rockefeller call me up and say how he really felt bad about tapping my phone above all, because we had been friends, and on the police force together. But hey, what are you going to do?"*

By the first week of March, the governor was offering to remove hashish from his list of hard drugs. Other modifications, including limited plea bargaining and parole followed by lifetime supervision, eased the way to senate passage on April 28. The legislation stalled in the assembly, where the decision had been made to proceed without Democratic support. After a few revisions (the dieting housewife saw her punishment for over-the-fence dealing reduced from life to a class D felony, with a maximum of seven years behind bars), the assembly acquiesced in a party-line vote of 80 to 65. At the signing ceremony on May 8, a boastful Rockefeller praised lawmakers for standing firm against "this strange alliance of vested establishment interests, political opportunists and misguided soft liners who joined forces and tried to stop this program."

Whatever short-term political advantage the new laws may have conferred, they did nothing for Rockefeller's historical reputation. Over the next three decades, New York's prison population exploded. As the costs of incarcerating drug offenders soared, successive governors, and legislatures, chipped away at the 1973 statute. Marijuana penalties were scaled back under Governor Hugh

---

* A Rockefeller loyalist points out possible justification for such wiretapping—in the wake of Attica, threats to the governor's safety were a staple of his visits to Buffalo, where state police routinely moved him to unannounced accommodations to minimize the danger. Under the circumstances, either the police or members of the state's Bureau of Criminal Investigation, on seeing Volker jab *his* finger into Rockefeller's chest, might well have overreacted, with or without Rockefeller's knowledge. Confidential source.

Carey. More significant changes took place during George Pataki's governor-ship and in 2009, when Governor David Paterson eliminated mandatory mini-mum sentences. (Laurance Rockefeller, who knew his brother's mind better than most, insisted that these and other revisions would have happened much faster had Nelson been elected to a fifth term in 1974. Seeing that his punitive methods were no more successful than earlier programs such as civil commit-ment, Nelson the empiricist would have devised yet another plan to combat drug use.)

Rockefeller hoped his final legislative session might be remembered for a radically different initiative, one whose benefits wouldn't be fully appreciated in his lifetime. Two weeks after codifying his frustrations over drugs, Rockefel-ler affirmed his stewardship of some six million acres of breathtaking scenery and bountiful wildlife in the Great Woods of New York's North Country by signing his name to the most sophisticated land use planning effort in the his-tory of American conservation—the Adirondack Park bill. It had been a long time coming. In the nineteenth century the wilderness area between Canada and the Mohawk River had inspired many a battle over water rights, lumbering, railroading, and the tourist trade. In 1885, the state legislature voted to establish the Adirondack Forest Preserve, approximately 2.3 million acres declared "for-ever wild" in the state's 1894 constitution.

The remainder of Adirondack Mountains State Park, twice the size of Yellowstone, included vast stretches of privately owned land. (As late as 1965, the state held title to less than 40 percent of the largest wilderness area east of the Mississippi.) Administering this hybrid was not easy, as the forest preserve coexisted with fifteen separate communities enforcing a patchwork of conflict-ing regulations. With completion of the Adirondack Northway linking Albany and the Canadian border, access to the formerly isolated park was greatly in-creased. A growing demand for private campgrounds, snowmobile trails, hous-ing tracts, and hydroelectric power brought Laurance Rockefeller into the picture. At his invitation, former National Park Service director Conrad Wirth undertook a study of the Adirondacks and their potential for conversion into a national park. Not surprisingly given his backgound, Wirth warmly endorsed the concept, which just as predictably sparked a firestorm of protest among North Country developers, logging companies, and local officials fearing the loss of autonomy and tax revenue.

Publicly, Nelson pronounced the result of Wirth's investigation "terrific." In truth, the national park idea was dead on arrival. Yet Laurance's report served as a catalyst for state and local action. Early in 1968, Nelson, whose personal attachment to the region dated to early summers he had spent there in boys' camps, announced plans for a Temporary Study Commission on the Future of the Adirondacks. Seeking the broadest possible political cover, he reached out not only to high-profile conservationists such as newscaster Lowell Thomas, but to Frederick O'Neal, the African American president of Actors' Equity Association. The governor's original preference to chair the group was Leo O'Brien, a former Albany newspaperman and Democratic congressman best known for his sponsorship of federal legislation conferring statehood on Alaska.

Unfortunately, O'Brien had an Alaska-sized thirst, which once led him to stage his very own Iditarod by mushing a dogsled team down the main street of Lake Placid. In his place, Rockefeller chose industrialist Harold Hochschild, founder of the Adirondack Museum and a major landowner in the area. Balancing "forever wild"–style preservation with an economically viable habitat for 130,000 permanent residents and up to ten million visitors a year, the commission fostered land use planning that protected some areas from so much as canoe traffic, while designating others for recreational and developmental purposes. In May 1971, Rockefeller accepted the commission's findings as a prelude to legislation expanding current park boundaries, providing state funding to offset local tax losses, and establishing an independent Adirondack Park Agency to administer public and private land management.

Shrewdly, Rockefeller minimized his public advocacy, recognizing that putting his stamp on the proposed agency would diminish its chances of enactment. Instead he worked backstage, coordinating strategy in unpublicized meetings with commission members at Fifty-fifth Street, twisting arms when needed. In a concession to local interests, a full year was to elapse between the agency's creation and implementation of its plans. Fears that developers would exploit this opportunity to initiate building projects wherever they could obtain ground to break led to special legislation conferring injunctive powers as temporary as the commission itself. A Rockefeller veto blocked last-ditch efforts to delay comprehensive land use plans from taking effect. Fifty or a hundred years hence, the governor declared in signing the final Adirondack Park bill into law, the 1973 legislative session would be remembered chiefly for its environmental statesmanship. The drug laws enacted at his insistence would demonstrate otherwise. In the twilight of his governorship, Rockefeller retained enough clout to secure passage of both initiatives. He had less influence over posterity's judgment.

7

WITHIN WEEKS OF his second inaugural, Richard Nixon was under siege, as congressional investigators probed alleged abuses of executive power lumped together under the umbrella label of Watergate. The atmosphere inside the White House was becoming toxic, with the president's personal secretary, Rose Mary Woods, convinced that the phones were tapped. John Mitchell, who two weeks after Nixon's landslide reelection had assured Happy Rockefeller that her husband would be the next president of the United States, was preparing for multiple trials arising from his conduct as attorney general. Careful to avoid criticism of the administration, Rockefeller justified his stance in language more revealing than he may have intended. His chief responsibility was to the people of New York, said Rockefeller. "You don't kick people in Washington in the shins if you expect them to do something for you."

Privately he displayed more curiosity, interrogating Ken Riland about the scandal and how near to the Oval Office it was likely to reach. At least to Mitchell, said Riland, if not beyond. (At this Nelson "blinked" in surprise, Riland recorded. Only a few weeks earlier, he had considered offering the Mitchells a house at Pocantico.) In mid-April, Nelson received one of Martha Mitchell's signature telephone calls, relaying rumors of Rockefeller anger over the failure of her husband while still in office to help in Riland's tax evasion case. "I'm not mad, Ken's not mad, nobody's mad at nothing or nobody," Nelson assured her. Aside from some grumbling over Nixon's seeming infatuation with his former Treasury secretary, John Connally—a potent rival in the succession contest already under way—Rockefeller kept his counsel regarding the embattled president.

He had good reason to practice discretion. "Nelson Rockefeller knew quite early that Agnew had problems," according to Jim Cannon. Another source claims that Rockefeller was aware as early as 1968, if not before, that Agnew as governor of Maryland was pocketing money from contractors and others doing business with the state. (This was apparently a long-standing practice around Annapolis, where it was said, only partly in jest, that the state's chief executives earned $25,000 a year, plus tips.)* On July 16, 1973, Haldeman assistant Alexander Butterfield revealed the existence of an elaborate White House taping system. Nixon invoked claims of executive privilege to forestall public disclosure of embarrassing or, worse, legally incriminating conversations. Simultaneously, it was revealed that Agnew was under investigation by Maryland prosecutors.

Peter Wallison, a politically astute young lawyer on the Rockefeller staff, raised with Cannon the distinct possibility that Agnew might be gone from the scene long before 1976 and that Rockefeller should be positioning himself to replace the vice president should it become necessary for Nixon to appoint a

---

* Rockefeller himself had, through a third party, supplied Agnew with $5,000 in cash prior to the 1968 campaign for the GOP presidential nomination, ostensibly to establish a headquarters operation in the period before Nelson's March 21 pullout. Ted Braun, HMI, 43.

successor under the never used Twenty-fifth Amendment. "So Peter and I contrived this plan on how we were going to do this," said Cannon. "Assemble the gang, people around the country urging Nixon to do it, and half a dozen other things—a press campaign, whatever." They committed their thoughts to paper, which Bill Ronan carried to a vacationing Rockefeller in Maine.

The governor agreed that Agnew had to go. "But Nixon has already made up his mind who it's going to be," said Nelson. Citing Henry Kissinger as his source, he added, "I'm not sure, but I think it's going to be John Connally." Fearing public embarrassment, Kissinger had discouraged his patron from actively pursuing the job. This didn't prevent most Republican governors, as well as many of Nixon's biggest campaign contributors, from rallying to his side. Then Rockefeller staffer Bob Armao got a hot tip from the vice president's office: Agnew was signing a letter of resignation. Armao hurried to Ann Whitman's desk; "Tell the governor the vice presidency's about to open up." For the next three days, Whitman monitored an open telephone line to Washington. Ultimately, Nixon's call went instead to House Republican leader Gerald Ford, identified by leaders of both parties as the most easily confirmable alternative to Connally.

Hiding his disappointment, insisting there was "very little governors can do about Watergate," Rockefeller continued his praise for Nixon's foreign policy achievements. When the president that same month fired Watergate special prosecutor Archibald Cox, Rockefeller spoke of a "national tragedy" rather than a crime. His own departure from office that December was strictly voluntary. Rockefeller offered multiple explanations of his decision to vacate the governorship a year before his term was up. "There's no more money," he told Ron Maiorana. "I couldn't stand to go to Albany and make any more deals," he acknowledged to Harry Albright. Originally cast as a political idealist wedded to pay-as-you-go fiscal policies, Nelson claimed that with the passage of time, "every time I wanted to do what I thought was the right thing," some legislator would condition his support on gaining a new thruway exit or other perk.

Ken Riland was nearer the mark, writing in the summer of 1973 that his friend was, quite simply, "fed up with state government." As always, Rockefeller had his sights fixed on bigger game. Long before Agnew's forced departure, Nelson was gearing up for a final lunge at the presidency. This was confirmed in August, when Malcolm Wilson learned that he would shortly become New York's fiftieth governor. A few key staffers were also notified. "There had been discussions," says Michael Whiteman, in the course of which Rockefeller expressed a desire that he and Budget Director Dick Dunham stay on. "I think he was a little bit worried that Malcolm would undo what he'd done." Such fears took root in Wilson's suburban background and daily devotions in a decidedly pre–Vatican II Catholicism. This Wilson invited caricature, with his unfashionably narrow ties, Latin quotations, and personal frugality that branded him a Westchester Coolidge. As governor, Wilson once invited a friendly journalist to lunch in his Manhattan office. "They bring out these two beautiful plates with the seal of the state of New York," recalls the scribe. "He reaches in his briefcase and brings out a Saratoga hard melon. He cuts it and says, 'Can I tempt you with some cottage cheese?'"

In the pool house behind the Executive Mansion one day in 1973, Wilson expressed genuine astonishment at the latest turn in international diplomacy. "You mean to tell me, Nelson, that Henry Kissinger has to share his Nobel Prize with a *Communist?*"* Yet Wilson was far more than the Rotarian orator dubbed "What's-his-name" by Albany cynics. His vast knowledge of the state and its government was equaled by his personal integrity and lack of pretense. Long after he and his wife, Katherine, moved to the Strathmore area of northeast Yonkers, a neighborhood with a tony Scarsdale address, Wilson continued to claim working-class Yonkers as his home. Wilson's insistence that federal revenue sharing was worth pursuing as an alternative to still higher taxes typified the sound counsel that Rockefeller valued as much as Wilson's devotion to the team.

As governor, Nelson did his best to return past favors. "He was always anxious to bring Malcolm in in different ways," recalls counsel Bob MacCrate. Having little interest himself in matters relating to the judiciary, Rockefeller was more than willing to leave these to the imaginary firm of Wilson and MacCrate. "One thing that every governor ordinarily likes to do is to call someone and ask them to set up an appointment to the bench. That was all delegated to me," says MacCrate. "And I'd come up with a recommendation. . . . Then he might say, 'Does Malcolm agree?' And I'd say yes, having reviewed the whole thing beforehand."† It could not have been easy for Wilson in May 1972 when legislators voted to reinstate New York's virtual ban on abortion. Rockefeller was out of the state the day the bill completed its successful passage through the legislature. As acting governor, Wilson was besieged with appeals from activists and supportive lawmakers who, sharing his strong pro-life convictions, pressured him to sign the restrictive measure in Rockefeller's absence. He re-

---

* Wilson's loyalty combined with a bone-dry sense of humor to produce some memorable observations. When Rockefeller as vice president famously delivered a one-finger salute to protesters at a campaign rally in Binghamton, Wilson told *Newsday*'s Dick Zander, "Nelson just got his fingers mixed up. I'm sure he meant to give them a thumbs-up sign."

† One area where the two men differed profoundly was art. For Rockefeller, the hardest part of returning to Albany during Wilson's brief tenure as governor was aesthetic—specifically, the Winslow Homer paintings that covered Executive Mansion walls once used to showcase the genius of Picasso, Pollock, and Motherwell.

jected their entreaties, reasoning that it was the governor's responsibility to decide the issue.

Rockefeller hoped to reciprocate by turning over the reins of government to his chosen successor in as politically favorable a climate as possible. For Rockefeller, 1973 was studded with ceremonial occasions that offered the departing governor architectural vindication. On a rain-spattered April day near the southern tip of Manhattan, he dedicated the World Trade Center he had saved from fiscal disaster by making the state of New York the principal tenant of the 110-story South Tower. In August, on a site originally suggested by his son Steven, he inaugurated Harlem River State Park, one of the first such recreation areas to be established in New York City. Finally, on November 21 Nelson consecrated the unfinished South Mall—renamed the Empire State Plaza—"as our generation's vision of what the capital of a great state should be." This alone should have tipped off the political class to Rockefeller's imminent departure. Hidden from public view, a final debate engulfed the governor and his advisers, as Rockefeller considered intervening in the Attica grand jury proceedings. To date, these had resulted in the indictment of sixty-one inmates or former inmates; among the state police and others who joined in retaking the prison, only one participant had been charged with a crime. Specifically, Rockefeller wished special prosecutor Robert Fischer to dismiss all the indictments and halt any further prosecution. His advisers talked him out of it, contending that such an act would be seen as intrusive and yet unlikely, as one put it, "to get the students off your back."

Rockefeller showed more finesse in handling the ghosts of Attica than in orchestrating his gubernatorial transition. His December 11 resignation announcement, to take effect one week later, consisted mostly of lavish praise for Malcolm Wilson. The next morning, Ken Riland discovered Rockefeller cavorting "like a kid out of school. I've never seen he or Happy so relaxed." The retiring governor's joy may have stemmed from more than his sense of pending release. Elsewhere in Manhattan that morning, a grand jury was voting to indict Perry Duryea, assembly Republican leader John Kingston, Queens assemblyman Alfred DelliBovi, and three GOP staffers for election law violations. The maneuverings behind the indictment were as murky as the alleged conspiracy by Republicans to promote Liberal Party candidates in marginal districts where they might tip the scales against the Democratic contender, and the improper identification of campaign literature that advanced the supposed plot.

Feeding the ensuing uproar was a near universal suspicion that Rockefeller, eager to clear the field for Wilson, was somehow responsible for Louis Lefkowitz's decision to deliver incriminating evidence in the case to Manhattan district attorney Frank Hogan. No hard proof of this has ever been produced, until now. A source close to Rockefeller, promised confidentiality by the author, described the scene as the governor harangued a reluctant Lefkowitz into doing "the right thing" by giving Hogan's investigators anything of a damning nature against Duryea. The sympathy this created among Duryea's political brethren, reinforced by a judge's summary dismissal of all charges in the case, could not undo the damage to the Speaker's gubernatorial hopes for 1974. But it generated bitter resentments that surfaced during Rockefeller's vice presidential confirmation hearings and beyond.

On December 17, his final full day as governor, Rockefeller spoke with Duryea by phone, though no details of their conversation were released. He consulted with Bill Ronan, his original tutor in state government, and appointed Al Marshall, Ronan's successor as secretary to the governor, to the new New York State Sports Authority, thereby swelling Marshall's state pension. (After fifteen years in office, Rockefeller himself was entitled to $21,000 a year in pension benefits.) The departing governor also announced a round of holiday season commutations. One of these was fifty-two-year-old Edward Young, an Attica inmate who had testified to impressive effect before the McKay Commission. In a final meeting with reporters, Rockefeller reminisced about a boyhood encounter with Theodore Roosevelt, insisting that, like TR, he had retained to the end his enthusiasm for the work entrusted to him by the people of New York.

The next day, he spoke five sentences of support for the new governor, then watched as Malcolm Wilson took the oath of office in the Red Room. From there the state's forty-ninth and fiftieth governors left for a Republican state committee luncheon, where Nelson ritualistically called for party unity. Restating his faith in the integrity and honor of Speaker Duryea and his associates, charged under a law "of doubtful validity," he devoted the balance of his remarks to extolling the virtues of Malcolm Wilson and Richard Nixon.

Twenty-Five
"THE CLOSEST I'M EVER GOING
TO GET. . . ."

Every vice president goes through hell—let's face it. He's an able man and he's sitting there and he can't do anything; can't express himself; he's got to follow the line. And it's a very frustrating experience.

—NELSON A. ROCKEFELLER

1

"FREE AT LAST!" Rockefeller cackled to a former staff member days after leaving Albany. Contributing to his happiness was a new building project, as he belatedly embarked on the Texas ranch venture first envisioned more than three decades earlier. A few days after Christmas 1973, Rockefeller loaded young Nelson and Mark into a Gulfstream II for the trip south to Port Mansfield, on the Gulf of Mexico. There being no ranch house on the six-thousand-acre property, father and sons roughed it in tents and sleeping bags. (There was a limit to their privation; according to a Secret Service agent who later accompanied them to the site, most of the hunting was done from the back of a jeep, while in the evening no fewer than nine chefs and waiters prepared a campsite dinner, complete with white linen tablecloths and candelabras.) The elder Nelson returned from his wilderness adventure covered with tick bites from his waist to his ankles; his nine-year-old namesake brought back two bucks, a wild boar, and a turkey, testament to his shooting prowess and extensive training by a Pocantico ranger.

Rockefeller's original ambition to join the landed gentry of the Lone Star State had foundered on the financial inadequacies of a youthful heir awaiting his legacy. Though his resources were much greater now, they never quite caught up to his enthusiasms. The Texas ranch, conceived as a private game preserve lavishly stocked with exotic creatures, was to impart a painful lesson. As recalled by one Rockefeller associate, "Poor Mary Kresky whose job it was to tell him, 'no, you can't do it,' really had a terrible time with him. He finally said to her one day, 'Mary, you are the only person who has made me understand that there are limits to what you can do with money.'"

This included a wing of the Metropolitan Museum of Art bearing the name of his late son, Michael. In addition to the "primitive" art collected by father and son, the new galleries would showcase the museum's impressive holdings from Africa, Oceania, and the Americas. Museum wings did not come cheap. "Instead of using marble or slate or such traditional materials," Nelson at one point suggested to Met officials, "why don't we use Astroturf?" It was durable, popular with the masses, "and this stuff would look great against that." Rockefeller's theory went untested, and the august precincts of the Met remained unsullied by artificial grass. Director Thomas Hoving publicly called Rockefeller a grifter for allegedly reneging on his $4 million pledge (an amount eventually cobbled together with help from Brooke Astor and the estate of Nelson's stepmother).

Rockefeller was a frequent visitor to the nation's capital during the first half of 1974. One day he welcomed Ann Whitman and Rose Mary Woods for drinks at Foxhall Road. Woods said it was the first time in months that anyone had treated her as a human being. To Ken Riland, in whose arms she broke down in tears, the president's confidential secretary appeared suicidal, "just waiting for something to happen." Nixon himself plied Riland with questions about his upcoming trial for tax evasion. "They won't send you to jail, will they?" he asked in a tone Riland thought unintentionally revealing. Rockefeller had long questioned Nixon's emotional stability. Now he was told by Henry Kissinger that the embattled chief executive was often drunk. Needless to say, this intelligence did not find its way into Nelson's comments before Republican audiences, as he traveled the country—logging eighty thousand miles between January and August—in a shadow campaign to succeed the president he still expected to serve out his term.

Wherever he went, Rockefeller told the GOP faithful what they wanted to hear. "I'm so tired of the tapes," Nelson informed a gathering of southern Republicans in Atlanta in December 1973. "Let us not forget what Richard Nixon did for this country. The Congress this year voted about $20 billion to $30 billion more in expenditures than we had in revenues—only Richard Nixon had the courage to stand up and cut back on these so we could live within our means." His private view of the presidential character was less generous. "I hope you're not seriously thinking of going to work for *him*," Rockefeller told Hugh Morrow when Morrow reported job feelers from the dying administration. Yet he stubbornly resisted attempts to hasten Nixon's involuntary departure from office. On *Meet the Press*, Johnny Apple of *The New York Times* pushed him hard, demanding to know why he didn't assemble a high-level group of Republicans and insist on the president's resignation. The heat was turned up further in April 1974, when both Barry Goldwater and Jim Buckley urged just such a course. At the end of the month, Nixon was hounded into releasing edited transcripts of his Oval Office conversations. That same day, making extensive use of the family plane, Rockefeller attended several previously scheduled events around the Empire State. Depressed by the tone of the Nixon tapes, recalls a fellow passenger, "He said nothing. He just stared out the window."

2

ON THE MORNING of August 7, Rockefeller and his family were in the driveway at Kykuit preparing to depart for coastal Maine, when Nelson was summoned inside to take a call from Mel Laird. The former defense secretary, known to be an intimate of Vice President Ford's, reiterated to Nelson what he had already told Hugh Morrow—that Rockefeller was under serious consideration to succeed Ford in the event of Nixon's resignation. "Don't pay any attention to it," Nelson had instructed Morrow. "Mel's just setting me up to be shot down." Morrow dissented. "I think this one is real," he said. An unlikely consensus soon formed around Laird's trial balloon. Writing in *The New York Times* on August 12, three days after Nixon boarded a White House helicopter to carry him into exile, liberal columnist William V. Shannon neatly summarized the case for Rockefeller's vice presidential selection. *Send for the old pro,* he argued. The same week, Nixon at San Clemente told his son-in-law Edward Cox, "Ford's got to make Rockefeller the Vice President."

This was a very different message from the one he had imparted to Henry Kissinger during the wrenching final hours of his presidency. Alternately cursing and crying, Nixon had lashed out at his prospective successor. "Tell your friend not to get mixed up with this Ford Administration," Nixon instructed Kissinger. "The worst mistake I made in my life was appointing this man Vice President." Predicting "total disaster" for a Ford presidency, Nixon added, "Nelson should have nothing to do with it, and I will support him in 1976 for President." This exchange was to have profound consequences later in the administration, when Rockefeller became convinced that agents of the former president, if not Nixon himself, were conspiring to validate his bleak forecast. Meanwhile Ford asked the FBI to run a background check on three vice presidential prospects: Rockefeller, GOP national chairman George H. W. Bush, and Donald Rumsfeld, a former Illinois congressman and Nixon White House official then serving as ambassador to NATO, to whom Ford had already entrusted major responsibilities for his Oval Office transition.

Rockefeller's credentials were never in question; if anything, he might be said to be overqualified, his record of executive leadership neatly complementing Ford's legislative background. Politically, the two men constituted a fusion ticket of sorts, with Rockefeller appealing to organized labor, urban America, and minorities, none of them natural elements in Ford's constituency. Time would call these assumptions into question, but in the shell-shocked atmosphere of August 1974, it was hard to argue against Rockefeller as a confidence builder, one whose colorful personality and hard-charging style only confirmed the new president's quiet self-assurance. At Ford's request, White House political adviser Bryce Harlow, the prototypical Washington Wise Man, weighed the strengths and shortcomings of sixteen prospective candidates, before coming down squarely in the Rockefeller camp. Choosing the New Yorker would surprise the media and provoke second thoughts among voters estranged from the GOP. Though Harlow didn't know it, Ford had already reached similar conclusions. Their shared efforts on federal revenue sharing and the Critical Choices Commission had given Ford ample opportunity to assess Rockefeller's collegiality and executive skills. Nothing in Nelson's background, or his unconcealed ambition, intimidated Ford, a man famously comfortable in his own skin.

On Friday, August 16, White House chief of staff Alexander Haig notified Rockefeller in Maine to expect a call from the president.

"That's it," Nelson told an aide as he put the phone down. "I've got to tell Happy."

Moments later, husband and wife were strolling through the pine-scented woods around the Anchorage, weighing their options, negotiating the future. It was not what Happy would have wished, or the boys either. (By promising that he would spend weekends with the family at Pocantico, Nelson defined himself as a commuting—in effect, part-time—vice president.) Others were even less enthusiastic. Bill Ronan cautioned him against taking the job if it was offered. With a firm grasp of Nelson's emotional makeup, Ronan recounted the misery his friend had experienced in the Eisenhower White House when called on to implement agendas not of his making. On Saturday afternoon, Ford himself called Seal Harbor with a conditional offer, hedged by queries about Rockefeller's health, potential skeletons in the closet, and his willingness to undergo exhaustive scrutiny by the FBI and IRS. In their hour-long conversation, the president emphasized Nelson's access to political and administrative talent with which to restock a depleted White House. Ford elicited a somewhat reluctant promise from Rockefeller to abandon his Foxhall Road residence in favor of Admiral's House off Massachusetts Avenue. Formerly home to the naval commandant, the turreted Victorian structure was being converted into a permanent vice presidential dwelling.*

This sacrifice was more than offset by Ford's assurance of a genuine partnership in place of the ceremonial fifth wheel that had caused earlier vice presidents such grief. He offered Rockefeller a level of domestic policy oversight comparable to Henry Kissinger's management of foreign relations. In subsequent discussions, Bill Ronan disputed the practical value of Ford's domestic policy pledge. This was prescient; both promises were to be revisited as Ford grew into the office he had never sought. Yet there was never any real doubt as to Rockefeller's acceptance. Saying no would undercut the unelected president struggling to establish his legitimacy in the midst of the country's worst constitutional crisis since the Civil War. In his own mind, a reluctant Rockefeller yielded to duty, though not without securing a Ford concession that he'd be what a skeptical Ann Whitman labeled "a new kind of vice president."

Others shared her doubts. Dick Dunham, the state budget official whom Rockefeller would bring with him into the Ford White House, echoed Ronan's arguments against taking a job for which Nelson was so temperamentally ill-suited. For twenty minutes, Dunham argued his case. Conceding the force of his objections, Rockefeller finally dismissed them for the most basic of reasons. "But Dick," he blurted out at last, "this is the closest I'm ever going to get. . . ." The formal announcement was set for Tuesday morning, August 20. Before striding into the Oval Office where television cameras were waiting to broadcast the news, Ford placed a phone call to Richard Nixon at San Clemente to inform him of his choice. "A big man for a big job," responded the former president. Rockefeller kept his formal remarks brief and deferential. With the cameras turned off, he was approached by White House congressional liaison Tom Korologos, the man charged with shepherding Nelson's nomination through the Senate. Korologos repeated to Rockefeller what he had told countless nominees before him. "What is there in your background . . . that's going to cause the president and you some consternation? I'm not asking you to tell me what it is, but I'm asking you to get an answer, because those sons of bitches up there are going to find it and ask you."

Rockefeller cleared his throat. There *was* something, he told Korologos. The

---

* As the FBI dispatched a small army of agents to conduct the most thorough investigation of any nominee in its history, Rockefeller offered to have his divorce proceedings unsealed and make available any information pertaining to his personal finances. Agents learned that he hadn't written a check in forty years and that he had deducted $274,704 in expenses relating to a 1964–1965 television series called *Executive Chamber* from his state and federal income taxes as a gift to the state. Among the most pointed criticisms lodged against him was a telegram from Perry Duryea's unforgiving wife, Betty. It castigated Rockefeller as undeserving of a job as dog-catcher. *New York Times*, October 27, 1974.

financial disclosure requirement—"It's going to get public, isn't it?" Korologos assured him that it would, either formally or by committee leak. In that case, the nominee had a confession to make. "How much I'm worth—it's not as much as everybody thinks." Back at Foxhall Road, Ken Riland raised a much more delicate subject. "I had to name names and Nelson couldn't remember that these episodes had taken place but I got the point across. . . . I talked to Happy about the smear that could possibly come up from various aspects of the press and she just had to not let it bother her. I went into no specifics but the rumors I've been asked about [and] haven't been able to honestly deny—would fill a book." Riland had reason to be concerned, even now. Jim Cannon recalled one "breathtaking" woman smuggled into the Foxhall Road estate under the noses of the Secret Service. "It was right after he was nominated for vice president," said Cannon, who was accustomed with other staff members to bunking there under normal circumstances, "but if he had a girl come in, we'd all have to stay downtown." On this particular occasion, Rockefeller's visitor was slipped in and out again the next morning, with no one the wiser. "I thought, You're really taking a gamble there, Governor," Cannon reflected.

Warning signs of another kind were detected by George Hinman, who criticized Nelson's unscheduled visit to Barry Goldwater's Senate office on the day of his nomination, television cameras in tow. Goldwater had refused to see him; indeed, said Hinman, the Arizona senator was "mad as hell" over his former rival's presumption. "You can kiss the Republican Party goodbye," Goldwater told White House operatives. "He left the party three times and now he gets the cream and sugar." Tennessee's Bill Brock reported calls to his office running fifty to one against Rockefeller. In neighboring Kentucky, Marlow Cook, locked in a tight reelection battle, was beside himself over Ford's back-to-back announcements of an amnesty program for Vietnam draft evaders and the Rockefeller selection. "Any way we can get Nixon back?" asked Cook.

Even Rockefeller's friends expressed dismay over his mishandling of a reporter's question about running with Ford in 1976—"instead of pledging complete support he left the door open," said one. Such lapses caused alarm within Nelson's kitchen cabinet. "All of us are concerned with what is commonly known as his arrogance and how he has a tendency to take over," wrote Ken Riland on August 22. Bill Jackson, the Milbank, Tweed attorney heading Rockefeller's confirmation team, minced no words. The rest of the group was just as frank. "We really laid it on the line as to just what he would have to do," Riland noted. "We pleaded with him to make as low [a] profile as possible. This is not going to be easy for Nelson Rockefeller." Sixty-six-year-old men are not known for their adaptability. At the Republican National Committee, Judy Harbaugh, assisting the vice president designate with the torrent of congratulatory letters that greeted his nomination, found only one of her drafts meeting any resistance. "Too effusive," said Rockefeller. Harbaugh duly toned down Nelson's words of appreciation to John Lindsay.

3

INITIAL PRESS RESPONSE to the nomination was positive, *The New York Times* calling it a "masterly political act," while *Newsweek* praised Ford for adding a "dollop of high style" to his "homespun presidency." On Friday, September 6, Rockefeller was back at the White House for briefings on U.S.-Soviet relations and the CIA. Twice that day he met with the president. One topic that did not come up was a subject Ford took understandable pains to conceal. Not until Saturday evening did he confide to Rockefeller his decision to grant Richard Nixon a full pardon for any crimes associated with Watergate. Recognizing that he was being informed, not consulted, Rockefeller confined his objections to the proposed return of Nixon's 880 White House tapes. "I said that they were done without the knowledge of the people who were present, that this was a violation of their privacy," he would recall. As for Nixon, "I think he will be in a position to blackmail half the people in this country." Ford spoke of a "legal responsibility" to return the tapes. Rockefeller pleaded with him to get another legal opinion. The next morning, Ken Riland observed his friend, dressed for church, with a familiar bulldog expression conveying suppressed anger. Publicly, Nelson defended the president's action for its statesmanship and compassion. He was learning to speak—if not think—like a vice president.*

September 23 marked the beginning of Rockefeller's confirmation hearings in the Senate. Exhaustively prepared for questions about Attica, his oil holdings, and New York State finances, Nelson breezed through four days of testimony before a national television audience. Even skeptics were impressed. "This time it was the witness who seemed in charge," concluded *The New York Times*. On September 26, his part in the hearings completed, Rockefeller took to his bed with a temperature of 101 degrees. Twenty-four hours later, he was chopping down trees on the Pocantico estate. He was much slower to recuperate from a series of damaging leaks that dominated headlines in the first days of October. These exposed a jaw-dropping series of gifts to associates on the pub-

---

* Ford ultimately agreed with Rockefeller—at least, he signed the 1974 Presidential Recordings and Materials Preservation Act, authorizing the federal government through the General Services Administration and the National Archives to seize Nixon's papers and tapes for preservation (not to mention use in legal proceedings) and eventual processing. Materials within the collection deemed private were to be returned to the former president. Nixon promptly sued to overturn the law, the constitutionality of which was upheld on a 7 to 2 Supreme Court ruling.

lic payroll, most in fact "loans" subsequently forgiven to get around New York's statutory ban on such payments. "He always used to say you can buy knowledge, but you can't buy loyalty," says one associate. Ultimately, this would be Rockefeller's line of defense: that his gifts were made to attract and retain public servants of the highest caliber. Among the beneficiaries were Henry Kissinger, who received $50,000 following a costly divorce settlement and coinciding with his appointment as national security adviser in the Nixon White House. More than $300,000 went to Al Marshall; $100,000 to Henry Diamond; a similar amount to labor consultant (and Dartmouth classmate) Victor Borella; and $135,000 to Hugh Morrow. Ed Logue was down for $176,389; Emmet Hughes, $155,000.

By far the greatest recipient of Rockefeller money was Bill Ronan, whose $625,000 in loans and gifts were forgiven when he left the Metropolitan Transportation Authority for the chairmanship of the Port Authority. In all, Rockefeller had bestowed almost $2 million on twenty individuals, augmented by $840,000 in gift taxes. A collective intake of breath was closely followed by a fresh round of stories questioning the nominee's record of tax compliance. Over the previous decade, Rockefeller had paid nearly half his total income, which averaged out to approximately $4.7 million annually, in federal, state, and local taxes. Another 30 percent went to philanthropic and charitable causes (admittedly, his repeated campaigns for office ranked high on his list of favored charities). In 1970, owing to stock transactions in one of the two trusts, totaling $116 million, that formed the bulk of his wealth, Rockefeller had paid no income taxes to Uncle Sam. He *did* return to the federal Treasury that year more than $6.2 million in capital gains taxes and an additional $814,701 in other levies.

Angered by the leaks, Rockefeller demanded an opportunity to refute the allegations before his senatorial inquisitors. Before he could do so, the focus of attention shifted abruptly from Nelson's taxes to his startling announcement on October 17 that Happy Rockefeller had undergone a radical mastectomy less than three weeks after Betty Ford had the same procedure. A self-professed "cocktail smoker" whose habit had intensified under the bright lights trained on New York's First Lady, Happy had voiced complaints during the family's August sojourn in Maine. "You know, my left side just doesn't seem to feel right," she remarked. A month later she lunched with Mrs. Ford, whose apparently robust health didn't prevent her from undergoing surgery for breast cancer at the end of September. Two weeks passed, during which Happy discovered a quarter-sized growth near her left armpit. Further tests led to her admission to New York's Memorial Sloan-Kettering Cancer Center and to the operating room for a procedure she hoped even then to avoid. Waking to find Nelson leaning over her, she was unprepared for the stiff, vestlike bandage that confirmed her worst fears. A second biopsy had confirmed traces of the disease in her right breast, requiring another operation as soon as she regained her strength. Nelson kept the news from her for a "blissfully ignorant" month of recuperation.

She had been home only a few days when a new wave of unflattering stories put Nelson on the defensive over his gift giving and the 1970 campaign biography, intended to hurt Arthur Goldberg, that now ironically threatened to derail Rockefeller's confirmation. Recalled by the Senate Rules Committee on November 13, he spent two days in damage control. Pausing to sip from a thermos full of Gatorade, Nelson supplied a moment of unintentional levity by justifying his high opinion of Bill Ronan as someone with "the balls" to fight for mass transit. As laughter swept the hearing room, an embarrassed-looking Rockefeller apologized for his language. As for the Goldberg book, he confessed, "Let's face it, I made a mistake. I made a hasty, ill-considered decision in the middle of a hectic campaign." The senators seemed satisfied. The House Judiciary Committee was less inclined to let him off the hook. In the vanguard of the movement to impeach Richard Nixon, the committee numbered in its ranks such liberal firebrands as Bella Abzug and Elizabeth Holtzman, both New Yorkers; Father Robert Drinan of Massachusetts; Jerome Waldie of California; and Michigan's John Conyers. But it was an Iowan, Edward Mezvinsky, who came closest to killing the Rockefeller nomination. On the eve of his November 21 appearance before the committee, Rockefeller learned that Mezvinsky had sent chairman Peter Rodino a letter demanding complete disclosure of all financial and property holdings by every member of the Rockefeller family, approximately seventy in all.

"I can't do that," Nelson told advisers assembled at Foxhall Road. The plain, if hidden, truth was that he had made differing financial provisions for each of his children. To reveal this tightly guarded secret now "will destroy the family."

"Governor," said Bobby Douglass, "this is your out, if you want to take it." Nelson rejected the idea of withdrawal—for now. He assigned Douglass the challenge of fashioning a workable compromise. This was far from a sure thing, as the hearings degenerated into what one Rockefeller supporter called "financial voyeurism. No one was interested in his qualifications for the job. They only wanted to know how much money the Rockefeller family had." Critics of the nomination found it easy to imagine a Vice President Rockefeller confronting conflicts of interest on a daily basis. They were further emboldened by the recent electoral landslide in which voters had punished the GOP for Watergate, the Nixon pardon, and a softening economy. Republican strength in the House fell to 1965 levels, insufficient to sustain a presidential veto. In New York's gubernatorial race, Hugh Carey crushed Malcolm Wilson by more than eight hundred thousand votes, restoring the Executive Mansion to Democratic hands for the first time in sixteen years.

Happy Rockefeller, only four days away from her second bout with the surgeon's knife, insisted on attending the opening round of Judiciary Committee questioning. Before he was sworn in, Nelson confided news of the still secret surgery to chairman Rodino, whose scheduling of evening sessions enabled the nominee to complete his testimony and be at his wife's side the following Monday morning. Otherwise the atmosphere in Room 2141 of the Rayburn House Office Building was notably more confrontational than in its Senate counterpart. Rockefeller defused some of the hostility by voicing regret over several actions taken during his governorship—Attica, the Goldberg book, the 1963 State Liquor Authority scandal and Jud Morhouse's subsequent disgrace, and his own unkept pledge not to raise taxes.* But he also clashed with Elizabeth Holtzman over CIA involvement in the 1973 military coup that toppled Chile's Marxist president Salvador Allende. And he sparred repeatedly with Father Drinan, who used the proceedings to denounce Rockefeller for inequities in the tax code and for remaining silent on Watergate and Vietnam.

The emotional flash point of the hearings came on the second day of testimony, when Drinan returned to the threat allegedly posed by Rockefeller family wealth and power. "Well, Father," Nelson interjected, "you belong to a very powerful organization which has much better discipline than the one I belong to." His riposte caught Drinan off guard, even as it brought smiles to the faces of Southern Democrats and other, more conservative members of the committee. The man of the cloth had no wish to see publicized his recent request for a $15,000 campaign contribution from a left-leaning Rockefeller niece in his district. Ultimately, Drinan had to settle for a promise from Rockefeller to abstain from personally supplementing any federal employee's salary. He had already offered to put his personal assets in a blind trust. As for the rest of the

---

* In retrospect, Rockefeller benefited from having his Senate hearings first. Although it didn't lessen the embarrassment caused by revelations about his gift giving and the Goldberg book, it meant that by the time members of the House Judicary Committee got to confront the nominee, these issues felt like old news. The failure of his adversaries to make more of Rockefeller's relationship with the disgraced Jud Morhouse seems surprising, especially given Nelson's 1970 pardon of his onetime political mentor on medical grounds (Morhouse was battling colon cancer and Parkinson's disease). For the same reason, Rockefeller forgave $86,000 still outstanding on his original loan to Morhouse. Cary Reich, no apologist for either man, concluded—as had New York State Supreme Court justice Samuel Gold and three of the seven judges on the New York State Court of Appeals—that Morhouse was wrongly convicted on the tainted testimony of two men, one a convicted felon seeking a reduced sentence in return for his cooperation, and the other contradicting what he had said under oath at an earlier trial arising out of the Playboy bribe of State Liquor Authority chairman Martin Epstein.

family, a majority of the committee accepted Bob Douglass's compromise formula, under which Room 5600 would supply their aggregate holdings to the last dollar, while restricting any individual breakdown of assets to Nelson's personal fortune.

Ford did not leave his nominee twisting in the wind. In addition to unwavering public support, he quietly leaned on Democratic Speaker Carl Albert and House majority leader Tip O'Neill to expedite the confirmation process. In return, O'Neill advised White House strategists to cultivate members of the Congressional Black Caucus and New York's heavily Democratic delegation. Spearheading the effort was Brooklyn's Shirley Chisholm, "Chizzy" to Rockefeller's handlers. Drawing on the talents of preacher-cum-speechwriter Thad Garrett, a member of her staff, Chisholm turned the tables on Nelson's accusers, demanding of her liberal brethren, "Where were you when Nelson Rockefeller was standing up for women's rights?" She didn't stop with women whose lives had been transformed by New York's pioneering abortion law. Chisholm singled out for mention environmentalists aided by Rockefeller's Pure Waters program; and organized labor, its position bolstered by the first state minimum wage law and the extension of collective bargaining to public employees. She wrote to each member of the House Rules Committee arguing against delay, as well as to the fifteen members of the Black Caucus. Chisholm's intervention stanched the bleeding over the Rockefeller nomination and may have helped swing the votes of Barbara Jordan, Andrew Young, and other prominent black lawmakers.*

On December 11, one day after the Senate voted to confirm Rockefeller 90 to 7, the House Judiciary Committee gave its somewhat grudging assent. The full House followed suit eight days later. During the interim, Rockefeller, mindful of his promise, once installed as vice president, to forgo substantial gifts to associates, handed Ken Riland a check for $153,000. For Rockefeller's swearing-in the evening of December 19, the Senate allowed live television cameras into its chamber for the first time. Sitting in the balcony beside Happy and the two boys was Averell Harriman, an ancient adversary invited as a guest of the new vice president. Harriman's presence was meant to send a signal, and it did, though not necessarily the right one. Henceforth Rockefeller's success would depend less on his ability to reconcile old enemies than on his deftness in avoiding new ones.

---

* Within days of Rockefeller's confirmation, Jim Cannon received a call from Representative Chisholm inquiring, "When are you going to hire Thad Garrett?" Though no one else could recall such a deal, neither were they willing to risk offending the lawmaker who had done so much to get Rockefeller confirmed. Garrett was duly employed as an urban affairs specialist reporting to Hugh Morrow. Jim Cannon, AI.

4

L ATER, WHEN IT became hard to imagine Nelson Rockefeller and Donald Rumsfeld as anything but antagonists, there was something almost cruelly ironic in Gerald Ford's proposed solution to the Washington housing needs of his chief of staff in all but name. "He said why don't I go and stay out at Rockefeller's," Rumsfeld noted in a memo to his youthful deputy Dick Cheney. "And I told him I just didn't think I should." Eager to differentiate himself from the Haldeman horrors, Rumsfeld was given the title of "Coordinator." In truth it mattered little what he was called, for his place in the Ford White House was scarcely less important than Al Haig's had been in ushering Richard Nixon offstage. The trajectory of Ford's presidency traced a learning curve in the differences between legislative and executive leadership, with Don Rumsfeld as chief instructor. The two men had a long-standing bond of trust, cemented in the 1965 contest among House Republicans that replaced aging, ineffectual minority leader Charlie Halleck with the vigorous, universally liked Jerry Ford. Perhaps because of that early mutiny in the ranks, compounded by his transparent eagerness to climb the greasy pole, Rumsfeld had been tagged ever since as a backroom intriguer. Attracting conspiracy theories like lint, his meritocratic demands offended some Ford loyalists—dubbed "the Michigan Mafia" by speechwriter Bob Hartman—accustomed to the more relaxed atmosphere of Capitol Hill or Grand Rapids.

More than simple rivals for place, Rocky and Rummy held diverging ideas of governance reflecting generational as much as philosophical differences. Hearkening back to his salad days in FDR's Washington, Rockefeller once confirmed was quick to invite Roosevelt accolytes Ben Cohen and Tommy Corcoran to Foxhall Road for dinner and some economic brainstorming. It was no accident that he used the Depression-era Reconstruction Finance Corporation as a model for government efforts to address the country's energy needs. Rumsfeld, at forty-two a full generation younger than his rival, held no brief for the New Deal. Having cut his teeth downsizing LBJ's Office of Economic Opportunity for Richard Nixon, Rumsfeld was firmly committed to reversing the flow of power to Washington on which Cohen and Corcoran had built their careers.

Yet Rockefeller and Rumsfeld also had more in common than either suspected. "You need Blacks in your Administration, including minorities in your personal office," Rumsfeld advised Ford in an early memo. Rockefeller could only nod in agreement. Sharing a powerful desire for change over continuity, each wanted Ford to put his personal stamp on the presidency by moving quickly to appoint a cabinet and White House staff loyal to him. Each felt a sense of urgency about ridding the administration of the former ad- and advancemen who had thrived under the Haldeman regime. Declining the role of doorkeeper between president and vice president, Rumsfeld said Rockefeller should have walk-in privileges to the Oval Office. Nelson needn't worry about including the chief of staff in his meetings with Ford. Ironically in light of subsequent developments, Rumsfeld himself had raised the prospect of designating the new vice president (then unchosen) "top man" for domestic, economic, or national security policy. He didn't rule out making him the head of a cabinet department as well, just as long as "he has something substantive to do."

Others wrestling with the same conundrum reached a different conclusion. "Everything depends on your ability to stay close to him [Ford] personally," George Hinman advised Rockefeller. Accordingly, Nelson should *not* take on an allegedly "significant" assignment in foreign affairs, economic policy, or the Domestic Council, the latter a Nixonian innovation designed to impose on domestic policy making the same order that the National Security Council under Henry Kissinger brought to foreign affairs. Rejecting such tasks as "sterile, divisive and destructive," Hinman urged Rockefeller instead to attach himself to Ford as trusted confidant and troubleshooter. "All you want is to sit in and help in his councils to the extent he thinks you can be helpful, keep yourself abreast of the issues so you can be prepared, and promote him and his policies with the party and the country to the extent he thinks you can be helpful. Nothing more."*

Hinman wasn't telling Rockefeller anything he hadn't learned clinging to FDR during his wartime apprenticeship. So why didn't he follow his old friend's counsel? Not for the first time, Rockefeller misjudged the strength of his position. Politically, he emerged from his protracted confirmation hearings a diminished figure. Worse, from an operational perspective, he had been effectively shut out of the administration's critical first four months. Like a transfer student enrolling at the beginning of sophomore year, he struggled to catch up with those who had bonded as freshmen. As for Rumsfeld, Rockefeller judged him "a very bright, able manipulator and maneuverer, but not an administrator. . . . I tried to negotiate with Mr. Rumsfeld as to how the Vice President could carry out the functions which the President wanted me to carry out." This was complicated, as Rockefeller saw it, by Rumsfeld's view of everyone else in the White House as "staff people at the beck and call of the President through him."

A notable exception to this rule was Henry Kissinger. Wearing two hats as

---

* Perhaps the best guidance Hinman ever gave Rockefeller, it was to prove just slightly ahead of its time. Prompted by the humiliation inflicted on his friend and mentor, Hubert Humphrey, Walter Mondale embraced the Hinman approach in the Carter White House. In doing so, Mondale became the first truly modern vice president, paving the way for assistant presidents such as Al Gore and Dick Cheney.

secretary of state and national security adviser, Kissinger operated outside the Rumsfeld orbit. He saw the president, alone, every morning. And he wasn't shy about urging Rockefeller to develop a similarly independent relationship with Ford. Rockefeller welcomed the opportunity once a week, if not more often, to give the president his frank assessment of events, personalities, and motives. "I have been a survivor as a minority party leader for four terms in New York and it wasn't because I was naive." Acknowledging his suspicious nature—"I am always sort of looking under stones and behind my back to see what is going on"—the vice president was hardly installed in his third-floor suite of the old Executive Office Building than he began to issue warnings: at least some of those Ford counted as friends, claimed Rockefeller, actually wished to see him fail.

Heading his list: Don Rumsfeld. By the end of 1974, Rumsfeld had put the finishing touches on a revised White House organization chart ("pure Jerry Ford," he called it) to replace the so-called spokes of the wheel model originally imported from Capitol Hill. Ford's August 17 promise to his putative vice president had likewise been superseded by events, though no one wanted to say as much out loud. "It was a mistake for Gerald Ford to think that he could give Rockefeller the power," concluded Jim Cannon, who admired both men. "When he said it, he didn't know what he was committing to. . . . Rumsfeld, whatever you may think of him, saw it better than Ford did, and said, 'It ain't going to work.'" As for the president, while he could not in good faith rescind his offer to Rockefeller, neither could he fully honor it. A compromise of sorts was arranged. On December 21, Ford assigned his newly confirmed vice president half a dozen tasks to complement his work with the Domestic Council. Besides a seat at the table in all national security discussions and an active role in personnel recruitment, Rockefeller was entrusted with the search for a White House science adviser, a review of federal pay scales, another dealing with issues of privacy, and a vague mandate to inject some fresh thinking into the nation's upcoming bicentennial.

"I wonder how he can fill all the shoes that Ford's handed him," speculated Ken Riland. This misread activity for purpose. In fact, Ford's to-do list offered up the antithesis of George Hinman's deputy president or Rockefeller's vicar of domestic policy. The first weeks of 1975 witnessed a classic turf war over the Domestic Council envisioned by Nelson as a White House think tank, an institutionalized, federally funded version of his National Commission on Critical Choices. To supplement a full-time staff of forty-five, he would draw on the best and brightest from outside government—employing nuclear experts Edward Teller and Dixy Lee Ray, for example, to help develop national energy policy. Let others put out fires (a potential swine flu epidemic, Boston's busing crisis); his interest was in averting future crises.

To Rumsfeld, already concerned that Rockefeller might overshadow his nominal superior, this was a profound misreading of how the White House functioned. Presidents require protection, sometimes from themselves, more often from the brainstorms of their subordinates. Consequently, any significant policy initiative must be staffed out for review by the White House counsel, press office, and those entrusted with congressional relations, not to mention political advisers, budget officials, cabinet departments, and agencies with relevant jurisdiction. So while Rockefeller stressed what President George H. W. Bush would call "the vision thing," Rumsfeld looked to the Domestic Council for more prosaic functions, the preparation of briefing papers and decision memos for the president, replies to inquiries from Congress, and liaison to governors and mayors. In Harvard Law School professor Phillip Areeda, already employed in the White House Counsel's Office, Rumsfeld had a ready-made candidate for executive director.*

Ford signed off on Areeda's promotion two weeks before Rockefeller was sworn into office, apparently without consulting his vice president in limbo. Rockefeller had nothing against Professor Areeda, except that he stood in the way of Nelson's plan to make himself executive director as well as council vice chairman. When legal objections were raised to a dual appointment, Rockefeller lobbied the president to install his trusted deputies Jim Cannon as executive director and Dick Dunham as deputy director in charge of long-range planning. Functioning as his agents, they would transform the council from a reactive body defined by the flow of paper into a permanent secretariat of original thinkers—not unlike the young program associates who had aided a rookie Governor Rockefeller in overcoming Albany's bureaucratic deadwood. Rockefeller's proposed executive order to implement these arrangements ran into fierce opposition, prompting him to send a sharply worded memo of complaint to Ford.

"The President didn't ask me to come down here to do paperwork," Nelson told Rumsfeld. "He wants advice and help on the major issues that face this country." It wasn't long before he was voicing second thoughts about his new position. "You know, Ken," Rockefeller told Riland at the end of January 1975, "we just play this one out for two years and then the hell with it." The defeatist mood didn't last; he had too much invested in the job, however imperfect, to walk away from it without a fight. By the first week of February, the president had reversed himself on the hiring of Areeda, who wasted no time in returning to Harvard. Rumsfeld was "sore as hell," Nelson reported, and taking out his resentment by leaking negative stories to *The New York Times*. On February 12,

---

* Though he was careful to attribute Areeda's candidacy to George Shultz, telling the president that Shultz had described the academic "in a way that leads me to believe he might not be a bad appointment."

the paper ran a piece minimizing Rockefeller's contributions to the administration to date. The next day, Ford used the occasion of a New York City dinner honoring the vice president to refute such claims. He announced the employment of Jim Cannon and Dick Dunham as part of a Domestic Council enlarged to include key advisers on economic and energy policy. Under Rockefeller's aegis, the revamped council would address both short- *and* long-term needs, establish national priorities, and craft options for meeting them.

Rockefeller, it appeared, had won a clean victory. This underestimated Rumsfeld's continuing closeness to Ford and the skillful play of his remaining cards, including a presidential mandate to reduce the White House payroll. As for Rockefeller, said one associate, "He would go over to the President, the President would promise him something, and he meant it. Just like the Domestic Council. We won the battle and lost the war. Rummy knocked us out of the budget on that thing." Thinking like a governor, Rockefeller assumed that by putting his people in critical positions, he could assure his control of the Domestic Council. Only they weren't "his" people anymore. While Jim Cannon might have the title of executive director, his promotion made him part of the chain of White House command reporting to Rumsfeld. Ultimately, of course, Cannon *worked* for the president, a situation lending itself to divided loyalties and wounded feelings, never more so than when Rumsfeld directed Cannon to staff out recommendations made by his former employer concerning a full-time science adviser in the White House.

"If the President didn't want to follow my recommendation," Nelson inquired, "why did he ask me to do it?" Cannon tried, as gently as possible, to convey the changes that went with his new role. "You forget what court politics is like when you're the emperor," muses Peter Wallison, the young lawyer originally hired to work on the Critical Choices Commission, "because everything revolves around you." After fifteen years in Albany, Rockefeller "never really got used to the idea that everything revolved around someone else in the Ford White House, and that was Ford." Nelson took another hit when Dick Dunham, unhappy with the Domestic Council's organizational setup, resigned to become chairman of the Federal Power Commission. His replacement was James Cavanaugh, a Nixon holdover whose current loyalty was to Rumsfeld. Thereafter, claimed Rockefeller, the Domestic Council ended up "just where Rumsfeld wanted it, namely handling the routine business coming from the departments, preparing memorandums on their positions, etc., on a most superficial, low level . . . but it was not the organization in any shape or form that the President had in mind."*

---

* This minimized the council's contributions to airline and trucking deregulation (Ford preferred the term *regulatory reform*); urban mass transit; the renewal of federal revenue sharing;

Rockefeller's critique wasn't all sour grapes, as evidenced by a decision, taken early in the administration, without input from either the vice president or the Domestic Council, decreeing a moratorium on new federal programs until Washington got a handle on spending and government did a better job of managing its existing docket. This policy of retrenchment, strongly endorsed by Rumsfeld, Budget Director Jim Lynn, and Council of Economic Advisers chairman Alan Greenspan, was communicated to Rockefeller by Jim Cannon. Nelson shook his head in something close to bewilderment.

"How does he expect to get elected if he offers nothing new?"

A flurry of less rhetorical questions followed, eliciting details of Cannon's exclusion from the process of advocacy and argument before the president.

"This is Rumsfeld again."

Rockefeller pressed Ford from the opposite direction to begin developing campaign themes for the 1976 election. Any hope for a government of national unity had died with the Nixon pardon, he contended. Besides, said Rockefeller, "umpires are not leaders." In New York, new programs targeted at specific constituencies were the mother's milk of successful electioneering. To rule out such initiatives at the federal level amounted to unilateral disarmament, ceding the policy argument to the Democrats while retreating to a veto-driven strategy that blamed unchecked government for 9 percent unemployment and accelerating inflation. In addition to budgetary concerns—Ford was determined to hold 1976 spending to $395 billion—the president was unprepared for the sheer volume of freshly hatched ideas Rockefeller brought to their weekly luncheon meetings. In the spring of 1975, these included a jobs program for inner-city youth affected by the current recession; another to spur housing construction; plus federal initiatives to restrain the cost of health care and to make the United States energy independent within ten years.

"He came to me once with a scheme that Edward Teller planted in his mind," recalls Kissinger deputy (and later national security adviser) Brent Scowcroft. "We were building the subway in Washington, and his scheme was to take a spur off the subway and build a deep underground shelter under the White House for the president. I said, 'We can't get there from here.' He wouldn't let go . . . when he had ideas he just kept pushing. But in a wonderful way." Rockefeller had no greater luck promoting a plan to buy Greenland from

and such financial innovations as electronic bank transfers, prerequisite to the nation's first ATM machines. Former Pennsylvania governor Raymond Shafer undertook a useful study of federal–state relations in tandem with a sweeping review of social welfare programs and the successful introduction of community development block grants. A task force on drug abuse led Ford to propose mandatory minimum sentences less stringent than in Rockefeller's New York. The same initiative promoted education and treatment as well as enhanced cooperation among the numerous agencies entrusted with drug policy.

Denmark for its supposed mineral riches. As his interest in running the Domestic Council flickered, Rockefeller looked for alternative means to influence
policy. He hired John Veneman, a former California legislator and HEW undersecretary, to conduct a systematic review of existing social programs, formu-
late innovative alternatives, and help craft a national energy strategy. In
addition, Veneman was entrusted with organizing half a dozen regional forums
around the country. Each of these gatherings was chaired by the vice president,
who brought with him several cabinet secretaries, plus the directors of the Office of Management and Budget and the Environmental Protection Agency.
The results were distilled in a presidential report of some eight hundred pages,
a sufficient length to practically ensure against its being read by anyone, most
of all those at which it was targeted—Gerald Ford, his speechwriters, and members of his staff responsible for the programmatic content of the president's 1976
State of the Union address. After a cursory review of the massive volume, Ford
handed it off to Jim Cannon, saying, "You keep it for me."

5

A S WARREN HARDING'S vice president and the Senate's presiding officer,
Calvin Coolidge had fully intended to study carefully the rules governing
the world's greatest deliberative body. He soon abandoned the effort, however,
on discovering that the Senate had but a single rule that mattered—namely,
that its members would do whatever they wanted whenever they wanted to.
Rockefeller approached Capitol Hill with a similarly open mind. On February 19, 1975, Ken Riland found Nelson in the library at Foxhall Road, boning
up on legislative precedents in advance of the next day's debate over Senate
Rule 22, a World War I–era provision requiring the votes of two-thirds of senators present to invoke cloture and thereby shut off a filibuster. Only twenty-one
times in Senate history had this daunting threshold been crossed. Now liberals
led by Democrat Walter Mondale of Minnesota and Kansas Republican James
Pearson undertook to reduce the two-thirds figure to three-fifths.

Any attempt to change the rules was sure to engender strong opposition
from conservatives of both parties, many of them southerners for whom the
filibuster had traditionally been their weapon of last resort to block the expansion of federal authority, especially in the field of civil rights. The Constitution
empowers Congress to make its own rules. This is simple for the House, which
is entirely reconstituted every two years, unlike the Senate, where only a third
of the membership faces the voters at any given time. Thus the determinative
question confronting Rockefeller as presiding officer: Could senators take ad-

vantage of a new Congress to change their rules by simple majority—or were they bound as a continuing body to observe the very Rule 22 they hoped to modify? For assistance in threading the labyrinth of parliamentary procedure, Rockefeller relied on Richard Parsons, his twenty-six-year-old assistant counsel.

Hardly your typical vice presidential adviser, Parsons had an unlikely Rockefeller connection—his maternal grandfather had once been employed as head grounds keeper at Kykuit. Born in Brooklyn to African American parents living a few blocks from Ebbets Field, Parsons left at age five for a black middle-class neighborhood in Queens. After skipping grades in both elementary and high school, he enrolled in the University of Hawaii at sixteen—inspired, he said, by a pretty girl of Hawaiian descent who was his bench partner in a physics lab. It was in Hawaii that Parsons met his future wife, Laura, who kept him from sleeping through his law school admission test, the first step toward finishing atop his class at Albany Law School. An internship with the New York State Legislature brought Parsons to the notice of Nelson Rockefeller's legal staff, and of the governor himself.

He would have been difficult to overlook in any case. Six feet four inches tall, Parsons cut a commanding figure, with a self-possession rare for his age. Rockefeller imagined the charismatic youth from Ozone Park a future Supreme Court justice. Others could already detect in Parsons hints of the formidable mix of political instinct, managerial talent, and personal salesmanship that would eventually rescue three floundering businesses—the Dime Savings Bank, AOL Time Warner, and Citigroup—in times of economic crisis. One of a handful of Albany alumni Rockefeller brought with him to Washington, Parsons quickly established himself as the vice president's guide through the dense thicket of senatorial precedent, a task complicated by Rockefeller's dyslexia. Exploiting his boss's preference for visual learning, Parsons devised an elaborate flow chart to assist Nelson in his rulings from the chair, while Parsons himself sat in the Senate gallery, nodding encouragement. The debate over Rule 22 tested these arrangements to the limit. The battle was joined on February 20, when Jim Pearson moved to cut off debate by simple majority vote and Majority Leader Mike Mansfield on his own point of order said this was a violation of Rule 22. Rockefeller told senators that if they rejected Mansfield's intervention, he would interpret that as an endorsement of Pearson's position.

By a margin of 51 to 42, the liberal position prevailed, or so its adherents thought. They underestimated the resourcefulness of Alabama's James Allen in gridlocking the Senate through a fresh barrage of parliamentary grapeshot. Strom Thurmond, the original Dixiecrat turned Republican, approached the vice president in his ceremonial office off the Senate floor to press the case for the status quo. "Apparently Rockefeller kept fobbing Thurmond off," according to White House counsel Jack Marsh, himself a former Democratic congressman from Virginia, "saying he was voting this way because his legal counsel told him that this was the way he had to vote." Another Rockefeller staffer picks up the story: "And so finally Strom says, 'Well, Mr. Vice President, I believe I better talk to your counsel.' So Rockefeller says, 'Fine—he's right over there.' And he points to Dick, this guy, six feet three or four, big, black as you can be, with a rather significant Afro haircut. It was a halo, really." Thurmond's face registered disbelief. His expression did not change noticeably after he engaged Parsons in a lively discussion of Senate rules, cut short when the young man exhibited a command of legislative minutiae comparable to Thurmond's own.

Frustrated conservatives led by John Tower then paid a visit to the White House, in which they suggested that his vice president should get with the program if Ford wished to see any of his legislative program become law. Declaring, "No one threatens Nelson Rockefeller," the vice president turned to Parsons for strategic advice on how to shut down the latest talkathon. Parsons outlined a scenario culminating in Jim Allen shouting for recognition on a point of order—and Rockefeller deliberately ignoring him. On February 26, with Allen and Tennessee's William Brock both clamoring for the chair's attention, and a red-faced Barry Goldwater shaking his head while charging the aisle in the direction of the rostrum, Rockefeller announced, "The clerk will call the roll." Those six seemingly innocuous words may well have sealed his fate as Ford's vice president. Although Rockefeller afterward said that he was just "trying to speed up action," conservatives interpreted his ruling as a grave breach of senatorial courtesy. Abuse rained down on the presiding officer. "It says right here in the precedents of the Senate," Rockefeller protested, "the Chair may decline to answer a parliamentary inquiry."

"That is correct," replied Goldwater. "That is what it says, but I never thought I would see the day when the Chair would take advantage of it."*

All this was but prologue to the main civil rights battle that year, involving renewal of the 1965 Voting Rights Act originally targeted at seven southern states. The 1975 debate revolved around efforts, incubated in the Nixon White House, to dilute the legislation by expanding it to include all fifty states. Both Rumsfeld and the ordinarily sympathetic attorney general Edward Levi encouraged Ford to support the revised formula. By this time, Parsons had moved over to the White House as counsel to the Domestic Council. In this capacity, he had drawn the assignment, highly offensive to him, of writing a brief justifying revision of the landmark legislation that had transformed southern politics. He was in his office when Rockefeller called from the Capitol.

"What do you think I should do?" asked the vice president.

"Well, it depends on what you want to do," Parsons replied.

---

* Rockefeller subsequently made a public apology to the senators, a touchy lot.

"I want to do the right thing. We haven't been engaged in this struggle for twenty years to blink now."

In that case, said Parsons, "you got to go against the southern strategy."

Should it come down to him, Rockefeller let it be known, he would cast a deciding vote to extend the Voting Rights Act in its current form. In the meantime, he could be counted on for sympathetic rulings from the chair. "It was those two things," maintains Parsons—Rockefeller's support for filibuster reform and a tough Voting Rights Act—"that cost him his place on the ticket in 1976."

6

DURING HIS GOVERNORSHIP, Rockefeller was once handed a text promoting his Pure Waters program as "a $1 billion" initiative. "That looks like one dollar," Nelson protested. "I want all the zeros!" This would come as no surprise to Frank Zarb, the onetime Wall Street prodigy who at thirty-seven had become Gerald Ford's federal energy administrator. "I used to tell people," reflects Zarb, "as much as I loved Nelson, his meter didn't start until you got to a billion dollars."* Keenly aware of the dangers posed by U.S. dependence on imported oil, much of it extracted from the volatile Middle East, Ford early in his presidency had asked Zarb and his team for a comprehensive energy strategy. On December 19, 1974, the same day Rockefeller was confirmed as vice president by the House, Zarb delivered to the president a 135-page game plan to increase and diversify energy supplies, while reducing their consumption. Heavily reliant on market forces, the package contained something to offend virtually every consumer and corporate interest group, not to mention a Congress that was allergic to sacrifice of any kind. In post-Watergate Washington, regional loyalties took precedence over institutional ones; individual self-promotion trumped both. No issue better illustrated these harsh new realities than energy. Reflecting popular skepticism, lawmakers in both parties dismissed the energy crisis as an artificial muddle crafted by Big Oil, the OPEC cartel, or both in a cynical attempt to pad their profits.

Rockefeller had a long-standing interest in the subject, as befitting a grandson of Standard Oil's founder. The topic of energy independence had preoccu-

---

* Rockefeller perfected his own verbal shorthand to illustrate the difference between a million and a billion dollars. The former, he explained, was a pile of thousand-dollar bills reaching to the top of his desk. The latter was a stack of the same currency as tall as the Empire State Building. Jerry Finkelstein, HMI, 63.

pied the Critical Choices Commission, with Edward Teller providing instruction in the vast, untapped potential of shale oil and gas, as well as wind power and coal deposits ripe for the taking. The amount of venture capital required to achieve energy independence dwarfed private resources. Thus Rockefeller's concept of a government corporation with sufficient backing to finance the massive undertaking. What became known as the Energy Independence Authority closely resembled Rockefeller's New York public authorities. Like them, it would exist off budget and be largely immune to legislative oversight. Endowed with up to $200 billion in borrowing authority, EIA was to make loans and loan guarantees, simplify the current tangle of bureaus and offices that delayed design and construction, and otherwise encourage the risky pursuit of new technologies. In some instances, the same agency would itself build nuclear generating plants and other energy-related facilities that could then be sold or leased back to private industry.

EIA was conceived as an emergency response with a lifetime to match. Having fulfilled its mission, it was supposed to go out of business after ten years, with the Treasury taking another decade or so to recover outstanding taxpayer investments. In a March 6, 1975, Oval Office meeting, Ford encouraged his vice president to further develop the concept. To supporters, EIA embodied the Hamiltonian tradition of an assertive federal government underwriting ventures as crucial to national development as the transcontinental railroad or interstate highway system. Free marketeers like Treasury Secretary Bill Simon, on the other hand, considered it economic and political heresy. To conservatives generally, his support for the EIA disproved any claim that Rockefeller had abandoned his liberal faith in government solutions. Frank Zarb, though no fan of Nelson's latest innovation, held a more nuanced view. "It was pure pragmatism," insists Zarb. "He just wanted to get the job done. And if we weren't going to get the government, the Congress to release [decontrol] prices . . . one way to get it done was what he was used to. Put up a pile of money and buy your way into it. You had to respect him for the initiative."

Respect, it hardly goes without saying, offered no guarantee of agreement. By the start of September 1975, Rockefeller and Zarb had reached an impasse over financing, autonomy, and efforts to restrict the corporation to experimental and demonstration projects (Rockefeller himself tried unsuccessfully to eliminate synthetic fuels as a drain on the EIA budget). Unable to resolve the stalemate, Nelson insisted on taking it to the president for his immediate decision. It did not matter that Ford was then bedridden with a high fever, the only day of his presidency he missed owing to illness. A no doubt groggy chief executive listened as his vice president and energy czar argued their conflicting views. Then he split the difference, letting the EIA go forward with $25 billion in equity and borrowing authority of $75 billion.

Rockefeller fought doggedly for his program, personally lobbying cabinet officers, economic advisers, members of Congress, and the Federal Reserve Board. At length he notified Ford that he had secured endorsements from all the major players. A wary president, by now well acquainted with Nelson's selective hearing, asked Don Rumsfeld to conduct his own survey of opinion regarding EIA. The responses he got varied sufficiently from Rockefeller's cheery consensus to warrant a more thorough discussion in the Cabinet Room. There emotions ran high, an agitated Bill Simon at one point turning to the president and warning him against letting Rockefeller "do to the United States of America what he did to the state of New York!" For a moment, Simon thought the vice president might physically strike him. After the meeting, he received a call from Ford.

"Bill, do me a favor. Lay off Nelson. I've got to throw him a bone. I am going to support it."

"Mr. President, you're not!"

"I don't want to get into screaming and yelling over this. We don't have to fight about things that have no prayer, and Nelson Rockefeller's idea about utilities has no prayer."

Ford may have harbored feelings of guilt over the unkept promise of a shared presidency. He may have wished to avoid alienating someone for whom he had a genuine fondness and whose sacrifice of family privacy to take on a mostly thankless job he hadn't forgotten. Or he may simply have empathized with Rockefeller, defying the odds in his attempt to make something constructive of a job that Ford himself described as the worst he ever held. Whatever the cause, Ford knew his former colleagues on Capitol Hill well enough to intuit that EIA would never see the light of day. Thus convinced, he prepared a bill for submission to Congress at the end of September. If nothing else, Ford rationalized, it would keep the spotlight on the energy issue and the heat on lawmakers taking advantage of a temporary oil glut to evade their responsibility to the future.

The AFL-CIO building trades convention, meeting in San Francisco on September 22, was chosen as the formal launching pad for the Energy Independence Authority. Yet that evening's network newscasts did not lead with the biggest, most daring government initiative since Project Apollo. That distinction was reserved for Sarah Jane Moore, a middle-aged housewife steeped in Bay Area fringe politics, who took it upon herself to assassinate the president as he left the St. Francis Hotel. At the last moment, Ms. Moore's bullet was deflected away from its intended target. Missing Gerald Ford, it brought the EIA trial balloon to earth with a thud.

7

ROCKEFELLER TOOK SOLACE in small victories. Warned by scientists that California could be devastated by a major earthquake, he convinced the president to restore funds for earthquake prediction efforts at the U.S. Geological Survey. His ideas on food stamp reform and consumer protection were taken up by Ford, though they failed to pass muster with an election year Congress. Submitting with relative grace to the funeral-going demands of the vice presidency, in April 1975 Rockefeller did make an unsuccessful attempt to substitute FDR, Jr., as U.S. representative to the services for Chiang Kai-shek. Nelson then used the long flight to and from Taiwan to repair his relationship with Barry Goldwater. "You know," he commented after a midflight breakfast the two men shared, "that's not a bad guy at all." (Less happily, he also waded into the diplomatic standoff between Greece and Turkey, his anger over a congressional cutoff of Turkish military aid exacerbated by five glasses of Mateus rosé.)*

Michigan's Guy Vander Jagt, chairman of the Republican Congressional Campaign Committee, was startled to receive a phone call from the vice president, asking if he could rent out the top floor of the Capitol Hill Club, a GOP watering hole facing foreclosure after years of mismanagement. Coming in the midst of the most severe recession since World War II, the club's shuttering would embarrass the administration and dull the contrast between Republican prudence and Democratic profligacy.

"Mr. Vice President, you shouldn't bother yourself with that sort of thing," said Vander Jagt. "You've got more important things to do."

Nonsense, replied Rockefeller. He was there to help the president in any way he could. "My first job out of Dartmouth was renting space for my dad in Rockefeller Center," said Nelson. "If I could do it in the middle of the Depression, I can do it now." Though saving the Capitol Hill Club was unlikely to secure Nelson's historical reputation, it beat foreign funerals (Saudi Arabia's King Faisal, Spain's Francisco Franco), natural disasters (an Italian earthquake), and mediating among a fractious staff whose nominal chief, Ann Whitman, was shipped back to New York after one too many admonitions that the White House did not function as Rockefeller supposed.

Publicly, Rockefeller downplayed his role, insisting he was a mere "staff man," or presidential assistant. His travel schedule suggested otherwise. A visit to Milwaukee showed he hadn't lost the campaigner's touch. Confronted by a

---

* At the start of April, as South Vietnam entered its death throes as an independent nation, a debate erupted among Ford's advisers: Should the president cut short an ill-timed vacation in Southern California? Rockefeller seemed oddly detached. "That's Rumsfeld's job . . . Rumsfeld's decision," Ken Riland quotes his friend in his diary for April 2.

youthful admirer aged nine or ten, he put his arm around the boy, said he had a son "just like you" at home, and invited him along on a TV interview. When the youngster said his mother would never believe he had been with the vice president, Nelson handed him a floral centerpiece from the set to take home as a souvenir of their visit. He was no less ingratiating during a call on George Meany at AFL-CIO headquarters near the White House. "Hello, Mr. Vice President," said the elevator operator before pressing the eighth-floor button for Meany's office suite. "We get to the eighth floor," recalls Bob Armao, "the doors open, Rockefeller turns to this guy and tells him, 'Aren't you nice? What a smooth ride! I really enjoyed it. Thank you so much.' We must have been there three minutes."

As the two men walked away from the elevator, Armao remarked, "Governor, for God's sake, all he did was push a button."

Rockefeller stopped in his tracks. "It never hurts to be nice."

At Pocantico, Rockefeller won the gratitude of Secret Service agents by replacing his underground Picasso tapestries with a table for pool and another for Ping-Pong. The whole family impressed agent Joseph Petro as "unbelievably down-to-earth" and unspoiled by wealth, notwithstanding the vice president's action in dispatching a Gulfstream jet to retrieve his sons' bicycles inadvertently left in Maine. Those with more long-standing acquaintance detected chinks in Rockefeller's normally upbeat temperament. Oscillating between thinking his place on the ticket in 1976 assured and telling friends he was tired of the whole business, Nelson speculated about events that might take Ford out of the picture. Ann Whitman referred to the First Lady's health as a factor in the president's political plans, and Rockefeller said no, he meant something "traumatic." Yet when Squeaky Fromme of the Manson gang tried to shoot Ford in September 1975, Rockefeller asked but one question: "What is the Manson Gang?"

His ambivalence extended to his domestic arrangements. He built a new pool at Foxhall Road for Happy's use, while acknowledging that "it's probably foolish to spend all this for two years." He dredged a lake on the property and had it stocked with fish, thinking it might provide Happy and the boys with an incentive to spend the month of June in the capital. "Not on your life, Ken," she told Riland. Fearful of making a misstep, underestimating her own charm, Happy was rarely seen in Washington. At a White House entertainment, remembered Bob Hartman, "the president was going to dance with her, and she was very shy about it . . . you practically had to push her onto the dance floor." Happy did host a Kennedy Center luncheon for the wife of visiting British prime minister Harold Wilson. On another occasion she led reporters on a tour of the vice presidential residence during its renovation. Later she welcomed hundreds of guests to a series of housewarming parties. While the press seemed fixated on a $35,000 mink-covered bed created by artist Max Ernst, Nelson gave pride of place to a huge eagle sculpture, originally used at Dwight Eisenhower's 1953 inaugural, which he bought for placement at the entrance to the property.*

In her absence, Nelson phoned his wife almost every night, their conversations frequently lasting half an hour or more. Of a generation, disproportionately male, easily defeated by the complexities of programming a VCR machine, Rockefeller complained to his Secret Service agents that he was unable to get through to the White House on the telephone. Not wishing to bother anyone, he'd looked up the number of the main switchboard in the phone book himself. Unfortunately, he continued, "every time I tell the operator that I'm the vice president, she hangs up on me." The agents directed Nelson's attention to the secure signal phone, or "drop line," already installed in the house on Foxhall Road next to his more conventional landline. All he needed to do was pick it up, they assured him, and the White House operator would put Rockefeller directly through to the president.

8

AT THEIR FIRST meeting following Nelson's confirmation, Ford had made no mention of the CIA. All that changed abruptly after Washington woke up the next morning to a sensational exposé by *New York Times* journalist Seymour Hersh. Domestic spying—explicitly outlawed by the National Security Act of 1947, which established the Cold War intelligence service—was just one of the illegal practices documented in a seventy-page dossier inexplicably handed over to congressional overseers by CIA director William Colby. Colby, in effect, blew the whistle on his own agency, never bothering to inform his superiors in the National Security Council, let alone the president, to whom he was legally accountable. (Rockefeller went to his grave believing Colby a latter-day Alger Hiss.) Whatever his motive, Colby's action plunged the CIA into the greatest crisis of its history. Multiple American presidents had used the agency to infiltrate antiwar and black radical groups; conduct surveillance on, and tap the phones of, government critics; and accumulate files on more than seven thousand American citizens and organizations deemed suspicious by the White House.

The CIA meltdown was Ford's presidency in miniature. Blindsided by the

---

* "That was the list price," said Rockefeller of the controversial Ernst bed. In fact he paid $22,000 for the piece.

illegalities of his predecessors, he must simultaneously reform a hidebound agency while ministering to its battered morale and preserving its ability to function within the law. Unable to avert congressional hearings, Ford hoped to at least limit their impact by launching his own inquiry, an administrative back-fire entrusted to a panel sufficiently distinguished as to guard against charges of an official cover-up. Joining Rockefeller, who chaired the commission, were Douglas Dillon, JFK's secretary of the Treasury; former solicitor general Erwin Griswold and commerce secretary John T. Connor from the Johnson adminis-tration; AFL-CIO president Lane Kirkland; University of Virginia president Edgar Shannon; former NATO commander General Lyman Lemnitzer; and Ronald Reagan, just days out of office as governor of California. Reagan enter-tained Rockefeller and other commission members with a seemingly endless supply of stories, some of them culturally dubious even by the standards of the time, such as the homosexual dog who gave himself away ("Bowsy wowsey") through his less than robust bark. Reagan's knack for devising often pithy lan-guage with which to bridge internal differences impressed Rockefeller. At one point, Nelson asked Reagan where he had perfected his literary skills.

"Labor negotiations," replied the former head of the Screen Actors Guild.

For his executive director, Rockefeller heeded the president's recommenda-tion and hired David Belin, an investigator with whom Ford had worked closely on the Warren Commission a decade before. The two men had an immediate falling-out, the consequence of Belin's refusal to forgo writing a book about the CIA probe. One Friday afternoon, before leaving the capital for a Pocantico weekend, Rockefeller told Peter Wallison that he intended to fire Belin. Walli-son urged caution. Given post-Watergate sensitivities and vivid memories of Richard Nixon's attempt to rid himself of special prosecutor Archibald Cox, did Rockefeller really want to put at risk the credibility of an investigation already viewed in some quarters as a whitewash?

Rockefeller was unmoved. "I just can't take this kind of behavior," he told Wallison, who pleaded with him to at least do nothing before Monday. A week-end of feverish negotiation among Wallison, Belin, and White House counsel Phil Buchan produced agreement that Belin, in addition to serving as the com-mission's executive director, was its de facto counsel. In the latter role, at least, he was bound by attorney-client privilege. The Rockefeller Commission would spend five months investigating past and current CIA practices. It absolved the agency of any prior knowledge of the Watergate break-in or involvement in the subsequent cover-up. But it was what the commission *didn't* probe that under-cut its reputation, while confirming Rockefeller's distrust of his White House colleagues. Asked by the president to examine possible links between CIA plots targeting foreign leaders such as Cuba's Fidel Castro and the assassination of President John F. Kennedy, Rockefeller warned Ford that nothing would come of such an investigation but political embarrassment. Astonishingly, he refused to accept a presidential letter formalizing these instructions. If forced to do so, Rockefeller told Ford, he would resign.

When Rumsfeld joined the discussion, Nelson's suspicions multiplied. "Then it was very clear to me what they wanted to do," he confided to a scholarly student of his vice presidency a year out of office. "This was another way of chopping my head off and of getting me out there where I was the one who was putting the finger on the Kennedys." Reiterating to Ford the political risks to which he was exposing himself, Rockefeller convinced the president to set aside his letter. In return for this, said Rockefeller, "we got this information and we put it together. . . ." He personally alerted Senator Edward Kennedy to what he was doing, insisting he was not out to embarrass anybody. Kennedy in return said he had only vague recollections of the subject, which had been briefly discussed "maybe once or twice" at Hyannis Port. Dismissing as "far-fetched speculation" rumors linking the CIA to the assassination of President Kennedy, Rockefeller cited executive privilege to thwart a request from Senator Frank Church for documents concerning possible U.S. complicity in the deaths of Vietnamese president Ngo Dinh Diem and the Congo's Patrice Lumumba.

In its report, the Rockefeller Commission made thirty recommendations designed to clarify organizational structure, improve oversight, limit covert operations, prohibit assassinations abroad, and reinstate a ban on surveillance of Americans on their own soil. Rockefeller pressed for the appointment of a White House director of national intelligence, an idea that was to be dusted off in the wake of the 9/11 terrorist attacks. For his part, Ford adhered closely to the commission's findings, implementing most of its reforms through executive order. Yet even this demonstrable success was marred by the administration's bungled release of Rockefeller's findings, after White House lawyers voiced concerns about unproven allegations in the 299-page document. Rumsfeld then ordered publication delayed. Press secretary Ron Nessen went a step further, telling reporters the report might not be made public at all. Anonymous sources blamed Rockefeller for the mix-up, prompting an angry vice president to pay an unscheduled visit to Rumsfeld's office.

By the time Ford released the report, it was minus eighty-five pages relating to CIA involvement in foreign assassination plots. Eventually, these too found their way into the hands of congressional investigators, which may well have been Rockefeller's intention all along (such a strategy, he boasted, "got the President off the hook, got me off the hook [and] got it right back to where it belonged in the Congress"). On July 8, Nelson's sixty-seventh birthday, Ford invited reporters into the Oval Office for a characteristically low-key announcement of his 1976 candidacy. The next day, his campaign manager, former Georgia congressman and army secretary Bo Callaway, stressed in press interviews that Ford was running alone. The ultimate choice of a running mate would be up to convention delegates. As if the message, intended to placate restive conservatives, weren't sufficiently explicit, Callaway in a subsequent meeting with reporters singled out Rockefeller as the campaign's "number one problem."

Although he made mention of the vice president's age, it was geography—specifically, Nelson's continuing unpopularity among southerners predisposed to Ronald Reagan's brand of conservatism—that influenced Callaway's unsubtle signals to Republicans in Dixie. Believing Reagan and his supporters could be talked into waiting until 1980, Callaway was guilty of wishful thinking. Others on the right accused him of far worse. When Louisiana governor David Treen called him a political traitor, Callaway demanded evidence. "Well, how about Rockefeller?" replied Treen. Such antipathy wasn't altogether rational, Callaway decided. Still less was it based on anything specific Rockefeller had done as vice president. Its roots went far deeper in the Republican psyche. "This was a guy they had hated since 1964. This was the New York liberal establishment. This guy had no business being vice president."*

Callaway adamantly denies that Rumsfeld encouraged him or anyone else to dump Rockefeller from the ticket. "In fact, he was pretty upset with me when this big flap happened." Ford's displeasure led to the most public display yet of loyalty to his vice president. Breaking precedent, the two men shared a helicopter ride to Andrews Air Force Base, from which Rockefeller saw Ford off on a diplomatic mission to Europe. To mark the administration's first anniversary, on August 9 Nelson and Happy dined alone with the Fords at the White House. After a heated discussion involving cabinet offices and other administration heavyweights, Rockefeller asked Ford if he had said or done anything inappropriate. Ford reassured him that he sought a variety of opinions. "I want you to speak and if I don't I will let you know." According to Nelson, "He never did, so I just kept it up."

None of this lessened tensions between Rockefeller and Rumsfeld. Petty differences were magnified, as vice presidential staff complained they were denied parking spaces by the chief of staff. A Rockefeller proposal on health care was returned by Rumsfeld with scant regard for the feelings of its author. Rockefeller asked Ford by executive order to restore the vice presidential seal to its appearance under FDR, replacing the eagle's drooping claws with a more militant look. Rumsfeld objected on grounds of cost. This was "perfectly absurd," said Rockefeller, given that the seal appeared only on matchbooks and trinkets

---

* Rockefeller had revenge of a sort by publicly labeling Callaway Ford's "pre-convention manager." In fact, Callaway didn't make it as far as Kansas City, falling victim to charges, later disproved, that he had improperly promoted a Colorado ski resort with officials of the U.S. Forest Service.

he distributed to visitors. Very well. "We will just use the old ones," Nelson told the president. "All I want is a flag and I will pay the cost of the flag." Later he would claim that changing the flag was his sole accomplishment as vice president. Rockefeller reciprocated in ways scarcely compatible with vice presidential dignity. The story would hardly be credible but for the testimony of those who insist it happened on their watch. On more than one occasion while passing Rumsfeld's White House office, Nelson in the-hell-with-it mode stuck his head inside the doorway and declared, "Rummy, you're never going to be Vice President."

9

ROCKEFELLER DIDN'T LACK for allies in the West Wing. Once a week he sat down to lunch with Bill Seidman, who chaired the Economic Policy Board, as well as Seidman's counterpart in the energy field. White House counsel Rod Hills frequently joined them. A more furtive relationship involved Bob Hartman, the polarizing Ford wordsmith who maintained a hideaway office in the same Executive Office Building where the vice president worked. Rumsfeld's eye for talent convinced them that the president required the services of a "caviar" speechwriter in the mold of Ray Price or Emmett Hughes. Needless to say, this did not endear him to the mercurial Hartman. On the time-tested theory that the enemy of my enemy is my friend, Rockefeller came to Hartman's defense when Rumsfeld allegedly tried to restrict his access to the Oval Office. Indeed, Nelson told the president that Hartman possessed the best political mind in the Ford White House.

Soon the two men were meeting regularly over lunch in the vice presidential suite. "And we would chew the fat," recalled Hartman. "He would find out what was going on through me . . . nobody else would tell him anything." It was at about this time that Susan Herter, who had replaced Ann Whitman as his chief of staff, became angry one day and told Rockefeller, "Sir, they're humiliating you." Not so, said Nelson. "Nobody humiliates you. You humiliate yourself. Or you allow yourself to be humiliated." Sometime late in the summer or early fall of 1975, Bill Seidman alerted Rockefeller to clandestine efforts aimed at replacing him on the 1976 ticket. Seidman refrained from mentioning his own chance attendance at a recent meeting of Ford's "old House buddies"—a group that included Rumsfeld, Mel Laird, John Byrnes of Wisconsin, and Michigan's Bob Griffin. The rump caucus was convened at the president's request to assess Ford's tardy and amateurish drive for Republican delegates. In Seidman's words, the response of those present boiled down to a simple conclusion: "We've got to dump Rockefeller or else we won't get the nomination." Nelson's initial reaction to the news was muted. "Either he didn't want one to know what the response was," mused Seidman, "or he didn't believe me . . . he may have thought it was more idle gossip going around."

It had been a rough summer for Rockefeller. Even as he did battle over energy policy and his place on the 1976 ticket, Albany ghosts resurfaced in a scandal involving the Rockefeller administration and a crash program to accommodate the state's nursing home population (swollen, ironically, by Rockefeller's release of elderly patients from state mental health facilities). The sheer scale of building, and the haste with which it was pursued, had invited abuse by politically connected scam artists. Some nursing home operators were accused of lining their pockets by inflating Medicaid costs while depriving elderly patients of decent care. An investigation was launched to determine what role, if any, was played by lobbyists friendly to the governor and his party. An initial probe was chaired by Andrew Stein, the politically ambitious son of Nelson's good friend Jerry Finkelstein. In February 1976, Moreland Act Commission chairman Morris Abram accused Rockefeller as governor of a lax attitude toward fraud and of sanctioning at least the appearance of inordinate influence by self-proclaiming insiders. Abram also pointed fingers of blame at Louis Lefkowitz, Malcolm Wilson, Norman Hurd, and Republican legislators. He didn't overlook Mayors Lindsay and Beame or Democratic assembly Speaker Stanley Steingut and his business partner Meade Esposito. In the end, Rockefeller escaped with a verbal slap on the wrist.

A much greater threat to his legacy was posed by New York City's pending bankruptcy, as a long postponed reckoning defied efforts by municipal officials— to call them leaders would be excessive—to pretend that everything was, in Rockefeller's words, "hunky-dory." The slide toward insolvency, decades in the making, had its immediate origins in a decision by Rockefeller's Albany successor, Malcolm Wilson, to repeal the 1962 covenant by which New York and New Jersey solemnly pledged to the Port Authority and its bondholders that they would never again be burdened with management of an unwanted mass transit system (the price New Jersey had exacted for authorizing the World Trade Center in lower Manhattan). To bankers already rattled by the Arab oil shock, mounting inflation, and the imploding Nixon presidency, Wilson's reversal raised doubts about the state's willingness or ability to honor its other financial commitments, including the moral obligation bonds that sustained Rockefeller's Urban Development Corporation.

In the six years since he rammed it through a balky legislature, the UDC had skirted the limits of political consensus and financial prudence. As governor, Rockefeller had assigned Stephen Lefkowitz, author of the UDC's enabling legislation, to keep a watchful eye on the force of nature that was Ed

Logue. "Ed was not satisfied to do one project at a time. . . . And so we didn't finance one by one. What we did—instead of twenty bond issues, for twenty projects, each having sufficient funds to complete its particular project—we issued basically nonspecific, nonproject bonds. We started, say, twenty projects and the bond issue would contain say, 10 percent of the funds required for each of those projects. This was an imaginative approach to the problem. . . . The problem, of course, came when we couldn't borrow the rest of the money." Logue the visionary lavished attention on unbuilt communities near Buffalo and Syracuse, and his most ambitious creation of all, Roosevelt Island in the turbulent East River, described by architecture critic Herbert Muschamp as "an economically and racially integrated new town of subsidized, market-rent and co-op housing."

Logue insisted that low-income housing be part of the island's initial mix, for the simple reason that were it to be left out, those who snapped up Roosevelt's middle-income dwellings would oppose any influx of the poor or racially diverse. An attempt to bring low- and middle-income housing to affluent Westchester County generated such fierce resistance from local inhabitants that the legislature voted to strip the agency of its signature power to override local zoning. A weakened Rockefeller had been compelled to accept the crippling amendment in order to avoid worse. Disregarding advice to scale back his construction schedule, Logue fell victim to the invisible hand of the marketplace. But the greatest blow to the UDC was struck by Richard Nixon. Fresh from his sweeping reelection, Nixon at the start of 1973 announced a suspension of Section 236 subsidies covering up to 90 percent of housing costs. Other state agencies reliant on moral obligation bonding could point to reliable income streams from student tuition or patient fees. To buttress a precarious flow of tenant dollars, the UDC depended on federal subsidies, bank loans, and the bulldozing charisma of Edward J. Logue. So when New York State disowned its covenant with the Port Authority, the investment community, for so long an uncritical beneficiary of UDC and other Rockefeller bond offerings, turned with a vengeance on its partners in government.

In January 1975, Malcolm Wilson yielded the governorship to Hugh Carey. "Poor Hugh," said Rockefeller at the time. "I drank the champagne and Hugh got the hangover." In his inaugural address, Carey famously proclaimed an end to the days of wine and roses. "We were in the lead car of the roller coaster going up," said the new governor, "and we are in the lead car coming down." How rough the ride would be was at the time beyond anyone's imagination. Six weeks into Carey's term, state legislators refused to appropriate more than $100 million to repay UDC notes. The resulting default led a frantic Carey to cobble together an emergency funding plan. But while the agency's solvency might be restored, its credibility was ruined. Although Ed Logue was replaced by Carey appointee Richard Ravitch, it wasn't enough to prevent the markets from seizing up in fear. By April 1975, New York City was on the brink of default. The UDC did not cause the city's financial spiral, the origins of which predated Rockefeller's time in Albany. Yet one is surely entitled to ask how much Nelson Rockefeller contributed to the fiscal storm about to overtake his beloved New York.

In announcing his candidacy for a fourth term early in 1970, Rockefeller seemed almost to anticipate the question. "I like to think of myself as an optimist, an idealist, an activist, and a doer . . . ," he reminded voters. While acknowledging errors over the preceding twelve years, he insisted that "most of them were the result of trying to move too fast or do too much. I suggest that these mistakes are preferable to those resulting from timidity or inertia." By any standard of measurement, the tangible results of his governorship were historic: a state university expanded from 38,000 to 244,000 students, 55 new state parks, 109 hospitals and nursing homes, and 200 water treatment plants; trails blazed in funding the arts, protecting the consumer, restoring the environment, and advancing transportation, human rights, highway safety, and a dozen other causes that led political and policy analyst Neal Peirce in his highly regarded 1972 work, *The Megastates of America*, to label Rockefeller "the most remarkable and innovative of the postwar governors."

Would Peirce have reached the same conclusions three years later, as the cost of Rockefeller's pioneering came into focus? The 1974 publication of Robert Caro's *The Power Broker* not only transformed how New Yorkers viewed legendary builder Robert Moses, but reinforced growing popular doubts about the competence, humanity, and reach of modern government in general. Since 1959, state spending had quadrupled, to $8.6 billion annually. And while New York's budget did not grow exponentially faster than those of other states, its tax burden did, along with the borrowing (much of it unsecured, or moral obligation, debt) required to sustain Rockefeller's vision of the activist state.

In 1977, Rockefeller family biographer Alvin Moscow posed his own defining question inspired by, but by no means limited to, the UDC debacle: "How does a capitalistic society, based upon private enterprise and profit, provide adequate housing (or other services) to the needy who cannot afford the price involved?" Ever since his wartime development efforts in Latin America, through his postwar creation of AIA and IBEC, and for fifteen years as governor of the nation's wealthiest state, Nelson Rockefeller had sought inventive ways to balance social responsibility and the bottom line. His failings were grounded in an aversion to failure itself, in the stubborn refusal to accept that it couldn't be done. As state government breached the limits of its problem-solving capacity during his stewardship, discrepancies cracked open: between revenue and spending, between economic productivity and government services, between individual need and the collective good. Clearly Rockefeller had left the Empire State in a vulnerable position whenever the economic cycle slowed or went into reverse. Yet it would be a mistake to conflate the challenges confronting the state and its largest city in the spring of 1975. New York State was solvent, if overextended, which was a great deal more than could be said of a municipal government forced at last to confront years of fiscal mismanagement, worsened by political buyoffs, endless borrowing, and fraudulent accounting.

John Lindsay's successor in Gracie Mansion, Abe Beame, was a faithful product of the Democratic organization. Faced with an immediate $1.5 billion budget shortfall, the new mayor resorted to all-too-familiar accounting tricks: raiding pension funds, advancing the collection date of sewer rent payments, hiding operating expenses in the city's capital budget, and yet more borrowing through something called the Stabilization Reserve Corporation. Announced layoffs were never implemented. The projected deficit grew. Bankers lost patience. Unions cracked the whip. Beame equivocated. Inevitably, the man whose proudest claim was "he knows the buck" passed it, first to Albany and then to Washington. In his first public comments on the crisis, Rockefeller on May 9, 1975, said the mayor had yet to convince the investment community that adequate financial controls were in place to make the city's bonds marketable.

At a May 13 Oval Office meeting in which both Carey and Beame petitioned Ford for a $1 billion short-term loan from Washington, Rockefeller suggested that the state could provide such a lifeline to the city. The state advanced $800 million to city hall. Yet even then, Rockefeller was uncomfortable with the approach urged on Ford by hard-liners such as Bill Simon. "Nelson never approved of the irresponsible fiscal policies that had been pursued in New York City," Ford told Hugh Morrow in 1979. "But Nelson had a love for New York City. The last thing that Nelson wanted was the City to go down the drain. He did not approve of some of my harsher statements vis-à-vis New York City. Yet he knew that to straighten New York City out, or to get them back on the right path, somebody had to be the bad guy. I think Nelson would have preferred that I let Bill Simon or some of the others be the focal point for the position that I took. But my feeling was that this was an issue that I had to face up to. Probably was too harsh in the rhetoric, but our fundamental position was not significantly different."*

When Beame proved unwilling to make politically ruinous spending cuts

---

* Prior to joining the government, Simon had profited handsomely as chief municipal bond dealer for Salomon Brothers—while simultaneously serving on a Technical Debt Advisory Committee reporting to Comptroller Abe Beame. Both were members in good standing of Ken Auletta's "community of interest," a polite term for the greedy confederacy stuffing its pockets while clamoring for even greater benefits.

and structural reforms, he was pushed aside by Carey and the newly formed Municipal Assistance Corporation (MAC), which sold its own bonds to help the city confront a mountain of short-term debt. With Rockefeller-like audacity, Carey secured legislation declaring a moratorium on principal payments so long as the state paid interest (in fact, Carey calculated that in the year before this was ruled unconstitutional by the courts, he could have in place a long-range response to the crisis that would pass legal muster). The focus shifted to Washington. Early in August, Rockefeller raised the possibility of a federal loan guarantee to help lagging MAC bond sales. Ford reiterated his opposition to any bailout, even after the state created the Emergency Financial Control Board to effectively supplant Abe Beame as the city's chief financial officer. On September 5, Rockefeller told reporters in Rochester, New York, that a default by New York City would have serious repercussions in the municipal bond market nationwide. By then administration unity was fraying, with conservatives led by Bill Simon seemingly relishing the opportunity to score points at New York's expense.

Rockefeller had no stomach for testing Simon's claim that default would have little effect on the American economy. Neither, Bill Seidman was convinced, did Gerald Ford: "Although we never said it, we both knew that he was going to give them something in the end, but we were going to get what we needed before that. Unfortunately there was a group in the White House, again led by Rumsfeld, who saw it as a big political opportunity in the rest of the country to dump on New York." Maneuvering within the narrow margins afforded by conflicting loyalties, Rockefeller proposed at the start of October to swap a federal loan to New York in return for a state-approved plan to balance the city's budget by June 1978. A week later, resolved to maintain the pressure on Mayor Beame for unpalatable austerities, Ford said it would be "premature" to comment on a possible veto of bailout legislation. Columnist James Reston accused the president of playing Grand Rapids politics. He quoted White House press secretary Ron Nessen's comparison of New York City to a wayward daughter hooked on heroin. "You don't give her $100 a day to support her habit," Nessen declared. "You make her go cold turkey to break the habit."

Publicly, Rockefeller minimized his differences with the president. This did not prevent him from telling a New York audience on Columbus Day that Congress should act "to avoid catastrophe" as soon as the state and city restored their fiscal credibility. "Nelson," Ford admonished his vice president after his latest comments, "we should not make things more confusing." As the debate within the White House intensified, Federal Reserve chairman Arthur Burns advised Ford that a New York City default could indeed have serious consequences for the national economy. A presidential address at the National Press Club on October 29 occasioned a wild in-house scramble over policy and politics. The question of aid to New York became a proxy for the pending Reagan challenge and Ford's need to demonstrate his conservative bona fides. On the right, Rumsfeld, Simon, and Alan Greenspan were pitted against moderates Bill Seidman and Bob Hartman in a rhetorical tug-of-war. "You don't call a whole state a bunch of clowns," Seidman maintained. "I guess Ford was running scared enough at that point, and all his old buddies kind of ganged up on him."

A high-stakes game of chicken was being played, with the presidency as well as the financial survival of the world's greatest city on the line. "If we go on spending more than we have," Ford told a national audience tuned in to the Press Club speech, "providing more benefits and more services than we can pay for, then a day of reckoning will come to Washington and the whole country, just as it has in New York City. . . . When that reckoning comes, who will bail out the United States of America?" Thirty years later, Seidman was still shaking his head in disbelief. "I don't know how that language got there in the end," he would recall. "We had taken out maybe three or four of the tough sentences, the ones that disparaged the people of New York, and Rumsfeld got them back in." History has been more generous in its assessment, with Hugh Carey himself acknowledging the effectiveness of tough love as practiced by the Ford administration. Ford claimed as much in noting the narrow margin by which Congress ultimately approved a financial aid package to the city. "It was touch-and-go . . . and the fact that I was tough brought along some of the more conservative members of Congress." Little of this is remembered on the sidewalks of New York. In popular memory, Ford is the man who told the world's greatest city to drop dead, in the iconic headline of the *New York Daily News*.

As the president spoke, Rockefeller was in Tampa, Florida, presiding over one of his Domestic Council forums. Acknowledging "some honest difference of opinion," he again stressed the need for New York City officials to adopt a more aggressive budget-cutting stance. By then the initiative had passed to Hugh Carey, who secured major concessions from municipal unions and banks to complement painful spending cuts and tax increases. The state legislature gave its approval. So did the White House. Adopting the course urged by Rockefeller in August, the U.S. Treasury would loan New York City $3.6 billion, all of it paid back with interest. Few achievements left a more sour aftertaste. The latest Gallup poll showed Ford with a 47 percent approval rating. Yet another poll informed the president that Rockefeller's presence in the 1976 ticket would cost him the support of one in four Republicans. Ford admitted to "a sleepless night or two" pondering how he might avail himself of Rockefeller's standing offer to stand down if it would advance the president's chances for a full term of his own. The issue came to a head at their weekly meeting on October 28. "Now, I have been talking with my political advisers," Nelson quoted

Ford, "and they feel that your presence on the ticket would be a liability in the nomination. And you know how much I like working with you and how much our friendship means and how"—here Rockefeller paused, as if the detailed recital of the words did them undeserved justice—"I think it would be helpful if you would withdraw."

"No problem, Mr. President, at all. I will write you a letter and you have no problem. I am here to help you and that's all I came down for and I have no ambitions, no anything." The next day, Ford delivered his National Press Club ultimatum to New York City. Rumors began to circulate about the vice president's future. Ken Riland asked Nelson if something was on his mind; the response he got was noncommittal. For the first time, Riland noticed, his friend looked his age. Rockefeller spent the weekend at Kykuit polishing his withdrawal letter. Around six thirty Sunday evening, Ford called him there. *Newsweek* was on to the story, said the president, part of a much larger White House reshuffle that had Bill Colby and Defense Secretary Jim Schlesinger out—the latter replaced by a reluctant Don Rumsfeld—Cheney promoted to Rumsfeld's old job, George H. W. Bush installed at the CIA, and Elliot Richardson taking over for Rogers Morton at Commerce. Ford asked Rockefeller if he could deliver his promised letter the following day.

Rockefeller complied with the request in a twelve-minute Oval Office meeting that spelled the end of a public life spanning thirty-five years. Two days later, the Rockefellers had the Fords to dinner at Admiral's House. Before they left, the First Lady told her husband he was "a damned fool" to jettison his vice president. Rallying his staff, Nelson put on his good-soldier face. "You have got fourteen months and we have got a hell-of-a-lot of things we are trying to do and if we stick together, we will do them." He maintained his upbeat demeanor before the press and in public. Only once did he let down his guard, in response to the verbal consolation offered by Maryland senator Charles "Mac" Mathias. For a moment, vestigial pride reasserted itself, even as he contemplated political divorce. "Who," Rockefeller asked Mathias, "would want to spend another four years with these shits today?"

Twenty-Six
THE DAY OF THE DEAD

You're either in it or out of it, and you really can't do both. So I got out. . . .
There's no sight worse, in my opinion, than some person who has been
active slowly petering out, trying to maintain a position of influence or
power.

—NELSON A. ROCKEFELLER

1

"I'M 67 YEARS OLD," Rockefeller told a friend days after his eviction from the 1976 ticket. "Why should I stay down here [in Washington] picking do-do with the chickens?" Freed by events to, in his own words, "tell it as it is," he chastised a group of southern GOP operatives assembled in Houston, telling them, "You SOBs got me off the ticket. Now you get off your asses and work for Ford and the party." Convinced that foreign agents were burrowing their way into Capitol Hill, Rockefeller said as much to Lance Morrow, Hugh's journalist son, who interviewed the vice president for *Time*. Startled by the claim, the younger Morrow pressed him for details. "Come on, Lanny," said Nelson, "you're a knowledgeable guy. You know the score." In April 1976, Rockefeller filled in the blanks by asserting his belief, in what he thought was an off-the-record conversation, that Communist sympathizers had infiltrated the office of Washington senator Henry "Scoop" Jackson. For this indiscretion, Nelson had to apologize to Jackson, his staff, and the full Senate.

By his own admission running out of activities to occupy his time, Rockefeller gained White House permission to give a series of speeches around the country, Ford asking only that he see his vice president's texts *after* they were delivered. Writing in the *National Journal*, one journalist compared Nelson with "an understudy who secretly hopes the star of the show breaks his leg." He didn't know the half of it. Hard on the heels of the so-called Halloween Massacre that numbered Rockefeller among its victims, Hubert Humphrey, in league with labor chieftain George Meany, floated a proposition anticipating a brokered Democratic convention the following July in New York. In the event of such a stalemate, would Rockefeller consider switching parties in return for their support? "It's like lightning striking a tree," Nelson said of the opposition feeler. It lasted about as long, as the old war-horse Humphrey waited until the following May to take himself out of the running. By then Democratic primary voters, eager for a fresh face to restore public confidence in post-Watergate Washington, had rallied to the candidacy of former Georgia governor Jimmy Carter.

Rockefeller remained on the fringes of the Ford reelection effort, hosting a cocktail party at 812 Fifth Avenue that raised $150,000 for the President Ford Committee and attending a Broadway performance of *Bubbling Brown Sugar* with the Fords. Even now he was scouting out fresh ideas with which to vitalize the Ford administration and campaign. Hungarian-born nuclear physicist Edward Teller was a $100-a-day consultant whose nearly indecipherable English led Rockefeller to draft his former state budget director, Dick Dunham, as interpreter. "Ed, you and Dick go into his office," he directed Teller. "If he can understand you, he'll come back and tell me." Teller outlined a plan to double American usage of coal in a decade. He also pitched, unsuccessfully, the cause of meteorological warfare. From Jesse Jackson and his Operation PUSH, Nelson borrowed "the work scholarship," a government jobs program that staked young applicants a fixed amount—say, $2,000—to be supplemented by a private employer who provided job training while evading minimum wage laws. The concept found few takers, even on the left.

By the spring of 1976, Rockefeller's policy prescriptions were as dispensable as his presence in the critical early primary states of New Hampshire, Florida, and Illinois. Telling reporters, "I would campaign if anybody asked me to," he instead left New York on March 19 for a two-week bicentennial tour of six nations, from Tunisia to Tahiti. The shah of Iran treated the Rockefellers to three days on his private Kish Island in the Persian Gulf, where the food was flown in daily from Paris. One night, Nelson produced a 35mm camera and snapped group pictures, interspersed with instructions familiar to any suburban shutterbug: "Hey, Shah, move to your right. . . . No, Shah, get closer." Forty-five years after his first visit, Nelson asked to see the famed Persian bazaar at Isfahan. Once transported there in the shah's private jet, Rockefeller scooped up enough bric-a-brac, it seemed, to fill Air Force Two several times over. Among his more curious acquisitions: a craftsman's anvil. "I'll say it was sculpted by Max Ernst and get $35,000 for it," he explained, presumably in jest, to mystified fellow travelers. Ken Riland thought his friend "mentally exhausted." Yet Riland was not the only one in the room moved to tears as Nelson in the Australian city of Sydney paid emotional tribute to the U.S.-Aussie relationship.

Rockefeller returned to a Washington consumed by presidential politics. A string of early primary successes had bred overconfidence in the Ford camp, raising doubts about Reagan's ability to contest the race through North Carolina on March 23. In the event, Reagan did that and much more, exploiting conservative opposition to any turnover of the Panama Canal to score an upset victory in the Tar Heel State, followed in rapid succession by wins in Texas, Alabama, Georgia, and Indiana. One week before the so-called Super Tuesday primaries on May 25, New York Republican Party chairman Richard Rosenbaum sent Rockefeller an SOS. Rosenbaum had done the math. By sweeping most of the southern and western states in the upcoming voting, as seemed likely, Reagan could overtake Ford in the delegate count nationally. Rosenbaum saw only one way to halt the challenger's momentum: New York must abandon its neutral stance and declare for Ford.

That evening, over dinner at Foxhall Road, the party boss dubbed "the Iron Chancellor" spelled out his plan (Operation Rescue) to commit the largest number possible of the state's 154 delegates to the president prior to Super Tuesday. Nelson was initially hesitant. "I realized what he was thinking," Rosenbaum said later. "Rockefeller really thought that Ford and Reagan could deadlock and he could come up the middle and get the nomination." Rosenbaum pleaded with him to consider the alternative. Were Ford to lose the nomination because New York held itself aloof, then surely Rockefeller would get the blame and, with it, the label of spoilsport permanently affixed to his name. Nelson signed on to Operation Rescue that night. Thereafter, he campaigned for Ford as he would have for himself, delivering 133 New York delegates to the president's column and orchestrating the simultaneous award of more than a hundred delegates from neighboring Pennsylvania and Connecticut. The run-up to the convention settled into trench warfare, interrupted on July 26 by Reagan's startling announcement that he had chosen a liberal Pennsylvania senator named Richard Schweiker to be his running mate.

The Schweiker selection angered many of those Rockefeller called "pureblood conservatives." At the same time, it opened the door, however narrowly, to reconsideration of Nelson himself as polling data pointed to a Democratic hammerlock on Jimmy Carter's South. Rockefeller had a different scenario in mind. Claiming that staff morale was slipping badly, he tendered his services to the president as chief of staff. "I can do a job for you both internally on the White House," he told Ford, "and in improving the morale of your Cabinet and the handling of the issues." Only if the two positions were combined would he consider staying on as vice president. Ford thanked Nelson for his offer but indicated that he was satisfied with the current setup. This reflected not only his regard for Dick Cheney—to Rockefeller "just a shadow of Mr. Rumsfeld"—but constitutional scruples identified earlier, when the possibility of Vice President Rockefeller joining the cabinet had been rejected by White House lawyers as a violation of the separation of powers. A few days later, Rockefeller handed the president a second letter, reiterating his withdrawal from consideration once and for all.

Declaring himself through with politics, by the end of June he was planning a return to New York, where the recent death of his sister, Abby, from cancer dramatized generational changes reshaping Room 5600 and the family whose interests it served. He removed his furniture from Admiral's House, in which he and Happy had spent two nights in as many years.* The identity of its next occupant mattered little to Rockefeller, with one notable exception. Blaming Don Rumsfeld for his fate, Nelson promised, "I will get this guy one way or another." After the fact, he told Bill Seidman of an offer he had allegedly made that the president could not refuse—either Rumsfeld stayed away from Kansas City or Ford risked losing the support of New York and Pennsylvania delegates critical to his nomination. Lending credence to his account, Rumsfeld did schedule some minor elective surgery to coincide with the opening of the convention. But the story has holes. Rockefeller made no mention of the ultimatum to trusted confidants such as Bill Ronan, Ken Riland, and Dick Rosenbaum. Rumsfeld dismissed the entire episode, which he himself brought up, in a 2008 interview with the author. So, before his death in 2006, did Gerald Ford.

That there *was* a strategy to exert regional, if not personal, pressure on the Ford White House is confirmed by a July 11 conversation between Rockefeller and George Hinman. The next day, Hinman urged the vice president to impress on Ford "bluntly and directly" the need to placate the Northeast if the resulting ticket was to have any hope of winning in November. In private, Rockefeller talked of releasing "his" delegates should Ford choose either Reagan or John Connally as a running mate. Whether this represented a genuine danger or mere grumbling by a neglected ally, Rockefeller's threats mattered less than his capacity to carry them out. And by the summer of 1976, more than his political powers were beginning to erode. Ann Whitman sensed a general deterioration in her boss, as if he were merely going through the motions of officeholding. Other staffers found him snappish and hard to please. "If you told Rockefeller what he wanted to hear," recalls one, "he didn't think you were of any use; and if you told him what he didn't want to hear, he didn't want to hear from you anymore." In Madrid for the funeral of Francisco Franco and coronation of King Juan Carlos, Hugh Morrow became so enraged by Rockefeller's conduct that he booked an early flight home.

Gaps in Nelson's cultural vocabulary caused as much head scratching as ever. One day, Guy Stever of the National Science Foundation briefed Rockefeller on the hazard posed by mankind to the earth's ozone layer. As recounted

---

* This was not out of pique, as some suspected, but a practical response to the navy's request to redo the air-conditioning and make other repairs to the old house.

by Peter Wallison, "They got on to the subject of chlorofluorocarbons and . . . Stever was telling him about how dangerous all these spray cans were. Then Stever left and Rockefeller says to me, 'Peter, wait a minute.' . . . I said, 'Yes, Governor.' He said, 'How do all those spray cans get up there?'" Ken Riland was more startled to hear four-letter words creeping into Nelson's conversation. The extroverted charmer who ushered members of the public into Capitol elevators marked "Senators Only" was still present. But he could turn waspish without warning, disparaging Commerce Secretary Elliot Richardson as "so stuffy, it's difficult to breathe when he's in the room" and saying of Ford, whose personal and political character he genuinely admired, "He's a grand guy, but Franklin D. Roosevelt he is not."

Never good at keeping official secrets, by 1976 Nelson was capable of stunning indiscretions. *New Times* magazine had him regaling a Washington dinner party with claims withheld from his CIA report—specifically, that JFK had been killed in retaliation for U.S. attempts, sanctioned by the late president's brother Bobby, to assassinate Fidel Castro. In an off-the-record discussion with the editors of *Time*, fully aware that his comments were being tape-recorded, Rockefeller disclosed, courtesy of the National Security Agency, exactly how the Soviets were monitoring American phone calls. What the hell was he supposed to do with such revelations? the magazine's Hedley Donovan asked Hugh Morrow. Was the vice president just sounding off?

Not at all, replied Morrow. "He got it from Henry Kissinger."

His distrust of Moscow left Rockefeller, paradoxically, closer to Rumsfeld's view of the Soviets than to that of his protégé Kissinger. Indeed, said Ford, on national security issues, arms control, and the defense budget, "Nelson and Don Rumsfeld were shoulder to shoulder." It wasn't enough to overcome their mutual mistrust or conflicting ambitions. And with only 34 percent of Americans polled expressing approval of Nelson's performance as vice president, Rumsfeld had plenty of company in viewing him as an electoral drag. None of this kept Rockefeller from playing the good soldier when GOP delegates gathered in Kansas City in August 1976. "He worked himself to the bone," recalls Brent Scowcroft. "I know because I was close to him at the convention . . . and he was twisting arms and delegations." Ironically, the week's most public embarrassment grew out of some successful troubleshooting by the vice president. Alerted to several wavering Ford supporters in the Iowa delegation, Nelson left his seat on the floor of the Kemper Arena and went off to charm the Hawkeyes back into the fold. Mission accomplished, he was returning to the New York standard when a Reagan partisan from nearby North Carolina thrust a sign promoting his candidate into Rockefeller's face. Nelson yanked the placard out of the man's hands and tossed it under Dick Rosenbaum's chair. Chaos ensued, as a second Reaganite, from Utah, threatened violence to New York's telephone unless Rockefeller returned the sign. Rosenbaum vowed retaliation in kind. The Utah delegate then grabbed the phone and fled, with Rosenbaum and the Secret Service on his heels. Eventually they retrieved the ruined instrument, which a grinning Rockefeller held aloft as a final ironic trophy in his long-running conflict with the Right over the future course of the Republican Party.

Declaring, "You've got to have *some* fun," Rockefeller urged everyone to lighten up. Away from the cameras, he was thoroughly businesslike. "He was discreet," says Jack Marsh. "He only tried to help Ford where he knew he could help him . . . where he thought his activities would hurt Ford, he acknowledged that and stayed the hell out." Rockefeller was instrumental in the fight against Rule 16c, a transparent attempt by Reagan supporters to compensate for the busted Schweiker ploy by requiring Ford to designate *his* running mate prior to the balloting for president on Wednesday night. At a reception for the New York delegation, Betty Ford declared that Nelson was still *her* candidate for vice president. The authors of 16c hoped the president would echo his wife's sentiments, since the advance selection of Rockefeller or some other northern liberal could prompt disillusioned conservatives in pivotal southern states such as Mississippi to take a fresh look at Reagan.

Yet by staking so much on a purely procedural question, Reagan strategists lessened the emotional impact of a second debate, this one involving the party platform and the administration's pursuit of détente with the Soviet Union. To many on the right, Henry Kissinger, unfairly blamed for the forced departure of cabinet hard-liner Jim Schlesinger, was seen as the architect of American decline. Reagan backers hoped to capitalize on this feeling by amending the platform to include a "Morality in Foreign Policy" plank. Their initiative left Ford and his advisers facing a Hobson's choice. "We felt that if we fought on the platform and lost, it would give to the Reagan people an added arrow in their quiver," recalled Ford. Recognizing the fragility of his lead, Ford decided, in effect, to concede the platform in order to clinch the nomination. His action did not sit well with the authors of the foreign policy going undefended before a national television audience. This included Rockefeller, who argued vigorously that the administration's honor was at stake, as well as its credibility beyond Kansas City. To White House political strategists, these abstractions mattered less than the hard numbers of their trade, above all the 1,130 figure required to put Ford over the top in his seesaw contest with Reagan. So when Kissinger issued one of his now threadbare threats to resign in protest, an irreverent member of the campaign team urged him to do so quickly, "because we can use the votes." In the end, Rockefeller, like Ford, swallowed his doubts and accepted the Reagan plank.

He had no intention of running up a white flag, however. Rather, he would co-opt the insurgents by recasting their complaint as an endorsement of what the administration was already doing overseas. The novice politician who had once needed to have explained to him the meaning of the word *chutzpah* showed just how much he had taken the lesson to heart. Hastily he scribbled out a verbal formula that Ford approved with minutes to spare. As John Tower rewrote Nelson's language to make it legible for Ford agents in the hall, Rockefeller appealed to Kissinger. "I told him that this was the best that could be done with the situation and for God's sake don't say anything." The subsequent adoption of the plank by voice vote provided the week's biggest anticlimax. Coupled with Ford's victory on Rule 16c, it reduced the outgeneraled Reagan forces to hoping for a miracle, much like Barry Goldwater's opponents twelve years earlier in San Francisco. Rockefeller, equally resolved to avoid a repeat of that televised bloodletting, instructed Dick Rosenbaum to make no complimentary podium references to his performance as vice president. As he put it, "If they start a demonstration, you could hurt Ford."

His self-denying strategy was vindicated on the evening of August 18, as Ford claimed his party's nomination with sixty votes to spare. Fittingly, it was New York that gave the president a roll call lead he never relinquished. Discussions over a running mate didn't begin in earnest until three in the morning. Ford confided to Rockefeller his preference for William Ruckelshaus, the former Environmental Protection Agency director and deputy attorney general whose refusal to fire Watergate special prosecutor Archibald Cox as ordered by the Nixon White House had earned him a reputation for putting principle above partisan loyalties. Rockefeller, figuring that Ruckelshaus would add to the ticket's appeal in the Northeast, welcomed the news. But Ford was also interested in hearing what others had to say. And virtually no one among the assembled party and campaign officials shared the president's enthusiasm for Ruckelshaus. The politicians talked in circles through the night. Campaign strategist Stu Spencer, part of the initial discussion group, was surprised to be called back two hours later. "We're rehashing the same stuff, and . . . I said, 'Why don't we forget about all this? We've gone through the primaries, we've beaten Reagan, let's put Nelson back on the ticket.'" It was a serious proposal, though not received as such.

Reminding Ford that he was no longer "a 25th Amendment President," Rockefeller decried the limits of consensus. "For Christ's sake," he groaned, "forget this Goddamned trial balloon stuff and just tell those so-and-sos on the floor who you want and they are going to nominate." More acceptable to the exhausted group was his suggestion to adjourn the meeting around six thirty in the morning. After an hour's sleep, Nelson went to a *Newsweek* breakfast, whose nominal host, publisher Kay Graham, was absent on account of the previous late night. While there, he received an urgent message from George Hinman conveying the sentiment of southern delegates for Reagan but offering the name of Bob Dole as an acceptable alternative. Back at the Crown Center Hotel, Rockefeller passed this information on to the president, not forgetting to add that Mississippi's Clarke Reed had been trying without success to reach Dick Cheney. The chief of staff acknowledged several messages from Reed, which he had been too busy to return. When he did get through to Reed, Cheney quickly validated Rockefeller's story. Ford then asked Nelson to contact Senators Jacob Javits and Hugh Scott for liberal reaction to their Kansas colleague. Within half an hour, the Dole nomination was buttoned up.

Rockefeller returned to his hotel suite. Ken Riland, on learning that his patient had gotten only four hours' sleep over the last two days, ordered him to bed after lunch. As he dozed, a note arrived from the president, asking Rockefeller to make the speech formally nominating Dole at that evening's concluding session. Rather than wake him, Riland and other staffers accepted on Nelson's behalf. Bill Ronan set to work writing a text. Rockefeller accepted it without a change, but when the time came to address the convention, he could hardly make himself heard above the din of the crowd. "Turn up the sound," he told a nearby technician. "I can't," replied the man. "It's up." Ken Riland, sitting in a nearby box with Ronan and his wife, strained to catch anything coming out of Nelson's mouth. Practically yelling into the microphone, Rockefeller hastened to the end of his remarks. Leaving the podium, he warned the next speaker, a blind girl who was to second Dole's nomination, that something was terribly wrong with the sound system. He directed Joe Canzeri to make sure the problem was fixed before the president's acceptance speech.

Before Canzeri could work his magic, someone else did. To Nelson's astonishment, the young woman who took his place onstage could be heard perfectly. From this he concluded that the sound had deliberately been turned down by convention managers to dampen early demonstrations and build anticipation for the president's prime-time appearance. Rockefeller's mood darkened as he recalled, none too philosophically, the affronts he had endured in the two years since he accepted Gerald Ford's offer of a substantive partnership. One final indignity remained. On the heels of Ford's well-received acceptance, a parade of officials, some accompanied by their families, prepared to take their places in a concluding tableau of orchestrated unity. Informed that his role in the convention's final act was to escort Bob Dole's mother, Rockefeller exploded. "Look, I am either going up following the President which is correct protocol . . . or I am leaving this convention hall right now." The campaign functionary to whom these angry words were directed spotted Dick Cheney among those milling around the holding area.

Now it was Cheney's turn to experience the chest-thumping fury earlier visited on recalcitrant New York legislators of both parties. "Of course you should go up," Cheney told Nelson. "I didn't know anything about this, but of course the Vice President will go up second." But Rockefeller wasn't through. "Look, you so and so," he raged, "I know what has been going on and I have been taking this all the way through and now it is over. You tell the President for me what has happened here. You tell him about turning down the mike when I made the speech, and you tell him I'm not going to Vail and I am not going to have anything further to do with his campaign. I have fulfilled my duties. He has now got a new Vice President. And I am finished." Watching the confrontation from a few feet away, Canzeri trembled visibly ("Don't ever do that to me," he told his boss afterward). Lynne Cheney was in tears.

Minutes later, Rockefeller lent his campaign face to the manger scene of ritualized harmony. Afterward he was invited to the president's hotel suite, where Ford made no mention of the convention hall meltdown. Instead he thanked Nelson in advance for being part of the Vail strategy session.

"Mr. President, didn't you get the message I sent? I am not going to Vail. I've finished. I got you the nomination. I worked with you in this thing for two years. I'll finish my duties as Vice President, but I am finished."

"This is terrible," said Ford. It was all a misunderstanding. He let Rockefeller vent. He would do anything he could to help the president win in November, said Nelson, but as for his White House enemies, "I am not going to work with these people. I am not going to sit in a room with them again." The tirade was interrupted by a congratulatory phone call from Henry Kissinger. Ford, no doubt grateful for its timing, invited Kissinger for an impromptu celebration. Rockefeller suggested asking the rest of the cabinet to join them. Even this somewhat strained festivity was marred by a confrontation between Nelson and Bill Simon regarding David Rockefeller and the Chase Bank. In his memoirs, Simon described an encounter with a tipsy vice president in which Rockefeller seized the Treasury secretary by the lapels and snarled, "You do anything to my brother David and you'll be sorry!" The threat was in apparent reference to rumors then circulating that Simon might replace the younger Rockefeller as chairman of Chase Manhattan Bank. Responding in character, the pugnacious Simon denied any interest in going to "a lousy bank like Chase . . . that's going to go broke."*

Nelson returned to his quarters around three in the morning, his resentment mingled with regret. "Kenny, I've never used such language in my life," he told Riland. The next day he left Kansas City for Jackson Hole, to which Happy had already fled on the second day of the convention. There he took another call from Ford renewing his appeal to attend the Vail meeting and

---

* Nelson's version of the face-off ended with him telling Simon, "One more peep out of you on the subject and I really am going to go out after you because the one thing our family has, we have loyalty." NROH, November 22, 1977, 56.

seeking Rockefeller's help in persuading an equally reluctant John Connally to participate. Nelson consented, but on one condition: "I am not going to sit down in a room with Cheney." A private, one-on-one session with the president in Vail was arranged—only to have Cheney cancel it in a phone call to Canzeri. Fine, said Rockefeller. "Tell them I'm not coming." Ford overruled his chief of staff, and the two men had their meeting. Later in the day, Rockefeller and Connally were coaxed into holding a joint press conference endorsing the Ford-Dole ticket. Neither man was to play a significant part in the fall campaign that Rockefeller had once expected to oversee. Illustrative of the new order was the vice president's parting request to John Deardourff, a junior member of the ground team that had organized Nelson's come-from-behind victory in the 1964 Oregon primary, now one-half of the hot political advertising firm Bailey, Deardourff & Associates, hired at the last minute to work on the Ford campaign.

"John," said Rockefeller, "would you mind if from time to time I call you up with ideas?"

2

THE PHONES IN the vice presidential offices rang less often that fall. Its chief occupant was yesterday's news. Yet Rockefeller hadn't lost his knack for making headlines, as he demonstrated on a mid-September campaign swing through upstate New York with Senator Bob Dole. In Binghamton, a group of about thirty students from the local SUNY campus greeted the pair with chants of "Attica killer!" and "Rocky, you traitor, we're going to get you later!" Rockefeller reminded the hecklers that he was responsible for the school in which they were enrolled. He introduced the Kansas senator as someone who had fought a war to protect their right to protest. This touched off fresh chanting, accompanied by a clutch of upraised fists and one-fingered salutes. Rockefeller reciprocated their body language, to the astonishment of the crowd, the delight of photographers, and the dismay of his entourage. He was just responding in kind, he told reporters. Ken Riland expressed surprise that his friend even knew the obscene gesture. Oh yeah, replied Nelson. "Happy taught me that."

A few days later, Peter Wallison, who had been assigned to the Dole campaign, dropped by Rockefeller's office to say hello. "And he's signing photographs of himself flipping the bird," he says in amazement. "You're the vice president of the United States," Wallison blurted out. Eventually, Nelson was dissuaded from autographing copies of the notorious photo, but not from marveling over the record amount of mail generated by the incident, second only to his televised confrontation with the Right at the 1964 Republican convention in San Francisco. By contrast, a single network reporter accompanied Rockefeller on his bicentennial visit to London in October 1976. For members of the vice presidential staff, many with even less on their plates, this was a time for résumé polishing. Certainly the third floor of the Executive Office Building was the last place in Washington to which any eager young job seeker would direct his or her attention. Then again, how many aspiring press aides appear for their job interview clutching a tray of Oreo cookies individually wrapped and tied in a festive bow?

Megan Marshack had done her homework. A twenty-two-year-old Californian, Marshack had long since outgrown her youthful shyness, but not her single-minded ambition to sample life beyond the Hollywood Hills. "I decided to become a White House correspondent at age twelve," Marshack told a reporter for the *San Fernando Valley News.* "I spent every waking moment and every dreaming moment trying to map out my strategy." When defense cutbacks cost her father his job as an aerospace engineer, the resulting financial difficulties may have fostered Megan's other life goal, to marry "somebody who will support me in the manner to which I would like to become accustomed." While still in college, Megan had written a piece on the White House press corps based near Richard Nixon's San Clemente home and sold it to *Coronet* magazine. "Megan would just show up on the press bus," one journalist told the *Washington Post's* Myra MacPherson. "She was always doing some freelance work." Her attraction to the press corps was more than professional. Her long-running affair with a considerably older reporter for a midwestern paper was common knowledge among the boys on the bus. "She was a groupie," says one.

Co-workers were divided over the tall—five-foot-eight—blonde with the oversize spectacles whom they variously labeled cherubic and matronly, caring and obsequious. Bright enough to skip a semester at Ulysses S. Grant High School, she was remembered by childhood friends for her competitiveness and drive. "Through bluff or bluster she always managed to be places she wasn't really credentialed to be," a former boyfriend told *People* magazine. According to speechwriter Joe Persico, "One had a sense of Megan's never having suppressed anything she had ever wanted to do or say in her life." Persico, her nominal supervisor in Rockefeller's vice presidential office, professed fondness for his exuberant new colleague, hired as a $138-a-day consultant at the end of a six-month, $225-a-week apprenticeship with Associated Press Radio, where her reputed tendency to panic over deadlines made a career in the news business problematic. Assigned to Persico's shop, Marshack uncomplainingly ground out birthday greetings and other messages before her promotion to assistant press secretary and subsequent move into an office next to the vice president's. Neither party concealed their growing intimacy. "I go over there one day on some business with him, and I detect a deference by him to her, and I heard on her part certain personal assumptions that were just unusual," says Jim Cannon. "Calling him Nelson, for example. We all called him Governor." On one occasion, with Rockefeller characteristically late for a speech at the National Press Club, he was confronted by Marshack, hands on her hips, demanding in a voice that would never be tolerated in Room 5600, "Nelson Rockefeller, where have you been?" Megan's Chevy Chase apartment housed an elegant Chinese jade horse sculpture, the first of many gifts to her from the vice president. When an office colleague took it upon himself to rewrite a Marshack draft, the vice president was said to have "raised hell" in demanding the letter go out as originally written.

Inevitably, there was gossip in an office with little of substance to discuss. Ray Shafer, the former Pennsylvania governor who had joined Rockefeller's vice presidential staff, warned Nelson that people were talking. "Get rid of her," Shafer advised. It was counsel Rockefeller had no intention of adopting, as Hugh Morrow could attest from awkward experience. Following dinner at Foxhall Road, Morrow made himself scarce for the rest of the evening. Eventually, he was awakened by a knock on the door of his room.

"Well, Hughie, I guess your friend wants to go home now." With that, the faithful Morrow got up and drove Marshack home.

Rockefeller's campaign travels that fall took him to a dozen states on behalf of Republican candidates. He barnstormed alone, as Happy spent the first half of October on a personal visit to the Soviet Union. Two days after her return from Moscow, Nelson learned that his oldest son, Rodman, had separated from his wife of a quarter century and that the couple planned to divorce—the last of his four surviving children by Tod to emulate their parents' marital breakup. Shut out of campaign debate preparations, Rockefeller offered Foxhall Road as a place for Bob Dole to rehearse in advance of his televised confrontation with Walter Mondale. He also gave the senator some friendly counsel following the publication of stories criticizing Dole and his campaign fund-raising. "I never read anything about myself in the papers," said Rockefeller. He advised Dole to do likewise. "Otherwise you'll spend half the day reading the criticism and the other half reacting." On election night, Henry Kissinger and a few friends joined Nelson at 812 Fifth Avenue. Early returns pointed to a Carter victory, though Ford narrowed the gap considerably as the Midwest and Pacific coast weighed in. Rockefeller's spirits picked up on the news that his nephew Jay (more formally, John D. Rockefeller IV) had been elected governor of West Virginia.

"Well," he observed, "it's a small state—but it's ours."

Two weeks after the election, Gerald and Betty Ford were overnight guests at Kykuit. The president took the occasion to formally declare the estate a national historic landmark. He played golf with Nelson and his brothers. The Fords also joined the Rockefellers for Sunday services at the tiny Union Church with its Matisse rose window memorializing Abby. Having abandoned his idea of writing a manual for vice presidents, Rockefeller did the next best thing: he invited Walter Mondale to dinner at Foxhall Road. In the course of the evening, Nelson expressed relief at the sound of a ringing telephone. "That happens so rarely now," he confided to his successor. In a second meeting, in his EOB office, he mentioned a receptionist—"a very attractive, bright young lady"—who hoped to continue in vice presidential service after January 20, 1977. Mondale promised to keep her on. Eager to thank the Secret Service agents who had protected him and his family, Nelson purchased handsome sets of cuff links for each member of his detail, only to be informed that they exceeded in value the government's annual gift limit. He got around the problem by presenting the agents with one link on December 31 and the other on January 1.

His parting gifts to the Senate included a copy of Anders Zorn's 1911 portrait of his grandfather Nelson Aldrich, as well as an Adam carved mahogany sideboard from the Rockefeller home on West Fifty-fourth Street in which Nelson had grown up. In a brief valedictory, Rockefeller saluted Ford for defusing the constitutional crisis of Watergate. As for himself, "These two unusual years, in all candor, cannot be said to have sorely tried either my talent or my stamina." He puckishly offered a motto to guide future vice presidents: "They also serve who merely sit and wait." On his last night in office, Nelson accepted the Fords' invitation to stay at the White House with Happy and the two boys. After dinner, the male members of the party adjourned to a third-floor putting green. Young Nelson, highly competitive, asked his father what President Ford would think of him after missing several shots. "President Ford is a very understanding man," replied Nelson, "and he understands exactly what happened and he thinks very well of you." The next day, Rockefeller led the applause at a farewell breakfast attended by seventy-five presidential aides and cabinet members. Following the ceremony that returned both Ford and Rockefeller to private citizenship, the two men and their wives boarded a helicopter for a final pass over Washington. At Andrews Air Force Base, they said their goodbyes to one another. Little more than a hour later, Air Force Two was on the ground in Westchester County. "I had a terrible feeling when we came home the day Carter was sworn in," says one who accompanied the prodigal son to Room 5600. "When he got out of the car downstairs, the first time I looked at him, I said to myself: He's aged unbelievably in such a short time. You could really see the fight was out of him."

3

O N JANUARY 29, ROCKEFELLER was back in the capital for a humorous turn before the self-regarding members of Washington's Alfalfa Club. "Having spent the last two years as Vice President," he noted archly, "I think it's time I returned to public life." He made sport of his unfulfilled presidential ambitions—"Recently, I thought I was dying, and Harold Stassen's life passed before my eyes"—his now infamous one-finger salute from the campaign trail, and the fleeting nature of power, "as I was saying only a minute ago to my waiter"—here he crossed out the name of Rogers Morton—"Donald Rumsfeld." Rockefeller's audience laughed heartily at his self-deprecatory jabs. Members of his family were treated to a less mellow side of Nelson, whose unsubtle efforts to reorganize Room 5600, redirect the Rockefeller Brothers Fund (RBF), and guarantee the future of Kykuit as a public museum would make him as polarizing to other Rockefellers as he had long been to other Republicans.

"Everybody was very nervous around here as to what he was going to do," conceded J. Richardson Dilworth, head of the family office since 1958. "Some of the family found it very difficult at that time to differentiate between a good idea, and the fact that Nelson was the proponent of it . . . it was a hell of a difficult situation for him, because he really was being attacked for his assumed motives rather than the actuality." Still more sympathetic was the view offered by Laurance Rockefeller: "He wanted to do a lot quickly and if there is any criticism of him, it is in just that. He came back to the family and he figured, I've been away twenty years and we don't have forever, now let's straighten this mess out." Characteristically, Nelson's first step was to commission a pair of studies examining operations in Room 5600 and the RBF. Over time, the family office had expanded with little formal oversight, reflecting demands from multiple generations while supplying a menu of useful services disproportionately underwritten by the Brothers. Nelson's solution was to incorporate the place, marketing to outside clients the same real estate and investment expertise previously reserved for descendants of John D. Rockefeller, Sr. "I thought what he was trying to do was in the family's long-term interest," concluded Dick Dilworth.

The RBF was more complex. John 3rd, conscientious to a fault, wished to set the philanthropic standard for compliance with the Tax Reform Act of 1969 by putting as much daylight as possible between his family and its charitable namesake. This meant an end to any privileged status for him or his siblings. Most of all, John wished to expedite a generational hand-off to the Cousins, as the next class of Rockefeller offspring were collectively known. Nelson acknowledged the need for an orderly transition, but not at the expense of the

Brothers in the Rockefeller Brothers Fund. His ideas of reform treated the rest of the RBF board, no less than the Cousins clamoring to take their place on it, as decidedly second-class citizens. RBF president Bill Dietel experienced for himself just how far Nelson—"he was a finger breaker"—would go to retain control. Refusing to sign a revised set of bylaws without first examining the document, Dietel learned that under the new rules the foundation was to be governed by a chairman, who would also double as CEO. "And he was going to become the chairman," said Dietel.

This blatant power grab fell by the wayside, one in a series of disappointments that clouded Nelson's homecoming. "The first year was difficult for him," acknowledges Richard Parsons, who had been asked by Nelson to review Room 5600 operations and to help patch up relations with his first family. Promised the same six months of Secret Service protection accorded Spiro Agnew following his resignation, Nelson saw his agents abruptly withdrawn by the Carter White House after a month. Later in the year, he was forced to deny a *New York* magazine article calling his CIA investigation a cover-up and linking him, falsely, to the agency's past mail intercepts and drug experiments. Such criticism was mild compared with the wounded feelings of his extended family. Many younger Rockefellers resented the loss of privacy, personal and financial, occasioned by Uncle Nelson's vice presidential hearings. They objected to his views on Vietnam, his handling of Attica, and his seemingly cavalier treatment of his brothers over the years.

All this and more had spilled embarrassingly into print in the spring of 1976, when several of the Cousins served as sources for Peter Collier and David Horowitz, who exploited family divisions to enliven their unabashedly critical history, *The Rockefellers: An American Dynasty*. As editors of *Ramparts* magazine, Collier and Horowitz were convinced Marxists before their subsequent migration to the new Right. They made much of their limited access to the family archives, a privilege accorded them based upon a reference from Laurance's daughter Marion. Appalled by the result, Nelson railed against the "disloyal, ungrateful, and irresponsible" Cousins, not excluding the children from his first marriage, who seized the opportunity to publicly credit their mother, Tod, for any interest they might have in books or learning. "Father likes his art and so forth," acknowledged Steven Rockefeller, "but even there his appreciation is completely intuitive, based only on immediate reaction."

In the tumultuous seventies, it wasn't unusual for Rockefeller women to hasten into marriage as the quickest way to shed a name they detested. Nelson's youngest daughter, Mary, went a step further by wedding Tom Morgan, John Lindsay's city hall press secretary and a journalist whose publications (*The Village Voice, New York* magazine) had little good to say about his new father-in-law. That he didn't know Morgan personally was irrelevant. "I know where he works," said Nelson. "That's all I need to know." As for her father, Mary Rockefeller Morgan told Collier and Horowitz, "I love him for his warmth. But he stands for power, and I think it is very important how one relates to power. It stands as a warning." At the least, she and her cousins hoped to revamp the RBF to better reflect their own priorities, such as opposition to companies doing business in white-ruled South Africa.

No one cheered them on more heartily than Uncle John. He just as strongly opposed plans by Nelson, determined to frustrate the Cousins' philanthropic pursuits, to liquidate most, if not all, RBF assets through a series of terminal grants to organizations whose association with the family went back to Senior's day. Tensions rose as the Brothers wrangled over how much of the RBF's roughly $200 million endowment should be retained for future giving. Nelson wanted key decisions reserved to himself and his siblings. John 3rd, by contrast, put his faith in trustees from outside the family exercising their independent judgment.

Hoping to thwart Nelson's ambitions, yet reluctant to wage a formal contest, John tried to direct his brother's attention elsewhere. Hugh Morrow spent much of 1977 denying rumors that Nelson might run for mayor of New York that fall. Morrow finally traced the whispering campaign to John—"a strange way to get him [Nelson] out of the office." Early in May, Nelson and John appeared to narrow their differences over a two-hour lunch at the Rainbow Room. (It didn't hurt that Nelson renounced his interest in the RBF chairmanship.) Nelson found other ways to incentivize fraternal cooperation. When his brothers each agreed to chip in $75,000 toward Kykuit's annual $430,000 maintenance bill, he offered them use of the big house for entertaining important guests. Nelson welcomed John's input to the planned reconstruction of Senior's birthplace on the Kykuit grounds, part of a larger effort to prepare the estate for eventual transfer to the National Park Service.

Unfortunately, whatever goodwill was fostered by such gestures did not survive a string of contentious RBF meetings. First Nelson opposed John's daughter Hope for reelection to the board. Then he blocked John's candidacy to chair the nominating committee, arguing that such recognition should be withheld until John accepted the Brothers' view of the RBF and their dominant role within it. Nelson scored another victory by engineering the election of both Henry Kissinger and Nancy Hanks to the RBF board (though trustees drew the line at Bill Ronan). At a board meeting on June 16, he overplayed his hand by proposing a $3 million gift to support the New York College of Osteopathic Medicine being established by his friend and personal physician, Kenneth Riland. Considerable opposition to the idea led to its being shelved pending review of the school's financial prospects.* As far as Nelson was concerned, this was merely a temporary delay; within forty-eight hours he was asking RBF trustees to raise, in addition to John's "very important questions," any concerns they might have regarding the osteopathic college project.

That same evening, in his self-described farewell to politics, Nelson introduced Gerald Ford at the annual dinner of the New York Republican State Committee. More than two thousand admirers packed a Waldorf ballroom to cheer the former governor, whose voice choked repeatedly as he responded to the praise heaped on him. And with that the curtain came down, though few New Yorkers, in either party, believed that Rockefeller was truly retired. Bob Armao discovered this for himself when confronted by some union elements hostile to Ed Koch's candidacy for mayor. Rockefeller had authorized Armao, on his own, to raise union money for the Koch campaign, as long as he clearly distinguished it from his own failed attempt four years earlier to restore Bob Wagner to city hall. Investigation revealed that the labor leaders in question believed they would be shut out of Gracie Mansion should Koch win the election against Mario Cuomo. What made them think so? asked Armao. Because, they replied, Rockefeller was sure to dominate any Koch mayoralty.

"I got bad news for you," Armao told the union men. As for influencing either the election or the administration that took office on January 1, 1978, "He couldn't care less, he's so bitter about politics." Later, as chief of protocol in the Koch administration ("There's no heavy lifting on that job," joked Nelson), Armao was approached by labor representatives keen to support a Rockefeller comeback. Would he consider a return to Albany in 1978? Out of the question, Nelson told Armao. "We had the golden years—oil, seven dollars a barrel. Easy to get our hands on money. Easy to build that trade center. Easy to build the state university. . . . Who wants to be a governor and cut, cut, cut? It's not my style. Let's look back with happiness, gratitude, and move on." His attitude was shared by the White House, where, for the first time since 1940, no one was interested in Nelson's opinion. In May, Rockefeller told a largely Jewish audience in New York that President Carter deserved bipartisan support for his human rights advocacy and Middle East peacemaking efforts. Later that year, testifying as a private citizen before the Senate Finance Committee, Nelson urged a second look at his ill-fated Energy Independence Authority. (The Carter administration did incorporate elements of the EIA into its Synthetic Fuels

---

* Nelson wasn't the only member of his family to swear by Riland's ministrations. His brother Laurance and sister, Babs, were equally devoted patients. Nelson liked to illustrate the benefits of osteopathy by describing his experience at the wedding of George Hinman's daughter, who was in tears on the dance floor owing to pain in her jaw. "I can fix that," he told her, and validated his claim by having the young woman bite down on a strategically placed pencil. Instantly the pain vanished. In osteopathic lingo, Dr. Rockefeller had corrected her dislocated jaw.

Corporation, whose brief, scandal-plagued existence was abruptly terminated when Ronald Reagan decontrolled oil prices in 1981.) Invited afterward to the Oval Office, Rockefeller welcomed a presidential request to lobby several Republican senators on behalf of Carter's unratified Panama Canal treaties. If he expected any additional assignment from Gerald Ford's successor, a prospect he discussed at some length with labor leader Lane Kirkland, Rockefeller was to be disappointed.

4

THE DAY AFTER RBF trustees tabled his osteopathic college proposal, Nelson wrote John a conciliatory letter touching on the proposed reconstruction of "Grandfather's house" and the Riland grant. "Despite a few differences," he felt the board discussion "went very well. . . . I appreciate the clear, simple and direct position you took in relation to the Riland request." This was vintage Nelson, employing flattery to dull the edge of disagreement. But then he ruined the effect at a dinner accompanying the Cousins' annual gathering on Father's Day weekend. Besides venting his anger over the Collier and Horowitz book, Nelson described his planned reorganization of the family office with scant regard for the feelings, or interests, of his already skeptical audience. The next day, the Cousins unanimously rejected his blueprint for change. At the same time, they insisted that Laurance stay on as chairman. On Sunday morning, June 19, the warring generations met at the Pocantico Playhouse. By all accounts it was a watershed in family history, as one cousin after another complained about Nelson's conduct toward them and professional staff at both the RBF and Room 5600. David thought the uprising, in whose dissatisfied ranks both Steven and Ann Rockefeller were prominent, left his brother "dumbfounded."

If so, it didn't take long for Nelson's initial surprise to morph into a play for fraternal solidarity. The two groups separated, the Brothers occupying the small card room, sitting on chairs embossed with their mother's needlepoint, and Abby's grandchildren gathering around the outdoor swimming pool. As David conducted shuttle diplomacy, Nelson exercised all his wiles to exploit the Cousins' inexperience and relative lack of organization. Looking on, Bill Dietel observed a master politician at work. "If you shut this door and you shut that door, he'd find a door around back here that he could escape through. He practiced divide and conquer with a passion, and with immense skill," Dietel claimed. "And every time they tried to gang up on him, he would thwart them. . . . And then they would get hurt." Ultimately a compromise was reached under which Nelson became chairman but not CEO of the family office. In return for this concession, voting on the new board of directors would henceforth be on a one-for-one basis, a significant change from the current system that was weighted according to the amount of family contribution.

At the last minute, even John reluctantly voted with his three siblings. The next morning, he and Nelson had what the latter called a "very helpful conversation." For ninety minutes, John compensated for his action the previous day, making plain his sympathy for the Cousins' insurgency. Nelson seemed oddly unaffected by the criticism, though he did at one point express disbelief that he could really be the figure so roundly denounced by the younger generation. The dispute escalated when John wrote his brother, likening the newfound assertiveness of the Cousins to Nelson's long-ago defiance of a Junior mired in tradition. "In those early days, you took leadership among us in a way that was appreciated. You appeared to care deeply about all of us and put the family interests above self. Then came your remarriage and the years away." His behavior since returning from Washington, claimed John, could be understood only as "an attempt to gain control of the RBF so that funds will be made available for projects of personal interest to you and other brothers regardless of the effect on the Fund's ongoing responsibilities and opportunities." To realize this objective, Nelson had resorted to tactics "which to my knowledge have never been employed within our family interests before and I hope never will be again. . . .

"You have had two ambitions in your life," John continued, "the presidency of the USA and the leadership of a united Rockefeller family which would carry forward the traditions we inherited: stewardship, public service and caring deeply about our country and its people. It would appear that the first was no longer attainable. In my opinion you are on the verge of losing any possibility of the second. It is a tragic situation as you have so much to offer and you care so much. Power politics just are not appropriate on the homefront. In-fighting, as you refer to it, in this setting can obviously win skirmishes but will lose the war." Declaring Nelson to be "on trial within the family," John said the outcome depended on his acceptance of two demands: withdrawing the osteopathic college from any further consideration by the RBF; and accepting John's latest recommendations guaranteeing sufficient capital to sustain future operations and assuring each member of the board an equal place at the table. "Please believe me, Nel, time is running out."

Nelson's point-scoring response to this ultimatum was never sent. Concerned that anything he wrote might be leaked to *The New York Times*—as had already happened in the wake of John Gardner's resignation from the RBF board—Nelson phoned his brother, urging him to withdraw his accusatory letter. In a follow-up message notable for its restraint, he spun the preceding six months as "a most productive period in bringing things out in the open for discussion." John retracted his letter, while Nelson revised his tactics to fit the mood of the board. On September 19, RBF trustees approved, over John's objection, a modest $111,000 grant to examine the fund-raising potential of Dr. Riland's college. Nelson had his bridgehead, which he quickly expanded as Henry Kissinger agreed to head up a $20 million fund-raising drive. Laurence and Nelson made separate gifts of $250,000. Following Nelson's death in January 1979, a memorial fund collected nearly $800,000, to be matched dollar for dollar as part of a $2.5 million RBF grant. Today's college, the second largest school of its kind in the country, enrolls more than a thousand students under the auspices of the New York Institute of Technology. Buildings named for Nelson Rockefeller and Ken Riland give evidence of Nelson's tenacity and to a talent for manipulation undiminished in the half century since a Dartmouth undergraduate, class of 1930, maneuvered his father into buying him a car much as Tom Sawyer glamorized fence painting.

5

HAVING NO NEED for a Washington residence, in the fall of 1977 Nelson put his Foxhall Road estate on the market. Listing the property, long coveted by developers, did not sit well with neighbors who feared the resulting loss of green space. A group of local residents appealed to Laurance Rockefeller as the family conservationist. He listened politely to the petitioners, acknowledging the merit of their environmental concerns. "But there is one factor you have left out of the equation," he observed dryly. "My brother needs the money." Like his father in the depressed 1930s, Nelson was not immune to the dismal economic currents of 1970s America, as inflation swelled the costs of maintaining Pocantico and his other homes, a lackluster stock market squeezed existing capital, and changes in tax law redefined the philanthropic landscape. Nelson's later years would be dogged by financial issues; at one point, he owed his trust $10 million. In 1978, the Foxhall Road estate sold for $5.5 million. (After his death, the thirty-room house was purchased separately for $750,000 by the Sargent Shrivers.) That same year, Nelson put his Seal Harbor summer home up for sale, with an asking price of $1 million. He unloaded one floor of his Fifth Avenue triplex, leaving him, Happy, and the boys to get along with twenty-two rooms. The need to replenish his personal fortune, no less than to regenerate the family's wealth, inspired both the downsizing and the launch of a characteristically audacious business venture. When CBS president Arthur Taylor, the latest would-be successor to fall afoul of network chairman Bill Paley, was forced out by his onetime mentor, it didn't take long for Taylor to be awakened by an early morning phone call.

"Art, have you taken another position?"

"Nelson, it's eight o'clock in the morning. I resigned at noon yesterday. I haven't taken one."

After inviting the newly unemployed broadcast executive to lunch with him and George Woods, Rockefeller signed off cheerily, "The new company's coming into being today at two o'clock." He was off by one hour. Over lunch at the West Fifty-fourth Street Clubhouse, the SARABAM Corporation took shape—"a typical Nelson Rockefeller operation," in Taylor's characterization. "Nelson was chairman, George was chairman of the executive committee. I was president. Funding was coming in, telexes going out." Described as "the development bank to end all development banks," SARABAM was conceived by Nelson as a partnership between the Rockefellers and the Saudi Arabian royal family. Together they would recycle billions of Western petrodollars to advance economic development in the Middle East, Africa, and Latin America. As explained by Arthur Taylor, the Saudis "wanted to stop the dole to their neighbors and they wanted an experienced group of people to supervise the reconstruction of those societies."

Envisioned as an alternative to the World Bank under Robert McNamara, SARABAM bore more than a passing resemblance to Nelson's postwar attempts to combine profit with philanthropy in Latin America. Indeed, SARABAM was IBEC by another name, with vastly wealthier investors and more tangible rewards for the Rockefellers as a family. So ran the theory. In practice, Nelson's closest relations, beginning with his brother Laurance, wanted nothing to do with the House of Saud. Nelson charged ahead anyway. In March 1977, he traveled to the Middle East with his SARABAM cofounders. In Jerusalem, they toured the Old City's Jewish Quarter with Mayor Teddy Kollek. Introducing himself as "a former politician," Rockefeller couldn't resist signing autographs or making an impromptu speech from a balcony near a Crusader ruin. Snapping endless photos, he asked one man on the street to pose for his camera because "you look like Barry Goldwater." Nelson had private talks with current and former Israeli leaders, including Yitzhak Rabin and Golda Meir. One evening, Rockefeller and Egyptian president Anwar Sadat sat on a bench overlooking the Pyramids and bonded while talking of their respective upbringings. In Jordan, King Hussein hosted a dinner at the royal palace for the American statesman.

Unfortunately, these courtesies were unaccompanied by Arab capital. In Riyadh, the Saudi crown prince kept the visitors cooling their heels for two days. When Nelson formally proposed a $20 billion joint venture, the prince expressed his thanks, promised to consult with his royal relations, and shook hands. The meeting was over. "It may never come to anything," Rockefeller conceded of SARABAM in the spring of 1978. "You can have ideas but unless the ideas click and make sense to all concerned, they remain just ideas." Though an economic failure, SARABAM served a useful purpose in helping Rockefeller transition to life after politics. This was largely because of George Woods. According to Arthur Taylor, the man Nelson called "Woodsy" was far more than a financial adviser. In the 1930s, Woods had assisted Rockefeller in filling the RCA building with commercial tenants. Now, consoling a friend who had yet to put the disappointments of the vice presidency behind him, "George was sort of talking Nelson into a view of himself, a view that although he did not achieve everything he wanted to achieve, he still was a historic figure."

The year 1978 was a definite improvement over its predecessor—"a rebuilding year," to Dick Parsons. Steven Rockefeller agreed. "In the last years of Father's life we had something of a reconciliation. I had gone my own way and was settling into an academic career that I found very rewarding. I was also beginning training in Zen and learning the art of letting go." Nelson got the message. "He stopped trying to impose his will on the family," says Parsons. "He retooled his approach and began to reconnect with people in the family on a less threatening basis." Parsons, who was being groomed to succeed Louis Lefkowitz as New York's attorney general, opted instead to enter private practice and spend more time with his young children. "And he looked at me," Parsons was to recall, "and he said, 'You're right.' He used to tell me what he had learned between his first family and second—you have to make time for your kids." In Rockefeller's case, that included fourteen grandchildren, many of them older than his two sons by Happy. After hearing boyish descriptions of campouts in the woods behind the coach barn at Pocantico, Nelson accepted an invitation to attend the next gathering. He showed his appreciation for the grilled hot dogs and fireside chat by hosting the entire group at his Venezuela ranch.

Reconciling himself to the fact he would never be president didn't immunize Rockefeller from regrets. "If only I did it the way Carter did it," he reflected after the Georgian's election. As economic and diplomatic challenges took their toll on Carter's poll numbers, Nelson reprimanded Joe Canzeri for mocking the man in the Oval Office. "Jimmy Carter is our president. I don't care whether you think he's good or bad . . . I don't ever want to hear you criticize him on my behalf." With the national GOP veering right, Rockefeller himself was increasingly relegated to the sidelines. Even in New York his influence declined along with his public profile. Plans to secure the 1978 Republican gubernatorial nomination for his protégé Dick Rosenbaum never got off the ground.

Riding in a helicopter bound for Pocantico one day that spring, Nelson brandished a newspaper clipping that quoted Brooklyn's Republican county chairman George Clark. A strong supporter of Ronald Reagan, Clark made it clear that Rockefeller could no longer expect to dictate Republican policies or candidates. Nelson smiled beatifically as the paper was handed back to him. "He simply does not understand how happy he has made me." Holding out his palms, the retired politician slammed shut an imaginary book. "That is my checkbook closing," he announced with a flourish. "If he does not want my support, so be it."

Although he and his brothers continued to have their disagreements, especially over the future of Kykuit as what John disparagingly called "a monument to Nelson," the bitter animosities of 1977 were replaced by a more civil tone. In January, Nelson attended the inauguration of his nephew Jay as governor of West Virginia. When a Russian-backed coup in Afghanistan prevented him from visiting the country with Happy, no one expressed greater concern for their safe return from the region than John. His note welcoming them home included thanks for a floral arrangement sent by the couple after John's long postponed ankle operation. The eldest Rockefeller brother wasn't sufficiently recovered to attend Nelson's seventieth birthday party, staged by Happy on May 27 as a simultaneous commemoration of their fifteenth wedding anniversary.* However, David and Laurance were on hand, joined by Gerald Ford, three governors of New York, the Bob Hopes, Danny Kayes, William Buckleys, Walter Annenbergs, Rupert Murdochs, Telly Savalas, Pierre Trudeau, and Barbara Walters. By the estimate of one partygoer, Nelson danced with no fewer than fourteen former girlfriends in the course of the evening. Away from the dance floor, he conducted tours of the big house, identifying well-loved artworks and showing off his vintage automobile collection. In the course of the evening, Laurance spoke movingly of his brother's lifelong ability "to be both statesman and artist. To endlessly bring order out of chaos—whether it be within the Family, the State, the Nation, or the World itself!"

Insisting, "I'm at the stage in life where nothing bothers me," Rockefeller sloughed off criticism of a second business venture, the by-product of five lavishly produced art books for which he had contracted with Alfred A. Knopf. *Masterpieces of Primitive Art*, set for release in October 1978, was already drawing rave notices. Companion volumes on modern and Mexican folk art were in the works, as was a book on architecture to be coauthored with Wally Harrison,

---

* Asked if his gift to Happy of a $33,000 Rolls-Royce for use in getting about the Pocantico estate wasn't extravagant, Nelson was unapologetic. "Well, you know, we're getting along. It's time to have a little fun." *New York Times*, January 28, 1979.

and another drawing on Nelson's experiences as a collector. Encouraged by the early response, he broadened the venture to include additional authors and subjects. He pondered a line of art-related books for young people. But it was a more prosaic—some said tacky—Rockefeller publication, specifically the five-hundred-thousand-copy run of a mail-order catalog promoting the Nelson Rockefeller Collection, that set tongues wagging among New York's art establishment. For $175 a plate, one could eat off a replica of Nelson's favorite Meissen dinner service. Twelve hundred dollars bought a faithfully reproduced Giacometti lamp from the living room of 812 Fifth Avenue. There were faux eighteenth-century candlesticks ($950 a pair); a sharkskin coffee table ($2,100); and Picasso's *Girl with a Mandolin*, framed in the newly devised Cibachrome process and available to any mail-order client for $850.

Arbiters of taste shuddered in revulsion. "That's just sad," says one. "You can't imagine why he did it." To be sure, "he had Picasso do some tapestries, but they were under Picasso's general purview, so you can say the hand of the artist is there somewhere. I mean, the Metropolitan Museum made copies of stuff and sells it in their thing. But that doesn't make it right for Nelson Rockefeller to be doing it. . . . You know, that's like, who cares? The game is over." Nonsense, replied Rockefeller, reveling in the controversy and no doubt grateful for the attention. "Five years from now this is going to be just as accepted as Beethoven's symphony on a recording to be played in your home." Bob Armao comes closer than either to explaining Nelson's decision to go into trade. "Makework," he concludes of the art reproduction business, in which Rockefeller invested $3.5 million. Armao tells of a Texas socialite who called him up one day and said she was in New York and would love to see the Rockefeller Collection, as would her traveling companion—"first cousin of the king of Bulgaria." They made arrangements to meet for lunch, before going to the temporary showroom on Fifty-seventh Street.

"So with that the governor came out of his office. 'What's going on?' I said, 'Governor, I'm going to try to sell antiques today . . . I've got Judy Gruff of Texas and the Countess of So-and-so.' He laughed, said, 'What time you going?'" After lunch, Armao appeared at the store with his out-of-town visitors, one of them wearing a 1950 vintage mink coat and an ice-cube-sized diamond. "She looked just like Gloria Swanson in *Sunset Boulevard*." Rockefeller proved the most seductive of salesmen. As Armao presented his minor Texan royalty, "He looks at her, took her hand—she had never met him before. He said, 'Oil?' Then he greeted the countess . . . he practically sold them the whole place. Still had the touch. Here we are, reduced to selling reproductions, the two of us working Fifty-seventh Street like yard salesmen. He got a kick out of it."

6

T O ANYONE WHO would listen, Nelson proclaimed his intention to live to a hundred, thereby surpassing even Senior's longevity record. He installed an elevator and a ramp in the low-slung Japanese House built for life after Kykuit, telling Joe Canzeri, "This is where you can push me up in my wheelchair when I get old." His credibility on the subject was undercut by cholesterol-heavy breakfasts—creamed chestnuts was a lifelong favorite—and a more sedentary lifestyle. "He stopped moving," says Happy Rockefeller. "He stopped exercising. And he used to be very rapid on his feet." His weight ballooned to a record 220 pounds. Old friends detected a loss of vitality, the source of which was not hard to trace. "It was over," says Canzeri. "He had had his last hurrah." Rockefeller himself said as much when, pondering the miscarriage of his presidential hopes, he characterized his life as a failure. "He spent the longest time ever up in Maine that summer," Happy recalls. "He knew, I swear to you, he knew." And what did she know? "I saw enough to know that things weren't right." Nelson's habit of rubbing his arm was a stoic's response to the angina pains caused by a failing heart. But there was only so much that could be done to mask his growing vulnerability. "We used to always take a path down to the Japanese gardens," remembers Joe Canzeri. "The last three or four months, he used to say, 'Joe, would you mind walking up and getting the car and coming back down with it. I had a rough week and I don't want to walk up that hill.'"

Happy persuaded Nelson to see her doctor, Ernest Esakof, who prescribed blood-thinning medication and put him on a diet. If his patient were anyone but Nelson Rockefeller, said Esakof, he would have ordered him to bed immediately for prolonged rest. This wasn't an option for Nelson, to whom claims of ill health were signs of weakness. Happy also reached out to Hugh Carey, the state's Democratic governor then locked in a tough reelection fight with Perry Duryea. Five weeks before Election Day, Carey announced the renaming of Albany's South Mall as the Nelson A. Rockefeller Empire State Plaza. On October 6, as the former and current governors publicly lavished praise on each other, it was said that the sound of brass balls clanking could be heard across the Hudson in Troy. "My God, it's beautiful," Rockefeller murmured as he took in the finished complex for the first and final time. "It's all come together." More than one hatchet was buried that day, as Nelson insisted on bringing along Robert Moses to see his completed monument. Duryea's presence went all but unnoticed.

Deliberately absenting himself from the campaign trail, at the end of October Nelson invited his eldest daughter, Ann, to join him for an impromptu weekend in Mexico coinciding with the country's colorful Day of the Dead observances. For three days he reconnected with a cherished culture, sampling local foods, haggling in open-air markets over black pottery, clay whistles, pungent wreaths of garlic—even an ox yoke whose lines he found pleasing. The attendant buying spree added considerably to his existing cache of Mexican folk art. More important, it restored a measure of joy to his emotional repertoire. After his death, Ann Rockefeller Roberts bought her father's entire collection, some three thousand pieces, from his estate. She donated five hundred objects to San Francisco's Mexican Museum and with the rest established an $11 million Latin American folk art museum in downtown San Antonio. Thus Nelson and his vocation, yet another cultural inheritance from his mother, were commemorated on a scale befitting Abby's shrine at Colonial Williamsburg.

Even before his Mexican adventure, thoughts of mortality had supplanted family acrimony. On July 20, John 3rd died instantly when a car driven by his secretary collided with a vehicle speeding out of control on an estate road. The day before her husband's funeral, Blanchette Rockefeller, accompanied by her sister-in-law Tod, visited the private cemetery where the Rockefellers memorialized their dead. At her request, Joe Canzeri promised to install a flowering dogwood tree in time for the obsequies. The two women headed for their car. Suddenly Tod halted. She turned around and made her way back to where Canzeri stood. "Mr. Canzeri, I've heard about you," she told him. "Believe me, I know how hard it is to work with this crowd." At the memorial service for his father, Jay Rockefeller spoke for the entire family. If Nelson took this as an affront, it was as nothing compared with his resentment over John's failure to include in his will a promised $5 million bequest to help fund the preservation of Kykuit for future visitors. The convoluted tale of how, a dozen years later, this objective finally came to pass more properly belongs to another narrative. Suffice it to say that it never would have happened but for the generosity and patience of surviving brothers Laurance and David, as well as the Rockefeller Brothers Fund.

Another separation marred Nelson's final months, rupturing a friendship of almost fifty years. As previously indicated, he had agreed to coauthor with Wally Harrison a book detailing their architectural partnership, from Rockefeller Center to Albany's South Mall. Conversations were taped, chapters outlined. Then, somewhere in the process of reclaiming their shared past, the two men had a falling-out. "Nelson isn't talking to me anymore," Harrison confided to friends. Professional jealousy played a part in their estrangement, as Harrison resented Rockefeller for switching his patronage to Philip Johnson. Thereafter he became a poignant sight, sitting by himself in the Rainbow Room, which was converted each noon into a lunch club for Rockefellers and their guests. Upset as he was over the breach, Harrison maintained a stoic front, or tried to, until one day when he spied Al Marshall entering the room and his emotions boiled over. Rising from his table, a teary-eyed Harrison confronted Marshall with a query as blunt as it was self-revealing.

"Did you tell Nelson that my buildings on Sixth Avenue look like brick shit-houses?"

Marshall denied making any such comment. The rage on Harrison's face was eclipsed by a look of recognition.

"Then it must have been that bitch Megan."

Harrison's unflattering estimate was shared by co-workers to whom Marshack seemed at once imperious and inseparable from Rockefeller. "She had a desk right outside his office," says one Room 5600 employee. "You had to go through her in order to see him." But it was her emotional proximity that came through in an interview granted a hometown newspaper in mid-January 1979. Even Marshack's harshest detractors conceded the warmth in her voice when she spoke of Nelson. "He wears us all out," she said of her septuagenarian employer, "the most caring man and considerate boss I've met." Acknowledging that the demands of her job left little time for anything else, privately she complained about being on "twenty-four-hour call"—a lament heard from countless Rockefeller retainers over the years. For all the resentment she generated, few questioned Marshack's dedication to the task of producing Rockefeller's art books on a schedule accelerated to meet his demands. Supervising a staff of six, she was reportedly paid $60,000 in salary, supplemented by an unlimited expense account, plus antiques and art with which to furnish an eighth-floor apartment in the Regent, a posh cooperative building at 25 West Fifty-fourth Street, separated only by the 1930s Rockefeller Apartments from the twin townhouses at 13 and 15 West Fifty-fourth that served as Nelson's Clubhouse and former home to his Museum of Primitive Art. Her purchase of the unit, facilitated by a $45,000 Rockefeller loan later forgiven in his will, was handled by Bill Ronan's real estate broker wife.

Rockefeller became a regular visitor. "He always carried a briefcase, and he would always send flowers before he arrived," a neighbor told the *New York Daily News*. "He seemed stooped, and his hands shook, and sometimes he looked as though he had trouble holding his eyes open," according to another resident. "But he was always polite." Marshack was invited to Pocantico, where she was given horseback-riding lessons with an English saddle. Press reports, some based on claims by admitted enemies, had her ordering household staff around as if she were Mrs. Rockefeller. None of this quelled speculation at the time of Nelson's death that Megan had been covering for someone else. Sophistication, breeding, and, above all, discretion were hallmarks of the Rockefeller Woman. These were not qualities that leapt to mind when thinking of Megan Marshack, who was known to appear in Room 5600 wearing army boots and spraying the air with profanities. To Rockefeller insiders, this simply confirmed Nelson's twilight disregard for appearances. "Never once did I see anything flaunted until the last one," claims Joe Canzeri. "And the reason the last one was—it was all over . . . he got a little reckless. He said, 'Screw it, I'm going to be me. I'm not going to do the things anymore I have to do.'" One frequent visitor to Fifty-fourth Street watched on several occasions as Rockefeller left a meeting without explanation, only to return an hour later, muttering, "I'm not as young as I used to be." Few were in doubt as to how he had passed the intervening time.

Evelyn Cunningham, in what was to be their last encounter, found an undiminished enthusiasm for ideas—in this case, an imagined mobile art gallery for Harlem. "He was really preoccupied with the African art that he had, and the fact that the people who would be most interested would never see it." Rockefeller's excitement did not conceal his obsession with growing old—too old for the presidency, but not, it appeared, for other pursuits. "What does an old man do?" asks Cunningham. "He finds a young broad, you know, to prove something. Almost hoping to get caught." That was how she explained the Rockefeller-Marshack pairing: an elderly suitor, powerless despite his wealth to stop the clock or compensate for thwarted ambition, matched to a Rubenesque young woman adept at flattery and acquisition. Cunningham left Room 5600 feeling at once energized and sad. "This poor man has nothing to do," she thought, "to spend time with me on a nothing kind of thing." Taking to heart his late brother's warning about time running out, Nelson moved that year's Christmas party for Room 5600 employees to Pocantico. For many in attendance, it was their first direct exposure to Kykuit. Inside the big house, he arranged for the older generation to greet their guests, while at the nearby Playhouse the Cousins did the honors. Even this bit of hospitality taxed his fading strength. At one point in the afternoon, an ashen-faced Nelson took a seat and asked for sherry, more stimulative than his customary Dubonnet.*

Rare was the Pocantico weekend that Rockefeller didn't survey his extensive property, in a golf cart or Mustang convertible, while simultaneously calling Joe Canzeri's attention to an errant shrub or footpath in need of widening. So when the local paper reported discovery of a body just outside the estate perimeter near the village of Pleasantville, it prompted the inevitable query: "Joe, do we have contingency plans in case it was on *our* side of the fence?"

---

* On this same occasion, Happy Rockefeller expressed alarm over Nelson's deteriorating health, causing Laurance to "blow up" at her, the only time he ever displayed such temper in her presence. To Happy, this was proof that her brother-in-law was in denial, unable to face the prospect of losing his best friend and unwilling to admit that more aggressive measures were called for than prescribed by Ken Riland. Happy Rockefeller, AI.

"Governor," replied the unflappable Canzeri, "I guess I would just wait until you were looking the other way, and throw it back over the fence."

At this Rockefeller let out a great honk of laughter. "Joe, you're *fabulous*, just *fabulous*." Their banter foreshadowed the night in January 1979 when Canzeri's resourcefulness would be tested in ways neither man had planned for. Halfway through the month, Rockefeller returned to New York from a post-holiday break in Puerto Rico, seventeen pounds lighter since Dr. Esakof had, in effect, taken charge of his case. More perversely, Nelson had stopped taking the medication prescribed for his extra heartbeat. Cheered by initial sales of his eponymous collection, he signed a five-year lease on retail store space at 11 East Fifty-seventh Street. A formal announcement to this effect was prepared for a major antiques conference on Saturday, January 27. Two years after it ended, he even appeared reconciled to his unhappy stint as vice president. Replying to a formal inquiry about the nation's second office from his friend Dick Rosenbaum, Rockefeller said he would advise a presidential veto should Congress attempt to restructure the vice presidency by legislating additional responsibilities for its occupant. As for the vice presidential selection process, it, too, should remain the exclusive prerogative of a presidential nominee *after* his nomination. "The President has enough problems to worry about in this really impossible job without having to cope with a recalcitrant or conniving Vice President at his side—which might be the case if the Vice President were chosen separately by the delegates of the party at the convention, on the basis of political expediency."

Rockefeller showed his more reflective side to Ed Kresky, one of his original program associates in Albany and a longtime champion of the New York State Council on the Arts. Late one day in January, Nelson called the Kreskys, looking for Ed's wife, Mary, another Albany veteran who more recently had been charged with the thankless task of balancing the Rockefeller books. In her absence, Nelson informed Ed that he had found a Japanese buyer willing to pay $850,000 for a Henry Moore sculpture displayed at Kykuit. Ed promised to share the good news with Mary. He couldn't help observing, however, that had it been *his* Henry Moore on the market, he would be mourning the loss. Nelson understood his feelings. He had enjoyed Moore's work every day since he bought it from the sculptor for $18,000 in 1956. "But now I have had my enjoyment out of it and it's over and I want to do other things and I decided to sell it." Noting again the handsome price he had gotten, Rockefeller concluded, "You have got to be able to turn off things . . . just turn it off." The unusually personal exchange prompted Kresky to mention some friends who had voiced admiration for the governor's seeming ability to walk away from politics without so much as a backward glance. "Well," said Rockefeller, "you've got to understand something. When you are a has-been you are a has-been. I am a has-been."

7

ROCKEFELLER MAY HAVE found it easier to shed the past because of his covert role in an unfolding drama—the race to rescue Iran's embattled shah, if not his Peacock Throne, from Islamic revolutionaries. A little more than a year had passed since Nelson joined Their Imperial Majesties in Tehran to dedicate a museum of contemporary art symbolic of the shah's Westernizing instincts. ("Never have a people gone through such a complete metamorphosis so rapidly, so smoothly, and with such little dislocation.") Their personal bonds were further strengthened when the shah employed Rockefeller assistant Bob Armao to handle his public relations in the West. Armao had his work cut out for him: by the fall of 1978, it wasn't a royal reputation he was trying to salvage, but the lives of Mohammad Reza Pahlavi and his immediate family. With the shah's days in power clearly numbered, Nelson volunteered to find him a suitable home in the United States. Inevitably, the search was entrusted to Joe Canzeri, who wasted no time in locating a spacious, secure estate on the grounds of Georgia's Callaway Gardens. The property won quick approval from the shah's representatives and the U.S. State Department. Nelson, self-professed has-been, was back at the center of events.

Unfortunately, the shah lacked Rockefeller's ability to "just turn it off." Blaming the United States for his downfall, he was in no haste to embrace his faithless ally. So he fled to Egypt, initial stop on a dismal odyssey, soon made desperate by the deposed monarch's previously undisclosed lymphatic cancer. On January 22 he left Cairo for Morocco, unaware that his strongest American advocate had less than a week to live. Even as the shah took to the road, Nelson was preparing for his own, less dramatic change of scene. The weekend before he died, he joined Happy and the boys in transferring family photo albums and other personal items from Kykuit to the recently completed Japanese House. Included was the dual portrait inscribed, "Dearest Happy, Here's to your 50th and time for us to really enjoy the years ahead. With a heart full of love and appreciation for your courage and understanding and strength for the tough years behind us." Guarding the fact of his declining health as jealously as his royal counterpart, he couldn't conceal it from Happy. One night while preparing for a dinner party they were hosting at 812 Fifth Avenue, she discovered him lying down and rubbing his chest in obvious discomfort. He made light of the incident, but her fears were reinforced. A few nights later, with Happy detained in Philadelphia, Nelson invited Malinda Murphy to dine in her mother's place. In the course of the meal, as matter-of-factly as possible, he informed the startled young woman that he wasn't afraid to die. "I just don't want to leave you all."

Before Wednesday, January 24, was over, Nelson had literally put his house in order, meeting with representatives from the National Trust for Historic Preservation, to whom he had decided to bequeath his share of Kykuit. A few weeks before, he had changed his will to eliminate the $5 million each of the Brothers had agreed to donate toward an operating endowment for the estate, a vengeful act that was to cause untold complications for his survivors, not to mention the insufficiently funded trust. Republican state chairman Bernie Kilbourn wanted a private meeting with Rockefeller, who was inclined to grant the request: after all, 1980 was an election year. It appeared the old war-horse might yet return to the track, especially if he could advance the undeclared senatorial candidacy of Henry Kissinger. That evening, Nelson and Happy entertained the Bill Ronans, Laurance and Mary Rockefeller, and other close friends. Though seen in retrospect as a farewell dinner, it didn't feel mournful at the time. To the contrary, when Oscar and Françoise de la Renta proposed to reassemble at their Dominican Republic vacation home in a month's time, Nelson jumped at the idea.

On January 26, he worked a full day at Room 5600, polishing remarks for the next day's antiques conference and laboring on several book projects. With Paul Anbinder, Knopf's director of special projects, he discussed the latest addition to the publishing schedule, a volume on Abby Aldrich Rockefeller's folk art collection at Colonial Williamsburg. Megan Marshack was in and out of their morning meeting. Later she accompanied Rockefeller to a working lunch with Dorothy Miller, the legendary MoMA curator whose impact on Nelson's collecting was scarcely less profound than her influence on the museum's galleries. Back at the office, Rockefeller reviewed a contemporary art volume in the late stages of development. Bob Armao, just back from Tehran, briefed him on the migratory shah. The two men agreed to meet the next day at the Park Avenue Armory, home to the winter New York Art and Antiques Show. Around five o'clock, Nelson departed Room 5600 for the Buckley School on East Seventy-fourth Street, where he was to introduce Henry Kissinger at a benefit for the institution attended by both Nelson Jr. and Mark Rockefeller. Happy was on hand, as were the ever loyal Laurance and Mary Rockefeller, but Kissinger was running late, and Nelson had to stretch his introductory remarks. At the reception that followed, some guests, noting his pallid color, wondered if he was ill. Repeating his request from the staff Christmas party, Rockefeller asked for sherry instead of Dubonnet.

By now it was seven thirty p.m. Two hours after he had arrived at the school, Nelson left to have dinner with his family. Throughout the meal, Happy would recall, "his hand was constantly roaming his chest." When finished he rose from the table and, with Happy in earshot, telephoned Megan Marshack, requesting that she meet him at 13 West Fifty-fourth to resume work on the contemporary art book. "And as he was going out the door of the apartment, he took my hand

and he looked at me and he said, 'Happy, the boys are okay.'" He told her that he loved her. And, "It won't be long." Reminded of her earlier, disregarded warning to Laurance, Happy sensed history repeating itself. Abby Aldrich Rockefeller, whose death from a massive coronary following a picture-perfect day with her loved ones was family legend, had been much on her son's mind that Friday, and not just because of her folk art. "He'd had a great time at the Buckley School. Maybe he wanted to go the way his mother went. Who knows?" On one point, Happy was insistent. "He did not want to drop dead in that apartment in front of young Nelson and myself." It was a little before nine o'clock when Rockefeller emerged from the Fifth Avenue entrance of 812. Accompanied by his driver, Lonnie Wilcher, and security man Andrew Hoffman, he traveled the short distance to Fifty-fifth Street. Wilcher remained in the car as Rockefeller threaded the familiar passage to his Fifty-fourth Street Clubhouse.

8

THE FIRST CALL came at 11:16 p.m.
"Could I have an ambulance at 13 West . . ." The caller's voice, distraught to the brink of incoherence, trailed off. The 911 operator asked for clarification. "It's death! It's immediate, please." A more complete address being given, the female caller was connected to an emergency medical services dispatcher. In her agitation, the caller repeated the address, adding, "Immediately, please." At length it was established that she was calling from a house, not an apartment.

"Miss, calm down. What's wrong there?"

"We need an ambulance immediately."

"Now listen. Before we can send an ambulance we've got to know what we're coming for. . . . Please, what happened?"

"A dying patient. Thirteen West Fifty-fourth Street, please."

The operator extracted from the nearly hysterical caller, who never identified herself, that the victim—also unidentified—was an unconscious cardiac patient. Within two minutes, a police patrol car from the Midtown North precinct was speeding to the scene. Inside were Officers Anthony Graffeo and George Frangos. Simultaneously, the dispatcher alerted paramedics from Roosevelt Hospital on West Fifty-ninth Street—a team from the nearer St. Clare's Hospital was responding to a reported shooting at Penn Station. At Roosevelt, it was close to a change of shift when Jim Paturas, twenty-six, took the call. "Oh shit!" thought Paturas as he and his partner, Randy Huff, pulled up to 13 West Fifty-fourth. Outside the elegant brownstone they were greeted by Rockefeller's security man and driver, neither of whom was any more forthcoming than the original caller in divulging the identity of the stricken man. Paturas climbed ten or twelve steps, entered the front door, and turned right into the salon, a sort of reception area, with two bay windows and French doors leading to the parlor and adjoining dining room.

Here memories diverge, with Paturas certain there were no cops inside the house, while contemporary news accounts cite the reaction of Officer Frangos on finding Rockefeller, fully clothed in suit and tie, lying on the floor. "He was still warm," said Frangos. "His face was reddish, not kind of polka dot blotches or bluish, the way they get a little later. . . . If he was dead at all, it was just before we got there." Feeling no pulse, he and his partner started pressing on Rockefeller's chest. In addition, the scene that greeted Paturas differed significantly from the one recounted by the police. They described a room littered with papers, consistent with the editorial labors attributed to Rockefeller by his official spokesman. Paturas's eyes were drawn to the profusion of paintings and sculpture throughout the room. He glimpsed unfinished boxes of Chinese food and a bottle of Dom Pérignon. And sprawled on the floor next to the coffee table he saw an apparently lifeless man, nude, bluish in color, without pulse or respiration. The man exhibited all the signs of full cardiac arrest. He had thrown up his last meal, complicating efforts to insert a plastic oxygen tube into his lung. Traces of his vomit clung to Megan's outfit, variously described as a black evening gown and a caftan, fully zipped.

"Is this who I think it is?" asked Paturas.

"Yes," someone answered.

Within four minutes of their arrival, Paturas and Huff radioed for a backup crew from St. Clare's Hospital. In the meantime, Paturas administered oxygen and hooked up intravenous tubes. At 11:37, William McCabe and Jim Rodgers arrived from St. Clare's. They reported finding Rockefeller "clad in dark trousers, but no shoes," according to *The New York Times*. (The paper of record was at this point unaware of frantic efforts to dress the body, whose feet were too swollen for conventional footwear.) Marshack told Paturas that for five minutes before his arrival, she had been performing heart massage on the victim. As an unnamed paramedic attempted mouth-to-mouth resuscitation, a hastily deployed portable electrocardiogram unit registered no heart activity of any kind. To combat the acidosis that develops when breathing stops, sodium bicarbonate was administered at ten-minute intervals. Epinephrine, a powerful heart stimulant, was injected. A faint wave, "just above the level of chemical death," briefly disturbed the flat green line on the monitor. Another dose of epinephrine was given, along with 500 milligrams of calcium chloride, an even stronger stimulant, plus dopamine to raise blood pressure.

"Is there any chance of saving him?" Megan asked. "Please save him, help him." By now the room was becoming crowded with medical personnel and their equipment. Rockefeller security man Andrew Hoffman juggled an intravenous tube in one hand and, in the other, a walkie-talkie. Overhearing Hoffman making arrangements to move the still unidentified victim to Lenox Hill Hospital on East Seventy-seventh Street, paramedic McCabe interrupted him. They were procedurally required to go to the nearest hospital, said McCabe, in this case St. Clare's at Fifty-first Street and Eighth Avenue. Hoffman leaned over and whispered in McCabe's ear: "Don't say anything about this, but this man here is the former vice president of the United States." Momentarily stunned, McCabe told his co-workers, "We'll go to Lenox Hill." Just before midnight, a small procession made its way down the stoop of Number 13 to a waiting ambulance. This was Megan Marshack's last opportunity to escape notoriety and to spare Nelson Rockefeller's reputation. She let it pass. "The only thing that bugged me," Hugh Morrow was to say afterward, "was she didn't simply turn the whole thing over to security and get out of there." Another insider made the same point still more bluntly, asking one of those on the scene, "What the hell was in your head? You should have locked her in a closet or something."*

It didn't escape Jim Paturas's notice that police had cordoned off both ends of Fifty-fourth Street and of *every* other block as they turned left on Park Avenue and, escorted by half a dozen patrol cars with flashing lights, raced for Lenox Hill. The shriek of sirens interrupted Evelyn Cunningham's dinner with some out-of-town friends at a restaurant on Fifty-third Street.

"Boy," said Cunningham, "somebody famous is in trouble."

Ernest Esakof was at Lenox Hill to meet the ambulance at 12:06 and to crisply instruct its crew, "All right, let's not talk about this." Jim Paturas stayed with Rockefeller in the treatment room until emergency staff called code. At 12:20, Esakof made it official, pronouncing Nelson dead of a massive heart attack. Happy Rockefeller arrived five minutes later. Laurance Rockefeller was en route. So was Hugh Morrow, roused from his bed by an ABC television reporter tipped off that Rockefeller was in an ambulance bound for Lenox Hill. Morrow verified the story by calling one of Nelson's security men. Moments later he was tearing up the road from Bronxville to East Seventy-seventh Street at eighty-five miles per hour. At the hospital, Morrow found Happy, in khaki slacks and sneakers, sharing a bench with Laurance just outside the treatment room.

Presently, Bob Armao arrived. An agitated Marshack, conspicuous in her vomit-stained black dress, ran over and threw her arms around him.

---

* What this cold-blooded assessment failed to consider was the possibility that Marshack rode in the ambulance because she was in love with the dying man—a better word being "infatuated," suggests Jim Cannon.

"Oh, Bob."

The look on Happy's and Laurance's faces only added to Armao's embarrassment. Wiping away tears, Happy told him, "Nelson has gone, Bob. It's our duty to carry on. I can't tell you how much he thought about you." By the time Louis Lefkowitz appeared in the doorway, gray with grief, Armao had drifted back to Hugh Morrow. With the clock pushing one a.m., Morrow couldn't ignore the swelling ranks of news media in the hospital driveway. The beast demanded its feeding. Morrow conducted a hurried inquest. He assumed Nelson had died at home. "No," Happy corrected him, gesturing in Megan's direction. "He was with *her*." From Nelson's driver, Lonnie Wilcher, Morrow learned that Rockefeller had died at "the office." To the grieving Lonnie, that meant Fifty-fourth Street, not Room 5600. Later, this discrepancy would be cited as justification for the disastrously botched narrative Morrow was about to offer the press. That his errors involved more than honest confusion—that they were in fact designed to spare Happy and her family public humiliation—was acknowledged by Morrow himself later that week, when he told a friend, "I just thought I'd do one more thing for Nelson." What's more, "We almost got away with it."

First things first. Before dealing with the ladies and gentlemen of the press, Morrow escorted Megan out to his car. Upon returning to the emergency room, he assured Happy, "Don't worry, she's not here." Mrs. Rockefeller nodded in acknowledgment, a gesture Morrow chose to interpret as tacit approval for what he did next. Brushing aside Bob Armao's suggestion that perhaps he should wait until he had all the facts, Morrow ventured outside to announce, in solemn tones, that Nelson Rockefeller had died, alone but for a security aide, while at his desk in Room 5600. Morrow gave the time of his seizure as 10:15. Paramedics, unsuccessful in their attempts at resuscitation, had then transported the former vice president to Lenox Hill, where he was admitted at 11:15 and pronounced dead shortly before his wife reached the scene. Morrow also claimed that Nelson had no history of heart disease. Believing he had acted in accordance with the family's wishes, Morrow then drove Megan to her apartment. The seeds of another controversy were planted when Megan subsequently told an AP caller around four a.m. that Morrow was with her. Morrow denied this. On the other hand, whether then or later, he also claimed to have heard Marshack relate three separate versions of what had occurred, none of which he found credible.

His doubts were soon shared by a growing number of New Yorkers, starting with the flock of reporters and cameramen mistakenly directed to Rockefeller Center. In the post-Watergate era, it was absurd to believe that Morrow's story would not be questioned, that lips would remain sealed as commanded by Dr. Esakof, or that the city's fiercely competitive media outlets would obligingly sweep any unpleasantness under the rug. Any cover-up was doomed. Indeed, the slightest evidence of deliberate misrepresentation was sure to inflame journalistic curiosity. Already Jimmy Breslin of the *Daily News* was talking to the paramedics at Roosevelt Hospital. Anna Quindlen, Bob McFadden, and other *New York Times* reporters were probing areas of potential embarrassment. Nor was it just the New York press that scented scandal. The idea of Nelson Rockefeller alone in his office on a Friday night, toiling manfully on an art book, struck John Goldman of the *Los Angeles Times* as risible. He tested his hunch by calling a police source, whose laughing response sent Goldman scurrying to the Midtown North precinct house. There he asked to see Rockefeller's 124 card. This was a police document routinely filled out at the scene of a death or accident, describing what had happened and including the names of any witnesses.

Goldman's request produced a round of smiles from the desk officers present. Eventually it produced the desired card, which Goldman photocopied. "And it was clear he had not died in his office." The reporter hastened to Roosevelt Hospital in hopes of interviewing Jim Paturas, only to be told that Jimmy Breslin had gotten there first. It didn't matter; Goldman learned more than enough from Paturas to justify the effort. What emerged was a story as delicate as it was suggestive, one sure to involve lawyers and questions of taste. On Saturday morning, Goldman telephoned Hugh Morrow.

"Hughie, Nelson didn't die at his office. He died at 13 West Fifty-fourth."

In the background, Goldman could hear Morrow's secretary burst into tears. He had what he needed. But he still faced the challenge of constructing a narrative to be read largely between the lines. So he built his account around the paramedic Jim Paturas and his belated recognition of a celebrated patient's identity as the struggle to save Rockefeller's life played out around him. This established Megan's role as eyewitness to the drama. That she might be more could only be guessed at, based on the information available. As he neared his deadline, Goldman's phone rang. On the other end was somebody calling himself "Doc." "You don't know me, but I was Megan Marshack's journalism teacher."

"Bless you," replied Goldman.

Whatever Doc told him in the next few minutes bolstered Goldman's confidence in his reporting, as it forced Hugh Morrow into a strategic retreat. Twice that Saturday he revised his original story, moving the death scene from Rockefeller Center to 13 West Fifty-fourth Street and doubling the roster of those present to include Nelson's chauffeur. Asked whether anyone else had been in the room, an evasive Morrow replied, "Not that I know of, not that I have been able to determine." This equivocation crumbled when anonymous callers to the *Times* helpfully reported seeing a woman in a black evening dress emerge from Number 13 and get into the ambulance transporting Rockefeller to Lenox

Hill. Sunday's papers produced fresh backtracking, with Marshack unmasked as the woman in black and Morrow mistakenly giving her age as thirty-one (she was actually twenty-five). Accepting 10:15 as the approximate time of death raised an obvious question: Why had Miss Marshack waited an hour to call 911? Morrow blamed it on confusion and stress experienced by "a very shaken aide." Marshack had simply misstated the time of the attack. "I don't know," he quoted her. "I was in shock. I probably am responsible."

Reporters would have to take Morrow's word for it, since the woman at the center of the storm had left New York for an unnamed country refuge. (In a remarkable display of generosity, Happy Rockefeller conveyed word that Megan should be allowed to pay her respects "when none of the family are around" at Tarrytown's Vanderbilt Funeral Home, where her husband's body had been taken prior to cremation at the nearby Ferncliff Cemetery in Hartsdale.) By Monday, January 29, his credibility in tatters, Morrow was understandably loath to comment further. "I've been through this thing over and over," he told an AP correspondent, "and I'm tired of it." He shouldn't expect any sympathy, least of all from the lordly *Times*. Al Marshall, long retired from Nelson's court but still a source by virtue of his position at Rockefeller Center, received an angry call from a top executive at the paper. *The New York Times* did not like being lied to, he admonished Marshall. Although no practitioner of keyhole journalism, "right now we have five people working this story." In addition, the original 911 call was being subjected to electronic analysis. A life may have ended on Fifty-fourth Street, but Hugh Morrow's ordeal was just beginning.

9

MEANWHILE, THERE WERE the rituals of public mourning to observe. Much of the press coverage was suffused with a theme of unfulfilled promise. *Time* called Rockefeller "The Champ Who Never Made It." Others portrayed a Republican Hubert Humphrey, the perennial also-ran who retained his exuberance while chiding his party for its rightward drift. Journalist Max Lerner likened the dead man to a figure out of the Renaissance—"the last Venetian doge we are likely to harbor on these American shores." Political leaders weighed in with sentiments appropriate to the occasion. "He knew how to lose with grace and with enthusiasm," said Jimmy Carter. "He drank deeply of life from a full cup." William F. Buckley, Jr., conceded Rockefeller's potential greatness as a president. The *Los Angeles Times* agreed—not that he wouldn't have made mistakes, but that, "more than most public men of his time he was equipped by experience, character and outlook to hold the office he so energetically went after, but which his own party firmly and at times vindictively denied him the chance for. . . ." John Lindsay said he would miss his longtime adversary "terribly." George Meany proclaimed, with somewhat greater credibility, that the trade union movement had lost a good friend, "one who understood the problems and aspirations of working people." Presumably these included the Pocantico housekeeper who remembered how Rockefeller had inquired after her sick husband. "He had a word for everybody," she maintained, "no matter how high or low his position was." An estate groundsman agreed. "Anytime he'd see you, he'd come up and shake your hand. He'd never turn his head and try to avoid you."

The most touching reaction came from Rockefeller's widow. Leaving their Fifth Avenue apartment for Pocantico—by bleak coincidence, January 27 was Mark Rockefeller's twelfth birthday—Happy spotted reporters keeping watch across Fifth Avenue. Without removing her dark glasses, she quickly straightened, smiled faintly, and mouthed the words *He was a great guy.* Monday morning, some sixty Rockefeller family members assembled on a snow-speckled hillside a mile from Kykuit. Though sheltered by maple and pine trees, they could not escape the prying eyes of news photographers in helicopters darkening already overcast skies. "Well, he's a public figure right to the end," reflected Steven Rockefeller, "right into the ground." The Reverend Dr. Marshall Smith, pastor of the nearby Union Church, read passages from the Book of Revelations, Paul's Letters to the Corinthians and the Romans, and Psalm 121. Nelson's eldest grandchild, twenty-three-year-old Meile Rockefeller, spoke of his influence on her generation. Then young Nelson approached the sixteen-inch-high bronze urn containing his father's ashes. "Dad, we know how much you love us. We know you know how much we're going to miss you. Your spirit will live with us forever. We'll try to live up to the example you've set as a father, as a husband, as a brother, as a statesman, and as a friend. But Dad, we're not saying goodbye, but until we meet again." As he finished, Laurance Rockefeller gently took the boy's arm and remarked, "Nelson, you've spoken for all of us." Twenty-seven minutes after it began, the service concluded with the 23rd Psalm and Lord's Prayer. Each family member took a handful of earth and tossed it in after the urn.

Only once that week did Happy interrupt her seclusion. On Tuesday, January 30, she received Richard Nixon, in town to see his daughter Tricia, who was expecting a child in March. For almost two hours they reminisced, with Nixon lavishing praise on his former antagonist. It was just as well that Happy remained within Kykuit's protective embrace. Outside its gates, press coverage leading up to Friday's memorial service turned decidedly lurid. Much was made of the fact that Nelson's body was cremated a day ahead of the original schedule. Had family tradition prevailed, it would have been consigned to the flames almost immediately. Only the desire of some younger members of the family to say their goodbyes in person led to the change. Dr. Michael Baden, the New York City medical examiner, was besieged with accusations masked as questions. Why had he allowed the cremation to go forward? Why was no autopsy conducted? Baden said he had "double-checked" with Dr. Esakof, who persuaded him that Rockefeller's death certificate accurately stated the facts. There was speculation that District Attorney Robert Morgenthau might launch his own investigation. In fact, the man nominated by Democrats to run against Rocky in 1962 *had* opened a preliminary inquiry based on information from police and unnamed "other sources." But he decided "early on," said Morgenthau, that there was no legal reason for his office to pursue the matter.

At *The New York Times*, metropolitan editor Sydney Schanberg raised the possibility of criminal negligence to justify his paper's intense focus on a story that continued to yield surprises more than a week after Rockefeller was laid to rest. On February 9, his will was made public. While the bequest to MoMA of twenty-three paintings and four pieces of sculpture might thrill curatorial staff, the public showed far more interest in the personal debts forgiven Rockefeller associates—including Megan Marshack. Two days earlier, the *Times* had produced a genuine bombshell. Utilizing state-of-the-art equipment, the police department had reevaluated recordings of the 911 call previously attributed to Marshack. Investigators now concluded that the caller was not Megan, but her friend and neighbor at 25 West Fifty-fourth Street, a thirty-six-year-old television journalist named Ponchitta Pierce. Long before she cohosted a Sunday morning WNBC program targeted at elderly viewers, Pierce had her own Rockefeller connection, having been appointed by the governor in 1968 to a study commission on news media and broadcasting. The latest revelations reportedly divided the Rockefeller family, between those who believed in a dignified silence as the best response and younger members—such as Steven Rockefeller—who publicly decried the atmosphere of secrecy that bred more questions than answers.

Amid mounting pressure from journalistic colleagues, Pierce tried to preserve both her silence and her dignity. Her prominence as an African American woman, a former network correspondent, and a frequent contributor to *McCall's* and other publications made her a victim of her own visibility. On February 10, Pierce issued a brief statement through her lawyer. Unfortunately, it did little to address the growing mystery. Pierce said that Megan had called her shortly before eleven p.m. on the night of January 26—the *Times* placed the call much earlier, around ten fifteen—to relate word of Governor Rockefeller's heart attack. She had hurriedly dressed and, at her friend's request, recruited their building doorman to summon the governor's chauffeur. On entering Number 13, Pierce observed Rockefeller "lying on a couch. I saw no one other than Megan and Governor Rockefeller in that room. Megan was administering mouth-to-mouth resuscitation. It seemed to me the best thing I could do was to call 911 [and] shortly after I made the 911 call I left." Walking back to her apartment, Pierce directed an approaching police car to the Rockefeller townhouse. She intended to say nothing more about the incident, Pierce concluded.

Why Pierce, a professional journalist, would leave her friend in such straits—not to mention Rockefeller, of whose condition at the time she professed ignorance—left many to scratch their heads. At the time, the potentially explosive introduction of a second woman into the story was attributed to "a Rockefeller family source." Another such source, interviewed a few years later for a Rockefeller biography that never materialized, would offer a possible rationale for Pierce's curious detachment. Careful analysis of the 911 call revealed striking informational gaps on the part of the caller. She seemed disoriented, unaware of her surroundings, unacquainted with the street address of the Rockefeller townhouse, and unable to provide a telephone number without turning to Marshack for the information. Moreover, she offered within the space of a brief call differing scenarios for what was transpiring around her—announcing at the outset, in evident distress, "It's death. It's immediate, please," and scarcely a minute later telling the emergency medical services operator, "It's a dying patient."

For all practical purposes, the police concluded, the call was made by two women, possibly from a pay phone deliberately chosen because the callers believed it would be harder to trace. This made sense given Rockefeller's lifelong fascination with clandestine operations. As coordinator of inter-American affairs in wartime Washington, keenly aware of the ease with which telephone messages could be traced or tapped, he had regularly employed the FBI to sweep his office and home phones for possible listening devices. In later years, candidate Rockefeller had hotels vetted for their electronic privacy. Under the circumstances, it would have been surprising had he failed to share his concerns with Marshack. In an interview with the author three years before his death in November 2004, Joe Canzeri declined to share details of Rockefeller's passing, though he dropped clues, identifying himself as one of three people who knew what happened on West Fifty-fourth Street that long-ago winter's night. And while the curtain of silence shielded the family from potentially embarrassing disclosures, it also sparked even wilder speculation. More recently, the fact that both women, and virtually everyone else who played a part in the drama of Rockefeller's final hours, have maintained radio silence for thirty-five years has done nothing to quash doubts surrounding this coldest of cold cases.

Fortunately, a variety of freshly plumbed archives and newly deposed witnesses can help to clear the fog. In his invaluable memoir, *The Imperial Rocke-*

feller, published in 1982, Joseph Persico eschewed graphic sensation for "just the facts" chronology. Persico's research notes, housed with the rest of his papers at SUNY's Albany campus, reveal just how much restraint he practiced in resisting the voyeuristic urge. They also corroborate what Marshack herself told a subsequent lover, the cartoonist Charles Addams, another neighbor at 25 West Fifty-fourth Street, who claimed to have bedded the suddenly notorious young woman the day after Nelson's death—"fast work, even for you," a female friend told the famously randy Addams. (Thereafter, according to his biographer, Linda H. Davis, Addams took macabre pleasure in recounting for listeners Marshack's frustrated efforts to get Nelson's shoes on his swollen feet.) The same notes, clearly reflecting the input of Hugh Morrow, make reference to the young woman's attempts at CPR. "She didn't act for 40–50 minutes," they read, noting a bit later, "She had to dress him up."

Enter Joe Canzeri. Publicly, he always maintained that he was in the country that night, where he learned of Rockefeller's death in a phone call from Laurance. He told a different story to trusted friends, describing a late night foray to Fifty-fourth Street and a rushed effort to re-dress the corpse. Later in the week, a grieving Canzeri, his tongue loosened by alcohol, told radio executive Bill O'Shaughnessy how Nelson's death *should* have been handled. Left to his own devices, said this preeminent fixer, he would have deposited the dead man in a taxicab, explaining to the driver that "my friend's had too much to drink." Escaping the jurisdiction of the New York City medical examiner, he would head straight to Westchester County, "where we had a little heft."*

Canzeri's comments matter, for the light they shed on the most enduring—and only historically significant—mystery surrounding Rockefeller's death. Did Nelson Rockefeller die instantly, from a burst heart, or needlessly, from a fatal concern for appearances? We may never know for sure. But the observations of Joe Canzeri, no less than the frantic efforts of paramedics to bring Rockefeller back from the dead, are consistent with Dr. Esakof's diagnosis of a massive unsurvivable coronary. Nelson had his mother's death, eerily enough in the same house where she had given birth to three of his siblings. Unless, that is, one accepts the claim that he died not in his townhouse at 13 West Fifty-fourth, but three doors down the street at Number 25. So asserted military historian Trumbull Higgins, a lifelong New Yorker who related to a colleague residing in the same building what he was told by two cops enrolled in a class he taught at

---

* The possibility of a state funeral for Rockefeller had occurred to the nation's congressional leadership. Jim Cannon, then working for Senate minority leader Howard Baker, was delegated to learn the family's wishes, in particular how they felt about having the former vice president lie in state in the Capitol Rotunda. On Saturday, Cannon was told to stand by. The next day, Canzeri called him back. They had best forget the Rotunda, said Canzeri. "He died in the saddle, in Megan's arms." Jim Cannon, AI.

John Jay College. One night the men offered Higgins a ride home. Approaching Fifty-fourth Street, they began to reminisce, sharing some highly personal memories of January 26, 1979, when they had been directed to the tony cooperative near Rockefeller's townhouse. There they had discovered his lifeless body in surroundings hardly compatible with his status in life. Hastily they dressed the dead man as best they could—all except for his shoes, which they could not get on his swollen feet. The officers then transported the former vice president of the United States the short distance to his neighboring residence. Later, they claimed, they were called back to the house, as if for the first time.

At first blush the tale sounds incredible, except that it is backed up by half a dozen current and former residents of Marshack's building who spoke to Rockefeller biographer Cary Reich or the present author. Moreover, this is not the first time an author has suggested in print that Rockefeller died somewhere other than his Fifty-fourth Street retreat. Richard Rosenbaum, in his unjustly overlooked memoir, *No Room for Democracy*, says of that night that "the governor was with his mistress in her Manhattan apartment. During the fatal heart attack she panicked and froze." (Rosenbaum based this claim, he says, on information gleaned from Hugh Morrow "and others.") Something else died that night, as the establishment press discarded traditional notions of privacy and keyhole journalism was redefined as the public's right to know. Countless political careers, from Gary Hart's to Anthony Weiner's, would not survive the ensuing culture of total disclosure. This, too, would become part of Nelson Rockefeller's legacy, and that of the ambitious woman who had dreamed of a career in journalism as her escape route from the Hollywood hills.

10

FRESH OFF BURYING his friend and patron, Joe Canzeri received his instructions for Rockefeller's memorial service. "Joe, this is your last advance for Nelson," Happy told him, "and I don't want anybody walking out of that church in tears." On Friday, February 2, twenty-two hundred mourners fought a bitter wind off the Hudson to fill Junior's industrial age Chartres. In the front row of pews, Jimmy Carter gently patted Happy's hand. Nearby sat Gerald Ford, tears streaking his face. They were joined by the chief justice and vice president of the United States, forty U.S. senators, and an even larger delegation of House members. The secretary-general of the United Nations was there, backed by representatives from forty-four nations. So were the widows of Lyndon Johnson, Hubert Humphrey, Robert Kennedy, and Martin Luther King, Jr. Mayors Koch, Lindsay, and Wagner sat together. A retired Pocantico houseman came down from the Berkshires for the invitation-only service. Agnes Roosa was there in place of her late husband, for fifty years a house carpenter on the estate. Roosa brought her own memories of playing baseball with Nelson as a boy. The American Brass Quintet was performing a prelude when Barry Goldwater, virtually unnoticed, slipped into a back pew.

Senior minister William Sloane Coffin presided over the seventy-five-minute program, customized to include favorite hymns ("A Mighty Fortress Is Our God") and performers such as Metropolitan Opera star Roberta Peters. Rising to the occasion, Henry Kissinger in his eulogy captured the contradictions of a man who loved caviar and hot dogs alike, "ebullient yet withdrawn, gregarious and lonely, joyful and driven." Kissinger credited Nelson with devising a policy agenda that was left to other men to implement. He acknowledged doubts in a leader "never quite sure that he had done enough to fulfill the moral obligations of his inheritance." Yet whatever inadequacies disturbed his Baptist conscience, they never diminished his view of American exceptionalism. Likening Rockefeller's role in American society to America's role in the world, Kissinger thought both "uniquely strong . . . idealistic, and a little inarticulate." Even at this time of reflection, Rockefeller would not want his countrymen to look back, much less be afraid or ashamed of their strength. It was not a burden but a blessing from God, conferring opportunities "to oppose tyranny, to defend the free, to lift up the poor, to give hope to the disadvantaged, and to walk truly in the paths of justice and compassion."

Later in the service, David and Rodman Rockefeller offered their own tributes. But the most moving words were spoken by Rockefeller's daughter Ann. She began by quoting Walt Whitman's poem "Excelsior," an unabashed celebration of self whose title doubles as New York State's motto. Of her father, said Ann, "He was what he was—exuberant, energetic, extravagant." To be the child of such a man was not always easy, Ann told mourners bathed in the murky colors filtered through February's stained glass, "but he filled our lives with excitement and he challenged us to reach beyond our grasp." Sitting in the second row, her son Steven beside her, Tod Rockefeller brushed away a tear as Ann remembered learning foreign languages during playtime; hanging pictures as a continuing exercise in art appreciation; and Nelson's insistence that his children assist in building a chicken coop or garden wall, "so as to learn the use of our hands and the dignity of work." She confided to feelings of surprise on seeing her father in his casket. He appeared so much smaller than remembered by Ann and her children. She thought she knew why. "The vibrant spirit that gave power to his presence was gone. To Father, life was meant to be lived. As we leave this church today, he would want us to get on with it—to go forward, to take our lives in our hands fully and joyfully, as he did."

The Reverend Martin Luther King, Sr.—Daddy King—offered a closing prayer, the one aspect of the service requested by Nelson in life. Then Reverend Coffin regained the pulpit. "The recessional is a bit unusual," he told the audience, hardly concealing his disapproval. "Rocky liked it." And with that, Lionel Hampton and his five-piece jazz band performed a rousing vibraphone rendition of "Sweet Georgia Brown," the toe-tapping anthem Nelson always used as his exit music.

11

ON FEBRUARY 14, ROCKEFELLER'S four surviving children from his first marriage sought to put the controversy over their father's death to rest. In a joint statement, they "accepted" Dr. Esakof's diagnosis of a massive heart attack and expressed satisfaction that Marshack "did her best" to save him. The same communication acknowledged errors in reporting, for which the younger Rockefellers conveyed regret. They singled out for gratitude Ponchitta Pierce.

To point out only the most obvious incongruity to emerge from the varying accounts cited here, why transport a clothed body from 25 to 13 West Fifty-fourth Street, only to have it discovered unclothed by paramedics? It's pure surmise, but if the corpse needed to be re-dressed, the process might have been interrupted by the arrival of Jim Paturas and other paramedics.

His professional credibility destroyed, Hugh Morrow was largely disowned by the Rockefellers (just as Joe Canzeri lost his Pocantico house and Nelson's two swimming pools and other modifications to the estate were undone). Morrow was pensioned off with an oral history project preserving memories of Nelson for unborn historians to puzzle over. Eventually he came to interview Blanchette Rockefeller, the widow of John 3rd and for many years a highly regarded successor to Nelson as president of MoMA. Near the end of their session, Blanchette offered a candid appraisal of the differences between her late husband and his controlling, endlessly creative younger brother. "Well, we miss them both," she told Morrow with a sigh, "but it is a lot more peaceful."

Acknowledgments

No author incurs more debts than a biographer or historian, drawing on the scholarship of his predecessors to inform, modify, and advance his own work. These obligations are necessarily magnified over fourteen years of research, writing, and rewriting. To cite just one factor prolonging the process in the present case: my decision to discard the first seventy thousand words of an early draft once the Rockefeller Archive Center opened more than a hundred boxes of paper labeled "Family and Friends." Among the previously untapped riches to be found in this collection within a collection are scores of letters written by Mary Todhunter Clark to her future husband during the years of their courtship. Funny, sensitive, and sometimes painful to read, the correspondence materially alters the popular image of an emotionally distant patrician at home exclusively on the Main Line. Now, belatedly, Tod Rockefeller can speak for herself.

In common with everyone who has an interest in Nelson Rockefeller, I owe a special debt to the late Cary Reich. Cary's *Worlds to Conquer*, the first in a planned two-volume Rockefeller biography, remains an essential source for students of the Rockefeller years and a model of the biographer's art: exhaustively researched, elegantly written, incisive in its conclusions, and well-nigh definitive in its treatment of Rockefeller's wartime diplomacy and subsequent frustrations under Eisenhower and John Foster Dulles. Cary's tragically premature death in 1998 deprived readers of a second volume, which would have encompassed Rockefeller's governorship, his divorce and remarriage, his frustrating turn as vice president, and his unending quest to occupy the place of leadership redefined by his youthful hero Franklin D. Roosevelt.

Though I never met Cary, I recall a most revealing telephone conversation I had with him. It concerned a footnote in my 1982 biography of Thomas E. Dewey, an obscure reference at best. As I hung up the phone, marveling at such attention to detail, I thought Nelson Rockefeller was fortunate indeed to have a biographer whose industry was equaled by his integrity. Early in the course of work on this book, I made arrangements with the Reich estate to gain access to Cary's research materials. At the time I could scarcely imagine the sixty thousand pages of primary source holdings that I would accumulate on my own, many (as in "Family and Friends") unavailable to Cary. Likewise with newly conducted or opened interviews that have done much to augment the documentary record. Besides two dozens of Cary's oral histories, I relied heavily on a series of legislative summaries, each detailing a year in the Rockefeller governorship Cary was working on at the time of his death. Beyond this, I have been careful in my endnotes to identify each instance wherein I have utilized information derived from Cary's research.

This book has its genesis in a seemingly endless automobile trip across the Kansas prairie in September 1989. On the eve of Dwight D. Eisenhower's centennial year, I had been asked by the National Archives to do double duty, combining oversight of the Eisenhower Library and attendant celebrations in Abilene, Kansas, with my regular duties as director of the Herbert Hoover Library in West Branch, Iowa. It was in Abilene, at an early organizational meeting on the centennial, that I met Jim Cannon, former national political correspondent, Howard Baker's deputy in the Reagan White House, and, for the better part of an eventful decade, employed by Nelson Rockefeller as adviser, strategist, and legislative lobbyist (his greatest triumph: passage of Richard Nixon's revenue-sharing program). Later that day, the long ride from Abilene to Kansas City's airport was enlivened by Jim's Rockefeller stories. That we should have this conversational bond was less surprising than one might expect, for I had my own Rockefeller connection. Of a sort. In August 1968, an annoyingly precocious fourteen-year-old, I took my place in the Rockefeller floor demonstration marching to its doom in the Miami convention hall where that year's Republican national convention was held.

I did not know it at the time, but Richard Nixon's first ballot victory in Miami merely confirmed a party in transformation. Four years had passed since the nationally televised confrontation in San Francisco's Cow Palace that pitted Nelson Rockefeller and a fading Eastern Establishment against the forefathers of today's Tea Party. My own subsequent career as an intern in Gerald Ford's White House and a speechwriter for Massachusetts senator Edward W. Brooke dovetailed with the decline of Rockefeller Republicanism. Following Brooke's defeat for a third term in 1978, I went to work for Senator Robert Dole. A conservative stalwart when he replaced Rockefeller on the Ford ticket two years earlier, Dole would, in time, see his ideological credentials called into question as the GOP migrated ever further from its midwestern roots and center-right instincts.

After 1987, I left politics altogether for an eighteen-year stint as director of four presidential libraries, including that of Gerald Ford, with whom I enjoyed numerous conversations touching upon his vice president. I was still at the Ford Library when I began this book in the spring of 2000. The work continued throughout my tenure as director of the Robert J. Dole Institute of Politics at the University of Kansas in Lawrence and again as founding director of the Abraham Lincoln Presidential Library and Museum in Springfield, Illinois.

My thanks to everyone associated with those facilities for allowing me to balance institutional administration with scholarly/literary pursuits.

In 2006 I accepted an invitation to become a scholar-in-residence, affiliated with the History Department at George Mason University. For this I am obliged to former GMU president Alan Merten and his successor, Ángel Cabrera; also to my GMU colleagues, students, and teaching assistants such as John Garnett, who signed on for a course on the American presidency and heard far more about Peronist Argentina and the Urban Development Corporation than he had bargained for. Throughout this same period, I was fortunate to serve as C-SPAN's in-house historian. In appreciation for the opportunity to work on such long-form series as *Presidential Libraries: History Uncovered, The Contenders,* and *First Ladies: Image & Influence* and, even more, for a personal friendship spanning more than twenty years, I have dedicated this book to Brian Lamb and all those who make up the C-SPAN family—on- and off-camera. In a time when our democracy is measured by decibels, they keep their voices down and their journalistic standards up.

The modest visibility generated by my involvement with C-SPAN, plus frequent appearances on *The NewsHour with Jim Lehrer* on PBS, prompted more than a few viewers to volunteer their own Rockefeller stories.

Elizabeth Skerritt was a Rochester, New York, widow, whose vital assistance included a thirty-three-page memoir of her service on the Rockefeller staff between 1943 and 1951. I was still savoring this encounter with one of the last survivors of the wartime coordinator's office when I was introduced to Paul Kramer, a Rhodes Scholar drafted to work for Rockefeller in the tinderbox summer of 1940. Besides a written memoir, Paul had unpublished stories—the best kind—to share. Speaking of which, I never would have met him but for the intervention of Tyler Abel, who with characteristic generosity also provided me entrée to the unpublished diaries of his legendary stepfather, Drew Pearson.

Among those who were closest to Rockefeller, his widow, Happy, devoted half a day in the post-9/11 autumn of 2001 to reliving distant events, some undoubtedly painful to recall. Mrs. Rockefeller also provided me with an unforgettable tour of Kykuit and nearby Japanese House. Since then I have had occasion to speak with her sons Nelson Jr. and Mark. And while Nelson's children from his first marriage declined to participate, Steven Rockefeller was kind enough to supply me with the full transcript of a revealing interview about his father that Steve did with Hugh Morrow.

My meeting with Laurance Rockefeller in his brother's office at Room 5600 was particularly memorable. At a critical point early in the life of the project, I took encouragement from some far-ranging conversations with Ed and Mary Kresky, as well as Oscar Ruebhausen. Mary and Oscar were Nelson Rockefeller's literary executors. In truth, they were far more than such a title conveys.

They enjoyed not only the friendship but the absolute trust of a man who gave sparingly of either. Harry Albright, though plagued with uncertain health, was a consistent champion of this project from its outset. He greatly aided my efforts by committing to paper some three hundred pages of personal recollections and insights into Rockefeller as governor and vice president. Al Marshall preferred to reconstruct the past over long, gossipy lunches atop the RCA Building (to me it will always be the RCA Building). I cherish their memory, and his. Al was one of several key Rockefeller staffers who sat down for multiple interviews. Bill Ronan, Robert Douglass, and Rod Perkins—you influenced my thinking more than you will ever know.

More firsthand history came over the transom, as it were. Two of Rockefeller's more distinguished appointees, gubernatorial counsels Sol Neil Corbin and Robert MacCrate, shared extensive documentation of their efforts culminating in New York's 1965 abolition of the death penalty. James Underwood, an eminent political scientist on the faculty of Union College in Schenectady, made it possible for me to see more than a dozen unpublished interviews conducted with his coauthor, William J. Daniels, for their book, *Governor Rockefeller in New York: The Apex of Pragmatic Liberalism in the United States.* Here I would be negligent as well as ungracious if I failed to single out Robert Connery and Gerald Benjamin, whose exhaustive studies of the Rockefeller years in Albany long ago established them as leading authorities on the period. Another generous donor to my growing archive was Irwin Gellman, himself an esteemed diplomatic historian and biographer of Richard Nixon, who passed on relevant documents from the Eisenhower and Nixon libraries. He also provided copies of extensive interviews he conducted with then vice president Rockefeller in 1976.

William Ringle, for many years Gannett's star reporter in Albany, wrote several pages out of the blue that helped me to understand how journalists steeped in Empire State politics might exaggerate a first-term governor's prospects for winning his party's 1960 presidential nomination. Bryce Nelson, another distinguished journalist before he joined the faculty of the Annenberg School for Communication and Journalism at USC, permitted me to observe Attica through his eyes and in the process helped me find my way back to that remote place, the 1970s. David Harris Engel, nationally noted landscape architect, described for me what it was like working with Rockefeller to fashion a Japanese garden at Pocantico. Rick Perlstein, the author of a superb trilogy (so far) tracing the evolution of American politics and culture from Eisenhower to Reagan, shared hundreds of pages from his research files. Few scholars are so generous. Christine Ward, New York State Archivist, and her colleague Jim Folts were more than generous in tracking down photographs, as was Stuart Lehman of the state's Office of General Services.

On a more poignant note, I still grieve for Steve Neal, Illinois's premier political journalist and a close friend, who handed me his extensive Rockefeller files just a few months before he took his own life in 2004. It is no accident that the disappearance of Steve's byline coincided with a severe outbreak of bipartisan corruption in the Land of Lincoln.

In describing biography as a collaborative venture, I am particularly mindful of the repositories we all mine for the elements of human portraiture and historical recreation. Since 2000, I have made more than fifty research trips to the Rockefeller Archive Center in Sleepy Hollow, New York. As someone with more than a passing acquaintance of the archival profession, I can say without exaggeration that the RAC sets the standard for personal and intellectual hospitality. That this book didn't take more than fourteen years to complete is largely due to Amy Fitch (and, before her, to John LeGloahec). Amy's knowledge of the Rockefeller Papers is unsurpassed. But so is her eagerness to be helpful to researchers—which in my case included identifying most of the photographs that illustrate this book. My admiration for her professionalism extends to Amy's RAC co-workers Robert Battaly, Monica Blank, Michele Hitzik, Mary Ann Quinn, and Charlotte Sturm. Much of what I have learned about Nelson Rockefeller was incubated in conversations with Harold Oakhill and Tom Rosenbaum. No less helpful were RAC executive directors Darwin Stapleton and Jack Myers and their administrative brethren Charles Bradley, Camilla Harris, Kenneth Rose, Roseann Variano, and James Washington.

At the Columbia Center for Oral History Collection, I am indebted to Erica Fugger and Breanne LaCamera for their aid in expediting my requests to cite CCOHC holdings. Mark Wolfe, of the M. E. Grenander Department of Special Collections & Archives at SUNY, Albany, went out of his way to extract important documents from Joseph Persico's papers housed there. (Joe himself, giving no hint of the heart condition that took his life at the end of August 2014, was unsparingly generous with his time and shrewd comments.) At Duke University's David M. Rubenstein Rare Book Manuscript and Special Collections Library I wish to acknowledge the assistance of Janie C. Morris and Tyler Gilmore. The same holds true for Barbara L. Krieger and her colleagues in the Rauner Special Collections Library at Dartmouth College. And a special word of thanks is in order to the helpful staff at Columbia's Avery Library, stewards of Wallace Harrison's archival legacy.

Probably no one appreciates more than I do the unique value of America's presidential libraries in the study of twentieth-century government and public policy. To Lynn Bassanese and her associates at FDR, Mark Updegrove and the superb archivists at LBJ, and Elaine Didier and my former colleagues at the Ford Library, a heartfelt thanks for supplying critical documentation, often in the face of approaching deadlines. Rafe Sagalyn remains the model literary agent, his commitment to substantive books undiminished in a creative partnership that exceeds three decades. At Random House, I benefited immensely from the editing skills of the legendary Robert Loomis, succeeded in the later stages of bookmaking by Jonathan Jao (dare I say, a legend in the making?). Jonathan's intellectual rigor is contagious. He has a talent for tactfully reminding his authors that good is never good enough. Jonathan's assistant, Molly Turpin, was just as helpful in steering an unwieldy manuscript toward publication. And this is a vastly better book for the meticulous copyediting of Sona Vogel.

After typing fifty or more drafts of a 332,000-word manuscript, Linda Kay Provo will understand the difficulty I have in finding the right words to recognize her superhuman labors. Without Linda, this book would not exist. Her contributions go far beyond its physical production. For she has lived many lives, and her wisdom is on a par with her word processing. More than once in the course of my research and writing I have tapped her sage viewpoint on human relations, those between men and women and those involving parent and child. She has never steered me wrong. The same holds true for Erik Nelson, Steve Chapman, Mike Waldinger, Kasey Pipes, Bob Rapp, Ed Cheffey, Jim Strock, and Elaine Richardson, friends for life who have not hesitated to remind me that there is more to life than Nelson Rockefeller.

My final acknowledgment is unavoidably personal. A decade into this project, I was unprepared for the knock on my apartment door the evening of November 30, 2010. I opened it to reveal John McConnell, a longtime friend and sometime neighbor, whose concerned expression penetrated the fog that had for several days blurred my consciousness of time, place, and Nelson Rockefeller. As it happened, John was one of several friends in the area who had invited me to Thanksgiving dinner. After a long weekend during which none of them was able to reach me, John volunteered to make a direct approach. Whatever he saw when I opened the door convinced him that I should go to the nearest hospital as fast as he could drive me there. His instinct saved my life. Having suffered one heart attack over the holiday, I had a second on my first full day in the hospital. An accompanying swarm of blood clots made things even more precarious. Fortunately, none of the clots headed north.

That first night at the Virginia Hospital Center, my thoughts revolved mainly around my unfinished book. Inevitably I thought about Cary Reich as well. Absurdly, I wondered if there was a curse on Rockefeller biographers. Yet even then I drew inspiration from Cary's example. Whatever he didn't live to complete is dwarfed by what he contributed to our knowledge of twentieth-century America. Nothing can subtract from that, any more than time or circumstance can ever diminish my gratitude to John McConnell for making it possible for me to write these words.

Notes

A Note on Sources

Documenting the sources from which a nonfiction book derives its authenticity presents the author with a range of choices. In the case of the current volume, for example, I had to weigh the impact of well over two thousand endnotes, on an already lengthy manuscript. Given the non-academic audience to which the book is chiefly directed, I employed the same system of notation I have used in earlier books (and, coincidentally, used by Peter Johnson and John Ensor Harr in their well-regarded two-volume history of the Rockefeller family). In practical terms, this means identifying all correspondence, diary entries, and official records by author, recipient, and date generated. Armed with this information, I believe researchers should have little if any difficulty locating relevant documents in the Rockefeller Archive Center (from which the bulk of my citations are drawn). In some instances, however, where the reference may not be self-evident, or the document in question is of unusual significance, I have gone further, encasing it within the full scholarly scaffolding of collections, archival series, individual boxes, and, wherever possible, folder numbers.

His dyslexia caused Nelson Rockefeller to look on the written word with suspicion. His natural caution reinforced a reluctance to commit sensitive information to paper. While such traits don't necessarily lower the evidentiary value of Rockefeller's papers, they do increase the returns from oral history. Here the documentary record is supplemented by approximately two hundred fifty interviews, including extensive conversations with Rockefeller himself used for the first time. A full accounting follows.

Richard Norton Smith Interviews

Bess Abell, Tyler Abell, Max Abramovitz, Harry Albright, Richard Allison, R. W. Apple, Robert Armao, Betsey Ashton, Dr. Michael Baden, Herman Badillo, Doug Bailey, Fred Barnes, Robert Bennett, Steve Berger, Betty Bixby, Burdell Bixby, Joseph Boyd, Douglas Brinkley, Bill Brinton, David Broder, Hal Bruno, Pat Buchanan, Kershaw Burbank, Howard "Bo" Callaway, John Camp, Jim Cannon, Lou Cannon, Joseph Canzeri, Hugh Carey, David Cargo, Robert Caro, William Coleman, Barber Conable, Chuck Conconi, Sol Corbin, Evelyn Cunningham, Alfonse D'Amato, John Deardourff, Henry Diamond, Robert J. Dole, Robert Douglass, George Dudley, Richard Dunham, John Dunne, Daniel Evans, Betty Ford, Gerald R. Ford, John Gardner, Jack Germond, Arch Gillies, David Goldberg, John Goldman, Andrew Goodpaster, Hugh Gregg, Paul Grindle, Paul Grondahl, June Hamersma, Kitty Carlisle Hart, Robert Hartman, Mark Hatfield, Ashton Hawkins, Rod Hills, Stewart Jacobson, David Kennerly, Bill Kent, Jim Kiepper, Henry Kissinger, Ed Koch, Tom Korologos, Paul Kramer, Edward Kresky, Mary Kresky, Melvin Laird, Cynthia Lefferts, Louis Lefkowitz, Kay Lockridge, John Lomenzo, John Love, Bob MacCrate, Ron Maiorana, John Marchi, George Marlin, Jack Marsh, Al Marshall, Arthur Massolo, Frank Mauro, John McConnell, Jack McGrath, Charles Metzner, Clifford Miller, Richard Miller, Walter Mondale, Vincent J. Moore, Lance Morrow, Richard Nathan, Victoria Newhouse, Lyn Nofziger, Robert Novak, Terry O'Donnell, Robert Orben, Bill O'Shaughnessy, Richard Parsons, Jim Paturas, Roswell Perkins, Rick Perlstein, Joseph Persico, Bill Plante, Robert Price, Bob Pyle, Happy Rockefeller, Larry Rockefeller, Laurance Rockefeller, Mark Rockefeller, Nelson Rockefeller, Jr., William J. Ronan, Rona Roob, Richard Rosenbaum, Patricia Rosenfield, Dan Rostenkowski, Oscar Ruebhausen, William Rusher, Michael Scelsi, Arthur Schlesinger, Brent Scowcroft, William Scranton, John Sears, William Seidman, Raymond Shafer, Elizabeth Skerritt, Ilene Slater, Les Slote, Stuart Spencer, Linda Jamieson Storrow, Robert Sweet, Bert Teague, Larry Temple, Craig Thorne, William Timmons, Jake Underhill, William vanden Heuval, Guy Vander Jagt, Dale Volker, Peter Wallison, Lawrence Walsh, Caspar Weinberger, Clifton Wharton, Michael Whiteman, Frank Zarb.

Cary Reich Interviews

ELIZA BLISS, JOSEPH Boyd, Kershaw Burbank, Victor Condello, Bill Dietel, Pauline Faulk, Ellen Harrison, Susan Herter, Philip Johnson, Henry Kissinger, Robert M. Morgenthau, Fulton Oursler, Jr., Ron Pedersen, Fioravante Perrotta, Tom Prideaux, Happy Rockefeller, William J. Ronan, Sheldon Stark, Stanley Steingut, Jim Wallis, Nadia Williams, Ted Ziegler.

Columbia Center for Oral History Collection

SHERMAN ADAMS, WILLIAM Benton, Spruille Braden, Bernard Gladieux, Barry Goldwater, Peter Grimm, Robert Hudgens, Francis Jamieson, Mary Lasker, Sam Lubell, Warren Moscow, Cliff Roberts, Arthur Taylor, Bob Wagner, Henry Wallace, F. Clifton White. The same Columbia facility is home to a pair of interviews with Rockefeller. In 1967, he shared memories of the Eisenhower administration as part of a larger oral history project devoted to the thirty-fourth president. A much more historically significant document, to which I have given the identifying initials NRI (for "Nelson Rockefeller Interviews"), CCOHC, is Rockefeller's personal history of his experiences in the Roosevelt and Truman administrations. More than seven hundred pages long, the memoir, based on interviews conducted in 1951–52, remained sealed for almost twenty years after Rockefeller's death.

Hugh Morrow Interviews

THESE ARE DIVIDED into two categories, both housed at the Rockefeller Archive Center. The Nelson Rockefeller Oral History Project (NROH) consists of nine separate interviews Morrow conducted with Governor Rockefeller after his return to New York early in 1977. Their combined transcripts exceed five hundred pages in length. A second group of interviews (HMI), approximately seventy-five in all, was compiled by Morrow in the eighteen months following Rockefeller's death.

These include: Harry Albright, Warren Anderson, Burdell Bixby, Ted Braun, Flor Brennan, Jim Cannon, Joseph Canzeri, Jerry Danzig, J. Richardson Dilworth, George Dudley, Meade Esposito, Gus Eyssell, Jerry Finkelstein, Gerald R. Ford, John French, Berent Friele, Nancy Hanks, George Hinman, Emmet Hughes, Norman Hurd, Ed Kresky, Louis Lefkowitz, Arthur Levitt, John Lockwood, John Lomenzo, Charles Metzner, Joseph Murphy, Harry O'Donnell, Fioravante Perrotta, Joseph Persico, William Pfeiffer, W. Kenneth Riland, Laurance Rockefeller, Steven Rockefeller, Isabelle Savell, Carl Spad, Gene Spagnoli, Linda Jamieson Storrow, Ann Whitman, Malcolm Wilson.

For many years, both collections of interviews were off limits to researchers. (They were unavailable to Cary Reich, for example.) With the passage of time, however, the cause of institutional credibility has outweighed fears of potential controversy. A majority of interview transcripts generated by Morrow, and all of those directly involving Rockefeller, have now been opened for research purposes.

ABBREVIATIONS

AAR	Abby Aldrich Rockefeller
AI	Author's interview
CCOHC	Columbia Center for Oral History Collection
CRI	Cary Reich interview
DDE	Dwight D. Eisenhower
DRA	Donald Rumsfeld Archive
FDR	Franklin D. Roosevelt
FDRL	Franklin D. Roosevelt Library

GRF	Gerald R. Ford
GRFL	Gerald R. Ford Library
HMI	Hugh Morrow interviews, RAC
HSTL	Harry S. Truman Library
JDR, Jr.	John D. Rockefeller, Jr.
JDR3rd	John D. Rockefeller 3rd
JFK	John F. Kennedy
JPP	Joseph Persico Papers, State University of New York at Albany
KRD	Kenneth Riland diary, RAC
LBJ	Lyndon Baines Johnson
LBJL	Lyndon Baines Johnson Library
LSR	Laurance S. Rockefeller
MTC	Mary Todhunter Clark
MTR	Mary Todhunter Rockefeller
NAR	Nelson Aldrich Rockefeller
NHOHP	Nancy Hanks Oral History Project
NRI, CCOHC	Nelson Rockefeller Interviews, Columbia Center for Oral History Collection
NROH	Nelson Rockefeller Oral Histories, RAC
NR, PP	Governor Nelson A. Rockefeller, Public Papers
RAC	Rockefeller Archive Center
RBM	Nelson Rockefeller–Adolf Berle manuscript (unpublished)
RMN	Richard M. Nixon
RNL	Richard M. Nixon Library
WHP	Wallace Harrison Papers, Avery Library, Columbia University

Prologue: "This Is Still a Free Country, Ladies and Gentlemen"

xv **There came down upon Rockefeller** Murray Kempton, "For Nelson Rockefeller," *New York World-Telegram and Sun,* March 25, 1966.

xv **"That's your problem, not mine"** Arthur Massolo, AI; Henry Kissinger, CRI.

xv **"He is like a perfect engine"** Wallace Harrison, "Builder," draft of Rockefeller book, Box 2, Folder 8, p. 4, WHP. Housed at Columbia's Avery Library, the Wallace Harrison Papers contain extensive notes, many based on taped reminiscences for a proposed biography of his friend and collaborator. Box 16 has a dozen preliminary chapters, as well as more polished treatments of Albany's South Mall and the 1945 San Francisco Conference of the United Nations.

xvi **"You don't know my name, do you?"** David Broder, "The Paradoxical Rockefeller," *Washington Post,* January 29, 1979.

xvi **"a WASP minestrone"** Joe Canzeri, AI.

xvi **dining on whitebait** Bill O'Shaughnessy, AI.

xvi **"I only wish we knew him"** Kershaw Burbank, CRI.

xvi **"Gregarious and outgoing"** William J. Ronan, AI.

xvi **a sixteen-slice pizza pie** Canzeri, AI.

xvii **"When most politicians are in campaign mode"** R. W. Apple, AI.

xvii **"My china"** Mark Hatfield, AI.

xvii **"Aldrich skin . . . you look like you just crawled out from under a stone"** Joseph Persico, *The Imperial Rockefeller: A Biography of Nelson A. Rockefeller* (New York: Simon & Schuster, 1982), 60.

xvii **"So glad you could come"** Robert Caro, AI.

xviii **"petrified" of the printed word** NAR, interview by Hugh Morrow on dyslexia, 7, RAC (hereafter referred to as "Morrow, Dyslexia").

xviii **"I'd like to win this goddamned election without New York"** Thruston Morton interview,

October 2, 1974, Thruston B. Morton Oral History Project, Louie B. Nunn Center for Oral History, University of Kentucky Libraries, Lexington, Kentucky, 49.

xix **"He's so square"** *Newsweek,* July 20, 1964.

xix **"I don't want to stand in the middle of the road too long"** *Life,* July 24, 1964.

xix **"I just wanted to tell Senator Goldwater"** *Time,* July 24, 1964.

xxi **"Forces are at work"** Richard Harris, A Reporter at Large, "Delegate," *New Yorker,* September 12, 1964.

xxi **"A Republican National Convention"** Robert D. Novak, *The Agony of the G.O.P. 1964* (New York: Macmillan, 1965), 452.

xxi **"You're looking at it, buddy"** Stuart Spencer, AI.

xxiii **"Forget it," said Rockefeller** Ibid.

xxiii **Now, yielding to the inevitable** Ike's efforts to promote a unified party are described in David Eisenhower and Julie Nixon Eisenhower, *Going Home to Glory: A Memoir of Life with Dwight D. Eisenhower, 1961–1969* (New York: Simon & Schuster, 2011), 146.

xxiii **His disquiet is shared** Arch Gillies, AI.

xxiv **"I had a hell of a time getting past the goons"** Ronan, AI.

xxiv **Meeting the new Mrs. Rockefeller for the first time** Theodore H. White, *The Making of the President, 1964* (New York: Atheneum, 1965), 81.

xxiv **"I don't know about that"** Caspar Weinberger, AI.

xxiv **"I don't think you're ever going to be President"** Ronan, AI.

xxv **"If you're a Rockefeller"** William Rusher, AI.

xxv **"If he hit a few golf balls"** Al Marshall, AI.

xxv **"Okay. You can turn the lights back on"** Jim Cannon, AI.

xxv **"Nelson is like a polar bear"** Nick Thimmesch, "Remembering the Unrelenting Drive of Nelson Rockefeller," *Washington Post,* January 29, 1979.

xxvi **"That's what I want"** George Dudley, AI.

xxvi **"I'm not interested in what I can't do"** Bob MacCrate, AI.

xxvii **"Governor, it's a great program"** Cannon, AI.

xxvii **"There's not enough money in the world"** Rona Roob, AI.

xxvii **Asked why he hasn't simply changed** Harry Albright, *An Affectionate Portrait of Nelson A. Rockefeller by an Unabashed Admirer* (hereafter identified as "Albright, *Portrait*"). In this unpublished memoir completed not long before his death in 2008, Harry Albright, entrusted by Rockefeller with responsibility for, among other sensitive matters, the state appointments process, offered much more than the fawning assessment hinted at in his title. Although acknowledging his regard for Rockefeller, he does not spare himself, his colleagues, or, ultimately, "the Governor." The result is a uniquely revealing insider's account, more than three hundred pages in length, from someone whose affection never overrode his intellectual integrity. On pages 253–54, Albright records Rockefeller's memories of tennis matches with New Deal figures such as Henry Wallace, Rexford Tugwell, and Tommy Corcoran. Of their subsequent policy discussions, said Rockefeller, "they scared the hell out of me." Consequently, he remained a Republican hopeful of leading the GOP in a more progressive direction—a course as perilous as entering into a marriage with a partner whose flaws one expects to correct.

xxviii **"I guess I really blew it"** Spencer, AI.

xxviii **"He would rather be Nelson Rockefeller"** Robert Hartman, AI.

xxviii **"Here's five dollars"** Joseph Boyd, AI.

xxix **"They were throwing paper at him"** Ibid.

xxix **"You try to push me"** Joseph Boyd, CRI. Over the years, Boyd offered slightly different versions of this encounter, including one to the author. Ultimately, I settled on the description he provided Cary Reich as sounding more authentically Rockefeller.

xxix **"Remember he was waging war"** Doug Bailey, AI.

xxx **"You goddamned Socialist"** *New Yorker,* September 12, 1964.

xxx **"That's it. We're going to shut him off"** *Newsweek,* July 20, 1964.

xxx "Look at that. It's America up there" Novak, *Agony*, 453.

xxx "I looked down at his arm" Bailey, AI.

xxx "Turn him loose, lady, turn him loose" Jackie Robinson, *I Never Had It Made* (New York: Putnam, 1972), 170.

xxxi "He couldn't have had a happier look on his face" Hatfield, AI.

xxxi "You look like the wrath of God" Gerald Ford, HMI, 34.

xxxi Out of the question, says Rockefeller Gillies, AI. Bob Novak, in his book on the 1964 campaign, reported tentative peace feelers from the Rockefeller camp to Goldwater manager Clif White early on the final night of the San Francisco convention. White in turn was amenable to burying the hatchet. Unfortunately for the GOP, any chance of unity exploded with Goldwater's fiery acceptance speech, the text of which had been kept even from White's eyes. Novak, *Agony*, 463.

xxxii "Les, I know exactly how you feel" Les Slote, AI.

xxxii In dedicating the Vatican Pavilion Francis Cardinal Spellman–NAR, December 7, 1963, RAC.

xxxii "That's my gift" Massolo, AI.

xxxii only to find himself owing $500,000 he didn't have Albright, *Portrait*, 281. The exact amount of Rockefeller's pledge differs in the retelling. Other versions of the story peg the number at $350,000. Several former advancemen testified to Rockefeller's aversion to physical contact; his disdain for both presidential suites and police sirens was confirmed to me by Joe Boyd.

xxxiii "There's no excuse for people to have to live like that" Steve Berger, AI.

xxxiii "Red. The hangman's color" KRD, September 18, 1971.

1: The House That Sugar Built

3 "I had a grandfather" Art lecture by Governor Nelson A. Rockefeller, New School for Social Research, March 15, 1967, RAC.

3 "He was so much the man of power" Nathaniel Stephenson, *Nelson W. Aldrich: A Leader in American Politics* (New York: Charles Scribner's Sons, 1930), 269.

3 "Most people don't know what they want!" Ibid., 41. Nelson Rockefeller, asked to define the essential Aldrich traits, replied "gregariousness, outgiving, fond of people, deeply interested in the arts, interested in politics, aware of and concerned about events and people." Transcript of interview with Nelson A. Rockefeller, July 19, 1977, 3, Folder 1, Box 1, Nelson A. Rockefeller Papers, RAC (part of a larger series of Rockefeller reflections henceforth referred to as "NROH").

4 "Come right to Warwick and stay" Stephenson, *Aldrich*, 173.

4 None of the several hundred invited guests Two very different accounts of Aldrich's formative years can be found in Stephenson's authorized life, commissioned by Abby and her siblings, and the harshly unofficial portrait drawn by the senator's great-great grandson Nelson W. Aldrich, Jr., in *Old Money: The Mythology of America's Upper Class* (New York: Alfred A. Knopf, 1988). Nelson Rockefeller preferred to remember his Aldrich grandfather as an influential lawmaker and art collector whose legislative efforts helped facilitate the flow of antiquities from the Old World to the New.

6 "Of all the sitters I ever had" Stephenson, *Aldrich*, 269.

6 Aldrich . . . invited caricature at odds with his complex motivations and personal magnetism For contemporary treatments, see "Senator Aldrich—The Most Influential Man in Congress," *Ainslee's Magazine*, December 1901, as well as David Graham Phillips's profile of Aldrich in his classic series *The Treason of the Senate*, in *Cosmopolitan*, March 1906, and Lincoln Steffens's "Rhode Island: A State for Sale," *McClure's Magazine*, February 1905. "He knows when to 'bluff,' when to bully, when to flatter and when to anger," concluded the *Baltimore Sun*. "The man who is lacking in alertness he bluffs, the timid man he bullies, the vain man he flatters, and the man whose judgment is overturned when angry he torments and

taunts until he loses his temper and is put at fault." See http://www.senate.gov/artandhistory/history/minute/Priority_Recognition_of_Floor_Leaders.htm.

6 **Now Big Sugar filled the Aldrich wallet** Jerome W. Sternstein, "Corruption in the Gilded Age Senate: Nelson W. Aldrich and the Sugar Trust," *Capitol Studies* 6, no. 1 (Spring 1973).

7 **"the best I have ever tasted in all my life"** Mary Ellen Chase, *Abby Aldrich Rockefeller* (New York: Macmillan, 1950), 11.

10 **"Who is entitled to better rebates from a railroad"** Ron Chernow, *Titan: The Life of John D. Rockefeller, Sr.* (New York: Random House, 1998), 116.

11 **"my precious jewels"** Grace Goulder, *John D. Rockefeller: The Cleveland Years* (Cleveland, OH: Western Reserve Historical Society, 1972), 140.

12 **"We have Baptist Fish, Mr. Rockefeller"** Allan Nevins, *John D. Rockefeller and the Heroic Age of American Enterprise*, vol. 2 (New York: Charles Scribner's Sons, 1940), 163.

12 **"But a lot of laws were passed because of him"** Stewart Alsop, *Nixon and Rockefeller: A Double Portrait* (Garden City, NY: Doubleday, 1960), 104.

14 **"Only three men had to be helped aboard"** "The Special Years of Johnny Rock," *Brown Alumni Monthly*, July 1960.

15 **"Tom, why did you come to see me?"** Raymond Fosdick, *John D. Rockefeller, Jr.: A Portrait* (New York: Harper & Brothers, 1956), 93.

15 **such frankly modern volumes as Sane Sex Life** Bernice Kert, *Abby Aldrich Rockefeller: The Woman in the Family* (New York: Random House, 1993), 74.

15 **"Great Caesar, but John is a trump!"** Fosdick, *John D. Rockefeller, Jr.*, 109. "Marriage either makes or breaks a life," Junior remarked in later years, "and I felt I couldn't afford to make a mistake. It isn't just a matter of affection, it's a matter of qualities and abilities you have to live with." Raymond Fosdick notes, May 19, 1953, RAC.

16 **"I can't believe that it is really true"** Chernow, *Titan*, 358.

16 **"Miss Abbie is not pretty"** *Town Topics*, August 24, 1901.

16 **The New York Telegraph wryly noted** Fosdick, *John D. Rockefeller, Jr.*, 102.

16 **Reporters described Junior's bachelor dinner** Junior's bachelor party and wedding are fully described in the *New York Journal*, October 9, 1901, and the *Providence Journal*, October 10, 1901.

17 **"I suppose that I shall have occasion"** Fosdick notes, Kenneth Chorley, June 4, 1952, RAC.

18 **This was too much for Senior** Charles D. Heydt, interview by Raymond Fosdick, February 4, 1953, RAC.

19 **"I did not seek nor choose"** Daniel Okrent, *Great Fortune: The Epic of Rockefeller Center* (New York: Viking, 2003), 172.

19 **At his fiftieth class reunion** Ibid., 35. "Before I entered Brown," Junior once observed., "I was known only as the son of my father; after I graduated, chiefly as the husband of Senator Aldrich's daughter." One can only speculate as to his desire, even subconsciously, to escape such anonymity.

19 **"He wanted her to be with him always"** David Rockefeller, *Memoirs* (New York: Random House, 2002), 16.

19 **"I'm sure the Lord made me"** Kert, *Abby Aldrich Rockefeller*, 110.

19 **"You know, I envy you"** Peter Collier and David Horowitz, *The Rockefellers: An American Dynasty* (New York: Holt, Rinehart & Winston, 1976), 174.

20 **"Father had no conception of art or beauty"** John D. Rockefeller, Jr., interview by Raymond Fosdick, September 26, 1952, RAC. The story of Kykuit's rather tortured creation is told in Robert F. Dalzell, Jr., and Lee Baldwin Dalzell, *The House the Rockefellers Built: A Tale of Money, Taste, and Power in Twentieth-Century America* (New York: Henry Holt & Co., 2007), 48–141; and in Ann Rockefeller Roberts, *The Rockefeller Family Home: Kykuit* (New York: Abbeville Press, 1998). See also "The Pocantico Correspondence," August 15, 1904–April 27, 1922, JDR, Personal, Box 57, Folder 500, RAC; and "Father's House at Pocantico Hills," January 1940, JDR, Jr., Box 7, Folder 72, RAC.

21 **"The President telegraphed for the Senators"** AAR–JDR, Jr., August 12, 1903, RAC.

21 **improving the spiritual and material lot of the African native** For the embarrassing African speculations of Junior and his father-in-law, see Jerome L. Sternstein, "King Leopold II, Senator Nelson W. Aldrich, and the Strange Beginnings of American Economic Penetration of the Congo," *African Historical Studies* 2, no. 2 (1969): 189–201.

21 **"Riches breed but sin"** "The Rockefellers," *The American Experience*, PBS, originally aired October 16, 2000, program transcript, 19.

2: Oil and Water

23 **"A man is fortunate"** Laura Spelman Rockefeller–JDR, Jr., October 1, 1902, RAC.

23 **"Pay attention to the filly"** Kert, *Abby Aldrich Rockefeller*, 102.

23 **"chairs made for lounge lizards"** Chase, *Abby Aldrich Rockefeller*, 46.

23 **"come in and laugh with me"** Ibid., 36–37.

24 **"I told him it proved the importance of having pleasant people in the world"** Collier and Horowitz, *The Rockefellers*, 156.

24 **"Marriage is an art and not an experiment"** Chase, *Abby Aldrich Rockefeller*, 74.

24 **"Nothing is as interesting or as beautiful"** AAR–JDR, Jr., March 19, 1922, RAC.

24 **"No, thank you, Tom"** Tom Pyle, *Pocantico: Fifty Years on the Rockefeller Domain* (New York: Duell, Sloan and Pearce, 1964), 12.

24 **"It was dear of you to telegraph me, sweetheart"** AAR–JDR, Jr., September 29, 1902, RAC.

25 **"I am so ashamed"** AAR–JDR, Jr., August 11, 1903, RAC.

25 **Her letter crossed with a wistful reply** JDR, Jr.–AAR, August 11, 1903, RAC.

25 **"writing to the girl I love"** JDR, Jr.–AAR, June 28, 1908, RAC.

25 **"To be with you, dear"** AAR–JDR, Jr., June 29, 1908, RAC.

25 **"Have you heard"** AAR–Lucy Aldrich [n.d.], AAR, Box 4, Folder 56, RAC.

25 **the fifteen-mile-long island offered a study in contrasts** The history of Mount Desert is admirably told by Ann Rockefeller Roberts, *Mr. Rockefeller's Roads* (Camden, ME: Down East Books, 1990), 47–71; see also G. W. Helfrich and Gladys O'Neil, *Lost Bar Harbor* (Camden, ME: Down East Books, 1982). For the idiosyncratic Joseph Pulitzer and his Tower of Silence, see Helfrich and O'Neil, 36.

26 **"very anxious to *see* the new baby"** AAR–JDR, Jr., July 2, 1908, RAC.

26 **"I have done my duty by this family"** Happy Rockefeller, AI.

26 **"My mother said to me"** Rockefeller told writer Alvin Moscow in 1976 that he had aspired to the presidency since the age of seven. He identified the broad, river-facing terrace of Kykuit as the spot where he revealed his childish presidential ambitions to his father. Junior's response is unrecorded. Canzeri, AI.

27 **his "very well and good baby"** JDR, Jr.–AAR, July 21, 1908, RAC.

27 **"I think I did pretty well if that is the poorest"** Ibid., July 29, 1908, RAC.

27 **"the flower of the family"** "My dear Lucy" [n.d.], AAR–Lucy Aldrich, AAR, Box 4, Folder 56, RAC.

27 **she, too, would like to "feel" him** AAR–JDR, Jr., October 11, 1911, RAC.

27 **"particularly Nelson, he is so observant"** Ibid., May 17, 1911, RAC.

28 **Of far greater entertainment value to a small boy** NROH, July 19, 1977, 20–21.

29 **"I can see him now sitting on the floor"** Ibid., 17–18.

29 **"And so I grew up in this atmosphere"** NAR, New School Lecture, March 1, 1967, RAC.

29 **"I would like to have the Sistine Madonna"** Cary Reich, *The Life of Nelson A. Rockefeller: Worlds to Conquer, 1908–1958* (New York: Doubleday, 1996), 64.

29 **While still a teenager, he looked on** Aline Saarinen, "The Nelson Rockefeller Collection," *McCall's*, January 1969.

30 **"I had a very sharp focus on making money"** NROH, July 12, 1977, 3.

30 **"a very nice black gentleman"** Ibid., 2.

30 **Even the rabbit trade** Ibid., 4.

31 "But we *planned* something else" D. Rockefeller, *Memoirs*, 17.

31 a horror of idleness Albright, *Portrait*, 12.

31 "If I want to be happy" NAR, March 12, 1917, Family and Friends, Box 27, Folder 350, RAC.

32 "He surely is a little devil" Wallace Worthley letter to his mother, August 25, 1919, excerpted in Alvin Moscow Papers (hereafter referred to as "Worthley, Moscow Papers"), RAC.

32 "just like a circus" Ibid., August 11, 1919.

32 "in his usual philosophical way" Florence Scales–AAR, November 2, 1915, Alvin Moscow Papers, Research Material, RAC.

32 "we really didn't do children's things with our parents" NROH, July 19, 1977, 25.

32 "She was beautiful" Ibid., 28.

33 "And then I finally got my courage" Ibid., 33.

33 "I asked somebody which is my left hand" Morrow, dyslexia, 3.

33 "I should be so lucky" Ron Maiorana, AI.

33 "Toilet paper" Richard Dunham, AI.

33 "we have the money" Fosdick interview with JDR, Jr., March 23, 1954, 99, RAC.

33 "If there's a phrase that sums him up" Berger, AI.

33 "He had great instincts" Maiorana, AI.

34 "Never show more surface than necessary" Cannon, AI.

35 "I told the children this afternoon" AAR–JDR, Jr., September 27, 1915, RAC; an excellent account of events surrounding the Ludlow Massacre is in Chernow, *Titan*, 571–90.

36 Her disdain for money snobbery Kert, *Abby Aldrich Rockefeller*, 170.

36 Though she enjoyed travel D. Rockefeller, *Memoirs*, 33–34.

36 "During the last few years" John Ensor Harr and Peter J. Johnson, *The Rockefeller Century: Three Generations of America's Greatest Family* (New York: Charles Scribner's Sons, 1988), 261.

37 their "million dollar outfield" Childhood Stories, Mr. and Mrs. William Baverstock, interview, April 8, 1968, Alvin Moscow Papers, RAC.

37 "Sister and I were very close friends" NROH, July 12, 1977, 17.

37 "a bit too strenuous" AAR–Lucy Aldrich, October 7, 1922, RAC.

37 Sharing rooms in each Rockefeller home Happy Rockefeller, AI.

37 "we were difficult for the nurse" NROH, July 19, 1977, 36–37.

37 Nelson promptly pulled the rug out from under the unfortunate woman Ibid., 27.

37 "Just a good regular guy name" Ibid., 6.

37 "I could get both of them going very easily" Ibid., July 12, 1977, 13.

37 "He loved to throw food at the table" LSR, HMI, 47.

38 "the only advantage of being rich" "The Rockefeller Boys," *Saturday Evening Post*, July 16, 1938.

38 "Mr. R behaved himself just like a kid" Worthley, Moscow Papers, August 15, 1919, RAC.

39 "It was not a very nice thing to do" NROH, July 12, 1977, 14.

39 "It was a Sunday morning" Ibid. "In retrospect I feel that I should have been much more considerate of Winnie," Nelson conceded. "Little children can be very tough on each other." His brother retained lifelong memories of his childish humiliation, pointing out to a friend a particular hemlock tree in a remote Mount Desert forest: "That's where Laurance and Nelson used to take me, and tie me up, and leave me." George Dudley, HMI, 90.

39 "I am so thankful we are not rich" AAR–Lucy Aldrich, AAR, "Letters to Her Sister Lucy," New York, 1957, 173.

39 "Because he's fat and lazy" Pyle, *Pocantico*, 78.

39 Phlegmatic by nature AAR–Lucy Aldrich, January 28, 1913, RAC.

40 "Perhaps it was eating your shoestrings" AAR–NAR, July 9, 1921, RAC.

40 Sixty years later, he could describe the French clock NROH, July 12, 1977, 53–54.

40 In later years, Abby told friends AAR–Lucy Aldrich, "Letters to Lucy," June 12, 1951, 209.

40 "It is great fun changing pictures" AAR–NAR, October 6, 1926, RAC.

40 "He couldn't sit five minutes" LSR, HMI, 10.

41 "No, you'd better not" Pyle, *Pocantico*, 83.

41 **"I am sorry that you were not here on Abby's birthday"** "Dear Mama," NAR–AAR, November 7, 1916, RAC.

41 **With a calculating charm worthy of a Tammany boss** NAR–AAR, April 22, 1920, RAC.

41 **"I'm not sure how much I was fooled by this Santa Claus stuff"** Michael S. Kramer and Sam Roberts, *"I Never Wanted to Be Vice President of Anything!": An Investigative Biography of Nelson Rockefeller* (New York: Basic Books, 1977), 36.

41 **At the age of twelve** NAR–AAR, April 10, 1920, RAC.

42 **"I blue up the *fut ball*"** NAR–"Dear John," December 14, 1920, RAC.

42 **Wallace Worthley reported to his family** Alvin Moscow, *The Rockefeller Inheritance* (Garden City, NY: Doubleday, 1977), 42–43.

42 **"I saw General Joffer yesterday evening"** NAR–AAR, May 10, 1917, RAC.

42 **On the Ocean Road** "Dear Ma and All," July 30, 1918, Worthley, Moscow Papers, RAC; Ruth Ann Hill, *Discovering Old Bar Harbor and Acadia National Park: An Unconventional History and Guide* (Camden, ME: Down East Books, 1996), 125.

42 **"Nelson had it very energetically"** AAR–Wallace Worthley, November 20, 1918, RAC.

43 **"I know people can't give me gifts like I can give them"** Cannon, AI.

43 **"The old man joked all the time"** "Dear Ma and All," July 8, 1919, Worthley, Moscow Papers, RAC.

43 **"Life is like a game of blind man's bluff"** LSR, AI.

43 **"I'm all right; save the women and children first"** Moscow, *Rockefeller Inheritance*, 59–60.

44 **"You should have had my grandfather for your grandfather"** Kramer and Roberts, *"I Never Wanted,"* 36.

44 **"Nelson didn't drink"** Kershaw Burbank, AI.

44 **"the snake oil salesman"** Cannon, AI.

44 **"Wasn't it wonderful of Grandfather to make all this lovely money?"** Ronan, AI.

44 **"I lived it"** James Desmond, *Nelson Rockefeller: A Political Biography* (New York: Macmillan, 1964), 11.

3: "What Are We Going to Learn Today That's *New*?"

45 **"I did not learn from somebody telling me you get burned"** NROH, July 12, 1977, 34.

45 **"I had known for a long time that Nelson is very deficient in reading"** Wallace Worthley–JDR, Jr., the Eyrie, Seal Harbor, Maine, August 11, 1920, RAC.

46 **"For his composition work"** Ibid.

46 **"No long sob story"** Morrow, Dyslexia, 20.

46 **"You have no idea how humiliating it is"** Steven Rockefeller, HMI, 22; Nelson A. Rockefeller, "Don't Accept Anyone's Verdict That You Are Lazy, Stupid, or Retarded," *TV Guide*, October 16, 1976.

46 **"a hell of a handicap"** Morrow, Dyslexia, 12; "Deconstructing Dyslexia," *Time*, March 26, 2001; "The New Science of Dyslexia," *Time*, July 28, 2003.

46 **"So I had a hard time balancing my accounts"** NROH, July 12, 1977, 10.

47 **Lincoln boasted significant representation** Nelson himself credited much of Lincoln's intellectual stimulation to the presence of Jewish students, "who mature rapidly and are very dedicated to their work." He estimated their numbers at 35 percent of the student body. Ibid., July 19, 1977, 11.

47 **"I never took an exam until I got into college"** Ibid., 12.

47 **"What are we going to learn today that's *new*?"** Robert Armao, AI. Nelson's redheaded classmate James Thomas Flexner never forgot the bullying he experienced at the hands of older students, two of whom administered an impromptu exam. "Father Uncle Cousin Kate," they wrote on a blackboard, taking care to underline each of the capitalized words. Did he know what the word thus formed meant? When Flexner replied in the negative, the bigger

boys told him to come back when he did. James Thomas Flexner, *Maverick's Progress: An Autobiography* (New York: Fordham University Press, 1996), 36.

48 "I was very good at sewing" NROH, July 12, 1977, 25.

48 "I explained all about rabbits" Ibid., 26.

48 "Even as a kid" *New York Post*, March 23, 1958.

48 "always sort of bouncing around" Linda Storrow, HMI, 1.

49 With the help of a purloined master key LSR–JDR3rd, March 9, 1925, RAC.

49 Nelson got into a fight with a Cuban boy Nelson's altercation with his Cuban classmate is described in NROH, July 12, 1977, 29–30.

49 "Come on, I want to show you something" Sheldon Stark, CRI.

49 "They weren't *treated* any differently" Pauline Faulk, CRI.

49 "I was seated between John D., Jr., and Old Dean Russell" Ibid.

50 "He was a very nice policeman" NROH, July 12, 1977, 28–29.

50 Though Lincoln frowned on overt competition Nelson emerged from a battery of athletic contests with a cumulative 877 points; the school record was 943.

50 "It was so funny about your getting stuck up the rope" "Dear Johnny," NAR–JDR3rd, Sunday [n.d.], RAC.

50 "You're new here" Noel F. Busch, "Nelson A. Rockefeller," *Life*, April 27, 1942.

51 "On Thursday we are giving a big dinner" AAR–NAR, December 13, 1926, RAC.

51 At a summer camp in upstate New York Joe Alex Morris, *Nelson Rockefeller: A Biography* (New York: Harper & Brothers, 1960), 23–24.

51 "You can telefone from New York" NAR–AAR, August 3, 1921, RAC.

51 "Home is not the same" JDR, Jr.–AAR, July 10, 1922, RAC.

52 "We got our marks the other day" NAR–JDR3rd, December 3, 1922, RAC.

52 "Nelson has been the family problem this winter" AAR–Lucy Aldrich, January 28, 1923, RAC.

52 "What a coincidence!" NAR–JDR3rd, February 10 [1925?], RAC.

52 "ash blond hair and an ash blond psyche" Tom Prideaux, CRI.

52 "Women are tratoures creatures" NAR–JDR3rd, December 9, 1923, RAC.

52 descending Pikes Peak NROH, July 12, 1977, 64.

53 "Another day they watched in horror" Father–Sister (Junior–Babs), July 15, 1924, RAC.

53 "I only got 37 wright" NAR–JDR3rd, October 6, 1924, RAC.

53 "I was just about to pass a man" NAR–JDR3rd, July 14, 1925, RAC.

53 a "peach Deb from Philadelphia" Ibid.

54 He was going out almost every evening AAR–Winthrop Rockefeller, August 21, 1925, RAC.

54 "If you only knew how good I've been" NAR–JDR3rd, Tuesday 5, 1925, RAC.

54 "I guess the affair between Gerry and I is about over" NAR–"Dear Mother and Father," November 7, 1925, RAC.

54 "If I can only get a durby now and a cane" NAR–JDR3rd, Tuesday 5, 1925, RAC.

55 "I really think that is a better all around college" NAR–"Dear Mother and Father," November 7, 1925, RAC.

55 "This means that I will not be able to go to Princeton" Ibid., November 21, 1925, RAC.

55 "I heard it was a place which let a person learn by his own experiences" Thimmesch, "Unrelenting Drive of Nelson Rockefeller," 99. In a 1977 oral history, Rockefeller explicitly credited President Hopkins as the motivating force behind his decision to attend Dartmouth. Charles E. Widmayer, *Hopkins of Dartmouth: The Story of Ernest Martin Hopkins and His Presidency of Dartmouth College* (Hanover, NH: University Press of New England, 1977), provides the fullest treatment of Hopkins's presidency.

55 "Leave me alone for fifteen minutes" Morris, *N. Rockefeller*, 30. In later years, Junior came to have second thoughts about the practical value of a Lincoln education. Recognizing what the school had done to foster "the creative spirit" in his sons who went there only muted his disappointment. Being Junior, he launched a study into the school's methods and manage-

ment. It never occurred to him that his sons' academic deficiencies might be genetic—that is, dyslexia. JDR, Jr.–Jesse H. Neulon, November 21, 1928, RAC.

56 **"I never had a long-term plan"** Kramer and Roberts, *"I Never Wanted,"* 43.

56 **"earpissers"** Marshall, AI.

57 **At the start of October 1926** NAR–JDR, October 2, 1926, RAC; the class of 1930 numbered approximately six hundred members, of whom 80 percent labeled themselves Protestant and 70 percent Republican.

57 **"Luckily it was warm"** NAR–"Dear Ma and Pa," Sunday evening, 1926, RAC.

57 **Deposited one night in unfamiliar country** Nelson's experiences on the spiral staircase and finding his way home armed with a Boy Scout knife are recounted in NROH, July 19, 1977, 40. Junior professed shock over the alcoholic excesses of hazing: "I am sorry your first impressions of Dartmouth should be clouded with this ugly realistic picture . . . and yet it is life, abhorrent as we find it." That said, Junior took comfort in knowing that his son would, by example, do his part in undermining such licentiousness. JDR, Jr.–NAR, September 30, 1926, RAC.

57 **"I thought it was a joke"** William Manchester, *A Rockefeller Family Portrait: From John D. to Nelson* (Boston: Little, Brown, 1958), 125.

57 **"How about tonight"** Busch, *Life,* April 27, 1940. Nelson was refused by a Hanover restaurateur when he attempted to cash a $2 check signed by his father. "Nothing doing," said the proprietor, "I've had students try to cash checks signed by everyone back to Christopher Columbus, but never before one by John D. Rockefeller."

58 **Nelson, by contrast, rose at five o'clock each morning** Morrow, Dyslexia, 7. Abby offered unorthodox encouragement in a December 1926 letter, telling her son how lucky he was to have gotten through a discussion of Thackeray's *Vanity Fair* with his English professor "without his knowing that you had not finished the book." AAR–NAR, December 7, 1926, RAC.

58 **"This is where I became very competitive"** NROH, July 19, 1977, 34.

58 **"If we get our picture in the paper"** Robert B. Graham, Dartmouth College News Service, "Nelson Rockefeller at Dartmouth," 2.

59 **"I didn't drink, I didn't smoke, I didn't like dirty stories"** In fact, according to Nelson, on more than one occasion he got into fights with other boys who told off-color stories. NROH, July 19, 1977, 33.

59 **"Time is pretty valuable at college"** NAR–"Dear Bill, Saturday" [n.d.]. In this same letter, Nelson coolly advised his brother against expending much time or energy reaching out to classmates: "You'll find that the fellows will come to you."

59 **he "always seemed to have minority people . . . on his mind"** Morris, *N. Rockefeller,* 36; In February 1928, Junior received a letter from the father of another youth in the class of 1930, praising Nelson for his modesty and the overall good example he set for his classmates. That his son was following the standards "of democracy and simplicity" set by his parents and grandparents was "most heartening," replied Junior. "Nelson is just a plain garden variety of boy, with a good heart, fine impulses, a tremendous interest in life and a real affection for his friends." JDR, Jr.–Frederick S. McClory, March 1, 1928, RAC. Young Robert McClory, for whom Nelson once substituted waiting on tables, would go on to represent central Illinois as a Republican in the U.S. House of Representatives, where he voted to impeach Richard Nixon and confirm his Dartmouth classmate as vice president.

59 **"Well, I got my first exams"** NAR–JDR3rd, March 6, 1927, RAC.

60 **"No one could be a bigger failure than I am"** "Dear Nelson," MTC–NAR, Thursday, [n.d.], 1926, RAC.

60 **"I am no success with the sick"** MTC–NAR, January 22, 1927.

60 **He was in "a bad way"** "Dear Johnny," NAR–JDR3rd, Sunday, [n.d.], RAC.

60 **Sorely missing "the sensitivity of the family and a co-educational school"** Harrison notes, December 2, 1975, 1:5, WHP.

60 **One Sabbath, taunted beyond endurance** Happy Rockefeller, AI.

61 **"Do what you think is right in this world"** Kramer and Roberts, *"I Never Wanted,"* 41.

61 **"I have a feeling as if your eyes had just been opened"** AAR–NAR, May 15, 1927, RAC.

61 "Shall I get you golf stockings" Ibid. Abby never concealed the special affection she felt for the son who bore her father's name. "I feel that one of the best things that ever happened to me was having you for a son," she wrote him at the time of his twenty-first birthday. AAR–NAR, July 14, 1929, RAC.

61 "Not backwoodsmen" "Dear Johnny, Saturday," NAR–JDR3rd, [n.d.], RAC.

62 On winter nights NROH, July 19, 1977, 36.

62 At Psi Upsilon he befriended Edwin Toothacher NAR–Arthur Roeder, April 6, 1932, RAC.

62 "to drink milk in" JDR3rd diary, July 11, 1927, RAC.

62 "and what a treat it turned out to be!" NAR–"Dear Father—Thursday," [n.d.], RAC.

62 "You know I really don't think I deserve" Ibid.

63 "He *had* to have a car to entertain girls" NAR–JDR3rd, May 22, 1927.

63 "Being cut in on by the girls was lots of fun" Ibid., Thursday, [n.d.], RAC. According to Peter Grimm, a longtime Rockefeller real estate agent, Nelson's initial request involved the purchase of a used car priced at $500. "What makes you think you've got a father who's got $500 more than anybody else has?" Reminiscences of Peter Grimm, CCOHC, 58–61.

63 "I have already won Ma over" "Dear Johnny, Thursday," NAR–JDR3rd, [n.d.], RAC.

63 "I don't expect you will be able to wear it much" NAR–AAR, [n.d.; back of Christmas card, almost certainly 1927], RAC.

63 He felt as if he were being introduced to a new world of beauty Ibid., January 2, 1928, RAC.

63 "I suppose I'll meet one some day" Ibid.

64 "It would be a great joy to me" AAR–NAR, January 7, 1928, RAC.

64 "Dear boy, your life, if it is to be really useful" Ibid., February 19, 1928, RAC.

64 From his father, he expected more tangible rewards NAR–JDR, Jr., April 15, April 30, May 24, 1928, RAC.

65 He was "happy beyond expression" JDR, Jr.–NAR, May 25, 1928, RAC.

4: "The Luckiest Person in the World"

66 "I always liked girls" NROH, July 12, 1977, 46.

66 "I was 18. She was about 35" Ibid., July 19, 1977, 41–42.

66 "8 or 10 rather nice girls" "Dear Johnny, Saturday," NAR–JDR3rd, [n.d].

67 "Of course I have chosen the Standard Oil Co. for my study" NAR–"Dear Ma and Pa," November 14, 1928, RAC.

67 "They could not hope to compete with us" Nelson A. Rockefeller, "The Standard Oil Company and Its Monopolistic Tendencies," 13–15, RAC. Nothing better illustrated Nelson's aggressively defensive posture toward Senior's legacy than a line he attributed to his grandfather: "that in the old days if a man would slip on a banana peel and fell down, he'd jump up and turn around and curse the Standard Oil Company," RAC.

67 "For the first time I felt that I really knew Grandfather" NAR–JDR, Jr., February 7, 1929, RAC.

68 "The more I know of life" AAR–NAR, Pocantico Hills, May 1928, RAC.

68 "Now I suppose you think I'm forgetting Tod" Morris, *N. Rockefeller*, 80.

68 "Tod has almost everything—as far as I can see" NAR–AAR, March 1, 1929, RAC.

68 "I wanted to get on with the business" NROH, July 12, 1977, 47.

69 "Mary is the life of the party" JDR, Jr.–NAR, January 19, 1929, RAC.

69 Abby agreed AAR–Lucy Aldrich, February 14, 1928, RAC.

69 "I've never seen so many prime ministers" MTC–NAR, January 31, 1929, RAC.

69 Acknowledging Tod to be "always pleasant and agreeable" JDR, Jr.–NAR, February 28, 1929, RAC.

69 "Sometimes I wish I had majored in Art" Morris, *N. Rockefeller*, 73.

70 "That's how I felt, but I could never do anything about it" Maiorana, AI.

70 "I think perhaps I'm beginning to acquire" Morris, *N. Rockefeller*, 74.

70 "Don't you think that you want to fall in love with me" MTC–NAR, June 25, 1929, RAC.

71 "For heaven's sake get all that flirtatiousness out of your system" Ibid.

71 "whatever being in love means" NAR–AAR, July 18, 1929, RAC.

71 "You have become a man" MTC–NAR, July 8, 1929, RAC.

71 "When men can no longer be theists" Ronald Steel, *Walter Lippmann and the American Century* (Boston: Little, Brown, 1980), 262.

71 "You worry me with all your careful thought out philosophy" MTC–NAR, July 8, 1919, RAC.

72 "The Captain said he couldn't take us back" Harrison notes, December 1, 1975, Chapter One, 7, WHP; ROHC, July 19, 1977, 45–46; LSR, AI.

72 He didn't relish the idea NAR–JDR, Jr., and AAR, July 8, 1929, RAC.

72 "Your letter came this morning" MTC–NAR, September 19, 1929, RAC.

72 "The more I get to know myself" Ibid., October 12, 1929.

72 Of *Radiant Motherhood* Ibid., "Darling," Tues. Eve [October 1929]. Nelson had John French obtain from a London bookstore two "very instructive" volumes that he highly recommended to family and friends—*Wise Parenthood* and *Truth About Venereal Disease*. NAR–LSR, July 8, 1931, RAC.

73 "I'm afraid I cause you much more trouble" NAR–JDR, Jr., November [n.d.] 1929, RAC.

73 "Because you are in that respect more like Mama" JDR, Jr.–NAR, November 15, 1929, RAC.

73 He offered Nelson and Tod Ibid.

74 "To have you and Pa for parents" NAR–AAR, November 23, 1929, RAC.

74 "Somebody you loved" NROH, July 12, 1977, 49, RAC.

74 "Nelson is so young" AAR–Winthrop Aldrich, June 10, 1930, RAC.

74 "Here is the plan" NROH, July 14, 1977, 3.

75 In a course popularly known as Universe I Art Lecture New School, March 15, 1967.

75 Only a son of Junior's Nelson A. Rockefeller, "The Uses of Leisure," *Dartmouth Alumni Magazine*, June 1930, 521–23.

75 In a talk before graduating seniors James Wiggins, CRI. Nelson had initially planned on skipping the commencement ceremonies and had urged his family to stay away from Hanover. President Hopkins had little difficulty persuading them to the contrary, not least of all in recognition of Nelson's achievements outside the classroom. "He came into an atmosphere when he entered Dartmouth that was ready to be suspicious of his type and of his antecedents, and . . . he has carried himself so as to win the respect and affection of all with whom he has come into contact." E. M. Hopkins–JDR, Jr., February 21, 1930, RAC.

76 "It doesn't seem possible" MTC–NAR, December 3, 1929, RAC.

77 "Of course our life shall be one long romance" Ibid., "Tues" [1930, otherwise n.d.], RAC.

77 "I don't know how I'd have managed it" Ibid., February 12, 1930, RAC.

77 If Nelson persisted in addressing her as Toady Ibid., December 13, 1929, RAC.

77 "Our children (when we have them)" Ibid., February 13, 1930, RAC.

77 "You have become so much the light of my life" Ibid., March 13, 1930, RAC.

77 "Tod certainly makes an ideal wife" NAR–JDR3rd, Monday [July 1930], Matson Line, RAC.

77 "Married life is a great success" Ibid., "Monday 6th—Between Shanghai and Hong Kong." RAC.

78 Adopting his worldliest tone Ibid. RAC.

78 "Not a very good omen" Ashton Hawkins, interview, AI.

78 At the time, however "Dear Johnny," NAR–JDR, Jr., Monday [n.d.], RAC.

78 "For over a month now" NAR–JDR3rd, December 11, 1930, RAC.

79 "For more than an hour" NRI, CCOHC, 3–6.

79 "I wish that I might transport myself to Paris" AAR–NAR, April 7, 1931, RAC.

79 "Wait 'til Nelson gets back" Ibid., February 12, 1931, RAC.

79 "Unfortunately the architects and contractors" Ibid., April 7, 1931, RAC; see also "53rd Street Patron," *Time*, January 27, 1936. An excellent modern view of the once reviled development is David Garrard Lowe, "The Triumph of Rockefeller Center," *City Journal*, Summer 1993.

82 "I walk the floor nights" Junior's perfectionism added greatly to his self-imposed burdens. "You know, I'm only interested in the ideal," he told Kenneth Chorley, his representative in Colonial Williamsburg. Then he informed Chorley that he was giving him an additional $15 million to avoid cutting corners. Conversation with Kenneth Chorley, May 1954, RAC.

82 "Life in New York is enormously interesting" AAR–NAR, January 7, 1931, RAC.

82 "We are doing a restoration" NROH, July 26, 1977, 15–16.

82 "I did not want to go on any boards" Ibid., 39.

83 "Soon he was able to report" NAR–JDR, Jr., April 25, 1932, RAC.

83 "I think she really loves it there" AAR–Lucy Aldrich, "Letters to Lucy," July 13, 1931, 173.

83 "If you had a connection with a company" NROH, July 26, 1977, 17.

83 "Father always had a very simple admonition" Ibid., 19.

84 Acknowledging that he was "continually in a state of flux" NAR–JDR, Jr., July 3, 1933.

85 "She weighs close to 200" Bill Alton–NAR, January 1, 1931, RAC.

85 Most of his $1,000 pledge NAR–AAR, September 27, 1932, RAC.

86 Among those he recruited Eliza Bliss, CRI.

86 "We tried to christen him Nelson" JDR, Jr.–Mary T. Rockefeller, April 27, 1932, RAC.

87 "If we threw it out" NROH, July 26, 1977, 21; Russell Lynes, *Good Old Modern: An Intimate Portrait of the Museum of Modern Art* (New York: Atheneum, 1973), 99–101.

87 "Portuguese Rococo" Carol Herselle Krinsky, *Rockefeller Center* (New York: Oxford University Press, 1978), 186.

87 "The show was an absolute bust" NROH, August 4, 1977, 4.

87 "one of the grimmest, most depressing meetings" Ibid.

88 "During the last two or three months" NAR–Lincoln Kirstein, January 9, 1933. To his father, Nelson wrote an abject apology: "I now see quite clearly how arrogant and conceited I was getting to be, and how difficult I have been making things for you. . . . I think my rocket has burst and that I have come back down to earth." NAR–JDR, Jr., December 28, 1932, RAC.

5: The Art of the Possible

89 "Nelson needs art more than any man I know" Alfred Barr, Jr. (essay), *The Nelson A. Rockefeller Collection: Masterpieces of Modern Art* (New York: Hudson Hills Press, 1981), 20.

89 "The freedom is absolute" Persico, *Rockefeller*, 177–78.

89 "I'm interested in art that relates to life in our own day" Rockefeller, *Modern Art*, 28.

90 "art is not a picture" Apple, AI.

90 "The more intellectual you get" NROH, July 26, 1977, 3.

90 "I like strong, simple painting" NAR, interview, *Archives of American Art*, Smithsonian Institution, July 24, 1972, 4.

90 "In this way the College could probably get the work more reasonably" NAR–Artemus Packard, November 11, 1931, RAC.

91 "Gentlemen, we seem to have reached an impasse" Reich, *Worlds to Conquer*, 106.

91 "Although I do not personally care for much of his work" Okrent, *Great Fortune*, 288–89.

92 "the hateful lined canvas" Diego Rivera–AAR, November 5, 1932, RAC.

92 "the best of all the work I have done up to this time" Kert, *Abby Aldrich Rockefeller*, 357.

93 "Since I shall not be able with complete satisfaction" Okrent, *Great Fortune*, 295.

94 "I'm a liberal to the nth degree in theory" NAR–LSR, April 8 [1934], RAC.

94 Rockefeller accepted appointment to the newly formed board A useful summary of Rockefeller's work with the Westchester County Health Board is the board's *Silver Anniversary Report*, NAR, Personal Projects, Box 262, Folder 2606.

94 "I have to spend my whole life being nice to people" Martin Duberman, *The Worlds of Lincoln Kirstein* (New York: Alfred A. Knopf, 2007), 132.

94 "an extra not contemplated in our arrangement" JDR, Jr.–"Dear Bab and Nelson," April 22, 1932, RAC.

94 "I was doing anywhere from four to six or eight things at the same time" NROH, July 12, 1977, 40.

94 "You can't be any more worried about me than I am myself" NAR–AAR, March 21, 1933, RAC.

95 "Nel suggested to Father" JDR3rd diary, April 6, 1933, RAC

95 On April 19 Lucienne Bloch, "On Location with Diego Rivera," Art in America, February 1986, 115.

95 "I'll have you in the chair before you come back" NAR–AAR, April 22, 1933, RAC.

96 "This is so sudden!" AAR–NAR, April 26, 1933, RAC.

96 "As we get older" NAR–JDR, Jr., May 1, 1933, RAC.

96 In response to this unsubtle appeal JDR, Jr.–NAR, May 28, 1933, RAC.

96 In his autobiography Diego Rivera, My Art, My Life: An Autobiography (Mineola, NY: Dover Publications, 1991), 124–26; a more recent, and dispassionate, account is Bertrand M. Patenaude, "The Battle of Rockefeller Center," Hoover Digest 3 (Summer 2013): 60–89.

97 On May 3, Nelson returned to the RCA Building Once Nelson received his marching orders from Junior, he quickly fell into line. Within days he shared with Hugh Robertson "the original sketch" made by Rivera. Countering the artist's claims that Lenin was always part of his vision, Nelson remembered things quite differently. Indeed, most of the conversation during their encounter revolved around Rivera's insistence on fresco over canvas. NAR–Hugh S. Robertson, May 15, 1933, RAC. Robertson's May 9 letter of dismissal mentions, almost in passing, "some other questions" he had discussed with Rivera's agent—a hint that the real reason the mural was doomed had less to do with politics than alleged obscenity.

97 "Frida was peeking in and out of the door" NAR, New School Lecture, March 15, 1967, RAC.

98 "I should prefer the physical destruction" Rivera, My Art, 127.

98 Using somewhat homelier language Harr and Johnson, Rockefeller Century, 334.

98 This didn't keep Nelson from devising a complex scenario NAR–Alan R. Blackburn, December 16, 1933, RAC.

99 By a twist of fate JDR, Jr.–AAR, May 19, 1933, RAC.

99 "You writers are all the same" Jake Underhill, AI.

99 it was not the artist who defined his work Canzeri, AI.

99 In the future, he would appreciate it if Nelson JDR, Jr.–NAR, July 3, 1933, RAC.

100 "We carefully avoided all the other passengers" NAR–"Dear Ma and Pa," September, Tuesday, [1933], RAC.

100 "All the companies that John is connected with" AAR–Lucy Aldrich, "Letters to Lucy," September 7, 1933, 20.

100 "Evidently the students of our great universities" JDR, Jr.–NAR, September 29, 1933, RAC.

101 "It seemed very silly to have my appendix out" NAR–Frederick Chase, October 9, 1933, RAC.

101 "Nelson is full of nervous energy" AAR–Allen O. Whipple, September 27, 1933, RAC.

101 The windfall came wrapped in cautionary advice JDR, Jr.–NAR, December 20, 1933, RAC.

102 The older man concluded with satisfaction Ibid., August 9, 1934, RAC.

102 "A most adorable person" AAR–Winthrop Rockefeller, June 1, 1934, RAC.

102 "My chief desire is that we as a family" NAR–AAR, July 25, 1934, RAC.

103 "a very attractive girl" Nelson chanced to meet in Dallas NROH, April 7, 1977, 28.

103 they opened his eyes NAR–E. M. Hopkins, March 9, 1935, RAC.

103 "an upheaval in the relations with the Managing Agents" Francis Christy, Rockefeller Center History, Business Interests, Box 82, Folder 619, 46, RAC.

104 "As you are still comparatively young" JDR, Jr.–NAR, December 18, 1934, RAC.

6: PROMETHEUS

105 **"Can I be of any help in pinning up the drawings?"** Okrent, *Great Fortune*, 150.

105 **To Harrison, he appeared** Victoria Newhouse, *Wallace K. Harrison: Architect* (New York: Rizzoli, 1989), 46.

105 **"Goddammit, Mr. Rockefeller"** Harrison, *Builder*, Box 2, 1, WHP; Nelson was more tactful, but no more reconciled to Junior's taste for ornament—what he called "Father's concession to the reactionary element." David Loth, *The City Within a City: The Romance of Rockefeller Center* (New York: William Morrow, 1966), 124.

105 **As described by his friend and fellow architect** Newhouse, *W. K. Harrison*, 85.

106 **To his partner, Max Abramovitz** Max Abramovitz, AI.

106 **"Whatever you do, you can't stand still"** Geoffrey T. Hellman, "Lucky If You Can Come Close," *New Yorker*, November 20, 1954 (the first of a three-part profile of Harrison).

106 **"I finally knew for sure"** Ibid.

107 **"a personal whim"** NAR interview, *Archives of American Art*, 2.

107 **"His mother wouldn't let him"** Kramer and Roberts, *"I Never Wanted,"* 49. Interestingly, Nelson's father took a more liberal approach toward his son's career aspirations, telling him that "unless one's whole heart is in one's work, one cannot do as good work." JDR, Jr.–NAR, July 25, 1928, RAC.

107 **"I've always taken money too seriously"** *New York Post Daily Magazine*, December 4, 1962.

107 **"He was a lot of fun"** Harrison notes, February 9, 1976, 3, WHP.

108 **"Do you want to have a cup of coffee?"** Ibid., 2.

108 **Why not sell the property** JDR3rd diary, June 12, 1934; for background on the Rockefeller Apartments, see Newhouse, *W. K. Harrison*, 68–70.

109 **Abby objected vigorously** AAR–NAR, July 26, 1935, RAC.

109 **"What with our growing family"** NAR–Mrs. W. V. S. Thorne, January 4, 1937, RAC.

110 **"I am afraid that he might be doing something crazy"** NAR–AAR, June 13, 1938, RAC.

110 **"I like moving things around"** "What Makes Rockefeller Run?," *American Weekly*, November 1, 1959.

110 **If Nelson had any fault** Harrison notes, Tape 1-A, February 9, 1976, 10.

110 **"If you wanted to reach him"** Gus Eyssell, HMI, 9.

110 **With an old man's candor** Harrison notes, February 9, 1972, 12, WHP.

111 **"Some day I should like to be on the board"** NAR–JDR, Jr., February 19, 1935.

111 **"For the first time in my life"** NAR–Joseph Rovensky, June 22, 1935, RAC.

112 **"What do the figures show?"** Frank Gervasi, *The Real Rockefeller: The Story of the Rise, Decline and Resurgence of the Presidential Aspirations of Nelson Rockefeller* (New York: Atheneum, 1964), 38.

112 **In return, Nelson gently ribbed his grandfather** NAR–JDR, January 17, 1936, RAC.

112 **"Father might not like having pagan figures on top of his grave"** NAR–AAR, August 7, 1935, RAC.

112 **"When I think of the way the people's money is being wasted"** AAR–"Dearest Lucy and David," July 27, 1935, RAC.

112 **"It seemed a perfect shame"** AAR–NAR, July 6, 1935, RAC.

112 **"He used to go to China every year"** NROH, July 26, 1977, 7.

113 **At the center of it all was Alfred Barr, Jr.** Dwight Macdonald, "Action on West Fifty-Third, Part One," *New Yorker*, December 12, 1953.

114 **The presumptive chairman** AAR–NAR, December 14, 1935; AAR–A. Conger Goodyear, December 13, 1935, RAC.

114 **Within three days of receiving Goodwin's initial draft** NAR–Philip Goodwin, January 20, 1936, RAC.

114 **Encouraged by Wally Harrison** Reminiscences of Wallace Harrison, CCOHC, April 1, 1978, 114–53.

114 **He had purposefully left out anyone associated with the search committee** Philip Goodwin–NAR, February 21, 1936, RAC.

115 **Barr made no attempt to hide his anxieties** Alfred Barr–NAR, May 12, 1936.

115 **Abby requested a delay** "Mother"–JDR3rd, July 6, 1936, RAC.

115 **MoMA "cannot afford"** Alfred Barr–Thomas Mabry, July 6, 1936, RAC.

115 **Reminding Nelson** Alfred Barr–NAR, July 7, 1936, RAC.

115 **It seemed desirable to keep the group small** NAR–Stephen Clark, October 24, 1936, RAC.

115 **Nelson assured his mother** NAR–AAR, February 22, 1936, RAC.

116 **"I don't know of any job"** NAR–Philip Goodwin, August 2, 1937, RAC.

117 **Agreeing there was something "fundamentally wrong" with the current approach** Thomas Debevoise–John R. Todd, December 30, 1935, Business Interests, Box 90, Folder 675, RAC.

118 **Sarnoff and Odlum expected "a pushover"** NROH, August 4, 1977, 8. Nelson portrayed his role in these negotiations in a far more modest light at the time, assuring his father's regent, Tom Debevoise, that he was only "sitting in" on the discussions, while leaving the negotiating to Hugh Robertson. NAR–Thomas Debevoise, July 15, 1936, RAC.

118 **"Don't go into something"** NROH, August 4, 1977, 9. Showing uncharacteristic introspection, Nelson pondered the reasons why his father, in so many ways his temperamental opposite, should entrust the completion of Rockefeller Center to him. In the end, he decided that it was due to his mother's reference, his own confidence, and his exhaustive preparation before any meeting between the two—in short, that he had become more like Junior himself.

118 **"I am imaginative"** Ibid., 14.

119 **"There were about eighty engineers on the job"** Desmond, *N. Rockefeller*, 49.

119 **"nobody is very enthusiastic"** John R. Todd–NAR, April 23, 1937, RAC.

7: A LATIN FROM MANHATTAN

123 **Prompted by stories in the** *London Illustrated News* NROH, July 26, 1977, 10.

123 **The two men had already clashed** Michael Gross, *Rogues' Gallery: The Secret History of the Moguls and the Money That Made the Metropolitan Museum* (New York: Broadway Books, 2009), 176.

124 **Nelson paid a courtesy call** NROH, July 26, 1977, 11–12.

124 **While the others dozed** NAR–"Dear Mother and Father," Saturday, [May 1, 1937], RAC.

125 **A seemingly unbridgeable chasm** Darlene Rivas, *Missionary Capitalist: Nelson Rockefeller in Venezuela* (Chapel Hill: University of North Carolina Press, 2002), 21–23.

125 **"This country is as sound and conservative"** NAR–"Dear Mother and Father," Thursday, [n.d.], Family and Friends, Box 30, Folder 376, RAC.

127 **"I didn't know we had a Communist in our midst"** NROH, July 26, 1977, 28.

127 **"He was a very attractive, very nice, intelligent guy"** Abramovitz, AI.

127 **"If it'll please you"** "The Lyons Den," *New York Post*, December 28, 1938.

127 **a month in Arizona** NROH, July 26, 1977, 22–23.

127 **"Everything went well and I got what we wanted"** "Dear Father," NAR–JDR, Jr., Friday, [n.d.], RAC.

128 **Adhering to family tradition** JDR, Jr.–NAR, May 18, 1938, RAC.

128 **"That brings the grandchildren up to an even dozen"** NAR–William Alton, September 23, 1938, RAC.

128 **"This time she has gotten clothes"** AAR–Lucy Aldrich, March 16, 1936, RAC.

128 **"We knew he liked women"** Abramovitz, AI.

129 **Nelson was less sexually potent than he appeared** Cary Reich notes on conversation with Philip Johnson, July 13, 1988.

129 **"I made all my mistakes with my first family"** Confidential source.

129 **"I caught their eye"** NROH, July 12, 1977, 50–51.

129 **Anna Rosenberg confirmed his judgment** For background on Anna Rosenberg, see Richard O. Boyer, "Middle Woman," *New Yorker*, April 23, 1938, and "New York Close-Up," *New York Herald Tribune*, September 16, 1949.

130 **"Your brain trusters"** JDR, Jr.–NAR, March 23, 1938, RAC.

131 **"I just signed a contract with a labor union"** Victor Borella notes, Alvin Moscow Research Materials, RAC.

131 **In the early thirties, he befriended Bob and Helen Kleberg** NROH, August 4, 1977, 30–33. True to form, Nelson hoped to combine ranching with art promotion—specifically, through the creation of a village of Mexican artisans to call attention to their country's distinctive art and handicrafts.

131 **Another unconventional academic snagged in the Rockefeller net** For Beardsley Ruml, see *New York Times* obituary, April 19, 1960.

133 **Eight years had passed** NROH, August 16, 1977, 2–3.

133 **In Venezuela, Nelson again encountered his countrymen as colonizers** NRI, CCOHC, 24.

133 **"I'm Nelson Rockefeller and I'd like to meet your editor"** Morris, *N. Rockefeller*, 118.

134 **"Nelson would ask us up to his apartment"** Martha Dalrymple, *The AIA Story: Two Decades of International Cooperation* (New York: American International Association for Economic and Social Development, 1968), 4.

134 **Rockefeller listened attentively** The story of the Avila Hotel is in Newhouse, *W. K. Harrison*, 93–96; see also Samuel E. Bleecker, *The Politics of Architecture: A Perspective on Nelson A. Rockefeller* (New York: Rutledge Press, 1981), 107–111.

135 **When he returned to New York** Beardsley Ruml–NAR, April 22, 1939, RAC.

135 **These were reinforced at a trustees dinner** Roob, AI; Lynes, *Good Old Modern*, 201–11. Nelson attributed his failure to mention Conger Goodyear in the radio broadcast to some advice from Lowell Thomas, who cautioned him against loading up the program with a lot of names unfamiliar to the listening audience. Whatever the source, it marred an already strained transition.

135 **Nelson was effusive in his thanks** NAR–FDR, May 29, 1939, RAC.

136 **Junior didn't think much of the idea** JDR, Jr.–NAR, July 22, 1939, RAC.

136 **Boarding a train** NROH, July 26, 1977, 29.

136 **Cárdenas impressed Nelson** NRI, CCOHC, 30–45.

137 **Cárdenas was surprisingly flexible** Memorandum of Conversation Between Cárdenas and Rockefeller, October 14–15, 1939, Series 4A, Box 20, Folder 125, RAC.

137 **The encounter taught Nelson** NROH, July 26, 1977, 32.

138 **"I got the job the way I get all my jobs"** Desmond, *N. Rockefeller*, 74.

138 **"sort of a catalyst"** Ibid., 75.

139 **"a typical Rockefeller presentation"** Ibid., 76.

140 **Memories of drunken ambassadors** Rockefeller never forgot the South American head of state who employed a special guard outside his official residence Saturday nights to ward off a drunken U.S. ambassador convinced that he had an appointment with the president. During his 1937 trip, the visiting American watched in embarrassment as his own country's ambassador, delayed an hour while trying to sober up his wife, gritted his teeth as the unfortunate woman navigated the room with a glass of Scotch on her head. NROH, August 4, 1977, 36–37.

140 **"I talked with all the enthusiasm and conviction"** NRI, CCOHC, 77.

141 **"Oh, Anna. Haven't I got enough Republicans on my hands?"** Contained in Cary Reich's research materials is a rough draft and several interview transcripts generated by an unfinished Rockefeller biography, dating to the early 1980s, the work of *Village Voice* writer Mary Perot Nichols. Ms. Nichols in turn employed Patricia Linden, a journalist best known for her work with *Town & Country*, to conduct interviews. The book ground to a halt when the collaborators parted company. Later, Nichols supplied Reich with much of the material compiled for the ill-fated project. This includes an interview with Anna Rosenberg, whose unfettered access to FDR and tireless advocacy of young Nelson Rockefeller make her a unique figure in the Rockefeller story.

141 **Eager to foster unity** Henry Wallace, CCOHC, February 7, 1940, 832.

141 **"Nelson has talked with his Uncle Winthrop"** JDR, Jr.–Thomas Debevoise, July 22, 1940, RAC.

141 "If I were President in a period of crisis" NROH, August 9, 1977, 4–5.

142 "Now look, I'm going to give him the job" Nichols draft, Anna Rosenberg interview.

142 "As far as I am concerned" I am deeply grateful to Professor Irwin F. Gellman, a leading scholar of FDR-era diplomacy, who was kind enough to share extensive interviews he conducted with Rockefeller in 1976. The NAR–Gellman interview on August 11, 1976, is the source for FDR's Oval Office comments at the time of Nelson's hiring. Barbara L. Gellman Papers, Box 3, folder labeled "Private Interview with Nelson Rockefeller," FDRL.

142 "What do I have in mind for a budget?" Ibid.

142 "I feel a great opportunity for service lies before us" NAR–James Forrestal, July 26, 1940.

8: At War

143 At Nelson's request NROH, August 18, 1977, 4.

143 "It was always going to louse somebody up" John Lockwood, HMI, 12–13.

144 Encountering Rockefeller for the first time Paul Kramer, AI. See also Paul Kramer, "Nelson Rockefeller and British Security Co-ordination," *Journal of Contemporary History* 16, no. 1 (January 1981): 573–88; Paul Kramer, *Memories of a Secret Agent* (Bloomington, IN: Xlibris Corp., 2006), 19–87.

144 He should never raise problems with the president NROH, August 9, 1977, 27.

145 At a tense State Department meeting Ibid., August 11, 1977, 11.

146 He had come to talk about Winthrop Ibid., August 9, 1977, 24–25.

146 "He was something of a Latino himself" John Camp, AI.

146 "The Latins love and will follow" NRI, CCOHC, 50.

146 "The purpose of this show" Rockefeller, *Modern Art*, 24

147 "Nelson ran an office" Harrison notes, Tape 4-B, January 28, 1976, 3, WHP.

147 Profligate with praise Geoffrey Hellman, "Best Neighbor—I," *New Yorker*, April 11, 1942.

147 "Okay, kids. Go run with it" Nadia Williams interview, Friends of Nancy Hanks Center Oral History Project, David M. Rubenstein Rare Book & Manuscript Library, Duke University, 11.

148 Reports that the llamas of Ecuador Harrison notes, December 1, 1975, Chapters Three, Six, WHP.

148 "to promote better feeling between the Americas" Anecdotes, Inter-American Period, Victor Borella–NAR, February 9, 1950, Series 4A, Box 17, Folder 109, RAC.

149 "It was like a marriage" Linda Storrow, HMI, 15.

149 "This guy is full of beans" John Lockwood, HMI, 4; the larger story of Nelson's involvement with the Lincoln School controversy and its long-term impact on his attitude toward Communism is best told by Reich, *Worlds to Conquer*, 156–62.

149 a phenomenal hit with Latin moviegoers Isabelle Savell, HMI, 4.

150 "They told me this fellow just had to see me" Persico, *Imperial Rockefeller*, 136.

150 "How would you like to have *American Weekly*" Myer Kutz, *Rockefeller Power* (New York: Simon & Schuster, 1974), 67. Kael's original articles on Kane are in *The New Yorker*, February 20, 27, 1971.

151 "A lot of jigaboos" Joseph McBride, *What Ever Happened to Orson Welles?: A Portrait of an Independent Career* (Lexington: University Press of Kentucky, 2006), 71.

151 "Nobody was ever more cowardly than Nelson, you know" Barbara Leaming, *Orson Welles: A Biography* (New York: Viking, 1985), 252.

152 "I'm not going to get into a public pissing contest" NAR–Gellman interview, August 11, 1976, 25–26, FDRL.

152 To Nelson, Welles appeared NROH, August 18, 1917, 14–15. Curiously enough, when speaking Spanish, Welles displayed an entirely different personality. Gone was the glacial formality that governed his official conduct.

152 "They put on a record" Linda Storrow, HMI, 14.

153 **"Nelson didn't stop to talk about it"** Joe Alex Morris, *Those Rockefeller Brothers: An Informal Biography of Five Extraordinary Young Men* (New York: Harper & Brothers, 1951), 52–53.

153 **Welles saw his opportunity** FDR–NAR, April 22, 1941, RAC; NRI, CCOHC, 248–49.

153 **"You've just got to get along with them"** Ibid. Rockefeller's experience undoubtedly shaped his later recommendation to establish the United States Information Agency under Dwight Eisenhower.

154 **"I would wake up at three or four in the morning"** NROH, July 12, 1977, 42–43.

154 **It took one visit** Ibid., 11.

154 **Education was reciprocal** Steven Rockefeller, HMI, 23.

154 **Hosting an outdoor cocktail party one evening** NROH, August 9, 1977, 14.

155 **"I have never seen a child more companionable"** JDR, Jr.–NAR, January 9, 1945, RAC.

155 **To another visitor** *Working with Nelson Rockefeller 1943–1952*, Elizabeth Skerritt memoir, 28.

155 **Tod Rockefeller is recalled** Kramer, AI.

155 **"I sometimes wonder"** JDR, Jr.–NAR, January 9, 1945, RAC.

155 **Taking their cue from the squire** Pyle, *Pocantico*, 169.

155 **"I don't have to worry about Nelson"** Bess Abel, AI; Skerritt memoir, 1–3.

156 **"His forte was solving problems"** Skerritt memoir, 4.

156 **"It was so outrageous"** Ibid., 5.

156 **"He got tired of always being expected to pick up the check"** Ibid., 6.

156 **"After he had put on pajamas"** Ibid., 7.

157 **Countering Anna Rosenberg's claim** Telephone conversation with Mrs. Rosenberg on Monday, July 14, internal CIAA memo, D.C. Files, Series 4, Box 5, RAC. In a telephone conversation with Pa Watson on March 7, 1942, Rockefeller threatened to resign if the White House followed through on its original intent to hand all communications and propaganda work to the Donovan agency. He subsequently enlisted Hull, Welles, and Wallace to argue his case before the president. Thus did the CIAA escape virtual annihilation at the hands of that master infighter Wild Bill Donovan.

158 **In a follow-up "Dear Bill" letter** NAR–W. J. Donovan, July 16, 1941, RAC.

158 **"Until I am quite sure"** Ibid., August 6, 1941, RAC.

159 **"Whom do I deal with"** John Lockwood, remarks concerning Colonel William Donovan, September 4, 1941, 4, RAC.

159 **As a practical matter** W. J. Donovan–NAR, October 9, 1941, RAC.

159 **Rockefeller appealed to Anna Rosenberg** NAR–Anna Rosenberg, October 11, 1941, RAC.

160 **At a tense encounter that afternoon** Internal CIAA memo, October 29, 1941, signed by Imogene Spencer, RAC.

160 **"When you talked to your father"** Ibid.

160 **"Father's too busy to be bothered with this sort of thing"** Ibid.

160 **"Bill, I think you're wrong"** Reminiscences of Bernard Gladieux, CCOHC, 272.

160 **"You know what you ought to do"** Spencer memo, October 9, 1941, RAC.

160 **"You don't have to tell me about Welles"** Ibid.; "How the Donovan Arrangement Finally Evolved," by WLC (internal CIAA memo), October 14, 1941, RAC.

161 **"an unlikely threesome"** NAR–Gellman interview, August 11, 1976, 53, FDRL. J. Edgar Hoover had his own methods of dealing with Donovan. NRI, CCOHC, 292–93.

161 **"Nelson doesn't expect you to be a yes-man"** Stewart Alsop, "The Rockefeller Nobody Knows," *Saturday Evening Post*, July 25, 1959.

161 **Hastening to see Perkins** NAR–Gellman interview, August 11, 1976, 55, FDRL; Paul Nitze, *From Hiroshima to Glasnost* (New York: Grove Weidenfeld, 1989), 13–15.

161 **"Never, but never, have all your eggs in one basket"** NROH, August 9, 1977, 22.

162 **"He was the one who told me"** Ibid., 26–27.

162 **"You can start the program with $25 million"** Ibid., August 18, 1977, 12–13; in the same interview, Rockefeller describes the *servicio* concept, its origins in the Rockefeller Foundation, and its successful application in Latin America, 17–23.

164 **Yet even Braden grudgingly acknowledged** Reminiscences of Spruille Braden, CCOHC, 1105.

164 **"We haven't had decent relations with the Latin Americans since"** John Lockwood, HMI, 14.

9: UNITED NATIONS

165 **As long as Stalin ruled in the Kremlin** Secret and Confidential Report on Conversation with President, May 19, 1943, DC File, RG3, Box 9, Folder 76, RAC.

165 **"whether it was Russia or anyone else"** Ibid.

166 **By the start of 1944** In his Columbia Oral History (189–90), Rockefeller contrasts Mexico's postwar planning with Brazil's dissipation of some $2 billion in wartime reserves on "yoyos and plastic suspenders."

166 **Congressman Sol Bloom of New York** Henry Wallace Diary, CCOHC, August 6, 1942.

166 **It was Nelson's salvation** FDR–NAR, June 11, 1943, RAC.

166 **That August, he sustained a major loss** NRI, CCOHC, 358–59. For Welles's downfall, see Irwin F. Gellman, *Secret Affairs: FDR, Cordell Hull, and Sumner Welles* (Baltimore: Johns Hopkins University Press, 1995), 302–331.

167 **"If you were close to the president"** NAR–Gellman interview, August 11, 1976, 5, FDRL.

167 **"It's been very informal and pleasant"** NAR–"Dear Father," Sunday, [November 7, 1943], RAC.

168 **"He was a bear for figures"** John Lockwood, HMI, 14. By no means everyone in Washington agreed with Rockefeller's numbers. A particularly harsh critique of the CIAA is contained in Senator Hugh Butler's "Our Deep Dark Secrets in Latin America," *Reader's Digest*, December 1943, 21–25.

168 **"I could not have begun to do as well"** JDR, Jr.–NAR, May 5, 1943, RAC.

168 **"again and again you have felt"** Ibid., marked "Personal and Confidential," September 24, 1943, RAC.

168 **Twice the coordinator had gone to FDR** Confidential Memorandum Concerning Lunch with the President, August 13, 1942, D.C. Files, Box 9, Folder 76, RAC.

169 **"The higher a man rises"** JDR, Jr.–NAR, January 18, 1945, RAC.

169 **The CIAA should be made permanent** "A Regional Structure for Hemisphere Unity," NAR memorandum to Edward Stettinius, January 14, 1944, RAC.

170 **"He and I just hit it off like gangbusters"** W. Kenneth Riland, HMI, 9.

170 **"I always treated him like one of the boys"** Ibid., 13.

170 **On the afternoon of June 5, 1944** Skerritt memoir, 11.

171 **Rockefeller again raised with Hull** NAR–Gellman interview, August 12, 1976, 61, FDRL; Henry Wallace Diary, CCOHC, January 8, 1944.

171 **Hull was unpersuaded** NRI, CCOHC, 368.

172 **"I reckon that if they know he is, they will"** Jonathan Daniels, *White House Witness, 1942–1945* (Garden City, NY: Doubleday, 1975), 164–65.

172 **"He was never able to establish himself"** Elizabeth Skerritt letter to author.

172 **Rockefeller calculated that by rationing soap and paint** NRI, CCOHC, 392–93.

173 **"How would you define attacked?"** NROH, July 14, 1977, 23; Memorandum of Conversation, January 9, 1943, NAR D.C. Files, Box 9, Folder 76, RAC.

174 **"These are the items we want on the agenda"** NRI, CCOHC, 419.

174 **"I can't turn the government over"** Ibid., 408–9.

174 **"It is going to be an interesting but hectic three weeks"** NAR–JDR, Jr., February 16, 1945, RAC.

175 **From FBI sources, he learned** NROH, July 14, 1977, 25.

175 **With a conspiratorial flourish** Harrison, *Builder*, 6–8, WHP.

175 **"I am not so sure"** NROH, July 14, 1977, 26.

177 "You have got your own conference in San Francisco" Ibid., 39.

177 Nelson had Frank Jamieson leak the story Ibid., 28.

177 "I'm afraid I can't" NRI, CCOHC, 487–88.

178 "For the first time I saw him" Ibid., 511–12.

178 the fertilizing virtues of hen versus horse manure Robert H. Jackson, *That Man: An Insider's Portrait of Franklin D. Roosevelt* (New York: Oxford University Press, 2003), 152–53.

179 "he knew even less than Ed did" NROH, August 16, 1977, 25–26.

179 "I remember you" Robert L. Beisner, *Dean Acheson: A Life in the Cold War* (New York: Oxford University Press, 2006), 568.

179 The exchange grew heated NROH, July 14, 1977, 36.

180 "Here are these two frightened and mousey guys" Harrison notes, taped conversation with NAR, December 1, 1975, Chapters Four, Three, WHP.

180 Now, as Rockefeller's eyes widened in disbelief RBM, part 5, chapter 4a, section 4, 6, FDRL.

180 "You are not going to be able to do anything" NROH, July 14, 1977, 37.

180 Nelson went "quietly but directly" to the War Department RBM, part 5, chapter 5, 2–5, FDRL.

181 early morning briefings from FBI agents NROH, July 14, 1977, 49.

182 Rockefeller left the hustling for votes to others Ibid., 39.

182 Arthur Vandenberg had agreed to participate Harrison, *Builder*, 12, WHP.

183 "I will support the admission of Argentina" NROH, July 14, 1977, 52.

183 "Get up and tell them" Ibid.

183 Leaked versions of his testimony Henry Wallace Diary, CCOHC, May 8, 1945.

184 "Look, this is easy" NROH, July 14, 1977, 41.

184 Upon returning to San Francisco May 5 Ibid., 42.

184 The mere sight of Rockefeller Bleecker, *Politics of Architecture*, 69.

185 "I was so mad by that time" NROH, July 14, 1977, 44.

185 "Harold, you have got it" Ibid.

185 "Either we have a world organization or we don't" Reich, *Worlds to Conquer*, 350.

185 "You have had it" NROH, July 14, 1977, 50. Nelson's cover story to the Latins involved the presence in San Francisco harbor of a Soviet vessel, disguised as a fishing boat, that was even then eavesdropping on their cable traffic. In their own interest as well as his, they must remain silent about anything he might say in their closed-door sessions.

186 "Will you come and talk to Truman" Ibid., 45.

186 "You can tell the young whippersnapper" Alsop, *Nixon and Rockefeller*, 89. Hull wasn't alone in his resentment of Rockefeller's role at San Francisco. Adlai Stevenson, another junior member of the U.S. delegation, expressed disappointment over the power bloc politics that emphasized hemispheric unity and left the Soviet Union feeling hopelessly outvoted in the new world organization. Henry Wallace Diary, CCOHC, May 3, 1945, 183.

187 "the usual Washington firing" NROH, September 27, 1977, 1–2.

187 Rockefeller's face hardened Ibid., 4.

188 "He wrote back one of the typical Truman letters" Ibid., 4–5.

188 "Well, gentlemen, here it is" Skerritt memoir, 22.

188 "I am all set to start the next conspiracy!" NAR–B. Ruml, September 19, 1945, RAC.

10: Too Much, Too Soon

189 "No soldier at the front" JDR, Jr. –NAR, August 25, 1945, RAC.

190 As a boy raised in blue-collar Brownsville Joshua B. Freeman, *Working Class New York: Life and Labor Since World War II* (New York: New Press, 2000), 26.

191 "what a city ought to be" Jed Perl, *New Art City: Manhattan at Mid-Century* (New York: Alfred A. Knopf, 2005), 37–38.

192 He defused a potential crisis NROH, September 27, 1977, 19.

192 **Even before the war** Ibid., July 26, 1977, 9–10.

193 **"I hope to be able to pull together"** NAR–Chester Bowles, September 28, 1945, RAC.

193 **Resorting to a familiar stratagem** NROH, September 27, 1977, 15.

194 **"I felt badly to walk out on you"** JDR3rd–NAR, Family and Friends, Box 46, Folder 500, January 11, 1946, RAC.

194 **On her first day in Room 5600** Skerritt memoir, 23–24.

194 **"Everything was equally exciting"** Linda Storrow, HMI, 42.

194 **"One *never* talked about what went on in the office"** Skerritt memoir, 25.

195 **She had been indiscreet** Ibid., 26.

195 **"I imagine you need money for a hotel"** Ibid., 24.

195 **"Mr. Nelson says you are to go home"** Ibid., 30.

195 **Gradually, it dawned on her** Elizabeth Skerritt, AI

196 **Introduced to Libby Shemwell** Skerritt letter to author.

196 **"After all, I had a degree in economics"** Joan Braden, *Just Enough Rope: An Intimate Memoir* (New York: Villard, 1989), 29.

197 **"She exuded IT"** Skerritt letter to author.

197 **"people in Room 5600 hated her"** Burbank, AI.

197 **"What would you say"** Braden, *Rope*, 30.

197 **"Joannie . . . I don't know enough about railroads"** Ibid., 40.

197 **"What Nelson wanted"** Ibid., 36.

198 **"We will never get divorced"** Ibid., 43.

198 **"Because Nelson was not suspicious of women"** Ibid., 35.

199 **"He never could quite understand"** John Lockwood, HMI, 16.

199 **"a better capitalism"** Ibid., 19.

200 **That there were limits** Ibid., 20–21.

200 **"We have to get Nelson to visit Brazil"** Berent Friele, HMI, 59.

201 **"You know what that man is thinking now?"** Reminiscences of Robert Hudgens, CCOHC, November 17, 1952, 220.

201 **"I have had no trouble in getting capital up to date"** NAR–Abby "Babs" Rockefeller, April 20, 1947, RAC.

201 **"You will be exploiting the people"** NROH, July 26, 1977, 38.

202 **"We couldn't get anybody to harvest"** Ibid., 41.

202 **"So we put motors in the sailboats"** Ibid., 39.

202 **"How do you get the fish up into the interior"** Ibid., 40.

203 **"I just showed you how"** Cannon, AI.

203 **"It was a case of too much, too soon"** *Christian Science Monitor*, September 23, 1952.

204 **vanity title "capital of the world"** There is a vast amount of literature concerning the UN site selection process. An interesting place to start is Charlene Mires, "The Search for the Capitol of the World," Research Reports from the Rockefeller Archive Center, Fall 2005, 1–3. Also see Newhouse, *W. K. Harrison*, 104–37.

205 **"Where is Nelson?"** Harrison notes, December 1, 1975, Chapters Five, Ten, WHP.

206 **"Nelson was aware of this going on"** George Dudley, HMI, 33. Zeckendorf claimed that his $8.5 selling price represented what he had himself paid for the future UN site. No so, said Dudley, who had worked on the proposed X City from its inception.

206 **an overflight of Pocantico** Newhouse, *W. K. Harrison*, 110.

207 **"Why, Pa!"** Ibid. See also Francis Jamieson, CCOHC, 192–204; and Morris, *Rockefeller Brothers*, 356–67.

207 **"He wants to give them the New York City property"** Harrison notes, December 1, 1975, Chapters Five, Eleven, WHP.

207 **"Wonderful, buy a bottle of champagne"** Ibid., 513. Junior remembered things differently, with his offer being made quite casually to Nelson face-to-face, while dressing for dinner. Raymond Fosdick conversation with JDR, Jr., April 1, 1952, RAC.

208 **"Wally, we've got to celebrate"** Aline B. Saarinen, *The Proud Possessors: The Lives, Times,*

and Tastes of Some Adventurous American Art Collectors (New York: Random House, 1958), 380.

208 **To the annoyance of her husband** Chase, *Abby Aldrich Rockefeller,* 91.

209 **On V-J Day** Ibid., 102.

209 **"I think Papa and I would feel very shut off"** AAR–NAR, February 14, 1947, RAC.

209 **Reverting to earlier habits** Skerritt memoir, 31.

209 **She was "deeply grieved"** AAR–John Abbott, February 21, 1947, AAR, OMR, Box 9, Folder 122, RAC.

209 **"She had a very strong personality"** Morrow, Dyslexia.

209 **"If Father was in favor of what you were doing"** Steven Rockefeller, HMI, 11.

210 **Having little enthusiasm for Junior's agent** AAR–NAR, February 12, 1948, RAC.

210 **"It was like the old days"** NROH, July 12, 1977, 55.

210 **"probably the only woman to whom he was totally devoted"** Steven Rockefeller, HMI, 19.

210 **Before the urn containing the cremated remains was sealed** Happy Rockefeller, AI.

11: THE GENERAL MANAGER

211 **"A very kind man who liked people"** NROH, October 4, 1977, 1.

211 **A month before Election Day** NAR–John S. Dickey, October 7, 1948, RAC.

211 **It was reassuring to know** LBJ–NAR, January 19, 1949, RAC.

211 **Within days of Truman's reelection** Harr and Johnson, *Rockefeller Century,* 443–44; see also Christine Hardy Little Oral History, 5–13, HSTL.

212 **"They took their hat off to it as they went by"** NRI, CCOHC, 710.

212 **"Do come and see me"** Ibid., 711.

213 **"You take it up with Acheson"** Ibid., 712.

213 **"The whole foreign economic picture in Washington"** NAR–Richard Aldrich, November 20, 1950, RAC.

213 **"A gentle, soft-voiced intellectual"** Cannon, AI.

213 **"Now that I like"** NROH, August 4, 1977, 16.

213 **"He would just call up"** Oscar Ruebhausen, AI.

214 **An adjoining dressing room** Ilene Slater, AI.

214 **"Many times I've been with him"** Ruebhausen, AI.

215 **"We cannot have a divided committee"** Ibid.

215 **"You know how it is"** NROH, September 27, 1977, 7–8; Claude Erb dissertation, 452–56.

216 **"I've been wandering around the country"** NAR–Lucy Aldrich, June 18, 1951, RAC.

216 **If India's crushing needs were to be addressed seriously** NAR–Chester Bowles, October 23, 1951, RAC.

217 **"I don't like this business"** Herbert Brownell, *Advising Ike: The Memoirs of Attorney General Herbert Brownell* (Lawrence: University Press of Kansas, 1993), 126.

217 **"an acceptance of the status quo"** NRI, Eisenhower Administration Project, CCOHC, 28.

217 **"a slow retreat"** NROH, October 4, 1977, 7.

217 **A treasured photograph of the late president** Albright, AI.

218 **"Everything about Roosevelt"** Richard Allison, AI.

218 **"The job is to convince, not publicize"** Paul Boller, *Presidential Campaigns* (New York: Oxford University Press, 2004), 295.

218 **Eisenhower appeared to Nelson** NROH, October 4, 1977, 2.

218 **Then he had been quick to congratulate Dulles** NAR–J. F. Dulles, March 27, 1952, RAC.

220 **"He has one hundred ideas"** Ann Whitman, HMI, 11.

220 **"Our little chat about the utilization of solar energy"** Vannevar Bush–NAR, April 13, 1953, RAC.

220 **He was happy to hear it** NAR–Vannevar Bush, [n.d.], RAC.

220 "We have been negotiating" NAR–Rodman Rockefeller, March 6, 1953, RAC; see also Stanley High, "Man Closest to the President," *Reader's Digest*, June 1953.

221 "This is Nelson Rockefeller calling" Charles Metzner, HMI, 14–15.

222 The most unlikely of bureaucrats Paul Healey, "Capitol Circus," *New York Daily News*, June 2, 1953.

222 "In the beginning he used the Chart Room" Nadia Williams, CRI.

223 "I'm up here," said Goldwater Nancy Hanks, HMI, 10–11.

223 "There's no question but that the federal government has just gotten too big" NAR–Lucy Aldrich, May 26, 1954, RAC.

223 One sultry Washington evening Braden, *Rope*, 65–66; Nadia Williams interview, NHOHP, Duke University, 30–31.

224 Nancy Hanks in turn credited Nelson Nancy Hanks, HMI, 36–37; the best single source for the Rockefeller-Hanks relationship is Michael Straight, *Nancy Hanks: An Intimate Portrait: The Creation of a National Commitment to the Arts* (Durham, NC: Duke University Press, 1988), 40–55.

224 Ordinarily the soul of courtesy Nancy Hanks, HMI, 8.

225 "Nancy once brought him around to my house" Williams, CRI.

225 "I can just imagine Bryan's mountain" NAR–"Dear Virginia and Bryan," "Sunday," November 16, 1954, RAC.

225 How different things might have been NROH, October 4, 1977, 12–14.

225 "It leaves the house very empty" NAR–Lucy Aldrich, October 22, 1952, RAC.

226 A younger visitor to the Fifth Avenue triplex Apple, AI.

226 "Six of us traveled in a station wagon" NAR–Lucy Aldrich, May 9, 1952, RAC.

226 Another spring he took the twins Ibid., July 7, 1949, RAC.

227 Clutching his father's briefcase Steven Rockefeller, HMI, 3.

227 "I can honestly say that being a Rockefeller" Collier and Horowitz, *The Rockefellers*, 544.

227 Within the family, Ann's adventurous outlook Lucy Aldrich–NAR, October 23, 1953, RAC.

228 "They are crazy about Mary" NAR–Rodman Rockefeller, November 10, 1952, RAC.

228 "We lived in a trailer" Collier and Horowitz, *The Rockefellers*, 351.

228 Back in New York Apple, AI.

228 "I wish your mother could see it" Lucy Aldrich–NAR, October 5, 1949, RAC.

228 "It was such fun to see you" NAR–Lucy Aldrich, February 23, 1954, RAC.

228 At Pocantico there appeared little Roberts, *Kykuit*, 22–29, 43.

229 According to David Rockefeller D. Rockefeller, *Memoirs*, 143; see also Harr and Johnson, *Rockefeller Century*, 527–29.

229 "The Republican party must be known as a progressive organization" Thomas E. Cronin, *Rethinking the Presidency* (Boston: Little, Brown, 1992), 113.

230 A meeting was scheduled for August 4, 1953 Reminiscences of Mary Lasker, CCOHC, 322–25.

231 "As far as I'm concerned" Stephen E. Ambrose, *Eisenhower* (New York: Simon & Schuster, 1984), 199.

233 "I don't think the Republicans have done a very good job" NAR–"Dear Rod and Barbie," October 26, 1954, RAC.

233 his relationship with Mrs. Hobby Roswell Perkins, AI.

233 "Tom Dewey doesn't want to pick anybody who will have a chance" NROH, July 14, 1977, 71.

12: Brainstorming

235 "The whole idea was that maybe Nelson could put some new ideas into the White House" Nadia Williams interview, NHOHP, Duke University.

235 "our enlightened national interests" Andrew Goodpaster, AI.

236 Tipped off that Ike's chief of staff NROH, August 18, 1977, 6–7.

236 "He was a great one for ordering memorandums" Ann Whitman, HMI, 164.

236 Capitol Hill was not overlooked JFK–NAR, January 10, 1955, RAC.

237 "He had the world in his head" NROH, October 4, 1977, 14.

237 "If I so much as took into account" Lloyd Free, "Open Skies—Then and Now," September 3, 1969, 3, RAC.

237 "Agricultural shortages promise to create internal dissatisfaction" Memorandum from the President, NAR–DDE, March 1, 1955, RAC. A still more chilling Rockefeller response came to an intelligence estimate of free world reaction should the United States use nuclear weapons against Communist China. Nelson thanked its author for "an interesting analysis of a very difficult opinion problem." NAR–Allan Evans, Intelligence Estimate Number 78, August 11, 1955, RAC.

238 George Humphrey was another story NROH, October 4, 1977, 8.

239 As speculation about his intentions mounted NAR–DDE, June 3, 1955, Memorandum for the President—Quantico, RAC.

240 "I doubt they will agree to it" Goodpaster, AI.

241 "If somebody said two words" Apple, AI.

241 No intellectual himself Free, "Open Skies," 4.

241 "Once decided that an idea is good" Ibid.

241 "a one-shot, off-the-top-of-the-head effort" C. D. Jackson—J. F. Dulles, June 13, 1955, RAC.

241 "Nelson is here and he has got a tremendous idea" NROH, July 14, 1977, 15.

241 He was more concerned Harrison notes, December 1, 1975, Chapters Five, Eighteen, WHP.

242 "God damn it, Nelson" Ibid.

242 "Eisenhower never showed all his cards" Goodpaster, AI.

243 "Maybe you've got something here, after all" Free, "Open Skies," 6.

244 "Harold, with your brains and my intuition, it's just a shame" NRI, Eisenhower Administration Project, CCOHC, 16.

244 "If I were to say this" Goodpaster, AI.

245 "You are trying to look into our bedrooms" Ibid.

245 "Now I know who's in charge" Ibid.

245 "Why, Mr. Dulles, your chauffeur must have gone" NROH, July 14, 1977, 56–57.

246 "We are having a moratorium" NAR Memorandum of Conversation, August 11, 1955, D.C. Files, Box 68, Folder 547, RAC.

246 "Why should I always have to be the one" NROH, October 4, 1977, 7.

247 "I feel very close to you" NAR–"Dearest," [n.d.], Nancy Hanks Papers, Duke University.

247 That fall, Nancy complained of Rockefeller's detachment Straight, Nancy Hanks, 53.

247 "I got off the elevator" Apple, AI.

248 "Then I got the idea of picking Picasso's paintings which I really was crazy about" NAR, interview, Smithsonian Archives of American Art, 5, July 24, 1972.

248 "I think I inherit my weakness for shopping" NAR–Lucy Aldrich, November 13, 1950, RAC.

249 "He came into the room with a broad smile on his face" Henry Kissinger, AI.

250 Nixon "had his feet cut right off" NROH, October 4, 1977, 18.

250 "one's spirits seem to come back" NAR–Milton Eisenhower, September 30, 1955, RAC.

250 "things have been a bit difficult in Washington" NAR–"Dear Virginia," November 1955, Nancy Hanks Papers, Duke University.

250 "the Rockefeller experiment" Reminiscences of Sherman Adams, CCOHC, 158.

251 "I can't wait for you to see me in my new red shirt" NAR–Percy L. Douglas, January 16, 1956, RAC.

251 "one of them is bound to work" Linda Storrow, HMI, 38.

251 "It doesn't make any sense" NAR–"Dear Virginia and Bryan," Sunday, [January 15, 1956], Nancy Hanks Papers, Duke University.

251 The alternative was worse Linda Storrow, HMI, 19.

252 "I don't think he ever stopped to rest" Morris, N. Rockefeller, 316.

252 "I don't need to go out" Cannon, AI.

252 "Oscar, I'm forty-eight" Ruebhausen, AI.

252 "Nelson had this . . . belief in his star" John Lockwood, HMI, 29.

252 "He really wants to run for President" Burbank, AI.

252 "What do you think Nelson really wants to be?" Linda Storrow, HMI, 18.

253 He hoped to continue his policy studies NAR–"Dear Virginia and Bryan," November 16, 1954, RAC.

253 "co-existence and atomic stalemate" Robert Kintner memorandum, "What Is to Be Done?," January 18, 1956, 3, RAC.

253 Still another project under discussion in Room 5600 Nancy Hanks–Frank Jamieson, March 8, 1956, RAC.

253 The only place big enough Nancy Hanks, HMI, 18.

254 "There is more than enough excitement" Rockefeller Brothers Fund, *The Power of the Democratic Idea*, America at Mid-Century series (New York: Doubleday, 1960), 16.

254 "I got Henry down from Harvard" NROH, July 14, 1977, 63.

255 "We had two papers for each panel" Ibid., 18.

255 the highest-paid proofreader in the country Slater, AI.

255 Behind Nelson's back Burbank, CRI.

255 "You have often deprecated your role" H. Kissinger–NAR, December 27, 1956, RAC.

255 He shared some complimentary references Ibid., August 21, 1957, RAC.

255 "The best way to read a book" Eleanor Harris, "What Makes Rockefeller Run?," *American Weekly*, November 1, 1959.

256 "I think Henry Kissinger is one of the real comers" NAR–William Benton, August 9, 1957, RAC.

256 To all outward appearances NROH, July 14, 1977, 65.

256 "They both need it and so do I!" NAR–"Dear Virginia and Bryan," December 31, 1956, RAC.

257 "Under you and the President" NAR–RMN, November 8, 1956, RAC.

257 "This issue has driven an unfortunate wedge" NAR–RMN, April 3, 1957, RAC.

258 a "nasty confrontation" Gerard Clarfield, *Security with Solvency: Dwight D. Eisenhower and the Shaping of the American Military Establishment* (Westport, CT: Praeger Publishers, 1999), 215.

259 "Our position a year or two hence" Rockefeller Brothers Fund, *International Security: The Military Aspect* (Garden City, NY: Doubleday, 1958), 19.

260 "Unless present trends are reversed" "Not Too Late," *Newsweek*, January 13, 1958.

260 "The willingness to engage in nuclear war" Kutz, *Rockefeller Power*, 210.

260 "Hey, Pierre, get the Rockefeller Brothers Studies" Collier and Horowitz, *The Rockefellers*, 329, fn.

13: ROLLIN' WITH ROCK

265 "I hope you are not going to let them persuade you" Natalie Davenport–NAR, March 27, 1957, RAC.

266 "You did an extraordinary job" NAR–A. Harriman, August 18, 1952, RAC; also see Harriman obituary, *New York Times*, June 27, 2000.

268 "It looks like an interesting year" L. J. Morhouse–NAR, January 10, 1956, RAC.

268 Most around Rockefeller were cool to the idea F. Jamieson–NAR, *Conversation with Frank Moore*, June 21, 1956, RAC.

268 "While this could have positive advantages" Ibid., *Constitutional Convention*, June 25, 1956, RAC.

269 "Harriman wasn't a weak governor" Ronan, AI.

269 "He saw Rockefeller" Ruebhausen, AI.

269 "My dear Mr. Secretary of State" Armao, AI.

269 Their role was to "hear and report" NAR–Alfred L. Rose, October 8, 1956, RAC.

269 "I am having fun" NAR–Zelia Ronan, [n.d.], NAR Personal Activities, Box 138, Folder 1523, RAC.

270 "You can't do that" Burbank, AI.

270 "We had an understanding" Ronan, AI.

270 To balance his executive director from New York City F. Jamieson–NAR, September 28, 1956, RAC; NROH, August 4, 1977, 12–13; Morris, N. Rockefeller, 311.

270 "Hinman had a very easy manner about him" Hatfield, AI.

271 Nelson said he would take his chances NROH, July 14, 1977, 68.

271 "You could have knocked me over with a feather" Ibid., 73.

271 "the New York grape" Ronan, AI.

271 "A lot of you are contenders" Edward Kresky, AI.

271 "Most politicians have to build themselves up" MacCrate, AI.

271 "Jamieson said to Nelson" Ruebhausen, AI.

272 According to one guest present Warren Anderson, HMI, 1.

272 Pollster Sam Lubell neatly summarized S. Lubell–F. Jamieson, October 31, 1957, RAC.

273 "unless you like controversy, oratory and vaudeville" New York World-Telegram and Sun, November 1, 1957.

273 "Your appearance at such a dinner" George Hinman–NAR, January 14, 1958, RAC.

274 But he wasn't running, said Wilson Malcolm Wilson, HMI, 6.

274 "Remember when we had our meeting with Herb?" Ibid., 8.

275 "This I hope to break" NAR–Richard Aldrich, June 25, 1958, RAC.

275 Also present, earning $40 a week Happy Rockefeller, AI.

275 "We came up with the idea of urban state parks" Ronan, AI.

276 Nelson was no pushover Eleanor Roosevelt, "My Day," New York Post, July 3, 1958.

276 "Nelson was his own best salesman" Malcolm Wilson, HMI, 15.

276 "In the car he would brief and prepare Father" Steven Rockefeller, HMI, 4.

276 "'there goes Len Hall with his platform'" Ibid. For Len Hall, see his obituary, New York Times, June 3, 1979.

277 Sometimes the candidate said nothing more Time, October 6, 1958.

277 "If we could get the voting age down to six" New York Times, October 10, 1958.

277 "They come out to see whether he's for real" Desmond, N. Rockefeller, 183.

277 "We went with him to a potato festival" Jack Germond, AI.

277 "I am glad to be here" Malcolm Wilson, HMI, 19.

278 "a sounder method of dealing with a mild recession" New York Herald Tribune, April 1, 1958.

278 Morhouse administered a firm rap on the knuckles L. J. Morhouse–F. Jamieson, July 15, 1958, RAC.

278 Nor was Morhouse shy about opposing Nelson's plan New York World-Telegram and Sun, August 1, 1958.

279 "I understand Harriman spent $27,000" "Political Whispers," New York Mirror, July 16, 1958.

279 He replaced the honey locust trees F. Cardinal Spellman–NAR, March 26, 1951, RAC.

279 Pfeiffer received a call from Nelson Rockefeller William Pfeiffer, HMI, 8–9.

279 Early in the campaign, Jud Morhouse forcibly denied Rochester Times-Union, June 11, 1958.

279 "I don't know how you handle those things around here" Malcolm Wilson, HMI, 9.

279 "I always dealt with him as if he were on welfare" Ibid.

280 "He would fly from Tarrytown to North Tarrytown" Ibid., 19–20.

280 "Who can compete with that kind of money?" Cannon, AI.

280 "Don't swap multimillionaires in midstream" New York Post, June 23, 1958.

280 Keynoting his party's convention in Buffalo on August 25 New York Times, August 26, 1958.

281 "You know, I have to tell you" NROH, July 14, 1977, 73.

281 "The job you have done" George Hinman–NAR, August 27, 1958, RAC.

281 "They gave old Ave a real Philadelphia rat fucking" Rudy Abramson, Spanning the Century: The Life of W. Averell Harriman, 1891–1986 (New York: William Morrow, 1992), 563.

281 **"That's it," said Frank Jamieson** Morris, N. *Rockefeller*, 177; see also Stewart Alsop, "The Battle of the Millionaires," *Saturday Evening Post*, October 25, 1958.

282 **"It is almost impossible not to like the man"** Robinson, *I Never Had It Made*, 162.

282 **"sort of running the state as it is"** *New York Times*, August 29, 1958.

283 **"Get Rollin' with Rock"** G. Hinman–L. J. Morhouse, September 16, 1958, RAC.

284 **Lunching with a conservative newspaper publisher** Morris, N. *Rockefeller*, 180–81.

284 **"He was for many of us a knight in shining armor then"** Steven Rockefeller, HMI, 5.

284 **"Mr. Rockefeller is trying a new campaign technique"** *New York Times*, October 2, 1958.

284 **"Hinman down to earth stuff"** G. Hinman–NAR, September 25, 1958, RAC. Rockefeller readily deferred to the experts around him, among them Burdell Bixby, Tom Dewey's law partner and a crack campaign scheduler. By contrast with the former governor, who had not allowed a single event to pass unjustified, Rockefeller offered no resistance whatever to Bixby's itineraries. "I don't want to waste my time. You do it and I'll go." Burdell Bixby, HMI, 15.

285 **As for the real problem, his dyslexia** Burbank, AI

285 **A solution was devised** Reich, *Worlds to Conquer*, 746–47. Arthur Levitt returned home one evening during the campaign only to have his wife inform him, "Harriman is done, he is finished." When asked why, she replied, "You should hear this man Rockefeller. He is superb, he is great." Arthur Levitt, HMI, 2.

285 **"just like Eisenhower was in Washington"** *New York Times*, October 2, 1958.

285 **"I ought to join a union"** Ibid., October 15, 1958.

285 **"a good fighting chance"** NAR–Oveta Culp Hobby, September 30, 1958, RAC.

285 **Attracting nearly as much attention as the players** *New York Times*, October 5, 1958.

286 **stooping to pick up a dime** *Time*, October 6, 1958.

286 **"I was worried he would be sick all night"** Louis Lefkowitz, HMI, 4–9. Rockefeller's "blintz tour" received extensive coverage in the daily press, especially the *Times* and *Herald Tribune*; see also *New Yorker*, "Talk of the Town," October 11, 1958.

286 **"Can I put hello in the bank?"** *New York Times*, October 2, 1958.

287 **By the third week of October** G. Hinman–L. J. Morhouse, October 14, 1958, RAC.

287 **"John 3rd was upset"** Burbank, AI.

288 **Tod accompanied Nelson on several trips around the state** For Tod's campaign activities, see *New York Times*, October 22, November 3, 1958.

288 **At an event in Rochester** Libby Shemwell, AI.

288 **Lubell began to speak of a rout in the making** Reminiscences of Samuel Lubell, CCOHC, 38–39.

289 **"Stay away from Eisenhower and Nixon"** "Talks Shelved by Rockefeller," *New York Times*, October 24, 1958.

289 **"I am running for Governor"** "Nixon Is Not Seen by Rockefeller," *New York Times*, October 24, 1958.

289 **"The governor is so accustomed"** *New York Times*, October 25, 1958.

290 **A reporter encountering Tom Dewey** Ibid., November 5, 1958.

291 **"He's been giving advice for fifty years"** *New York Daily News*, November 5, 1958.

291 **Privately, he expressed gratitude to his son Steven** Steven Rockefeller, HMI, 21.

291 **"You have mixed emergency capital expenditures"** NAR–R. Harnoncourt, November 8, 1958, RAC.

14: PAY AS YOU GO

293 **Nelson launches into his fourteen-minute inaugural address** Inaugural Address, January 1, 1959, Public Papers of Nelson A. Rockefeller (hereafter cited as "NR, PP [year]"), 11–14.

294 **"They look like they're all scribbled up"** *New York Herald Tribune*, January 2, 1959.

295 **A light snow is falling** *Time*, January 12, 1959.

295 **"He loved big challenges"** Isabelle Savell statement (in lieu of an interview), HMI. For an

excellent introduction to New York's governorship and how it evolved from colonial times, see Robert H. Connery and Gerald Benjamin, *Rockefeller of New York: Executive Power in the Statehouse* (Ithaca, NY: Cornell University Press, 1979), 23–26; Donald M. Roper, "The Governorship in History," in Robert H. Connery and Gerald Benjamin, eds., *Governing New York State: The Rockefeller Years* (New York: Academy of Political Science, 1974), 16–30; Robert H. Connery, "Nelson A. Rockefeller as Governor," *Proceedings of the Academy of Political Science* 31, no. 3 (May 1974): 1–16. Also see Alan G. Hevesi, *Legislative Politics in New York State: A Comparative Analysis* (New York: Praeger Publishers, 1975), 81–128.

297 **As one of its first acts** *New York Times,* January 7, 1959.

297 **On a postelection visit to Pocantico** Malcolm Wilson, HMI, 9–10.

297 **The first-floor press office** Betty Bixby, AI.

297 **Because his office was in one townhouse** Ronan, AI.

297 **"The floors were covered"** Persico, AI.

297 **"It was a rabbit warren"** MacCrate, AI.

298 **That Rockefeller's workdays sometimes began** Albright, AI.

298 **"How I love it here when it snows"** Richard Norton Smith, *Thomas E. Dewey and His Times: The First Full-Scale Biography of the Maker of the Modern Republican Party* (New York: Simon & Schuster, 1982), 359.

298 **"Other than eating, drinking, and politics"** Bixby, AI.

298 **"The legislature convened"** Slater, AI.

299 **"Neither do I"** Ronan, AI.

299 **Unknown to the public** George Dudley, AI.

299 **On being presented with an old Civil War cannon** Robert Bennett, AI. The same source recalled a house fire that destroyed the wooden balcony of a nearby property. Rockefeller, ever sensitive to local aesthetics, offered to send over a couple of painters to repair the resulting eyesore.

299 **Struck by the barren appearance** Albright, *Portrait,* 137–38.

299 **Some preferences were communicated nonverbally** Cynthia Lefferts, AI.

300 **"The governor loved meetings"** Robert J. Donovan, *Confidential Secretary* (Boston: Dutton Adult, 1988), 169.

300 **"Nelson would never tolerate"** Malcolm Wilson, HMI, 1.

300 **"In our staff meetings"** MacCrate, AI.

300 **"Be the best governor of New York you can be"** Burbank, AI.

300 **"Isn't this fun?"** William V. Shannon, "The Live One," *New York Post,* June 4, 1958.

301 **"On second thought"** *New York Herald Tribune,* April 3, 1959.

301 **"Whose show is this?"** Ibid., January 18, 1959.

301 **Rockefeller's pet peeves** Cynthia Lefferts, Bill Ronan, Harry Albright, and Les Slote testified to Rockefeller's office habits.

301 **Besides a leg of lamb** Bennett, AI.

301 **"I'm aware . . . that you have some independent resources"** "The Lyons Den," *New York Post,* January 29, 1959. The Friday Report, initiated by Bill Ronan in 1962 and reinstated nine years later by Norman Hurd, is described in Connery and Benjamin, *Rockefeller of New York,* 158–59.

302 **"I'm Nelson Rockefeller"** *New York World-Telegram and Sun,* January 13, 1959.

302 **"You feel at ease in his presence"** Gay Talese, "Impressionistic Sketch of a Governor," *New York Times Magazine,* March 29, 1959.

303 **"I don't know how they used to do things around here"** Harry O'Donnell, HMI, 43.

303 **"That's difficult politically"** NRI, Eisenhower Administration Project, CCOHC, 30; Malcolm Wilson, HMI, 3.

304 **"If my grandfather could only see me now"** Joseph Murphy, HMI, 10.

305 **"You seem to have quickly become a controversial figure"** DDE–NAR, February 17, 1959, RAC.

305 **Rockefeller was loudly booed** "Politicians' Spurs," *Time,* March 16, 1959.

306 **He had no intention of scraping by** *New York Times,* February 20, 1959.

306 "Every man in public life" "No Status Quo Guy, This Gov. Rockefeller," *New York Herald Tribune*, [n.d.].

306 The Boy Scout in him truly believed Norman Hurd, HMI, 10–11.

306 a massive shake-up of the state's Republican organization *New York Times*, January 12, 1959; *Christian Science Monitor*, April 9, 1959.

307 "the Wunderkind of American politics" *BusinessWeek*, March 21, 1959.

307 To columnist Joseph Alsop "The Rockefeller Phenomenon," *New York Herald Tribune*, [n.d.]; see also James Desmond, "Rockefeller's Fast Start," *The Nation*, April 25, 1959.

308 "It's a completely abstract painting" Talese, "Sketch of a Governor."

308 "He starts mouthing off about Nelson's taxes" Victor Condello, CRI.

309 "Dear Nelson" Walter J. Mahoney–NAR, July 1, 1959, RAC.

309 two weeks at his Venezuela ranch *New York Times*, May 19, 1959.

309 "I'm going to stay in Albany" *New York Journal-American*, June 12, 1959.

310 "Cal-Rocks" *Newsweek*, April 6, 1959.

310 George Gallup reported *U.S. News & World Report*, August 17, 1959.

310 warning of the GOP's "emasculation" Frank C. Hanighen–A. G. Berry, August 11, 1959 (referred to Rod Perkins by Bob McManus, August 27, 1959), RAC.

310 "One of the toughest things about Nelson" Lefferts, AI.

311 "Stop the presses" Nancy Hanks, HMI, 26–29.

311 By the fall of 1959 *New York Times*, December 24, 1959. Henry Kissinger himself urged Rockefeller to take a hard line against Eisenhower's peacemaking efforts—specifically faulting Ike's popular invitation to Nikita Khrushchev to visit the United States in the autumn of 1959. "I am not impressed by the ovations for the President," Kissinger told Rockefeller. "The same was true after Munich." H. Kissinger–NAR, September 3, 1959, RAC.

312 a publicity stunt Joseph Alsop column of August 15, 1959, as reported in *Brownwood Texas Bulletin*, August 31, 1959.

313 where she polished her English Anne-Marie Rasmussen, *There Was Once a Time* (New York: Bantam, 1976), 18.

313 "I had to take my husband to Hamburger Heaven" Ibid.

313 If she stayed another year Ibid., 28.

313 he did not love Ibid., 45.

313 "I almost feel pity for him" Ibid., 47.

314 A two-day visit to Chicago *San Antonio Express*, October 25, 1959.

314 even down to Len Hall's vigorous opposition The long arm of a vengeful Hall could be seen in stunts like the one reported by Rockefeller operatives in the fall of 1959—at an American Legion convention, a Nixon supporter from Wisconsin showed up with pictures of Rockefeller in front of a Picasso canvas and the caption "Wouldn't it be better if he were standing before a framed honorable discharge?" L. J. Morhouse–Mr. Hinman, September 15, 1959, RAC.

315 "It always bugged him" George Hinman, HMI, 4.

315 "If Jesus Christ came down off the cross today" Letter to author from William Ringle.

316 "Here we are again" KRD, November 12, 1959.

316 By the time he finished W. Kenneth Riland, HMI, 96–97.

316 In Oklahoma City KRD, December 16, 1959.

316 "he has friends in Texas" Morris, *N. Rockefeller*, 238.

317 Were Rockefeller to upset the vice president Robert Novak, AI.

317 "He had the meeting" Happy Rockefeller, AI.

317 "Nelson turns to me" Ronan, AI.

318 Nixon thought reporters were joking *New York Herald Tribune*, December 27, 1959.

318 "You never know what will happen to Dick" KRD, December 29, 1959.

318 Henry Kissinger acknowledged feelings of despair H. Kissinger–NAR, December 28, 1959, RAC.

318 "All of us who love you" Lincoln Kirstein–NAR, December 27, 1959, RAC.

318 **A dying Frank Jamieson** Linda Storrow, AI.

318 **Rockefeller emphasized the need** KRD, December 29, 1959.

318 **Joe Alsop came closest to the truth** "Rockefeller: Background Report," *Washington Post*, December 30, 1959.

319 **After the fact, Rockefeller attributed his withdrawal** Desmond, N. *Rockefeller*, 245.

319 **A decade later, he was more explicit** NRI, Eisenhower Administration Project, CCOHC, 39.

319 **"The party was locked up"** George Hinman, HMI, 10.

319 **"The national party and Nelson"** Ibid., 3.

319 **"When I became insecure"** NROH, October 4, 1977, 10.

319 **"No man can run for the White House"** Ruebhausen, AI.

15: In and Out

320 **"Nelson's mistake in 1960"** George Hinman, HMI, 10.

320 **"But you will never find another Frankie"** Max Ascoli–NAR, February 1, 1960, RAC.

321 **"I am happy with the time we spent together"** E. J. Hughes–NAR, October 18, 1959, RAC.

321 **"I remember him in a black cape"** Happy Rockefeller, AI.

321 **"an explosion of temperament"** Emmet Hughes, HMI, 7.

321 **his engraved card** John Goldman, AI.

322 **"He expected Emmet to do for him"** Cannon AI.

322 **his "remarkable inability to spell"** Morris, N. *Rockefeller*, 13.

322 **Inadequate preparation or physical exhaustion** Canzeri, AI.

322 **"He can't keep his pecker in his pants"** Massolo, AI.

322 **"You better give the key back to the girls"** *New York Post*, May 6, 1959.

322 **A Freudian slip, perhaps** Dan Rostenkowski, AI.

323 **"It wasn't that he used women"** Jack McGrath, AI.

323 **To a photographer asking her to pose** *New York Times*, November 7, 1958.

323 **"I am learning to fend off embarrassing questions"** MTR–F. Jamieson, April 30, 1959, RAC.

323 **"I liked being with her"** John Gardner, AI.

323 **"I always suspected"** Germond, AI.

323 **"Nelson never realized"** Malcom Wilson, HMI, 24.

323 **"I think the Albany setting"** Marshall, AI.

323 **"Nelson abhorred smoking"** Henry Diamond, AI.

323 **"She was terribly embittered"** Burbank, AI.

324 **"New England lockjaw"** Hatfield, AI.

324 **Only a handful of intimates knew** Burbank, AI.

324 **"Jamieson was like a guard"** Marshall, AI.

324 **a "simple, rustic guesthouse"** *New York World-Telegram*, March 12, 1959.

324 **"What had become an empty marriage"** White, *Making of President, 1964*, 80.

325 **"I knew both Tod and Happy"** William Scranton, AI.

326 **"I had this aunt"** Happy Rockefeller, AI; "The Guarded Tranquil World Happy Rockefeller Is Giving Up," *People*, September 9, 1974.

326 **A childhood friend remembered Happy** "Guarded, Tranquil World."

326 **her "bright smile and perpetual good humor"** *Washington Post*, May 1, 1968.

326 **According to the 1944 class yearbook** *New York Times*, May 5, 1963.

326 **"If you want to know how sheltered my upbringing was"** Happy Rockefeller, CRI.

327 **"At the reception following the wedding"** Elizabeth Shemwell, letter to the author.

327 **no stranger to the Rockefellers** Happy Rockefeller, AI.

328 **David Rockefeller was instrumental** D. Rockefeller, *Memoirs*, 191.

328 **"They were so delighted with the plans"** NAR–George Dudley, December 5, 1956, RAC.

328 **a controlling husband** White, *Making of President, 1964*, 81–82.

328 **"I first met her in 1958"** Burbank, AI.

328 "Rockefeller didn't want to record anything" Boyd, AI.

329 "The people who say they knew" Germond, AI.

329 "The dot is Nelson" Jerry Danzig, HMI, 24.

329 "He always insisted I have a phone connected to him" Ronan, AI.

329 "Nelson had a weakness" Harry O'Donnell, HMI, 38.

330 "A couple of times I would say to him" Ronan, AI.

330 "I saw him angry several times" Lefferts, AI.

330 "program associates" E. Kresky, AI.

330 Prompted by a similar effort in Hawaii Vincent J. Moore, AI.

331 he startled Sol Corbin Sol Corbin, AI.

331 "He talked to me about nothing but bomb shelters" Collier and Horowitz, *The Rockefellers*, 344, fn.

332 "It was disgraceful" Ronan, AI.

333 "Withholding was the greatest bonanza" Joseph Murphy, HMI, 14.

333 "My basic pitch was" MacCrate, AI.

333 "Shortcomings in the administration of our laws" NR, PP 1960, 191.

333 "Fuck the governor" Kramer and Roberts, "*I Never Wanted*," 106.

334 "Atta boy, Rocky!" Ken Auletta, *The Streets Were Paved with Gold* (New York: Vintage, 2011), 49.

335 With his dumpy physique *New York Times*, February 13, 1991; Harry O'Donnell, HMI, 70. An excellent portrait of Wagner as mayor is in Robert A. Caro, *The Power Broker: Robert Moses and the Fall of New York* (New York: Vintage, 1975), 799–806. See also *New York Times*, February 13, 1991.

336 "Don't horseshit me" Reminiscences of Warren Moscow, CCOHC, 43.

336 "An arrogant son of a bitch" Ibid., 44.

337 "Did he say what place?" Desmond, *N. Rockefeller*, 254.

337 What could his boss do Burdell Bixby notes of talk with Robert Finch, March 9, 1959, RAC.

337 Nixon's strong showing in the primaries G. Hinman–NAR, Convention Offer Decision, May 12, 1960, RAC.

337 On May 11, his father died *New York Times*, May 12, 1960.

338 On the day of Junior's memorial service June Hamersma, AI.

338 "In view of the many beautiful editorials" NAR–JDR3rd, May 26, 1960, RAC.

338 More than once that spring John French, HMI, 19.

338 A replay of the 1958 scrimmage *New York Times*, May 19, 1960.

338 "There is a real and imminent danger" G. Hinman–NAR, May 12, 1960. As evidence of Rockefeller's diminished clout, pollster Lou Harris found Rockefeller's job approval ratings sharply lower in the wake of his 1959 tax increases. Harris, "Why the Odds Are Against a Governor's Becoming President," *Public Opinion Quarterly* (Fall 1959): 368–69. One might write off Harris as a Democratic-leaning pollster but for the fact that Rockefeller's own public opinion oracle, Sam Lubell, was simultaneously telling Nelson in the summer of 1959 that he was nationally known "either as a rich man or as that fellow who raised taxes." S. Lubell–F. Jamieson, July 23, 1959, RAC.

339 Recognizing something had to be done Desmond, *N. Rockefeller*, 256.

339 Hinman met with Ken Keating G. Hinman–NAR, May 12, 1960, RAC.

339 "By frankness, realism and magnanimity" Ibid., May 20, 1960, RAC.

339 "the 1964 argument" E. Hughes–NAR, May 31, 1960, RAC.

339 "That's irrelevant" Moscow, *Rockefeller Inheritance*, 346.

339 "We have come to a time" NR, PP 1960, 1044–50.

340 Rockefeller's "buckshot indictment" *New York Herald Tribune*, June 12, 1960.

340 Grand Old Patricide *New York Journal-American*, June 13, 1960.

341 "a good swift kick" *New York Post*, June 15, 1960.

341 "I see the fine hand of Emmet in this" Alan Levy, "Today's Writing: Art or Séance?," *The Tech* (MIT), April 25, 1962.

341 "off again, on again, gone again, Finnegan" Donovan, *Confidential Secretary*, 167–68.

341 "Don't let anyone else write your speeches" Ambrose, *Eisenhower*, 595.

341 "Nelson felt he could be the conscience" Emmet Hughes, HMI, 2.

341 "one of the most remarkable collections" Theodore White, *The Making of the President, 1960* collections (New York: Atheneum, 1964), 185; see also *Memorandum for the 1960 Republican Party Platform*, NR, PP 1960, 1108–19.

342 George Hinman met in New York G. Hinman–NAR, June 17, 1960, RAC.

342 His candidate's withdrawal in December Bill Brinton, AI.

342 "I had to get my hands on the decision-making apparatus" White, *Making of President, 1960*, 185.

342 "I knew there would never be a draft" Desmond, *N. Rockefeller*, 256.

343 Percy flew to New York Ann Whitman's diary for July 5, housed at the Dwight Eisenhower Library in Abilene, Kansas, quotes Gabriel Hauge, the White House economist who accompanied Percy to the platform review session: "He said he felt Nelson was a little bewildered that his recent stand had caused so little enthusiasm."

343 "My God, isn't it awful" Malcolm Wilson, HMI, 22.

343 "You couldn't find them with a search warrant" George Hinman, HMI, 10.

343 "I'm always willing to take a chance" Alsop, *Nixon and Rockefeller*, 178.

344 "Tell Dick to call me" *Time*, August 1, 1960.

344 "I want to go all the way with you" Ibid.

344 "Nixon feared Rockefeller's power" John Sears, AI.

344 Without informing his staff Don Hughes, AI.

344 Nelson, more than slightly miffed NRI, Eisenhower Administration Project, CCOHC, 35; also helping to re-create that surreal encounter for me was Ilene Slater, who was pressed into service to take dictation over the phone from Emmet Hughes in Chicago and between the two principals in the study at 810 Fifth Avenue.

344 Nixon sweetened his offer Arthur Schlesinger, Jr., *Journals: 1952–2000* (New York: Penguin Press, 2007), 84.

345 "We are sitting here with a pair of 3's" Emmet Hughes, HMI, 3.

345 The only real snag of the evening NRI, Eisenhower Administration Project, CCOHC, 32.

345 a lawyerly distinction Richard Nixon, *Six Crises* (New York: Doubleday, 1962), 315.

346 In private, he accused Rockefeller W. J. Rorabaugh, *The Real Making of the President: Kennedy, Nixon, and the 1960 Election* (Lawrence: University Press of Kansas, 2012), 111.

346 Members of the platform committee Drew Pearson diary, July 23, 1960.

346 "a damned sellout" *Time*, August 1, 1960.

346 Tom Dewey said *New York Times*, July 25, 1960.

346 "Both Nelson and I were quite shortsighted at the time" Emmet Hughes, HMI, 3.

347 Had Rockefeller only waited a day Joseph W. Alsop and Adam Platt, *"I've Seen the Best of It": Memoirs* (New York: W. W. Norton, 1992), 416–18.

347 Taking a cue from Ike The fight over the civil rights plank is re-created by Rick Perlstein in his seminal *Before the Storm: Barry Goldwater and the Unmaking of the American Consensus* (New York: Hill & Wang, 2001), 86–91.

347 Rockefeller carried the fight to the Liberty Baptist Church *New York Times*, July 25, 1960.

347 Their pleas did not go entirely unheard White, *Making of President*, 1960, 187; "GOP: How Drafty?," *Newsweek*, July 15, 1960.

348 "Progress is not their business" *New York Times*, July 27, 1960.

348 Ken Riland was doing a slow burn W. Kenneth Roland, HMI, 65.

16: LOSS AND RENEWAL

349 Henry Kissinger found his patron Schlesinger, *Journals*, 84.

349 This did not prevent him *Newsweek*, November 14, 1960.

349 **Addressing one Wall Street rally** *New Yorker*, November 5, 1960.

349 **Rockefeller was quick to blame Nixon** Novak, *Agony*, 11–15.

350 **Nelson let a week pass** NAR–RMN, November 15, 1960, RAC.

350 **a search for scapegoats** "Nixon's Lonely Battle," *Wall Street Journal*, October 28, 1960; for a counterview, see "Rockefeller and the Republicans," *New York Post*, November 28, 1960.

350 **"I need hardly tell you"** JFK–NAR, January 24, 1961, RAC.

350 **By pumping an additional $40 million** Unsent letter, NAR–JFK, November 1960; *New York Herald Tribune*, January 5, 1961; Perkins, AI.

352 **"If Shorty Knox says it's OK"** Kitty Carlisle Hart, AI.

352 **"I know where Queens is"** E. Kresky, AI.

352 **He wasn't through with the fair** Philip Johnson, CRI.

353 **There things stood for the next decade** Rockefeller's long struggle to establish a university worthy of the Empire State was extensively covered, both in the daily press of the period and in his own public papers. Robert Connery and Gerald Benjamin provide an excellent over-view of the private versus public school battle in their *Rockefeller of New York*, 282–313; see also Donald Axhod's essay "Higher Education," in Connery and Benjamin, *Governing New York State*, 131–45; and "Private Colleges in New York Get the Nod," *Newsday*, April 26, 1992. I owe a special debt to Bob MacCrate for his insider's perspective on how SUNY came to be trans-formed.

355 **"It's necessary"** Germond, AI.

355 **"Only Nelson Rockefeller could have pulled it off"** Clifton Wharton, AI.

356 **Rockefeller should stick to Albany** G. Hinman–NAR, "Washington Intelligence," Decem-ber 12, 1960, RAC.

356 **At the White House, JFK readily acknowledged** *Time*, March 10, 1961.

356 **Within days of the inauguration** NAR–Rod Perkins, February 13, 1961, RAC.

356 **Dave Garroway related a presidential promise** Hugh Morrow–The Governor, February 15, 1961, RAC.

356 **Rockefeller urged public support** *Washington Post*, April 26, 1961.

356 **"Hinman understood people very well"** Robert Douglass, AI.

357 **Even Eisenhower sounded a reassuring note** G. Hinman–NAR, "Ike," September 10, 1961, RAC.

357 **Gratified by the progress he was making** G. Hinman–L. J. Morhouse, July 19, 1961. A perfect illustration of Hinman's top-down approach to the forthcoming campaign was his excitement over Harvard's invitation for Rockefeller to deliver the 1962 Godkin Lectures—"a tremendous opportunity" for the New York governor to advance conservative principles of local responsi-bility within a revitalized federal system. G. Hinman–NAR, July 26, 1961, RAC.

357 **Assailing Kennedy for playing racial politics** Drew Pearson diary, February 4, 1962; Peter Maas, "Nelson Rockefeller: Does He Have a Future with the GOP?," *Saturday Evening Post*, September 15, 1962.

357 **"he's really not such a bad fellow"** Perlstein, *Before the Storm*, 162. In December 1961, Gold-water reiterated in no uncertain terms that he had no intention of running for president. "Hell," he told George Hinman, "if I wanted to run for President, I would hire you and start you out organizing things." G. Hinman–NAR, December 14, 1961, RAC.

357 **Nelson had leaned hard on Jacob Javits** Novak, *Agony*, 36–39.

358 **"We want Barry!"** *Time*, March 10, 1961.

358 **"He's made it respectable"** Novak, *Agony*, 45.

358 **It was shortly before eleven o'clock** Bennett, AI; *Newsweek*, March 13, 1961; *Time*, March 10, 1961.

359 **"A fight wouldn't have changed anything"** Desmond, *N. Rockefeller*, 291.

359 **About this time** Ibid., 289.

359 **Emmet Hughes knew better** Emmet Hughes, HMI, 4–5.

360 **His preferred candidate** John Hay Whitney–NAR, April 14, 1961, RAC.

360 **Acting a familiar part** "Searching Party," *Time*, May 19, 1961.

361 **At the height of the campaign** Mrs. JDR3rd–"Dear Nel," October 4, 1961, RAC.

361 **Early in September** Milt Machlin, *The Search for Michael Rockefeller* (Pleasantville, NY: Akadine Press, 2000), 182–84.

361 **Brew put the expedition in context** J. O. Brew–Michael Rockefeller, June 2, 1960, RAC.

361 **up to $50,000** Michael Rockefeller–J. O. Brew, July 5, 1960, RAC.

361 **the strange molar music** *New York World-Telegram*, April 25, 1961, RAC.

362 **"It's *unbelievable*"** Kevin Bubriski, *Michael Rockefeller: New Guinea Photographs, 1961* (Cambridge, MA: Peabody Museum Press, 2006), 3; for additional background on the Asmat, see *Newsweek*, September 10, 1962.

362 **"I can think of nothing better for Americans"** M. Rockefeller–JDR3rd, July 25, 1961, RAC.

362 **"The key to my fascination"** Adrian A. Gerbrands, ed., *The Asmat of New Guinea: The Journal of Michael Clark Rockefeller* (New York: Museum of Primitive Art, 1968), 44; Gerbrands's introductory essay (11–39) provides a superb overview of the Asmat and their art.

362 **"a mammoth exhibition"** Ibid., 45. Books about Michael's final days continue to appear, most recently a well-reviewed volume, *Savage Harvest*, by journalist Carl Hoffman. By now Nelson Rockefeller's youngest son has taken his place alongside Amelia Earhart and James Hoffa, more famous for his disappearance than for the life preceding his mysterious loss.

363 **Laurance alone held out** LSR, HMI, 51–52.

363 **One evening in November** Malcolm Wilson, HMI, 10; *Newsweek* (November 27, 1961) said the only greater surprise would be if Rockefeller had filed for bankruptcy.

364 **To another friend** Confidential source.

364 **At the stroke of six p.m.** *Time*, November 24, 1961.

364 **George Hinman was in Atlanta** "Reports Southern View of Rockefeller Divorce," WNBC *Monitor*, November 18, 1961; G. Hinman–NAR, "Republican Southern Conference, November 17th and 18th," RAC.

364 **"if there were anything like that in the picture"** G. Hinman–NAR, "Republican Mid-Western States Conference," December 4, 1961, RAC.

364 **Drawing on personal experience** William Benton–NAR, November 20, 1961, RAC.

365 **In a snidely amusing commentary** "Too Much," *Syracuse Herald-Journal*, November 20, 1961.

365 **"I don't believe it"** Drew Pearson diary, December 28, 1961.

366 **He shouldn't expect too much** NROH, July 26, 1977, 48.

366 **"I pride myself on being a realist"** Desmond, *N. Rockefeller*, 297.

366 **During his first twenty-four hours** Desmond, *N. Rockefeller*, 300–01.

366 **"I warned him about the crocodiles"** "Father and Son," *Newsweek*, December 4, 1961.

367 **"Reasonable chance Michael reached shore"** NAR cable to Louise Boyer, November 22, 1961, RAC.

367 **He fixed his hopes** *Newsweek*, December 4, 1961.

367 **"They know what to look for"** Desmond, *N. Rockefeller*, 302.

367 **"No. Have you?"** Machlin, *Search for Michael Rockefeller*, 223.

367 **Rockefeller took comfort** Mary R. Morgan, *Beginning with the End: A Memoir of Twin Loss and Healing* (New York: Vantage Point, 2012), 18.

367 **"Ever since he was little"** Nick Thimmesch, *Milwaukee Journal*, June 18, 1968.

368 **"Hello, Nels"** Rasmussen, *There Was Once*, 148.

368 **"I hope Michael meets Mother in Heaven"** Happy Rockefeller, AI.

368 **"The only picture he had on his desk"** Slote, AI.

368 **Before settling Michael's $660,000 estate** *New York Times*, January 17, 1964.

368 **Among the first visitors to the show** G. Gardner–NAR, September 28, 1962, RAC.

369 **Even so, her mail had to be sifted** Jim Wallis, CRI.

369 **"I don't think anybody will ever know the truth"** Happy Rockefeller, AI.

369 **His son "gambled and lost"** NROH, July 26, 1977, 48.

369 **"He was one of those intuitive people"** *New York Times*, February 27, 1968.

369 **Within days of Nelson's death** *New York Post*, April 22, 1979.

370 **on the brink of resignation** *New York Times*, December 13, 1961.

370 **"those on the fringes of our society"** *Newsweek*, December 4, 1961.

370 **Meeting in Dallas that same week** Ibid.

371 **Hinman felt confident** MacCrate, AI.

371 **Hinman hardly needed to spell out** G. Hinman–NAR, "The Great Republican Issue," December 11, 1961, RAC.

372 **As delivered on February 15, 1962** NR, PP 1962, 1208–12.

372 **Rockefeller all but read out of the GOP** Ibid.

372 **Rockefeller injected himself into a dispute** NR, PP 1962, 1036–39.

373 **Rockefeller credited atomic weapons** *New York Mirror*, May 13, 1962.

373 **"I don't care if I burn"** Richard Jacoby, *Conversations with the Capeman: The Untold Story of Salvador Agron* (Madison: University of Wisconsin Press, 2004), 3; *New York Daily News*, September 6, 2009.

374 **Going into the hearing** MacCrate, AI.

375 **"It is just using some imagination"** Frank Lynn, "The Rockefeller Years," *Newsday*, April 15, 1969.

375 **Levitt found the idea repugnant** Arthur Levitt, HMI, August 27, 1979, 8.

376 **"I have been busy every waking hour"** MTR–Blanchette Rockefeller, January 23, 1962, RAC.

377 **"I just don't know what to do"** Joan Crawford–NAR, April 12, 1962, RAC. A different side of Miss Crawford's personality showed itself when, unable to have her call to the governor put through immediately (or at all), she spewed profanities at the offending secretary. Paul Grondahl, "Longtime Secretary Recalls Rockefeller," *Albany Times Union*, January 16, 2012.

377 **In Reno, Tod was accompanied** Morgan, *Beginning with the End*, 60–61.

377 **"This is a great break for Reno"** *New York Daily News*, March 17, 1962.

377 **Having no need for thirty-plus rooms** "810 Fifth Avenue," *Parade*, June 28, 1964.

378 **"Can Rocky be licked"** Warren Moscow, CCOHC, 45.

378 **JFK had some advice** Benjamin C. Bradlee, *Conversations with Kennedy* (New York: W. W. Norton, 1984), 74.

378 **"Where was Old Nels"** Ibid., 75.

378 **"I got a call from the IRS"** Ronan, AI; Corbin, AI.

379 **"Old Lou is full of shit on this one"** Bradlee, *Conversations*, 74. For Robert M. Morgenthau, see "The Lamb Who Won," *Time*, September 28, 1962; "Robert Morgenthau," Jewish Virtual Library, www.jewishvirtuallibrary.org; Geoffrey Gray, "Morgenthau Gets Witchy About Leslie Crocker Snyder," *New York*, November 6, 2005.

380 **"He had never run for anything"** William vanden Heuval, AI; *New York Herald Tribune*, November 7, 1962.

380 **Privately, he called him "a prick"** Underhill, AI.

381 **To run against Javits for the Senate** George J. Marlin, *Fighting the Good Fight: A History of the New York Conservative Party* (South Bend, IN: St. Augustine's Press, 2002), 51.

381 **At the eleventh hour** *New York Times*, October 2, 1962.

381 **"There's an election going on"** "Rocky Running Like It's '64," *New York Journal-American*, November 1, 1962.

382 **"Understand this now"** William Pfeiffer, HMI, 12.

382 **Once again the candidate made a point** "How Far Can Rocky Run?," *Look*, December 18, 1962.

382 **In dairy country, Rockefeller blamed** *New York World-Telegram*, May 4, 1962.

382 **On street corners in the Bronx** *New York Times*, November 3, 1962.

382 **Even *The New York Times* questioned Rocky's arithmetic** *Newsweek*, May 14, 1962.

382 **At Bill Ronan's instigation** Ronan, AI.

383 **"Don't put it out"** Ibid.

383 **Rockefeller restated his support for the administration** NR, PP 1962, 1120; interview of NAR by Martin Agronsky, *Today* show, October 29, 1962, 1132–35.

384 **Rockefeller versus Kennedy** *New York Times*, October 19, 1962.

384 **"You know, I'm fucking your first wife"** Robert Morgenthau, CRI.

17: SECOND CHANCES

385 **"There are two things you must remember"** Jerry Danzig, HMI, 23.

385 **In the postmidnight haze** John Lomenzo, HMI, 8–10.

385 **Throughout the boy's illness** Lance Morrow, *The Chief: A Memoir of Fathers and Sons* (New York: Random House, 1984), 13; Lance Morrow, AI. Rockefeller once dispatched his personal photographer, a Barbados native, to represent him at the inauguration of that island's new prime minister—"official greetings, chauffeured limousine," and all. Notes from Cary Reich's interview with Bert Smith. Amid rumors that an alcoholic judge and former state GOP official was about to be forced from the bench, Rockefeller visited the man in the hospital, expressed sympathy for his condition, offered help toward his recovery, and guaranteed that he would be retained in his present position "as long as I am Governor." The man died two days later. Confidential source.

386 **"You admire it. . . . I got it"** Lefferts, AI.

386 **"You better stay"** When gubernatorial speech-writing duties prevented Morrow from joining his wife for a New Year's Eve party in Washington, Rockefeller telephoned his aide's wife and "laid it on eighteen feet thick," in Morrow's words. The next day, Carol Morrow received two bottles of vintage champagne, courtesy of Governor Rockefeller. Harry O'Donnell, HMI, 91. Rockefeller's repeated assertion that "I'm only as good as the people who work for me" didn't hurt his staff relationships. Cannon, AI.

386 **"Nelson wanted to be a man of the people"** Goldman, AI.

386 **"It's deliberate . . . to keep you off balance"** Donovan, *Confidential Secretary*, 174.

386 **"People expect you to be stuck-up"** Steward Alsop–F. Jamieson, text of interview with NAR, May 7, 1959, RAC.

386 **"Did you have dinner?"** Louis Lefkowitz, HMI, 30.

386 **"imagine going through life never knowing who your friends really are"** Michael Whiteman, AI.

386 **"The thing about Nelson is that he had no friends"** Ann Whitman, HMI, 33.

387 **"he's my doctor, not my friend"** Ibid.

387 **a classic extrovert** Happy Rockefeller, AI.

387 **"And this pallid, exhausted man"** Jerry Danzig, HMI, 22.

387 **"I wonder what the hell's the matter with that soldier?"** Joseph Murphy, HMI, 21–22.

387 **Rockefeller established a trust fund** Confidential source.

387 **For her sixty-fifth birthday** Donovan, *Confidential Secretary*, 179.

388 **"Would you mind opening the door, please?"** Joseph Murphy, HMI, 22–23.

388 **He showed similar forbearance** Jerry Danzig, HMI, 5.

388 **he was not always so considerate** Slote, AI.

388 **"Am I going to make this speech or are you?"** "A Political Puzzle," *New York Times*, March 22, 1968.

388 **"Aren't the trains running?"** Joseph Murphy, HMI, 16–17.

388 **"Look at that memorandum"** Diamond, AI.

389 **"I want you to look down and see what they're doing"** Underhill, AI.

390 **He flew into a rage** Ronan, AI; Caro, *The Power Broker*, 1072–81.

390 **"It is regrettable"** NR, PP 1962, 1159.

390 **He sent his trusted deputy** Ronan, AI.

391 **scandal involving the State Liquor Authority** *Life*, April 5, 1963; *New York Mirror*, April 17, 1963; William Rodgers, *Rockefeller's Follies: An Unauthorized View of Nelson A. Rockefeller* (New York: Stein & Day, 1966), 46–55.

391 **"I heard some rumors"** Ronan, AI.

391 **"Why didn't he ask me"** Drew Pearson, "Scandals Shock Rockefeller," *Washington Post*, May 7, 1963.

392 **He left the criminal investigation** *New York Mirror*, June 1, 1963.

392 **acting under the state's Moreland Act** Lawrence Walsh, AI.

392 Rockefeller's second term began much like his first Oren Root, *Persons and Persuasions* (New York: W. W. Norton, 1974), 150–51.

393 Rockefeller faulted the Kennedy White House *New York Times*, April 7, 1963.

394 Only a few months after the Cuban missile crisis *New York Herald Tribune*, April 14, 1963.

394 he railed against "domination from Washington" *New York Times*, April 8, 1963; *Christian Science Monitor*, April 9, 1963.

395 the Conservative Society of America *New York Times*, April 14, 1963.

395 Clarence Jones was summoned to the vault Taylor Branch, *Parting the Waters: America in the King Years 1954–63* (New York: Simon & Schuster, 1988), 789. I am indebted to my colleague Douglas Brinkley for calling this incident to my attention and for sharing his own research on the Jones-Rockefeller connection. Diane McWhorter, in her searing memoir, *Carry Me Home* (New York: Simon & Schuster, 2001), 403, suggests a Rockefeller contribution to Dr. King's bail fund of around $90,000.

395 The Executive Mansion was ablaze with light Bleecker, *Politics of Architecture*, 150–51.

395 "That's not modern" At least Rockefeller's architects limited their comments to the age of his paintings. One upstate legislator, roped into joining a similar tour led by the governor, glanced at a particularly colorful abstract canvas and declared, "That's the way the world looked to me on the day I discovered sex." Warren Weaver, "Nelson Aldrich Rockefeller Remembered," *New York Times*, January 28, 1979.

396 Not content to expedite the process Bleecker, *Politics of Architecture*, 142–46.

396 As Rockefeller made good Ibid., 151–75.

397 "We needed space for state office buildings" Ronan, AI.

397 "Start building a monument to yourself" Burdell Bixby, HMI, 19.

398 The two men had a history Paul Grondahl, *Mayor Corning: Albany Icon, Albany Enigma* (Albany, NY: Washington Park Press, 1997), 454–57.

398 Nelson ordered sycamore trees planted Albright, AI.

398 That Rockefeller had his own ideas on the subject MacCrate, AI.

398 On a Sunday evening in January 1962 Ronan, AI; Bleecker, *Politics of Architecture*, 187–88.

399 Decrying the "sterile monument" Grondahl, *Mayor Corning*, 458.

399 "I had a lot to do with everything Nelson didn't do" Newhouse, *W. K. Harrison*, 252.

399 "it looked pretty good to me" Ibid., 251.

400 What happened next has long been enshrouded Bleecker, *Politics of Architecture*, 191–92.

401 "I had Nelson by the balls" Grondahl, *Mayor Corning*, 489.

401 "He had an almost pathetic belief" Norman Hurd, HMI, 82.

402 "He liked to get fairly detailed position papers" Deardourff, AI.

402 "Henry, this is just superb" Ronan, AI.

402 "When you go to Spain" Bailey, AI.

403 It would give her much pleasure Martha Rockefeller–NAR, January 30, 1962, RAC.

403 David proposed to replicate the lottery system D. Rockefeller, *Memoirs*, 192–93.

403 the canary-yellow De La Courtille porcelain dessert service NAR–LSR, February 1, 1963, RAC.

403 "Typically, once he had lost the battle" D. Rockefeller, *Memoirs*, 193.

404 Nelson planted a double row Letter from David Harris Engel to author.

404 Nelson in full curatorial mode Deardourff, AI.

405 "some kind of a consultant" Marshall, AI.

405 "Suddenly I felt this grip on my thigh" Corbin, AI.

405 "She seemed typical of her class" Underhill, AI.

405 "She was a gorgeous woman" Goldman, AI.

405 "She was just dazzling in those days" Collier and Horowitz, *The Rockefellers*, 350.

405 "He was the pursuer" Happy Rockefeller, AI.

406 "The mother would not consider divorce" Ibid.

406 "Happy added a wonderful kind of exuberance" Lefferts, AI.

406 "Did that man ever need to be loved" Evelyn Cunningham, AI.

406 "Discretion wasn't in him" Pyle, AI.

407 "If he marries Mrs. Murphy" *BusinessWeek*, May 4, 1963.

407 "You have so needed a partner" W. Alton–NAR, August 28, 1963, RAC.

408 William Rusher had no doubt Rusher, AI.

408 Doctor of Romance Languages *New York Journal-American*, June 13, 1963.

408 Barber Conable . . . chuckled approvingly Barber Conable, AI.

408 Liberal theologian Reinhold Niebuhr Novak, *Agony*, 145.

408 "He is through" *New Republic*, June 8, 1968.

408 The Pulitzer Prize board Perlstein, *Before the Storm*, 197.

408 "Have we come to the point in our life as a nation" *Time*, June 14, 1963.

408 Hinman and other Rockefeller strategists Evans and Novak, "Hinman to the Rescue," *Washington Post*, May 20, 1963.

408 "She's another Jackie Kennedy" Fulton Lewis, Jr., "Capitol Report," *New York Mirror*, June 12, 1963.

409 At one early reception Cunningham, AI.

409 the Woman's Exchange William Kennedy, *O Albany!: Improbable City of Political Wizards, Fearless Ethnics, Spectacular Aristocrats, Splendid Nobodies, and Underrated Scoundrels* (New York: Penguin Books, 1985), 13.

410 George Hinman had a new partner Harry O'Donnell, HMI, 96.

410 "They left arm in arm" Ibid.

410 "There's an insanity in the air around here" Novak, *Agony*, 176–77.

410 Tactics of delay and disruption The Young Republican convention is widely regarded as a turning point in the conservative takeover of the GOP. For Rockefeller's reaction, see *U.S. News & World Report*, September 23, 1963. The convention is described in Novak, *Agony*, 195–201.

411 "Mr. Rockefeller intends to work diligently" *New York Herald Tribune*, May 17, 1963.

411 "Had he been born poor" Cannon, AI.

412 drove Rockefeller to unload on his right-wing tormentors Strident as it was, Rockefeller's July 14 blast at his party's right wing was originally even harsher in its language; George Hinman's draft came replete with explicit references to Fascism, edited out of the text by Hugh Morrow. Fioravante G. Perrotta, HMI, 45.

412 "You conservatives are picking on me for marrying Happy" Barry Goldwater, *With No Apologies: The Personal and Political Memoirs of United States Senator Barry M. Goldwater* (New York: William Morrow, 1979), 158.

412 "Political success cannot be divorced from political morality" NR, PP 1963, 853–57.

412 "There'll be no more breakfasts" Novak, *Agony*, 212.

413 "if he were a captive of the radical right" Novak, *Agony*, 216.

413 "New York was his dukedom" Gillies, AI.

414 "And don't forget to write the book" Edward Heath, *The Course of My Life* (London: Hodder & Stoughton, 1998), 244.

414 One rain-swept autumn evening Roob, AI.

414 In near desperation Wells's interview at the RAC is useful; see also his *New York Times* obituary, April 15, 1980.

414 Once, JFK had expressed fear Cannon, AI.

414 "I can beat Goldwater" Gore Vidal, *Palimpsest: A Memoir* (New York: Random House, 1995), 360.

415 When talk turned briefly to Rockefeller Theodore Sorenson, *Kennedy* (New York: Harper Perennial Political Classics, 2009), 754.

18: The Road to San Francisco

416 "Rockefeller's wife ain't going to let him get off the ground" Perlstein, *Before the Storm*, 32.

416 "the people will not accept a wife swapper" *Life*, November 1, 1963.

416 "I believe that there is a publisher who has less regard for the truth" Robert David Johnson, *All the Way with LBJ: The 1964 Presidential Election* (New York: Cambridge University Press, 2009), 69.

417 Richard Nixon settles into the backseat White, *Making of President, 1964*, 6–7.

417 Rockefeller telephones each of his children Lefferts, AI.

418 "was it one of the right wing nuts?" Richard Nixon, *RN: The Memoirs of Richard Nixon* (New York: Warner Books, 1978), 312.

418 Nelson recalls a recent governors' conference NAR, Lyndon B. Johnson Oral History Project, LBJL, 7–8.

418 "Lyndon thinks it's going to be like chasing the deer off the Pedernales" Happy Rockefeller, AI.

419 "New Deal Republicans" Hy Rosen and Peter Slocum, *From Rocky to Pataki: Character and Caricatures in New York Politics* (Syracuse, NY: Syracuse University Press, 1998), 44.

419 Early polls in pivotal New Hampshire *Confidential*, Lloyd Free–NAR, November 8, 1963, RAC; Harris poll, *Washington Post*, November 26, 1963.

419 "They say Nelson is too much like Kennedy was" "The Reassessment," *Time*, December 13, 1963.

419 he railed against LBJ as a treacherous wheeler-dealer J. William Middendorf II, *A Glorious Disaster: Barry Goldwater's Presidential Campaign and the Origins of the Conservative Movement* (New York: Basic Books, 2006), 64.

420 On December 8, a small group of friends Lee Edwards, *Goldwater: The Man Who Made a Revolution* (Washington, DC: Regnery Publishing, 1995), 198–99. Len Hall rejected overtures from the Rockefeller camp, though not before complaining that Nelson "turns you on and off like a faucet." Burdell Bixby, HMI, 26.

420 "If I'd said no" Barry Goldwater, CCOHC, 72–73.

420 Deception, Deceit, and Divorce Daniel Ford, "The Nation's Primary Primary," *Reporter*, February 27, 1964.

421 Ten days after this initial meeting Hugh Gregg, AI.

421 For twenty-eight days I benefited greatly from reading Thomas Sliney's Dartmouth senior thesis, *The 1964 New Hampshire Primary*. I wish to thank him for permission to cite his work, as well as the helpful staff at the university archives for bringing it to my attention. Hugh Gregg, Bert Teague, and Jim Kiepper generously shared their memories of the same contest and of the sometimes treacherous crosscurrents of Granite State politics.

421 Gregg, mindful of a slipping schedule Jerry Danzig, HMI, 32. A more brittle side of Rockefeller was displayed outside Portsmouth's historic Strawberry Bank restoration, which refused to open its doors, even for a Rockefeller. "Maybe they won't come to the Rockefeller Foundation for a contribution," said Nelson. Hugh Gregg, *The Candidates—See How They Run* (Portsmouth, NH: Peter E. Randall, 1990), 22.

422 At his first press conference in Concord White, *Making of President, 1964*, 109.

422 Goldwater's ordeal by candor F. Clifton White, *Suite 3505: The Story of the Draft Goldwater Movement* (New Rochelle, NY: Arlington House, 1967), 288–90; Middendorf, *Glorious Disaster*, 80–85.

422 Quick to pounce on his opponent's gaffes Sliney, *1964 New Hampshire Primary*, 39.

422 At a January 24 dinner in Concord Ibid., 46–48.

423 Rockefeller began talking of a "leadership gap" *Portland Oregonian*, May 12, 1964.

424 "Henry Sabotage" Paul Grindle and David Goldberg graciously relived their own children's crusade on behalf of a candidate even they didn't take altogether seriously. In a characteristically irreverent conversation with the author in 2001, Grindle compared his "draft Lodge" activities with the celebrated prank by a group of Harvard undergraduates at the turn of the twentieth century. The youthful scholars had succeeded in matriculating a purebred mule through four years of college (it graduated with honors). Paul Grindle, AI; David Goldberg, AI.

424 his favorite snack of skinned Portuguese sardines *Newsweek*, April 20, 1964.

425 "For Christ's sake, if this is going to really piss you off" Grindle, AI.

425 The plan went awry Sliney, *1964 New Hampshire Primary*, 65.

425 "I've got it made" *New York Times*, March 11, 1964.

426 more free advice than claims of responsibility Charles Moore–NAR, March 23, 1964.

426 "Our candidate's image is not coming through" William L. Pfeiffer–John A. Wells, March 17, 1964, RAC.

426 "You don't win too many wars" Goldberg, AI.

427 a "victim of his resources" Grindle, AI.

427 "The focus on Goldwater was temporary" Deardourff, AI. Rockefeller's focus on the fall campaign explains the excessive attention his camp gave to a poll of African American voters in the District of Columbia—nearly 40 percent of whom voiced support for Rockefeller over LBJ in a fall matchup. *New York Times*, April 14, 1964.

427 "They were all alike" Canzeri, AI.

428 This was George Hinman's constituency Gillies, AI.

428 "Nelson is going to take this state hands down" G. Hinman–Homer Capehart, February 5, 1964, RAC.

428 "I run the campaign, and I have 51 percent of the vote" Robert Price, AI.

429 Now Rockefeller himself came calling Ibid.

429 "What we need now are firemen and surgeons" Robert Price–Charles F. Moore, Jr., April 22, 1964, RAC.

429 "Read from your notes" Price, AI.

430 "I can afford it" Ibid.

431 "You'd be surprised what that does at airports" Price, AI.

431 Hoping to put twenty telephones in each county Ibid.

432 Price pleaded with his East Coast bosses Specifically, Price urged a four-minute coda to a half-hour national broadcast. In a second, undated, memo arguing for such an appeal, Price emphasized the need to disprove any "abandonment" of the Murphy children, while stressing the joint custody arrangement between their parents—a stretching of facts that may help to explain Rockefeller's continued silence on the matter. Price–Charles F. Moore, April 11, 1964; "Possible Content of National TV Statement by Governor Rockefeller," [n.d.], RAC; see also *New York Times*, March 21, 1964.

433 "It is difficult to know Lodge's stand" Rockefeller's own position on Vietnam remained murky. On April 27, 1964, he told a Portland audience that the United States should follow a policy of hot pursuit into Communist sanctuaries in Laos, Cambodia, and North Vietnam— but relying on South Vietnamese troops and air strikes to accomplish the mission. That said, Rockefeller opposed any further withdrawals of U.S. forces already in Southeast Asia, in contradiction of JFK's intent to pull out a thousand American advisory and related forces.

433 "He'd go to tank towns where they grew berries and nothing else" E. Kresky, AI.

433 Just as Tom Dewey in 1948 *Time*, May 22, 1964.

433 When fog forced Rockefeller to reroute his plane Nick Thimmesch, "Remembering the Unrelenting Drive of Nelson Rockefeller," *Washington Post*, January 19, 1979.

434 "So we're on our way back from Portland" Deardourff, AI.

434 "This is my primary responsibility" *New York Times*, March 21, 1964.

435 Nelson braved the wrath of civil libertarians Civil rights groups joined the New York State Bar Association in declaring both no-knock and "stop and frisk" unconstitutional. The latter resurfaced as a subject of controversy during the mayoralty of Michael Bloomberg, another wealthy neophyte in politics prior to his first election in 2001.

435 "a wide-open market, a dumping ground" *New York Times*, April 26, 1964.

435 "Rocky accused me of being a tool of the liquor lobby" Conable, AI.

436 "I've never seen a legislature I couldn't buy" Theodore H. White, *The Making of the President, 1968* (New York: Atheneum, 1969), 264. In an interview with Cary Reich, Bronfman was identified as the lobbyist in question by former assembly Speaker Joseph Carlino. I found

Bronfman's name recorded on Rockefeller's desk calendar during the period of maximum gubernatorial pressure on legislators to enact reforms in the state's liquor laws.

436 **On the last night of the 1964 legislative session** *New York Times*, March 27, 1964.

436 **It was no secret that . . . Charles Buckley badly wanted revisions** Ibid., April 26, 1964.

437 **"If you're behind in the polls"** *Portland Oregonian*, May 9, 1964.

437 **"What do the absent advocate?"** Ibid., May 14, 1964.

437 **At the end he even unbent a little** Ibid., May 10, 1964.

437 **By the second week of May** Ibid., May 13, 1964. Alone among pollsters, Sam Lubell detected the massive shift of voter sentiment in the campaign's final days. Behind the numbers were voters, their emotions in flux. Typical of Lubell's sample was a retired utilities worker who had several weeks earlier made it clear to the pollster that "my wife and I won't vote to put a divorced woman into the White House." His wife told Lubell of their last minute change of heart. "The country is more important than who his [Rockefeller's] wife is."

438 **"We retired with CBS at midnight"** *Time*, May 22, 1964.

438 **Barry Goldwater dismissed the results** *Washington Star*, May 17, 1964.

438 **"Where the hell have you been?"** Price, AI.

438 **"If you had gone from Oregon to California"** Ibid.

439 **"Bill is very good at taking an established candidate"** Stuart Spencer interview, Government History Documentation Project, Regional Oral History Office, Bancroft Library, University of California, Berkeley, 7.

439 **"I don't care about the issues"** "The Backroom Boys," *Newsweek*, March 22, 1976.

439 **"we had to bring Barry back down to us"** Stuart Spencer interview, Miller Center, University of Virginia, Ronald Reagan Presidential Oral History Project, 6; Spencer, AI.

439 **"I've got him by myself now"** *Time*, May 22, 1964.

440 **he had "to get that 70% stirred up"** Ibid.

440 **The next day in Los Angeles** *New York Herald Tribune*, April 30, 1964.

440 **"We used the Rockefeller magic"** Spencer, AI; that there were limits to even Rockefeller's multilingual ability to connect to voters was demonstrated during a campus visit to Berkeley, where a student with a pronounced accent cried out his support of the governor. *"Gracias mil veces,"* Rockefeller shot back. ("A thousand thanks.") "I'm not Spanish," said the youthful admirer. "I'm Egyptian." *New York Times*, March 13, 1964.

441 **"The Chandlers weren't wild about Rockefeller"** Spencer, AI.

441 **Whatever the incentive** *Los Angeles Times*, May 17, 1964.

441 **"The Goldwater people were really so god-awful"** Grindle, AI.

442 **Telephone receptionists in several Rockefeller offices** Deardourff, AI; Rockefeller himself claimed that his Los Angeles–area campaign offices received more than two hundred telephone bomb threats.

442 **"We didn't have any troops"** Spencer interview, Government History Documentation Project, 22.

442 **"Periodically we would need money"** Spencer, AI.

442 **Perhaps a few hundred thousand dollars** Ibid.

442 **Traveling in style** Grindle, AI.

443 **They met at Margate** Ibid.

443 **The impact of Ike's intervention** F. Clifton White, Goldwater's canny delegate hunter, nipped the Eisenhower insurgency—if that is what it was—in the bud by enlisting the aid of Ike's onetime Treasury secretary George Humphrey. The former president was to stay under Humphrey's roof when he visited the Republican Governors' Conference in Cleveland. Alerted by White in advance, Humphrey telephoned his former boss, informed him that no "traitors" were welcome at the Humphrey residence, and maintained a close watch on Ike— and close liaison with Clif White—throughout the Eisenhower visit. F. Clifton White, CCOHC, 168–69.

444 **"You got to remember this"** Spencer, AI.

444 **That he was conflicted over the newly cautious approach** Williams Roberts interview, Gov-

ernment History Documentation Project, Regional Oral History Office, Bancroft Library, University of California, Berkeley, 5.

445 **The film was shrill and counterproductive** Ronan, AI.

445 **a last minute opposition ad barrage** Deardourff, AI.

445 **The patrician Leonard Firestone** Jerry Danzig, HMI, 13.

445 **"I killed it"** Ronan, AI.

446 **"I have a show opening"** Lee Edwards, *The Conservative Revolution: The Movement That Remade America* (New York: Free Press, 1999), 121.

446 **"Hinman had come to us a week out"** Spencer, AI.

446 **"'Is it going to happen?'"** Spencer interview, Miller Center, 7.

446 **"My suggestion would be that it would be nice to have the baby on Wednesday"** Roberts interview, Government History Documentation Project, 7. Jack McGrath recalls a barroom discussion revolving around the imminent birth of Nelson Rockefeller, Jr. "Why don't you just not announce it?" McGrath asked Spencer and the others present. "Let her go some place and have the baby quietly." McGrath, AI.

446 **"The New York people thought"** Spencer interview, Miller Center, 7.

446 **Even now, it is hard to believe** Confidential source.

446 **"that he was a wife-stealer"** Roberts interview, Government History Documentation Project, 7.

446 **"On Friday he had won"** Boyd AI.

447 **"I think we've blown it"** Germond, AI.

19: CHANGE OF COURSE

451 **"Hell . . . I don't want to talk to that son of a bitch"** Perlstein, *Before the Storm*, 389.

451 **"How many lawyers from Niagara Falls get to run for Vice President?"** Jack W. Germond, *Fat Man in the Middle Seat: Forty Years of Covering Politics* (New York: Random House, 2002), 54.

452 **Rockefeller missed the speech** *Time*, July 24, 1964.

452 **The Albany mailbag held balm** William Scranton–NAR, August 3, 1964; NAR–Hugh Scott, August 28, 1964, RAC.

452 **"they had nothing to offer the people but themselves"** Novak, *Agony*, 468–69.

452 **"There were those of us around him"** Malcolm Wilson, HMI, 31.

453 **"I think I would have been punished had we won"** Michael Scelsi, AI.

454 **"We've got plenty to talk about"** *New York Post*, August 10, 1964; *Newsweek*, August 31, 1964. For coverage of Happy's courtroom testimony, see *New York Times* and *New York Herald Tribune* for September 3, 1964.

454 **In the end, he deferred to expert opinion** *New York Post*, October 2, 1964; *Time*, October 9, 1964.

454 **Before the case faded from the headlines** *Newsweek*, October 12, 1964.

454 **a startling visual resemblance** Cannon, AI.

455 **a tone of knowing irony** KRD, April 3, 1976.

455 **an open secret among Rockefeller associates** Ellen Harrison, CRI.

455 **Happy categorically denied** Happy Rockefeller, CRI.

456 **A Gallup poll taken one week after the election** Johnson, *All the Way with LBJ*, 302.

456 **"I'm afraid of Vietnam"** Perlstein, *Before the Storm*, 512.

456 **"It's a rule of life"** *Albany Times Union*, November 6, 1964.

456 **"you would hardly say it was won"** NR, PP 1964, 876.

456 **The Empire State would have its own Great Society** David Lawrence, "Rockefeller's Great Society Plan," *New York Herald Tribune*, January 8, 1965.

457 **"It isn't the end of a policy"** *New York Herald Tribune*, January 7, 1965.

458 **a gesture of solidarity** Rockefeller's total contributions to the Ebenezer Baptist Church ex-

ceeded $140,000. This included a $100,000 gift made two years after Dr. King's 1968 assassination.

458 **On a visit to New York** Happy Rockefeller, AI.

458 **Too busy *doing* to entertain doubt** Ronan, AI.

458 **Rockefeller had scant patience** Gerald Benjamin and T. Norman Hurd, eds., *Rockefeller in Retrospect: The Governor's New York Legacy* (Albany, NY: Nelson A. Rockefeller Institute of Government, 1984), 225.

459 **"I'm gonna do it"** Douglass, AI.

459 **"I've got the program"** *Newsweek*, July 12, 1965.

459 ROCKEFELLER WANTS MORE OF EVERYTHING *New York World-Telegram*, January 7, 1965.

460 **"I feel worse about this than anything since I've been in office"** *New York Times*, January 30, 1965.

461 **"I have a letter which begins 'Dear Nelson'"** Braden, *Just Enough Rope*, 264.

461 **Rockefeller had castigated Kennedy** NR, PP 1964, 866.

461 **A victorious Kennedy used the occasion of his maiden Senate floor speech** *New York Herald Tribune*, January 7, 1965. Rockefeller also got into a public spat with Kennedy over funding for mental health programs, a dispute that did neither man credit. *New York Times*, December 19, 1965.

462 **Sometimes these were scrawled across the back of a plain envelope** Albright, AI.

462 **"It's time that we settle this"** Robert Wagner, CCOHC, 1069; see also *Economist*, February 13, 1965; Hevesi, *Legislative Politics in New York State*, 99–101; the backstairs lobbying of Rockefeller agents Spad and Young is in *New York Times*, February 5, 1968.

462 **"a Rockefeller-Wagner sellout of the people"** *New York Times*, February 5, 1965.

463 **"Zaretzki was a good friend of his"** Gene Spagnoli, HMI, 35–36.

463 **"Governor, I know that one"** Benjamin and Hurd, *Rockefeller in Retrospect*, 266.

463 **"I never have trouble with the Democrats"** Jerry Danzig, HMI, 34.

463 **"We made a swap with the city"** Ronan, AI.

464 **He left confident of what he had come for** Underhill, AI.

464 **"He was impatient with the federal government"** Marshall, AI.

465 **"We used to joke about putting barbwire around the Adirondack Mountains"** Ibid.

465 **Flying back to New York** Ibid.

466 **"as indispensable as the right to a fair trial"** NR, PP 1965, 622.

466 **"They picked it up 100 percent"** *New York Herald Tribune*, March 27, 1966.

467 **"Our problem [in New York] is not that we have too little water"** Rosen and Slocum, *From Rocky to Pataki*, 21.

467 **"first in the nation, first in the world"** Nelson A. Rockefeller, *Our Environment Can Be Saved* (New York: Doubleday, 1970), 51.

467 **"His example triggered Lyndon Johnson"** LSR, HMI, 20.

467 **"Where's Lady Bird?"** Bess Abell, AI.

468 **A paradigm of sixties hubris** The Storm King saga is covered at length by Robin Winks, *Laurance S. Rockefeller: Catalyst for Conservation* (Washington, DC: Island Press, 1997); Collier and Horowitz, *The Rockefellers*; and Connery and Benjamin, *Rockefeller of New York*. The fullest account by a legislative opponent of Storm King is William Rodgers, *Rockefeller's Follies*, 84–118. See also Laurance Pringle, "Storm over Storm King," *Audubon*, August 1968.

468 **"The world needs visionaries"** Whiteman, AI.

469 **"I don't see any point in going through a useless gesture"** Rodgers, *Rockefeller's Follies*, 109.

470 **the modern Headless Horseman rode a bulldozer** Ibid., 162–92. Assemblyman Lawrence Cabot, though initially frustrated in efforts to defeat the Rockefeller highway projects, did manage to uncover the shabby tactics employed to misrepresent their origins. Though he refused to meet with a group of petitioning mayors, the governor saw Cabot, who brought with him a representative sampling of protest mail. "That's odd," Rockefeller said airily, "I haven't heard a single objection to the expressway." Joseph L. Sax, "Rocky's Road," *American Heritage*, February 1971.

471 **In moments of pique** Boyd, AI.

471 **"Look at Javits"** Letter to author from William Ringle.

471 **"That double-crossing S.O.B."** Richard M. Rosenbaum, *No Room for Democracy: The Triumph of Ego over Common Sense* (Rochester, NY: RIT Press, 2008), 114–15.

471 **"All right then, why don't *you* run for Mayor?"** Jacob K. Javits, *Javits: The Autobiography of a Public Man* (Boston: Houghton Mifflin, 1981), 372–77.

472 **Price had convinced himself** Ibid.

472 **"Nelson would love it"** Price, AI.

473 **"Abe, run the story"** Ibid.

473 **"There was a danger when he 'lent' you money"** Marshall, AI.

473 **His differences with Jacob Javits** For Rockefeller's side of the dispute involving Javits and Lindsay, see Emmet John Hughes, "An Untold Tale," *Newsweek*, July 12, 1965.

473 **"Where are they going to go?"** *New York Herald Tribune*, November 21, 1965.

474 **Not content to boo their governor** Underhill, AI.

474 **"We did it"** Vincent J. Cannato, *The Ungovernable City: John Lindsay and His Struggle to Save New York* (New York: Basic Books, 2001), 21.

474 **"I get buried so often I'm used to it"** Murray Kempton, "Lindsay and Rockefeller," *New York World-Telegram and Sun*, November 5, 1965.

475 **"I am the greatest ham in the world"** Curiously, this was one point on which Lindsay and his most bitter antagonist agreed. "If you elect a matinee-idol mayor," Robert Moses told associates shortly after Lindsay's election, "you're going to get a musical-comedy administration." Caro, *Power Broker*, 1117–18.

475 **"the Congressman from the Constitution"** Cannato, *Ungovernable City*, 10.

475 **"One of the most important things I've learned"** Nat Hentoff, *A Political Life: The Education of John V. Lindsay* (New York: Alfred A. Knopf, 1969), 42.

475 **"John Lindsay looked at Mike Quill and he saw the past"** Sam Roberts, "City in Crisis I," from *America's Mayor: John V. Lindsay and the Reinvention of New York* (New York: Museum of the City of New York; Columbia University Press, 2010), 25. This volume, published by the Museum of the City of New York in conjunction with a major retrospective of the Lindsay years, is a model of its kind, employing the sometimes harsh light of perspective while honoring the era's aspirations and the man's essential decency.

476 **"Wagner had a deal with Quill"** Slote, AI; an excellent account of the strike and its impact on Lindsay's first days in office is Woody Klein, *Lindsay's Promise: The Dream That Failed* (New York: Macmillan, 1970), 36–80.

476 **Lindsay's gratitude was muted** *New York Times*, February 17, 1966.

477 **Resentful of the governor's stranglehold** Hentoff, *A Political Life*, 44.

477 **"Rockefeller wouldn't drink"** Price, AI.

477 **That Lindsay held Rockefeller in minimal high regard** Bill Kent, AI.

478 **"That was quite a bombshell, wasn't it?"** *New York Herald Tribune*, November 21, 1965.

478 **"He's interesting," Nelson said of Lindsay** Murray Kempton, "There's Only One Winner," *New York Post*, June 16, 1966.

478 **During a break in the talks** Hentoff, *A Political Life*, 129.

478 **"I've never been involved in anything like this"** Klein, *Lindsay's Promise*, 181.

478 **"These are the toughest negotiations I've ever been in"** Characteristic of the mistrust that pervaded the Rockefeller-Lindsay relationship was a secret meeting held at the New York apartment of David Lindsay, the mayor's twin brother, and attended by George Hinman and state tax commissioner Joseph Murphy. Preceding more formal negotiations in Albany over the mayor's latest tax package, the meeting almost ended before it began when David Lindsay suggested a quid pro quo involving an infusion of Lindsay campaign talent into Rockefeller's upcoming reelection effort in return for gubernatorial support of the mayor's commuter tax. Hinman nearly walked out then and there. Eventually tempers cooled, and sufficient progress was made to warrant Rockefeller's public invitation to move the discussions to the Executive Mansion in Albany. Joseph Murphy, HMI, 29–30.

478 "Eventually the mayor joined the others at the table" Bennett, AI.
479 Leaving the Plaza hotel one evening McGrath, AI.

20: ROCK BOTTOM

480 "I tell you, they were not going to make me walk out" *New York World Journal Tribune*, November 9, 1966.
480 Even George Hinman, the ultimate loyalist "Rocky's Family Triumph," *New York Post*, November 9, 1966.
480 "you've done so damn much for the state" Ronan, AI.
480 An early poll showed *Wall Street Journal*, November 2, 1966.
480 "I know what's going to happen if I lose" Douglass, AI.
481 "Tell us what we're doing wrong" *New York Times*, November 22, 1965; see also *Christian Science Monitor*, November 10, 1965, and *New York Times*, December 5, 1967. In Syracuse, breeding ground of his most strident opposition from the Right, the alleged spendthrift governor had the satisfaction of telling an audience hungry for government largesse, "Money doesn't grow on trees."
481 "I was the third child" Gene Spagnoli, HMI, 8.
481 "You've never had to go hungry" Marshall, AI.
483 "There were lots of things that could be traded" Whiteman, AI.
483 "I could find half a dozen things" Marshall, AI.
484 "New York's Gigantic Giveaway" Tom Wilkinson, "Doctoring Up Medicaid," *New Leader*, April 8, 1968.
484 "If you don't have good education and good health" *New York Post*, September 10, 1966.
484 "My God, Nelson, at the rate you're going" Persico, *Imperial Governor*, 208.
484 "If I had known what was in this legislation" NR, PP 1973, 1319.
484 "Great, Congressman" Ibid., 1295.
484 "God, the first year was $1.3 billion" Rosen and Slocum, *From Rocky to Pataki*, 31–32.
485 In a reception line McGrath, AI.
486 "When it got late at night" Ibid.
486 "A good Baptist never lies" Armao, AI.
486 On this point, Wells was emphatic Mary Wells Lawrence, *A Big Life (in advertising)* (New York: Simon & Schuster, 2003), 39–44; Jerry Danzig, HMI, 27.
487 "I don't think it cost that much" Deardourff, AI. In a postelection message, Bill Pfeiffer assured Rockefeller that the campaign had stayed within legal spending limits, "but it was rough going." Pfeiffer–NAR, November 14, 1966, RAC. An excellent appraisal of the Rockefeller high command that made his 1966 campaign one for the textbooks is Tom Buckley, "The Three Men Behind Rockefeller," *New York Times Magazine*, October 30, 1966.
488 More New Deal than New Frontier Sidney Zion, "Frank O'Connor Takes the High Road," *New York Times Magazine*, January 16, 1966.
488 If willing to take orders in the mayor's race Mitchel Levitas, "Rise, Fall and—of FDR, Jr.," *New York Times Magazine*, October 23, 1966. The same author related the sardonic observation made by Bob Wagner following a postelection visit to the headquarters shared by O'Connor and his 1965 running mates, Abe Beame and Mario Procaccino: "All the people I thought I knocked out in 1961 are sitting there studying the Green Book"—the bible of municipal job seekers.
489 "the big blooper I made in politics" *New York Post*, September 6, 1966.
489 "He looks better than some of the lifeguards" *New York Times*, September 6, 1966.
489 "You raise taxes so well" *New York Herald Tribune*, March 27, 1966.
489 "taxing too much and doing too little" *New York Times*, September 20, 1966.
490 "Ask them which highways they are going to curtail" Ibid., September 19, 1966.
490 "It was like running against a ghost" McGrath, AI.
490 "¡Viva O'Connor!" Underhill, AI.

490 **A reporter visiting campaign headquarters** Evans and Novak, "Rocky Off the Mat," *Washington Post*, October 6, 1966. The painstaking preparation of Rockefeller's substantive campaign was equaled only by the spontaneity of his interaction with voters. Besides an impromptu dip in the Atlantic or lifting weights with men three decades his junior, Rockefeller invited himself onto a Harlem stage in the middle of a performance by music legend James Brown (whom he had confused with the football legend of the same name). Sometimes even the fabled Rockefeller organization came up short, as when the governor suddenly decided to spend the night on Long Island, only to have the state police veto a hastily reserved motel, which turned out to be one of Suffolk County's more notorious love nests. *New York Post*, November 10, 1966.

491 **"You have been the greatest inspiration to all of us"** G. Hinman–NAR, Monday p.m., [n.d.], RAC.

491 **Swallowing his pride** William Safire, *Before the Fall: An Inside View of the Pre-Watergate White House* (Garden City, NY: Doubleday, 1975), 30–31.

491 **In a weird reversal of form** *New York Post*, October 27, 1966. At the time, some upstate polls showed FDR, Jr., polling up to 17 percent of the vote.

492 **"Go back to Africa"** Cannato, *Ungovernable City*, 125.

492 **Against this menacing backdrop** A comprehensive treatment of the Civilian Complaint Review Board, and its implications for political realignment beyond the borders of New York City, is in ibid., 155–88.

492 **Though Rockefeller had at one point expressed "complete agreement"** *New York Times*, October 5, 1966; *New York Daily News*, September 15, 1966.

492 **Confronted by reporters** NROH, August 16, 1977, 6.

492 **"Politics is a rough business"** Ibid., 5–7.

493 **"If you want to keep crime rates high"** Jack Newfield, "The Case Against Nelson," *New York*, March 9, 1970.

493 **"to mug, to purse-snatch, to steal"** *New York Times*, October 29, 1966.

493 **"Do you *really* think I'm going to win"** Ronan, AI.

493 **"this is just the most exciting damn thing I've ever heard"** *New York World Journal Tribune*, November 9, 1966.

493 **"You're a good guy"** Ibid.

494 **"Oh my God"** *New York Post*, November 9, 1966.

494 **Winkler's antivivisectionist passion for "the little animals"** Dunham, AI.

495 **"I just don't think you should be lecturing the people of New York"** Ronan, AI.

495 **"The governor liked unconventional approaches"** Armao, AI.

495 **"These are the loyal troops"** Douglass, AI.

495 **"Mondays were always an adventure"** Marshall, AI.

495 **"You can't have junkies running around the *Queen Mary*"** Ibid.

495 **"When that red button flashed"** Dunham, AI.

496 **"He had his yellow pad"** Slote, AI.

496 **"You now have a unique position"** G. Hinman–NAR, December 28, 1966, RAC.

497 **Seeking an alternative to the status quo** William Seidman, AI.

497 **"The day that Romney made his brainwashed remark"** Ibid.

498 **At an early meeting** Douglass, AI.

498 **"When he gets engaged"** *Time*, October 20, 1967.

498 **Seeking common ground** "NAR–Dear Ronald," January 12, 1968, RAC.

498 **"One of the advantages of getting older"** Larry King, "The Cool World of Nelson Rockefeller," *Harper's Magazine*, February, 1968.

498 **"If you had stood in front of that convention"** Ibid.

498 **He sent Les Slote to Annapolis** Slote, AI.

498 **"out on the end of the ice floe"** *Washington Post*, July 1, 1967.

499 **Romney proposed a joint campaign swing** G. Hinman–NAR, January 23, 1968, RAC.

499 **At a Palm Beach golf weekend** G. Hinman–"Dear Nelson," July 7, 1967, RAC.

499 **"It's a time to keep our feet on the ground"** "Nelson" undated, handwritten memo from George Hinman. Hinman compared Rockefeller's prospective influence at the upcoming party convention with the "exquisite flora that you observe under water when snorkeling. They instantly vanish if you touch them." RAC.

499 **"His judgment is the last to be trusted"** G. Hinman–NAR, October 6, 1967, RAC. "The doves are not serving peace," wrote Hinman. "They are prolonging the war." These words were mild compared with his indictment of Hughes and his confrontational strategy—the polar opposite of Hinman's painstaking diplomacy to win over a party fundamentally hostile to Rockefeller's brand of politics. Of course, it was Rockefeller himself who had entrusted his presidential hopes to this oddest of couples.

499 **City hall wasn't blind to the problem** "Call from Bob Sweet," G. Hinman–NAR, October 19, 1967, RAC.

499 **"Lindsay was absolutely intractable"** Fioravante G. Perrotta, CRI.

500 **"Nelson knew how to co-opt everybody"** William vanden Heuvel, AI.

500 **"If New York City was dumb enough to become a state"** Benjamin and Hurd, *Rockefeller in Retrospect*, 157.

500 **More cutting still** Gene Spagnoli, HMI, 26.

500 **"I wish Lindsay would become an actor"** Rosenbaum, *No Room for Democracy*, 129.

500 **Within months of Lindsay's election** David L. A. Gordon, *Battery Park City: Politics and Planning on the New York Waterfront* (Amsterdam: Gordon and Breach, 1997), 1–19.

500 **Lindsay returned the favor** *New York Times*, December 6, 7, 1967; Robert Sweet, AI.

501 **"Oh, we never got into politics"** Harry O'Donnell, HMI, 37.

501 **"So, four or five days later we're up in Albany for the inauguration"** Ibid., 49–51; *New York Times*, May 1, 1967.

503 **"I like to get a thing started"** Notes on Al Marshall interview, JPP; Raymond O. Horton, "Public Employee Labor Relations Under the Taylor Law," in Connery and Benjamin, *Governing New York State*, 161–74.

504 **In the wake of the transit strike** Caro, *Power Broker*, 1119–31. Lindsay, hearing what he wanted to hear, believed that he had Rockefeller's support for his proposed merger of Moses's Triborough and the existing Transit Authority. He badly underestimated Moses's ability to stop the scheme in its tracks. Perkins, AI.

504 **"Lots of governors have built highways"** Neal R. Peirce, *The Megastates of America: People, Politics, and Power in the Ten Great States* (New York: W. W. Norton, 1972), 31; Joseph F. Zimmerman, "Public Transportation," in Connery and Benjamin, *Governing New York State*, 214–24.

505 **"When we created the MTA"** Ronan, AI.

507 **At a meeting in Rockefeller's office** Ibid.; Caro, *Power Broker*, 1134–44.

507 **"I think he hoped to see"** Arthur Schlesinger, Jr., was kind enough to share with me pages from his unpublished journals dealing with the New York sanitation workers' strike. This passage, edited out of the published *Journals*, is dated February 19, 1968; my chief source for the strike is an unpublished chronology of events compiled at the time by Harry Albright of the Rockefeller staff. Interviews with Albright and other participants on both sides of the dispute are supplemented by Roger Kahn's superb instant history, "On the Brink of Chaos," in the July 27, 1968, issue of *The Saturday Evening Post*.

507 **"I'll shut this town down so tight even babies won't get milk"** Marshall, AI.

507 **Rockefeller took the threat seriously enough** Ted Braun, HMI, 18–19.

508 **there was the memory of Ludlow** Bemoaning his seeming helplessness—"I can't do anything or say anything without making matters worse"—Rockefeller tearfully recalled the long-ago labor dispute. "My father called the guard out once, and a lot of people got killed." Kahn, "On the Brink"; Marshall, AI.

508 **"Don't they remember the Colorado Fuel and Iron strike?"** Schlesinger, unpublished journal, February 19, 1968.

508 **"And he just yells over"** Cunningham, AI.

508 **The real action that morning** Marshall, AI; Sweet, AI.

508 **"He would have had to be Jesus Christ"** Ted Braun, HMI, 21.

508 **"a proud, touchy man"** Ibid.

509 **In a phone conversation with the governor** Albright strike diary, 6–9.

509 **Nelson asked Lindsay to repeat his statement** Ibid., 9–10.

509 **With state health officials warning** Ibid., 12–13.

509 **"You mean that the Mayor of the City of New York won't meet with the Governor"** Ibid.

510 **"Will he have negotiating power?"** Kahn, "On the Brink."

510 **"We got Lindsay on the phone"** Canzeri, AI.

510 **That night, Rockefeller remained holed up in his office** Whiteman, AI.

510 **"They think I'm too tired to negotiate"** Kahn, "On the Brink"; Albright strike diary, 15.

510 **Lindsay returned to the airwaves** When a lawyer for the state informed Rockefeller that his proposed takeover of the New York City Sanitation Department was illegal, the governor replied, "It certainly is, and there is no legal way to settle this strike. But the garbage is on the streets. Monday I'm going to try to get the legislature to pass a bill that will make this illegal act legal." Kahn, "On the Brink."

511 **"He didn't call me Johnny this time"** Nick Thimmesch, *The Condition of Republicanism* (New York: W. W. Norton, 1980) 220.

21: Too Much, Too Late

512 **"I'll accept anyone making a mistake once"** Boyd, AI.

512 **"His people think I am double-crossing him"** Schlesinger, unpublished journal, February 19, 1968.

512 **"There are eighteen Republican governors who want me"** Ibid. In the same meeting, Schlesinger quoted a recent remark made by Bobby Kennedy to Walter Lippmann, to the effect that none of the Republicans seeking their party's nomination represented an improvement over LBJ—"I make an exception, of course, for Nelson Rockefeller." Hearing this, noted Schlesinger, Nelson seemed "touched."

512 **if the French couldn't prevail in Indochina** Happy Rockefeller, AI.

512 **"You know, I have my roots in the New Deal"** Schlesinger, *Journals*, 278.

513 **As his options narrowed** G. Hinman–NAR, "Bill Scranton," January 29, 1968, RAC.

513 **Rockefeller was the only Republican** Jackie Robinson, Confidential Memo to NAR, February 26, 1968, RAC.

513 **"Your position of non-candidacy"** G. Hinman–NAR, "Our Dilemma—Its Possible Resolution," [n.d.], RAC. In the same memo, Hinman warned Rockefeller against discussing issues: "You can only strip away the illusions, get controversial and bore when you start talking too much." By this standard, even Hinman should have been pleased by Nelson's contribution to the January 1968 issue of *Foreign Affairs*. He somehow contrived to write ten pages for the current events journal without once mentioning Vietnam, the war tearing his own nation apart.

513 **Rockefeller convened a gathering** The minutes of this February 21 meeting make clear both the would-be candidate's reluctance to actively contest Oregon and George Hinman's belief that the Romney candidacy was doomed. Hinman had access to Rockefeller-financed polls that showed Nixon trouncing Romney in Wisconsin by a margin of nearly two to one.

513 **He turned to one of his latest hired guns** Clifford Miller, AI.

514 **"He didn't know the difference between *Newsday* and *Newsweek*"** Underhill, AI.

514 **Even this "availability strategy" was questioned** Ronan, AI. An invaluable insider's account of Rockefeller's torturous debate with himself is Ted Braun's "History of Events Immediately Prior to and Leading Up to Rockefeller's Decision and Statement of March 21, 1968," RAC. Written within twenty-four hours of Nelson's formal withdrawal from the race, Braun's narrative gains credibility by the author's unique combination of proximity and detachment.

514 **On the last day of February** Scarcely a month before his withdrawal from the race, Romney asked Rockefeller to join him in a joint campaign visit to Oregon. The idea smacked of desperation; Rockefeller and his agents pointed out that such a paring would only stimulate press speculations about Romney's relative weakness as a candidate. To dark hints of betrayal, George Hinman replied that "the trouble here is not with us but with our candidate George who had fallen on his face," prompting a flurry of calls for Rockefeller to get into the race. While Romney's initial bitterness would fade, his family was slower to forgive. Years later, Mitt Romney spoke of Rockefeller's treachery as an accepted truth. G. Hinman–NAR, January 24, 1968, RAC.

514 **Never, wrote Riland, had he seen his friend so indecisive** KRD, March 17, 1968.

514 **Lindsay described a country coming unhinged** *New York Post*, March 11, 1968.

514 **Spiro Agnew urged him** Minutes of March 10, 1968, meeting, RAC.

514 **"I went out there, and I worked my butt off"** Deardourff, AI.

515 **On Saturday morning, Rockefeller went over a draft statement** Braun, "History," 1.

515 **They needn't take his word for it** Deardourff, AI.

515 **For three hours that Sunday morning** KRD, March 17, 1968.

515 **"an awful lot of vague promises"** Ronan, AI.

515 **"I think Nelson's going"** Deardourff, AI. The next day, Rockefeller wrote Agnew to thank him for coming to the meeting and for his "major contribution" to the discussion. "I'll be in touch within the next week or ten days," he promised. Ten days later, he announced his withdrawal from the race—without first communicating his intent to Agnew. NAR–Spiro Agnew, March 11, 1968, RAC; Thruston Morton interview, 66–69, Thruston B. Morton Oral History Project.

516 **Nelson grabbed the positive announcement** Emmet Hughes, HMI, 5.

516 **That evening, Thruston Morton left a Foxhall Road dinner** *Newsweek*, April 1, 1968.

516 **Coffee had hardly been poured** KRD, March 20, 1968.

516 **the day's second unwelcome surprise** Braun, "History," 4.

516 **Seeming confirmation of this view** Emmet Hughes, HMI, 6.

516 **"If I'm not caught up in an enthusiasm I'm not any good"** Albright, *Portrait*, 283.

517 **Ted Braun . . . specifically excluded Spiro Agnew** Ted Braun, HMI, 43. New Mexico governor David Cargo insists he *was* called prior to Rockefeller's announcement and that Agnew was also on the call list. Yet as late as eleven o'clock that morning, campaign planners Doug Bailey and John Deardourff were assured that Rockefeller was running. "Too bad about your man," Theodore White remarked to Joe Canzeri ten minutes prior to the start of Rockefeller's press conference. It was news to Canzeri.

517 **Ted Agnew never forgave Rockefeller** Sears, AI.

517 **"It was the polls"** Safire, *Before the Fall*, 18.

518 **Pat Buchanan, then a young Nixon speechwriter** Pat Buchanan, AI.

518 **Employing the oblique language of the period** *Newsweek*, April 1, 1968.

518 **The day before his withdrawal** KRD, March 20, 1968. At the White House, LBJ was tipped off to a recent dinner meeting of high-profile journalists at which Hugh Morrow attempted to lay to rest "Nixon crowd stories" about Rockefeller's "new girlfriend." Memorandum for the President from Mike Manatos, March 27, 1968, LBJL.

518 **"Nelson was just compulsive"** Schlesinger, *Journals*, 514.

518 **Professional gossips such as author Truman Capote** Gerald Clarke, ed., *Too Brief a Treat: The Letters of Truman Capote* (New York: Random House, 2004), 358.

518 **Nelson tested the patience** KRD, July 9, 1968.

518 **Campaigning in East Harlem** Confidential source.

518 **he had long been the object of pursuit** Ruebhausen, AI.

519 **Rockefeller conducted himself** O'Shaughnessy, AI.

519 **By early December** Schlesinger, *Journals*, 266.

519 **"He made Happy go through the misery of a divorce"** Ibid., 514.

519 **the rumors held center stage** Drew Pearson diary, December 19, 1967.

519 **"I heard several reporters discuss it"** Sears, AI.

519 **"Every other birthday Happy has been having a baby"** *New York Times*, January 10, 1967.

520 **"Nelson could barely sit at the table"** Roberts, *Kykuit*, 31.

520 **"I got Bill Blass to work on that"** Happy Rockefeller, AI.

520 **Her influence made itself felt** Cannon, AI.

521 **More sympathetic observers traced Happy's insecurities** Lefferts, AI.

521 **"She'd be fine when talking to the governor of Ohio"** McGrath, AI.

521 **Pocantico was Nelson's favorite place** "A Pleasant Day with the Rockefellers," *Good Housekeeping*, February 1968.

522 **"The true memorial to Martin Luther King"** KRD, April 6, 1968; "Statement by Governor Nelson A. Rockefeller, April 5, 1968," NR, PP 1968, 1039.

522 **"I'm sitting at the bedside of Coretta King"** Canzeri, AI; KRD, May 23, 1968; Lucien Warren, "An Untold Drama: Rocky's Help to Martin Luther King's Family," *Buffalo Evening News*, January 11, 1969.

522 **"Do what you have to do"** Canzeri, AI.

522 **Bobby Kennedy appeared deeply distressed** Joseph Persico diary of the 1968 campaign, JPP, 1–2.

523 **Before wheels up** Douglass, AI. Stephen Lefkowitz, who played a major role in drafting the original legislation and later seeing to its implementation, explained to me the origins of the UDC; for more on the subject, see Frank S. Kristol's chapter on housing in Connery and Benjamin, *Governing New York State*, 188–99; also see Connery and Benjamin, *Rockefeller of New York*, 258–66.

523 **"David, I've got the twenty cents"** Ibid., 262.

523 **By the late sixties** Alton G. Marshall–The Governor, "Delays in Urban Renewal and Housing Construction," February 20, 1968, RAC.

524 **"And he gets me, and he just pours it on"** Benjamin and Hurd, *Rockefeller in Retrospect*, 207–08.

524 **Logue mentioned unpaid campaign debts** Persico, *Imperial Rockefeller*, 113.

525 **His confidence was well-placed** Slote, AI.

525 **"And Rocky would ply him with martinis"** John Dunne, AI.

525 **something of a dilettante** Confidential source.

525 **"Perry was an extremely proud guy"** Maiorana, AI.

525 **"I got bad news"** Douglass, AI.

525 **"It better pass by the time my plane lands"** Albright, AI.

525 **"I had never seen him so angry"** Albright, *Portrait*, 202.

526 **"He thought his mother had died or something"** Douglass, AI.

526 **Rockefeller personally threatened** Confidential source.

526 **"Now I don't like to take this position"** Kramer and Roberts, *"I Never Wanted,"* 86–87.

526 **He solicited Jackie Robinson's help** Sam (Singletary) to Jackie Robinson, April 12, 1968, RAC. Singletary, another African American Rockefeller staff member, related the governor's concerns regarding Lindsay's opposition to the UDC.

527 **"I am a great believer in waiting"** *U.S. News & World Report*, April 15, 1968.

527 **the message "of confidence, creativity, and stability"** Persico diary, 1968, 1.

528 **"I finally came to realize"** Ted Braun, HMI, 32.

528 **He wanted to make four major speeches** Slote, AI.

528 **"another Emmet Hughes peroration"** Albright, *Portrait*, 195.

528 **Mindful of Republican sensitivities** "The Making of a Just America," NR, PP 1968, 1303–08.

528 **the biggest bomb since Hiroshima** Persico diary, 1968, 6.

528 **Nelson and Happy were smuggled into the White House** Larry Temple, AI.

528 **"He told me he could not sleep at night"** *Washington Star*, January 28, 1979.

528 **"The confidence implicit in your conversation"** NAR–LBJ, April 25, 1968, RAC.

529 **"It was a non-primary campaign"** Emmet Hughes, HMI, 6. Asked long after why the 1968 campaign failed, Hughes blamed it on Nelson's inability to delegate. The remark sounds

self-serving, yet a larger need for control undoubtedly factored into Rockefeller's refusal to grant a request from Hughes and others in the campaign's high command for a copy of the governor's daily schedule. They should be informed of "official appointments" only, replied Rockefeller—"just fill in the rest," he instructed Ann Whitman, "with office work or speech writing." The Governor, from Ann, [n.d., but clearly sometime during the first half of May 1968], RAC.

529 **"That whole headquarters was such a mess"** James Cannon, HMI, 42–43.

529 **"In 1960 they say I dropped out too soon"** *Newsday*, April 18, 1969.

530 **"A man named Warren Harding"** "Dear Nelson," G. Hinman–NAR, "Saturday morning," [n.d.], RAC.

530 **When bad weather scrubbed a speech at Penn State** *New York Times*, May 17, 1968. Jack McGrath took advantage of the lull in the schedule to survey local delegates chosen to attend the party's upcoming convention. Together with a colleague, McGrath made a number of cold calls to those who would choose their party's candidate for president. To his dismay none of the delegates had been contacted by anyone else from the Rockefeller camp. McGrath, AI.

530 **Jackie Robinson took him to task** Jackie Robinson–Robert Douglass, May 17, 1968, RAC.

530 **"To have visited the poor people's march"** "Dear Nelson," G. Hinman–NAR, "Saturday morning," [n.d.]. Hinman blamed press secretary Les Slote—"an unprincipled genuinely vicious son of a bitch"—for the story in question. In the same ten-page handwritten screed, Hinman reiterated that Rockefeller's hopes for victory in Miami rested almost wholly on his fellow governors, RAC.

530 **"Governor Rockefeller: No Direct Answers"** *New York Times*, May 17, 1968.

530 **Rockefeller strategists took heart** Graham T. Molitor–John Deardourff, May 3, 1968, RAC; *U.S. News & World Report*, April 29, 1968.

530 **On a four-day swing through the region** *Time*, May 31, 1968; *Washington Star*, May 23, 1968.

531 **While retracting his earlier characterization** *Christian Science Monitor*, June 29, 1968.

531 **"Reagan was very careful"** Lyn Nofziger, AI.

531 **The low point of the Rockefeller campaign** Ibid.; "Story Bob Finch Got from Clark—Reagan's AA," May 20, 1968, PPS 501.1, 72, RNL; Evans and Novak, "The Reagan Strategy," *New York Post*, May 23, 1968.

531 **A week after his ill-fated meeting with Reagan** KRD, May 27, 1968.

531 **Rushed into print was *Votepower*** Persico diary, 1968, 13–14.

531 **"Nelson kept changing his own leadership"** In summing up the 1968 campaign, Joe Persico captured perfectly the curse of too much: "Nelson Rockefeller is over advised. He has the good quality of seeking the opinions of other people. But the failing of heeding too many. The collision of high level advisers becomes inevitable. And the necessity to compromise differences and accommodate diversity fuzzes positions." Ibid., 47.

532 **Identifying "a vast reservoir of uneasiness"** H. Kissinger–NAR, "Where Are We Now in the Campaign?," June 9, 1968, RAC.

533 **"I know how bad it is for you"** Judy Michaelson, "Woman in the News: Joan Braden," *New York Post Weekend Magazine*, July 13, 1968.

533 **White, too, was caught up in the Rockefeller surge** White, *Making of President, 1968*, 272; see also "Rocky: Out of the Trance," *Newsweek*, June 21, 1968.

533 **Rockefeller himself seemed liberated** At the rhetorical heart of Rockefeller's newfound dovishness was a phrase others would soon pick up: "We must never again find ourselves with a commitment looking for a justification." Persico diary, 1968, 27.

533 **America's cities, he insisted, would never be saved** *New York Times*, June 14, 1968.

533 **"Nixon's the One"** *Time*, July 26, 1968.

533 **The day after Bobby Kennedy was shot** Steven Rockefeller, HMI, 12–13.

534 **"We ran Nelson Rockefeller"** Marshall, AI.

534 **"I sometimes wondered whether Father really wanted that nomination"** Steven Rockefeller, HMI, 14.

534 **Desperate to prevent Spiro Agnew** Agnew was particularly susceptible to flattery. According to Wilson, one of the things that most impressed him about Nixon was that the former vice president invariably returned his phone calls "within forty minutes." Malcolm Wilson–George Hinman, "Maryland," June 13, 1968, RAC.

534 **an airborne birthday party** KRD, July 8, 1968.

534 **The festivities culminated** White, *Making of President, 1968*, 273–74.

534 **Emmet Hughes missed the party** Ibid., 275.

535 **He couldn't maintain the grueling pace** KRD, June 21, 1968.

535 **Vocal cords worn ragged** Ibid., May 23, 1968.

535 **"We write you as a brother and a friend"** JDR3rd diary, June 16, 1968; NAR–Winthrop Rockefeller, June 17, 1968, RAC.

535 **"Joe, why do people drink?"** Canzeri, AI.

535 **Rockefeller's continuing inability to remember names** Marshall, AI.

535 **"You know, George"** David Cargo, AI.

536 **"a Protestant church bazaar"** Persico diary, 1968, 43.

536 **Jimmy Breslin, returning from the convention floor** Ibid., 42.

536 **That night, Happy asked a radio reporter** "The Party of Abraham Lincoln," WVOX radio commentaries by William O'Shaughnessy, 1, RAC.

536 **"I knew a hell of a lot about counting delegates"** Cannon, AI.

537 **"Strom would take delegates"** Howard "Bo" Callaway, AI.

537 **George Hinman orchestrated a vice presidential search** Oscar Ruebhausen–NAR, August 3, 1968; Appendix A of this document includes Hinman's "post-nomination points," including the quest for a running mate, RAC.

537 **"During the last days of the campaign"** Albright, *Portrait*, 265–66.

537 **Ken Riland left a meeting** KRD, August 7, 1968.

538 **"Not a single vote"** Elia Kazan, "Face to Face with the GOP," *New York*, August 26, 1968.

538 **A few minutes later New Jersey broke wide open** KRD, August 28, 1968.

538 **"What's the use?"** WVOX commentaries, 3.

538 **"Have you ever been to a Republican national convention?"** *Washington Post*, January 28, 1979.

538 **"It's just like Dick"** Richard Reeves, "Is That Really Nelson Rockefeller Crawling to Richard Nixon?," *New York*, October 18, 1971.

538 **Around the hotel swimming pool** Persico diary, 1968, 46.

538 **"He must have meant you"** KRD, August 8, 1968; Ted Braun, HMI, 45–46.

539 **"Lord, he must really feel sorry for himself"** Albright, AI.

539 **Two days later he fought back tears** René d'Harnoncourt eulogy, August 15, 1968, RAC; Canzeri, AI; Sarah d'Harnoncourt–NAR, September 11, 1968, RAC.

539 **The distraction of grief** Endicott Peabody–NAR, August 13, 1968, RAC.

539 **Peabody wasn't acting alone** Slote, AI.

540 **Peabody renewed his pitch** Endicott Peabody–NAR, August 20, 1968, RAC.

540 **Had he prevailed in Miami** KRD, June 24, 1968.

540 **Rockefeller was free to pick** *New York Times*, June 11, 1968; Oscar Ruebhausen–The Governor, "Senatorial Vacancy," June 7, 1968, RAC.

540 **But first Lindsay would have to ask him for the job** *New York Times*, June 30, 1968.

540 **"Tell me why I should appoint you to the Senate, John"** Hentoff, *A Political Life*, 207–10.

540 **Another account of what happened** McGrath, AI. Yet another version of events comes from Lindsay's deputy mayor Robert Sweet. He maintains that an offer was conveyed through seconds Tom Dewey (for Rockefeller) and Herb Brownell (for Lindsay) and that Lindsay rejected it.

541 **Bowing to the inevitable** Slote, AI.

542 **Mississippi would have migrated to Reagan** Callaway, AI.

542 **"He was always in the wrong church"** Marshall, AI.

542 **"Well now, don't go picking my Cabinet for me, Gene"** Gene Spagnoli, HMI, 20.

542 "Is there any law that says you have to have one?" Safire, *Before the Fall*, 33.

542 "Dear Ted" NAR–Spiro T. Agnew, January 19, 1969, RAC.

22: LEANING RIGHT

543 "Ours is a turbulent world" NAR–RMN, June 20, 1969, RAC.

543 "Do you realize" *New York Times*, January 21, 1969.

543 "an old tomcatting partner of his" Cannon, AI.

543 During the same period Critics of the Alliance pointed to no fewer than sixteen military coups in Latin America since JFK first undertook his regional initiative. "Rocky Road for Mr. Rockefeller," *Economist*, May 22, 1969.

544 Weary of being studied "Why the Latins Don't Love Us," *Life*, July 18, 1969; "Rockefeller's Tour: Painful Reappraisal of the Neighbors," *Time*, July 11, 1969.

544 "Nixon thought of Rockefeller" Kissinger, *White House Years*, 7.

544 "Nixon's basic problem" NROH, October 4, 1977, 37–38.

544 Shortly after Nixon's election Slote, AI.

544 Gone, too, were the red phones NROH, October 4, 1977, 42.

545 "Nixon said to me one day" W. Kenneth Riland, HMI, 77–78.

545 "no party is big enough" Reeves, "Is That Really Nelson Rockefeller Crawling to Richard Nixon?"

545 only three men in America Safire, *Before the Fall*, 498.

545 "He seems to feel quite close to the President" JDR3rd diary, November 4, 1969.

546 As early as December 1967 NR, PP 1967, 1189.

546 Employing language not heard for ten years or more *New York Daily News*, January 26, 1969.

546 Skinflint Rocky *New York Post*, February 5, 1969.

546 the Syracuse Tea Party Ibid., February 19, 1969.

546 "I don't like you" *New York Times*, February 1, 1969.

546 Rockefeller appeared before Nixon Ibid., February 13, 1969.

547 "Nixon himself got me aside" Cannon, AI.

547 "I'm not adopting an ideology" "Who Should Pay the Bill," *New York Times*, January 12, 1969.

547 "Yours was an excellent presentation" *New York Times*, January 17, 1969.

548 "It's a good example of Rockefeller's high-handedness" Gloria Steinem, "Nelson Rockefeller: The Sound of One Hand Clapping," *New York*, August 11, 1969.

548 The announcement of his Latin America message *Christian Science Monitor*, February 4, 1969.

549 Old habits die hard KRD, May 11, 1969.

549 "a man who did what he said he would do" Steinem, "One Hand Clapping."

549 The first signs of serious trouble KRD, May 14, 15, 1969.

550 "Thank you very much" Flor Brennan, HMI, 43.

550 "I'm trying to get understanding going both ways" Kutz, *Rockefeller Power*, 225.

550 That evening, a well-lubricated stenotypist Flor Brennan, HMI, 45.

550 "So they burned the flag" Ibid.

550 "You don't understand" Rockefeller similarly defied Secret Service instructions to keep his car windows tightly closed—a necessary precaution against a grenade tossed from the crowd.

550 "We ought to call the whole thing 'Sneaking Down to Rio'" Steinem, "One Hand Clapping."

550 "I bring no new programs" "Rocky's Second State," *Time*, June 6, 1969.

550 the talks had to be moved *New York Daily News*, May 31, 1969.

550 Having set fire *New York Times*, May 30, 31, 1969.

551 "I had to tell him the news" Cannon, AI.

551 "Well, Nelson, you're a wonderful guy to hook up with" Ibid.

551 "He's a qualified man" *Christian Science Monitor*, July 10, 1969.

551 "You've gotten us off the back pages" *Time*, June 13, 1969.

552 "In most of our countries" *New York Post*, June 12, 1969.

552 Sidestepping a military decoration ceremony *New York Times*, June 18, 19, 1969.

552 Rockefeller's stay in the Paraguayan capital Ibid., June 20, 1969.

552 "You've got a lot of courage" NAR remarks, National Conference of UPI Editors and Publishers, October 7, 1969, RAC.

553 Anticipating such a gesture *Newsweek*, July 14, 1969; W. Kenneth Riland, HMI, 15; Cannon, AI. In fact, both Cannon and Ken Riland shared the balcony with the Haitian dictator—and were either cropped or airbrushed out of the resulting photo.

553 Raising Duvalier's arm above his head W. Kennneth Riland, HMI, 15.

553 "I'm only happy when I'm reacting to people" Steinem, "One Hand Clapping."

554 "Let's face it" NAR remarks, UPI editors and publishers.

554 "Hugh Morrow was a gift to Nelson Rockefeller" Cannon, AI.

554 Rockefeller's military views John W. Sloan, "Three Views of Latin America: President Nixon, Governor Rockefeller, and the Latin American Consensus of Vina Del Mar," *Orbis* 14, no. 4 (Winter 1971): 934–50.

555 Nixon offered reassurances RMN–NAR, December 26, 1969, RAC.

555 "a good man with a good heart" Steinem, "One Hand Clapping."

556 "I wish you could have known Mother" Cannon, AI.

556 "You were in a house by yourself" Ibid.

556 Dispensing with a chauffeur Canzeri, AI. By his own estimate, Canzeri was personally involved in the purchase of thirty-seven Rockefeller automobiles.

556 Weekends he played dollar-a-hole golf Nelson Rockefeller, Jr., AI.

556 Holidays were observed in style Happy Rockefeller, AI.

556 Sibling rivalries simmered JDR3rd–NAR, June 9, 1969, RAC.

556 On weekends Nelson liked to stroll the grounds Canzeri, AI.

557 "I think there was a lot of bitterness" Ibid.

557 "If he'd only done a little bit of this" KRD, June 1, 1970.

557 "He'd fly down [from Albany]" Cannon, AI.

557 Frugal to the point of self-caricature Cunningham, AI.

557 "He struggled to be a Rockefeller" Marshall, AI.

557 much of the tension around Kykuit Lynne Baranski, "Post Divorce and Breakdowns, the Cinderella Once Wed to a Rockefeller Finds a New Career," *People*, October 9, 1971.

558 "If the Kennedys can do it" Rasmussen, *There Was Once*, 199.

558 "Are you campaigning for Father or for yourself?" Ibid., 201.

558 Cannon hid messages from Nelson Rockefeller Cannon, AI.

558 At about the same time KRD, "The week of the 20th July, 1970."

558 "Live, Mrs. Astor. Live" Rasmussen, *There Was Once*, 222.

558 "Here, Hughie" Lance Morrow, AI.

559 "My heart is as black as yours" Cannato, *Ungovernable City*, 429.

559 Blaming Albany for his city's financial woes Ron Maiorana–NAR, April 14, 1970, RAC.

559 "the cupboard is bare" *Albany Times Union*, August 2, 1969.

559 "My generation is tired of confrontations" Hugh Morrow, "Memo to Monday Breakfast Group," March 24, 1969, RAC.

560 Thus he erupted in anger Rosen and Slocum, *From Rocky to Pataki*, 36; Marshall, AI.

560 The same message NR, PP 1970, 14.

560 "I have a deep, real, abiding conviction" Richard Perez-Pena, "'70 Abortion Law: New York Said Yes, Stunning the Nation," *New York Times*, April 9, 2000.

560 Moments before the official tally could be announced *Albany Times Union*, April 10, 1970.

561 "New York State did it again!" JDR3rd–NAR, April 15, 1970, RAC.

561 "What are phosphates?" Mary Kresky, AI.

562 **"Race you, Gov"** Gene Spagnoli, HMI, 12–13.

562 **"We wanted him out"** Marshall, AI.

562 **"We couldn't have a white hand show"** Ibid.

562 **Summoned to the second-floor executive suite** Charles B. Rangel, *And I Haven't Had a Bad Day Since: From the Streets of Harlem to the Halls of Congress* (New York: Thomas Dunne Books, 2007), 139.

562 **"He loved the job"** Louis Lefkowitz, HMI, 38–39.

563 **According to Free** Lloyd Free–NAR, "Your Forthcoming Legislative Program," December 23, 1969, RAC.

563 **"I had an exaggerated opinion"** David L. Stebenne, *Arthur J. Goldberg: New Deal Liberal* (New York: Oxford University Press, 1996), 348–51.

563 **A frequently told joke** Confidential source.

564 **At the state Democratic convention** vanden Heuval, AI.

564 **"Well, you know when Goldberg was nominated"** Edward Koch, AI.

564 **"Mr. Goldberg, I hope you win"** *Albany Times Union*, August 5, 1970.

564 **"By inviting him up there"** Kramer and Roberts, *"I Never Wanted,"* 342–43.

564 **"the Manhattan Monopoly"** *New York Daily News*, September 28, 1970.

564 **"You sons of bitches"** Marshall, AI.

564 **The incumbent again ruled the airwaves** Peirce, *Megastates of America,* 49–50; *New York Times*, August 18, 1970.

565 **Rockefeller media efforts** Fred Powledge, "The Marketing of Nelson Rockefeller," *New York*, November 30, 1970.

565 **his emphasis on family stability** Samuel Lubell–NAR, October 11, 1970, RAC.

565 **A *New York Times* Daniel Yankelovich survey** *New York Times*, October 11, 1970.

565 **"the Germans are very athletic"** Powledge, "Marketing of Nelson Rockefeller."

565 **"a war that no one wants"** *Albany Times Union*, May 17, 1970.

566 **Speaking before a less youthful crowd** Ibid., May 7, 1970.

566 **"the shabbiest kind of pandering"** *New York Daily News*, September 30, 1970.

566 **"I'd like a piece of that Italian hot dog"** Joe Persico–The Governor, August 31, 1970, RAC; John Lomenzo, HMI, 16–17.

566 **Rockefeller declared August 24** *New York Times*, August 28, 1970.

567 **"The governor desperately wanted"** Armao, AI.

567 **Hoping to forestall a roll call** Kramer and Roberts, *"I Never Wanted,"* 347–49; Burt Glinn, "Making a Mensch of Arthur," *New York*, October 12, 1970.

567 **In an emotional appeal** Armao, AI.

568 **"How about that?"** Ibid.

568 **The futuristic towers and sweeping vistas** William J. Ronan, CRI.

568 **Rockefeller announced a $75 million increase** *Albany Times Union*, February 24, 1970.

568 **platform builders complained** Kutz, *Rockefeller Power,* 93–94.

568 **Another recurring problem** Kennedy, *O Albany!,* 317; see also Bleecker, *Politics of Architecture,* 197–212.

568 **Dangerously high water tables** Isabelle Savell, "The South Mall," Rockefeller Book, Box 2, WHP. Far more critical is Lo Faber's "Rocky's Last Erection: The Making of Empire State Plaza," http://www.lofaber.com/albany/essaymaking.html.

569 **"the greatest thing to happen in this country in a hundred years"** "Governor Defends Mall Costs," *Albany Times Union*, January 29, 1971.

569 **John Marchi remembers walking** John Marchi, AI.

569 **"They used to laugh at my grandfather"** Gene Spagnoli, HMI, 31.

569 **Repeatedly his requests were turned down** *Remembering Al Marshall, 1921–2008* (Albany, NY: Nelson A. Rockefeller Institute of Government, 2009), 9–10.

569 **Thanks to advances in computer design** Newhouse, *W. K. Harrison,* 271.

569 **"turning a slug of a town"** Kennedy, *O Albany!,* 307.

570 **"What the hell do I do with them?"** Perrotta, CRI.

570 **dropping off thousands of copies** Craig Thorne, AI.
570 **Initially denying any personal involvement** Collier and Horowitz, *The Rockefellers*, 492.
570 **"I'm going to go down fighting"** Perrotta, CRI.
570 **"*You* have a son who is graduating from law school?"** Alfonse D'Amato, AI.
571 **Speaking before a men's group in Harlem** KRD, September 16, 1970; Pete Hamill, "The Heart of the Matter," *New York Post*, September 17, 1970.
571 **"I only saw Nelson that one night get loaded"** McGrath, AI.
571 **"Hello, Ned"** Harry O'Donnell, HMI, 89.
571 **"The wheels are beginning to slow down"** KRD, October 30, 1970.
571 **The first week in September** KRD, September 3, 1970.
572 **After Rockefeller appeared wearing a Goodell button** Timothy J. Sullivan, *New York State and the Rise of Modern Conservatism: Redrawing Party Lines* (Albany: State University of New York Press, 2009), 129.
572 **Formally, he remained in Goodell's corner** *New York Daily News*, September 30, 1970.
572 **"I really am a conservative, you know"** Sullivan, *New York State and the Rise of Modern Conservatism*, 122.
572 **And so, despite the trauma and the shock** Ibid., 124.
573 **By mid-October** KRD, October 19, 20, 1970.
573 **The concept was at least as old** *Time*, February 1, 1971.
574 **"I am not going to be a tax collector"** Ibid. For an excellent treatment of Rockefeller's campaign for revenue sharing, see Connery and Benjamin, *Rockefeller of New York*, 393–417.
574 **Then Lindsay took the podium** Armao, AI.

23: ATTICA

575 **On the heels of his reelection** *New York Times*, November 11, 1970.
575 **"Governor Rockefeller buried a dream yesterday"** Ibid., January 2, 1971, quoted in Peirce, *Megastates of America*, 35.
575 **"Perhaps this is my real role in politics"** KRD, January 26, 1971.
577 **Publicly, her death was attributed to a heart attack** Ibid., January 24, 29, 1971.
577 **"I'm in a spot"** Dunham, AI.
577 **Perry Duryea declared his opposition** *New York Times*, February 9, 1977.
577 **By mid-March, he was offering** Ibid., March 16, 1971.
577 **a chastened Rockefeller** Rosen and Slocum, *From Rocky to Pataki*, 142–43.
578 **"Regrettably, I was simply wrong"** Albright, *Portrait*, 164–65.
578 **Incentives for Independence** See Blanche Bernstein's chapter, "The State and Social Welfare," in Connery and Benjamin, *Governing New York State*, 146–60.
579 **"I cannot fight any longer"** Jackie Robinson–NAR, May 2, 1972, RAC.
579 **"Putting on the brakes"** NAR–Jackie Robinson, May 8, 1972, RAC.
579 **It was almost midnight** *New York Times*, April 2, 1971. As part of his strategic retreat on the budget, Rockefeller cut a deal with Senator James Donovan, a passionate foe of abortion, who insisted on deleting Medicaid funds earmarked for the procedure. Rockefeller agreed to sign an executive order suspending such funding for ninety days—and promised to sign a permanent law if one was to pass the legislature. *Albany Times Union*, April 2, 1971. There were limits to Rockefeller's economizing. For example, he was outraged to learn that Al Marshall had sold off a state-owned Packard touring car once used by Franklin Roosevelt. "You got to get it back," he ordered Marshall, whose success hardly compensated for his costly faux pas. Harry Albright, HMI, 109–11.
580 **Rockefeller appealed to the medical profession** *Albany Times Union*, May 3, 1971.
580 **a number, Rockefeller noted archly** *New York Times*, April 20, 1971.
580 **"What in the world are we going to be able to do about this?"** KRD, May 26, 1971.

580 "tell Nelson he's got all the help in the world" Ibid.

581 Provoked by the mayor's repeated charges *New York Times*, June 4, 1971.

581 Lindsay returned the fire "Should New York City Be the Next State?," *Time*, June 21, 1971.

581 "He's not responsible for what he's saying" *New York Times*, June 11, 1971.

581 "Too hot to use—by me!" Undated note, NAR–W. Kenneth Randall, KRD, Box 1, Folder 2, RAC.

582 "I became increasingly concerned" NAR testimony before McKay Commission, April 5, 1972, RAC, 9.

582 "When I lay my head on the pillow at night" Dunne, AI.

582 "Why don't you get going on this right away" Russell G. Oswald, *Attica—My Story* (Garden City, NY: Doubleday, 1972), 181–84.

583 His immediate predecessor had warned *Attica: The Official Report of the New York State Special Commission on Attica* (New York: Bantam Books, 1972), 130 (hereafter referred to as *McKay Report*).

583 "This was not a classic prison riot" January 15, 1971, RAC; it is unclear who is the author of this eleven-page report, though it is filed with counsel Michael Whiteman's papers, Box 44, Folder 464, RAC.

584 "convict's paradise" *McKay Report*, 15. The same volume is notable for its extended description of the deadening routines, substandard clothing and cuisine, and daily assaults on individual dignity that marked life behind bars. "A Look at Attica," 21–102.

584 Oswald ordered dietary improvements Ibid., 47. What Superintendent Mancusi called "meals which are tasty, possess eye appeal and contain the necessary nutritional ingredients to provide a balanced diet" struck McKay Commission members as heavy on starch, poorly prepared, and sometimes inedible.

584 At Attica this position was filled by *New York Times*, July 21, 2005.

585 With Rockefeller's approval Oswald, *My Story*, 202–05.

585 "The status quo is anathema to all" Russell Oswald–NAR, May 10, 1971. That Oswald was an unhappy man long before Attica exploded is documented by Norman Hurd in advance of the commissioner's May 19 meeting with the governor. Portraying Oswald as "quite discouraged" by the magnitude of his task, and the relative scarcity of state resources, Hurd advised Rockefeller to substitute verbal praise for the additional staff and program funds sought by the commissioner. Hurd–NAR, May 19, 1971, RAC.

585 the Attica Liberation Faction Tom Wicker, *A Time to Die* (New York: Quadrangle/New York Times Book Company, 1975), 6.

586 "no other state agency holds the potential for disaster" Oswald, *My Story*, 210.

586 officer William Quinn, convinced that major trouble was brewing Jennifer Gonnerman, "Remembering Attica," *Village Voice*, September 12, 2001.

587 Around ten thirty he was handed a note NAR testimony, McKay Commission, 12. Much of what follows is based on the testimony of Rockefeller and others before the commission. Also helpful: a detailed chronology of events developed by Rockefeller assistant Harry Albright and reproduced as Appendix D of his aforementioned *Portrait*, RAC.

587 "We'll get you in the morning" Wicker, *A Time to Die*, 11.

588 Almost none of this reached the state's chief executive NAR testimony, McKay Commission, 12–13.

588 there might have been a different outcome Albright, AI.

588 the "fatal decision" Norman Hurd, HMI, 55. Strongly opposed to having Rockefeller visit Attica during the crisis, Hurd was equally reluctant to blame Oswald for letting Friday's counterattack fizzle. "By the time Russ got there, it was too late," Hurd concluded. Ibid., 58.

588 "As long as I am here there will be no compromise" Governor Lehman's response to the uprising at Auburn State Prison is described in Allan Nevins, *Herbert H. Lehman and His Era* (New York: Charles Scribner's Sons, 1963), 111–13.

589 Years were to pass Malcolm Wilson, HMI, 44.

589 Once in D Yard Wicker, *A Time to Die*, 27–28.

589 **The governor affirmed the decision** NAR testimony, McKay Commission, 14–15.

590 **sitting in Sing Sing's electric chair** Dunne, AI.

590 **Oswald . . . had his hopes dashed** Report from inside Attica, "We'll win or die together," interview with Tom Soto, [n.d.], RGIII, Series 26, Box 6, 8, Folder 53, RAC.

591 **Picking up where Soto left off** Wicker, *A Time to Die*, 39–40.

591 **Rockefeller had begun to entertain doubts** NAR testimony, McKay Commission, 19–20.

591 **"It got out of hand"** Dunne, AI.

591 **It might even be necessary** NAR testimony, McKay Commission, 20–21.

592 **Within minutes of first entering D Yard** Herman Badillo interview with McKay Commission, November 9, 1971, 2–4, RA.

592 **Having proclaimed his solidarity** Wicker, *A Time to Die*, 80.

592 **"Russ went in there and got beat up real bad"** Dunne, AI.

593 **"They wanted to have more showers"** Herman Badillo, AI.

593 **"we were now moving into a political area"** NAR testimony, McKay Commission, 22. RAC.

593 **Rockefeller had plans to retake the prison** KRD, September 11, 1971.

594 **"And then we got to the tough one"** Badillo, AI.

594 **fearing he might destabilize a situation** Wicker, *A Time to Die*, 155.

594 **Fearing for their safety** NAR testimony, McKay Commission, 23–24.

594 **The publisher from Harlem** *McKay Report*, 262–63.

594 **Then it was Kunstler's turn** Reverend Franklin D. R. Florence, interview with McKay Commission, December 10, 1971, 7. RAC.

595 **a unifying imperative** The appeal to Rockefeller, Tom Wicker acknowledged, was born "out of desperation" as much as anything else. Wicker, *A Time to Die*, 200.

595 **"If the governor does not come"** Oswald, *My Story*, 232.

595 **"What am I coming for?"** Douglass, AI. Needless to say, many of the observers would have taken issue with the way Douglass framed the issues being negotiated.

595 **"Russ had tried"** Oswald, *My Story*, 232–33.

595 **At one point Happy Rockefeller asked** Maiorana, AI.

596 **"Why don't you tell them"** Ibid.

596 **"We have to get Rocky to come here"** Wicker, *A Time to Die*, 213.

596 **For over an hour** Just as participants in the call differed as to its duration, so they took away conflicting views of what had been said. Clarence Jones sincerely believed that Rockefeller might come to Attica, while John Dunne was certain the governor had closed the door to such intervention.

597 **"Listen, Governor"** Badillo, AI. Badillo told representatives of the McKay Commission that by Sunday afternoon attitudes were hardening. At a tent providing hot dogs for the camp followers assembled outside the prison gates, he was denied service. Corrections officers on the scene labeled Badillo "the enemy," fueling his growing concerns about the violence likely to be inflicted by the forces of lawful authority in any operation to retake the prison. Rockefeller at this point shared his fears. Had he been on the scene, it seems more likely than not that his order to limit the next day's operation to state troopers and National Guardsman would have been carried out.

597 **"I can't do that"** Ibid.

597 **"Why not?"** Ibid.

597 **"Well, if it's more time you want"** NAR testimony, McKay Commission, 28. RAC.

598 **"Wouldn't you assume"** Ibid., 29.

598 **"I'm under great pressure to go to Attica"** Linda Storrow, HMI, 17.

598 **"John Lindsay would have been up there five days ago"** Ibid. Interestingly, Badillo also invoked Lindsay's name, along with bitter memories of the 1968 garbage strike, by telling Rockefeller that a decision to retake the prison on Sunday would undoubtedly elicit a request from the mayor for National Guardsmen with which to control the resulting street violence. Wicker, *A Time to Die*, 219.

598 **"Man, you and the Governor"** Herman Badillo and Milton Haynes, *A Bill of No Rights: Attica and the American Prison System* (New York: Outerbridge & Lazard, 1972), 84.

598 **"There are four Third World and African country people"** *McKay Report*, 290; Wicker, *A Time to Die*, 241.

598 **At ten twenty, Wyatt Tee Walker phoned** Wyatt Tee Walker interview with the McKay Commission, December 20, 1971, 8. RAC.

599 **"Do you feel it will be productive?"** *McKay Report*, 322.

599 **"In life it's not easy to face a hard decision"** Ibid., 323.

599 **"He got convinced that if he went there"** W. Kenneth Riland, HMI, 53; Oswald, *My Story*, 234.

599 **he wished Wilson had been there** Malcolm Wilson, HMI, 44.

599 **"I think we got some bad advice"** Cannon, AI.

600 **"I have done what I regard as the very best thing"** James E. Underwood and William J. Daniels, *Governor Rockefeller in New York: The Apex of Pragmatic Liberalism in the United States* (Westport, CT: Greenwood Press, 1982), 235.

600 **"In every other crisis"** Dunham, AI.

600 **Even the McKay Commission** *McKay Report*, 323–25.

601 **"If you came something might happen"** Underwood and Daniels, *Governor Rockefeller in New York*, 236.

601 **On the other end of the line** Maiorana, AI.

602 **Minimal force was to be used** Douglass, AI.

602 **General O'Hara's two-way radio** Wicker, *A Time to Die*, 277.

602 **"It's getting worse"** Maiorana, AI.

602 **"I don't think it will work"** Ibid.

602 **"You're the governor"** Confidential source.

603 **"Hang on a second"** Maiorana, AI.

603 **"The retaking of the prison"** Douglass, AI.

603 **"My God!" Rockefeller rasped** James Cannon, HMI, 102; *Time*, September 27, 1971.

604 **stories were already beginning to circulate** Dunham, AI.

604 **Rockefeller contributed to the confusion** *New York Times*, September 14, 1971.

604 **"these poor fellows"** Carolyn Thompson, Associated Press, "Nixon, Rockefeller Discuss Attica in New Tapes," September 13, 2011.

604 **"It really was a beautiful operation"** *Democracy Now*, NPR, September 16, 2011.

605 **"If Governor Rockefeller had come to Attica"** Bryce Nelson, *New York Times Book Review*, December 17, 1972.

605 **In his conversation with Nixon** *Democracy Now*.

605 **Yet there were just two doctors** Nelson, *New York Times Book Review*.

605 **An errant Oswald gesture** Oswald, *My Story*, 295–96.

605 **there had been no "indiscriminate fire"** *Time*, September 27, 1971.

606 **"make men worse rather than better"** Tom Wicker, *New York Times*, September 14, 1972; for a very different assessment of the McKay Commission, its methods and conclusions, see Roger Starr, "Prisons, Politics and the Attica Report," *Commentary*, March 1973.

606 **Bell resigned in protest** *New York Times*, September 12, 1971. By his own acknowledgment, Bell was prepared to indict several of the state troopers who stormed the prison exactly a decade before he wrote his *Times* retrospective. Taken off the case by his superiors, Bell quit, but not before relating his findings to state attorney general Louis Lefkowitz. The AG promised to get back to Bell within ten days, and he did, via a letter accepting his resignation and wishing him well in any future endeavors.

607 **"You did what had to be done"** NAR–Russell Oswald, September 17, 1971, RAC.

607 **"I don't think Governor Rockefeller, if he had been there"** John Lomenzo, HMI, 30–31.

24: The Boss of New York

611 "Rocky—this is his first crisis" KRD, September 22, 1971.

611 "Sit down," said Nelson Ron Maiorana, email to author, August 9, 2006.

611 "Nelson Rockefeller wants one thing" New York Post, September 17, 1971.

612 In abandoning his earlier pay-as-you-go approach to budgeting New York Daily News, May 2, 1972.

612 Enter Jerry Finkelstein For Jerry Finkelstein, see his obituaries in the New York Times, November 28, 2012, and the New York Law Journal, November 30, 2012. Finkelstein's habit of befriending the famous and powerful did not endear him to the Rockefeller staff, for whom he personified Al Marshall's dreaded "earpisser."

613 The Runyonesque pol ingratiated himself Kramer and Roberts, "I Never Wanted," 118.

613 "I don't know you except by reputation" Underwood and Daniels, Governor Rockefeller in New York, 145. A wonderful portrait of Esposito is in Assemblyman Daniel L. Feldman's 2010 memoir, Tales from the Sausage Factory: Making Laws in New York State (Albany: State University of New York Press, 2010). Shortly after winning a hotly contested Democratic primary, the reform politician Feldman paid a courtesy call to Esposito's office at 16 Court Street. Pleasantries out of the way, Esposito imparted some advice to the young reformer: "I think he should say fuck more often."

613 "I'm here with the governor" Rosen and Slocum, From Rocky to Pataki, 34.

614 "Governor, we have nothing to threaten him with" Cannon, AI.

614 By dangling the prospect of a $100 million loan New York Times, December 5, 1971.

614 "You are the wise old owl" Meade Esposito, HMI, 3.

614 "I will get you my tailor" Ibid., 9.

615 "Rocky, if you ever get gonorrhea" Ibid.

615 "I taught him more four letter words" Ibid., 16.

615 a rare exception to this rule was "sleazy" bankers Harry Albright, HMI, 114.

615 "Let's get out of here" Jerry Finkelstein, HMI, 30.

615 Finkelstein was surprised Ibid., 33.

615 "If you ever crossed that man" Meade Esposito, HMI, 8.

615 "There are certain legislators" New York Times, January 16, 1972.

616 When it was suggested, sotto voce Ibid., January 29, 1972.

617 "Nobody wants to hold shares in America anymore" Cannon, AI.

617 It was his custom to stand Harry Albright, HMI, 114.

618 Getting there entailed a hair-raising trip NROH, August 16, 1977, 8–9.

618 "In this library" NR, PP 1972, 1259–60.

619 Conversing with one staff member Ron Pedersen, CRI.

619 He presented this as a compromise New York Times, May 21, 1972.

619 An eleventh-hour intervention Ibid., May 9, 1972.

619 "the very intensity of this debate" NR, PP 1972, 179–80.

620 "He was too liberal for the Republicans" Meade Esposito, HMI, 13.

620 "We started talking Attica" Berger, AI.

621 "we're not going to make it easy for them" Ibid.

622 Rockefeller continued to seek outside advice Jerry Danzig, HMI, 6–7.

622 "These fellows smuggled in a cameraman" NAR, PP 1972, 1238–39.

623 "You little son of a bitch" Stanley Steingut, CRI.

623 "But let me ask you a question" Albright, Portrait, 169.

624 eager to discard his spoiler image Comments by Catherine Bertini, in Conversation on the Public Service (Albany, NY: Nelson A. Rockefeller Institute of Government, 2007), 32–33.

624 "We had committed to carrying the state for Nixon" Cannon, AI.

624 based on John Mitchell's own indiscretions Ibid.

624 "What the hell is this all about?" Ibid.

625 "They know it's going on all the time" Richard Reeves, President Nixon: Alone in the White House (New York: Simon & Schuster, 2002), 526.

625 He also recorded in his diary Ibid.

625 "A couple months later we were having lunch at Pocantico" Dunham, AI.

625 "It is a task as important and historic as that of the founding fathers" NAR–RMN, November 8, 1972, RAC.

626 Jim Cannon wasn't so sure Cannon, AI.

626 Initially conceived as an examination of the modern state NAR–RMN, May 3, 1972, RAC.

626 Embracing activity for its own sake Berger, AI.

627 An ill-advised attempt at kingmaking *Time*, May 9, 1973.

627 Eight years out of Gracie Mansion *New York Times*, March 26, 1973.

627 "Do you think he'll run?" Koch, AI.

627 Nelson claimed to have the necessary pledges of support KRD, March 12, 1973.

628 "I've never been a puppet" *Newsweek*, April 2, 1973; *Time*, April 9, 1973.

628 "I'm responsible for a lot of Winthrop's problems" Linda Storrow, HMI, 3.

628 In the years since, he had tried to make amends Flor Brennan, HMI, 60.

628 "I'm never going to get through this" Linda Storrow, HMI, 3.

628 In his verbal tribute Nelson's eulogy for his brother is reproduced in NR, PP 1973, 1273–75; *New York Times*, March 4, 1973.

629 "All he wants is to get out and do graduate work at Vassar" *Albany Times Union*, January 4, 1973.

629 "Jerry, do you know I wasted a billion dollars" Jerry Finkelstein, HMI, 16; see also Alan Chartock's essay "Narcotics Addiction: The Politics of Frustration," in Connery and Benjamin, *Governing New York State*, 239–49.

630 ROCKY ASKS LIFE FOR PUSHERS *New York Daily News*, January 4, 1973.

630 "The only way to deter this commerce" NR, PP 1973, 43.

631 Rockefeller himself credited Happy's children William Kennedy, "Rocky Is 64, Going on 35," *New York Times Magazine*, April 29, 1973.

631 "I think it distorted his thinking" Whiteman, AI.

631 No one did more to shape Rockefeller's views Kennedy, "Rocky Is 64."

631 "He saw one feature and he brought that back" Whiteman, AI.

631 Rockefeller first shared his thinking Joseph Persico, AI.

631 "What do I do?" Maiorana, AI.

631 "I have only one client here" Whiteman, AI.

632 "I find it's an emotional thing" *Albany Times Union*, January 1, 1973.

632 "It's only unconstitutional if you call them a Supreme Court judge" NR, PP 1973, 869 (April 26, 1973, news conference, Albany).

632 "Your son is giving me a really hard time" Dale Volker, AI.

632 "Next thing I know, I'm walking around" Ibid.

633 "If mine is tapped . . . I'll bet yours is tapped too" Ibid.

633 Rockefeller praised lawmakers NAR, PP 1973, 893–97.

634 the most sophisticated land use planning effort in the history of American conservation The long struggle over the Adirondacks is covered in Albright, *Portrait*, 107–34, and in the relevant volumes of Rockefeller's Public Papers. See also Connery and Benjamin, *Rockefeller of New York*, 343–48.

635 Unfortunately, O'Brien had an Alaska-sized thirst Albright, *Portrait*, 122; Henry Diamond, "Nelson Rockefeller: The Improbable Tree Hugger," Rockefeller Institute of Government, Albany, NY, January 2009 (available online at http://www.rockinst.org/observations/diamondh/2009-01-improbable_tree-hugger.aspx).

635 The atmosphere inside the White House KRD, February 14, 1973.

636 "You don't kick people in Washington in the shins" Art Buchwald, *Ellensburg Daily Record*, May 8, 1975.

636 At least to Mitchell, said Riland KRD, March 24, 1972; the same document describes Martha Mitchell's accusatory phone call and Nelson's response.

636 "Nelson Rockefeller knew quite early" Cannon, AI.

636 **Another source claims** Confidential source.

637 **"So Peter and I contrived this plan"** Cannon, AI; Peter Wallison, AI.

637 **"But Nixon has already made up his mind"** Cannon, AI.

637 **"Tell the governor the vice presidency's about to open up"** Armao, AI.

637 **"There's no more money"** Maiorana, AI.

637 **"I couldn't stand to go to Albany"** Albright, *Portrait*, 104.

637 **"fed up with state government"** KRD, July 21, 1973.

637 **"There had been discussions"** Whiteman, AI.

637 **This Wilson invited caricature** *New York Times*, March 14, 2000.

638 **As governor, Wilson once invited a friendly journalist to lunch** O'Shaughnessy, AI.

638 **"You mean to tell me, Nelson"** Norman Hurd, HMI, 76.

638 **Long after he and his wife** *Westchester Journal News*, March 14, 2000.

638 **"He was always anxious to bring Malcolm in"** MacCrate, AI.

638 **Rockefeller was out of the state** Malcolm Wilson, HMI, 40.

639 **Hidden from public view** Hugh Morrow, NAR, "Attica Indictments," November 27, 1973, RGIII, Series 15, Box 27, RAC.

639 **"like a kid out of school"** KRD, December 12, 1973.

639 **Elsewhere in Manhattan that morning** *New York Times*, December 13, 1973.

640 **the governor harangued a reluctant Lefkowitz** Confidential source.

640 **his final full day as governor** *New York Times*, December 18, 1973.

25: "The Closest I'm Ever Going to Get. . . ."

641 **"Every vice president goes through hell"** NRI, Eisenhower Administration Project, CCOHC, 32.

641 **"Free at last!"** Lefferts, AI.

641 **There was a limit to their privation** Joseph Petro, *Standing Next to History: An Agent's Life Inside the Secret Service* (New York: Thomas Dunne Books, 2005), 112.

641 **"Poor Mary Kresky"** Jerry Finkelstein, HMI, 63.

642 **"Instead of using marble or slate"** Hawkins, AI.

642 **Hoving publicly called Rockefeller a grifter** Gross, *Rogues' Gallery*, 343.

642 **Woods said it was the first time in months** KRD, January 24, 1974.

642 **"They won't send you to jail, will they?"** Ibid.

642 **Now he was told** Jerry Danzig, HMI, 30.

642 **"I'm so tired of the tapes"** Richard Reeves, *Old Faces of 1976* (New York: Harper & Row, 1976), 102.

643 **"He just stared out the window"** Canzeri, AI.

643 **"Don't pay any attention to it"** Gerald Ford, HMI, 2.

643 *Send for the old pro* *New York Times*, August 12, 1974.

643 **"Ford's got to make Rockefeller the Vice President"** Edward Cox, in *Conversation on the Public Service*, 38.

643 **"Tell your friend not to get mixed up"** NROH, November 22, 1977, 30. Rockefeller related the same tale, with only slight variations, to Bob Hartman and other interviewers after he left office.

644 **"That's it"** "A Natural Force on a National Stage," *Time*, September 2, 1974.

644 **With a firm grasp of Nelson's emotional makeup** Ronan, AI.

645 **He offered Rockefeller a level of domestic policy oversight** NAR interview with Bob Hartman, December 2, 1977, James M. Cannon Papers, Box 35, 7 (hereafter referred to as "NAR, BH"), GRFL.

645 **In subsequent discussions, Bill Ronan** James Cannon, *Gerald R. Ford: An Honorable Life* (Ann Arbor: University of Michigan Press, 2013), 337.

645 **"a new kind of vice president"** Donovan, *Confidential Secretary*, 182.

645 **Others shared her doubts** Dunham, AI.

645 **"A big man for a big job"** *Time*, September 2, 1979.

645 **With the cameras turned off** Tom Korologos, AI.

646 **"It's going to get public, isn't it?"** Ibid.

646 **"I had to name names"** KRD, September 2, 1974.

646 **"It was right after he was nominated for vice president"** Cannon, AI.

646 **Goldwater had refused to see him** KRD, August 28, 1974.

646 **"You can kiss the Republican Party goodbye"** Memorandum to the President, from William E. Timmons, August 21, 1974, phw 19740822-08.pdf.

646 **"Any way we can get Nixon back?"** Ibid.

646 **Even Rockefeller's friends expressed dismay** KRD, August 28, 1974.

646 **"All of us are concerned"** Ibid., August 22, 1974.

647 **"Too effusive," said Rockefeller** Judy Harbaugh, AI.

647 **Rockefeller confined his objections** NROH, November 22, 1977, 6–7.

647 **"I think he will be in a position to blackmail"** NAR interview with Trevor Armbrister, October 21, 1977, James M. Cannon Papers, Box 35, 19 (hereafter referred to as "NAR, TA"), GRFL.

647 **Publicly, Nelson defended the president's action** KRD, September 8, 1974.

647 **"This time it was the witness who seemed in charge"** Moscow, *Rockefeller Inheritance*, 371.

648 **"He always used to say you can buy knowledge"** Armao, AI; "A Little Help for His Friends," *Time*, October 21, 1974; *New York Times*, October 6, 1974.

648 **A self-professed "cocktail smoker"** Happy Rockefeller, "If It Happens to You," as told to Elanor Harris, *Reader's Digest*, May 1976, 131–34.

649 **As laughter swept the hearing room** KRD, November 13, 1974.

649 **"Let's face it, I made a mistake"** "A Matter of Sharing Apples," *Time*, November 25, 1974.

649 **"I can't do that"** Cannon, AI.

649 **To reveal this tightly guarded secret** NAR interview with Michael Turner, December 21, 1977, James M. Cannon Papers, Box 35, 14 (hereafter referred to as "NAR, MT"), GRFL.

649 **"this is your out"** Ibid.

650 **The man of the cloth had no wish to see publicized** Ibid., 12.

651 **In addition to unwavering public support** Jack Marsh, AI.

651 **"Chizzy" to Rockefeller's handlers** Cannon, AI; *New York Times*, December 17, 1974.

651 **During the interim** KRD, December 13, 1974.

652 **"He said why don't I go and stay out at Rockefeller's?"** In conjunction with the publication of his memoir, *Known and Unknown*, former secretary of defense Donald Rumsfeld established his own online archive at papers.rumsfeld.com. Memo: Meeting with the President, October 11, 1974, Donald Rumsfeld Archive (hereafter referred to as "DRA").

652 **"You need Blacks in your Administration"** Memo: Personnel, Donald Rumsfeld–GRF, August 20, 1974, DRA.

653 **Rumsfeld himself had raised the prospect** Ibid.

653 **"Everything depends on your ability"** Memo: Relationship with President, George Hinman–NAR, September 4, 1974, RAC.

653 **"a very bright, able manipulator"** NROH, November 22, 1977, 11.

653 **"I tried to negotiate with Mr. Rumsfeld"** Ibid., 3.

654 **"I have been a survivor"** NAR, MT, 19.

654 **"pure Jerry Ford"** "Rocky and Rummy: Getting Organized," *Time*, December 30, 1974.

654 **"It was a mistake for Gerald Ford"** Cannon, AI; Meeting with the President, December 21, 1974, DRA.

654 **"I wonder how he can fill all the shoes"** Meeting with the President, January 3, 1975, DRA; KRD, January 3, 1975.

655 **"The President didn't ask me to come down here"** NAR, BH, 27. A complete account of the

battle to define, and control, the Domestic Council is in Robert T. Hartman, *Palace Politics* (New York: McGraw-Hill, 1980) 308–14.

655 "we just play this one out for two years" KRD, January 29, 1975.

655 Rumsfeld was "sore as hell" Ibid., February 9, 1975; *New York Times*, February 9, 1975.

656 "He would go over to the President" Joseph Canzeri, HMI, 44.

656 "If the President didn't want to follow my recommendation" Cannon, *An Honorable Life*, 342.

656 "You forget what court politics is like" Wallison, AI.

656 the Domestic Council ended up NROH, November 22, 1975, 8.

657 "This is Rumsfeld again" Cannon, *An Honorable Life*, 355–56; "The Growling on Ford's Right," *Time*, March 17, 1975. The insistence on a programming moratorium may well have originated in an Oval Office visit by more conservative Republican lawmakers disenchanted by Ford's Vietnam amnesty program, his continuing support for détente with the Soviet Union—and his selection of Nelson Rockefeller to be vice president.

657 "umpires are not leaders" NAR political memo to GRF, May 8, 1975, RAC. Along with a more decisive use of executive powers, shorter, more dynamic speeches, and a legislative program he called Vision, Not Veto, Rockefeller boiled his policy recommendations down into the five E's: energy-economy-employment-ecology-efficiency. A week later, he directed the president's attention to an array of topics, from the cost of health care to a summary of national eating habits.

657 "He came to me once with a scheme" Brent Scowcroft, AI; see Michael Turner, *The Vice President as Policy Maker: Rockefeller in the Ford White House* (Westport, CT: Greenwood Press, 1982), 22–86. Turner's book benefits greatly from his extensive interviews with Rockefeller.

658 "You keep it for me" Cannon, AI.

659 He would have been difficult to overlook "New Boss for a Media Giant Is an Old Hand at New York," *New York Times*, December 9, 2001; Devin Leonard, "Dick Parsons, Captain Emergency," *Bloomberg Businessweek*, March 24, 2011.

659 The battle was joined *Congressional Quarterly Almanac 1975* (Washington, DC: CQ Press, 1976), 35–38.

659 "Apparently Rockefeller kept fobbing Thurmond off" Marsh, AI.

660 "And so finally Strom says" Cannon, AI.

660 "No one threatens Nelson Rockefeller" Richard Parsons, AI.

660 "It says right here" Mary McGrory, "Barry and Rocky," *Washington Star*, February 26, 1975.

660 "What do you think I should do?" Parsons, AI.

661 "That looks like one dollar" Joseph Persico, in *Conversation on the Public Service*, 30.

661 "I used to tell people" Frank Zarb, AI; an excellent overview of Rockefeller's activities in the energy field is Dennis Farney, "On the Move," *Wall Street Journal*, August 15, 1975.

662 "It was pure pragmatism" Frank Zarb, AI; Nelson A. Rockefeller, "Toward Energy Independence," *New York Times*, February 24, 1976.

663 At length he notified Ford Cannon, *An Honorable Life*, 366–68.

663 "Bill, do me a favor" William E. Simon, *A Time for Reflection: An Autobiography* (Washington, DC: Regnery Publishing, 2004), 144.

664 Rockefeller took solace in small victories NAR meeting with Ford, notes, February 5, 1976.

664 "that's not a bad guy at all" Gerald Ford, HMI, 29.

664 he also waded into the diplomatic standoff On a 1976 around-the-world tour as part of the America bicentennial, Rockefeller accused the Soviets of turning the Indian Ocean into a Russian lake—without first checking his bellicose language with Kissinger or anyone else in the administration. W. Kenneth Riland, HMI, 45.

664 Nonsense, replied Rockefeller Guy Vander Jagt, AI.

664 A visit to Milwaukee KRD, October 24, 1975.

665 He was no less ingratiating Armao, AI.

665 At Pocantico, Rockefeller won the gratitude Petro, *Standing Next to History*, 111.

665 **Nelson speculated about events** Jerry Finkelstein, HMI, 49.

665 **"What is the Manson Gang?"** Persico, *Imperial Rockefeller*, 266–67.

665 **He built a new pool** KRD, May 7, 1975.

665 **"Not on your life, Ken"** Ibid., June 12, 1975.

666 **Rockefeller complained to his Secret Service agents** Petro, *Standing Next to History*, 116.

667 **Reagan entertained Rockefeller** Gerald Ford, HMI, 27–28.

667 **"Labor negotiations"** Cannon, *An Honorable Life*, 350.

667 **The two men had an immediate falling-out** Wallison, AI.

668 **Astonishingly, he refused to accept** NAR, MT, 35.

668 **"Then it was very clear to me what they wanted to do"** Ibid.

668 **White House lawyers voiced concerns** Rod Hills, AI.

668 **Rumsfeld then ordered publication delayed** *The Washington Post, Evans and Novak,* June 27, 1975. Ford invited his vice president for a Camp David weekend, sans Rumsfeld, at which the two men might have confronted the broken relationship head-on. But Rockefeller chose instead to go home to Pocantico. KRD, June 4, 1975.

668 **such a strategy, he boasted** NAR, MT, 36; "Rocky's Probe: Bringing the CIA to Heel," *Time,* June 23, 1975.

669 **"Well, how about Rockefeller?"** Callaway, AI.

669 **"In fact, he was pretty upset with me"** Ibid.

669 **Ford reassured him that he sought a variety of opinions** NAR, TA, 26.

670 **On more than one occasion** Albright, *Portrait*, 231.

670 **Rumsfeld's eye for talent** Meeting with the President, December 7, 1974, DRA.

670 **"And we would chew the fat"** Hartman, AI.

670 **"Sir, they're humiliating you"** Susan Herter, CRI.

670 **Sometime late in the summer** Seidman, AI.

671 **a scandal involving the Rockefeller administration** *New York Times*, December 19, 1974, February 26, 1976.

672 **"Ed was not satisfied to do one project at a time"** Stephen Lefkowitz remarks, "How UDC Began," June 10, 2005, Policy and Design for Housing, City of New York Graduate Center.

672 **Logue the visionary** "Herbert Muschamp, from an Era When Equality Mattered," *New York Times*, February 20, 2000.

672 **"Poor Hugh . . . I drank the champagne"** Rosen and Slocum, *From Rocky to Pataki*, 62.

673 **"I like to think of myself"** Ibid., 38.

673 **"the most remarkable and innovative of the postwar governors"** Peirce, *Megastates of America*, 25. Peirce did not stop there. He credited Rockefeller with building "the most complex, fascinating, and socially advanced state government in U.S. history."

673 **"How does a capitalistic society"** Moscow, *Rockefeller Inheritance*, 343.

674 **Faced with an immediate $1.5 billion budget shortfall** Auletta, *Streets Paved with Gold*, 81–85.

674 **"Nelson never approved of the irresponsible fiscal policies"** Gerald Ford, HMI, 31.

675 **"Although we never said it"** Seidman, AI.

675 **Columnist James Reston accused the president** *New York Times*, October 18, 1975.

675 **This did not prevent him** NAR, BH, 46–47.

675 **"Nelson," Ford admonished his vice president** *Time*, November 17, 1975.

676 **"You don't call a whole state a bunch of clowns"** Seidman, AI.

676 **"If we go on spending more than we have"** *New York Times*, October 30, 1975.

676 **"I don't know how that language got there"** Seidman, AI. Profoundly depressed on first hearing the president's public reaction, Hugh Carey and Felix Rohatyn perked up considerably that evening at Elaine's on East Eighty-eighth Street when they saw the freshly printed *Daily News* with its famous headline. "We're going to win this thing!" declared Carey. Rosen and Slocum, *From Rocky to Pataki*, 72.

676 **History has been more generous in its assessment** Carey, AI.

676 **"It was touch-and-go"** Gerald Ford, HMI, 32.

676 **Acknowledging "some honest difference of opinion"** *New York Times*, October 31, 1975; **"a sleepless night or two"** Ford, AI. In an interview with Hugh Morrow, Ford revealed his long held belief—part rationalization, part shrewd insight—that Rockefeller didn't want another four years in so confining a job as the vice presidency. His current restlessness would only be exacerbated, even if being dropped from the ticket wounded his pride.

676 **"Now, I have been talking with my political advisers"** NROH, November 22, 1977, 35. **"Ford's Costly Purge,"** *Time*, November 17, 1975.

677 **"No problem, Mr. President, at all"** NROH, November 22, 1977, 35.

677 **for the first time, Riland noticed** KRD, November 2, 1975.

677 **the First Lady told her husband** Confidential source.

677 **"You have got fourteen months"** Address by the Vice President to his Staff, November 5, 1975, RAC.

677 **Only once did he let down his guard** Albright, *Portrait*, 232.

26: THE DAY OF THE DEAD

678 **"I'm 67 years old"** Rosenbaum, *No Room for Democracy*, 149.

678 **"You SOBs got me off the ticket"** KRD, December 13, 1975.

678 **"Come on, Lanny"** Morrow, *Chief*, 234.

678 **"an understudy who secretly hopes"** Don Bonefide, "The Forgotten Man," *National Journal*, February 14, 1976.

679 **"It's like lightning striking a tree"** KRD, November 19, 1976.

679 **"Ed, you and Dick go into his office"** Dunham, AI.

679 **"I would campaign if anybody asked me to"** *New York Times*, February 17, 1976.

679 **"Hey, Shah, move to your right"** Petro, *Standing Next to History*, 119.

679 **"I'll say it was sculpted by Max Ernst"** Persico, *The Imperial Rockefeller*, 180.

679 **Riland thought his friend** KRD, March 3–April 3, 1976 folder, RAC. Eight-page journal of Rockefeller's 1976 bicentennial trip around the world.

680 **"I realized what he was thinking"** Rosen and Slocum, *From Rocky to Pataki*, 40.

680 **Were Ford to lose the nomination** Rosenbaum, *No Room for Democracy*, 7.

680 **Reagan's startling announcement** For the Schweiker nomination, see "A Gamble Gone Wrong," *Time*, August 9, 1976.

680 **"I can do a job for you"** NAR, BH, 45.

680 **"just a shadow of Mr. Rumsfeld"** NAR, TA, 35.

681 **"I will get this guy one way or another"** Seidman, AI.

681 **So, before his death in 2006** Gerald Ford, AI.

681 **That there *was* a strategy** George Hinman–NAR, July 12, 1976, RAC.

681 **In private, Rockefeller talked** KRD, July 14, 1976.

681 **Ann Whitman sensed** Donovan, *Confidential Secretary*, 187.

681 **"If you told Rockefeller what he wanted to hear"** Wallison, AI.

682 **"They got on to the subject of chlorofluorocarbons"** Ibid.

682 **"So stuffy, it's difficult to breathe"** Rosenbaum, *No Room for Democracy*, 149.

682 **"He's a grand guy"** Albright, *Portrait*, 276.

682 ***New Times* magazine had him regaling a Washington dinner party** *Newsweek*, September 27, 1976.

682 **In an off-the-record discussion** Jerry Danzig, HMI, 29.

682 **"Nelson and Don Rumsfeld were shoulder to shoulder"** Gerald Ford, HMI, 39.

682 **"He worked himself to the bone"** Scowcroft, AI.

682 **the week's most public embarrassment** Rosenbaum, *No Room for Democracy*, 14–15. In an interview with the author, White House operative Tom Korologos described semi-frantic efforts by Ford's managers to hustle the vice president off the convention floor and away from the television cameras.

683 "You've got to have *some* fun" *Newsweek*, September 27, 1976.

683 "He was discreet" Marsh, AI.

683 "We felt that if we fought on the platform and lost" Gerald Ford, HMI, 35–36.

683 "because we can use the votes" Korologos, AI.

684 "I told him that this was the best" NAR, BH, 65.

684 "If they start a demonstration" Richard Rosenbaum, AI.

684 Ford confided to Rockefeller NAR, BH, 56.

684 "We're rehashing the same stuff" Spencer, AI.

684 "For Christ's sake . . . forget this Goddamned trial balloon stuff" NAR, BH, 58. Rockefeller related his part in Bob Dole's nomination to multiple interviewers. The fullest account is in his interview with Ford ghostwriter Trevor Armbrister, October 21, 1977, James M. Cannon Papers, Box 35, 38–43, GRFL.

685 a note arrived from the president KRD, August 19, 1976 (part of a larger text, "1976 Republican National Convention, Kansas City, Saturday, August 14, to Friday 20th August").

685 "Turn up the sound" NAR, BH, 64; NROH, November 22, 1977, 51–52.

685 "Look, I am either going up following the President" NAR, BH, 67.

685 "Of course you should go up" Ibid.

686 "Look, you so and so" Ibid., 68. The same sequence of events is described by Joe Canzeri and Hugh Morrow—the latter in conversation with Fioravante Perrotta—as part of Morrow's oral history venture undertaken after Rockefeller's death. In his memoir, *In My Time*, Cheney himself adopted a semi-humorous attitude to the Rockefeller tantrum. Years later, accused of inflating his position in the Bush administration, Cheney joked that he knew an "imperial" vice president when he saw one. Interestingly, Cheney recalls Howard Baker as the presumptive favorite to be Ford's running mate. Doug Bailey was just as convinced that William Ruckelshaus was a consensus choice.

686 "Don't ever do that to me" Canzeri, AI.

686 "Mr. President, didn't you get the message I sent?" NROH, November 22, 1977, 54.

686 "I am not going to work with these people" Ibid., 55.

686 "You do anything to my brother David and you'll be sorry!" Simon, *A Time for Reflection*, 158–59.

686 "Kenny, I've never used such language in my life" KRD, August 19, 1976.

687 "I am not going to sit down in a room with Cheney" NAR, BH, 70.

687 "Tell them I'm not coming" Joseph Canzeri, HMI, 83.

687 "John, would you mind" Deardourff, AI.

687 "Rocky, you traitor" *Washington Star*, September 17, 1976.

687 "Happy taught me that" KRD, September 17, 1976.

687 "And he's signing photographs of himself" Wallison, AI.

688 "I decided to become a White House correspondent" "Megan Marshack's Instant Celebrity," *Washington Post*, February 16, 1979.

688 "She was a groupie" Confidential source.

688 Bright enough to skip a semester *People* magazine, February 26, 1979.

688 "One had a sense of Megan's never having suppressed anything" Persico, *Imperial Rockefeller*, 276.

689 "I go over there one day on some business with him" Cannon, AI.

689 the vice president was said to have "raised hell" Hugh Morrow interview notes, JPP; "From the Balcony," January 14, 2009, Dr. Bob's Nightmare, http://gabbyhyman.blogspot.com/2009_01_01_archive.html.

689 "Get rid of her" Raymond Shafer, AI.

689 "Well, Hughie, I guess your friend wants to go home now" Morrow, *Chief*, 237–38.

689 "I never read anything about myself" Bob Dole, AI.

689 Rockefeller's spirits picked up Rosenbaum, *No Room for Democracy*, 162.

690 In the course of the evening Walter Mondale, AI.

690 "a very attractive, bright young lady" NAR, MT, 2.

690 **Eager to thank the Secret Service agents** John McConnell, AI.

690 **His parting gifts to the Senate** NAR–Robert Byrd, Howard Baker, February 4, 1977, RAC.

690 **On his last night in office** NAR, MT, 3–4.

690 **The next day, Rockefeller led the applause** *Time*, January 31, 1977; William Coleman, AI.

690 **"I had a terrible feeling"** Armao, AI.

691 **"Having spent the last two years as Vice President"** NAR remarks before the Alfalfa Club, January 29, 1977. These were largely crafted by Paul Keyes, gag writer for Bob Hope, Jack Paar, and other show business luminaries.

691 **"Everybody was very nervous around here"** J. Richardson Dilworth, HMI, 4–5.

691 **"He wanted to do a lot quickly"** Laurance Rockefeller, HMI, 25.

692 **"he was a finger breaker"** Bill Dietel, CRI.

692 **"The first year was difficult for him"** Parsons, AI.

692 **Promised the same six months** *New York Times*, April 5, 1977.

692 **Later in the year** Statement by NAR before the Senate Finance Committee, September 13, 1977, RAC.

693 **"I know where he works"** Hugh Morrow interview notes, JPP.

693 **"I love him for his warmth"** Collier and Horowitz, *The Rockefellers*, 587.

693 **Hugh Morrow spent much of 1977** J. Richardson Dilworth, HMI, 6.

693 **he offered them use of the big house** NAR–JDR3rd, June 14, 1977. Nelson was serious about making Pocantico more cost-efficient. At his behest, Joe Canzeri slashed the estate workforce from 240 to 183, much of it by mechanizing the place. Joseph Canzeri, HMI, 48.

693 **Nelson welcomed John's input** NAR–JDR3rd, June 17, 1977, RAC.

694 **As far as Nelson was concerned** NAR–RBF Board of Trustees, June 22, 1977, RAC.

694 **Bob Armao discovered this for himself** Armao, AI.

694 **"I got bad news for you"** Ibid.

694 **Rockefeller told a largely Jewish audience** *New York Daily News*, May 10, 1977. Richard Parsons is convinced that Rockefeller lost no sleep over White House neglect. "He had put all that behind him by then." Other Rockefeller associates are equally certain that he longed for a presidential assignment, particularly in the area of foreign policy.

695 **"Despite a few differences"** NAR–JDR3rd, June 17, 1977, RAC.

695 **By all accounts it was a watershed** D. Rockefeller, *Memoirs*, 336–50. David's narrative of what he calls "brotherly conflicts" is surprisingly frank and scrupulously balanced.

695 **"If you shut this door and you shut that door"** Dietel, CRI.

696 **a "very helpful conversation"** NAR–JDR3rd, June 20, 1977. RAC.

696 **Nelson seemed oddly unaffected** JDR3rd diary, June 20, 1977, RAC.

696 **"In those early days"** JDR3rd–NAR, July 15, 1978, RAC.

696 **"You have had two ambitions in your life"** Ibid.

696 **In a follow-up message** NAR–JDR3rd, August 12, 1977, RAC.

697 **A group of local residents** "Rockefeller Sale Stirs Protest," *New York Times*, October 20, 1977.

697 **"My brother needs the money"** Abell, AI.

698 **"Art, have you taken another position?"** Arthur Taylor, CCOHC, 13.

698 **Introducing himself as "a former politician"** *New York Times*, March 24, 1977.

699 **"It may never come to anything"** Carey Winfrey, "Rockefeller, Out of Politics, Focuses on Art and Family," *New York Times*, May 9, 1978.

699 **far more than a financial adviser** Arthur Taylor, CCOHC, 29.

699 **"a rebuilding year"** Parsons, AI.

699 **"In the last years of Father's life"** Steven Rockefeller, HMI, 8.

699 **Nelson accepted an invitation** Roberts, *Kykuit*, 38.

699 **"If only I did it the way Carter did it"** George Hinman interview notes, JPP.

699 **"Jimmy Carter is our president"** Canzeri, AI; *Kansas City Times*, May 9, 1978.

700 **"He simply does not understand how happy he has made me"** Albright, *Portrait*, 261–62.

700 **His note welcoming them home** JDR3rd–NAR, May 11, 1978, RAC.

700 **By the estimate of one partygoer** Confidential source.

700 **In the course of the evening** *New York Daily News*, May 28, 1978.

700 **"I'm at the stage in life where nothing bothers me"** Winfrey, "Rockefeller, Out of Politics."

701 **"That's just sad"** Gillies, AI.

701 **"Five years from now"** NAR press conference, July 25, 1978.

701 **"Makework"** Armao, AI; see also Helen Duwar, "Nelson Now," *New York*, September 25, 1978.

701 **"She looked just like Gloria Swanson in *Sunset Boulevard*"** Armao, AI.

702 **"This is where you can push me"** Canzeri, AI.

702 **"He stopped moving"** Happy Rockefeller, AI.

702 **Rockefeller himself said as much** Larry Rockefeller, AI.

702 **If his patient were anyone but Nelson Rockefeller** Happy Rockefeller; AI, *Newsday*, October 8, 1978.

702 **it was said that the sound of brass balls clanking** Edward Kresky, HMI, 70–71.

702 **"My God, it's beautiful"** Joseph Murphy, HMI, 27.

702 **Deliberately absenting himself from the campaign trail** Marion Oettinger, Jr., *Folk Treasures of Mexico: The Nelson A. Rockefeller Collection in the San Antonio Museum of Art and the Mexican Museum, San Francisco* (New York: Harry N. Abrams, 1990), 58–65.

703 **an $11 million Latin American folk art museum in downtown San Antonio** For the history of the San Antonio folk art museum bearing his name, see *New York Times*, October 20, 1993.

703 **"Mr. Canzeri, I've heard about you"** Canzeri, AI.

703 **the preservation of Kykuit for future visitors** For the story of Kykuit's preservation, see Dalzell and Dalzell, *House the Rockefellers Built*, 228–77.

703 **"Nelson isn't talking to me anymore"** Abramovitz, AI.

704 **"She had a desk right outside his office"** Confidential source.

704 **"He wears us all out"** McPherson, "Instant Celebrity," *Washington Post*, February 16, 1979.

704 **She was reportedly paid $60,000** *New York Post*, February 12, 1979.

704 **Rockefeller became a regular visitor** *New York Daily News*, February 14, 1979.

704 **Marshack was invited to Pocantico** *New York Post*, February 12, 1979.

705 **"Never once did I see anything flaunted"** Canzeri, AI.

705 **"I'm not as young as I used to be"** Confidential source.

705 **"What does an old man do?"** Cunningham, AI.

705 **At one point in the afternoon** Happy Rockefeller, AI.

706 **"I guess I would just wait"** Canzeri, AI.

706 **Two years after it ended** NAR–Richard Rosenbaum, January 18, 1979 (reproduced as Appendix E in Rosenbaum, *No Room for Democracy*, 268–71).

706 **"You have got to be able to turn off things"** Edward Kresky, HMI, 48–49.

707 **A little more than a year had passed** NAR remarks at opening of the Museum of Contemporary Arts, Tehran, Iran, October 13, 1977, United States Mission to AK. Huldrum, Room 5600, 30 Rockefeller Plaza, RAC.

707 **Nelson volunteered to find him a suitable home** Persico, *Imperial Rockefeller*, 286–87.

707 **The weekend before he died** Happy Rockefeller, AI.

707 **"I just don't want to leave you all"** Ibid.

708 **Bernie Kilbourn wanted a private meeting** Canzeri, AI.

708 **Though seen in retrospect as a farewell dinner** *New York Daily News*, January 28, 1979.

708 **he worked a full day at Room 5600** Roob, AI.

708 **The two men agreed to meet the next day** Armao, AI.

708 **Around five o'clock, Nelson departed** Alfred L. Malabre, Jr., "A Brief Encounter with Nelson Rockefeller," *Wall Street Journal*, January 30, 1979.

708 **"his hand was constantly roaming his chest"** Happy Rockefeller, AI.

709 **"It won't be long"** Ibid.

709 **"He did not want to drop dead in that apartment"** Ibid.

709 **"Could I have an ambulance at 13 West . . ."** *New York Post*, January 30, 1979.

709 **Within two minutes, a police patrol car** *New York Times*, January 28, 1979.

709 **At Roosevelt, it was close to a change of shift** Jim Paturas, AI.

710 **"He was still warm"** *New York Times*, January 29, 1979.

710 **He glimpsed unfinished boxes of Chinese food** Ibid.

710 **They reported finding Rockefeller** *New York Times*, February 7, 1979.

710 **Marshack told Paturas** Paturas, AI.

710 **"Is there any chance of saving him?"** *New York Post*, January 29, 1979.

711 **Overhearing Hoffman making arrangements** Jimmy Breslin, *New York Daily News*, January 28, 1979.

711 **"The only thing that bugged me"** W. Kenneth Riland, HMI, 62.

711 **"What the hell was in your head?"** Armao, AI.

711 **"somebody famous is in trouble"** Cunningham, AI.

711 **"All right, let's not talk about this"** "Spin r.i.p Nelson Rockefeller," *New York Daily News*, November 6, 1998.

712 **"Oh, Bob".** Armao, AI.

712 **"Nelson has gone, Bob"** Ibid.

712 **He assumed Nelson had died at home** Morrow, *Chief*, 237–38.

712 **"I just thought I'd do one more thing for Nelson"** Cannon, AI.

712 **"Don't worry, she's not here"** Hugh Morrow interview notes, JPP.

712 **three separate versions of what had happened** W. Kenneth Riland, HMI, 62.

713 **The idea of Nelson Rockefeller alone in his office** Goldman, AI.

713 **"And it was clear he had not died in his office"** Ibid.

713 **"You don't know me, but I was Megan Marshack's journalism teacher"** Ibid.

713 **"Not that I know of"** Alexander Coburn, "Death in Action," *Village Voice*, February 5, 1979.

714 **In a remarkable display of generosity** Confidential source.

714 **"I've been through this thing over and over"** *New York Daily News*, January 30, 1979.

714 *The New York Times* **did not like being lied to** Marshall, AI.

714 **"The Champ Who Never Made It"** *Time*, February 5, 1979.

714 **"The last Venetian doge"** *New York Post*, January 31, 1979.

714 **William F. Buckley, Jr., conceded Rockefeller's potential greatness** William Buckley's tribute appeared in the *New York Post*, February 1, 1979.

714 **"more than most public men of his time"** *Los Angeles Times*, January 29, 1979.

714 **John Lindsay said** *New York Times*, January 29, 1979.

715 **George Meany proclaimed** *Washington Post*, January 28, 1979.

715 **"He had a word for everybody"** *New York Post*, January 29, 1979.

715 *He was a great guy* *New York Daily News*, January 28, 1979.

715 **"Well, he's a public figure right to the end"** "Farewell to Rocky," *Newsweek*, February 12, 1979.

715 **"Dad, we know how much you love us"** *New York Daily News*, January 30, 1979.

715 **For almost two hours they reminisced** Happy Rockefeller, AI.

716 **Why had he allowed the cremation to go forward?** Michael Baden, AI; *Newsday*, January 31, 1979; "Questions Still Cloud Rocky's Death," *New York Post*, February 8, 1979.

716 **There was speculation that District Attorney Robert Morgenthau** *New York Post*, February 15, 1979.

716 **Sydney Schanberg raised the possibility** "Catching Up on the Rocky Story," *Newsday*, February 4, 1979.

716 **On February 9, his will was made public** *New York Times*, February 10, 1979. The will, dated December 6, 1978, makes scant provision for Nelson's children by Tod, since they had already benefited from the trusts established by Junior.

716 **Investigators now concluded that the caller was not Megan** "Rockefeller Aide Did Not Make Call to 911," *New York Times*, February 9, 1979.

716 **The latest revelations** *New York Post*, February 9, 1979.

716 **On February 10, Pierce issued a brief statement** *New York Daily News*, February 11, 1979.

716 **the *Times* placed the call much earlier** *New York Times*, February 7, 1979. This story, like much *Times* reporting about Rockefeller's death, carries the byline of Robert McFadden, whose aggressive pursuit of the facts was equaled by his deftness in presenting them in ways more suggestive than salacious.

717 **"a Rockefeller family source"** Ibid., February 9, 1979.

717 **Another such source** Confidential source.

717 **For all practical purposes, the police concluded** Angered by Morrow's clumsy deception, the *Times* demanded the 911 tape be tested—if only to clear up an obvious discrepancy between the caller's panic-stricken demeanor and the relative calm displayed in person by Miss Marshack.

717 **one of three people who knew** Canzeri, AI.

718 **what Marshack herself told a subsequent lover** Linda H. Davis, *Charles Addams: A Cartoonist's Life* (New York: Random House, 2006), 253–55. She may have maintained an unbroken silence with the press, yet one of the author's former colleagues vividly recalls her sole meeting with Marshack while both were working for CBS in New York—an encounter prefaced by Megan's cheerful identification of herself as the woman who was with Nelson Rockefeller at the time of his death.

718 **"She didn't act for 40–50 minutes"** Hugh Morrow interview notes, JPP.

718 **Publicly, he always maintained** William O'Shaughnessy, *It All Comes Back to Me Now: Character Portraits from the "Golden Apple"* (New York: Fordham University Press, 2001), 130.

718 **He told a different story** Bill Plante, Chuck Conconi, AI.

718 **Later in the week** O'Shaughnessy, AI.

718 **So asserted military historian** Confidential source. It bears noting that at least two other residents of 25 West Fifty-fourth Street gave Cary Reich detailed accounts confirming Rockefeller's death in their building.

719 **"the governor was with his mistress"** Rosenbaum, *No Room for Democracy*, 173.

719 **"Joe, this is your last advance for Nelson"** Canzeri, AI.

719 **On Friday, February 2, twenty-two hundred mourners** For coverage of the memorial service, see *New York Times*, February 3, 1979.

720 **Rising to the occasion** Kissinger's eulogy was excerpted in *The New York Times*, February 3, 1979, and entered into the *Congressional Record* for February 5, 1979.

720 **"He was what he was"** Ibid.

721 **"Well, we miss them both"** Jerry Finkelstein, HMI, 59.

Select Bibliography

Abramson, Rudy, *Spanning the Century: The Life of W. Averell Harriman, 1891–1986* (New York: William Morrow, 1992)

Albright, Harry, *An Affectionate Portrait of Nelson A. Rockefeller by an Unabashed Admirer* (unpublished)

Aldrich, Nelson W., Jr., *Old Money: The Mythology of America's Upper Class* (New York: Alfred A. Knopf, 1988)

Alsop, Joseph W., and Adam Platt, *"I've Seen the Best of It": Memoirs* (New York: W. W. Norton, 1992)

Alsop, Stewart, *Nixon and Rockefeller: A Double Portrait* (Garden City, NY: Doubleday, 1960)

Ambrose, Stephen E., *Eisenhower* (New York: Simon & Schuster, 1984)

Andrews, John A., 3rd, *The Other Side of the Sixties* (New Brunswick, NJ: Rutgers University Press, 1997)

Auletta, Ken, *The Streets Were Paved with Gold* (New York: Vintage, 2011)

Badillo, Herman, and Milton Haynes, *A Bill of No Rights: Attica and the American Prison System* (New York: Outerbridge & Lazard, 1972)

Barr, Alfred, Jr. (essay), *The Nelson A. Rockefeller Collection: Masterpieces of Modern Art* (New York: Hudson Hills Press, 1981)

Beisner, Robert L., *Dean Acheson: A Life in the Cold War* (New York: Oxford University Press, 2006)

Bell, Malcolm, *The Turkey Shoot* (New York: Grove Press, 1985)

Benjamin, Gerald, and Robert T. Nakamura, *The Modern New York State Legislature* (Albany, NY: Nelson A. Rockefeller Institute of Government, 1991)

Benjamin, Gerald, and T. Norman Hurd, eds., *Rockefeller in Retrospect: The Governor's New York Legacy* (Albany, NY: Nelson A. Rockefeller Institute of Government, 1984)

Bleecker, Samuel E., *Politics of Architecture: A Perspective on Nelson A. Rockefeller* (New York: Rutledge Press, 1981)

Boller, Paul, *Presidential Campaigns* (New York: Oxford University Press, 2004)

Braden, Joan, *Just Enough Rope: An Intimate Memoir* (New York: Villard, 1989)

Bradlee, Benjamin C., *Conversations with Kennedy* (New York: W. W. Norton, 1984)

Branch, Taylor, *At Canaan's Edge: America in the King Years 1965–68* (New York: Simon & Schuster, 2007)

———, *Parting the Waters: America in the King Years 1954–63* (New York: Simon & Schuster, 1988)

Brownell, Herbert, *Advising Ike: The Memoirs of Attorney General Herbert Brownell* (Lawrence: University Press of Kansas, 1993)

Bubriski, Kevin, *Michael Rockefeller: New Guinea Photographs 1961* (Cambridge, MA: Peabody Museum Press, 2006)

Buckley, William F., Jr., *Flying High: Remembering Barry Goldwater* (New York: Basic Books, 2008)

Cannato, Vincent J., *The Ungovernable City: John Lindsay and His Struggle to Save New York* (New York: Basic Books, 2001)

Cannon, James, *Gerald R. Ford: An Honorable Life* (Ann Arbor: University of Michigan Press, 2013)

Caro, Robert, *The Power Broker: Robert Moses and the Fall of New York* (New York: Vintage, 1975)

Chase, Mary Ellen, *Abby Aldrich Rockefeller* (New York: Macmillan, 1950)

Cheney, Richard, *In My Time* (New York: Simon & Schuster, 2011)

Chernow, Ron, *Titan* (New York: Random House, 1998)

Clarke, Gerald, ed., *Too Brief a Treat: The Letters of Truman Capote* (New York: Random House, 2004)

Cobbs, Elizabeth A., *The Rich Neighbor Policy: Rockefeller and Kaiser in Brazil* (New Haven, CT: Yale University Press, 1992)

Collier, Peter, and David Horowitz, *The Rockefellers: An American Dynasty* (New York: Holt, Rinehart & Winston, 1976)

Connery, Robert H., and Gerald Benjamin, *Rockefeller of New York: Executive Power in the Statehouse* (Ithaca, NY: Cornell University Press, 1979)

——, eds., *Governing New York State: The Rockefeller Years* (New York: Academy of Political Science, 1974)

Dalrymple, Martha, *The AIA Story: Two Decades of International Cooperation* (New York: American International Association for Economic and Social Development, 1968)

Dalzell, Robert F., Jr., and Lee Baldwin Dalzell, *The House the Rockefellers Built* (New York: Henry Holt, 2007)

Daniels, Jonathan, *White House Witness, 1942–1945* (Garden City, NY: Doubleday, 1975)

Davis, Linda H., *Charles Addams: A Cartoonist's Life* (New York: Random House, 2006)

Desmond, James, *Nelson Rockefeller: A Political Biography* (New York: Macmillan, 1964)

Doig, Jameson W., *Empire on the Hudson* (New York: Columbia University Press, 2002)

Donovan, Robert, *Confidential Secretary* (Boston: Dutton Adult, 1988)

Duberman, Martin, *The Worlds of Lincoln Kirstein* (New York: Alfred A. Knopf, 2007)

Edwards, Lee, *The Conservative Revolution: The Movement That Remade America* (New York: Free Press, 1999)

——, *Goldwater: The Man Who Made a Revolution* (Washington, DC: Regnery Publishing, 1997)

Eisenhower, David, and Julie Nixon Eisenhower, *Going Home to Glory: A Memoir of Life with Dwight D. Eisenhower, 1961–1969* (New York: Simon & Schuster, 2011)

Ferrell, Robert, ed., *The Eisenhower Diaries* (New York: W. W. Norton, 1981)

Flexner, James Thomas, *Maverick's Progress: An Autobiography* (New York: Fordham University Press, 1996)

Fosdick, Raymond, *John D. Rockefeller, Jr.: A Portrait* (New York: Harper & Brothers, 1956)

Freeman, Joshua B., *Working Class New York: Life and Labor Since World War II* (New York: New Press, 2000)

Gerbrands, Adrian A., ed., *The Asmat of New Guinea: The Journal of Michael Clark Rockefeller* (New York: Museum of Primitive Art, 1968)

Germond, Jack W., *Fat Man in the Middle Seat: Forty Years of Covering Politics* (New York: Random House, 2002)

Gervasi, Frank, *The Real Rockefeller: The Story of the Rise, Decline and Resurgence of the Presidential Aspirations of Nelson Rockefeller* (New York: Atheneum, 1964)

Gilder, George, and Bruce Chapman, *The Party That Lost Its Head* (New York: Alfred A. Knopf, 1966)

Goldwater, Barry, *With No Apologies: The Personal and Political Memoirs of United States Senator Barry M. Goldwater* (New York: William Morrow, 1979)

Gordon, David L. A., *Battery Park City: Politics and Planning on the New York Waterfront* (Amsterdam: Gordon and Breach, 1997)

Goulder, Grace, *John D. Rockefeller: The Cleveland Years* (Cleveland, OH: Western Reserve Historical Society, 1972)

Gregg, Hugh, *The Candidates—See How They Run* (Portsmouth, NH: Peter E. Randall, 1990)

Grondahl, Paul, *Mayor Corning: Albany Icon, Albany Enigma* (Albany, NY: Washington Park Press, 1977)

Gross, Michael, *Rogues' Gallery: The Secret History of the Moguls and the Money That Made the Metropolitan Museum* (New York: Broadway Books, 2009)

Haldeman, H. R., *The Haldeman Diaries: Inside the Nixon White House* (New York: G. P. Putnam's Sons, 1994)

Hamill, Pete, *Diego Rivera* (New York: Harry N. Abrams, 1999)

Harr, John Ensor, and Peter J. Johnson, *The Rockefeller Century: Three Generations of America's Greatest Family* (New York: Charles Scribner's Sons, 1988)

Hartman, Robert T., *Palace Politics: An Insider's Account of the Ford Years* (New York: McGraw-Hill, 1980)

Hatfield, Mark, *Vice Presidents of the United States, 1789–1993* (Washington, DC: U.S. Government Printing Office, 1997)

Heath, Edward, *The Course of My Life* (London: Hodder & Stoughton, 1998)

Helfrich, G. W., and Gladys O'Neil, *Lost Bar Harbor* (Camden, ME: Down East Books, 1982)

Hentoff, Nat, *A Political Life: The Education of John V. Lindsay* (New York: Alfred A. Knopf, 1969)

Hevesi, Alan G., *Legislative Politics in New York State: A Comparative Analysis* (New York: Praeger Publishers, 1975)

Hill, Ruth Ann, *Discovering Old Bar Harbor and Acadia National Park: An Unconventional History and Guide* (Camden, ME: Down East Books, 1996)

Hoffman, Carl, *Savage Harvest: A Tale of Cannibals, Colonialism, and Michael Rockefeller's Tragic Quest for Primitive Art* (New York: HarperCollins, 2014)

Hoving, Thomas, *Making the Mummies Dance: Inside the Metropolitan Museum of Art* (New York: Simon & Schuster, 1993)

Jackson, Robert H., *That Man: An Insider's Portrait of Franklin D. Roosevelt* (New York: Oxford University Press, 2003)

Jacoby, Richard, *Conversations with the Capeman: The Untold Story of Salvador Agron* (Madison: University of Wisconsin Press, 2004)

Javits, Jacob K., *Javits: The Autobiography of a Public Man* (Boston: Houghton Mifflin, 1981)

Johnson, Robert David, *All the Way with LBJ: The 1964 Presidential Election* (New York: Cambridge University Press, 2009)

Kennedy, William, *O Albany!: Improbable City of Political Wizards, Fearless Ethnics, Spectacular Aristocrats, Splendid Nobodies, and Underrated Scoundrels* (New York: Penguin Books, 1985)

Kert, Bernice, *Abby Aldrich Rockefeller: The Woman in the Family* (New York: Random House, 1993)

Kissinger, Henry, *White House Years* (New York: Little, Brown, 1979)

Klein, Milton, *The Empire State: A History of New York* (Ithaca, NY: Cornell University Press, 2001)

Klein, Woody, *Lindsay's Promise: The Dream That Failed* (New York: Macmillan, 1970)

Kramer, Michael, and Sam Roberts, *"I Never Wanted to Be Vice President of Anything!": An Investigative Biography of Nelson Rockefeller* (New York: Basic Books, 1977)

Kramer, Paul, *Memories of a Secret Agent* (Bloomington, IN: Xlibris Corp., 2006)

Krinsky, Carol Herselle, *Rockefeller Center* (New York: Oxford University Press, 1978)

Kutz, Myer, *Rockefeller Power* (New York: Simon & Schuster, 1974)

Lachman, Seymour P., with Robert Polner, *Three Men in a Room: The Inside Story of Power and Betrayal in an American Statehouse* (New York: New Press, 2006)

Lawrence, Mary Wells, *A Big Life (in advertising)* (New York: Simon & Schuster, 2003)

Leaming, Barbara, *Orson Welles: A Biography* (New York: Viking, 1985)

Loebl, Suzanne, *America's Medicis: The Rockefellers and Their Astonishing Cultural Legacy* (New York: HarperCollins, 2010)

Long, Michael G., ed., *First Class Citizenship: The Civil Rights Letters of Jackie Robinson* (New York: Times Books, 2007)

Loth, David, *The City Within a City: The Romance of Rockefeller Center* (New York: William Morrow, 1966)

Lowi, Theodore, *The End of Liberalism: Ideology, Policy and the Crisis of Public Authority* (New York: W. W. Norton, 1969)

Lynes, Russell, *Good Old Modern: An Intimate Portrait of the Museum of Modern Art* (New York: Atheneum, 1973)

Machlin, Milt, *The Search for Michael Rockefeller* (Pleasantville, NY: Akadine Press, 2000)

Manchester, William, *A Rockefeller Family Portrait: From John D. to Nelson* (Boston: Little, Brown, 1958)

Marlin, George J., *Fighting the Good Fight: A History of the New York Conservative Party* (South Bend, IN: St. Augustine's Press, 2002)

McBride, Joseph, *What Ever Happened to Orson Welles?: A Portrait of an Independent Career* (Lexington: University Press of Kentucky, 2006)

McKay Commission, *Attica: The Official Report of the New York State Special Commission on Attica* (New York: Bantam Books, 1972)

Middendorf, J. William, II, *A Glorious Disaster: Barry Goldwater's Presidential Campaign and the Origins of the Conservative Movement* (New York: Basic Books, 2006)

Mieczkowski, Yanek, *Gerald Ford and the Challenges of the 1970s* (Lexington: University Press of Kentucky, 2005)

Miller, Howard F. (introduction), *The Executive Budget of New York State* (Albany: New York State Division of the Budget, 1981)

Morgan, Mary R., *Beginning with the End: A Memoir of Twin Loss and Healing* (New York: Vantage Point, 2012)

Morgan, Thomas B., *Self-Creations: 13 Impersonalities* (London: Michael Joseph, 1966)

Morris, Jan, *Manhattan '45* (Baltimore: Johns Hopkins University Press, 1998)

Morris, Joe Alex, *Those Rockefeller Brothers: An Informal Biography of Five Extraordinary Young Men* (New York: Harper & Brothers, 1951)

———, *Nelson Rockefeller: A Biography* (New York: Harper & Brothers, 1960)

Morrow, Lance, *The Chief: A Memoir of Fathers and Sons* (New York: Random House, 1984)

Moscow, Alvin, *The Rockefeller Inheritance* (Garden City, NY: Doubleday, 1977)

Moscow, Warren, *The Last of the Big-Time Bosses: The Life and Times of Carmine De Sapio* (New York: Stein and Day, 1971)

Nevins, Allan, *Herbert H. Lehman and His Era* (New York: Charles Scribner's Sons, 1963)

———, *John D. Rockefeller: The Heroic Age of American Enterprise*, vol. 2 (New York: Charles Scribner's Sons, 1940)

———, *Study in Power: John D. Rockefeller, Industrialist and Philanthropist* (New York: Charles Scribner's Sons, 1953)

Newhouse, Victoria, *Wallace K. Harrison: Architect* (New York: Rizzoli, 1989)

Newton, Ronald C., *The "Nazi Menace" in Argentina, 1931–1947* (Stanford, CA: Stanford University Press, 1992)

Nitze, Paul, *From Hiroshima to Glasnost* (New York: Grove Weidenfeld, 1989)

Nixon, Richard, *RN: The Memoirs of Richard Nixon* (New York: Warren Books, 1978)

Novak, Robert D., *The Agony of the G.O.P. 1964* (New York: Macmillan, 1965)

Oettinger, Marion, Jr., *Folk Treasures of Mexico: The Nelson A. Rockefeller Collection* (New York: Harry N. Abrams, 1990)

Okrent, Daniel, *Great Fortune: The Epic of Rockefeller Center* (New York: Viking, 2003)

O'Shaughnessy, William, *It All Comes Back to Me Now: Character Portraits from the "Golden Apple"* (New York: Fordham University Press, 2001)

Oswald, Russell G., *Attica—My Story* (Garden City, NY: Doubleday, 1972)

Peirce, Neal R., *The Megastates of America: People, Politics, and Power in the Ten Great States* (New York: W. W. Norton, 1972)

Perlstein, Rick, *Before the Storm: Barry Goldwater and the Unmaking of the American Consensus* (New York: Hill & Wang, 2001)

Persico, Joseph, *The Imperial Rockefeller: A Biography of Nelson A. Rockefeller* (New York: Simon & Schuster, 1982)

Petro, Joseph, *Standing Next to History: An Agent's Life Inside the Secret Service* (New York: Thomas Dunne Books, 2005)

Pietrusza, David, *1960: LBJ vs. JFK vs. Nixon* (New York: Union Square Press, 2008)

Pyle, Tom, *Pocantico: Fifty Years on the Rockefeller Domain* (New York: Duell, Sloan and Pearce, 1964)

Rangel, Charles, *And I Haven't Had a Bad Day Since: From the Streets of Harlem to the Halls of Congress* (New York: Thomas Dunne Books, 2007)

Rasmussen, Anne-Marie, *There Was Once a Time* (New York: Bantam, 1976)

Reeves, Richard, *Old Faces of 1976* (New York: Harper & Row, 1976)

Reich, Cary, *The Life of Nelson Rockefeller: Worlds to Conquer, 1908–1958* (New York: Doubleday, 1996)

Remembering Al Marshall, 1921–2008 (Albany, NY: Nelson A. Rockefeller Institute of Government, 2009)

Rivas, Darlene, *Missionary Capitalist: Nelson Rockefeller in Venezuela* (Chapel Hill: University of North Carolina Press, 2002)

Rivera, Diego, *My Art, My Life: An Autobiography* (Mineola, NY: Dover Publications, 1991)

Roberts, Ann Rockefeller, *Kykuit: The Rockefeller Family Home* (New York: Abbeville Press, 1998)

——, *Mr. Rockefeller's Roads* (Camden, ME: Down East Books, 1990)

Roberts, Sam, *America's Mayor: John V. Lindsay and the Reinvention of New York* (New York: Museum of the City of New York; Columbia University Press, 2010)

Robinson, Jackie, *I Never Had It Made: An Autobiography of Jackie Robinson* (New York: Putnam, 1972)

Rockefeller, Abby Aldrich, *Abby Aldrich Rockefeller's Letters to Her Sister Lucy* (New York: John D. Rockefeller, Jr., 1957)

Rockefeller Brothers Fund, *Prospect for America: The Rockefeller Panel Reports* (Garden City, NY: Doubleday, 1961)

Rockefeller, David, *Memoirs* (New York: Random House, 2002)

Rockefeller, Nelson A., *The Future of Federalism* (Cambridge, MA: Harvard University Press, 1962)

——, *Our Environment Can Be Saved* (New York: Doubleday, 1970)

Rockefeller Report on the Americas, The, (Chicago: Quadrangle Books, 1969)

Rodgers, William, *Rockefeller's Follies: An Unauthorized View of Nelson A. Rockefeller* (New York: Stein & Day, 1966)

Root, Oren, *Persons and Persuasions* (New York: W. W. Norton, 1974)

Rorabaugh, W. J., *The Real Making of the President: Kennedy, Nixon, and the 1960 Election* (Lawrence: University Press of Kansas, 2012)

Rosen, Hy, and Peter Slocum, *From Rocky to Pataki: Character and Caricatures in New York Politics* (Syracuse, NY: Syracuse University Press, 1998)

Rosen, James, *The Strong Man: John Mitchell and the Secrets of Watergate* (New York: Doubleday, 2008)

Rosenbaum, Richard M., *No Room for Democracy: The Triumph of Ego over Common Sense* (Rochester, NY: RIT Press, 2008)

Rumsfeld, Donald, *Known and Unknown* (New York: Penguin, 2011)

Saarinen, Aline B., *The Proud Possessors: The Lives, Times, and Tastes of Some Adventurous American Art Collectors* (New York: Random House, 1958)

Safire, William, *Before the Fall: An Inside View of the Pre-Watergate White House* (Garden City, NY: Doubleday, 1975)

Sander, Irving (introduction), *The Empire State Collection: Art for the Public* (New York: Harry N. Abrams, 1987)

Savell, Isabelle Keating, *The Governor's Mansion in Albany* (Albany, NY: [government publication], 1962)

Schlesinger, Arthur, Jr., *Journals: 1952–2000* (New York: Penguin Press, 2007)

Schneier, Edward, and John Brian Murtaugh, *New York Politics: A Tale of Two States* (Armonk, NY: M. E. Sharpe, 2009)

Simon, William E., *A Time for Reflection: An Autobiography* (Washington, DC: Regnery Publishing, 2004)

Skerritt, Elizabeth, *Working with Nelson Rockefeller 1943–1952* (unpublished memoir)

Smith, Richard Norton, *Thomas E. Dewey and His Times: The First Full-Scale Biography of the Maker of the Modern Republican Party* (New York: Simon & Schuster, 1982)

Sorenson, Theodore, *Kennedy* (New York: Harper Perennial Political Classics, 2009)

Stebenne, David L., *Arthur J. Goldberg: New Deal Liberal* (New York: Oxford University Press, 1996)

Steel, Ronald, *Walter Lippmann and the American Century* (Boston: Little, Brown, 1980)

Stephenson, Nathaniel, *Nelson W. Aldrich: A Leader in American Politics* (New York: Charles Scribner's Sons, 1930)

Straight, Michael, *Nancy Hanks: An Intimate Portrait: The Creation of a National Commitment to the Arts* (Durham, NC: Duke University Press, 1988)

Sullivan, Timothy J., *New York State and the Rise of Modern Conservatism: Redrawing Party Lines* (Albany: State University of New York Press, 2009)

Thimmesch, Nick, *The Condition of Republicanism* (New York: W. W. Norton, 1980)

Turner, Michael, *The Vice President as Policy Maker: Rockefeller in the Ford White House* (Westport, CT: Greenwood Press, 1982)

Underwood, James E., and William J. Daniels, *Governor Rockefeller in New York: The Apex of Pragmatic Liberalism in the United States* (Westport, CT: Greenwood Press, 1982)

Vidal, Gore, *Palimpsest: A Memoir* (New York: Random House, 1995)

Welles, Benjamin, *Sumner Welles: FDR's Global Strategist* (New York: St. Martin's Press, 1977)

Werth, Barry, *31 Days: Gerald Ford, the Nixon Pardon, and a Government in Crisis* (New York: Random House, 2006)

White, F. Clifton, *Suite 3505: The Story of the Draft Goldwater Movement* (New Rochelle, NY: Arlington House, 1967)

White, Theodore H., *The Making of the President, 1960* (New York: Atheneum, 1964)

———, *The Making of the President, 1964* (Boston: Atheneum, 1965)

———, *The Making of the President, 1968* (New York: Atheneum, 1969)

Wicker, Tom, *A Time to Die* (New York: Quadrangle/New York Times Book Company, 1975)

Widmayer, Charles E., *Hopkins of Dartmouth: The Story of Ernest Martin Hopkins and His Presidency of Dartmouth College* (Hanover, NH: University Press of New England, 1977)

Wills, Garry, *Nixon Agonistes: The Crisis of the Self-Made Man* (Boston: Houghton Mifflin, 1969)

Wolfe, Bertram D., *The Fabulous Life of Diego Rivera* (New York: Stein & Day, 1963)

Wyckoff, Gene, *The Image Candidates: American Politics in the Age of Television* (New York: Macmillan, 1968)

Index

About the Author

RICHARD NORTON SMITH is the author of *Thomas E. Dewey and His Times*, for which he was a finalist for the Pulitzer Prize in 1983, as well as *An Uncommon Man: The Triumph of Herbert Hoover; The Harvard Century: The Making of a University to a Nation; The Colonel: The Life and Legend of Robert R. McCormick, 1880–1955*; and *Patriarch: George Washington and the New American Nation.* He has served as director of several presidential libraries, including those of Presidents Herbert Hoover, Dwight Eisenhower, Gerald Ford, and Ronald Reagan. He was founding director of the Abraham Lincoln Presidential Library in Springfield, Illinois. A frequent guest on C-SPAN and *The NewsHour with Jim Lehrer* (and, later, *The PBS NewsHour*) and a former presidential historian for ABC News, he has spent fourteen years researching and writing *On His Own Terms: A Life of Nelson Rockefeller.*

About the Type

This book was set in Electra, a typeface designed for Linotype by renowned type designer W. A. Dwiggins (1880–1956). Electra is a fluid typeface, avoiding the contrasts of thick and thin strokes that are prevalent in most modern typefaces.